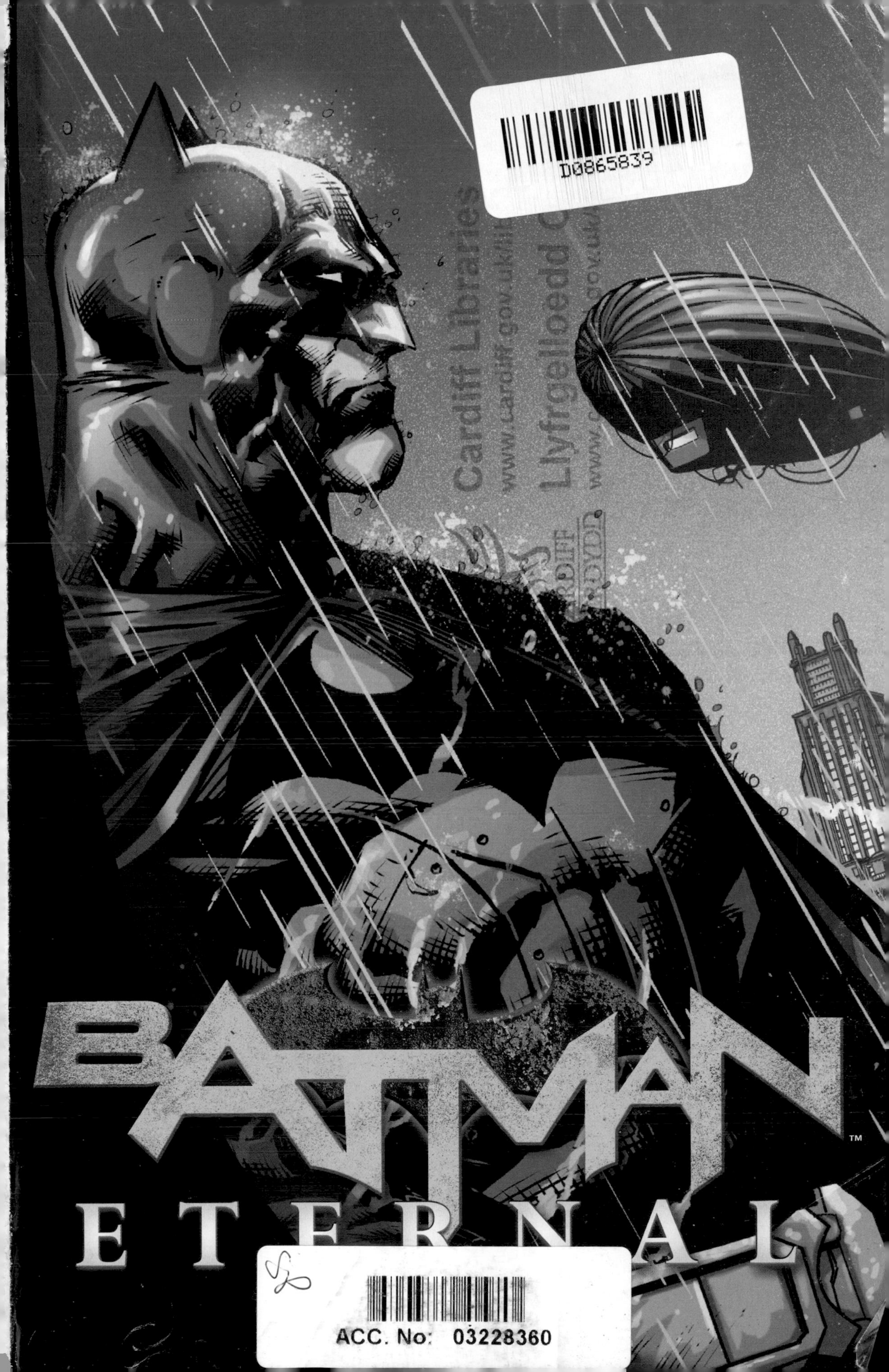
BATMAN™
ETERNAL

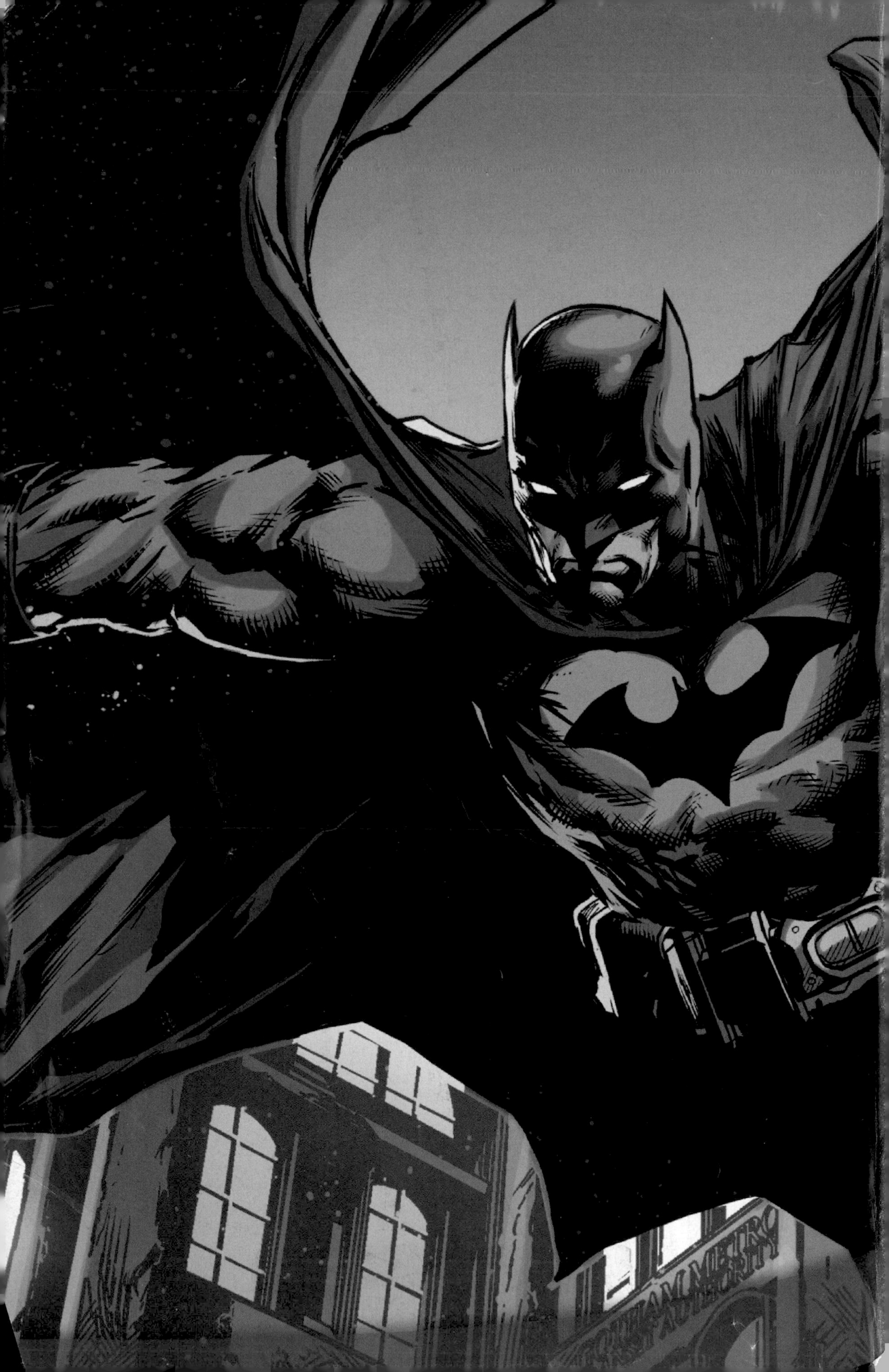

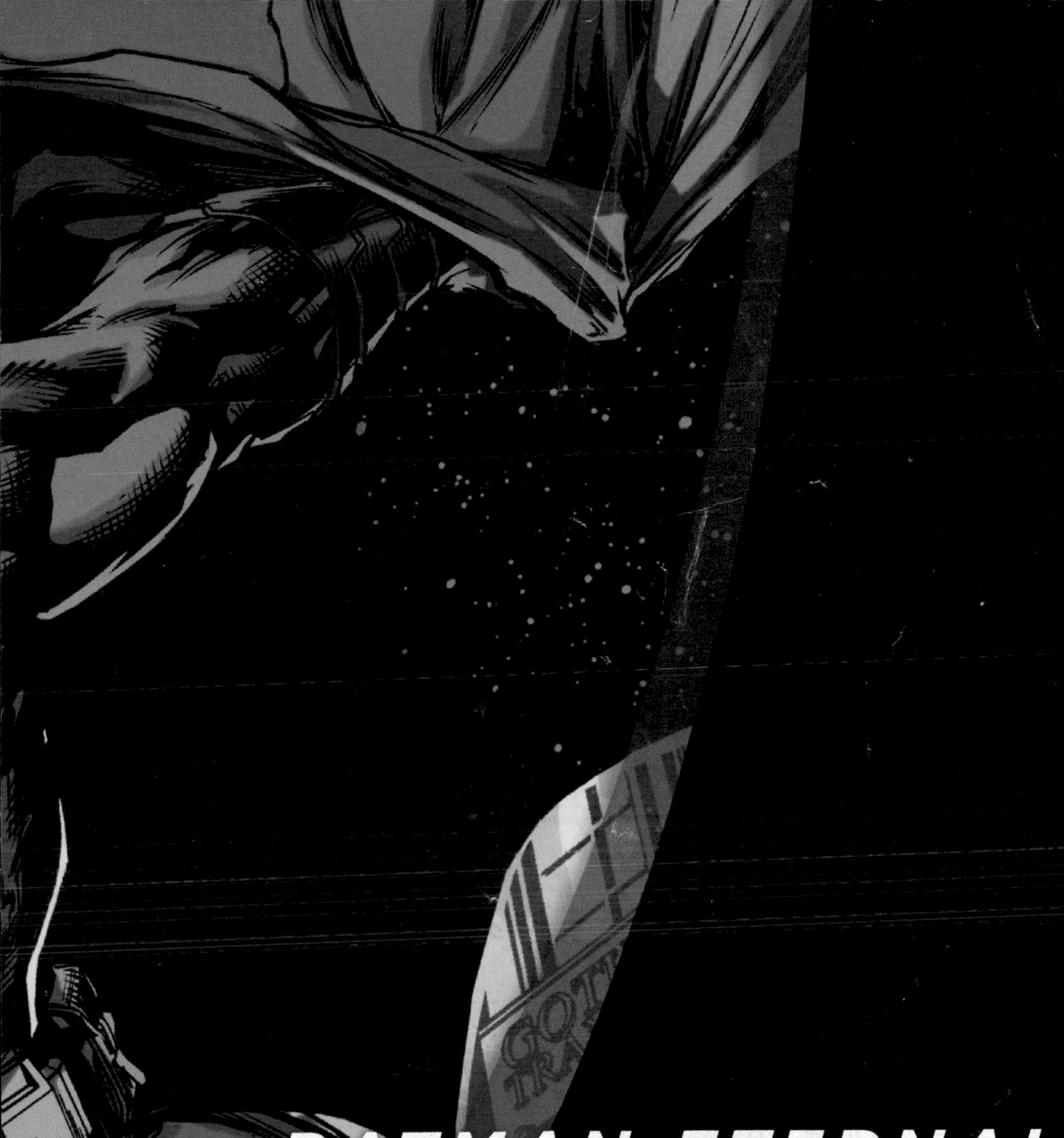

BATMAN ETERNAL
VOLUME 1

SCOTT **SNYDER** JAMES **TYNION IV** story

JAMES **TYNION IV** JOHN **LAYMAN** RAY **FAWKES**
TIM **SEELEY** SCOTT **SNYDER** KYLE **HIGGINS** writers

JASON **FABOK** DUSTIN **NGUYEN** MIKEL **JANIN** GUILLEM **MARCH**
IAN **BERTRAM** RICCARDO **BURCHIELLI** ANDY **CLARKE** TREVOR **McCARTHY**
EMANUEL **SIMEONI** DEREK **FRIDOLFS** GUILLERMO **ORTEGO** artists

BRAD **ANDERSON** JOHN **KALISZ** **BLOND** JEROMY **COX** TOMEU **MOREY** GUY **MAJOR**
DAVE **McCAIG** DAVE **STEWART** colorists

TAYLOR **ESPOSITO** ROB **LEIGH** NICK J. **NAPOLITANO** STEVE **WANDS**
DEZI **SIENTY** CARLOS M. **MANGUAL** letterers

BATMAN created by BOB **KANE**

KATIE KUBERT CHRIS CONROY Editors – Original Series MATT HUMPHREYS DAVE WIELGOSZ Assistant Editors – Original Series
ROBIN WILDMAN Editor ROBBIN BROSTERMAN Design Director – Books ROBBIE BIEDERMAN Publication Design

BOB HARRAS Senior VP – Editor-in-Chief, DC Comics

DIANE NELSON President DAN DIDIO and JIM LEE Co-Publishers GEOFF JOHNS Chief Creative Officer
AMIT DESAI Senior VP – Marketing and Franchise Management
AMY GENKINS Senior VP – Business and Legal Affairs NAIRI GARDINER Senior VP – Finance
JEFF BOISON VP – Publishing Planning MARK CHIARELLO VP – Art Direction and Design
JOHN CUNNINGHAM VP – Marketing TERRI CUNNINGHAM VP – Editorial Administration
LARRY GANEM VP – Talent Relations and Services ALISON GILL Senior VP – Manufacturing and Operations
HANK KANALZ Senior VP – Vertigo and Integrated Publishing JAY KOGAN VP – Business and Legal Affairs, Publishing
JACK MAHAN VP – Business Affairs, Talent NICK NAPOLITANO VP – Manufacturing Administration SUE POHJA VP – Book Sales
FRED RUIZ VP – Manufacturing Operations COURTNEY SIMMONS Senior VP – Publicity BOB WAYNE Senior VP – Sales

BATMAN ETERNAL VOLUME 1

DC Comics, 1700 Broadway, New York, NY 10019
A Warner Bros. Entertainment Company.
Printed by RR Donnelley, Salem, VA, USA. 10/31/14. First Printing.

ISBN: 978-1-4012-5173-4

Library of Congress Cataloging-in-Publication Data

Snyder, Scott, author.
Batman eternal volume 1 / Scott Snyder, James Tynion IV, writers ; Ray Fawkes, John Layman, Tim Seeley, artists.
pages cm
ISBN: 978-1-4012-5173-4
1. Graphic novels. I. Tynion, James, IV, author. II. Fawkes, Ray, illustrator. III. Layman, John, 1967- illustrator. IV. Seeley, Tim, illustrator. V. Title.

PN6728.B36S659 2014
741.5'973—dc23

2014026870

SUSTAINABLE
FORESTRY
INITIATIVE

Certified Chain of Custody
20% Certified Forest Content,
80% Certified Sourcing
www.sfiprogram.org
SFI-01042
APPLIES TO TEXT STOCK ONLY

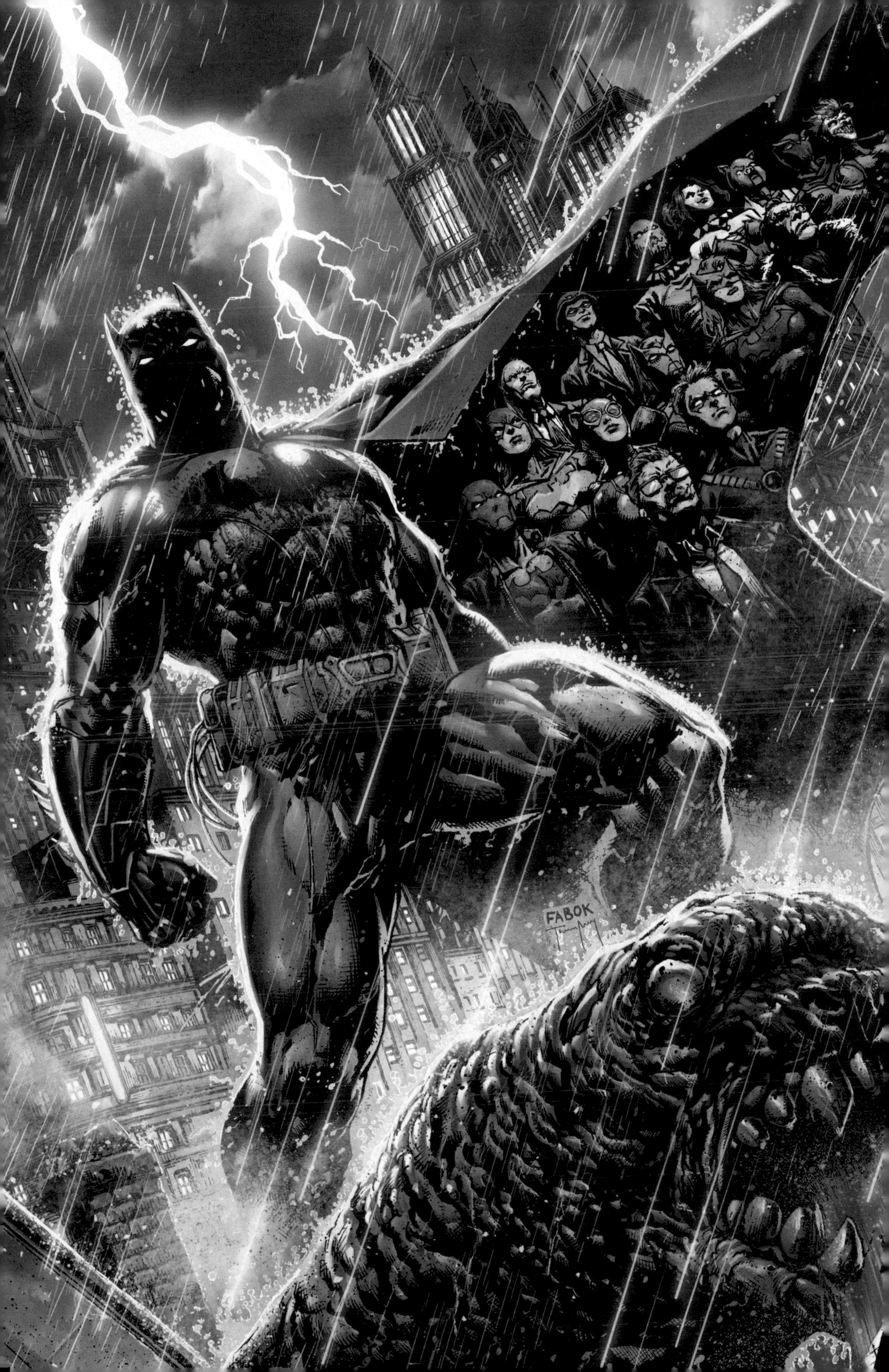
FABOK

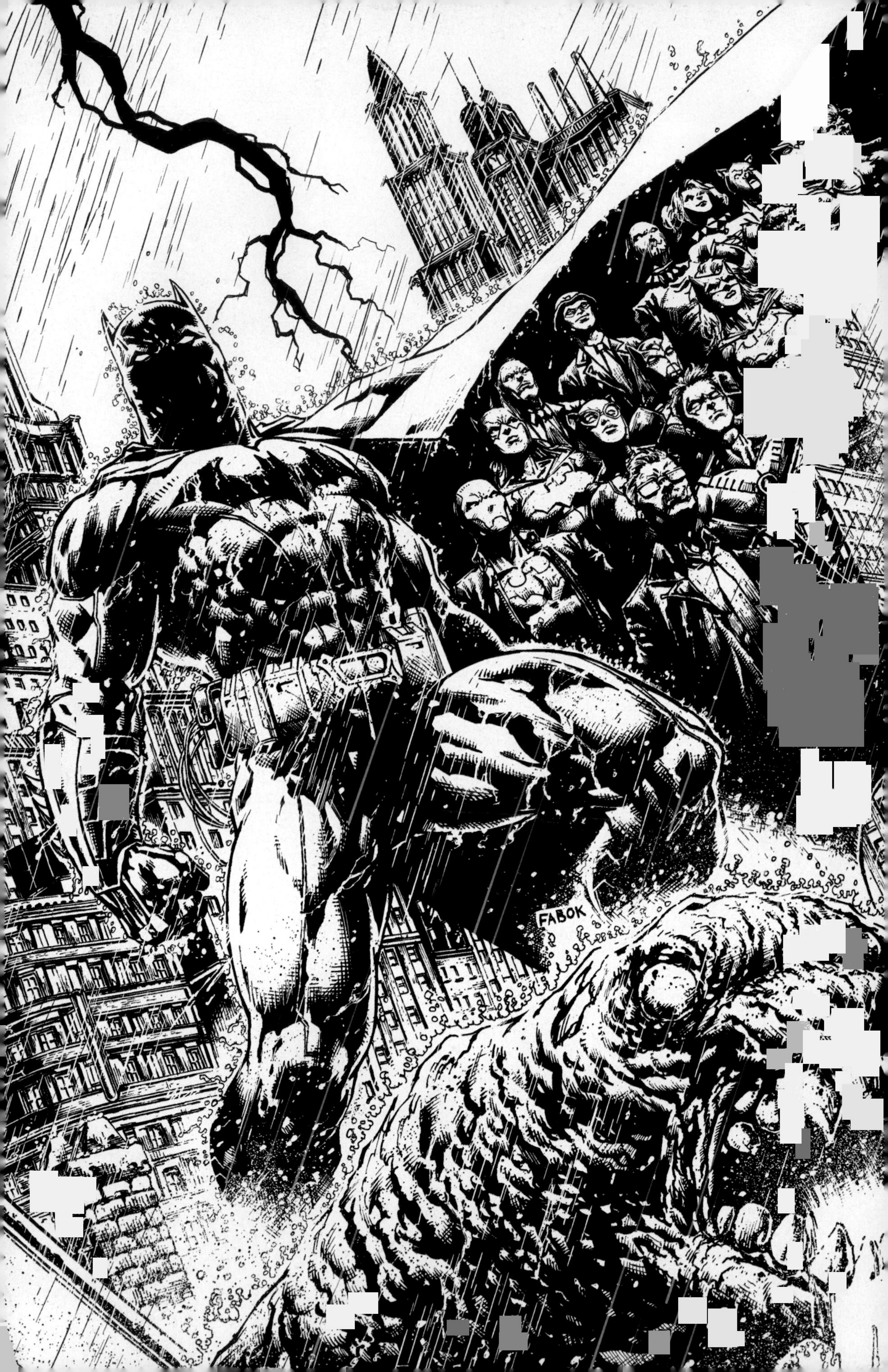
FABOK

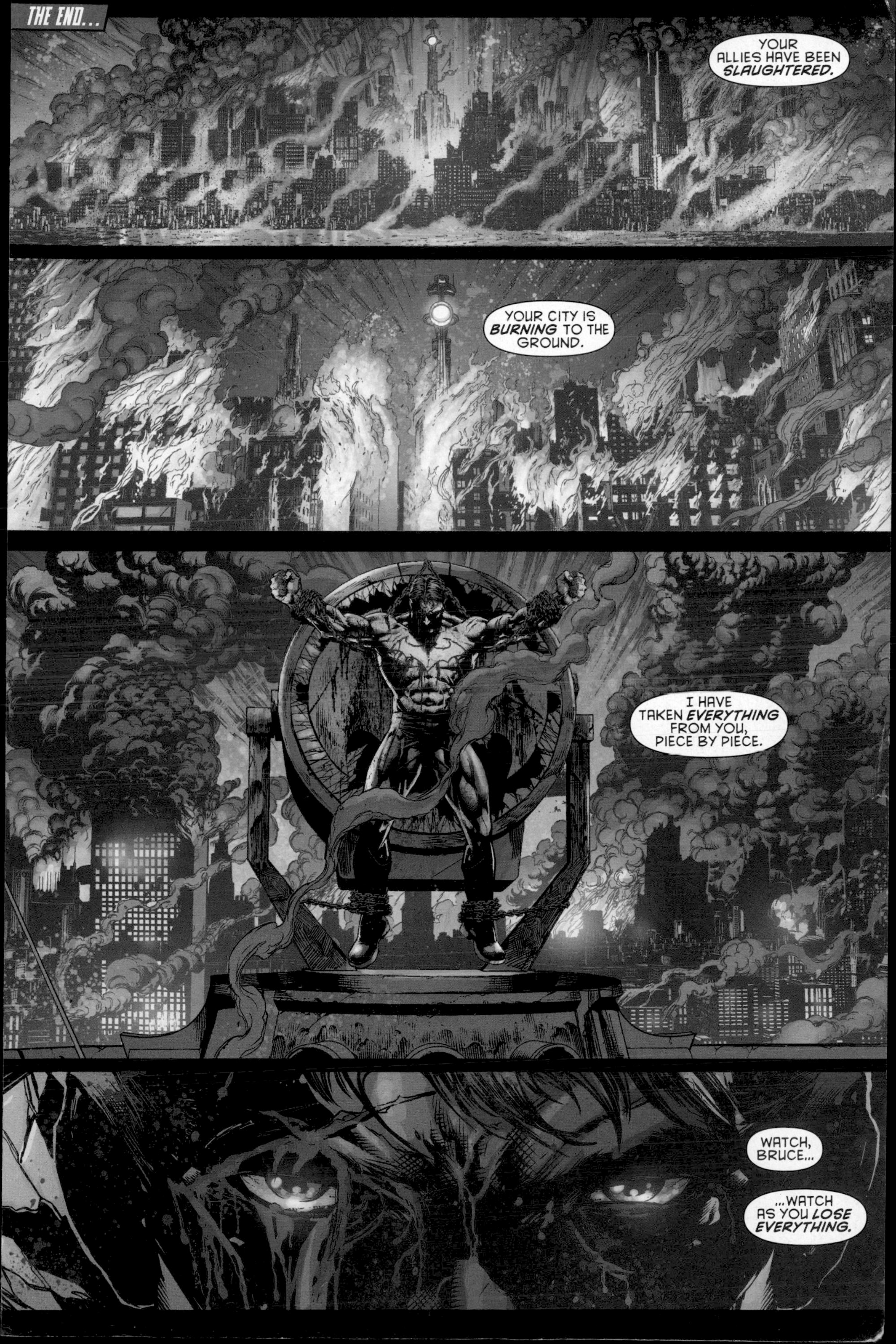
THE END...
YOUR ALLIES HAVE BEEN SLAUGHTERED.
YOUR CITY IS BURNING TO THE GROUND.
I HAVE TAKEN EVERYTHING FROM YOU, PIECE BY PIECE.
WATCH, BRUCE...
...WATCH AS YOU LOSE EVERYTHING.

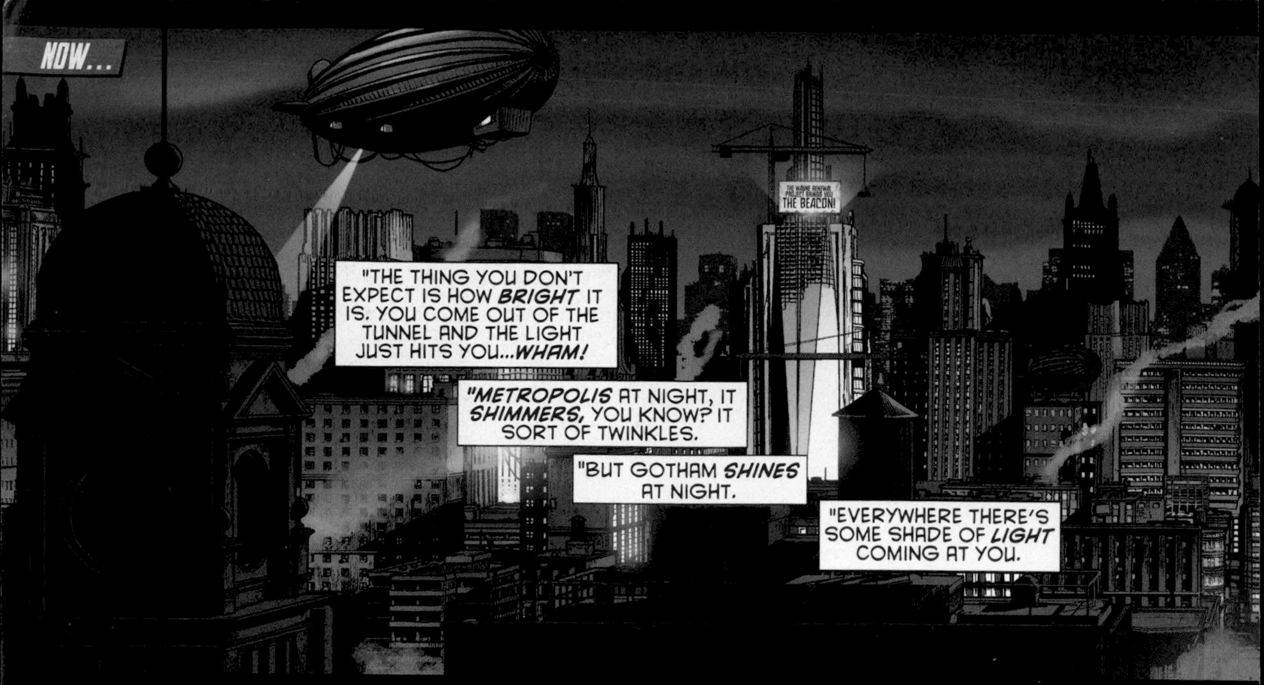
NOW...
THE BEACON!
"THE THING YOU DON'T EXPECT IS HOW BRIGHT IT IS. YOU COME OUT OF THE TUNNEL AND THE LIGHT JUST HITS YOU...WHAM!
"METROPOLIS AT NIGHT, IT SHIMMERS, YOU KNOW? IT SORT OF TWINKLES.
"BUT GOTHAM SHINES AT NIGHT.
"EVERYWHERE THERE'S SOME SHADE OF LIGHT COMING AT YOU.

SCOTT SNYDER & JAMES TYNION IV STORY & SCRIPT
CONSULTING WRITERS: RAY FAWKES, JOHN LAYMAN & TIM SEELEY
ART BY: JASON FABOK

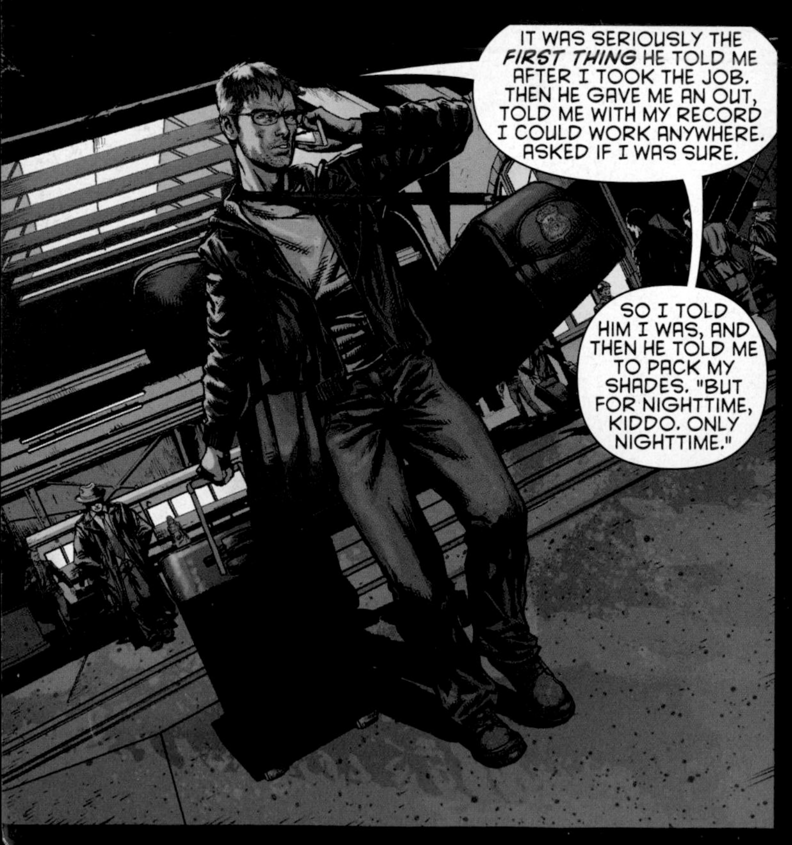
IT WAS SERIOUSLY THE FIRST THING HE TOLD ME AFTER I TOOK THE JOB. THEN HE GAVE ME AN OUT, TOLD ME WITH MY RECORD I COULD WORK ANYWHERE. ASKED IF I WAS SURE.
SO I TOLD HIM I WAS, AND THEN HE TOLD ME TO PACK MY SHADES. "BUT FOR NIGHTTIME, KIDDO. ONLY NIGHTTIME."

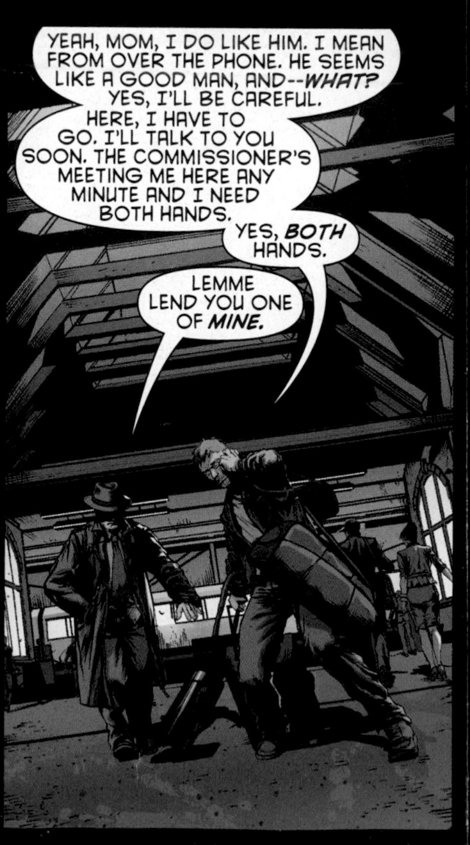
YEAH, MOM, I DO LIKE HIM. I MEAN FROM OVER THE PHONE. HE SEEMS LIKE A GOOD MAN, AND--WHAT? YES, I'LL BE CAREFUL.
HERE, I HAVE TO GO. I'LL TALK TO YOU SOON. THE COMMISSIONER'S MEETING ME HERE ANY MINUTE AND I NEED BOTH HANDS.
YES, BOTH HANDS.
LEMME LEND YOU ONE OF MINE.

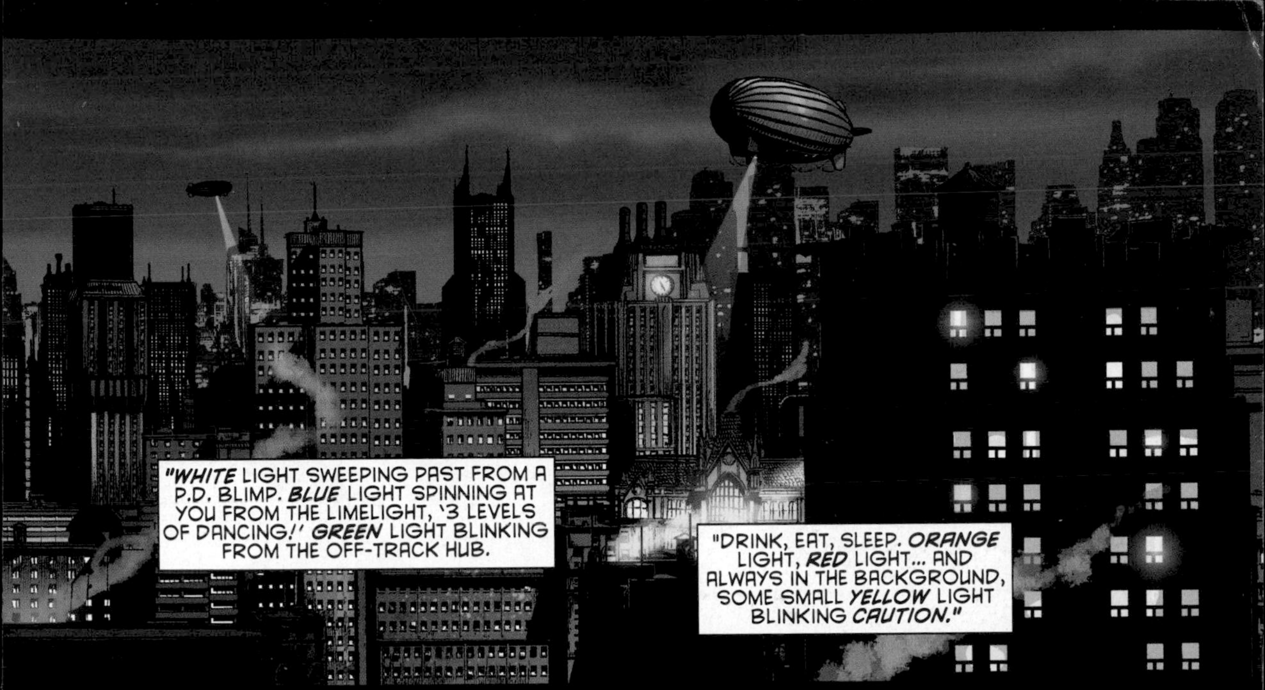
"WHITE LIGHT SWEEPING PAST FROM A P.D. BLIMP. BLUE LIGHT SPINNING AT YOU FROM THE LIMELIGHT, '3 LEVELS OF DANCING!' GREEN LIGHT BLINKING FROM THE OFF-TRACK HUB.
"DRINK, EAT, SLEEP. ORANGE LIGHT, RED LIGHT... AND ALWAYS IN THE BACKGROUND, SOME SMALL YELLOW LIGHT BLINKING CAUTION."

COLORS BY: BRAD ANDERSON LETTERING BY: NICK J. NAPOLITANO
COVER BY: JASON FABOK & TOMEU MOREY

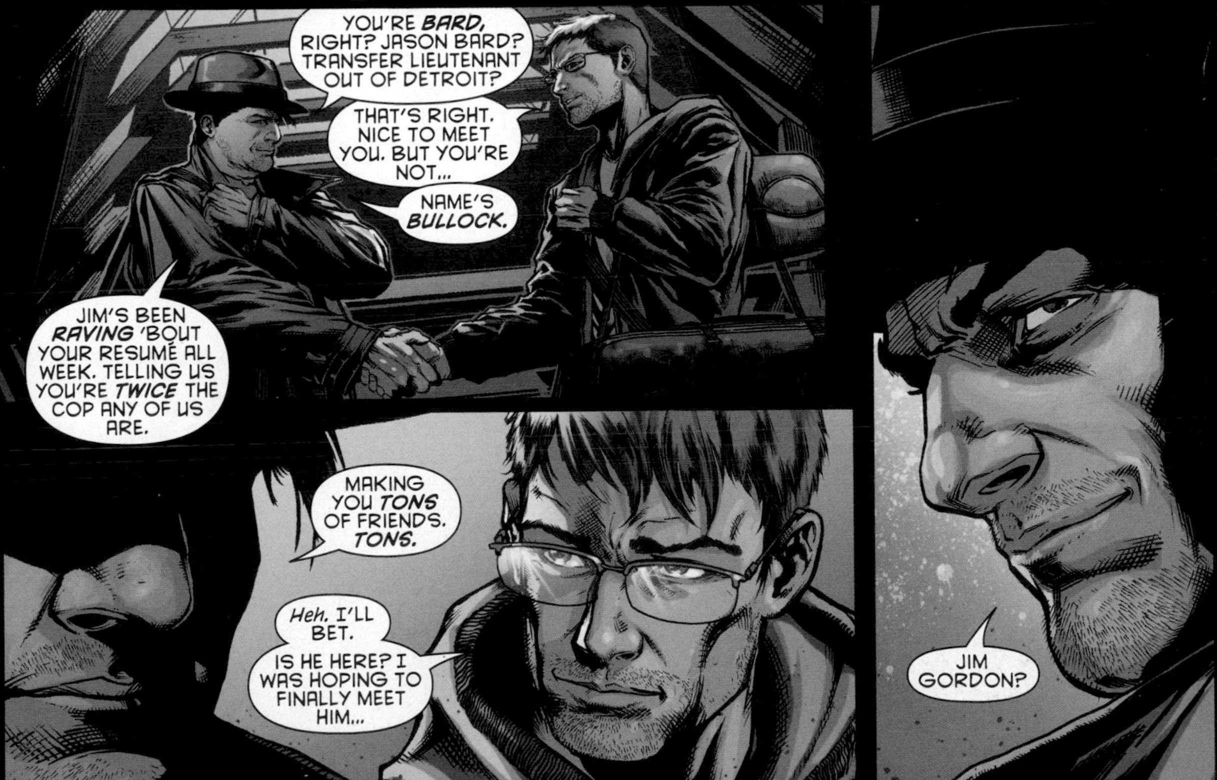
YOU'RE BARD, RIGHT? JASON BARD? TRANSFER LIEUTENANT OUT OF DETROIT?
THAT'S RIGHT. NICE TO MEET YOU. BUT YOU'RE NOT...
NAME'S BULLOCK.
JIM'S BEEN RAVING 'BOUT YOUR RESUMÉ ALL WEEK. TELLING US YOU'RE TWICE THE COP ANY OF US ARE.
MAKING YOU TONS OF FRIENDS. TONS.
Heh. I'LL BET.
IS HE HERE? I WAS HOPING TO FINALLY MEET HIM...
JIM GORDON?

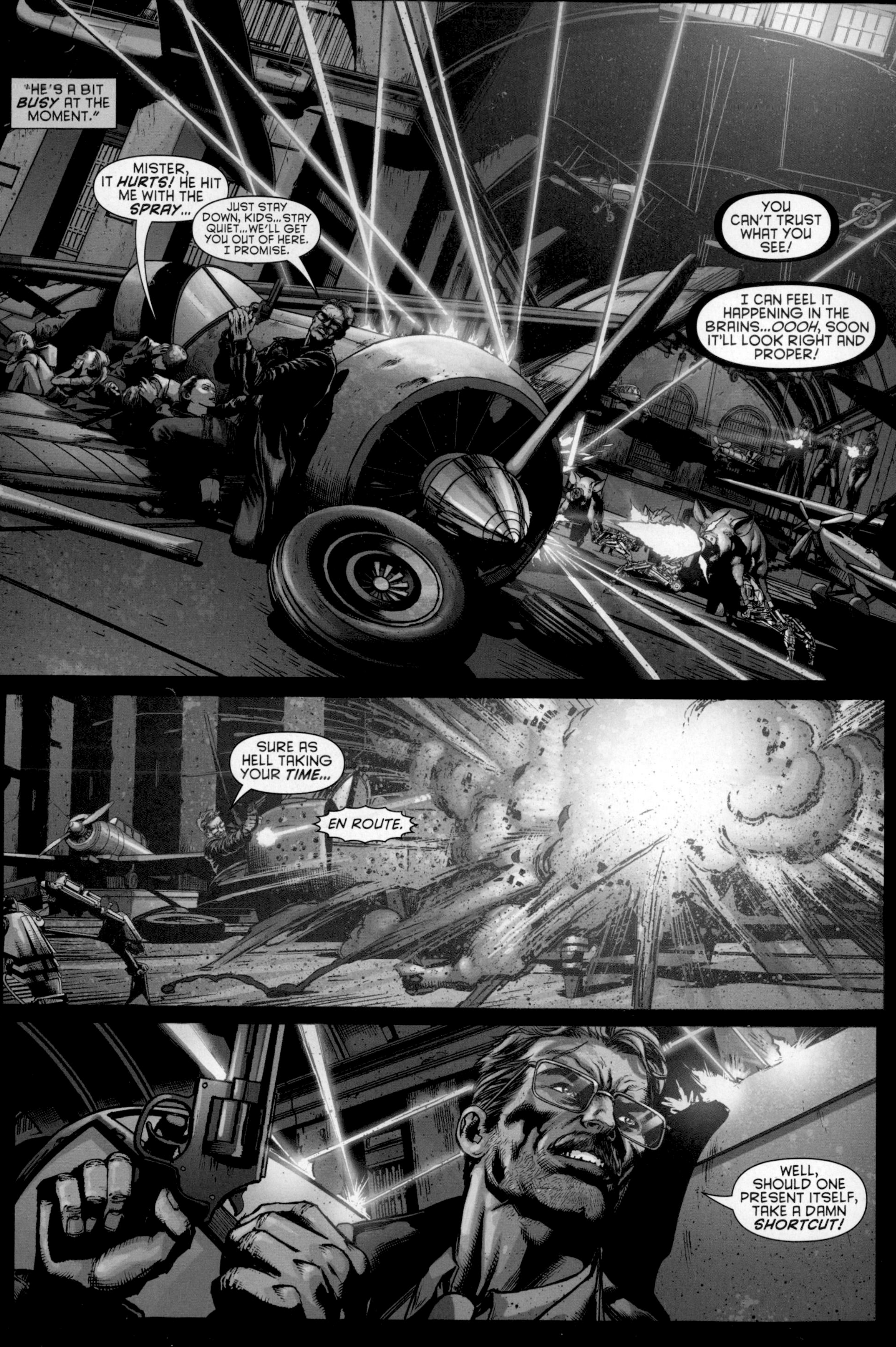
"HE'S A BIT *BUSY* AT THE MOMENT."
MISTER, IT *HURTS!* HE HIT ME WITH THE *SPRAY*...
JUST STAY DOWN, KIDS... STAY QUIET... WE'LL GET YOU OUT OF HERE. I PROMISE.
YOU CAN'T TRUST WHAT YOU SEE!
I CAN FEEL IT HAPPENING IN THE BRAINS... *OOOH*, SOON IT'LL LOOK RIGHT AND PROPER!
SURE AS HELL TAKING YOUR *TIME*...
EN ROUTE.
WELL, SHOULD ONE PRESENT ITSELF, TAKE A DAMN *SHORTCUT!*

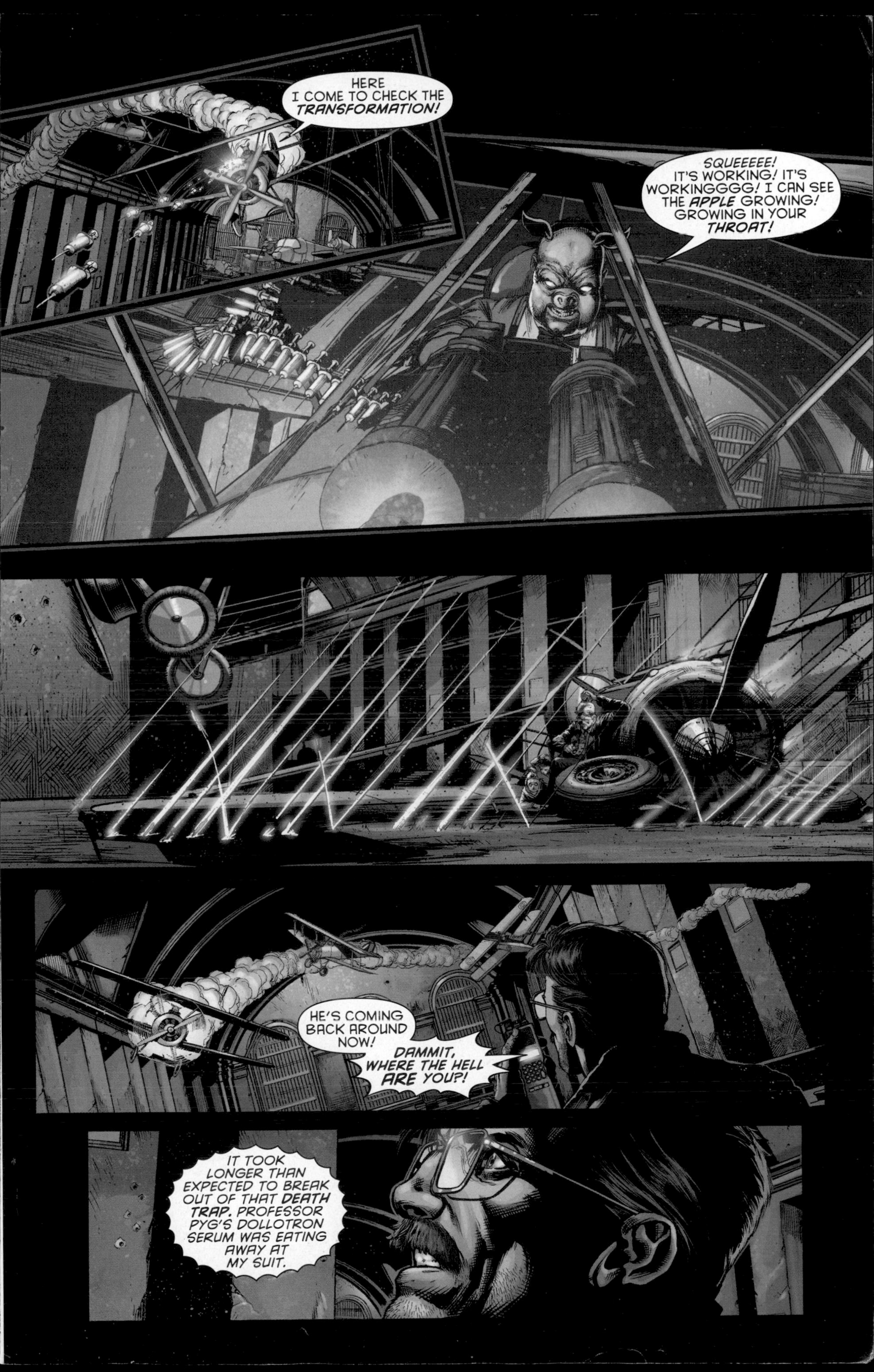
HERE I COME TO CHECK THE TRANSFORMATION!
SQUEEEEE! IT'S WORKING! IT'S WORKINGGGG! I CAN SEE THE APPLE GROWING! GROWING IN YOUR THROAT!
HE'S COMING BACK AROUND NOW!
DAMMIT, WHERE THE HELL ARE YOU?!
IT TOOK LONGER THAN EXPECTED TO BREAK OUT OF THAT DEATH TRAP. PROFESSOR PYG'S DOLLOTRON SERUM WAS EATING AWAY AT MY SUIT.

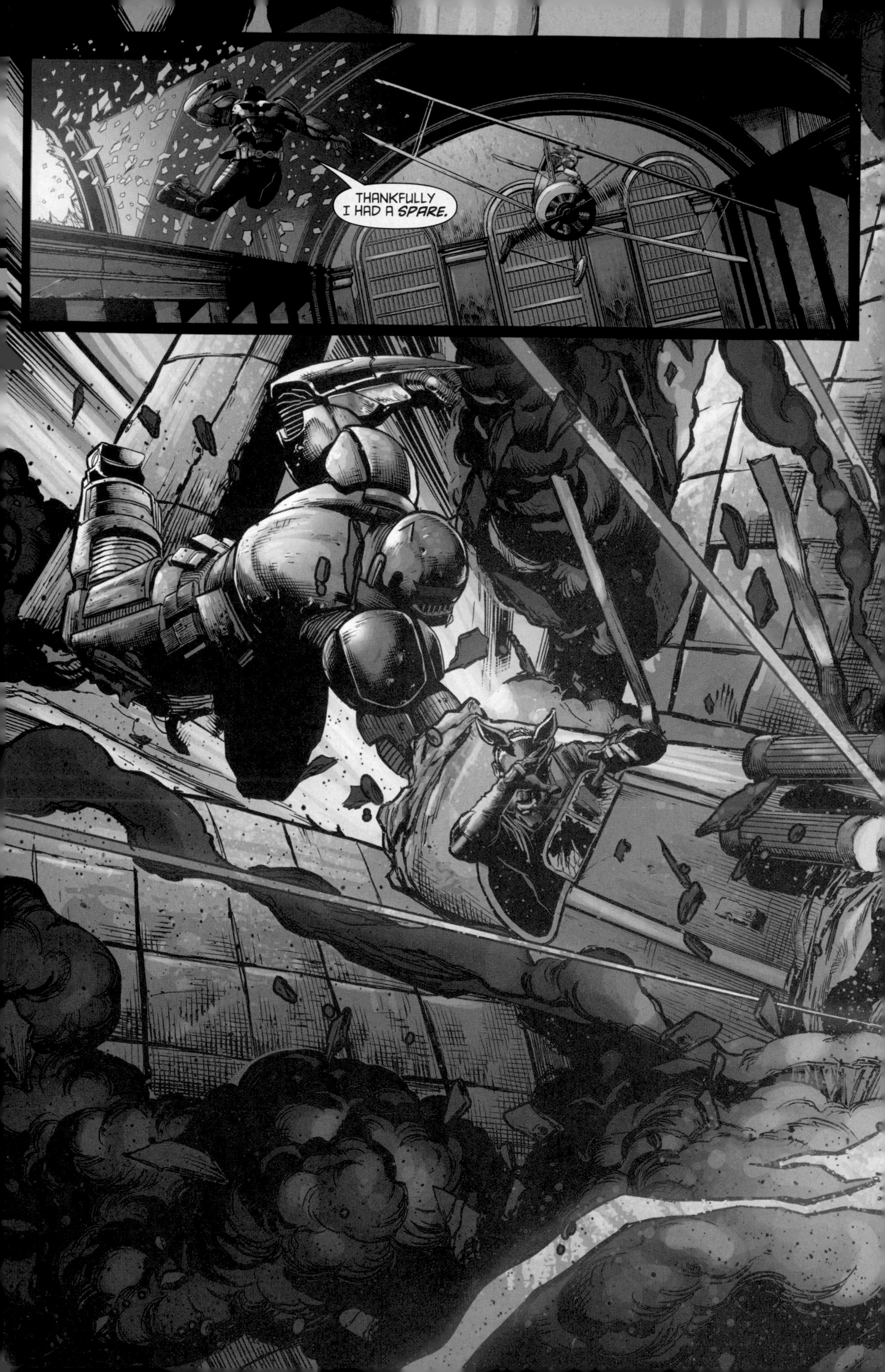
THANKFULLY I HAD A *SPARE.*

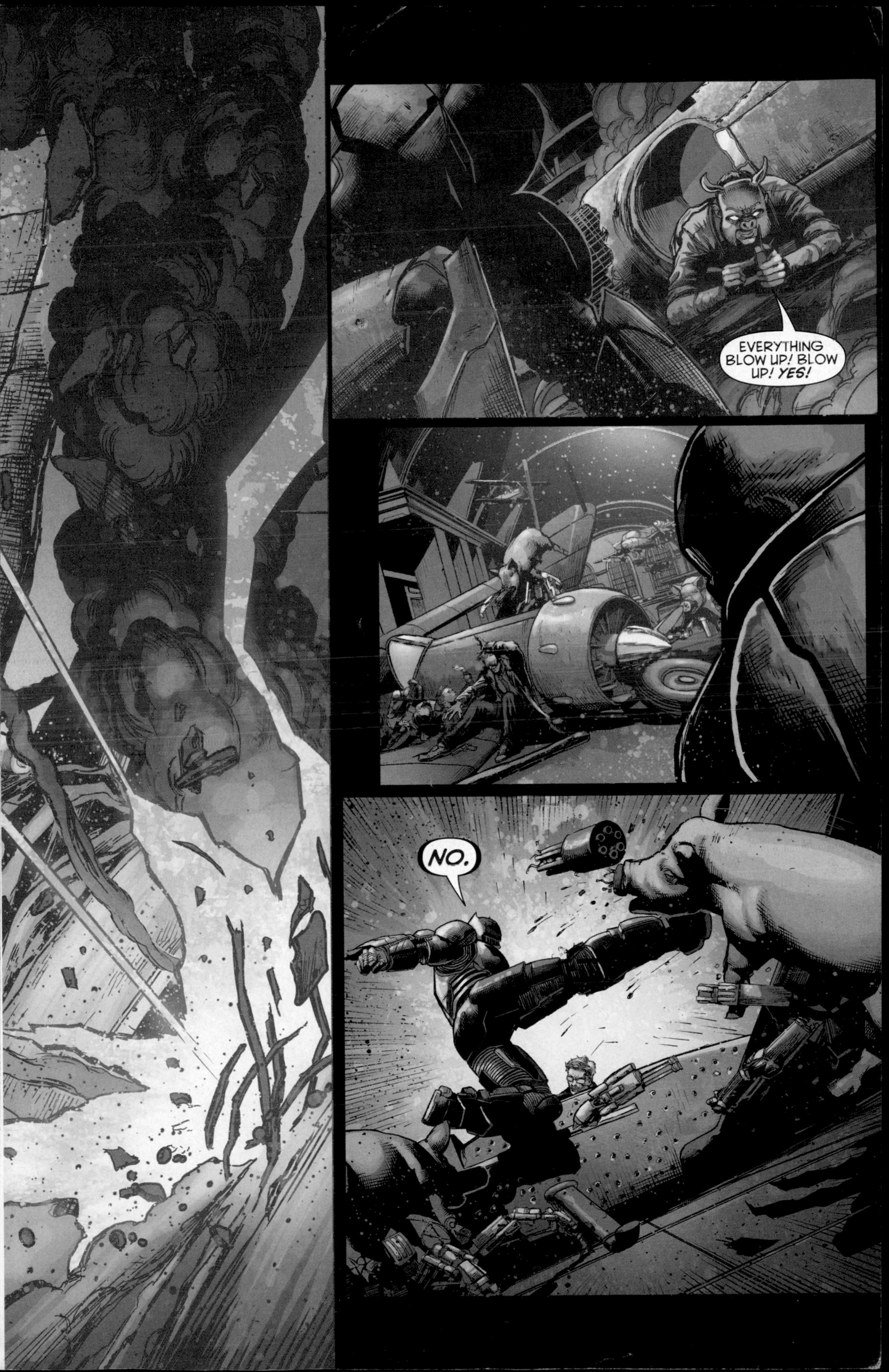
EVERYTHING BLOW UP! BLOW UP! YES!
NO.

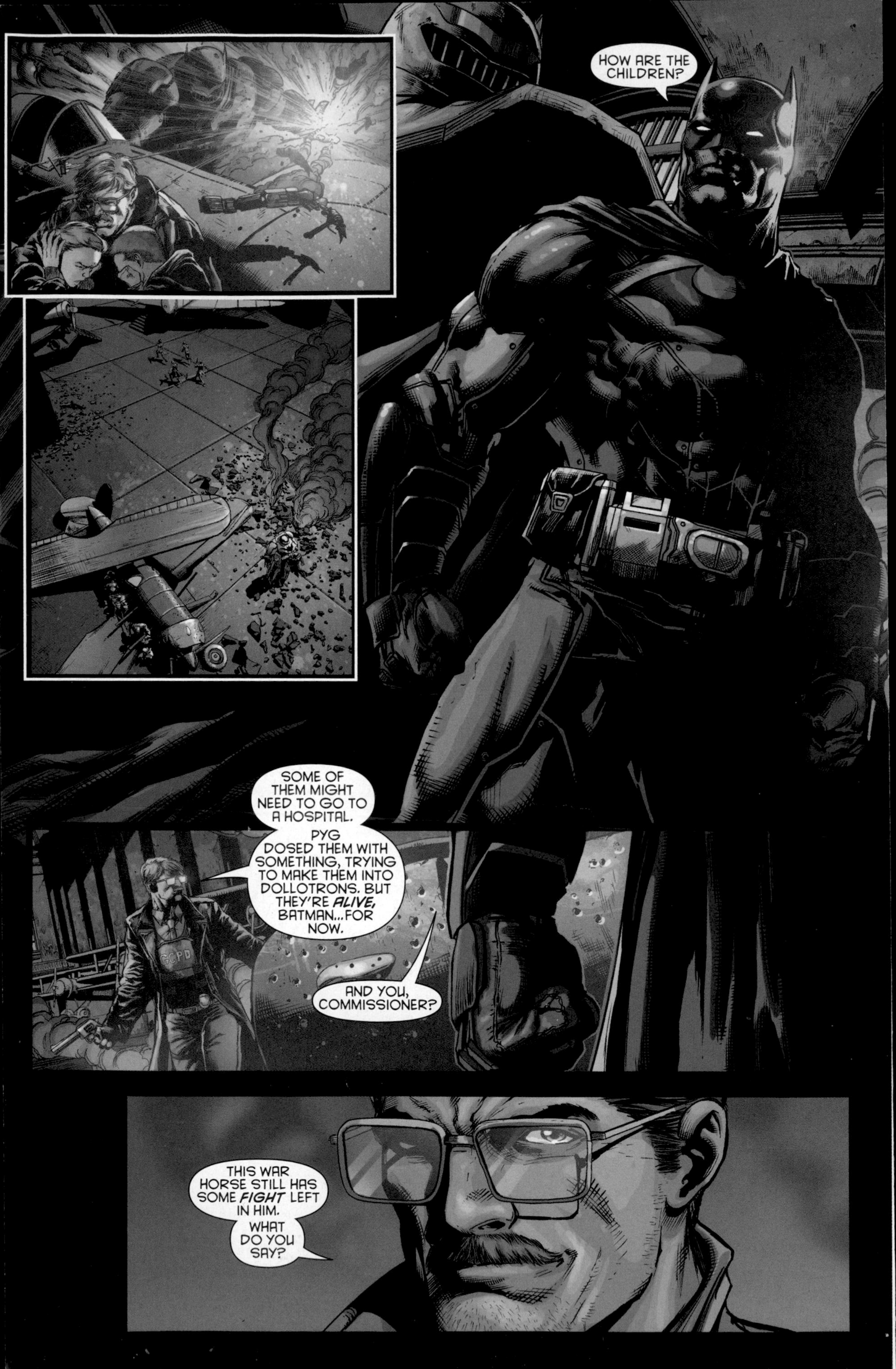
HOW ARE THE CHILDREN?
SOME OF THEM MIGHT NEED TO GO TO A HOSPITAL.
PYG DOSED THEM WITH SOMETHING, TRYING TO MAKE THEM INTO DOLLOTRONS. BUT THEY'RE *ALIVE,* BATMAN...FOR NOW.
AND YOU, COMMISSIONER?
THIS WAR HORSE STILL HAS SOME *FIGHT* LEFT IN HIM.
WHAT DO YOU SAY?

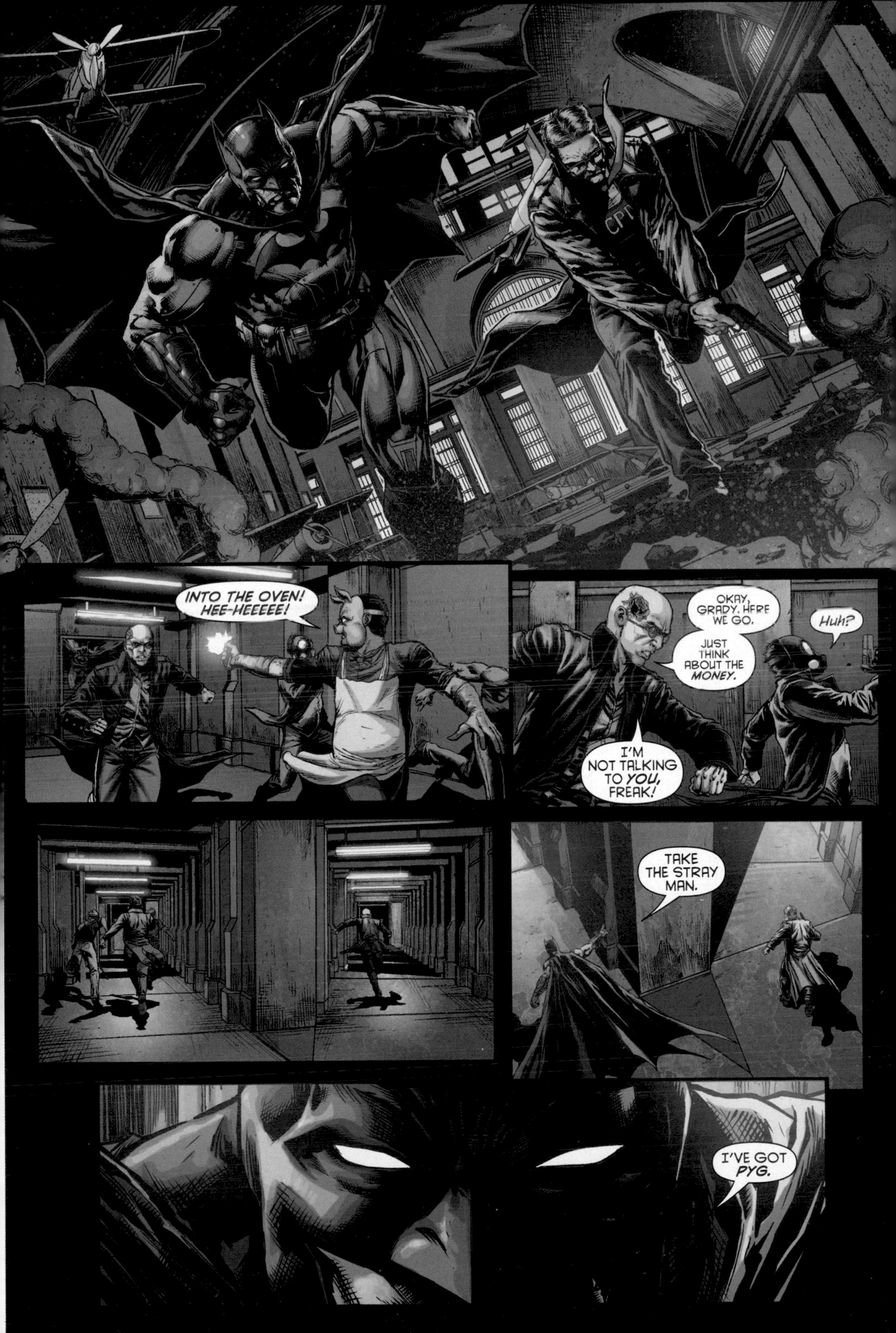
INTO THE OVEN! HEE-HEEEEE!
OKAY, GRADY. HERE WE GO.
JUST THINK ABOUT THE MONEY.
Huh?
I'M NOT TALKING TO YOU, FREAK!
TAKE THE STRAY MAN.
I'VE GOT PYG.

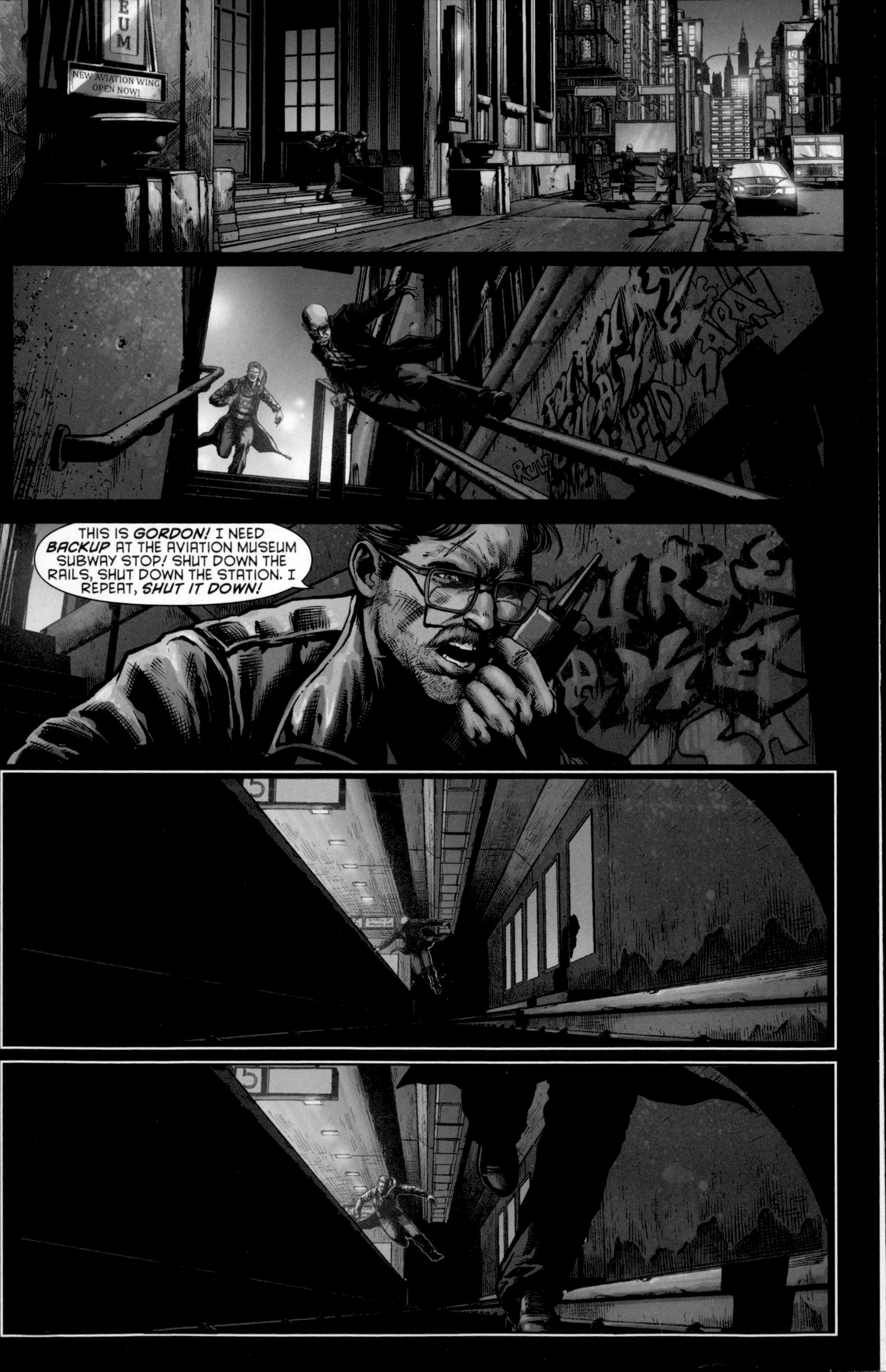

EUM
NEW AVIATION WING OPEN NOW!
THIS IS GORDON! I NEED BACKUP AT THE AVIATION MUSEUM SUBWAY STOP! SHUT DOWN THE RAILS, SHUT DOWN THE STATION. I REPEAT, SHUT IT DOWN!

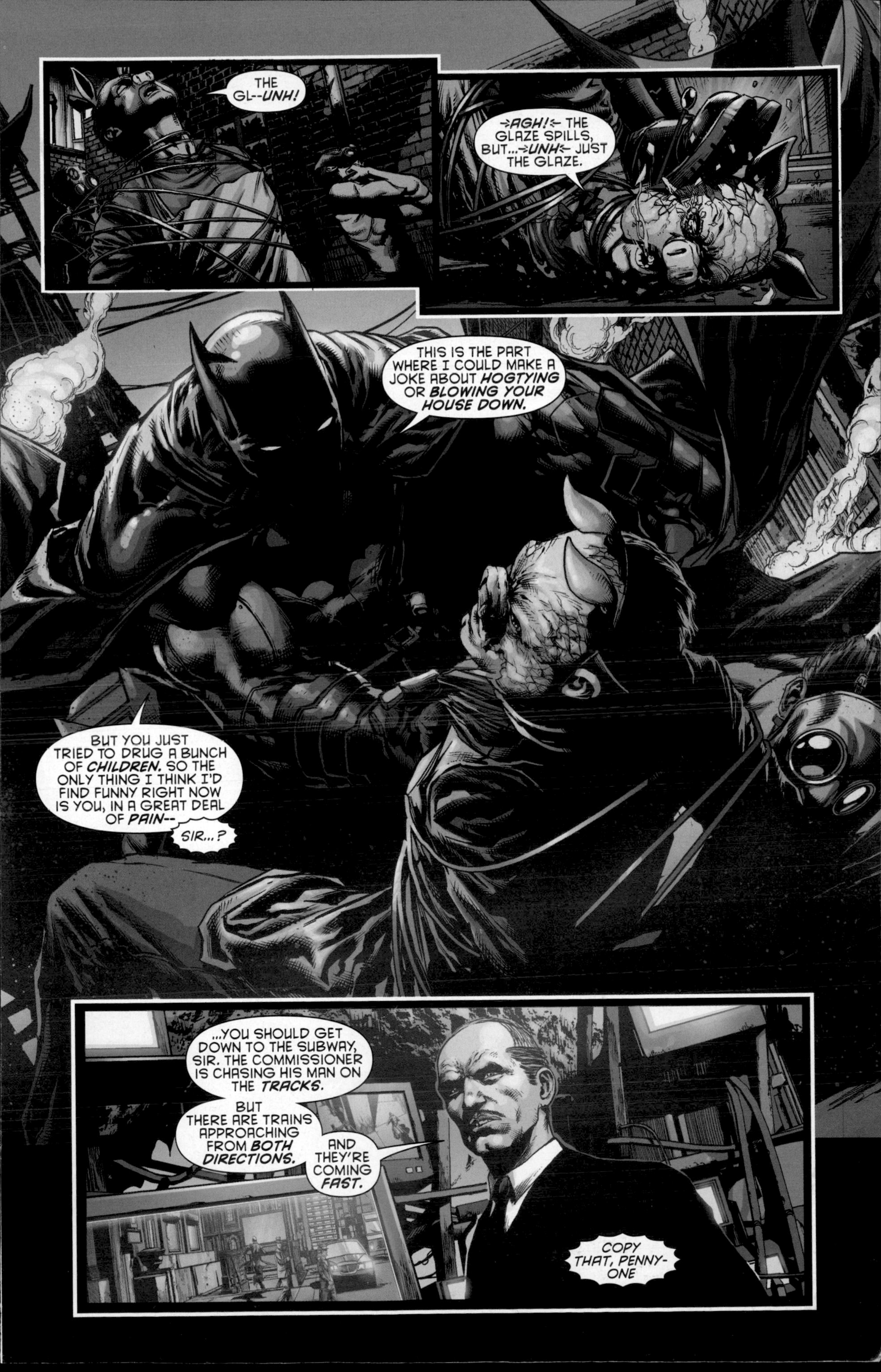
THE GL--UNH!
>AGH!< THE GLAZE SPILLS, BUT...>UNH< JUST THE GLAZE.
THIS IS THE PART WHERE I COULD MAKE A JOKE ABOUT HOGTYING OR BLOWING YOUR HOUSE DOWN.
BUT YOU JUST TRIED TO DRUG A BUNCH OF CHILDREN. SO THE ONLY THING I THINK I'D FIND FUNNY RIGHT NOW IS YOU, IN A GREAT DEAL OF PAIN--
SIR...?
...YOU SHOULD GET DOWN TO THE SUBWAY, SIR. THE COMMISSIONER IS CHASING HIS MAN ON THE TRACKS.
BUT THERE ARE TRAINS APPROACHING FROM BOTH DIRECTIONS.
AND THEY'RE COMING FAST.
COPY THAT, PENNY-ONE

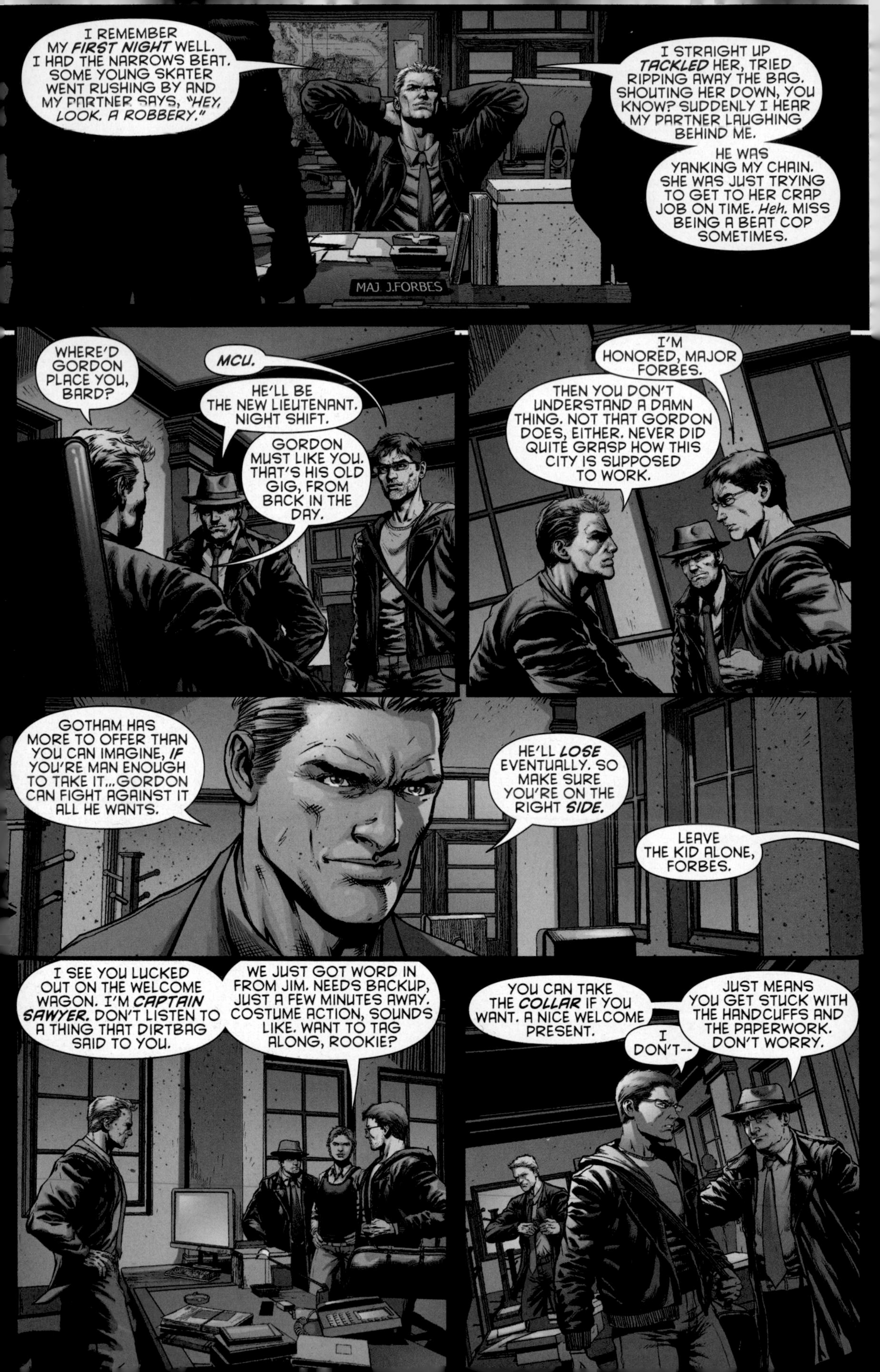
I REMEMBER MY FIRST NIGHT WELL. I HAD THE NARROWS BEAT. SOME YOUNG SKATER WENT RUSHING BY AND MY PARTNER SAYS, "HEY, LOOK. A ROBBERY."
I STRAIGHT UP TACKLED HER, TRIED RIPPING AWAY THE BAG. SHOUTING HER DOWN, YOU KNOW? SUDDENLY I HEAR MY PARTNER LAUGHING BEHIND ME.
HE WAS YANKING MY CHAIN. SHE WAS JUST TRYING TO GET TO HER CRAP JOB ON TIME. Heh. MISS BEING A BEAT COP SOMETIMES.
MAJ. J.FORBES
WHERE'D GORDON PLACE YOU, BARD?
MCU.
HE'LL BE THE NEW LIEUTENANT. NIGHT SHIFT.
GORDON MUST LIKE YOU. THAT'S HIS OLD GIG, FROM BACK IN THE DAY.
I'M HONORED, MAJOR FORBES.
THEN YOU DON'T UNDERSTAND A DAMN THING. NOT THAT GORDON DOES, EITHER. NEVER DID QUITE GRASP HOW THIS CITY IS SUPPOSED TO WORK.
GOTHAM HAS MORE TO OFFER THAN YOU CAN IMAGINE, IF YOU'RE MAN ENOUGH TO TAKE IT...GORDON CAN FIGHT AGAINST IT ALL HE WANTS.
HE'LL LOSE EVENTUALLY. SO MAKE SURE YOU'RE ON THE RIGHT SIDE.
LEAVE THE KID ALONE, FORBES.
I SEE YOU LUCKED OUT ON THE WELCOME WAGON. I'M CAPTAIN SAWYER. DON'T LISTEN TO A THING THAT DIRTBAG SAID TO YOU.
WE JUST GOT WORD IN FROM JIM. NEEDS BACKUP, JUST A FEW MINUTES AWAY. COSTUME ACTION, SOUNDS LIKE. WANT TO TAG ALONG, ROOKIE?
YOU CAN TAKE THE COLLAR IF YOU WANT. A NICE WELCOME PRESENT.
I DON'T--
JUST MEANS YOU GET STUCK WITH THE HANDCUFFS AND THE PAPERWORK. DON'T WORRY.

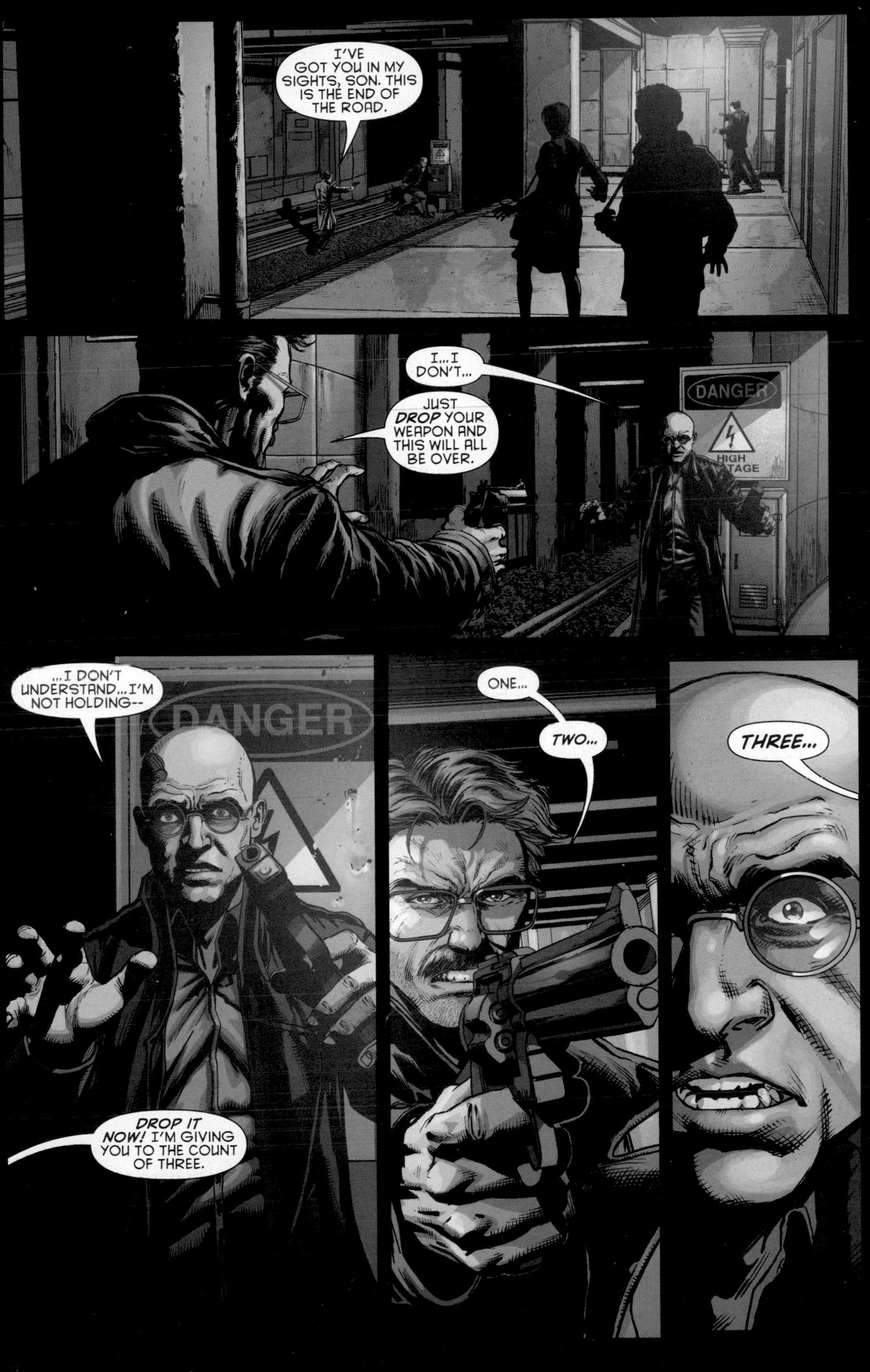

I'VE GOT YOU IN MY SIGHTS, SON. THIS IS THE END OF THE ROAD.
I...I DON'T...
JUST *DROP* YOUR WEAPON AND THIS WILL ALL BE OVER.
DANGER
HIGH
...I DON'T UNDERSTAND...I'M NOT HOLDING--
DANGER
DROP IT NOW! I'M GIVING YOU TO THE COUNT OF THREE.
ONE...
TWO...
THREE...

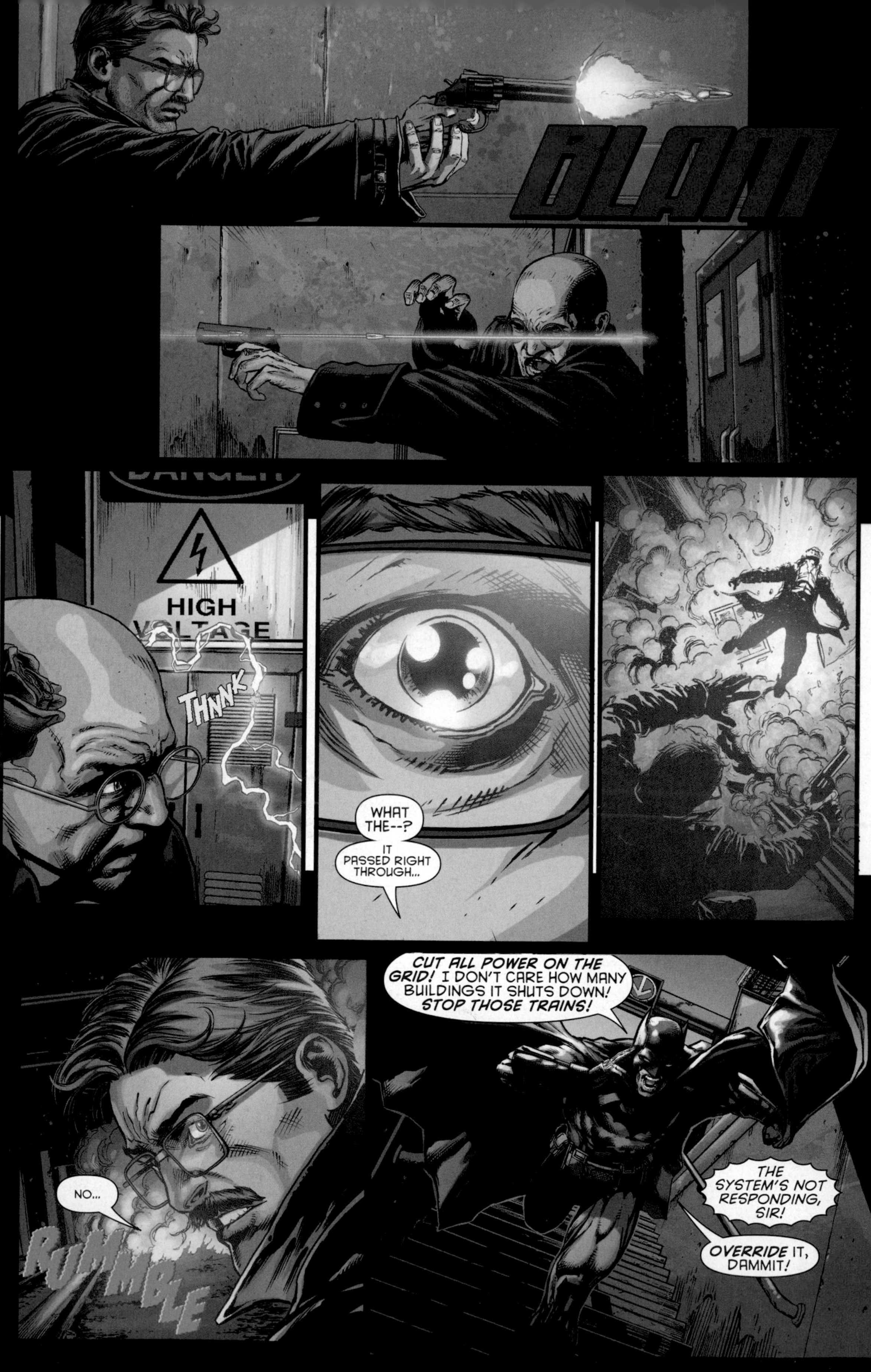
BLAM
DANGER
HIGH VOLTAGE
THNNK
WHAT THE--? IT PASSED RIGHT THROUGH...
NO...
RUMMBLE
CUT ALL POWER ON THE GRID! I DON'T CARE HOW MANY BUILDINGS IT SHUTS DOWN! STOP THOSE TRAINS!
THE SYSTEM'S NOT RESPONDING, SIR!
OVERRIDE IT, DAMMIT!

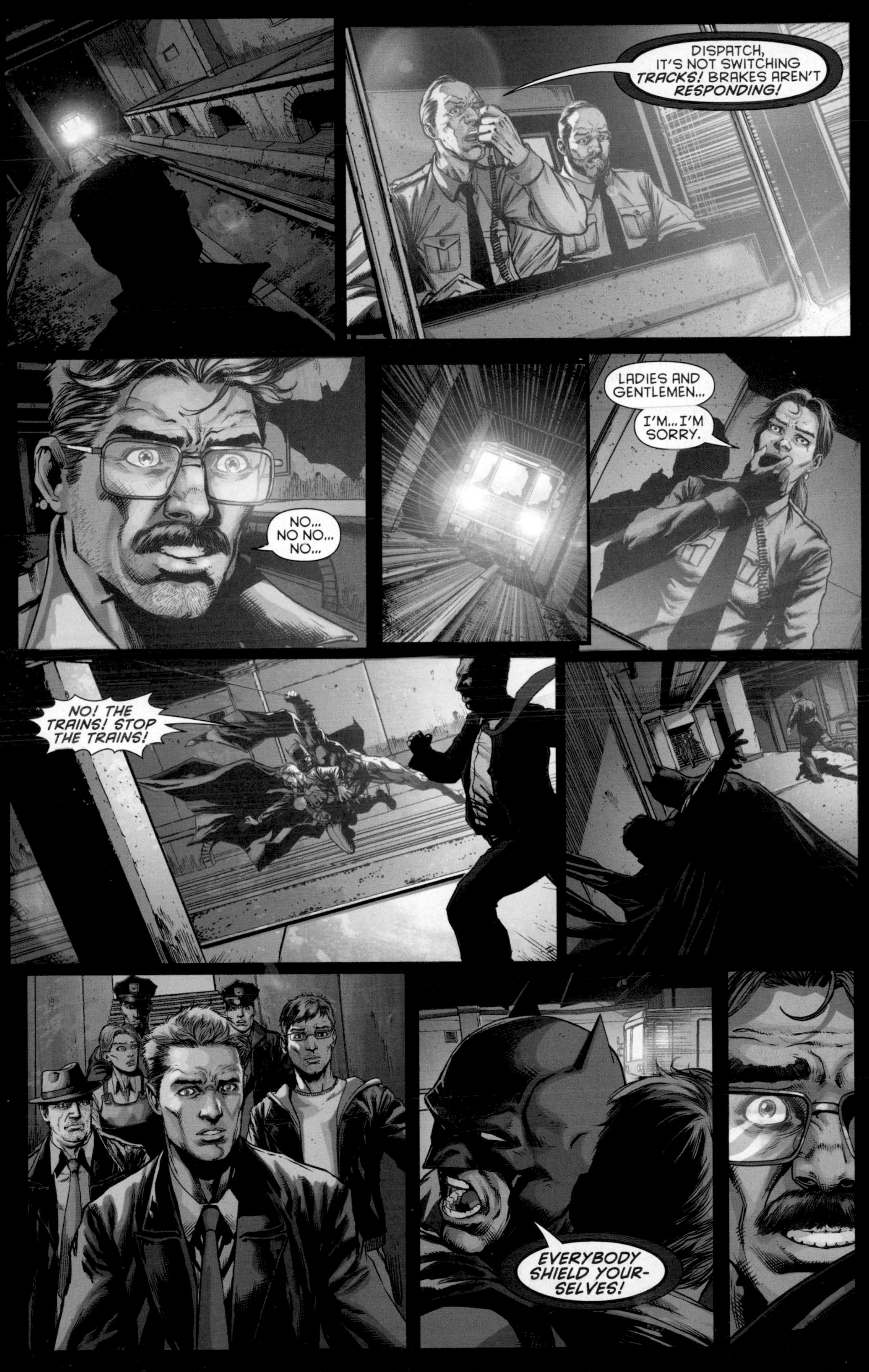
DISPATCH, IT'S NOT SWITCHING TRACKS! BRAKES AREN'T RESPONDING!
NO... NO NO... NO...
LADIES AND GENTLEMEN...
I'M... I'M SORRY.
NO! THE TRAINS! STOP THE TRAINS!
EVERYBODY SHIELD YOUR-SELVES!

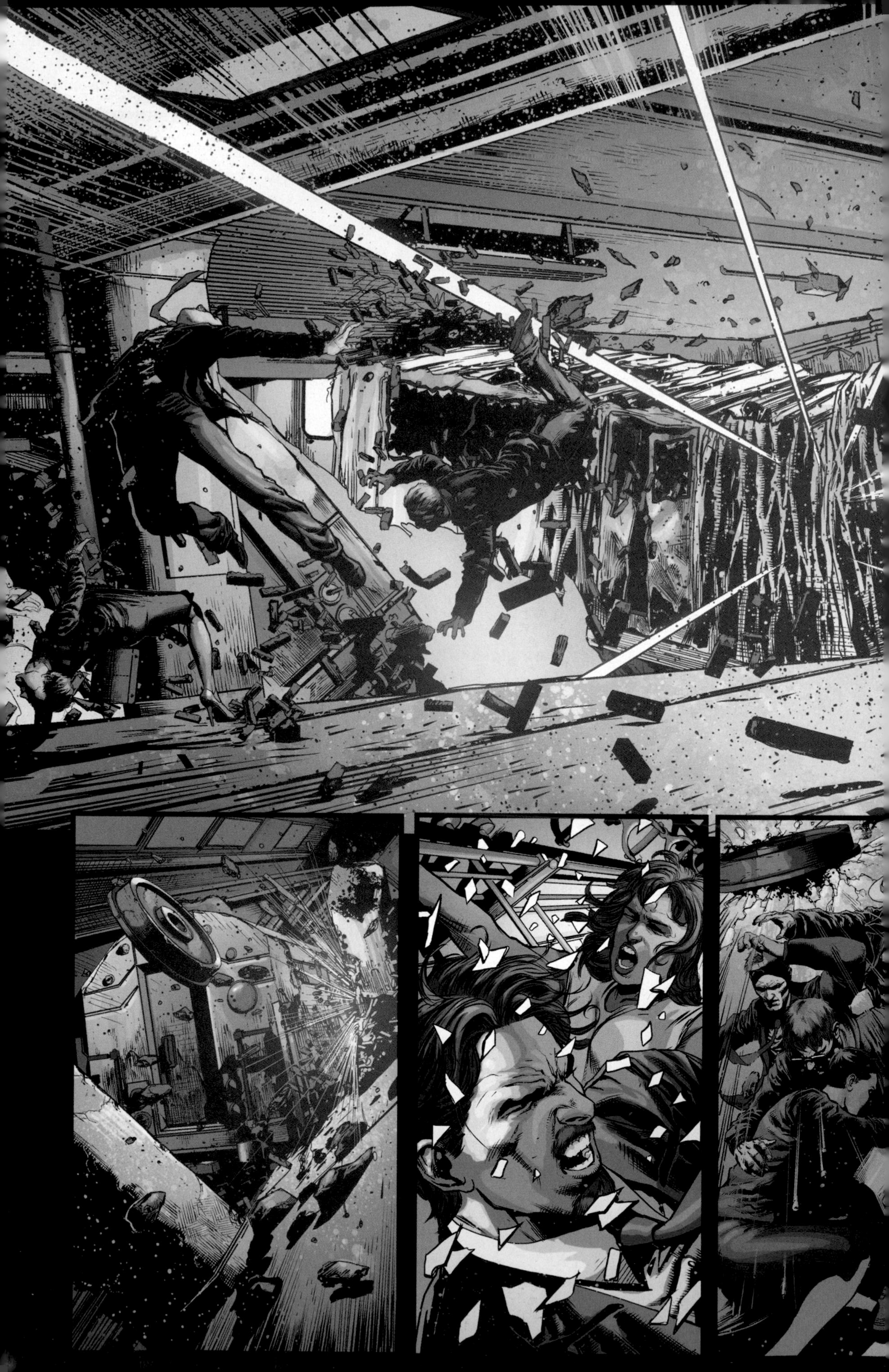

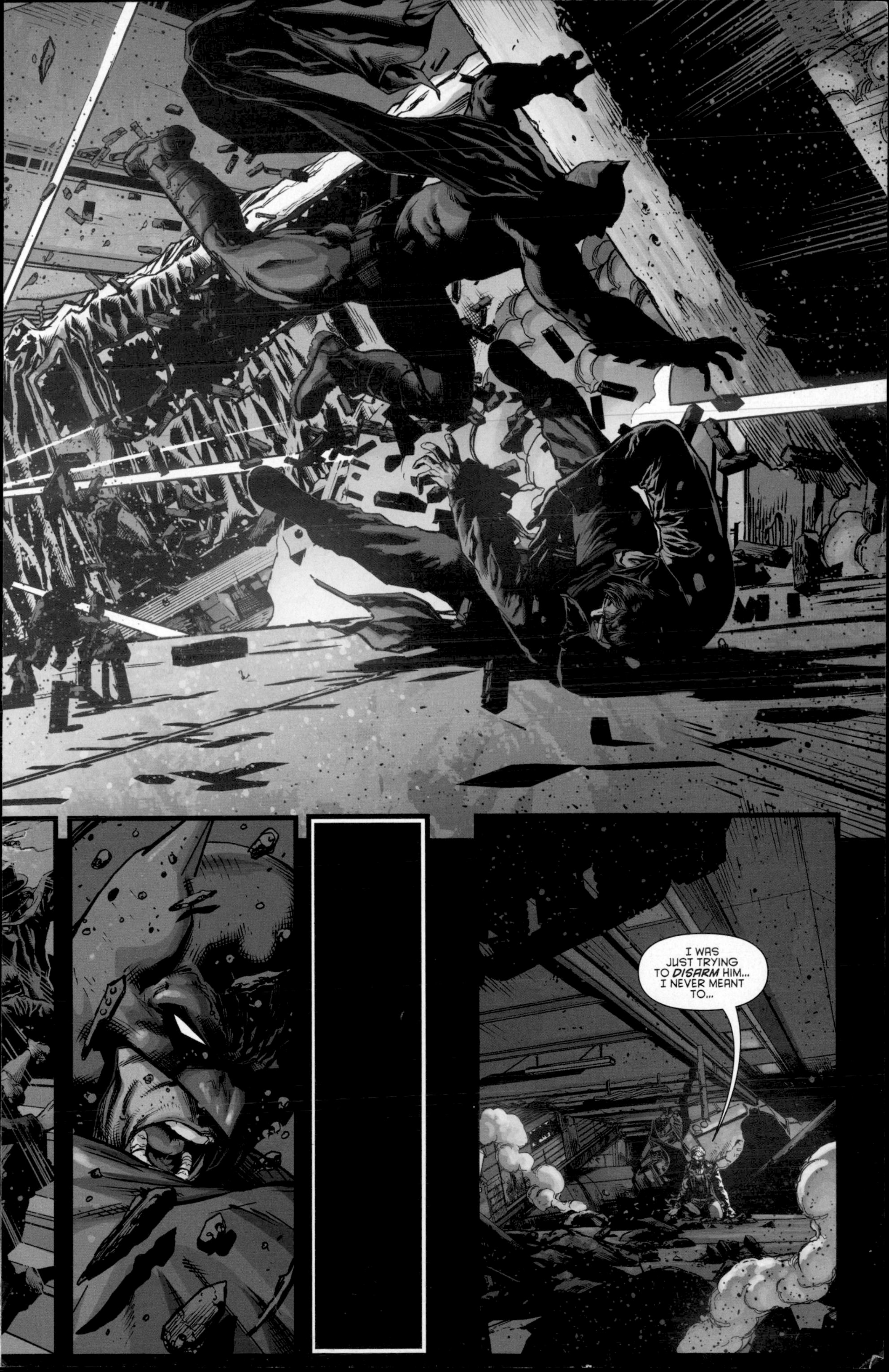
I WAS JUST TRYING TO *DISARM* HIM... I NEVER MEANT TO...

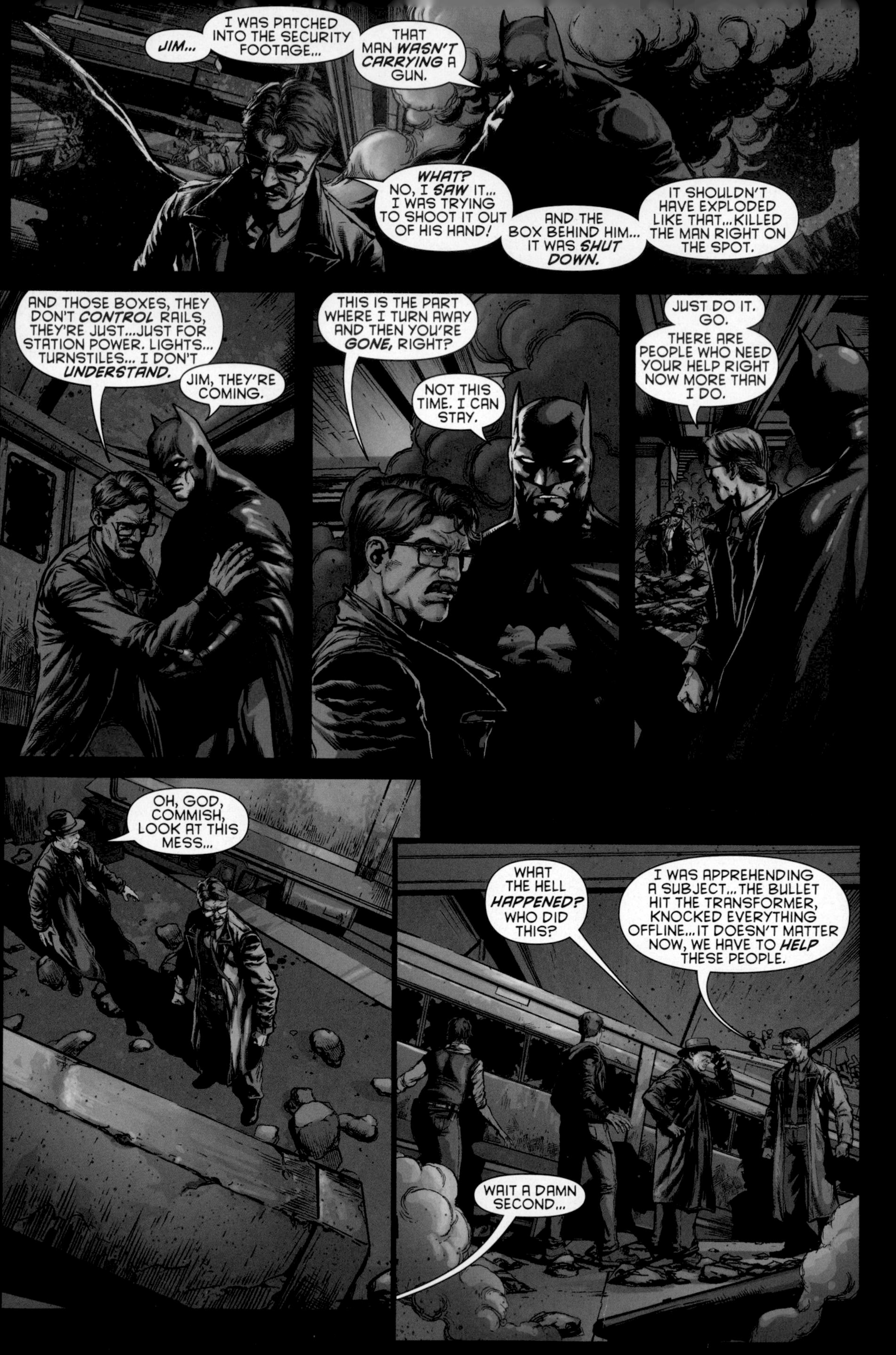
JIM...
I WAS PATCHED INTO THE SECURITY FOOTAGE...
THAT MAN WASN'T CARRYING A GUN.
WHAT? NO, I SAW IT... I WAS TRYING TO SHOOT IT OUT OF HIS HAND!
AND THE BOX BEHIND HIM... IT WAS SHUT DOWN.
IT SHOULDN'T HAVE EXPLODED LIKE THAT...KILLED THE MAN RIGHT ON THE SPOT.
AND THOSE BOXES, THEY DON'T CONTROL RAILS, THEY'RE JUST...JUST FOR STATION POWER. LIGHTS... TURNSTILES... I DON'T UNDERSTAND.
JIM, THEY'RE COMING.
THIS IS THE PART WHERE I TURN AWAY AND THEN YOU'RE GONE, RIGHT?
NOT THIS TIME. I CAN STAY.
JUST DO IT. GO.
THERE ARE PEOPLE WHO NEED YOUR HELP RIGHT NOW MORE THAN I DO.
OH, GOD, COMMISH, LOOK AT THIS MESS...
WHAT THE HELL HAPPENED? WHO DID THIS?
I WAS APPREHENDING A SUBJECT...THE BULLET HIT THE TRANSFORMER, KNOCKED EVERYTHING OFFLINE...IT DOESN'T MATTER NOW, WE HAVE TO HELP THESE PEOPLE.
WAIT A DAMN SECOND...

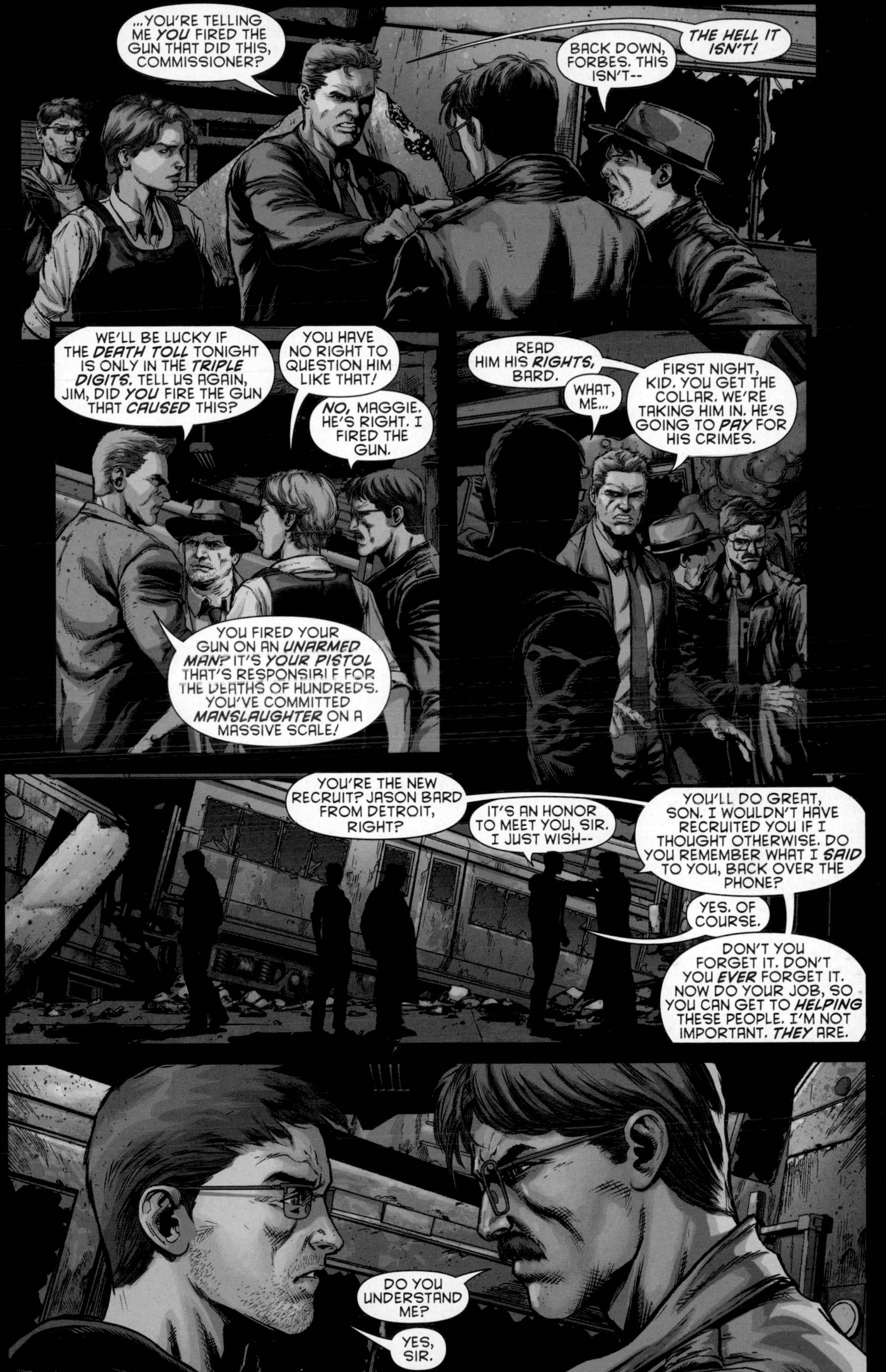
...YOU'RE TELLING ME YOU FIRED THE GUN THAT DID THIS, COMMISSIONER?
BACK DOWN, FORBES. THIS ISN'T--
THE HELL IT ISN'T!
WE'LL BE LUCKY IF THE DEATH TOLL TONIGHT IS ONLY IN THE TRIPLE DIGITS. TELL US AGAIN, JIM, DID YOU FIRE THE GUN THAT CAUSED THIS?
YOU HAVE NO RIGHT TO QUESTION HIM LIKE THAT!
NO, MAGGIE. HE'S RIGHT. I FIRED THE GUN.
YOU FIRED YOUR GUN ON AN UNARMED MAN? IT'S YOUR PISTOL THAT'S RESPONSIBLE FOR THE DEATHS OF HUNDREDS. YOU'VE COMMITTED MANSLAUGHTER ON A MASSIVE SCALE!
READ HIM HIS RIGHTS, BARD.
WHAT, ME...
FIRST NIGHT, KID. YOU GET THE COLLAR. WE'RE TAKING HIM IN. HE'S GOING TO PAY FOR HIS CRIMES.
YOU'RE THE NEW RECRUIT? JASON BARD FROM DETROIT, RIGHT?
IT'S AN HONOR TO MEET YOU, SIR. I JUST WISH--
YOU'LL DO GREAT, SON. I WOULDN'T HAVE RECRUITED YOU IF I THOUGHT OTHERWISE. DO YOU REMEMBER WHAT I SAID TO YOU, BACK OVER THE PHONE?
YES. OF COURSE.
DON'T YOU FORGET IT. DON'T YOU EVER FORGET IT. NOW DO YOUR JOB, SO YOU CAN GET TO HELPING THESE PEOPLE. I'M NOT IMPORTANT. THEY ARE.
DO YOU UNDERSTAND ME?
YES, SIR.

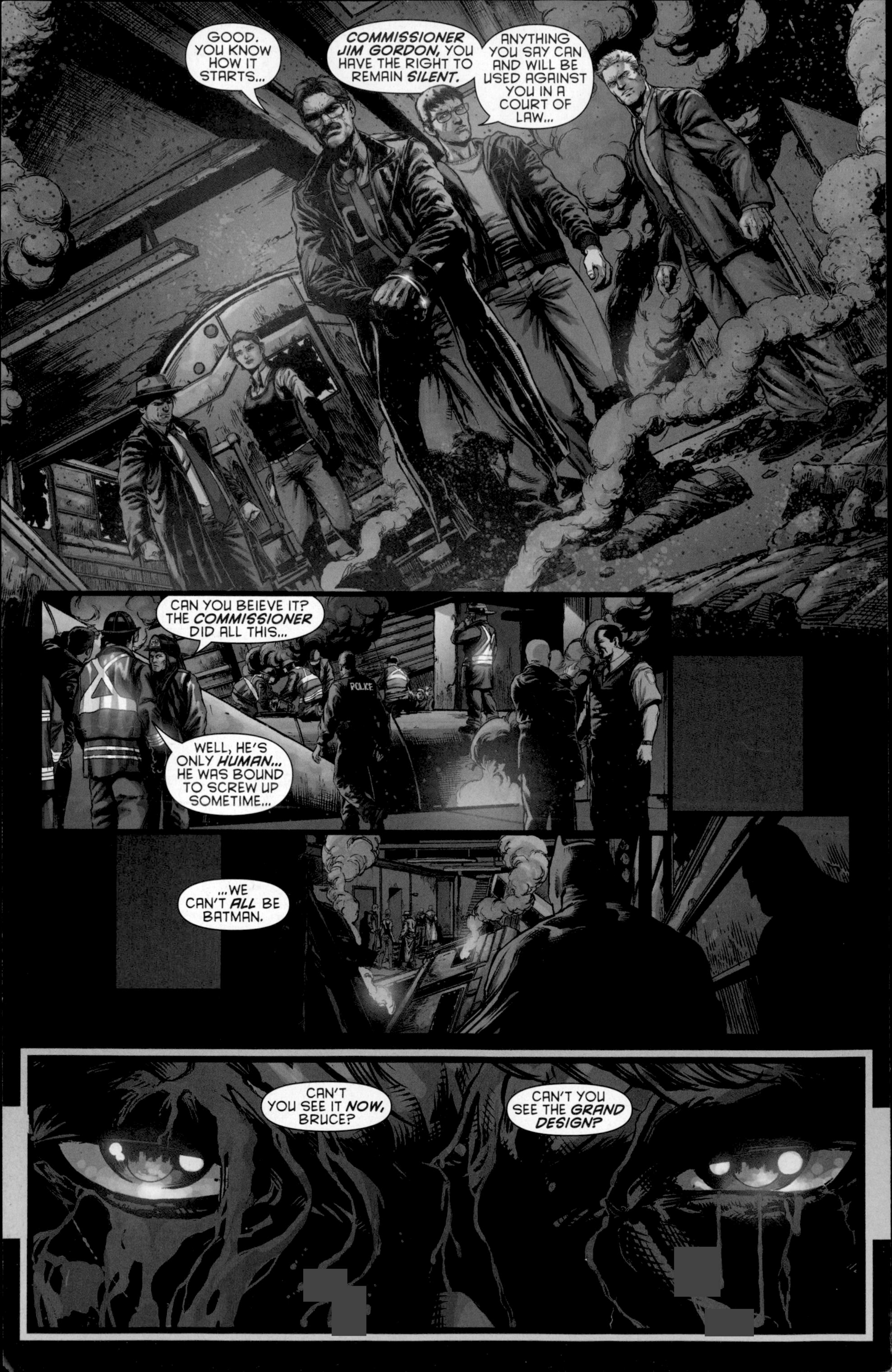
GOOD. YOU KNOW HOW IT STARTS...
COMMISSIONER JIM GORDON, YOU HAVE THE RIGHT TO REMAIN SILENT.
ANYTHING YOU SAY CAN AND WILL BE USED AGAINST YOU IN A COURT OF LAW...
CAN YOU BEIEVE IT? THE COMMISSIONER DID ALL THIS...
POLICE
WELL, HE'S ONLY HUMAN... HE WAS BOUND TO SCREW UP SOMETIME...
...WE CAN'T ALL BE BATMAN.
CAN'T YOU SEE IT NOW, BRUCE?
CAN'T YOU SEE THE GRAND DESIGN?

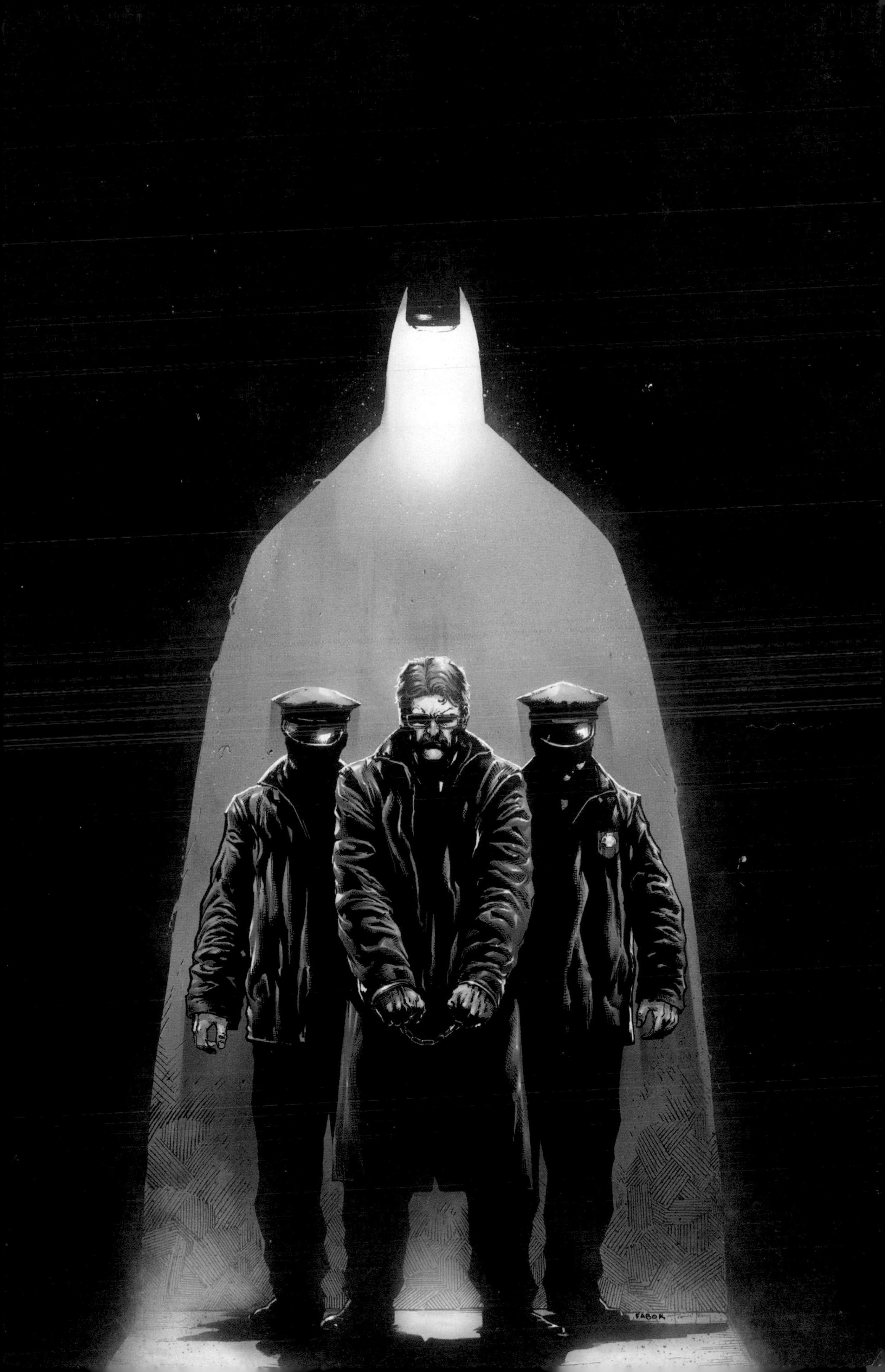
FABOK

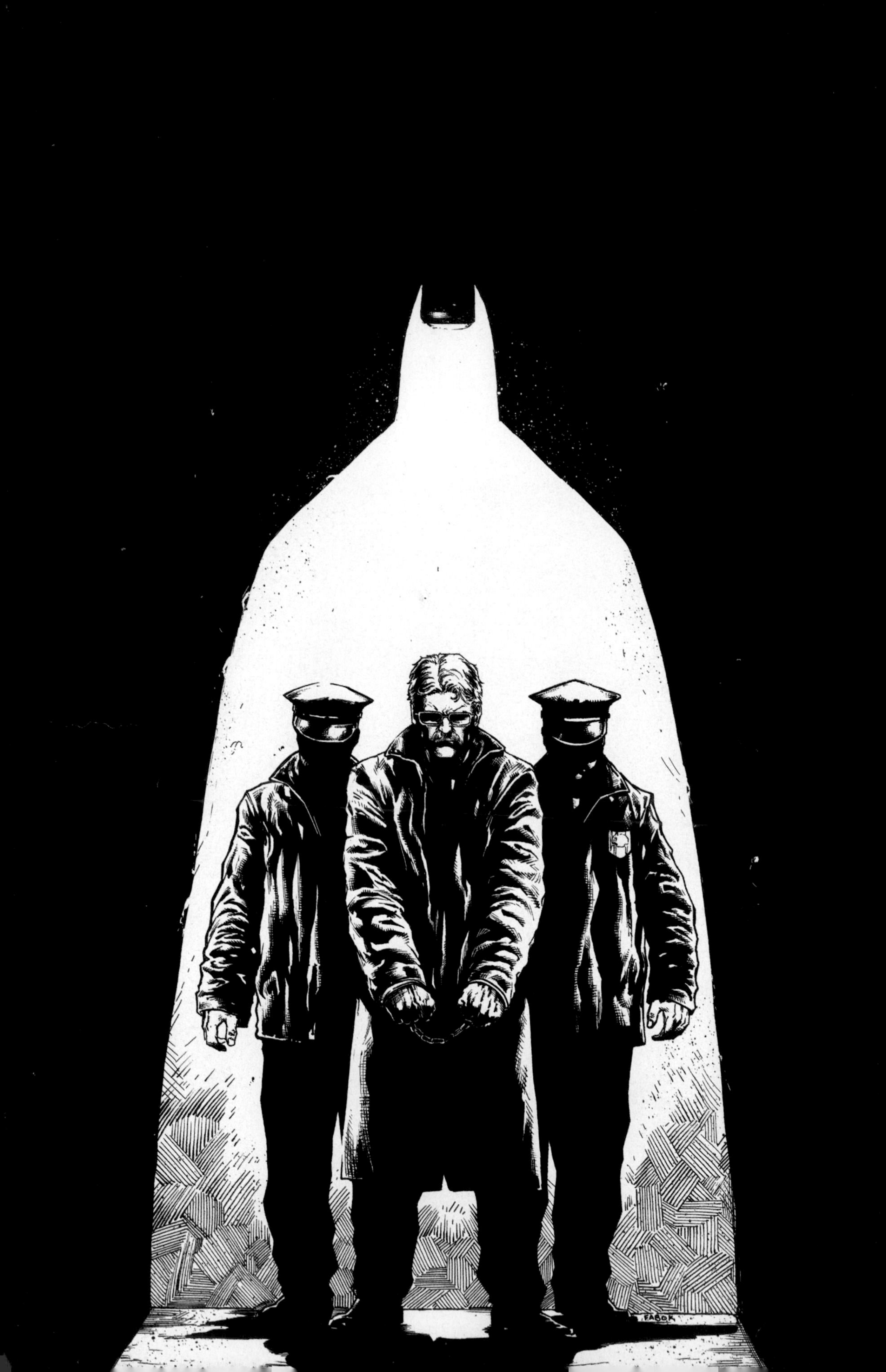
FABOK

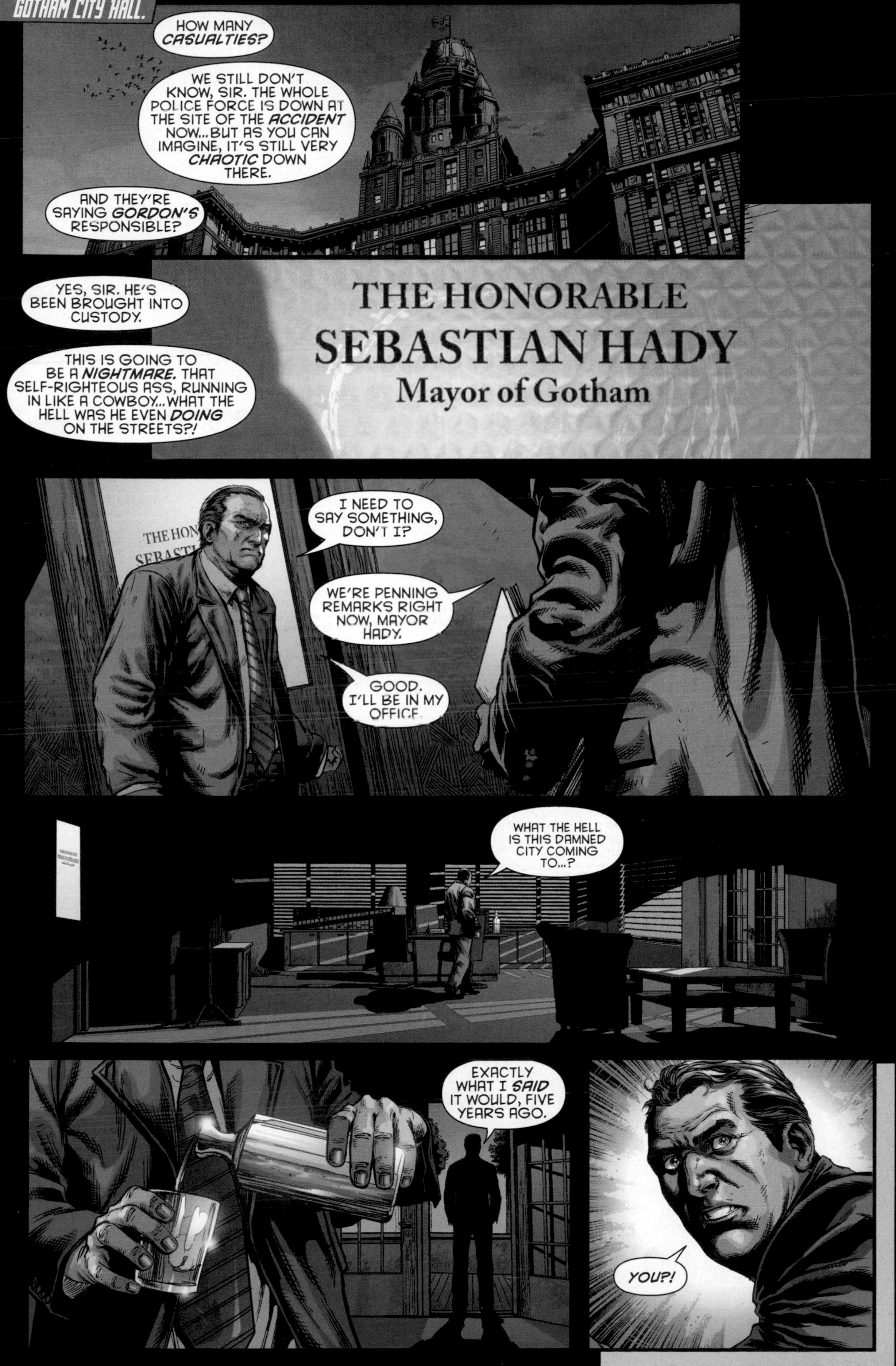
GOTHAM CITY HALL.
HOW MANY CASUALTIES?
WE STILL DON'T KNOW, SIR. THE WHOLE POLICE FORCE IS DOWN AT THE SITE OF THE ACCIDENT NOW...BUT AS YOU CAN IMAGINE, IT'S STILL VERY CHAOTIC DOWN THERE.
AND THEY'RE SAYING GORDON'S RESPONSIBLE?
YES, SIR. HE'S BEEN BROUGHT INTO CUSTODY.
THIS IS GOING TO BE A NIGHTMARE. THAT SELF-RIGHTEOUS ASS, RUNNING IN LIKE A COWBOY...WHAT THE HELL WAS HE EVEN DOING ON THE STREETS?!
THE HONORABLE
SEBASTIAN HADY
Mayor of Gotham
I NEED TO SAY SOMETHING, DON'T I?
WE'RE PENNING REMARKS RIGHT NOW, MAYOR HADY.
GOOD. I'LL BE IN MY OFFICE.
WHAT THE HELL IS THIS DAMNED CITY COMING TO...?
EXACTLY WHAT I SAID IT WOULD, FIVE YEARS AGO.
YOU?!

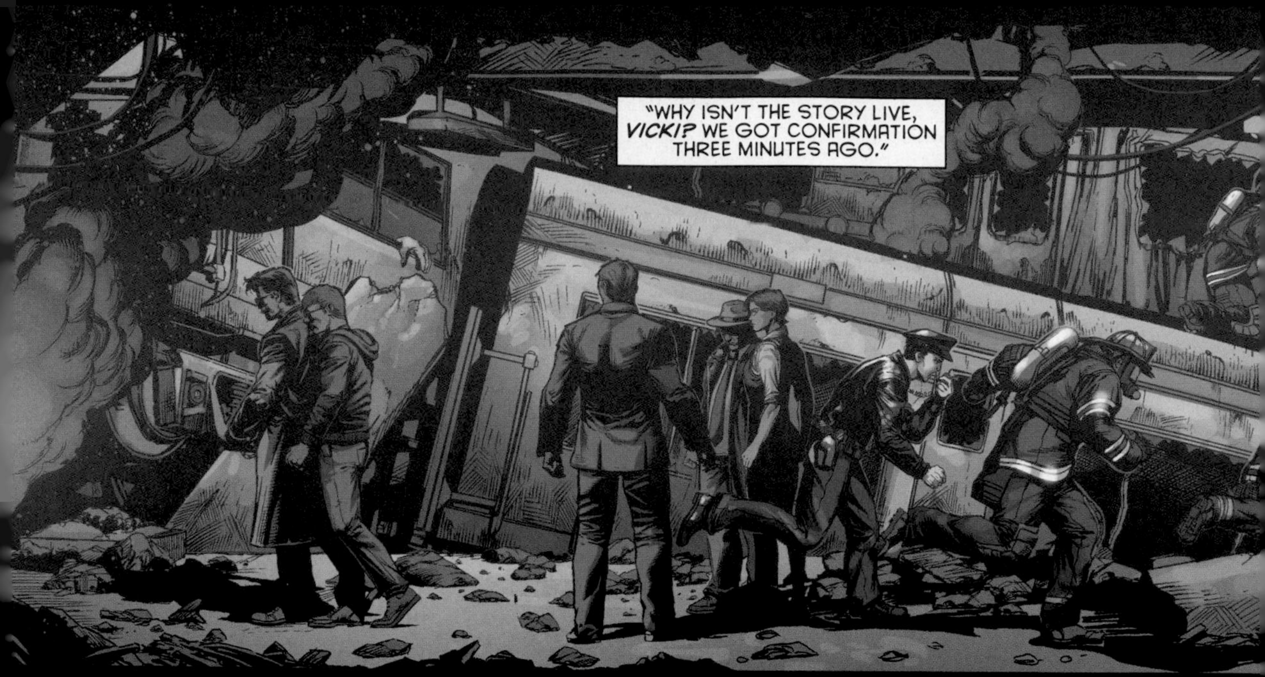
"WHY ISN'T THE STORY LIVE, VICKI? WE GOT CONFIRMATION THREE MINUTES AGO."

SCOTT SNYDER & JAMES TYNION IV STORY & SCRIPT
CONSULTING WRITERS: RAY FAWKES, JOHN LAYMAN & TIM SEELEY
ART BY: JASON FABOK

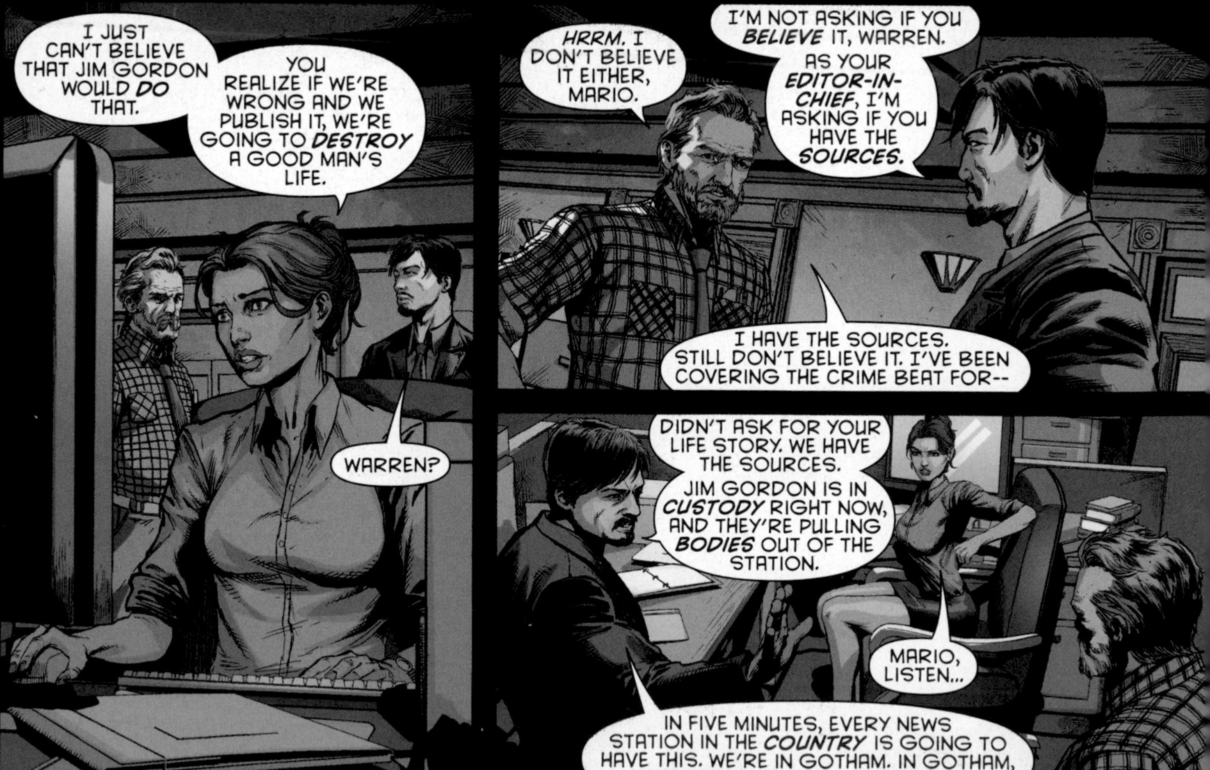
I JUST CAN'T BELIEVE THAT JIM GORDON WOULD DO THAT.
YOU REALIZE IF WE'RE WRONG AND WE PUBLISH IT, WE'RE GOING TO DESTROY A GOOD MAN'S LIFE.
WARREN?
HRRM. I DON'T BELIEVE IT EITHER, MARIO.
I'M NOT ASKING IF YOU BELIEVE IT, WARREN.
AS YOUR EDITOR-IN-CHIEF, I'M ASKING IF YOU HAVE THE SOURCES.
I HAVE THE SOURCES. STILL DON'T BELIEVE IT. I'VE BEEN COVERING THE CRIME BEAT FOR--
DIDN'T ASK FOR YOUR LIFE STORY. WE HAVE THE SOURCES.
JIM GORDON IS IN CUSTODY RIGHT NOW, AND THEY'RE PULLING BODIES OUT OF THE STATION.
MARIO, LISTEN...
IN FIVE MINUTES, EVERY NEWS STATION IN THE COUNTRY IS GOING TO HAVE THIS. WE'RE IN GOTHAM. IN GOTHAM, THE GAZETTE BREAKS THE NEWS.

COLORS BY: BRAD ANDERSON   LETTERING BY: NICK J. NAPOLITANO
COVER BY: JASON FABOK & TOMEU MOREY

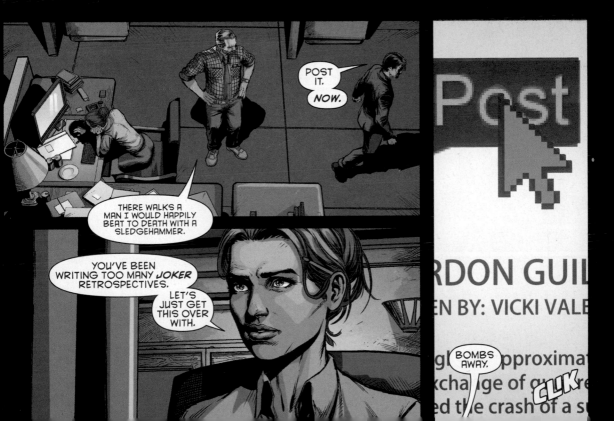

POST IT.
NOW.

THERE WALKS A MAN I WOULD HAPPILY BEAT TO DEATH WITH A SLEDGEHAMMER.

YOU'VE BEEN WRITING TOO MANY JOKER RETROSPECTIVES.

LET'S JUST GET THIS OVER WITH.

Post

RDON GUIL

EN BY: VICKI VALE

gh pproximat
xch ge of
d the crash of a s

BOMBS AWAY.

CLIK

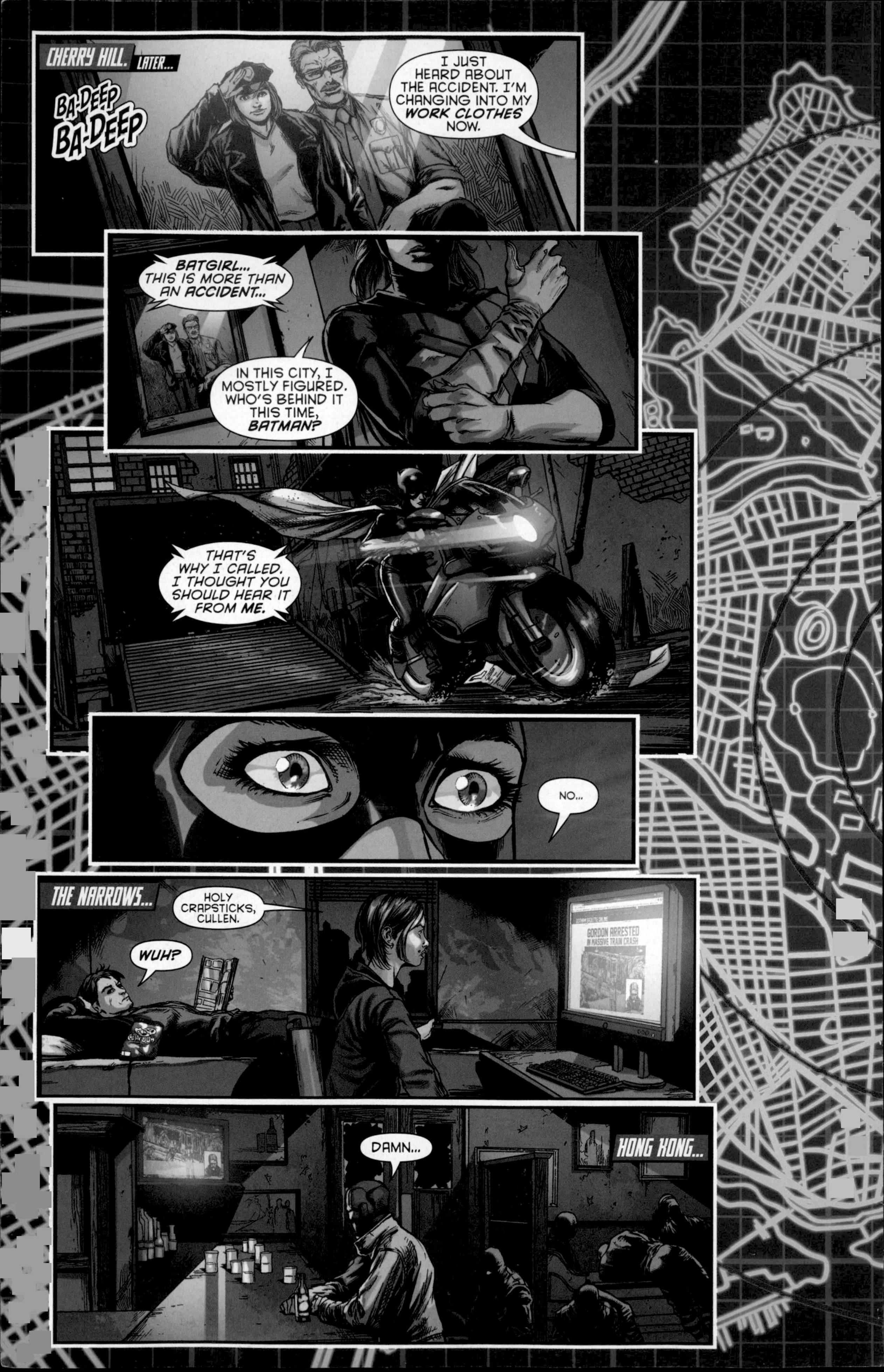

CHERRY HILL. LATER...
BA-DEEP BA-DEEP
I JUST HEARD ABOUT THE ACCIDENT. I'M CHANGING INTO MY WORK CLOTHES NOW.
BATGIRL... THIS IS MORE THAN AN ACCIDENT...
IN THIS CITY, I MOSTLY FIGURED. WHO'S BEHIND IT THIS TIME, BATMAN?
THAT'S WHY I CALLED. I THOUGHT YOU SHOULD HEAR IT FROM ME.
NO...
THE NARROWS...
HOLY CRAPSTICKS, CULLEN.
WUH?
GORDON ARRESTED
IN MASSIVE TRAIN CRASH
HONG KONG...
DAMN...

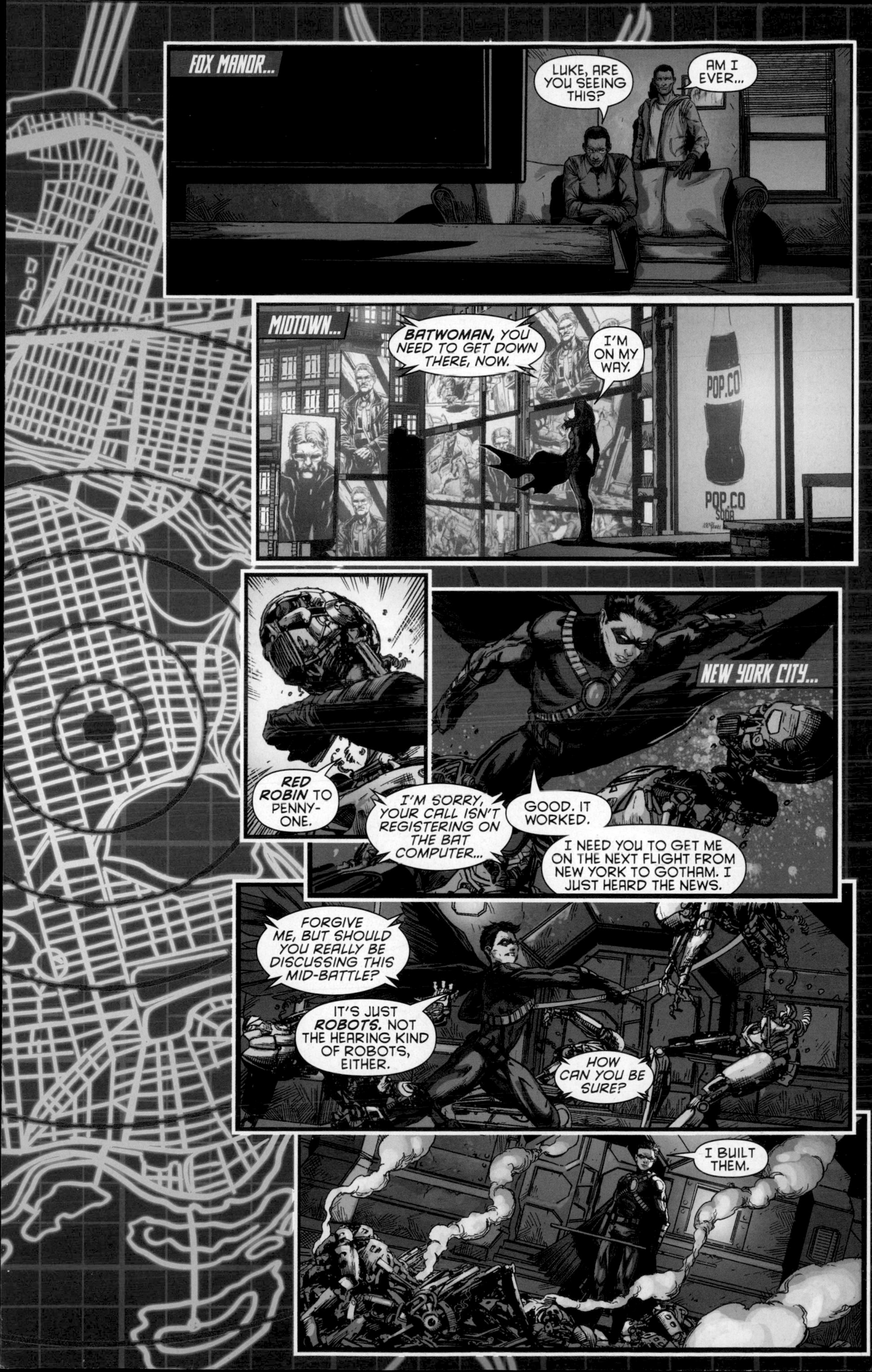
FOX MANOR...
LUKE, ARE YOU SEEING THIS?
AM I EVER...
MIDTOWN...
BATWOMAN, YOU NEED TO GET DOWN THERE, NOW.
I'M ON MY WAY.
POP.CO
POP.CO SODA
NEW YORK CITY...
RED ROBIN TO PENNY-ONE.
I'M SORRY, YOUR CALL ISN'T REGISTERING ON THE BAT COMPUTER...
GOOD. IT WORKED.
I NEED YOU TO GET ME ON THE NEXT FLIGHT FROM NEW YORK TO GOTHAM. I JUST HEARD THE NEWS.
FORGIVE ME, BUT SHOULD YOU REALLY BE DISCUSSING THIS MID-BATTLE?
IT'S JUST ROBOTS. NOT THE HEARING KIND OF ROBOTS, EITHER.
HOW CAN YOU BE SURE?
I BUILT THEM.

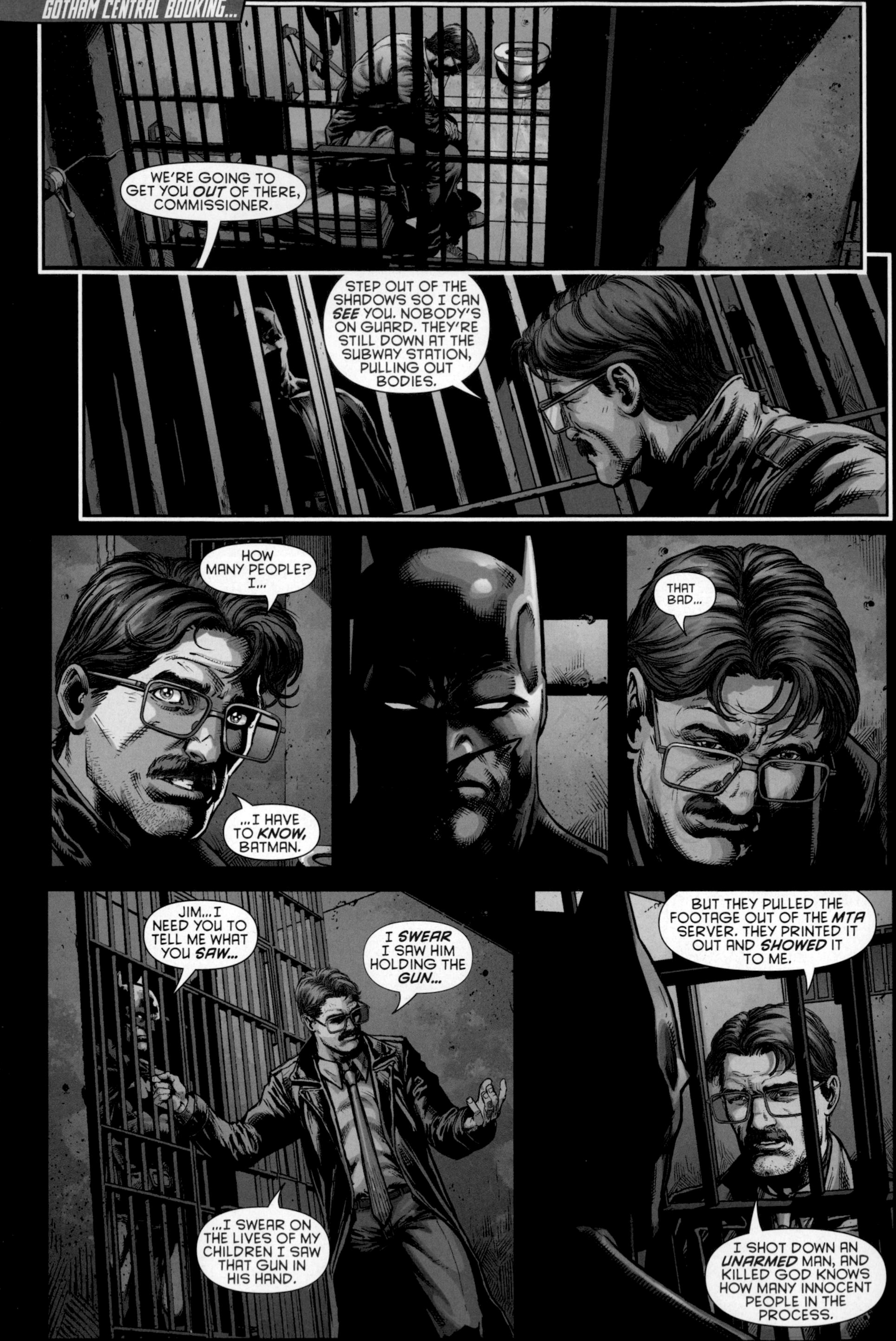
GOTHAM CENTRAL BOOKING...
WE'RE GOING TO GET YOU OUT OF THERE, COMMISSIONER.
STEP OUT OF THE SHADOWS SO I CAN SEE YOU. NOBODY'S ON GUARD. THEY'RE STILL DOWN AT THE SUBWAY STATION, PULLING OUT BODIES.
HOW MANY PEOPLE? I...
...I HAVE TO KNOW, BATMAN.
THAT BAD...
JIM...I NEED YOU TO TELL ME WHAT YOU SAW...
I SWEAR I SAW HIM HOLDING THE GUN...
...I SWEAR ON THE LIVES OF MY CHILDREN I SAW THAT GUN IN HIS HAND.
BUT THEY PULLED THE FOOTAGE OUT OF THE MTA SERVER. THEY PRINTED IT OUT AND SHOWED IT TO ME.
I SHOT DOWN AN UNARMED MAN, AND KILLED GOD KNOWS HOW MANY INNOCENT PEOPLE IN THE PROCESS.

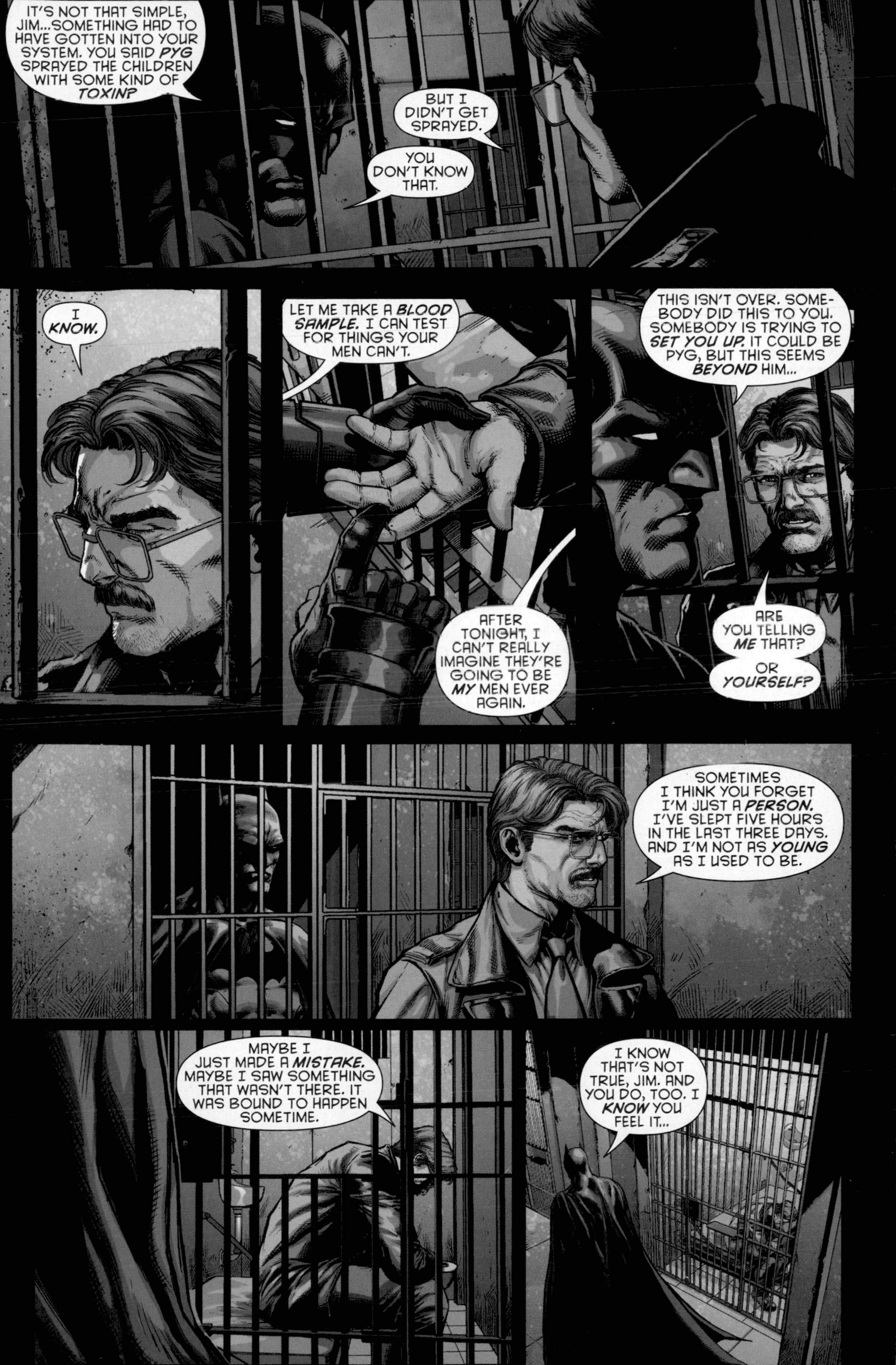
IT'S NOT THAT SIMPLE, JIM...SOMETHING HAD TO HAVE GOTTEN INTO YOUR SYSTEM. YOU SAID PYG SPRAYED THE CHILDREN WITH SOME KIND OF TOXIN?
BUT I DIDN'T GET SPRAYED.
YOU DON'T KNOW THAT.
I KNOW.
LET ME TAKE A BLOOD SAMPLE. I CAN TEST FOR THINGS YOUR MEN CAN'T.
AFTER TONIGHT, I CAN'T REALLY IMAGINE THEY'RE GOING TO BE MY MEN EVER AGAIN.
THIS ISN'T OVER. SOMEBODY DID THIS TO YOU. SOMEBODY IS TRYING TO SET YOU UP. IT COULD BE PYG, BUT THIS SEEMS BEYOND HIM...
ARE YOU TELLING ME THAT?
OR YOURSELF?
SOMETIMES I THINK YOU FORGET I'M JUST A PERSON. I'VE SLEPT FIVE HOURS IN THE LAST THREE DAYS. AND I'M NOT AS YOUNG AS I USED TO BE.
MAYBE I JUST MADE A MISTAKE. MAYBE I SAW SOMETHING THAT WASN'T THERE. IT WAS BOUND TO HAPPEN SOMETIME.
I KNOW THAT'S NOT TRUE, JIM. AND YOU DO, TOO. I KNOW YOU FEEL IT...

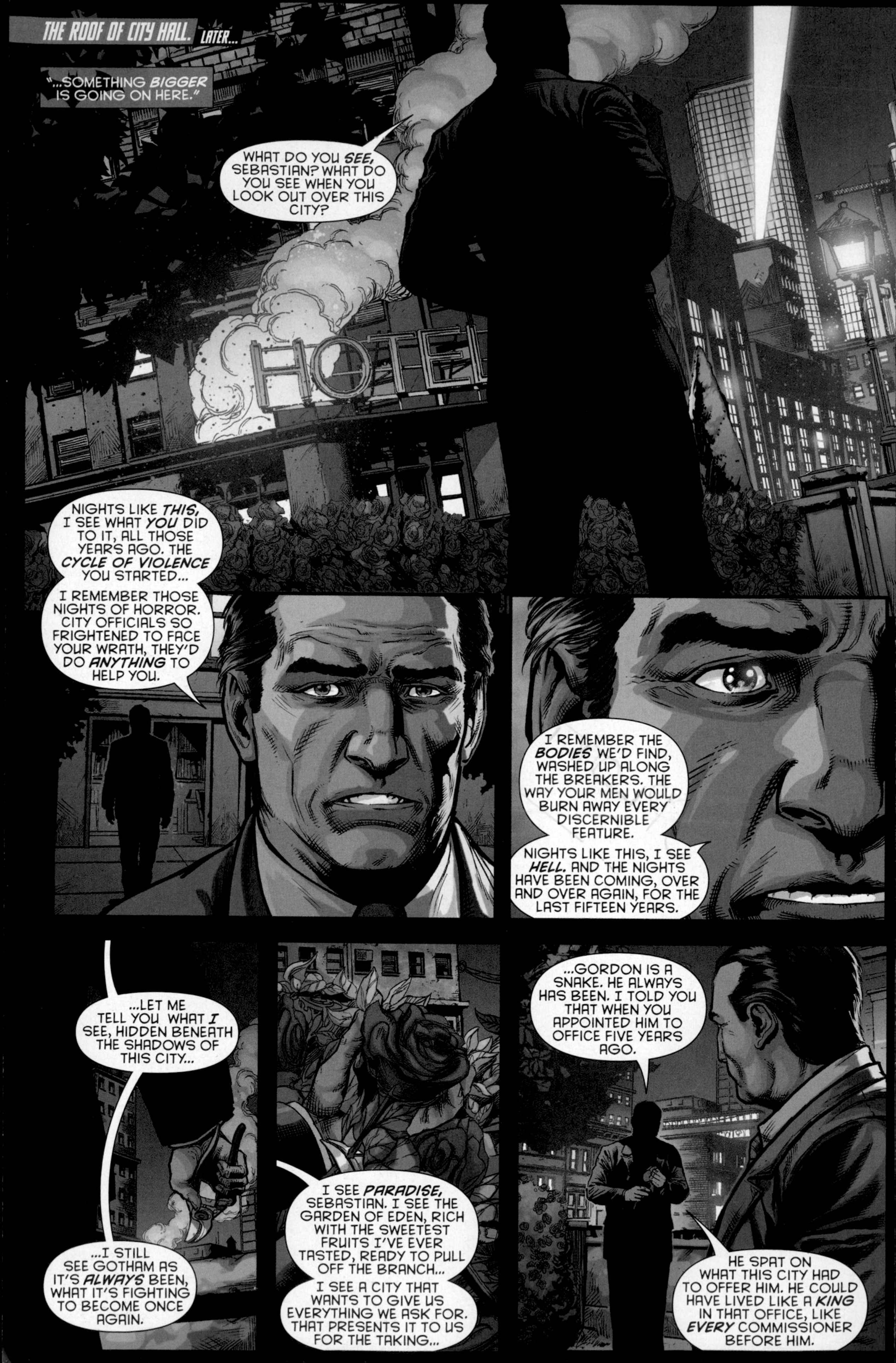
THE ROOF OF CITY HALL. LATER...
"...SOMETHING BIGGER IS GOING ON HERE."
WHAT DO YOU SEE, SEBASTIAN? WHAT DO YOU SEE WHEN YOU LOOK OUT OVER THIS CITY?
HOTEL
NIGHTS LIKE THIS, I SEE WHAT YOU DID TO IT, ALL THOSE YEARS AGO. THE CYCLE OF VIOLENCE YOU STARTED...
I REMEMBER THOSE NIGHTS OF HORROR. CITY OFFICIALS SO FRIGHTENED TO FACE YOUR WRATH, THEY'D DO ANYTHING TO HELP YOU.
I REMEMBER THE BODIES WE'D FIND, WASHED UP ALONG THE BREAKERS. THE WAY YOUR MEN WOULD BURN AWAY EVERY DISCERNIBLE FEATURE.
NIGHTS LIKE THIS, I SEE HELL. AND THE NIGHTS HAVE BEEN COMING, OVER AND OVER AGAIN, FOR THE LAST FIFTEEN YEARS.
...LET ME TELL YOU WHAT I SEE, HIDDEN BENEATH THE SHADOWS OF THIS CITY...
...I STILL SEE GOTHAM AS IT'S ALWAYS BEEN, WHAT IT'S FIGHTING TO BECOME ONCE AGAIN.
I SEE PARADISE, SEBASTIAN. I SEE THE GARDEN OF EDEN, RICH WITH THE SWEETEST FRUITS I'VE EVER TASTED, READY TO PULL OFF THE BRANCH...
I SEE A CITY THAT WANTS TO GIVE US EVERYTHING WE ASK FOR. THAT PRESENTS IT TO US FOR THE TAKING...
...GORDON IS A SNAKE. HE ALWAYS HAS BEEN. I TOLD YOU THAT WHEN YOU APPOINTED HIM TO OFFICE FIVE YEARS AGO.
HE SPAT ON WHAT THIS CITY HAD TO OFFER HIM. HE COULD HAVE LIVED LIKE A KING IN THAT OFFICE, LIKE EVERY COMMISSIONER BEFORE HIM.

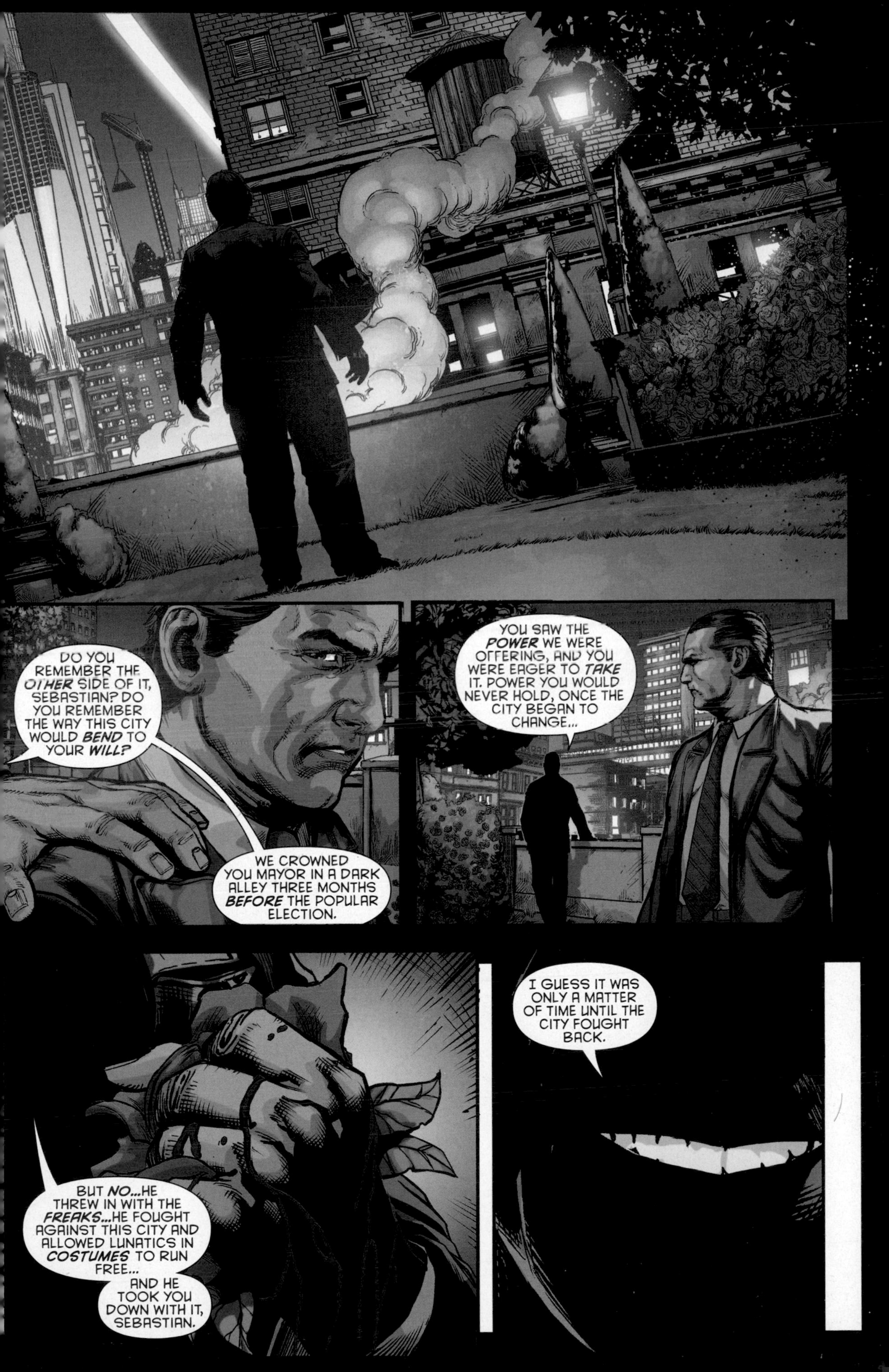
DO YOU REMEMBER THE OTHER SIDE OF IT, SEBASTIAN? DO YOU REMEMBER THE WAY THIS CITY WOULD BEND TO YOUR WILL?
WE CROWNED YOU MAYOR IN A DARK ALLEY THREE MONTHS BEFORE THE POPULAR ELECTION.
YOU SAW THE POWER WE WERE OFFERING, AND YOU WERE EAGER TO TAKE IT. POWER YOU WOULD NEVER HOLD, ONCE THE CITY BEGAN TO CHANGE...
BUT NO...HE THREW IN WITH THE FREAKS...HE FOUGHT AGAINST THIS CITY AND ALLOWED LUNATICS IN COSTUMES TO RUN FREE...
AND HE TOOK YOU DOWN WITH IT, SEBASTIAN.
I GUESS IT WAS ONLY A MATTER OF TIME UNTIL THE CITY FOUGHT BACK.

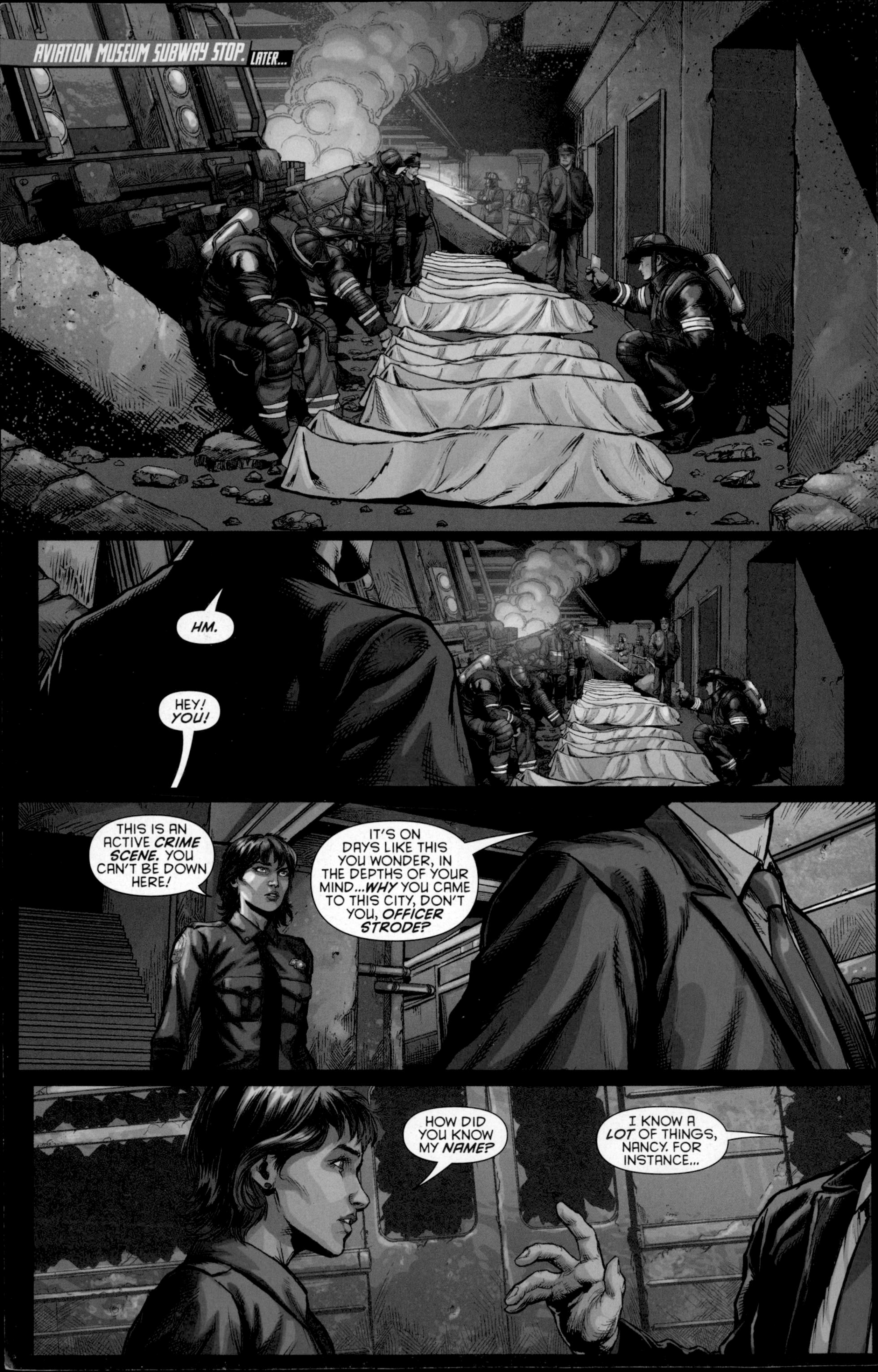
AVIATION MUSEUM SUBWAY STOP. LATER...
HM.
HEY! YOU!
THIS IS AN ACTIVE CRIME SCENE. YOU CAN'T BE DOWN HERE!
IT'S ON DAYS LIKE THIS YOU WONDER, IN THE DEPTHS OF YOUR MIND...WHY YOU CAME TO THIS CITY, DON'T YOU, OFFICER STRODE?
HOW DID YOU KNOW MY NAME?
I KNOW A LOT OF THINGS, NANCY. FOR INSTANCE...

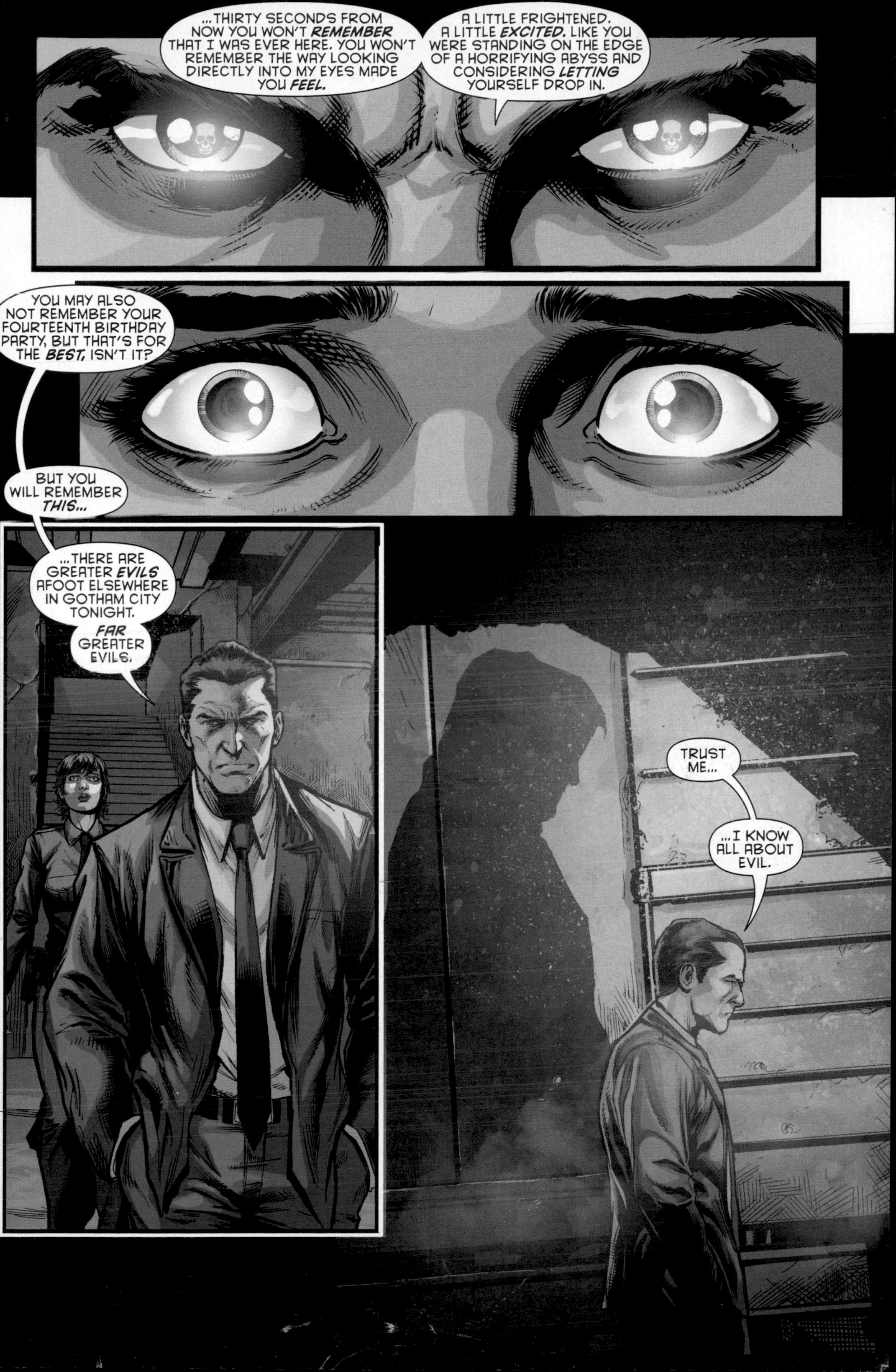

...THIRTY SECONDS FROM NOW YOU WON'T REMEMBER THAT I WAS EVER HERE. YOU WON'T REMEMBER THE WAY LOOKING DIRECTLY INTO MY EYES MADE YOU FEEL.
A LITTLE FRIGHTENED. A LITTLE EXCITED. LIKE YOU WERE STANDING ON THE EDGE OF A HORRIFYING ABYSS AND CONSIDERING LETTING YOURSELF DROP IN.
YOU MAY ALSO NOT REMEMBER YOUR FOURTEENTH BIRTHDAY PARTY, BUT THAT'S FOR THE BEST, ISN'T IT?
BUT YOU WILL REMEMBER THIS...
...THERE ARE GREATER EVILS AFOOT ELSEWHERE IN GOTHAM CITY TONIGHT.
FAR GREATER EVILS.
TRUST ME...
...I KNOW ALL ABOUT EVIL.

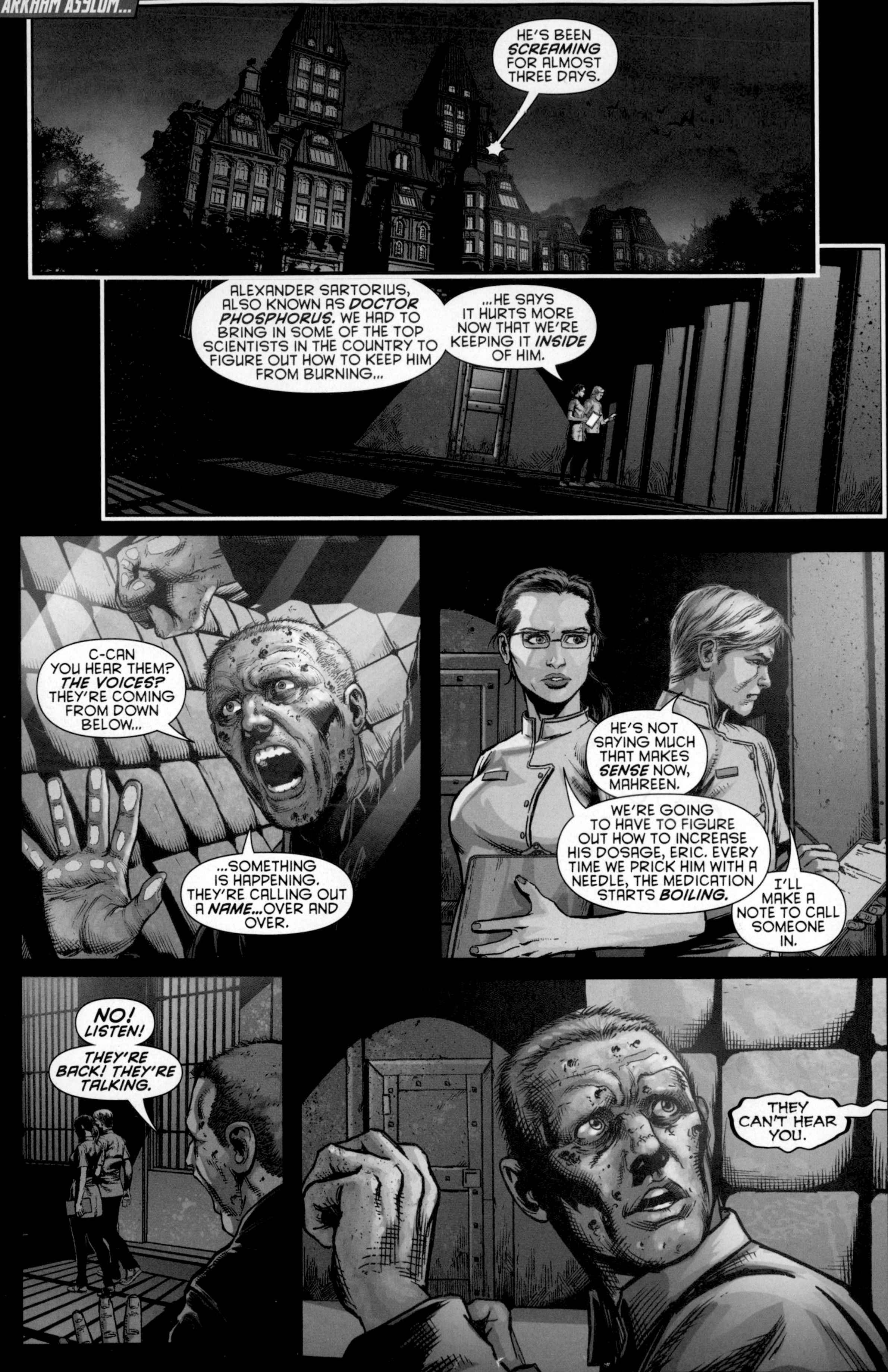

ARKHAM ASYLUM...
HE'S BEEN SCREAMING FOR ALMOST THREE DAYS.
ALEXANDER SARTORIUS, ALSO KNOWN AS DOCTOR PHOSPHORUS. WE HAD TO BRING IN SOME OF THE TOP SCIENTISTS IN THE COUNTRY TO FIGURE OUT HOW TO KEEP HIM FROM BURNING...
...HE SAYS IT HURTS MORE NOW THAT WE'RE KEEPING IT INSIDE OF HIM.
C-CAN YOU HEAR THEM? THE VOICES? THEY'RE COMING FROM DOWN BELOW...
...SOMETHING IS HAPPENING. THEY'RE CALLING OUT A NAME...OVER AND OVER.
HE'S NOT SAYING MUCH THAT MAKES SENSE NOW, MAHREEN.
WE'RE GOING TO HAVE TO FIGURE OUT HOW TO INCREASE HIS DOSAGE, ERIC. EVERY TIME WE PRICK HIM WITH A NEEDLE, THE MEDICATION STARTS BOILING.
I'LL MAKE A NOTE TO CALL SOMEONE IN.
NO! LISTEN!
THEY'RE BACK! THEY'RE TALKING.
THEY CAN'T HEAR YOU.

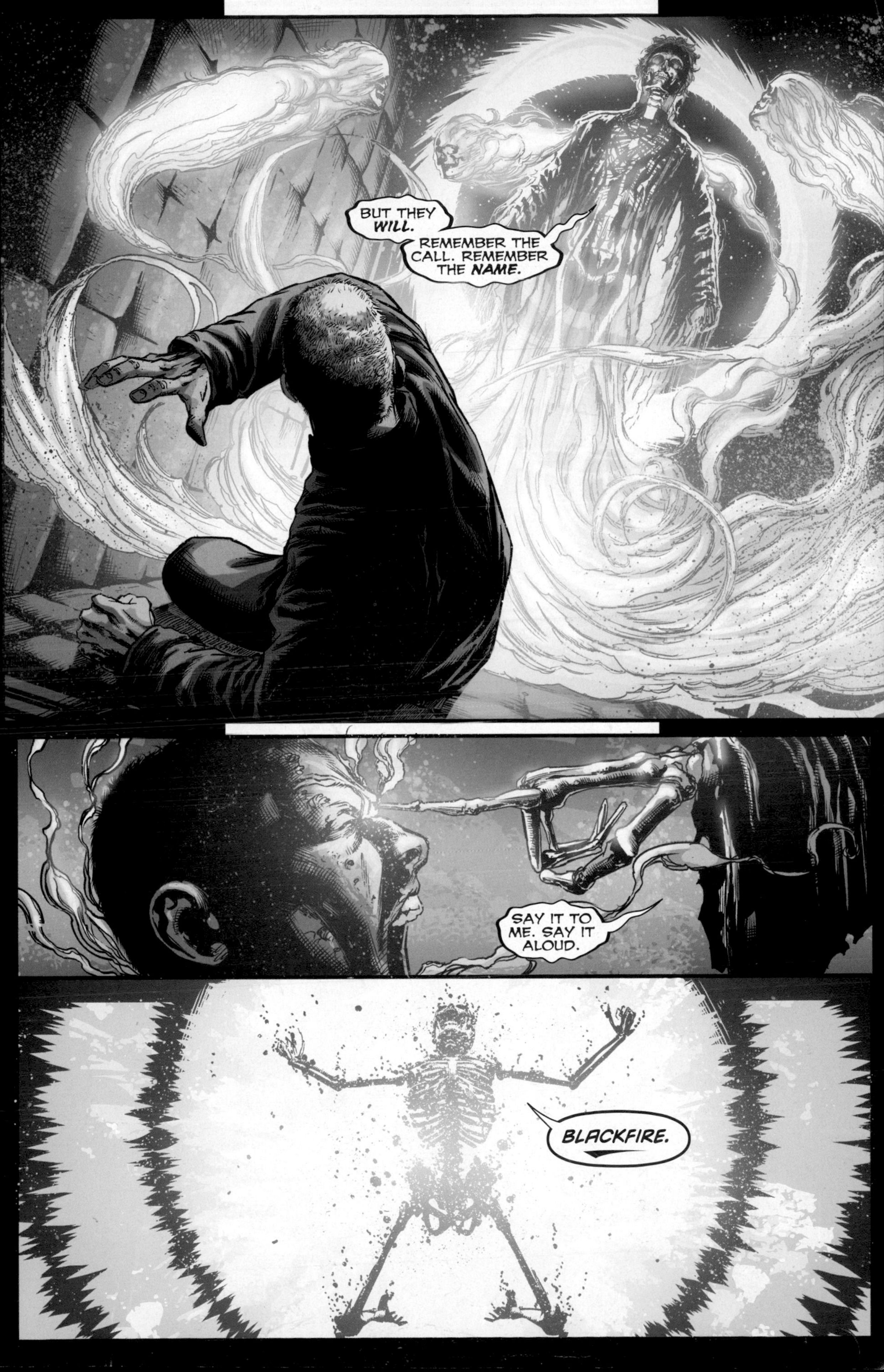
BUT THEY WILL.
REMEMBER THE CALL. REMEMBER THE NAME.
SAY IT TO ME. SAY IT ALOUD.
BLACKFIRE.

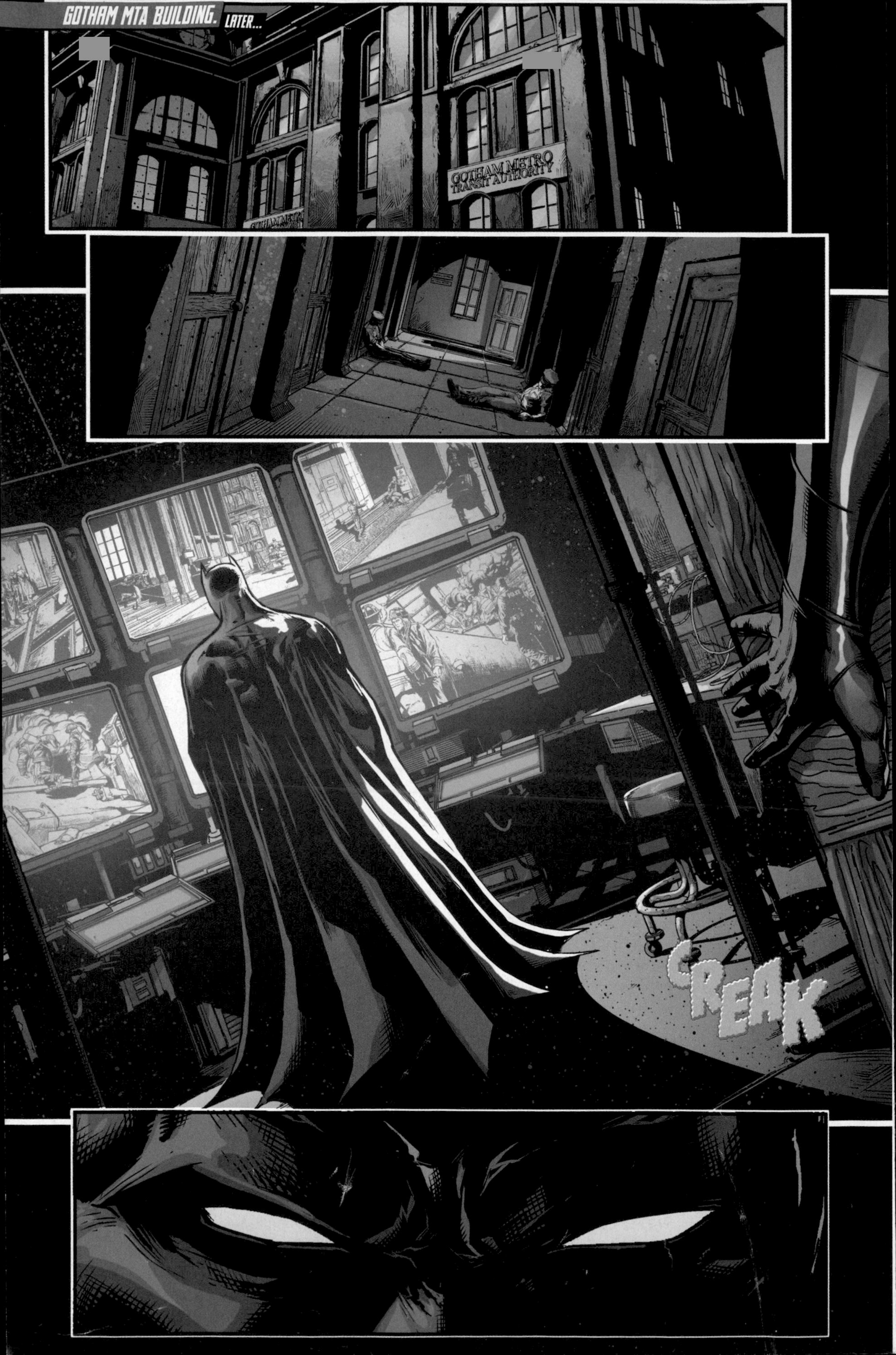

GOTHAM MTA BUILDING.
LATER...
GOTHAM METRO TRANSIT AUTHORITY
CREAK

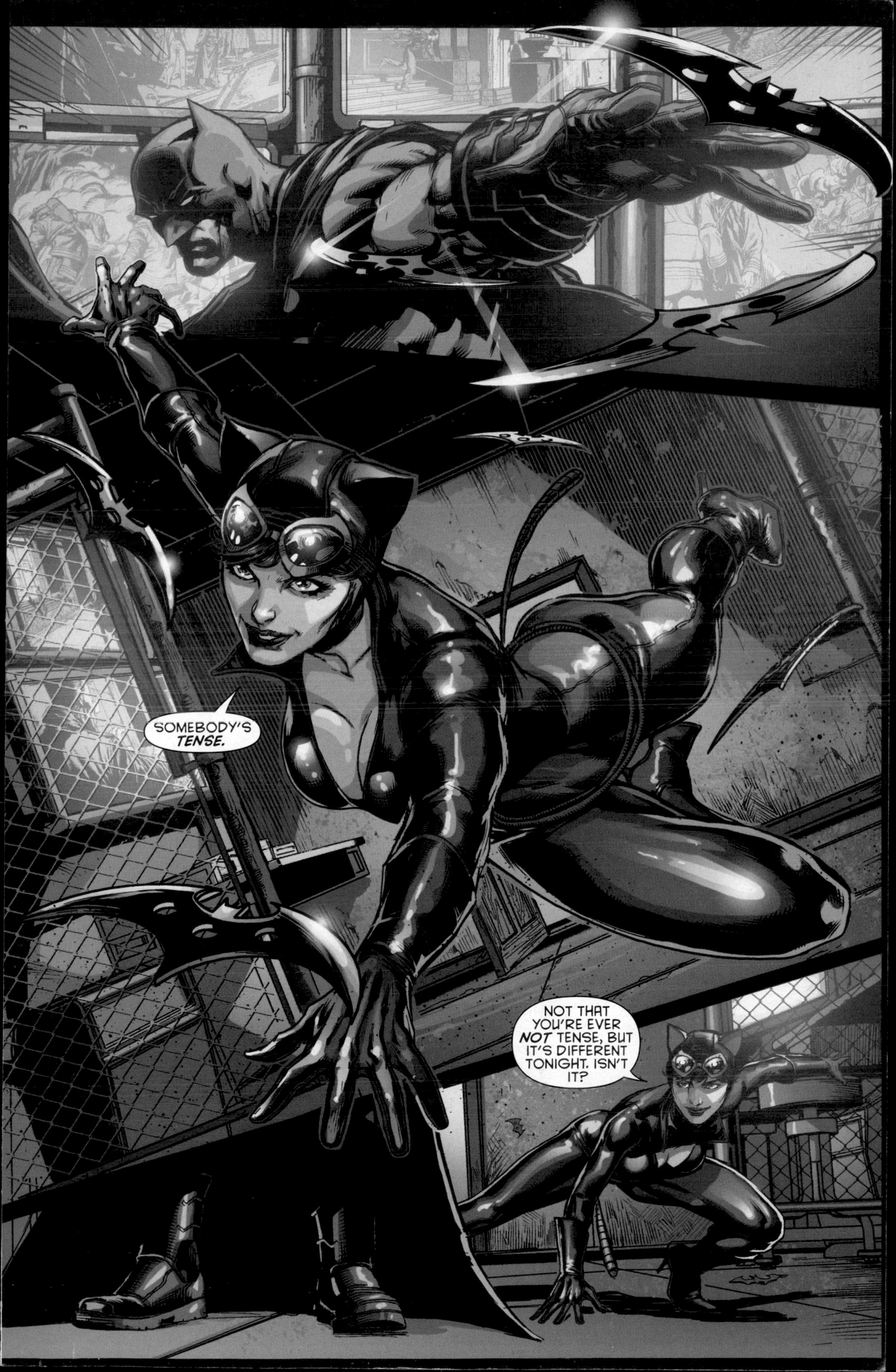
SOMEBODY'S *TENSE.*
NOT THAT YOU'RE EVER ***NOT*** TENSE, BUT IT'S DIFFERENT TONIGHT. ISN'T IT?

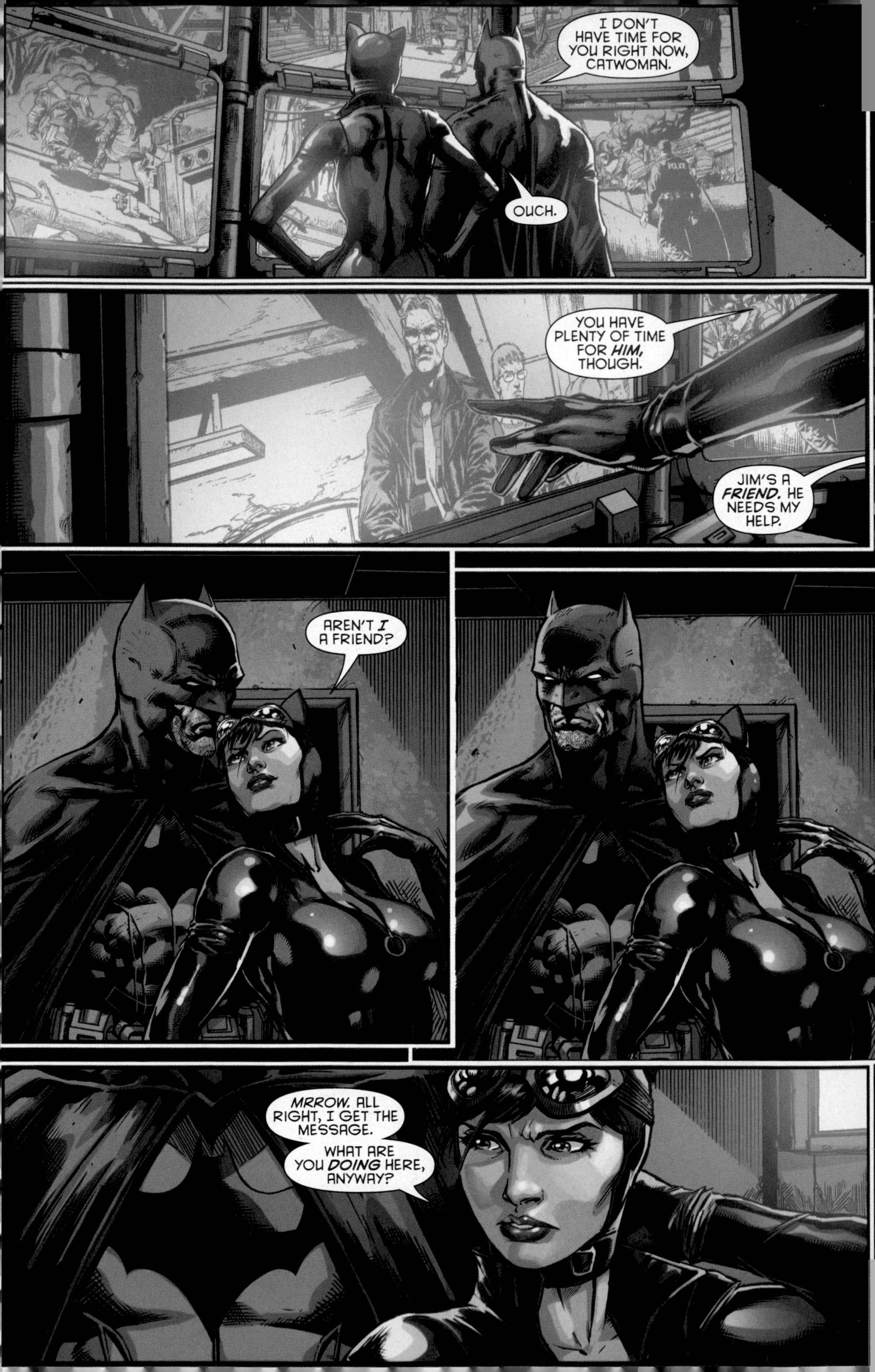
I DON'T HAVE TIME FOR YOU RIGHT NOW, CATWOMAN.
OUCH.
POLICE
YOU HAVE PLENTY OF TIME FOR *HIM,* THOUGH.
JIM'S A *FRIEND.* HE NEEDS MY HELP.
AREN'T *I* A FRIEND?
MRROW. ALL RIGHT, I GET THE MESSAGE.
WHAT ARE YOU *DOING* HERE, ANYWAY?

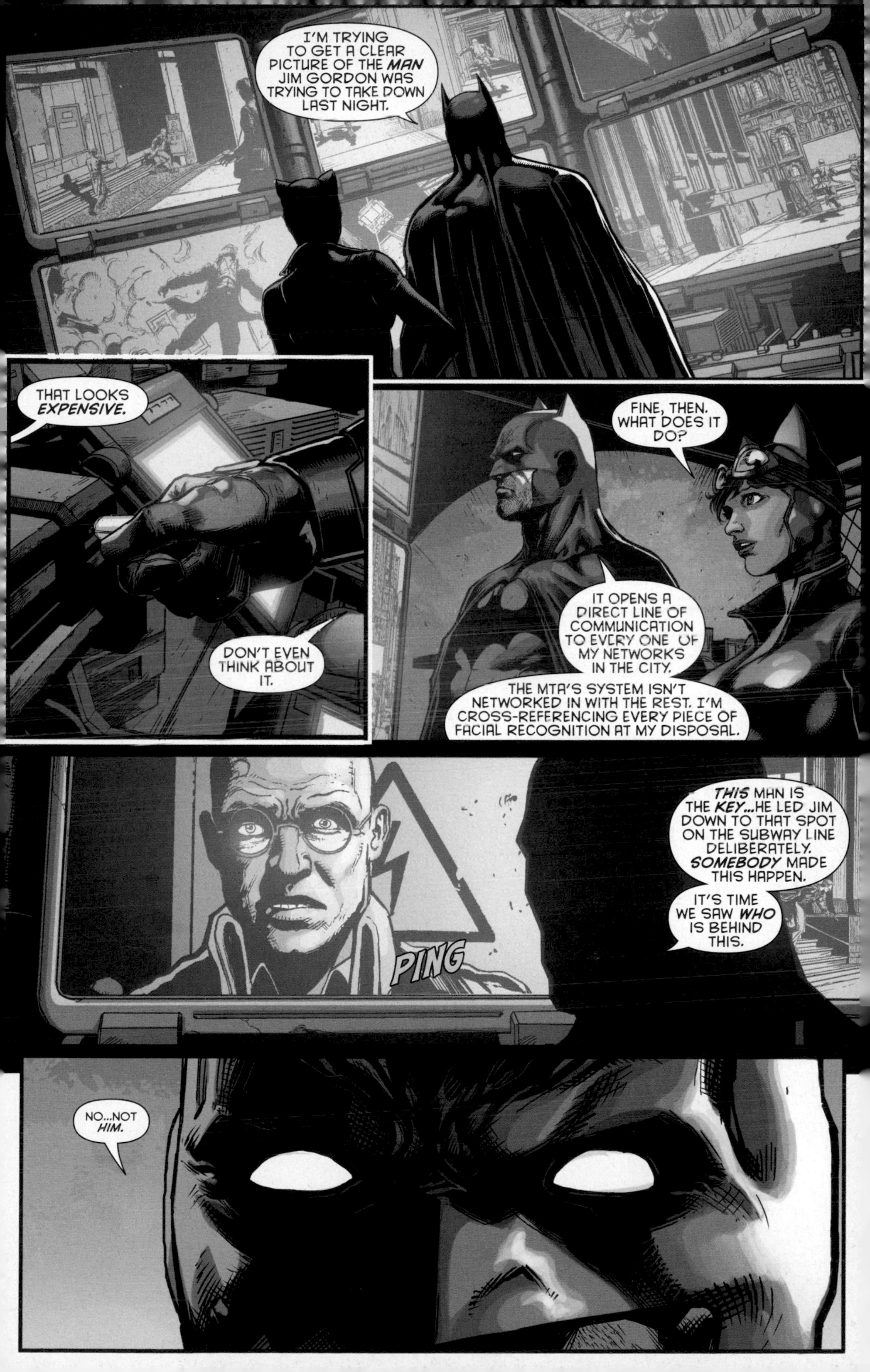
I'M TRYING TO GET A CLEAR PICTURE OF THE MAN JIM GORDON WAS TRYING TO TAKE DOWN LAST NIGHT.
THAT LOOKS EXPENSIVE.
DON'T EVEN THINK ABOUT IT.
FINE, THEN. WHAT DOES IT DO?
IT OPENS A DIRECT LINE OF COMMUNICATION TO EVERY ONE OF MY NETWORKS IN THE CITY.
THE MTA'S SYSTEM ISN'T NETWORKED IN WITH THE REST. I'M CROSS-REFERENCING EVERY PIECE OF FACIAL RECOGNITION AT MY DISPOSAL.
THIS MAN IS THE KEY...HE LED JIM DOWN TO THAT SPOT ON THE SUBWAY LINE DELIBERATELY. SOMEBODY MADE THIS HAPPEN.
IT'S TIME WE SAW WHO IS BEHIND THIS.
PING
NO...NOT HIM.

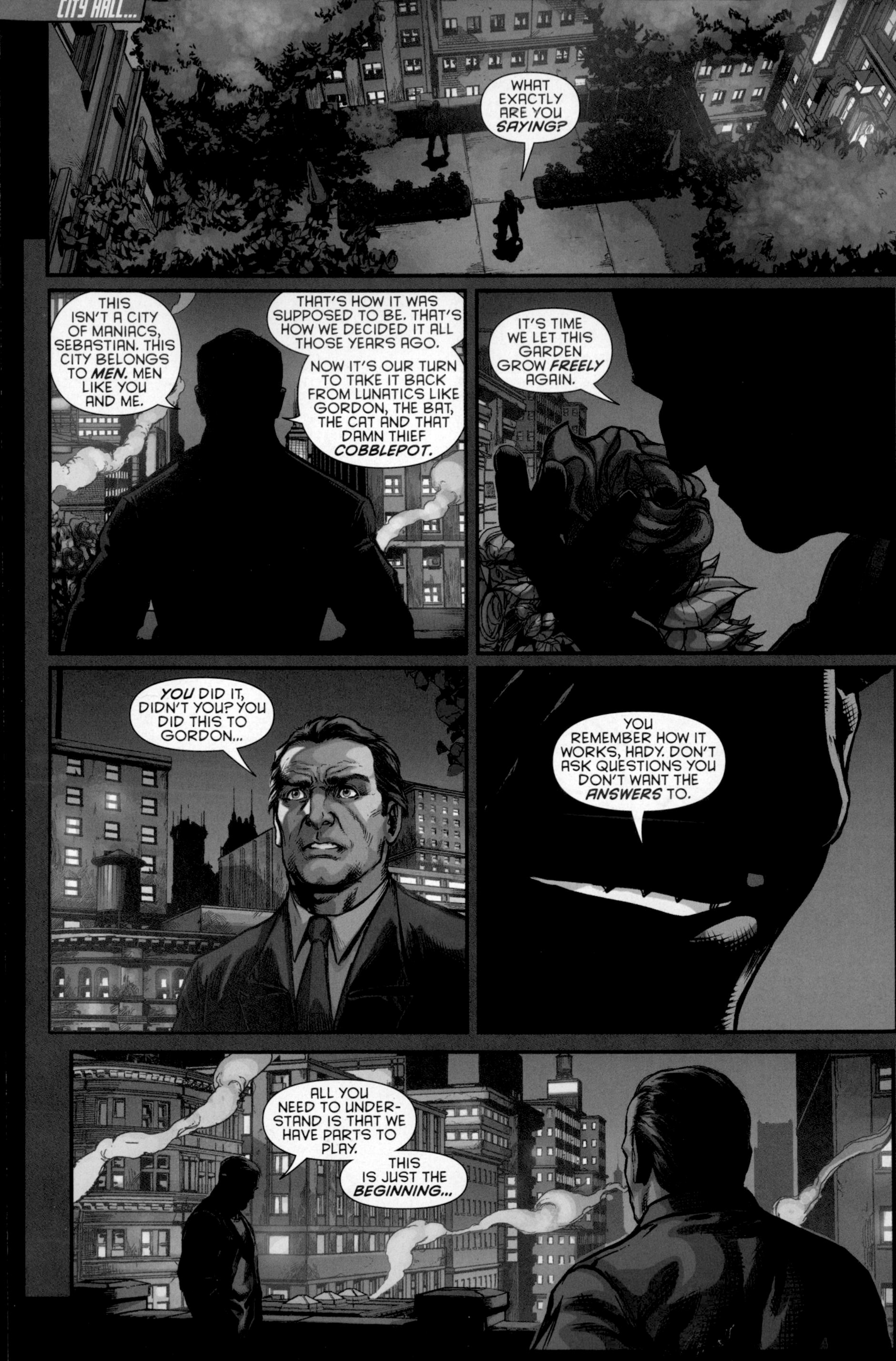
CITY HALL...
WHAT EXACTLY ARE YOU SAYING?
THIS ISN'T A CITY OF MANIACS, SEBASTIAN. THIS CITY BELONGS TO MEN. MEN LIKE YOU AND ME.
THAT'S HOW IT WAS SUPPOSED TO BE. THAT'S HOW WE DECIDED IT ALL THOSE YEARS AGO.
NOW IT'S OUR TURN TO TAKE IT BACK FROM LUNATICS LIKE GORDON, THE BAT, THE CAT AND THAT DAMN THIEF COBBLEPOT.
IT'S TIME WE LET THIS GARDEN GROW FREELY AGAIN.
YOU DID IT, DIDN'T YOU? YOU DID THIS TO GORDON...
YOU REMEMBER HOW IT WORKS, HADY. DON'T ASK QUESTIONS YOU DON'T WANT THE ANSWERS TO.
ALL YOU NEED TO UNDERSTAND IS THAT WE HAVE PARTS TO PLAY.
THIS IS JUST THE BEGINNING...

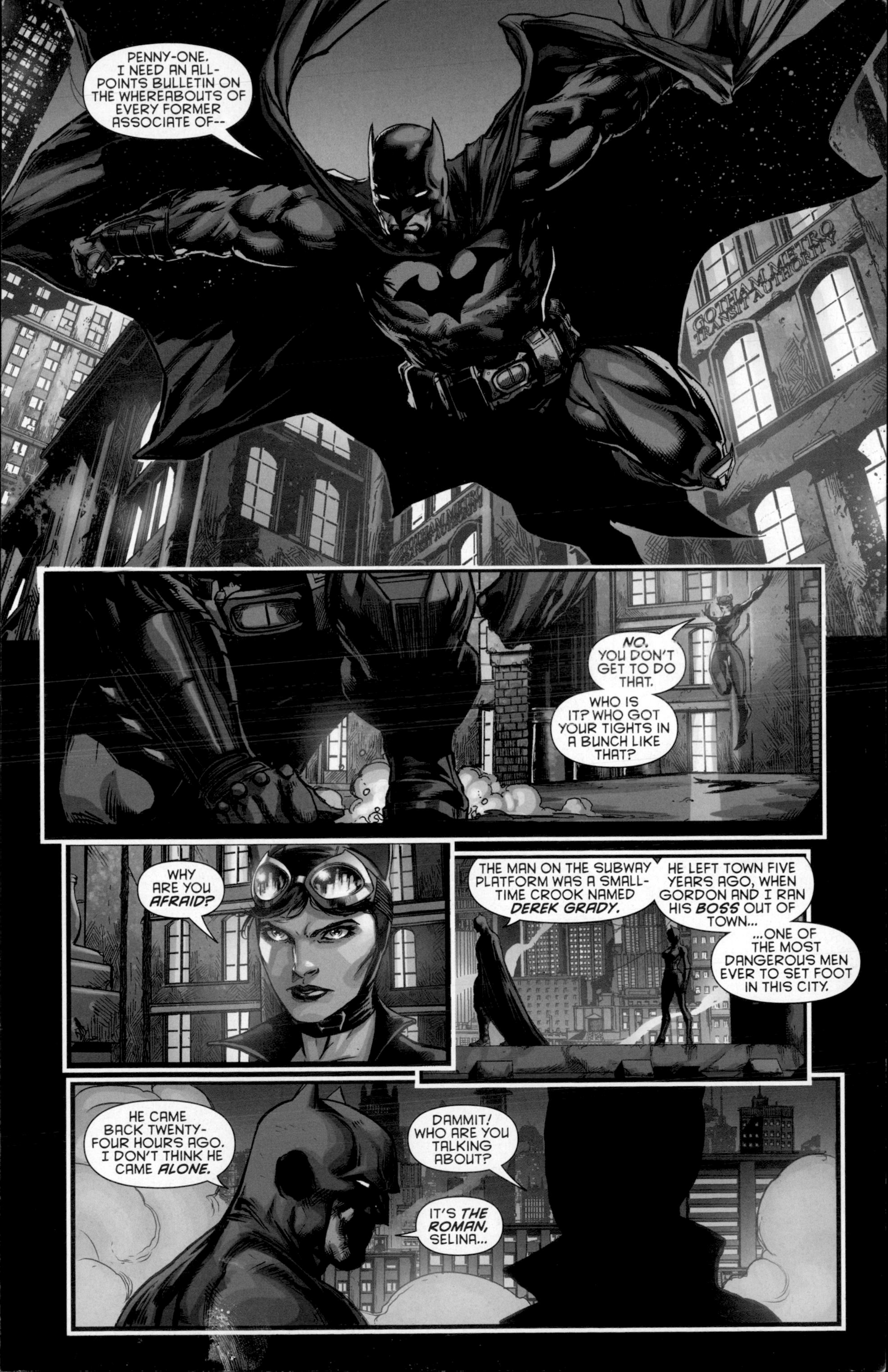
PENNY-ONE. I NEED AN ALL-POINTS BULLETIN ON THE WHEREABOUTS OF EVERY FORMER ASSOCIATE OF--
GOTHAM METRO TRANSIT AUTHORITY
NO. YOU DON'T GET TO DO THAT.
WHO IS IT? WHO GOT YOUR TIGHTS IN A BUNCH LIKE THAT?
WHY ARE YOU *AFRAID?*
THE MAN ON THE SUBWAY PLATFORM WAS A SMALL-TIME CROOK NAMED ***DEREK GRADY.***
HE LEFT TOWN FIVE YEARS AGO, WHEN GORDON AND I RAN HIS ***BOSS*** OUT OF TOWN...
...ONE OF THE MOST DANGEROUS MEN EVER TO SET FOOT IN THIS CITY.
HE CAME BACK TWENTY-FOUR HOURS AGO. I DON'T THINK HE CAME ***ALONE.***
DAMMIT! WHO ARE YOU TALKING ABOUT?
IT'S ***THE ROMAN,*** SELINA...

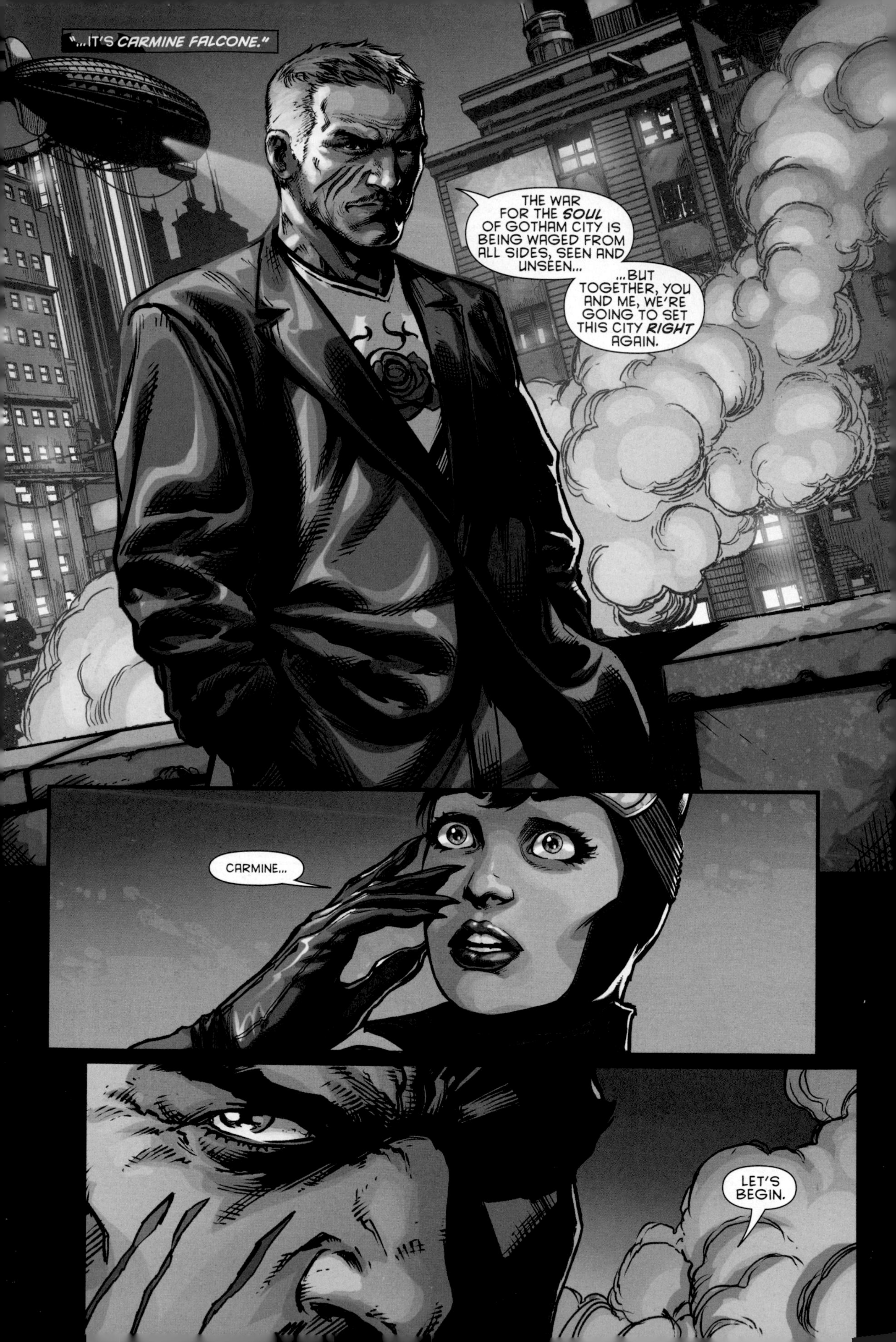
"...IT'S CARMINE FALCONE."
THE WAR FOR THE SOUL OF GOTHAM CITY IS BEING WAGED FROM ALL SIDES, SEEN AND UNSEEN...
...BUT TOGETHER, YOU AND ME, WE'RE GOING TO SET THIS CITY RIGHT AGAIN.
CARMINE...
LET'S BEGIN.

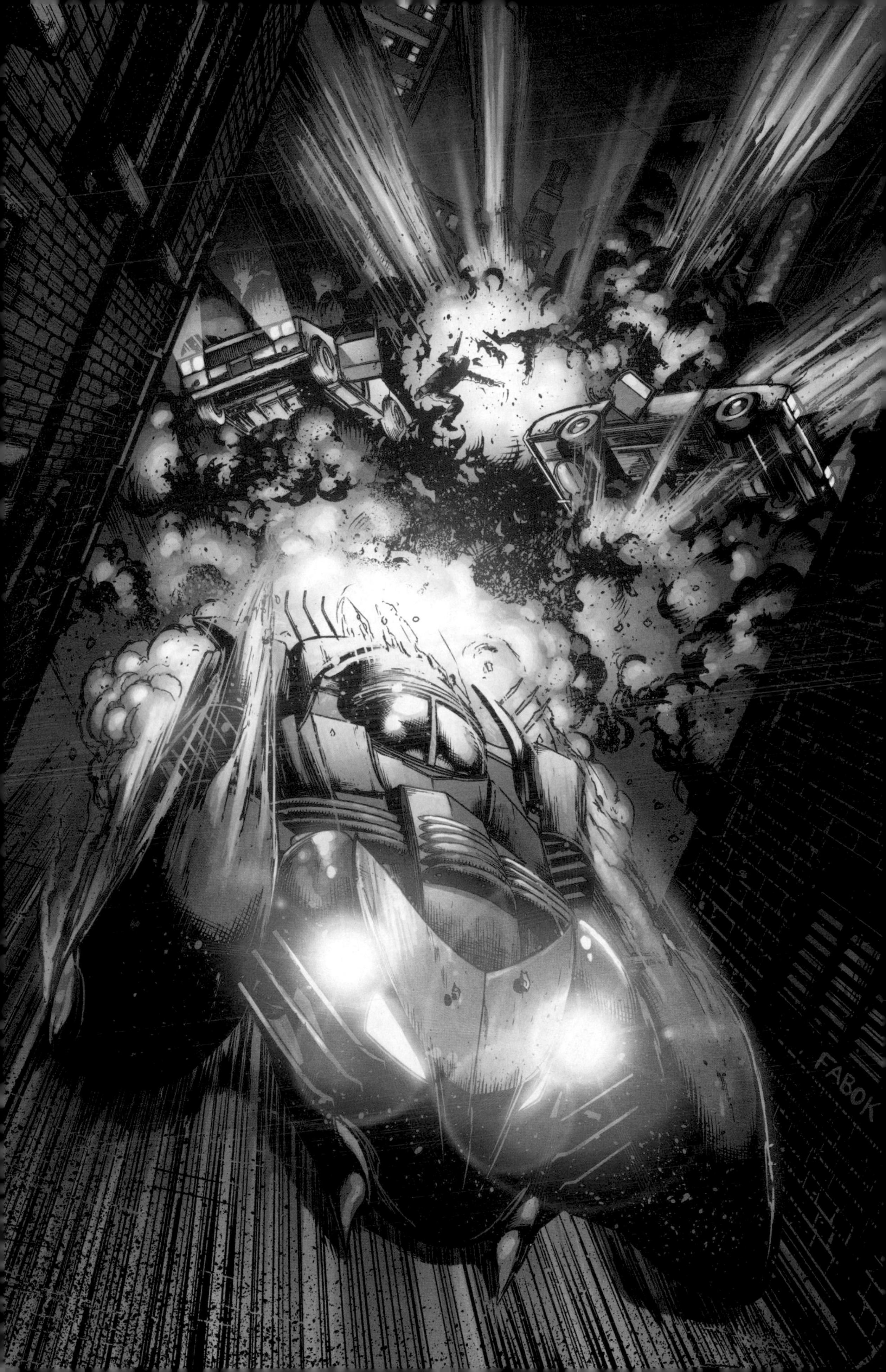
FABOK

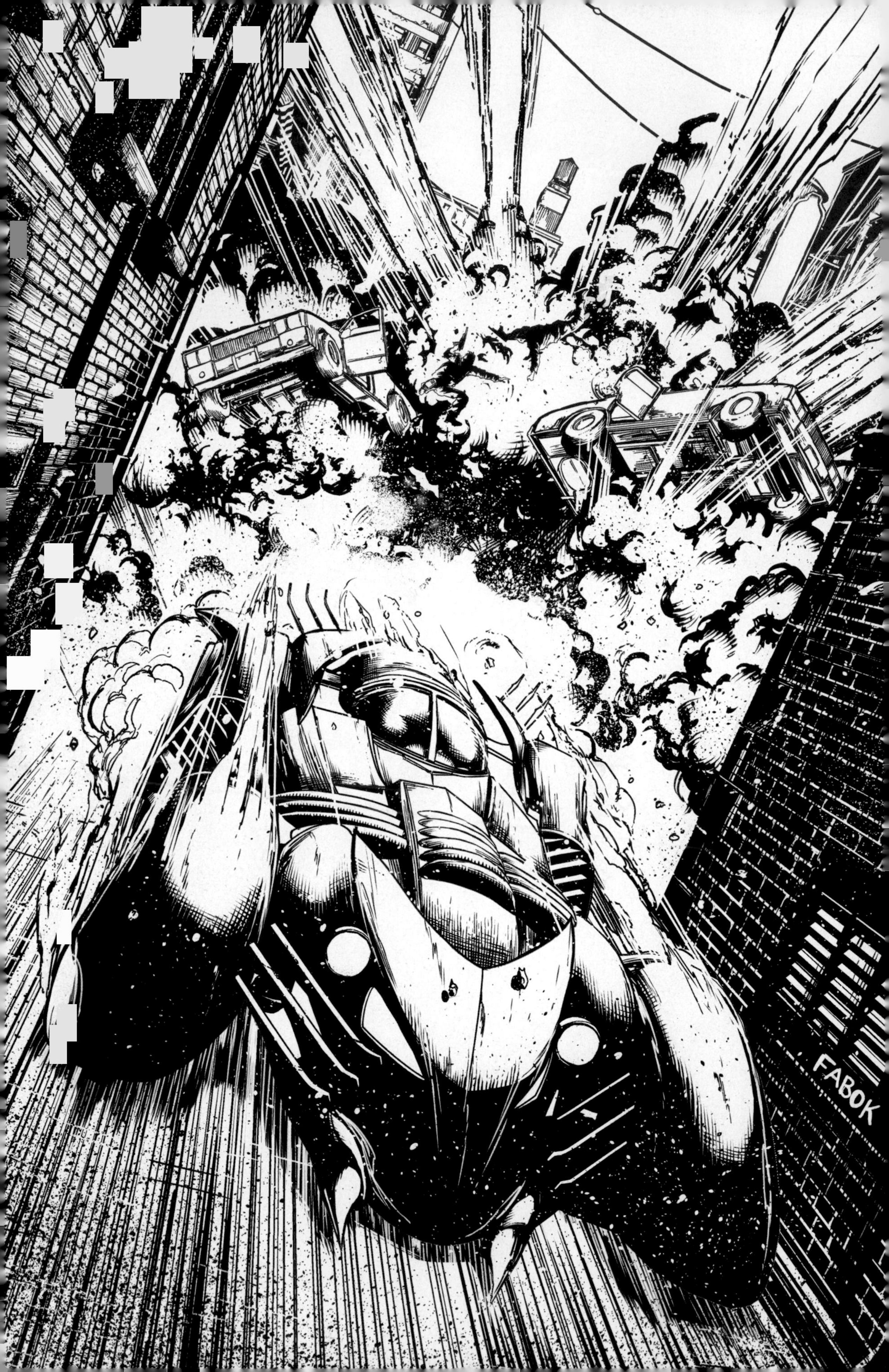
FABOK

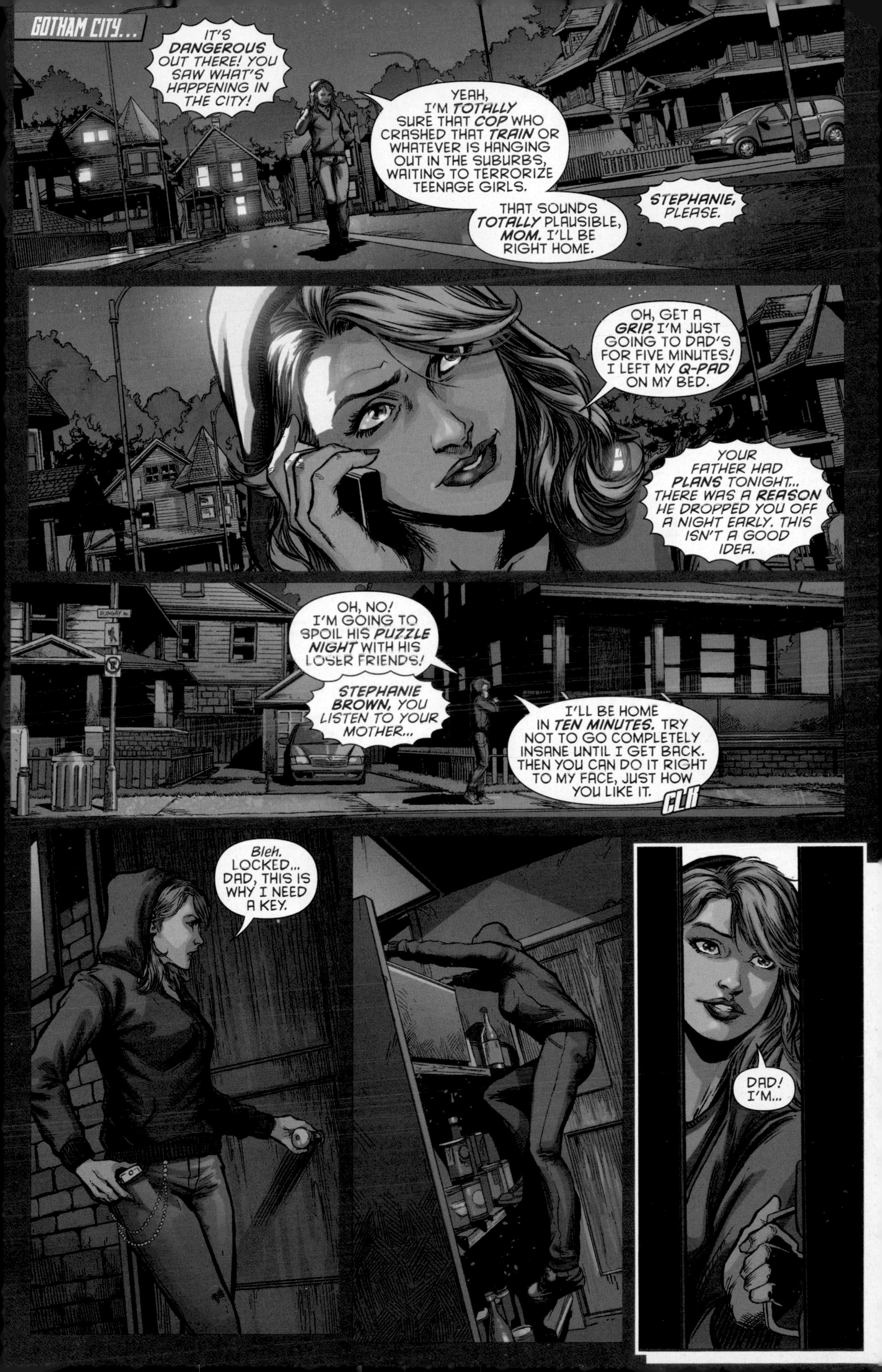
GOTHAM CITY...
IT'S DANGEROUS OUT THERE! YOU SAW WHAT'S HAPPENING IN THE CITY!
YEAH, I'M TOTALLY SURE THAT COP WHO CRASHED THAT TRAIN OR WHATEVER IS HANGING OUT IN THE SUBURBS, WAITING TO TERRORIZE TEENAGE GIRLS.
THAT SOUNDS TOTALLY PLAUSIBLE, MOM. I'LL BE RIGHT HOME.
STEPHANIE, PLEASE.
OH, GET A GRIP. I'M JUST GOING TO DAD'S FOR FIVE MINUTES! I LEFT MY Q-PAD ON MY BED.
YOUR FATHER HAD PLANS TONIGHT... THERE WAS A REASON HE DROPPED YOU OFF A NIGHT EARLY. THIS ISN'T A GOOD IDEA.
OH, NO! I'M GOING TO SPOIL HIS PUZZLE NIGHT WITH HIS LOSER FRIENDS!
STEPHANIE BROWN, YOU LISTEN TO YOUR MOTHER...
I'LL BE HOME IN TEN MINUTES. TRY NOT TO GO COMPLETELY INSANE UNTIL I GET BACK. THEN YOU CAN DO IT RIGHT TO MY FACE, JUST HOW YOU LIKE IT.
CLK
Bleh. LOCKED... DAD, THIS IS WHY I NEED A KEY.
DAD! I'M...

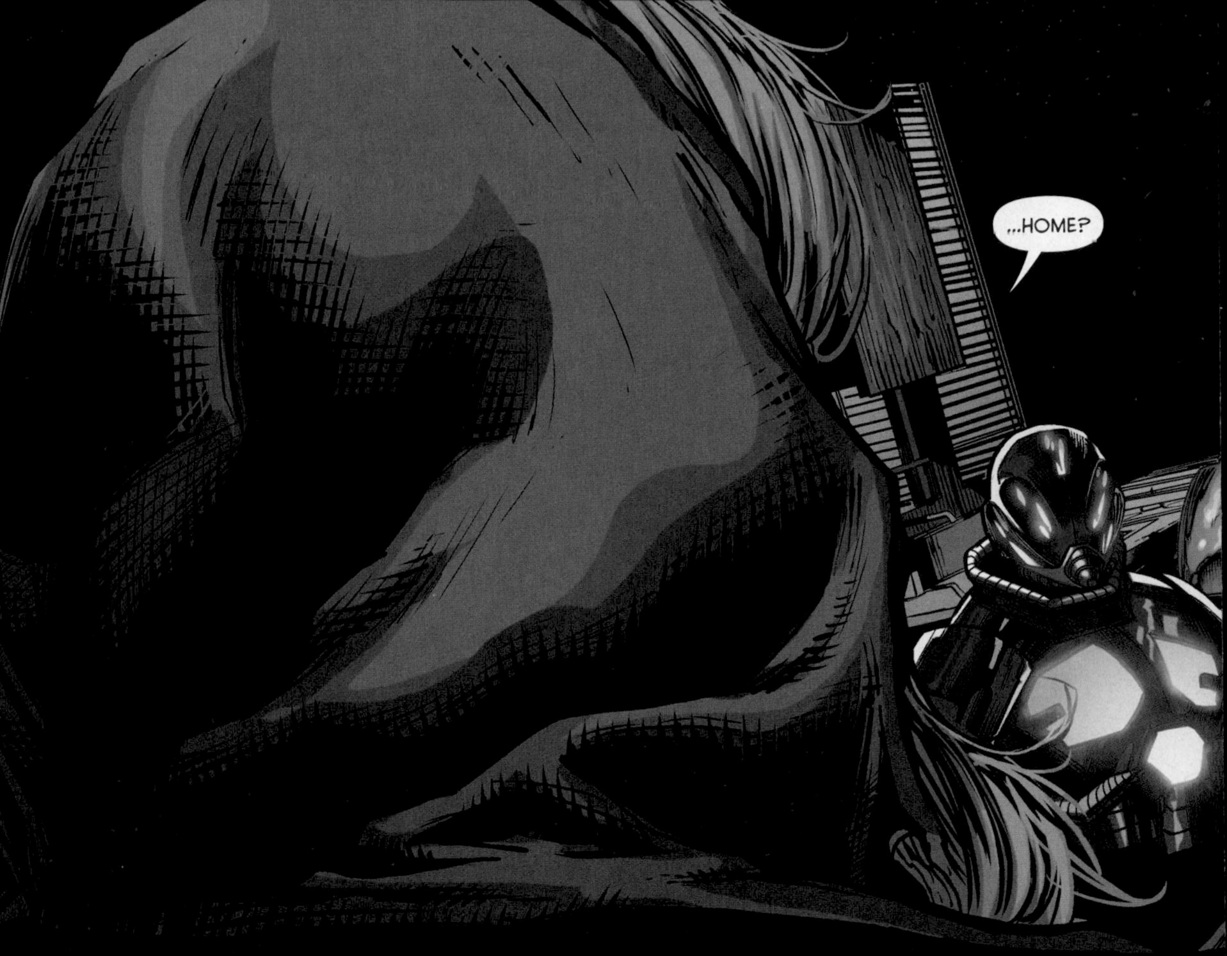
...HOME?

SCOTT SNYDER & JAMES TYNION IV
STORY & SCRIPT
CONSULTING WRITERS: RAY FAWKES,
JOHN LAYMAN & TIM SEELEY

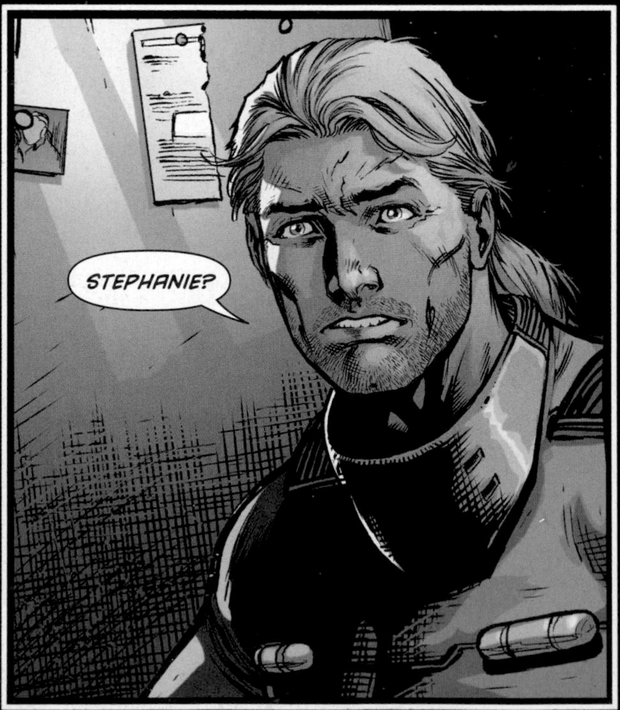
STEPHANIE?

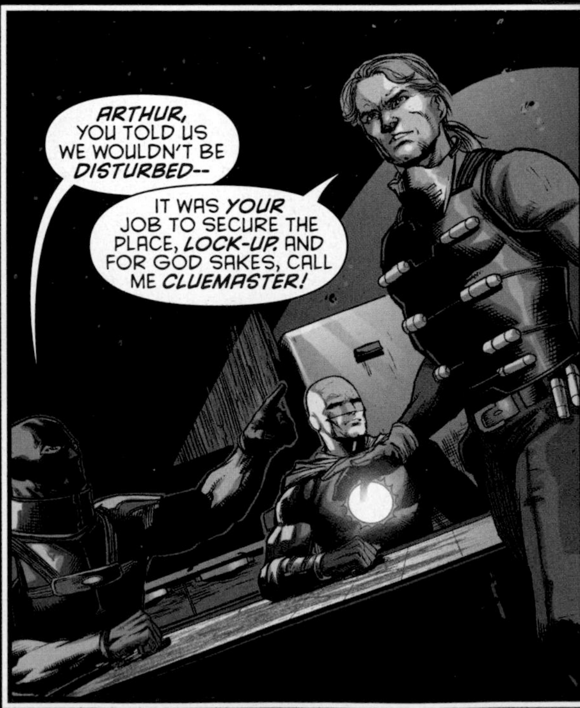
ARTHUR, YOU TOLD US WE WOULDN'T BE DISTURBED--
IT WAS YOUR JOB TO SECURE THE PLACE, LOCK-UP, AND FOR GOD SAKES, CALL ME CLUEMASTER!

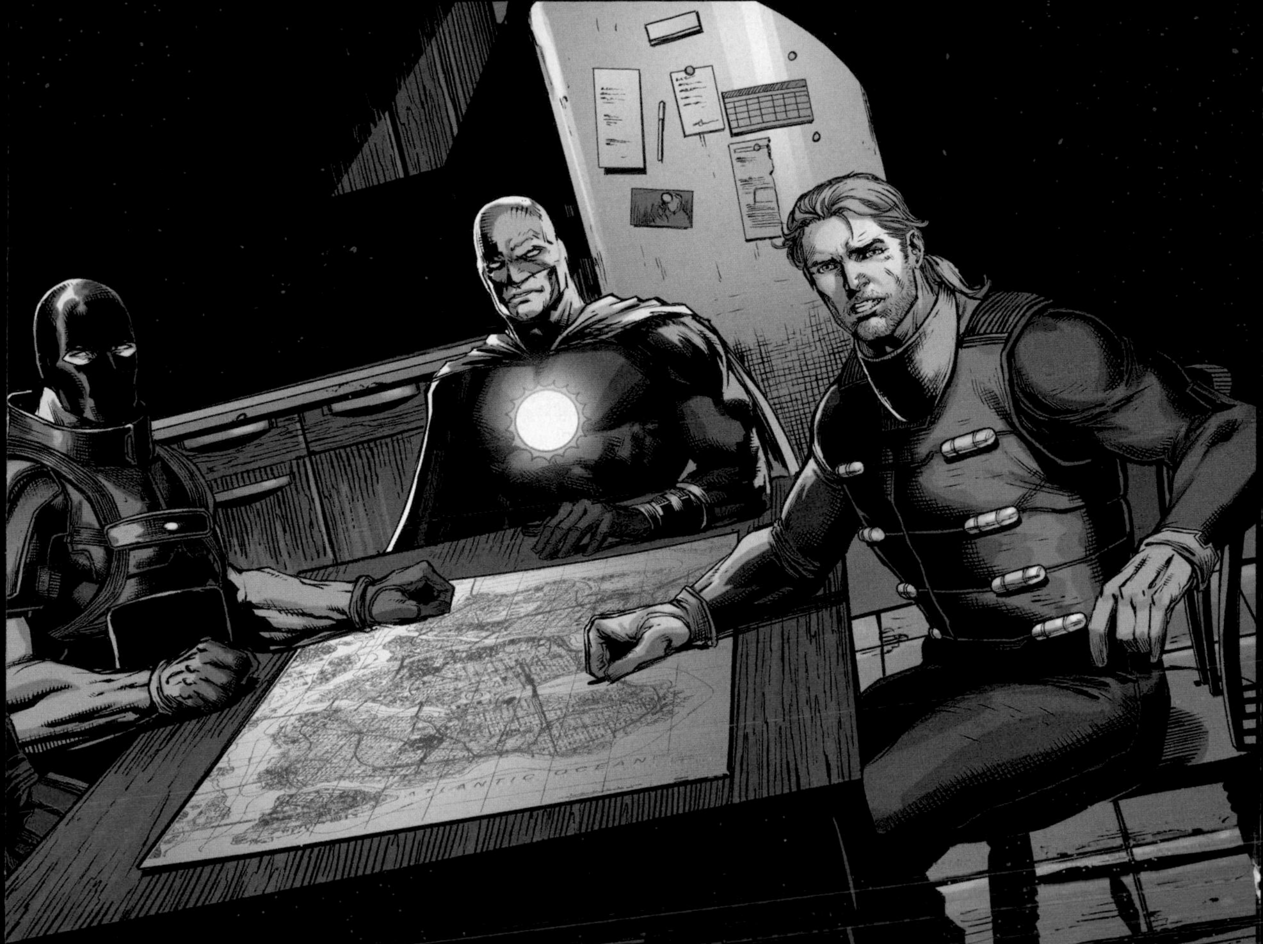

ART BY: JASON FABOK
COLORS BY: BRAD ANDERSON • LETTERING BY: TAYLOR ESPOSITO
COVER BY: FABOK & ANDERSON

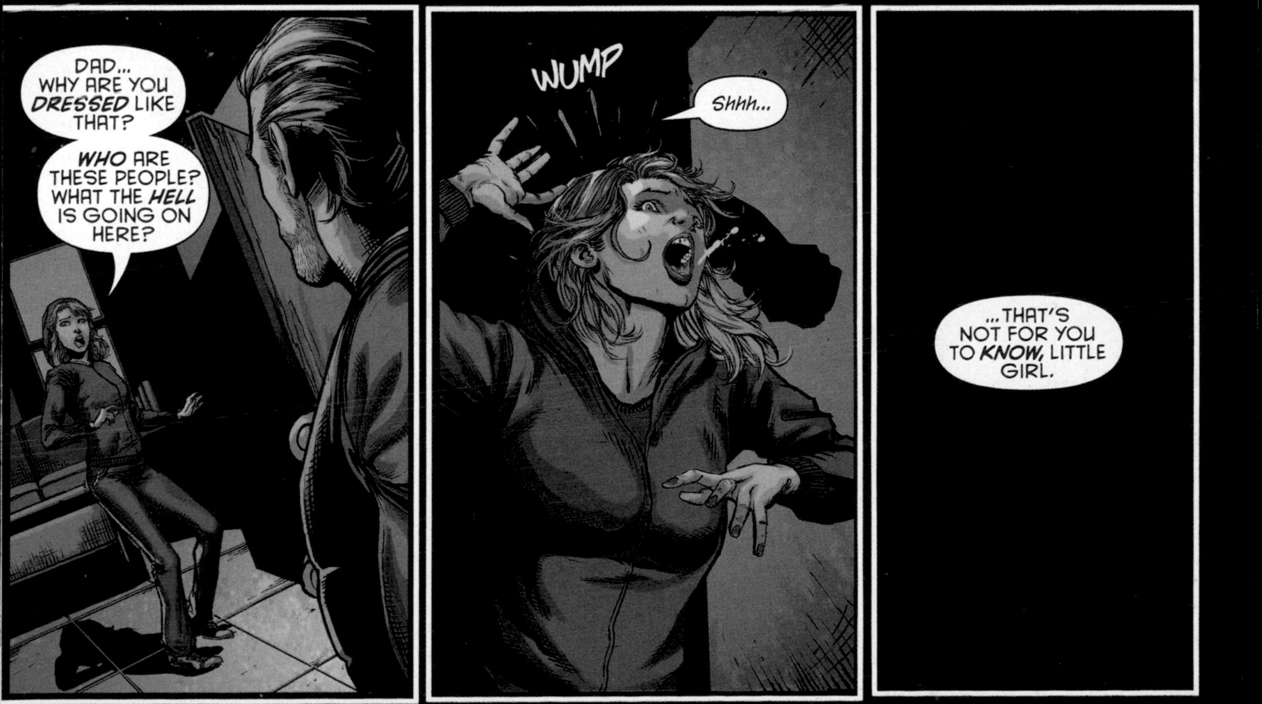

DAD... WHY ARE YOU *DRESSED* LIKE THAT?
WHO ARE THESE PEOPLE? WHAT THE *HELL* IS GOING ON HERE?
WUMP
Shhh...
...THAT'S NOT FOR YOU TO *KNOW,* LITTLE GIRL.

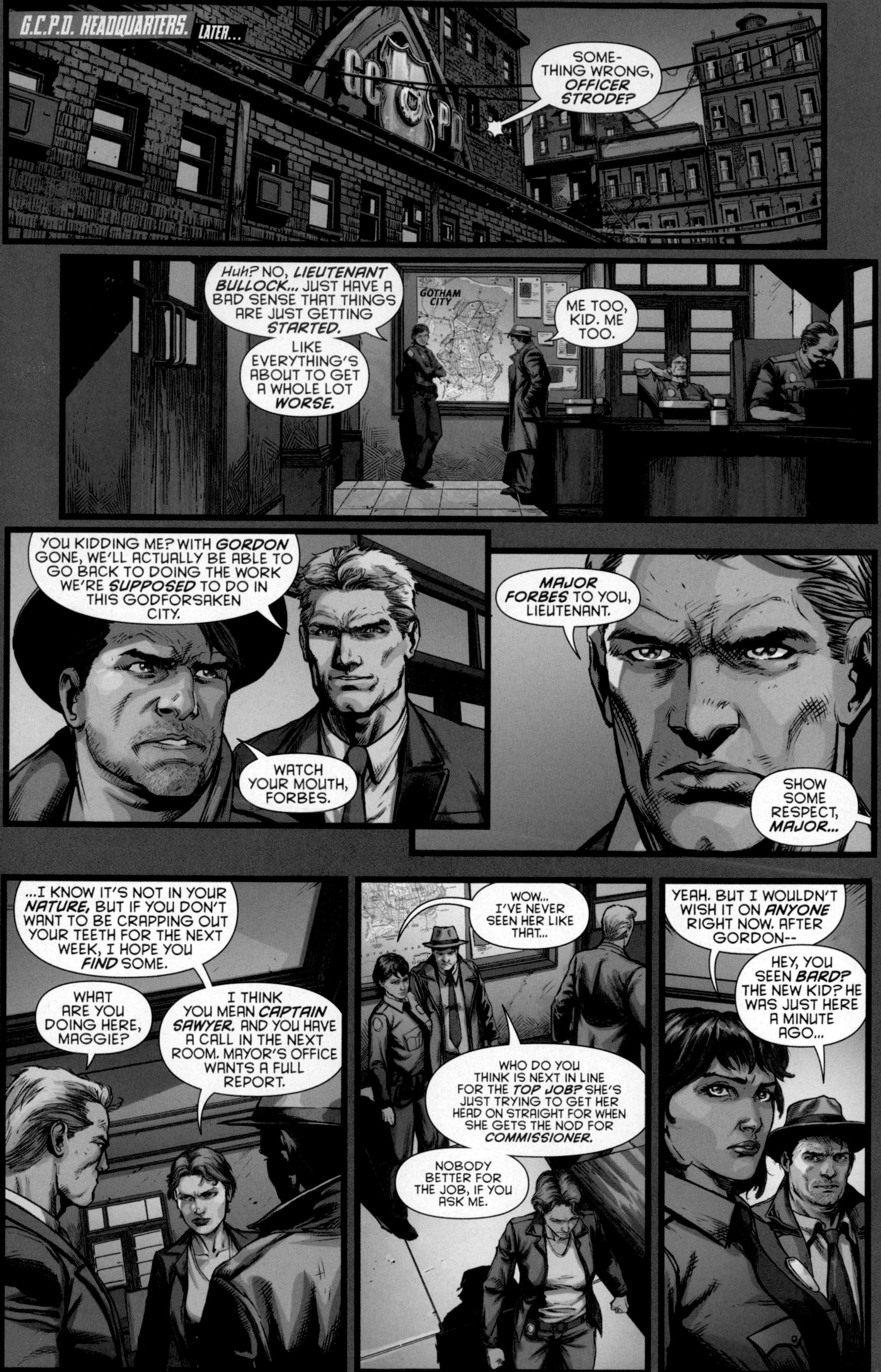
G.C.P.D. HEADQUARTERS.
LATER...
SOME-THING WRONG, OFFICER STRODE?
Huh? NO, LIEUTENANT BULLOCK... JUST HAVE A BAD SENSE THAT THINGS ARE JUST GETTING STARTED.
LIKE EVERYTHING'S ABOUT TO GET A WHOLE LOT WORSE.
ME TOO, KID. ME TOO.
GOTHAM CITY
YOU KIDDING ME? WITH GORDON GONE, WE'LL ACTUALLY BE ABLE TO GO BACK TO DOING THE WORK WE'RE SUPPOSED TO DO IN THIS GODFORSAKEN CITY.
WATCH YOUR MOUTH, FORBES.
MAJOR FORBES TO YOU, LIEUTENANT.
SHOW SOME RESPECT, MAJOR...
...I KNOW IT'S NOT IN YOUR NATURE, BUT IF YOU DON'T WANT TO BE CRAPPING OUT YOUR TEETH FOR THE NEXT WEEK, I HOPE YOU FIND SOME.
WHAT ARE YOU DOING HERE, MAGGIE?
I THINK YOU MEAN CAPTAIN SAWYER. AND YOU HAVE A CALL IN THE NEXT ROOM. MAYOR'S OFFICE WANTS A FULL REPORT.
WOW... I'VE NEVER SEEN HER LIKE THAT...
WHO DO YOU THINK IS NEXT IN LINE FOR THE TOP JOB? SHE'S JUST TRYING TO GET HER HEAD ON STRAIGHT FOR WHEN SHE GETS THE NOD FOR COMMISSIONER.
NOBODY BETTER FOR THE JOB, IF YOU ASK ME.
YEAH. BUT I WOULDN'T WISH IT ON ANYONE RIGHT NOW. AFTER GORDON--
HEY, YOU SEEN BARD? THE NEW KID? HE WAS JUST HERE A MINUTE AGO...

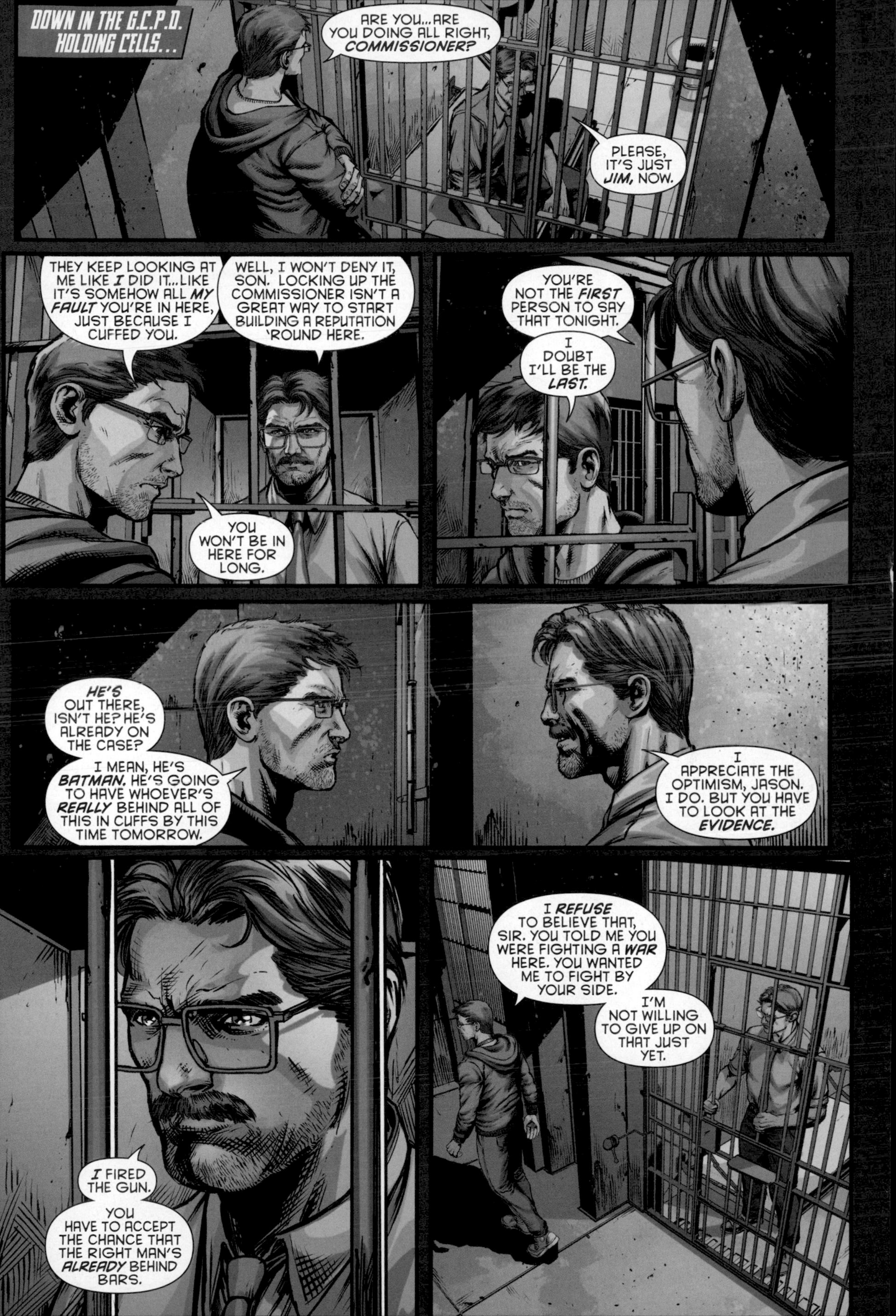
DOWN IN THE G.C.P.D. HOLDING CELLS...
ARE YOU...ARE YOU DOING ALL RIGHT, COMMISSIONER?
PLEASE, IT'S JUST JIM, NOW.
THEY KEEP LOOKING AT ME LIKE I DID IT...LIKE IT'S SOMEHOW ALL MY FAULT YOU'RE IN HERE, JUST BECAUSE I CUFFED YOU.
WELL, I WON'T DENY IT, SON. LOCKING UP THE COMMISSIONER ISN'T A GREAT WAY TO START BUILDING A REPUTATION 'ROUND HERE.
YOU WON'T BE IN HERE FOR LONG.
YOU'RE NOT THE FIRST PERSON TO SAY THAT TONIGHT.
I DOUBT I'LL BE THE LAST.
HE'S OUT THERE, ISN'T HE? HE'S ALREADY ON THE CASE?
I MEAN, HE'S BATMAN. HE'S GOING TO HAVE WHOEVER'S REALLY BEHIND ALL OF THIS IN CUFFS BY THIS TIME TOMORROW.
I APPRECIATE THE OPTIMISM, JASON. I DO. BUT YOU HAVE TO LOOK AT THE EVIDENCE.
I FIRED THE GUN.
YOU HAVE TO ACCEPT THE CHANCE THAT THE RIGHT MAN'S ALREADY BEHIND BARS.
I REFUSE TO BELIEVE THAT, SIR. YOU TOLD ME YOU WERE FIGHTING A WAR HERE. YOU WANTED ME TO FIGHT BY YOUR SIDE.
I'M NOT WILLING TO GIVE UP ON THAT JUST YET.

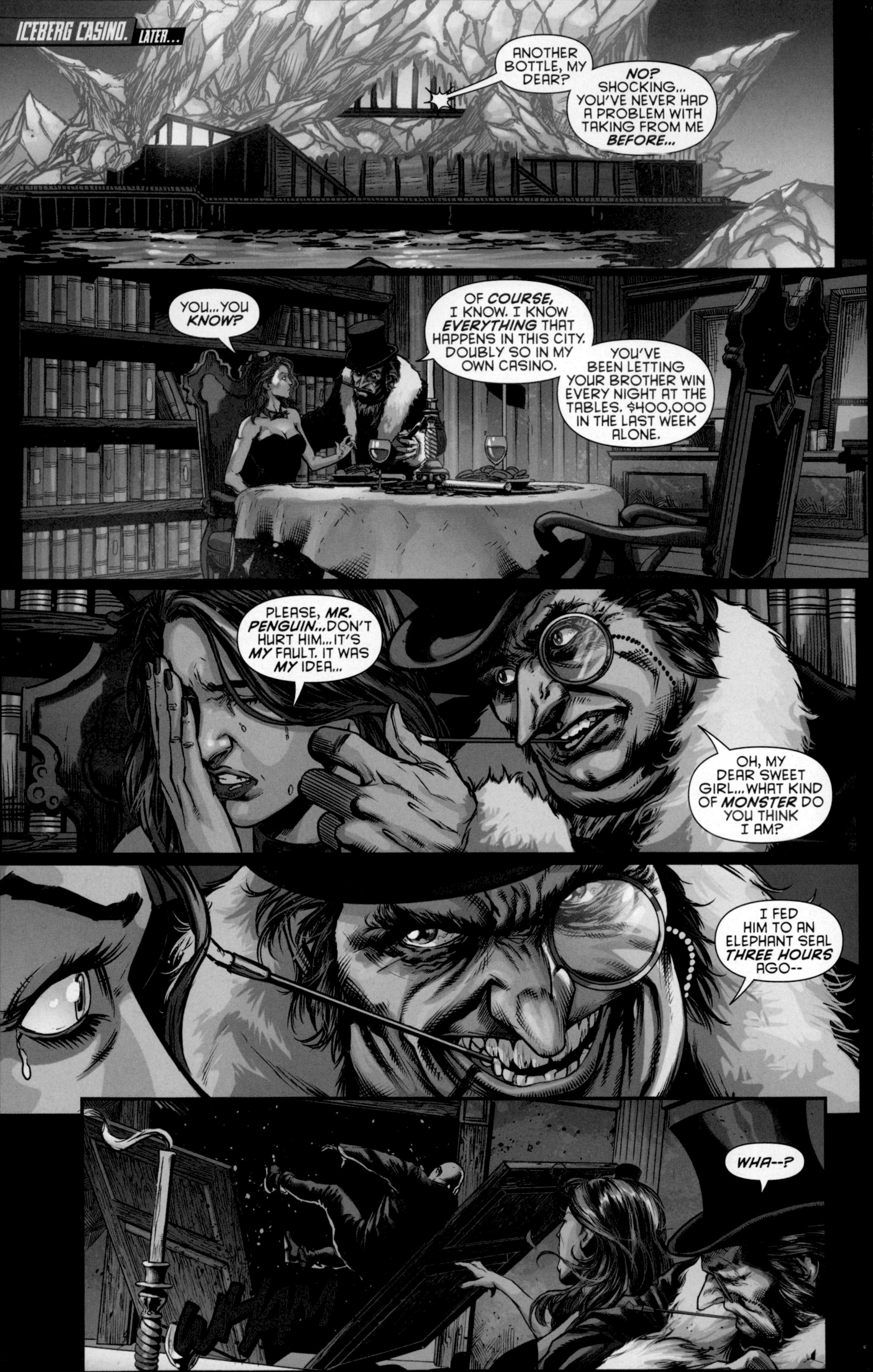
ICEBERG CASINO. LATER...
ANOTHER BOTTLE, MY DEAR?
NO? SHOCKING... YOU'VE NEVER HAD A PROBLEM WITH TAKING FROM ME BEFORE...
YOU...YOU KNOW?
OF COURSE, I KNOW. I KNOW EVERYTHING THAT HAPPENS IN THIS CITY. DOUBLY SO IN MY OWN CASINO.
YOU'VE BEEN LETTING YOUR BROTHER WIN EVERY NIGHT AT THE TABLES. $400,000 IN THE LAST WEEK ALONE.
PLEASE, MR. PENGUIN...DON'T HURT HIM...IT'S MY FAULT. IT WAS MY IDEA...
OH, MY DEAR SWEET GIRL...WHAT KIND OF MONSTER DO YOU THINK I AM?
I FED HIM TO AN ELEPHANT SEAL THREE HOURS AGO--
WHA--?

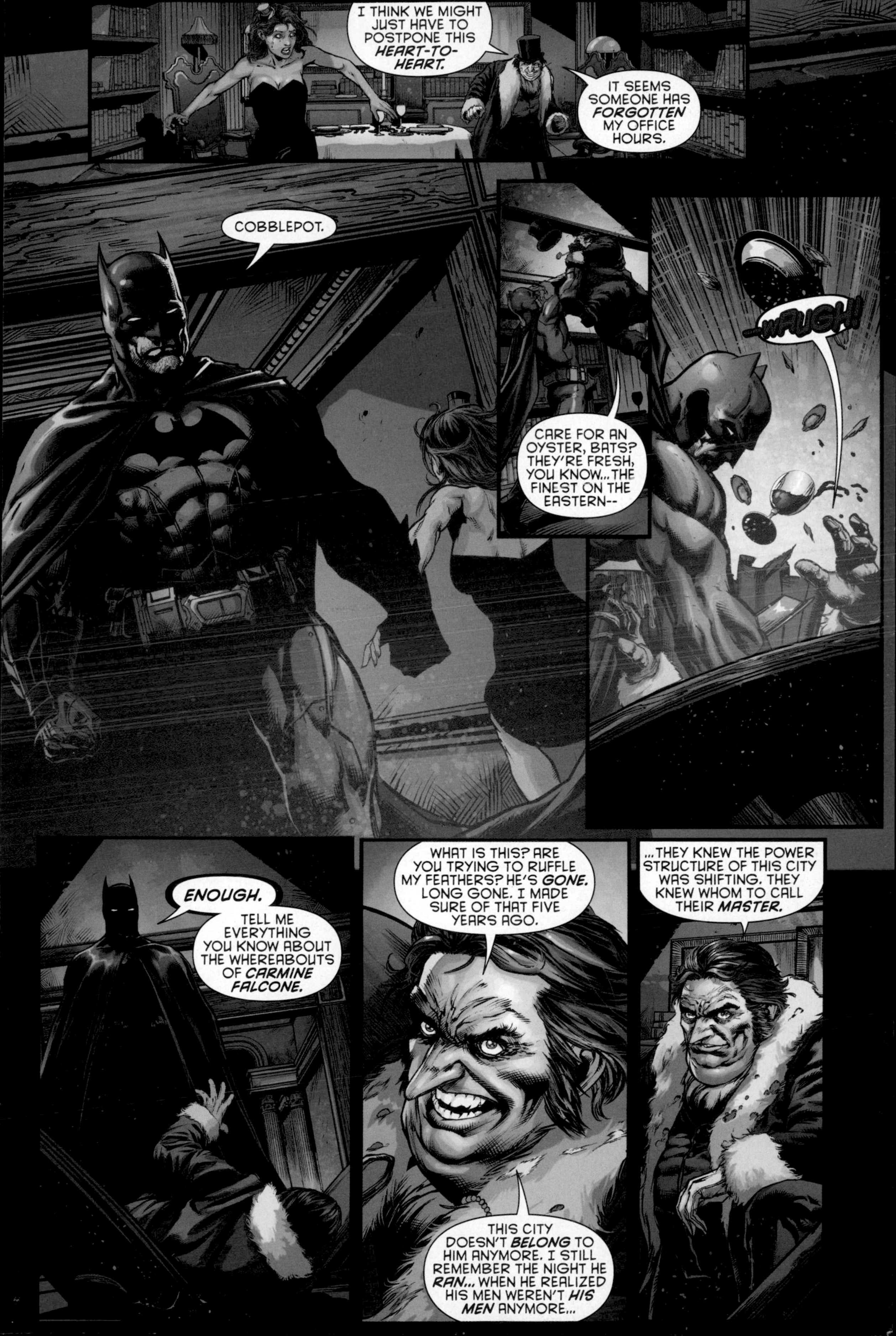
I THINK WE MIGHT JUST HAVE TO POSTPONE THIS *HEART-TO-HEART.*
IT SEEMS SOMEONE HAS *FORGOTTEN* MY OFFICE HOURS.
COBBLEPOT.
CARE FOR AN OYSTER, BATS? THEY'RE FRESH, YOU KNOW... THE FINEST ON THE EASTERN--
--WAUGH!
ENOUGH.
TELL ME EVERYTHING YOU KNOW ABOUT THE WHEREABOUTS OF *CARMINE FALCONE.*
WHAT IS THIS? ARE YOU TRYING TO RUFFLE MY FEATHERS? HE'S *GONE.* LONG GONE. I MADE SURE OF THAT FIVE YEARS AGO.
THIS CITY DOESN'T *BELONG* TO HIM ANYMORE. I STILL REMEMBER THE NIGHT HE *RAN*... WHEN HE REALIZED HIS MEN WEREN'T *HIS MEN* ANYMORE...
...THEY KNEW THE POWER STRUCTURE OF THIS CITY WAS SHIFTING. THEY KNEW WHOM TO CALL THEIR *MASTER.*

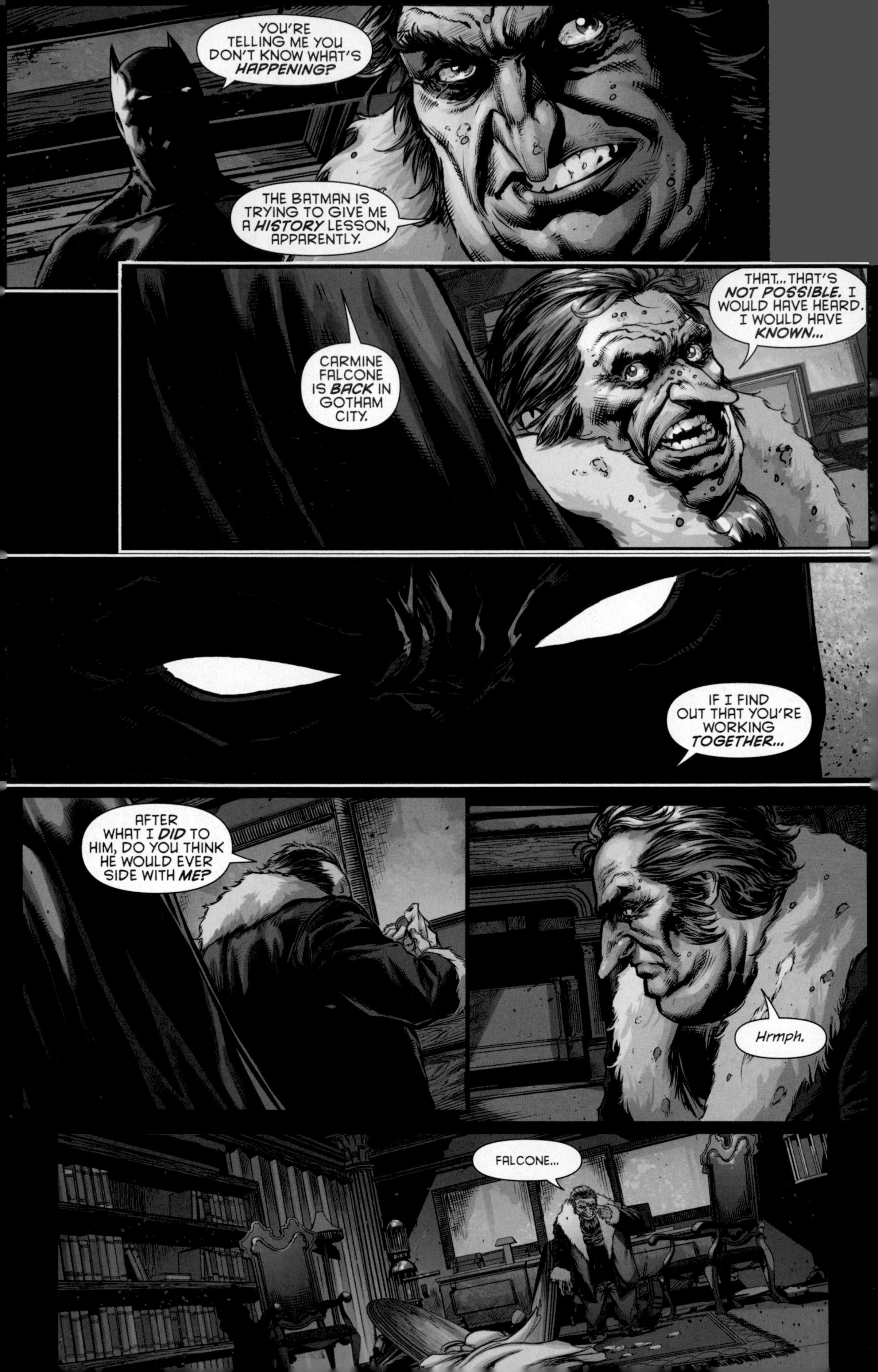

YOU'RE TELLING ME YOU DON'T KNOW WHAT'S HAPPENING?
THE BATMAN IS TRYING TO GIVE ME A HISTORY LESSON, APPARENTLY.
CARMINE FALCONE IS BACK IN GOTHAM CITY.
THAT... THAT'S NOT POSSIBLE. I WOULD HAVE HEARD. I WOULD HAVE KNOWN...
IF I FIND OUT THAT YOU'RE WORKING TOGETHER...
AFTER WHAT I DID TO HIM, DO YOU THINK HE WOULD EVER SIDE WITH ME?
Hrmph.
FALCONE...

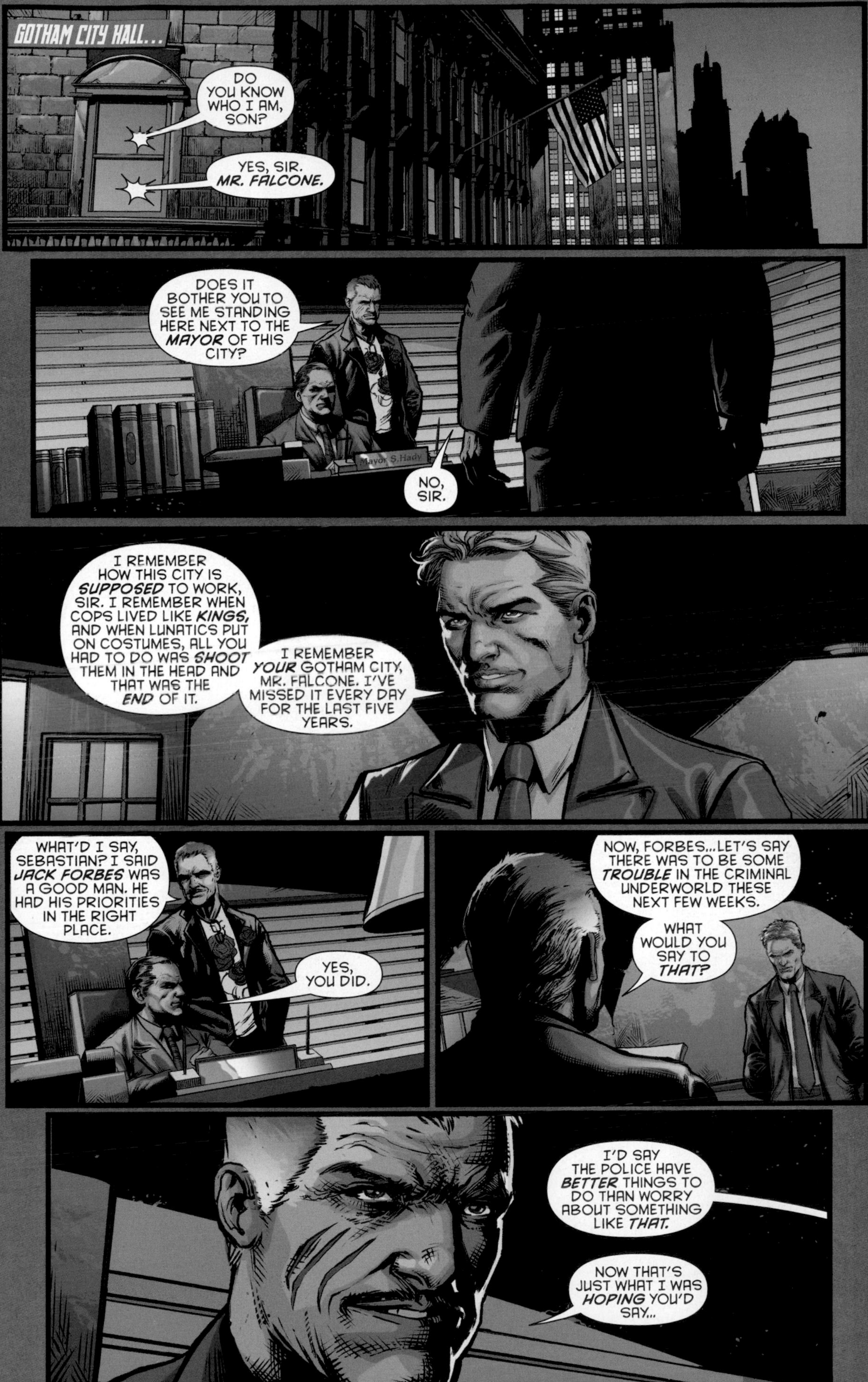
GOTHAM CITY HALL...
DO YOU KNOW WHO I AM, SON?
YES, SIR. MR. FALCONE.
DOES IT BOTHER YOU TO SEE ME STANDING HERE NEXT TO THE MAYOR OF THIS CITY?
Mayor S.Hady
NO, SIR.
I REMEMBER HOW THIS CITY IS SUPPOSED TO WORK, SIR. I REMEMBER WHEN COPS LIVED LIKE KINGS, AND WHEN LUNATICS PUT ON COSTUMES, ALL YOU HAD TO DO WAS SHOOT THEM IN THE HEAD AND THAT WAS THE END OF IT.
I REMEMBER YOUR GOTHAM CITY, MR. FALCONE. I'VE MISSED IT EVERY DAY FOR THE LAST FIVE YEARS.
WHAT'D I SAY, SEBASTIAN? I SAID JACK FORBES WAS A GOOD MAN. HE HAD HIS PRIORITIES IN THE RIGHT PLACE.
YES, YOU DID.
NOW, FORBES...LET'S SAY THERE WAS TO BE SOME TROUBLE IN THE CRIMINAL UNDERWORLD THESE NEXT FEW WEEKS.
WHAT WOULD YOU SAY TO THAT?
I'D SAY THE POLICE HAVE BETTER THINGS TO DO THAN WORRY ABOUT SOMETHING LIKE THAT.
NOW THAT'S JUST WHAT I WAS HOPING YOU'D SAY...

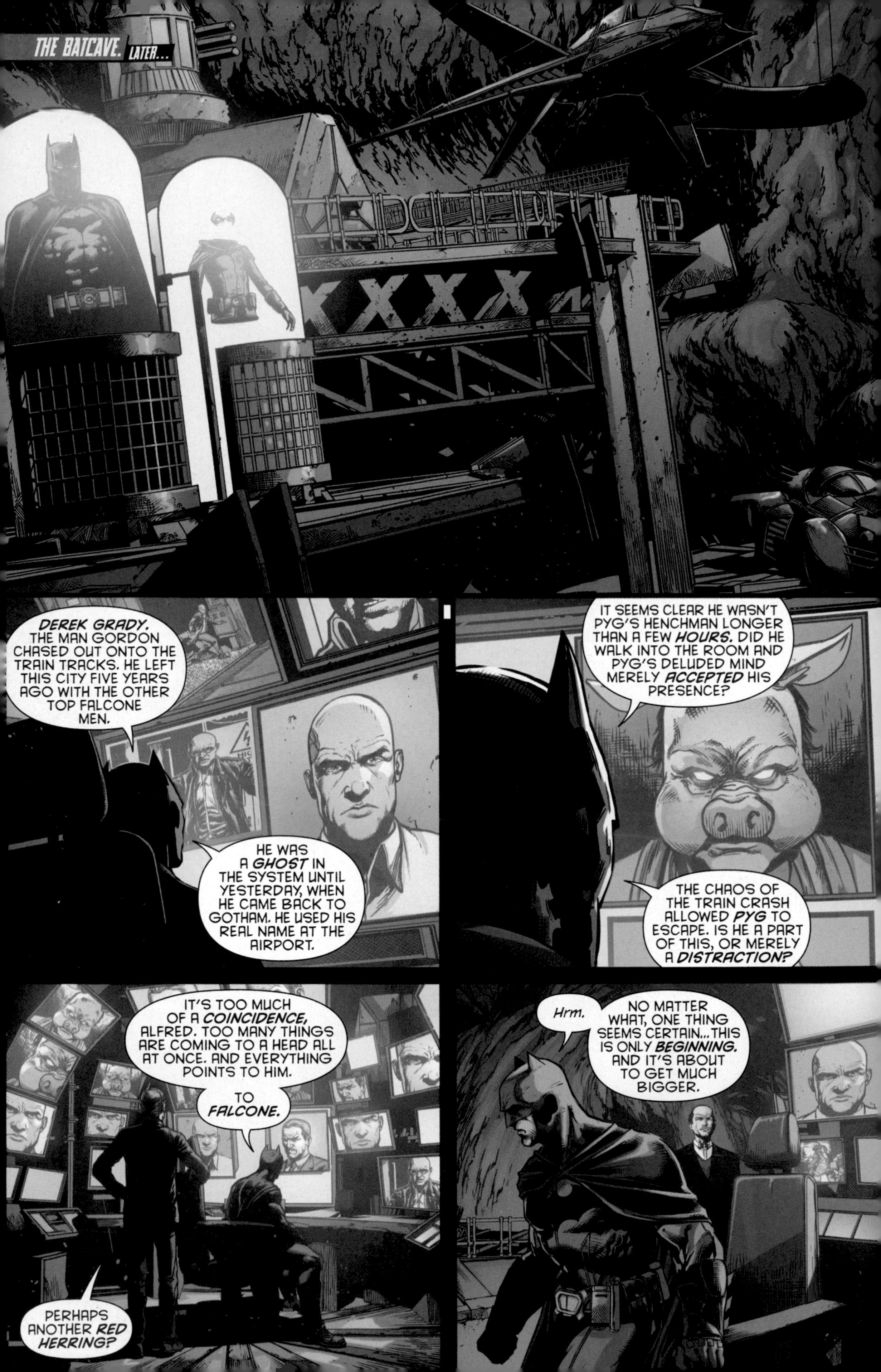
THE BATCAVE. LATER...
DERECK GRADY. THE MAN GORDON CHASED OUT ONTO THE TRAIN TRACKS. HE LEFT THIS CITY FIVE YEARS AGO WITH THE OTHER TOP FALCONE MEN.
HE WAS A GHOST IN THE SYSTEM UNTIL YESTERDAY, WHEN HE CAME BACK TO GOTHAM. HE USED HIS REAL NAME AT THE AIRPORT.
IT SEEMS CLEAR HE WASN'T PYG'S HENCHMAN LONGER THAN A FEW HOURS. DID HE WALK INTO THE ROOM AND PYG'S DELUDED MIND MERELY ACCEPTED HIS PRESENCE?
THE CHAOS OF THE TRAIN CRASH ALLOWED PYG TO ESCAPE. IS HE A PART OF THIS, OR MERELY A DISTRACTION?
IT'S TOO MUCH OF A COINCIDENCE, ALFRED. TOO MANY THINGS ARE COMING TO A HEAD ALL AT ONCE. AND EVERYTHING POINTS TO HIM.
TO FALCONE.
PERHAPS ANOTHER RED HERRING?
Hrm.
NO MATTER WHAT, ONE THING SEEMS CERTAIN... THIS IS ONLY BEGINNING. AND IT'S ABOUT TO GET MUCH BIGGER.

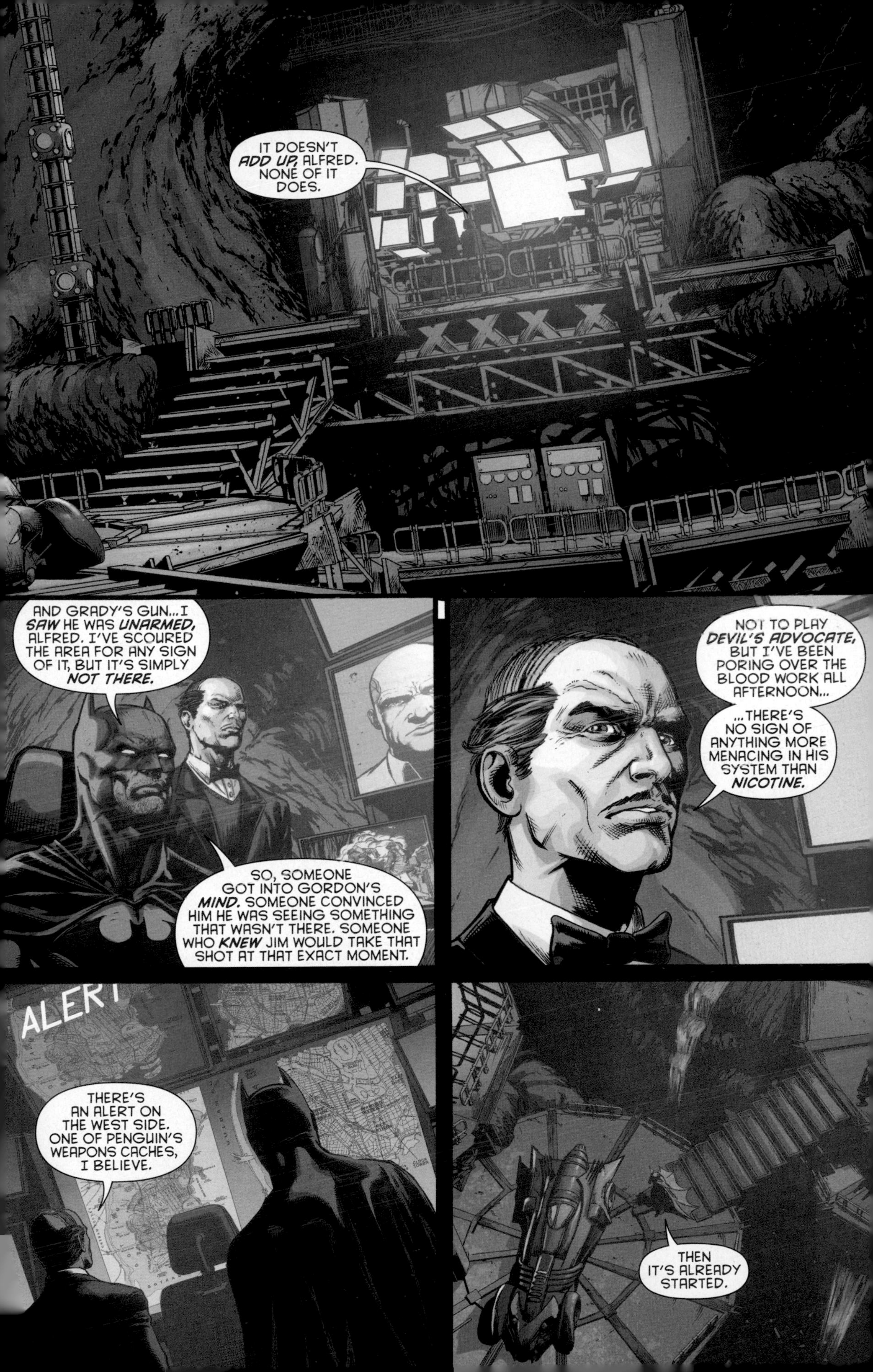

IT DOESN'T ADD UP, ALFRED. NONE OF IT DOES.
AND GRADY'S GUN...I SAW HE WAS UNARMED, ALFRED. I'VE SCOURED THE AREA FOR ANY SIGN OF IT, BUT IT'S SIMPLY NOT THERE.
SO, SOMEONE GOT INTO GORDON'S MIND. SOMEONE CONVINCED HIM HE WAS SEEING SOMETHING THAT WASN'T THERE. SOMEONE WHO KNEW JIM WOULD TAKE THAT SHOT AT THAT EXACT MOMENT.
NOT TO PLAY DEVIL'S ADVOCATE, BUT I'VE BEEN PORING OVER THE BLOOD WORK ALL AFTERNOON...
...THERE'S NO SIGN OF ANYTHING MORE MENACING IN HIS SYSTEM THAN NICOTINE.
ALERT
THERE'S AN ALERT ON THE WEST SIDE. ONE OF PENGUIN'S WEAPONS CACHES, I BELIEVE.
THEN IT'S ALREADY STARTED.

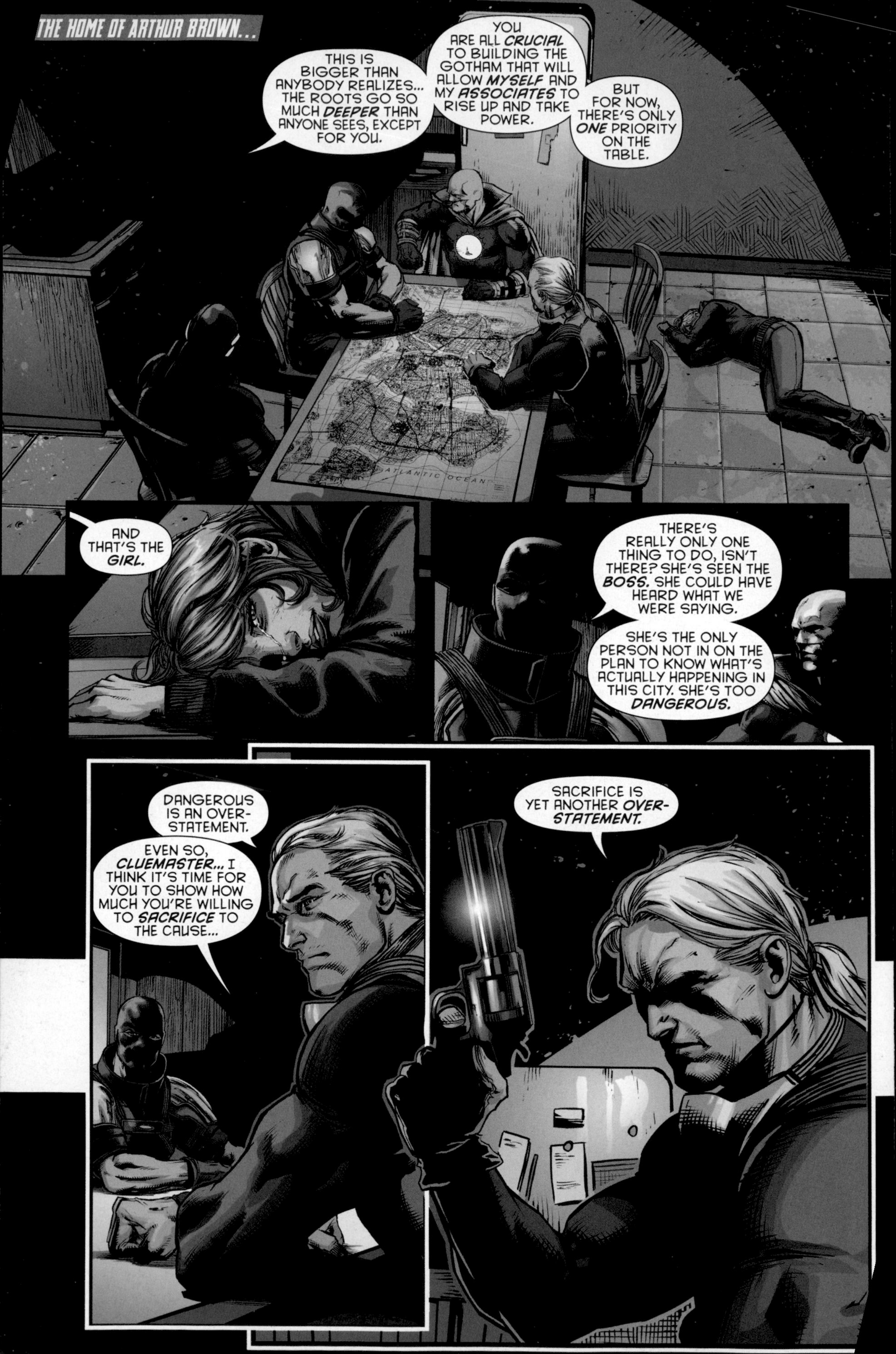
THE HOME OF ARTHUR BROWN...
THIS IS BIGGER THAN ANYBODY REALIZES... THE ROOTS GO SO MUCH DEEPER THAN ANYONE SEES, EXCEPT FOR YOU.
YOU ARE ALL CRUCIAL TO BUILDING THE GOTHAM THAT WILL ALLOW MYSELF AND MY ASSOCIATES TO RISE UP AND TAKE POWER.
BUT FOR NOW, THERE'S ONLY ONE PRIORITY ON THE TABLE.
ATLANTIC OCEAN
AND THAT'S THE GIRL.
THERE'S REALLY ONLY ONE THING TO DO, ISN'T THERE? SHE'S SEEN THE BOSS. SHE COULD HAVE HEARD WHAT WE WERE SAYING.
SHE'S THE ONLY PERSON NOT IN ON THE PLAN TO KNOW WHAT'S ACTUALLY HAPPENING IN THIS CITY. SHE'S TOO DANGEROUS.
DANGEROUS IS AN OVER-STATEMENT.
EVEN SO, CLUEMASTER... I THINK IT'S TIME FOR YOU TO SHOW HOW MUCH YOU'RE WILLING TO SACRIFICE TO THE CAUSE...
SACRIFICE IS YET ANOTHER OVER-STATEMENT.

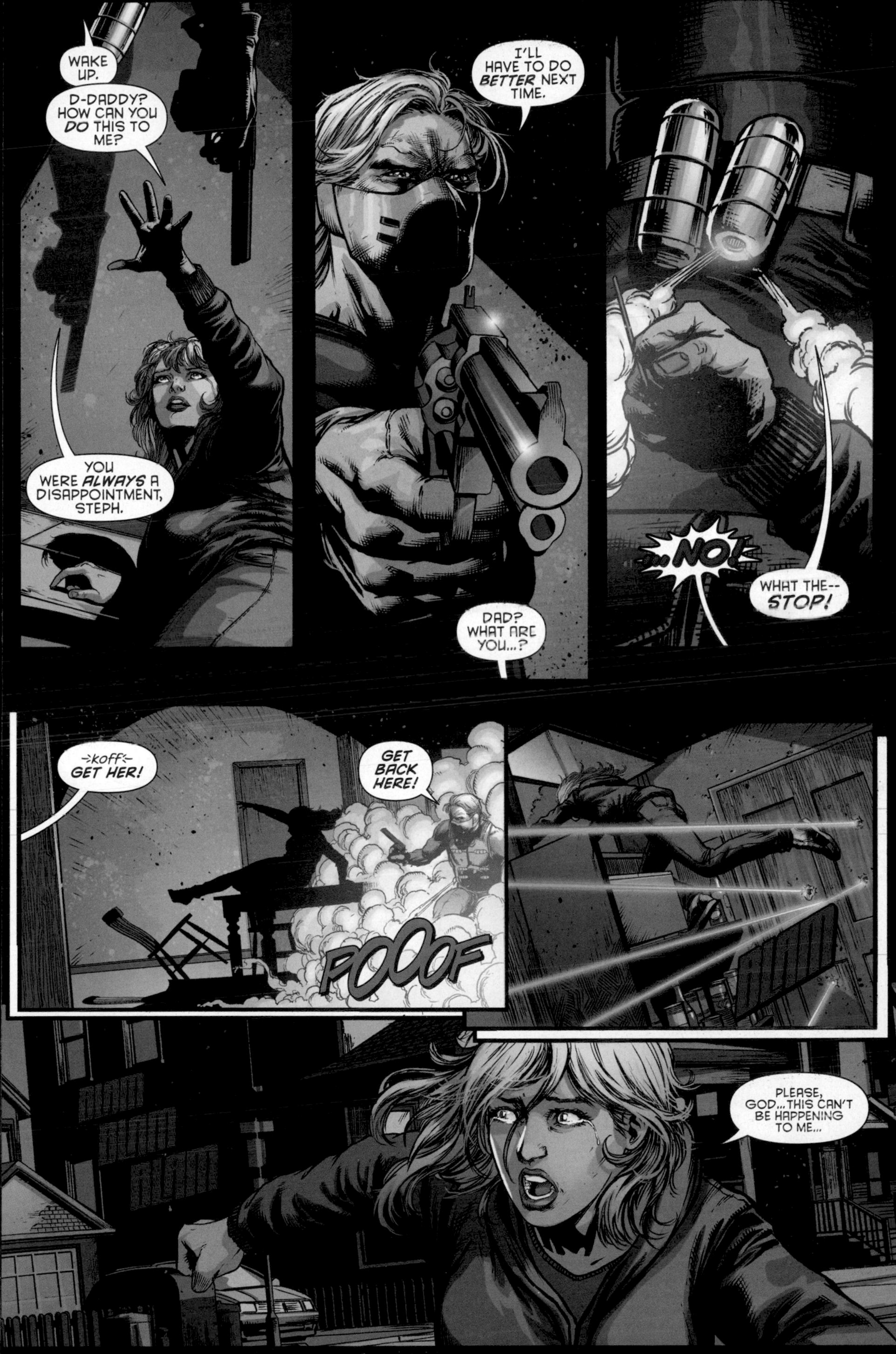
WAKE UP.
D-DADDY? HOW CAN YOU DO THIS TO ME?
YOU WERE ALWAYS A DISAPPOINTMENT, STEPH.
I'LL HAVE TO DO BETTER NEXT TIME.
DAD? WHAT ARE YOU...?
...NO!
WHAT THE-- STOP!
-koff- GET HER!
GET BACK HERE!
POOOF
PLEASE, GOD... THIS CAN'T BE HAPPENING TO ME...

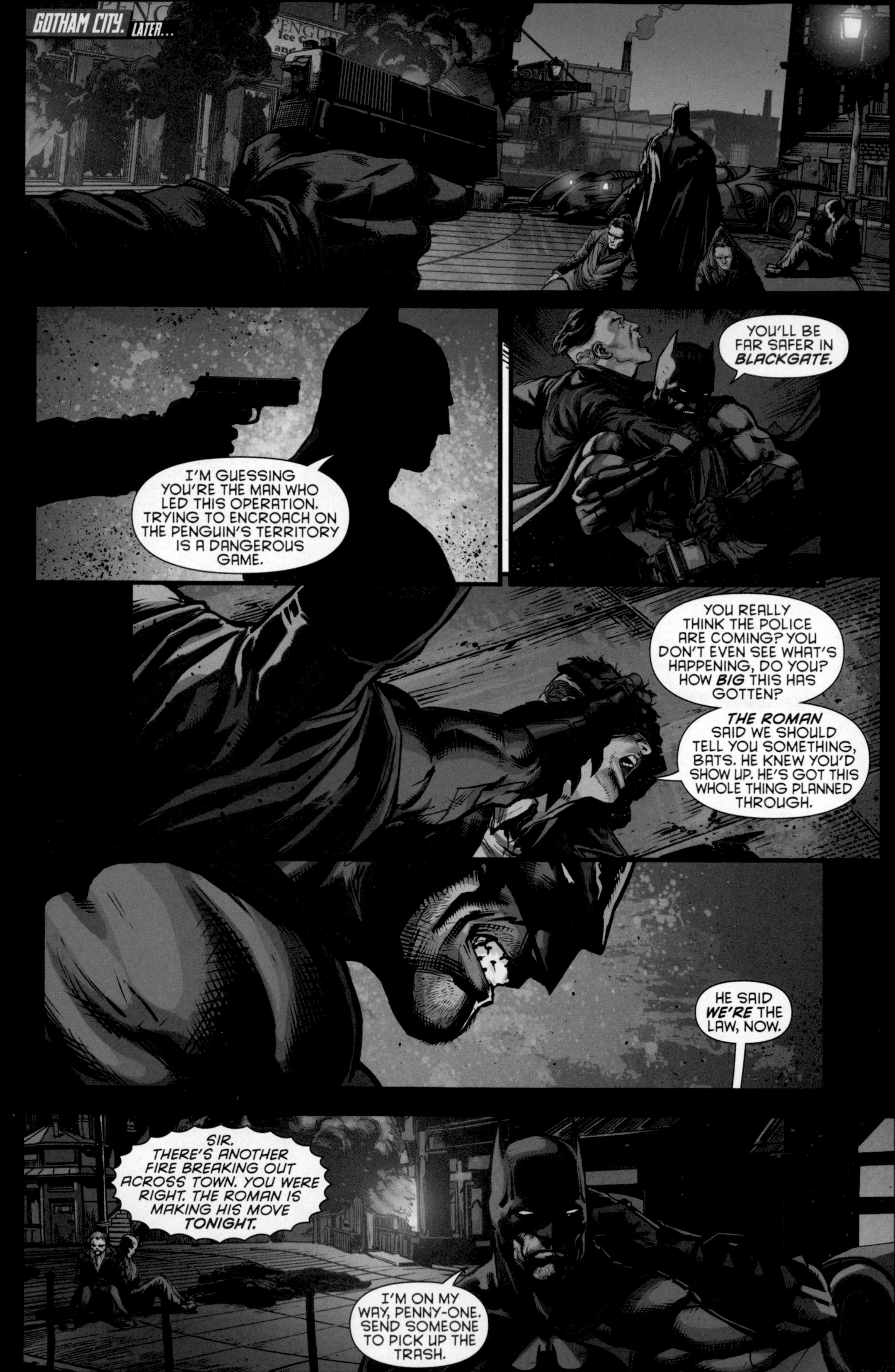
GOTHAM CITY. LATER...
PENGUIN Ice Cream and
I'M GUESSING YOU'RE THE MAN WHO LED THIS OPERATION. TRYING TO ENCROACH ON THE PENGUIN'S TERRITORY IS A DANGEROUS GAME.
YOU'LL BE FAR SAFER IN BLACKGATE.
YOU REALLY THINK THE POLICE ARE COMING? YOU DON'T EVEN SEE WHAT'S HAPPENING, DO YOU? HOW BIG THIS HAS GOTTEN?
THE ROMAN SAID WE SHOULD TELL YOU SOMETHING, BATS. HE KNEW YOU'D SHOW UP. HE'S GOT THIS WHOLE THING PLANNED THROUGH.
HE SAID WE'RE THE LAW, NOW.
SIR. THERE'S ANOTHER FIRE BREAKING OUT ACROSS TOWN. YOU WERE RIGHT. THE ROMAN IS MAKING HIS MOVE TONIGHT.
I'M ON MY WAY, PENNY-ONE. SEND SOMEONE TO PICK UP THE TRASH.

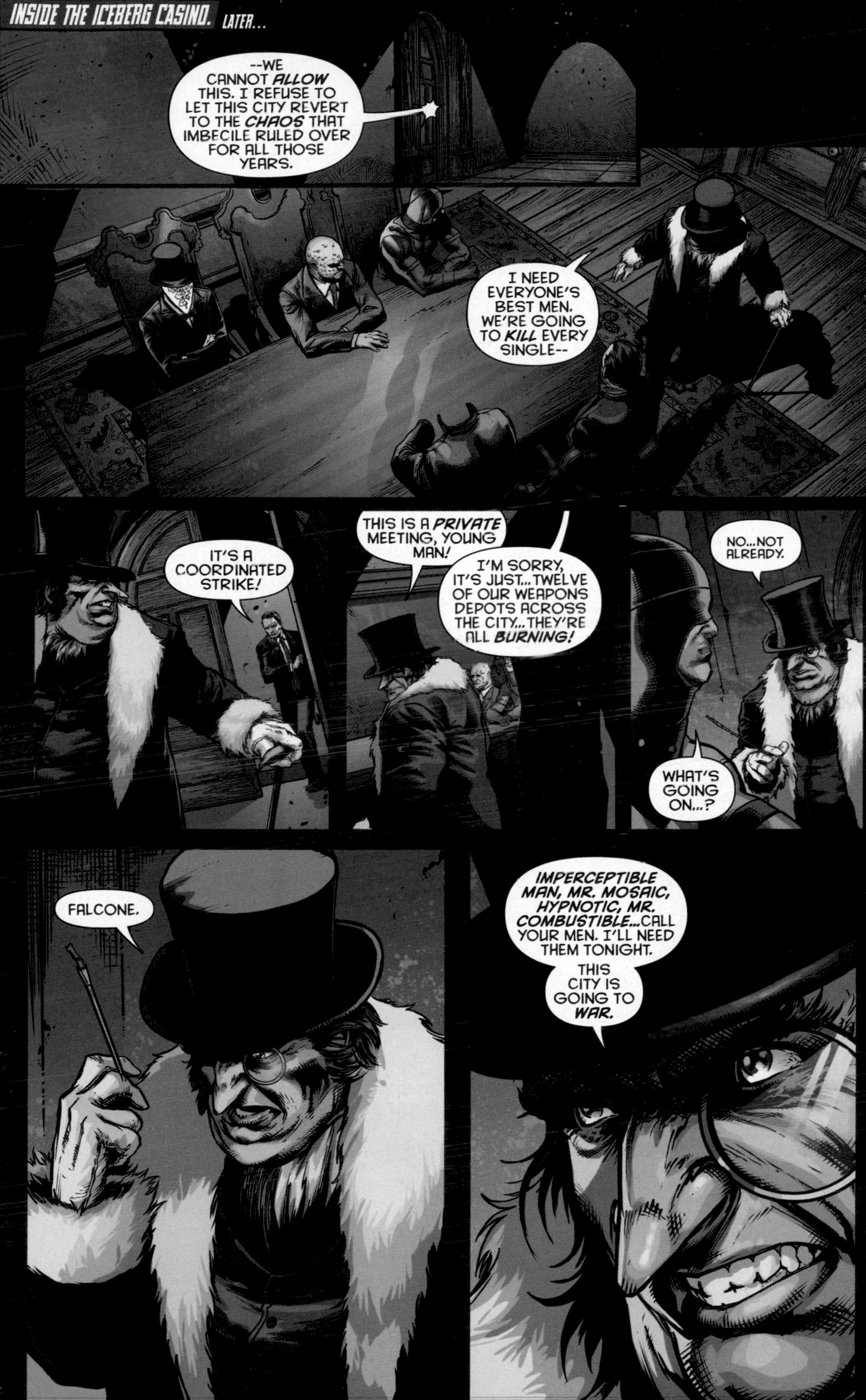
INSIDE THE ICEBERG CASINO. LATER...
--WE CANNOT ALLOW THIS. I REFUSE TO LET THIS CITY REVERT TO THE CHAOS THAT IMBECILE RULED OVER FOR ALL THOSE YEARS.
I NEED EVERYONE'S BEST MEN. WE'RE GOING TO KILL EVERY SINGLE--
IT'S A COORDINATED STRIKE!
THIS IS A PRIVATE MEETING, YOUNG MAN!
I'M SORRY, IT'S JUST... TWELVE OF OUR WEAPONS DEPOTS ACROSS THE CITY... THEY'RE ALL BURNING!
NO... NOT ALREADY.
WHAT'S GOING ON...?
FALCONE.
IMPERCEPTIBLE MAN, MR. MOSAIC, HYPNOTIC, MR. COMBUSTIBLE... CALL YOUR MEN. I'LL NEED THEM TONIGHT.
THIS CITY IS GOING TO WAR.

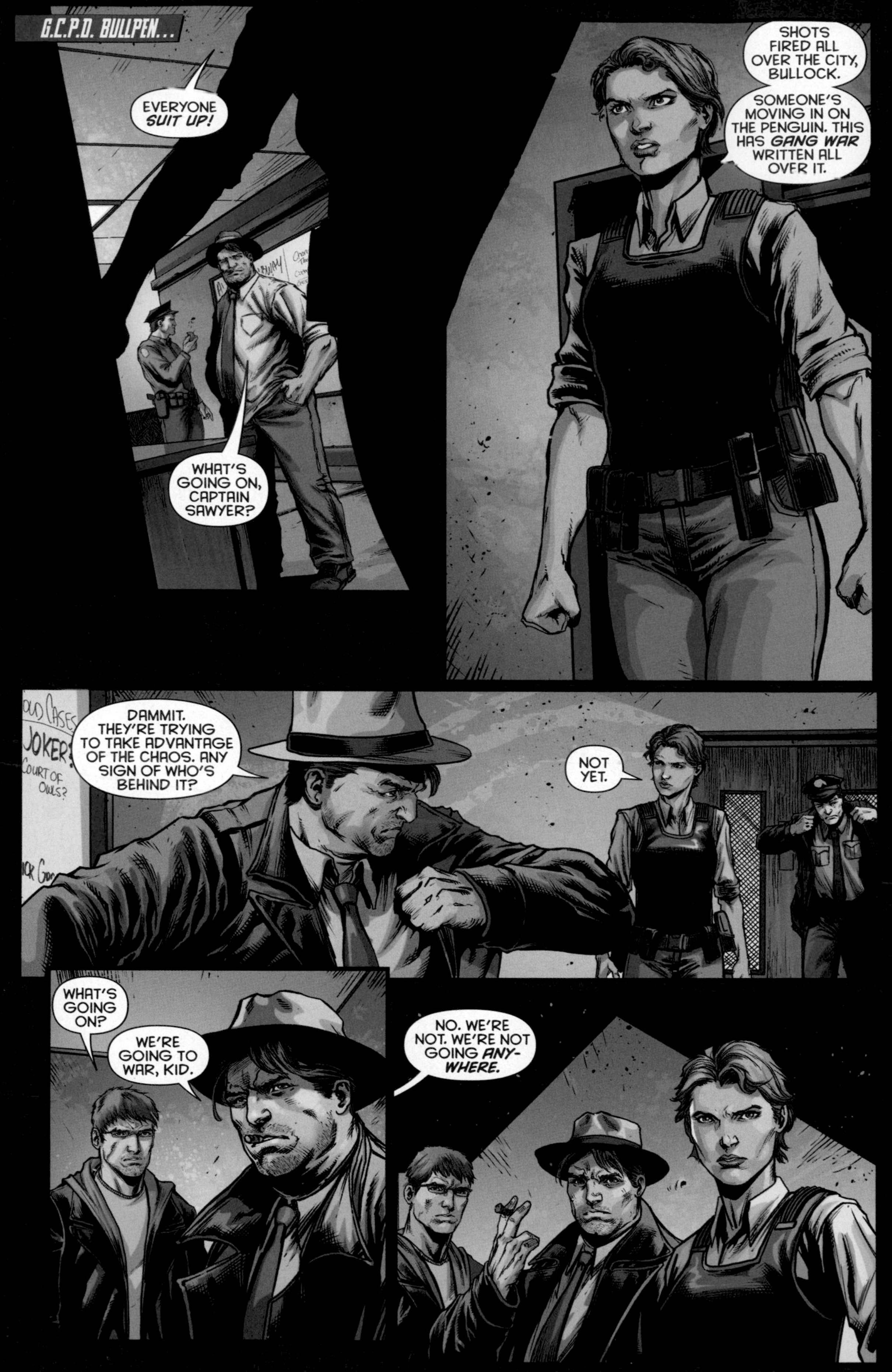
G.C.P.D. BULLPEN...
EVERYONE SUIT UP!
WHAT'S GOING ON, CAPTAIN SAWYER?
SHOTS FIRED ALL OVER THE CITY, BULLOCK.
SOMEONE'S MOVING IN ON THE PENGUIN. THIS HAS GANG WAR WRITTEN ALL OVER IT.
DAMMIT. THEY'RE TRYING TO TAKE ADVANTAGE OF THE CHAOS. ANY SIGN OF WHO'S BEHIND IT?
NOT YET.
WHAT'S GOING ON?
WE'RE GOING TO WAR, KID.
NO. WE'RE NOT. WE'RE NOT GOING ANYWHERE.

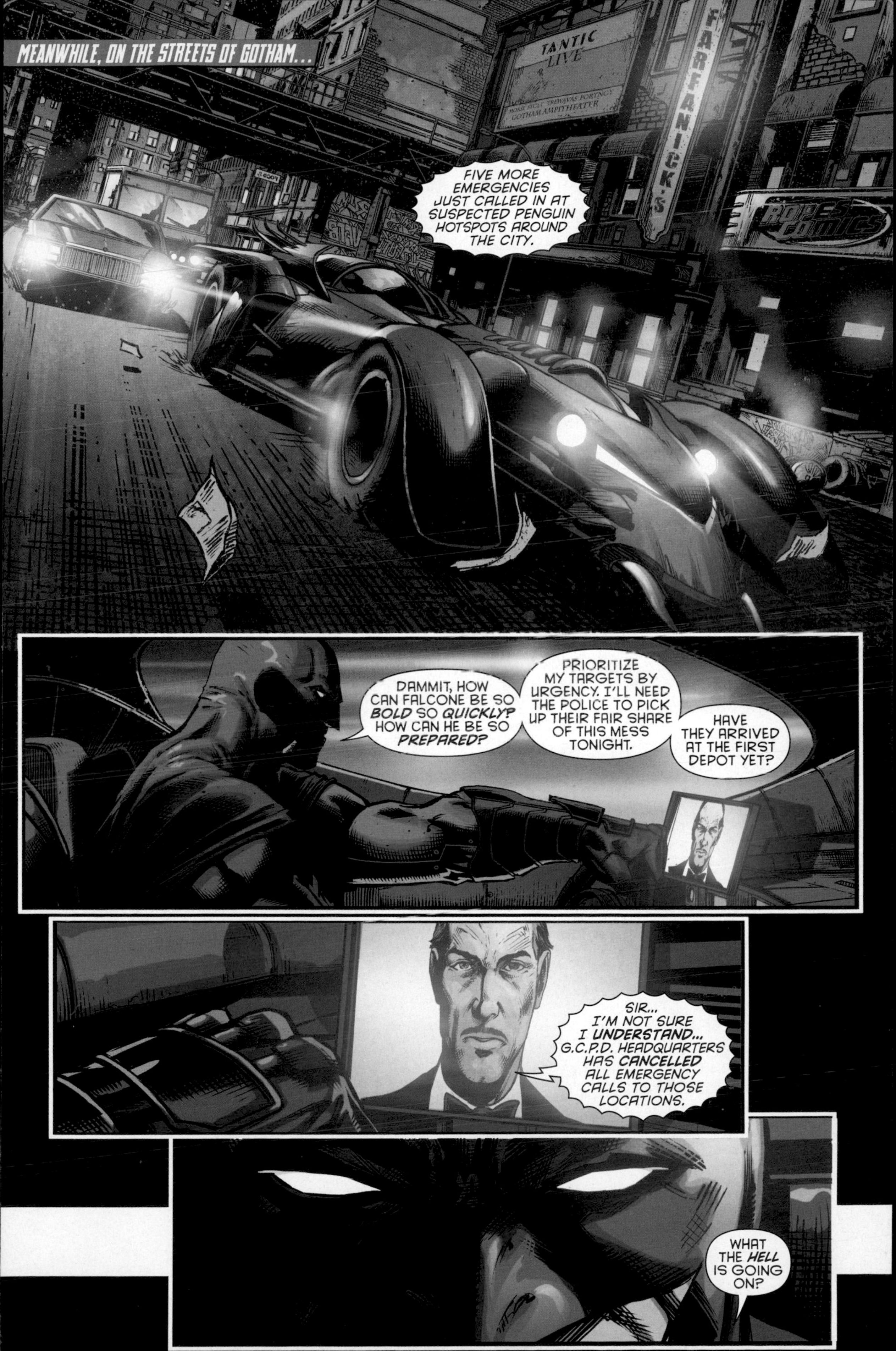
MEANWHILE, ON THE STREETS OF GOTHAM...
FIVE MORE EMERGENCIES JUST CALLED IN AT SUSPECTED PENGUIN HOTSPOTS AROUND THE CITY.
DAMMIT, HOW CAN FALCONE BE SO BOLD SO QUICKLY? HOW CAN HE BE SO PREPARED?
PRIORITIZE MY TARGETS BY URGENCY. I'LL NEED THE POLICE TO PICK UP THEIR FAIR SHARE OF THIS MESS TONIGHT.
HAVE THEY ARRIVED AT THE FIRST DEPOT YET?
SIR... I'M NOT SURE I UNDERSTAND... G.C.P.D. HEADQUARTERS HAS CANCELLED ALL EMERGENCY CALLS TO THOSE LOCATIONS.
WHAT THE HELL IS GOING ON?

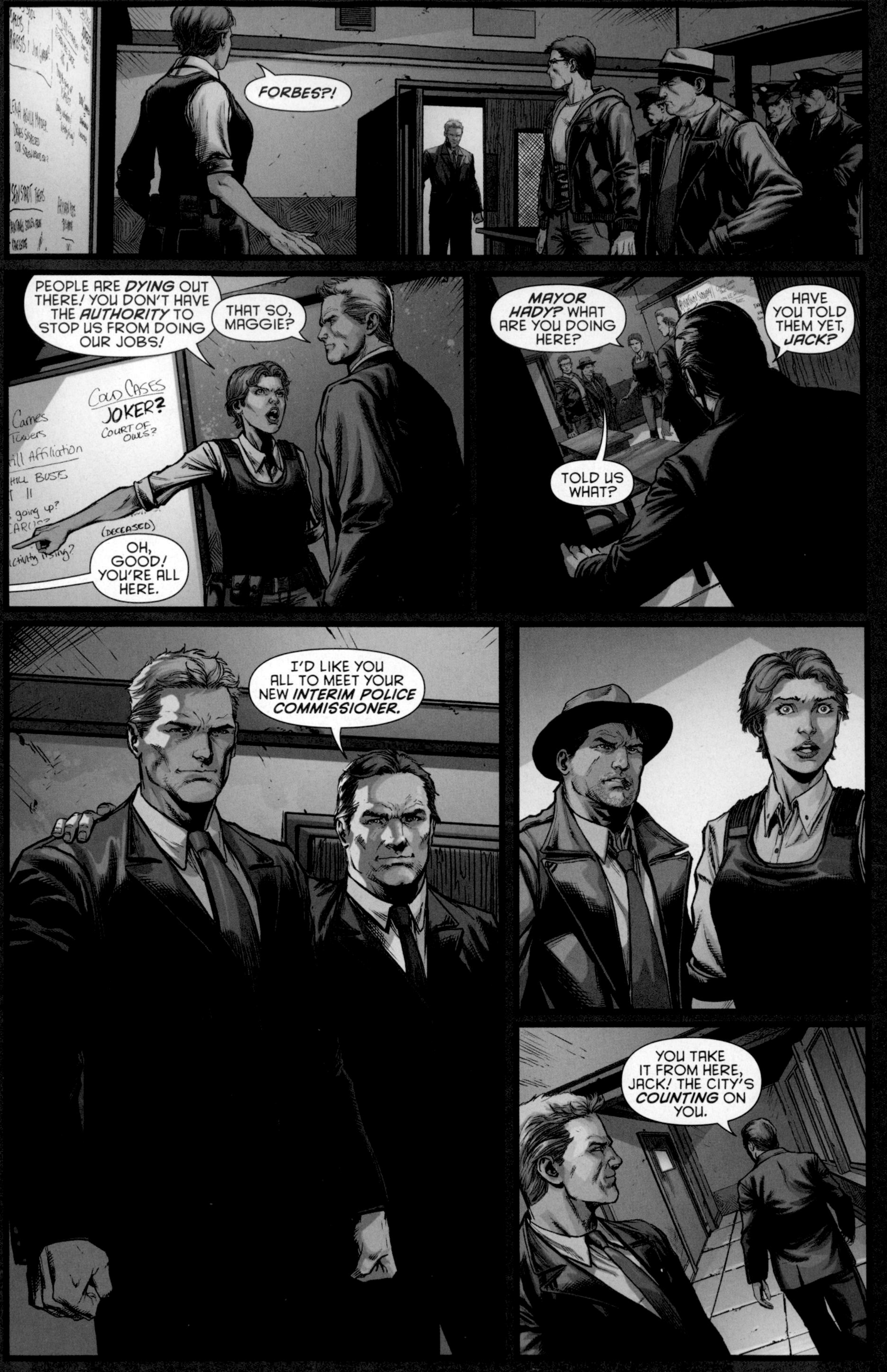
FORBES?!
PEOPLE ARE DYING OUT THERE! YOU DON'T HAVE THE AUTHORITY TO STOP US FROM DOING OUR JOBS!
THAT SO, MAGGIE?
COLD CASES
JOKER?
COURT OF OWLS?
(DECEASED)
OH, GOOD! YOU'RE ALL HERE.
MAYOR HADY? WHAT ARE YOU DOING HERE?
HAVE YOU TOLD THEM YET, JACK?
TOLD US WHAT?
I'D LIKE YOU ALL TO MEET YOUR NEW INTERIM POLICE COMMISSIONER.
YOU TAKE IT FROM HERE, JACK! THE CITY'S COUNTING ON YOU.

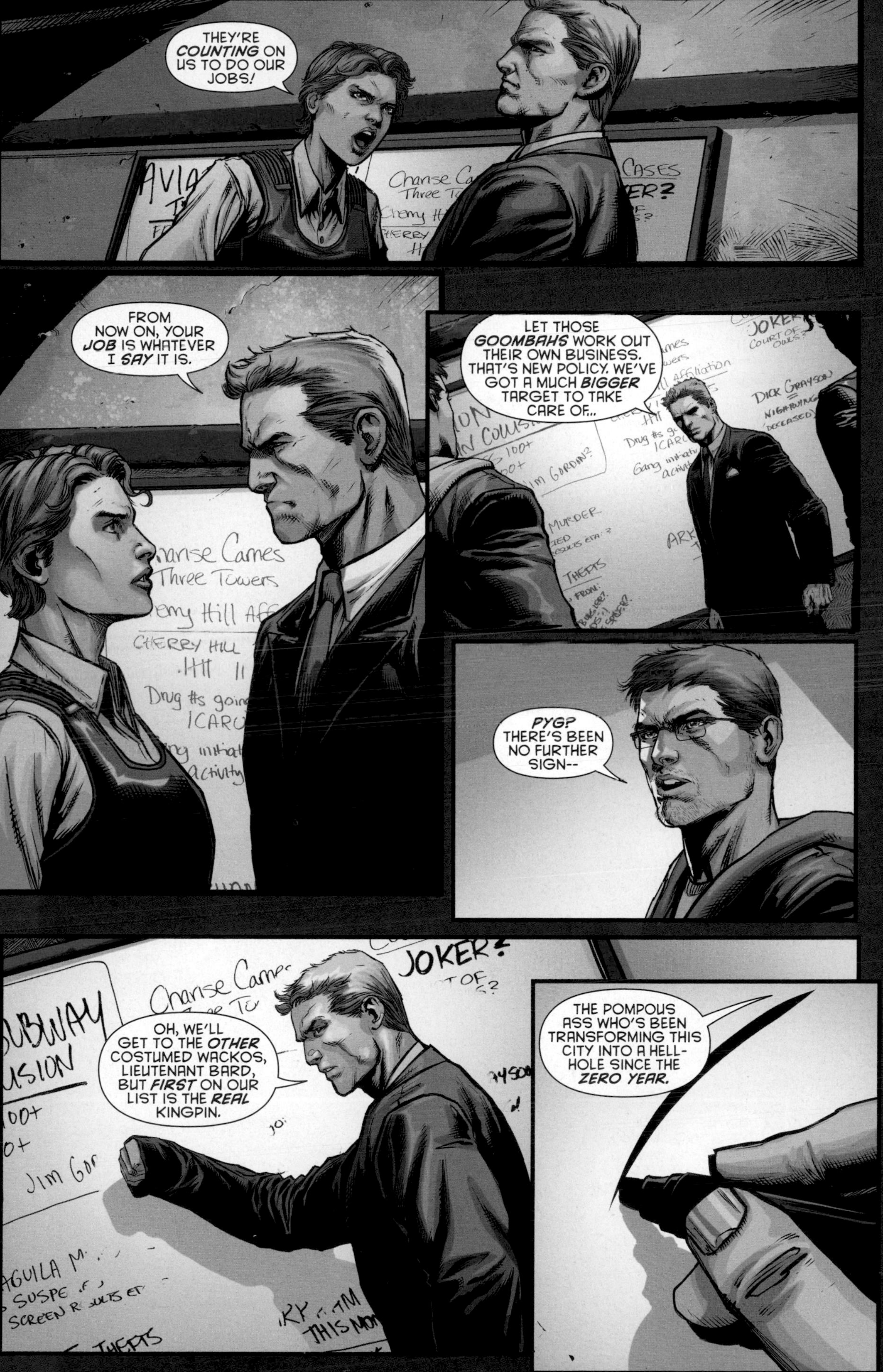
THEY'RE COUNTING ON US TO DO OUR JOBS!
FROM NOW ON, YOUR JOB IS WHATEVER I SAY IT IS.
LET THOSE GOOMBAHS WORK OUT THEIR OWN BUSINESS. THAT'S NEW POLICY. WE'VE GOT A MUCH BIGGER TARGET TO TAKE CARE OF...
PYG? THERE'S BEEN NO FURTHER SIGN--
OH, WE'LL GET TO THE OTHER COSTUMED WACKOS, LIEUTENANT BARD, BUT FIRST ON OUR LIST IS THE REAL KINGPIN.
THE POMPOUS ASS WHO'S BEEN TRANSFORMING THIS CITY INTO A HELL-HOLE SINCE THE ZERO YEAR.

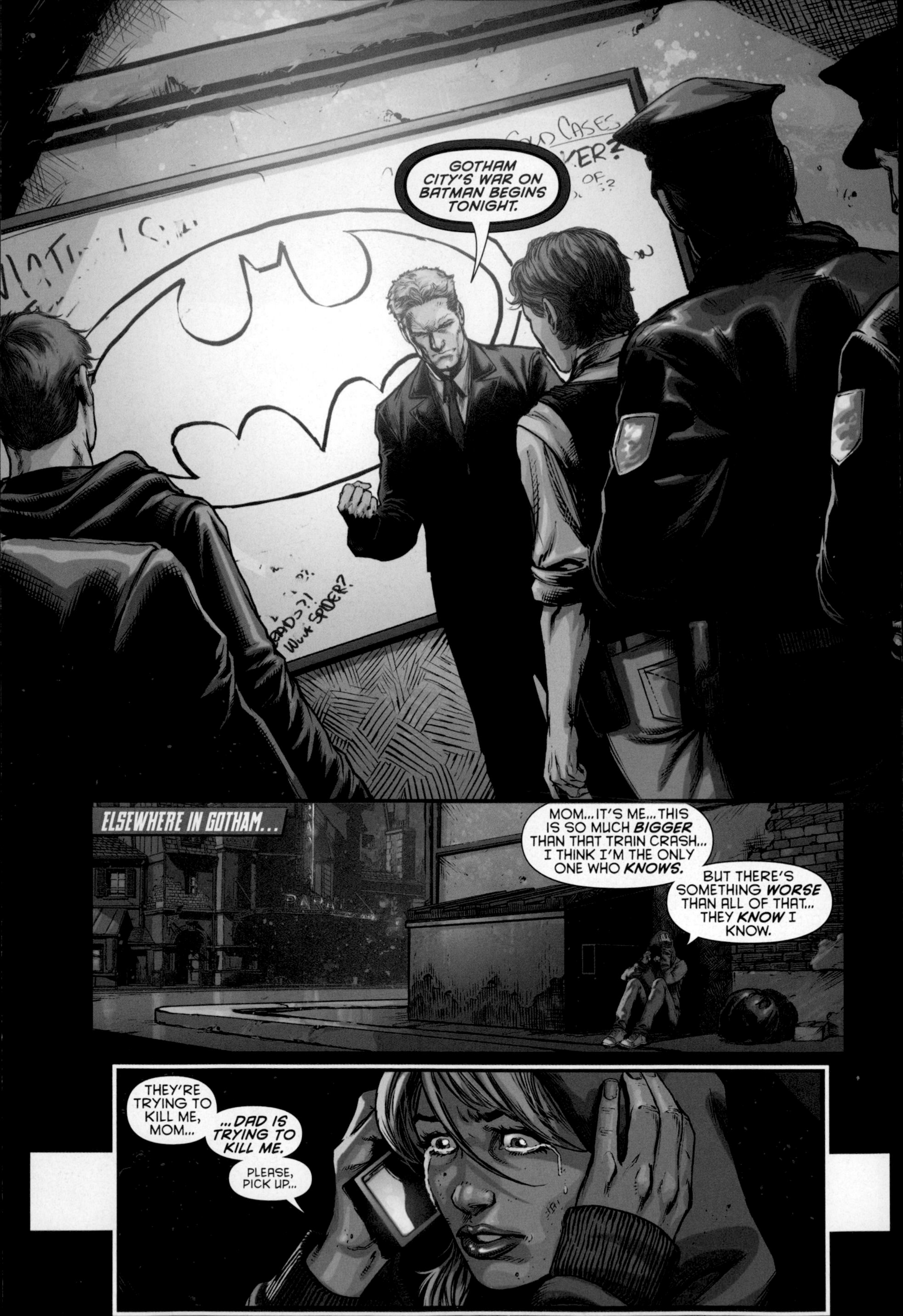
GOTHAM CITY'S WAR ON BATMAN BEGINS TONIGHT.
COLD CASES
ELSEWHERE IN GOTHAM...
MOM...IT'S ME...THIS IS SO MUCH BIGGER THAN THAT TRAIN CRASH... I THINK I'M THE ONLY ONE WHO KNOWS.
BUT THERE'S SOMETHING WORSE THAN ALL OF THAT... THEY KNOW I KNOW.
THEY'RE TRYING TO KILL ME, MOM...
...DAD IS TRYING TO KILL ME.
PLEASE, PICK UP...

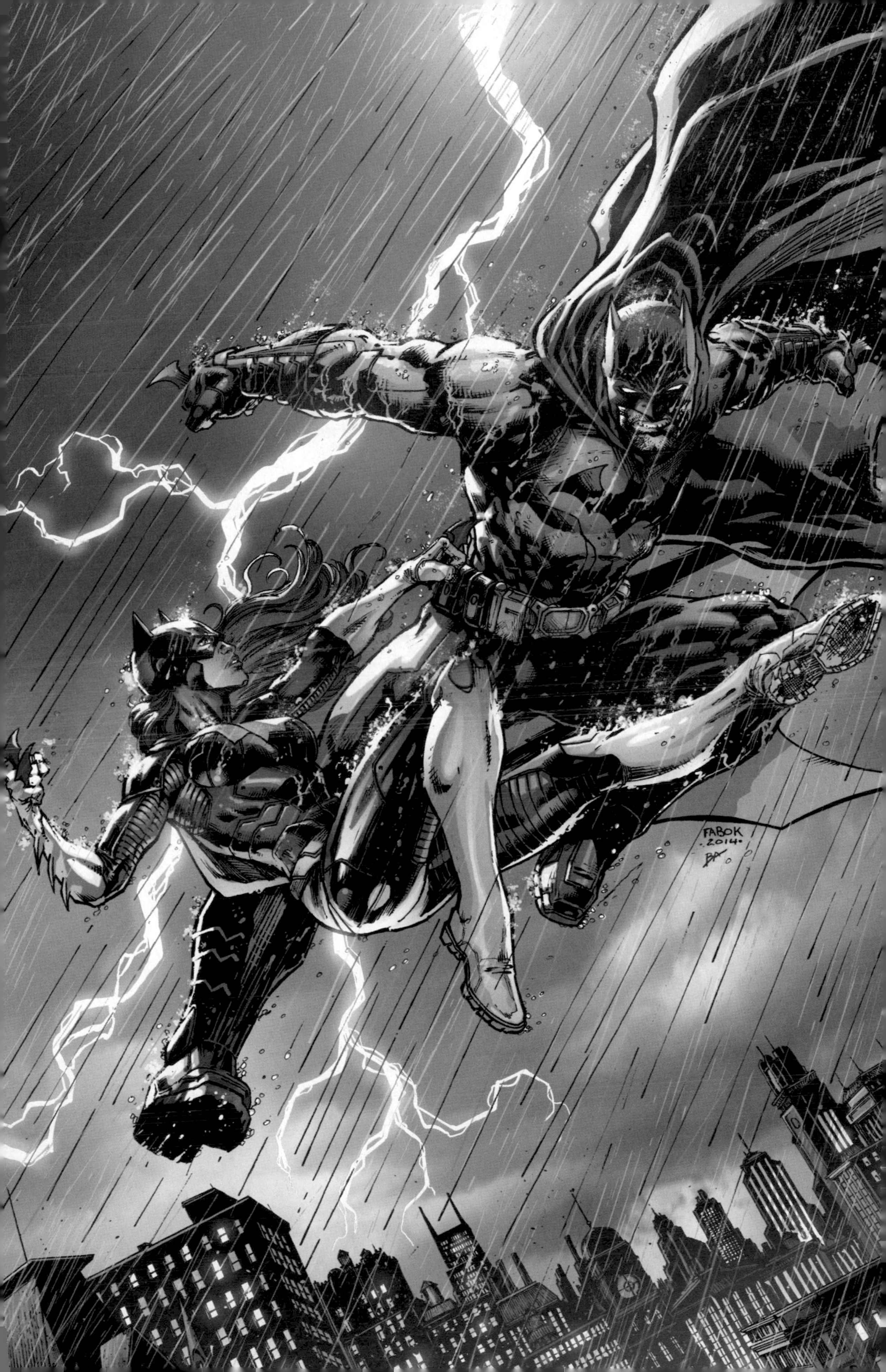
FABOK
2014
BA

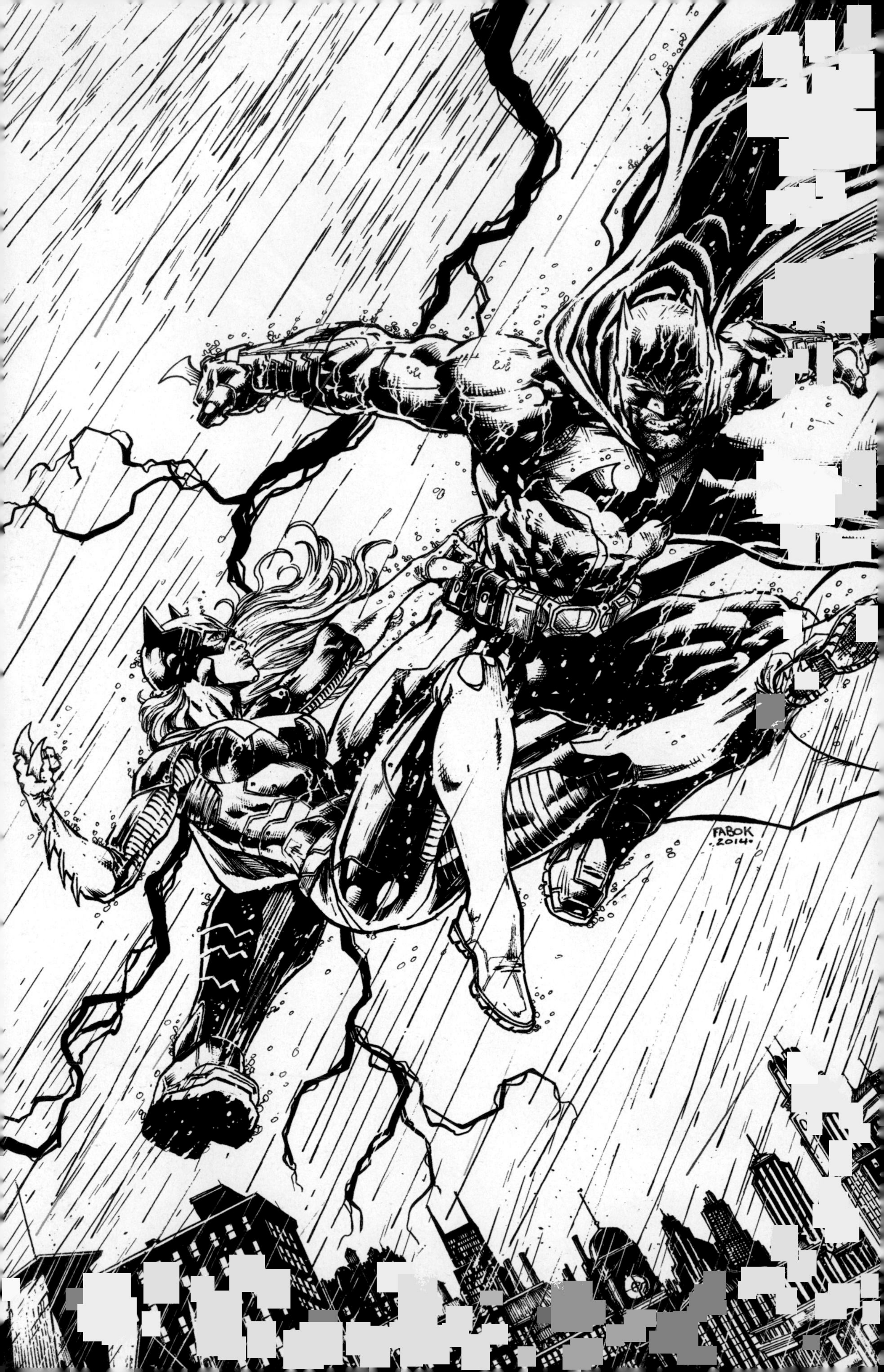
FABOK
2014

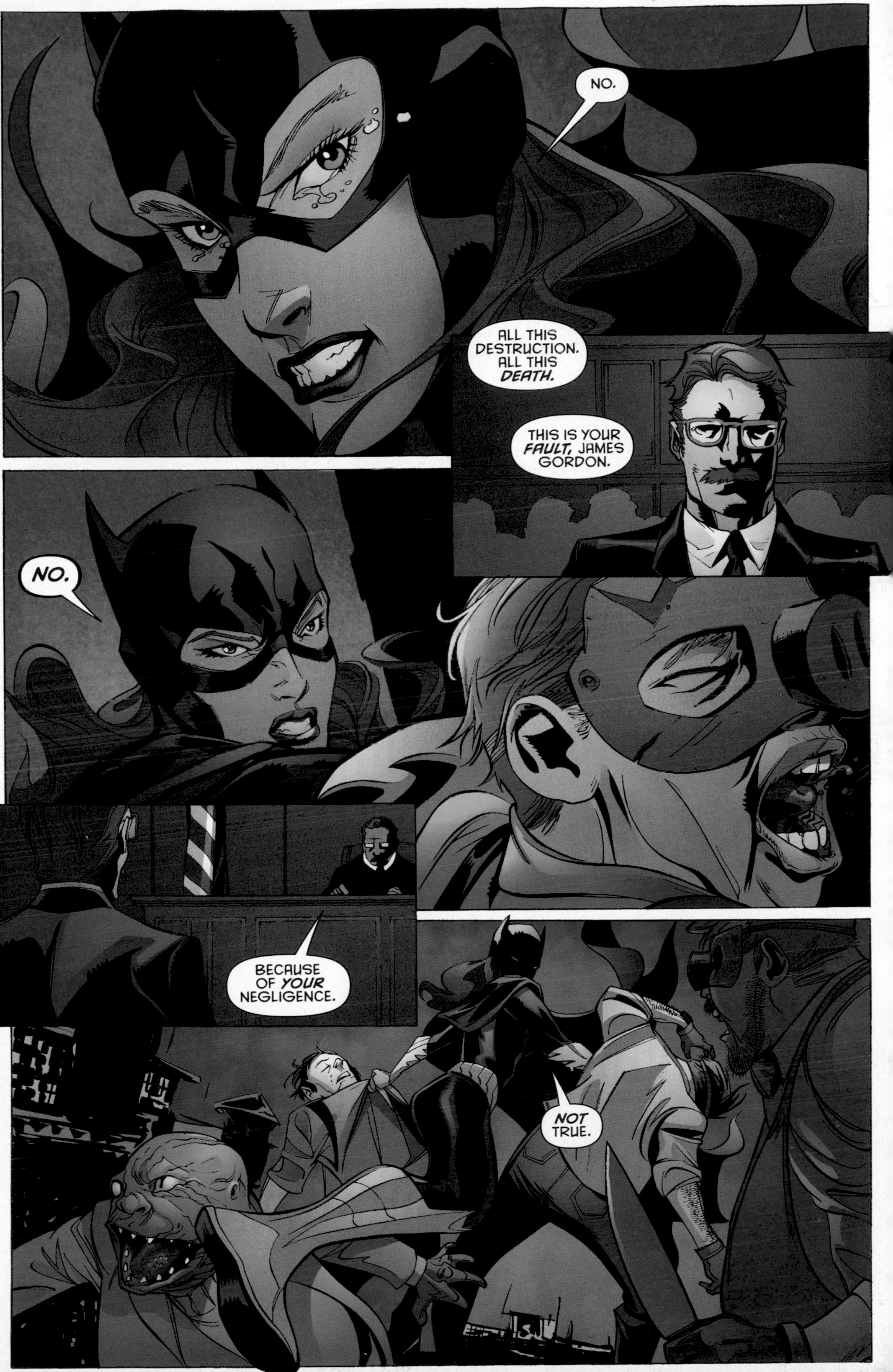
NO.
ALL THIS DESTRUCTION. ALL THIS *DEATH.*
THIS IS YOUR *FAULT,* JAMES GORDON.
NO.
BECAUSE OF *YOUR* NEGLIGENCE.
NOT TRUE.

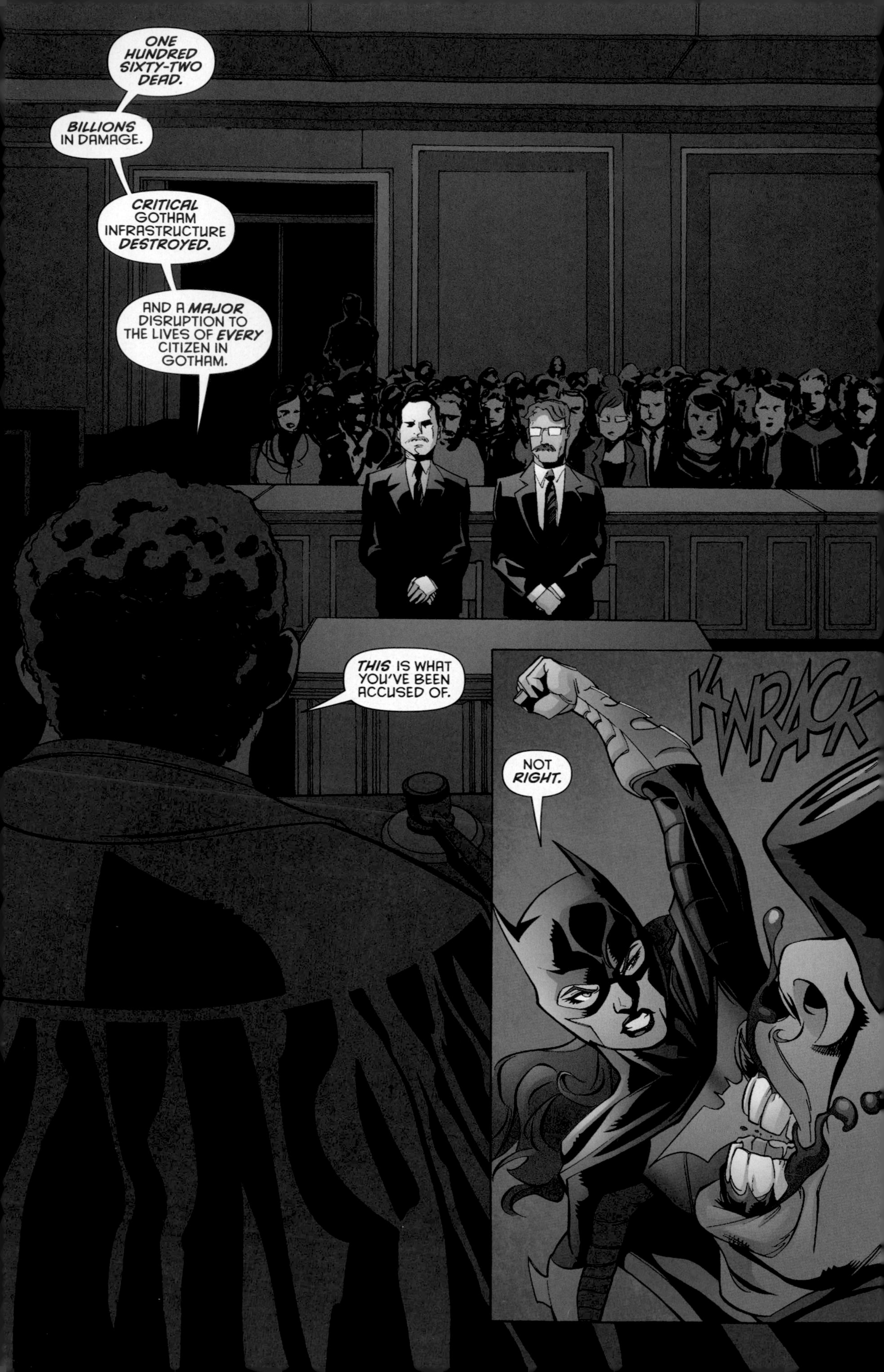

ONE HUNDRED SIXTY-TWO DEAD.
BILLIONS IN DAMAGE.
CRITICAL GOTHAM INFRASTRUCTURE DESTROYED.
AND A MAJOR DISRUPTION TO THE LIVES OF EVERY CITIZEN IN GOTHAM.
THIS IS WHAT YOU'VE BEEN ACCUSED OF.
KWRACK
NOT RIGHT.

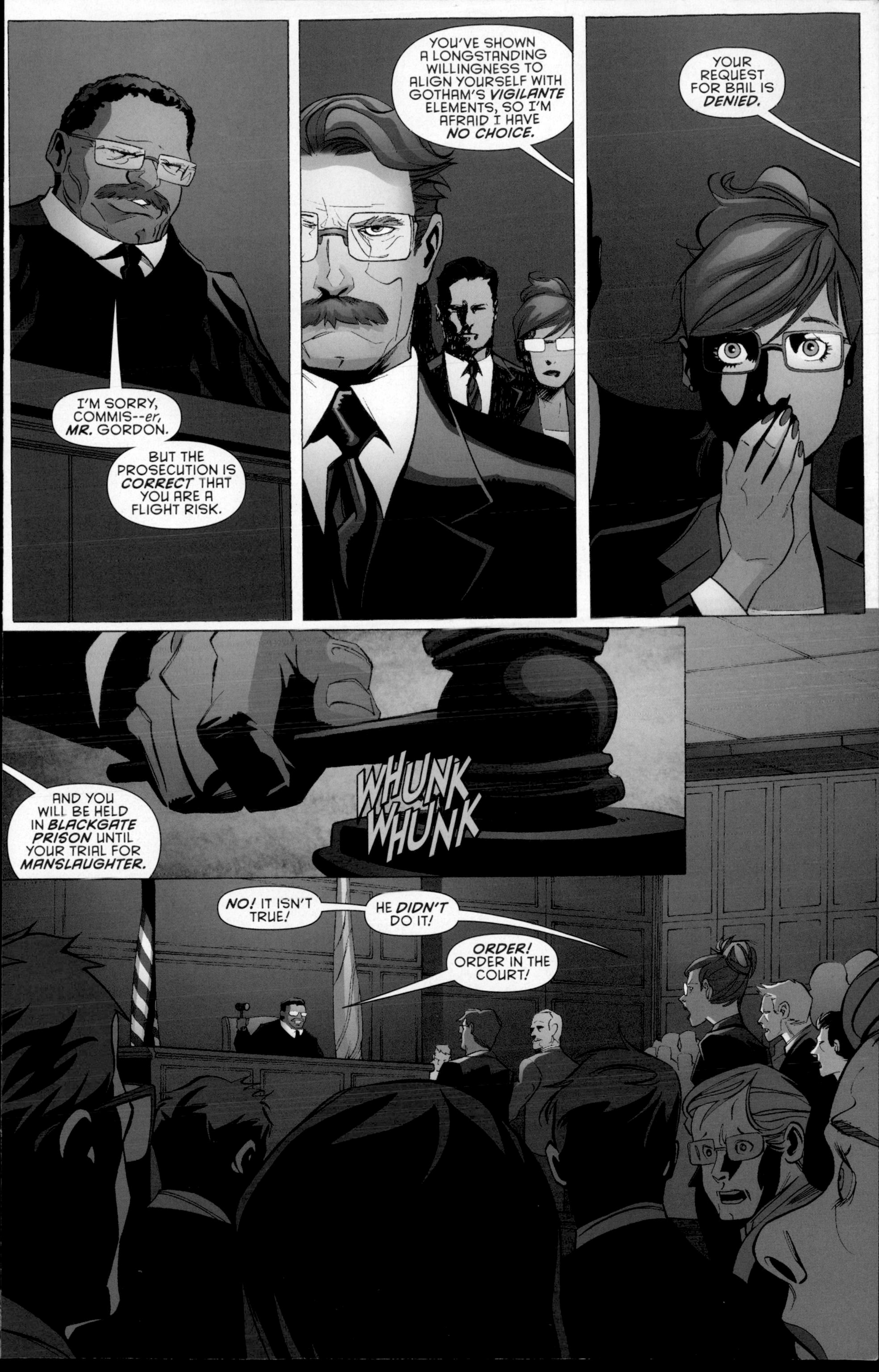
I'M SORRY, COMMIS--er, MR. GORDON.
BUT THE PROSECUTION IS CORRECT THAT YOU ARE A FLIGHT RISK.
YOU'VE SHOWN A LONGSTANDING WILLINGNESS TO ALIGN YOURSELF WITH GOTHAM'S VIGILANTE ELEMENTS, SO I'M AFRAID I HAVE NO CHOICE.
YOUR REQUEST FOR BAIL IS DENIED.
AND YOU WILL BE HELD IN BLACKGATE PRISON UNTIL YOUR TRIAL FOR MANSLAUGHTER.
WHUNK WHUNK
NO! IT ISN'T TRUE!
HE DIDN'T DO IT!
ORDER! ORDER IN THE COURT!

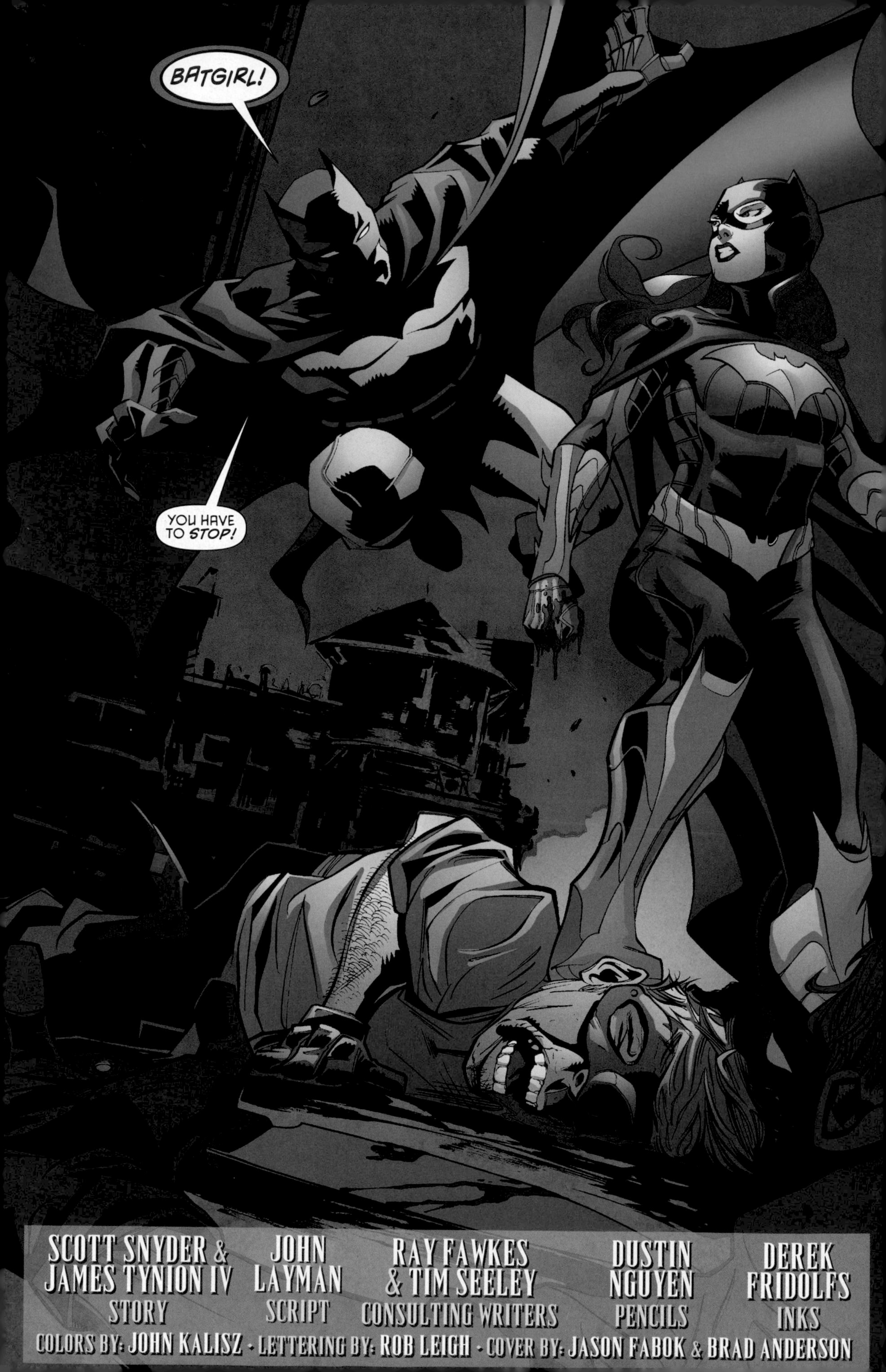
BATGIRL!
YOU HAVE TO STOP!
SCOTT SNYDER & JAMES TYNION IV STORY
JOHN LAYMAN SCRIPT
RAY FAWKES & TIM SEELEY CONSULTING WRITERS
DUSTIN NGUYEN PENCILS
DEREK FRIDOLFS INKS
COLORS BY: JOHN KALISZ • LETTERING BY: ROB LEIGH • COVER BY: JASON FABOK & BRAD ANDERSON

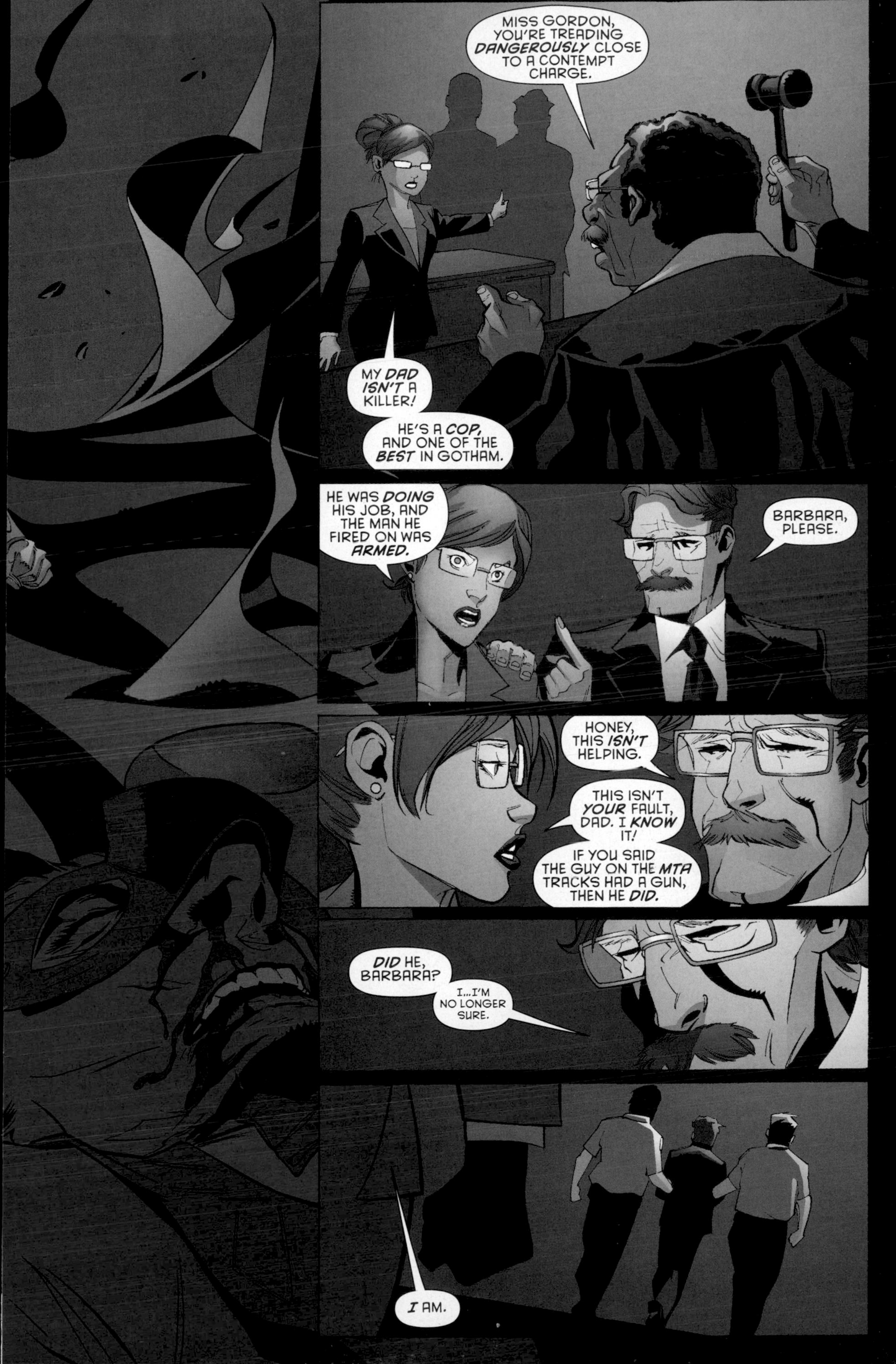
MISS GORDON, YOU'RE TREADING DANGEROUSLY CLOSE TO A CONTEMPT CHARGE.
MY DAD ISN'T A KILLER!
HE'S A COP, AND ONE OF THE BEST IN GOTHAM.
HE WAS DOING HIS JOB, AND THE MAN HE FIRED ON WAS ARMED.
BARBARA, PLEASE.
HONEY, THIS ISN'T HELPING.
THIS ISN'T YOUR FAULT, DAD. I KNOW IT!
IF YOU SAID THE GUY ON THE MTA TRACKS HAD A GUN, THEN HE DID.
DID HE, BARBARA?
I...I'M NO LONGER SURE.
I AM.

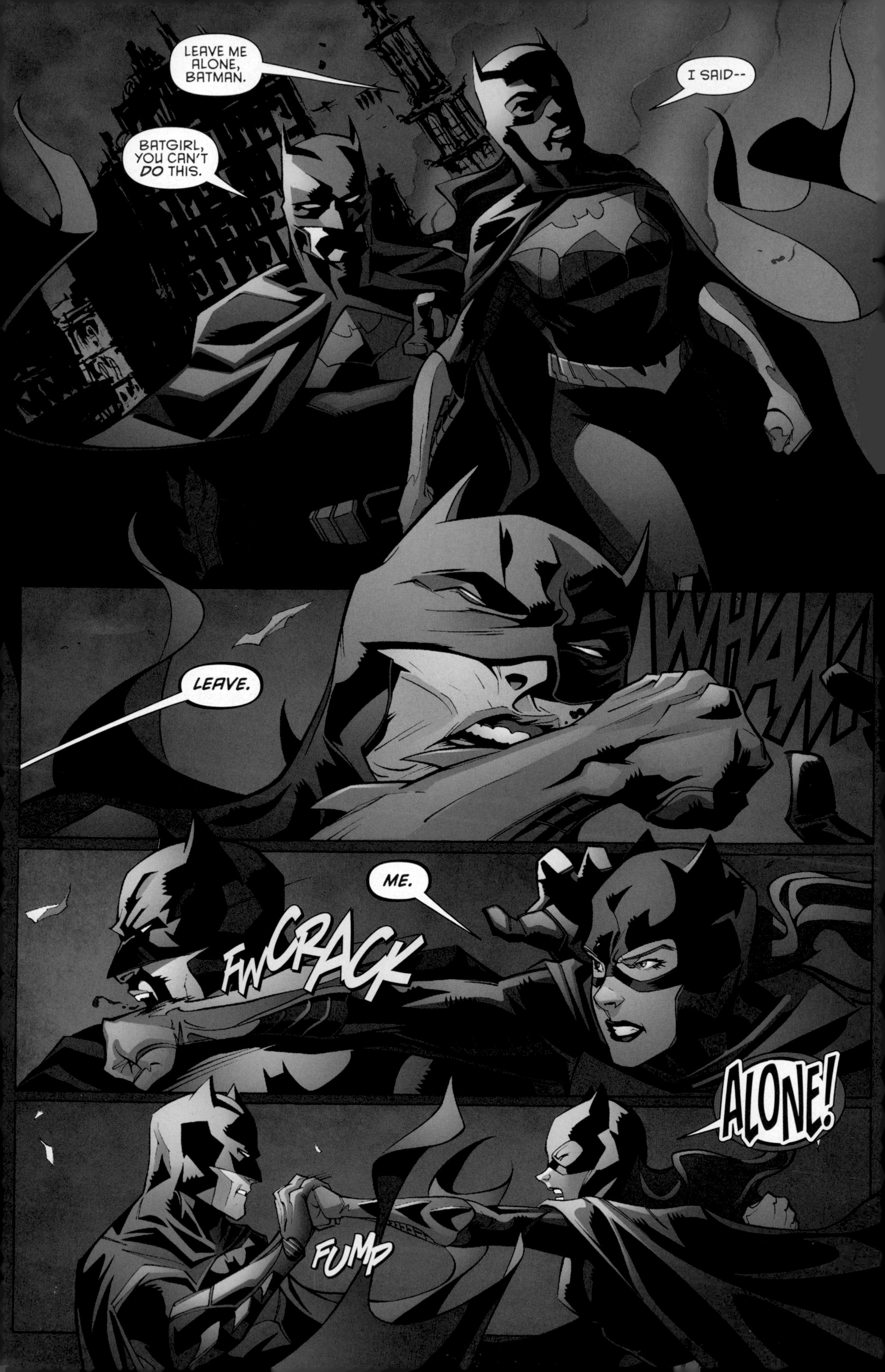
LEAVE ME ALONE, BATMAN.
BATGIRL, YOU CAN'T DO THIS.
I SAID--
LEAVE.
WHAM
ME.
FWCRACK
ALONE!
FUMP

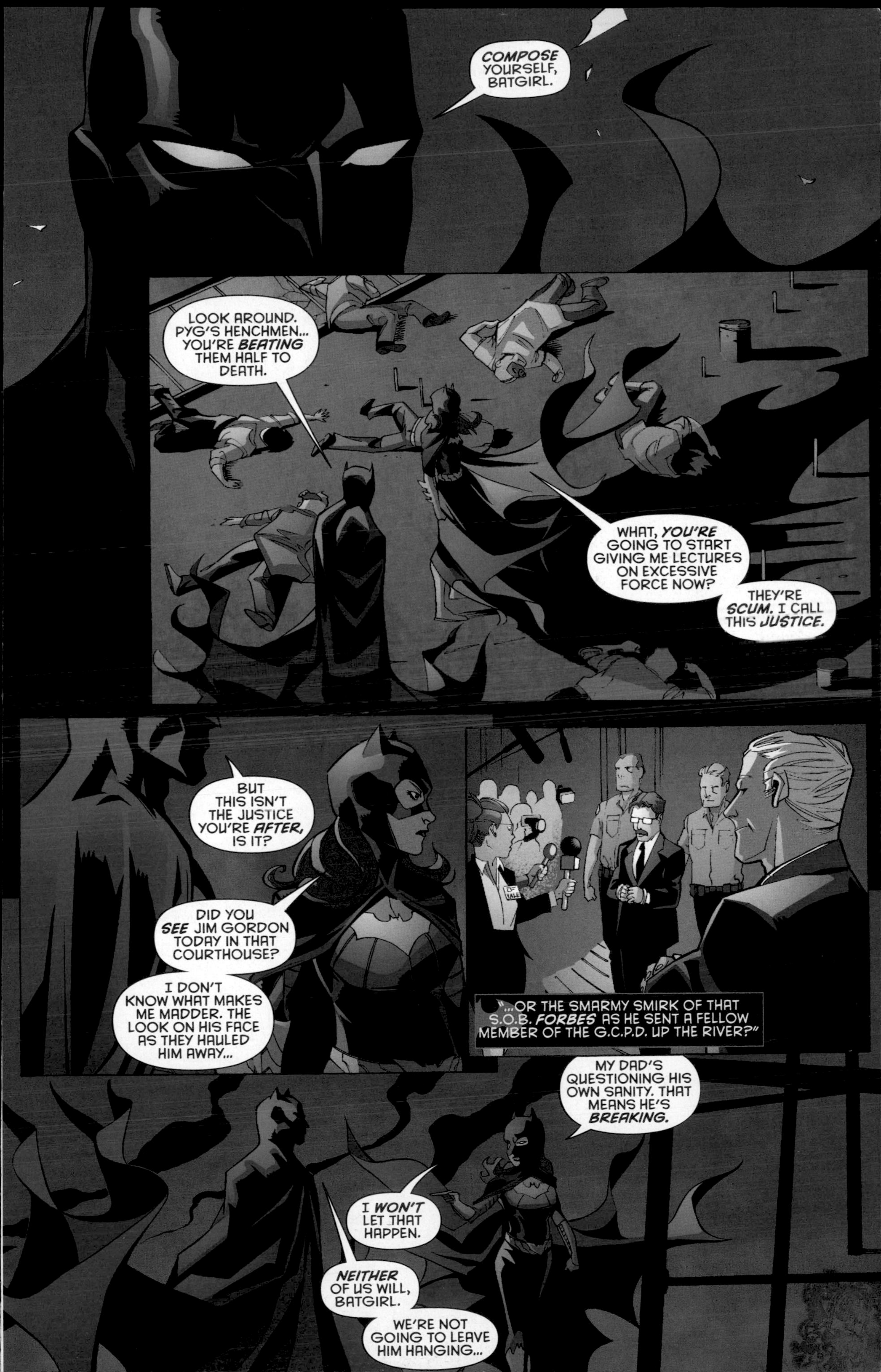
COMPOSE YOURSELF, BATGIRL.
LOOK AROUND. PYG'S HENCHMEN... YOU'RE BEATING THEM HALF TO DEATH.
WHAT, YOU'RE GOING TO START GIVING ME LECTURES ON EXCESSIVE FORCE NOW?
THEY'RE SCUM. I CALL THIS JUSTICE.
BUT THIS ISN'T THE JUSTICE YOU'RE AFTER, IS IT?
DID YOU SEE JIM GORDON TODAY IN THAT COURTHOUSE?
I DON'T KNOW WHAT MAKES ME MADDER. THE LOOK ON HIS FACE AS THEY HAULED HIM AWAY...
"...OR THE SMARMY SMIRK OF THAT S.O.B. FORBES AS HE SENT A FELLOW MEMBER OF THE G.C.P.D. UP THE RIVER?"
MY DAD'S QUESTIONING HIS OWN SANITY. THAT MEANS HE'S BREAKING.
I WON'T LET THAT HAPPEN.
NEITHER OF US WILL, BATGIRL.
WE'RE NOT GOING TO LEAVE HIM HANGING...

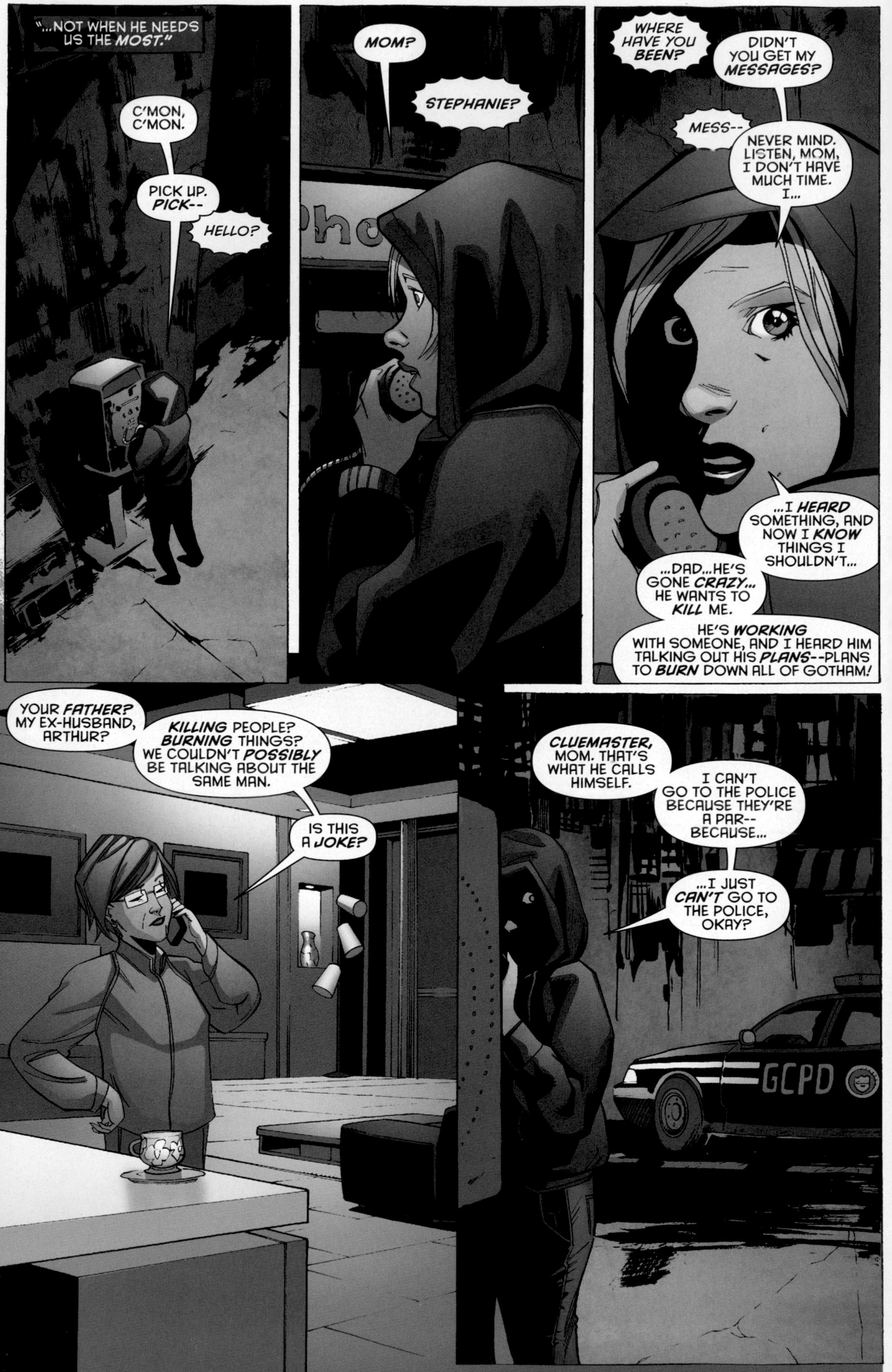
"...NOT WHEN HE NEEDS US THE *MOST.*"
C'MON, C'MON.
PICK UP. *PICK--*
HELLO?
MOM?
STEPHANIE?
WHERE HAVE YOU BEEN?
DIDN'T YOU GET MY *MESSAGES?*
MESS--
NEVER MIND. LISTEN, MOM, I DON'T HAVE MUCH TIME. I...
...I *HEARD* SOMETHING, AND NOW I *KNOW* THINGS I SHOULDN'T...
...DAD...HE'S GONE *CRAZY...* HE WANTS TO *KILL* ME.
HE'S *WORKING* WITH SOMEONE, AND I HEARD HIM TALKING OUT HIS *PLANS*--PLANS TO *BURN* DOWN ALL OF GOTHAM!
YOUR *FATHER?* MY EX-HUSBAND, ARTHUR?
KILLING PEOPLE? *BURNING* THINGS? WE COULDN'T *POSSIBLY* BE TALKING ABOUT THE SAME MAN.
IS THIS A *JOKE?*
CLUEMASTER, MOM. THAT'S WHAT HE CALLS HIMSELF.
I CAN'T GO TO THE POLICE BECAUSE THEY'RE A PAR-- BECAUSE...
...I JUST *CAN'T* GO TO THE POLICE, OKAY?
GCPD

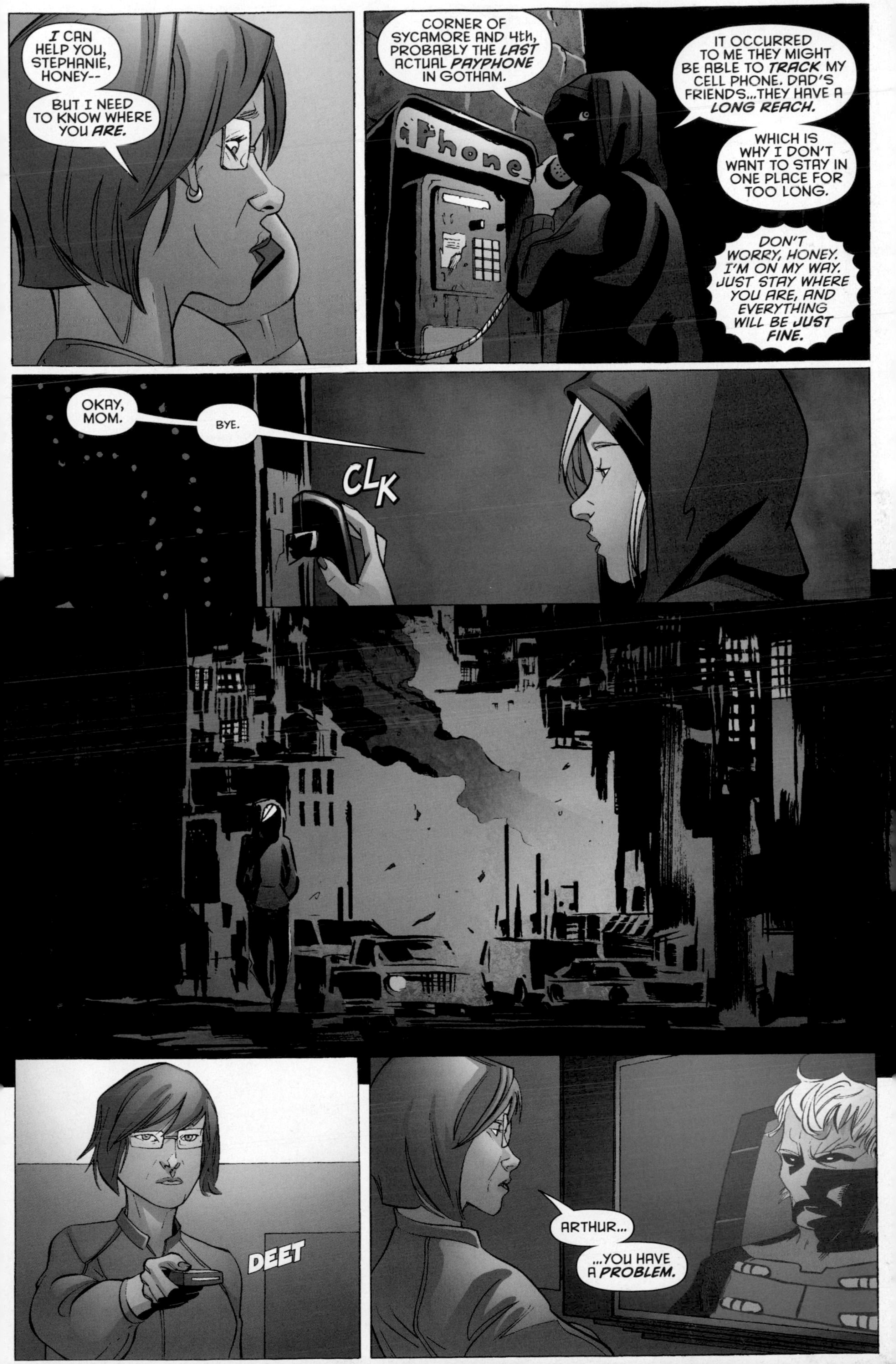
I CAN HELP YOU, STEPHANIE, HONEY--
BUT I NEED TO KNOW WHERE YOU ARE.
CORNER OF SYCAMORE AND 4th, PROBABLY THE LAST ACTUAL PAYPHONE IN GOTHAM.
Phone
IT OCCURRED TO ME THEY MIGHT BE ABLE TO TRACK MY CELL PHONE. DAD'S FRIENDS...THEY HAVE A LONG REACH.
WHICH IS WHY I DON'T WANT TO STAY IN ONE PLACE FOR TOO LONG.
DON'T WORRY, HONEY. I'M ON MY WAY. JUST STAY WHERE YOU ARE, AND EVERYTHING WILL BE JUST FINE.
OKAY, MOM.
BYE.
CLK
DEET
ARTHUR...
...YOU HAVE A PROBLEM.

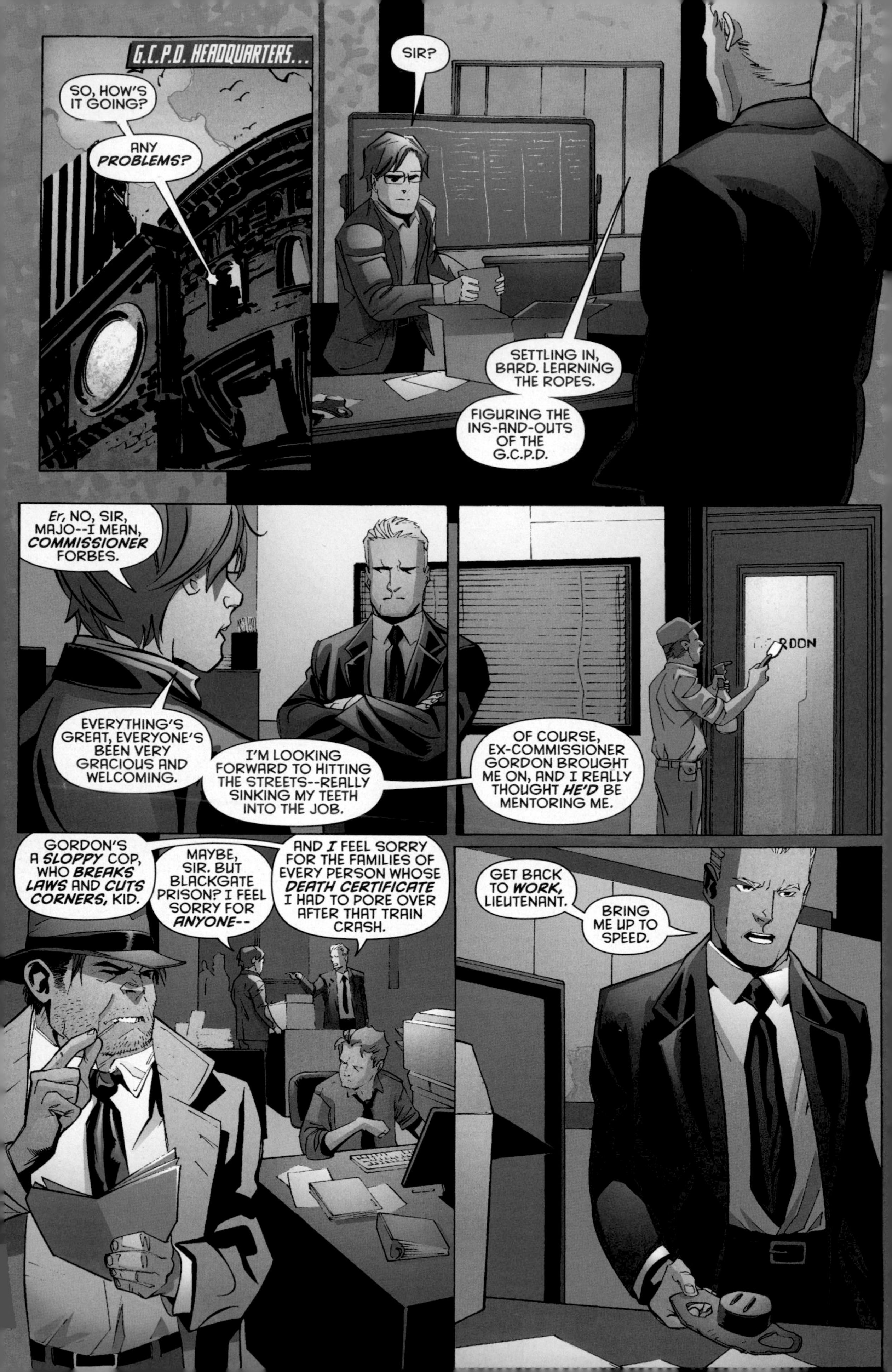

G.C.P.D. HEADQUARTERS...
SO, HOW'S IT GOING?
ANY *PROBLEMS?*
SIR?
SETTLING IN, BARD. LEARNING THE ROPES.
FIGURING THE INS-AND-OUTS OF THE G.C.P.D.
Er, NO, SIR, MAJO--I MEAN, ***COMMISSIONER*** FORBES.
EVERYTHING'S GREAT, EVERYONE'S BEEN VERY GRACIOUS AND WELCOMING.
I'M LOOKING FORWARD TO HITTING THE STREETS--REALLY SINKING MY TEETH INTO THE JOB.
OF COURSE, EX-COMMISSIONER GORDON BROUGHT ME ON, AND I REALLY THOUGHT ***HE'D*** BE MENTORING ME.
GORDON
GORDON'S A ***SLOPPY*** COP, WHO ***BREAKS LAWS*** AND ***CUTS CORNERS,*** KID.
MAYBE, SIR. BUT BLACKGATE PRISON? I FEEL SORRY FOR ***ANYONE***--
AND ***I*** FEEL SORRY FOR THE FAMILIES OF EVERY PERSON WHOSE ***DEATH CERTIFICATE*** I HAD TO PORE OVER AFTER THAT TRAIN CRASH.
GET BACK TO ***WORK,*** LIEUTENANT.
BRING ME UP TO SPEED.

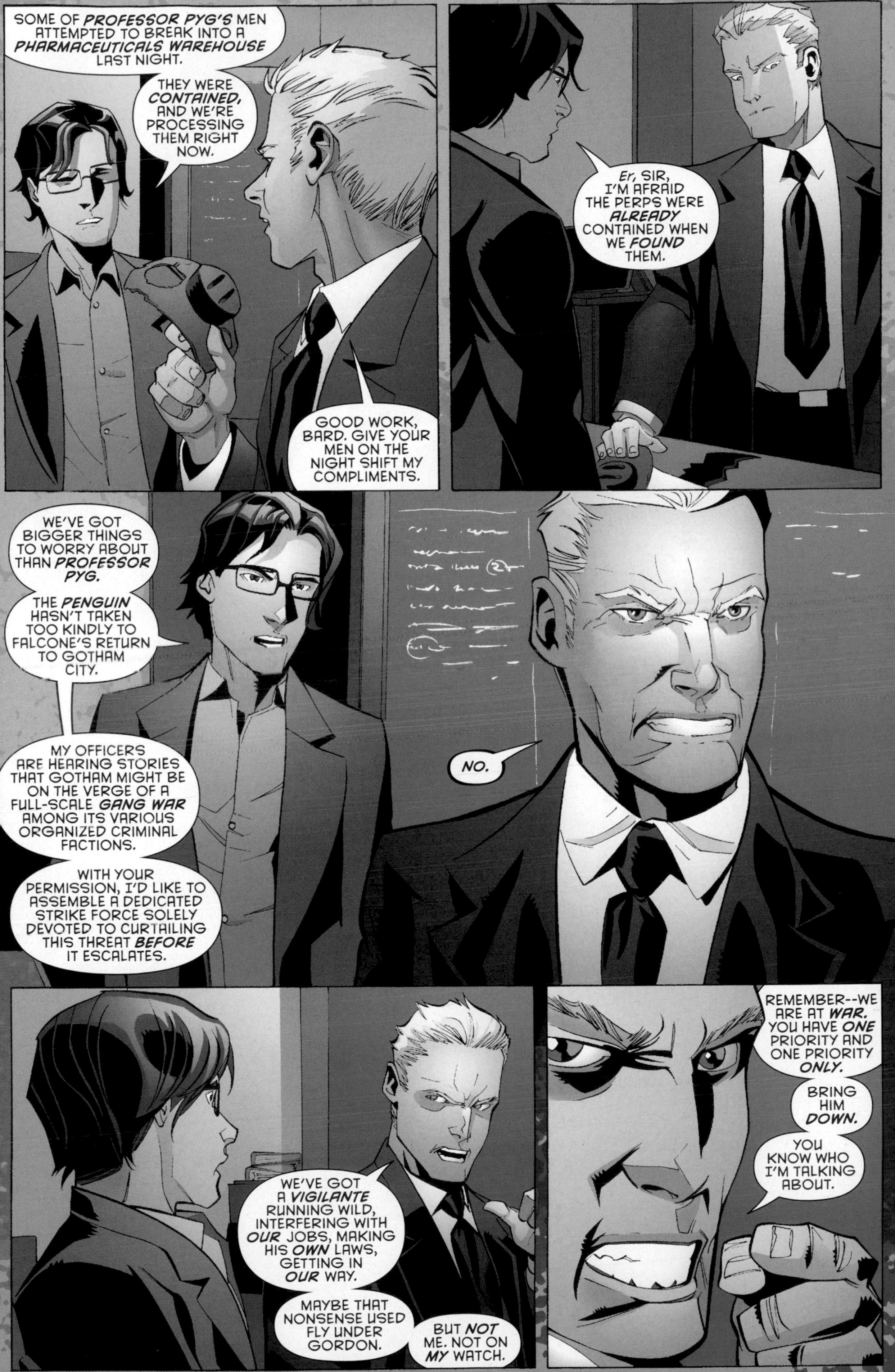
SOME OF PROFESSOR PYG'S MEN ATTEMPTED TO BREAK INTO A PHARMACEUTICALS WAREHOUSE LAST NIGHT.
THEY WERE CONTAINED, AND WE'RE PROCESSING THEM RIGHT NOW.
GOOD WORK, BARD. GIVE YOUR MEN ON THE NIGHT SHIFT MY COMPLIMENTS.
Er, SIR, I'M AFRAID THE PERPS WERE ALREADY CONTAINED WHEN WE FOUND THEM.
WE'VE GOT BIGGER THINGS TO WORRY ABOUT THAN PROFESSOR PYG.
THE PENGUIN HASN'T TAKEN TOO KINDLY TO FALCONE'S RETURN TO GOTHAM CITY.
MY OFFICERS ARE HEARING STORIES THAT GOTHAM MIGHT BE ON THE VERGE OF A FULL-SCALE GANG WAR AMONG ITS VARIOUS ORGANIZED CRIMINAL FACTIONS.
WITH YOUR PERMISSION, I'D LIKE TO ASSEMBLE A DEDICATED STRIKE FORCE SOLELY DEVOTED TO CURTAILING THIS THREAT BEFORE IT ESCALATES.
NO.
WE'VE GOT A VIGILANTE RUNNING WILD, INTERFERING WITH OUR JOBS, MAKING HIS OWN LAWS, GETTING IN OUR WAY.
MAYBE THAT NONSENSE USED FLY UNDER GORDON.
BUT NOT ME. NOT ON MY WATCH.
REMEMBER--WE ARE AT WAR. YOU HAVE ONE PRIORITY AND ONE PRIORITY ONLY.
BRING HIM DOWN.
YOU KNOW WHO I'M TALKING ABOUT.

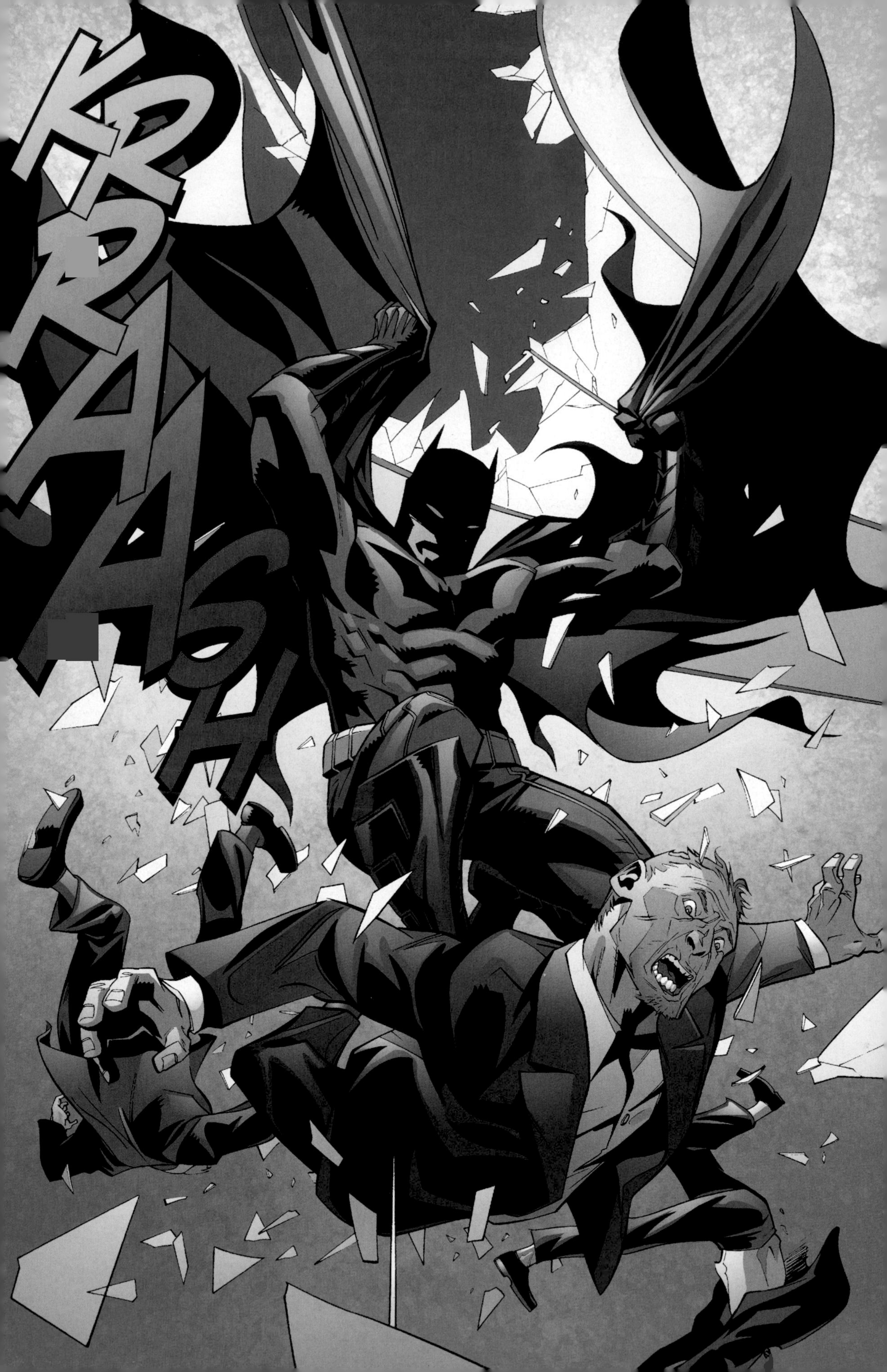
KRRAAASH

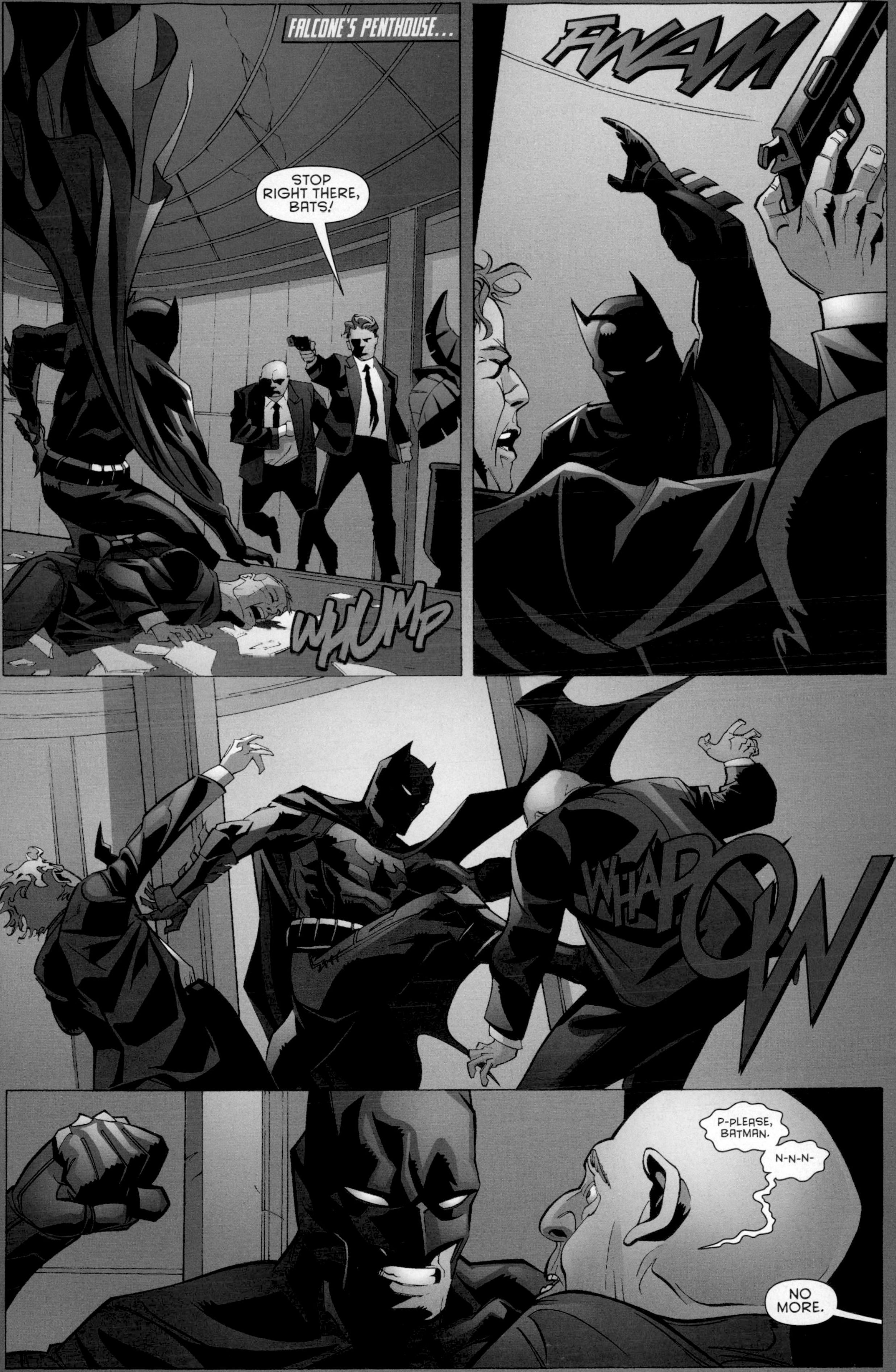
FALCONE'S PENTHOUSE...
STOP RIGHT THERE, BATS!
WHUMP
FWAM
WHAPOW
P-PLEASE, BATMAN.
N-N-N-
NO MORE.

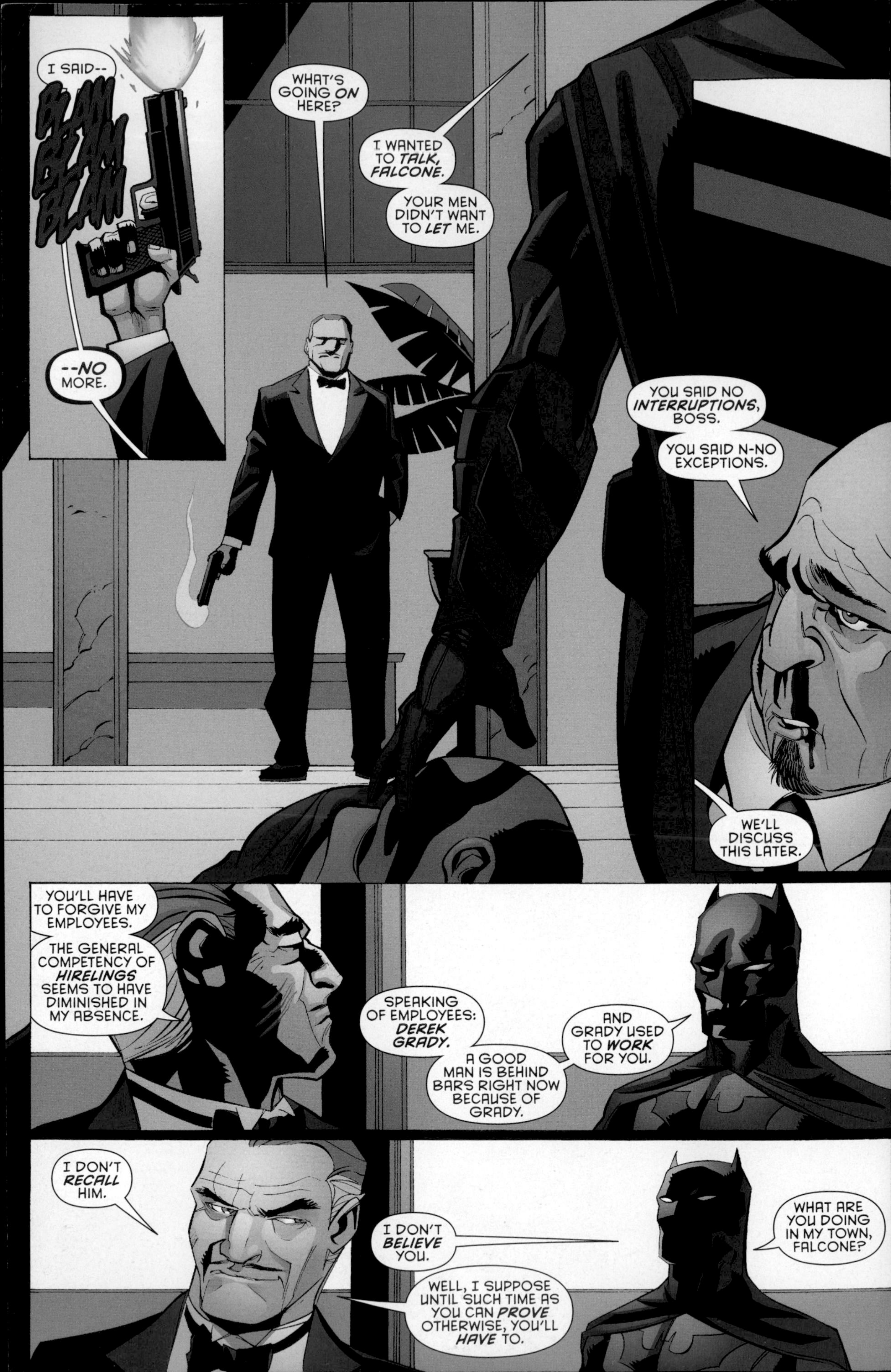

I SAID--
BLAM BLAM BLAM
--NO MORE.
WHAT'S GOING ON HERE?
I WANTED TO TALK, FALCONE.
YOUR MEN DIDN'T WANT TO LET ME.
YOU SAID NO INTERRUPTIONS, BOSS.
YOU SAID N-NO EXCEPTIONS.
WE'LL DISCUSS THIS LATER.
YOU'LL HAVE TO FORGIVE MY EMPLOYEES.
THE GENERAL COMPETENCY OF HIRELINGS SEEMS TO HAVE DIMINISHED IN MY ABSENCE.
SPEAKING OF EMPLOYEES: DEREK GRADY.
A GOOD MAN IS BEHIND BARS RIGHT NOW BECAUSE OF GRADY.
AND GRADY USED TO WORK FOR YOU.
I DON'T RECALL HIM.
I DON'T BELIEVE YOU.
WELL, I SUPPOSE UNTIL SUCH TIME AS YOU CAN PROVE OTHERWISE, YOU'LL HAVE TO.
WHAT ARE YOU DOING IN MY TOWN, FALCONE?

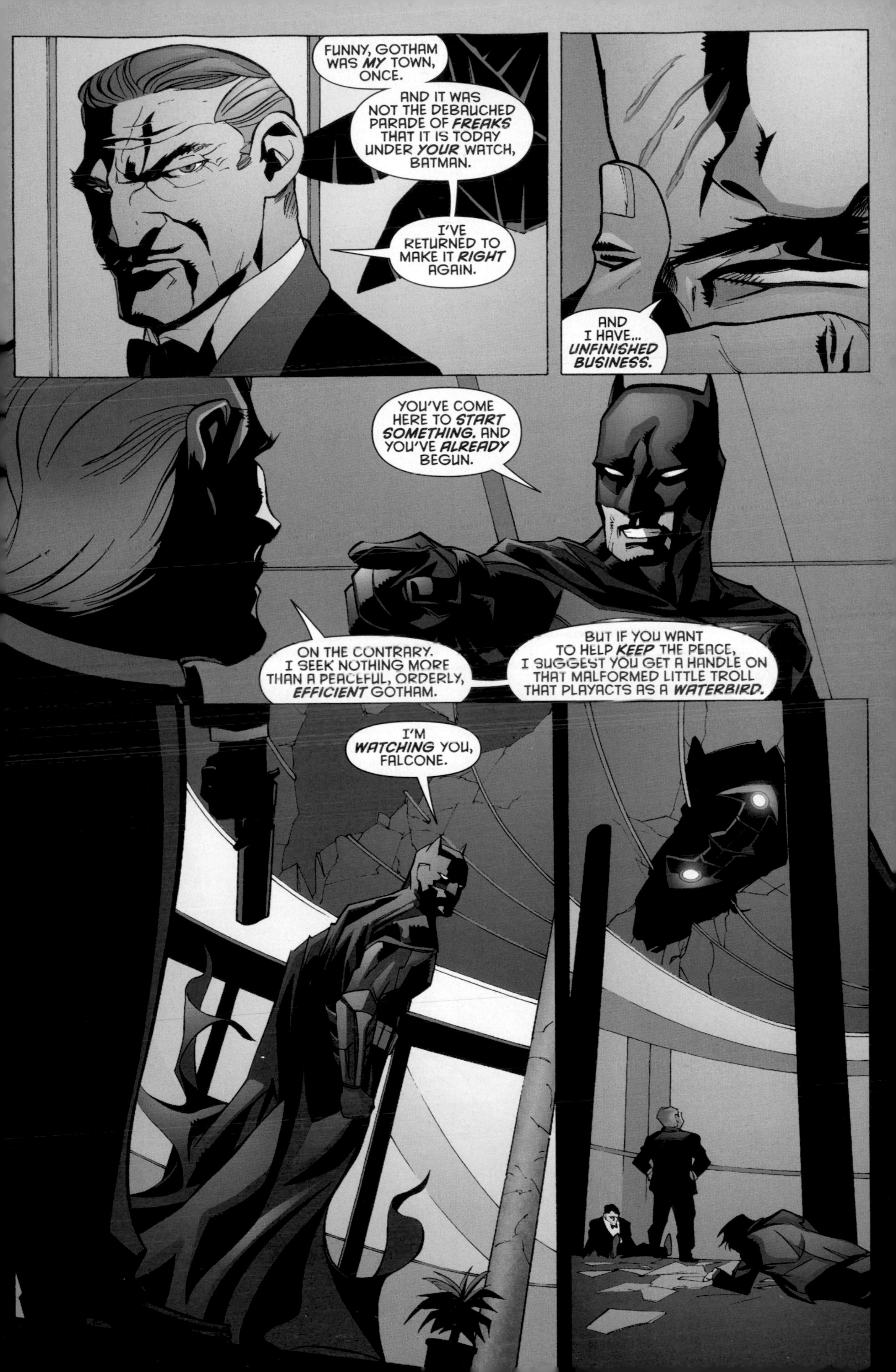
FUNNY, GOTHAM WAS MY TOWN, ONCE.
AND IT WAS NOT THE DEBAUCHED PARADE OF FREAKS THAT IT IS TODAY UNDER YOUR WATCH, BATMAN.
I'VE RETURNED TO MAKE IT RIGHT AGAIN.
AND I HAVE... UNFINISHED BUSINESS.
YOU'VE COME HERE TO START SOMETHING. AND YOU'VE ALREADY BEGUN.
ON THE CONTRARY. I SEEK NOTHING MORE THAN A PEACEFUL, ORDERLY, EFFICIENT GOTHAM.
BUT IF YOU WANT TO HELP KEEP THE PEACE, I SUGGEST YOU GET A HANDLE ON THAT MALFORMED LITTLE TROLL THAT PLAYACTS AS A WATERBIRD.
I'M WATCHING YOU, FALCONE.

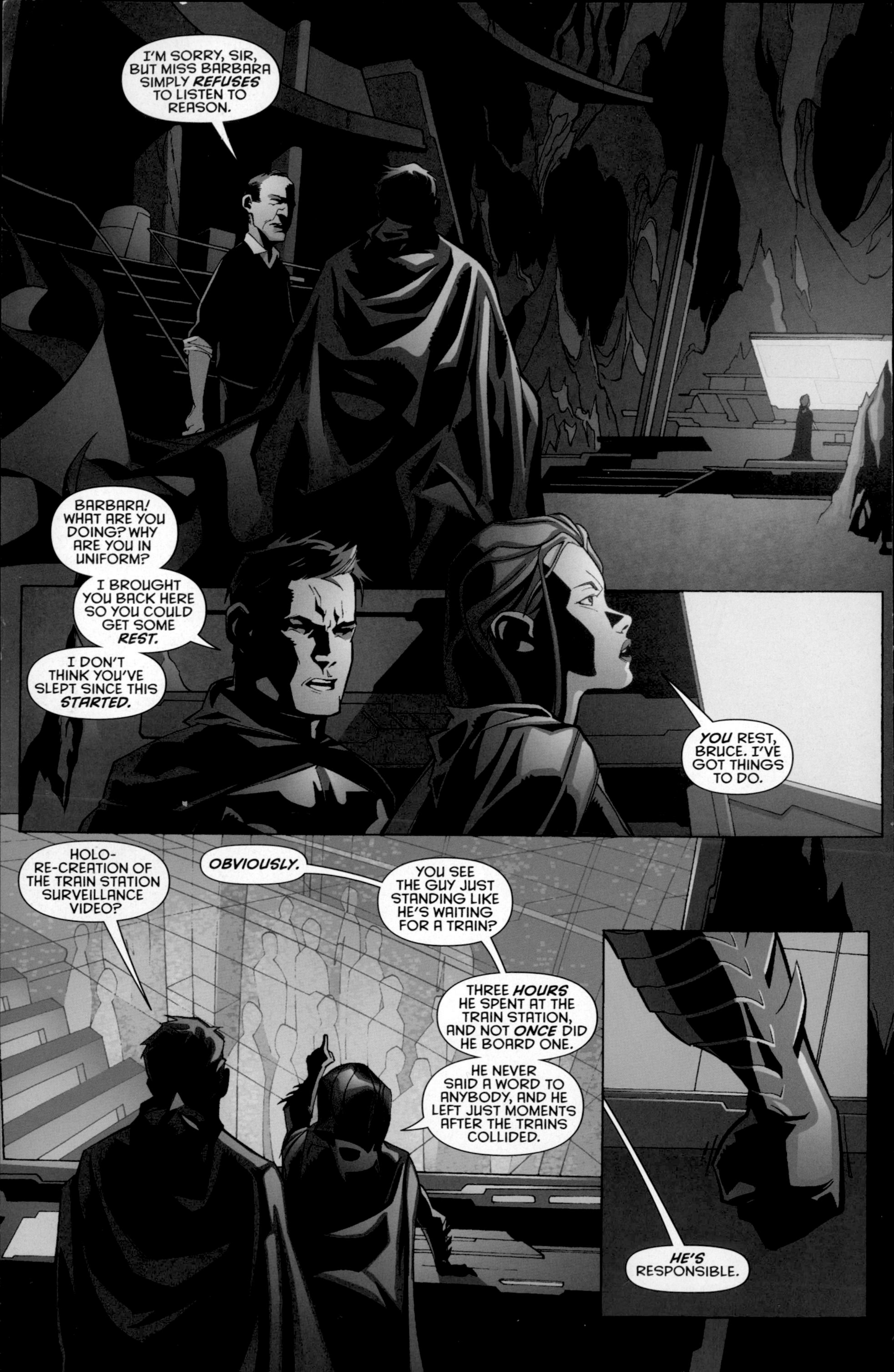
I'M SORRY, SIR, BUT MISS BARBARA SIMPLY *REFUSES* TO LISTEN TO REASON.
BARBARA! WHAT ARE YOU DOING? WHY ARE YOU IN UNIFORM?
I BROUGHT YOU BACK HERE SO YOU COULD GET SOME *REST.*
I DON'T THINK YOU'VE SLEPT SINCE THIS *STARTED.*
YOU REST, BRUCE. I'VE GOT THINGS TO DO.
HOLO-RE-CREATION OF THE TRAIN STATION SURVEILLANCE VIDEO?
OBVIOUSLY.
YOU SEE THE GUY JUST STANDING LIKE HE'S WAITING FOR A TRAIN?
THREE *HOURS* HE SPENT AT THE TRAIN STATION, AND NOT *ONCE* DID HE BOARD ONE.
HE NEVER SAID A WORD TO ANYBODY, AND HE LEFT JUST MOMENTS AFTER THE TRAINS COLLIDED.
HE'S RESPONSIBLE.

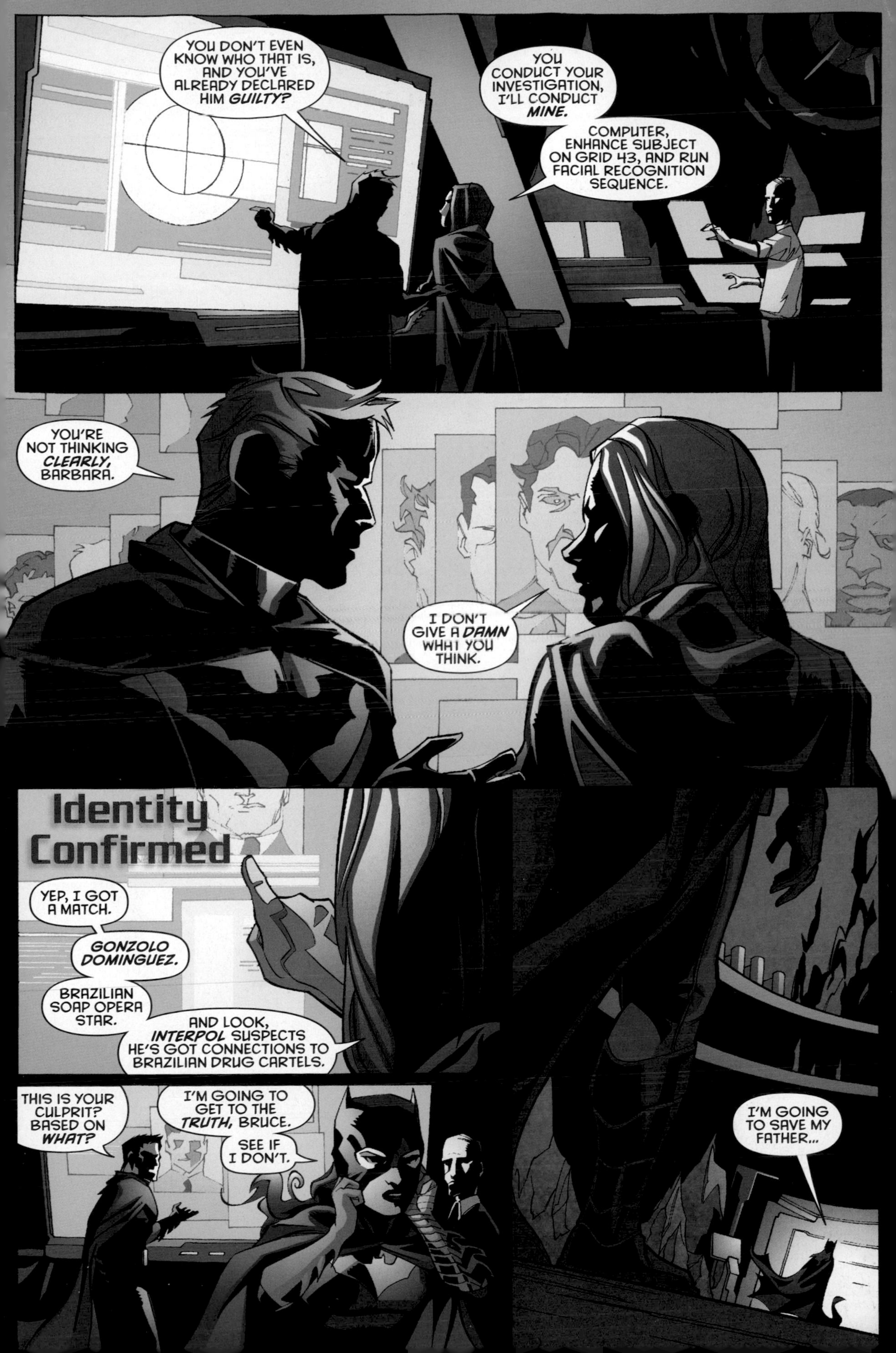
YOU DON'T EVEN KNOW WHO THAT IS, AND YOU'VE ALREADY DECLARED HIM GUILTY?
YOU CONDUCT YOUR INVESTIGATION, I'LL CONDUCT MINE.
COMPUTER, ENHANCE SUBJECT ON GRID 43, AND RUN FACIAL RECOGNITION SEQUENCE.
YOU'RE NOT THINKING CLEARLY, BARBARA.
I DON'T GIVE A DAMN WHAT YOU THINK.
Identity Confirmed
YEP, I GOT A MATCH.
GONZOLO DOMINGUEZ.
BRAZILIAN SOAP OPERA STAR.
AND LOOK, INTERPOL SUSPECTS HE'S GOT CONNECTIONS TO BRAZILIAN DRUG CARTELS.
THIS IS YOUR CULPRIT? BASED ON WHAT?
I'M GOING TO GET TO THE TRUTH, BRUCE.
SEE IF I DON'T.
I'M GOING TO SAVE MY FATHER...

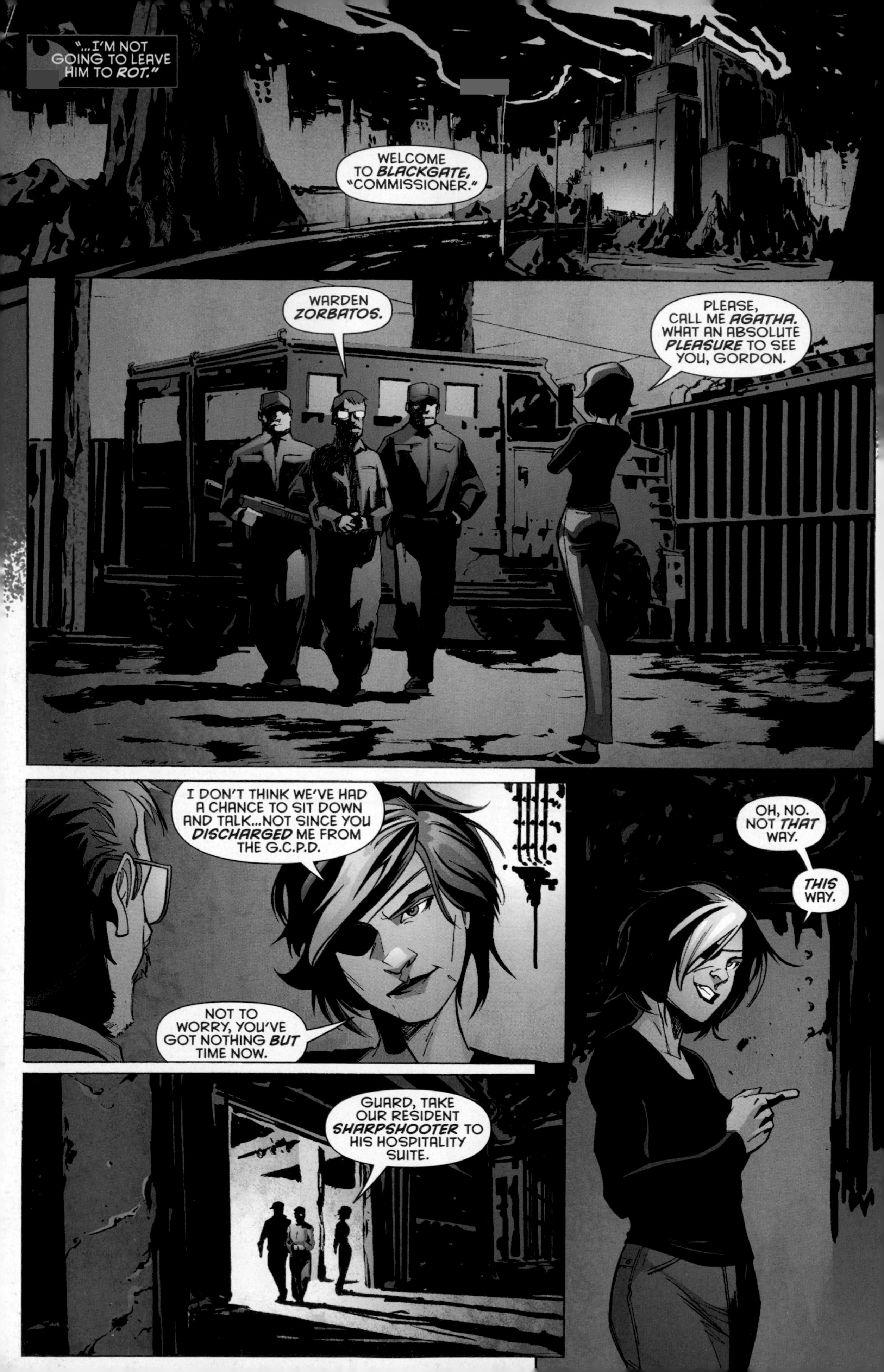
"...I'M NOT GOING TO LEAVE HIM TO ROT."
WELCOME TO BLACKGATE, "COMMISSIONER."
WARDEN ZORBATOS.
PLEASE, CALL ME AGATHA. WHAT AN ABSOLUTE PLEASURE TO SEE YOU, GORDON.
I DON'T THINK WE'VE HAD A CHANCE TO SIT DOWN AND TALK...NOT SINCE YOU DISCHARGED ME FROM THE G.C.P.D.
NOT TO WORRY, YOU'VE GOT NOTHING BUT TIME NOW.
GUARD, TAKE OUR RESIDENT SHARPSHOOTER TO HIS HOSPITALITY SUITE.
OH, NO. NOT THAT WAY.
THIS WAY.

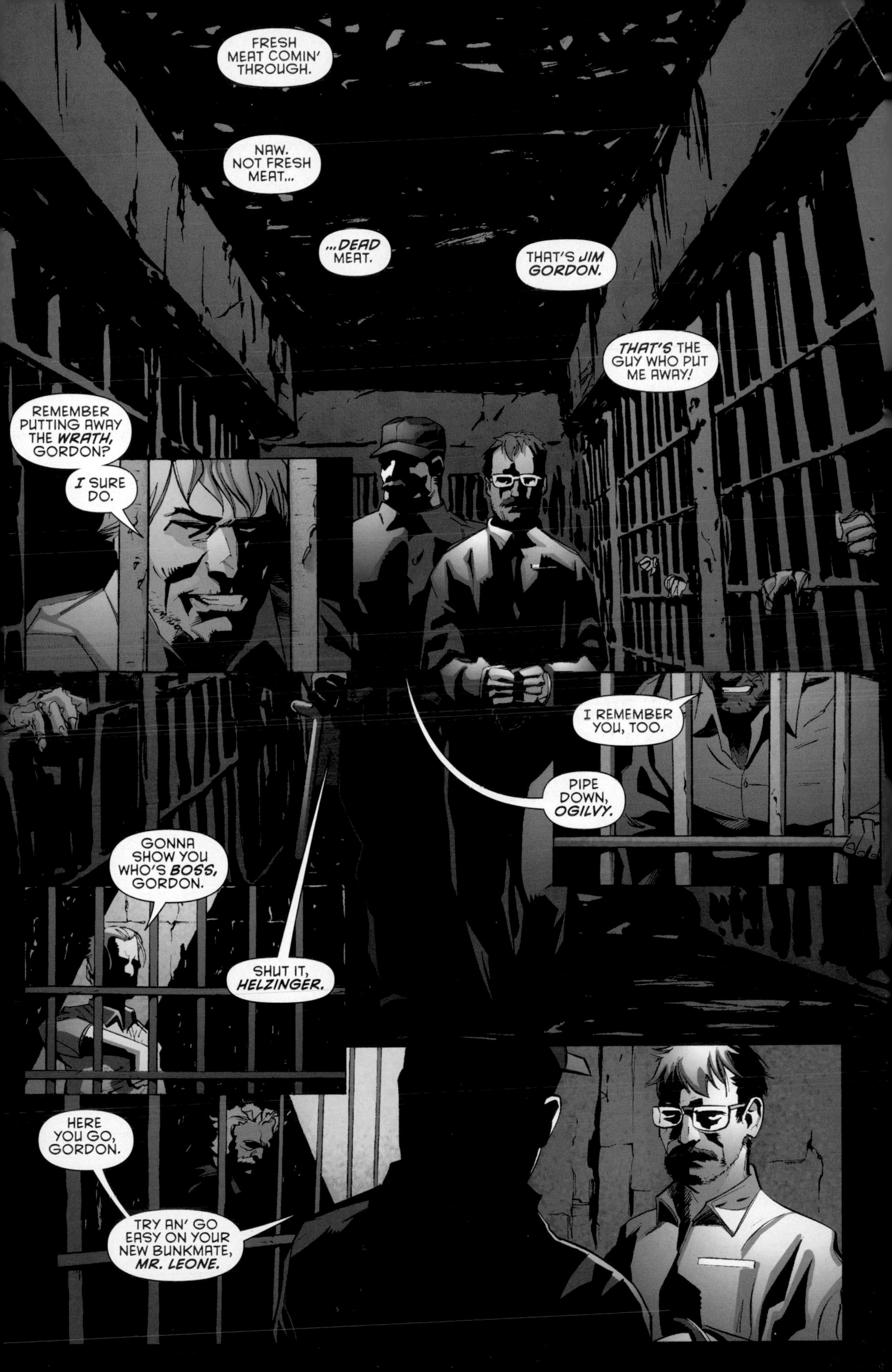
FRESH MEAT COMIN' THROUGH.
NAW. NOT FRESH MEAT...
...DEAD MEAT.
THAT'S JIM GORDON.
THAT'S THE GUY WHO PUT ME AWAY!
REMEMBER PUTTING AWAY THE WRATH, GORDON?
I SURE DO.
I REMEMBER YOU, TOO.
PIPE DOWN, OGILVY.
GONNA SHOW YOU WHO'S BOSS, GORDON.
SHUT IT, HELZINGER.
HERE YOU GO, GORDON.
TRY AN' GO EASY ON YOUR NEW BUNKMATE, MR. LEONE.

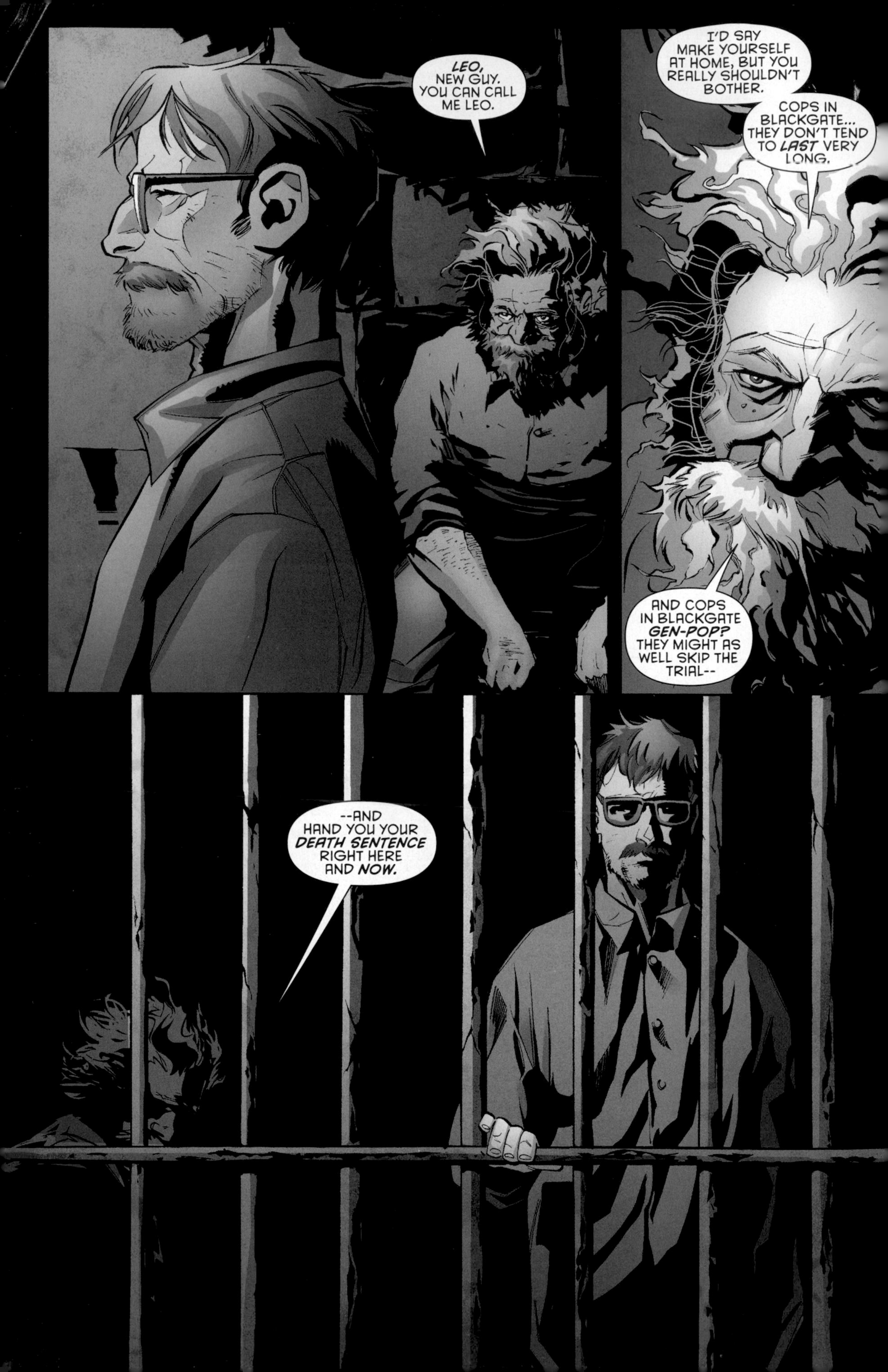
LEO, NEW GUY. YOU CAN CALL ME LEO.
I'D SAY MAKE YOURSELF AT HOME, BUT YOU REALLY SHOULDN'T BOTHER.
COPS IN BLACKGATE... THEY DON'T TEND TO LAST VERY LONG.
AND COPS IN BLACKGATE GEN-POP? THEY MIGHT AS WELL SKIP THE TRIAL--
--AND HAND YOU YOUR DEATH SENTENCE RIGHT HERE AND NOW.

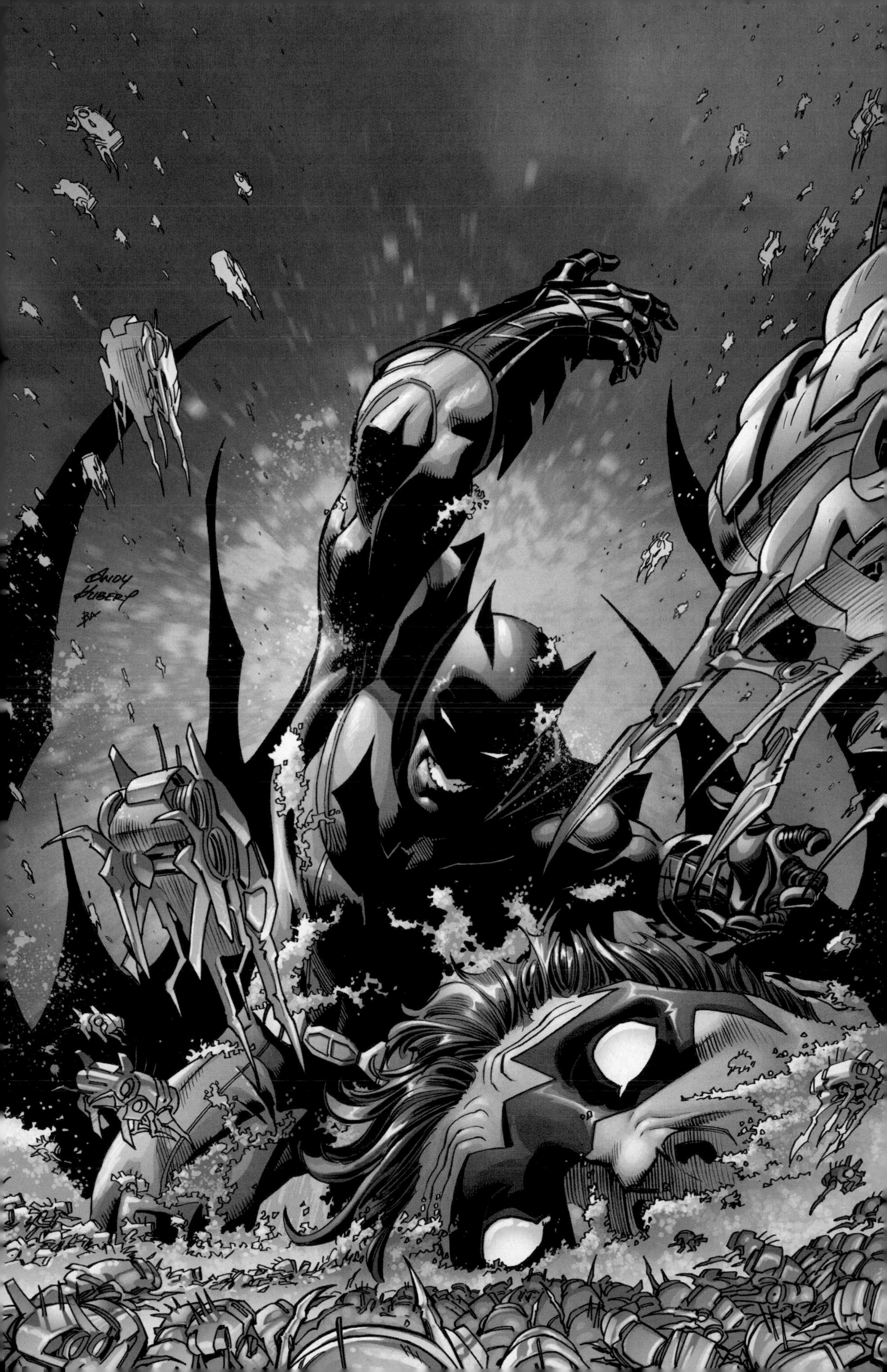

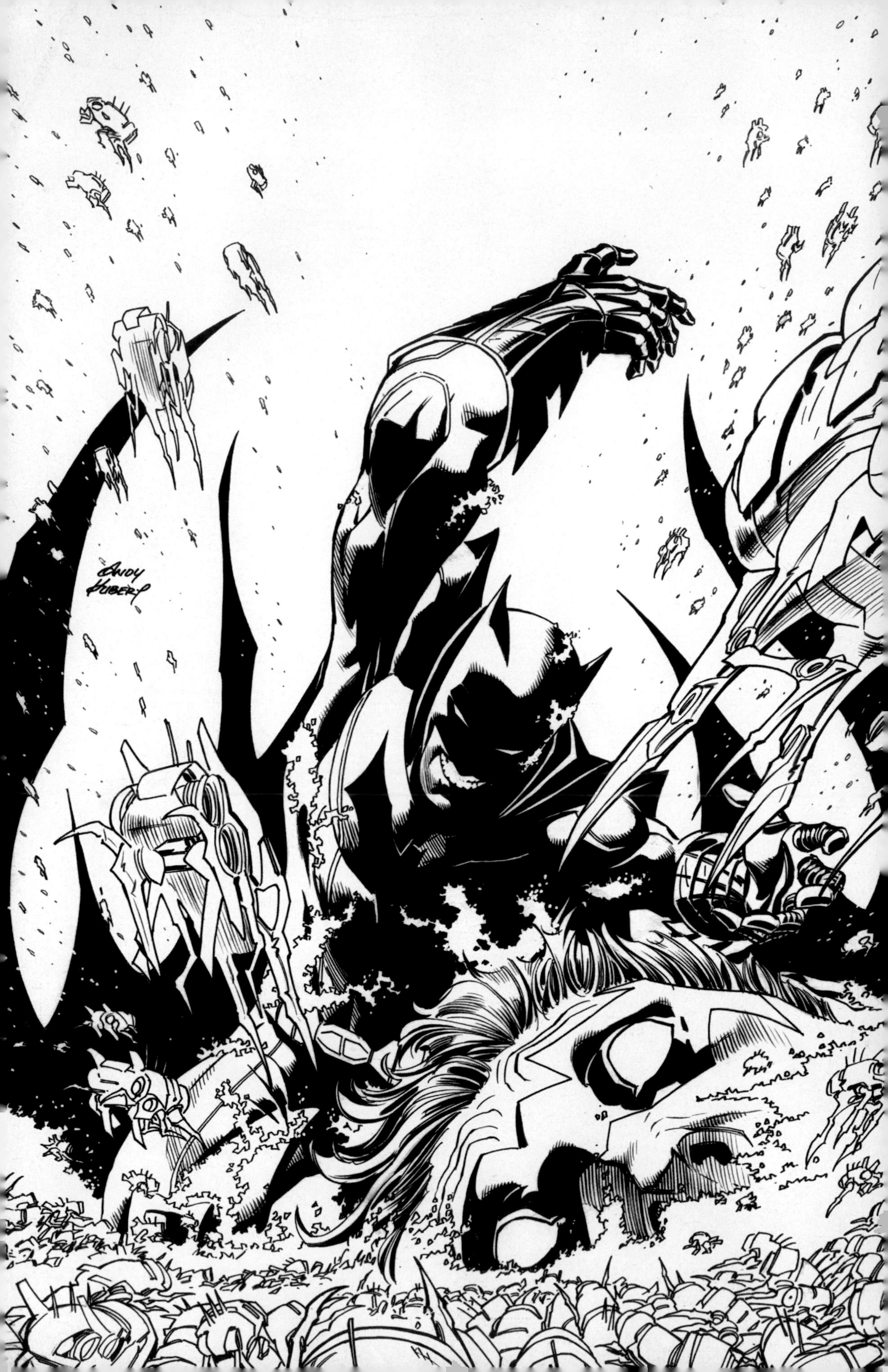
ANDY KUBERT

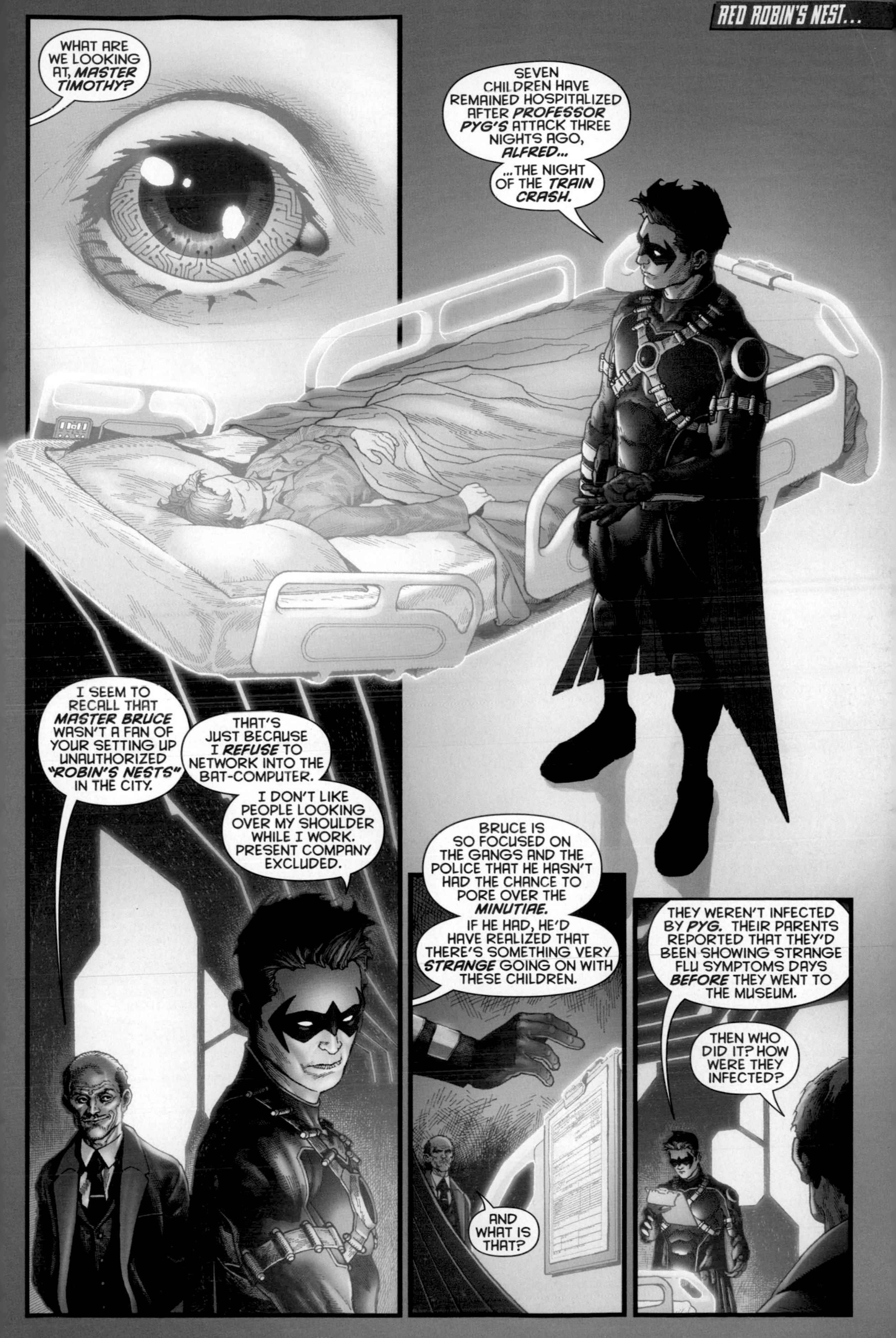
RED ROBIN'S NEST...
WHAT ARE WE LOOKING AT, MASTER TIMOTHY?
SEVEN CHILDREN HAVE REMAINED HOSPITALIZED AFTER PROFESSOR PYG'S ATTACK THREE NIGHTS AGO, ALFRED...
...THE NIGHT OF THE TRAIN CRASH.
I SEEM TO RECALL THAT MASTER BRUCE WASN'T A FAN OF YOUR SETTING UP UNAUTHORIZED "ROBIN'S NESTS" IN THE CITY.
THAT'S JUST BECAUSE I REFUSE TO NETWORK INTO THE BAT-COMPUTER.
I DON'T LIKE PEOPLE LOOKING OVER MY SHOULDER WHILE I WORK. PRESENT COMPANY EXCLUDED.
BRUCE IS SO FOCUSED ON THE GANGS AND THE POLICE THAT HE HASN'T HAD THE CHANCE TO PORE OVER THE MINUTIAE.
IF HE HAD, HE'D HAVE REALIZED THAT THERE'S SOMETHING VERY STRANGE GOING ON WITH THESE CHILDREN.
AND WHAT IS THAT?
THEY WEREN'T INFECTED BY PYG. THEIR PARENTS REPORTED THAT THEY'D BEEN SHOWING STRANGE FLU SYMPTOMS DAYS BEFORE THEY WENT TO THE MUSEUM.
THEN WHO DID IT? HOW WERE THEY INFECTED?

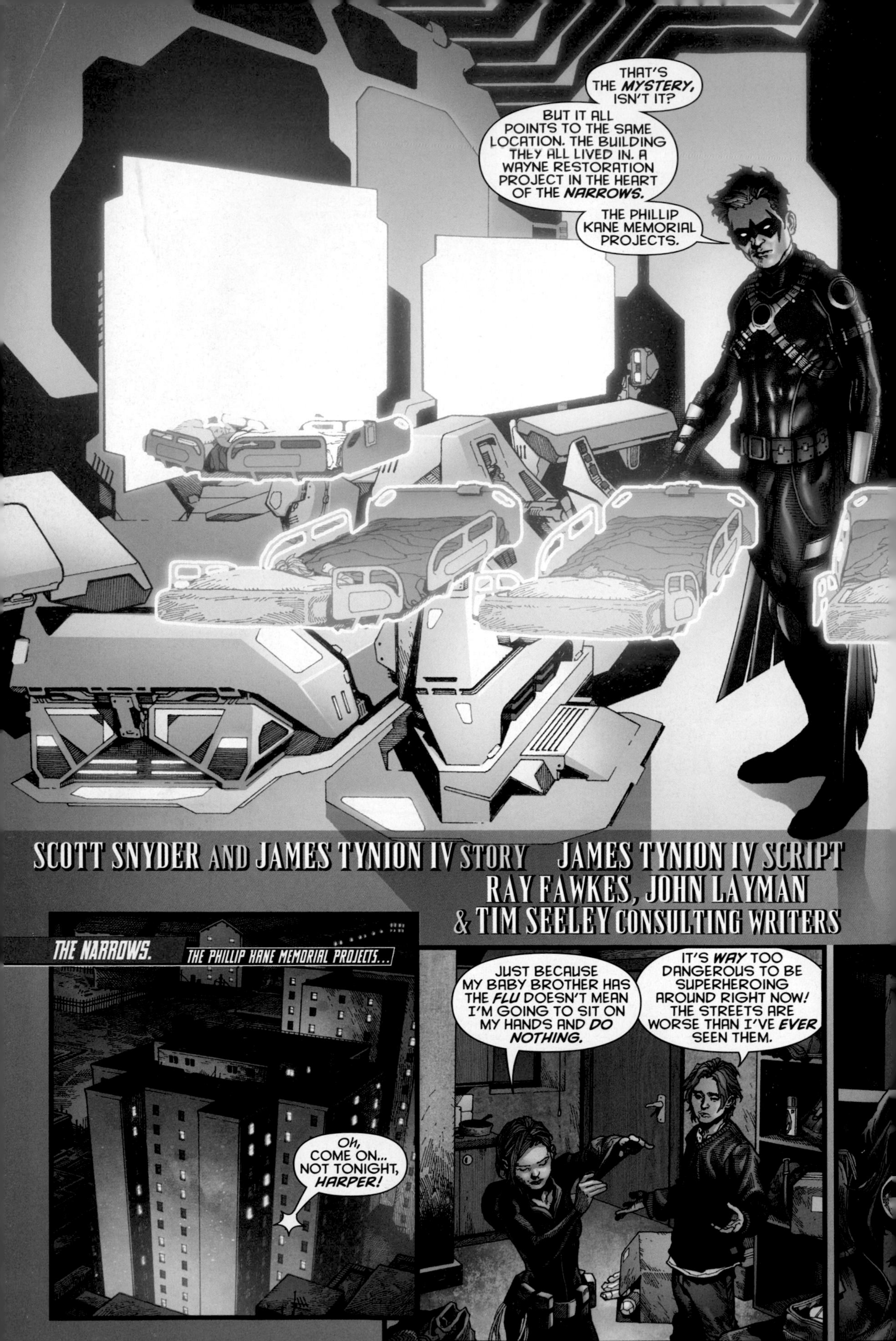
THAT'S THE MYSTERY, ISN'T IT?
BUT IT ALL POINTS TO THE SAME LOCATION. THE BUILDING THEY ALL LIVED IN. A WAYNE RESTORATION PROJECT IN THE HEART OF THE NARROWS.
THE PHILLIP KANE MEMORIAL PROJECTS.
SCOTT SNYDER AND JAMES TYNION IV STORY JAMES TYNION IV SCRIPT
RAY FAWKES, JOHN LAYMAN & TIM SEELEY CONSULTING WRITERS
THE NARROWS.
THE PHILLIP KANE MEMORIAL PROJECTS...
Oh, COME ON... NOT TONIGHT, HARPER!
JUST BECAUSE MY BABY BROTHER HAS THE FLU DOESN'T MEAN I'M GOING TO SIT ON MY HANDS AND DO NOTHING.
IT'S WAY TOO DANGEROUS TO BE SUPERHEROING AROUND RIGHT NOW! THE STREETS ARE WORSE THAN I'VE EVER SEEN THEM.

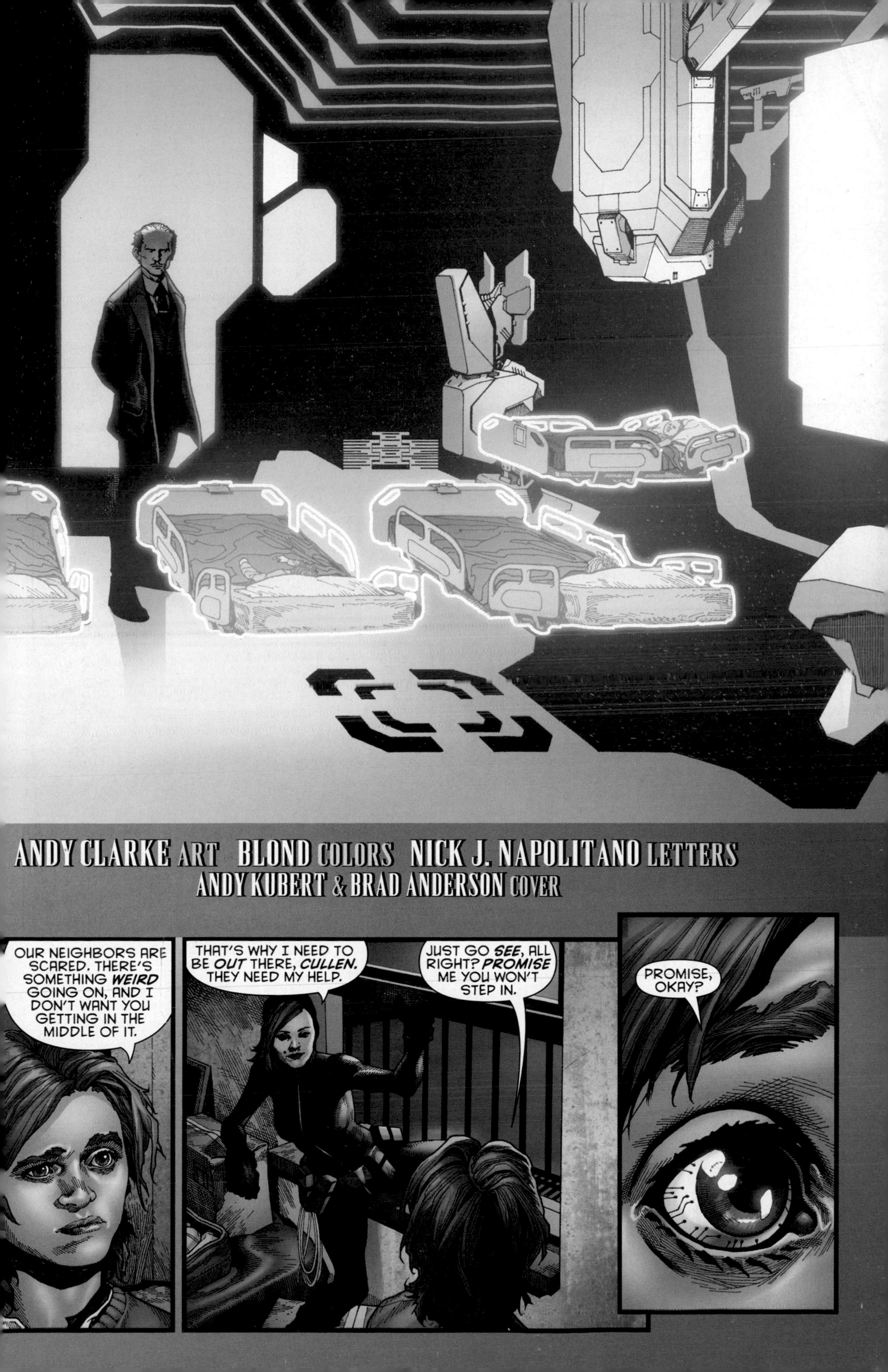
ANDY CLARKE ART BLOND COLORS NICK J. NAPOLITANO LETTERS
ANDY KUBERT & BRAD ANDERSON COVER
OUR NEIGHBORS ARE SCARED. THERE'S SOMETHING *WEIRD* GOING ON, AND I DON'T WANT YOU GETTING IN THE MIDDLE OF IT.
THAT'S WHY I NEED TO BE *OUT* THERE, *CULLEN.* THEY NEED MY HELP.
JUST GO *SEE,* ALL RIGHT? *PROMISE* ME YOU WON'T STEP IN.
PROMISE, OKAY?

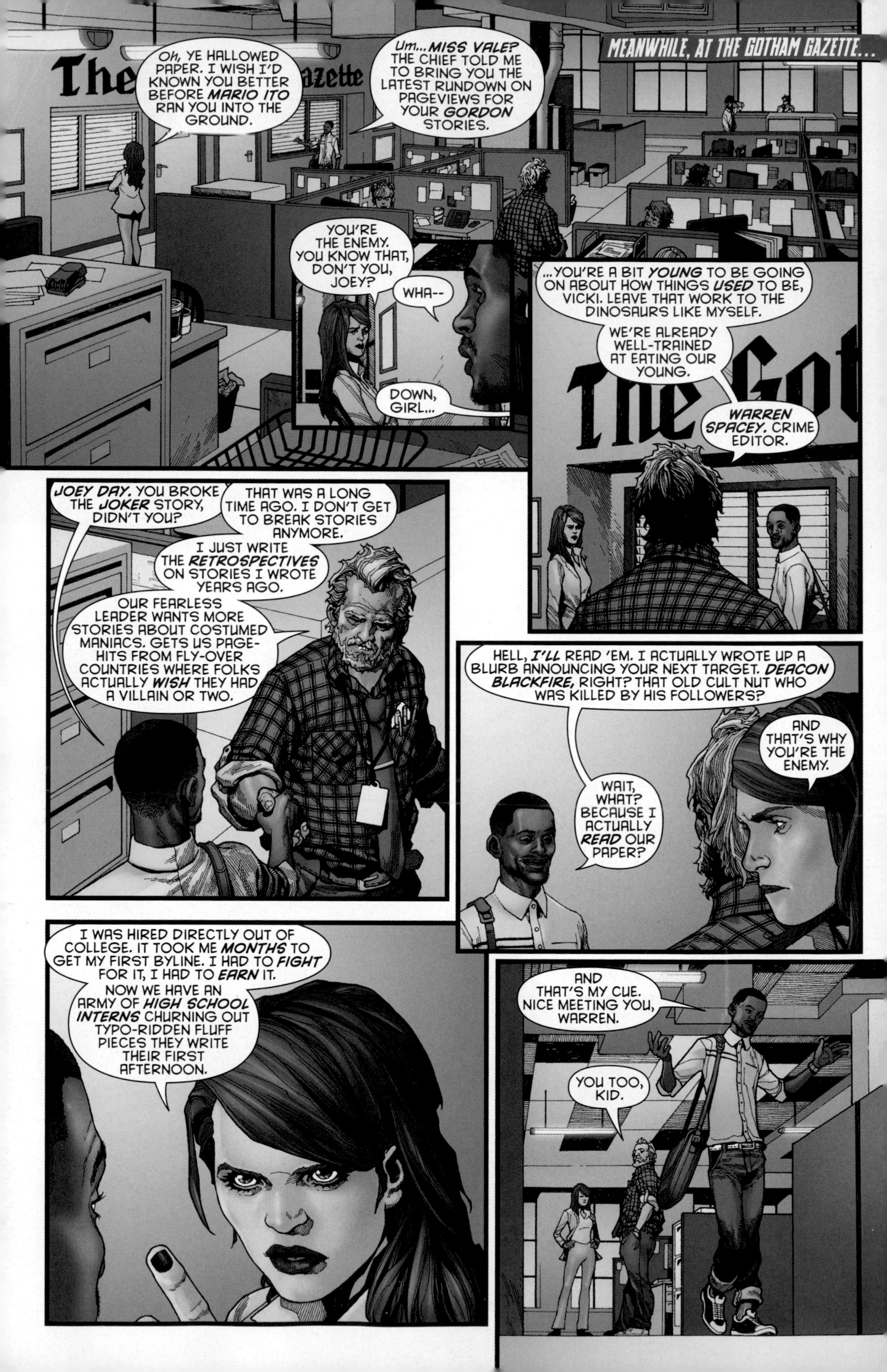
MEANWHILE, AT THE GOTHAM GAZETTE...
Oh, YE HALLOWED PAPER. I WISH I'D KNOWN YOU BETTER BEFORE MARIO ITO RAN YOU INTO THE GROUND.
Um...MISS VALE? THE CHIEF TOLD ME TO BRING YOU THE LATEST RUNDOWN ON PAGEVIEWS FOR YOUR GORDON STORIES.
YOU'RE THE ENEMY. YOU KNOW THAT, DON'T YOU, JOEY?
WHA--
DOWN, GIRL...
...YOU'RE A BIT YOUNG TO BE GOING ON ABOUT HOW THINGS USED TO BE, VICKI. LEAVE THAT WORK TO THE DINOSAURS LIKE MYSELF.
WE'RE ALREADY WELL-TRAINED AT EATING OUR YOUNG.
WARREN SPACEY. CRIME EDITOR.
JOEY DAY. YOU BROKE THE JOKER STORY, DIDN'T YOU?
THAT WAS A LONG TIME AGO. I DON'T GET TO BREAK STORIES ANYMORE.
I JUST WRITE THE RETROSPECTIVES ON STORIES I WROTE YEARS AGO.
OUR FEARLESS LEADER WANTS MORE STORIES ABOUT COSTUMED MANIACS. GETS US PAGE-HITS FROM FLY-OVER COUNTRIES WHERE FOLKS ACTUALLY WISH THEY HAD A VILLAIN OR TWO.
HELL, I'LL READ 'EM. I ACTUALLY WROTE UP A BLURB ANNOUNCING YOUR NEXT TARGET. DEACON BLACKFIRE, RIGHT? THAT OLD CULT NUT WHO WAS KILLED BY HIS FOLLOWERS?
AND THAT'S WHY YOU'RE THE ENEMY.
WAIT, WHAT? BECAUSE I ACTUALLY READ OUR PAPER?
I WAS HIRED DIRECTLY OUT OF COLLEGE. IT TOOK ME MONTHS TO GET MY FIRST BYLINE. I HAD TO FIGHT FOR IT, I HAD TO EARN IT.
NOW WE HAVE AN ARMY OF HIGH SCHOOL INTERNS CHURNING OUT TYPO-RIDDEN FLUFF PIECES THEY WRITE THEIR FIRST AFTERNOON.
AND THAT'S MY CUE. NICE MEETING YOU, WARREN.
YOU TOO, KID.

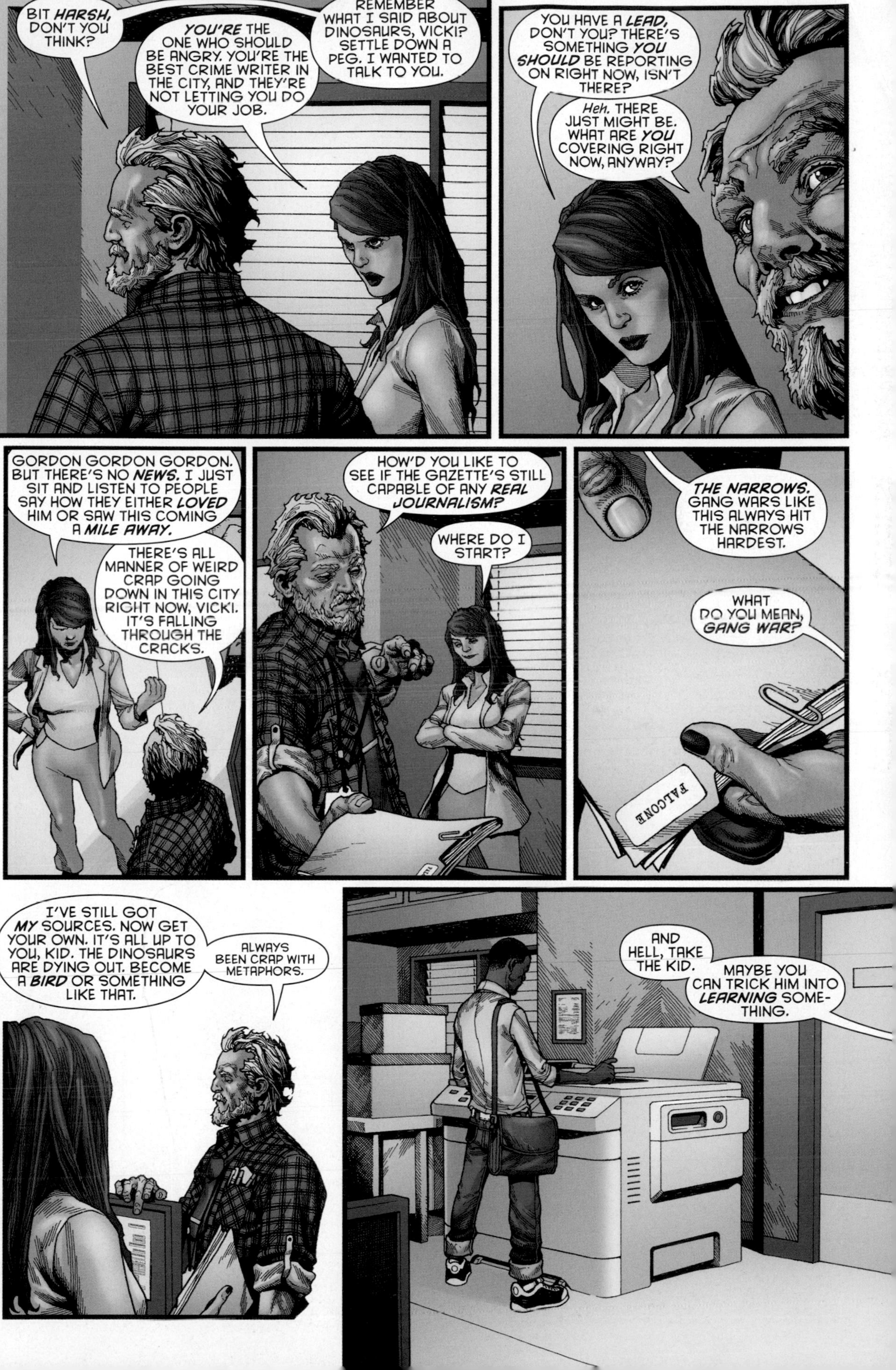
BIT HARSH, DON'T YOU THINK?
REMEMBER WHAT I SAID ABOUT DINOSAURS, VICKI? SETTLE DOWN A PEG. I WANTED TO TALK TO YOU.
YOU'RE THE ONE WHO SHOULD BE ANGRY. YOU'RE THE BEST CRIME WRITER IN THE CITY, AND THEY'RE NOT LETTING YOU DO YOUR JOB.
YOU HAVE A LEAD, DON'T YOU? THERE'S SOMETHING YOU SHOULD BE REPORTING ON RIGHT NOW, ISN'T THERE?
Heh. THERE JUST MIGHT BE. WHAT ARE YOU COVERING RIGHT NOW, ANYWAY?
GORDON GORDON GORDON. BUT THERE'S NO NEWS. I JUST SIT AND LISTEN TO PEOPLE SAY HOW THEY EITHER LOVED HIM OR SAW THIS COMING A MILE AWAY.
THERE'S ALL MANNER OF WEIRD CRAP GOING DOWN IN THIS CITY RIGHT NOW, VICKI. IT'S FALLING THROUGH THE CRACKS.
HOW'D YOU LIKE TO SEE IF THE GAZETTE'S STILL CAPABLE OF ANY REAL JOURNALISM?
WHERE DO I START?
THE NARROWS. GANG WARS LIKE THIS ALWAYS HIT THE NARROWS HARDEST.
WHAT DO YOU MEAN, GANG WAR?
FALCONE
I'VE STILL GOT MY SOURCES. NOW GET YOUR OWN. IT'S ALL UP TO YOU, KID. THE DINOSAURS ARE DYING OUT. BECOME A BIRD OR SOMETHING LIKE THAT.
ALWAYS BEEN CRAP WITH METAPHORS.
AND HELL, TAKE THE KID.
MAYBE YOU CAN TRICK HIM INTO LEARNING SOMETHING.

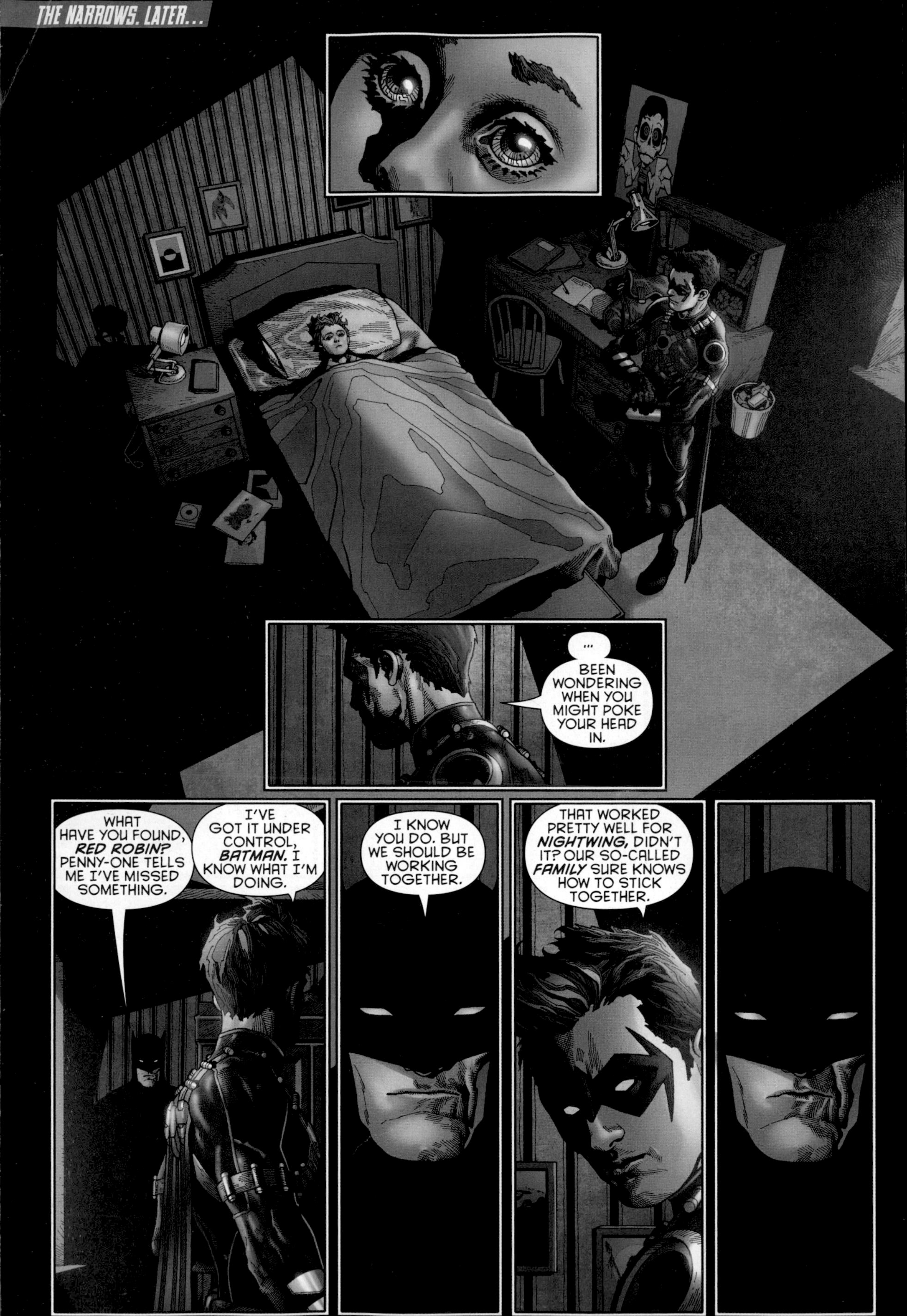
THE NARROWS. LATER...
...
BEEN WONDERING WHEN YOU MIGHT POKE YOUR HEAD IN.
WHAT HAVE YOU FOUND, RED ROBIN? PENNY-ONE TELLS ME I'VE MISSED SOMETHING.
I'VE GOT IT UNDER CONTROL, BATMAN. I KNOW WHAT I'M DOING.
I KNOW YOU DO. BUT WE SHOULD BE WORKING TOGETHER.
THAT WORKED PRETTY WELL FOR NIGHTWING, DIDN'T IT? OUR SO-CALLED FAMILY SURE KNOWS HOW TO STICK TOGETHER.

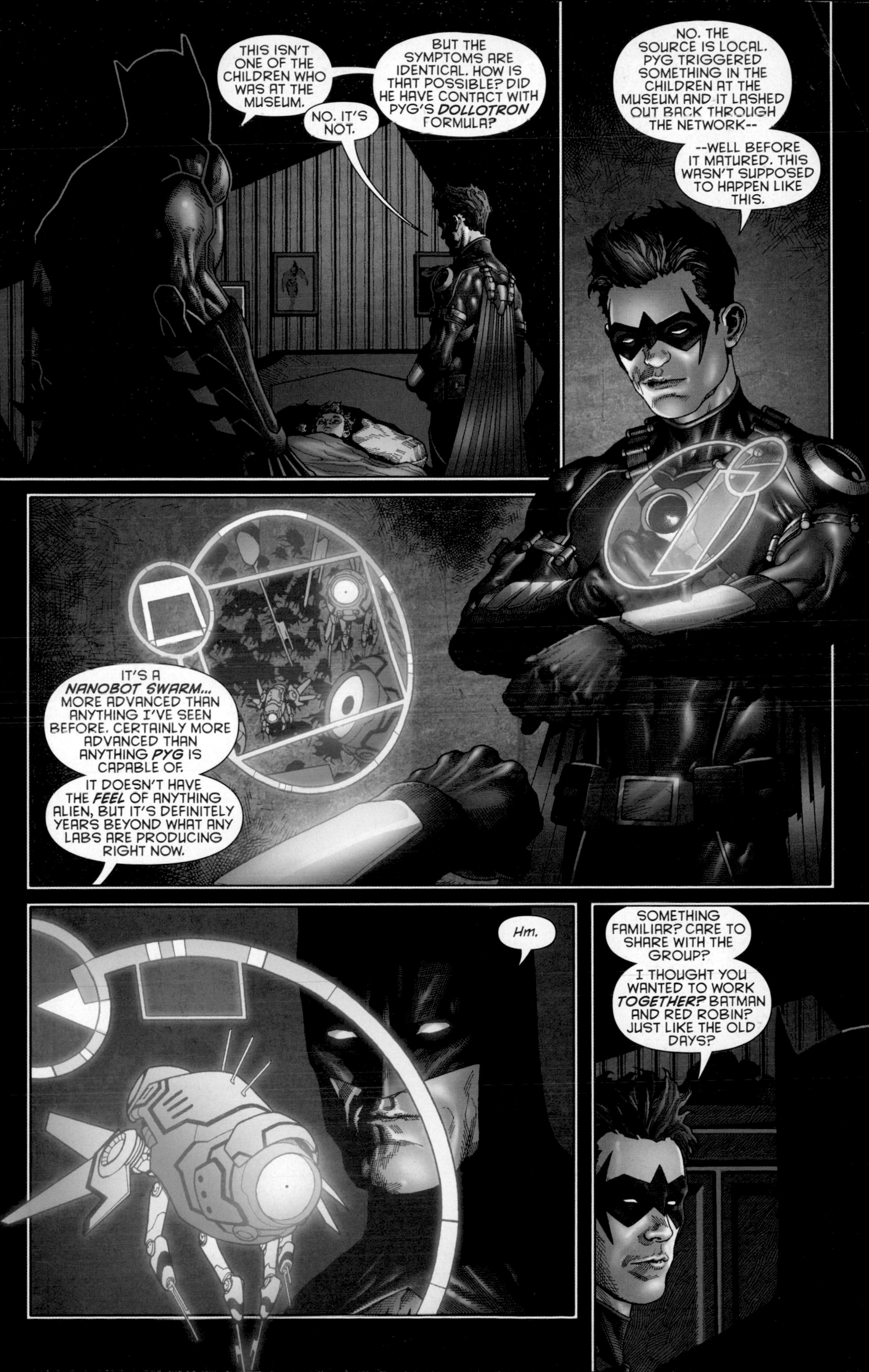
THIS ISN'T ONE OF THE CHILDREN WHO WAS AT THE MUSEUM.
BUT THE SYMPTOMS ARE IDENTICAL. HOW IS THAT POSSIBLE? DID HE HAVE CONTACT WITH PYG'S DOLLOTRON FORMULA?
NO. IT'S NOT.
NO. THE SOURCE IS LOCAL. PYG TRIGGERED SOMETHING IN THE CHILDREN AT THE MUSEUM AND IT LASHED OUT BACK THROUGH THE NETWORK--
--WELL BEFORE IT MATURED. THIS WASN'T SUPPOSED TO HAPPEN LIKE THIS.
IT'S A NANOBOT SWARM... MORE ADVANCED THAN ANYTHING I'VE SEEN BEFORE. CERTAINLY MORE ADVANCED THAN ANYTHING PYG IS CAPABLE OF.
IT DOESN'T HAVE THE FEEL OF ANYTHING ALIEN, BUT IT'S DEFINITELY YEARS BEYOND WHAT ANY LABS ARE PRODUCING RIGHT NOW.
Hm.
SOMETHING FAMILIAR? CARE TO SHARE WITH THE GROUP?
I THOUGHT YOU WANTED TO WORK TOGETHER? BATMAN AND RED ROBIN? JUST LIKE THE OLD DAYS?

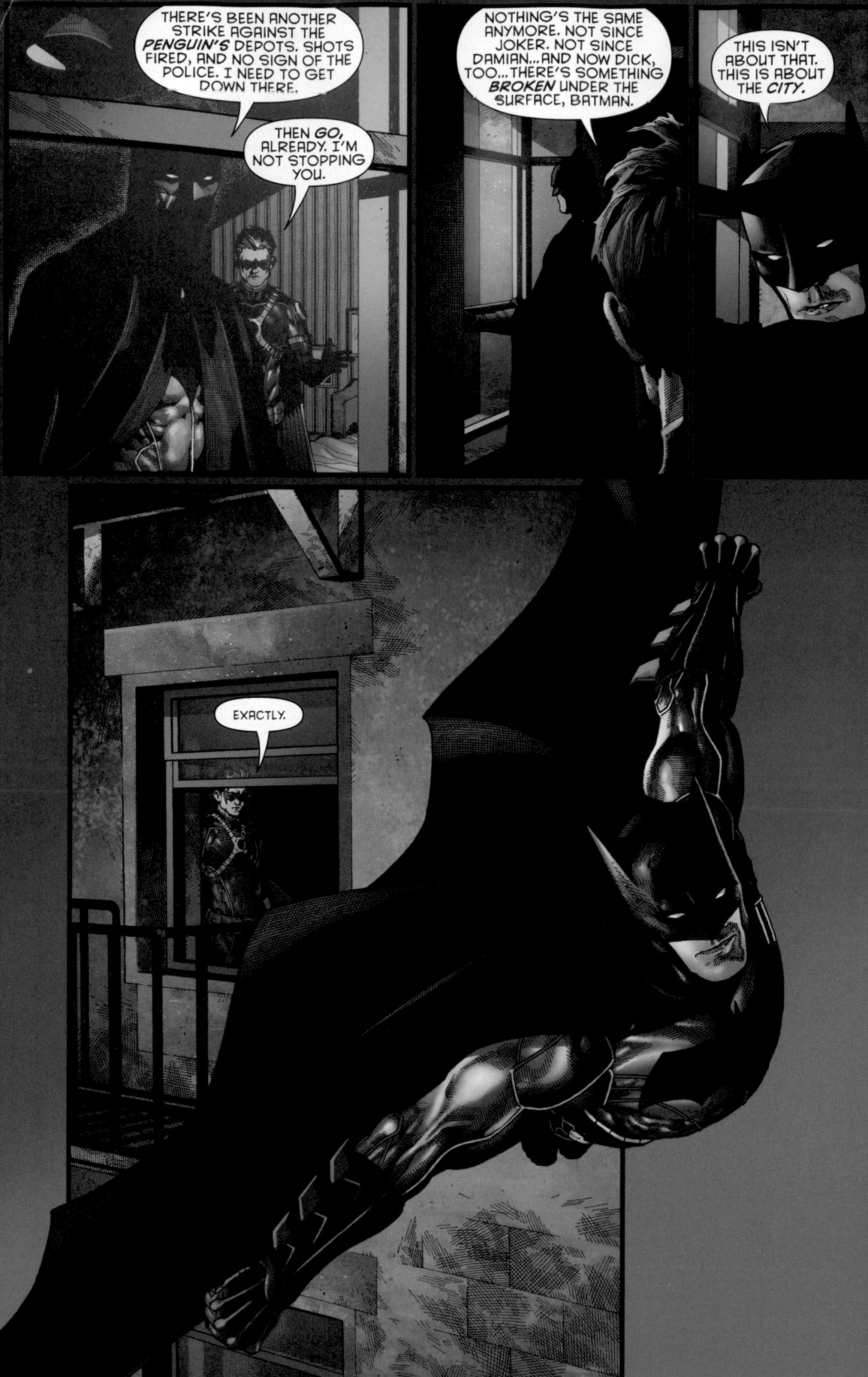
THERE'S BEEN ANOTHER STRIKE AGAINST THE PENGUIN'S DEPOTS. SHOTS FIRED, AND NO SIGN OF THE POLICE. I NEED TO GET DOWN THERE.
THEN GO, ALREADY. I'M NOT STOPPING YOU.
NOTHING'S THE SAME ANYMORE. NOT SINCE JOKER. NOT SINCE DAMIAN...AND NOW DICK, TOO...THERE'S SOMETHING BROKEN UNDER THE SURFACE, BATMAN.
THIS ISN'T ABOUT THAT. THIS IS ABOUT THE CITY.
EXACTLY.

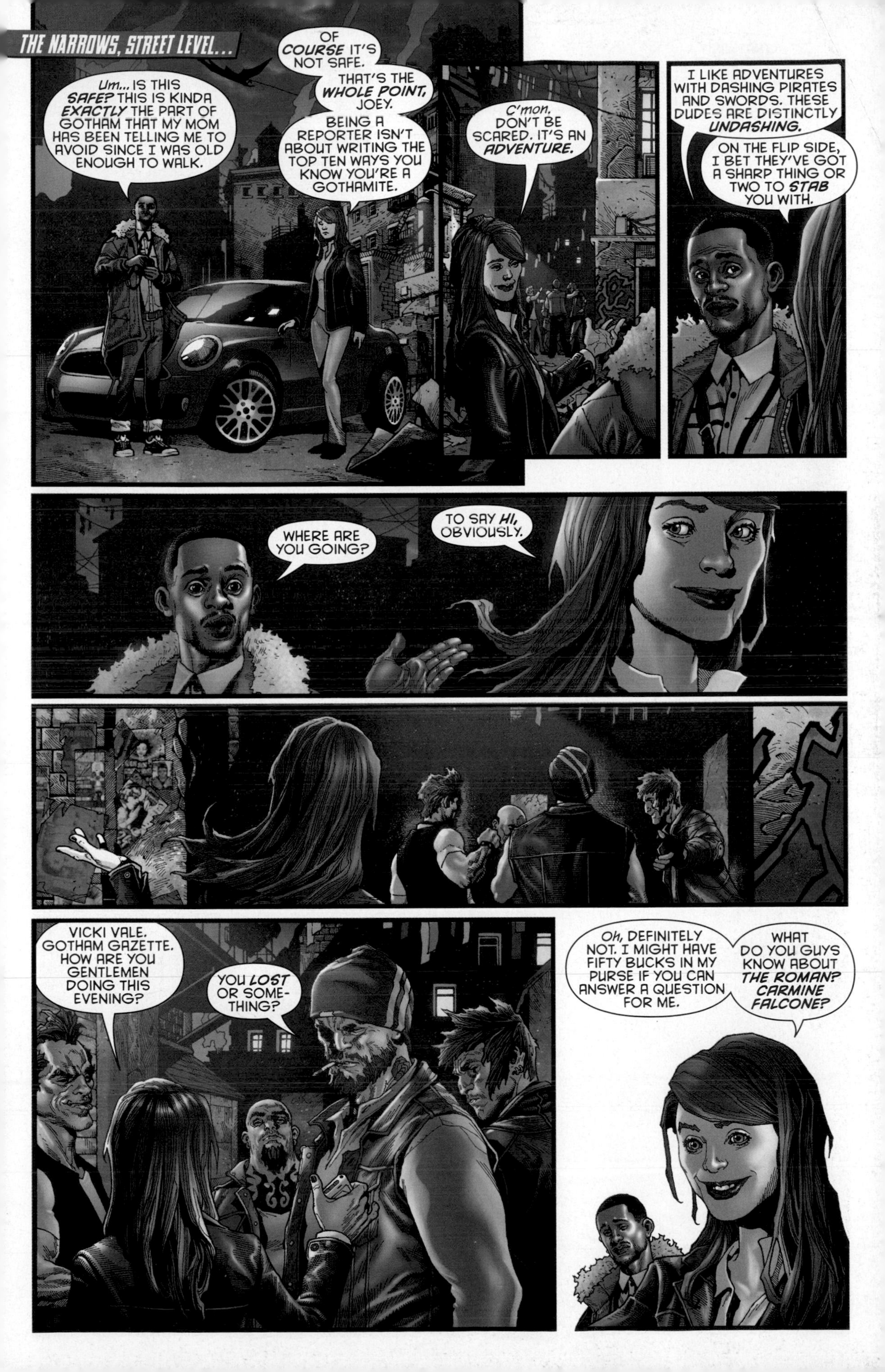
THE NARROWS, STREET LEVEL...
Um... IS THIS SAFE? THIS IS KINDA EXACTLY THE PART OF GOTHAM THAT MY MOM HAS BEEN TELLING ME TO AVOID SINCE I WAS OLD ENOUGH TO WALK.
OF COURSE IT'S NOT SAFE.
THAT'S THE WHOLE POINT, JOEY.
BEING A REPORTER ISN'T ABOUT WRITING THE TOP TEN WAYS YOU KNOW YOU'RE A GOTHAMITE.
C'mon. DON'T BE SCARED. IT'S AN ADVENTURE.
I LIKE ADVENTURES WITH DASHING PIRATES AND SWORDS. THESE DUDES ARE DISTINCTLY UNDASHING.
ON THE FLIP SIDE, I BET THEY'VE GOT A SHARP THING OR TWO TO STAB YOU WITH.
WHERE ARE YOU GOING?
TO SAY HI, OBVIOUSLY.
VICKI VALE. GOTHAM GAZETTE. HOW ARE YOU GENTLEMEN DOING THIS EVENING?
YOU LOST OR SOME-THING?
Oh, DEFINITELY NOT. I MIGHT HAVE FIFTY BUCKS IN MY PURSE IF YOU CAN ANSWER A QUESTION FOR ME.
WHAT DO YOU GUYS KNOW ABOUT THE ROMAN? CARMINE FALCONE?

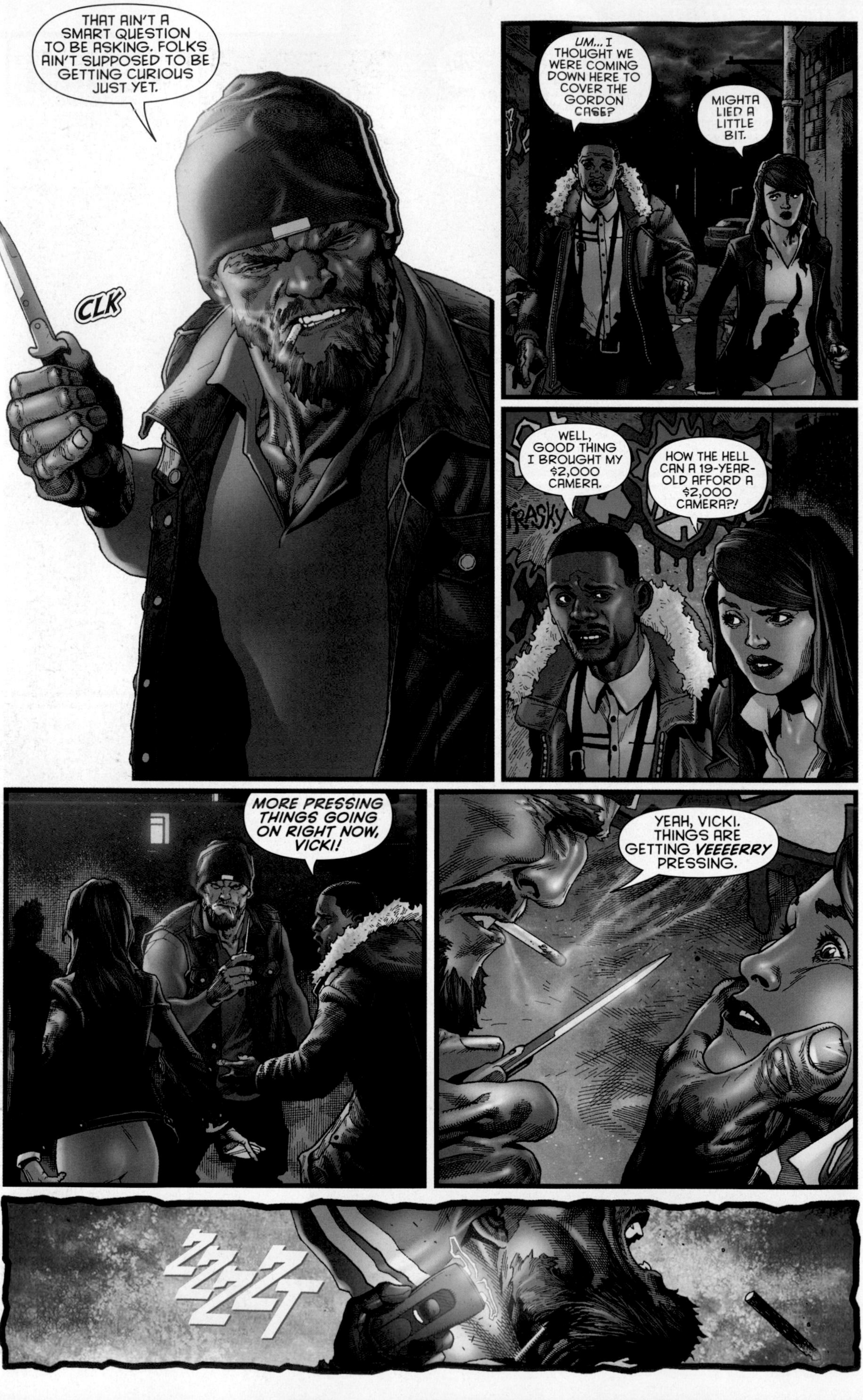
THAT AIN'T A SMART QUESTION TO BE ASKING. FOLKS AIN'T SUPPOSED TO BE GETTING CURIOUS JUST YET.
CLK
UM... I THOUGHT WE WERE COMING DOWN HERE TO COVER THE GORDON CASE?
MIGHTA LIED A LITTLE BIT.
WELL, GOOD THING I BROUGHT MY $2,000 CAMERA.
HOW THE HELL CAN A 19-YEAR-OLD AFFORD A $2,000 CAMERA?!
MORE PRESSING THINGS GOING ON RIGHT NOW, VICKI!
YEAH, VICKI. THINGS ARE GETTING VEEEERRY PRESSING.
ZZZZT

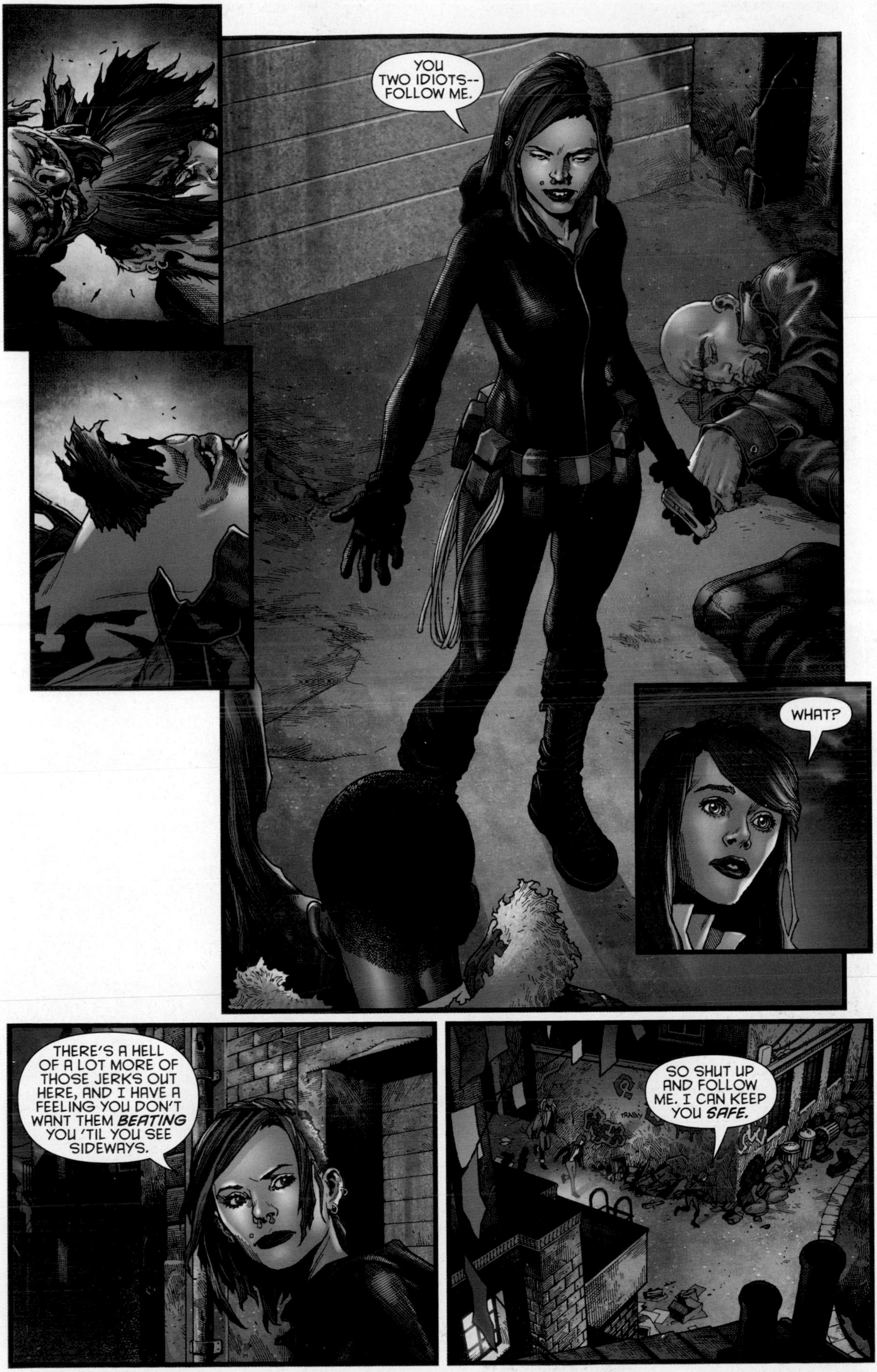
YOU TWO IDIOTS-- FOLLOW ME.
WHAT?
THERE'S A HELL OF A LOT MORE OF THOSE JERKS OUT HERE, AND I HAVE A FEELING YOU DON'T WANT THEM *BEATING* YOU 'TIL YOU SEE SIDEWAYS.
SO SHUT UP AND FOLLOW ME. I CAN KEEP YOU *SAFE.*

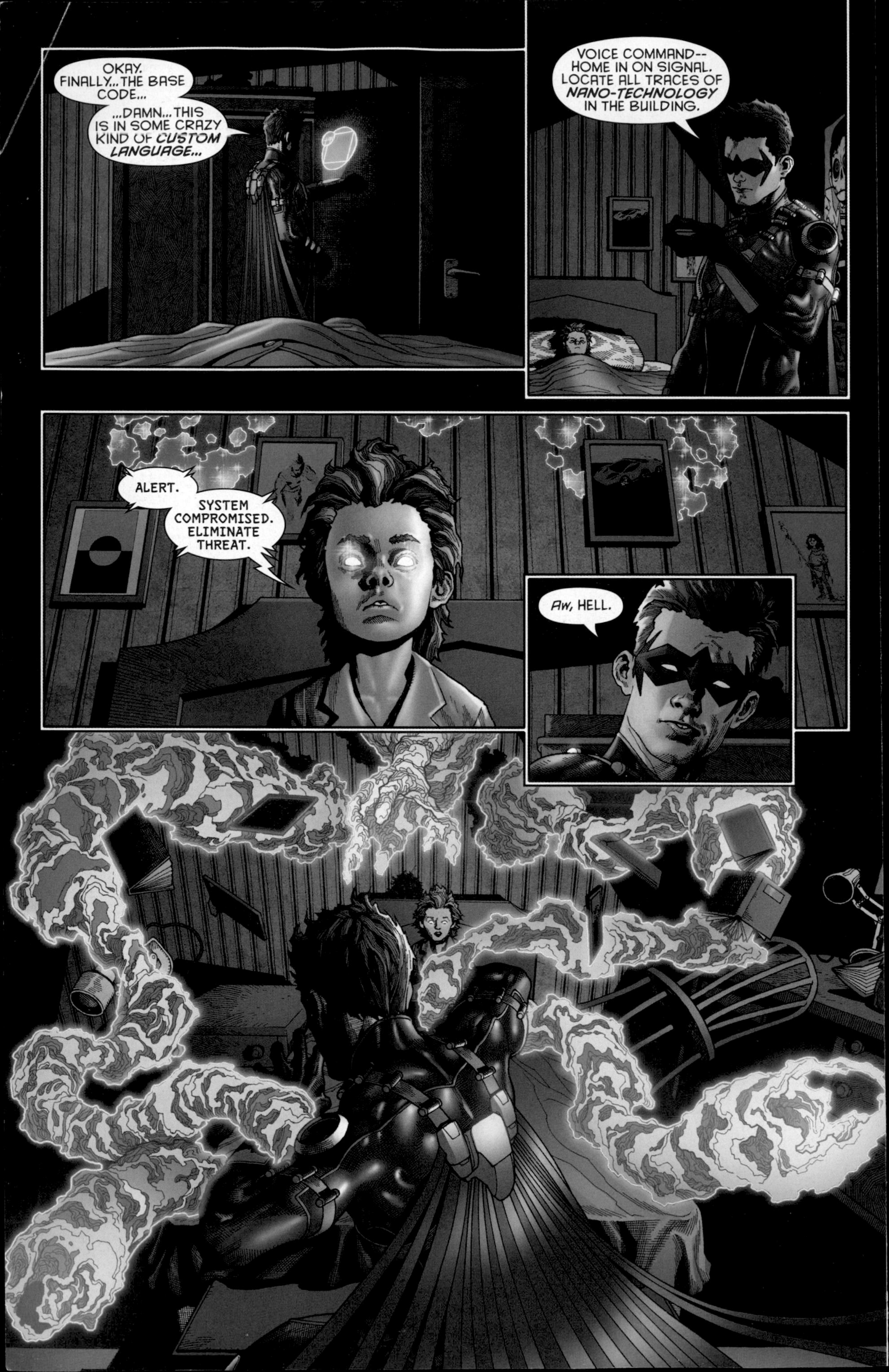
OKAY. FINALLY... THE BASE CODE...
...DAMN... THIS IS IN SOME CRAZY KIND OF *CUSTOM LANGUAGE*...
VOICE COMMAND-- HOME IN ON SIGNAL. LOCATE ALL TRACES OF *NANO-TECHNOLOGY* IN THE BUILDING.
ALERT.
SYSTEM COMPROMISED. ELIMINATE THREAT.
Aw, HELL.

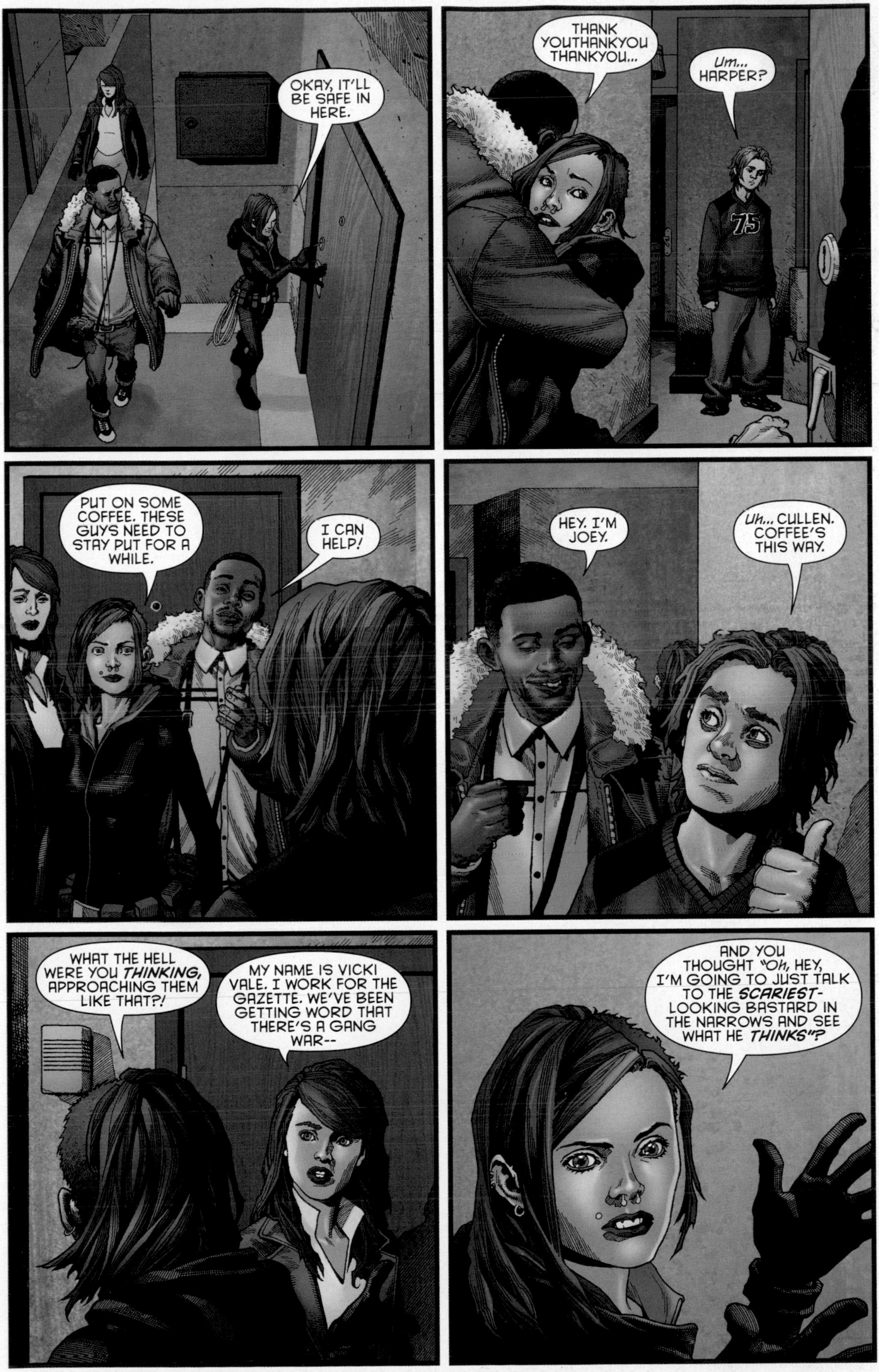
OKAY, IT'LL BE SAFE IN HERE.
THANK YOUTHANKYOU THANKYOU...
Um... HARPER?
PUT ON SOME COFFEE. THESE GUYS NEED TO STAY PUT FOR A WHILE.
I CAN HELP!
HEY. I'M JOEY.
Uh... CULLEN. COFFEE'S THIS WAY.
WHAT THE HELL WERE YOU THINKING, APPROACHING THEM LIKE THAT?!
MY NAME IS VICKI VALE. I WORK FOR THE GAZETTE. WE'VE BEEN GETTING WORD THAT THERE'S A GANG WAR--
AND YOU THOUGHT "Oh, HEY, I'M GOING TO JUST TALK TO THE SCARIEST-LOOKING BASTARD IN THE NARROWS AND SEE WHAT HE THINKS"?

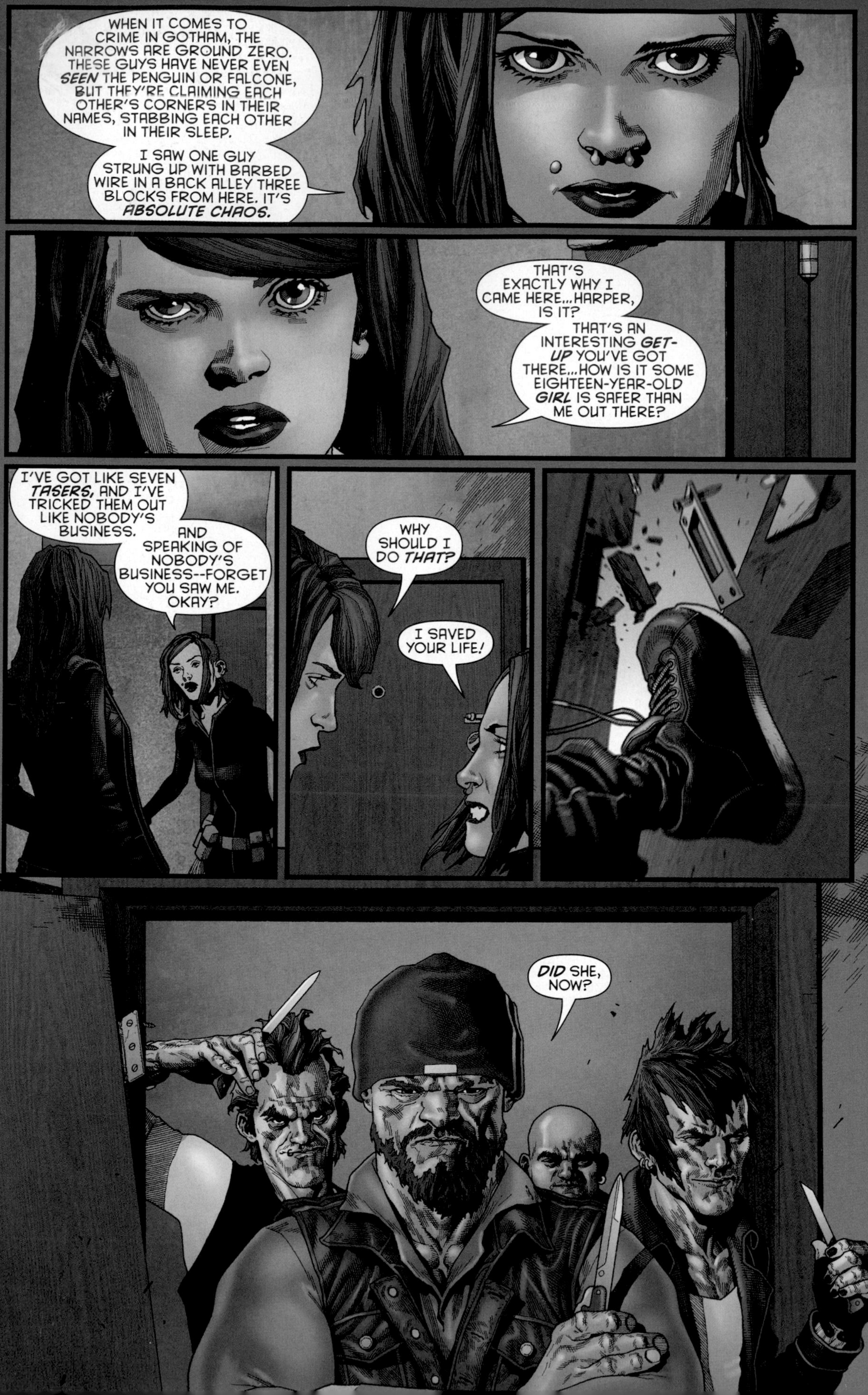
WHEN IT COMES TO CRIME IN GOTHAM, THE NARROWS ARE GROUND ZERO. THESE GUYS HAVE NEVER EVEN *SEEN* THE PENGUIN OR FALCONE, BUT THEY'RE CLAIMING EACH OTHER'S CORNERS IN THEIR NAMES, STABBING EACH OTHER IN THEIR SLEEP.
I SAW ONE GUY STRUNG UP WITH BARBED WIRE IN A BACK ALLEY THREE BLOCKS FROM HERE. IT'S ***ABSOLUTE CHAOS.***
THAT'S EXACTLY WHY I CAME HERE...HARPER, IS IT?
THAT'S AN INTERESTING ***GET-UP*** YOU'VE GOT THERE...HOW IS IT SOME EIGHTEEN-YEAR-OLD ***GIRL*** IS SAFER THAN ME OUT THERE?
I'VE GOT LIKE SEVEN ***TASERS,*** AND I'VE TRICKED THEM OUT LIKE NOBODY'S BUSINESS.
AND SPEAKING OF NOBODY'S BUSINESS--FORGET YOU SAW ME. OKAY?
WHY SHOULD I DO ***THAT?***
I SAVED YOUR LIFE!
DID SHE, NOW?

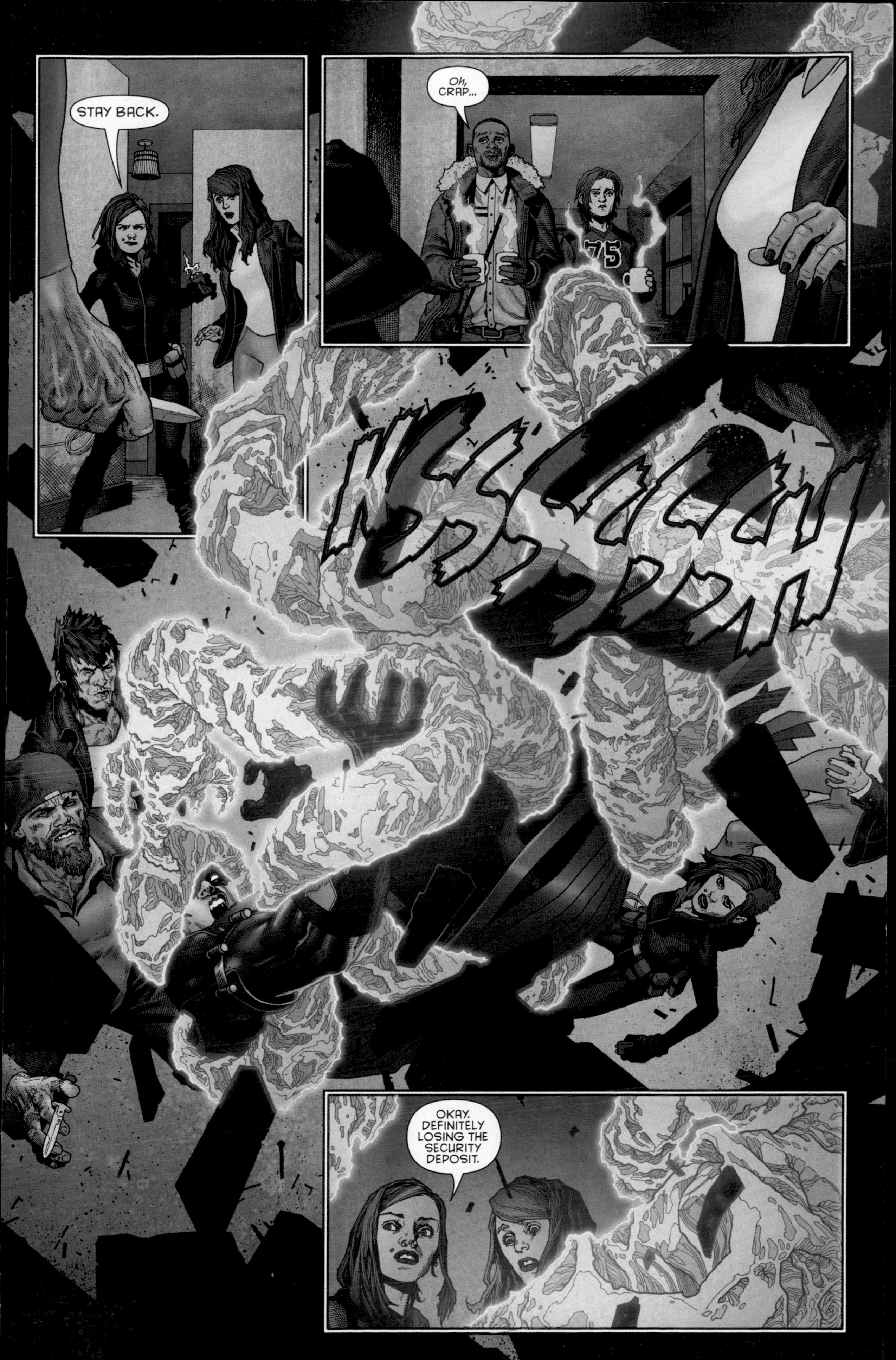
STAY BACK.
Oh, CRAP...
OKAY. DEFINITELY LOSING THE SECURITY DEPOSIT.

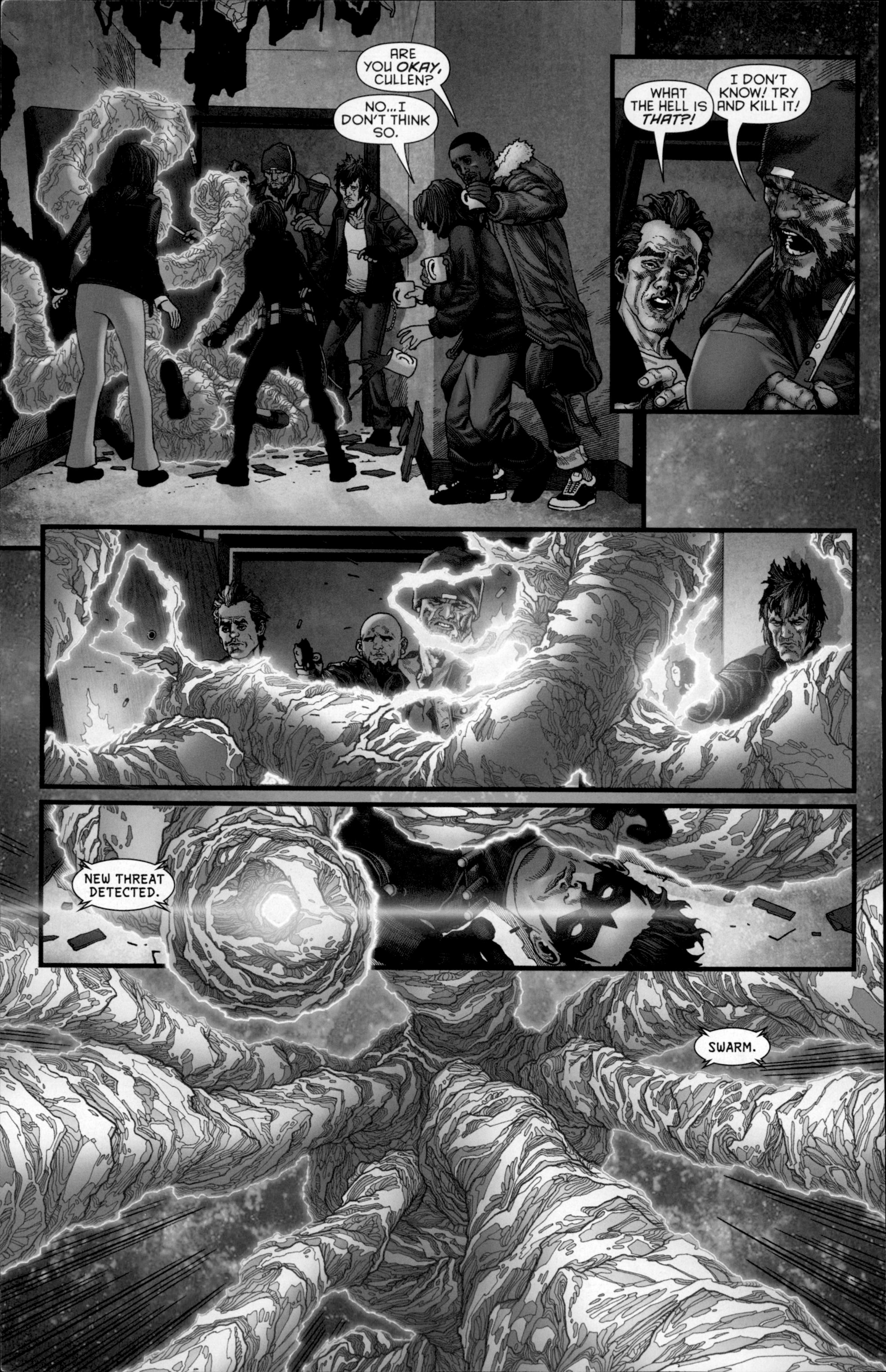
ARE YOU OKAY, CULLEN?
NO... I DON'T THINK SO.
WHAT THE HELL IS THAT?!
I DON'T KNOW! TRY AND KILL IT!
NEW THREAT DETECTED.
SWARM.

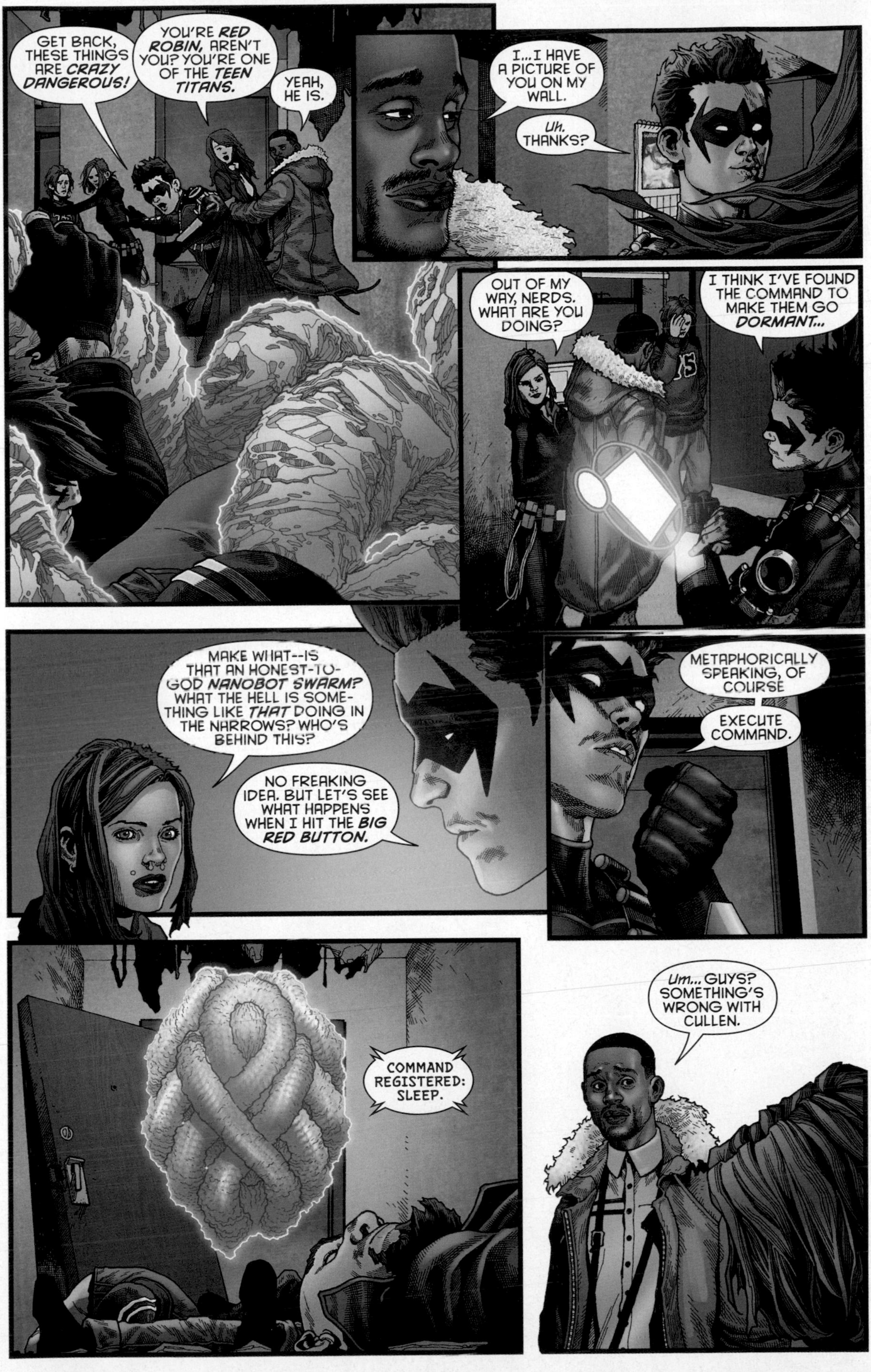
GET BACK, THESE THINGS ARE CRAZY DANGEROUS!
YOU'RE RED ROBIN, AREN'T YOU? YOU'RE ONE OF THE TEEN TITANS.
YEAH, HE IS.
I...I HAVE A PICTURE OF YOU ON MY WALL.
Uh. THANKS?
OUT OF MY WAY, NERDS. WHAT ARE YOU DOING?
I THINK I'VE FOUND THE COMMAND TO MAKE THEM GO DORMANT...
MAKE WHAT--IS THAT AN HONEST-TO-GOD NANOBOT SWARM? WHAT THE HELL IS SOMETHING LIKE THAT DOING IN THE NARROWS? WHO'S BEHIND THIS?
NO FREAKING IDEA. BUT LET'S SEE WHAT HAPPENS WHEN I HIT THE BIG RED BUTTON.
METAPHORICALLY SPEAKING, OF COURSE
EXECUTE COMMAND.
COMMAND REGISTERED: SLEEP.
Um... GUYS? SOMETHING'S WRONG WITH CULLEN.

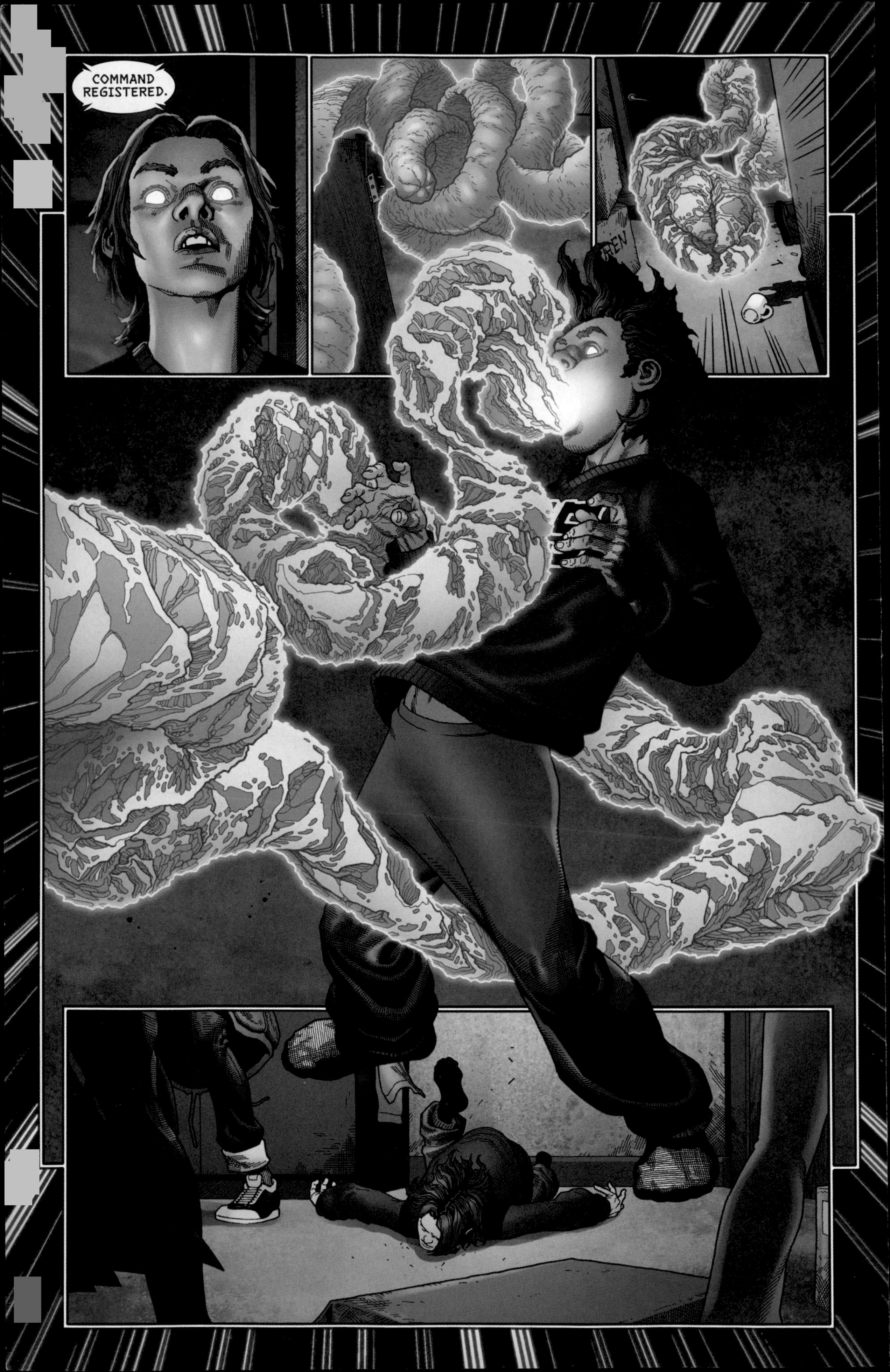
COMMAND REGISTERED.

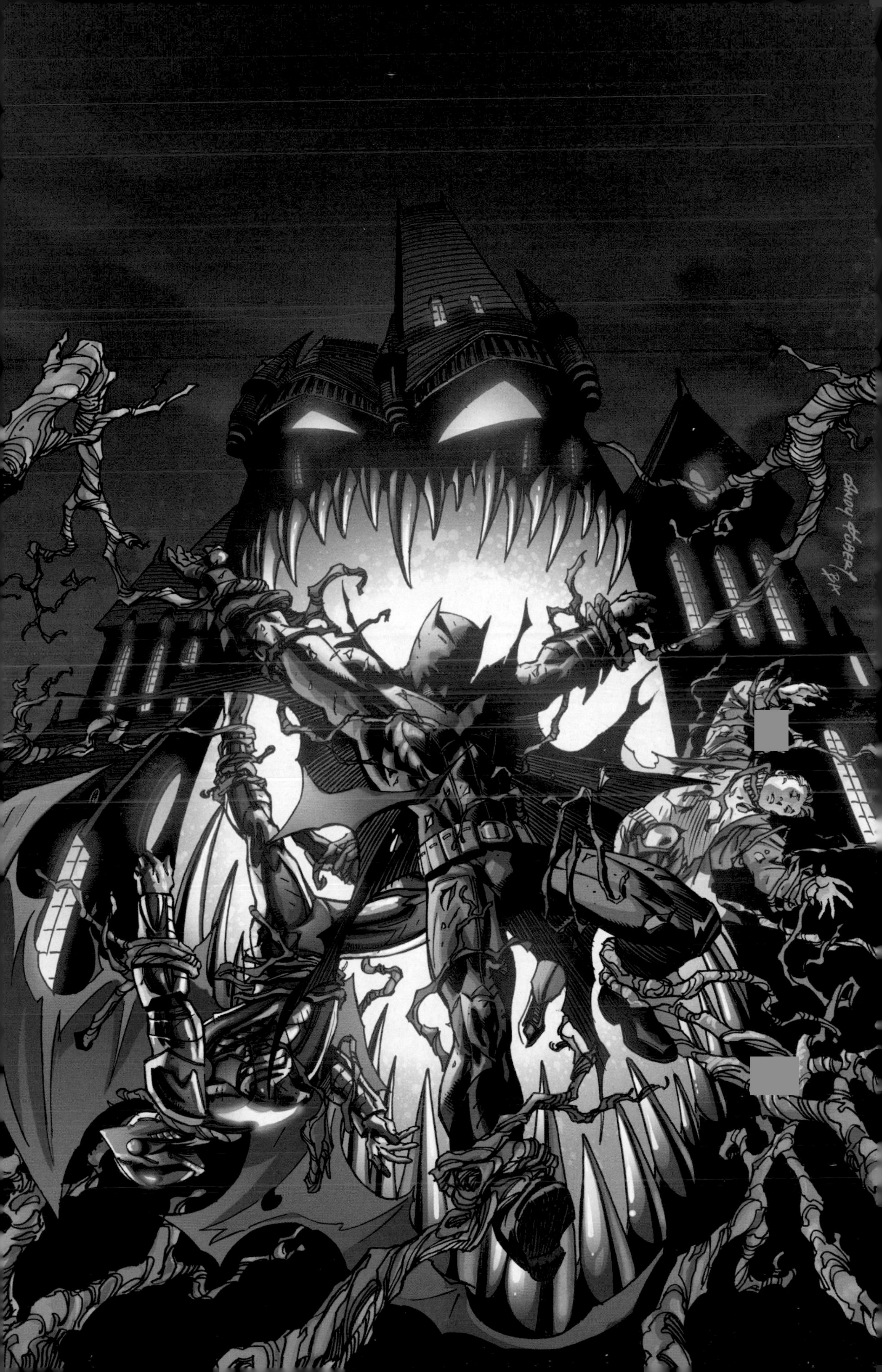

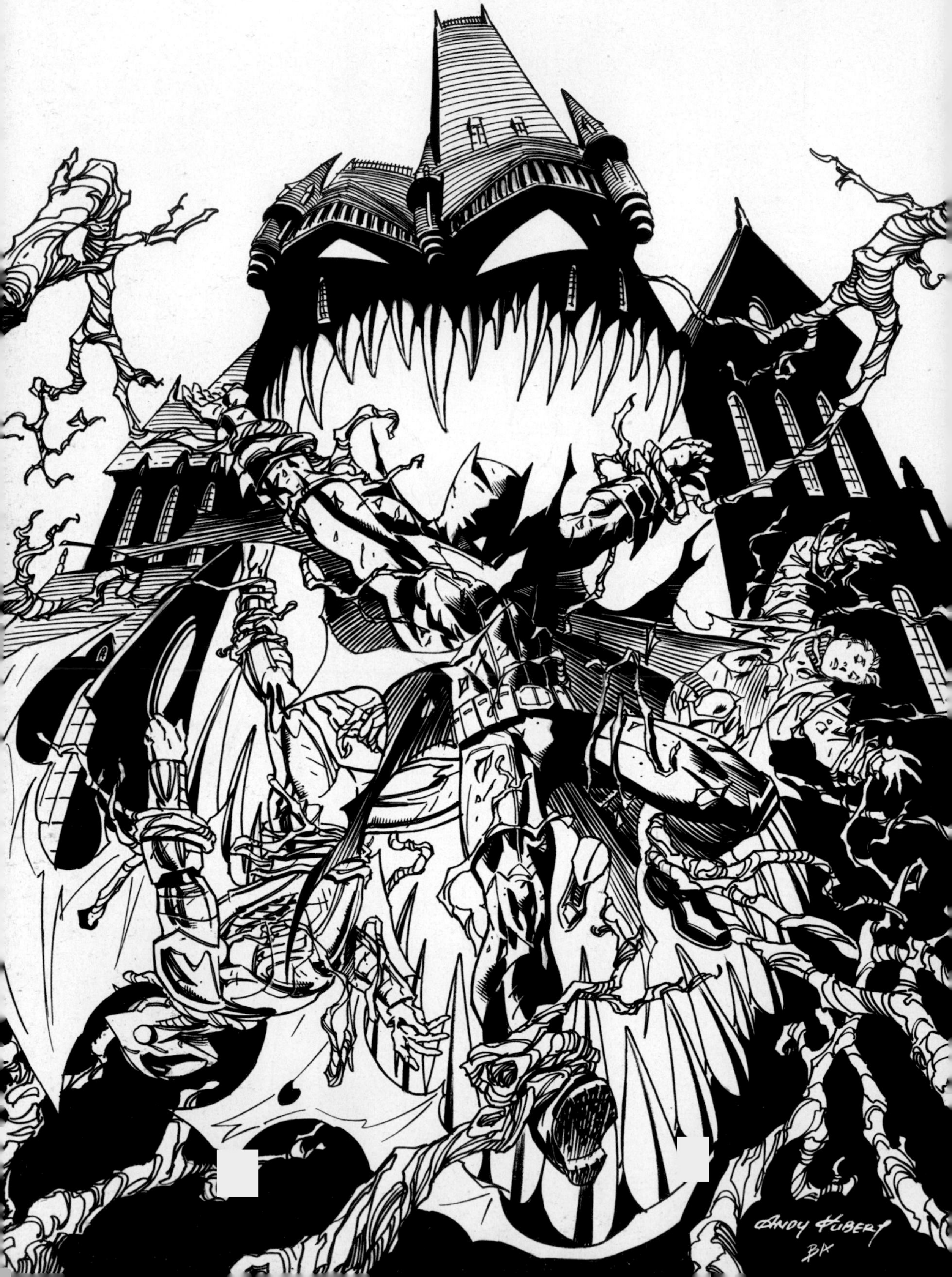
ANDY KUBERT
BA

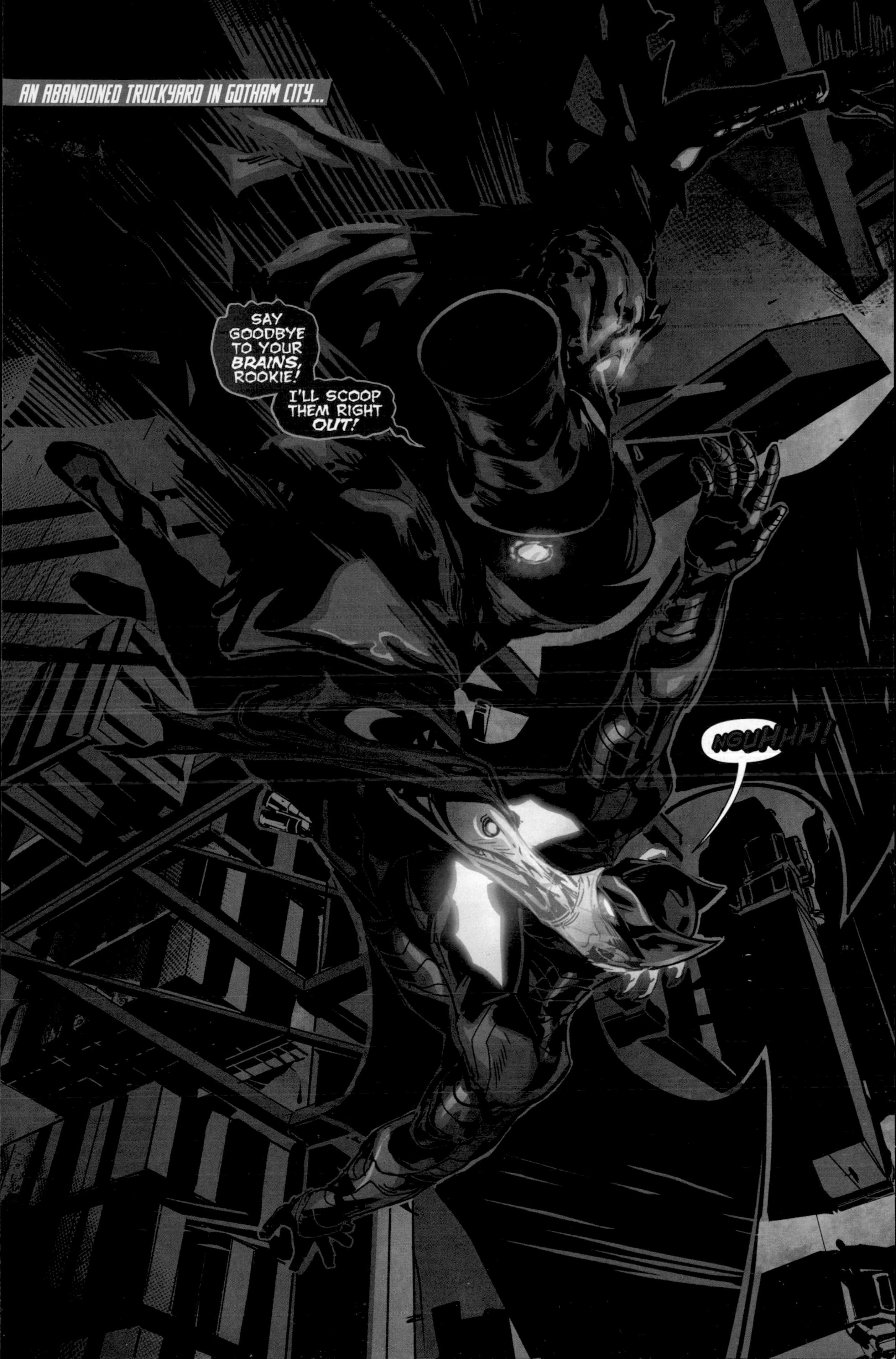
AN ABANDONED TRUCKYARD IN GOTHAM CITY...
SAY GOODBYE TO YOUR BRAINS, ROOKIE!
I'LL SCOOP THEM RIGHT OUT!
NGUHHH!

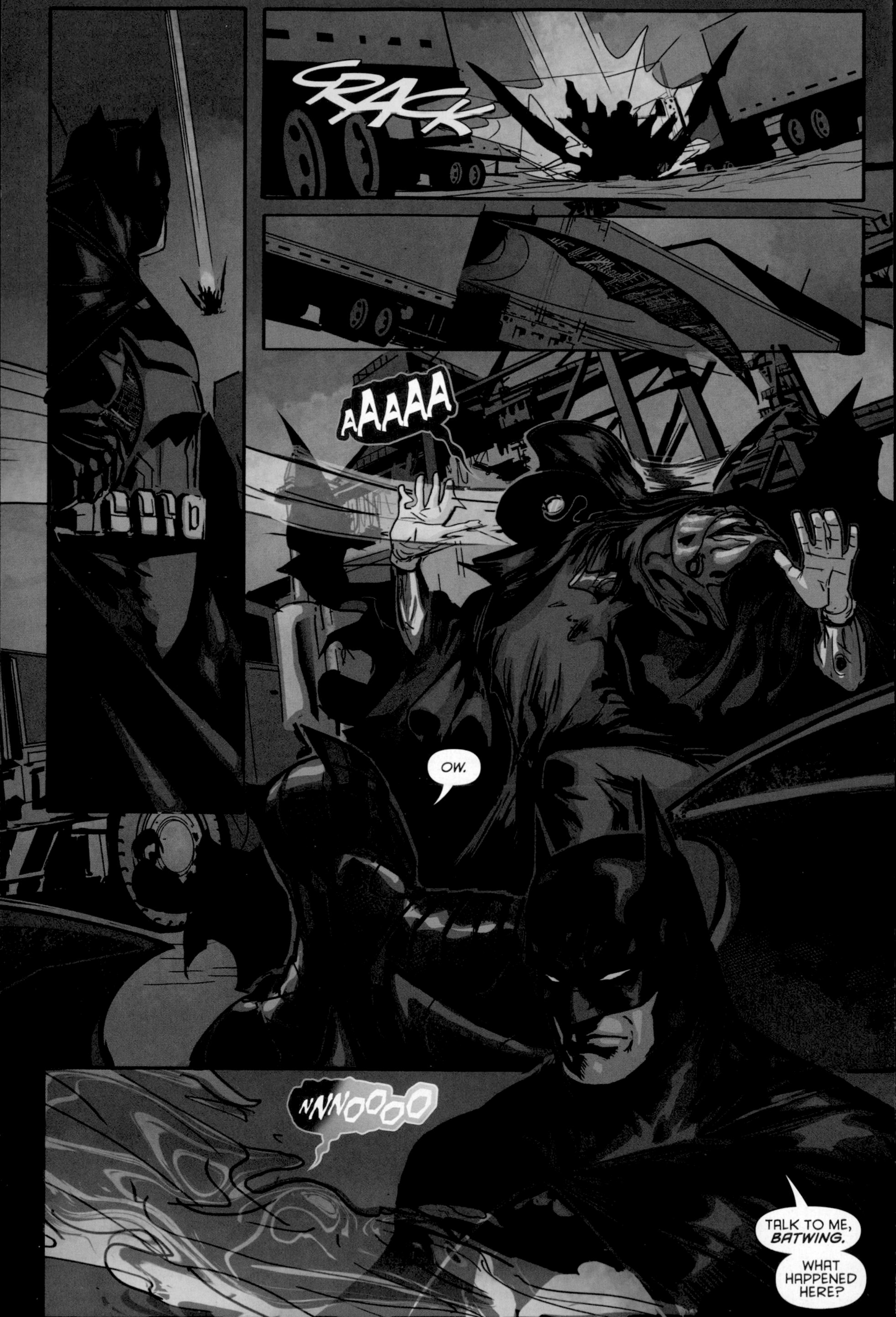
CRACK
AAAAA
OW.
NNNOOOOO
TALK TO ME, *BATWING.*
WHAT HAPPENED HERE?

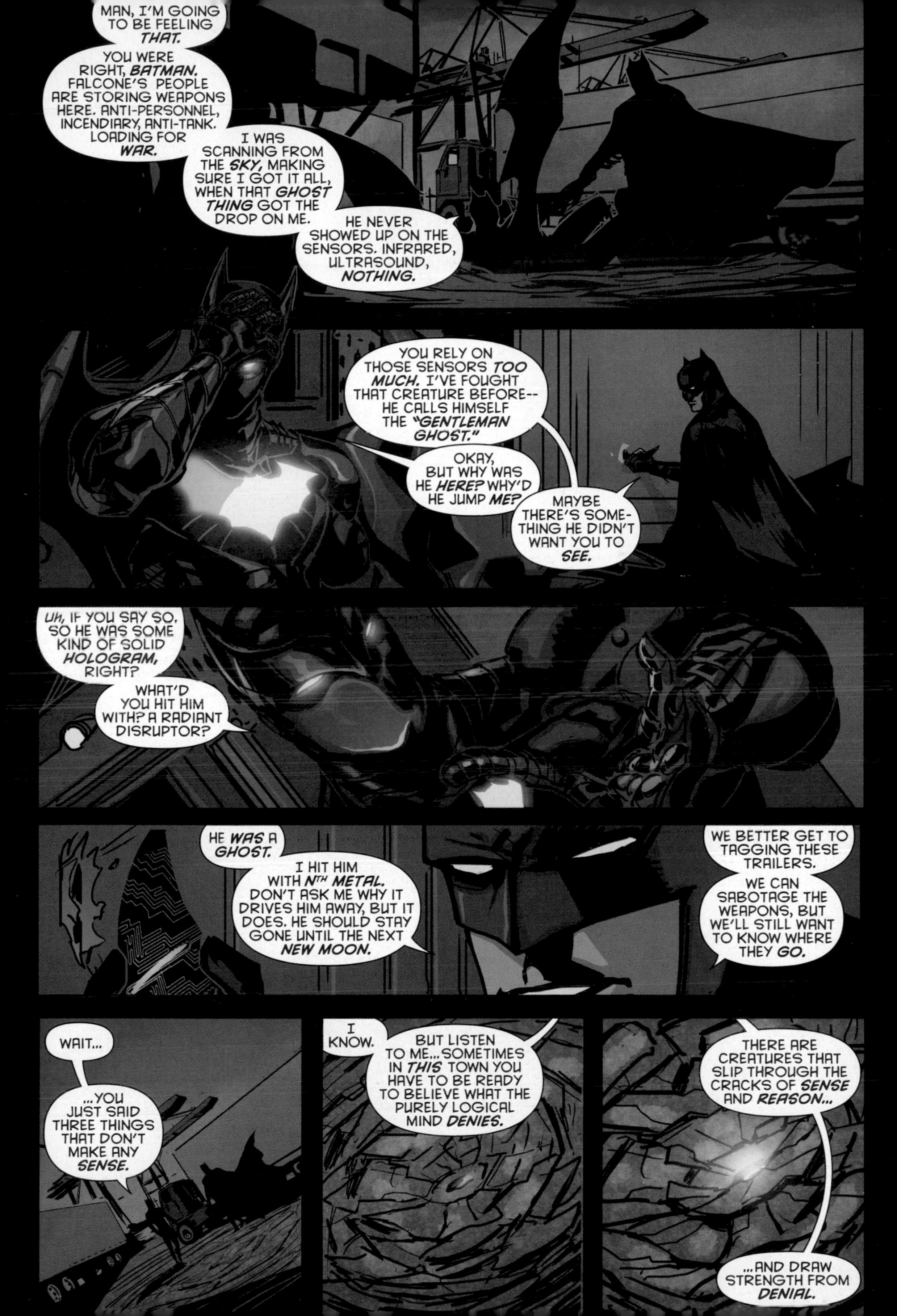
MAN, I'M GOING TO BE FEELING THAT.
YOU WERE RIGHT, BATMAN. FALCONE'S PEOPLE ARE STORING WEAPONS HERE. ANTI-PERSONNEL, INCENDIARY, ANTI-TANK. LOADING FOR WAR.
I WAS SCANNING FROM THE SKY, MAKING SURE I GOT IT ALL, WHEN THAT GHOST THING GOT THE DROP ON ME.
HE NEVER SHOWED UP ON THE SENSORS. INFRARED, ULTRASOUND, NOTHING.
YOU RELY ON THOSE SENSORS TOO MUCH. I'VE FOUGHT THAT CREATURE BEFORE-- HE CALLS HIMSELF THE "GENTLEMAN GHOST."
OKAY, BUT WHY WAS HE HERE? WHY'D HE JUMP ME?
MAYBE THERE'S SOME-THING HE DIDN'T WANT YOU TO SEE.
UH, IF YOU SAY SO. SO HE WAS SOME KIND OF SOLID HOLOGRAM, RIGHT?
WHAT'D YOU HIT HIM WITH? A RADIANT DISRUPTOR?
HE WAS A GHOST.
I HIT HIM WITH Nth METAL. DON'T ASK ME WHY IT DRIVES HIM AWAY, BUT IT DOES. HE SHOULD STAY GONE UNTIL THE NEXT NEW MOON.
WE BETTER GET TO TAGGING THESE TRAILERS.
WE CAN SABOTAGE THE WEAPONS, BUT WE'LL STILL WANT TO KNOW WHERE THEY GO.
WAIT...
...YOU JUST SAID THREE THINGS THAT DON'T MAKE ANY SENSE.
I KNOW.
BUT LISTEN TO ME...SOMETIMES IN THIS TOWN YOU HAVE TO BE READY TO BELIEVE WHAT THE PURELY LOGICAL MIND DENIES.
THERE ARE CREATURES THAT SLIP THROUGH THE CRACKS OF SENSE AND REASON...
...AND DRAW STRENGTH FROM DENIAL.

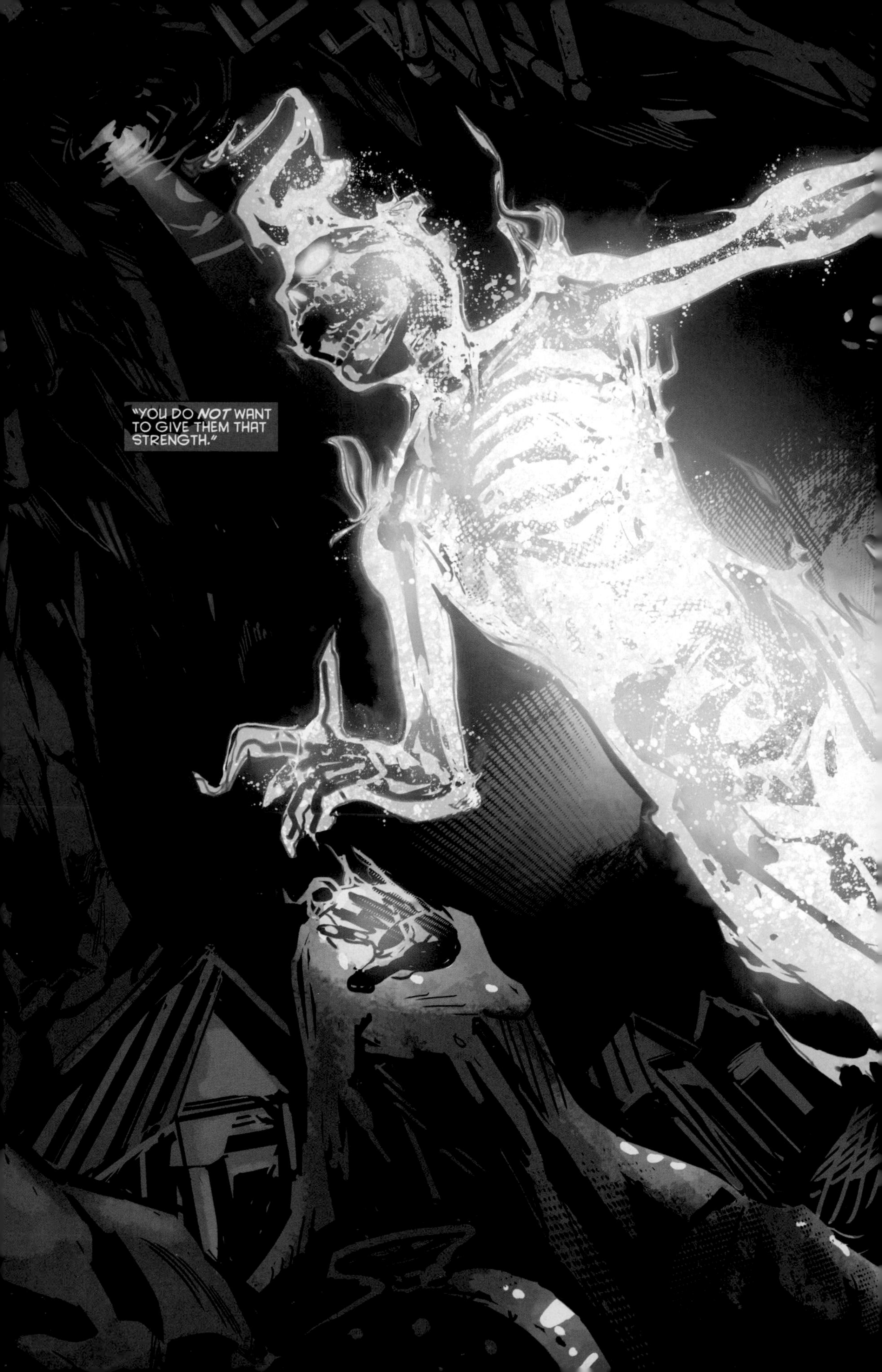
"YOU DO *NOT* WANT TO GIVE THEM THAT STRENGTH."

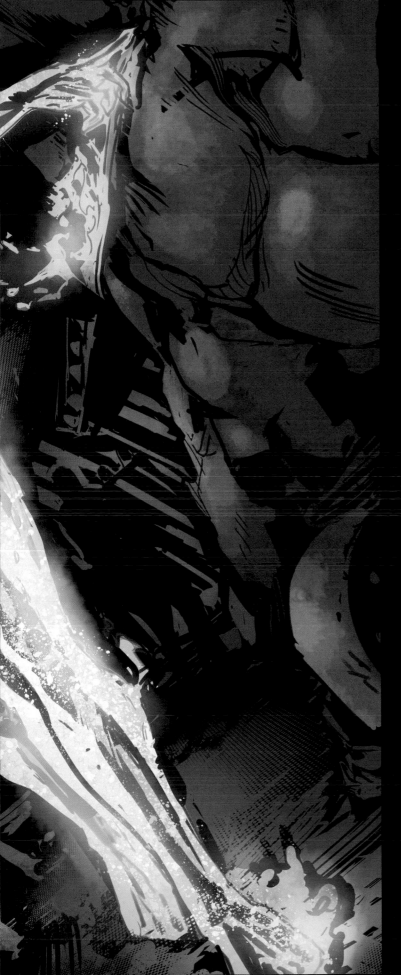

SCOTT SNYDER &
JAMES TYNION IV
STORY

SCRIPT:
RAY FAWKES

CONTRIBUTING WRITERS:
JOHN LAYMAN &
TIM SEELEY

ART BY:
TREVOR McCARTHY

COLORS BY:
GUY MAJOR

LETTERING BY:
TAYLOR ESPOSITO

COVER BY:
ANDY KUBERT &
BRAD ANDERSON

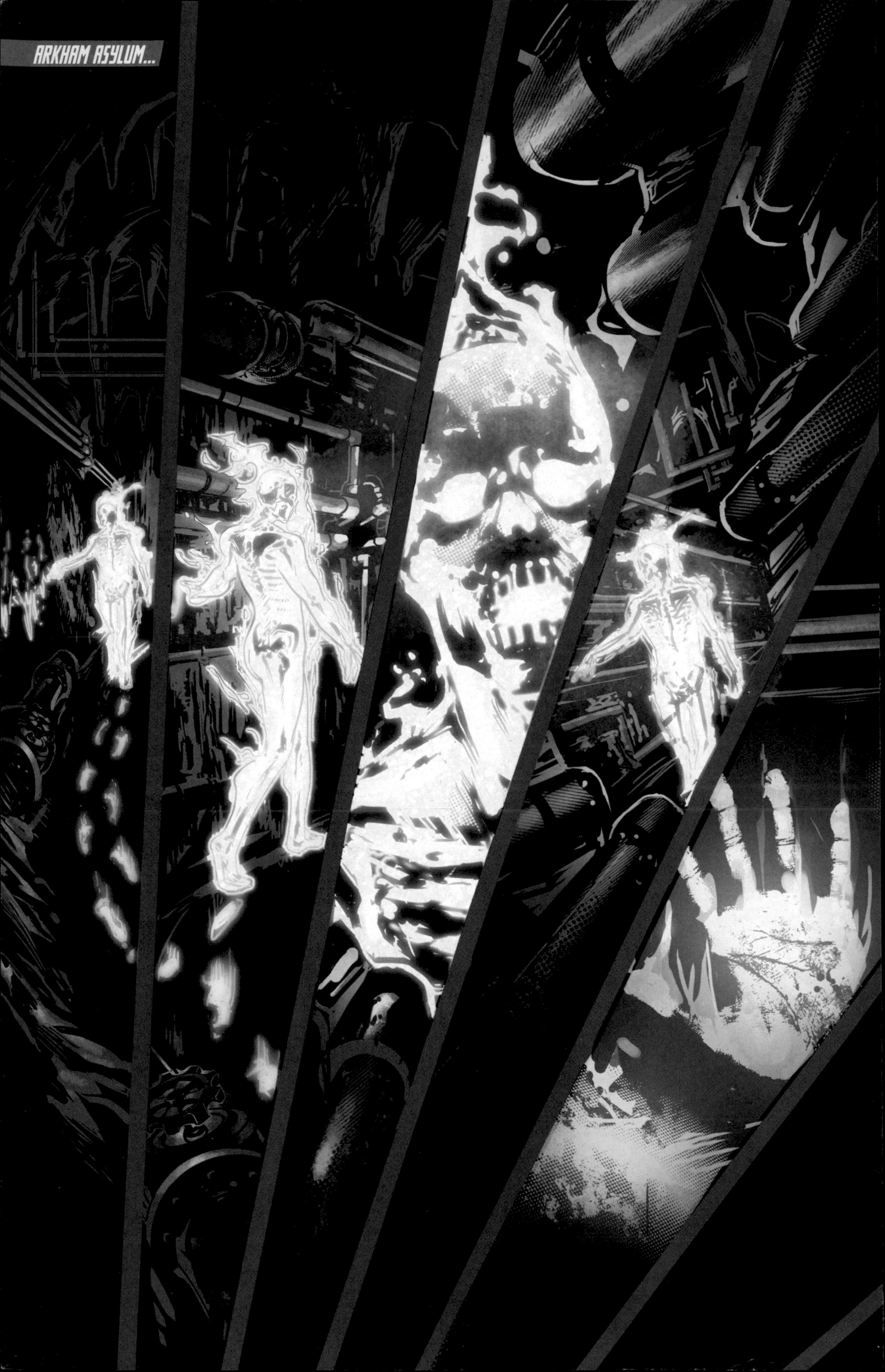
ARKHAM ASYLUM...

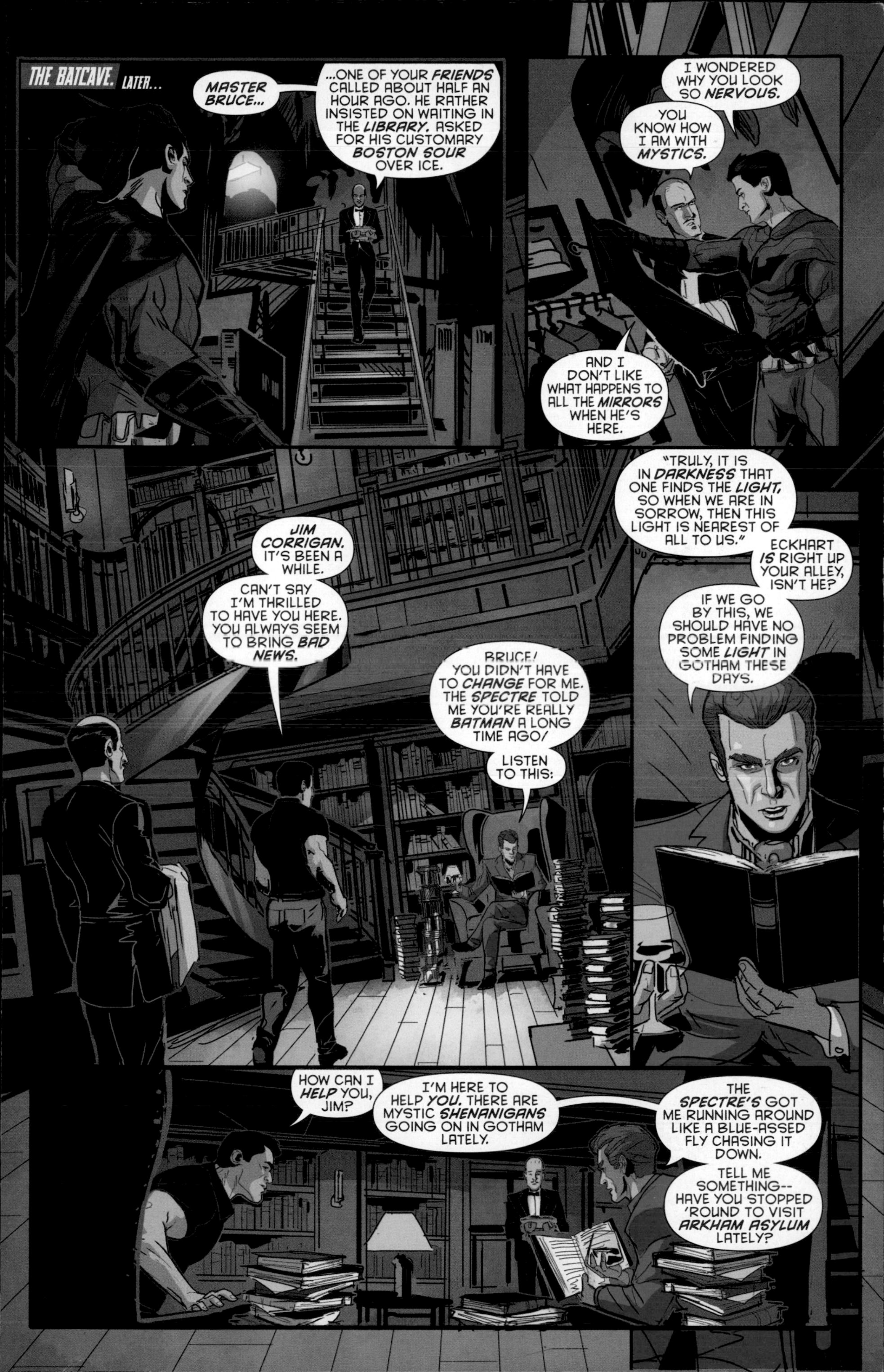
THE BATCAVE. LATER...
MASTER BRUCE...
...ONE OF YOUR FRIENDS CALLED ABOUT HALF AN HOUR AGO. HE RATHER INSISTED ON WAITING IN THE LIBRARY. ASKED FOR HIS CUSTOMARY BOSTON SOUR OVER ICE.
I WONDERED WHY YOU LOOK SO NERVOUS.
YOU KNOW HOW I AM WITH MYSTICS.
AND I DON'T LIKE WHAT HAPPENS TO ALL THE MIRRORS WHEN HE'S HERE.
JIM CORRIGAN. IT'S BEEN A WHILE.
CAN'T SAY I'M THRILLED TO HAVE YOU HERE. YOU ALWAYS SEEM TO BRING BAD NEWS.
BRUCE! YOU DIDN'T HAVE TO CHANGE FOR ME. THE SPECTRE TOLD ME YOU'RE REALLY BATMAN A LONG TIME AGO!
LISTEN TO THIS:
"TRULY, IT IS IN DARKNESS THAT ONE FINDS THE LIGHT, SO WHEN WE ARE IN SORROW, THEN THIS LIGHT IS NEAREST OF ALL TO US."
ECKHART IS RIGHT UP YOUR ALLEY, ISN'T HE?
IF WE GO BY THIS, WE SHOULD HAVE NO PROBLEM FINDING SOME LIGHT IN GOTHAM THESE DAYS.
HOW CAN I HELP YOU, JIM?
I'M HERE TO HELP YOU. THERE ARE MYSTIC SHENANIGANS GOING ON IN GOTHAM LATELY.
THE SPECTRE'S GOT ME RUNNING AROUND LIKE A BLUE-ASSED FLY CHASING IT DOWN.
TELL ME SOMETHING-- HAVE YOU STOPPED 'ROUND TO VISIT ARKHAM ASYLUM LATELY?

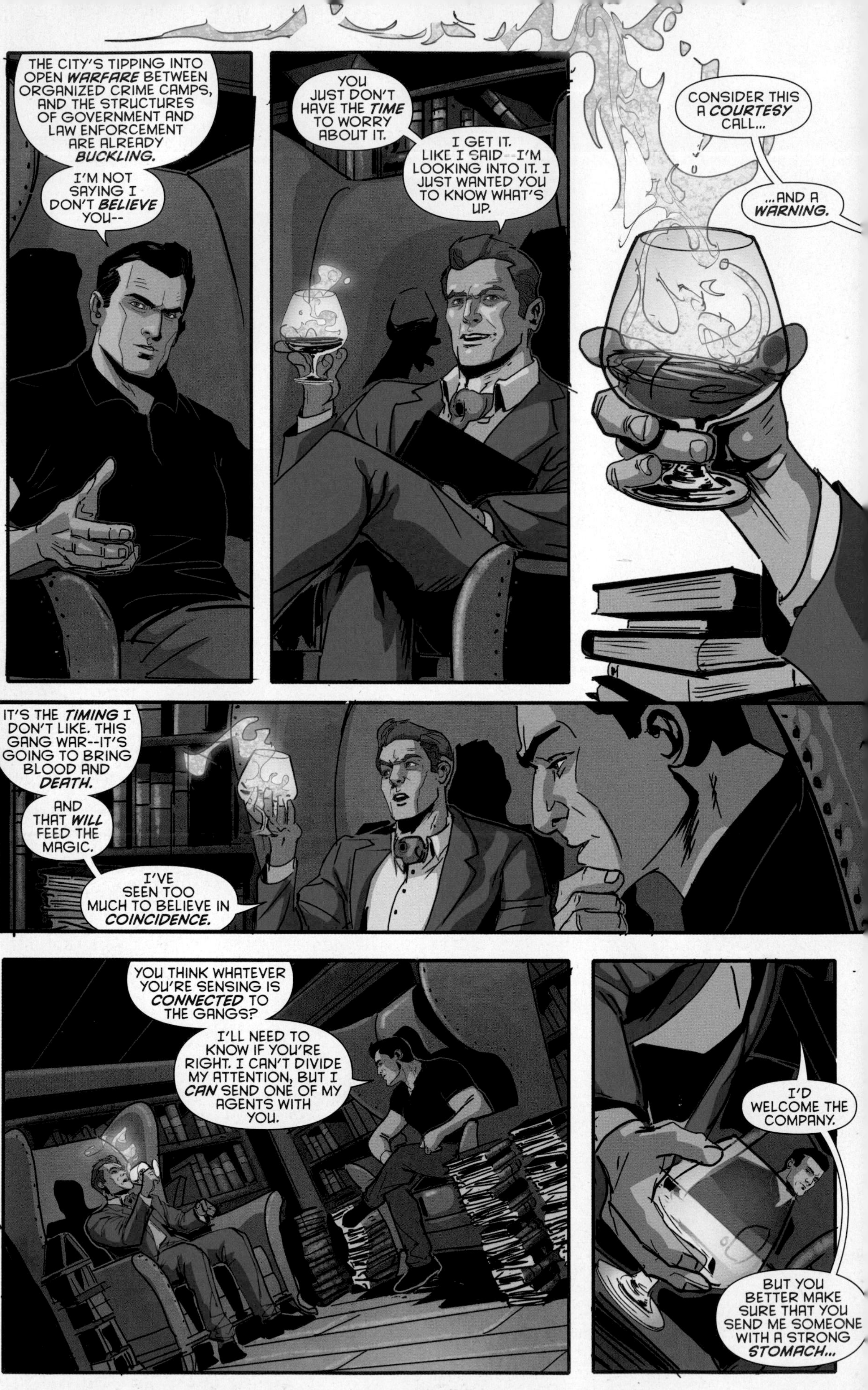
THE CITY'S TIPPING INTO OPEN *WARFARE* BETWEEN ORGANIZED CRIME CAMPS, AND THE STRUCTURES OF GOVERNMENT AND LAW ENFORCEMENT ARE ALREADY *BUCKLING.*
I'M NOT SAYING I DON'T *BELIEVE* YOU--
YOU JUST DON'T HAVE THE *TIME* TO WORRY ABOUT IT.
I GET IT. LIKE I SAID--I'M LOOKING INTO IT. I JUST WANTED YOU TO KNOW WHAT'S UP.
CONSIDER THIS A *COURTESY* CALL...
...AND A *WARNING.*
IT'S THE *TIMING* I DON'T LIKE. THIS GANG WAR--IT'S GOING TO BRING BLOOD AND *DEATH.*
AND THAT *WILL* FEED THE MAGIC.
I'VE SEEN TOO MUCH TO BELIEVE IN *COINCIDENCE.*
YOU THINK WHATEVER YOU'RE SENSING IS *CONNECTED* TO THE GANGS?
I'LL NEED TO KNOW IF YOU'RE RIGHT. I CAN'T DIVIDE MY ATTENTION, BUT I *CAN* SEND ONE OF MY AGENTS WITH YOU.
I'D WELCOME THE COMPANY.
BUT YOU BETTER MAKE SURE THAT YOU SEND ME SOMEONE WITH A STRONG *STOMACH...*

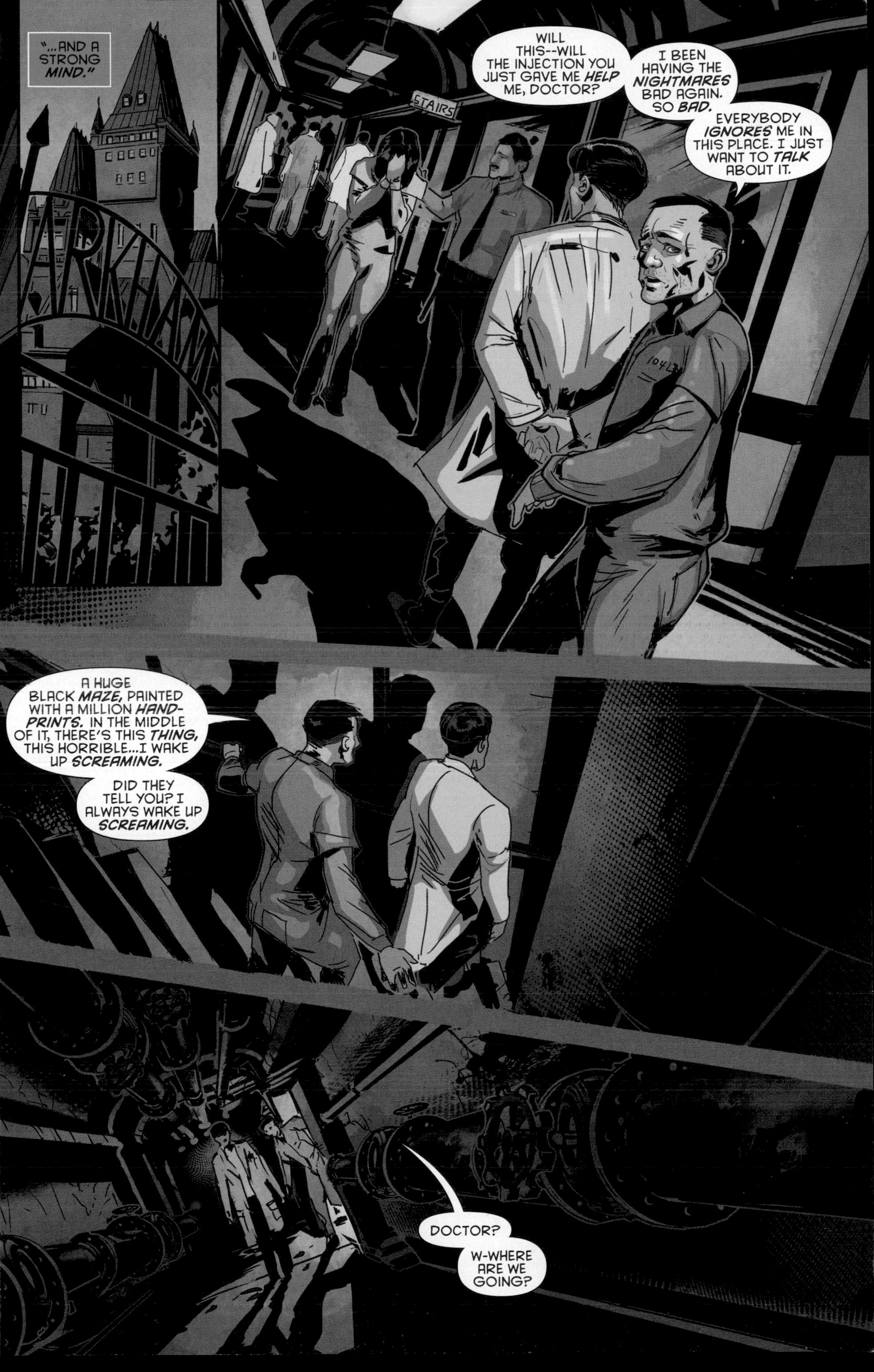
"...AND A STRONG MIND."
STAIRS
WILL THIS--WILL THE INJECTION YOU JUST GAVE ME HELP ME, DOCTOR?
I BEEN HAVING THE NIGHTMARES BAD AGAIN. SO BAD.
EVERYBODY IGNORES ME IN THIS PLACE. I JUST WANT TO TALK ABOUT IT.
A HUGE BLACK MAZE, PAINTED WITH A MILLION HAND-PRINTS. IN THE MIDDLE OF IT, THERE'S THIS THING, THIS HORRIBLE...I WAKE UP SCREAMING.
DID THEY TELL YOU? I ALWAYS WAKE UP SCREAMING.
DOCTOR?
W-WHERE ARE WE GOING?

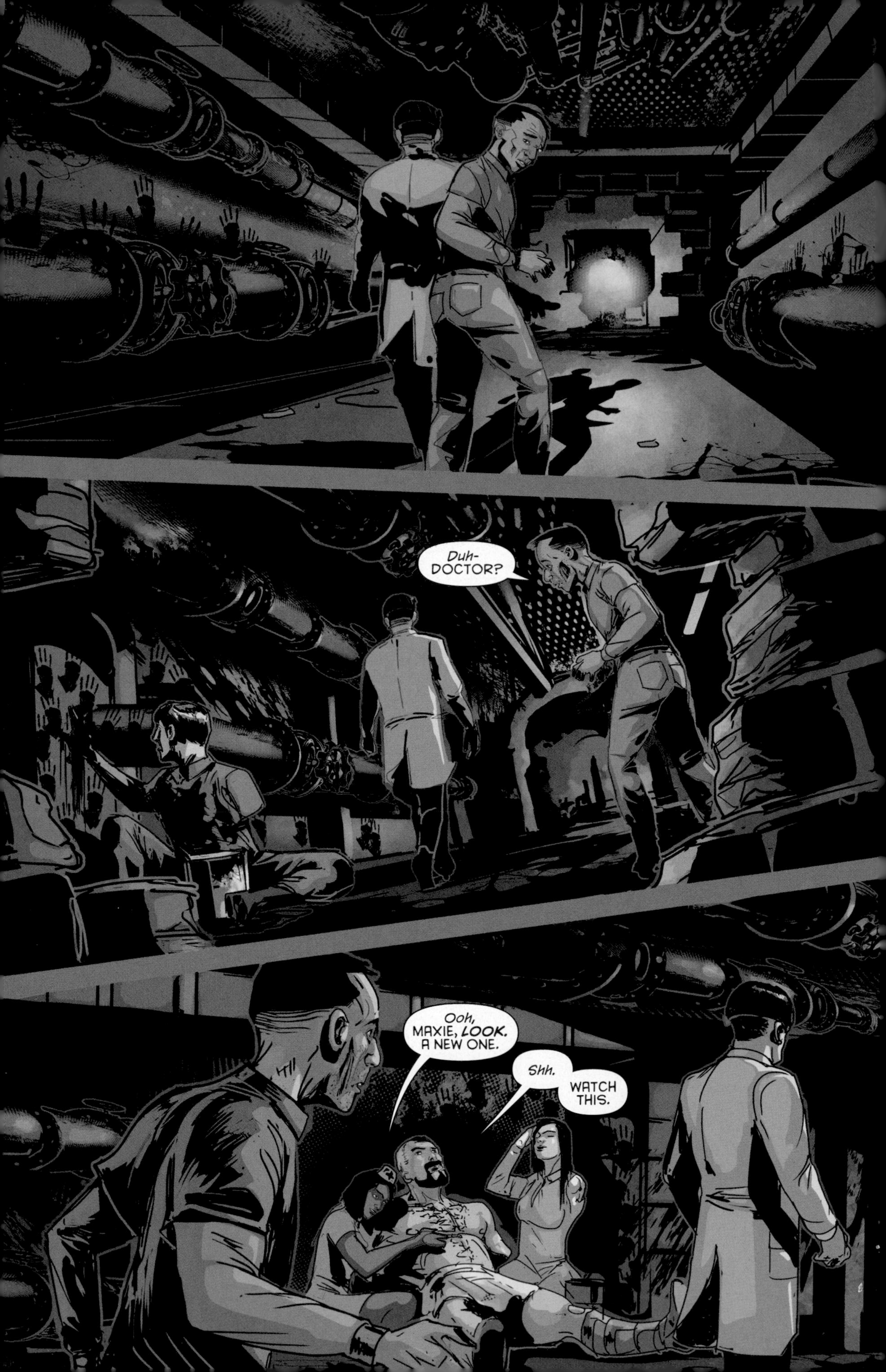
Duh-
DOCTOR?
Ooh, MAXIE, LOOK. A NEW ONE.
Shh.
WATCH THIS.

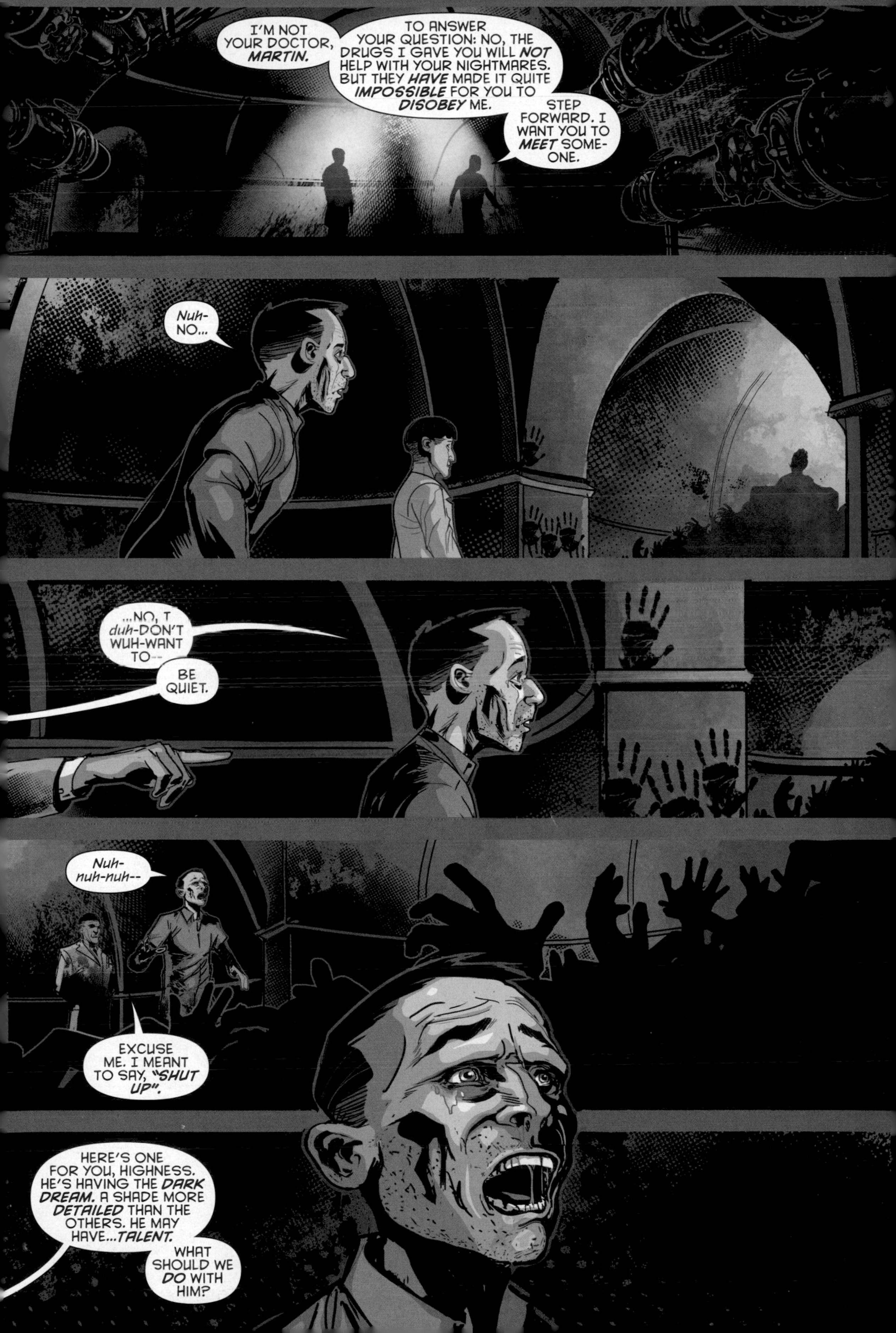
I'M NOT YOUR DOCTOR, MARTIN.
TO ANSWER YOUR QUESTION: NO, THE DRUGS I GAVE YOU WILL NOT HELP WITH YOUR NIGHTMARES. BUT THEY HAVE MADE IT QUITE IMPOSSIBLE FOR YOU TO DISOBEY ME.
STEP FORWARD. I WANT YOU TO MEET SOME-ONE.
Nuh-NO...
...NO, I duh-DON'T WUH-WANT TO--
BE QUIET.
Nuh-nuh-nuh--
EXCUSE ME. I MEANT TO SAY, "SHUT UP".
HERE'S ONE FOR YOU, HIGHNESS. HE'S HAVING THE DARK DREAM. A SHADE MORE DETAILED THAN THE OTHERS. HE MAY HAVE...TALENT.
WHAT SHOULD WE DO WITH HIM?

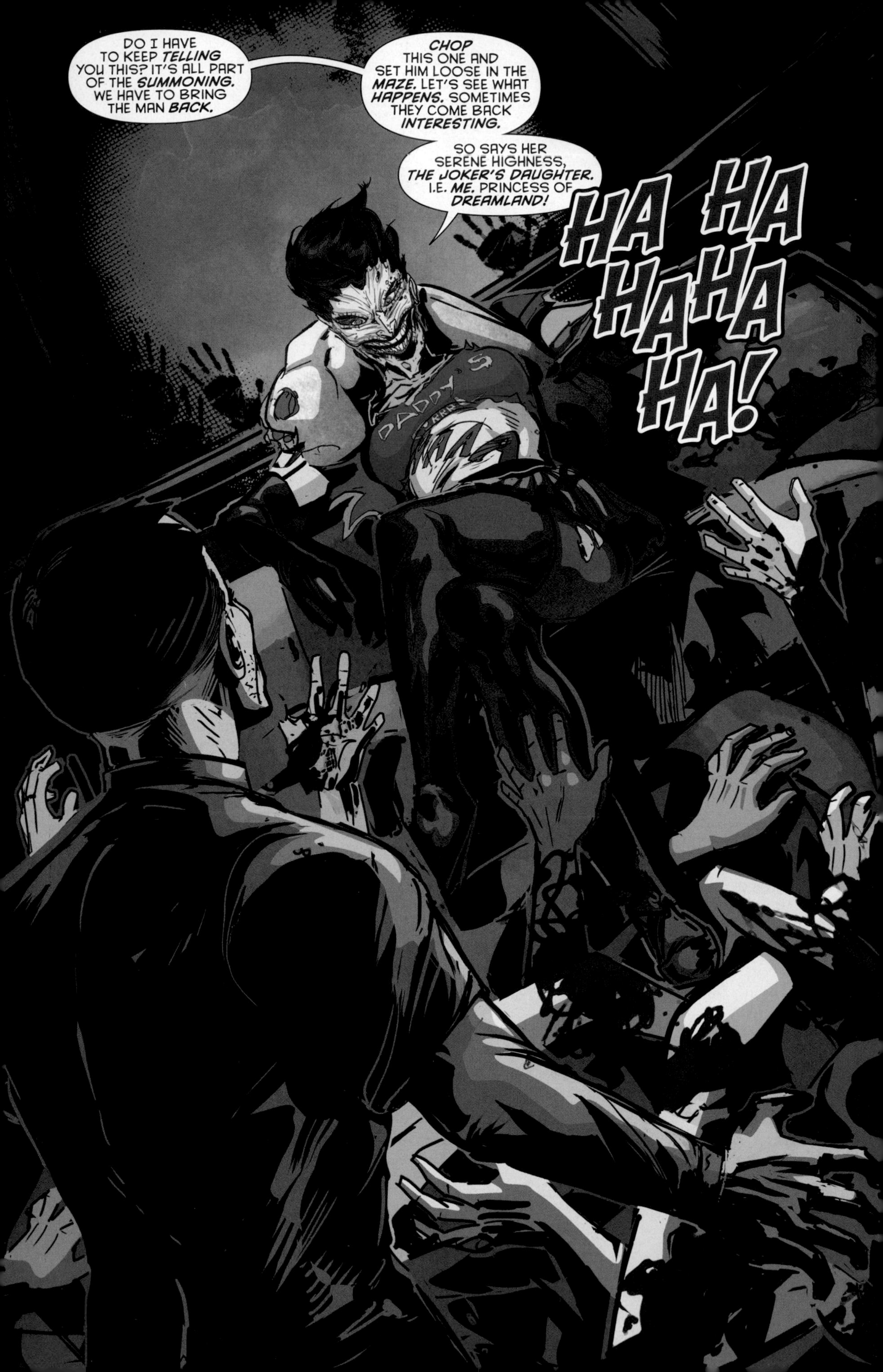
DO I HAVE TO KEEP TELLING YOU THIS? IT'S ALL PART OF THE SUMMONING. WE HAVE TO BRING THE MAN BACK.
CHOP THIS ONE AND SET HIM LOOSE IN THE MAZE. LET'S SEE WHAT HAPPENS. SOMETIMES THEY COME BACK INTERESTING.
SO SAYS HER SERENE HIGHNESS, THE JOKER'S DAUGHTER. I.E. ME. PRINCESS OF DREAMLAND!
HA HA HAHAHA HA!

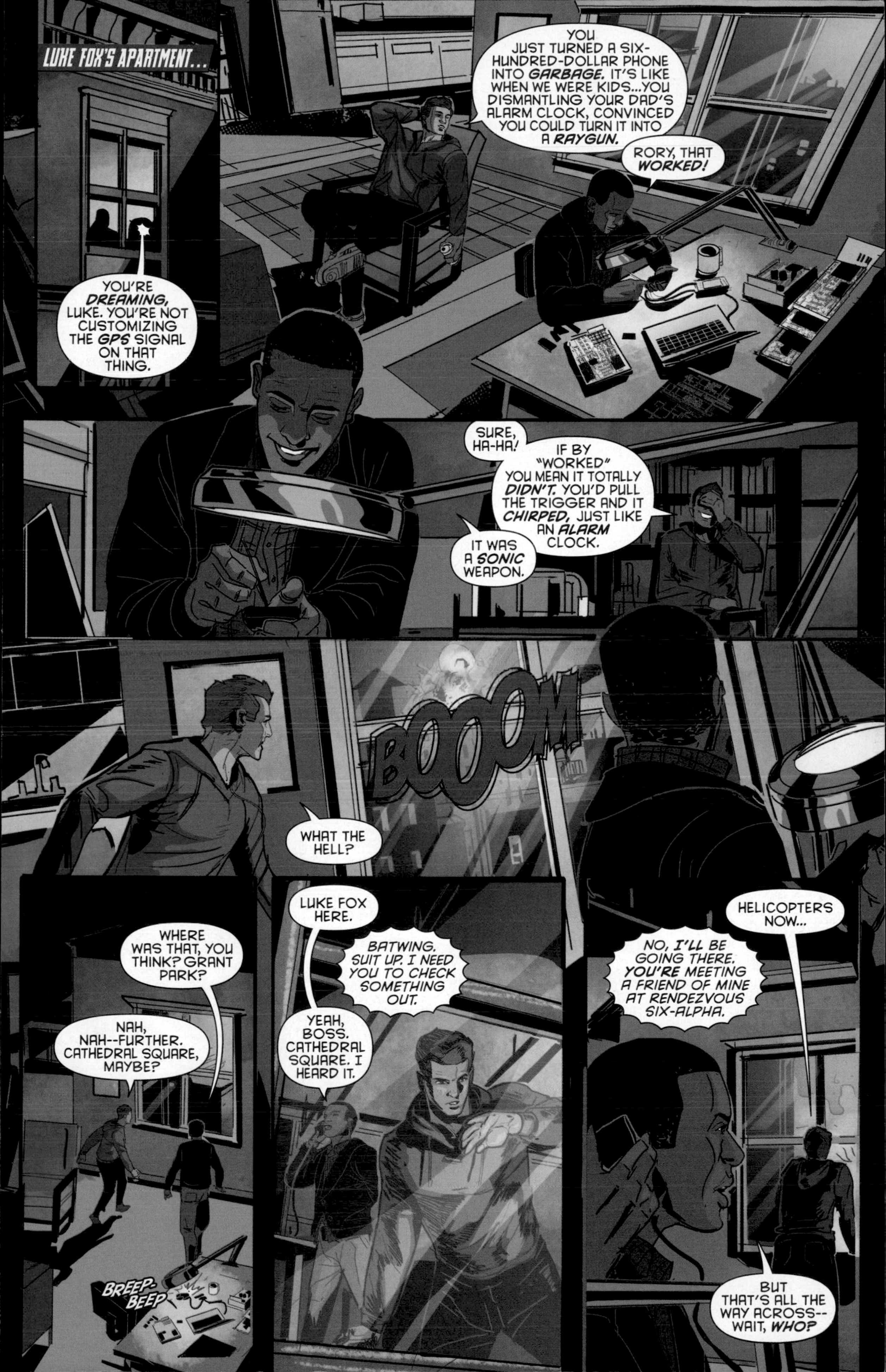
LUKE FOX'S APARTMENT...
YOU JUST TURNED A SIX-HUNDRED-DOLLAR PHONE INTO GARBAGE. IT'S LIKE WHEN WE WERE KIDS...YOU DISMANTLING YOUR DAD'S ALARM CLOCK, CONVINCED YOU COULD TURN IT INTO A RAYGUN.
RORY, THAT WORKED!
YOU'RE DREAMING, LUKE. YOU'RE NOT CUSTOMIZING THE GPS SIGNAL ON THAT THING.
SURE, HA-HA!
IF BY "WORKED" YOU MEAN IT TOTALLY DIDN'T. YOU'D PULL THE TRIGGER AND IT CHIRPED, JUST LIKE AN ALARM CLOCK.
IT WAS A SONIC WEAPON.
BOOOM
WHAT THE HELL?
WHERE WAS THAT, YOU THINK? GRANT PARK?
NAH, NAH--FURTHER. CATHEDRAL SQUARE, MAYBE?
BREEP-BEEP
LUKE FOX HERE.
BATWING. SUIT UP. I NEED YOU TO CHECK SOMETHING OUT.
YEAH, BOSS. CATHEDRAL SQUARE. I HEARD IT.
HELICOPTERS NOW...
NO, I'LL BE GOING THERE. YOU'RE MEETING A FRIEND OF MINE AT RENDEZVOUS SIX-ALPHA.
BUT THAT'S ALL THE WAY ACROSS--WAIT, WHO?

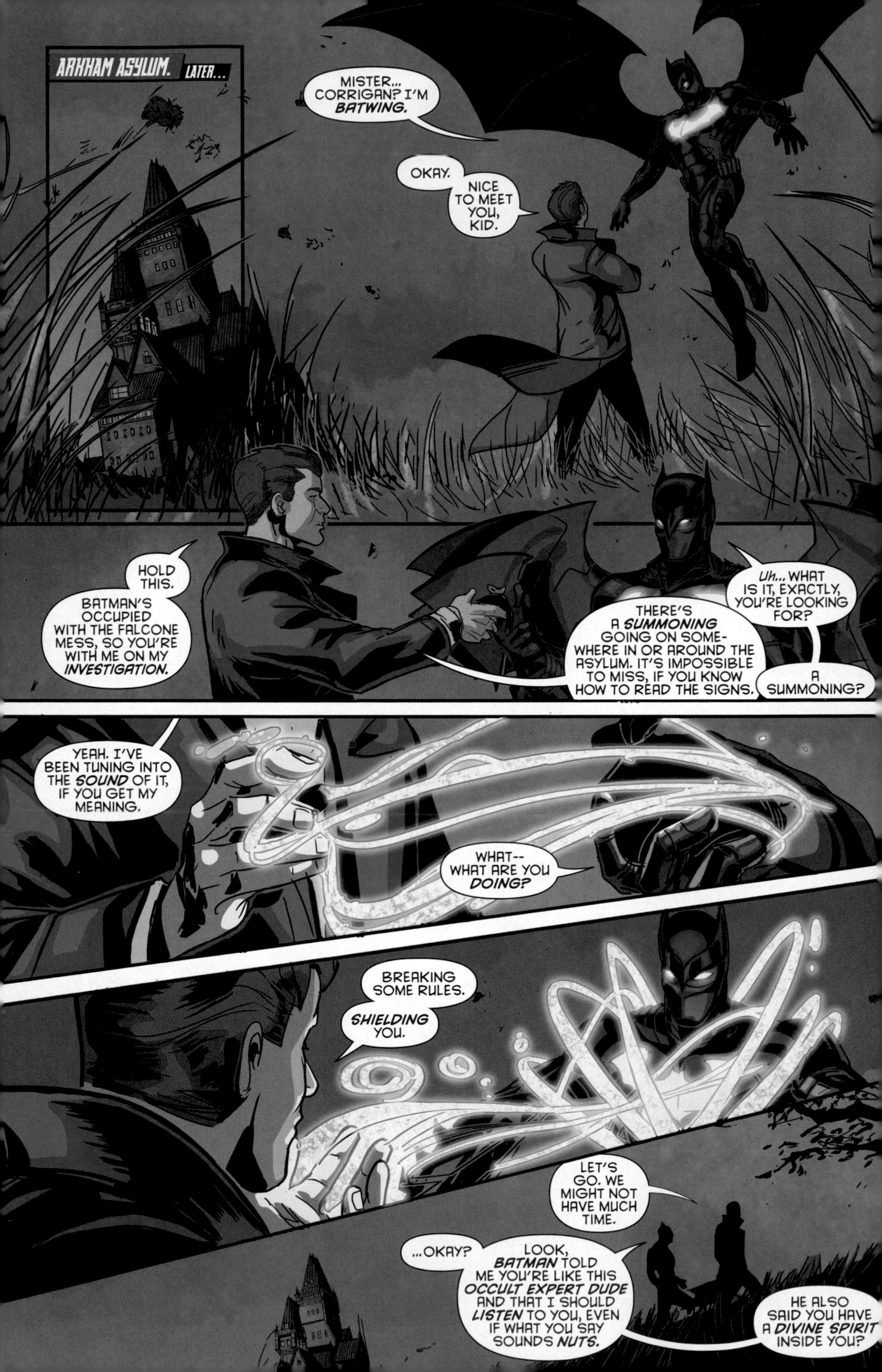
ARKHAM ASYLUM. LATER...
MISTER... CORRIGAN? I'M BATWING.
OKAY.
NICE TO MEET YOU, KID.
HOLD THIS.
BATMAN'S OCCUPIED WITH THE FALCONE MESS, SO YOU'RE WITH ME ON MY INVESTIGATION.
UH... WHAT IS IT, EXACTLY, YOU'RE LOOKING FOR?
THERE'S A SUMMONING GOING ON SOME-WHERE IN OR AROUND THE ASYLUM. IT'S IMPOSSIBLE TO MISS, IF YOU KNOW HOW TO READ THE SIGNS.
A SUMMONING?
YEAH. I'VE BEEN TUNING INTO THE SOUND OF IT, IF YOU GET MY MEANING.
WHAT-- WHAT ARE YOU DOING?
BREAKING SOME RULES.
SHIELDING YOU.
LET'S GO. WE MIGHT NOT HAVE MUCH TIME.
...OKAY?
LOOK, BATMAN TOLD ME YOU'RE LIKE THIS OCCULT EXPERT DUDE AND THAT I SHOULD LISTEN TO YOU, EVEN IF WHAT YOU SAY SOUNDS NUTS.
HE ALSO SAID YOU HAVE A DIVINE SPIRIT INSIDE YOU?

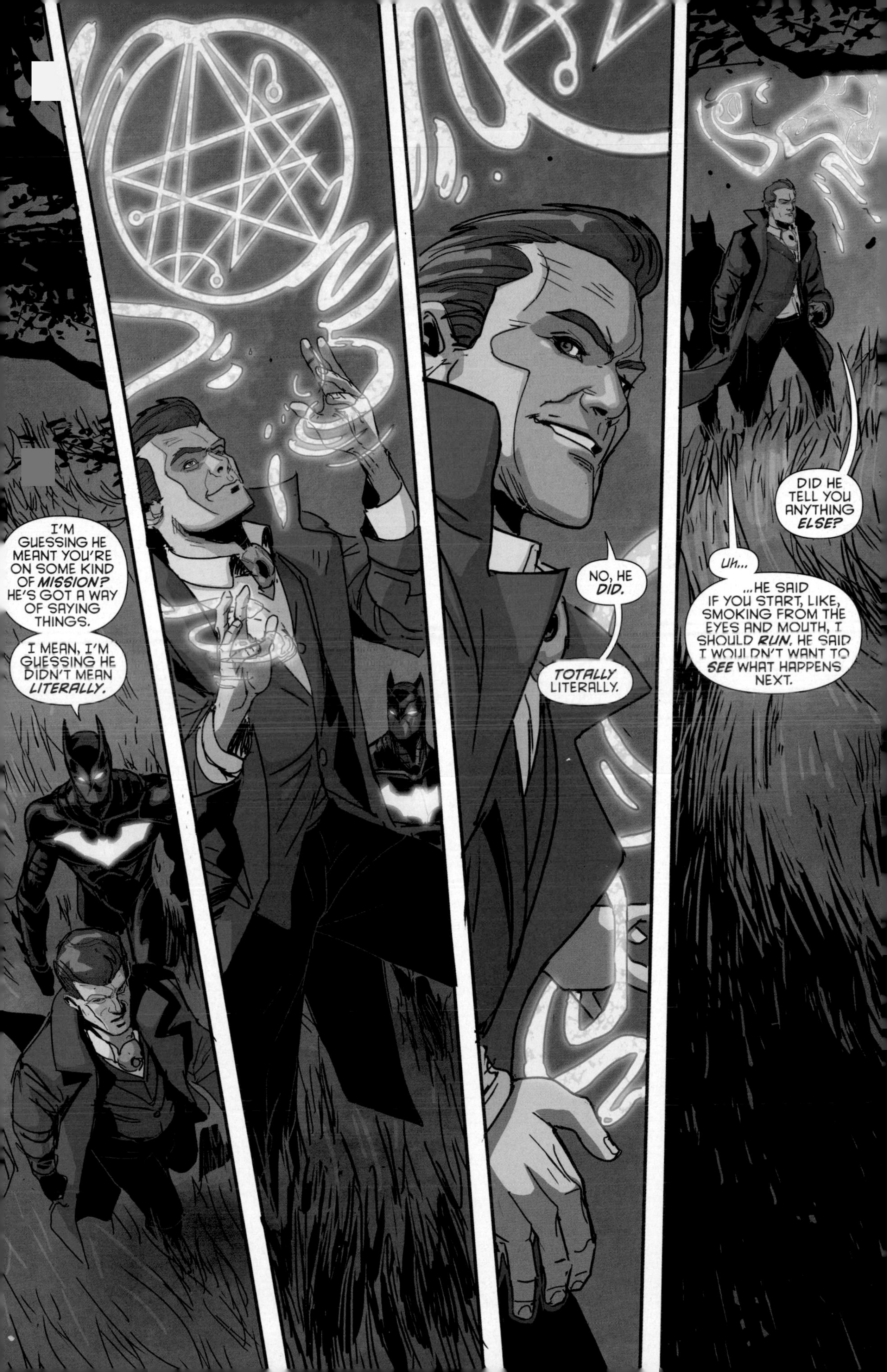
I'M GUESSING HE MEANT YOU'RE ON SOME KIND OF MISSION? HE'S GOT A WAY OF SAYING THINGS.
I MEAN, I'M GUESSING HE DIDN'T MEAN LITERALLY.
NO, HE DID.
TOTALLY LITERALLY.
DID HE TELL YOU ANYTHING ELSE?
Uh...
...HE SAID IF YOU START, LIKE, SMOKING FROM THE EYES AND MOUTH, I SHOULD RUN. HE SAID I WOULDN'T WANT TO SEE WHAT HAPPENS NEXT.

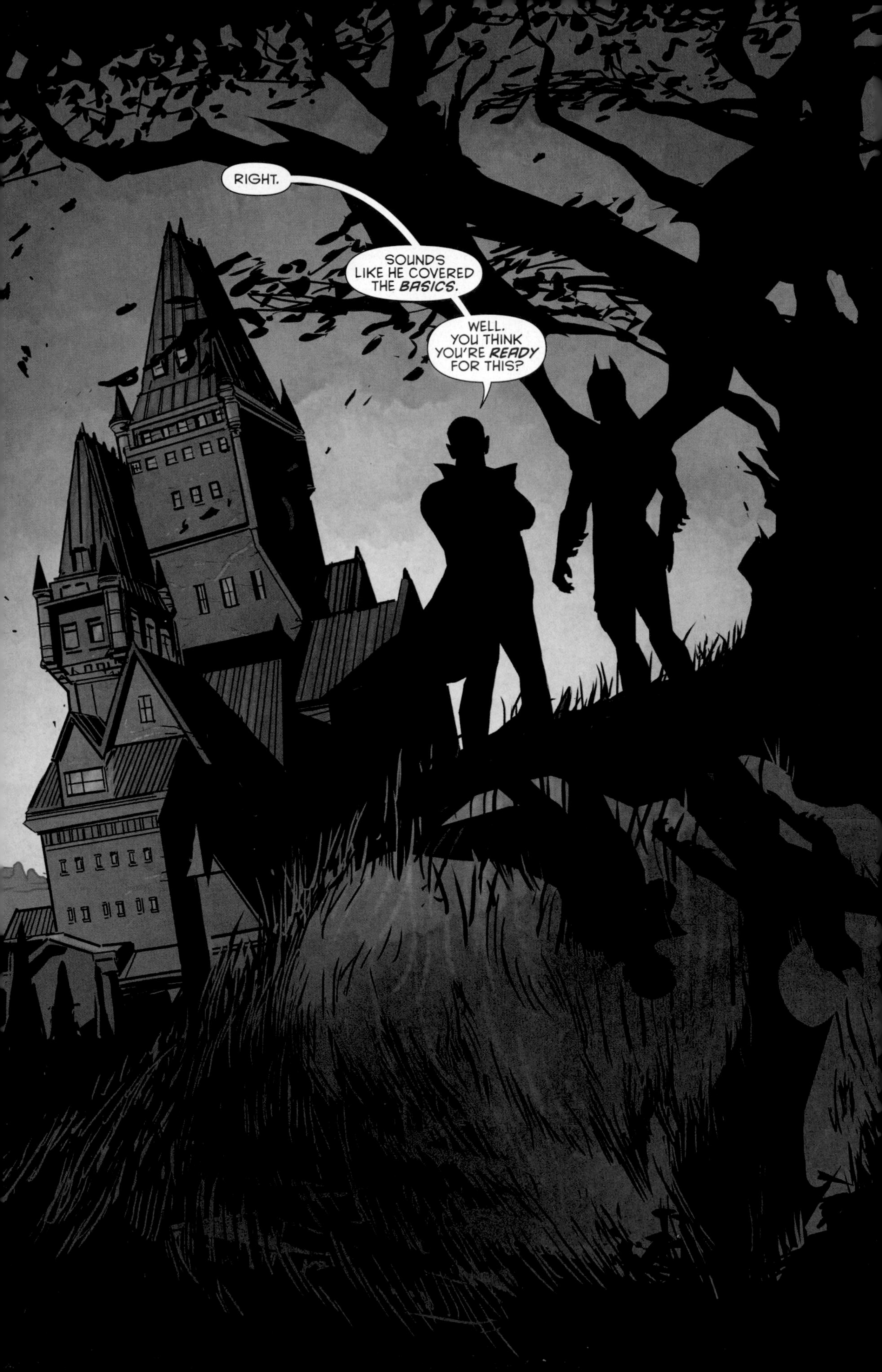
RIGHT.
SOUNDS LIKE HE COVERED THE *BASICS*.
WELL. YOU THINK YOU'RE *READY* FOR THIS?

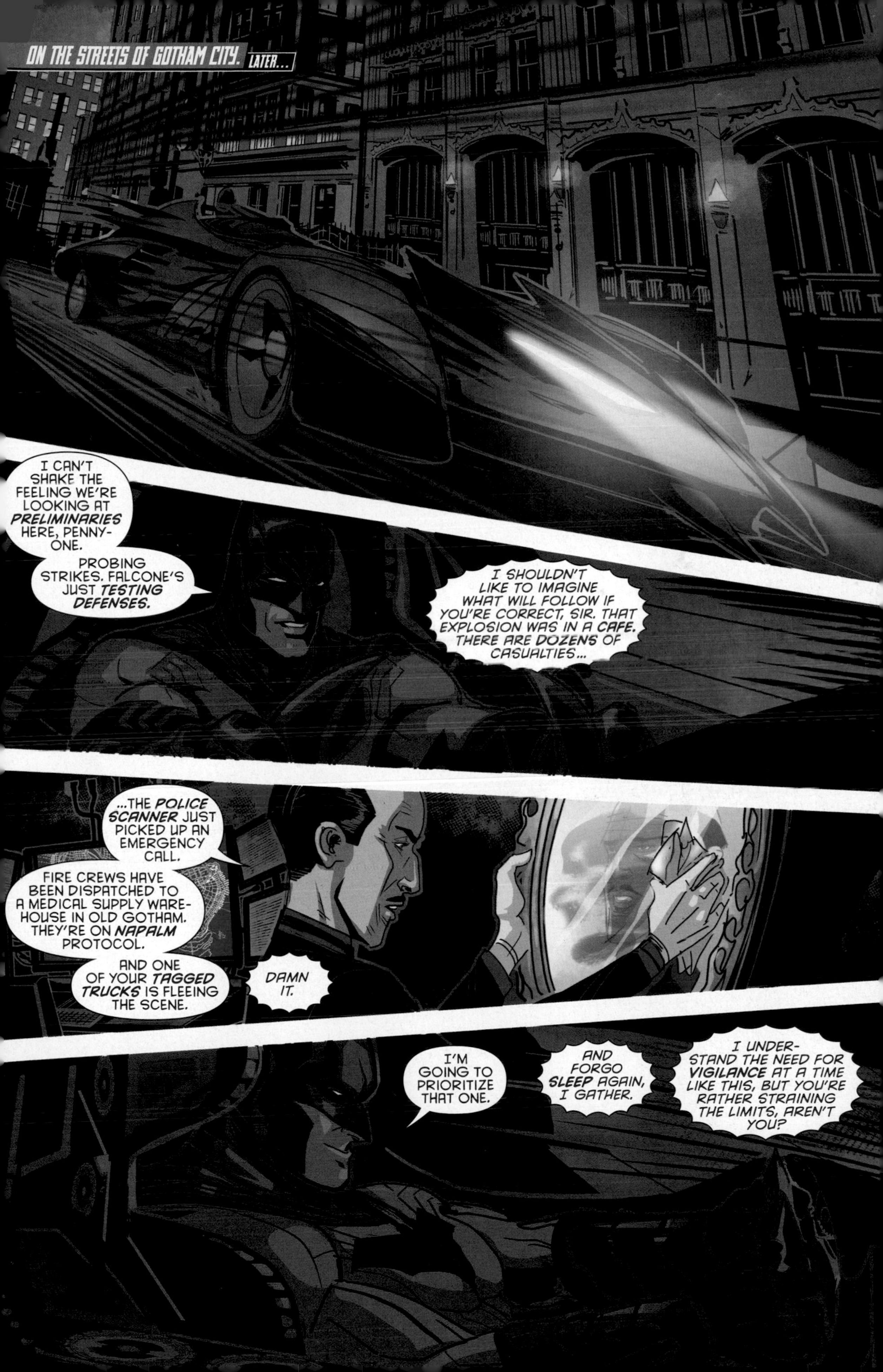
ON THE STREETS OF GOTHAM CITY. LATER...
I CAN'T SHAKE THE FEELING WE'RE LOOKING AT PRELIMINARIES HERE, PENNY-ONE.
PROBING STRIKES. FALCONE'S JUST TESTING DEFENSES.
I SHOULDN'T LIKE TO IMAGINE WHAT WILL FOLLOW IF YOU'RE CORRECT, SIR. THAT EXPLOSION WAS IN A CAFE. THERE ARE DOZENS OF CASUALTIES...
...THE POLICE SCANNER JUST PICKED UP AN EMERGENCY CALL.
FIRE CREWS HAVE BEEN DISPATCHED TO A MEDICAL SUPPLY WAREHOUSE IN OLD GOTHAM. THEY'RE ON NAPALM PROTOCOL.
AND ONE OF YOUR TAGGED TRUCKS IS FLEEING THE SCENE.
DAMN IT.
I'M GOING TO PRIORITIZE THAT ONE.
AND FORGO SLEEP AGAIN, I GATHER.
I UNDERSTAND THE NEED FOR VIGILANCE AT A TIME LIKE THIS, BUT YOU'RE RATHER STRAINING THE LIMITS, AREN'T YOU?

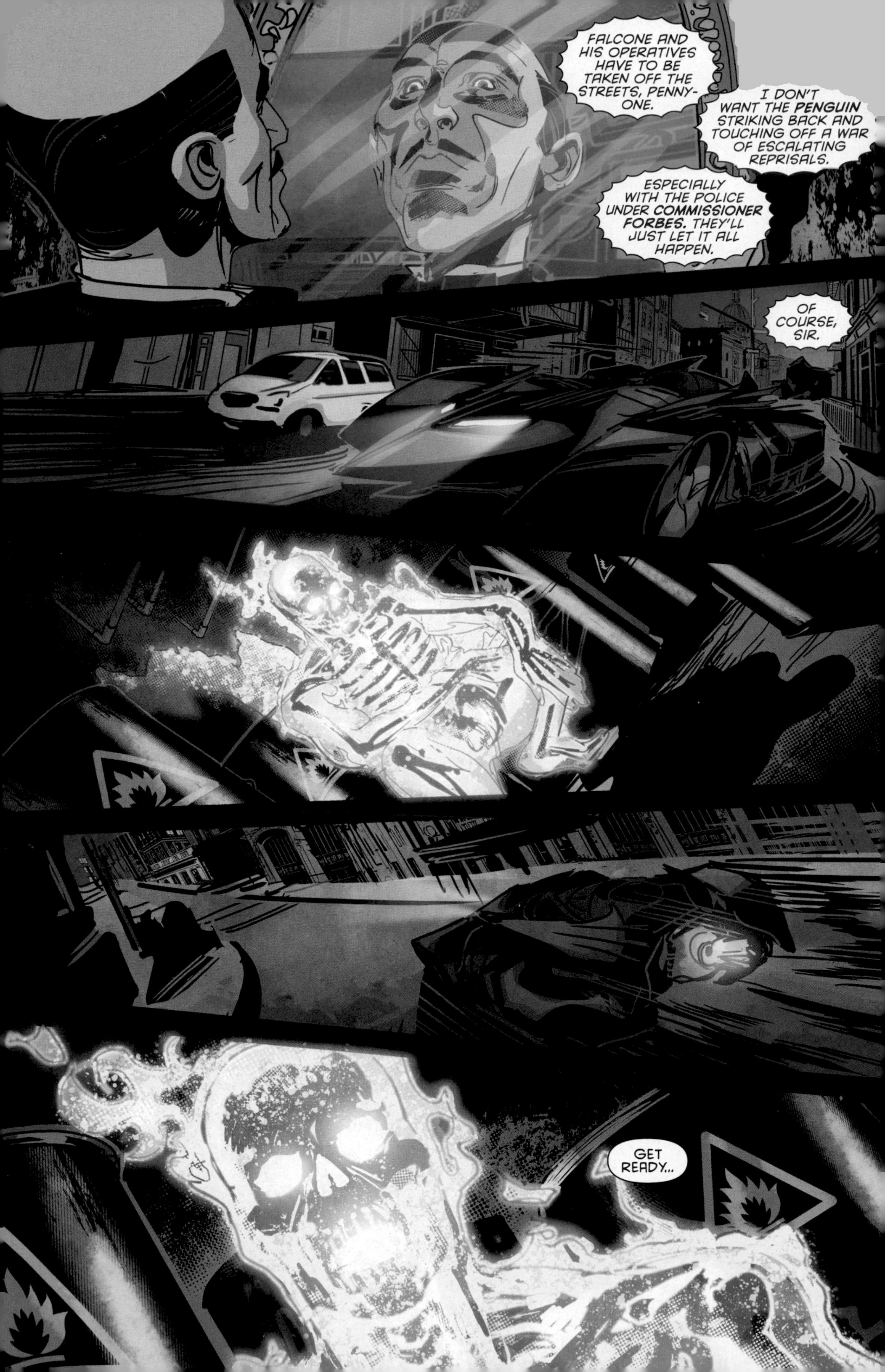
FALCONE AND HIS OPERATIVES HAVE TO BE TAKEN OFF THE STREETS, PENNY-ONE.
I DON'T WANT THE **PENGUIN** STRIKING BACK AND TOUCHING OFF A WAR OF ESCALATING REPRISALS.
ESPECIALLY WITH THE POLICE UNDER **COMMISSIONER FORBES.** THEY'LL JUST LET IT ALL HAPPEN.
OF COURSE, SIR.
GET READY...

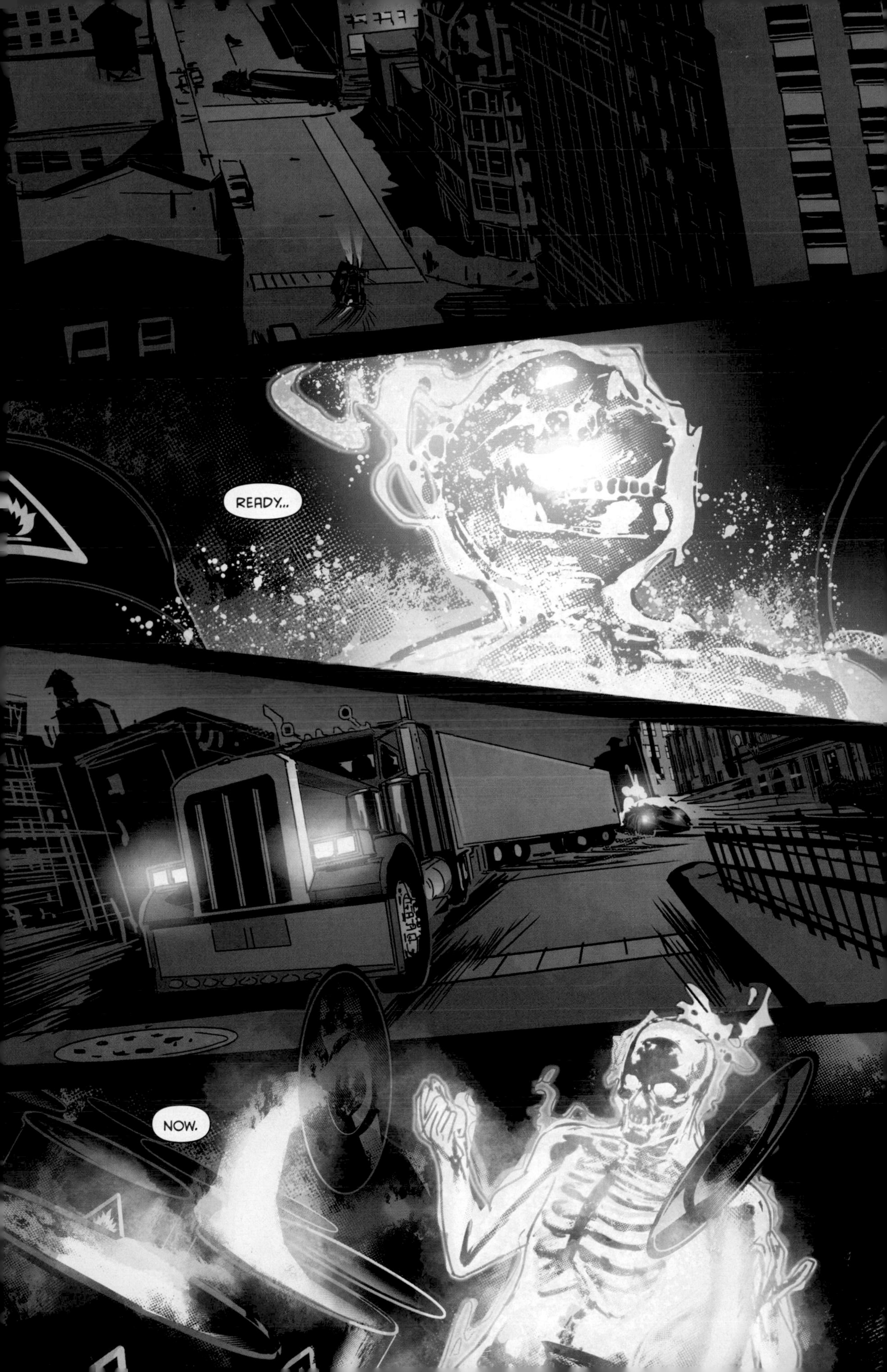
READY...
NOW.

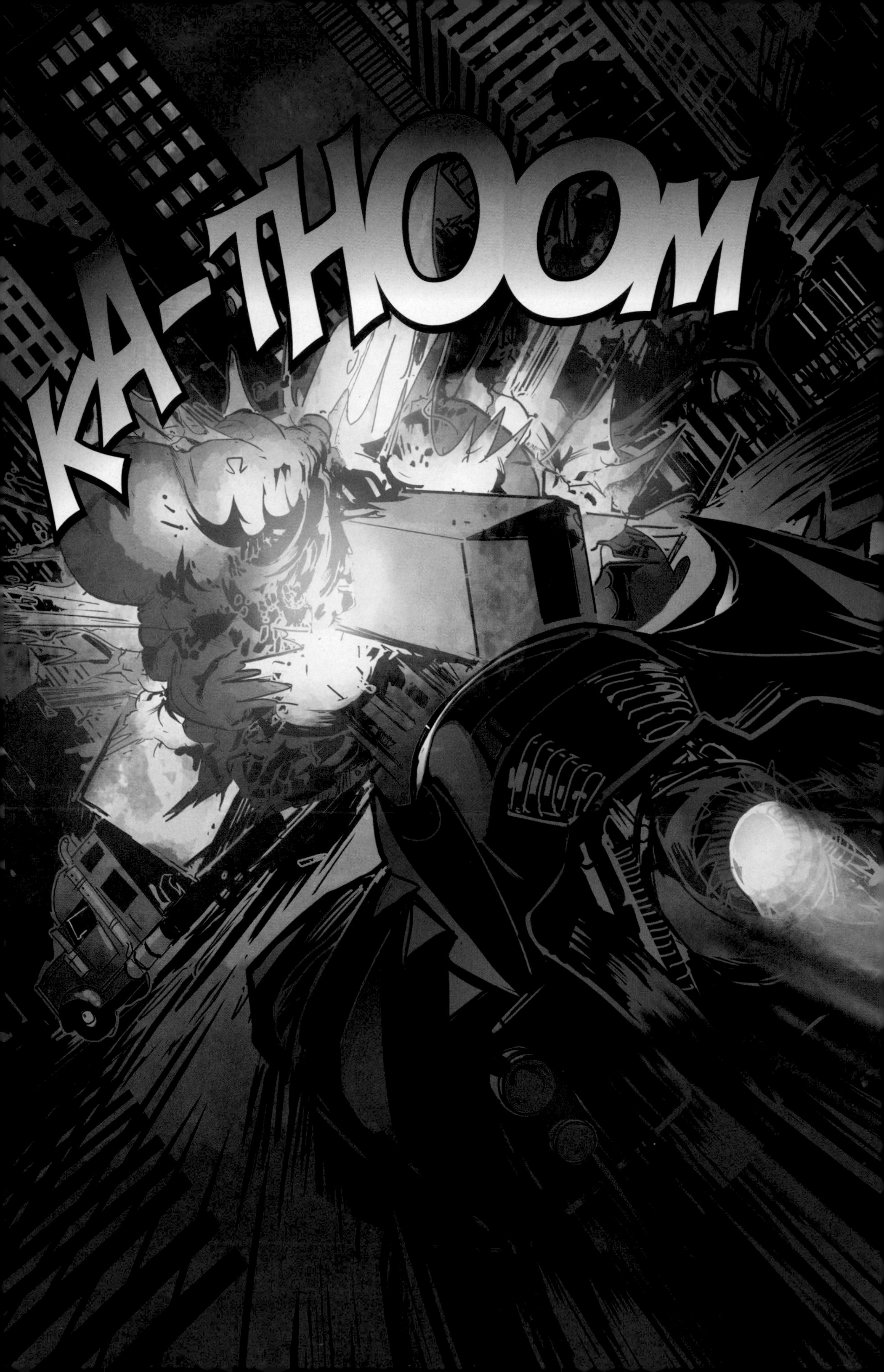
KA-THOOM

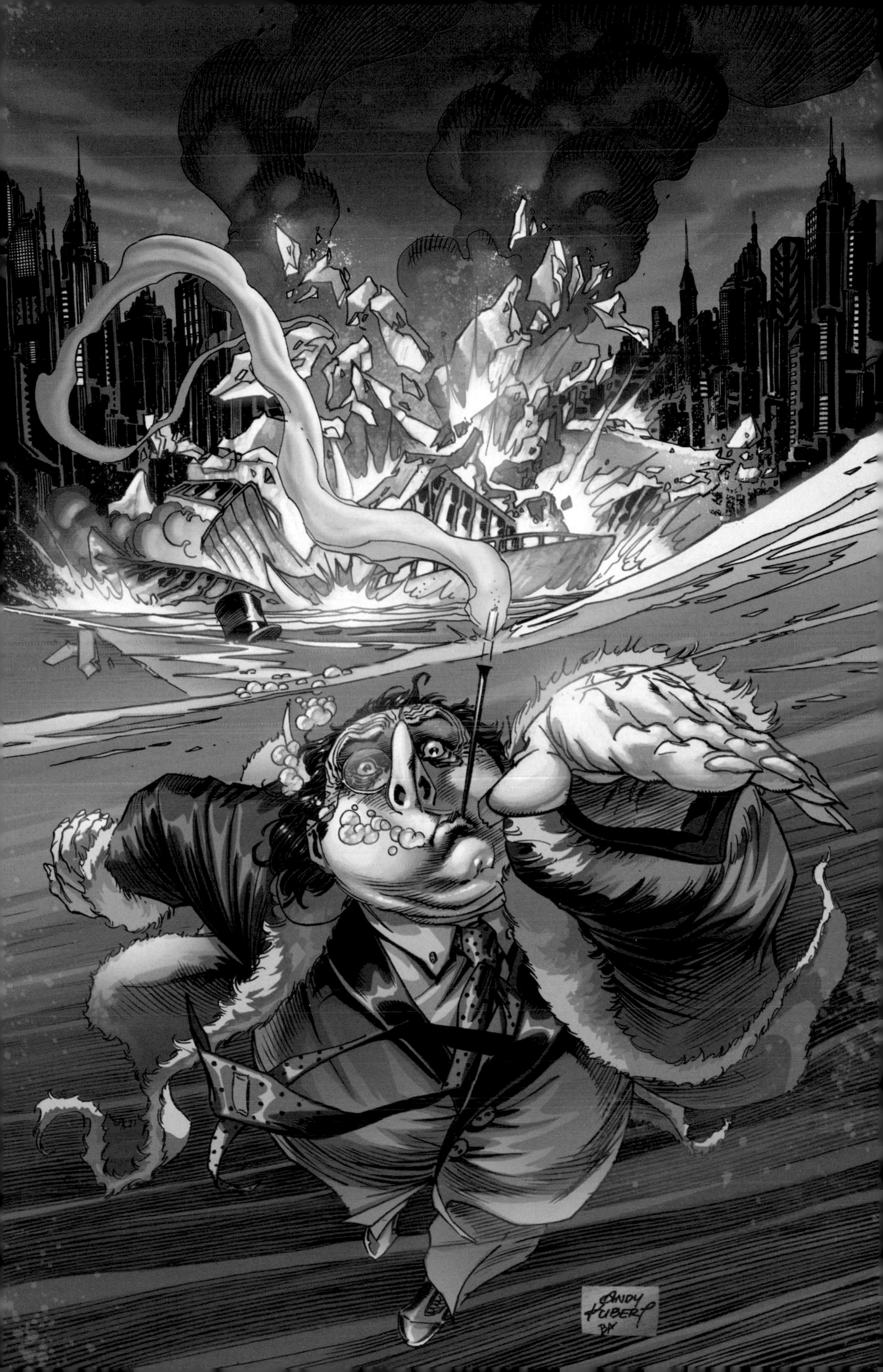
ANDY KUBERT
BA

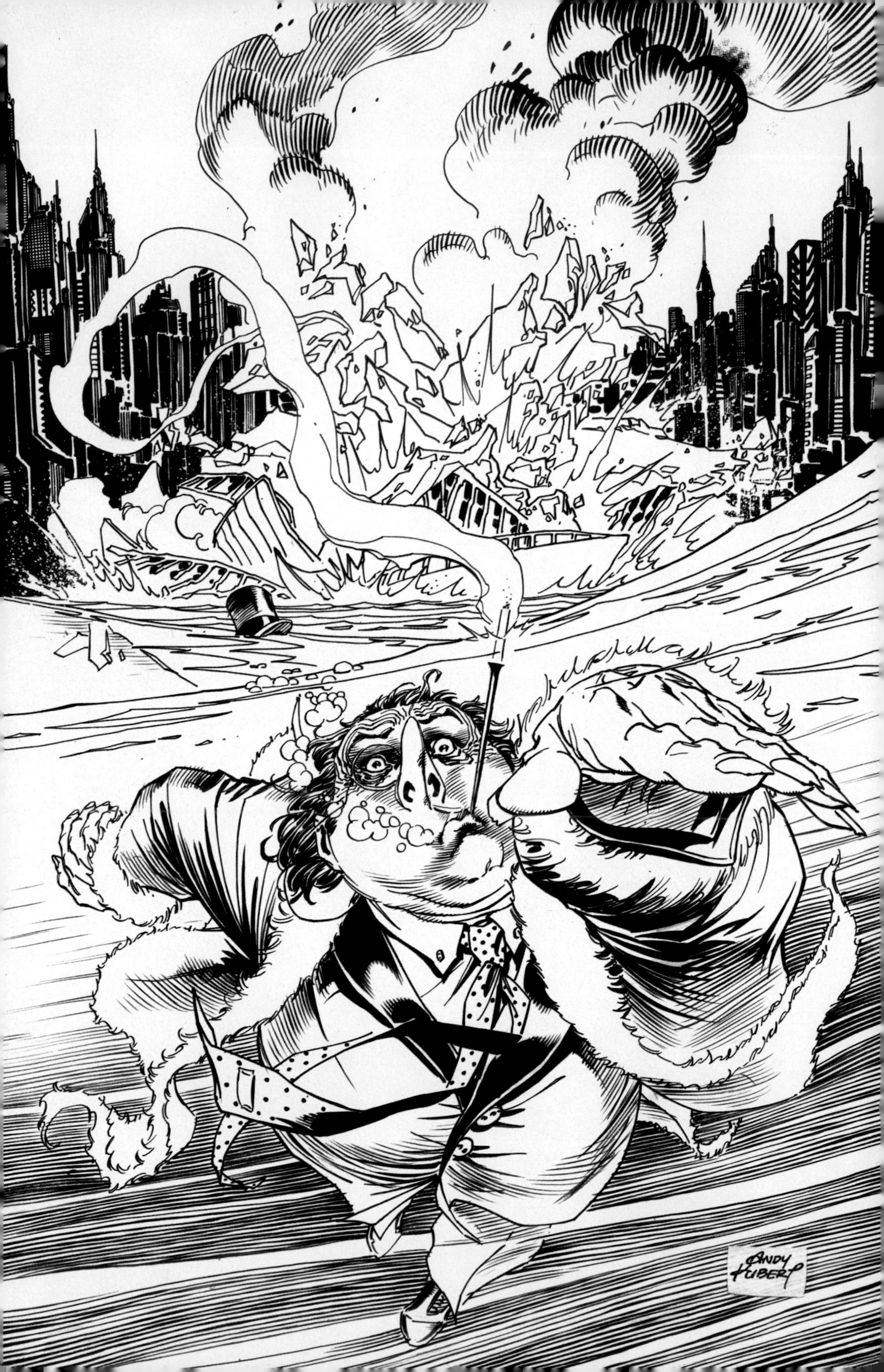
ANDY KUBERT

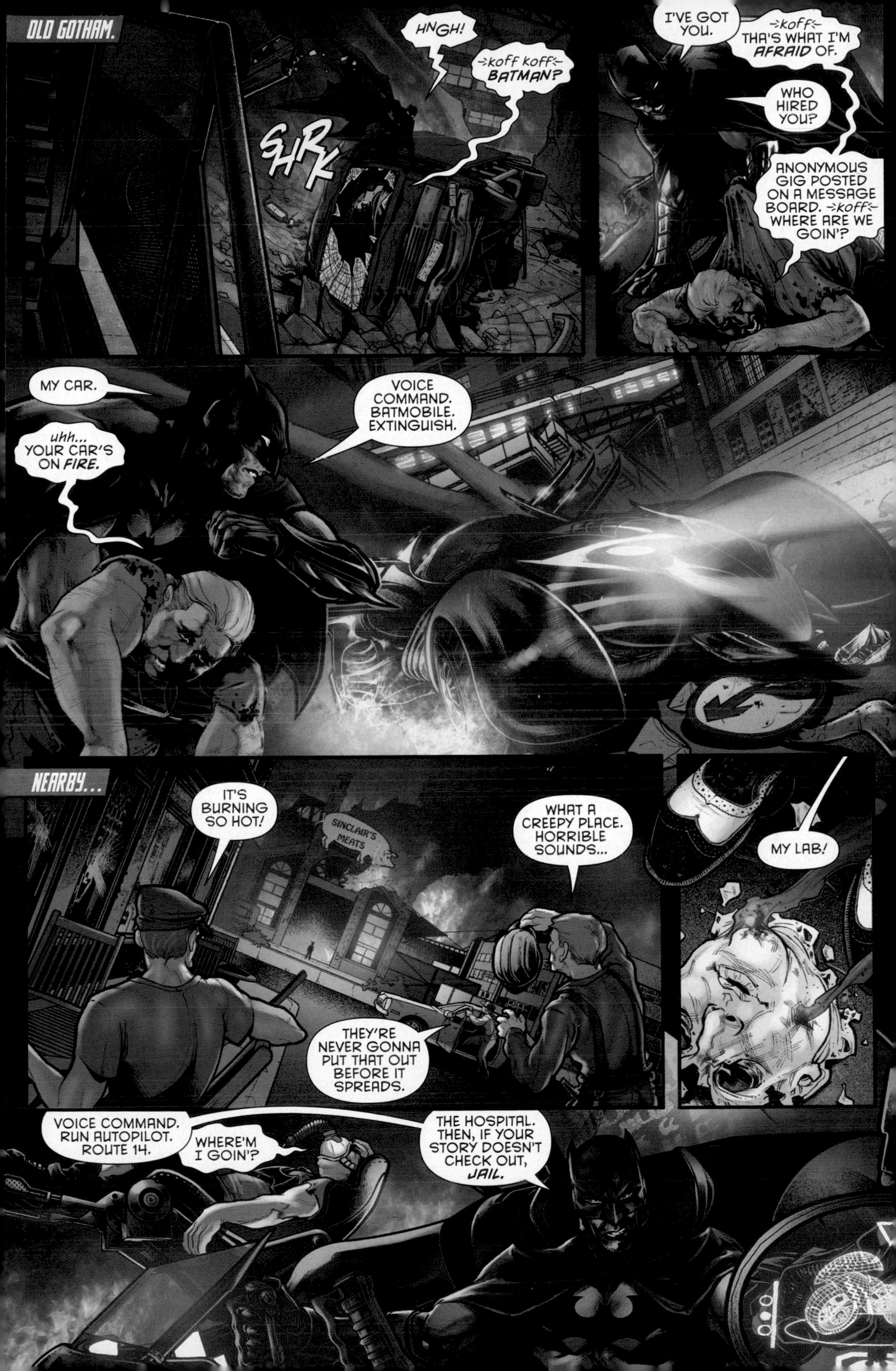
OLD GOTHAM.
HNGH!
-koff koff- BATMAN?
SHRK
I'VE GOT YOU.
-koff- THA'S WHAT I'M AFRAID OF.
WHO HIRED YOU?
ANONYMOUS GIG POSTED ON A MESSAGE BOARD. -koff- WHERE ARE WE GOIN'?
MY CAR.
uhh... YOUR CAR'S ON FIRE.
VOICE COMMAND. BATMOBILE. EXTINGUISH.
NEARBY...
IT'S BURNING SO HOT!
SINCLAIR'S MEATS
WHAT A CREEPY PLACE. HORRIBLE SOUNDS...
THEY'RE NEVER GONNA PUT THAT OUT BEFORE IT SPREADS.
MY LAB!
VOICE COMMAND. RUN AUTOPILOT. ROUTE 14.
WHERE'M I GOIN'?
THE HOSPITAL. THEN, IF YOUR STORY DOESN'T CHECK OUT, JAIL.

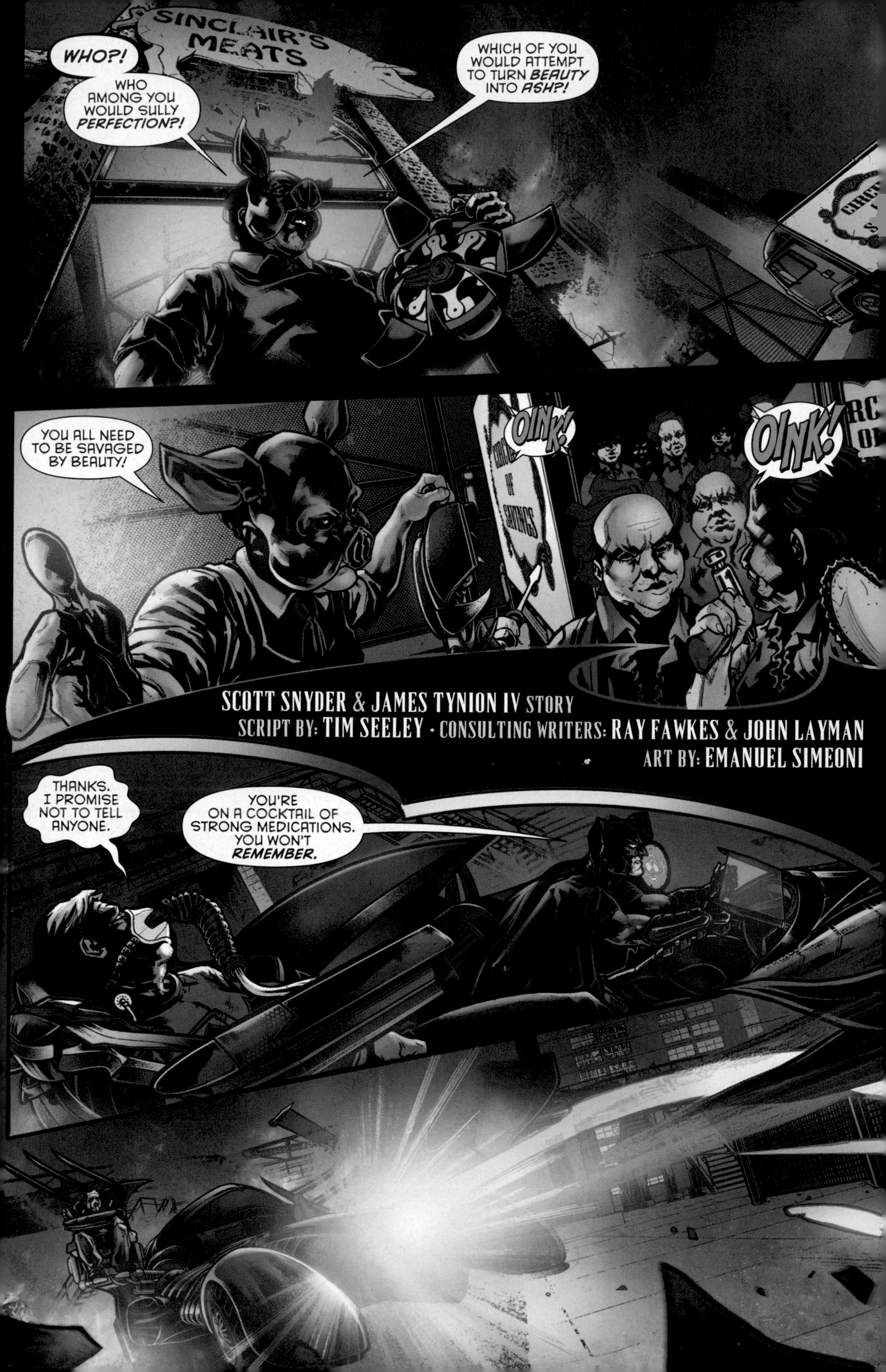
SINCLAIR'S MEATS
WHO?!
WHO AMONG YOU WOULD SULLY PERFECTION?!
WHICH OF YOU WOULD ATTEMPT TO TURN BEAUTY INTO ASH?!
YOU ALL NEED TO BE SAVAGED BY BEAUTY!
OINK!
OINK!
SCOTT SNYDER & JAMES TYNION IV STORY
SCRIPT BY: TIM SEELEY • CONSULTING WRITERS: RAY FAWKES & JOHN LAYMAN
ART BY: EMANUEL SIMEONI
THANKS. I PROMISE NOT TO TELL ANYONE.
YOU'RE ON A COCKTAIL OF STRONG MEDICATIONS. YOU WON'T REMEMBER.

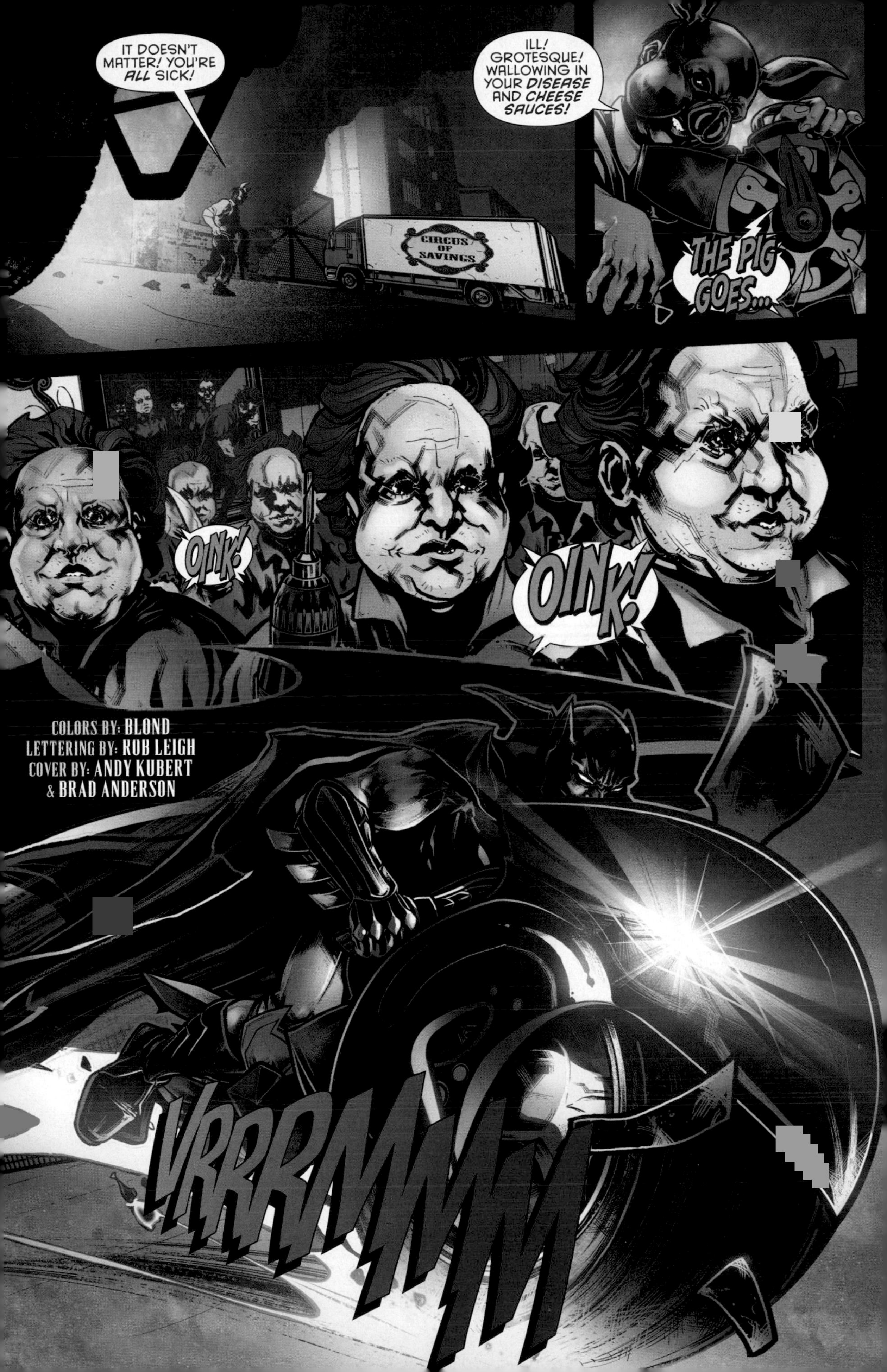
IT DOESN'T MATTER! YOU'RE *ALL* SICK!
CIRCUS OF SAVINGS
ILL! GROTESQUE! WALLOWING IN YOUR *DISEASE* AND *CHEESE SAUCES!*
THE PIG GOES...
OINK!
OINK!
COLORS BY: BLOND
LETTERING BY: ROB LEIGH
COVER BY: ANDY KUBERT
& BRAD ANDERSON
VRRRMMMM

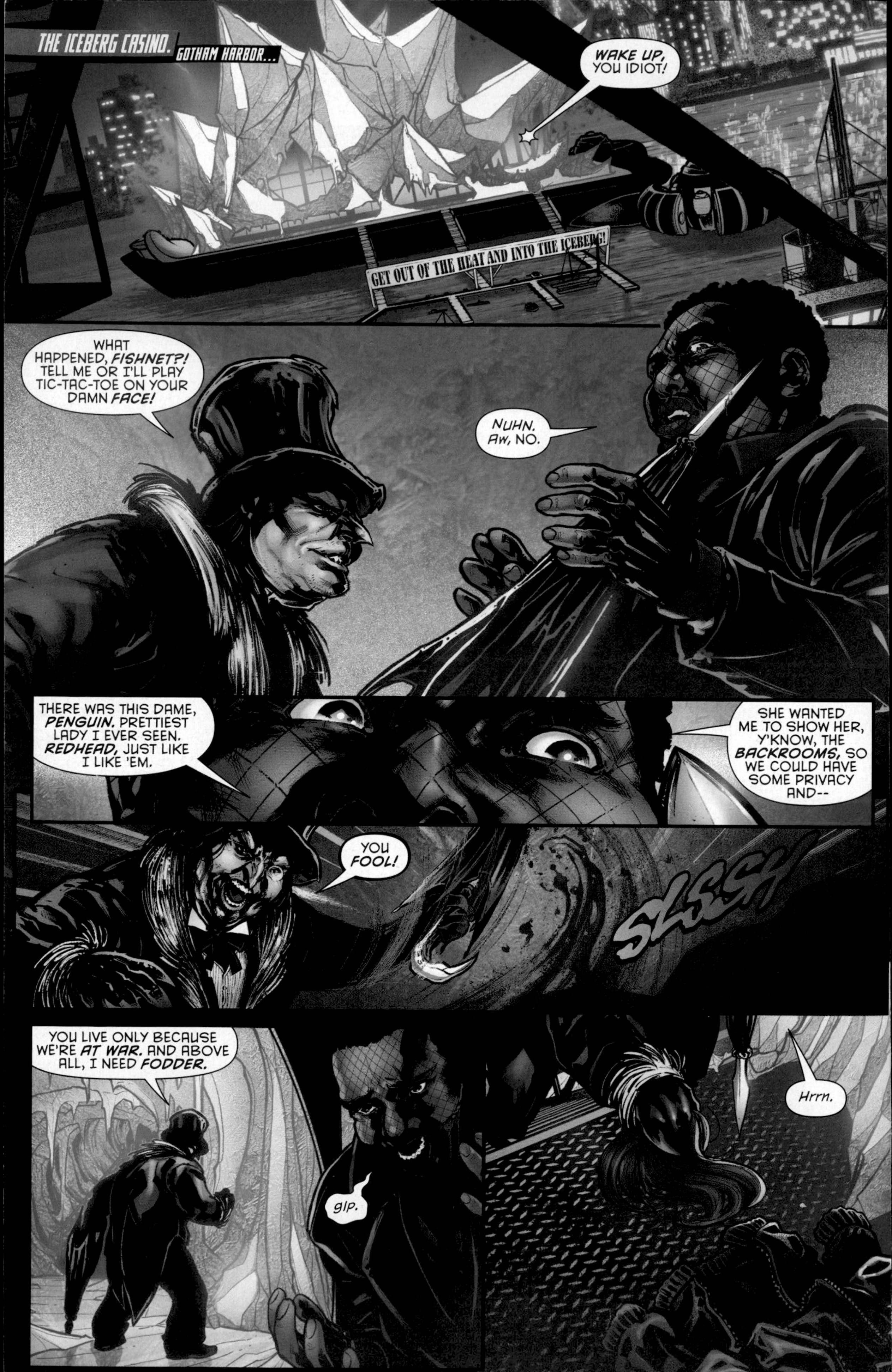
THE ICEBERG CASINO. GOTHAM HARBOR...
WAKE UP, YOU IDIOT!
GET OUT OF THE HEAT AND INTO THE ICEBERG!
WHAT HAPPENED, FISHNET?! TELL ME OR I'LL PLAY TIC-TAC-TOE ON YOUR DAMN FACE!
NUHN. AW, NO.
THERE WAS THIS DAME, PENGUIN. PRETTIEST LADY I EVER SEEN. REDHEAD, JUST LIKE I LIKE 'EM.
SHE WANTED ME TO SHOW HER, Y'KNOW, THE BACKROOMS, SO WE COULD HAVE SOME PRIVACY AND--
YOU FOOL!
SLSSH
YOU LIVE ONLY BECAUSE WE'RE AT WAR. AND ABOVE ALL, I NEED FODDER.
glp.
Hrrn.

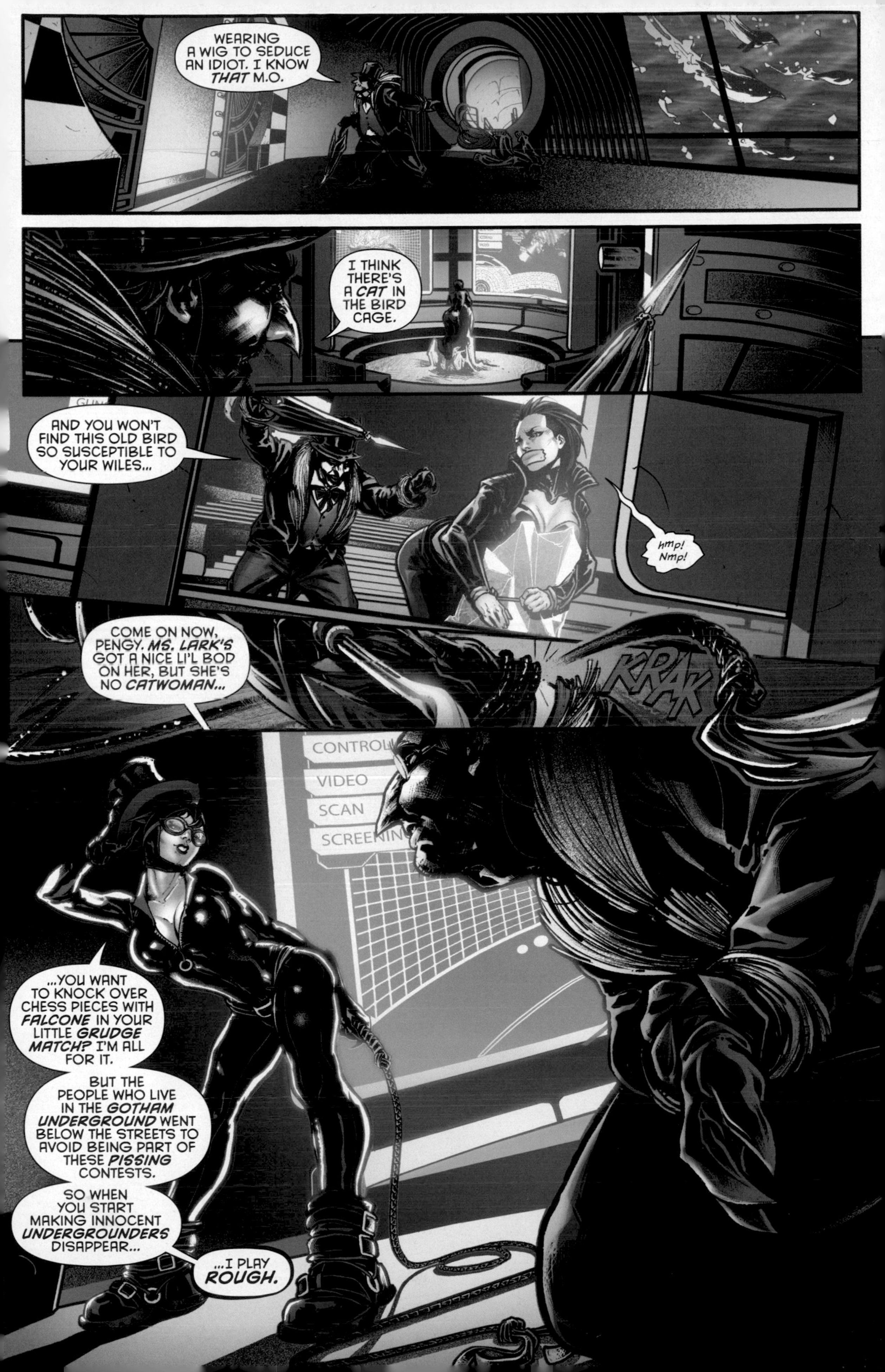
WEARING A WIG TO SEDUCE AN IDIOT. I KNOW THAT M.O.
I THINK THERE'S A CAT IN THE BIRD CAGE.
AND YOU WON'T FIND THIS OLD BIRD SO SUSCEPTIBLE TO YOUR WILES...
Hmp! Nmp!
COME ON NOW, PENGY. MS. LARK'S GOT A NICE LI'L BOD ON HER, BUT SHE'S NO CATWOMAN...
KRAK
CONTROL
VIDEO
SCAN
SCREENIN
...YOU WANT TO KNOCK OVER CHESS PIECES WITH FALCONE IN YOUR LITTLE GRUDGE MATCH? I'M ALL FOR IT.
BUT THE PEOPLE WHO LIVE IN THE GOTHAM UNDERGROUND WENT BELOW THE STREETS TO AVOID BEING PART OF THESE PISSING CONTESTS.
SO WHEN YOU START MAKING INNOCENT UNDERGROUNDERS DISAPPEAR...
...I PLAY ROUGH.

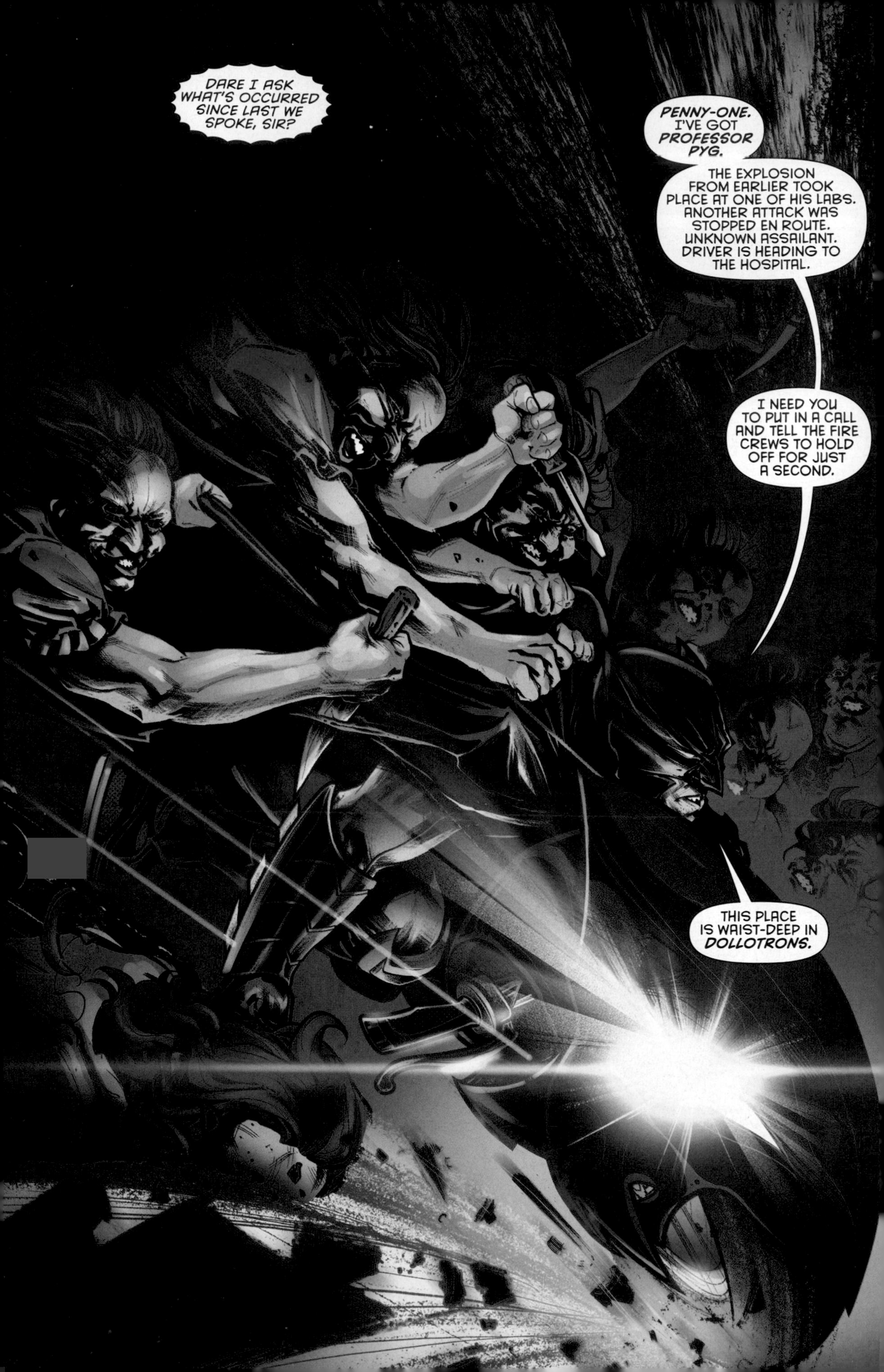
DARE I ASK WHAT'S OCCURRED SINCE LAST WE SPOKE, SIR?
PENNY-ONE. I'VE GOT PROFESSOR PYG.
THE EXPLOSION FROM EARLIER TOOK PLACE AT ONE OF HIS LABS. ANOTHER ATTACK WAS STOPPED EN ROUTE. UNKNOWN ASSAILANT. DRIVER IS HEADING TO THE HOSPITAL.
I NEED YOU TO PUT IN A CALL AND TELL THE FIRE CREWS TO HOLD OFF FOR JUST A SECOND.
THIS PLACE IS WAIST-DEEP IN DOLLOTRONS.

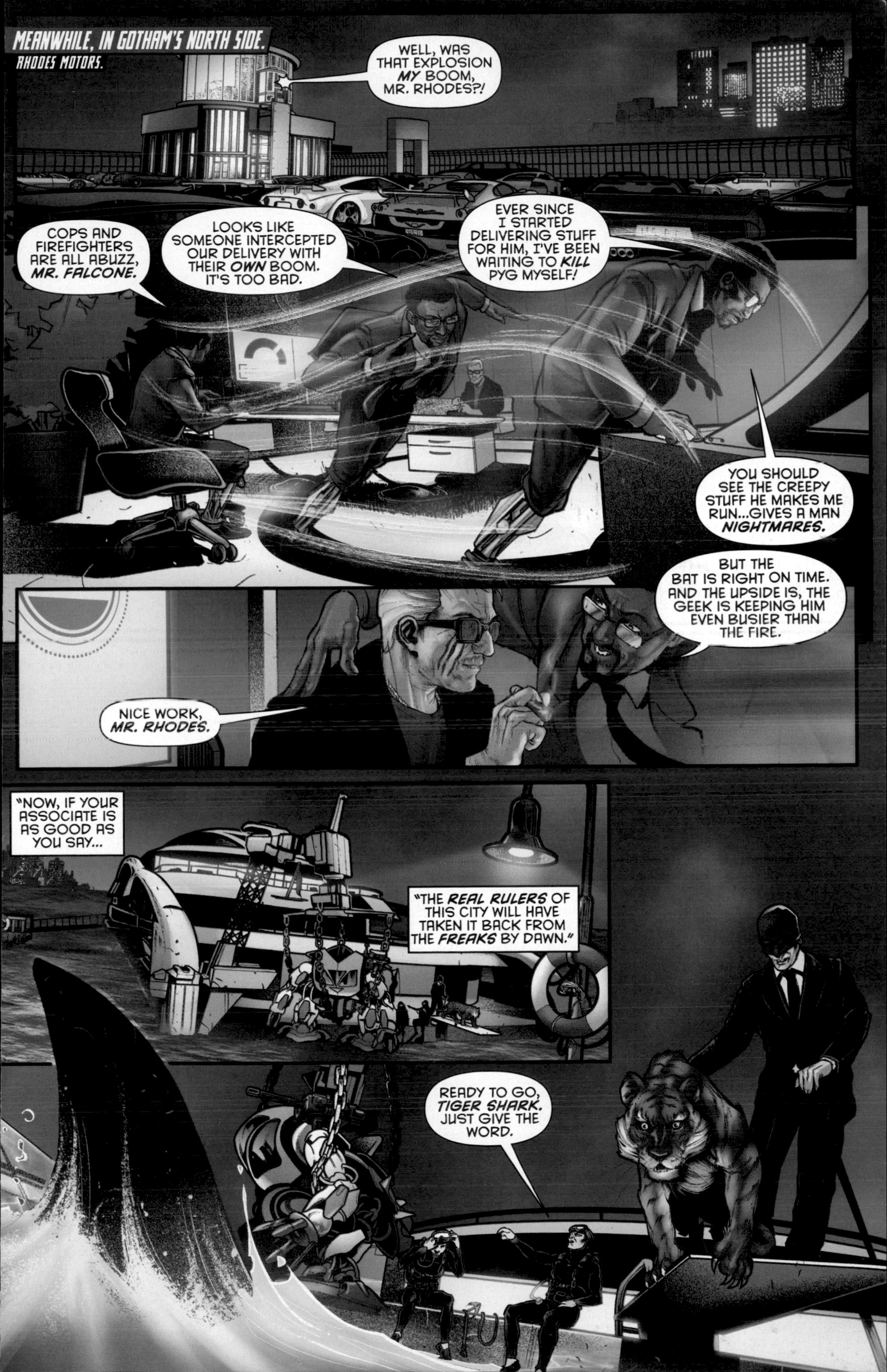
MEANWHILE, IN GOTHAM'S NORTH SIDE.
RHODES MOTORS.
WELL, WAS THAT EXPLOSION MY BOOM, MR. RHODES?!
COPS AND FIREFIGHTERS ARE ALL ABUZZ, MR. FALCONE.
LOOKS LIKE SOMEONE INTERCEPTED OUR DELIVERY WITH THEIR OWN BOOM. IT'S TOO BAD.
EVER SINCE I STARTED DELIVERING STUFF FOR HIM, I'VE BEEN WAITING TO KILL PYG MYSELF!
YOU SHOULD SEE THE CREEPY STUFF HE MAKES ME RUN...GIVES A MAN NIGHTMARES.
BUT THE BAT IS RIGHT ON TIME. AND THE UPSIDE IS, THE GEEK IS KEEPING HIM EVEN BUSIER THAN THE FIRE.
NICE WORK, MR. RHODES.
"NOW, IF YOUR ASSOCIATE IS AS GOOD AS YOU SAY...
"THE REAL RULERS OF THIS CITY WILL HAVE TAKEN IT BACK FROM THE FREAKS BY DAWN."
READY TO GO, TIGER SHARK. JUST GIVE THE WORD.

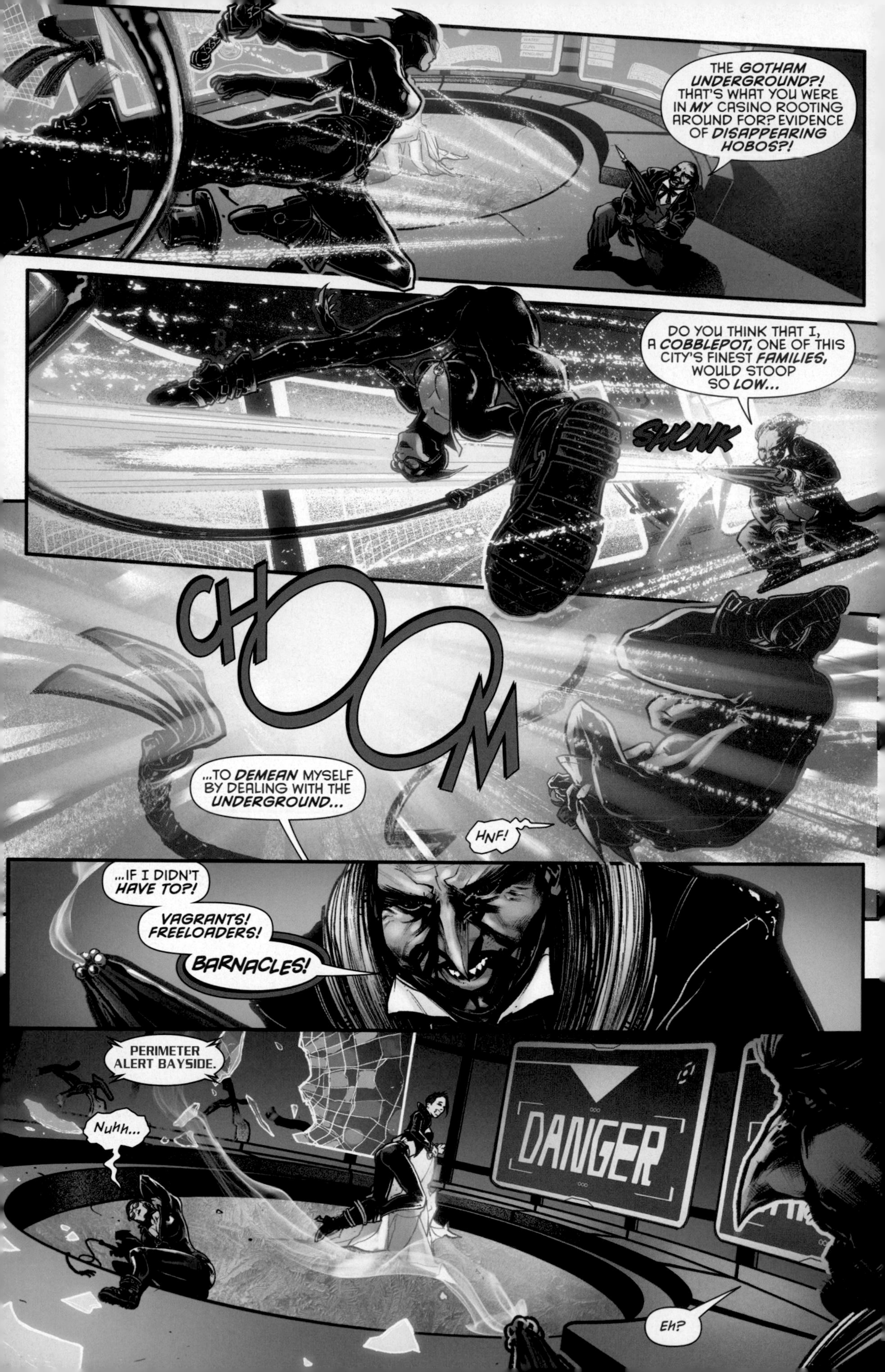

THE GOTHAM UNDERGROUND?! THAT'S WHAT YOU WERE IN MY CASINO ROOTING AROUND FOR? EVIDENCE OF DISAPPEARING HOBOS?!
DO YOU THINK THAT I, A COBBLEPOT, ONE OF THIS CITY'S FINEST FAMILIES, WOULD STOOP SO LOW...
SHUNK
CHOOM
...TO DEMEAN MYSELF BY DEALING WITH THE UNDERGROUND...
HNF!
...IF I DIDN'T HAVE TO?!
VAGRANTS! FREELOADERS!
BARNACLES!
PERIMETER ALERT BAYSIDE.
Nuhh...
DANGER
Eh?

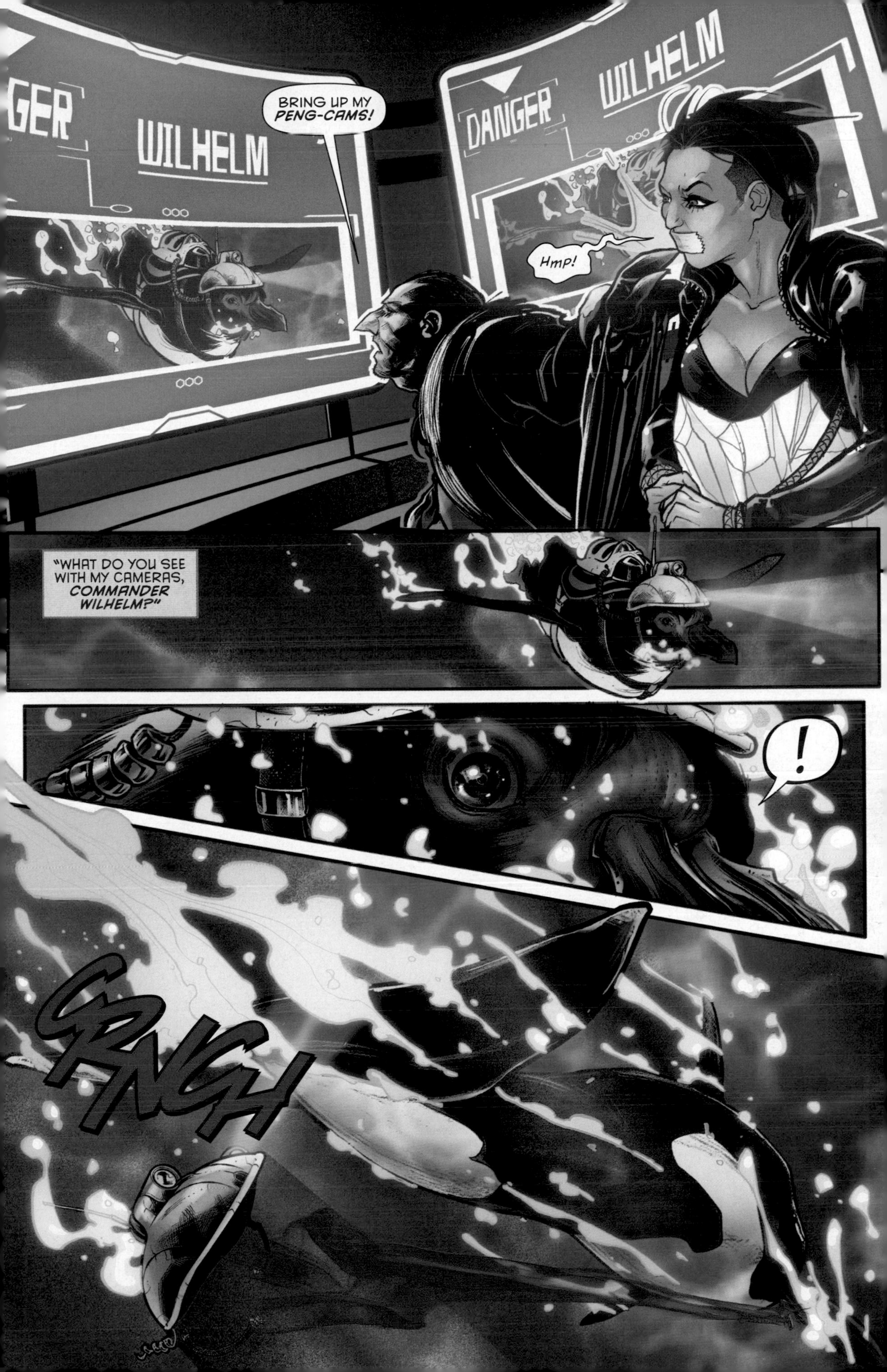

GER
WILHELM
BRING UP MY PENG-CAMS!
DANGER
WILHELM
Hmp!
"WHAT DO YOU SEE WITH MY CAMERAS, COMMANDER WILHELM?"
!
CRNCH

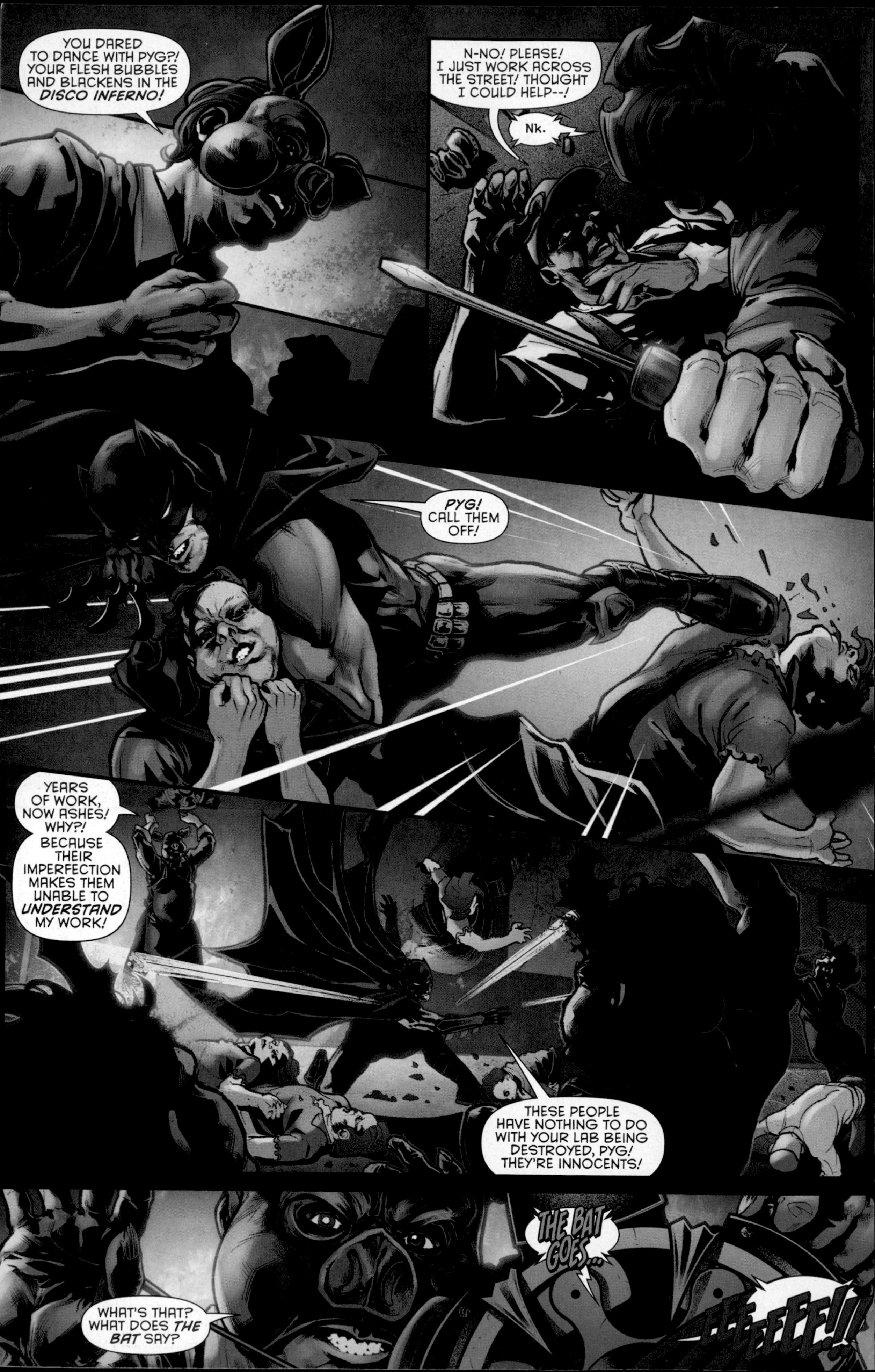

YOU DARED TO DANCE WITH PYG?! YOUR FLESH BUBBLES AND BLACKENS IN THE DISCO INFERNO!
N-NO! PLEASE! I JUST WORK ACROSS THE STREET! THOUGHT I COULD HELP--!
Nk.
PYG! CALL THEM OFF!
YEARS OF WORK, NOW ASHES! WHY?!
BECAUSE THEIR IMPERFECTION MAKES THEM UNABLE TO UNDERSTAND MY WORK!
THESE PEOPLE HAVE NOTHING TO DO WITH YOUR LAB BEING DESTROYED, PYG! THEY'RE INNOCENTS!
WHAT'S THAT? WHAT DOES THE BAT SAY?
THE BAT GOES...
EEEEEEEE!!!

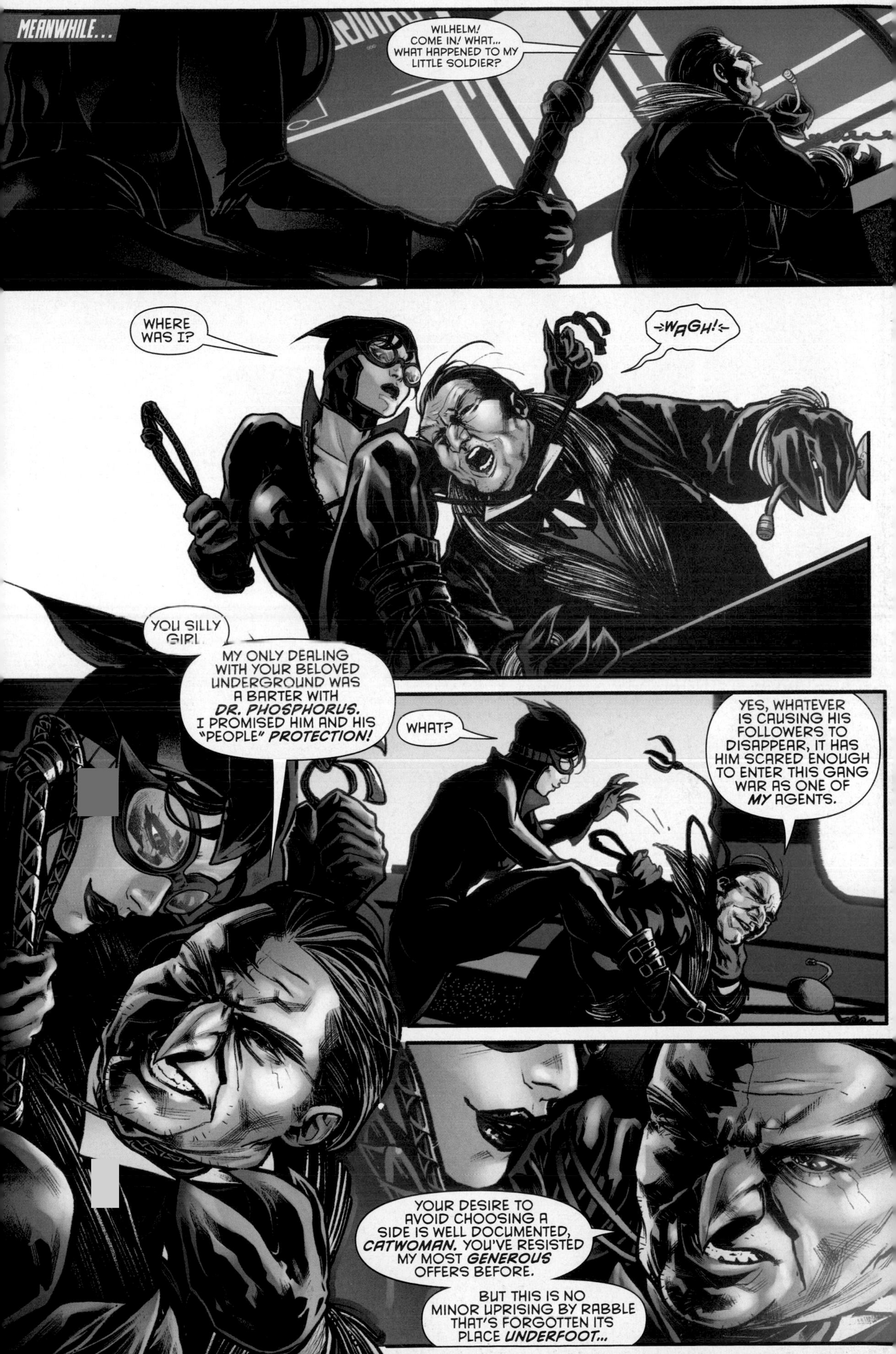
MEANWHILE...
WILHELM! COME IN! WHAT... WHAT HAPPENED TO MY LITTLE SOLDIER?
WHERE WAS I?
WAGH!
YOU SILLY GIRL.
MY ONLY DEALING WITH YOUR BELOVED UNDERGROUND WAS A BARTER WITH DR. PHOSPHORUS. I PROMISED HIM AND HIS "PEOPLE" PROTECTION!
WHAT?
YES, WHATEVER IS CAUSING HIS FOLLOWERS TO DISAPPEAR, IT HAS HIM SCARED ENOUGH TO ENTER THIS GANG WAR AS ONE OF MY AGENTS.
YOUR DESIRE TO AVOID CHOOSING A SIDE IS WELL DOCUMENTED, CATWOMAN. YOU'VE RESISTED MY MOST GENEROUS OFFERS BEFORE.
BUT THIS IS NO MINOR UPRISING BY RABBLE THAT'S FORGOTTEN ITS PLACE UNDERFOOT...

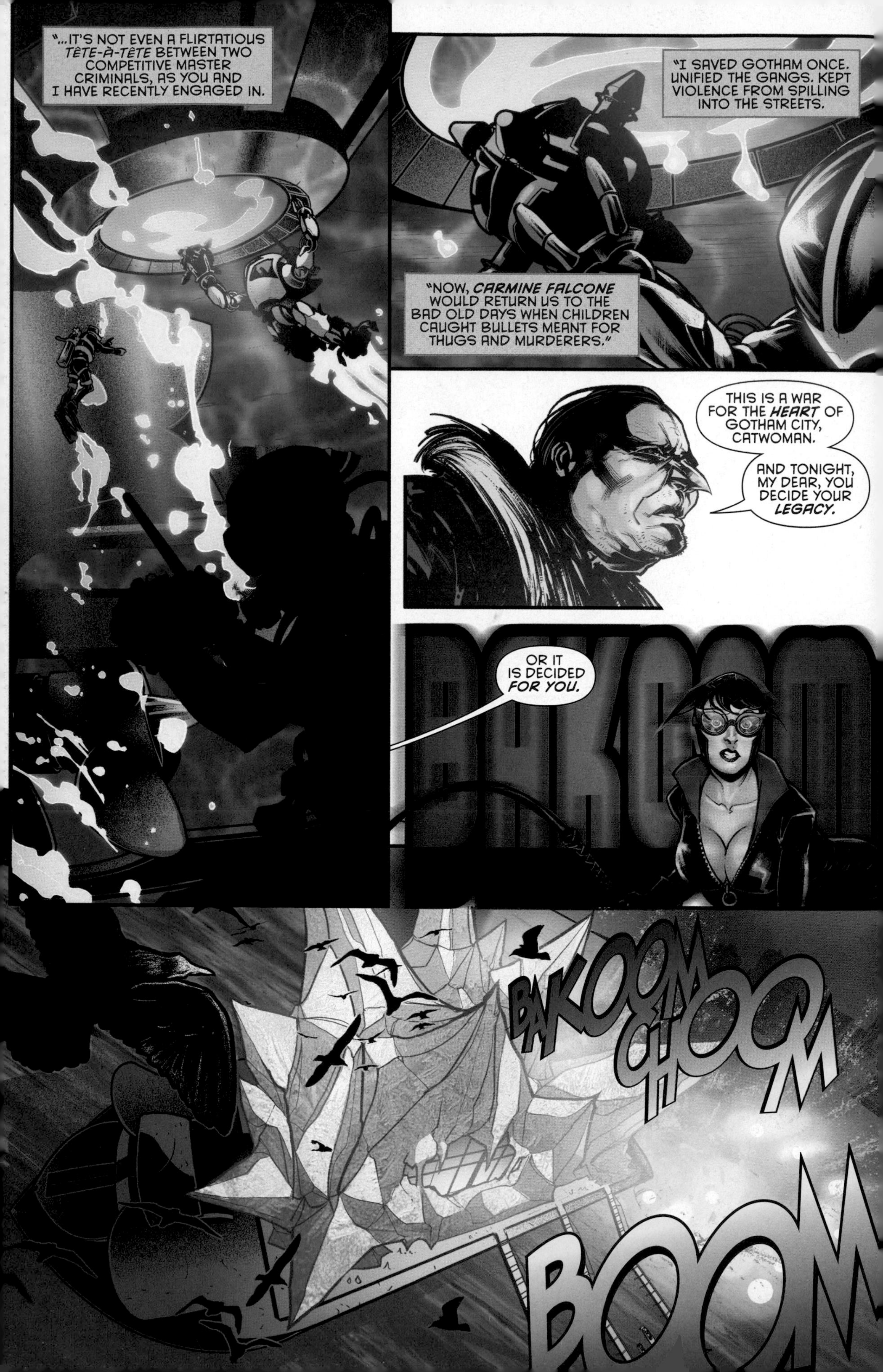
"...IT'S NOT EVEN A FLIRTATIOUS *TÊTE-À-TÊTE* BETWEEN TWO COMPETITIVE MASTER CRIMINALS, AS YOU AND I HAVE RECENTLY ENGAGED IN.
"I SAVED GOTHAM ONCE. UNIFIED THE GANGS. KEPT VIOLENCE FROM SPILLING INTO THE STREETS.
"NOW, *CARMINE FALCONE* WOULD RETURN US TO THE BAD OLD DAYS WHEN CHILDREN CAUGHT BULLETS MEANT FOR THUGS AND MURDERERS."
THIS IS A WAR FOR THE *HEART* OF GOTHAM CITY, CATWOMAN.
AND TONIGHT, MY DEAR, YOU DECIDE YOUR *LEGACY.*
OR IT IS DECIDED *FOR YOU.*
BAKOOM
BAKOOM
CHOOM
BOOM

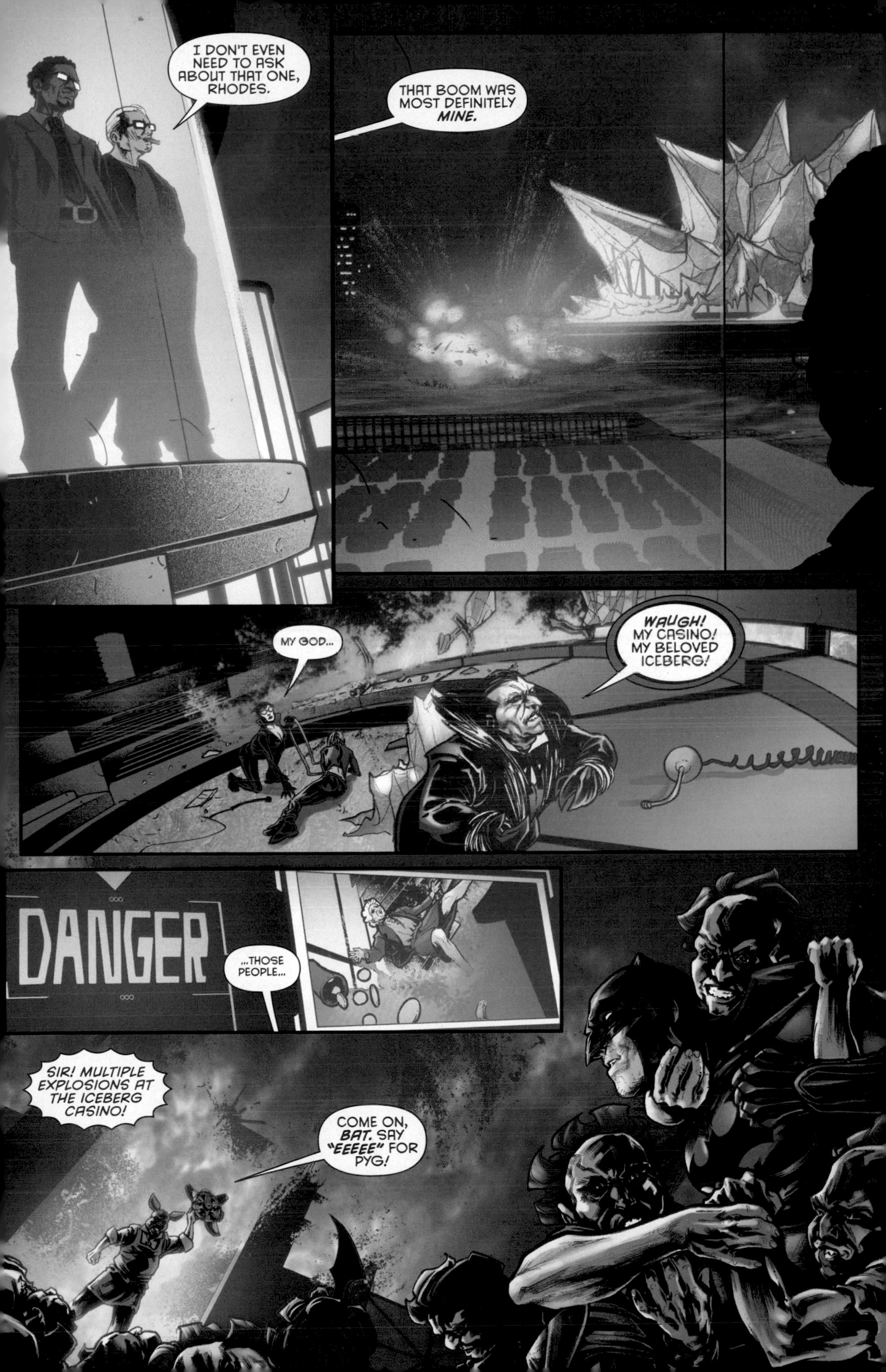
I DON'T EVEN NEED TO ASK ABOUT THAT ONE, RHODES.
THAT BOOM WAS MOST DEFINITELY *MINE.*
MY GOD...
WAUGH! MY CASINO! MY BELOVED ICEBERG!
DANGER
...THOSE PEOPLE...
SIR! MULTIPLE EXPLOSIONS AT THE ICEBERG CASINO!
COME ON, *BAT.* SAY *"EEEEE"* FOR PYG!

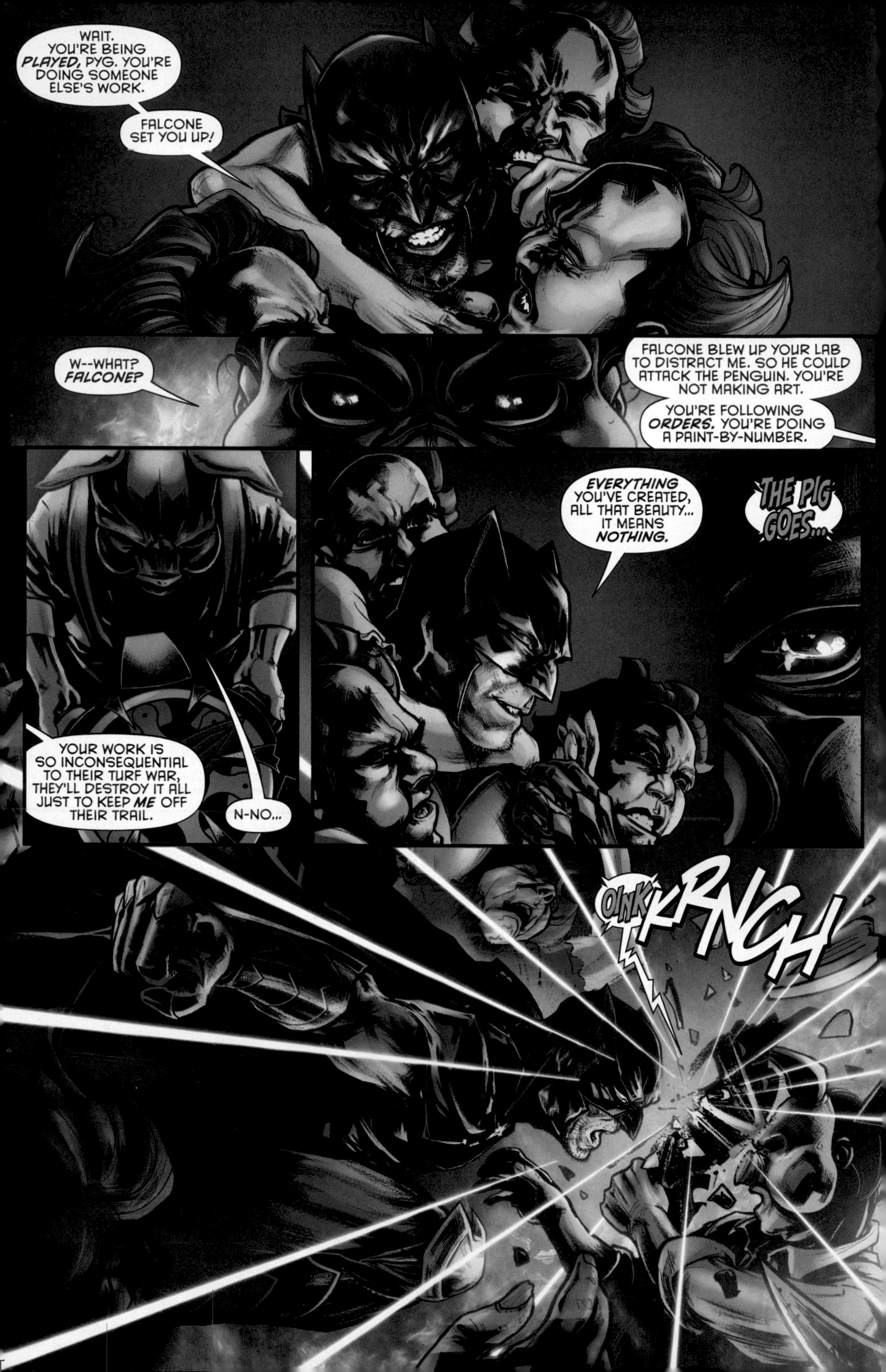
WAIT. YOU'RE BEING *PLAYED,* PYG. YOU'RE DOING SOMEONE ELSE'S WORK.
FALCONE SET YOU UP!
W--WHAT? *FALCONE?*
FALCONE BLEW UP YOUR LAB TO DISTRACT ME. SO HE COULD ATTACK THE PENGUIN. YOU'RE NOT MAKING ART.
YOU'RE FOLLOWING *ORDERS.* YOU'RE DOING A PAINT-BY-NUMBER.
YOUR WORK IS SO INCONSEQUENTIAL TO THEIR TURF WAR, THEY'LL DESTROY IT ALL JUST TO KEEP *ME* OFF THEIR TRAIL.
N-NO...
EVERYTHING YOU'VE CREATED, ALL THAT BEAUTY... IT MEANS *NOTHING.*
THE PIG GOES...
OINK
KRNCH

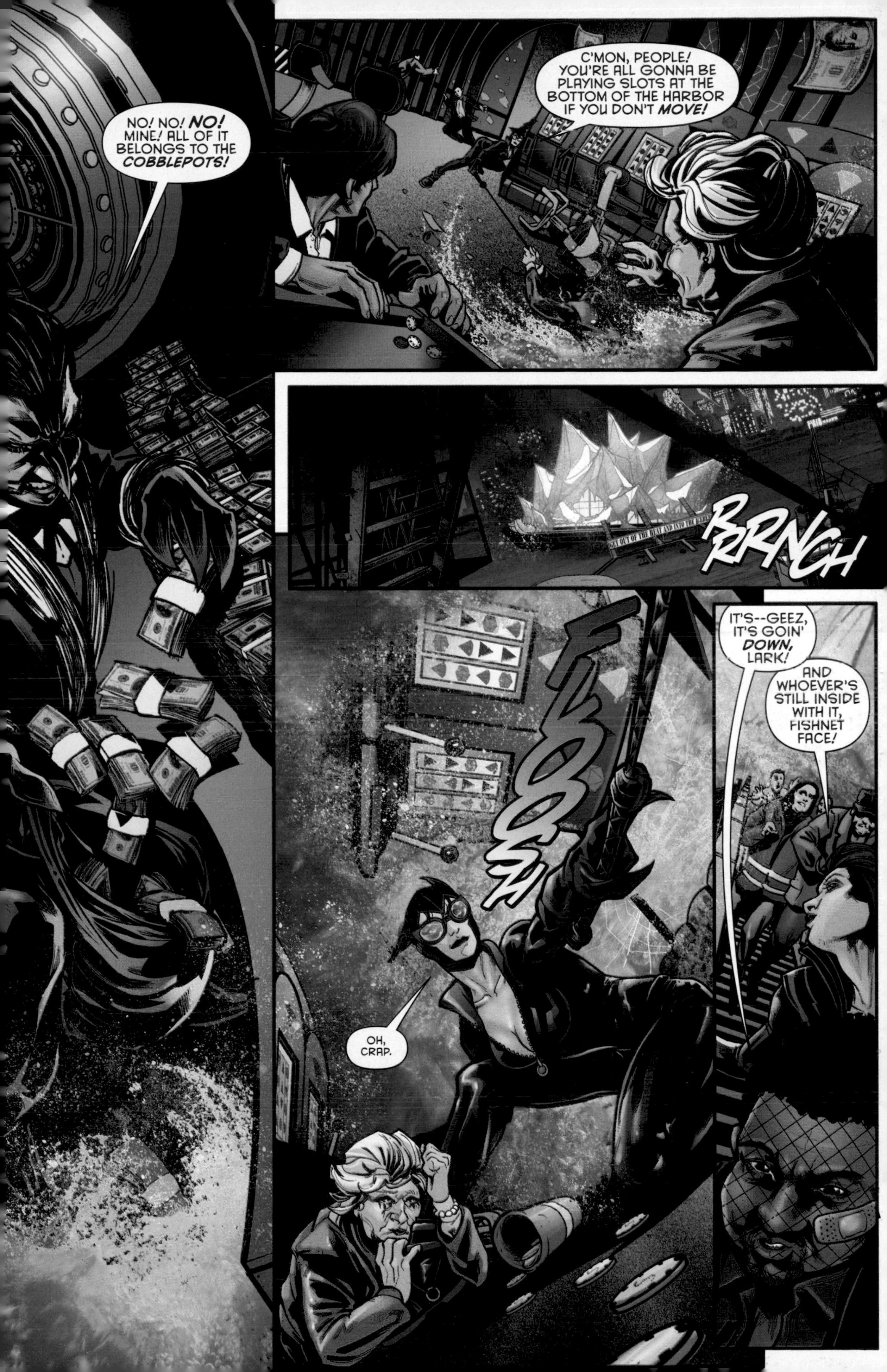
NO! NO! NO! MINE! ALL OF IT BELONGS TO THE COBBLEPOTS!
C'MON, PEOPLE! YOU'RE ALL GONNA BE PLAYING SLOTS AT THE BOTTOM OF THE HARBOR IF YOU DON'T MOVE!
BRRNCH
FWOOOSH
OH, CRAP.
IT'S--GEEZ, IT'S GOIN' DOWN, LARK!
AND WHOEVER'S STILL INSIDE WITH IT, FISHNET FACE!

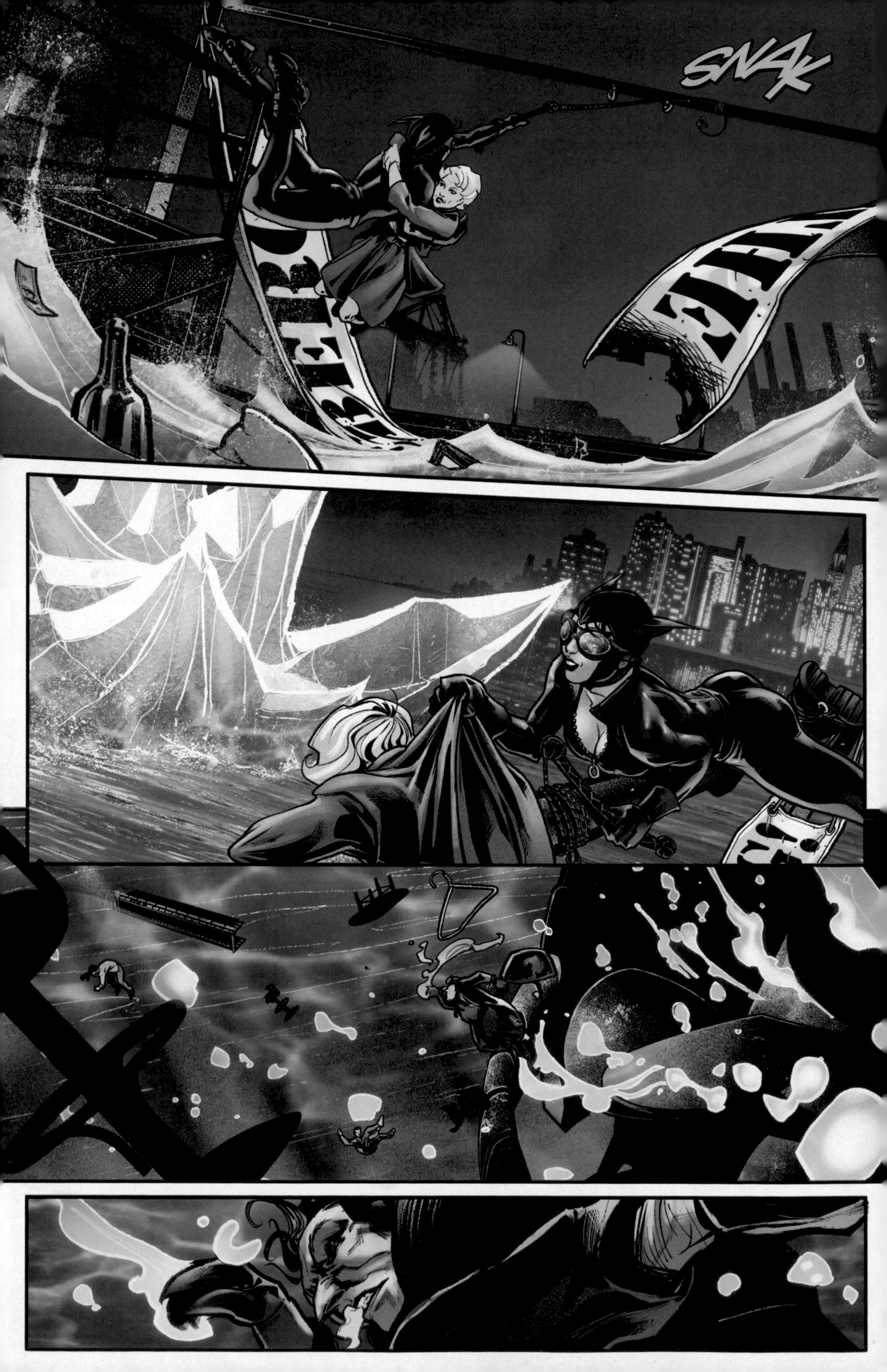
SNAK

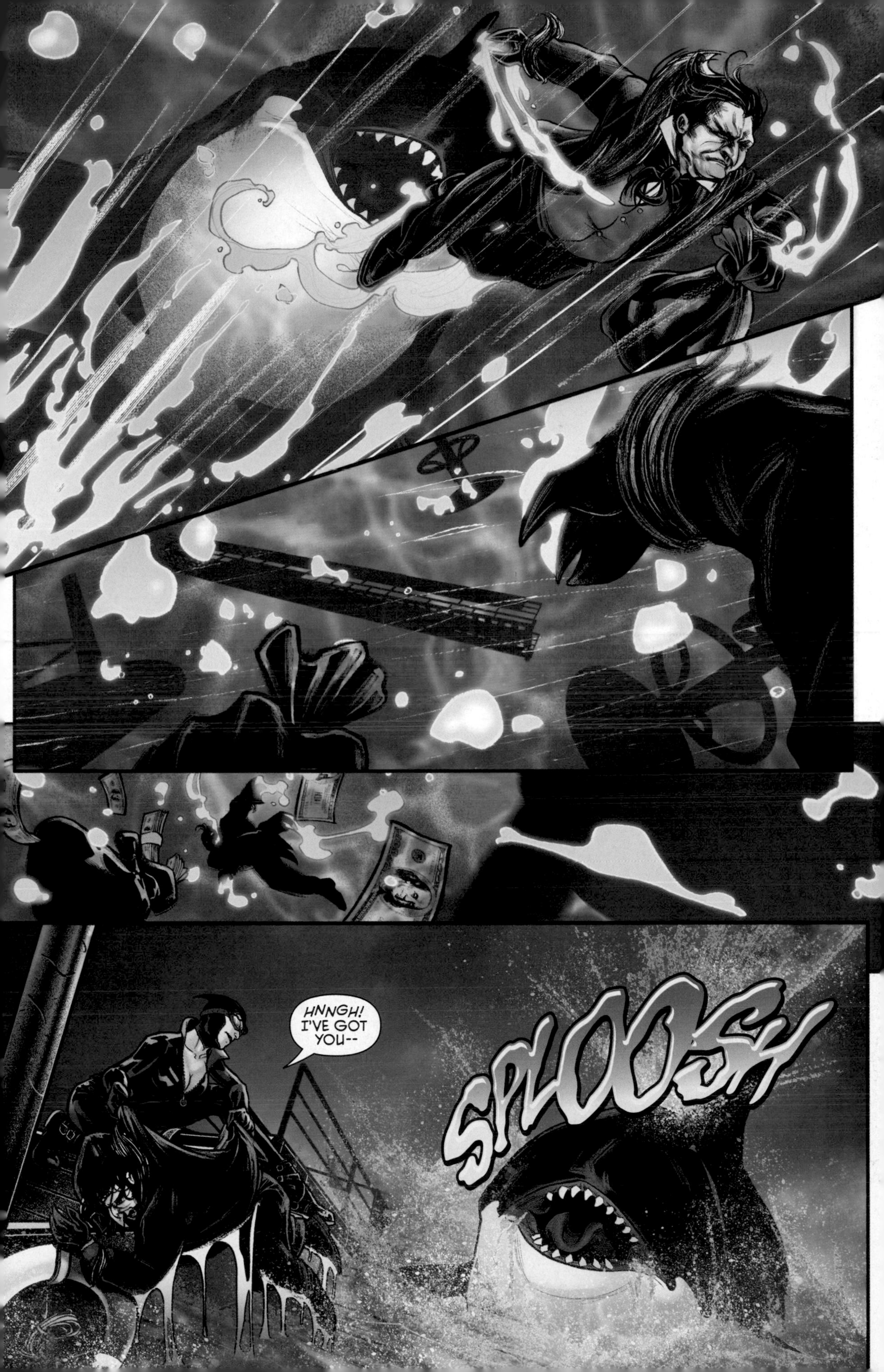
HNNGH! I'VE GOT YOU--
SPLOOSH

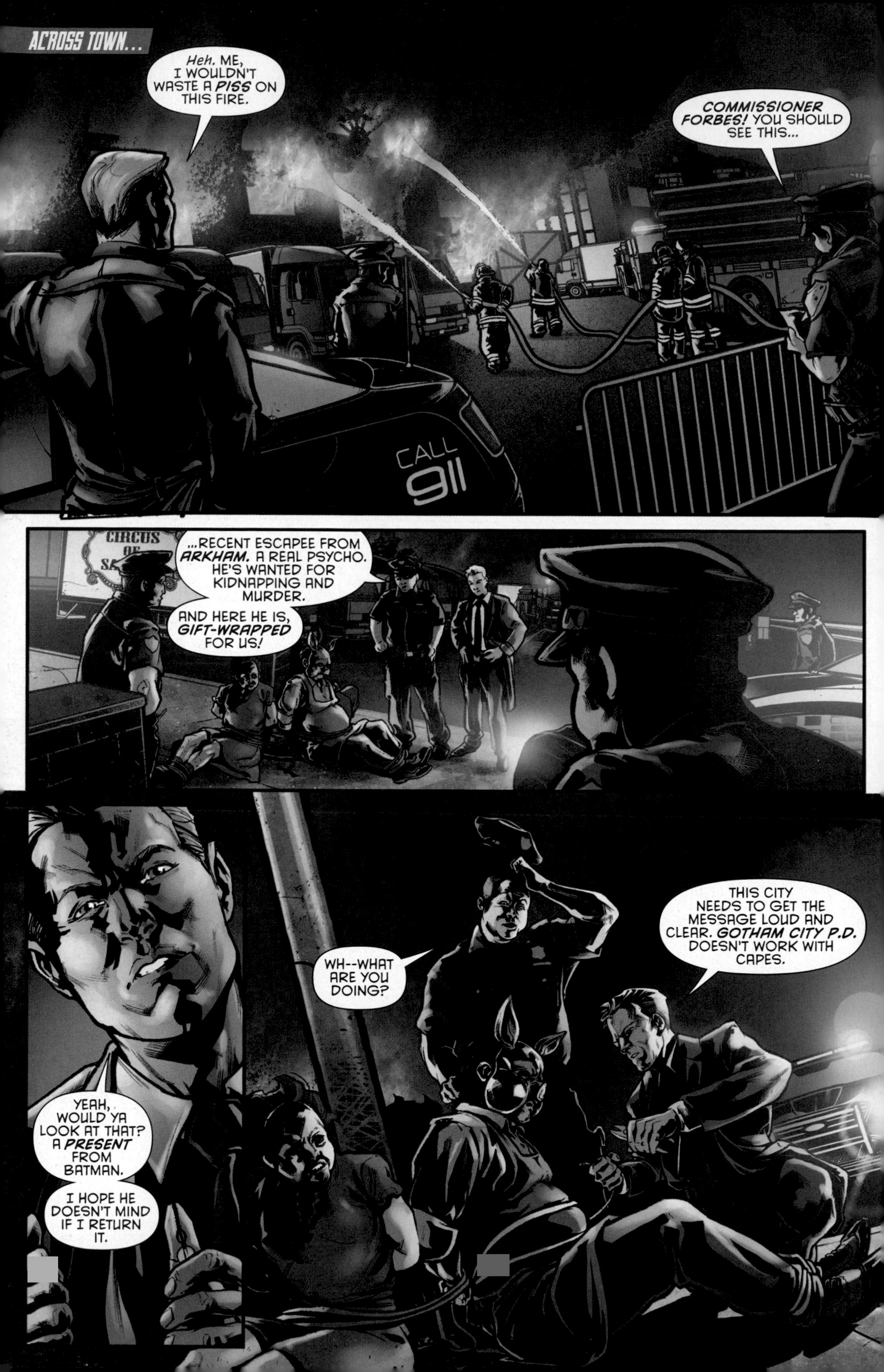
ACROSS TOWN...
Heh. ME, I WOULDN'T WASTE A PISS ON THIS FIRE.
COMMISSIONER FORBES! YOU SHOULD SEE THIS...
CALL 911
...RECENT ESCAPEE FROM ARKHAM. A REAL PSYCHO. HE'S WANTED FOR KIDNAPPING AND MURDER.
AND HERE HE IS, GIFT-WRAPPED FOR US!
YEAH, WOULD YA LOOK AT THAT? A PRESENT FROM BATMAN.
I HOPE HE DOESN'T MIND IF I RETURN IT.
WH--WHAT ARE YOU DOING?
THIS CITY NEEDS TO GET THE MESSAGE LOUD AND CLEAR. GOTHAM CITY P.D. DOESN'T WORK WITH CAPES.

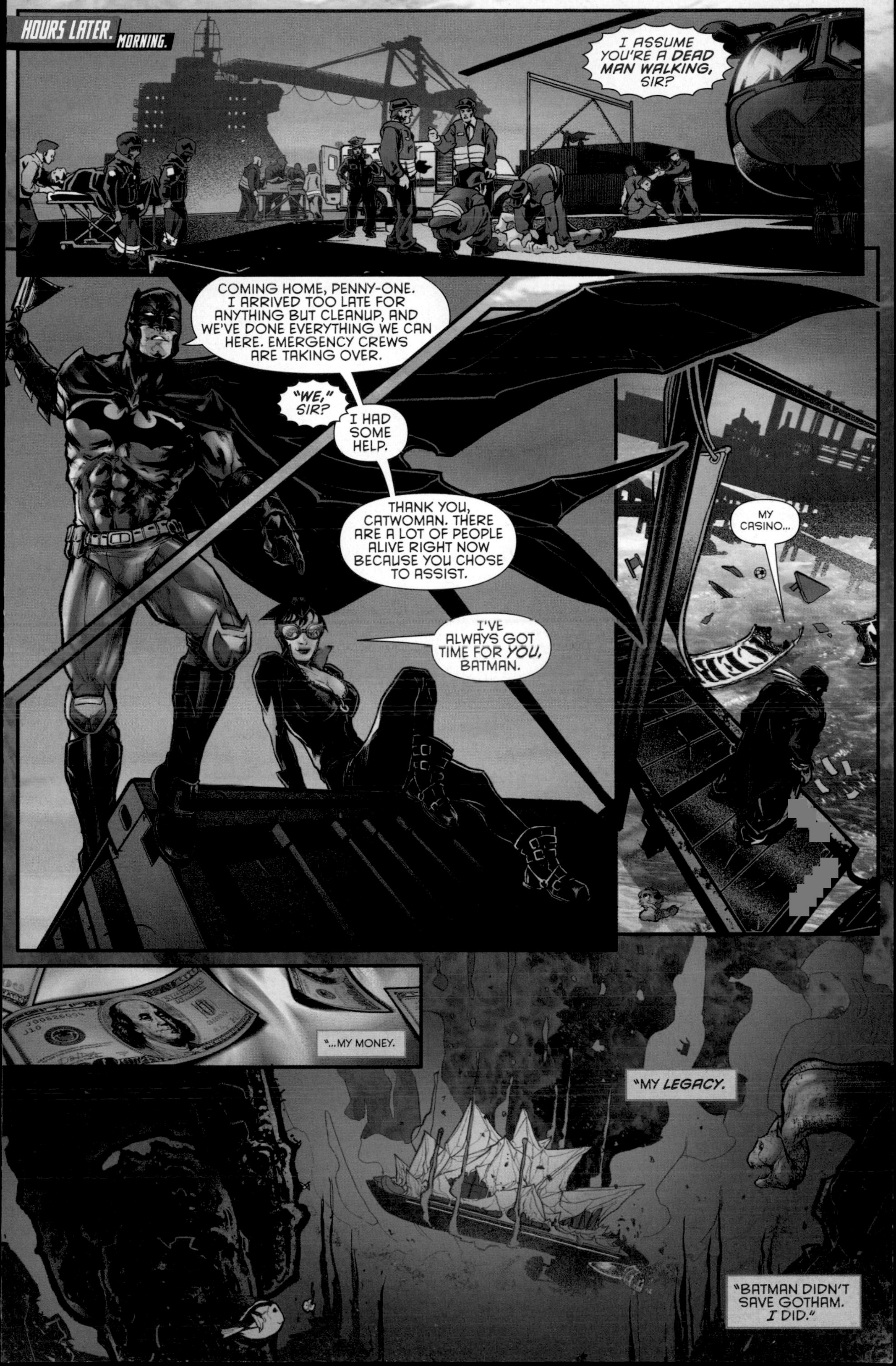
HOURS LATER. MORNING.
I ASSUME YOU'RE A DEAD MAN WALKING, SIR?
COMING HOME, PENNY-ONE. I ARRIVED TOO LATE FOR ANYTHING BUT CLEANUP, AND WE'VE DONE EVERYTHING WE CAN HERE. EMERGENCY CREWS ARE TAKING OVER.
"WE," SIR?
I HAD SOME HELP.
THANK YOU, CATWOMAN. THERE ARE A LOT OF PEOPLE ALIVE RIGHT NOW BECAUSE YOU CHOSE TO ASSIST.
I'VE ALWAYS GOT TIME FOR YOU, BATMAN.
MY CASINO...
"...MY MONEY.
"MY LEGACY.
"BATMAN DIDN'T SAVE GOTHAM. I DID."

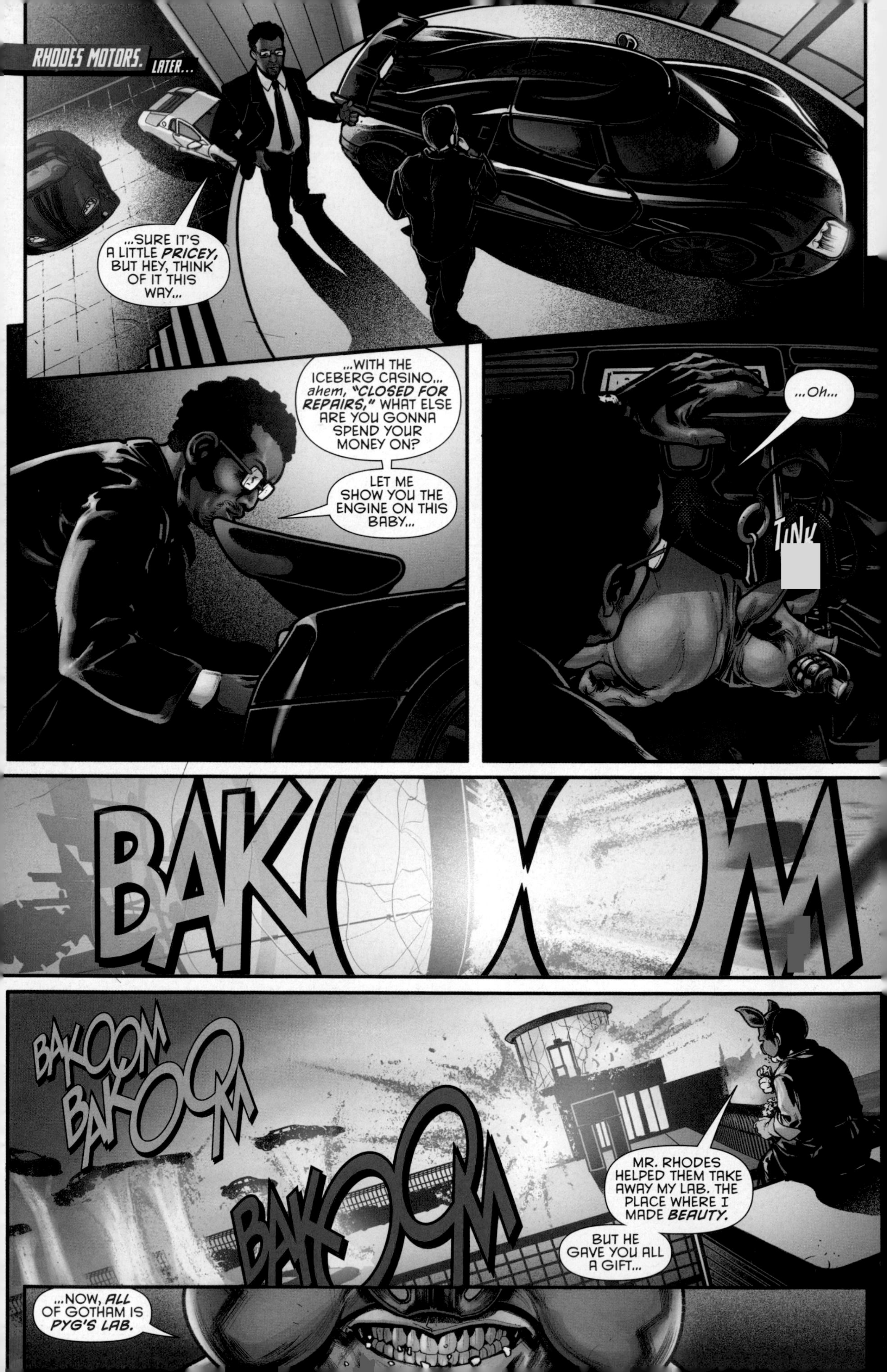
RHODES MOTORS. LATER...
...SURE IT'S A LITTLE PRICEY, BUT HEY, THINK OF IT THIS WAY...
...WITH THE ICEBERG CASINO... ahem, "CLOSED FOR REPAIRS," WHAT ELSE ARE YOU GONNA SPEND YOUR MONEY ON?
LET ME SHOW YOU THE ENGINE ON THIS BABY...
...Oh...
TINK
BAKOOM
BAKOOM
BAKOOM
BAKOOM
MR. RHODES HELPED THEM TAKE AWAY MY LAB. THE PLACE WHERE I MADE BEAUTY.
BUT HE GAVE YOU ALL A GIFT...
...NOW, ALL OF GOTHAM IS PYG'S LAB.

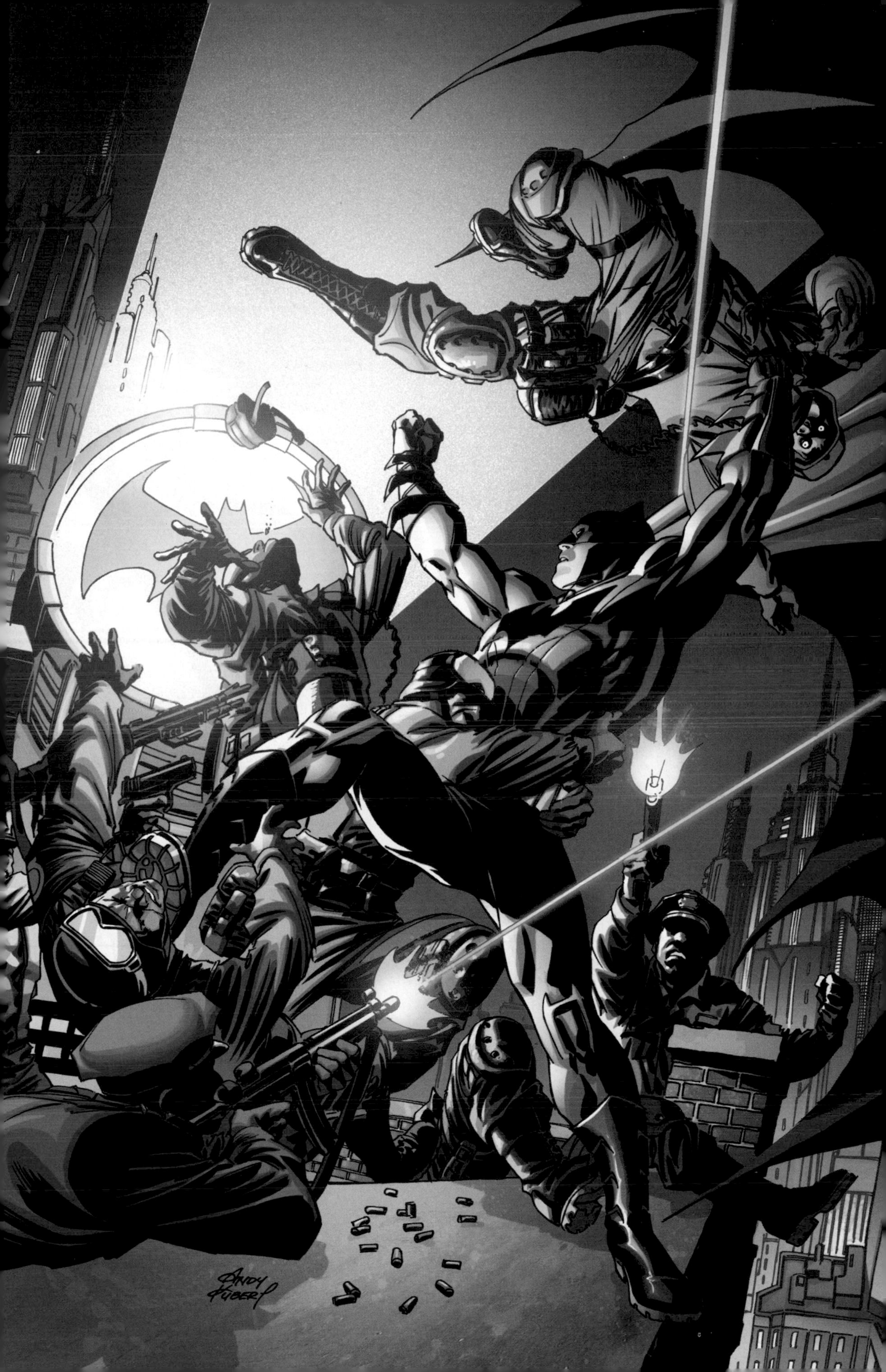
ANDY KUBERT

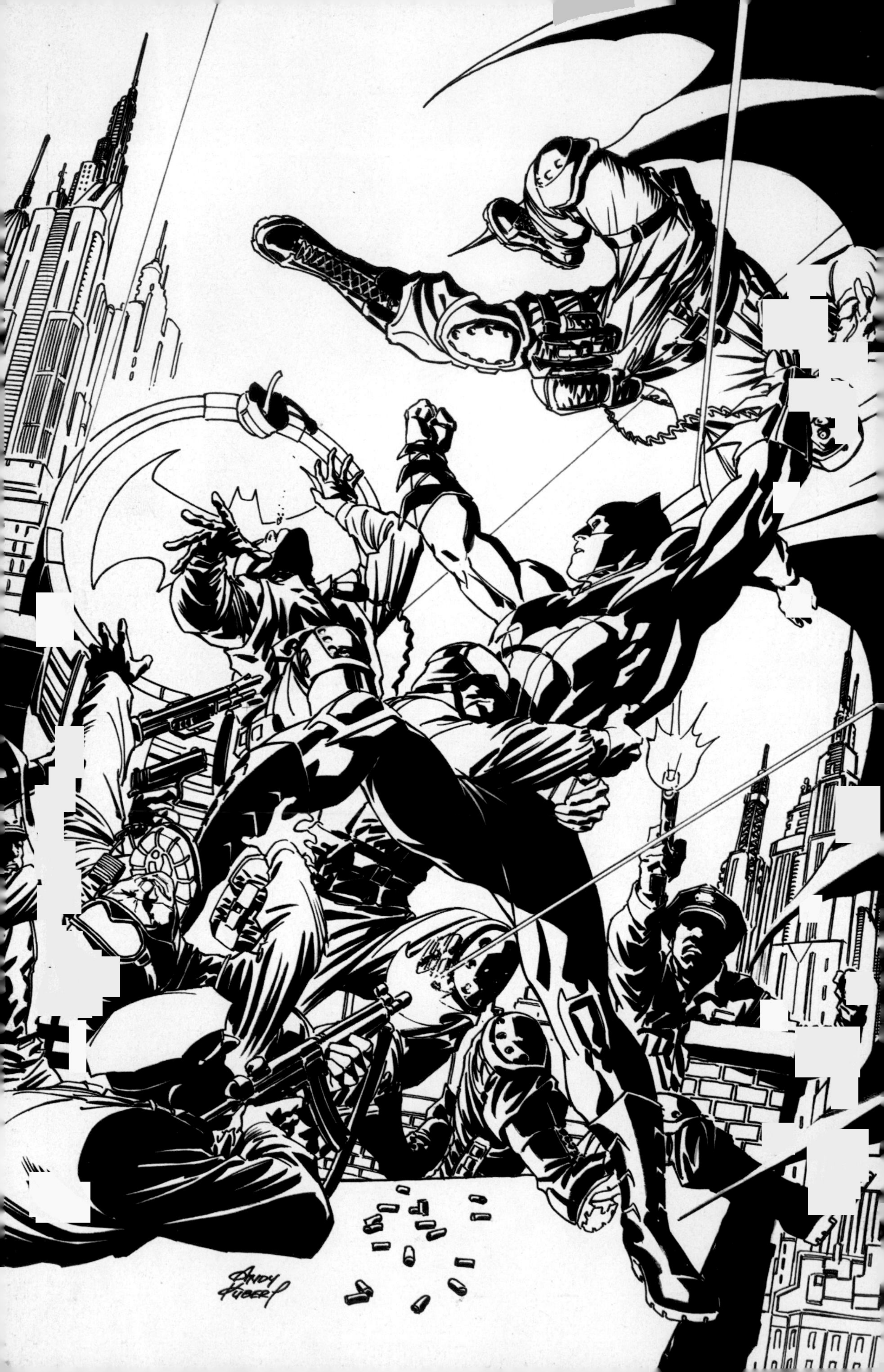
ANDY KUBERT

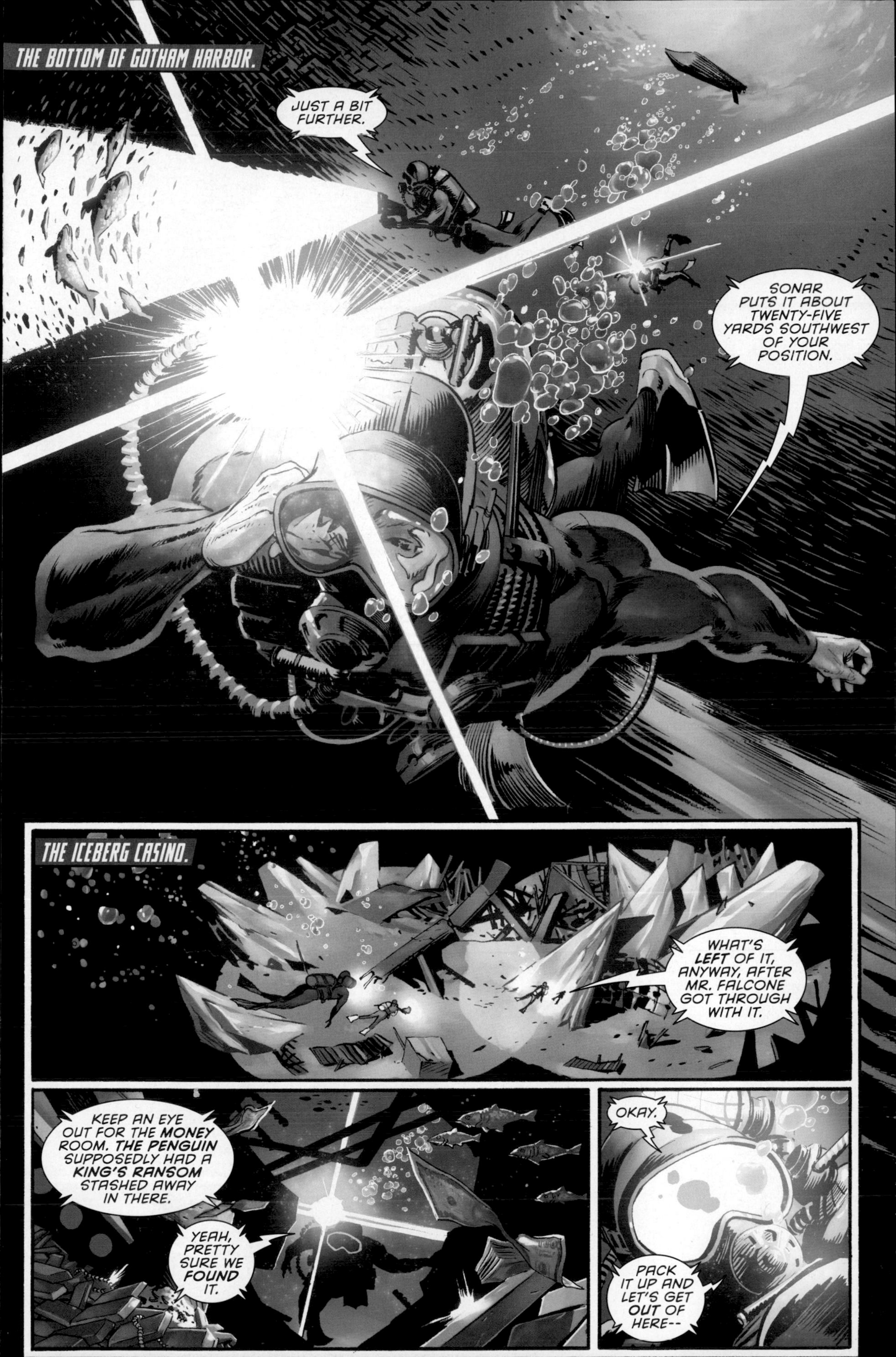
THE BOTTOM OF GOTHAM HARBOR.
JUST A BIT FURTHER.
SONAR PUTS IT ABOUT TWENTY-FIVE YARDS SOUTHWEST OF YOUR POSITION.
THE ICEBERG CASINO.
WHAT'S LEFT OF IT, ANYWAY, AFTER MR. FALCONE GOT THROUGH WITH IT.
KEEP AN EYE OUT FOR THE MONEY ROOM. THE PENGUIN SUPPOSEDLY HAD A KING'S RANSOM STASHED AWAY IN THERE.
YEAH, PRETTY SURE WE FOUND IT.
OKAY.
PACK IT UP AND LET'S GET OUT OF HERE--

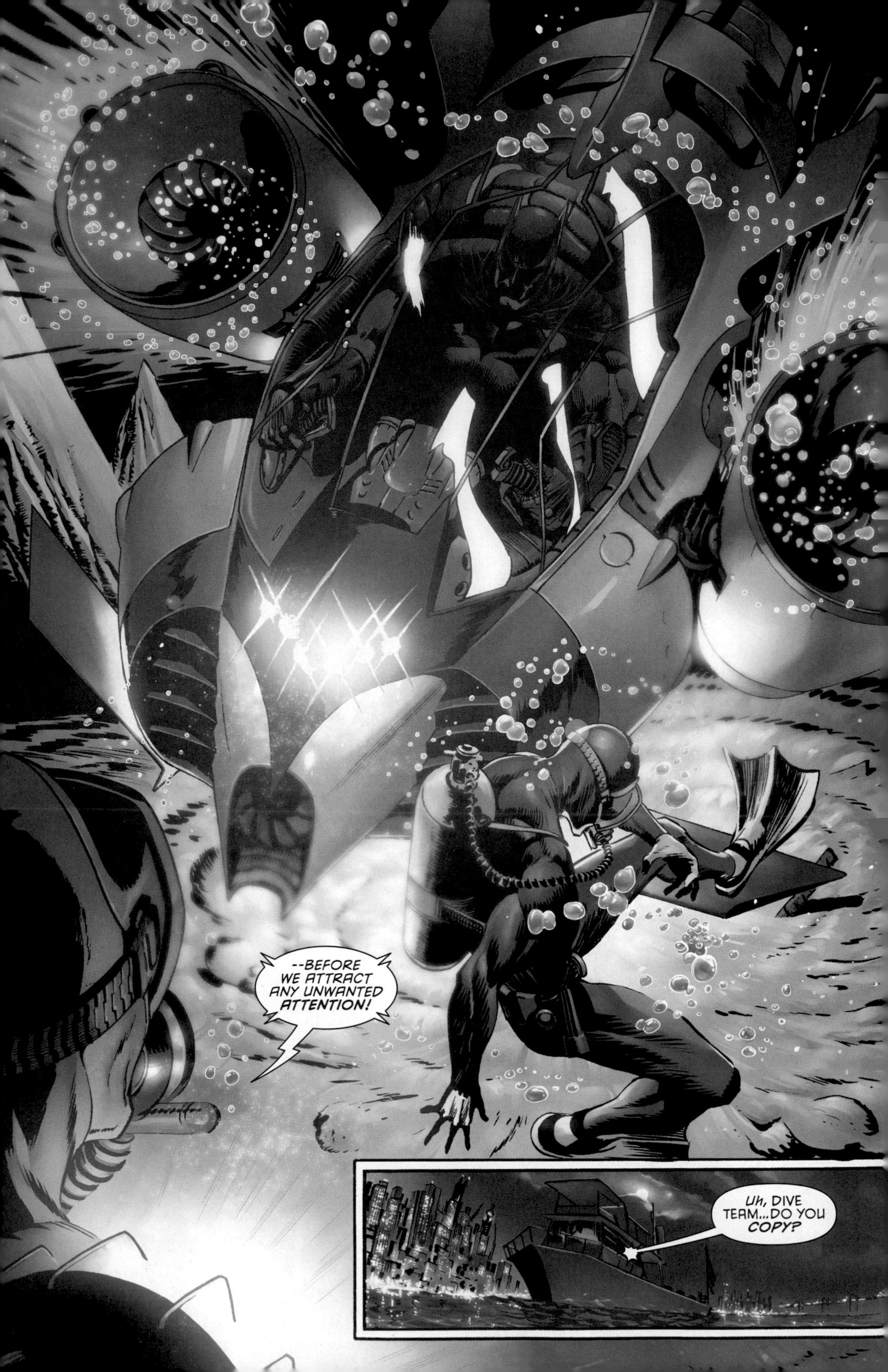
--BEFORE WE ATTRACT ANY UNWANTED ATTENTION!
Uh, DIVE TEAM...DO YOU COPY?

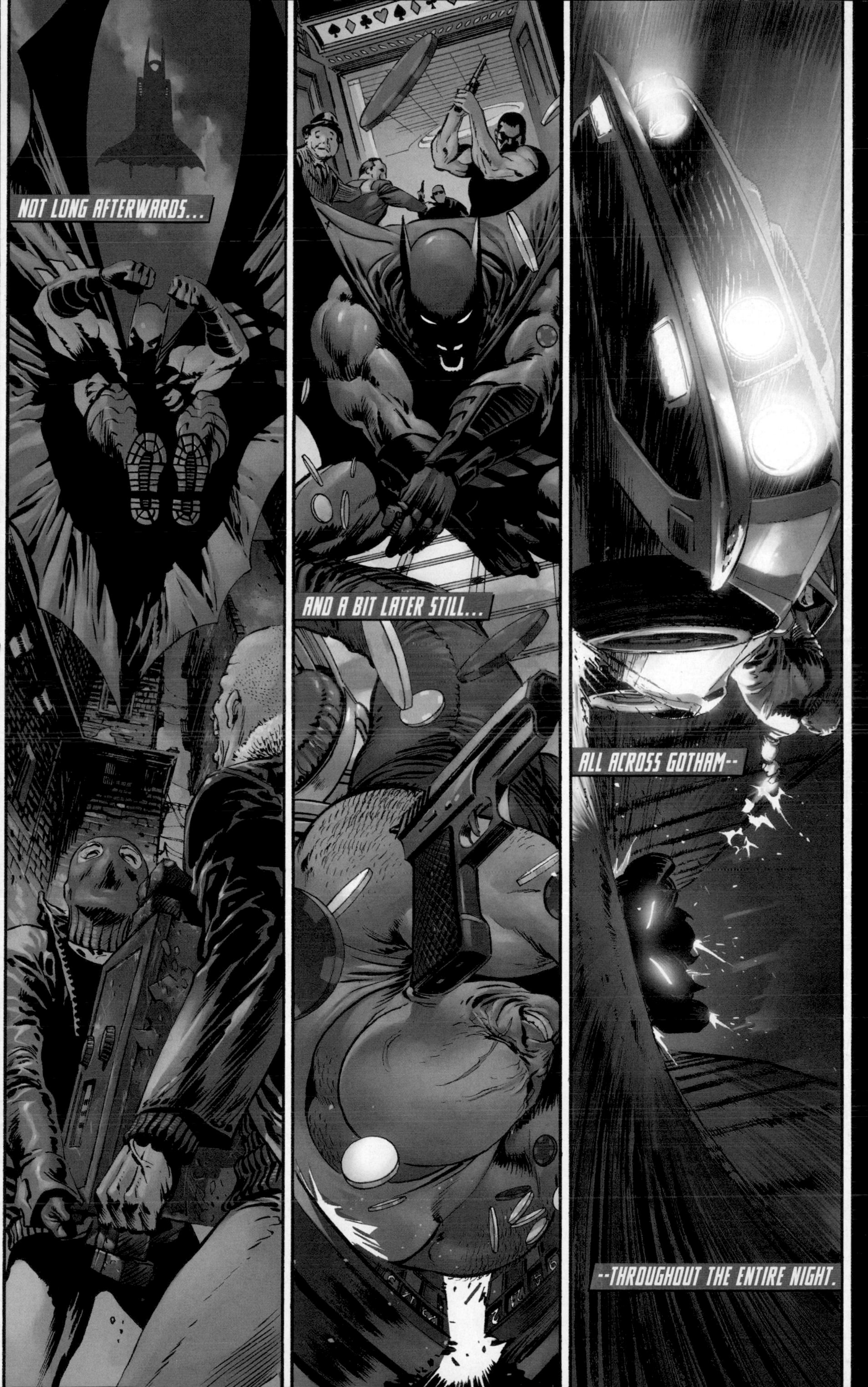
NOT LONG AFTERWARDS...
AND A BIT LATER STILL...
ALL ACROSS GOTHAM--
--THROUGHOUT THE ENTIRE NIGHT.

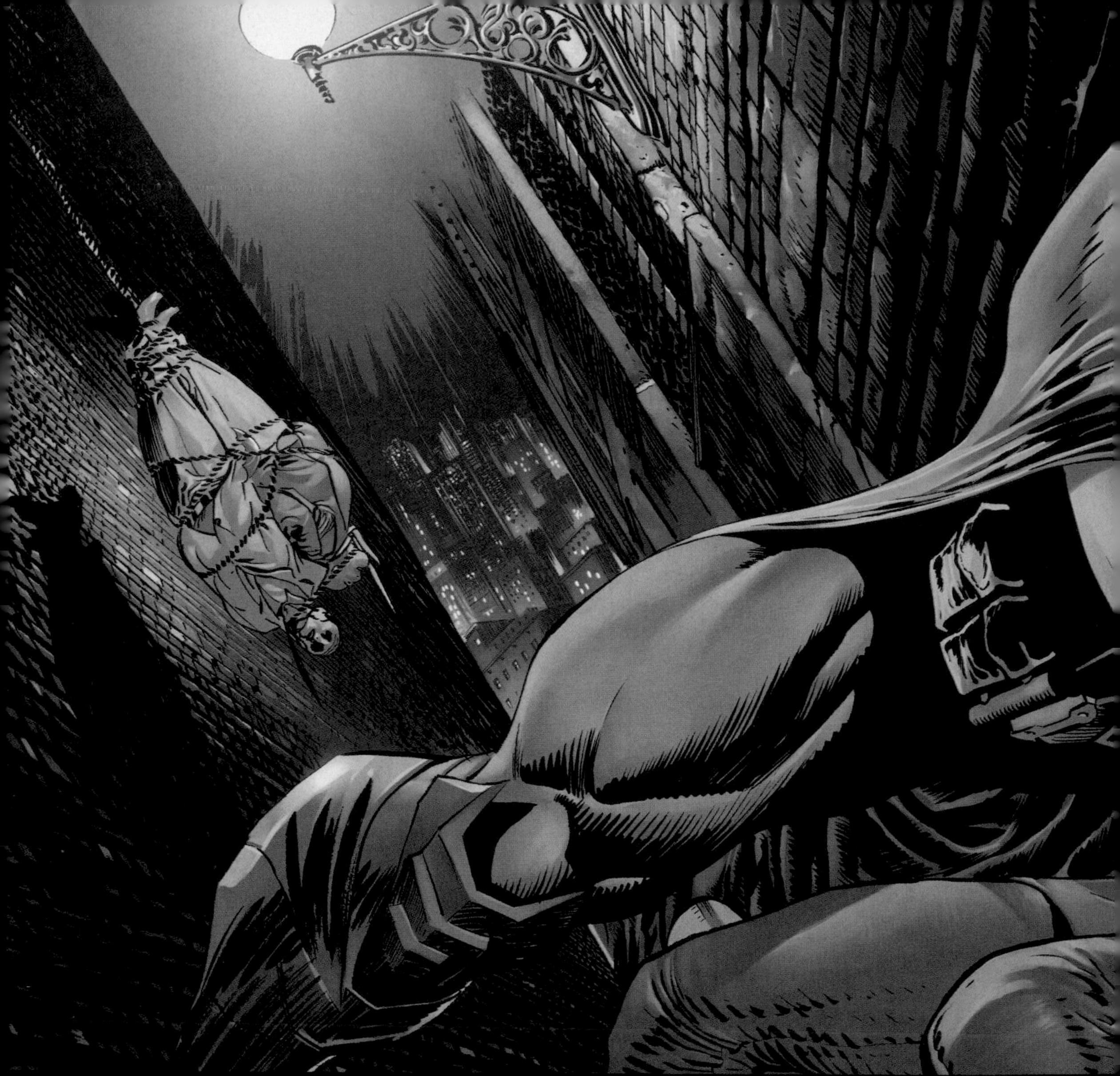

SCOTT SNYDER & JAMES TYNION IV STORY

JOHN LAYMAN SCRIPT   RAY FAWKES & TIM SEELEY CONTRIBUTING WRITERS

GUILLEM MARCH ART

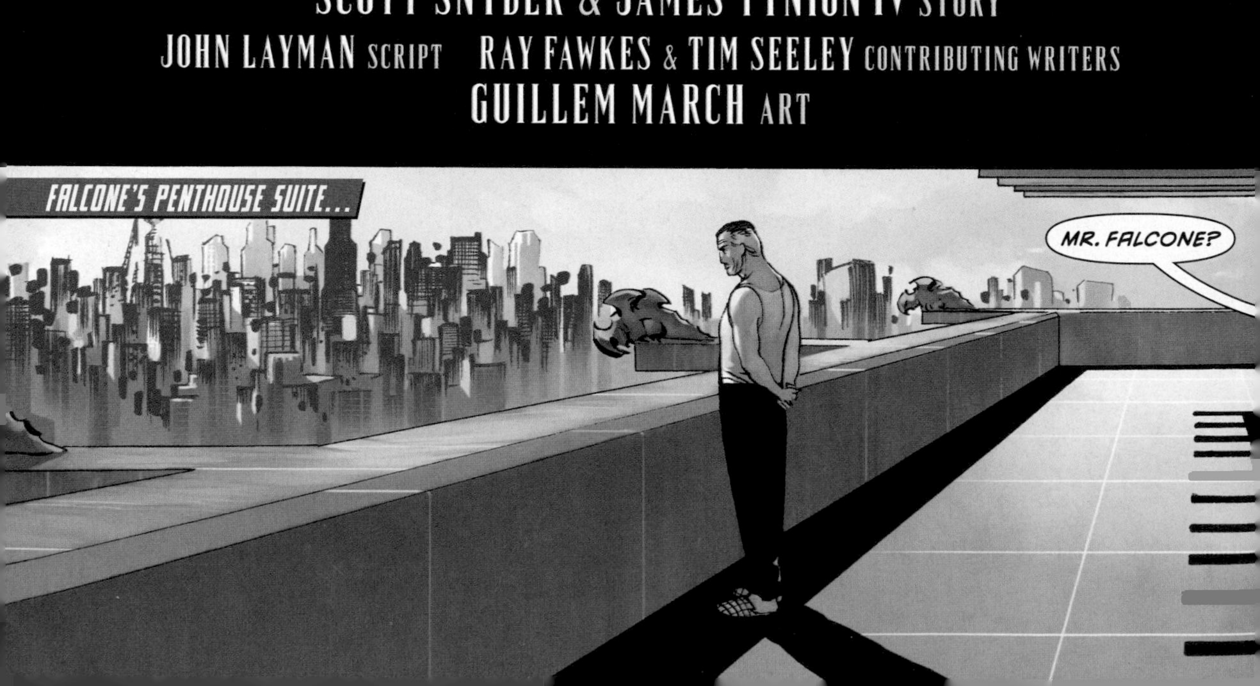
FALCONE'S PENTHOUSE SUITE...
MR. FALCONE?

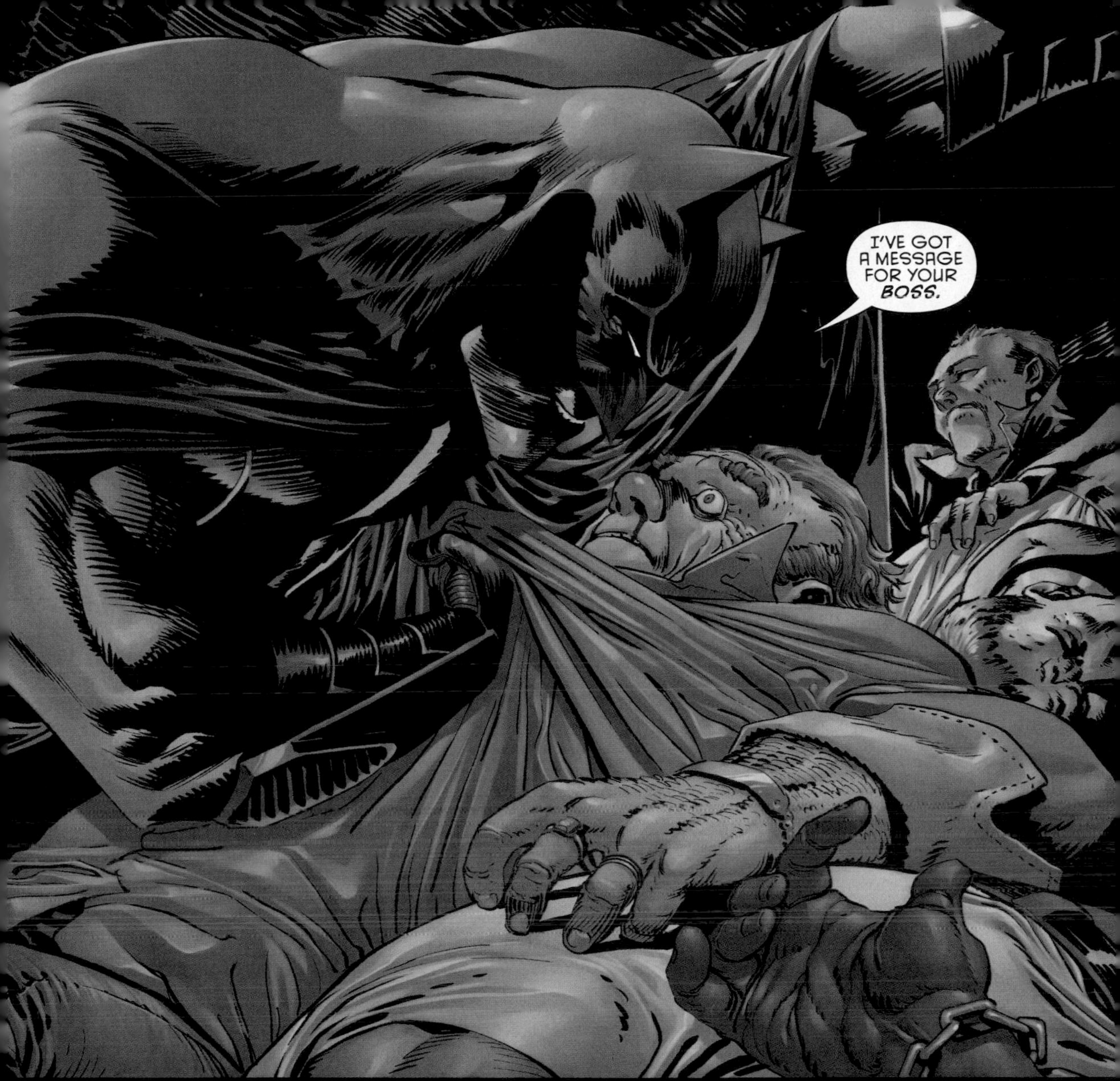
I'VE GOT A MESSAGE FOR YOUR *BOSS.*

TOMEU MOREY COLORS STEVE WANDS LETTERS
ANDY KUBERT & BRAD ANDERSON COVER

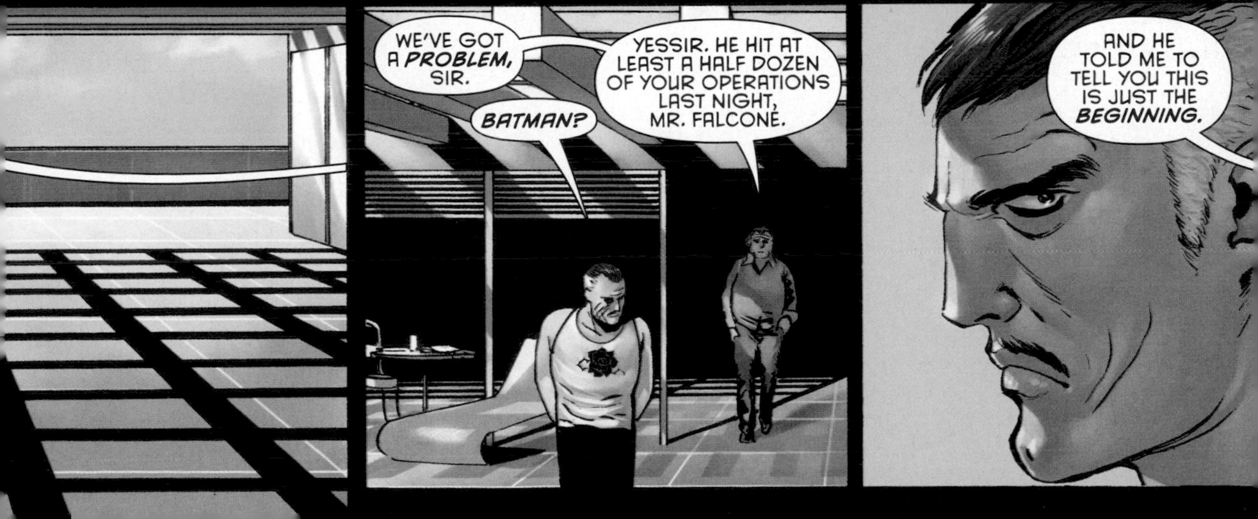
WE'VE GOT A *PROBLEM,* SIR.
BATMAN?
YESSIR. HE HIT AT LEAST A HALF DOZEN OF YOUR OPERATIONS LAST NIGHT, MR. FALCONE.
AND HE TOLD ME TO TELL YOU THIS IS JUST THE *BEGINNING.*

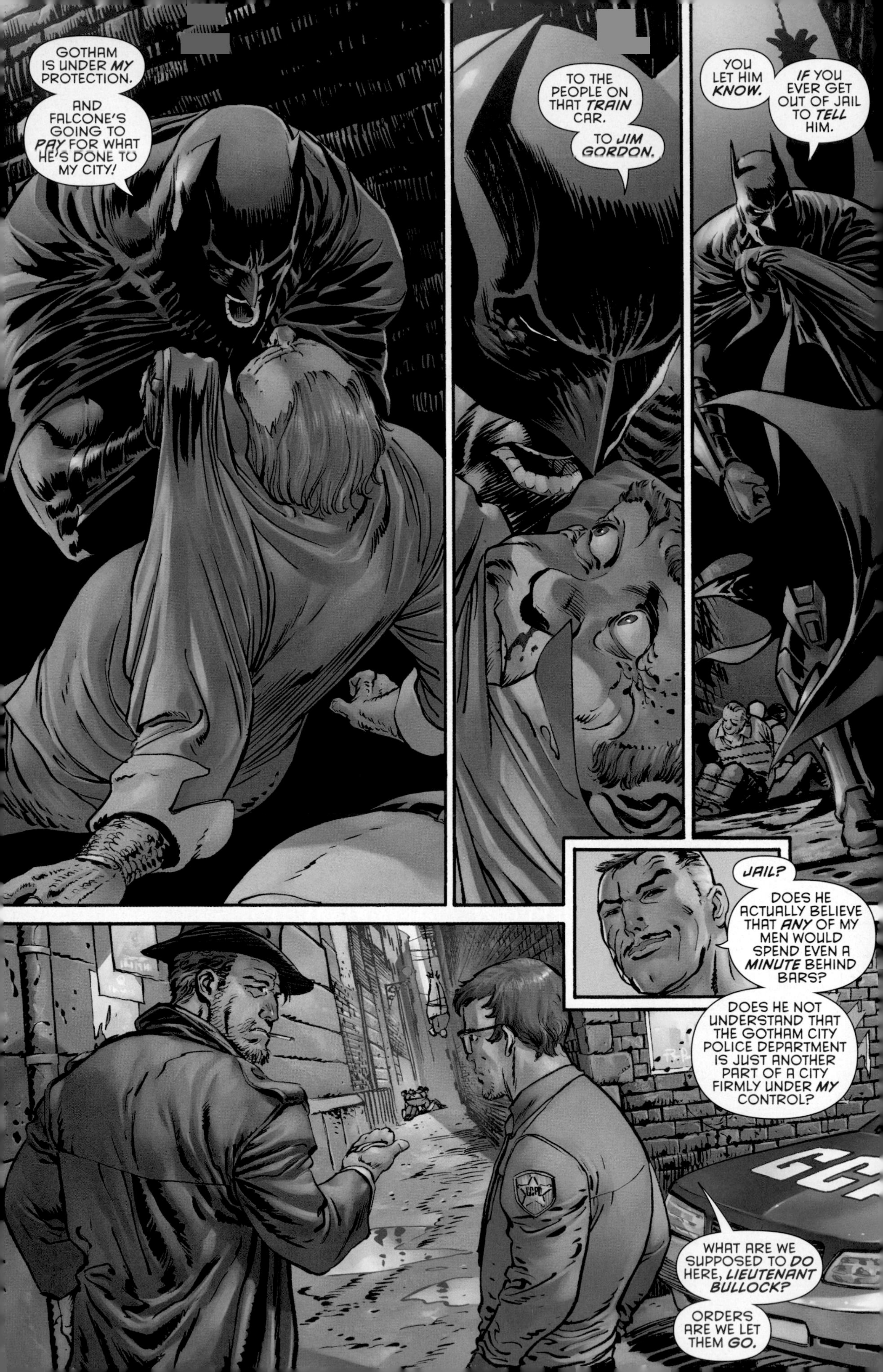
GOTHAM IS UNDER MY PROTECTION.
AND FALCONE'S GOING TO PAY FOR WHAT HE'S DONE TO MY CITY!
TO THE PEOPLE ON THAT TRAIN CAR.
TO JIM GORDON.
YOU LET HIM KNOW.
IF YOU EVER GET OUT OF JAIL TO TELL HIM.
JAIL?
DOES HE ACTUALLY BELIEVE THAT ANY OF MY MEN WOULD SPEND EVEN A MINUTE BEHIND BARS?
DOES HE NOT UNDERSTAND THAT THE GOTHAM CITY POLICE DEPARTMENT IS JUST ANOTHER PART OF A CITY FIRMLY UNDER MY CONTROL?
WHAT ARE WE SUPPOSED TO DO HERE, LIEUTENANT BULLOCK?
ORDERS ARE WE LET THEM GO.

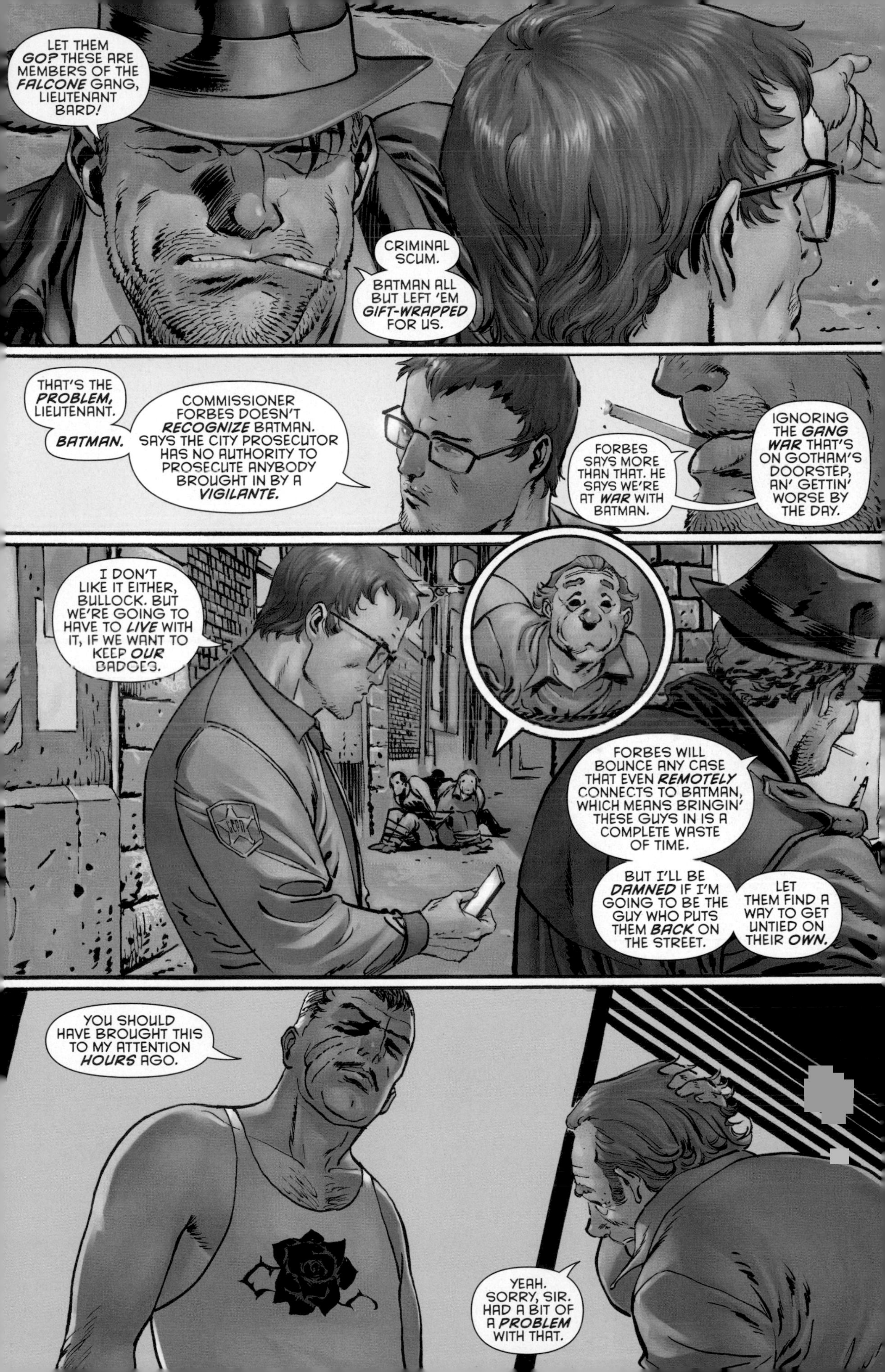
LET THEM GO? THESE ARE MEMBERS OF THE FALCONE GANG, LIEUTENANT BARD!
CRIMINAL SCUM.
BATMAN ALL BUT LEFT 'EM GIFT-WRAPPED FOR US.
THAT'S THE PROBLEM, LIEUTENANT.
BATMAN.
COMMISSIONER FORBES DOESN'T RECOGNIZE BATMAN. SAYS THE CITY PROSECUTOR HAS NO AUTHORITY TO PROSECUTE ANYBODY BROUGHT IN BY A VIGILANTE.
FORBES SAYS MORE THAN THAT. HE SAYS WE'RE AT WAR WITH BATMAN.
IGNORING THE GANG WAR THAT'S ON GOTHAM'S DOORSTEP, AN' GETTIN' WORSE BY THE DAY.
I DON'T LIKE IT EITHER, BULLOCK. BUT WE'RE GOING TO HAVE TO LIVE WITH IT, IF WE WANT TO KEEP OUR BADGES.
FORBES WILL BOUNCE ANY CASE THAT EVEN REMOTELY CONNECTS TO BATMAN, WHICH MEANS BRINGIN' THESE GUYS IN IS A COMPLETE WASTE OF TIME.
BUT I'LL BE DAMNED IF I'M GOING TO BE THE GUY WHO PUTS THEM BACK ON THE STREET.
LET THEM FIND A WAY TO GET UNTIED ON THEIR OWN.
YOU SHOULD HAVE BROUGHT THIS TO MY ATTENTION HOURS AGO.
YEAH. SORRY, SIR. HAD A BIT OF A PROBLEM WITH THAT.

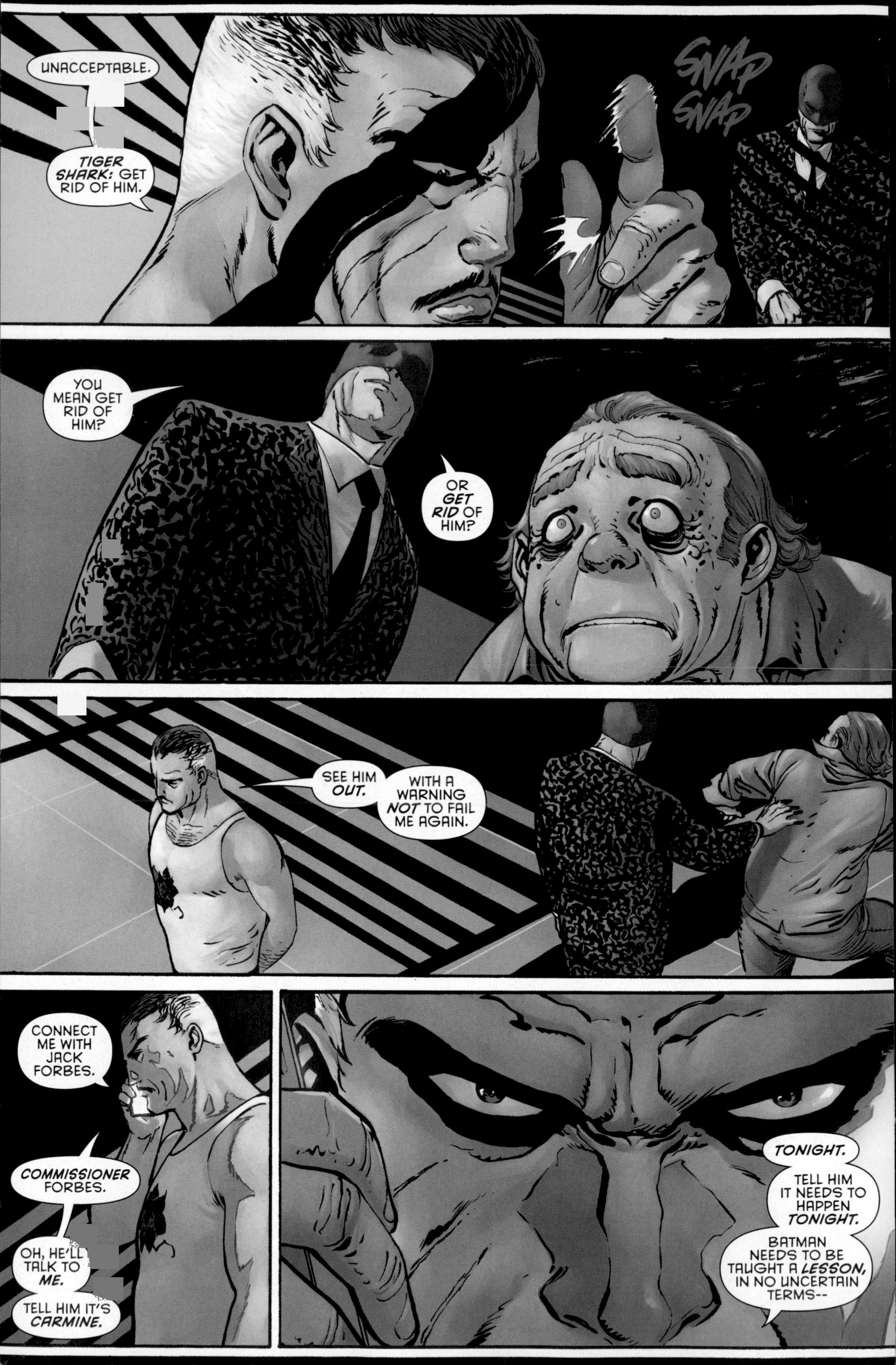
UNACCEPTABLE.
TIGER SHARK: GET RID OF HIM.
SNAP SNAP
YOU MEAN GET RID OF HIM?
OR GET RID OF HIM?
SEE HIM OUT.
WITH A WARNING NOT TO FAIL ME AGAIN.
CONNECT ME WITH JACK FORBES.
COMMISSIONER FORBES.
OH, HE'LL TALK TO ME.
TELL HIM IT'S CARMINE.
TONIGHT.
TELL HIM IT NEEDS TO HAPPEN TONIGHT.
BATMAN NEEDS TO BE TAUGHT A LESSON, IN NO UNCERTAIN TERMS--

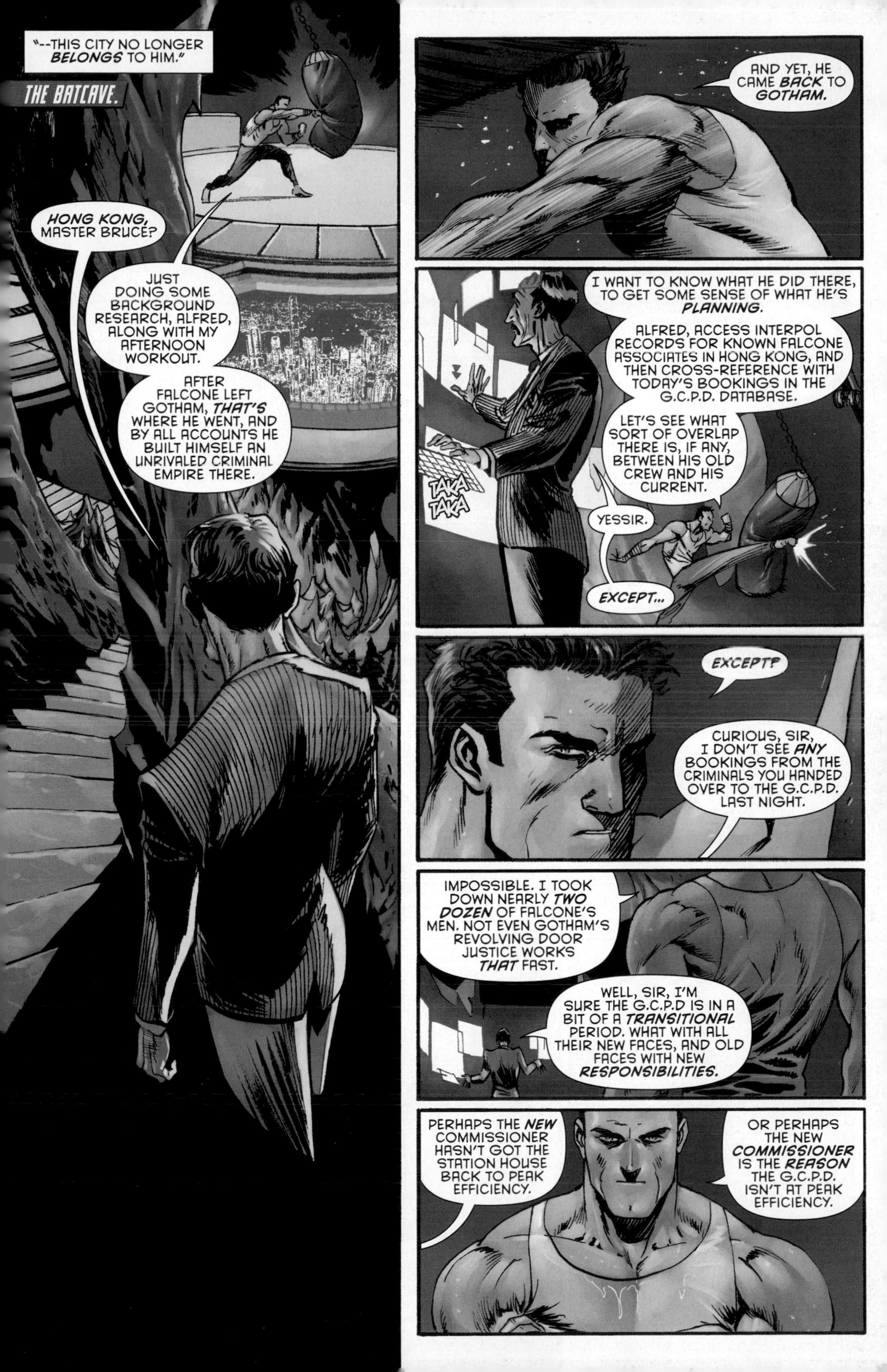
"--THIS CITY NO LONGER BELONGS TO HIM."
THE BATCAVE.
HONG KONG, MASTER BRUCE?
JUST DOING SOME BACKGROUND RESEARCH, ALFRED, ALONG WITH MY AFTERNOON WORKOUT.
AFTER FALCONE LEFT GOTHAM, THAT'S WHERE HE WENT, AND BY ALL ACCOUNTS HE BUILT HIMSELF AN UNRIVALED CRIMINAL EMPIRE THERE.
AND YET, HE CAME BACK TO GOTHAM.
I WANT TO KNOW WHAT HE DID THERE, TO GET SOME SENSE OF WHAT HE'S PLANNING.
ALFRED, ACCESS INTERPOL RECORDS FOR KNOWN FALCONE ASSOCIATES IN HONG KONG, AND THEN CROSS-REFERENCE WITH TODAY'S BOOKINGS IN THE G.C.P.D. DATABASE.
LET'S SEE WHAT SORT OF OVERLAP THERE IS, IF ANY, BETWEEN HIS OLD CREW AND HIS CURRENT.
TAKA TAKA
YESSIR.
EXCEPT...
EXCEPT?
CURIOUS, SIR, I DON'T SEE ANY BOOKINGS FROM THE CRIMINALS YOU HANDED OVER TO THE G.C.P.D. LAST NIGHT.
IMPOSSIBLE. I TOOK DOWN NEARLY TWO DOZEN OF FALCONE'S MEN. NOT EVEN GOTHAM'S REVOLVING DOOR JUSTICE WORKS THAT FAST.
WELL, SIR, I'M SURE THE G.C.P.D IS IN A BIT OF A TRANSITIONAL PERIOD. WHAT WITH ALL THEIR NEW FACES, AND OLD FACES WITH NEW RESPONSIBILITIES.
PERHAPS THE NEW COMMISSIONER HASN'T GOT THE STATION HOUSE BACK TO PEAK EFFICIENCY.
OR PERHAPS THE NEW COMMISSIONER IS THE REASON THE G.C.P.D. ISN'T AT PEAK EFFICIENCY.

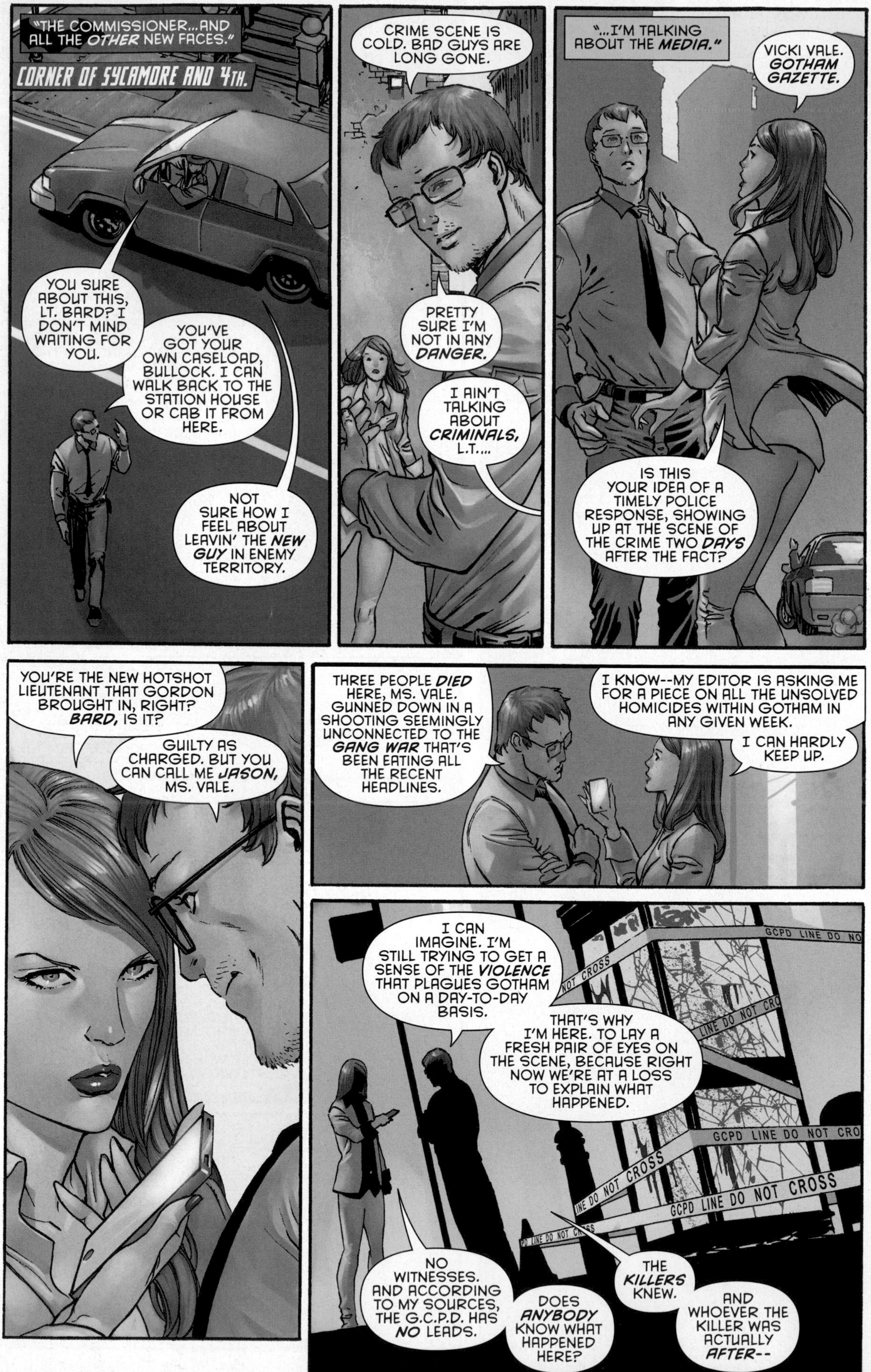
"THE COMMISSIONER...AND ALL THE OTHER NEW FACES."
CORNER OF SYCAMORE AND 4TH.
YOU SURE ABOUT THIS, LT. BARD? I DON'T MIND WAITING FOR YOU.
YOU'VE GOT YOUR OWN CASELOAD, BULLOCK. I CAN WALK BACK TO THE STATION HOUSE OR CAB IT FROM HERE.
NOT SURE HOW I FEEL ABOUT LEAVIN' THE NEW GUY IN ENEMY TERRITORY.
CRIME SCENE IS COLD. BAD GUYS ARE LONG GONE.
PRETTY SURE I'M NOT IN ANY DANGER.
I AIN'T TALKING ABOUT CRIMINALS, L.T....
"...I'M TALKING ABOUT THE MEDIA."
VICKI VALE. GOTHAM GAZETTE.
IS THIS YOUR IDEA OF A TIMELY POLICE RESPONSE, SHOWING UP AT THE SCENE OF THE CRIME TWO DAYS AFTER THE FACT?
YOU'RE THE NEW HOTSHOT LIEUTENANT THAT GORDON BROUGHT IN, RIGHT? BARD, IS IT?
GUILTY AS CHARGED. BUT YOU CAN CALL ME JASON, MS. VALE.
THREE PEOPLE DIED HERE, MS. VALE. GUNNED DOWN IN A SHOOTING SEEMINGLY UNCONNECTED TO THE GANG WAR THAT'S BEEN EATING ALL THE RECENT HEADLINES.
I KNOW--MY EDITOR IS ASKING ME FOR A PIECE ON ALL THE UNSOLVED HOMICIDES WITHIN GOTHAM IN ANY GIVEN WEEK.
I CAN HARDLY KEEP UP.
I CAN IMAGINE. I'M STILL TRYING TO GET A SENSE OF THE VIOLENCE THAT PLAGUES GOTHAM ON A DAY-TO-DAY BASIS.
THAT'S WHY I'M HERE. TO LAY A FRESH PAIR OF EYES ON THE SCENE, BECAUSE RIGHT NOW WE'RE AT A LOSS TO EXPLAIN WHAT HAPPENED.
GCPD LINE DO NOT CROSS
NO WITNESSES. AND ACCORDING TO MY SOURCES, THE G.C.P.D. HAS NO LEADS.
DOES ANYBODY KNOW WHAT HAPPENED HERE?
THE KILLERS KNEW.
AND WHOEVER THE KILLER WAS ACTUALLY AFTER--

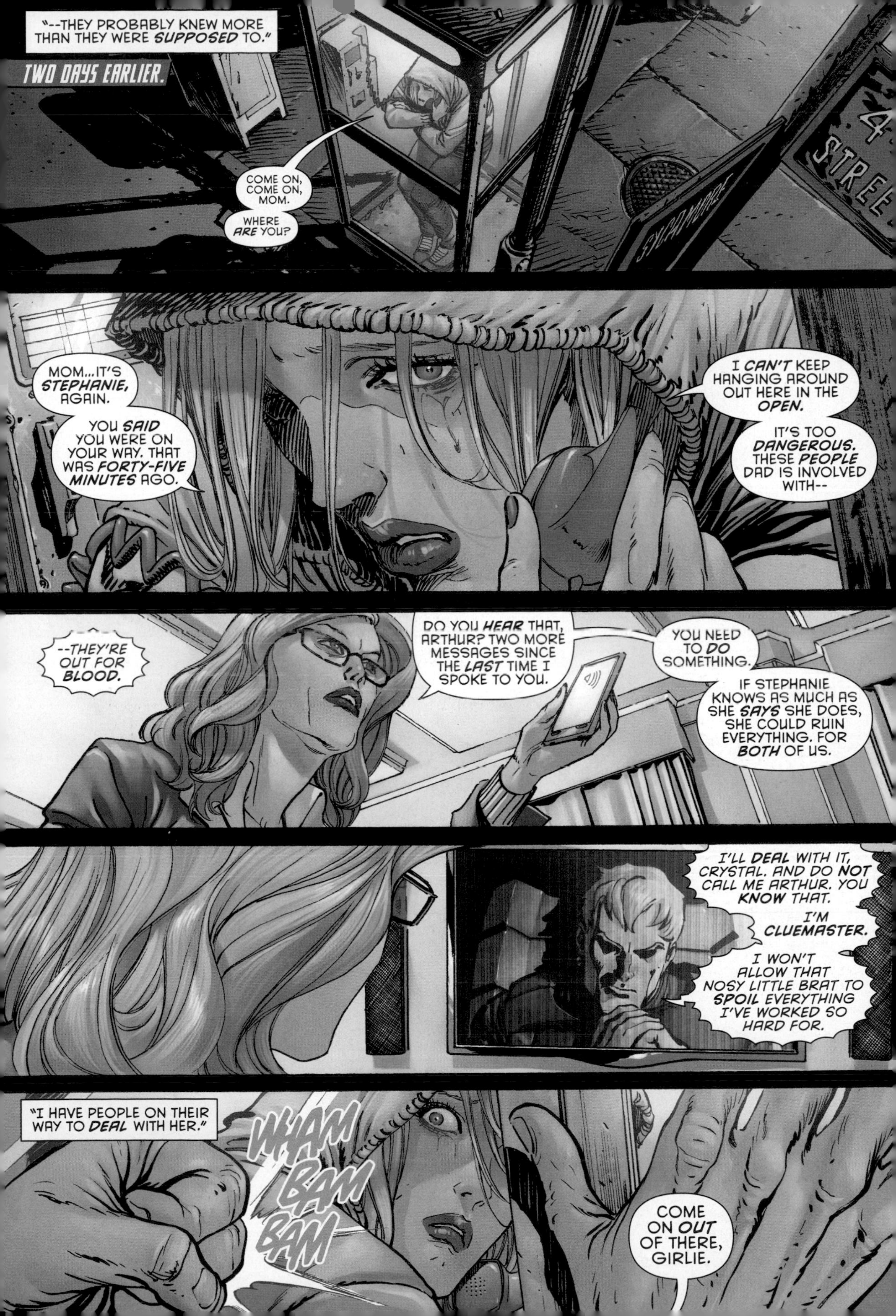
"--THEY PROBABLY KNEW MORE THAN THEY WERE SUPPOSED TO."
TWO DAYS EARLIER.
COME ON, COME ON, MOM.
WHERE ARE YOU?
MOM...IT'S STEPHANIE, AGAIN.
YOU SAID YOU WERE ON YOUR WAY. THAT WAS FORTY-FIVE MINUTES AGO.
I CAN'T KEEP HANGING AROUND OUT HERE IN THE OPEN.
IT'S TOO DANGEROUS. THESE PEOPLE DAD IS INVOLVED WITH--
--THEY'RE OUT FOR BLOOD.
DO YOU HEAR THAT, ARTHUR? TWO MORE MESSAGES SINCE THE LAST TIME I SPOKE TO YOU.
YOU NEED TO DO SOMETHING.
IF STEPHANIE KNOWS AS MUCH AS SHE SAYS SHE DOES, SHE COULD RUIN EVERYTHING. FOR BOTH OF US.
I'LL DEAL WITH IT, CRYSTAL. AND DO NOT CALL ME ARTHUR. YOU KNOW THAT.
I'M CLUEMASTER.
I WON'T ALLOW THAT NOSY LITTLE BRAT TO SPOIL EVERYTHING I'VE WORKED SO HARD FOR.
"I HAVE PEOPLE ON THEIR WAY TO DEAL WITH HER."
WHAM BAM BAM
COME ON OUT OF THERE, GIRLIE.

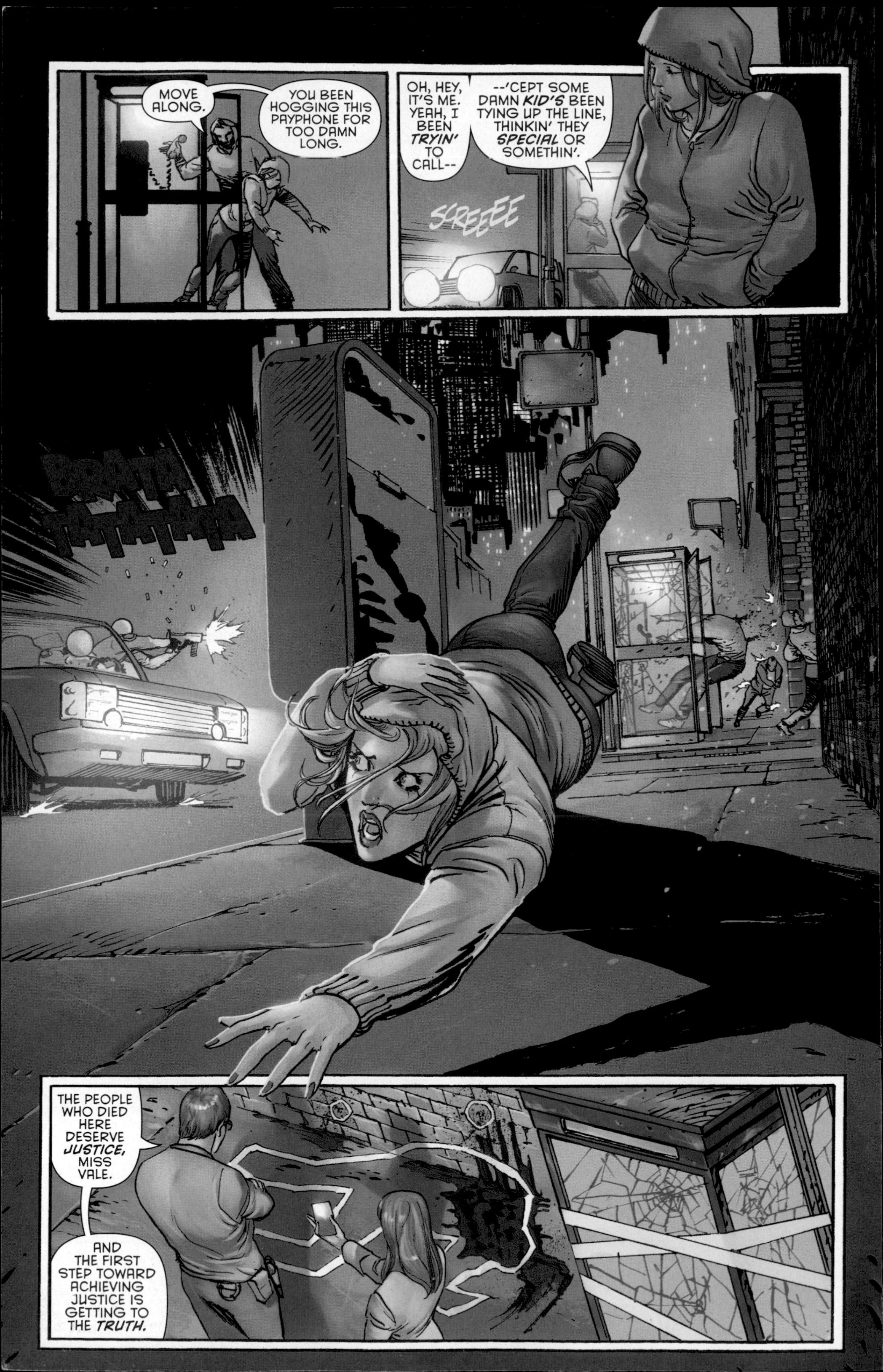
MOVE ALONG.
YOU BEEN HOGGING THIS PAYPHONE FOR TOO DAMN LONG.
OH, HEY, IT'S ME. YEAH, I BEEN *TRYIN'* TO CALL--
--'CEPT SOME DAMN *KID'S* BEEN TYING UP THE LINE, THINKIN' THEY *SPECIAL* OR SOMETHIN'.
SCREEEEE
BRATTA
THE PEOPLE WHO DIED HERE DESERVE *JUSTICE,* MISS VALE.
AND THE FIRST STEP TOWARD ACHIEVING JUSTICE IS GETTING TO THE *TRUTH.*

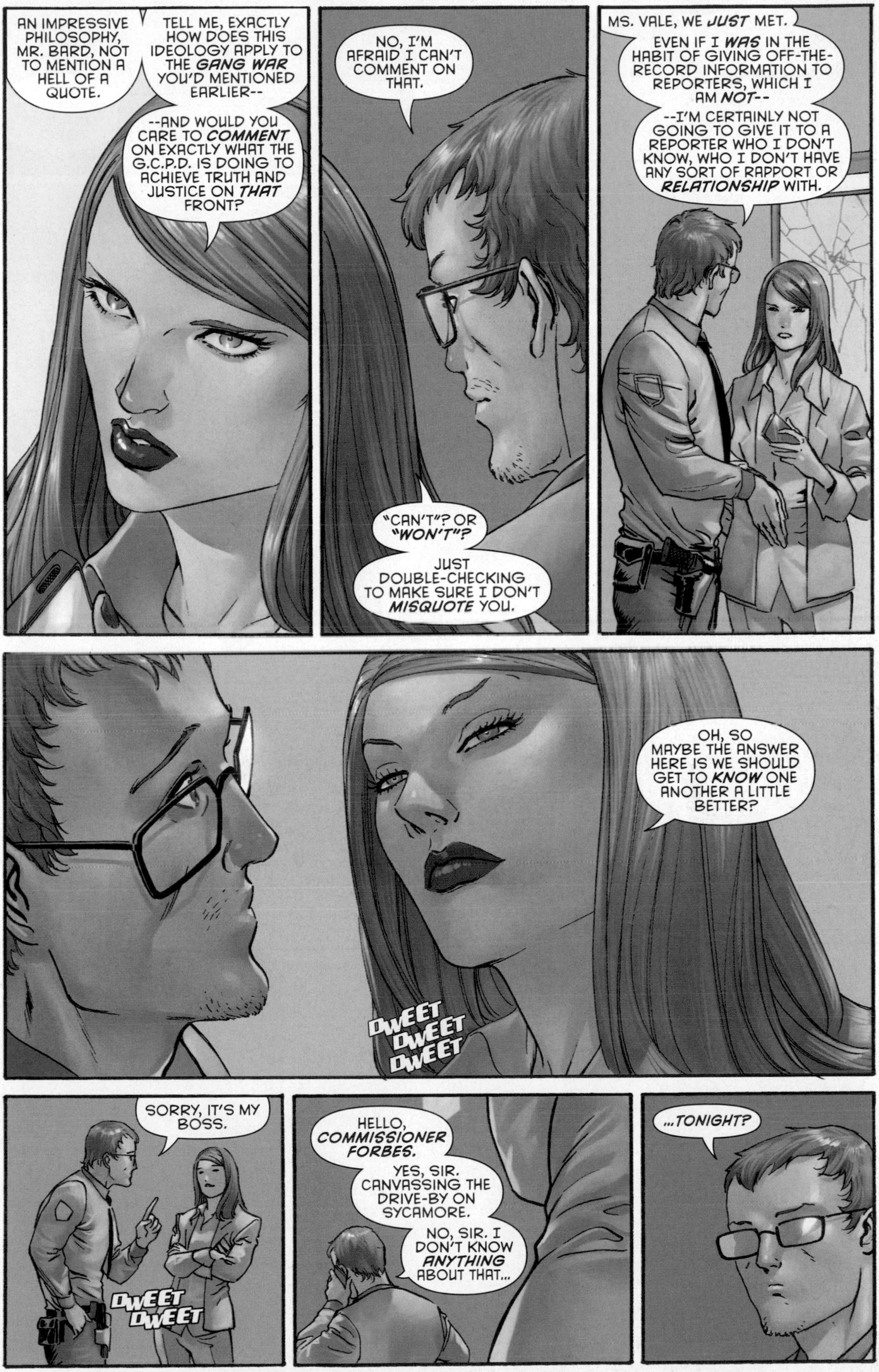
AN IMPRESSIVE PHILOSOPHY, MR. BARD, NOT TO MENTION A HELL OF A QUOTE.
TELL ME, EXACTLY HOW DOES THIS IDEOLOGY APPLY TO THE GANG WAR YOU'D MENTIONED EARLIER--
--AND WOULD YOU CARE TO COMMENT ON EXACTLY WHAT THE G.C.P.D. IS DOING TO ACHIEVE TRUTH AND JUSTICE ON THAT FRONT?
NO, I'M AFRAID I CAN'T COMMENT ON THAT.
"CAN'T"? OR "WON'T"?
JUST DOUBLE-CHECKING TO MAKE SURE I DON'T MISQUOTE YOU.
MS. VALE, WE JUST MET.
EVEN IF I WAS IN THE HABIT OF GIVING OFF-THE-RECORD INFORMATION TO REPORTERS, WHICH I AM NOT--
--I'M CERTAINLY NOT GOING TO GIVE IT TO A REPORTER WHO I DON'T KNOW, WHO I DON'T HAVE ANY SORT OF RAPPORT OR RELATIONSHIP WITH.
OH, SO MAYBE THE ANSWER HERE IS WE SHOULD GET TO KNOW ONE ANOTHER A LITTLE BETTER?
DWEET DWEET DWEET
SORRY, IT'S MY BOSS.
DWEET DWEET
HELLO, COMMISSIONER FORBES.
YES, SIR. CANVASSING THE DRIVE-BY ON SYCAMORE.
NO, SIR. I DON'T KNOW ANYTHING ABOUT THAT...
...TONIGHT?

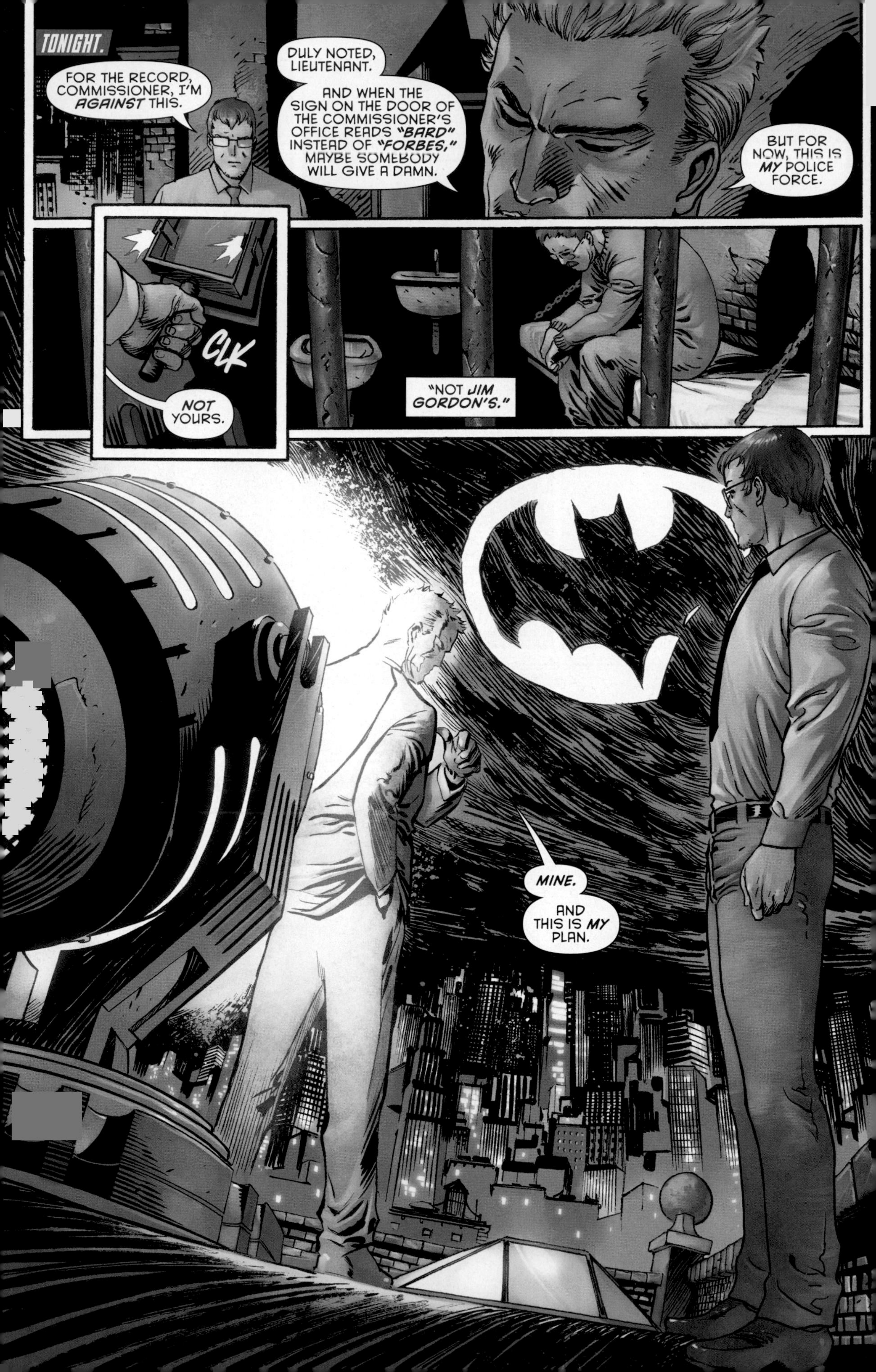
TONIGHT.
FOR THE RECORD, COMMISSIONER, I'M AGAINST THIS.
DULY NOTED, LIEUTENANT.
AND WHEN THE SIGN ON THE DOOR OF THE COMMISSIONER'S OFFICE READS "BARD" INSTEAD OF "FORBES," MAYBE SOMEBODY WILL GIVE A DAMN.
BUT FOR NOW, THIS IS MY POLICE FORCE.
CLK
NOT YOURS.
"NOT JIM GORDON'S."
MINE.
AND THIS IS MY PLAN.

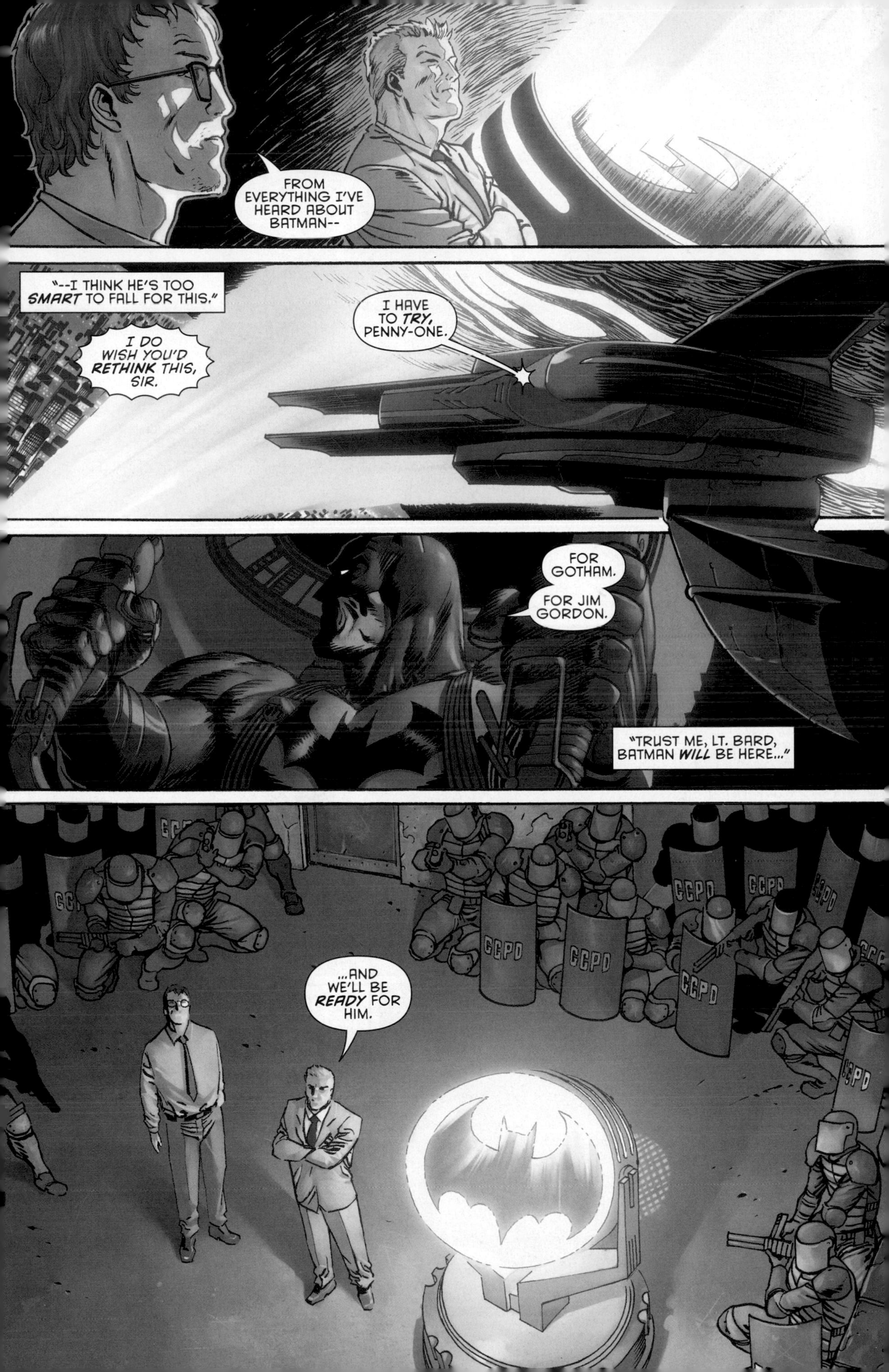
FROM EVERYTHING I'VE HEARD ABOUT BATMAN--
"--I THINK HE'S TOO SMART TO FALL FOR THIS."
I DO WISH YOU'D RETHINK THIS, SIR.
I HAVE TO TRY, PENNY-ONE.
FOR GOTHAM.
FOR JIM GORDON.
"TRUST ME, LT. BARD, BATMAN WILL BE HERE..."
GCPD
...AND WE'LL BE READY FOR HIM.

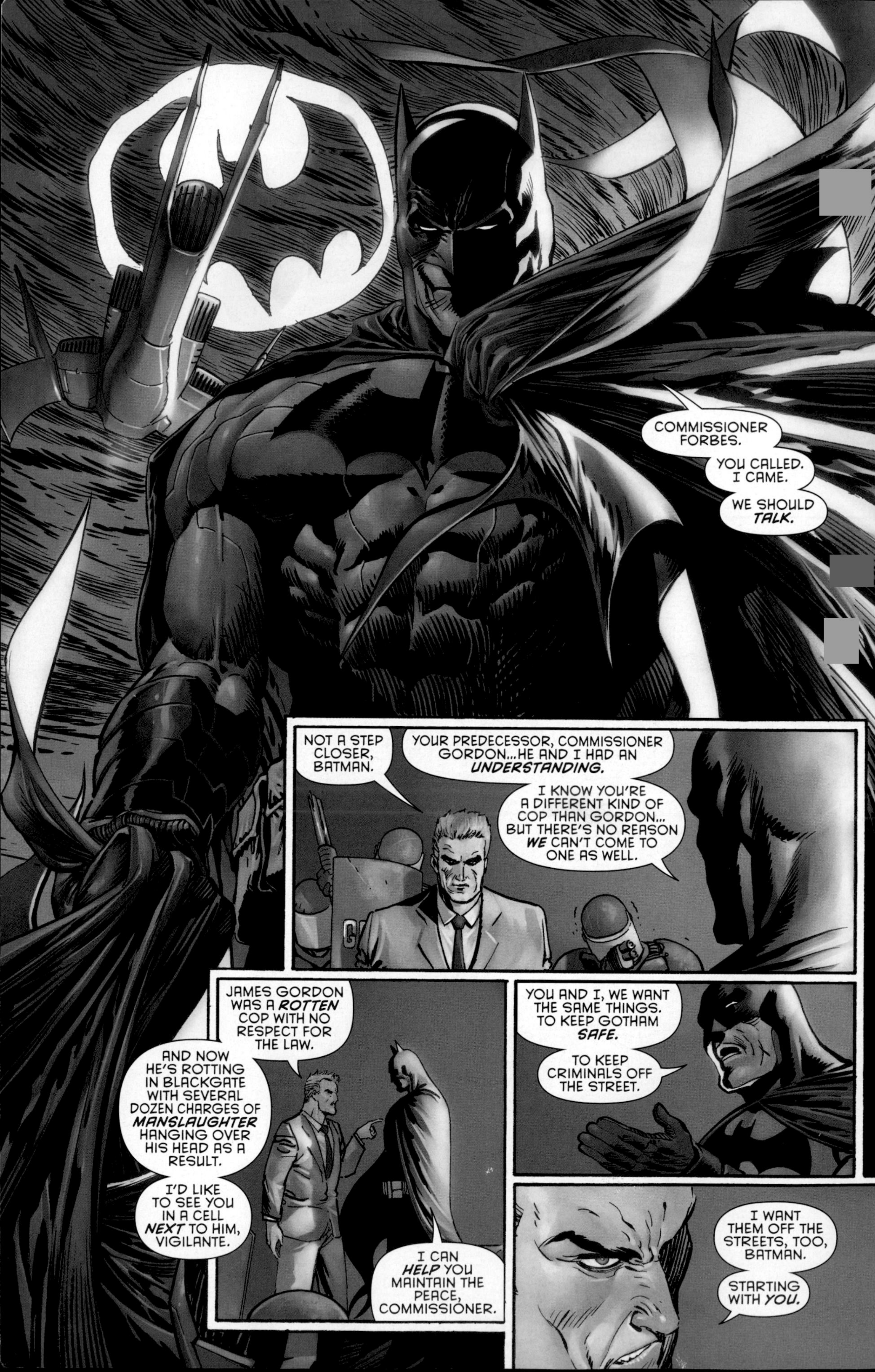
COMMISSIONER FORBES.
YOU CALLED. I CAME.
WE SHOULD TALK.
NOT A STEP CLOSER, BATMAN.
YOUR PREDECESSOR, COMMISSIONER GORDON...HE AND I HAD AN UNDERSTANDING.
I KNOW YOU'RE A DIFFERENT KIND OF COP THAN GORDON... BUT THERE'S NO REASON WE CAN'T COME TO ONE AS WELL.
JAMES GORDON WAS A ROTTEN COP WITH NO RESPECT FOR THE LAW.
AND NOW HE'S ROTTING IN BLACKGATE WITH SEVERAL DOZEN CHARGES OF MANSLAUGHTER HANGING OVER HIS HEAD AS A RESULT.
I'D LIKE TO SEE YOU IN A CELL NEXT TO HIM, VIGILANTE.
I CAN HELP YOU MAINTAIN THE PEACE, COMMISSIONER.
YOU AND I, WE WANT THE SAME THINGS. TO KEEP GOTHAM SAFE.
TO KEEP CRIMINALS OFF THE STREET.
I WANT THEM OFF THE STREETS, TOO, BATMAN.
STARTING WITH YOU.

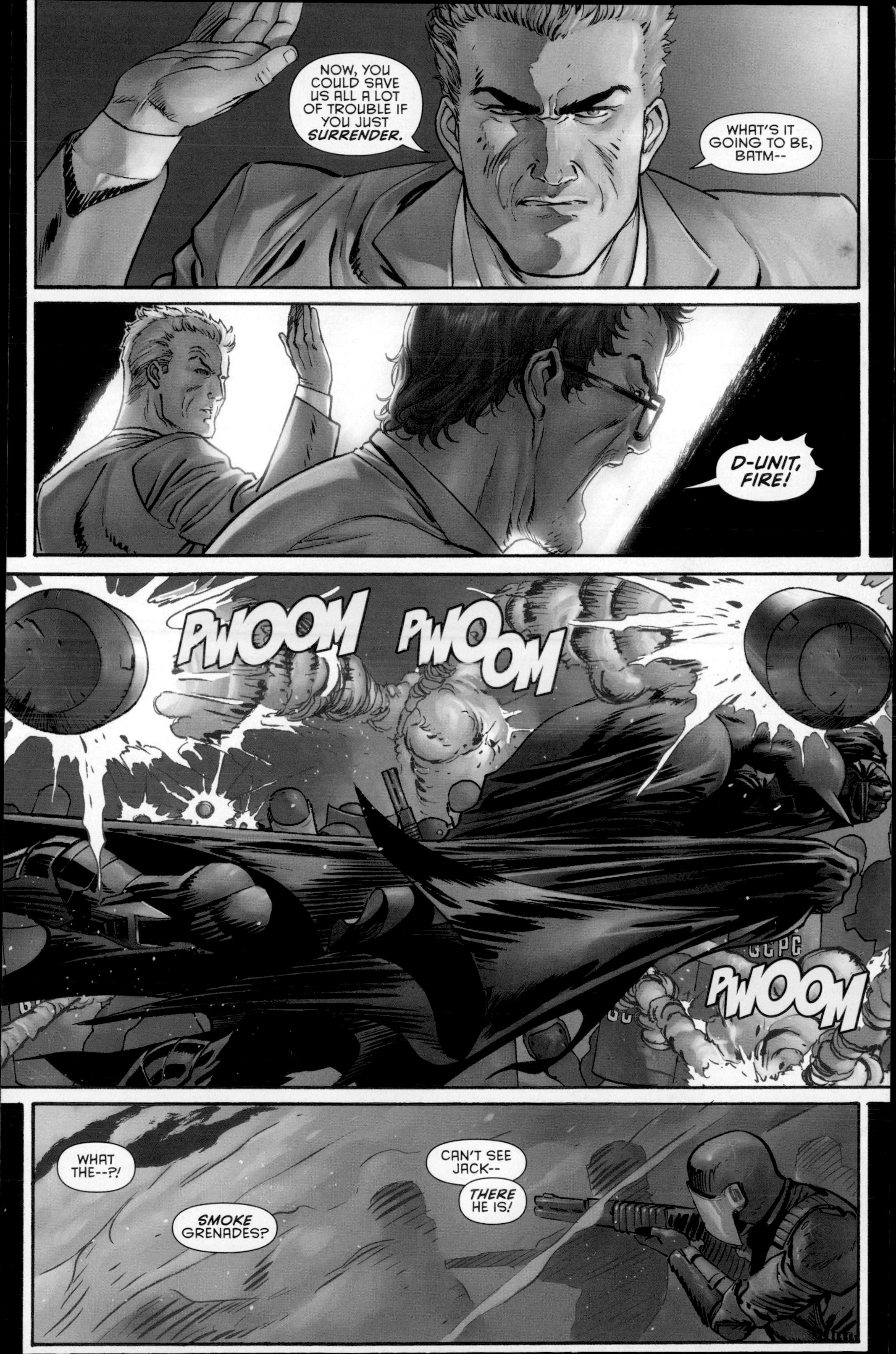

NOW, YOU COULD SAVE US ALL A LOT OF TROUBLE IF YOU JUST SURRENDER.
WHAT'S IT GOING TO BE, BATM--
D-UNIT, FIRE!
PWOOM PWOOM
GCPC
PWOOM
WHAT THE--?!
SMOKE GRENADES?
CAN'T SEE JACK--
THERE HE IS!

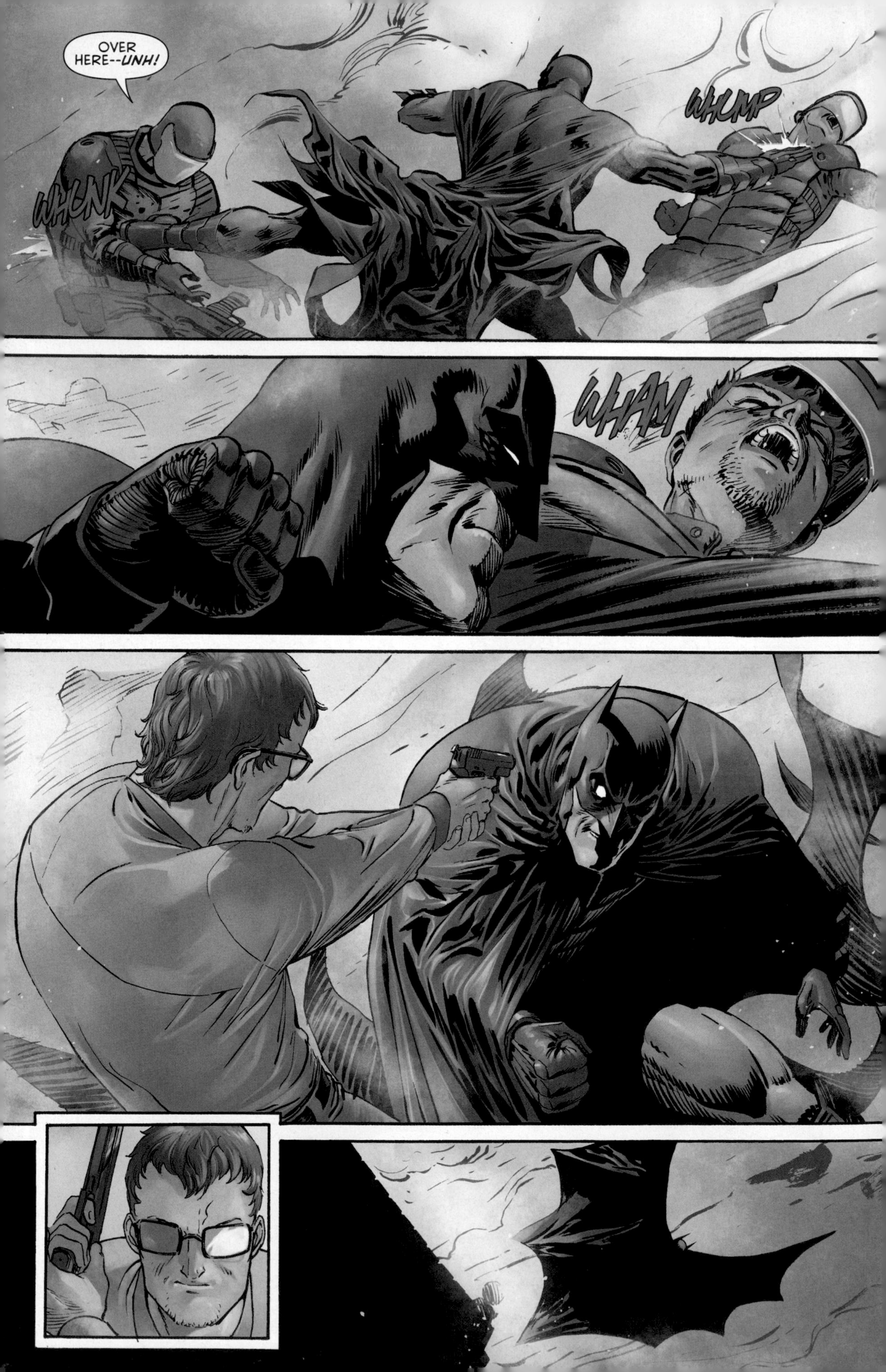
OVER HERE--UNH!
WHUNK
WHUMP
WHAM

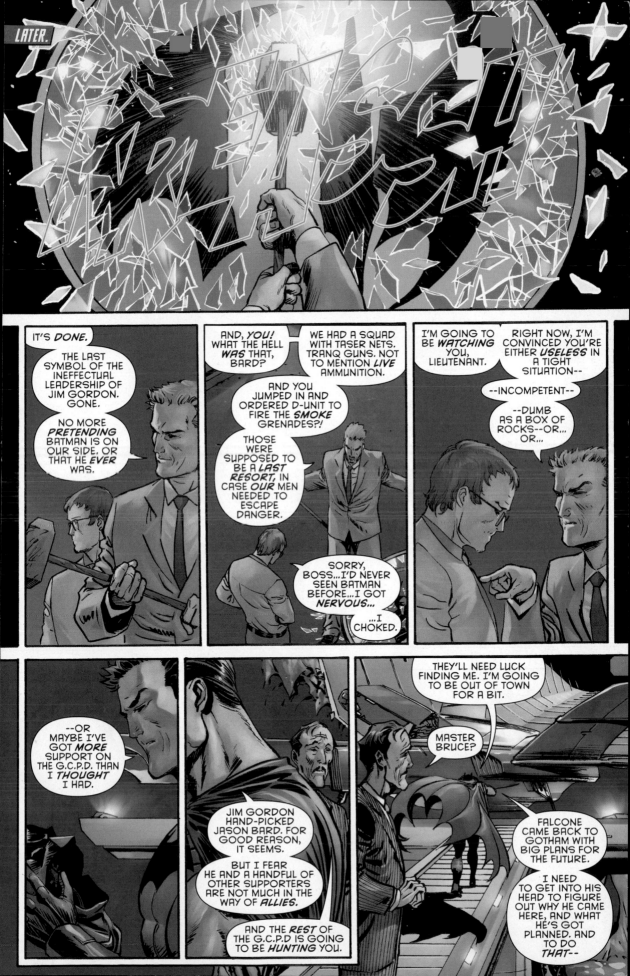

IT'S **DONE.**

THE LAST SYMBOL OF THE INEFFECTUAL LEADERSHIP OF JIM GORDON. GONE.

NO MORE **PRETENDING** BATMAN IS ON OUR SIDE. OR THAT HE **EVER** WAS.

AND, **YOU!** WHAT THE HELL **WAS** THAT, BARD?

WE HAD A SQUAD WITH TASER NETS. TRANQ GUNS. NOT TO MENTION **LIVE** AMMUNITION.

AND YOU JUMPED IN AND ORDERED D-UNIT TO FIRE THE **SMOKE** GRENADES?!

THOSE WERE SUPPOSED TO BE A **LAST RESORT,** IN CASE **OUR** MEN NEEDED TO ESCAPE DANGER.

SORRY, BOSS...I'D NEVER SEEN BATMAN BEFORE...I GOT **NERVOUS...**

...I CHOKED.

I'M GOING TO BE **WATCHING** YOU, LIEUTENANT.

RIGHT NOW, I'M CONVINCED YOU'RE EITHER **USELESS** IN A TIGHT SITUATION--

--INCOMPETENT--

--DUMB AS A BOX OF ROCKS--OR... OR...

--OR MAYBE I'VE GOT **MORE** SUPPORT ON THE G.C.P.D. THAN I **THOUGHT** I HAD.

JIM GORDON HAND-PICKED JASON BARD. FOR GOOD REASON, IT SEEMS.

BUT I FEAR HE AND A HANDFUL OF OTHER SUPPORTERS ARE NOT MUCH IN THE WAY OF **ALLIES.**

AND THE **REST** OF THE G.C.P.D IS GOING TO BE **HUNTING** YOU.

THEY'LL NEED LUCK FINDING ME. I'M GOING TO BE OUT OF TOWN FOR A BIT.

MASTER BRUCE?

FALCONE CAME BACK TO GOTHAM WITH BIG PLANS FOR THE FUTURE.

I NEED TO GET INTO HIS HEAD TO FIGURE OUT WHY HE CAME HERE, AND WHAT HE'S GOT PLANNED. AND TO DO **THAT--**

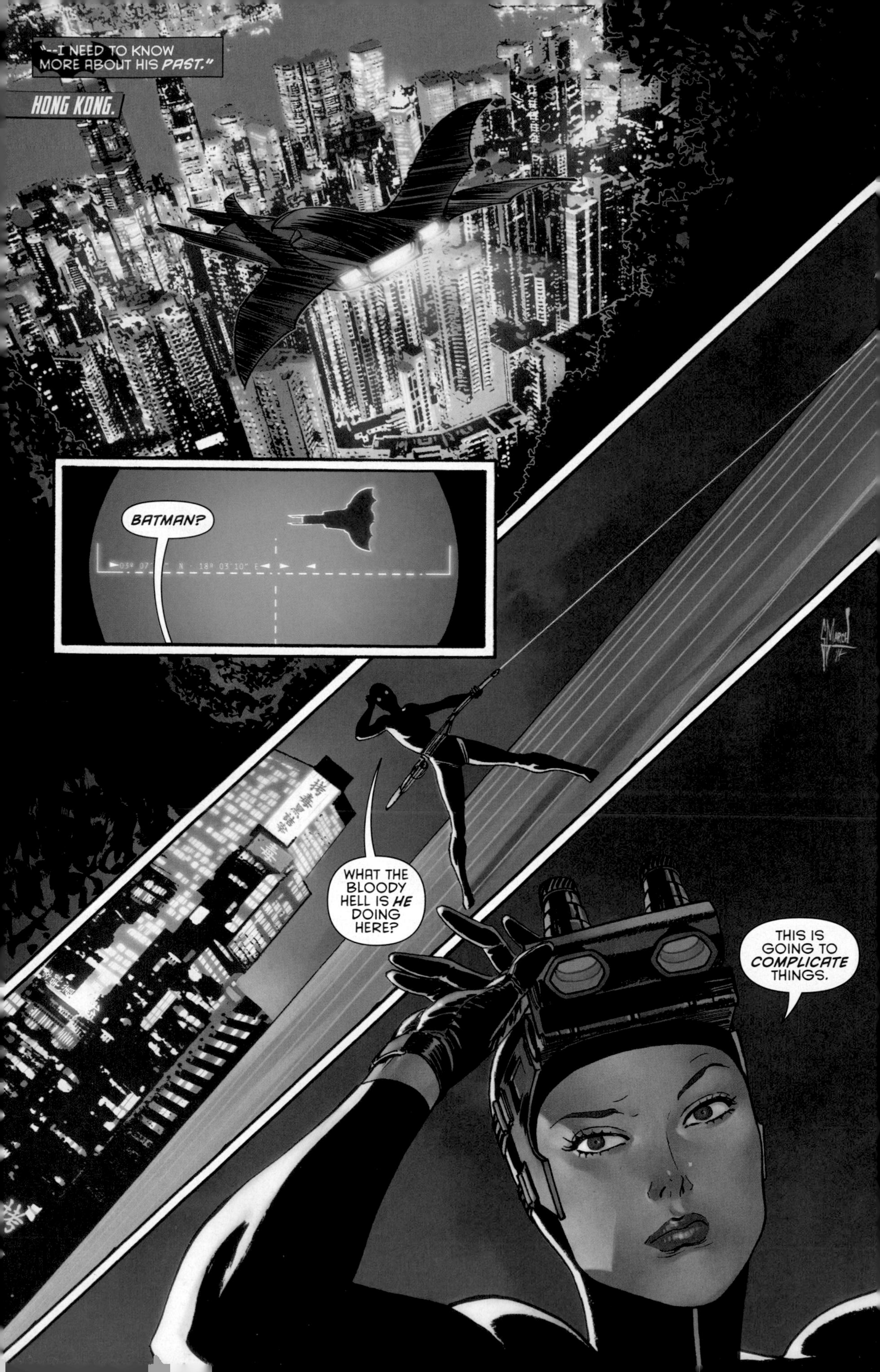
"--I NEED TO KNOW MORE ABOUT HIS PAST."
HONG KONG.
BATMAN?
WHAT THE BLOODY HELL IS HE DOING HERE?
THIS IS GOING TO COMPLICATE THINGS.

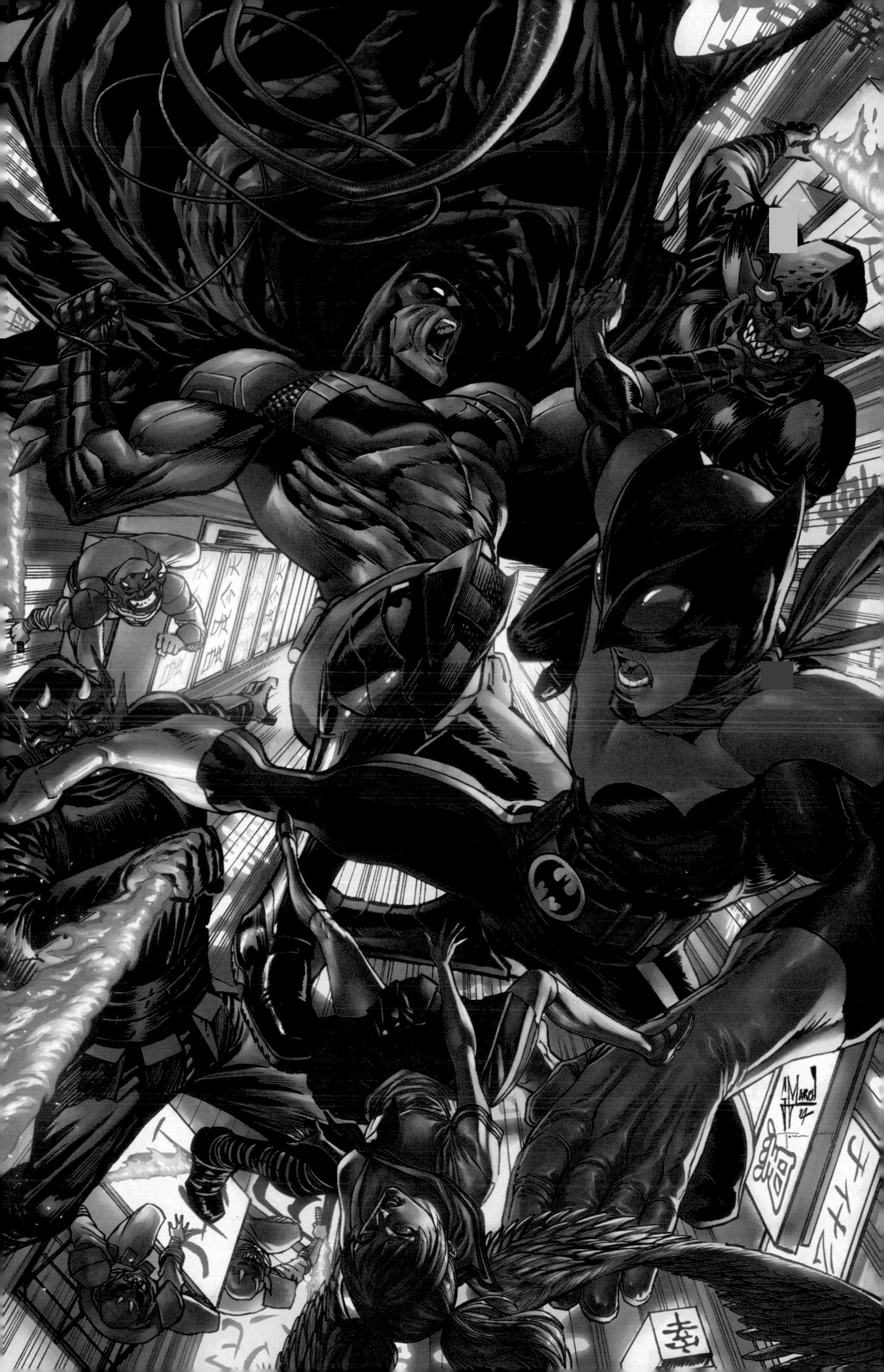

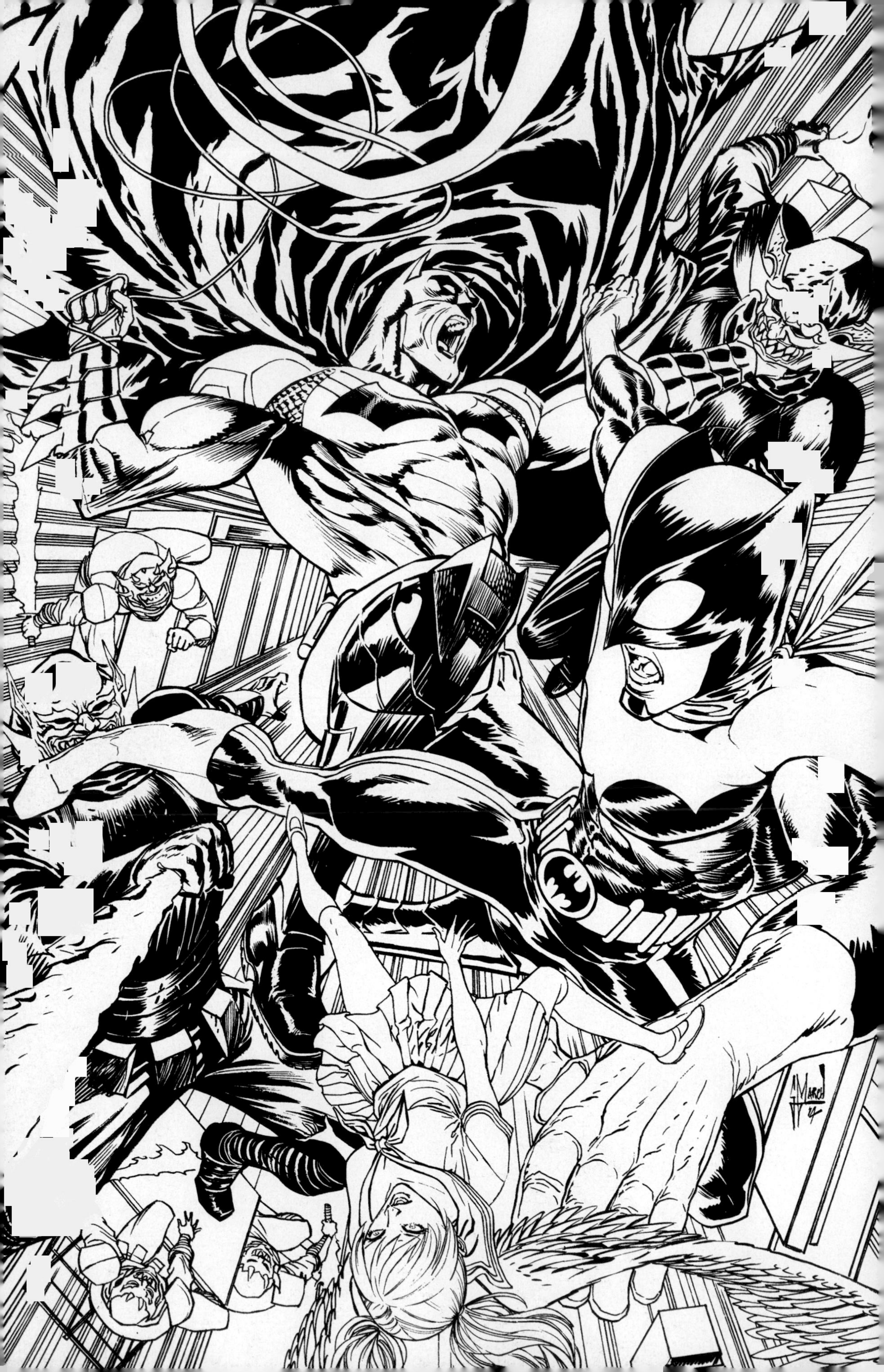

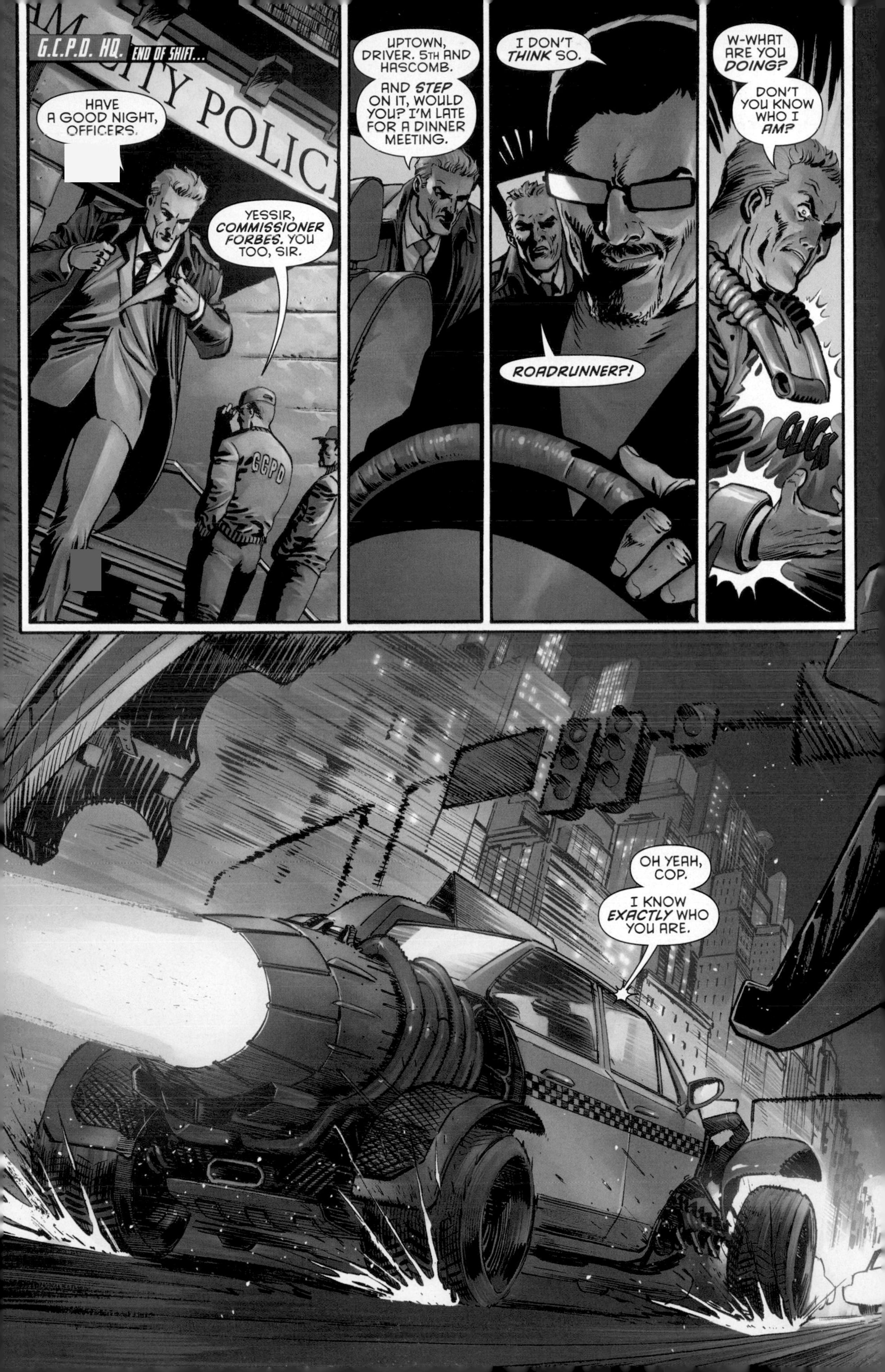

G.C.P.D. HQ.
END OF SHIFT...
HAVE A GOOD NIGHT, OFFICERS.
YESSIR, COMMISSIONER FORBES. YOU TOO, SIR.
UPTOWN, DRIVER. 5TH AND HASCOMB.
AND STEP ON IT, WOULD YOU? I'M LATE FOR A DINNER MEETING.
I DON'T THINK SO.
ROADRUNNER?!
W-WHAT ARE YOU DOING?
DON'T YOU KNOW WHO I AM?
CLICK
OH YEAH, COP.
I KNOW EXACTLY WHO YOU ARE.

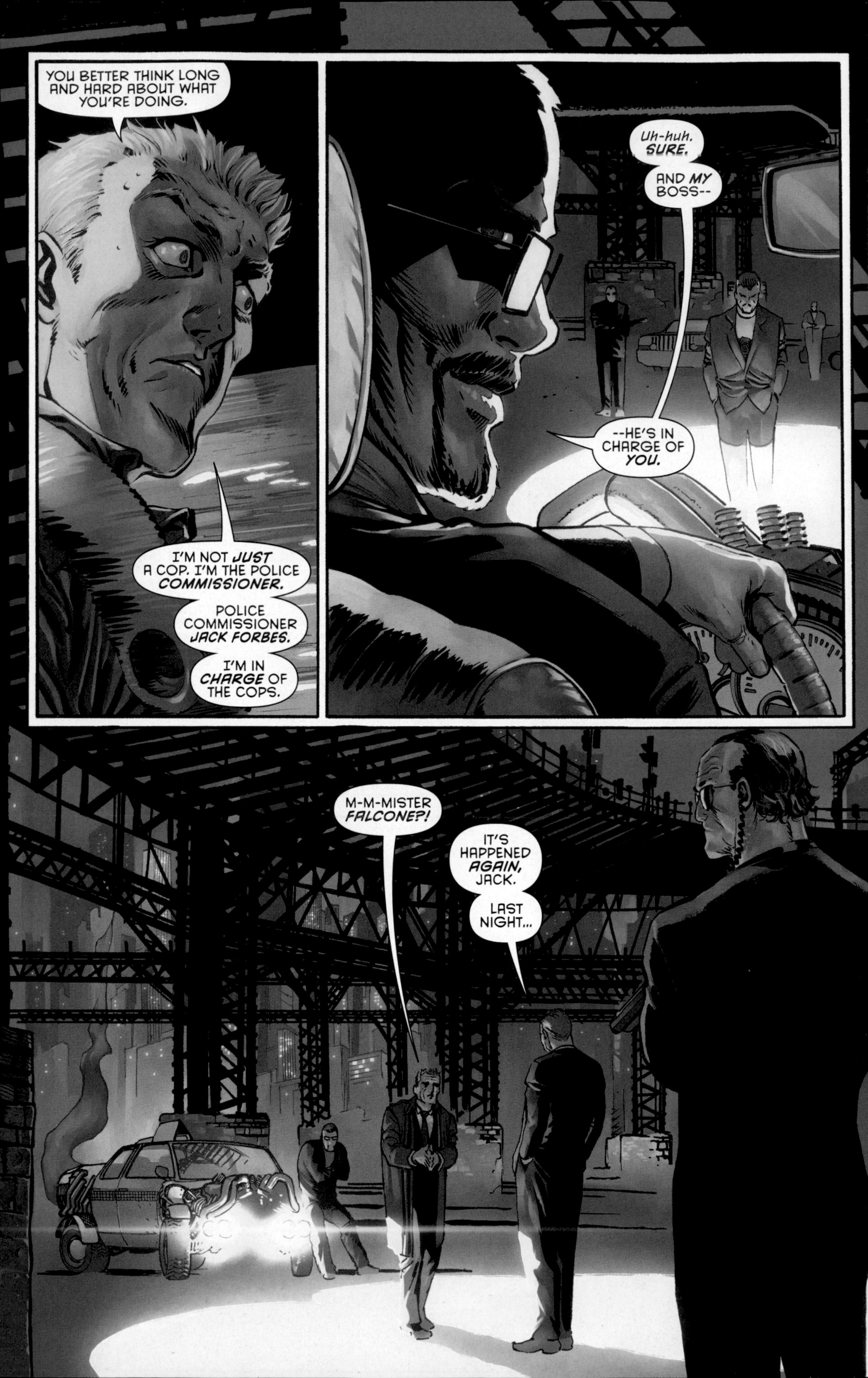
YOU BETTER THINK LONG AND HARD ABOUT WHAT YOU'RE DOING.
I'M NOT *JUST* A COP. I'M THE POLICE *COMMISSIONER.*
POLICE COMMISSIONER *JACK FORBES.*
I'M IN *CHARGE* OF THE COPS.
Uh-huh. SURE.
AND *MY* BOSS--
--HE'S IN CHARGE OF *YOU.*
M-M-MISTER *FALCONE?!*
IT'S HAPPENED *AGAIN,* JACK.
LAST NIGHT...

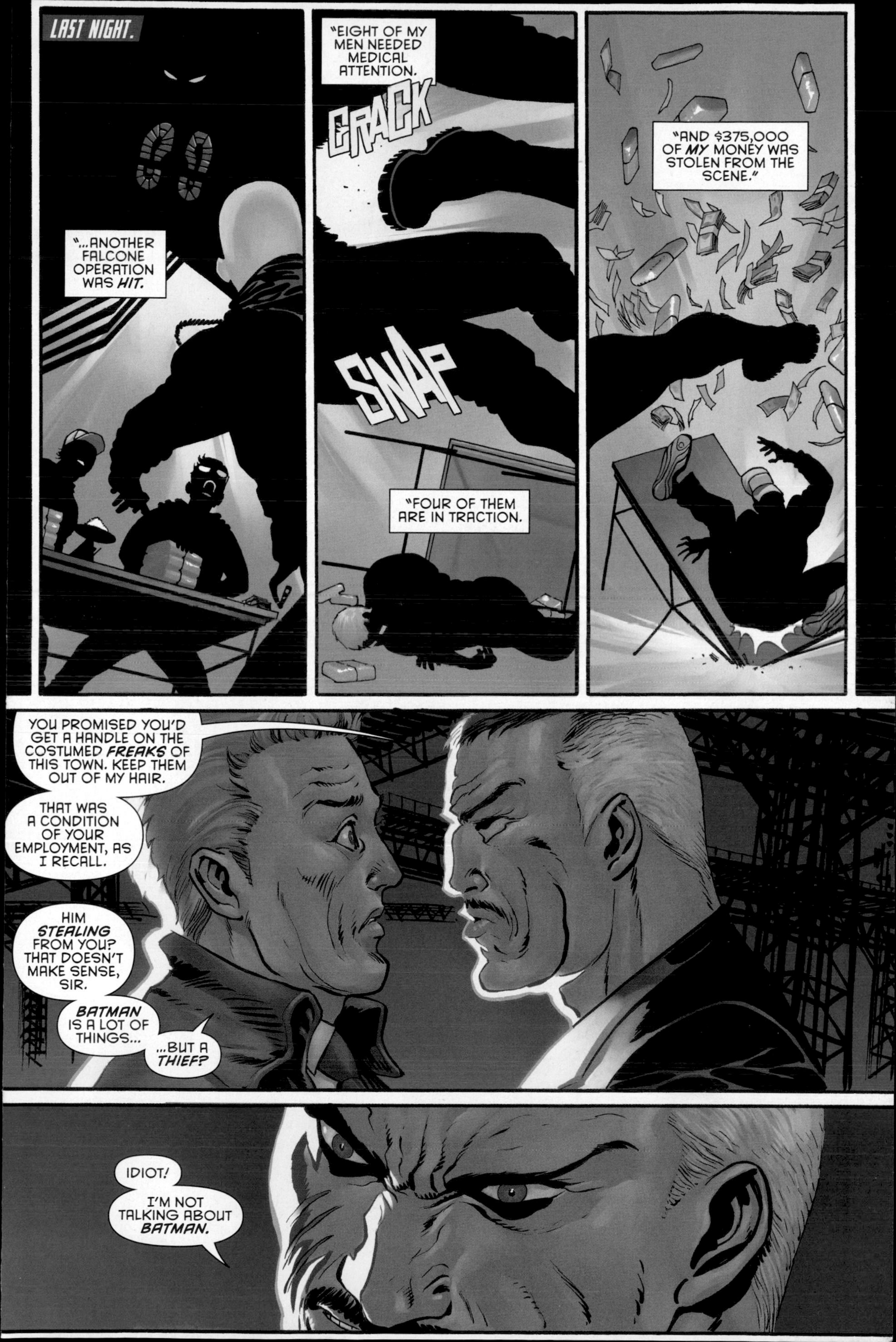

LAST NIGHT.
"...ANOTHER FALCONE OPERATION WAS HIT.
"EIGHT OF MY MEN NEEDED MEDICAL ATTENTION.
CRACK
SNAP
"FOUR OF THEM ARE IN TRACTION.
"AND $375,000 OF MY MONEY WAS STOLEN FROM THE SCENE."
YOU PROMISED YOU'D GET A HANDLE ON THE COSTUMED FREAKS OF THIS TOWN. KEEP THEM OUT OF MY HAIR.
THAT WAS A CONDITION OF YOUR EMPLOYMENT, AS I RECALL.
HIM STEALING FROM YOU? THAT DOESN'T MAKE SENSE, SIR.
BATMAN IS A LOT OF THINGS...
...BUT A THIEF?
IDIOT!
I'M NOT TALKING ABOUT BATMAN.

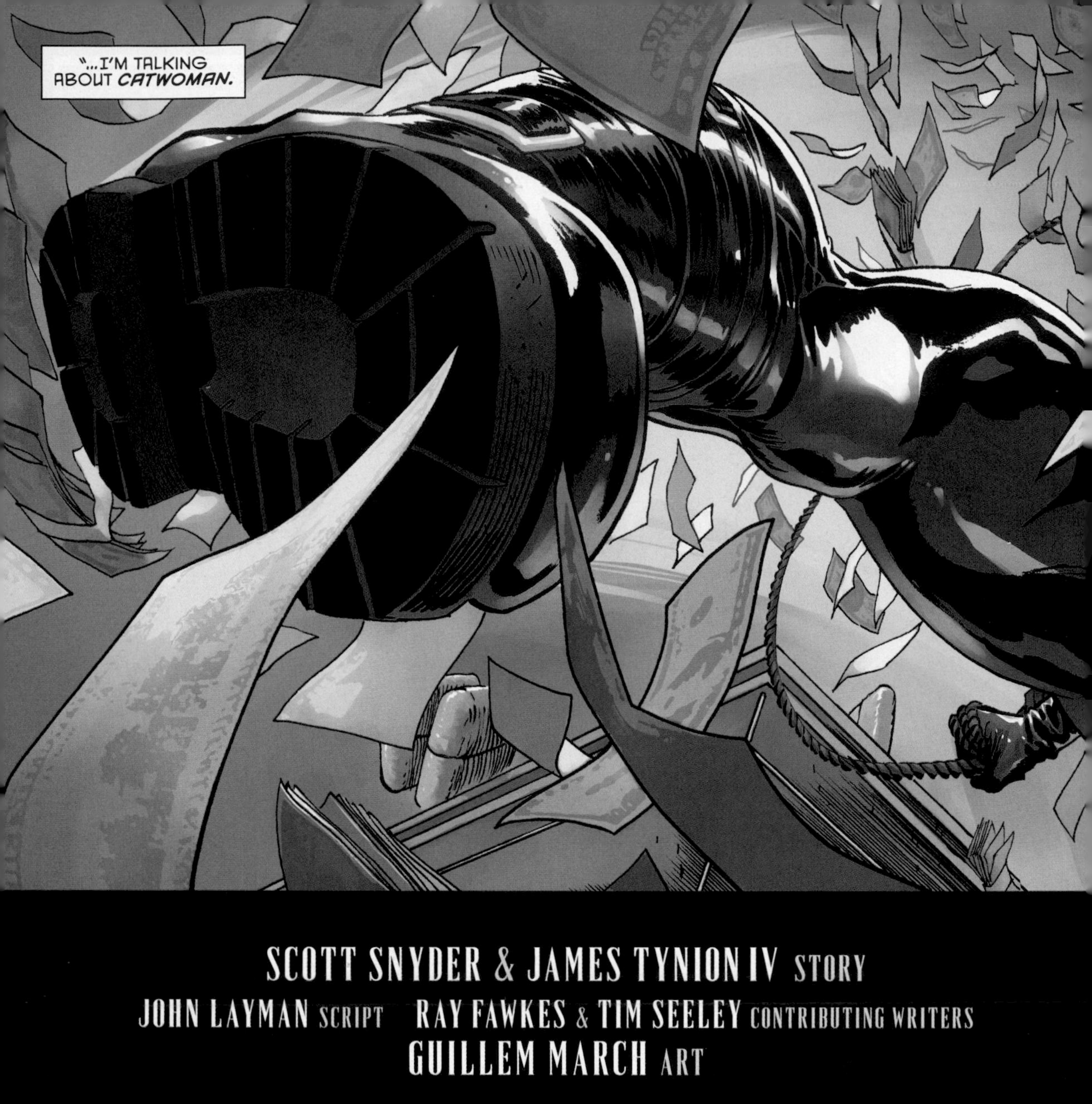
"...I'M TALKING ABOUT CATWOMAN.

SCOTT SNYDER & JAMES TYNION IV STORY
JOHN LAYMAN SCRIPT RAY FAWKES & TIM SEELEY CONTRIBUTING WRITERS
GUILLEM MARCH ART

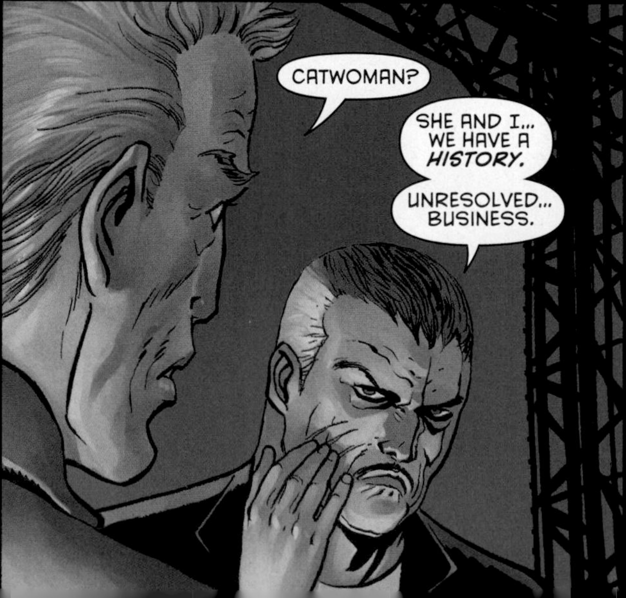
CATWOMAN?
SHE AND I... WE HAVE A HISTORY.
UNRESOLVED... BUSINESS.

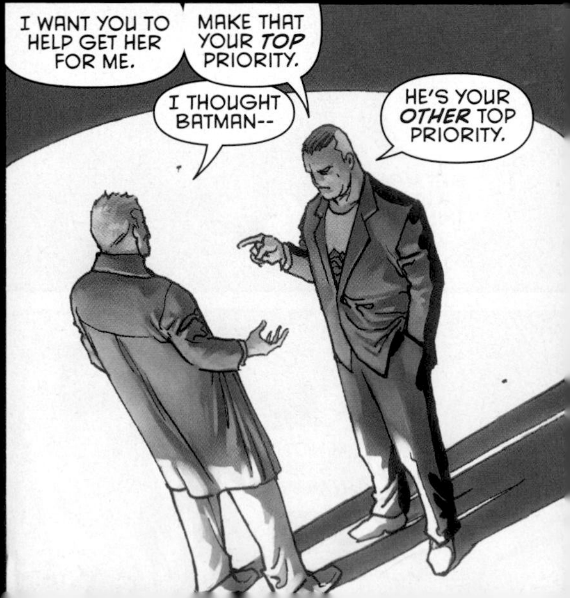
I WANT YOU TO HELP GET HER FOR ME.
MAKE THAT YOUR TOP PRIORITY.
I THOUGHT BATMAN--
HE'S YOUR OTHER TOP PRIORITY.

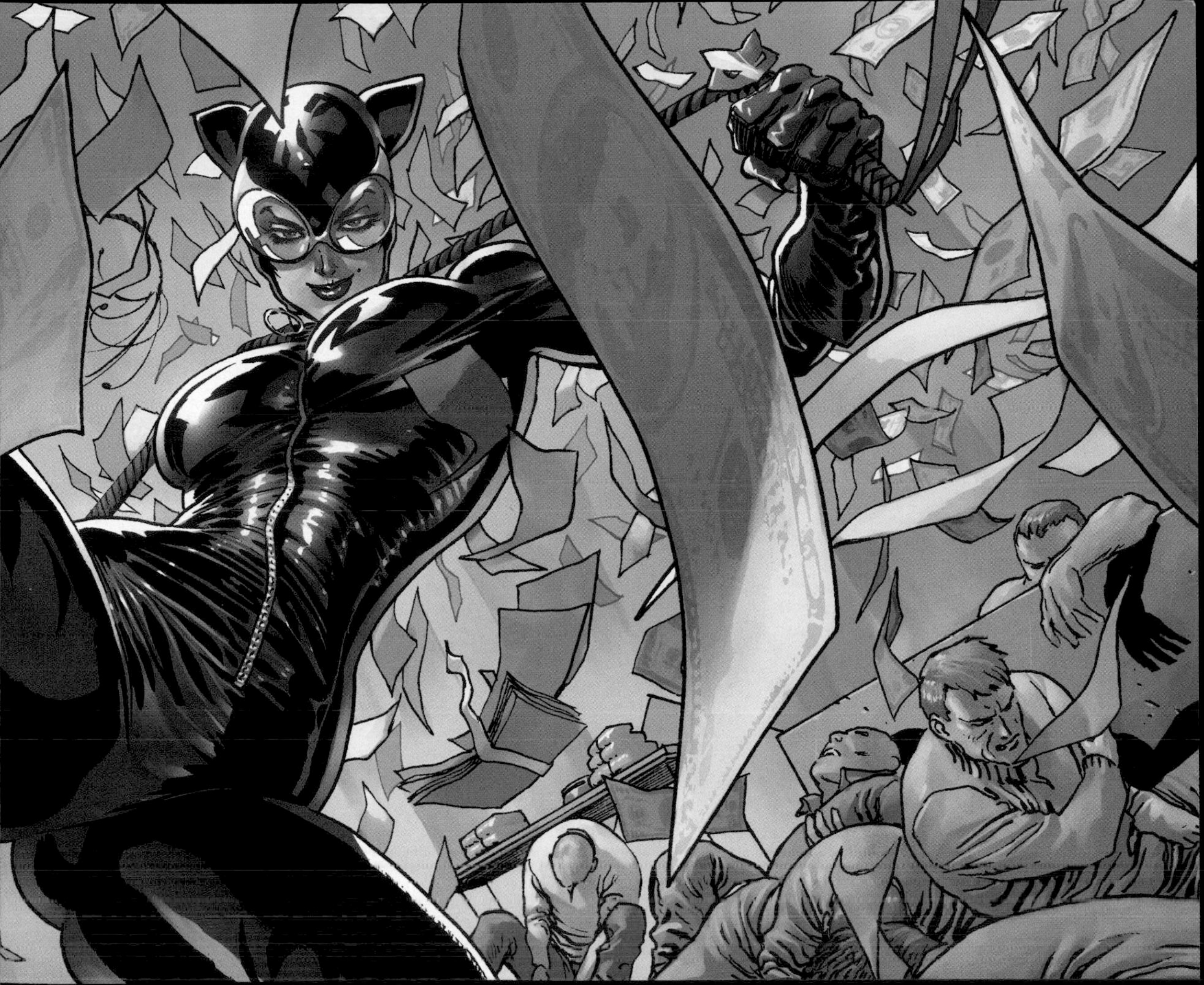

TOMEU MOREY COLORS STEVE WANDS LETTERS
GUILLEM MARCH & TOMEU MOREY COVER

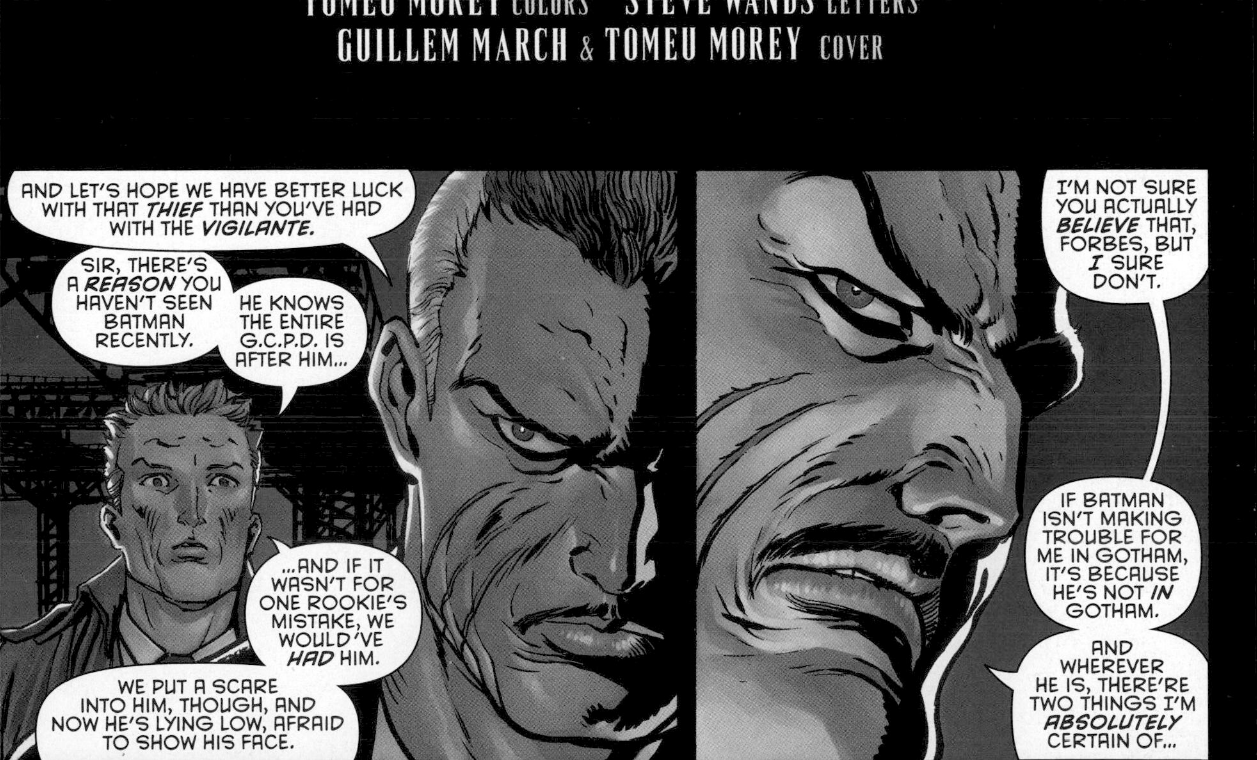

AND LET'S HOPE WE HAVE BETTER LUCK WITH THAT *THIEF* THAN YOU'VE HAD WITH THE *VIGILANTE.*
SIR, THERE'S A *REASON* YOU HAVEN'T SEEN BATMAN RECENTLY.
HE KNOWS THE ENTIRE G.C.P.D. IS AFTER HIM...
...AND IF IT WASN'T FOR ONE ROOKIE'S MISTAKE, WE WOULD'VE *HAD* HIM.
WE PUT A SCARE INTO HIM, THOUGH, AND NOW HE'S LYING LOW, AFRAID TO SHOW HIS FACE.
I'M NOT SURE YOU ACTUALLY *BELIEVE* THAT, FORBES, BUT *I* SURE DON'T.
IF BATMAN ISN'T MAKING TROUBLE FOR ME IN GOTHAM, IT'S BECAUSE HE'S NOT *IN* GOTHAM.
AND WHEREVER HE IS, THERE'RE TWO THINGS I'M *ABSOLUTELY* CERTAIN OF...

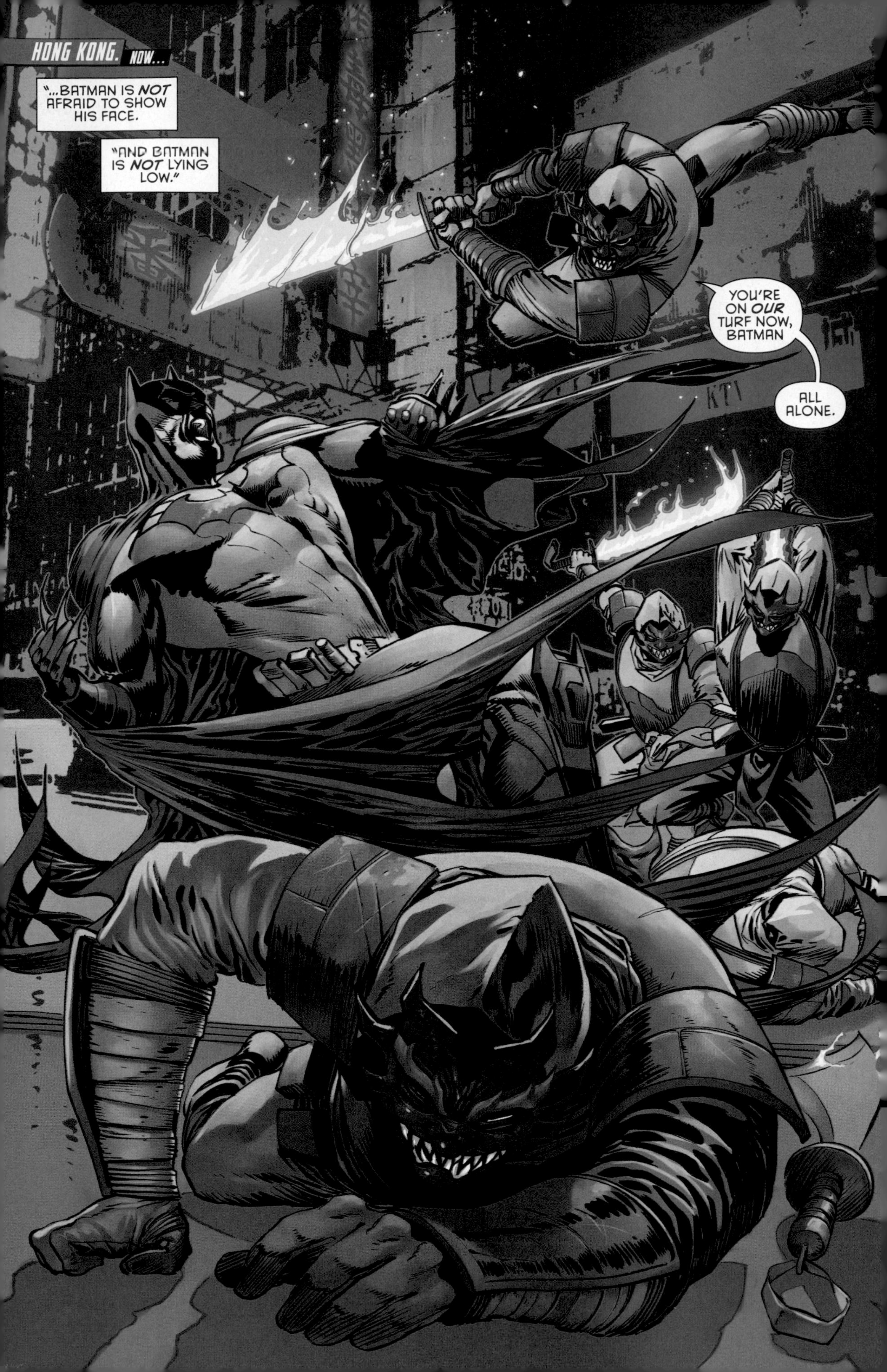
HONG KONG. NOW...
"...BATMAN IS NOT AFRAID TO SHOW HIS FACE.
"AND BATMAN IS NOT LYING LOW."
YOU'RE ON OUR TURF NOW, BATMAN
ALL ALONE.

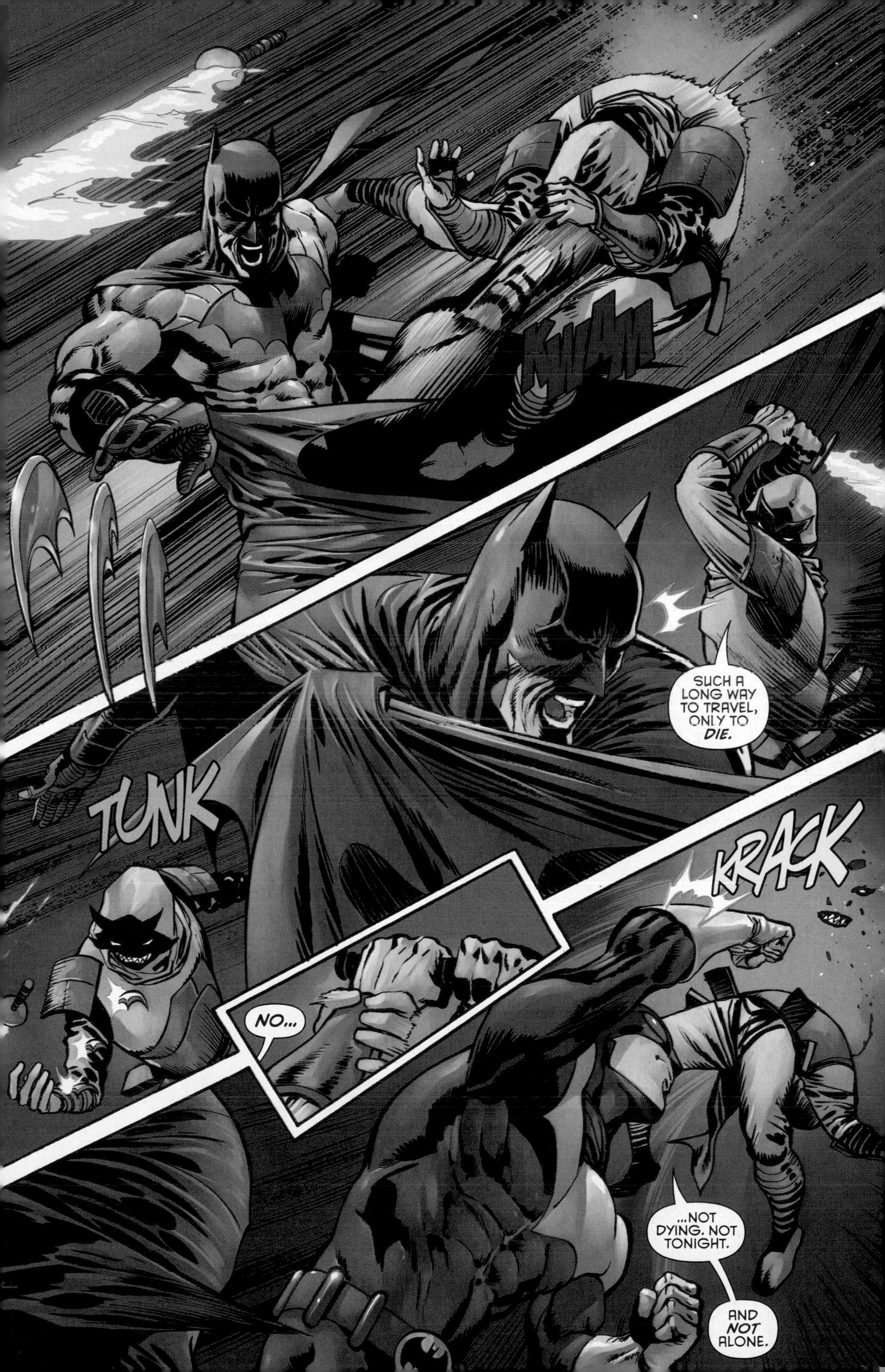
KWAM
SUCH A LONG WAY TO TRAVEL, ONLY TO *DIE.*
TUNK
KRACK
NO...
...NOT DYING. NOT TONIGHT.
AND *NOT* ALONE.

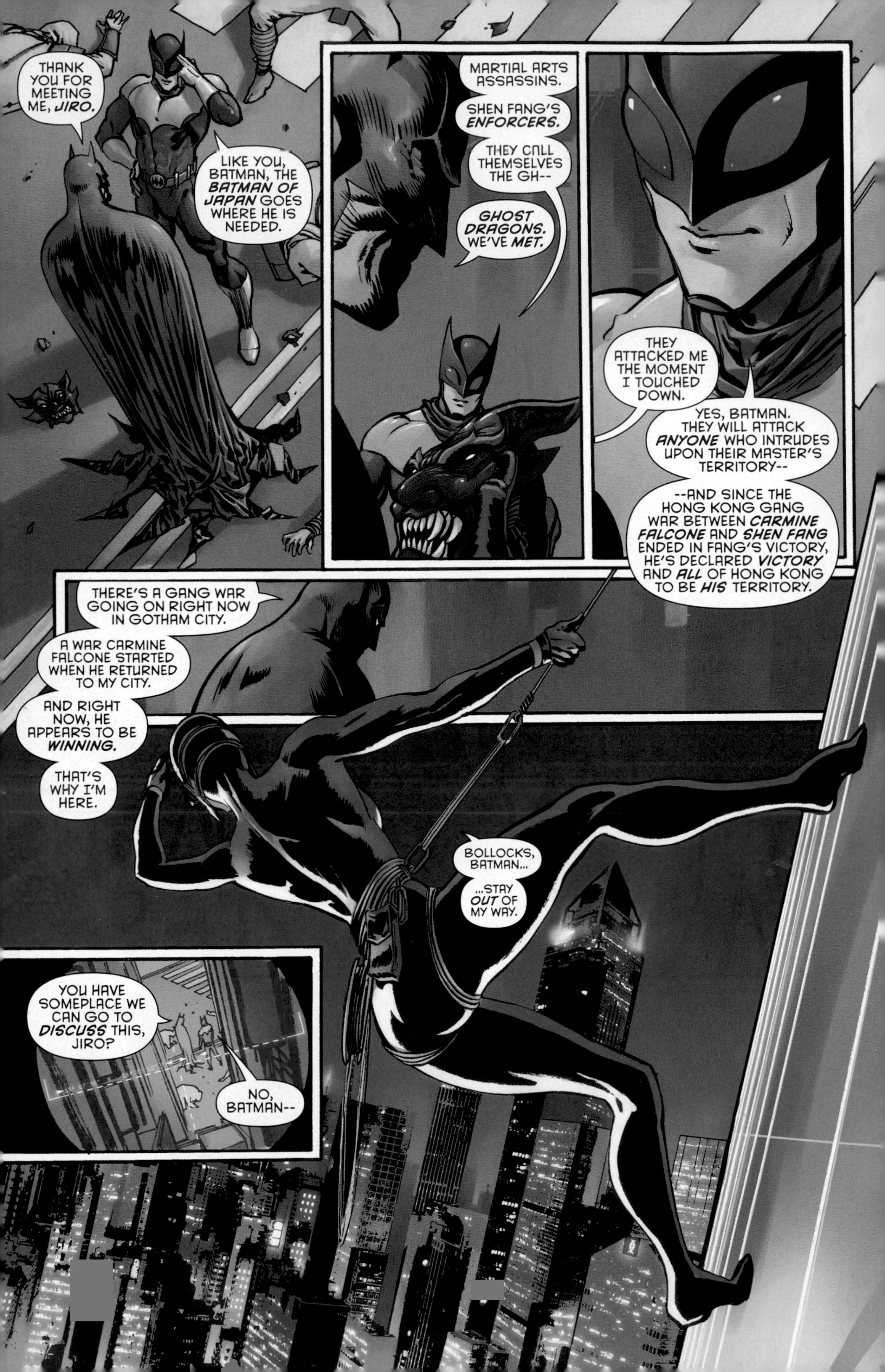
THANK YOU FOR MEETING ME, JIRO.
LIKE YOU, BATMAN, THE BATMAN OF JAPAN GOES WHERE HE IS NEEDED.
MARTIAL ARTS ASSASSINS.
SHEN FANG'S ENFORCERS.
THEY CALL THEMSELVES THE GH--
GHOST DRAGONS. WE'VE MET.
THEY ATTACKED ME THE MOMENT I TOUCHED DOWN.
YES, BATMAN. THEY WILL ATTACK ANYONE WHO INTRUDES UPON THEIR MASTER'S TERRITORY--
--AND SINCE THE HONG KONG GANG WAR BETWEEN CARMINE FALCONE AND SHEN FANG ENDED IN FANG'S VICTORY, HE'S DECLARED VICTORY AND ALL OF HONG KONG TO BE HIS TERRITORY.
THERE'S A GANG WAR GOING ON RIGHT NOW IN GOTHAM CITY.
A WAR CARMINE FALCONE STARTED WHEN HE RETURNED TO MY CITY.
AND RIGHT NOW, HE APPEARS TO BE WINNING.
THAT'S WHY I'M HERE.
BOLLOCKS, BATMAN...
...STAY OUT OF MY WAY.
YOU HAVE SOMEPLACE WE CAN GO TO DISCUSS THIS, JIRO?
NO, BATMAN--

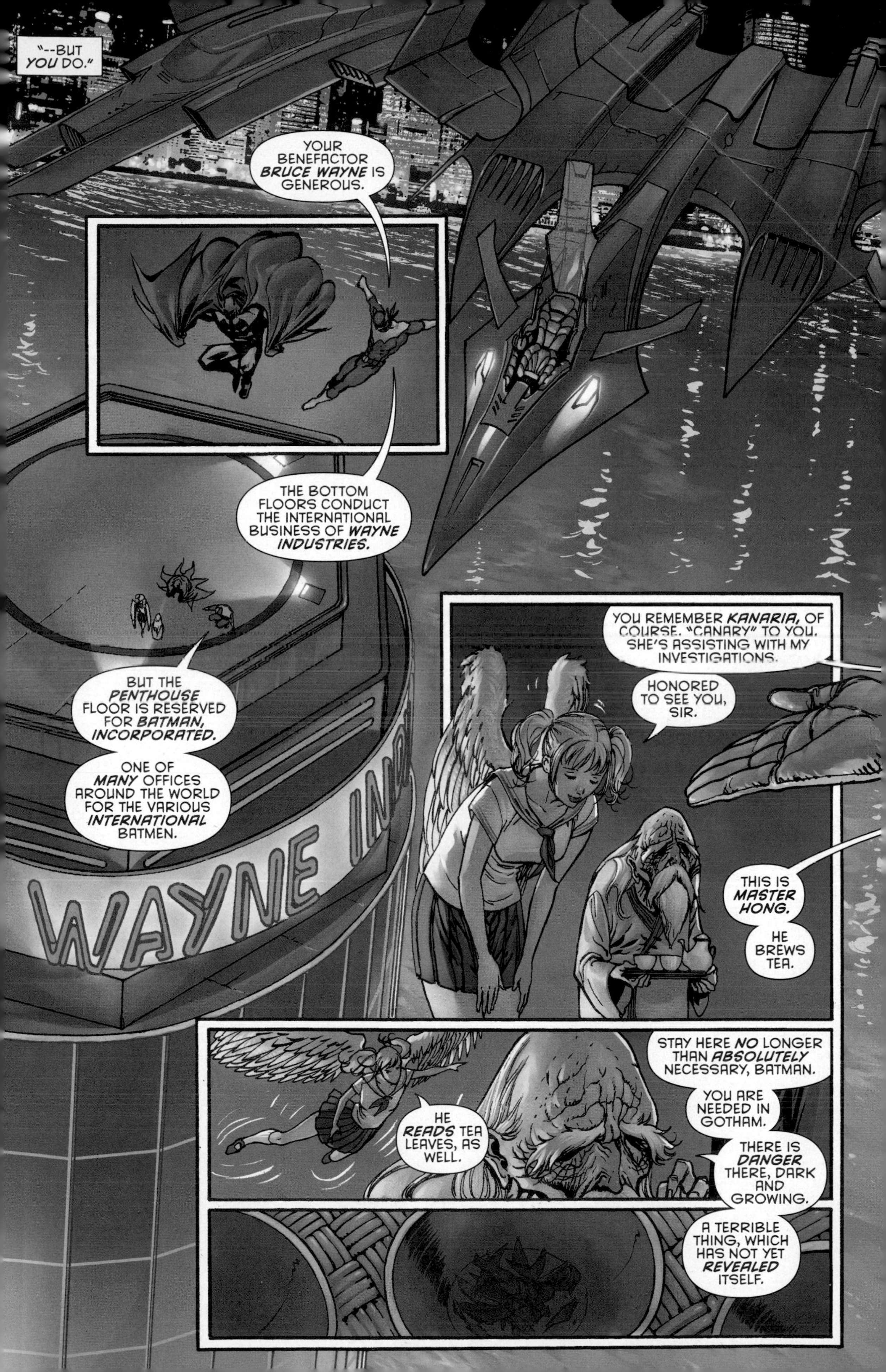
"--BUT YOU DO."
YOUR BENEFACTOR BRUCE WAYNE IS GENEROUS.
THE BOTTOM FLOORS CONDUCT THE INTERNATIONAL BUSINESS OF WAYNE INDUSTRIES.
BUT THE PENTHOUSE FLOOR IS RESERVED FOR BATMAN, INCORPORATED.
ONE OF MANY OFFICES AROUND THE WORLD FOR THE VARIOUS INTERNATIONAL BATMEN.
WAYNE IND
YOU REMEMBER KANARIA, OF COURSE. "CANARY" TO YOU. SHE'S ASSISTING WITH MY INVESTIGATIONS.
HONORED TO SEE YOU, SIR.
THIS IS MASTER HONG.
HE BREWS TEA.
HE READS TEA LEAVES, AS WELL.
STAY HERE NO LONGER THAN ABSOLUTELY NECESSARY, BATMAN.
YOU ARE NEEDED IN GOTHAM.
THERE IS DANGER THERE, DARK AND GROWING.
A TERRIBLE THING, WHICH HAS NOT YET REVEALED ITSELF.

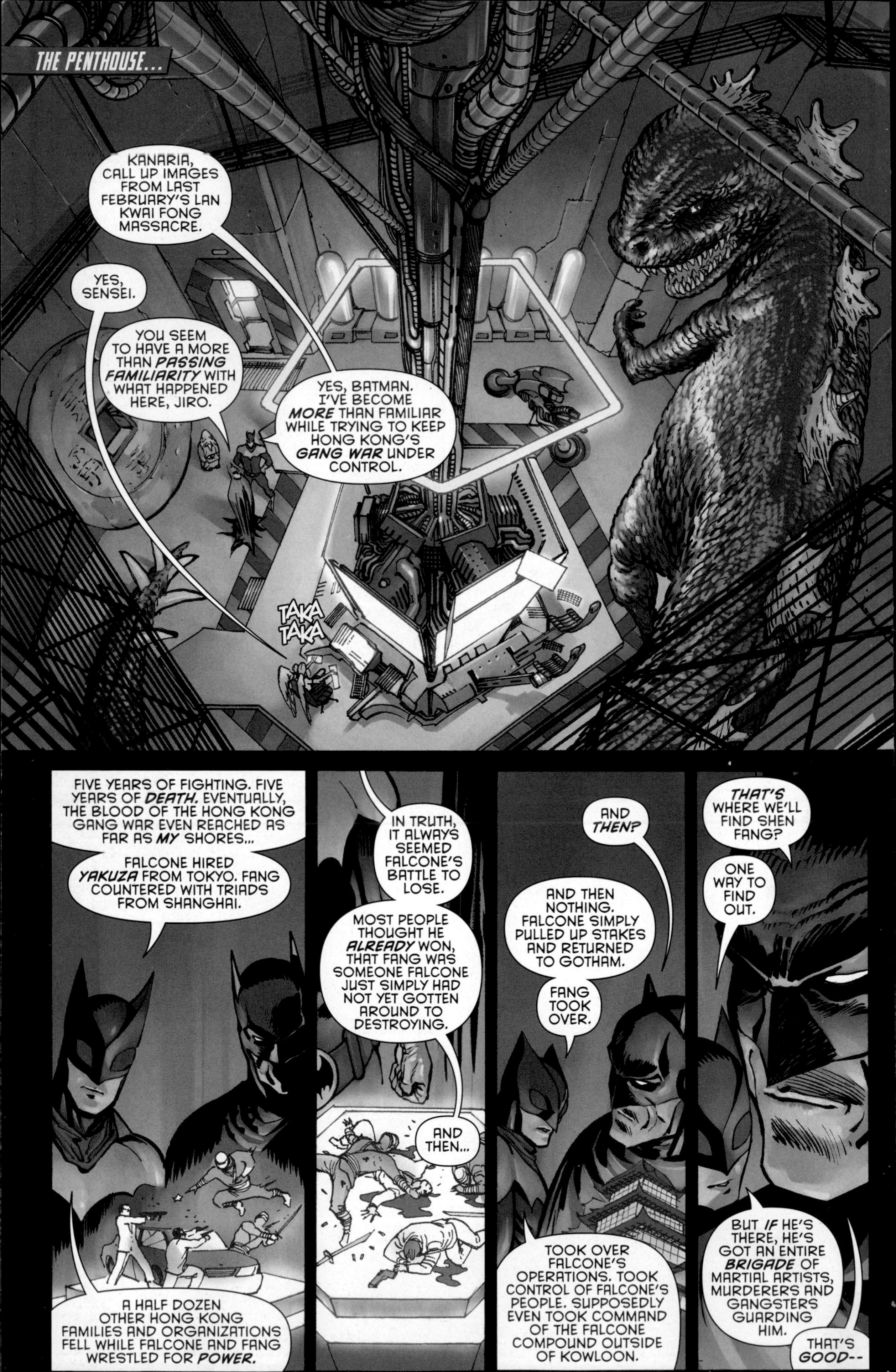
THE PENTHOUSE...
KANARIA, CALL UP IMAGES FROM LAST FEBRUARY'S LAN KWAI FONG MASSACRE.
YES, SENSEI.
YOU SEEM TO HAVE A MORE THAN PASSING FAMILIARITY WITH WHAT HAPPENED HERE, JIRO.
YES, BATMAN. I'VE BECOME MORE THAN FAMILIAR WHILE TRYING TO KEEP HONG KONG'S GANG WAR UNDER CONTROL.
TAKA TAKA
FIVE YEARS OF FIGHTING. FIVE YEARS OF DEATH. EVENTUALLY, THE BLOOD OF THE HONG KONG GANG WAR EVEN REACHED AS FAR AS MY SHORES...
FALCONE HIRED YAKUZA FROM TOKYO. FANG COUNTERED WITH TRIADS FROM SHANGHAI.
A HALF DOZEN OTHER HONG KONG FAMILIES AND ORGANIZATIONS FELL WHILE FALCONE AND FANG WRESTLED FOR POWER.
IN TRUTH, IT ALWAYS SEEMED FALCONE'S BATTLE TO LOSE.
MOST PEOPLE THOUGHT HE ALREADY WON, THAT FANG WAS SOMEONE FALCONE JUST SIMPLY HAD NOT YET GOTTEN AROUND TO DESTROYING.
AND THEN...
AND THEN?
AND THEN NOTHING. FALCONE SIMPLY PULLED UP STAKES AND RETURNED TO GOTHAM.
FANG TOOK OVER.
TOOK OVER FALCONE'S OPERATIONS. TOOK CONTROL OF FALCONE'S PEOPLE. SUPPOSEDLY EVEN TOOK COMMAND OF THE FALCONE COMPOUND OUTSIDE OF KOWLOON.
THAT'S WHERE WE'LL FIND SHEN FANG?
ONE WAY TO FIND OUT.
BUT IF HE'S THERE, HE'S GOT AN ENTIRE BRIGADE OF MARTIAL ARTISTS, MURDERERS AND GANGSTERS GUARDING HIM.
THAT'S GOOD--

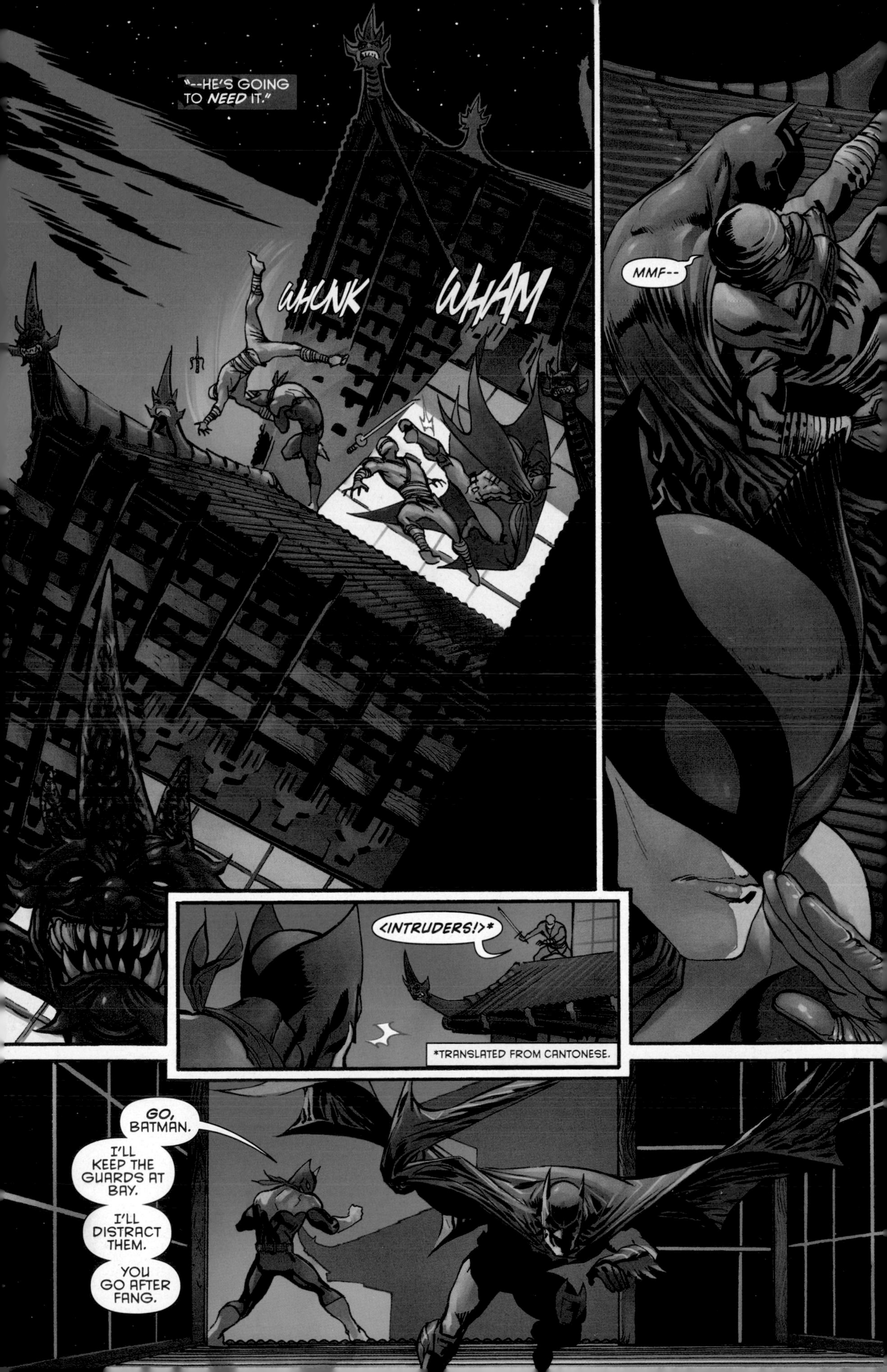
"--HE'S GOING TO NEED IT."
WHUNK
WHAM
MMF--
<INTRUDERS!>*
*TRANSLATED FROM CANTONESE.
GO, BATMAN.
I'LL KEEP THE GUARDS AT BAY.
I'LL DISTRACT THEM.
YOU GO AFTER FANG.

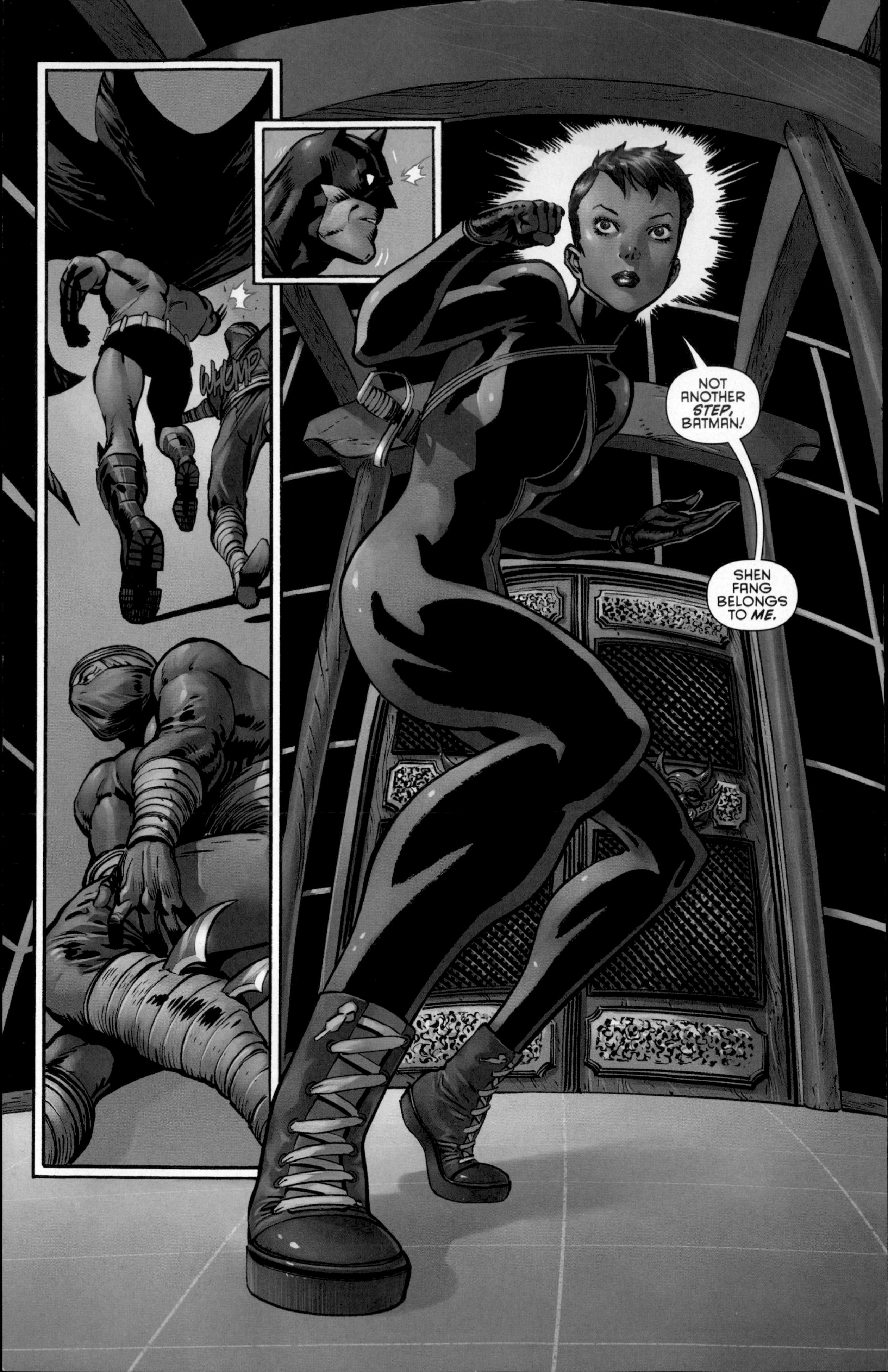
WHUMP
NOT ANOTHER STEP, BATMAN!
SHEN FANG BELONGS TO ME.

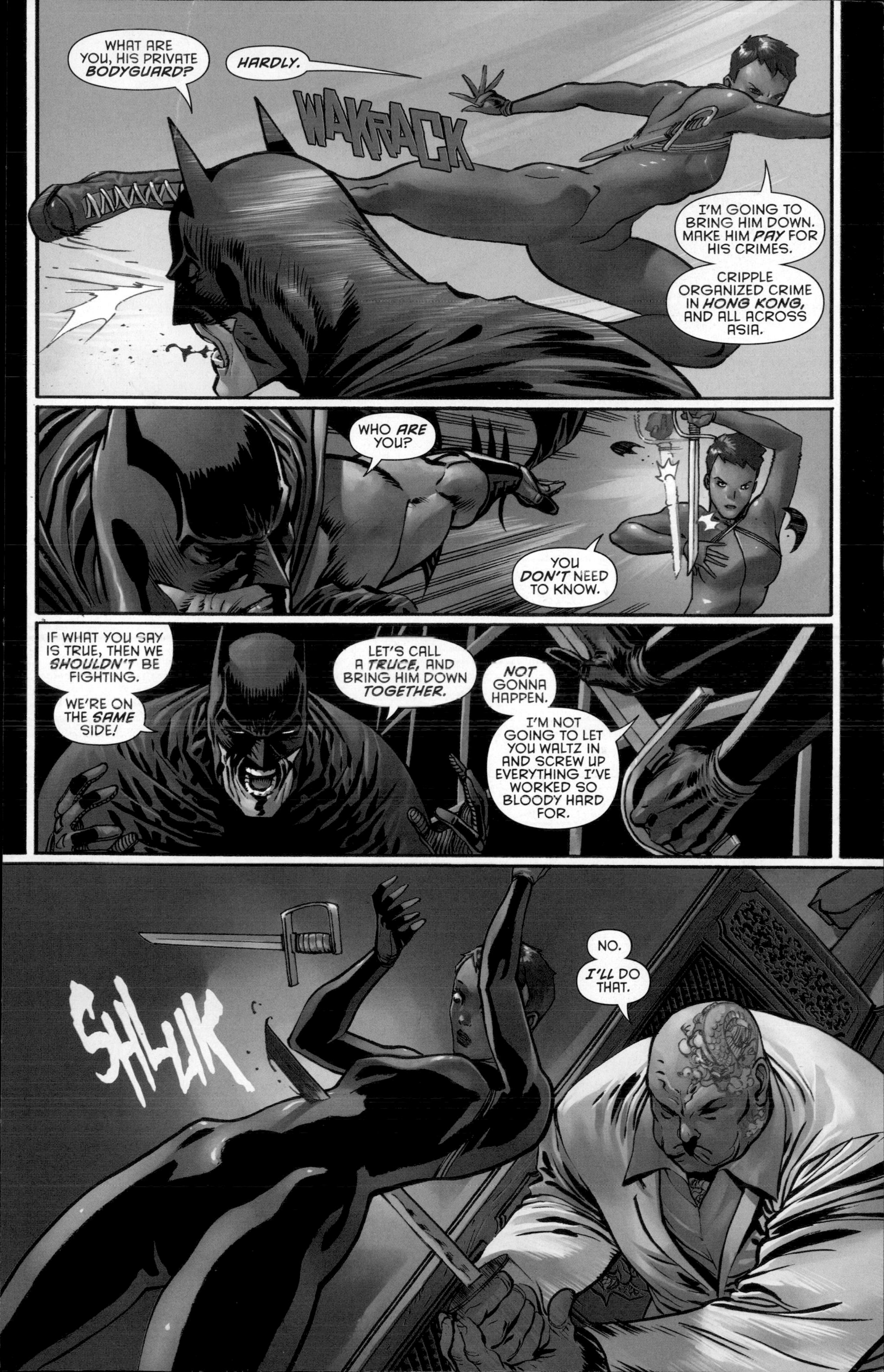
WHAT ARE YOU, HIS PRIVATE BODYGUARD?
HARDLY.
WAKRACK
I'M GOING TO BRING HIM DOWN. MAKE HIM PAY FOR HIS CRIMES.
CRIPPLE ORGANIZED CRIME IN HONG KONG, AND ALL ACROSS ASIA.
WHO ARE YOU?
YOU DON'T NEED TO KNOW.
IF WHAT YOU SAY IS TRUE, THEN WE SHOULDN'T BE FIGHTING.
WE'RE ON THE SAME SIDE!
LET'S CALL A TRUCE, AND BRING HIM DOWN TOGETHER.
NOT GONNA HAPPEN.
I'M NOT GOING TO LET YOU WALTZ IN AND SCREW UP EVERYTHING I'VE WORKED SO BLOODY HARD FOR.
SHLUK
NO.
I'LL DO THAT.

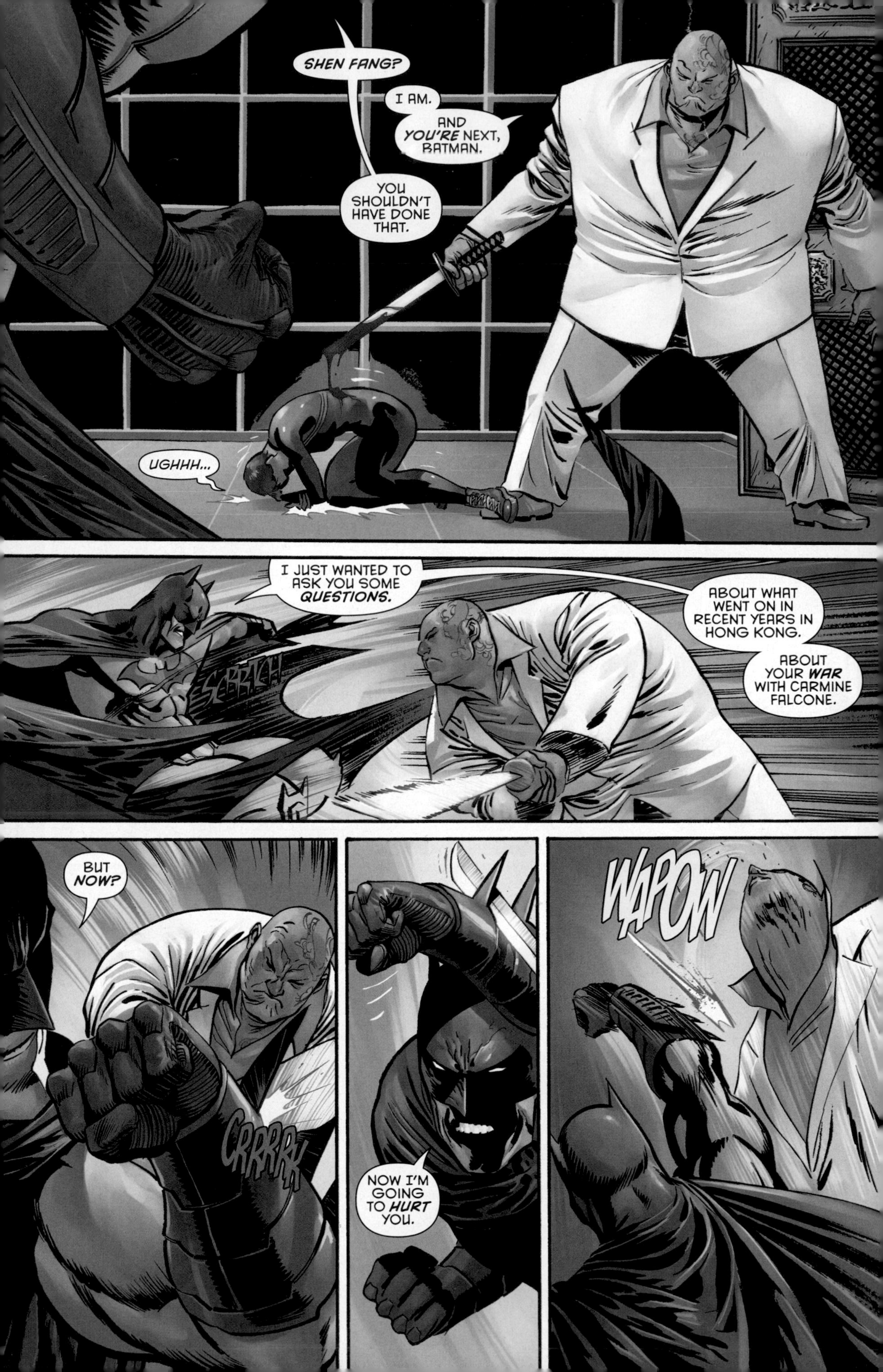
SHEN FANG?
I AM.
AND YOU'RE NEXT, BATMAN.
YOU SHOULDN'T HAVE DONE THAT.
UGHHH...
I JUST WANTED TO ASK YOU SOME QUESTIONS.
ABOUT WHAT WENT ON IN RECENT YEARS IN HONG KONG.
ABOUT YOUR WAR WITH CARMINE FALCONE.
SCRATCH
BUT NOW?
CRRRRK
NOW I'M GOING TO HURT YOU.
WAPOW

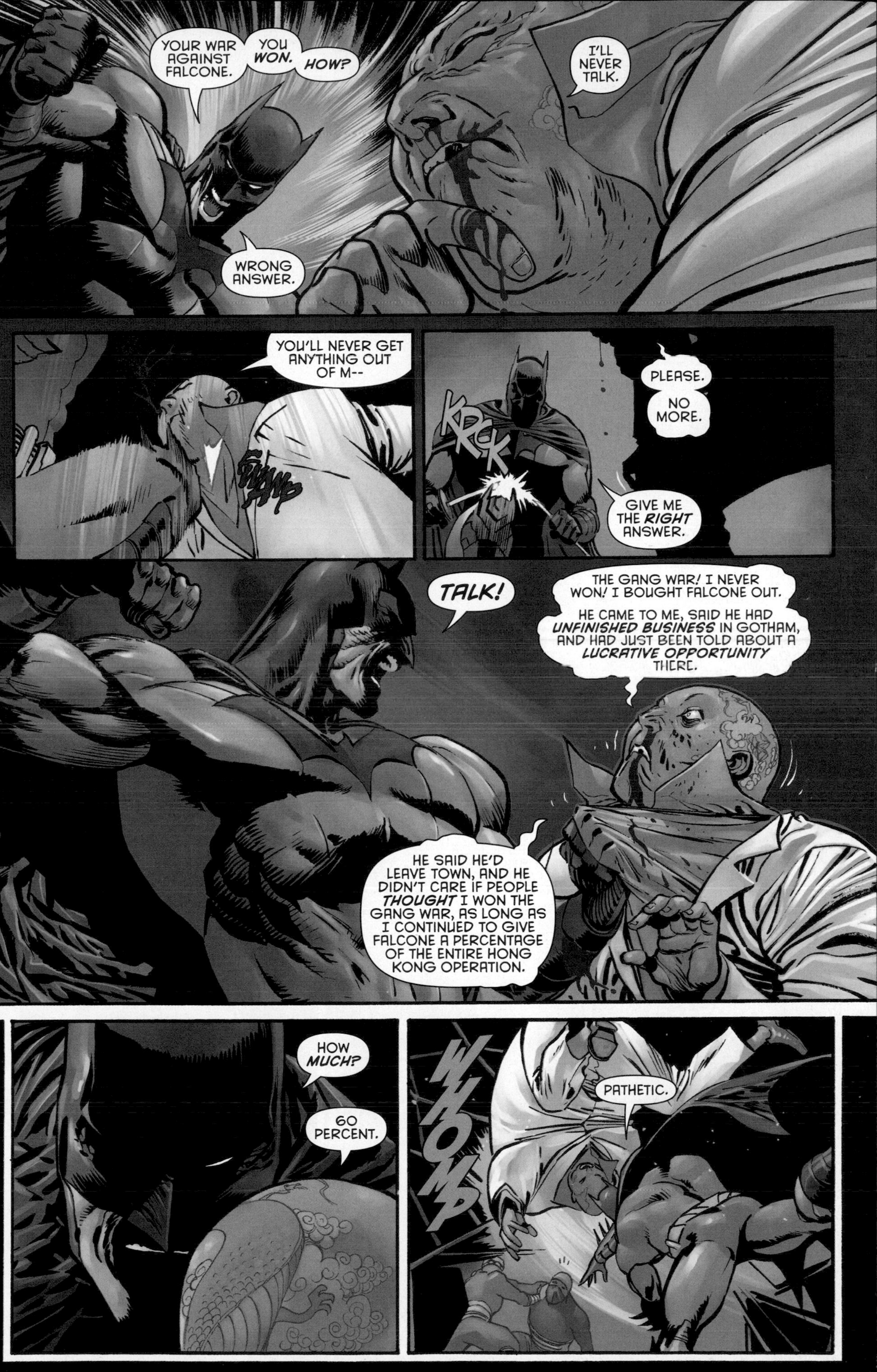
YOUR WAR AGAINST FALCONE.
YOU WON.
HOW?
I'LL NEVER TALK.
WRONG ANSWER.
YOU'LL NEVER GET ANYTHING OUT OF M--
KRCK
PLEASE.
NO MORE.
GIVE ME THE RIGHT ANSWER.
TALK!
THE GANG WAR! I NEVER WON! I BOUGHT FALCONE OUT.
HE CAME TO ME, SAID HE HAD UNFINISHED BUSINESS IN GOTHAM, AND HAD JUST BEEN TOLD ABOUT A LUCRATIVE OPPORTUNITY THERE.
HE SAID HE'D LEAVE TOWN, AND HE DIDN'T CARE IF PEOPLE THOUGHT I WON THE GANG WAR, AS LONG AS I CONTINUED TO GIVE FALCONE A PERCENTAGE OF THE ENTIRE HONG KONG OPERATION.
HOW MUCH?
60 PERCENT.
WHOMP
PATHETIC.

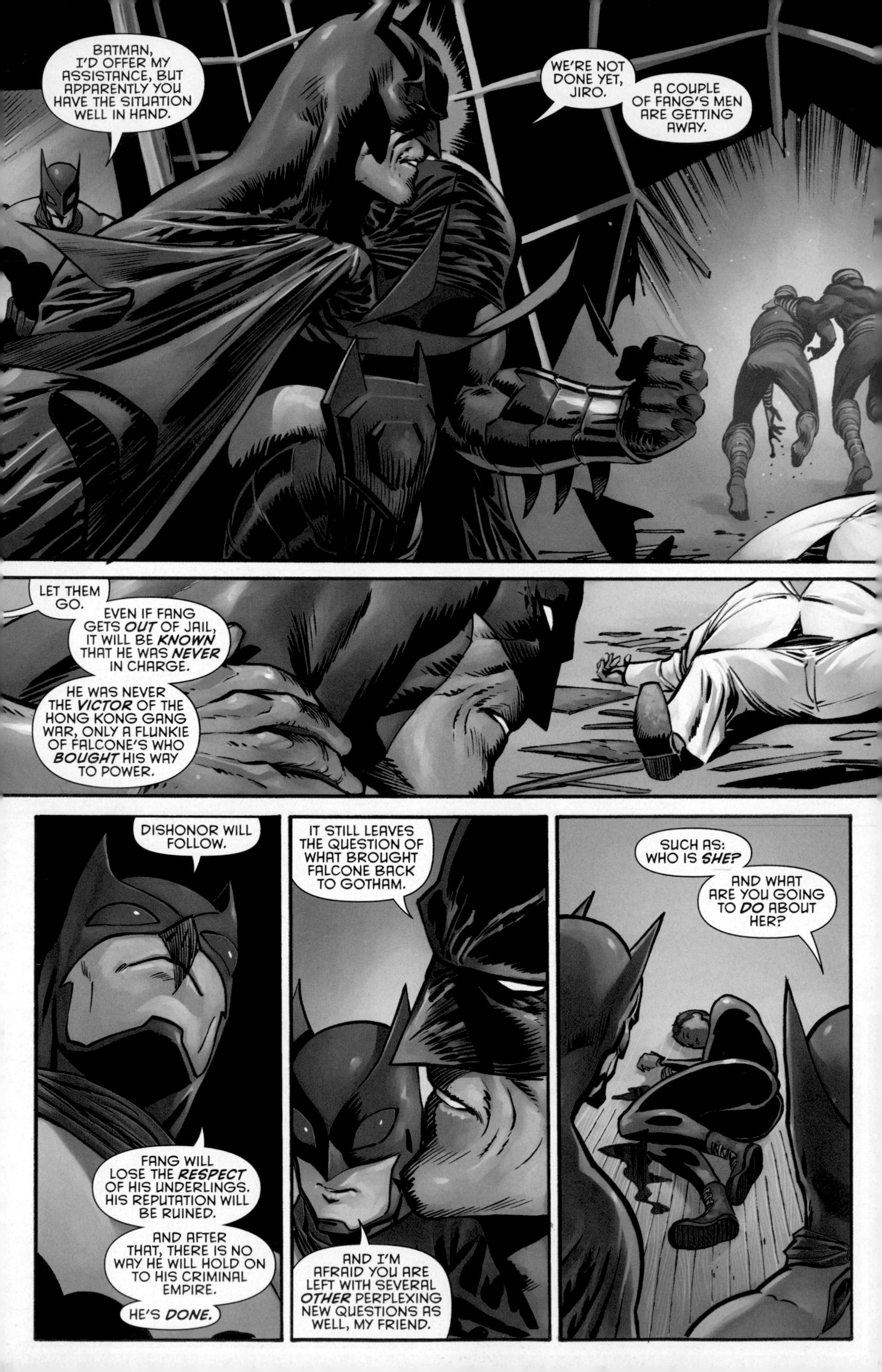
BATMAN, I'D OFFER MY ASSISTANCE, BUT APPARENTLY YOU HAVE THE SITUATION WELL IN HAND.
WE'RE NOT DONE YET, JIRO.
A COUPLE OF FANG'S MEN ARE GETTING AWAY.
LET THEM GO.
EVEN IF FANG GETS OUT OF JAIL, IT WILL BE KNOWN THAT HE WAS NEVER IN CHARGE.
HE WAS NEVER THE VICTOR OF THE HONG KONG GANG WAR, ONLY A FLUNKIE OF FALCONE'S WHO BOUGHT HIS WAY TO POWER.
DISHONOR WILL FOLLOW.
FANG WILL LOSE THE RESPECT OF HIS UNDERLINGS. HIS REPUTATION WILL BE RUINED.
AND AFTER THAT, THERE IS NO WAY HE WILL HOLD ON TO HIS CRIMINAL EMPIRE.
HE'S DONE.
IT STILL LEAVES THE QUESTION OF WHAT BROUGHT FALCONE BACK TO GOTHAM.
AND I'M AFRAID YOU ARE LEFT WITH SEVERAL OTHER PERPLEXING NEW QUESTIONS AS WELL, MY FRIEND.
SUCH AS: WHO IS SHE?
AND WHAT ARE YOU GOING TO DO ABOUT HER?

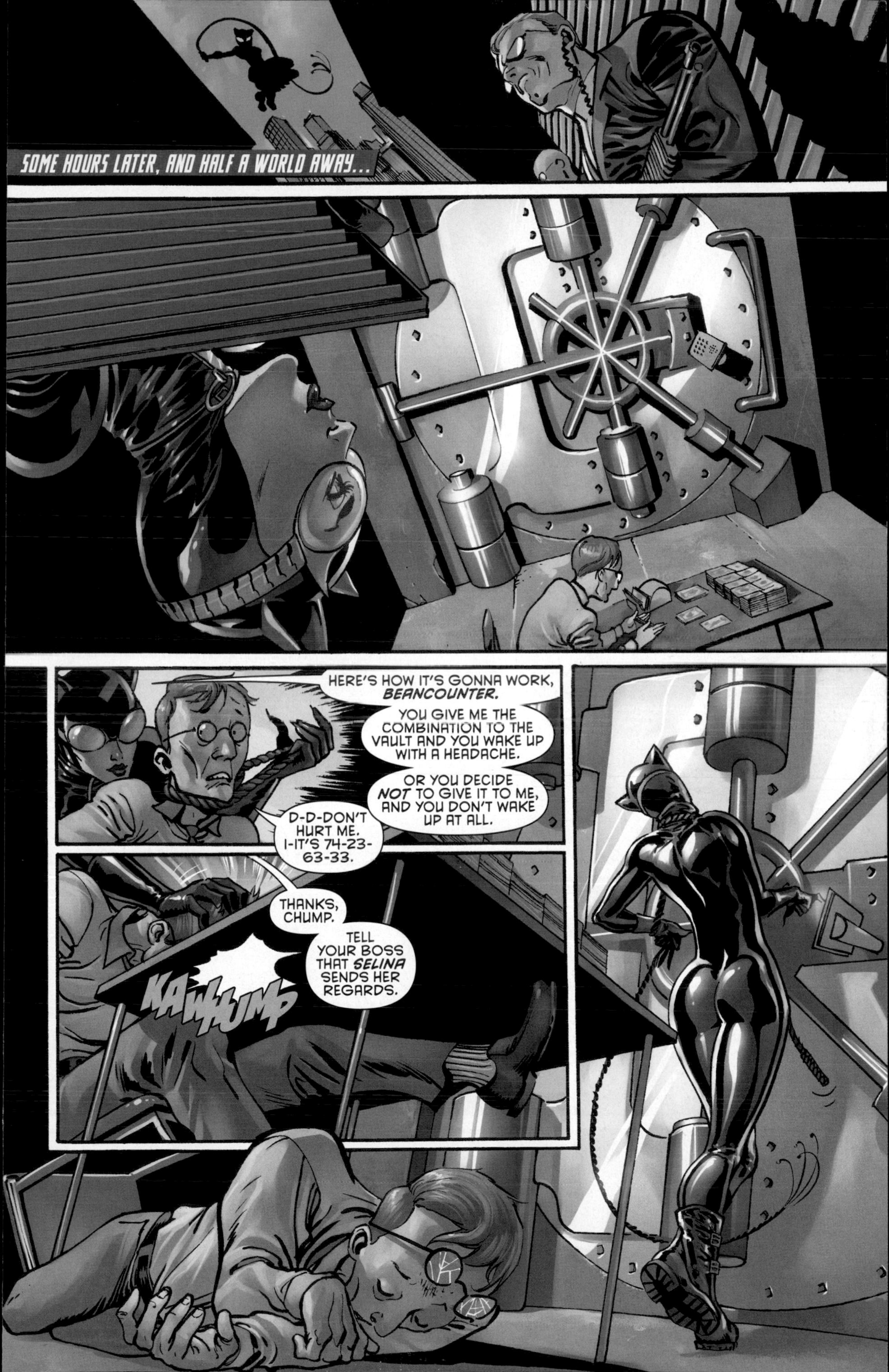
SOME HOURS LATER, AND HALF A WORLD AWAY...
HERE'S HOW IT'S GONNA WORK, BEANCOUNTER.
YOU GIVE ME THE COMBINATION TO THE VAULT AND YOU WAKE UP WITH A HEADACHE.
OR YOU DECIDE NOT TO GIVE IT TO ME, AND YOU DON'T WAKE UP AT ALL.
D-D-DON'T HURT ME. I-IT'S 74-23-63-33.
THANKS, CHUMP.
TELL YOUR BOSS THAT SELINA SENDS HER REGARDS.
KAWHUMP

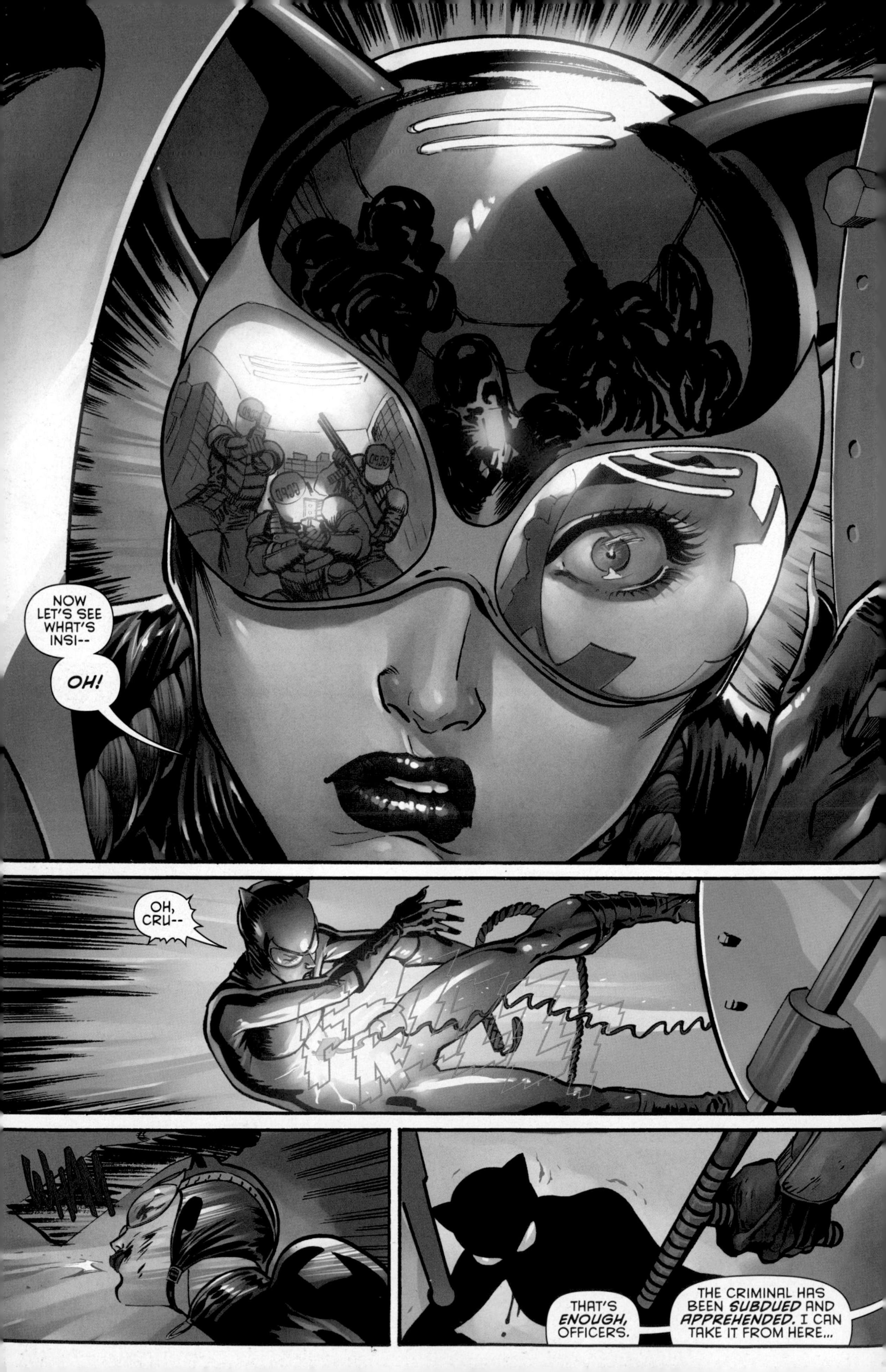
NOW LET'S SEE WHAT'S INSI--
OH!
OH, CRU--
THAT'S ENOUGH, OFFICERS.
THE CRIMINAL HAS BEEN SUBDUED AND APPREHENDED. I CAN TAKE IT FROM HERE...

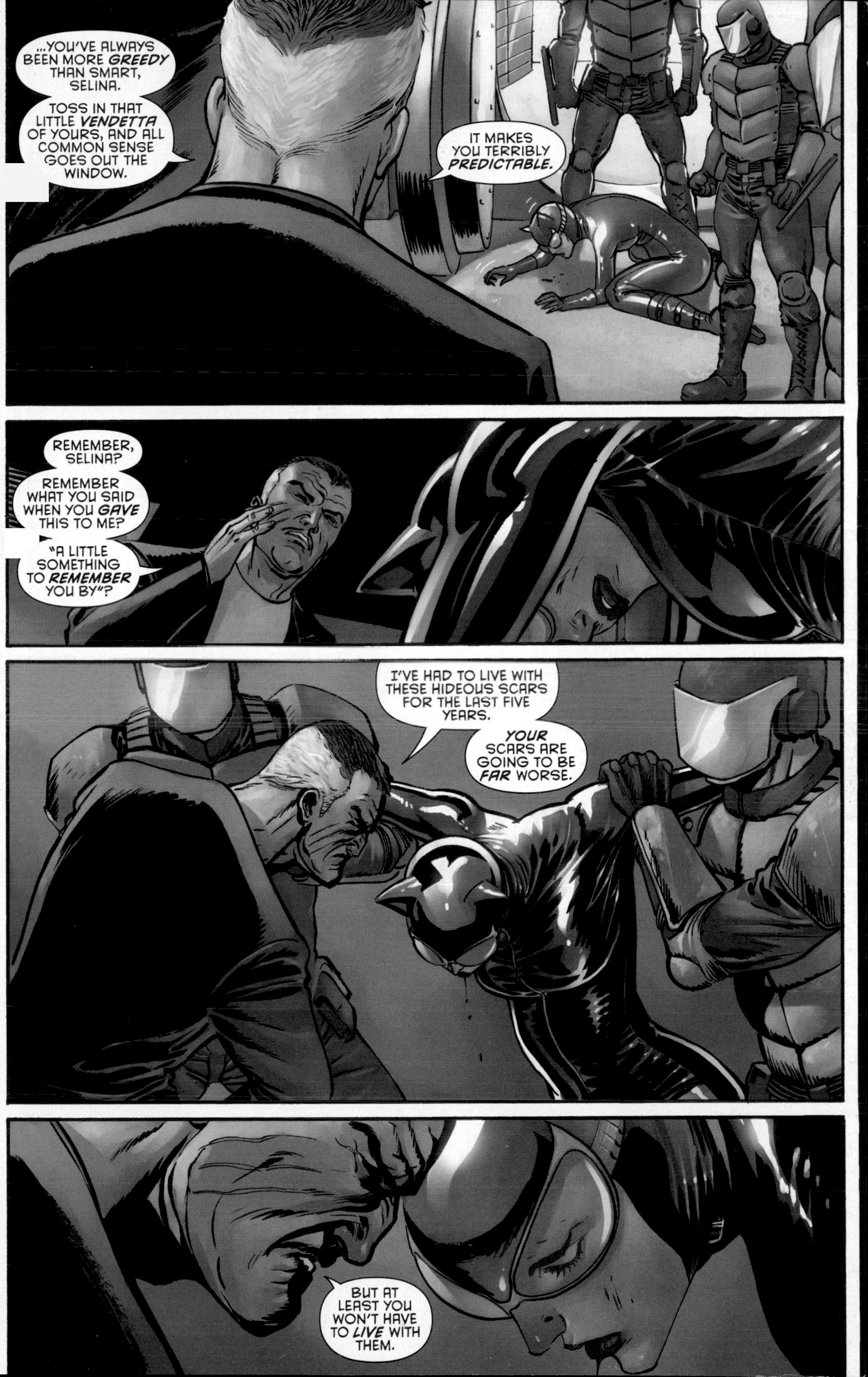
...YOU'VE ALWAYS BEEN MORE GREEDY THAN SMART, SELINA.
TOSS IN THAT LITTLE VENDETTA OF YOURS, AND ALL COMMON SENSE GOES OUT THE WINDOW.
IT MAKES YOU TERRIBLY PREDICTABLE.
REMEMBER, SELINA?
REMEMBER WHAT YOU SAID WHEN YOU GAVE THIS TO ME?
"A LITTLE SOMETHING TO REMEMBER YOU BY"?
I'VE HAD TO LIVE WITH THESE HIDEOUS SCARS FOR THE LAST FIVE YEARS.
YOUR SCARS ARE GOING TO BE FAR WORSE.
BUT AT LEAST YOU WON'T HAVE TO LIVE WITH THEM.

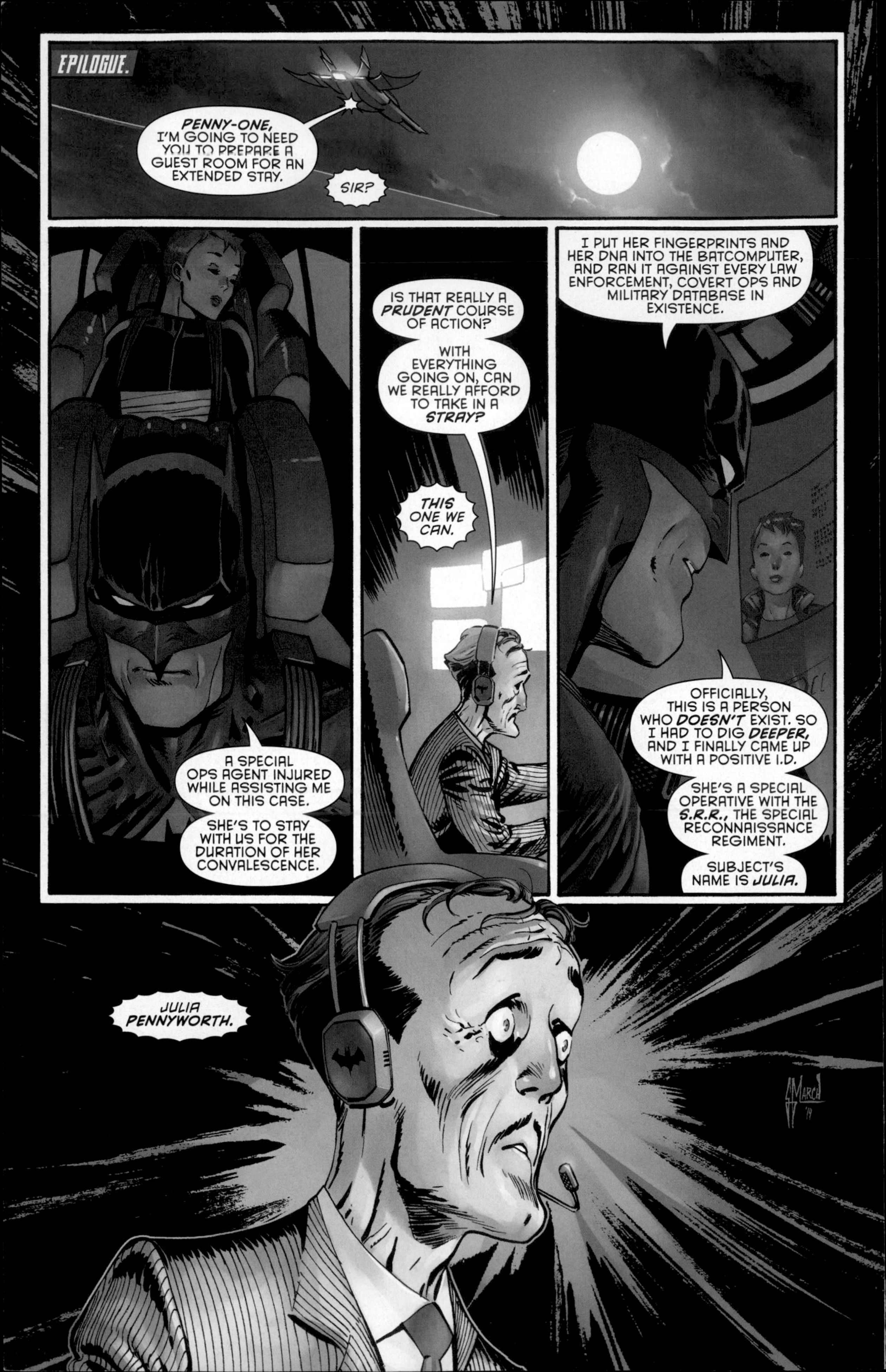
EPILOGUE.
PENNY-ONE, I'M GOING TO NEED YOU TO PREPARE A GUEST ROOM FOR AN EXTENDED STAY.
SIR?
A SPECIAL OPS AGENT INJURED WHILE ASSISTING ME ON THIS CASE.
SHE'S TO STAY WITH US FOR THE DURATION OF HER CONVALESCENCE.
IS THAT REALLY A PRUDENT COURSE OF ACTION?
WITH EVERYTHING GOING ON, CAN WE REALLY AFFORD TO TAKE IN A STRAY?
THIS ONE WE CAN.
I PUT HER FINGERPRINTS AND HER DNA INTO THE BATCOMPUTER, AND RAN IT AGAINST EVERY LAW ENFORCEMENT, COVERT OPS AND MILITARY DATABASE IN EXISTENCE.
OFFICIALLY, THIS IS A PERSON WHO DOESN'T EXIST. SO I HAD TO DIG DEEPER, AND I FINALLY CAME UP WITH A POSITIVE I.D.
SHE'S A SPECIAL OPERATIVE WITH THE S.R.R., THE SPECIAL RECONNAISSANCE REGIMENT.
SUBJECT'S NAME IS JULIA.
JULIA PENNYWORTH.

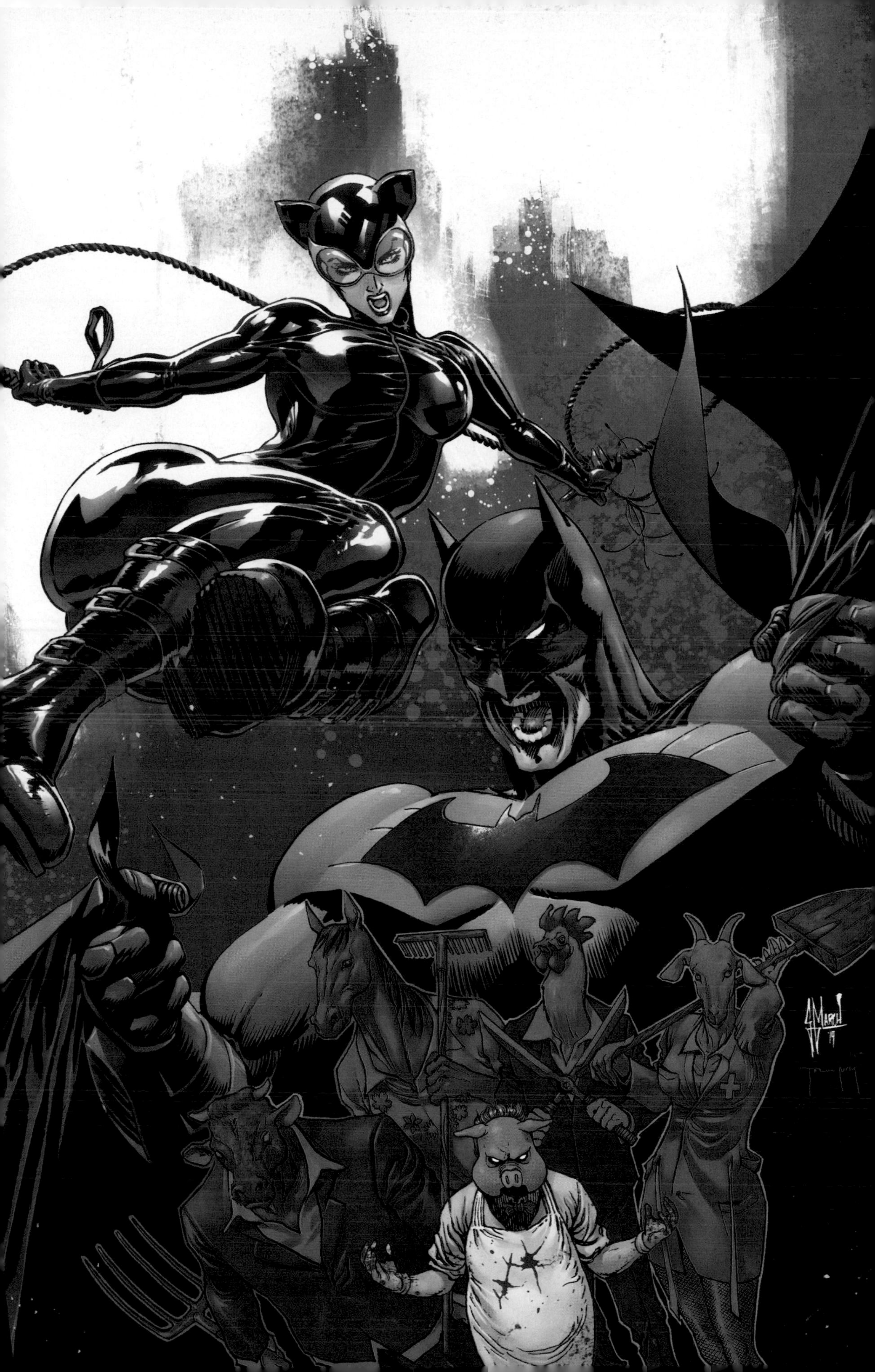

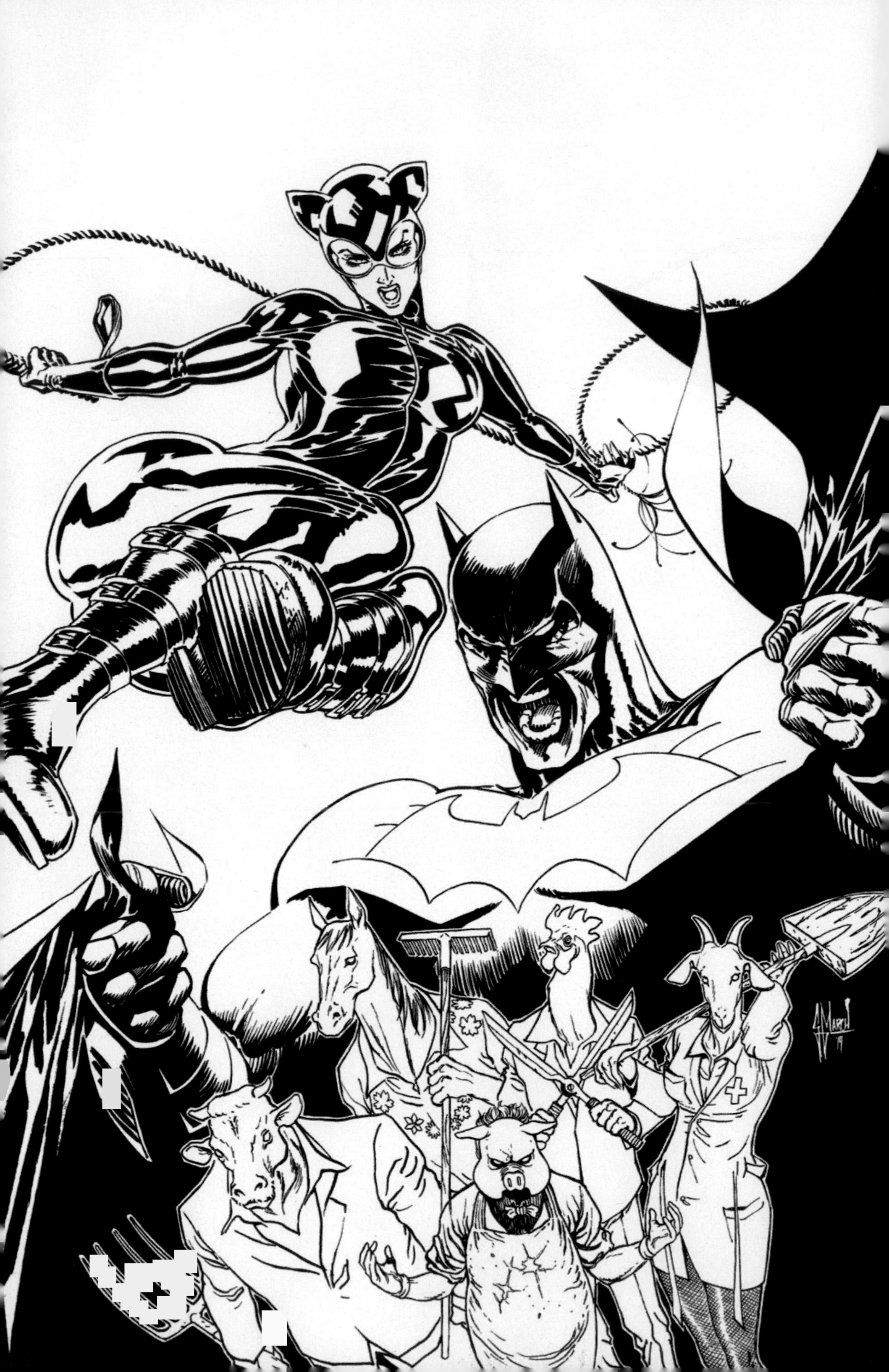

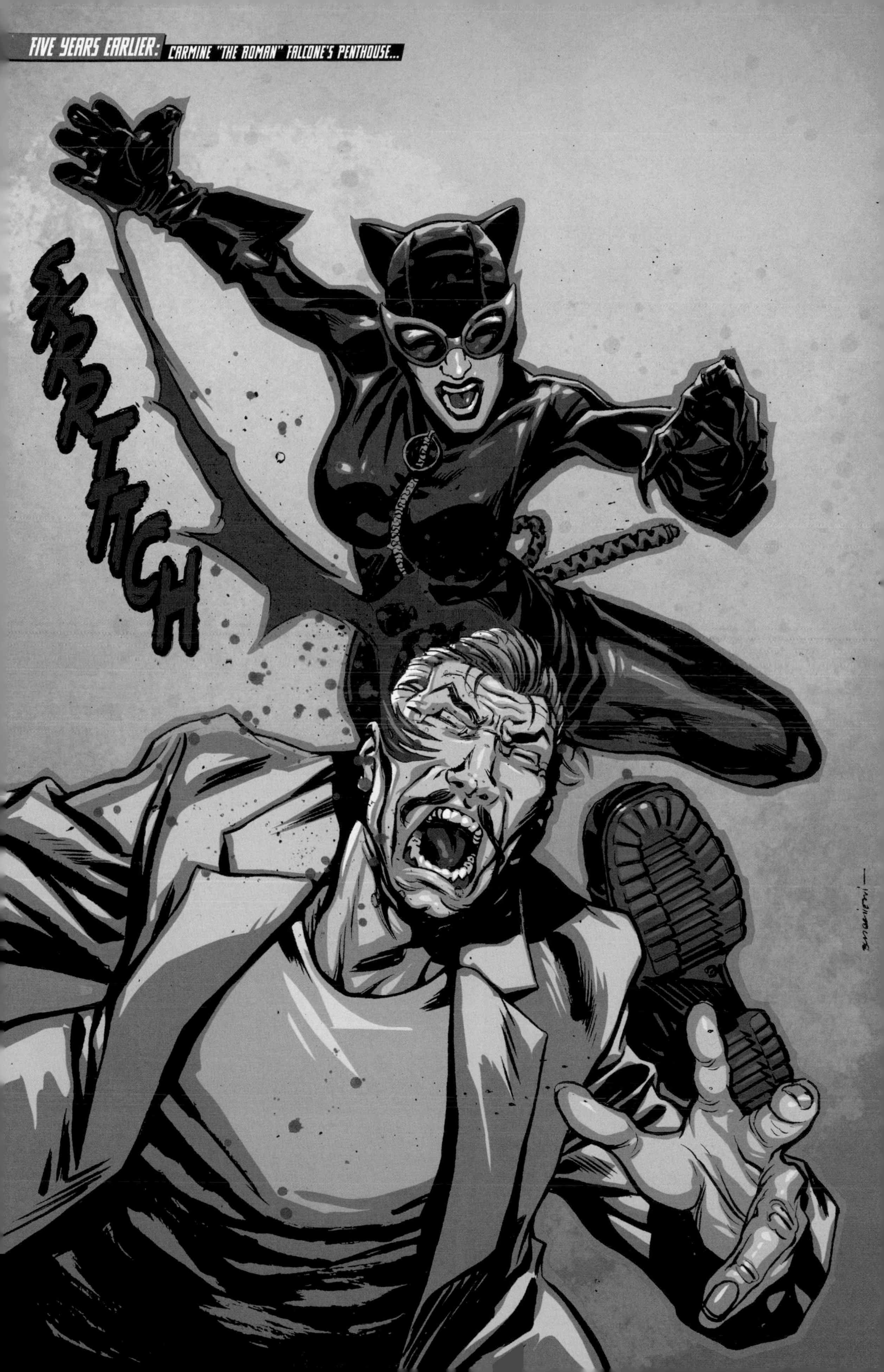
FIVE YEARS EARLIER: CARMINE "THE ROMAN" FALCONE'S PENTHOUSE...
SKRRTTCH

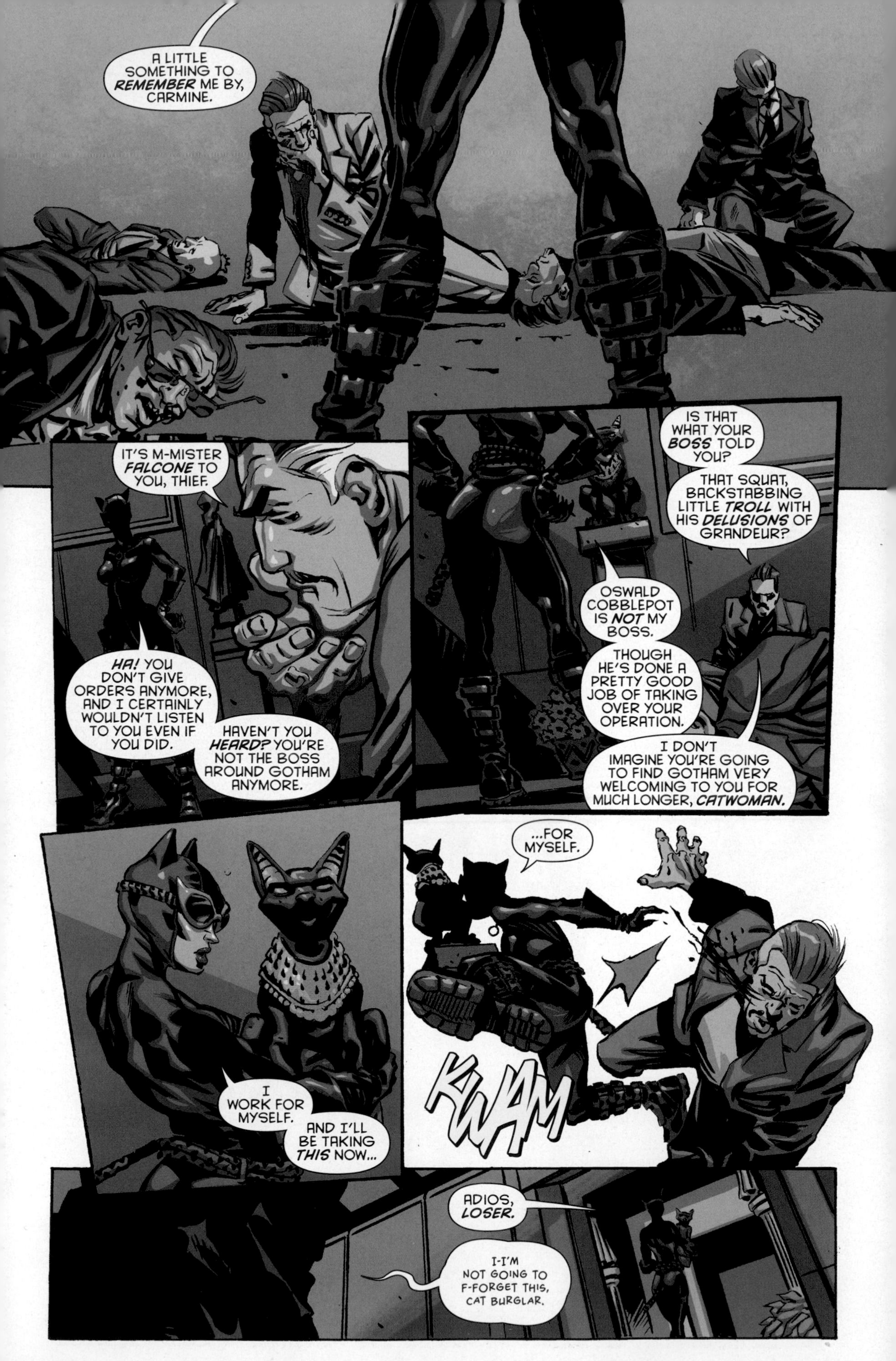
A LITTLE SOMETHING TO REMEMBER ME BY, CARMINE.
IT'S M-MISTER FALCONE TO YOU, THIEF.
HA! YOU DON'T GIVE ORDERS ANYMORE, AND I CERTAINLY WOULDN'T LISTEN TO YOU EVEN IF YOU DID.
HAVEN'T YOU HEARD? YOU'RE NOT THE BOSS AROUND GOTHAM ANYMORE.
IS THAT WHAT YOUR BOSS TOLD YOU?
THAT SQUAT, BACKSTABBING LITTLE TROLL WITH HIS DELUSIONS OF GRANDEUR?
OSWALD COBBLEPOT IS NOT MY BOSS.
THOUGH HE'S DONE A PRETTY GOOD JOB OF TAKING OVER YOUR OPERATION.
I DON'T IMAGINE YOU'RE GOING TO FIND GOTHAM VERY WELCOMING TO YOU FOR MUCH LONGER, CATWOMAN.
I WORK FOR MYSELF.
AND I'LL BE TAKING THIS NOW...
...FOR MYSELF.
KWAM
ADIOS, LOSER.
I-I'M NOT GOING TO F-FORGET THIS, CAT BURGLAR.

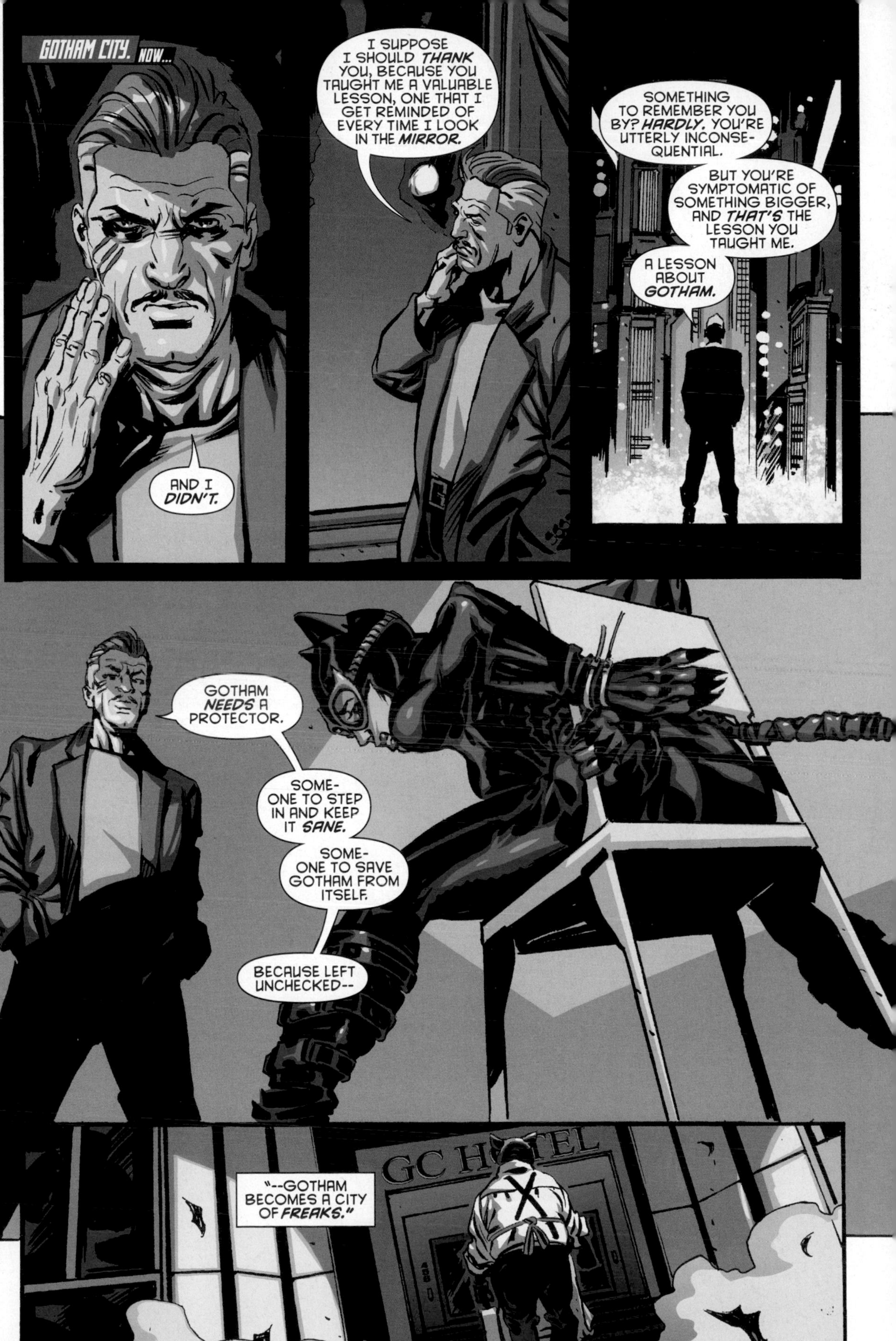
GOTHAM CITY. NOW...
AND I DIDN'T.
I SUPPOSE I SHOULD THANK YOU, BECAUSE YOU TAUGHT ME A VALUABLE LESSON, ONE THAT I GET REMINDED OF EVERY TIME I LOOK IN THE MIRROR.
SOMETHING TO REMEMBER YOU BY? HARDLY. YOU'RE UTTERLY INCONSE- QUENTIAL.
BUT YOU'RE SYMPTOMATIC OF SOMETHING BIGGER, AND THAT'S THE LESSON YOU TAUGHT ME.
A LESSON ABOUT GOTHAM.
GOTHAM NEEDS A PROTECTOR.
SOME- ONE TO STEP IN AND KEEP IT SANE.
SOME- ONE TO SAVE GOTHAM FROM ITSELF.
BECAUSE LEFT UNCHECKED--
"--GOTHAM BECOMES A CITY OF FREAKS."
GC HOTEL

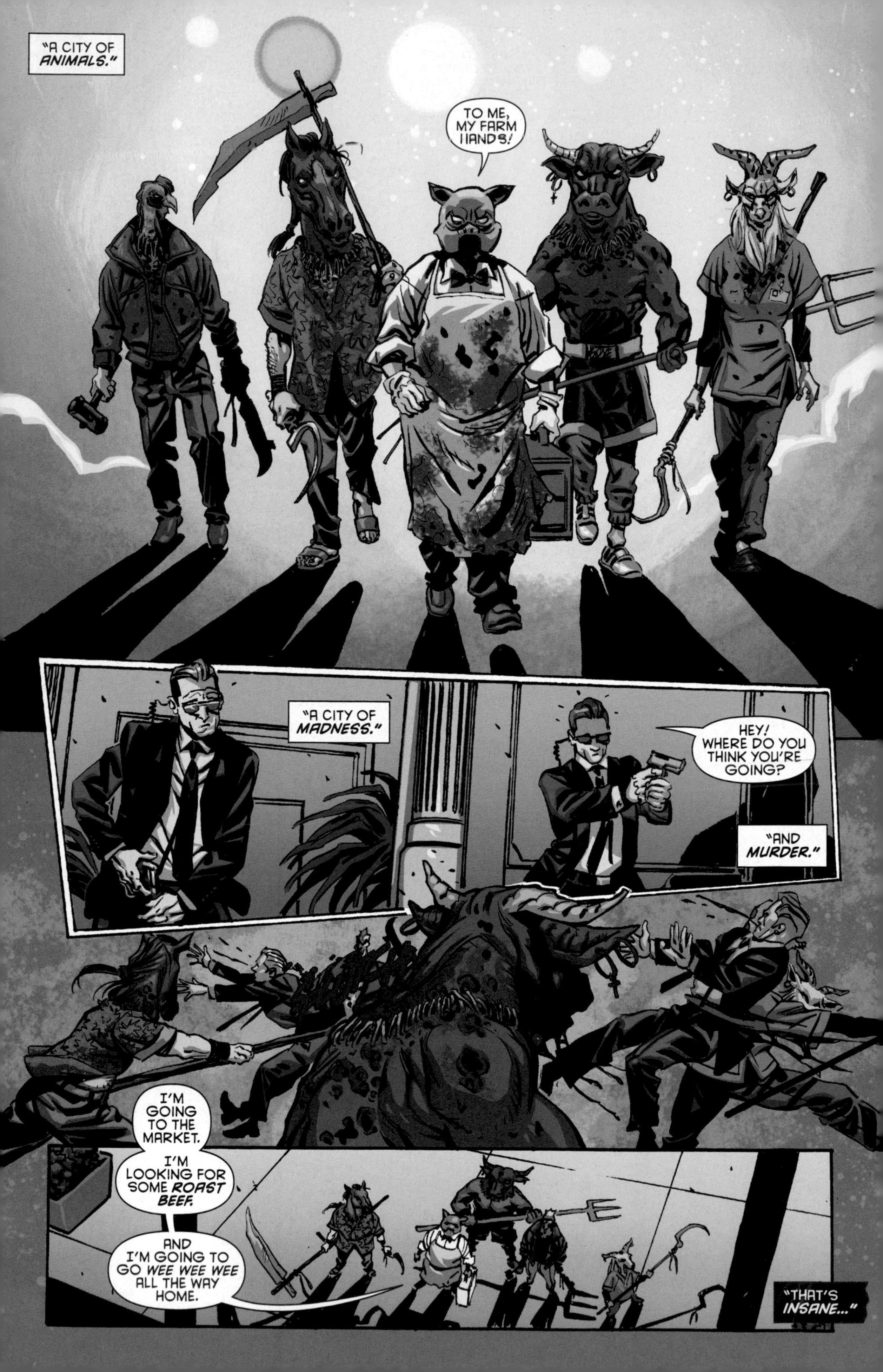
"A CITY OF ANIMALS."
TO ME, MY FARM HANDS!
"A CITY OF MADNESS."
HEY! WHERE DO YOU THINK YOU'RE GOING?
"AND MURDER."
I'M GOING TO THE MARKET.
I'M LOOKING FOR SOME ROAST BEEF.
AND I'M GOING TO GO WEE WEE WEE ALL THE WAY HOME.
"THAT'S INSANE..."

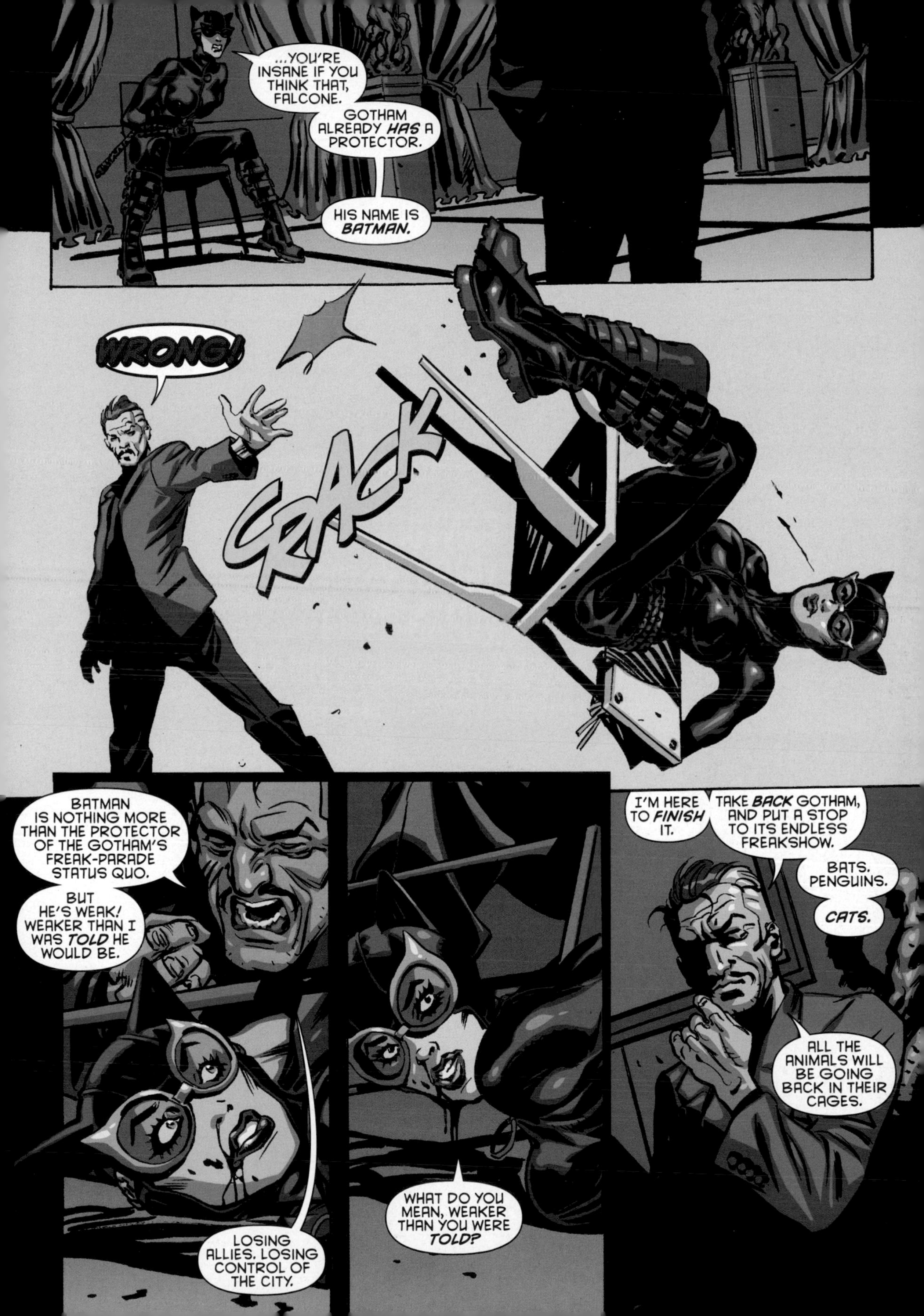
...YOU'RE INSANE IF YOU THINK THAT, FALCONE.
GOTHAM ALREADY HAS A PROTECTOR.
HIS NAME IS BATMAN.
WRONG!
CRACK
BATMAN IS NOTHING MORE THAN THE PROTECTOR OF THE GOTHAM'S FREAK-PARADE STATUS QUO.
BUT HE'S WEAK! WEAKER THAN I WAS TOLD HE WOULD BE.
LOSING ALLIES. LOSING CONTROL OF THE CITY.
WHAT DO YOU MEAN, WEAKER THAN YOU WERE TOLD?
I'M HERE TO FINISH IT.
TAKE BACK GOTHAM, AND PUT A STOP TO ITS ENDLESS FREAKSHOW.
BATS. PENGUINS.
CATS.
ALL THE ANIMALS WILL BE GOING BACK IN THEIR CAGES.

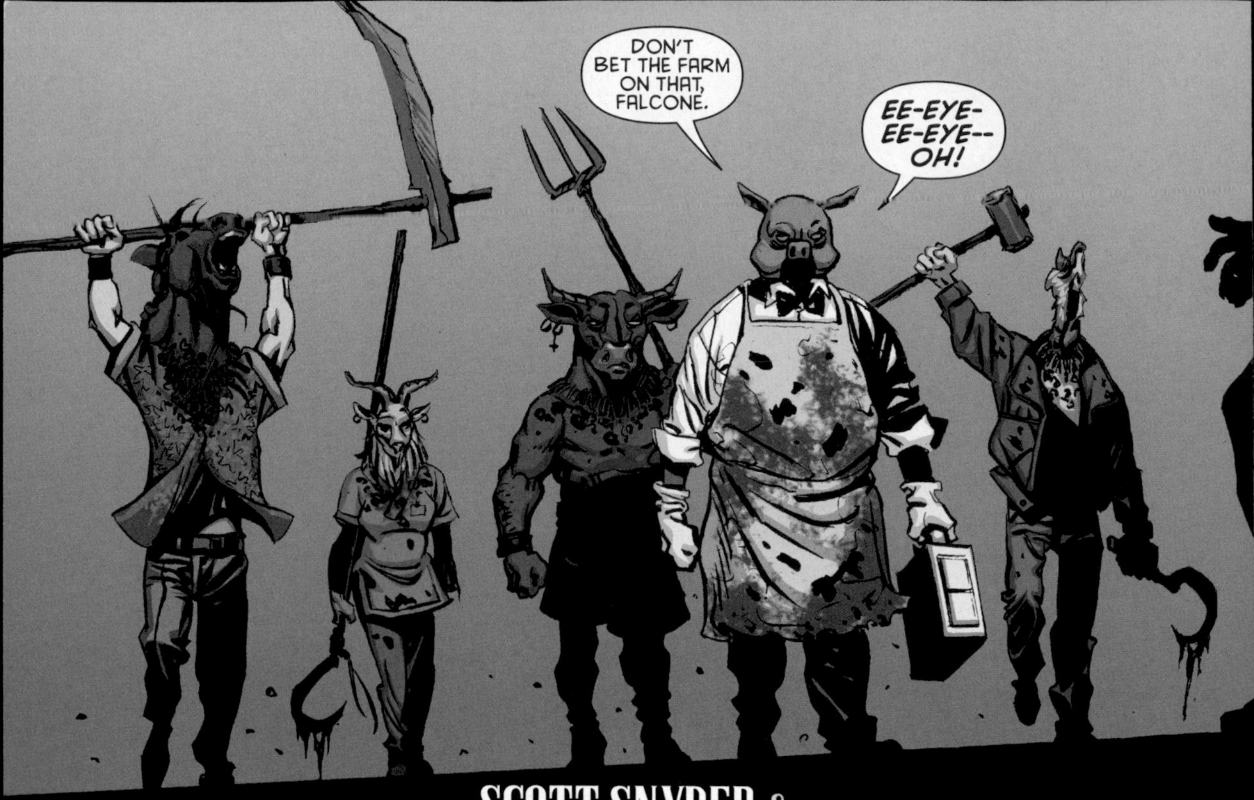
DON'T BET THE FARM ON THAT, FALCONE.
EE-EYE-EE-EYE--OH!

SCOTT SNYDER &
JAMES TYNION IV STORY
JOHN LAYMAN SCRIPT
CONSULTING WRITERS: RAY FAWKES & TIM SEELEY

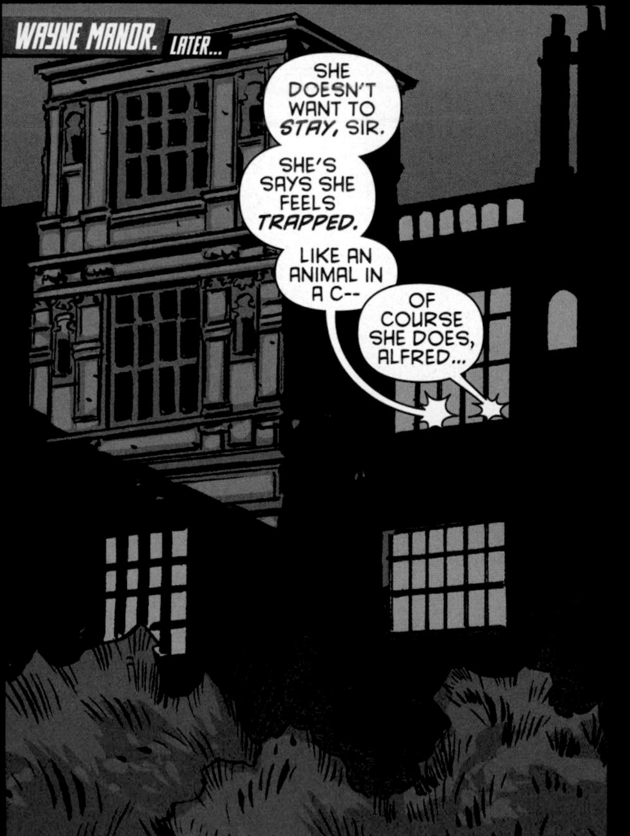
WAYNE MANOR. LATER...
SHE DOESN'T WANT TO STAY, SIR.
SHE'S SAYS SHE FEELS TRAPPED.
LIKE AN ANIMAL IN A C--
OF COURSE SHE DOES, ALFRED...

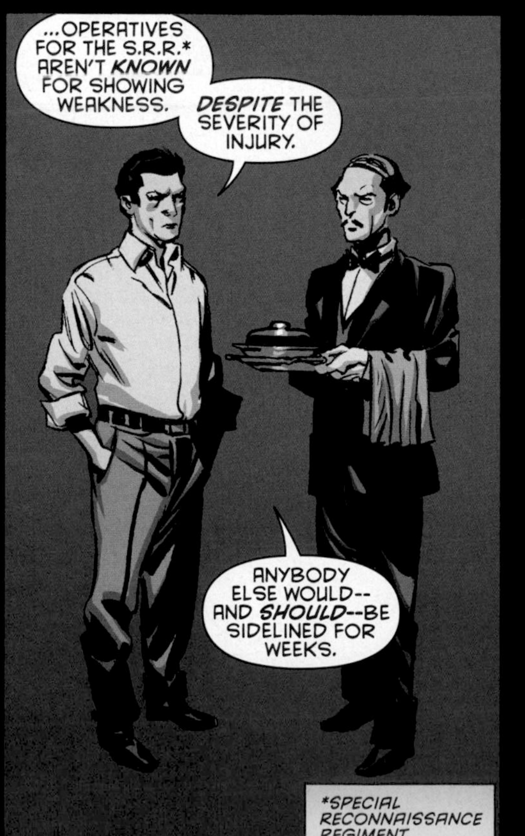
...OPERATIVES FOR THE S.R.R.* AREN'T KNOWN FOR SHOWING WEAKNESS.
DESPITE THE SEVERITY OF INJURY.
ANYBODY ELSE WOULD--AND SHOULD--BE SIDELINED FOR WEEKS.
*SPECIAL RECONNAISSANCE REGIMENT.

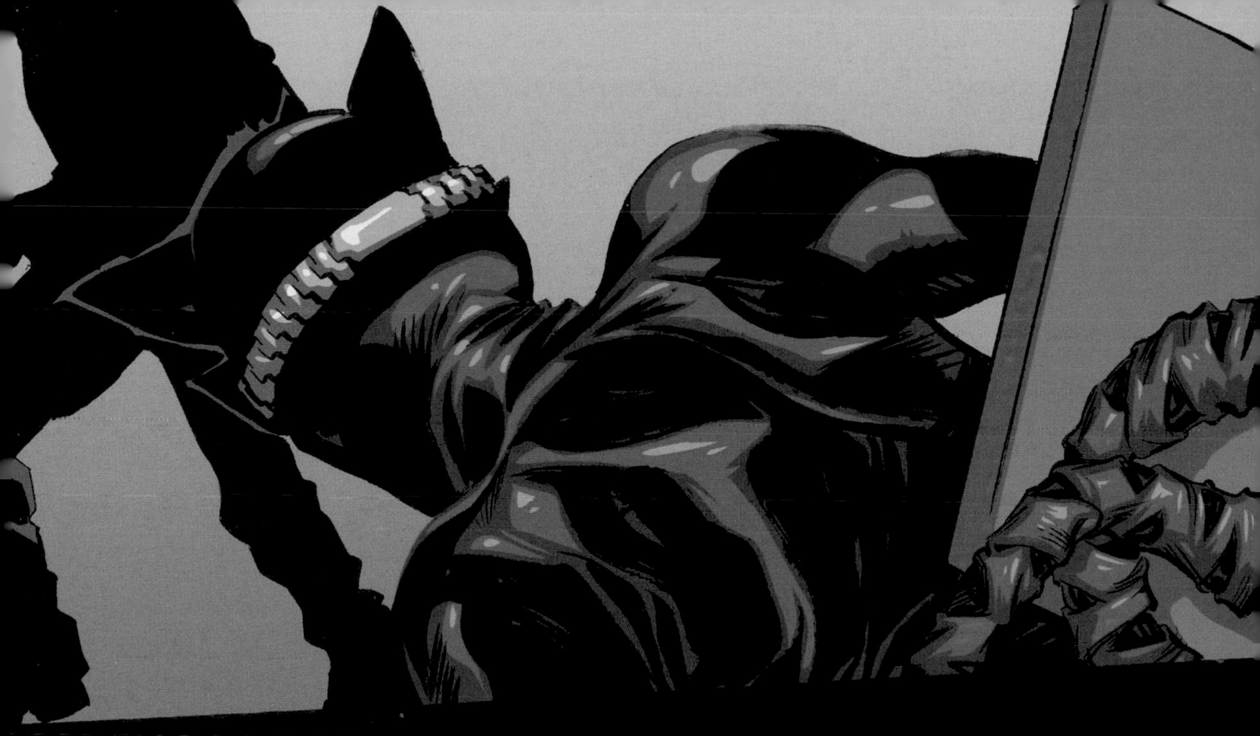

ART BY: RICCARDO BURCHIELLI
COLORS BY: DAVE McCAIG • LETTERING BY: TAYLOR ESPOSITO
COVER BY: GUILLEM MARCH & TOMEU MOREY

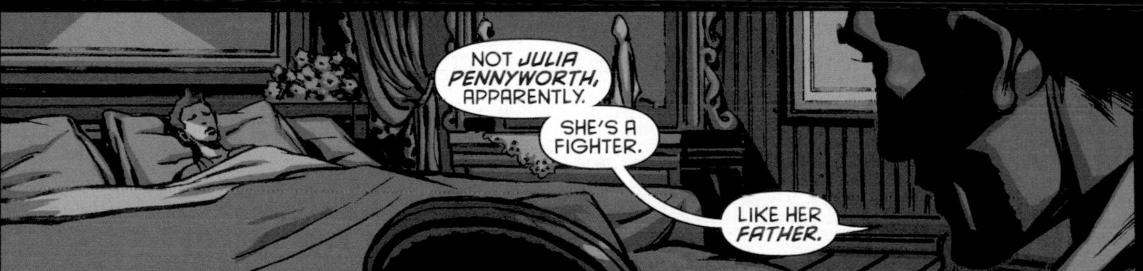
NOT JULIA PENNYWORTH, APPARENTLY.
SHE'S A FIGHTER.
LIKE HER FATHER.

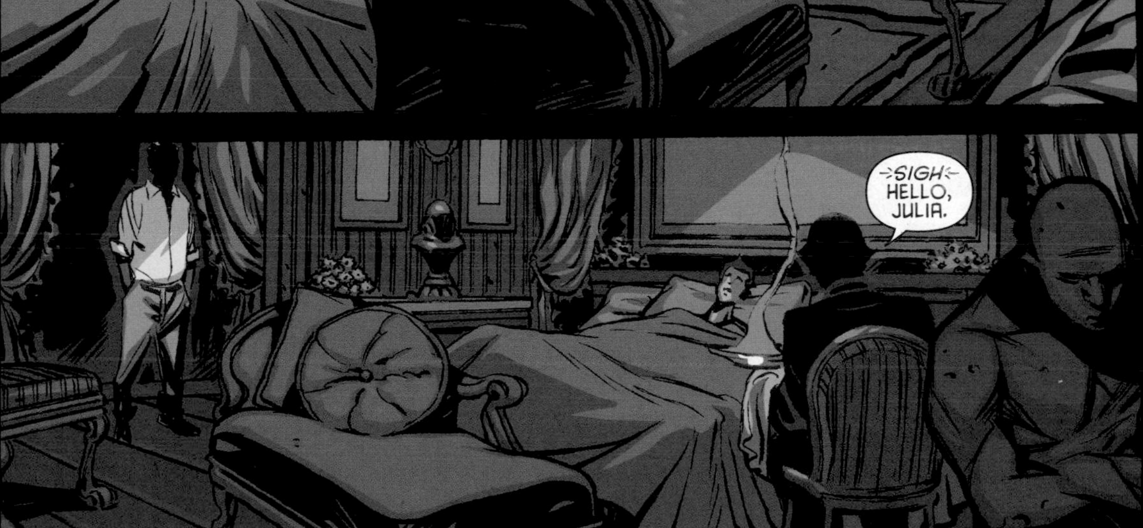
SIGH HELLO, JULIA.

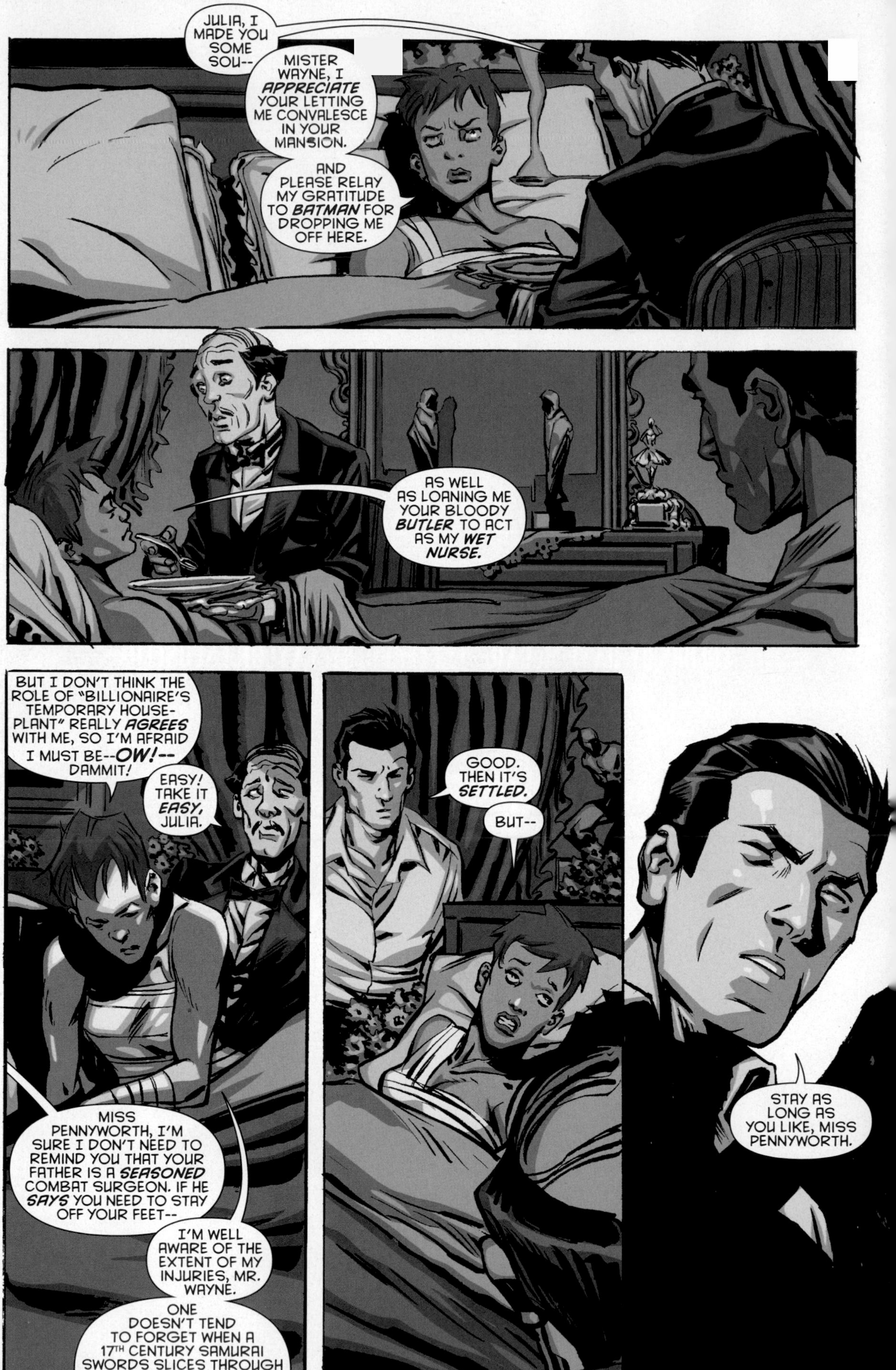
JULIA, I MADE YOU SOME SOU--
MISTER WAYNE, I APPRECIATE YOUR LETTING ME CONVALESCE IN YOUR MANSION.
AND PLEASE RELAY MY GRATITUDE TO BATMAN FOR DROPPING ME OFF HERE.
AS WELL AS LOANING ME YOUR BLOODY BUTLER TO ACT AS MY WET NURSE.
BUT I DON'T THINK THE ROLE OF "BILLIONAIRE'S TEMPORARY HOUSE-PLANT" REALLY AGREES WITH ME, SO I'M AFRAID I MUST BE--OW!--DAMMIT!
EASY! TAKE IT EASY, JULIA.
MISS PENNYWORTH, I'M SURE I DON'T NEED TO REMIND YOU THAT YOUR FATHER IS A SEASONED COMBAT SURGEON. IF HE SAYS YOU NEED TO STAY OFF YOUR FEET--
I'M WELL AWARE OF THE EXTENT OF MY INJURIES, MR. WAYNE.
ONE DOESN'T TEND TO FORGET WHEN A 17TH CENTURY SAMURAI SWORDS SLICES THROUGH ONE'S INTERNAL ORGANS.
GOOD. THEN IT'S SETTLED.
BUT--
STAY AS LONG AS YOU LIKE, MISS PENNYWORTH.

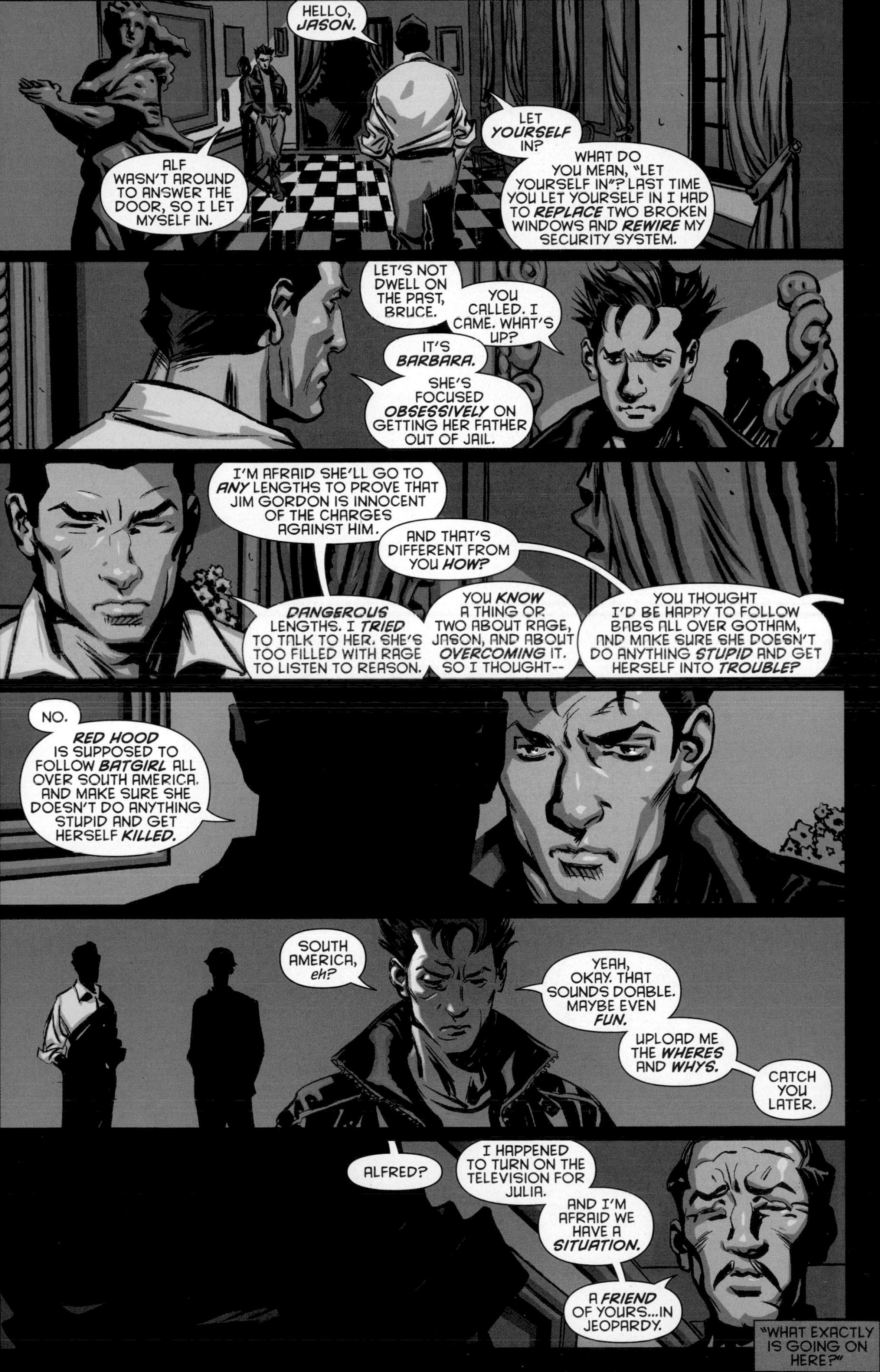
HELLO, JASON.
ALF WASN'T AROUND TO ANSWER THE DOOR, SO I LET MYSELF IN.
LET YOURSELF IN?
WHAT DO YOU MEAN, "LET YOURSELF IN"? LAST TIME YOU LET YOURSELF IN I HAD TO REPLACE TWO BROKEN WINDOWS AND REWIRE MY SECURITY SYSTEM.
LET'S NOT DWELL ON THE PAST, BRUCE.
YOU CALLED. I CAME. WHAT'S UP?
IT'S BARBARA.
SHE'S FOCUSED OBSESSIVELY ON GETTING HER FATHER OUT OF JAIL.
I'M AFRAID SHE'LL GO TO ANY LENGTHS TO PROVE THAT JIM GORDON IS INNOCENT OF THE CHARGES AGAINST HIM.
AND THAT'S DIFFERENT FROM YOU HOW?
DANGEROUS LENGTHS. I TRIED TO TALK TO HER. SHE'S TOO FILLED WITH RAGE TO LISTEN TO REASON.
YOU KNOW A THING OR TWO ABOUT RAGE, JASON, AND ABOUT OVERCOMING IT. SO I THOUGHT--
YOU THOUGHT I'D BE HAPPY TO FOLLOW BABS ALL OVER GOTHAM, AND MAKE SURE SHE DOESN'T DO ANYTHING STUPID AND GET HERSELF INTO TROUBLE?
NO.
RED HOOD IS SUPPOSED TO FOLLOW BATGIRL ALL OVER SOUTH AMERICA. AND MAKE SURE SHE DOESN'T DO ANYTHING STUPID AND GET HERSELF KILLED.
SOUTH AMERICA, eh?
YEAH, OKAY. THAT SOUNDS DOABLE. MAYBE EVEN FUN.
UPLOAD ME THE WHERES AND WHYS.
CATCH YOU LATER.
ALFRED?
I HAPPENED TO TURN ON THE TELEVISION FOR JULIA.
AND I'M AFRAID WE HAVE A SITUATION.
A FRIEND OF YOURS...IN JEOPARDY.
"WHAT EXACTLY IS GOING ON HERE?"

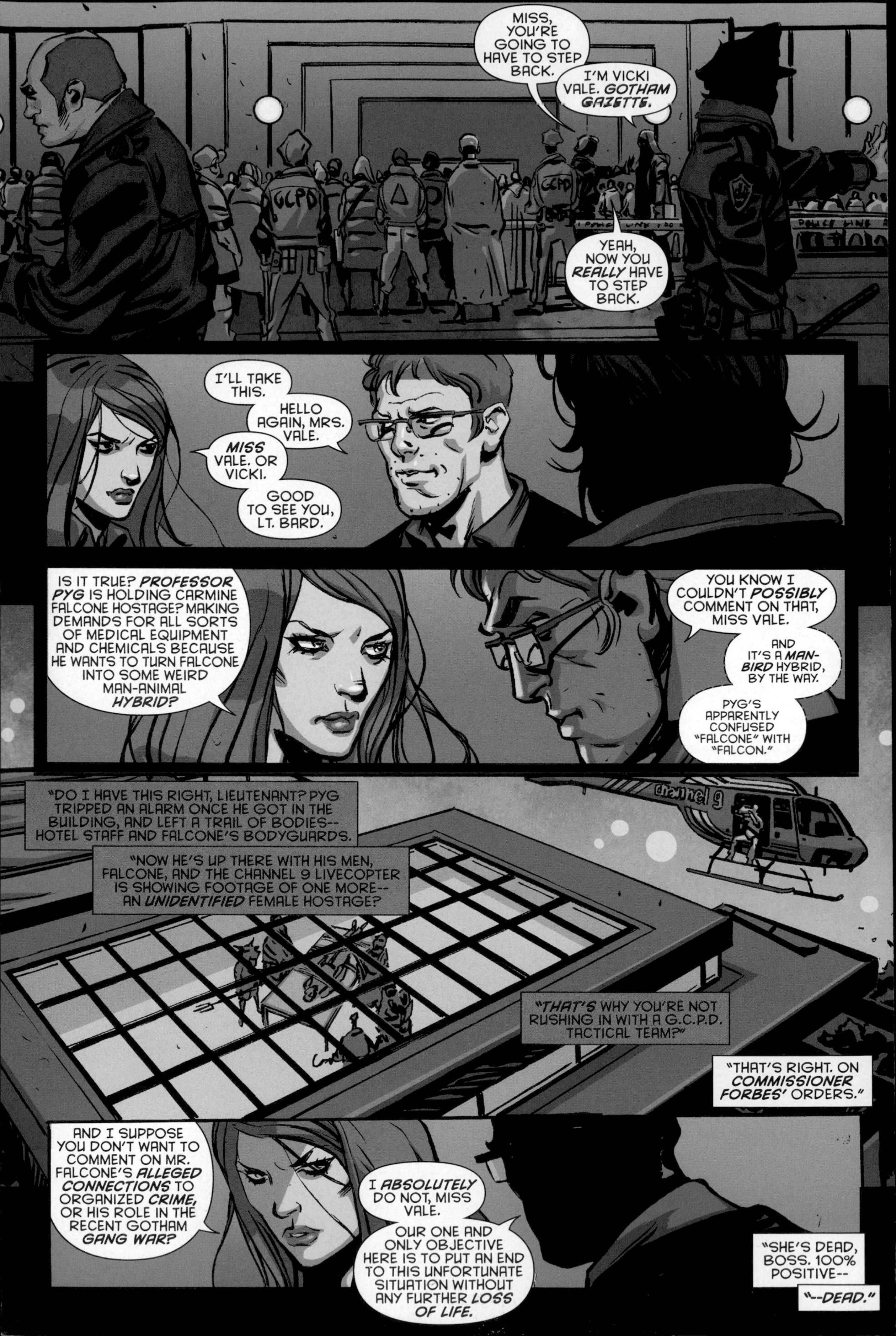
MISS, YOU'RE GOING TO HAVE TO STEP BACK.
I'M VICKI VALE. GOTHAM GAZETTE.
YEAH, NOW YOU REALLY HAVE TO STEP BACK.
GCPD
POLICE LINE
I'LL TAKE THIS.
HELLO AGAIN, MRS. VALE.
MISS VALE. OR VICKI.
GOOD TO SEE YOU, LT. BARD.
IS IT TRUE? PROFESSOR PYG IS HOLDING CARMINE FALCONE HOSTAGE? MAKING DEMANDS FOR ALL SORTS OF MEDICAL EQUIPMENT AND CHEMICALS BECAUSE HE WANTS TO TURN FALCONE INTO SOME WEIRD MAN-ANIMAL HYBRID?
YOU KNOW I COULDN'T POSSIBLY COMMENT ON THAT, MISS VALE.
AND IT'S A MAN-BIRD HYBRID, BY THE WAY.
PYG'S APPARENTLY CONFUSED "FALCONE" WITH "FALCON."
channel 9
"DO I HAVE THIS RIGHT, LIEUTENANT? PYG TRIPPED AN ALARM ONCE HE GOT IN THE BUILDING, AND LEFT A TRAIL OF BODIES-- HOTEL STAFF AND FALCONE'S BODYGUARDS.
"NOW HE'S UP THERE WITH HIS MEN, FALCONE, AND THE CHANNEL 9 LIVECOPTER IS SHOWING FOOTAGE OF ONE MORE-- AN UNIDENTIFIED FEMALE HOSTAGE?
"THAT'S WHY YOU'RE NOT RUSHING IN WITH A G.C.P.D. TACTICAL TEAM?"
"THAT'S RIGHT. ON COMMISSIONER FORBES' ORDERS."
AND I SUPPOSE YOU DON'T WANT TO COMMENT ON MR. FALCONE'S ALLEGED CONNECTIONS TO ORGANIZED CRIME, OR HIS ROLE IN THE RECENT GOTHAM GANG WAR?
I ABSOLUTELY DO NOT, MISS VALE.
OUR ONE AND ONLY OBJECTIVE HERE IS TO PUT AN END TO THIS UNFORTUNATE SITUATION WITHOUT ANY FURTHER LOSS OF LIFE.
"SHE'S DEAD, BOSS. 100% POSITIVE--
"--DEAD."

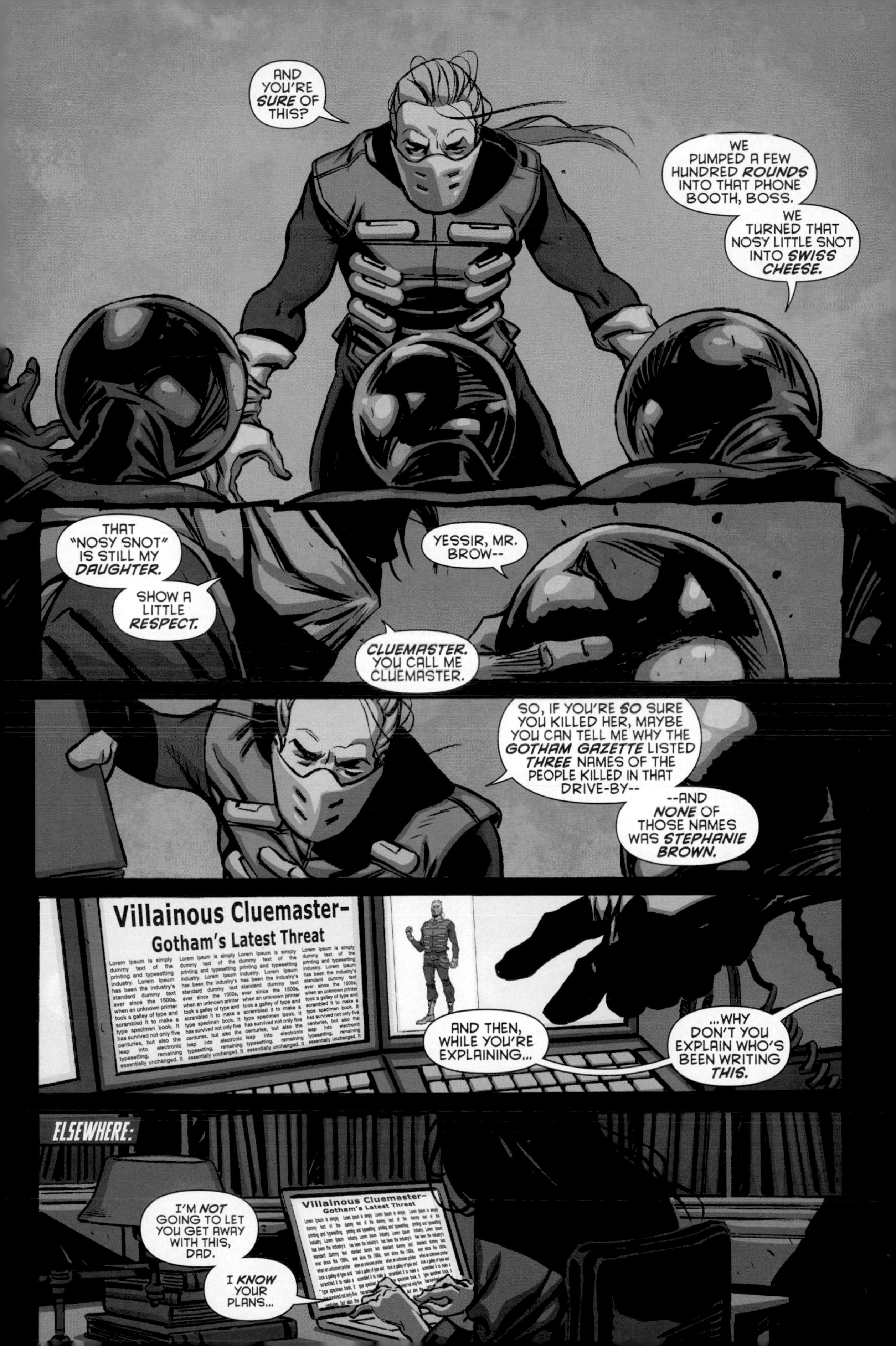
AND YOU'RE SURE OF THIS?
WE PUMPED A FEW HUNDRED ROUNDS INTO THAT PHONE BOOTH, BOSS.
WE TURNED THAT NOSY LITTLE SNOT INTO SWISS CHEESE.
THAT "NOSY SNOT" IS STILL MY DAUGHTER.
SHOW A LITTLE RESPECT.
YESSIR, MR. BROW--
CLUEMASTER. YOU CALL ME CLUEMASTER.
SO, IF YOU'RE SO SURE YOU KILLED HER, MAYBE YOU CAN TELL ME WHY THE GOTHAM GAZETTE LISTED THREE NAMES OF THE PEOPLE KILLED IN THAT DRIVE-BY--
--AND NONE OF THOSE NAMES WAS STEPHANIE BROWN.
Villainous Cluemaster-
Gotham's Latest Threat
AND THEN, WHILE YOU'RE EXPLAINING...
...WHY DON'T YOU EXPLAIN WHO'S BEEN WRITING THIS.
ELSEWHERE:
Villainous Cluemaster-
Gotham's Latest Threat
I'M NOT GOING TO LET YOU GET AWAY WITH THIS, DAD.
I KNOW YOUR PLANS...

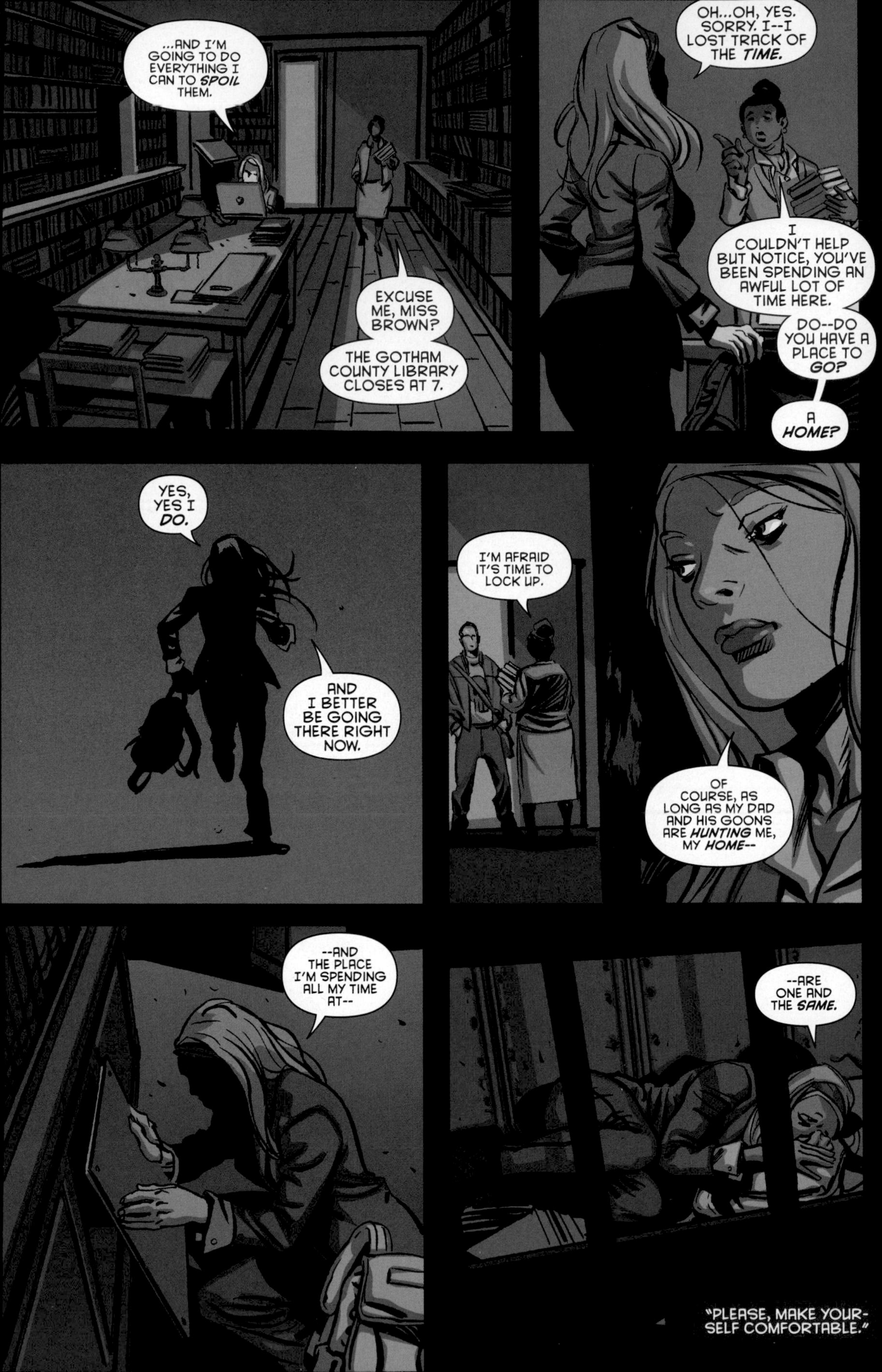
...AND I'M GOING TO DO EVERYTHING I CAN TO SPOIL THEM.
EXCUSE ME, MISS BROWN?
THE GOTHAM COUNTY LIBRARY CLOSES AT 7.
OH...OH, YES. SORRY. I--I LOST TRACK OF THE TIME.
I COULDN'T HELP BUT NOTICE, YOU'VE BEEN SPENDING AN AWFUL LOT OF TIME HERE.
DO--DO YOU HAVE A PLACE TO GO?
A HOME?
YES, YES I DO.
AND I BETTER BE GOING THERE RIGHT NOW.
I'M AFRAID IT'S TIME TO LOCK UP.
OF COURSE, AS LONG AS MY DAD AND HIS GOONS ARE HUNTING ME, MY HOME--
--AND THE PLACE I'M SPENDING ALL MY TIME AT--
--ARE ONE AND THE SAME.
"PLEASE, MAKE YOURSELF COMFORTABLE."

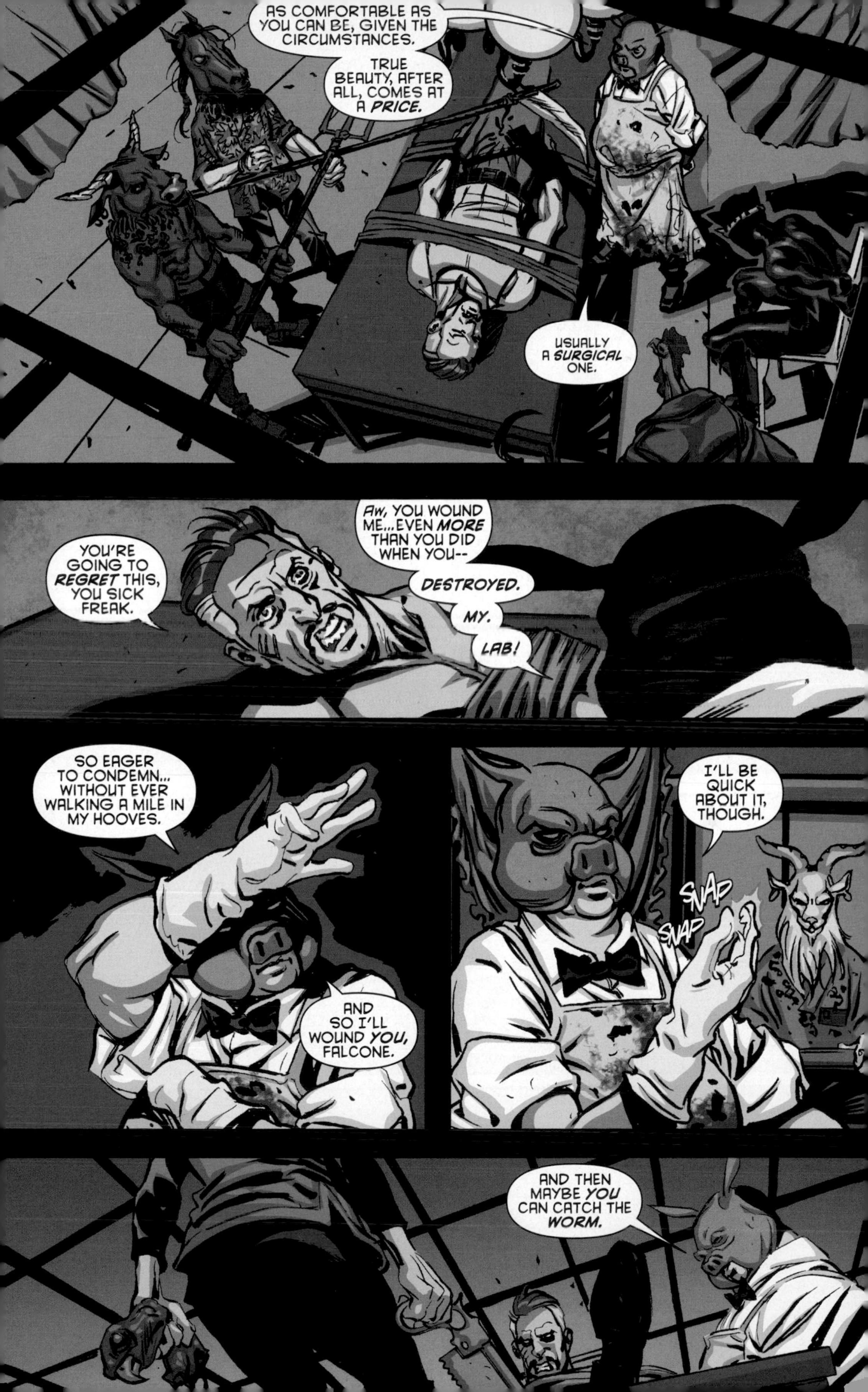
AS COMFORTABLE AS YOU CAN BE, GIVEN THE CIRCUMSTANCES.
TRUE BEAUTY, AFTER ALL, COMES AT A *PRICE*.
USUALLY A *SURGICAL* ONE.
YOU'RE GOING TO *REGRET* THIS, YOU SICK FREAK.
AW, YOU WOUND ME...EVEN *MORE* THAN YOU DID WHEN YOU--
DESTROYED.
MY.
LAB!
SO EAGER TO CONDEMN... WITHOUT EVER WALKING A MILE IN MY HOOVES.
AND SO I'LL WOUND *YOU*, FALCONE.
I'LL BE QUICK ABOUT IT, THOUGH.
SNAP
SNAP
AND THEN MAYBE *YOU* CAN CATCH THE *WORM.*

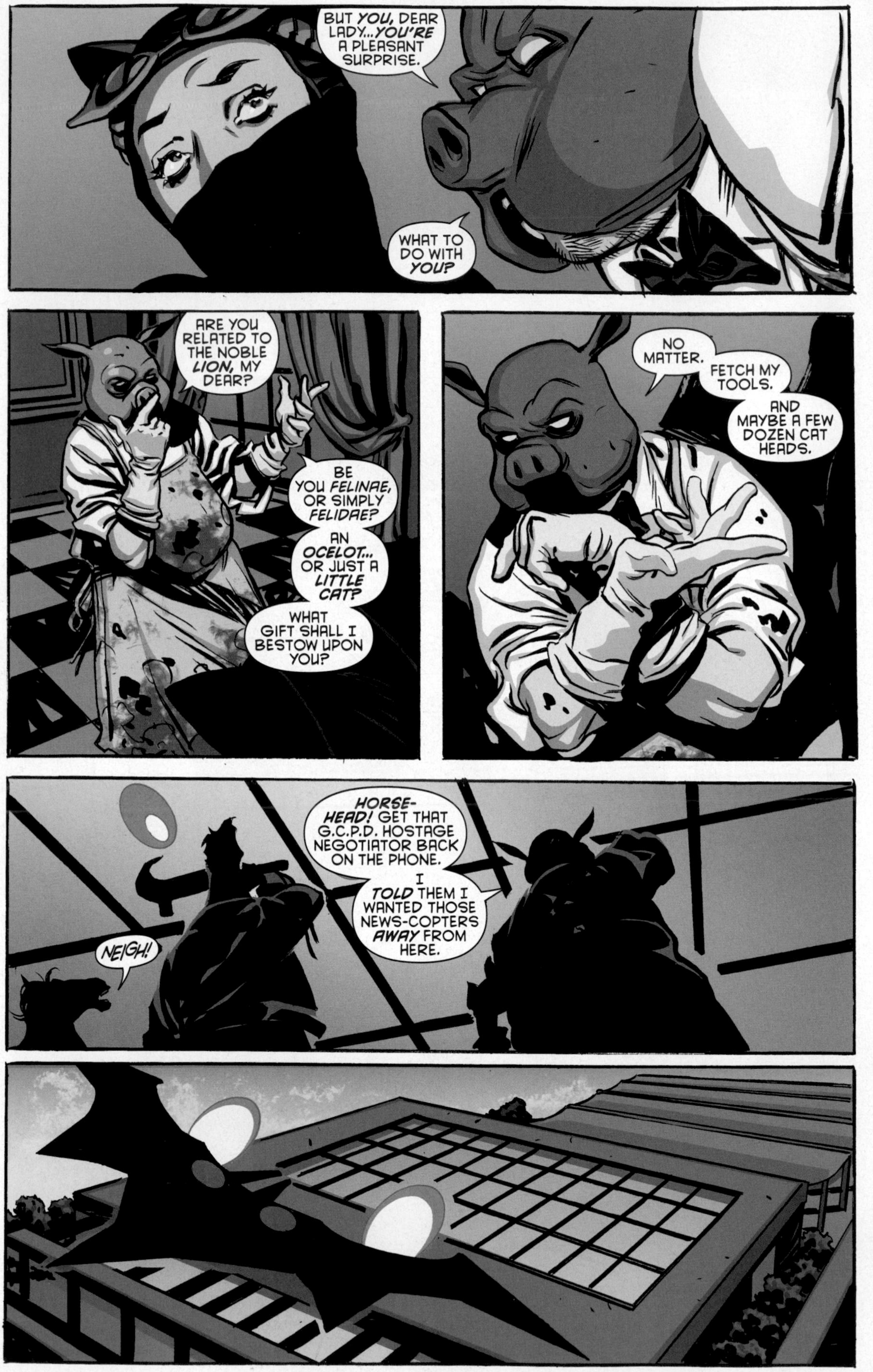
BUT YOU, DEAR LADY...YOU'RE A PLEASANT SURPRISE.
WHAT TO DO WITH YOU?
ARE YOU RELATED TO THE NOBLE LION, MY DEAR?
BE YOU FELINAE, OR SIMPLY FELIDAE?
AN OCELOT... OR JUST A LITTLE CAT?
WHAT GIFT SHALL I BESTOW UPON YOU?
NO MATTER.
FETCH MY TOOLS.
AND MAYBE A FEW DOZEN CAT HEADS.
HORSE-HEAD! GET THAT G.C.P.D. HOSTAGE NEGOTIATOR BACK ON THE PHONE.
I TOLD THEM I WANTED THOSE NEWS-COPTERS AWAY FROM HERE.
NEIGH!

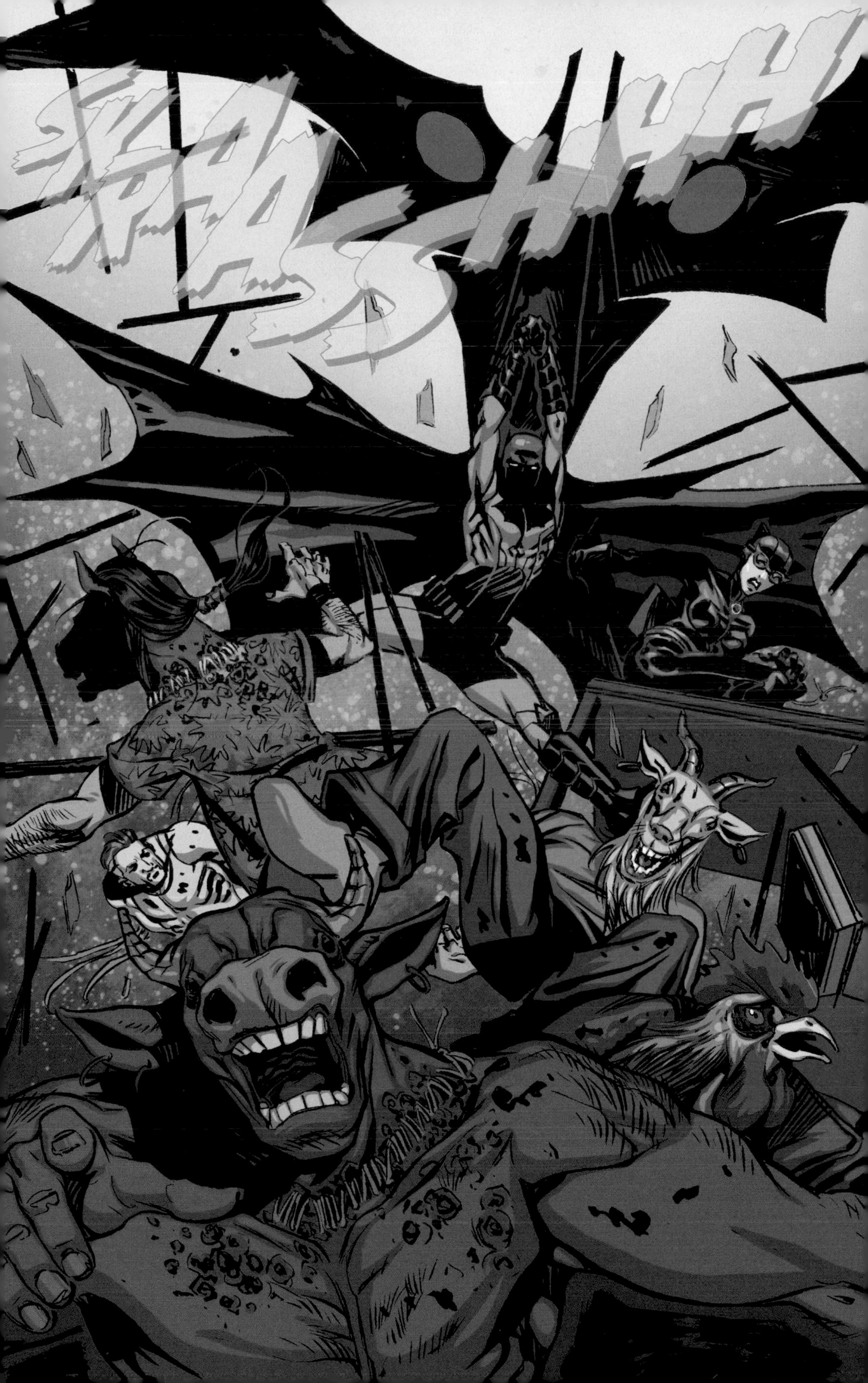

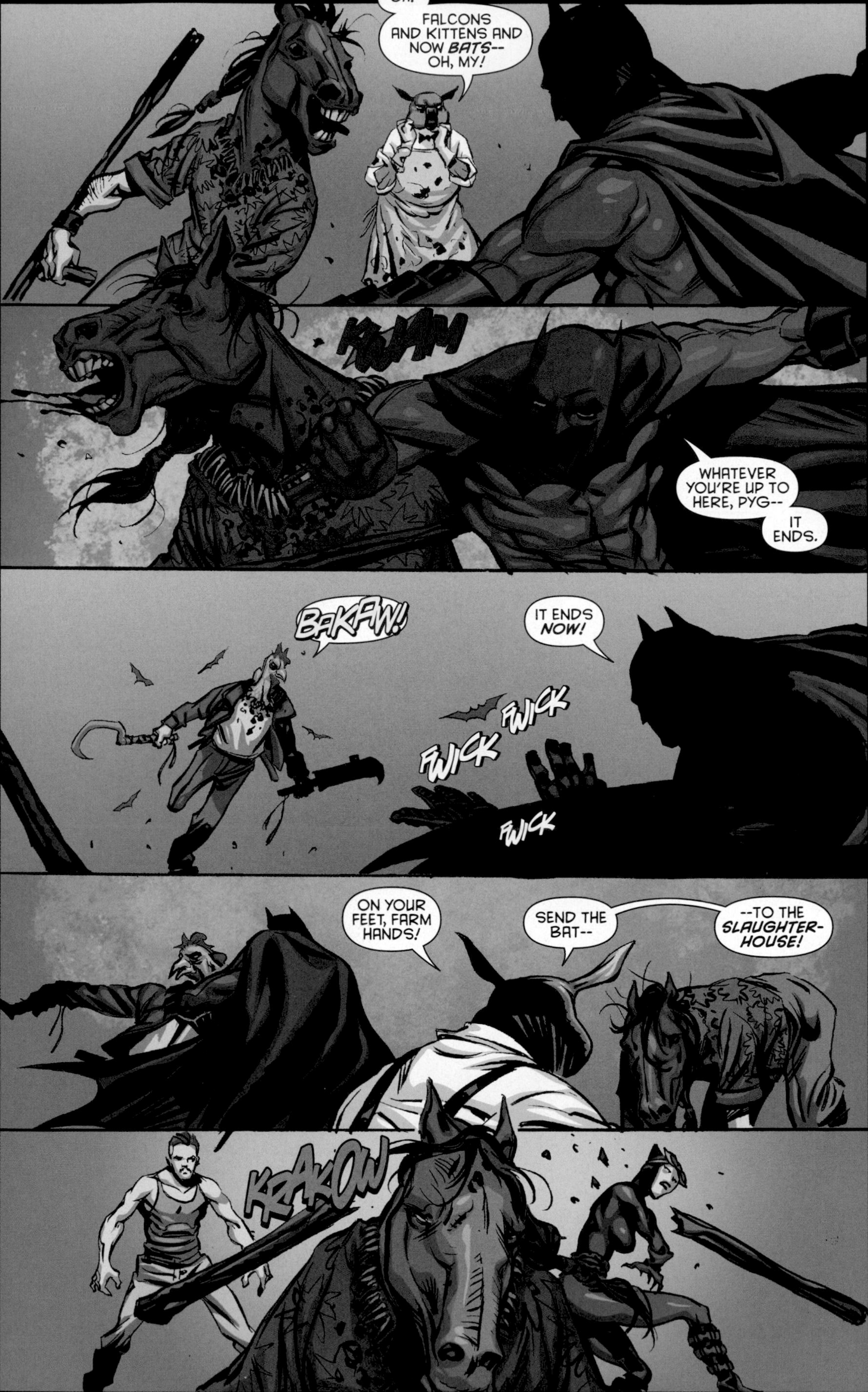
Oh!
FALCONS AND KITTENS AND NOW BATS-- OH, MY!
KWAM
WHATEVER YOU'RE UP TO HERE, PYG--
IT ENDS.
BAKAW!
IT ENDS NOW!
FWICK
FWICK
FWICK
ON YOUR FEET, FARM HANDS!
SEND THE BAT--
--TO THE SLAUGHTER-HOUSE!
KRAKOW

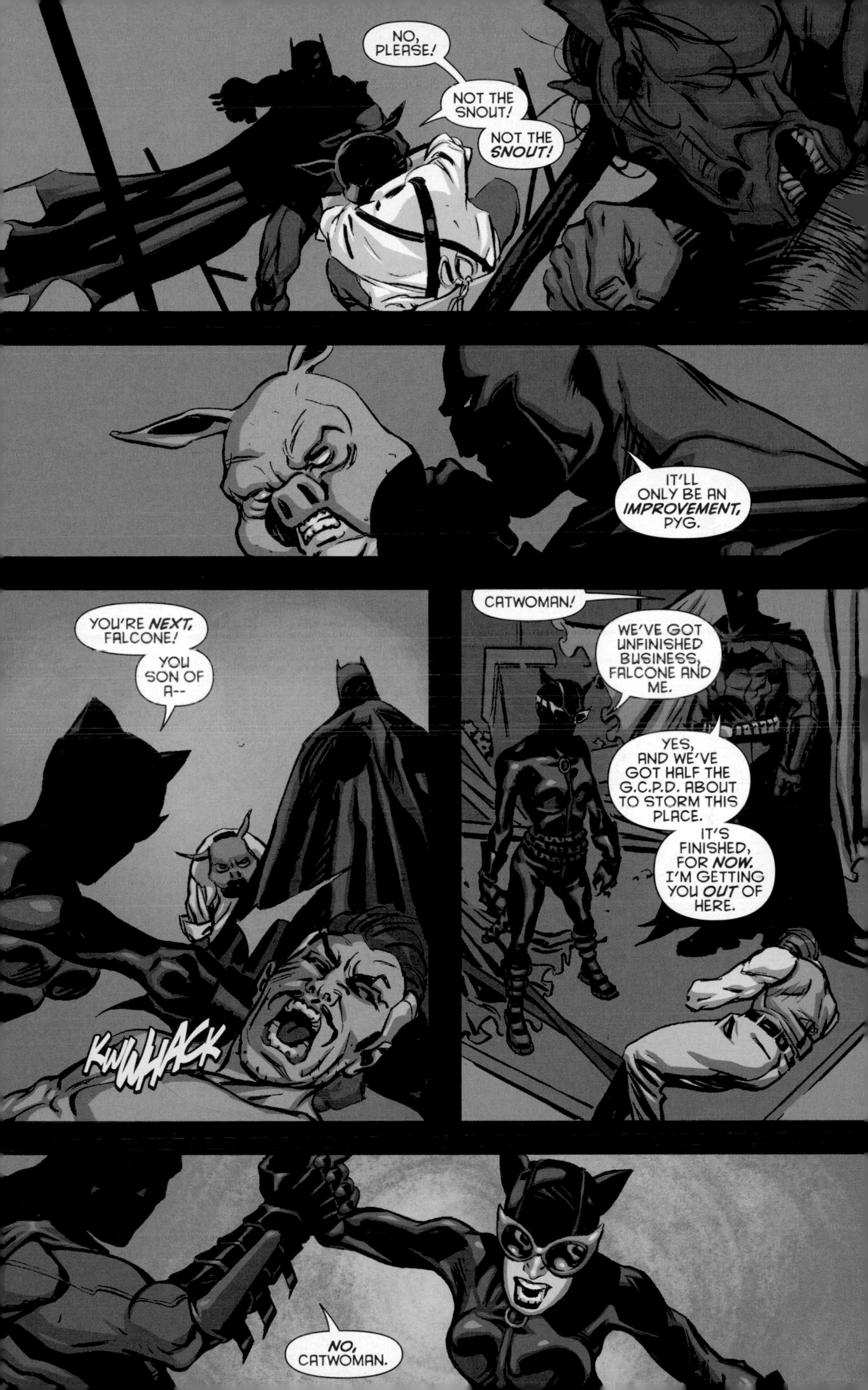
NO, PLEASE!
NOT THE SNOUT!
NOT THE *SNOUT!*
IT'LL ONLY BE AN *IMPROVEMENT,* PYG.
YOU'RE *NEXT,* FALCONE!
YOU SON OF A--
KWWHACK
CATWOMAN!
WE'VE GOT UNFINISHED BUSINESS, FALCONE AND ME.
YES, AND WE'VE GOT HALF THE G.C.P.D. ABOUT TO STORM THIS PLACE.
IT'S FINISHED, FOR *NOW.* I'M GETTING YOU *OUT* OF HERE.
NO, CATWOMAN.

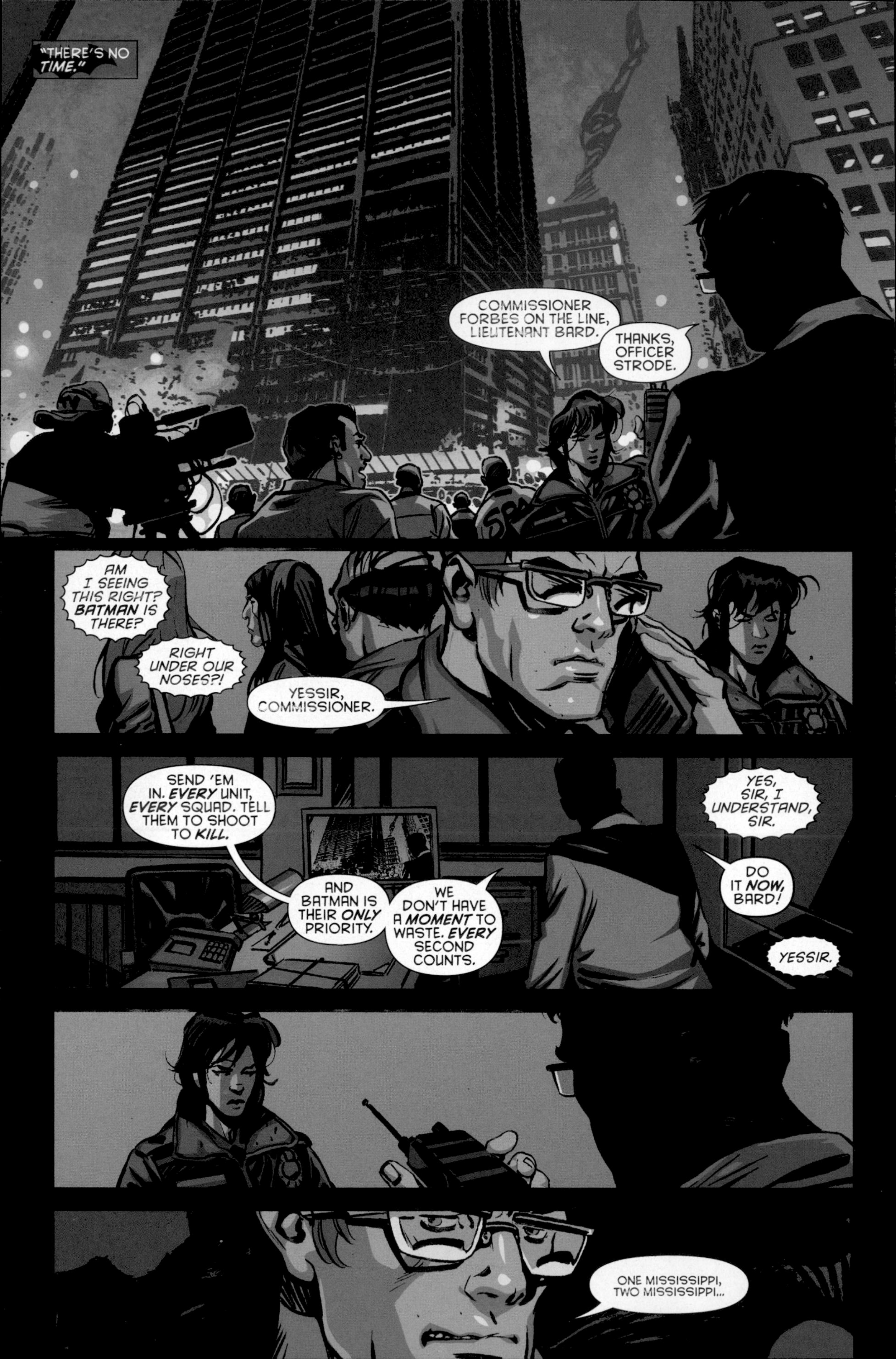
"THERE'S NO TIME."
COMMISSIONER FORBES ON THE LINE, LIEUTENANT BARD.
THANKS, OFFICER STRODE.
AM I SEEING THIS RIGHT? BATMAN IS THERE?
RIGHT UNDER OUR NOSES?!
YESSIR, COMMISSIONER.
SEND 'EM IN. EVERY UNIT, EVERY SQUAD. TELL THEM TO SHOOT TO KILL.
AND BATMAN IS THEIR ONLY PRIORITY.
WE DON'T HAVE A MOMENT TO WASTE. EVERY SECOND COUNTS.
YES, SIR, I UNDERSTAND, SIR.
DO IT NOW, BARD!
YESSIR.
ONE MISSISSIPPI, TWO MISSISSIPPI...

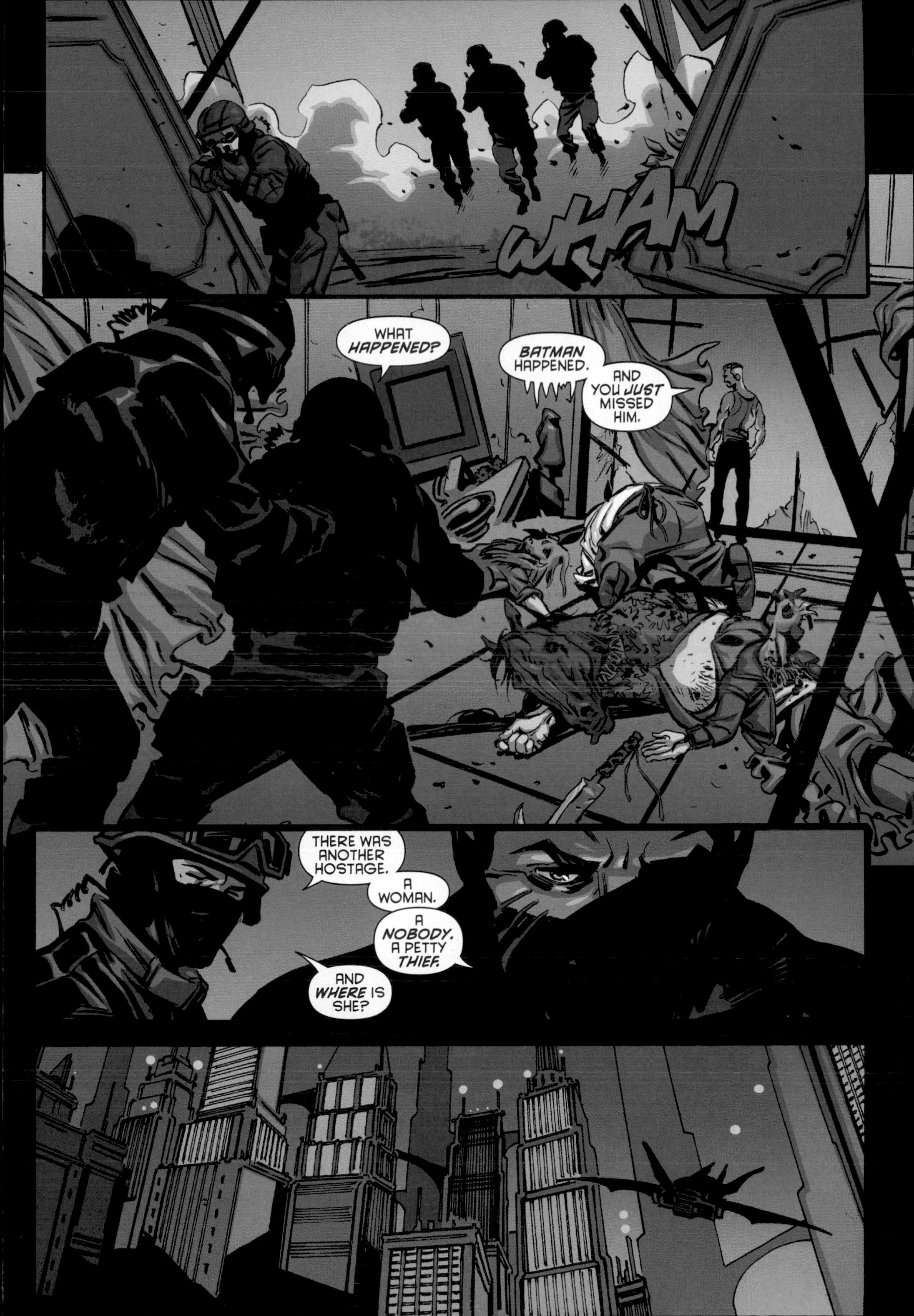
WHAM
WHAT HAPPENED?
BATMAN HAPPENED.
AND YOU JUST MISSED HIM.
THERE WAS ANOTHER HOSTAGE.
A WOMAN.
A NOBODY. A PETTY THIEF.
AND WHERE IS SHE?

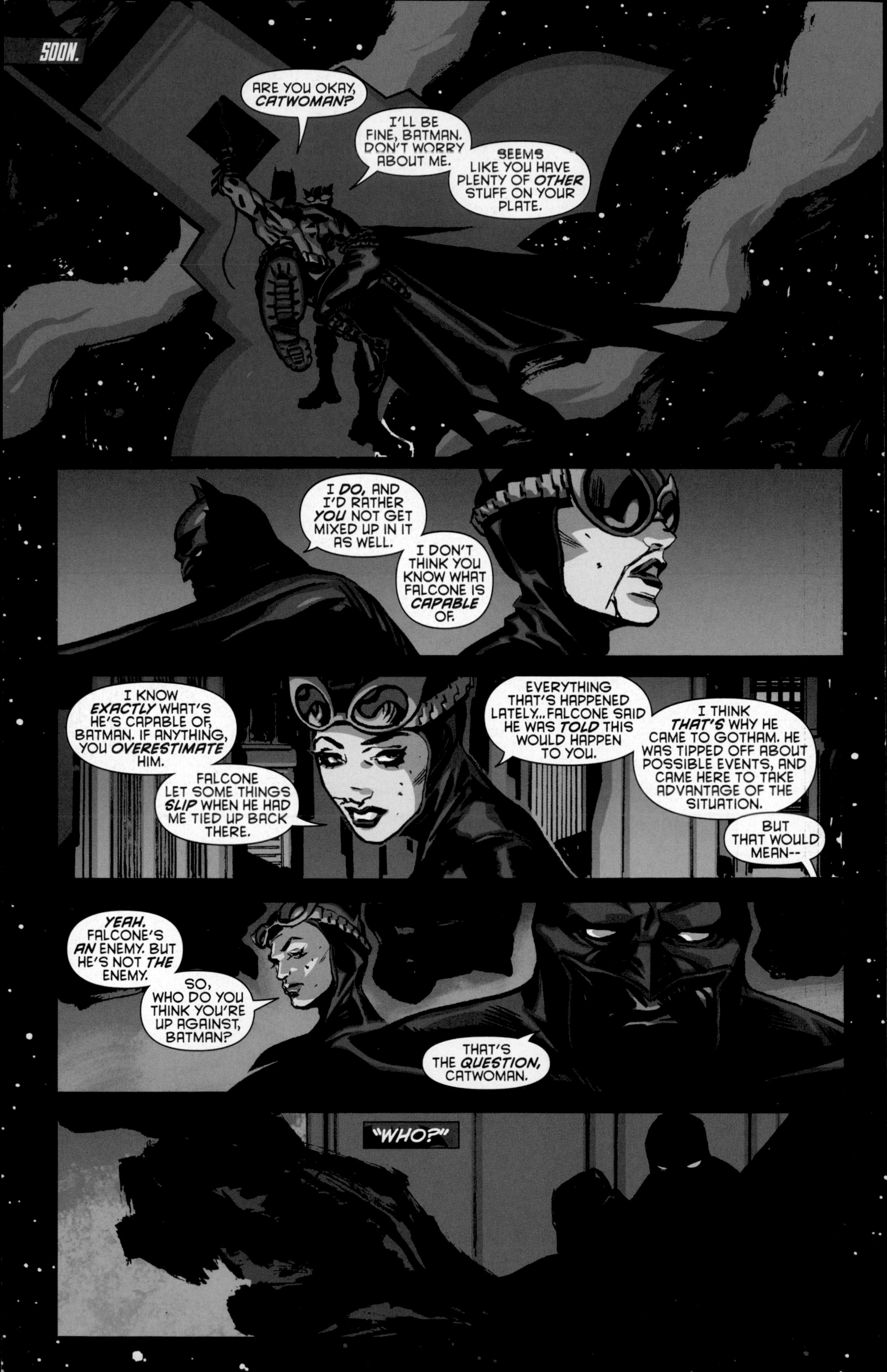
SOON.
ARE YOU OKAY, CATWOMAN?
I'LL BE FINE, BATMAN. DON'T WORRY ABOUT ME.
SEEMS LIKE YOU HAVE PLENTY OF OTHER STUFF ON YOUR PLATE.
I DO, AND I'D RATHER YOU NOT GET MIXED UP IN IT AS WELL.
I DON'T THINK YOU KNOW WHAT FALCONE IS CAPABLE OF.
I KNOW EXACTLY WHAT'S HE'S CAPABLE OF, BATMAN. IF ANYTHING, YOU OVERESTIMATE HIM.
FALCONE LET SOME THINGS SLIP WHEN HE HAD ME TIED UP BACK THERE.
EVERYTHING THAT'S HAPPENED LATELY...FALCONE SAID HE WAS TOLD THIS WOULD HAPPEN TO YOU.
I THINK THAT'S WHY HE CAME TO GOTHAM. HE WAS TIPPED OFF ABOUT POSSIBLE EVENTS, AND CAME HERE TO TAKE ADVANTAGE OF THE SITUATION.
BUT THAT WOULD MEAN--
YEAH. FALCONE'S AN ENEMY. BUT HE'S NOT THE ENEMY.
SO, WHO DO YOU THINK YOU'RE UP AGAINST, BATMAN?
THAT'S THE QUESTION, CATWOMAN.
"WHO?"

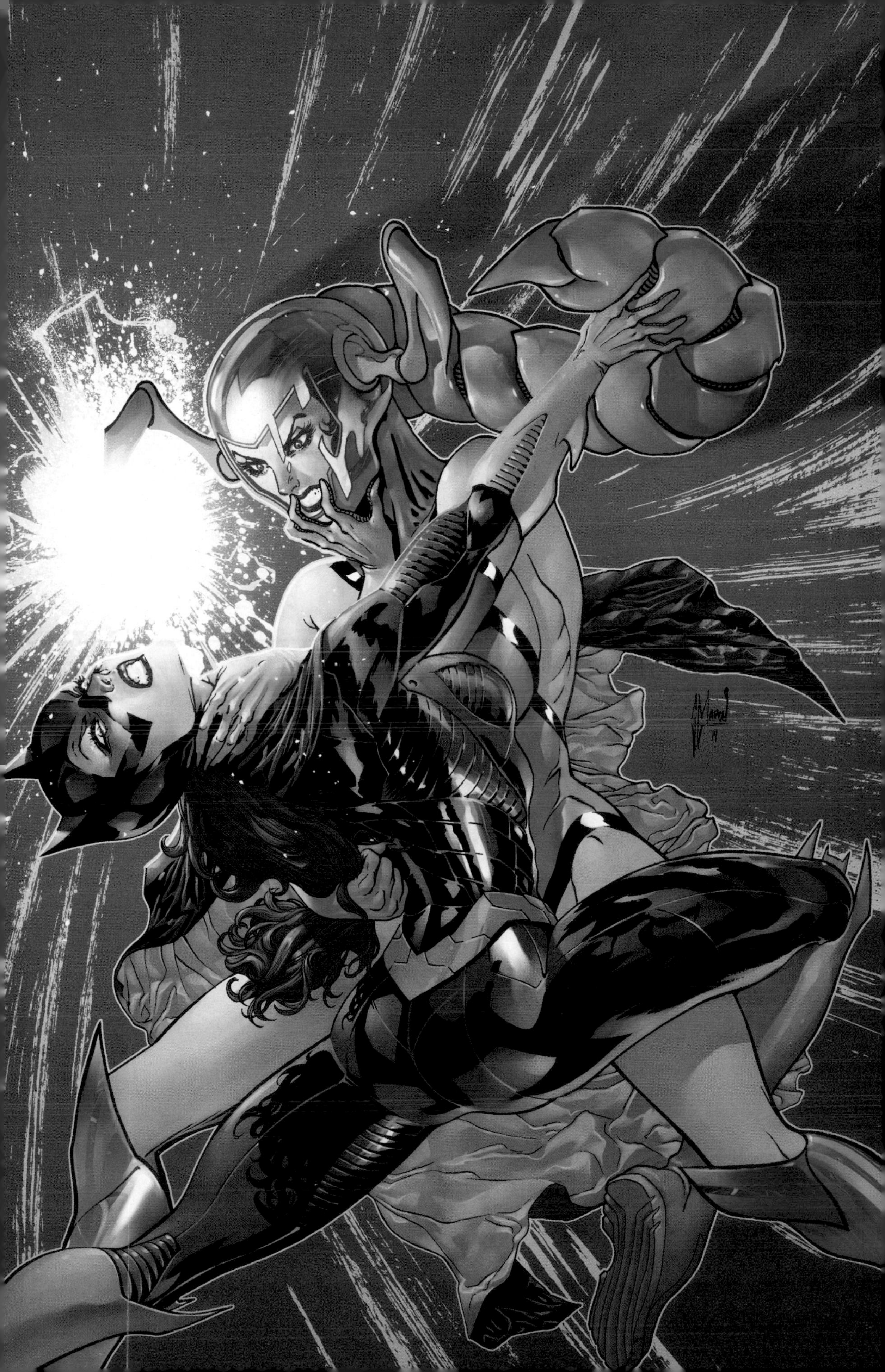

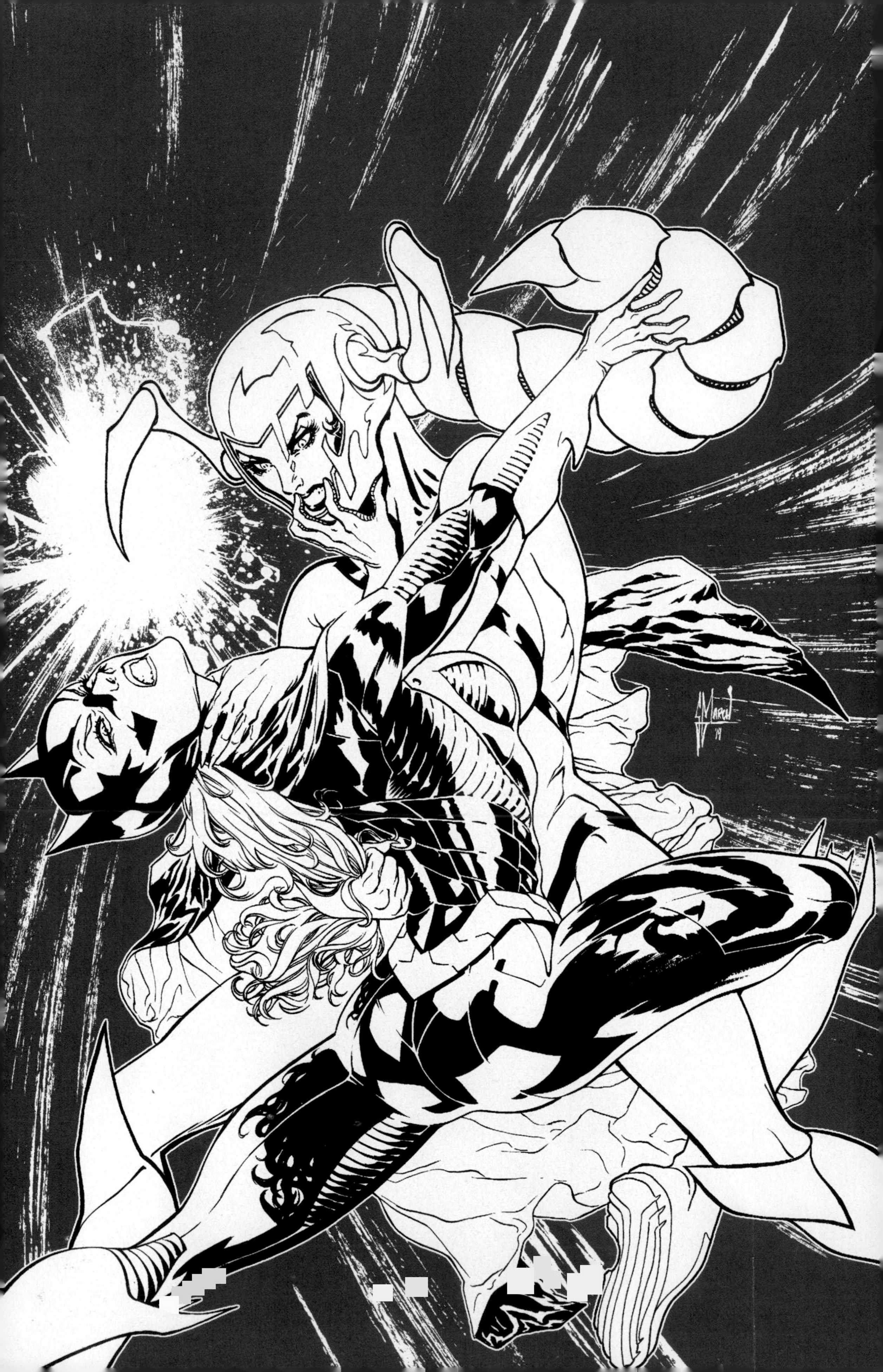

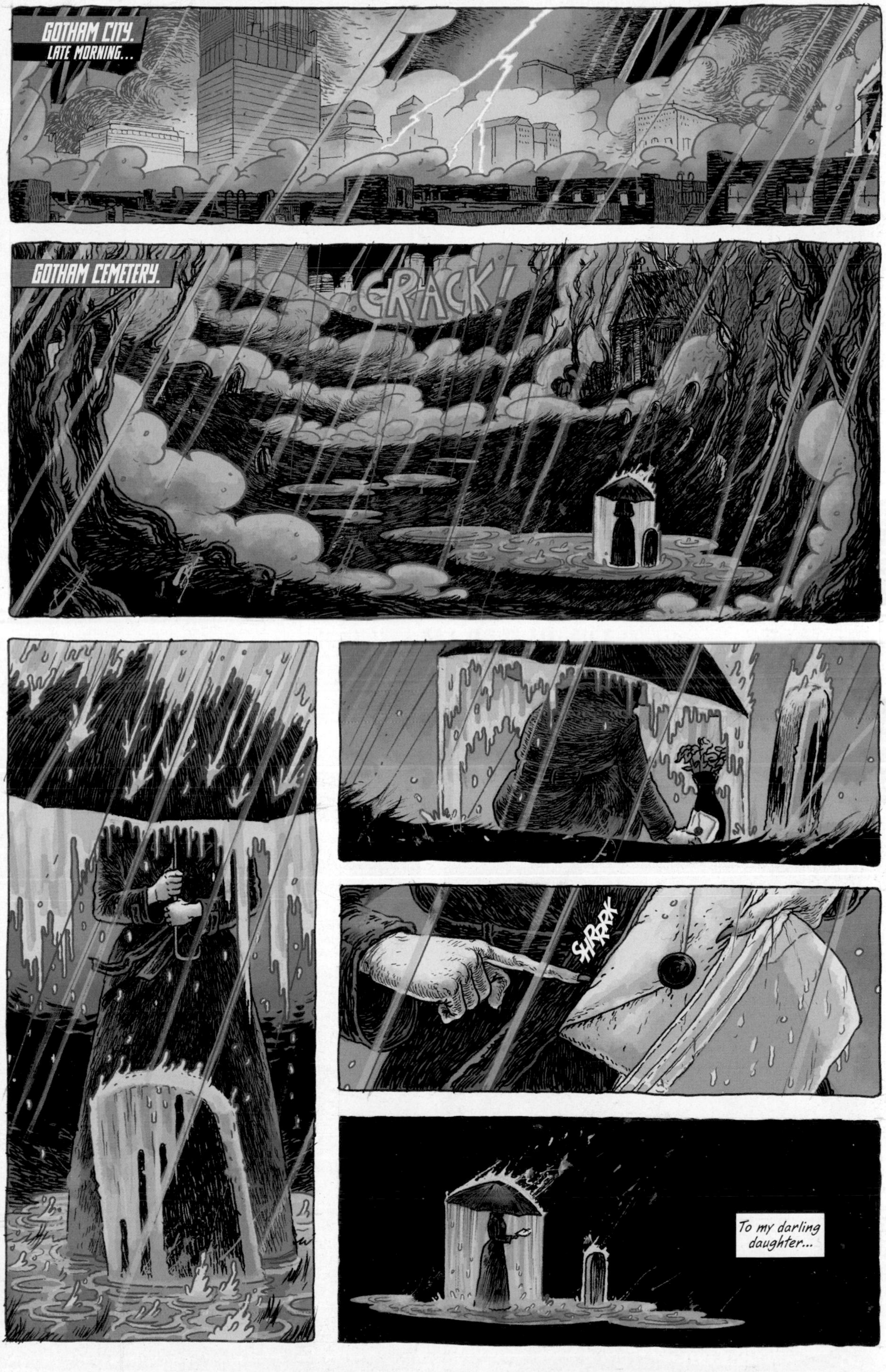
GOTHAM CITY.
LATE MORNING...
GOTHAM CEMETERY.
CRACK!
SHRRRK
To my darling daughter...

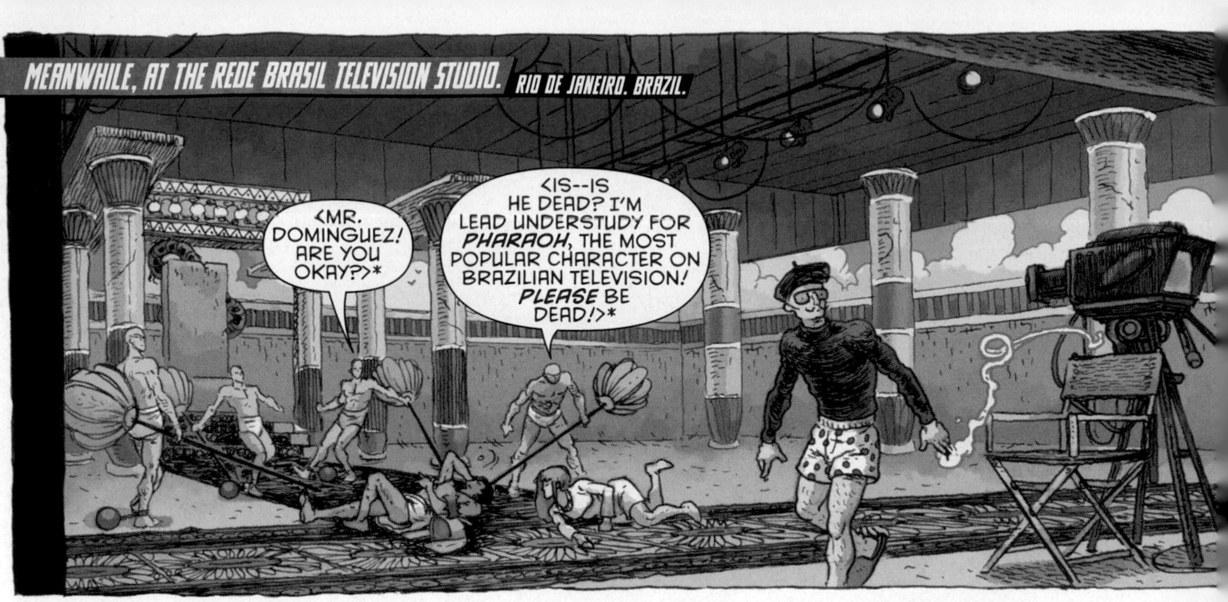
MEANWHILE, AT THE REDE BRASIL TELEVISION STUDIO.
RIO DE JANEIRO. BRAZIL.
<MR. DOMINGUEZ! ARE YOU OKAY?>*
<IS--IS HE DEAD? I'M LEAD UNDERSTUDY FOR PHARAOH, THE MOST POPULAR CHARACTER ON BRAZILIAN TELEVISION! PLEASE BE DEAD!>*

SCOTT SNYDER & JAMES TYNION IV STORY TIM SEELEY SCRIPT
RAY FAWKES & JOHN LAYMAN CONSULTING WRITERS
IAN BERTRAM ARTIST

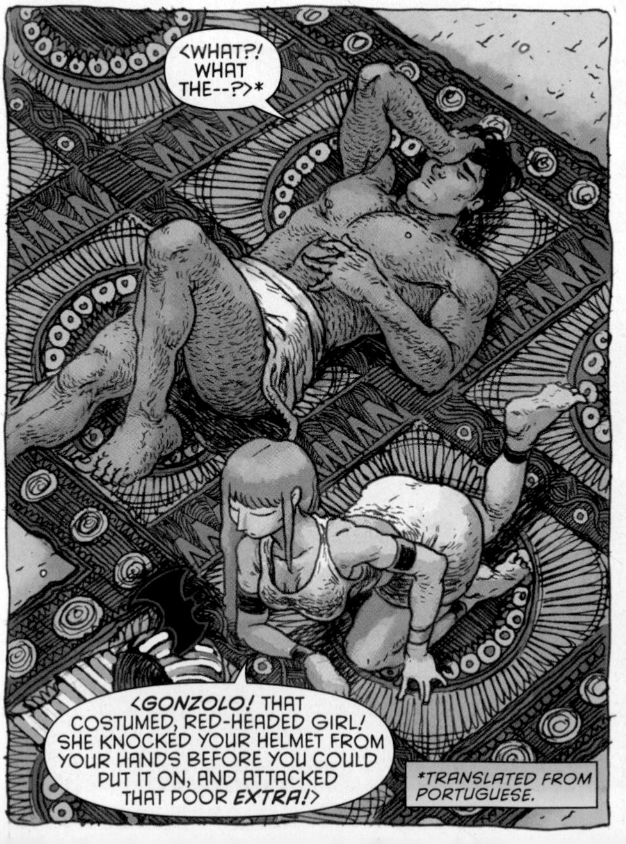
<WHAT?! WHAT THE--?>*
<GONZOLO! THAT COSTUMED, RED-HEADED GIRL! SHE KNOCKED YOUR HELMET FROM YOUR HANDS BEFORE YOU COULD PUT IT ON, AND ATTACKED THAT POOR EXTRA!>
*TRANSLATED FROM PORTUGUESE.

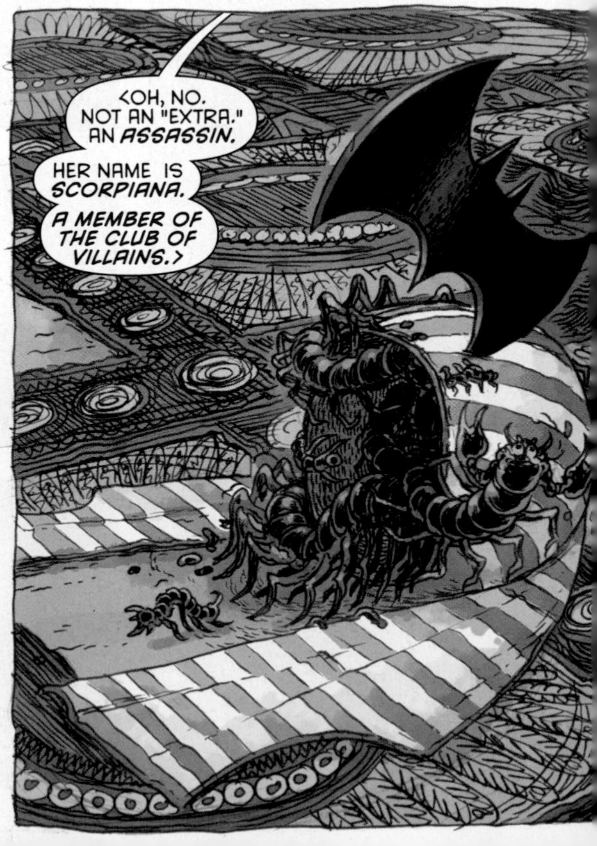
<OH, NO. NOT AN "EXTRA." AN ASSASSIN.
HER NAME IS SCORPIANA.
A MEMBER OF THE CLUB OF VILLAINS.>

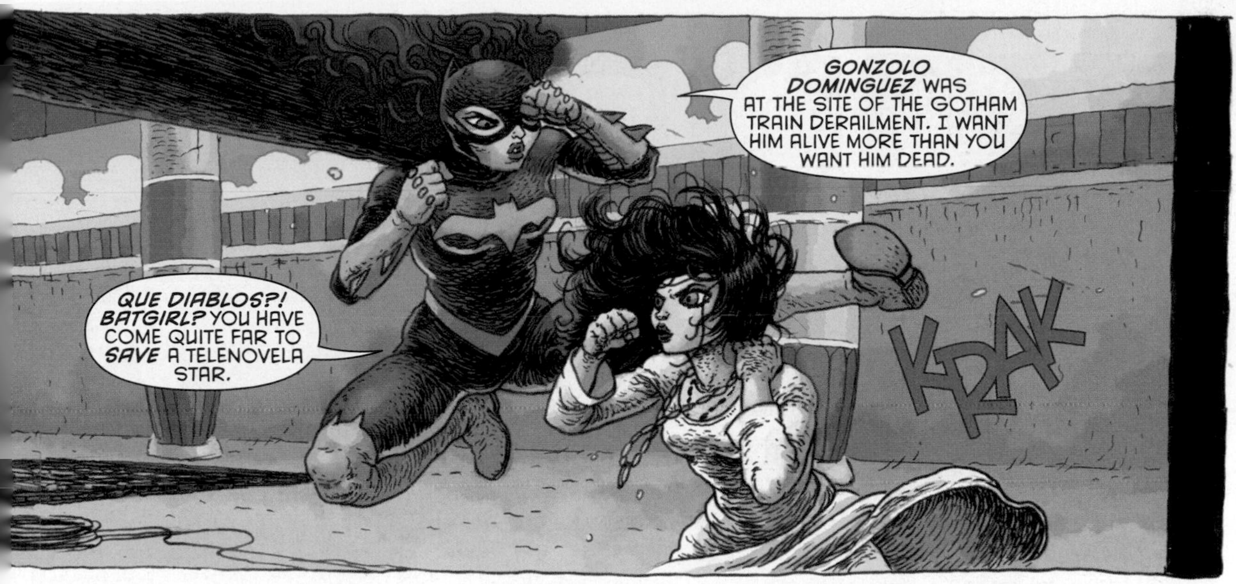
GONZOLO DOMINGUEZ WAS AT THE SITE OF THE GOTHAM TRAIN DERAILMENT. I WANT HIM ALIVE MORE THAN YOU WANT HIM DEAD.
QUE DIABLOS?! BATGIRL? YOU HAVE COME QUITE FAR TO SAVE A TELENOVELA STAR.
KRAK

COLORS BY DAVE STEWART LETTERING BY DEZI SIENTY
COVER BY GUILLEM MARCH & TOMEU MOREY

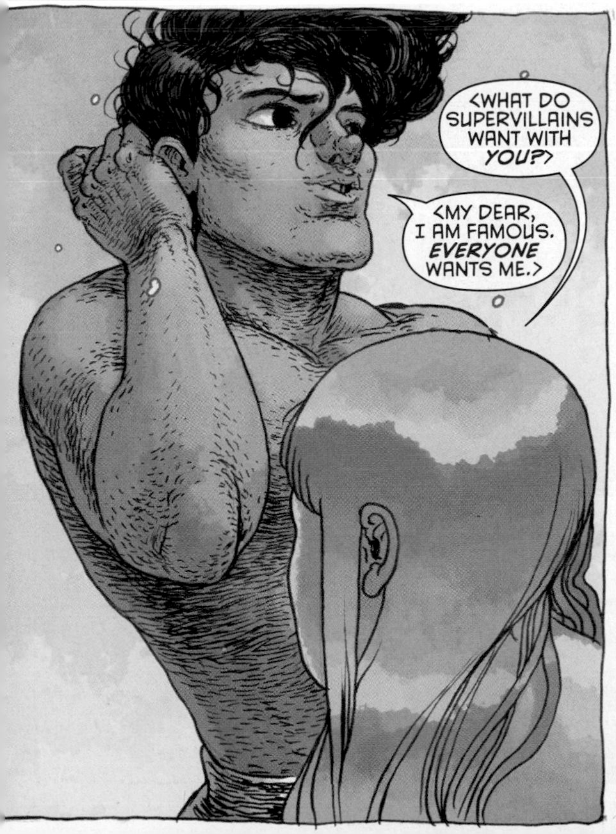
<WHAT DO SUPERVILLAINS WANT WITH YOU?>
<MY DEAR, I AM FAMOUS. EVERYONE WANTS ME.>

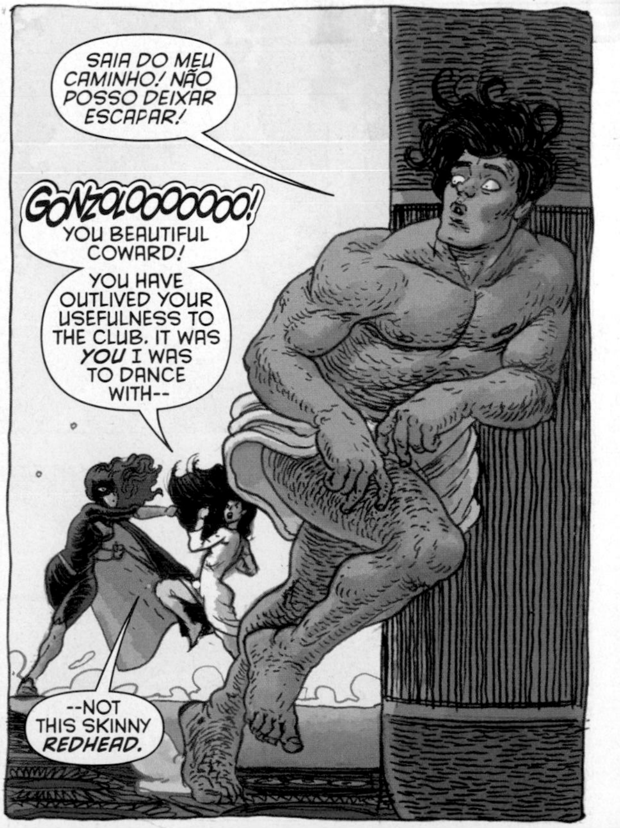
SAIA DO MEU CAMINHO! NÃO POSSO DEIXAR ESCAPAR!
GONZOLOOOOOOO! YOU BEAUTIFUL COWARD!
YOU HAVE OUTLIVED YOUR USEFULNESS TO THE CLUB. IT WAS YOU I WAS TO DANCE WITH--
--NOT THIS SKINNY REDHEAD.

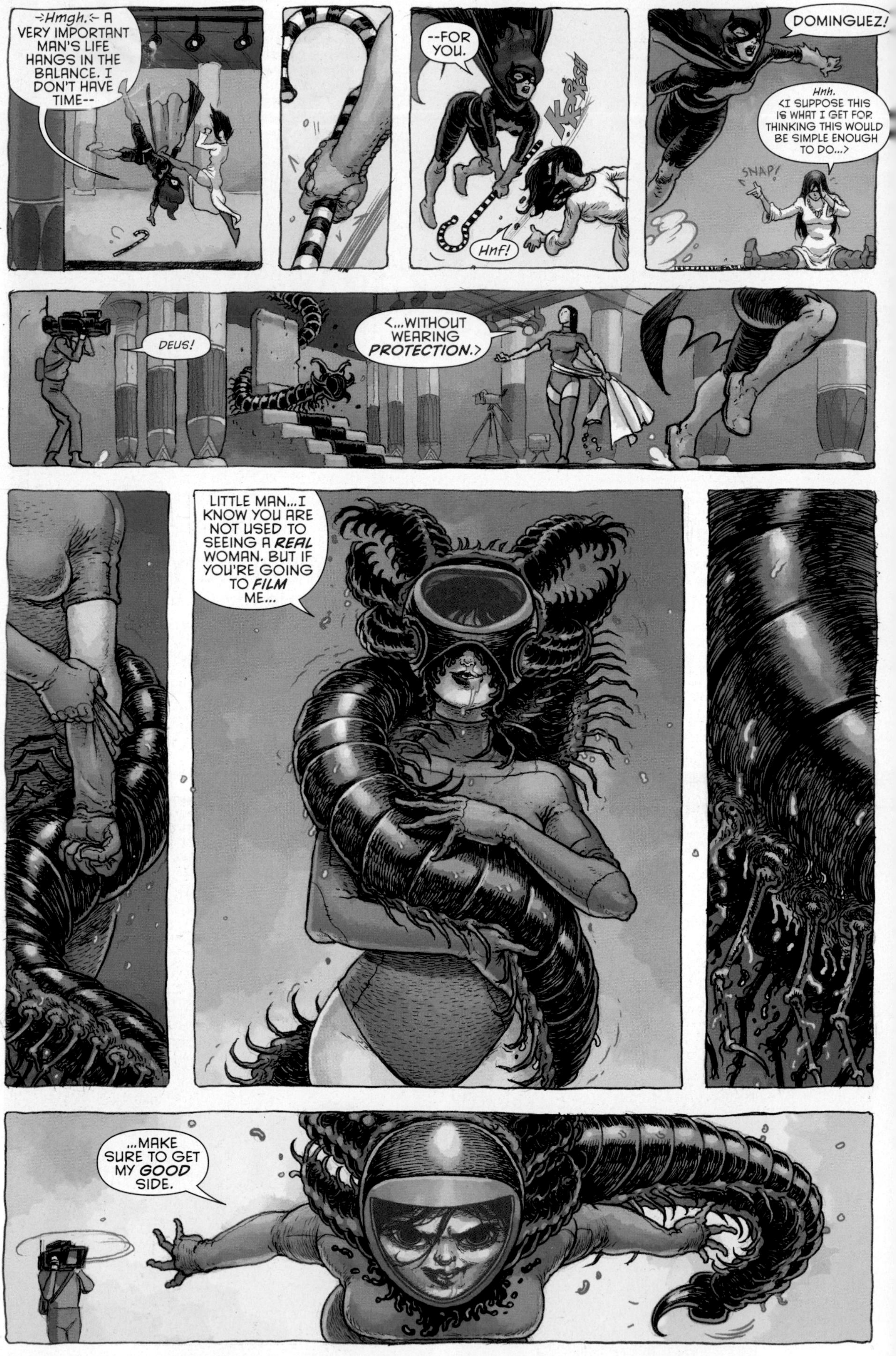

Hmgh. A VERY IMPORTANT MAN'S LIFE HANGS IN THE BALANCE. I DON'T HAVE TIME--
--FOR YOU.
Hnf!
DOMINGUEZ!
Hnh. <I SUPPOSE THIS IS WHAT I GET FOR THINKING THIS WOULD BE SIMPLE ENOUGH TO DO...>
SNAP!
DEUS!
<...WITHOUT WEARING PROTECTION.>
LITTLE MAN...I KNOW YOU ARE NOT USED TO SEEING A REAL WOMAN. BUT IF YOU'RE GOING TO FILM ME...
...MAKE SURE TO GET MY GOOD SIDE.

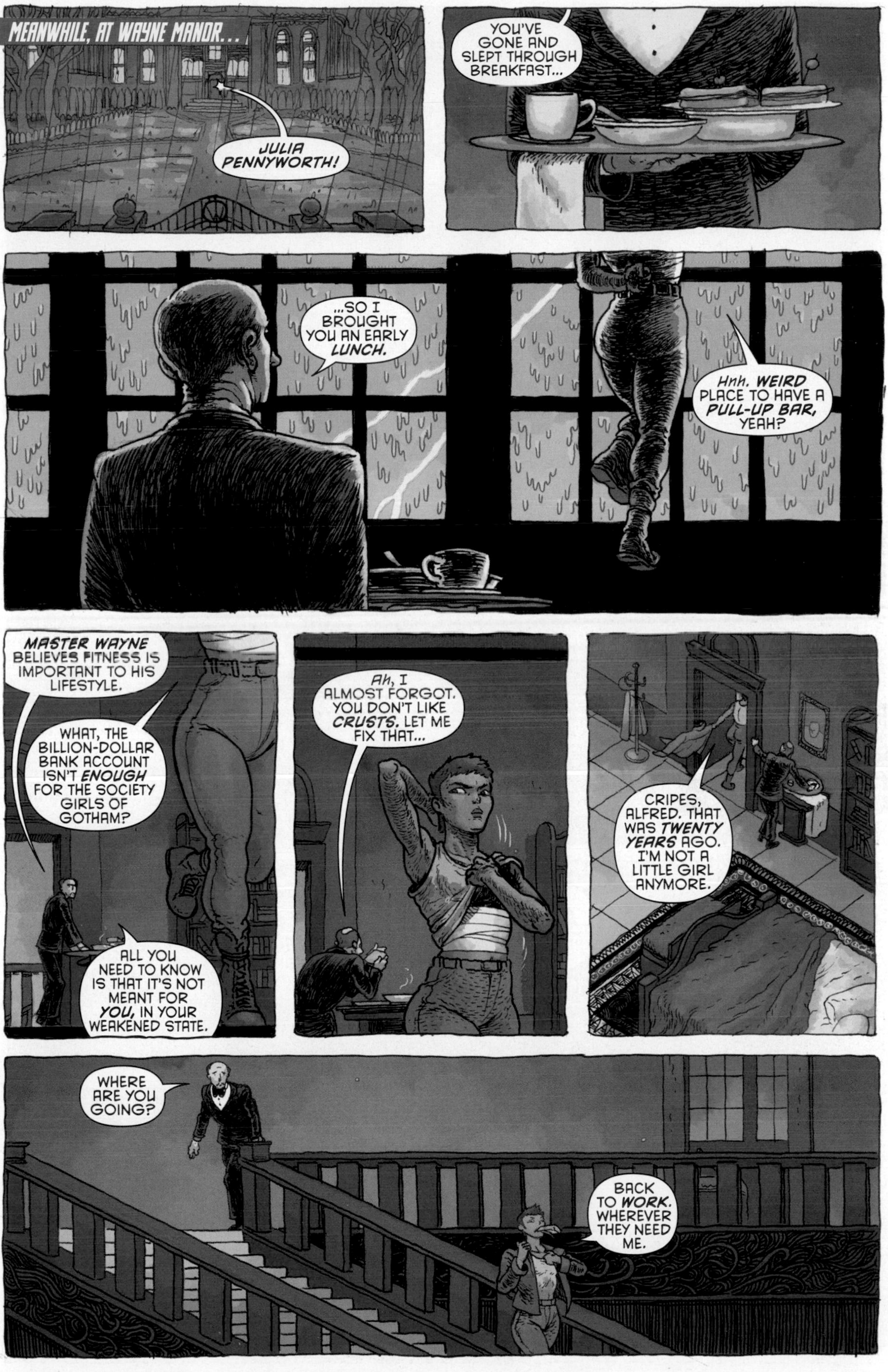
MEANWHILE, AT WAYNE MANOR...
JULIA PENNYWORTH!
YOU'VE GONE AND SLEPT THROUGH BREAKFAST...
...SO I BROUGHT YOU AN EARLY LUNCH.
Hnh. WEIRD PLACE TO HAVE A PULL-UP BAR, YEAH?
MASTER WAYNE BELIEVES FITNESS IS IMPORTANT TO HIS LIFESTYLE.
WHAT, THE BILLION-DOLLAR BANK ACCOUNT ISN'T ENOUGH FOR THE SOCIETY GIRLS OF GOTHAM?
ALL YOU NEED TO KNOW IS THAT IT'S NOT MEANT FOR YOU, IN YOUR WEAKENED STATE.
Ah, I ALMOST FORGOT. YOU DON'T LIKE CRUSTS. LET ME FIX THAT...
CRIPES, ALFRED. THAT WAS TWENTY YEARS AGO. I'M NOT A LITTLE GIRL ANYMORE.
WHERE ARE YOU GOING?
BACK TO WORK. WHEREVER THEY NEED ME.

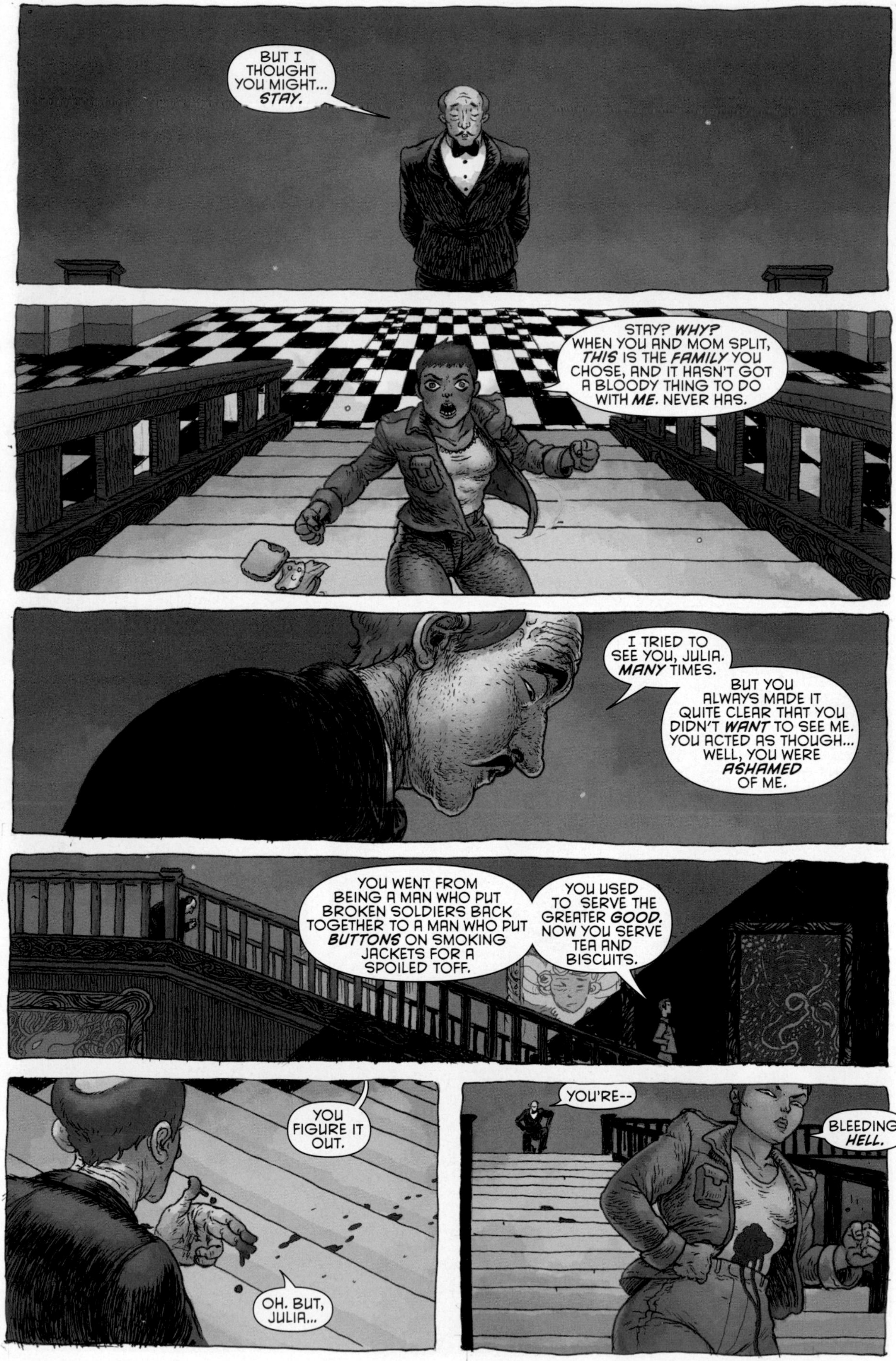
BUT I THOUGHT YOU MIGHT... STAY.
STAY? WHY? WHEN YOU AND MOM SPLIT, THIS IS THE FAMILY YOU CHOSE, AND IT HASN'T GOT A BLOODY THING TO DO WITH ME. NEVER HAS.
I TRIED TO SEE YOU, JULIA. MANY TIMES.
BUT YOU ALWAYS MADE IT QUITE CLEAR THAT YOU DIDN'T WANT TO SEE ME. YOU ACTED AS THOUGH... WELL, YOU WERE ASHAMED OF ME.
YOU WENT FROM BEING A MAN WHO PUT BROKEN SOLDIERS BACK TOGETHER TO A MAN WHO PUT BUTTONS ON SMOKING JACKETS FOR A SPOILED TOFF.
YOU USED TO SERVE THE GREATER GOOD. NOW YOU SERVE TEA AND BISCUITS.
YOU FIGURE IT OUT.
OH. BUT, JULIA...
YOU'RE--
BLEEDING. HELL.

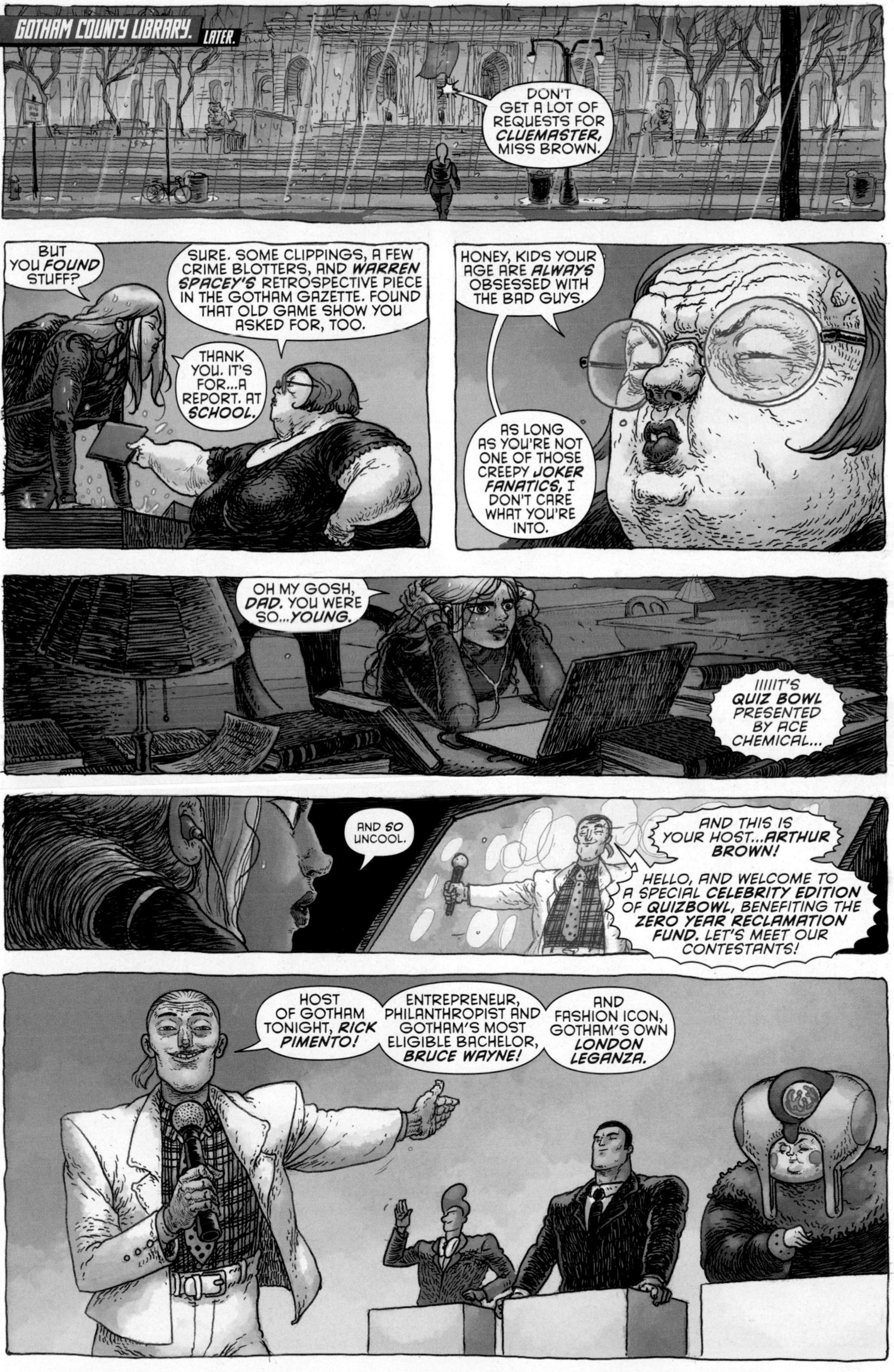

GOTHAM COUNTY LIBRARY.
LATER.
DON'T GET A LOT OF REQUESTS FOR CLUEMASTER, MISS BROWN.
BUT YOU FOUND STUFF?
SURE. SOME CLIPPINGS, A FEW CRIME BLOTTERS, AND WARREN SPACEY'S RETROSPECTIVE PIECE IN THE GOTHAM GAZETTE. FOUND THAT OLD GAME SHOW YOU ASKED FOR, TOO.
THANK YOU. IT'S FOR...A REPORT. AT SCHOOL.
HONEY, KIDS YOUR AGE ARE ALWAYS OBSESSED WITH THE BAD GUYS.
AS LONG AS YOU'RE NOT ONE OF THOSE CREEPY JOKER FANATICS, I DON'T CARE WHAT YOU'RE INTO.
OH MY GOSH, DAD. YOU WERE SO...YOUNG.
IIIIIT'S QUIZ BOWL PRESENTED BY ACE CHEMICAL...
AND SO UNCOOL.
AND THIS IS YOUR HOST...ARTHUR BROWN!
HELLO, AND WELCOME TO A SPECIAL CELEBRITY EDITION OF QUIZBOWL, BENEFITING THE ZERO YEAR RECLAMATION FUND. LET'S MEET OUR CONTESTANTS!
HOST OF GOTHAM TONIGHT, RICK PIMENTO!
ENTREPRENEUR, PHILANTHROPIST AND GOTHAM'S MOST ELIGIBLE BACHELOR, BRUCE WAYNE!
AND FASHION ICON, GOTHAM'S OWN LONDON LEGANZA.

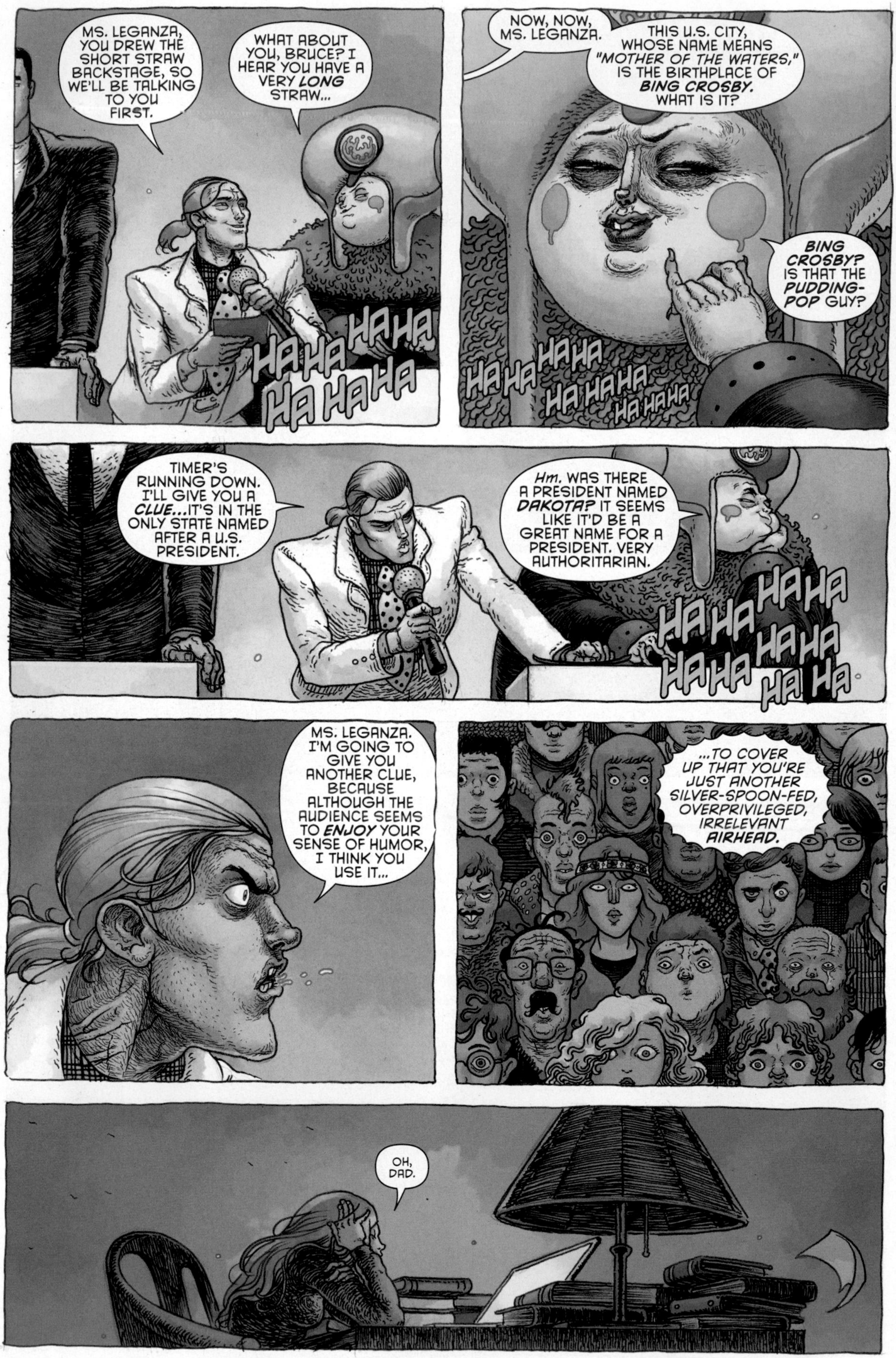
MS. LEGANZA, YOU DREW THE SHORT STRAW BACKSTAGE, SO WE'LL BE TALKING TO YOU FIRST.
WHAT ABOUT YOU, BRUCE? I HEAR YOU HAVE A VERY *LONG* STRAW...
HA HA HA HA HA HA HA HA
NOW, NOW, MS. LEGANZA.
THIS U.S. CITY, WHOSE NAME MEANS *"MOTHER OF THE WATERS,"* IS THE BIRTHPLACE OF **BING CROSBY.** WHAT IS IT?
BING CROSBY? IS THAT THE ***PUDDING-POP*** GUY?
HA HA HA HA HA HA HA HA HA HA
TIMER'S RUNNING DOWN. I'LL GIVE YOU A *CLUE...*IT'S IN THE ONLY STATE NAMED AFTER A U.S. PRESIDENT.
Hm. WAS THERE A PRESIDENT NAMED ***DAKOTA?*** IT SEEMS LIKE IT'D BE A GREAT NAME FOR A PRESIDENT. VERY AUTHORITARIAN.
HA HA HA HA HA HA HA HA HA HA
MS. LEGANZA. I'M GOING TO GIVE YOU ANOTHER CLUE, BECAUSE ALTHOUGH THE AUDIENCE SEEMS TO *ENJOY* YOUR SENSE OF HUMOR, I THINK YOU USE IT...
...TO COVER UP THAT YOU'RE JUST ANOTHER SILVER-SPOON-FED, OVERPRIVILEGED, IRRELEVANT ***AIRHEAD.***
OH, DAD.

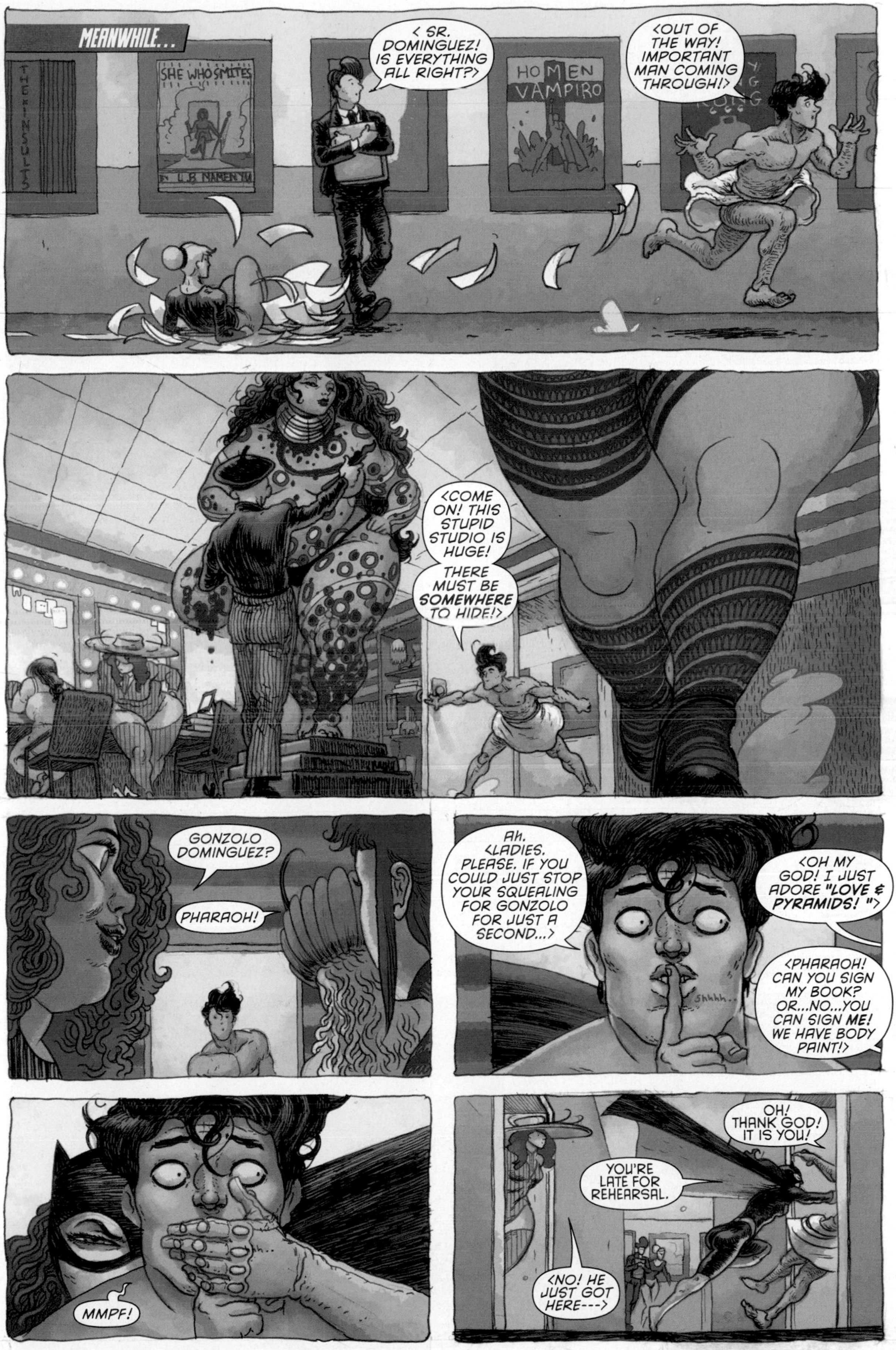
MEANWHILE...
THE INSULTS
SHE WHO SMITES
L.B. NAMENYU
< SR. DOMINGUEZ! IS EVERYTHING ALL RIGHT?>
HOMEN VAMPIRO
<OUT OF THE WAY! IMPORTANT MAN COMING THROUGH!>
<COME ON! THIS STUPID STUDIO IS HUGE!
THERE MUST BE SOMEWHERE TO HIDE!>
GONZOLO DOMINGUEZ?
PHARAOH!
Ah. <LADIES. PLEASE. IF YOU COULD JUST STOP YOUR SQUEALING FOR GONZOLO FOR JUST A SECOND...>
Shhhh...
<OH MY GOD! I JUST ADORE "LOVE & PYRAMIDS!">
<PHARAOH! CAN YOU SIGN MY BOOK? OR...NO...YOU CAN SIGN ME! WE HAVE BODY PAINT!>
MMPF!
OH! THANK GOD! IT IS YOU!
YOU'RE LATE FOR REHEARSAL.
<NO! HE JUST GOT HERE--->

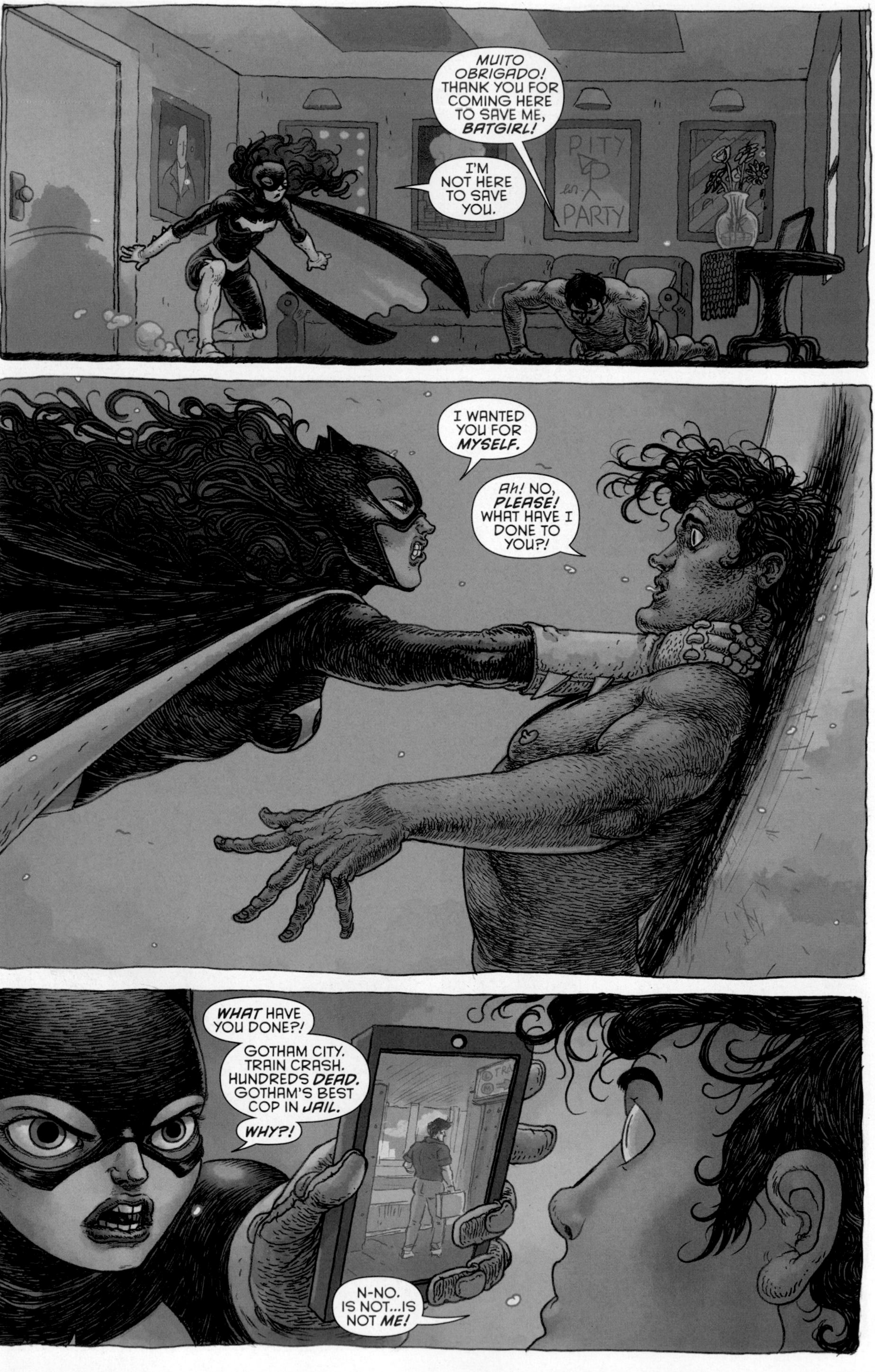
MUITO OBRIGADO! THANK YOU FOR COMING HERE TO SAVE ME, BATGIRL!
I'M NOT HERE TO SAVE YOU.
PITY
PARTY
I WANTED YOU FOR MYSELF.
AH! NO, PLEASE! WHAT HAVE I DONE TO YOU?!
WHAT HAVE YOU DONE?!
GOTHAM CITY. TRAIN CRASH. HUNDREDS DEAD. GOTHAM'S BEST COP IN JAIL.
WHY?!
N-NO. IS NOT...IS NOT ME!

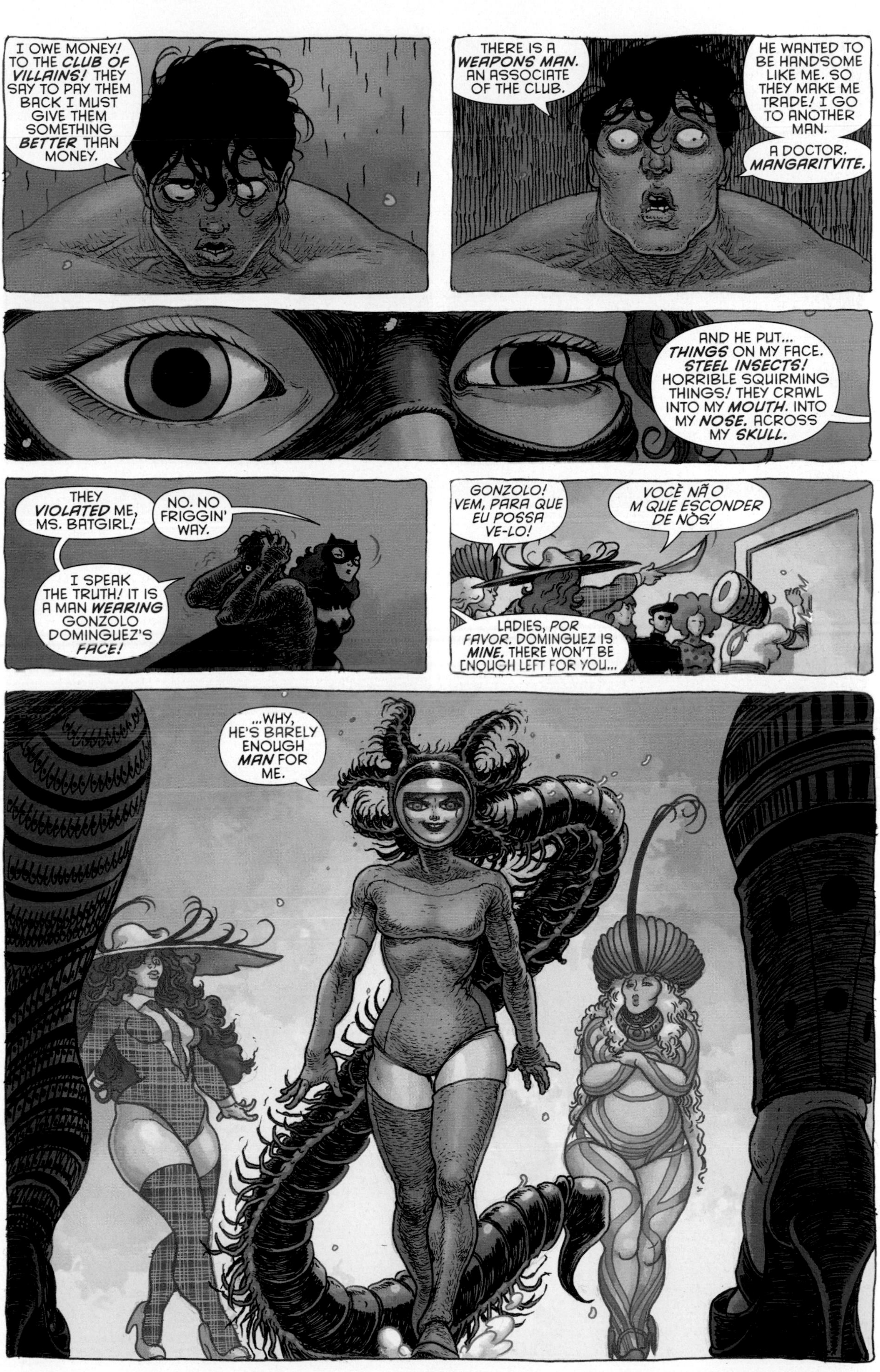

I OWE MONEY! TO THE CLUB OF VILLAINS! THEY SAY TO PAY THEM BACK I MUST GIVE THEM SOMETHING BETTER THAN MONEY.
THERE IS A WEAPONS MAN. AN ASSOCIATE OF THE CLUB.
HE WANTED TO BE HANDSOME LIKE ME. SO THEY MAKE ME TRADE! I GO TO ANOTHER MAN.
A DOCTOR. MANGARITVITE.
AND HE PUT... THINGS ON MY FACE. STEEL INSECTS! HORRIBLE SQUIRMING THINGS! THEY CRAWL INTO MY MOUTH. INTO MY NOSE. ACROSS MY SKULL.
THEY VIOLATED ME, MS. BATGIRL!
NO. NO FRIGGIN' WAY.
I SPEAK THE TRUTH! IT IS A MAN WEARING GONZOLO DOMINGUEZ'S FACE!
GONZOLO! VEM, PARA QUE EU POSSA VE-LO!
VOCÈ NÃO M QUE ESCONDER DE NÒS!
LADIES, POR FAVOR. DOMINGUEZ IS MINE. THERE WON'T BE ENOUGH LEFT FOR YOU...
...WHY, HE'S BARELY ENOUGH MAN FOR ME.

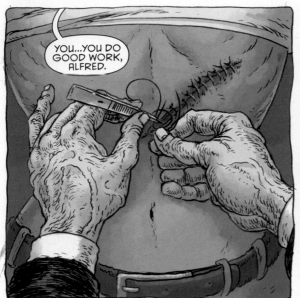

YOU...YOU DO GOOD WORK, ALFRED.

I SPOKE TO MASTER WAYNE.

WHATEVER YOU MAY THINK OF HIM, HE LOVES GOTHAM, WITH ALL HIS HEART. HE WANTS *CARMINE FALCONE* OUT OF HIS CITY, AND IN PRISON WHERE HE BELONGS.

HE SAYS, IF THE *S.R.R.* IS KEEN, YOU CAN STAY HERE. HE'LL PROVIDE WHATEVER YOU NEED.

I WILL GET THE *TIME* WITH MY DAUGHTER I DID NOT HAVE. AND I CAN *ASSIST* YOU IN YOUR MISSIONS.

BECAUSE, UNFORTUNATELY, MY DEAR, FIXING BROKEN SOLDIERS IS NOT A SKILL I'VE HAD THE LIBERTY TO *FORGET*.

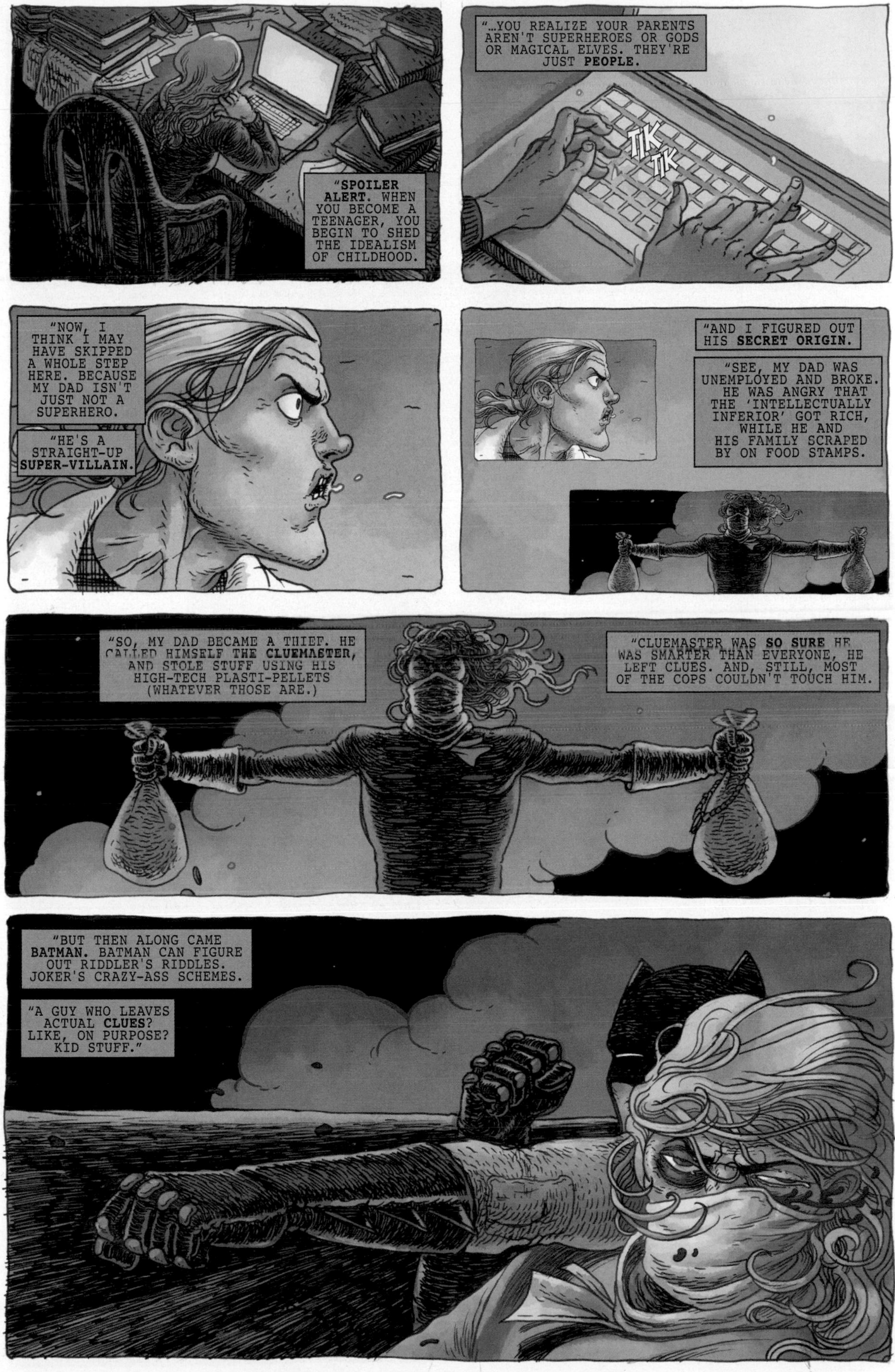
"SPOILER ALERT. WHEN YOU BECOME A TEENAGER, YOU BEGIN TO SHED THE IDEALISM OF CHILDHOOD.
"...YOU REALIZE YOUR PARENTS AREN'T SUPERHEROES OR GODS OR MAGICAL ELVES. THEY'RE JUST PEOPLE.
TIK TIK
"NOW, I THINK I MAY HAVE SKIPPED A WHOLE STEP HERE. BECAUSE MY DAD ISN'T JUST NOT A SUPERHERO.
"HE'S A STRAIGHT-UP SUPER-VILLAIN.
"AND I FIGURED OUT HIS SECRET ORIGIN.
"SEE, MY DAD WAS UNEMPLOYED AND BROKE. HE WAS ANGRY THAT THE 'INTELLECTUALLY INFERIOR' GOT RICH, WHILE HE AND HIS FAMILY SCRAPED BY ON FOOD STAMPS.
"SO, MY DAD BECAME A THIEF. HE CALLED HIMSELF THE CLUEMASTER, AND STOLE STUFF USING HIS HIGH-TECH PLASTI-PELLETS (WHATEVER THOSE ARE.)
"CLUEMASTER WAS SO SURE HE WAS SMARTER THAN EVERYONE, HE LEFT CLUES. AND, STILL, MOST OF THE COPS COULDN'T TOUCH HIM.
"BUT THEN ALONG CAME BATMAN. BATMAN CAN FIGURE OUT RIDDLER'S RIDDLES. JOKER'S CRAZY-ASS SCHEMES.
"A GUY WHO LEAVES ACTUAL CLUES? LIKE, ON PURPOSE? KID STUFF."

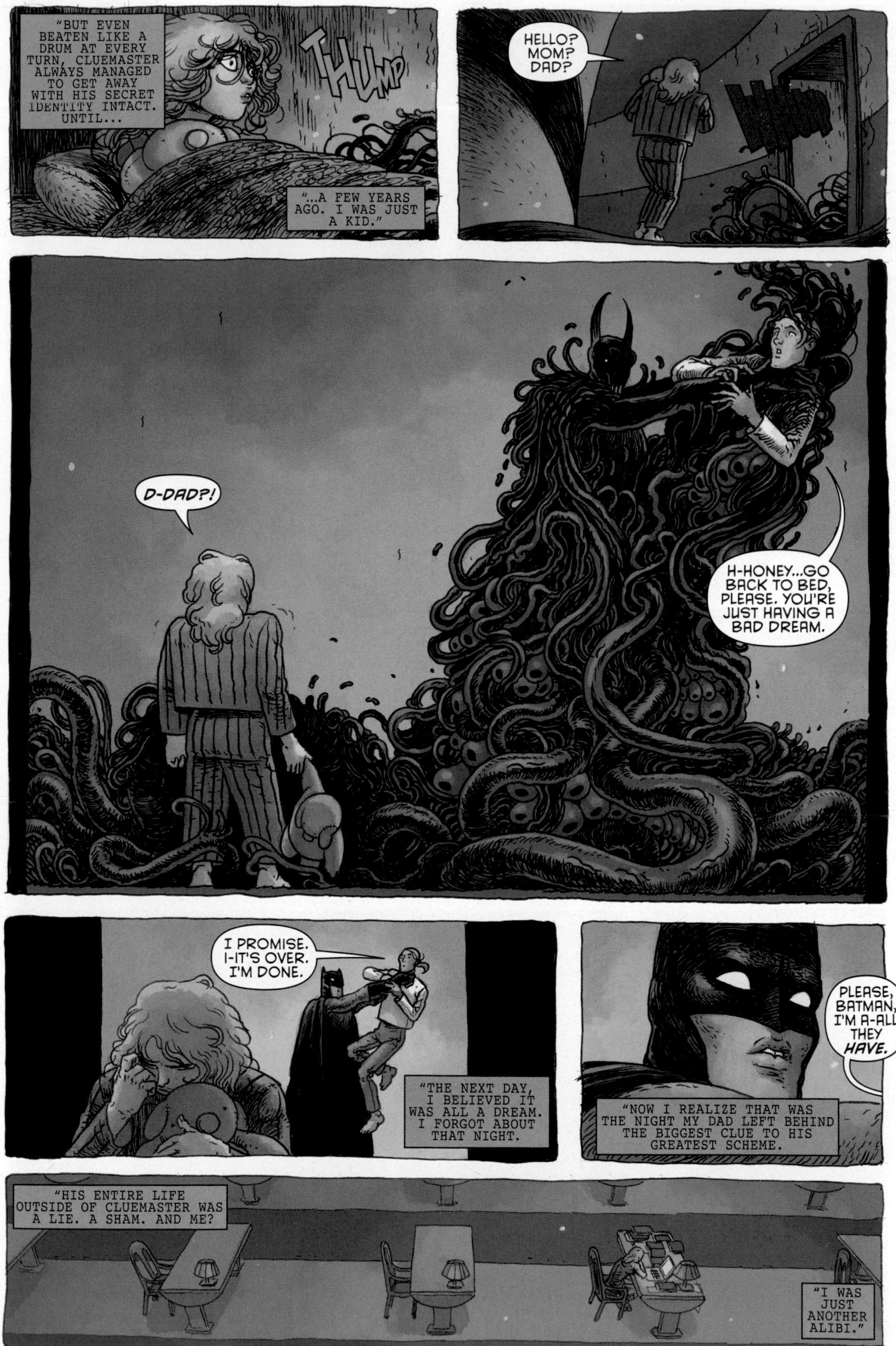
"BUT EVEN BEATEN LIKE A DRUM AT EVERY TURN, CLUEMASTER ALWAYS MANAGED TO GET AWAY WITH HIS SECRET IDENTITY INTACT. UNTIL...
THUMP
"...A FEW YEARS AGO. I WAS JUST A KID."
HELLO? MOM? DAD?
D-DAD?!
H-HONEY...GO BACK TO BED, PLEASE. YOU'RE JUST HAVING A BAD DREAM.
I PROMISE. I-IT'S OVER. I'M DONE.
"THE NEXT DAY, I BELIEVED IT WAS ALL A DREAM. I FORGOT ABOUT THAT NIGHT.
PLEASE, BATMAN, I'M A-ALL THEY HAVE.
"NOW I REALIZE THAT WAS THE NIGHT MY DAD LEFT BEHIND THE BIGGEST CLUE TO HIS GREATEST SCHEME.
"HIS ENTIRE LIFE OUTSIDE OF CLUEMASTER WAS A LIE. A SHAM. AND ME?
"I WAS JUST ANOTHER ALIBI."

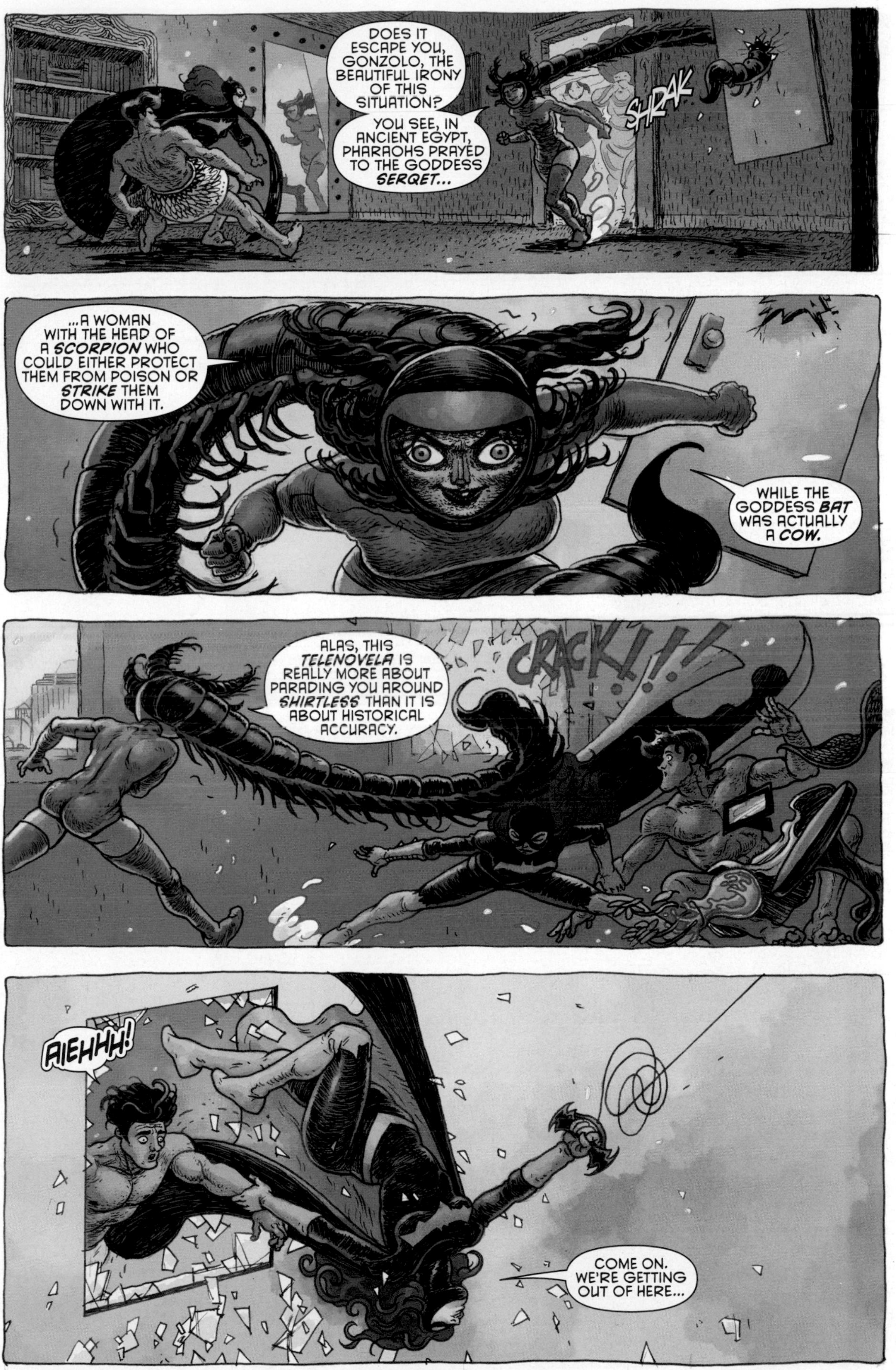

DOES IT ESCAPE YOU, GONZOLO, THE BEAUTIFUL IRONY OF THIS SITUATION?
YOU SEE, IN ANCIENT EGYPT, PHARAOHS PRAYED TO THE GODDESS SERQET...
SHRAK
...A WOMAN WITH THE HEAD OF A SCORPION WHO COULD EITHER PROTECT THEM FROM POISON OR STRIKE THEM DOWN WITH IT.
WHILE THE GODDESS BAT WAS ACTUALLY A COW.
ALAS, THIS TELENOVELA IS REALLY MORE ABOUT PARADING YOU AROUND SHIRTLESS THAN IT IS ABOUT HISTORICAL ACCURACY.
CRACK!!!
AIEHHH!
COME ON. WE'RE GETTING OUT OF HERE...

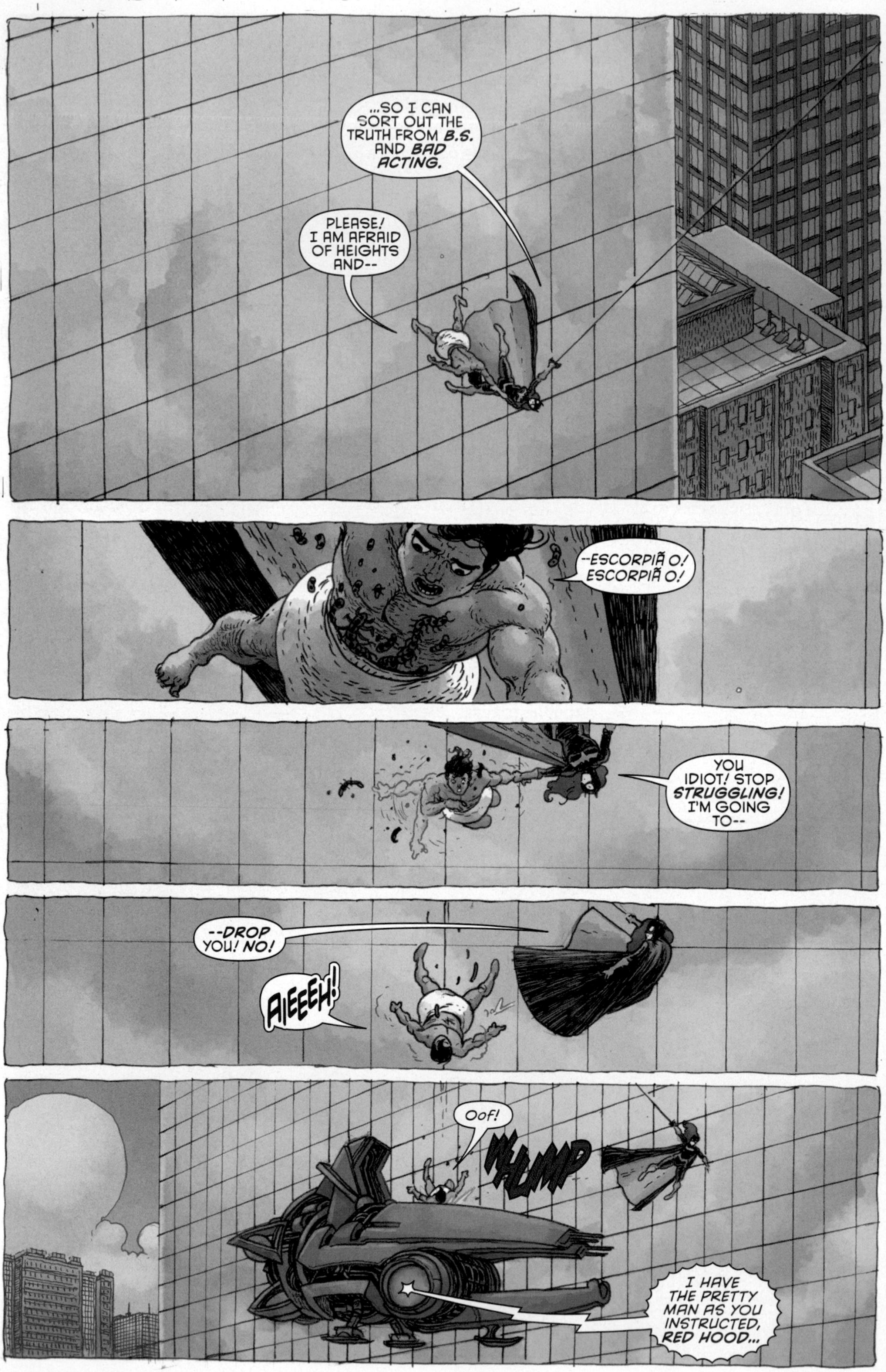
...SO I CAN SORT OUT THE TRUTH FROM B.S. AND BAD ACTING.
PLEASE! I AM AFRAID OF HEIGHTS AND--
--ESCORPIÃ O! ESCORPIÃ O!
YOU IDIOT! STOP STRUGGLING! I'M GOING TO--
--DROP YOU! NO!
AIEEEH!
Oof!
WHUMP
I HAVE THE PRETTY MAN AS YOU INSTRUCTED, RED HOOD...

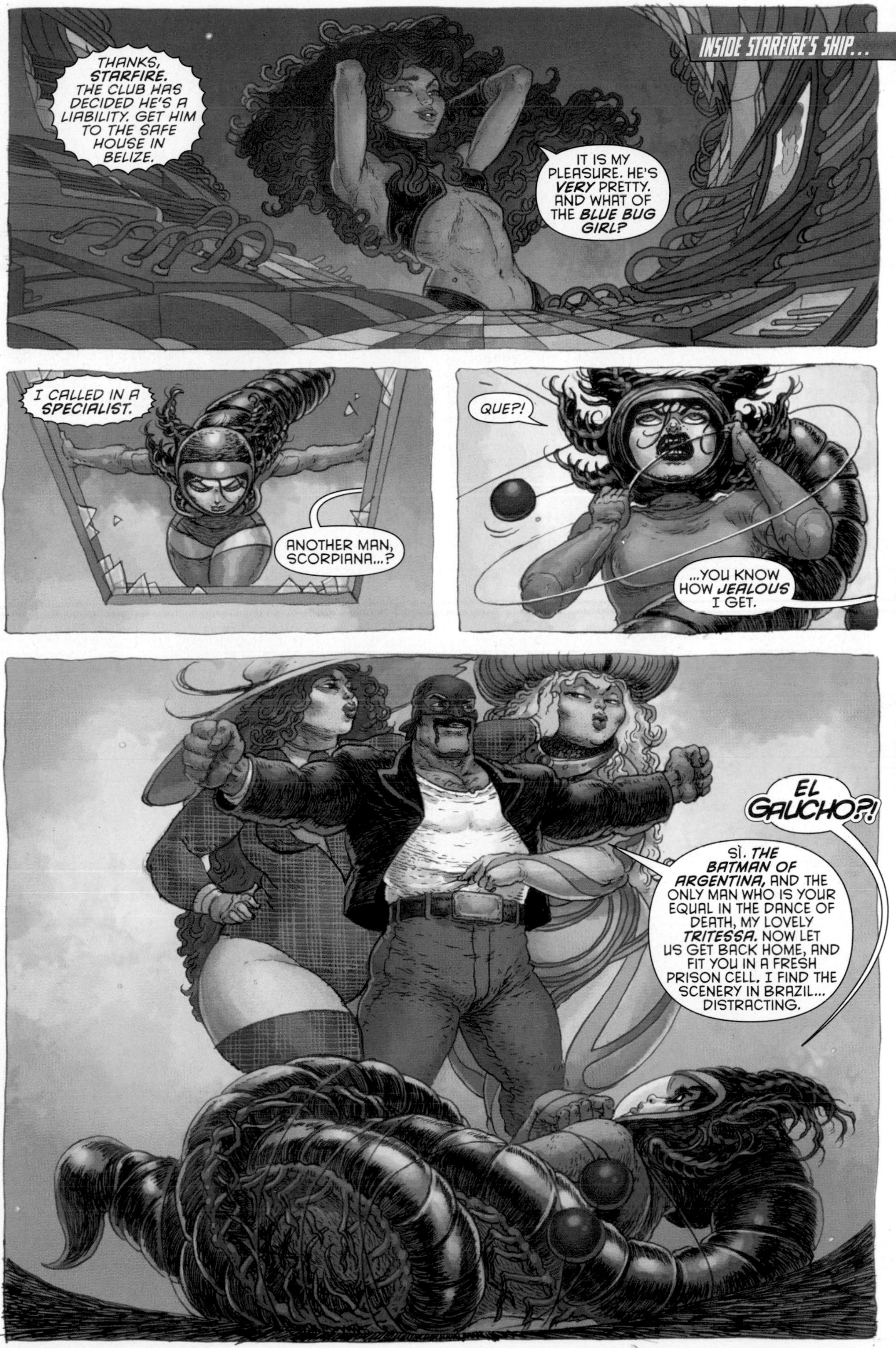
INSIDE STARFIRE'S SHIP...
THANKS, STARFIRE. THE CLUB HAS DECIDED HE'S A LIABILITY. GET HIM TO THE SAFE HOUSE IN BELIZE.
IT IS MY PLEASURE. HE'S VERY PRETTY. AND WHAT OF THE BLUE BUG GIRL?
I CALLED IN A SPECIALIST.
ANOTHER MAN, SCORPIANA...?
QUE?!
...YOU KNOW HOW JEALOUS I GET.
EL GAUCHO?!
SÌ. THE BATMAN OF ARGENTINA, AND THE ONLY MAN WHO IS YOUR EQUAL IN THE DANCE OF DEATH, MY LOVELY TRITESSA. NOW LET US GET BACK HOME, AND FIT YOU IN A FRESH PRISON CELL. I FIND THE SCENERY IN BRAZIL... DISTRACTING.

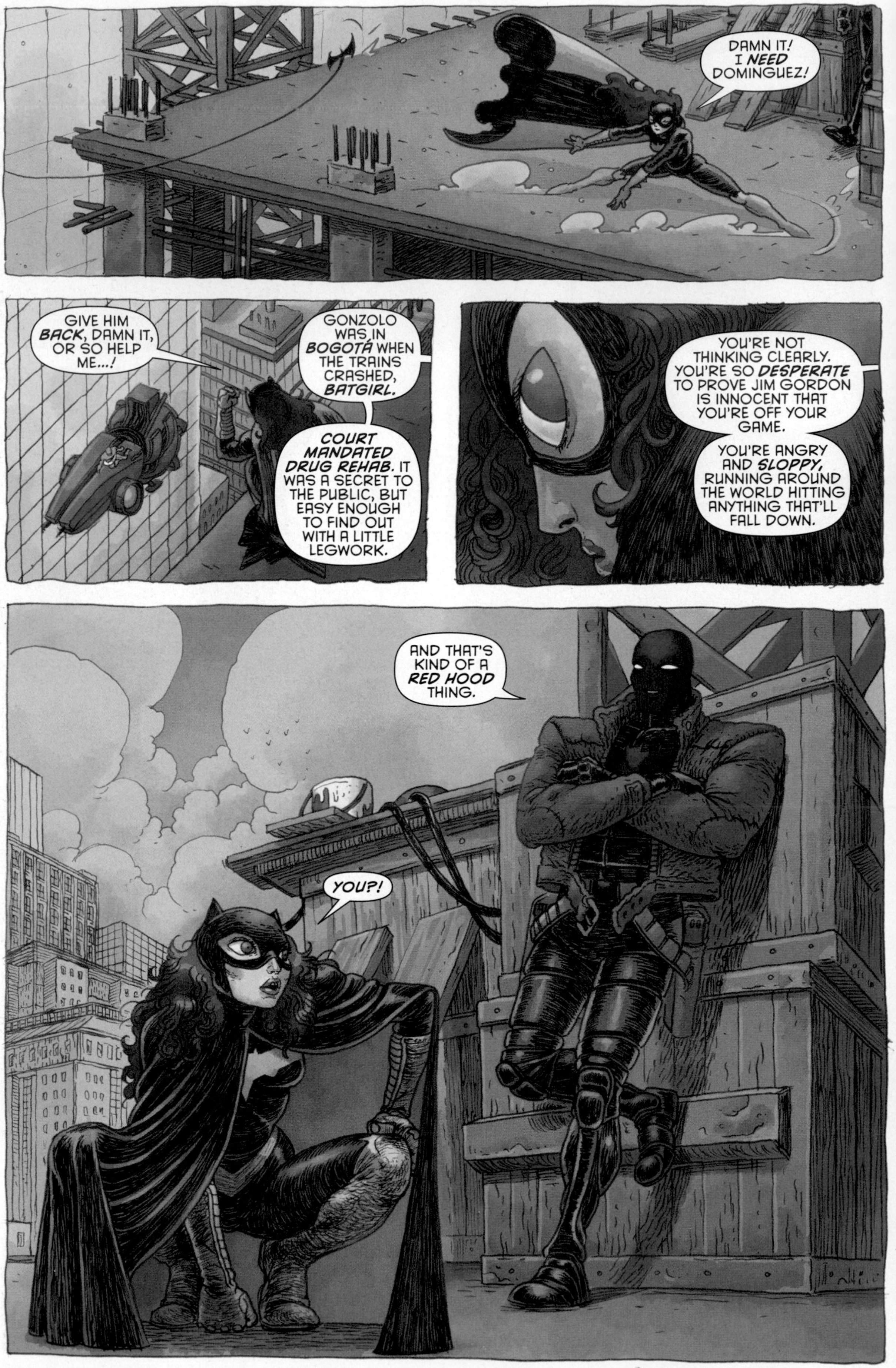
DAMN IT! I NEED DOMINGUEZ!
GIVE HIM BACK, DAMN IT, OR SO HELP ME...!
GONZOLO WAS IN BOGOTÁ WHEN THE TRAINS CRASHED, BATGIRL.
COURT MANDATED DRUG REHAB. IT WAS A SECRET TO THE PUBLIC, BUT EASY ENOUGH TO FIND OUT WITH A LITTLE LEGWORK.
YOU'RE NOT THINKING CLEARLY. YOU'RE SO DESPERATE TO PROVE JIM GORDON IS INNOCENT THAT YOU'RE OFF YOUR GAME.
YOU'RE ANGRY AND SLOPPY, RUNNING AROUND THE WORLD HITTING ANYTHING THAT'LL FALL DOWN.
AND THAT'S KIND OF A RED HOOD THING.
YOU?!

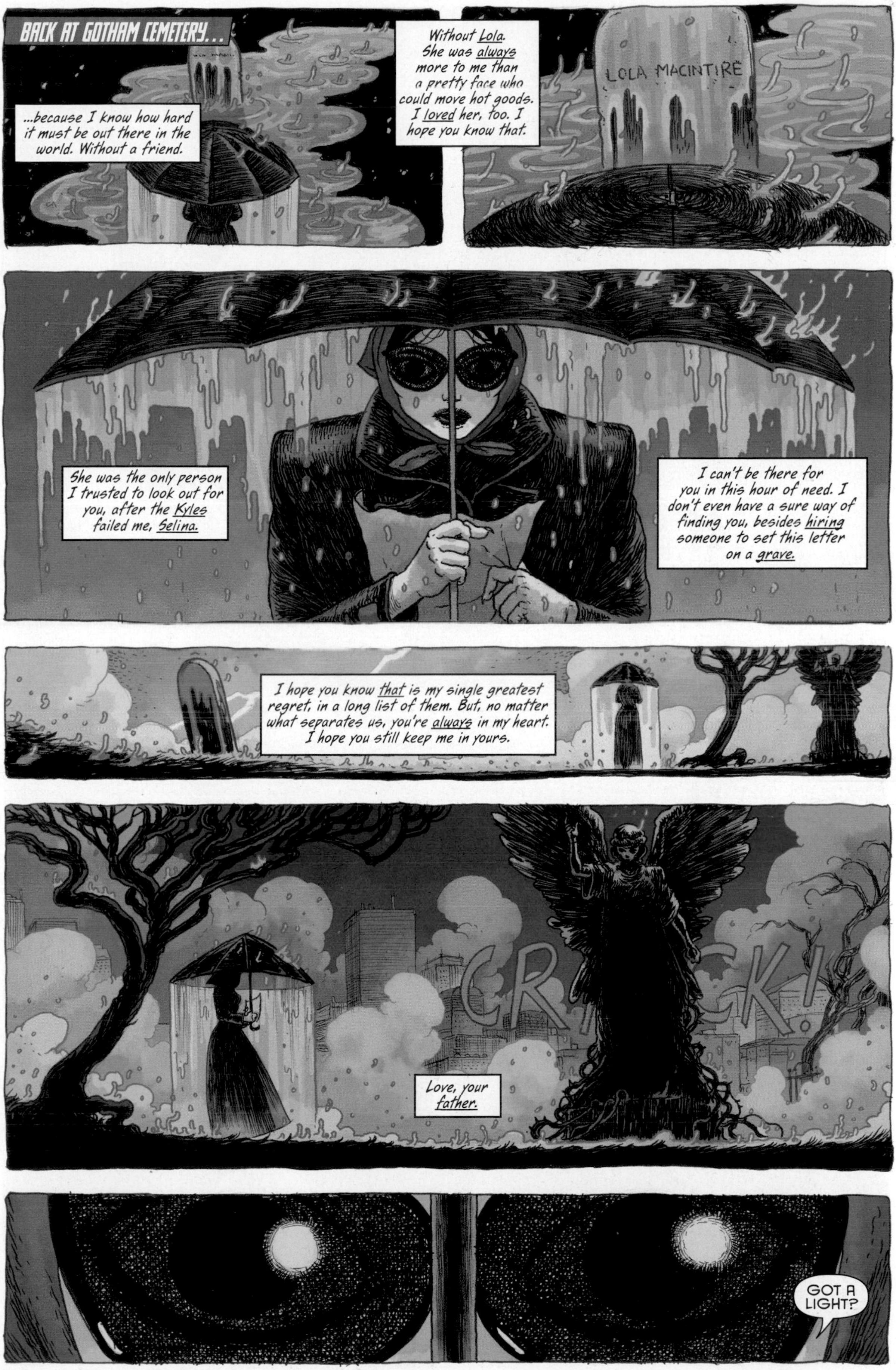
BACK AT GOTHAM CEMETERY...
...because I know how hard it must be out there in the world. Without a friend.
Without Lola. She was always more to me than a pretty face who could move hot goods. I loved her, too. I hope you know that.
LOLA MACINTIRE
She was the only person I trusted to look out for you, after the Kyles failed me, Selina.
I can't be there for you in this hour of need. I don't even have a sure way of finding you, besides hiring someone to set this letter on a grave.
I hope you know that is my single greatest regret, in a long list of them. But, no matter what separates us, you're always in my heart. I hope you still keep me in yours.
CRACK!
Love, your father.
GOT A LIGHT?

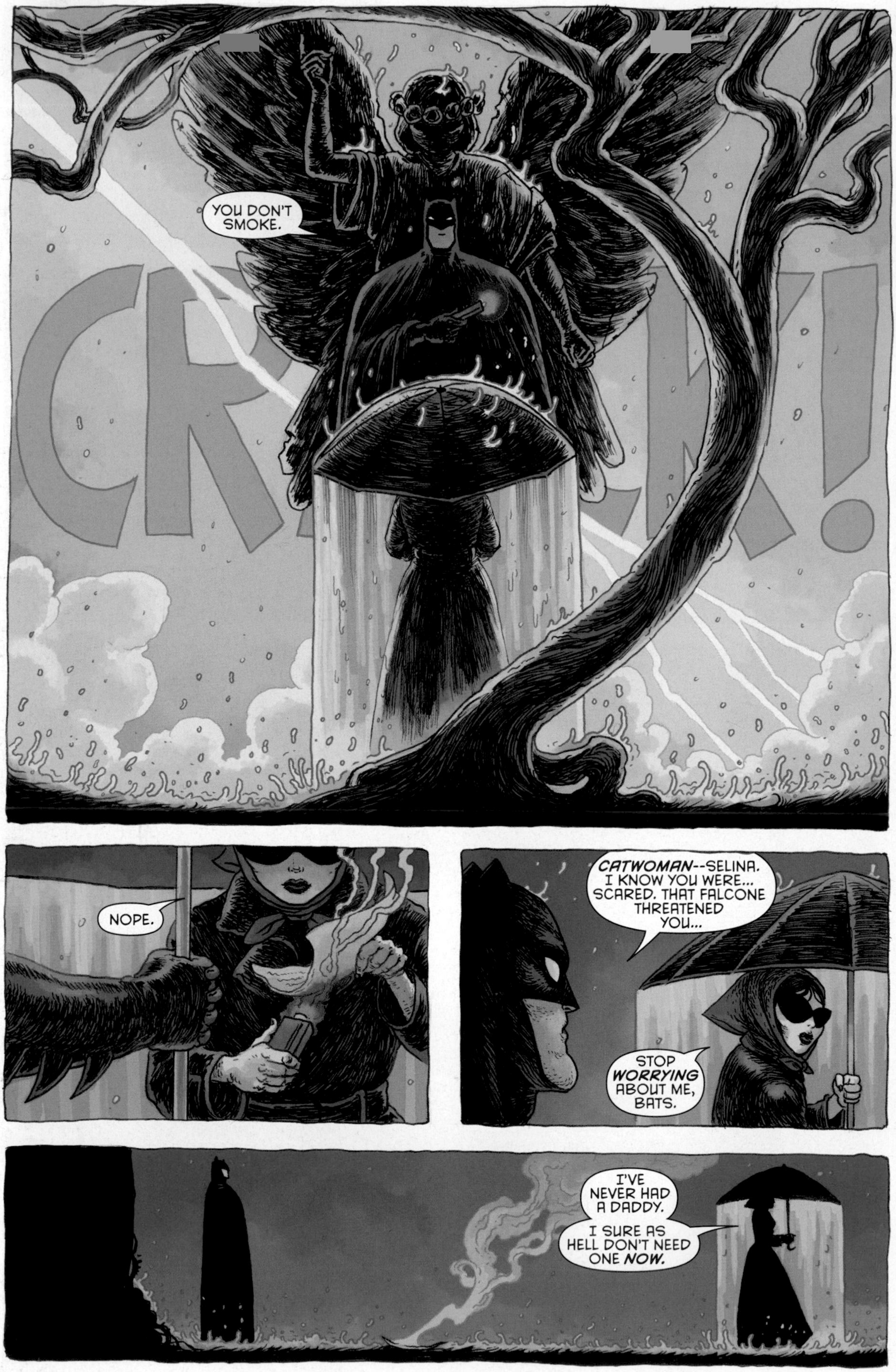

YOU DON'T SMOKE.
NOPE.
CATWOMAN--SELINA. I KNOW YOU WERE... SCARED. THAT FALCONE THREATENED YOU...
STOP *WORRYING* ABOUT ME, BATS.
I'VE NEVER HAD A DADDY.
I SURE AS HELL DON'T NEED ONE *NOW.*

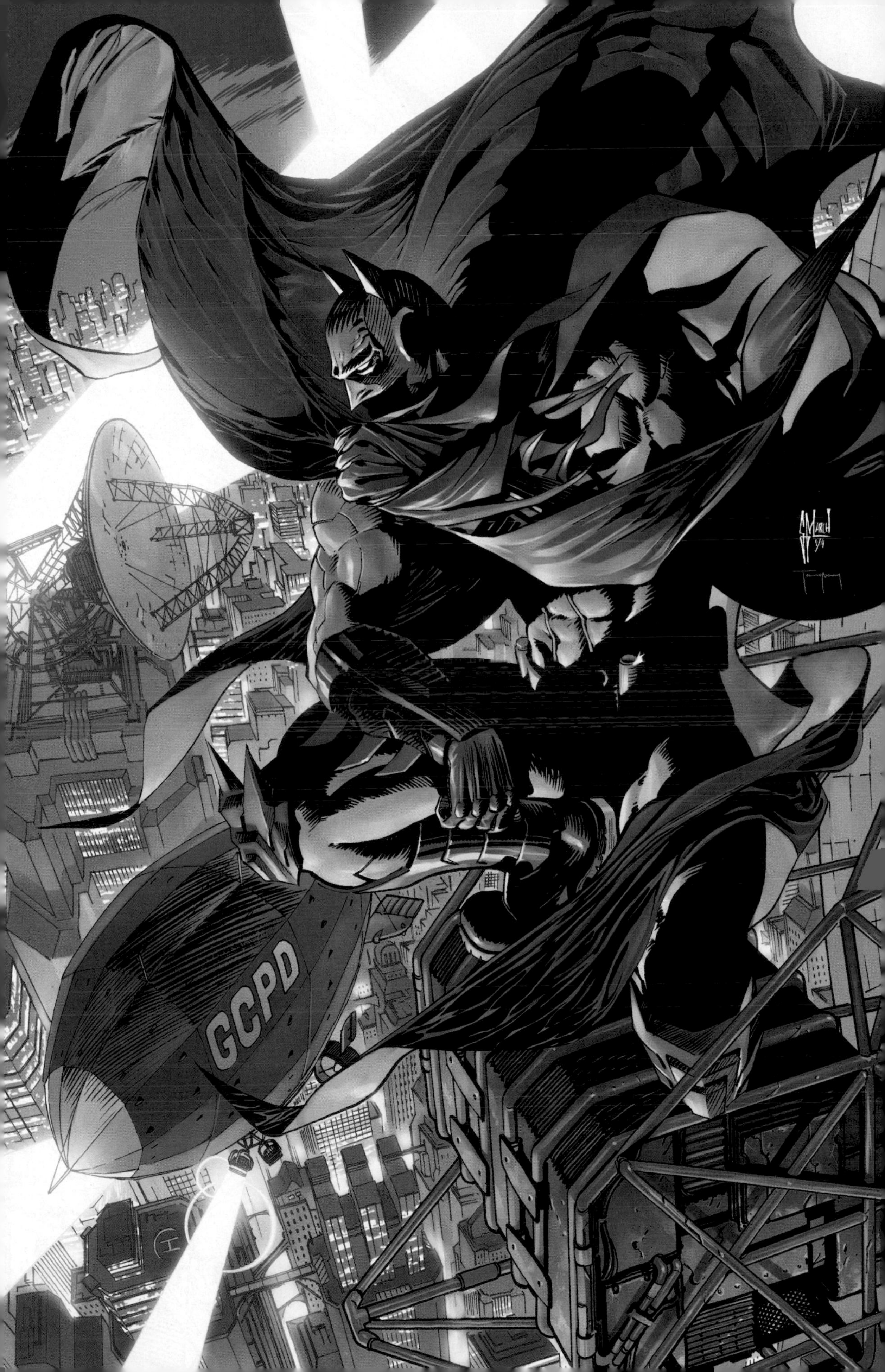
GCPD

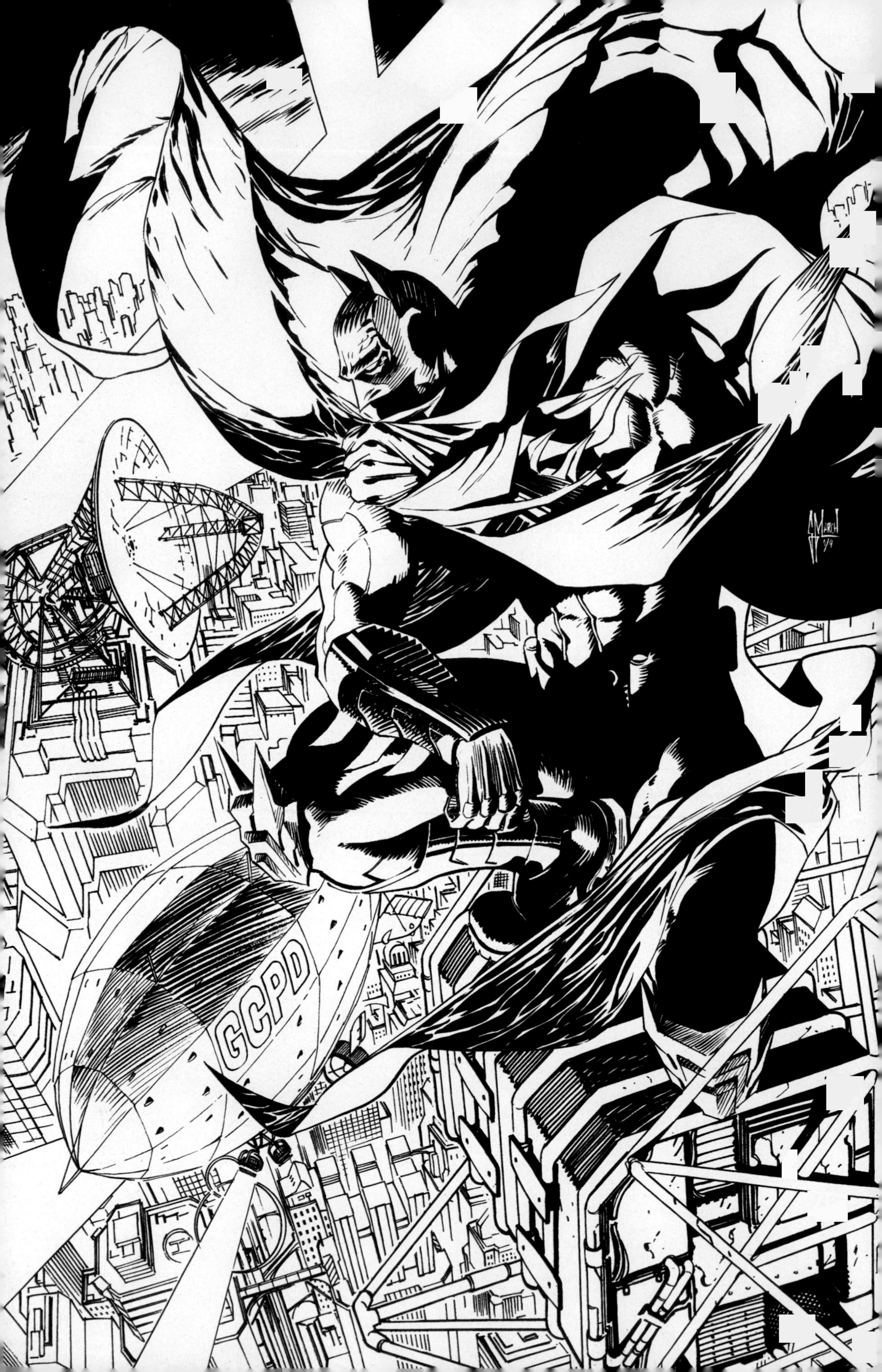
GCPD

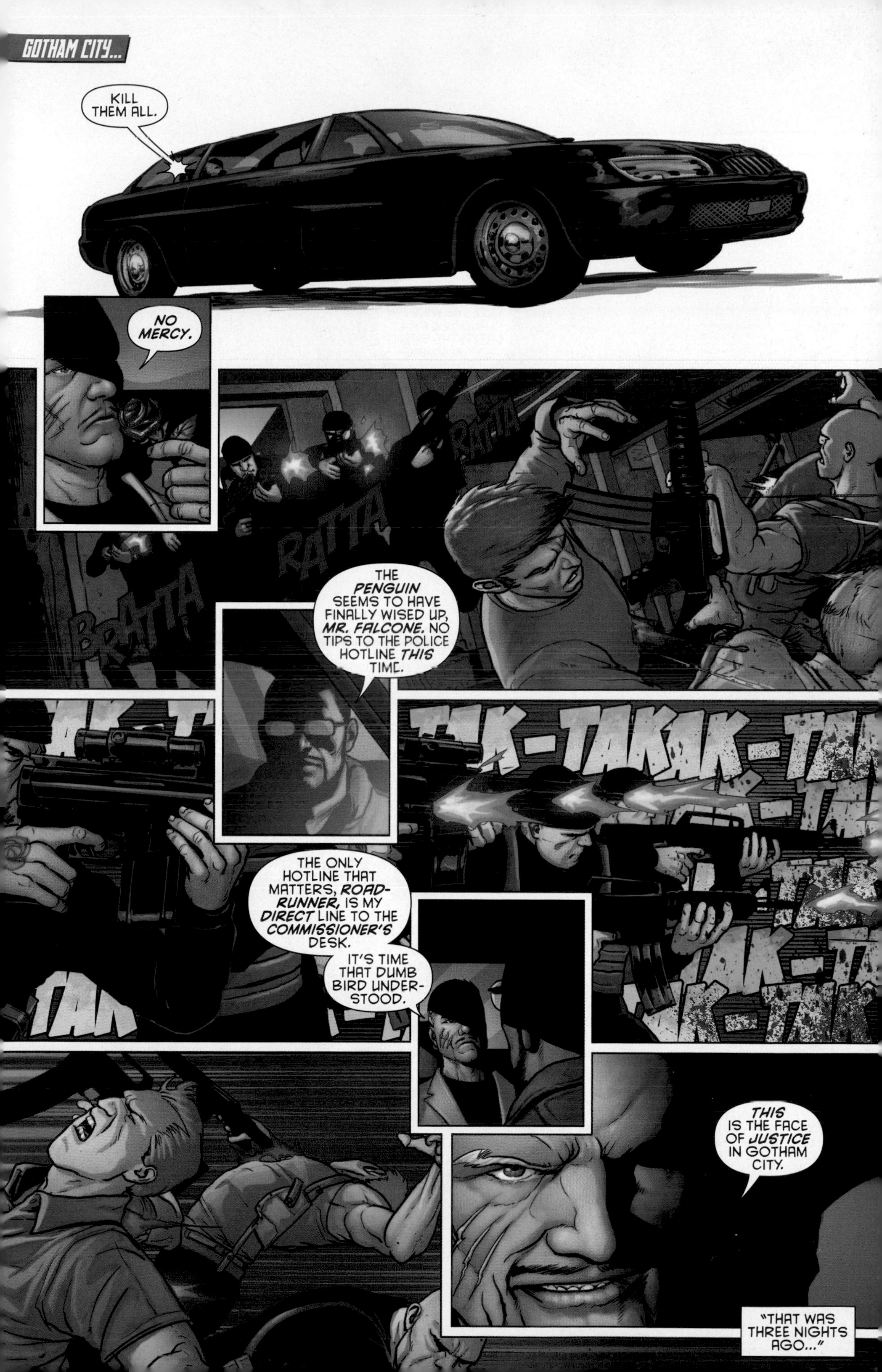
GOTHAM CITY...
KILL THEM ALL.
NO MERCY.
RATTA
RATTA
RATTA
BRATTA
THE PENGUIN SEEMS TO HAVE FINALLY WISED UP, MR. FALCONE. NO TIPS TO THE POLICE HOTLINE THIS TIME.
TAK-TAKAK-TAK
THE ONLY HOTLINE THAT MATTERS, ROAD-RUNNER, IS MY DIRECT LINE TO THE COMMISSIONER'S DESK.
IT'S TIME THAT DUMB BIRD UNDER-STOOD.
THIS IS THE FACE OF JUSTICE IN GOTHAM CITY.
"THAT WAS THREE NIGHTS AGO..."

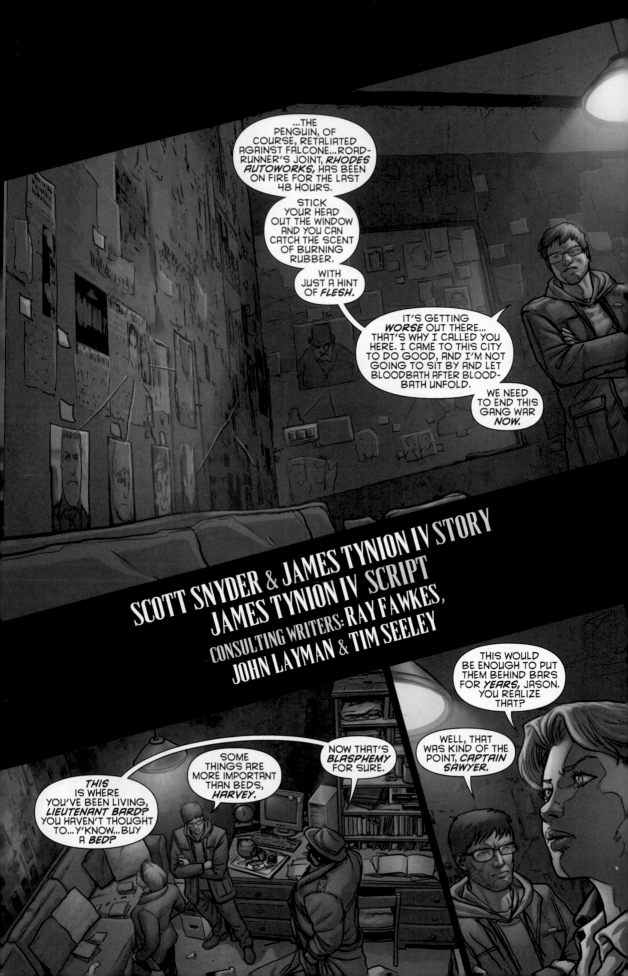

...THE PENGUIN, OF COURSE, RETALIATED AGAINST FALCONE...ROADRUNNER'S JOINT, *RHODES AUTOWORKS,* HAS BEEN ON FIRE FOR THE LAST 48 HOURS.

STICK YOUR HEAD OUT THE WINDOW AND YOU CAN CATCH THE SCENT OF BURNING RUBBER.

WITH JUST A HINT OF *FLESH.*

IT'S GETTING *WORSE* OUT THERE... THAT'S WHY I CALLED YOU HERE. I CAME TO THIS CITY TO DO GOOD, AND I'M NOT GOING TO SIT BY AND LET BLOODBATH AFTER BLOODBATH UNFOLD.

WE NEED TO END THIS GANG WAR *NOW.*

SCOTT SNYDER & JAMES TYNION IV STORY
JAMES TYNION IV SCRIPT
CONSULTING WRITERS: RAY FAWKES,
JOHN LAYMAN & TIM SEELEY

THIS WOULD BE ENOUGH TO PUT THEM BEHIND BARS FOR *YEARS,* JASON. YOU REALIZE THAT?

WELL, THAT WAS KIND OF THE POINT, *CAPTAIN SAWYER.*

THIS IS WHERE YOU'VE BEEN LIVING, *LIEUTENANT BARD?* YOU HAVEN'T THOUGHT TO...Y'KNOW...BUY A *BED?*

SOME THINGS ARE MORE IMPORTANT THAN BEDS, *HARVEY.*

NOW THAT'S *BLASPHEMY* FOR SURE.

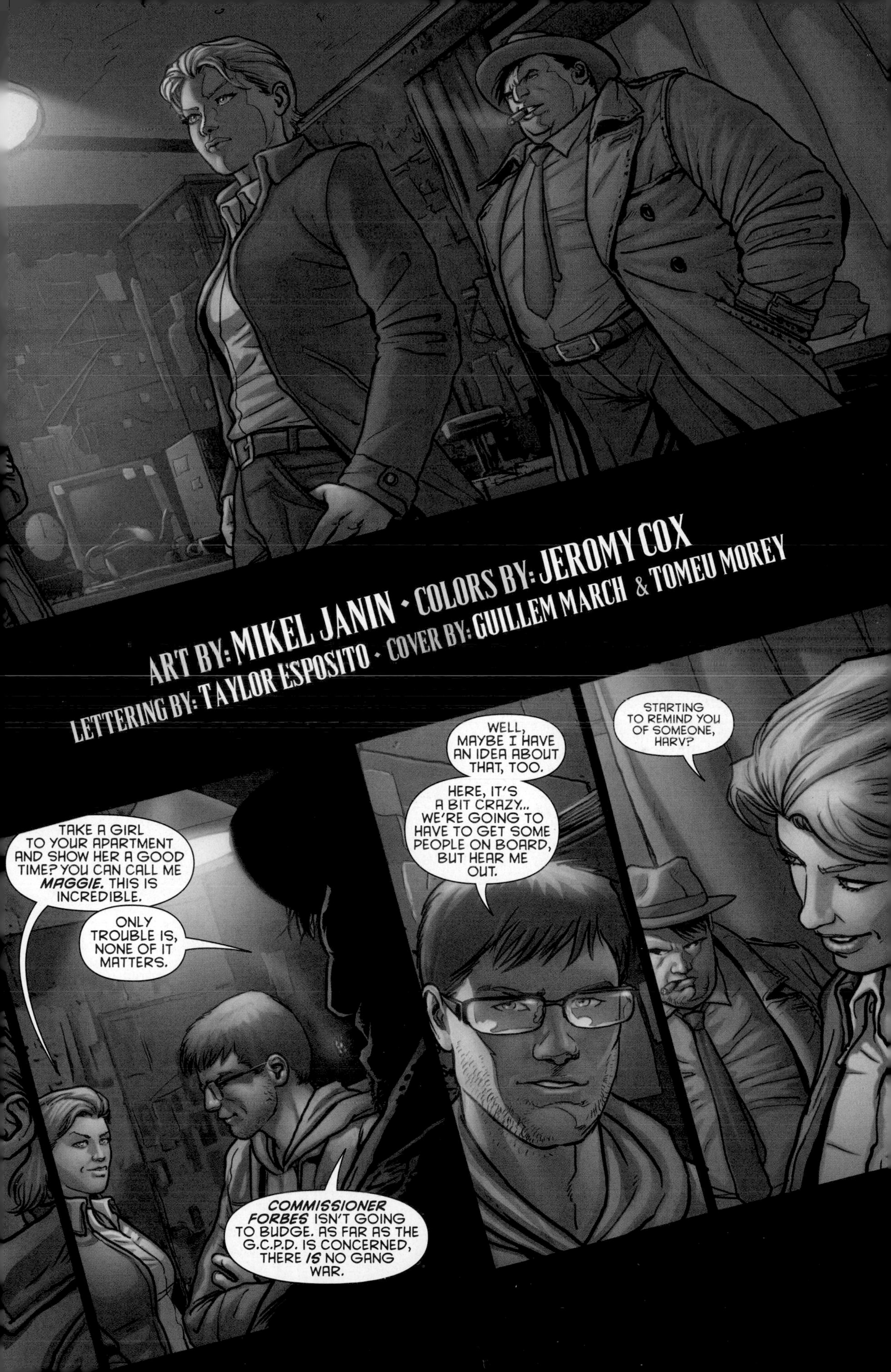

ART BY: MIKEL JANIN • COLORS BY: JEROMY COX
LETTERING BY: TAYLOR ESPOSITO • COVER BY: GUILLEM MARCH & TOMEU MOREY
TAKE A GIRL TO YOUR APARTMENT AND SHOW HER A GOOD TIME? YOU CAN CALL ME MAGGIE. THIS IS INCREDIBLE.
ONLY TROUBLE IS, NONE OF IT MATTERS.
COMMISSIONER FORBES ISN'T GOING TO BUDGE. AS FAR AS THE G.C.P.D. IS CONCERNED, THERE IS NO GANG WAR.
WELL, MAYBE I HAVE AN IDEA ABOUT THAT, TOO.
HERE, IT'S A BIT CRAZY... WE'RE GOING TO HAVE TO GET SOME PEOPLE ON BOARD, BUT HEAR ME OUT.
STARTING TO REMIND YOU OF SOMEONE, HARV?

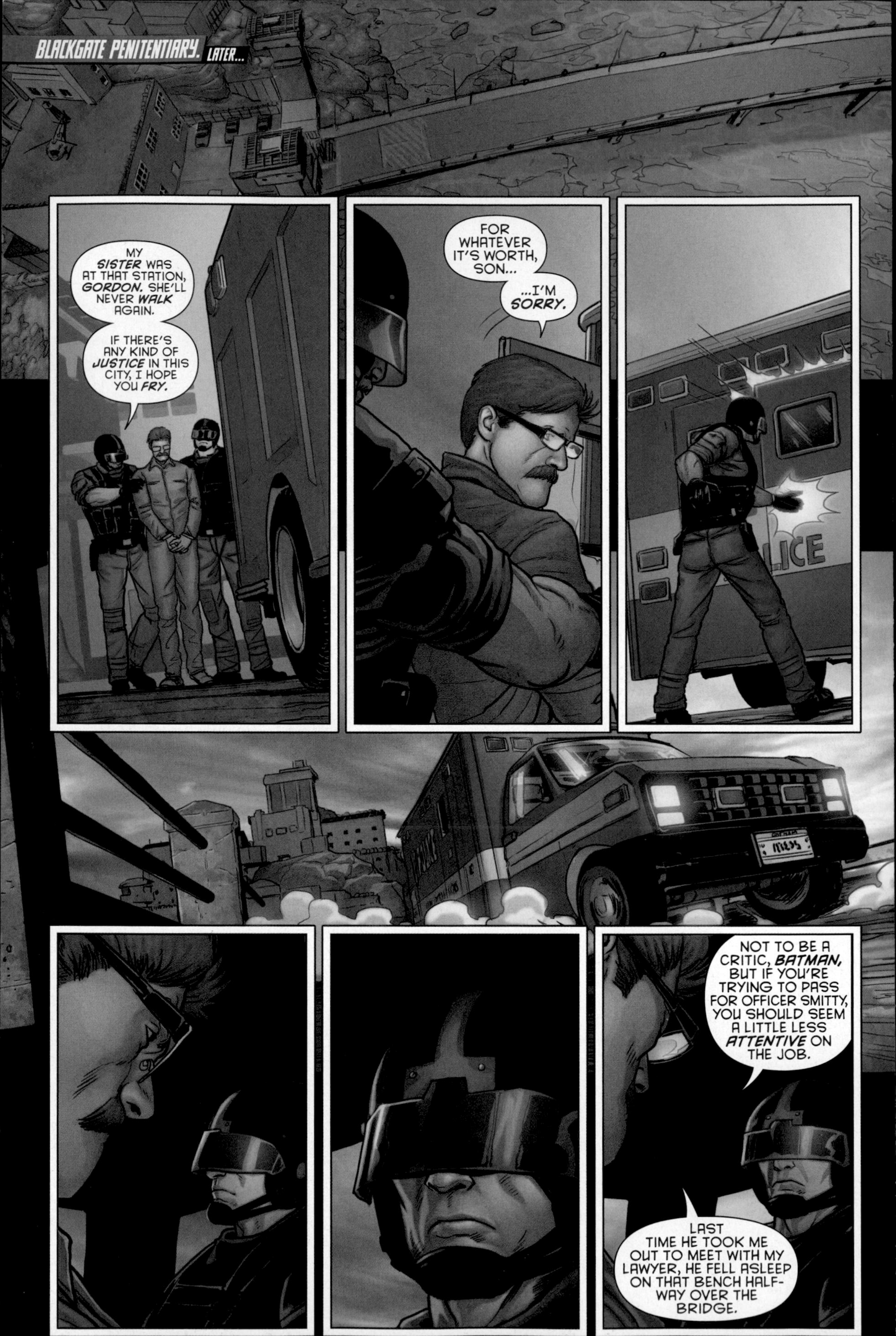
BLACKGATE PENITENTIARY. LATER...
MY SISTER WAS AT THAT STATION, GORDON. SHE'LL NEVER WALK AGAIN.
IF THERE'S ANY KIND OF JUSTICE IN THIS CITY, I HOPE YOU FRY.
FOR WHATEVER IT'S WORTH, SON...
...I'M SORRY.
LICE
NOT TO BE A CRITIC, BATMAN, BUT IF YOU'RE TRYING TO PASS FOR OFFICER SMITTY, YOU SHOULD SEEM A LITTLE LESS ATTENTIVE ON THE JOB.
LAST TIME HE TOOK ME OUT TO MEET WITH MY LAWYER, HE FELL ASLEEP ON THAT BENCH HALF-WAY OVER THE BRIDGE.

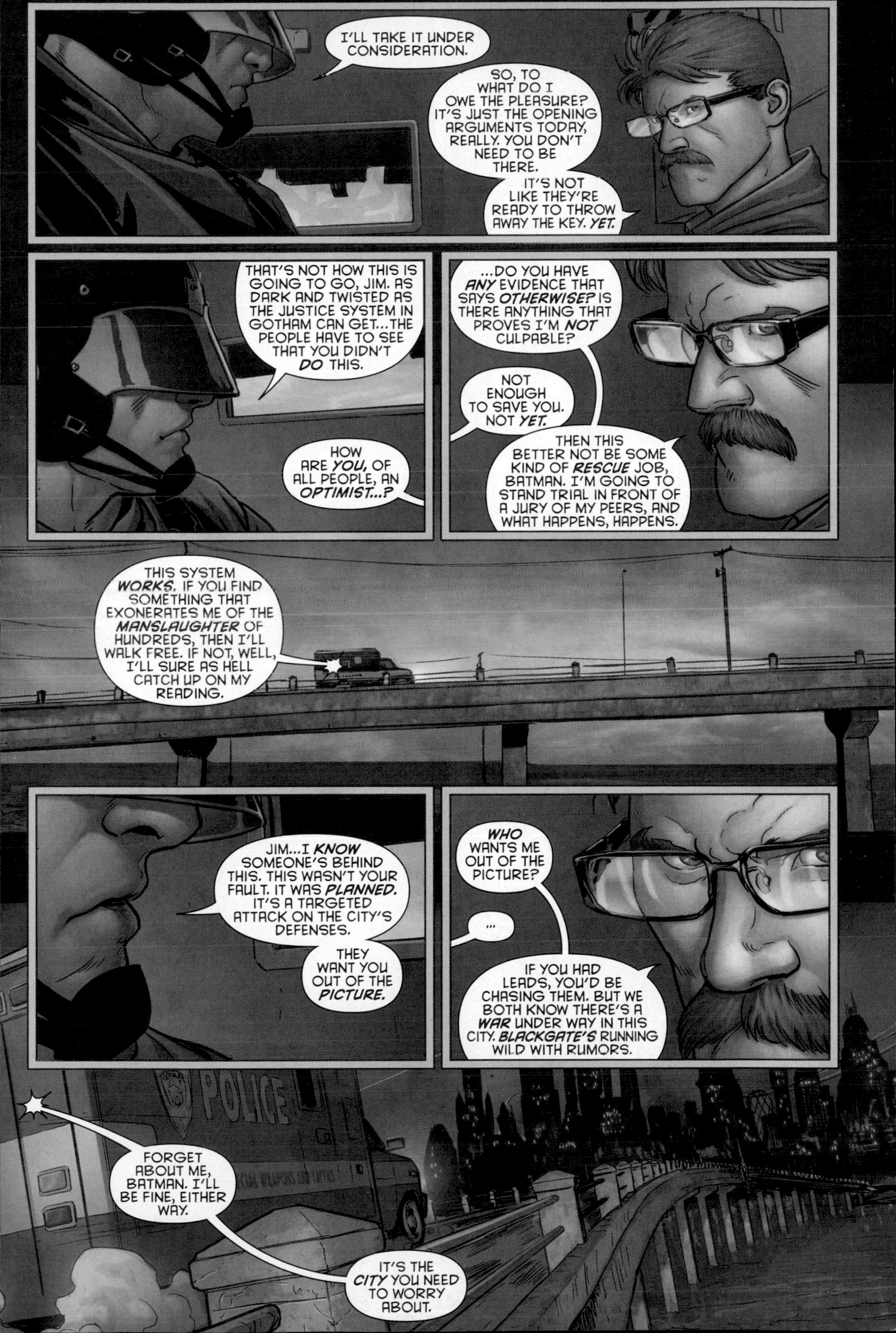
I'LL TAKE IT UNDER CONSIDERATION.
SO, TO WHAT DO I OWE THE PLEASURE? IT'S JUST THE OPENING ARGUMENTS TODAY, REALLY. YOU DON'T NEED TO BE THERE.
IT'S NOT LIKE THEY'RE READY TO THROW AWAY THE KEY. YET.
THAT'S NOT HOW THIS IS GOING TO GO, JIM. AS DARK AND TWISTED AS THE JUSTICE SYSTEM IN GOTHAM CAN GET...THE PEOPLE HAVE TO SEE THAT YOU DIDN'T DO THIS.
...DO YOU HAVE ANY EVIDENCE THAT SAYS OTHERWISE? IS THERE ANYTHING THAT PROVES I'M NOT CULPABLE?
NOT ENOUGH TO SAVE YOU. NOT YET.
THEN THIS BETTER NOT BE SOME KIND OF RESCUE JOB, BATMAN. I'M GOING TO STAND TRIAL IN FRONT OF A JURY OF MY PEERS, AND WHAT HAPPENS, HAPPENS.
HOW ARE YOU, OF ALL PEOPLE, AN OPTIMIST...?
THIS SYSTEM WORKS. IF YOU FIND SOMETHING THAT EXONERATES ME OF THE MANSLAUGHTER OF HUNDREDS, THEN I'LL WALK FREE. IF NOT, WELL, I'LL SURE AS HELL CATCH UP ON MY READING.
JIM...I KNOW SOMEONE'S BEHIND THIS. THIS WASN'T YOUR FAULT. IT WAS PLANNED. IT'S A TARGETED ATTACK ON THE CITY'S DEFENSES.
THEY WANT YOU OUT OF THE PICTURE.
WHO WANTS ME OUT OF THE PICTURE?
...
IF YOU HAD LEADS, YOU'D BE CHASING THEM. BUT WE BOTH KNOW THERE'S A WAR UNDER WAY IN THIS CITY. BLACKGATE'S RUNNING WILD WITH RUMORS.
POLICE
FORGET ABOUT ME, BATMAN. I'LL BE FINE, EITHER WAY.
IT'S THE CITY YOU NEED TO WORRY ABOUT.

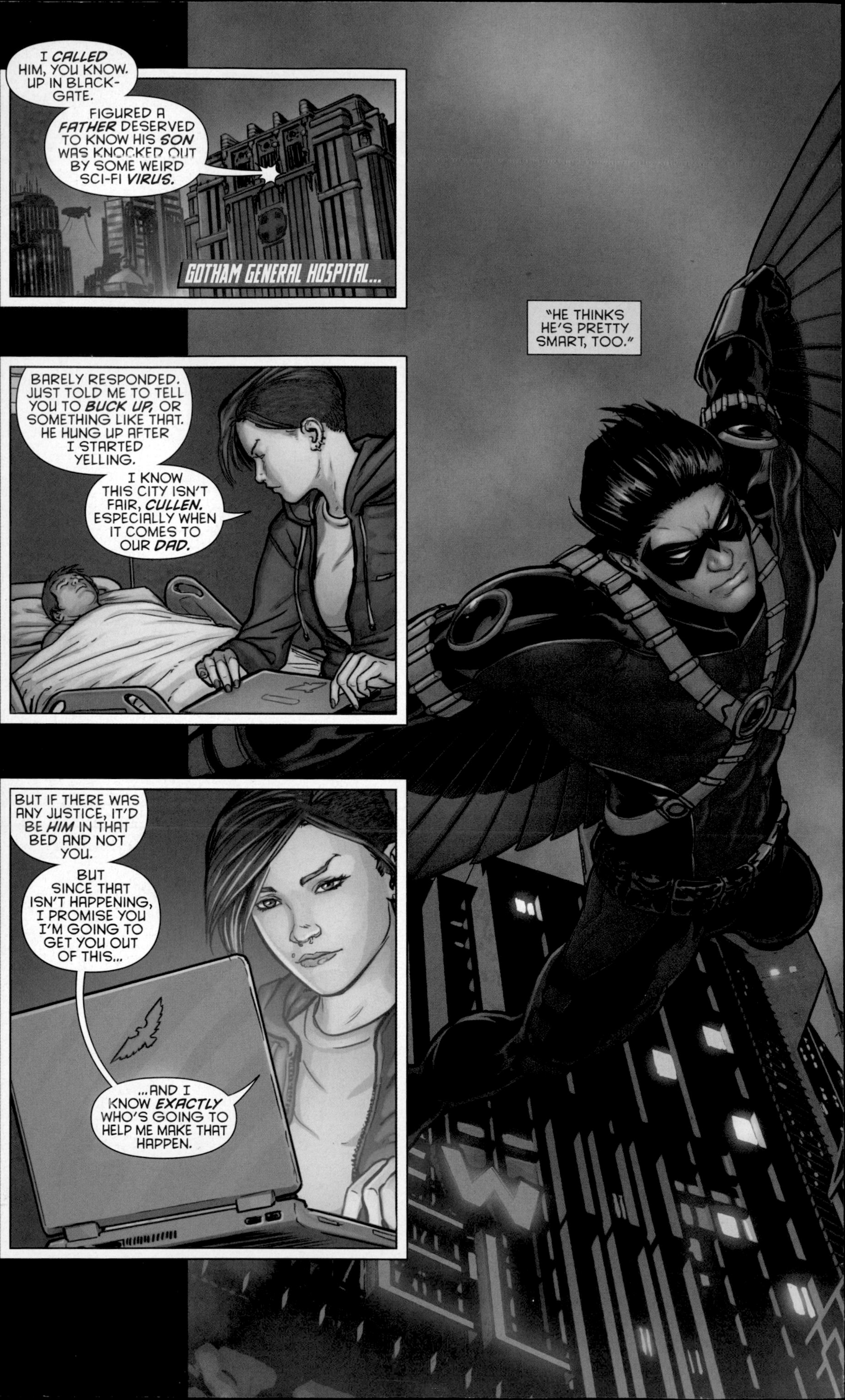
I CALLED HIM, YOU KNOW. UP IN BLACK-GATE.
FIGURED A FATHER DESERVED TO KNOW HIS SON WAS KNOCKED OUT BY SOME WEIRD SCI-FI VIRUS.
GOTHAM GENERAL HOSPITAL...
"HE THINKS HE'S PRETTY SMART, TOO."
BARELY RESPONDED. JUST TOLD ME TO TELL YOU TO BUCK UP, OR SOMETHING LIKE THAT. HE HUNG UP AFTER I STARTED YELLING.
I KNOW THIS CITY ISN'T FAIR, CULLEN. ESPECIALLY WHEN IT COMES TO OUR DAD.
BUT IF THERE WAS ANY JUSTICE, IT'D BE HIM IN THAT BED AND NOT YOU.
BUT SINCE THAT ISN'T HAPPENING, I PROMISE YOU I'M GOING TO GET YOU OUT OF THIS...
...AND I KNOW EXACTLY WHO'S GOING TO HELP ME MAKE THAT HAPPEN.

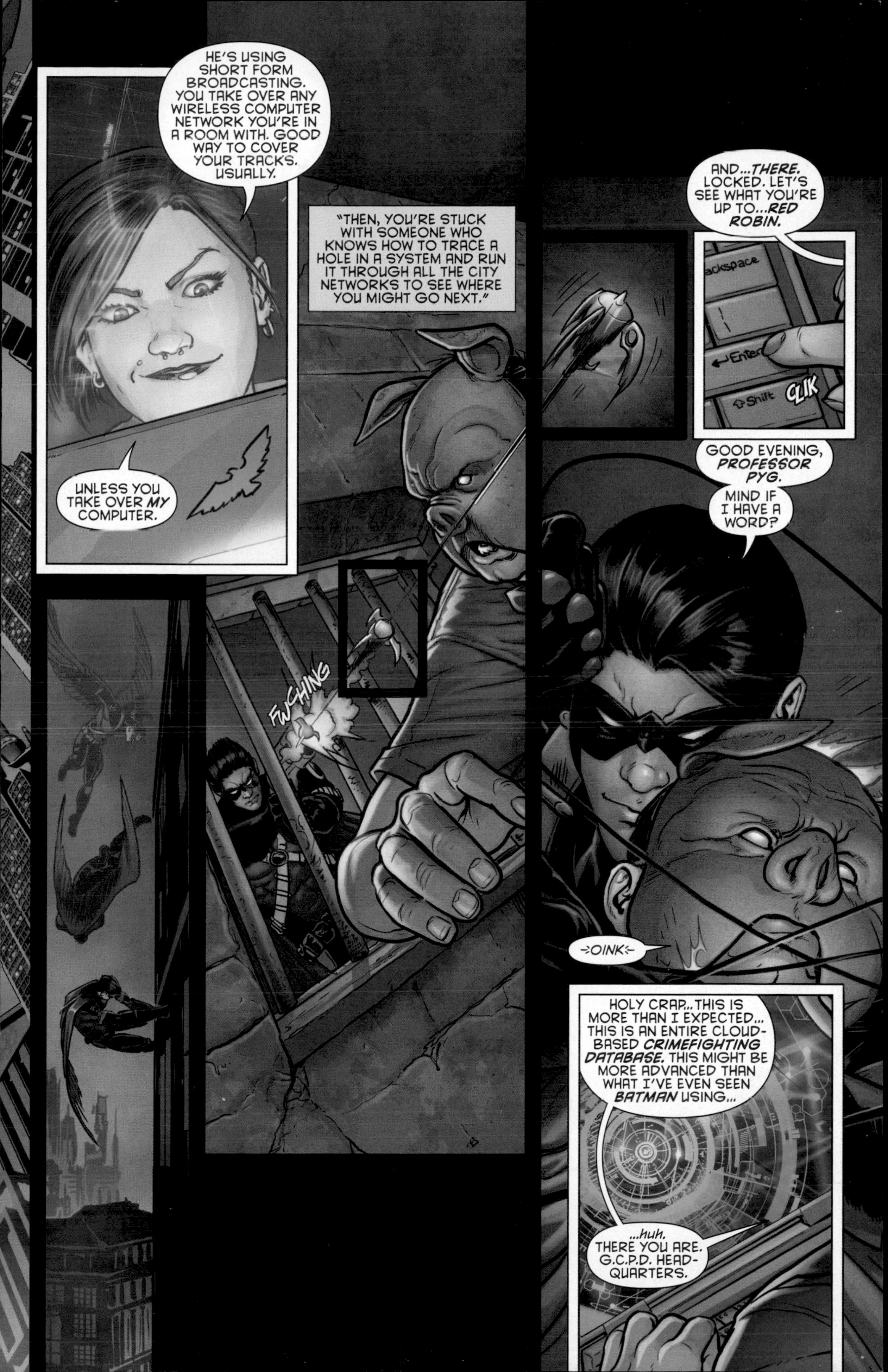
HE'S USING SHORT FORM BROADCASTING. YOU TAKE OVER ANY WIRELESS COMPUTER NETWORK YOU'RE IN A ROOM WITH. GOOD WAY TO COVER YOUR TRACKS. USUALLY.
UNLESS YOU TAKE OVER MY COMPUTER.
"THEN, YOU'RE STUCK WITH SOMEONE WHO KNOWS HOW TO TRACE A HOLE IN A SYSTEM AND RUN IT THROUGH ALL THE CITY NETWORKS TO SEE WHERE YOU MIGHT GO NEXT."
FWCHING
AND...THERE. LOCKED. LET'S SEE WHAT YOU'RE UP TO...RED ROBIN.
ackspace
Enter
Shift
CLIK
GOOD EVENING, PROFESSOR PYG.
MIND IF I HAVE A WORD?
OINK
HOLY CRAP... THIS IS MORE THAN I EXPECTED... THIS IS AN ENTIRE CLOUD-BASED CRIMEFIGHTING DATABASE. THIS MIGHT BE MORE ADVANCED THAN WHAT I'VE EVEN SEEN BATMAN USING...
...huh. THERE YOU ARE. G.C.P.D. HEADQUARTERS.

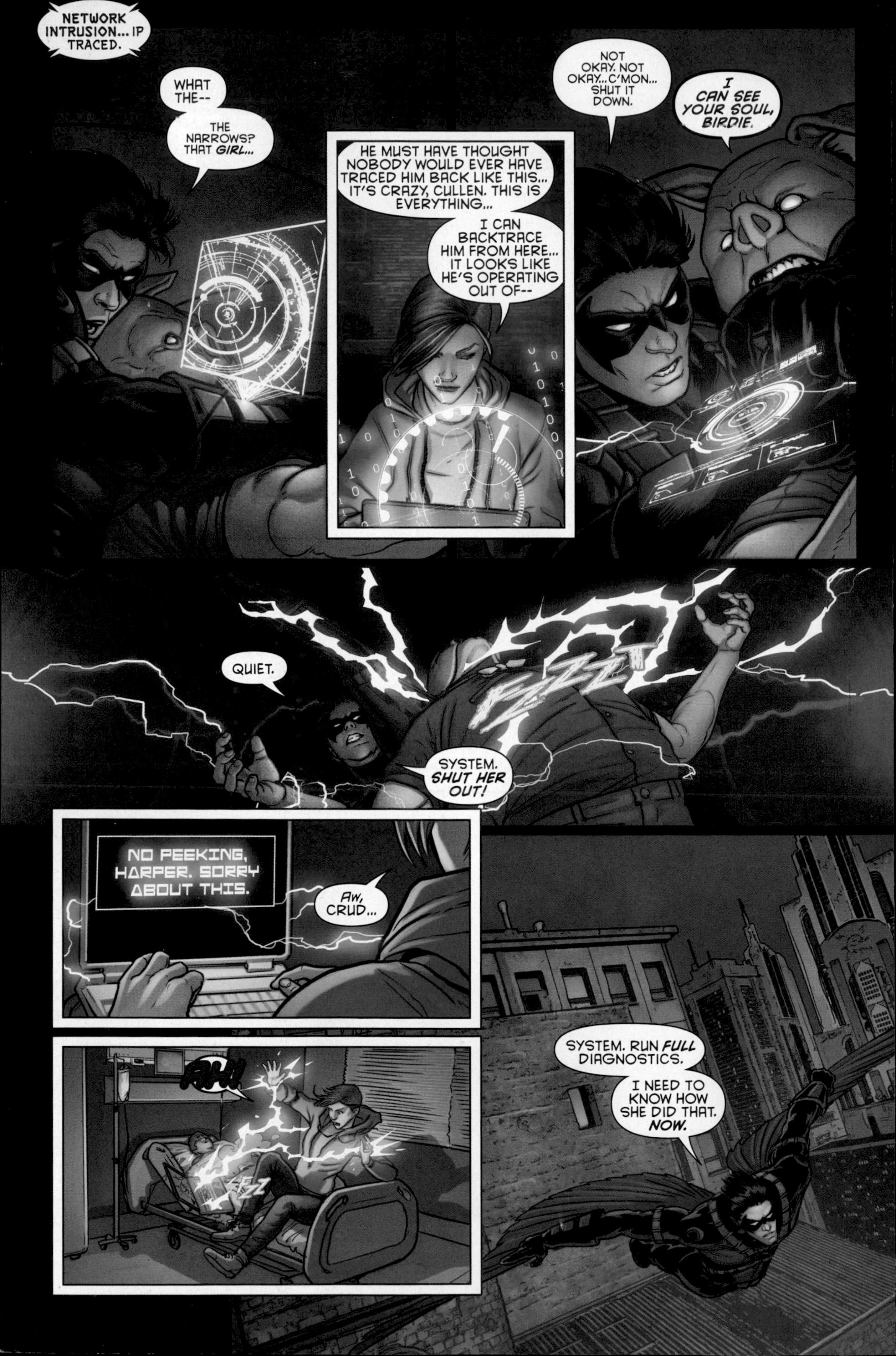

NETWORK INTRUSION... IP TRACED.
WHAT THE--
THE NARROWS? THAT GIRL...
HE MUST HAVE THOUGHT NOBODY WOULD EVER HAVE TRACED HIM BACK LIKE THIS... IT'S CRAZY, CULLEN. THIS IS EVERYTHING...
I CAN BACKTRACE HIM FROM HERE... IT LOOKS LIKE HE'S OPERATING OUT OF--
NOT OKAY. NOT OKAY... C'MON... SHUT IT DOWN.
I CAN SEE YOUR SOUL, BIRDIE.
QUIET.
SYSTEM. SHUT HER OUT!
NO PEEKING, HARPER. SORRY ABOUT THIS.
AW, CRUD...
SYSTEM. RUN FULL DIAGNOSTICS.
I NEED TO KNOW HOW SHE DID THAT. NOW.

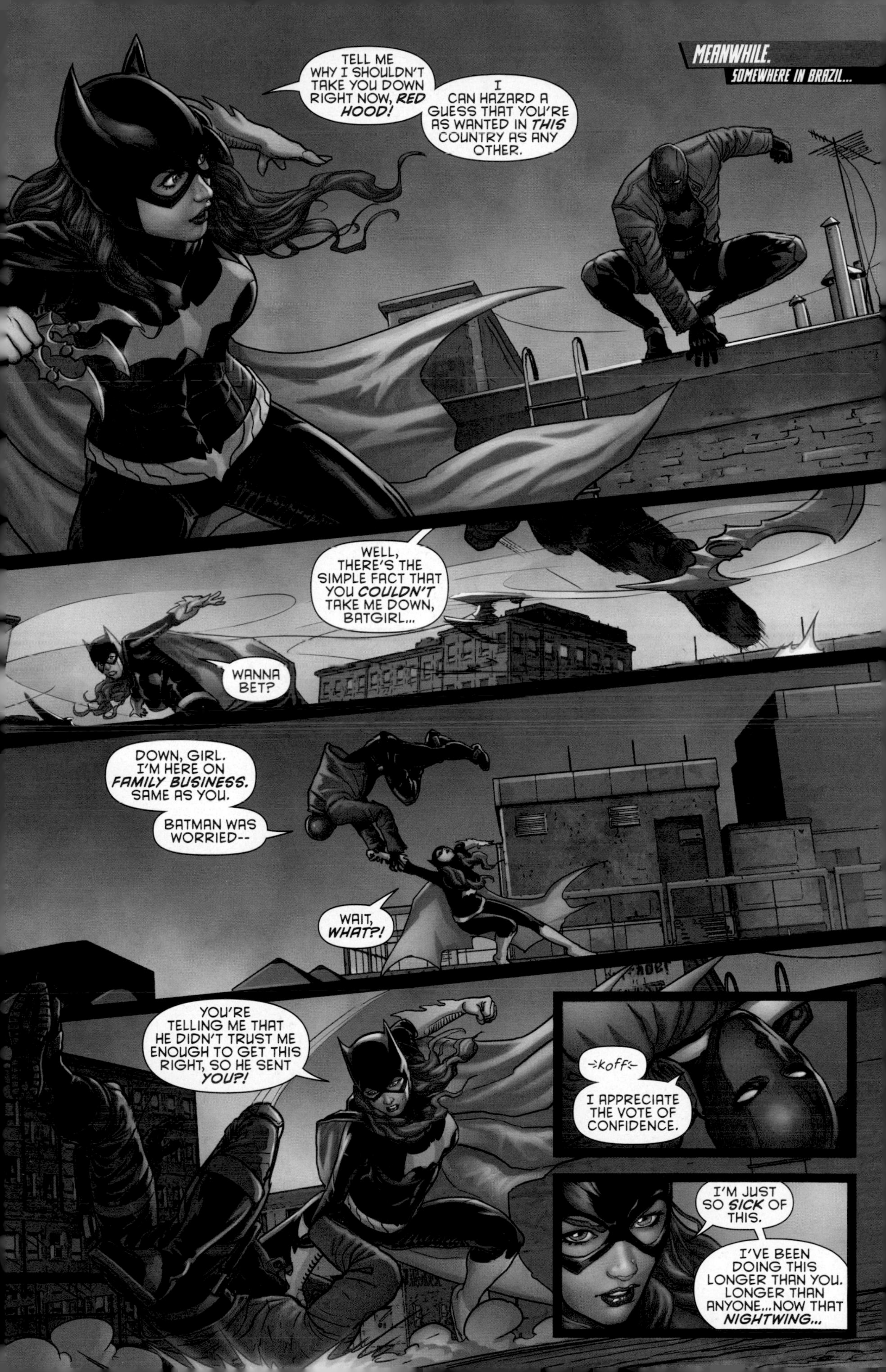
MEANWHILE.
SOMEWHERE IN BRAZIL...
TELL ME WHY I SHOULDN'T TAKE YOU DOWN RIGHT NOW, RED HOOD!
I CAN HAZARD A GUESS THAT YOU'RE AS WANTED IN THIS COUNTRY AS ANY OTHER.
WELL, THERE'S THE SIMPLE FACT THAT YOU COULDN'T TAKE ME DOWN, BATGIRL...
WANNA BET?
DOWN, GIRL. I'M HERE ON FAMILY BUSINESS. SAME AS YOU.
BATMAN WAS WORRIED--
WAIT, WHAT?!
YOU'RE TELLING ME THAT HE DIDN'T TRUST ME ENOUGH TO GET THIS RIGHT, SO HE SENT YOU?!
koff
I APPRECIATE THE VOTE OF CONFIDENCE.
I'M JUST SO SICK OF THIS.
I'VE BEEN DOING THIS LONGER THAN YOU. LONGER THAN ANYONE...NOW THAT NIGHTWING...

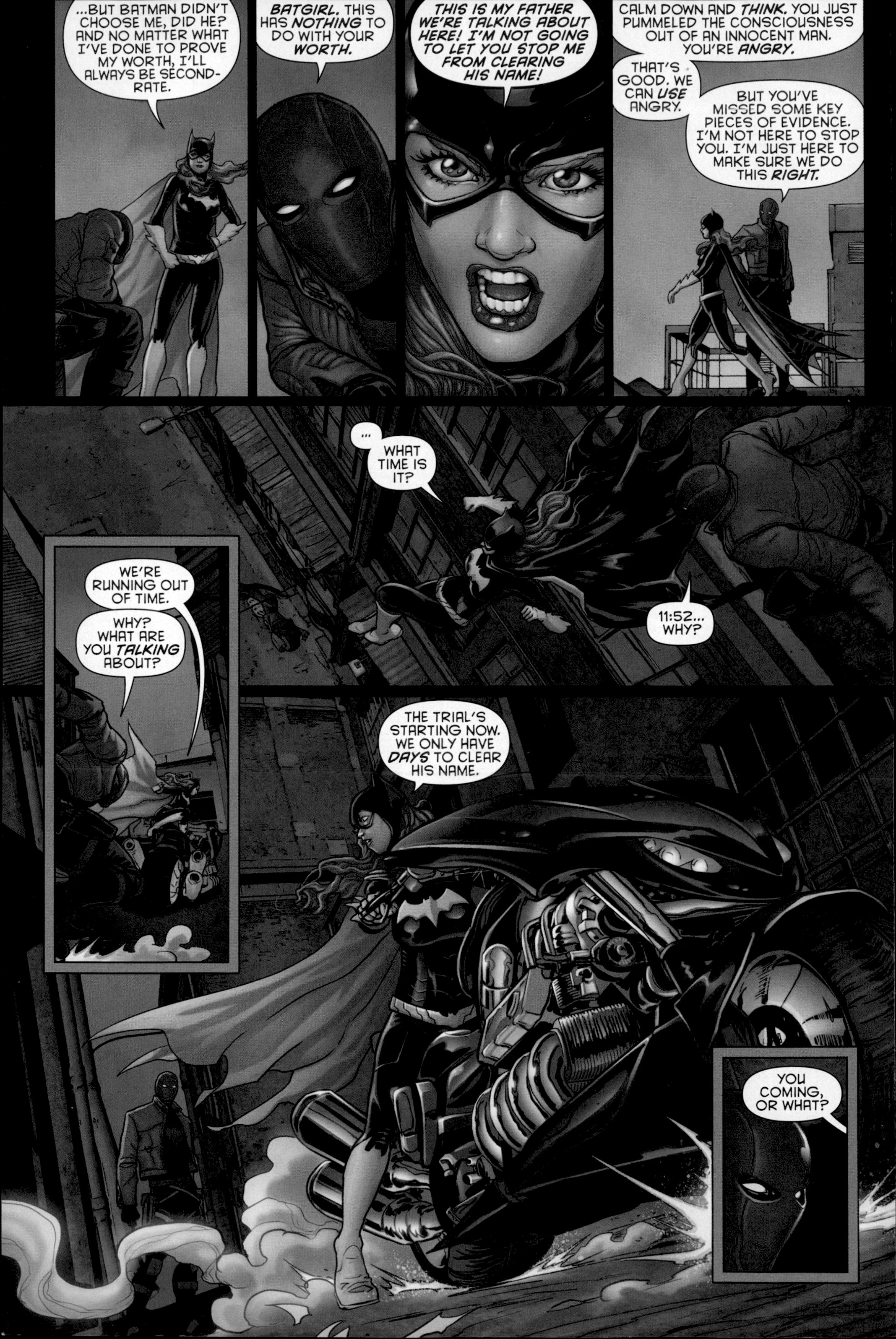
...BUT BATMAN DIDN'T CHOOSE ME, DID HE? AND NO MATTER WHAT I'VE DONE TO PROVE MY WORTH, I'LL ALWAYS BE SECOND-RATE.
BATGIRL. THIS HAS NOTHING TO DO WITH YOUR WORTH.
THIS IS MY FATHER WE'RE TALKING ABOUT HERE! I'M NOT GOING TO LET YOU STOP ME FROM CLEARING HIS NAME!
CALM DOWN AND THINK. YOU JUST PUMMELED THE CONSCIOUSNESS OUT OF AN INNOCENT MAN. YOU'RE ANGRY.
THAT'S GOOD. WE CAN USE ANGRY.
BUT YOU'VE MISSED SOME KEY PIECES OF EVIDENCE. I'M NOT HERE TO STOP YOU. I'M JUST HERE TO MAKE SURE WE DO THIS RIGHT.
... WHAT TIME IS IT?
11:52... WHY?
WE'RE RUNNING OUT OF TIME.
WHY? WHAT ARE YOU TALKING ABOUT?
THE TRIAL'S STARTING NOW. WE ONLY HAVE DAYS TO CLEAR HIS NAME.
YOU COMING, OR WHAT?

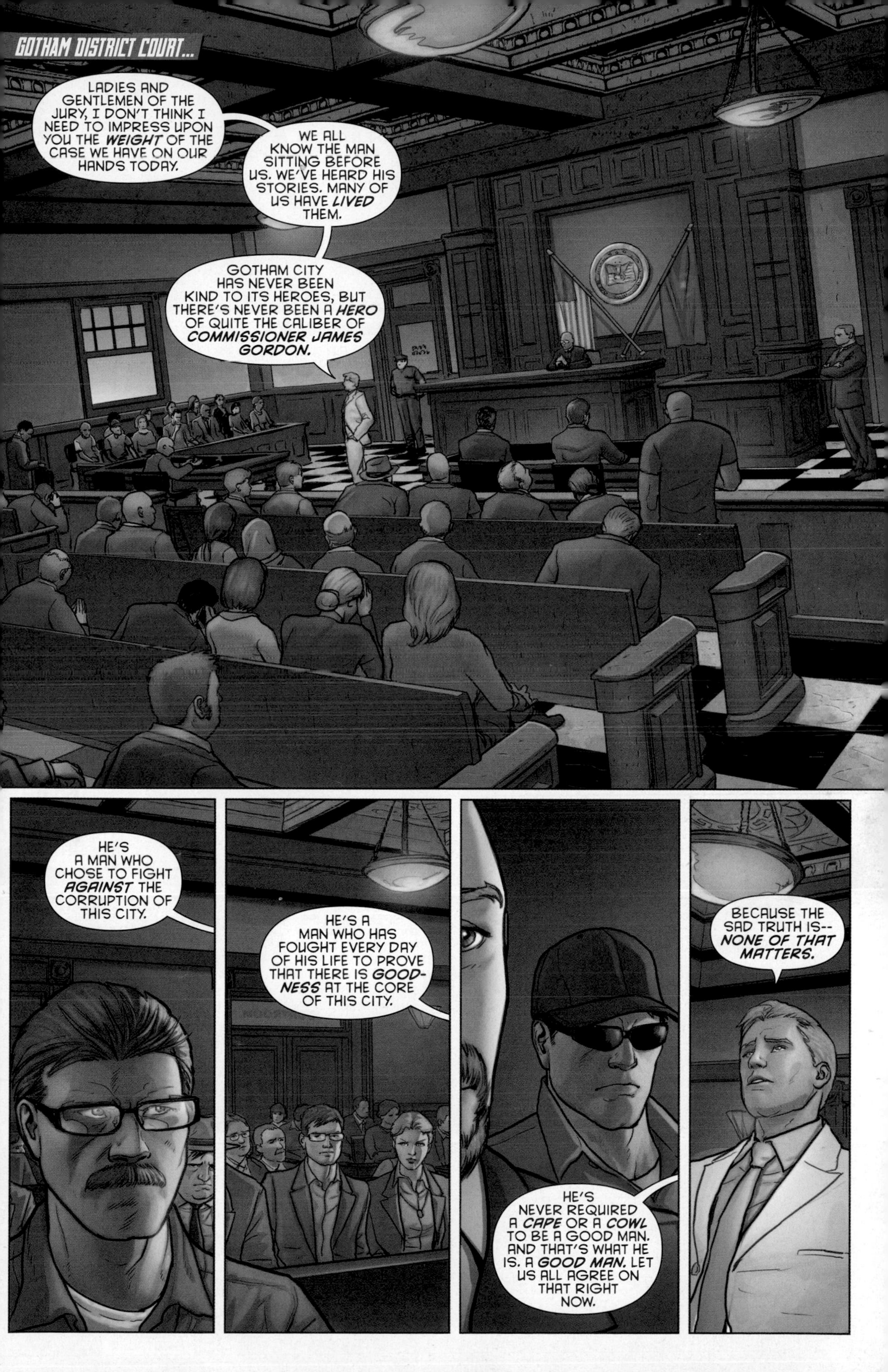
GOTHAM DISTRICT COURT...
LADIES AND GENTLEMEN OF THE JURY, I DON'T THINK I NEED TO IMPRESS UPON YOU THE WEIGHT OF THE CASE WE HAVE ON OUR HANDS TODAY.
WE ALL KNOW THE MAN SITTING BEFORE US. WE'VE HEARD HIS STORIES. MANY OF US HAVE LIVED THEM.
GOTHAM CITY HAS NEVER BEEN KIND TO ITS HEROES, BUT THERE'S NEVER BEEN A HERO OF QUITE THE CALIBER OF COMMISSIONER JAMES GORDON.
HE'S A MAN WHO CHOSE TO FIGHT AGAINST THE CORRUPTION OF THIS CITY.
HE'S A MAN WHO HAS FOUGHT EVERY DAY OF HIS LIFE TO PROVE THAT THERE IS GOODNESS AT THE CORE OF THIS CITY.
HE'S NEVER REQUIRED A CAPE OR A COWL TO BE A GOOD MAN. AND THAT'S WHAT HE IS. A GOOD MAN. LET US ALL AGREE ON THAT RIGHT NOW.
BECAUSE THE SAD TRUTH IS-- NONE OF THAT MATTERS.

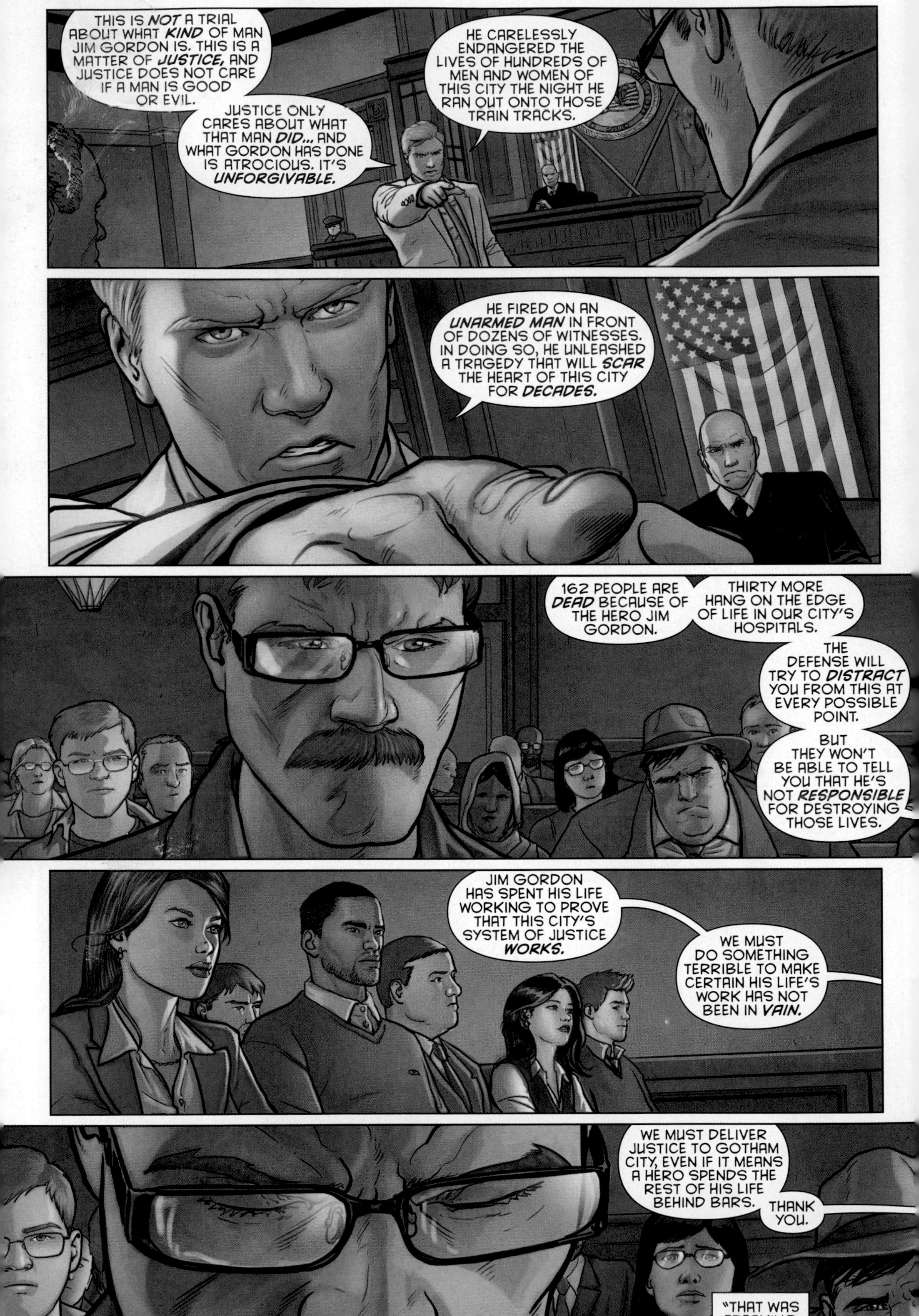
THIS IS NOT A TRIAL ABOUT WHAT KIND OF MAN JIM GORDON IS. THIS IS A MATTER OF JUSTICE, AND JUSTICE DOES NOT CARE IF A MAN IS GOOD OR EVIL.
JUSTICE ONLY CARES ABOUT WHAT THAT MAN DID... AND WHAT GORDON HAS DONE IS ATROCIOUS. IT'S UNFORGIVABLE.
HE CARELESSLY ENDANGERED THE LIVES OF HUNDREDS OF MEN AND WOMEN OF THIS CITY THE NIGHT HE RAN OUT ONTO THOSE TRAIN TRACKS.
HE FIRED ON AN UNARMED MAN IN FRONT OF DOZENS OF WITNESSES. IN DOING SO, HE UNLEASHED A TRAGEDY THAT WILL SCAR THE HEART OF THIS CITY FOR DECADES.
162 PEOPLE ARE DEAD BECAUSE OF THE HERO JIM GORDON.
THIRTY MORE HANG ON THE EDGE OF LIFE IN OUR CITY'S HOSPITALS.
THE DEFENSE WILL TRY TO DISTRACT YOU FROM THIS AT EVERY POSSIBLE POINT.
BUT THEY WON'T BE ABLE TO TELL YOU THAT HE'S NOT RESPONSIBLE FOR DESTROYING THOSE LIVES.
JIM GORDON HAS SPENT HIS LIFE WORKING TO PROVE THAT THIS CITY'S SYSTEM OF JUSTICE WORKS.
WE MUST DO SOMETHING TERRIBLE TO MAKE CERTAIN HIS LIFE'S WORK HAS NOT BEEN IN VAIN.
WE MUST DELIVER JUSTICE TO GOTHAM CITY, EVEN IF IT MEANS A HERO SPENDS THE REST OF HIS LIFE BEHIND BARS.
THANK YOU.
"THAT WAS FREAKING BRUTAL..."

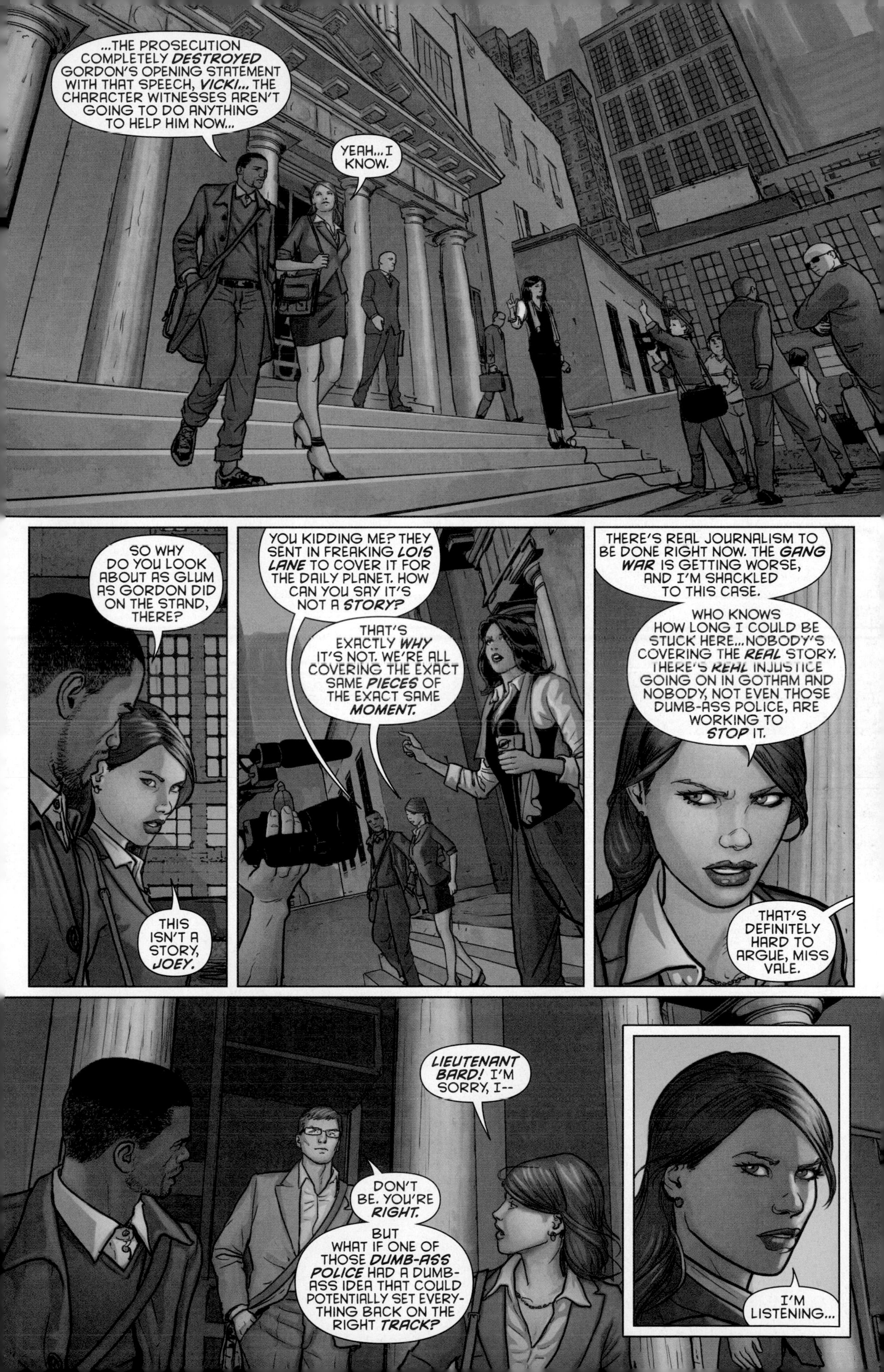
...THE PROSECUTION COMPLETELY DESTROYED GORDON'S OPENING STATEMENT WITH THAT SPEECH, VICKI... THE CHARACTER WITNESSES AREN'T GOING TO DO ANYTHING TO HELP HIM NOW...
YEAH... I KNOW.
SO WHY DO YOU LOOK ABOUT AS GLUM AS GORDON DID ON THE STAND, THERE?
THIS ISN'T A STORY, JOEY.
YOU KIDDING ME? THEY SENT IN FREAKING LOIS LANE TO COVER IT FOR THE DAILY PLANET. HOW CAN YOU SAY IT'S NOT A STORY?
THAT'S EXACTLY WHY IT'S NOT. WE'RE ALL COVERING THE EXACT SAME PIECES OF THE EXACT SAME MOMENT.
THERE'S REAL JOURNALISM TO BE DONE RIGHT NOW. THE GANG WAR IS GETTING WORSE, AND I'M SHACKLED TO THIS CASE.
WHO KNOWS HOW LONG I COULD BE STUCK HERE...NOBODY'S COVERING THE REAL STORY. THERE'S REAL INJUSTICE GOING ON IN GOTHAM AND NOBODY, NOT EVEN THOSE DUMB-ASS POLICE, ARE WORKING TO STOP IT.
THAT'S DEFINITELY HARD TO ARGUE, MISS VALE.
LIEUTENANT BARD! I'M SORRY, I--
DON'T BE. YOU'RE RIGHT.
BUT WHAT IF ONE OF THOSE DUMB-ASS POLICE HAD A DUMB-ASS IDEA THAT COULD POTENTIALLY SET EVERYTHING BACK ON THE RIGHT TRACK?
I'M LISTENING...

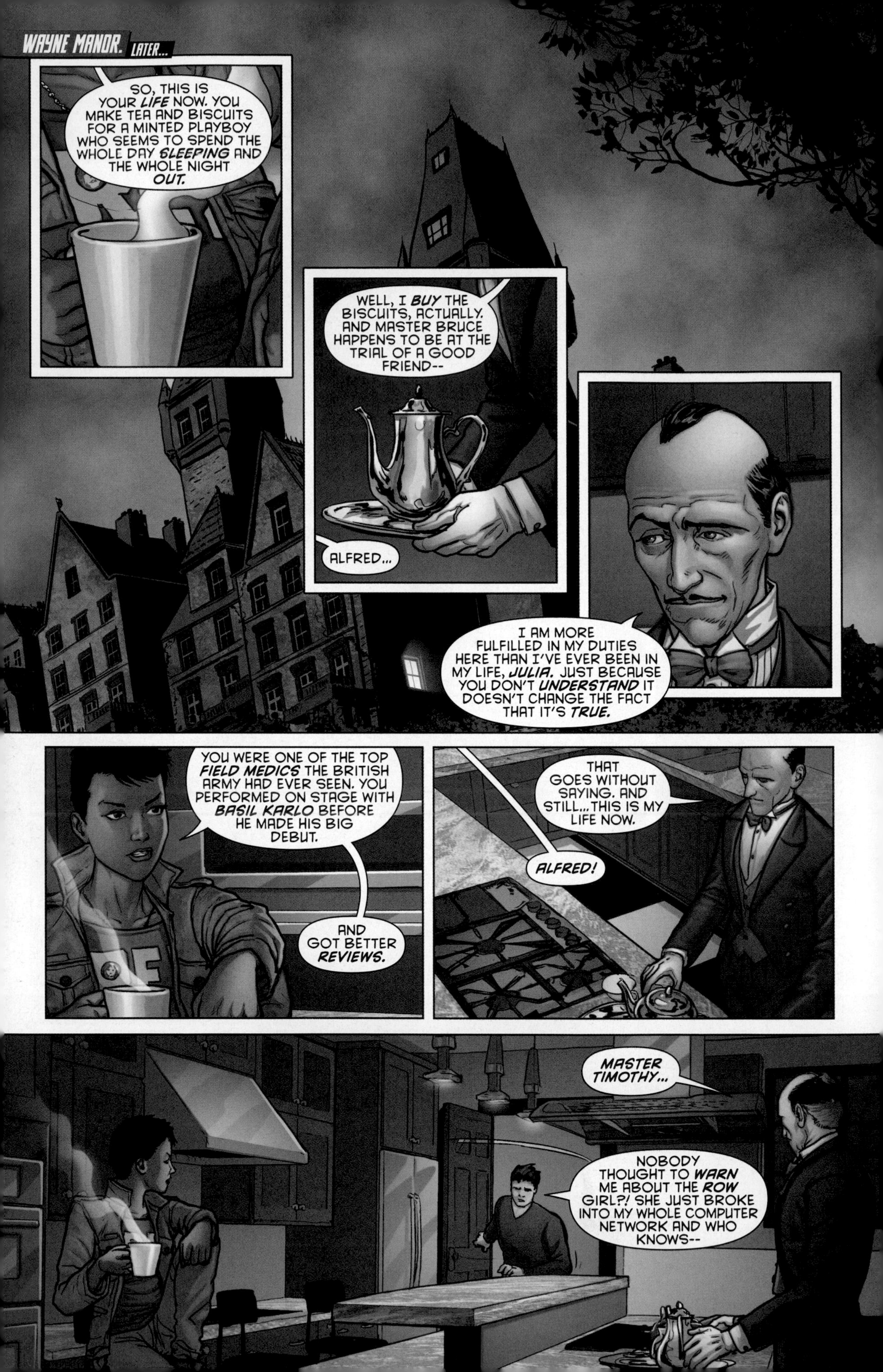
WAYNE MANOR. LATER...
SO, THIS IS YOUR LIFE NOW. YOU MAKE TEA AND BISCUITS FOR A MINTED PLAYBOY WHO SEEMS TO SPEND THE WHOLE DAY SLEEPING AND THE WHOLE NIGHT OUT.
WELL, I BUY THE BISCUITS, ACTUALLY. AND MASTER BRUCE HAPPENS TO BE AT THE TRIAL OF A GOOD FRIEND--
ALFRED...
I AM MORE FULFILLED IN MY DUTIES HERE THAN I'VE EVER BEEN IN MY LIFE, JULIA. JUST BECAUSE YOU DON'T UNDERSTAND IT DOESN'T CHANGE THE FACT THAT IT'S TRUE.
YOU WERE ONE OF THE TOP FIELD MEDICS THE BRITISH ARMY HAD EVER SEEN. YOU PERFORMED ON STAGE WITH BASIL KARLO BEFORE HE MADE HIS BIG DEBUT.
AND GOT BETTER REVIEWS.
THAT GOES WITHOUT SAYING. AND STILL...THIS IS MY LIFE NOW.
ALFRED!
MASTER TIMOTHY...
NOBODY THOUGHT TO WARN ME ABOUT THE ROW GIRL?! SHE JUST BROKE INTO MY WHOLE COMPUTER NETWORK AND WHO KNOWS--

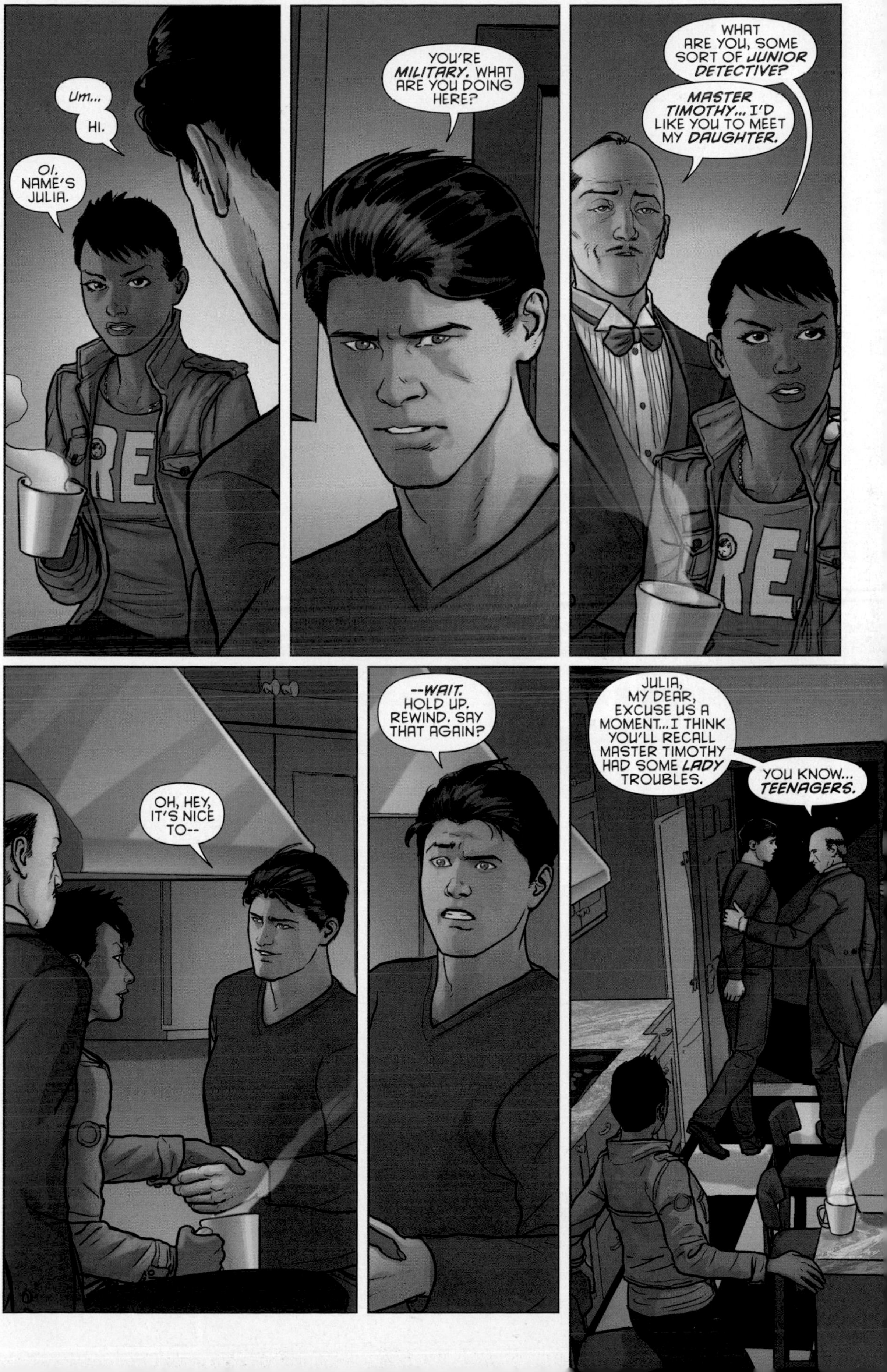
Um...
HI.
OI. NAME'S JULIA.
YOU'RE MILITARY. WHAT ARE YOU DOING HERE?
WHAT ARE YOU, SOME SORT OF JUNIOR DETECTIVE?
MASTER TIMOTHY... I'D LIKE YOU TO MEET MY DAUGHTER.
OH, HEY, IT'S NICE TO--
--WAIT. HOLD UP. REWIND. SAY THAT AGAIN?
JULIA, MY DEAR, EXCUSE US A MOMENT... I THINK YOU'LL RECALL MASTER TIMOTHY HAD SOME LADY TROUBLES.
YOU KNOW... TEENAGERS.

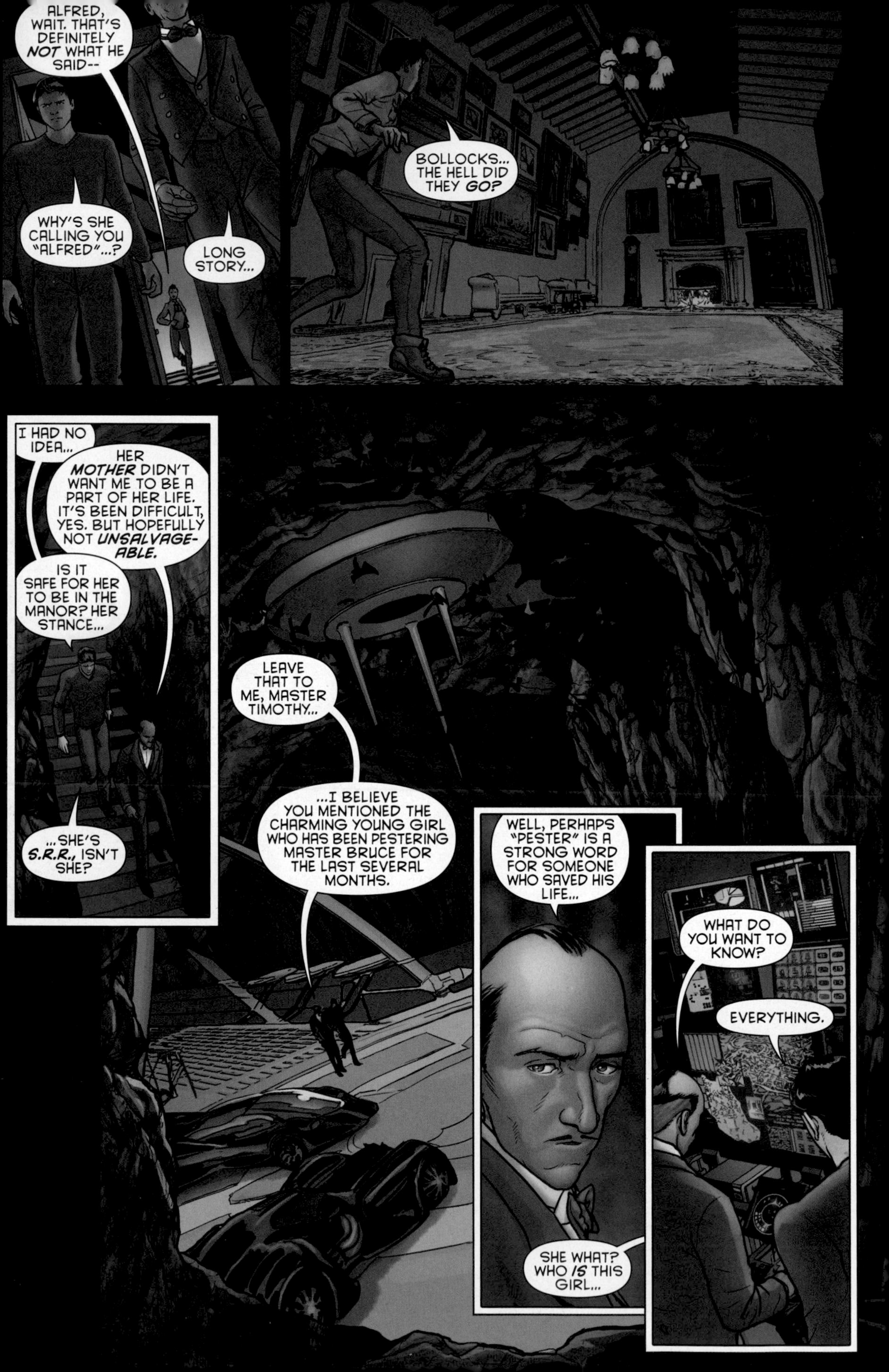
ALFRED, WAIT. THAT'S DEFINITELY NOT WHAT HE SAID--
WHY'S SHE CALLING YOU "ALFRED"...?
LONG STORY...
BOLLOCKS... THE HELL DID THEY GO?
I HAD NO IDEA...
HER MOTHER DIDN'T WANT ME TO BE A PART OF HER LIFE. IT'S BEEN DIFFICULT, YES. BUT HOPEFULLY NOT UNSALVAGE-ABLE.
IS IT SAFE FOR HER TO BE IN THE MANOR? HER STANCE...
...SHE'S S.R.R., ISN'T SHE?
LEAVE THAT TO ME, MASTER TIMOTHY...
...I BELIEVE YOU MENTIONED THE CHARMING YOUNG GIRL WHO HAS BEEN PESTERING MASTER BRUCE FOR THE LAST SEVERAL MONTHS.
WELL, PERHAPS "PESTER" IS A STRONG WORD FOR SOMEONE WHO SAVED HIS LIFE...
SHE WHAT? WHO IS THIS GIRL...
WHAT DO YOU WANT TO KNOW?
EVERYTHING.

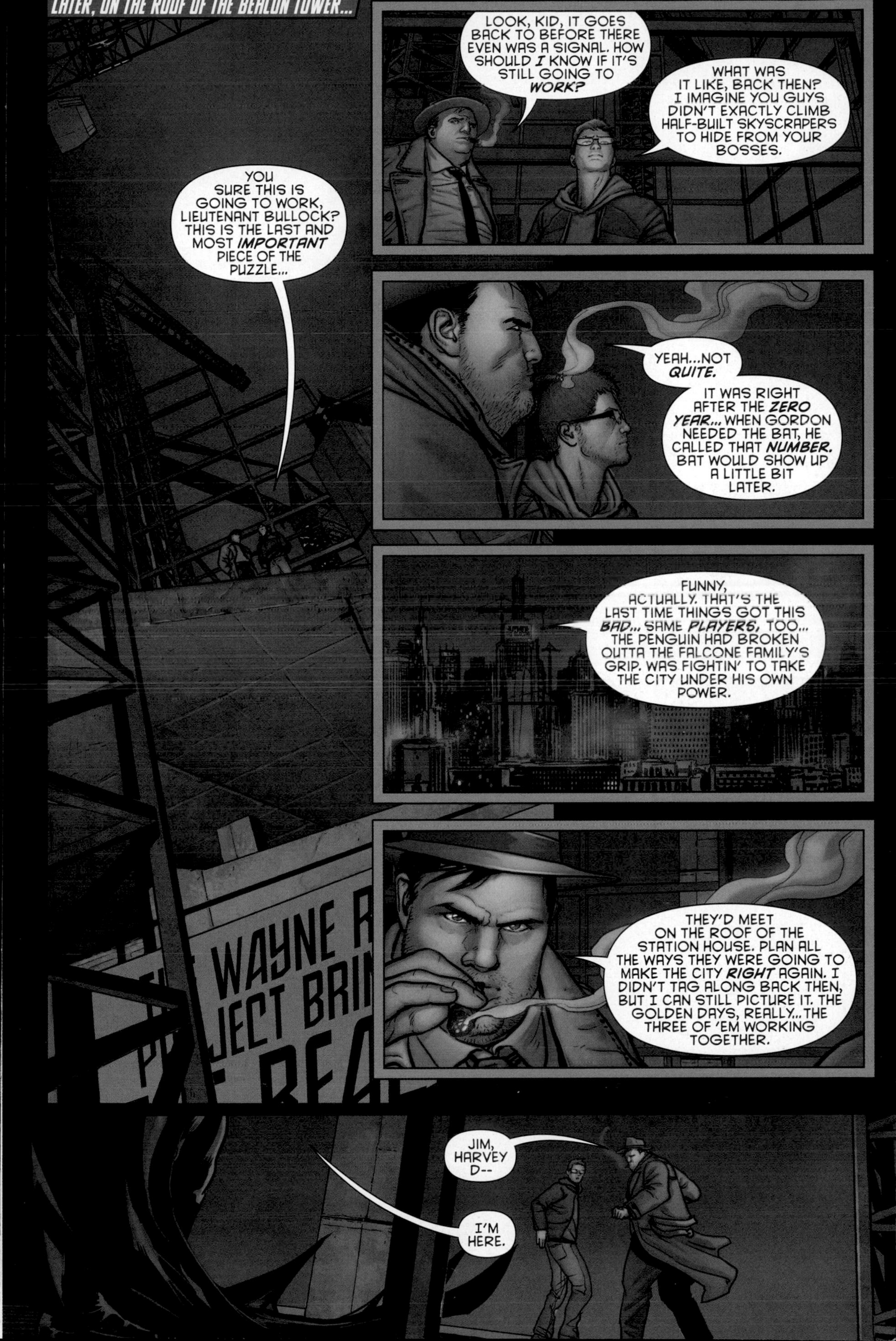
LATER, ON THE ROOF OF THE BEACON TOWER...
YOU SURE THIS IS GOING TO WORK, LIEUTENANT BULLOCK? THIS IS THE LAST AND MOST IMPORTANT PIECE OF THE PUZZLE...
LOOK, KID, IT GOES BACK TO BEFORE THERE EVEN WAS A SIGNAL. HOW SHOULD I KNOW IF IT'S STILL GOING TO WORK?
WHAT WAS IT LIKE, BACK THEN? I IMAGINE YOU GUYS DIDN'T EXACTLY CLIMB HALF-BUILT SKYSCRAPERS TO HIDE FROM YOUR BOSSES.
YEAH...NOT QUITE.
IT WAS RIGHT AFTER THE ZERO YEAR... WHEN GORDON NEEDED THE BAT, HE CALLED THAT NUMBER. BAT WOULD SHOW UP A LITTLE BIT LATER.
FUNNY, ACTUALLY. THAT'S THE LAST TIME THINGS GOT THIS BAD... SAME PLAYERS, TOO... THE PENGUIN HAD BROKEN OUTTA THE FALCONE FAMILY'S GRIP. WAS FIGHTIN' TO TAKE THE CITY UNDER HIS OWN POWER.
THEY'D MEET ON THE ROOF OF THE STATION HOUSE. PLAN ALL THE WAYS THEY WERE GOING TO MAKE THE CITY RIGHT AGAIN. I DIDN'T TAG ALONG BACK THEN, BUT I CAN STILL PICTURE IT. THE GOLDEN DAYS, REALLY... THE THREE OF 'EM WORKING TOGETHER.
THE WAYNE R
PROJECT BRIN
BEA
JIM, HARVEY D--
I'M HERE.

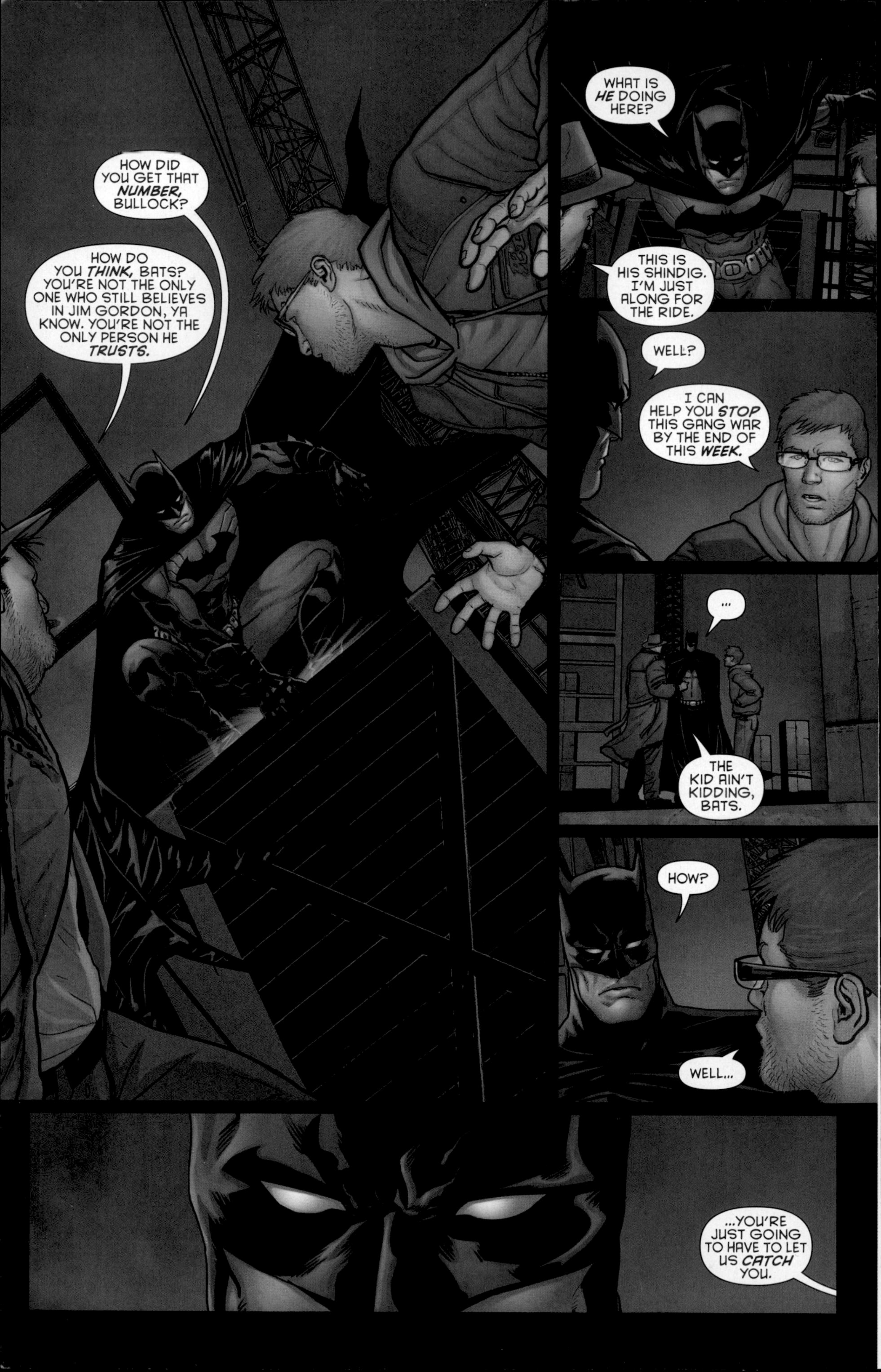
HOW DID YOU GET THAT NUMBER, BULLOCK?
HOW DO YOU THINK, BATS? YOU'RE NOT THE ONLY ONE WHO STILL BELIEVES IN JIM GORDON, YA KNOW. YOU'RE NOT THE ONLY PERSON HE TRUSTS.
WHAT IS HE DOING HERE?
THIS IS HIS SHINDIG. I'M JUST ALONG FOR THE RIDE.
WELL?
I CAN HELP YOU STOP THIS GANG WAR BY THE END OF THIS WEEK.
...
THE KID AIN'T KIDDING, BATS.
HOW?
WELL...
...YOU'RE JUST GOING TO HAVE TO LET US CATCH YOU.

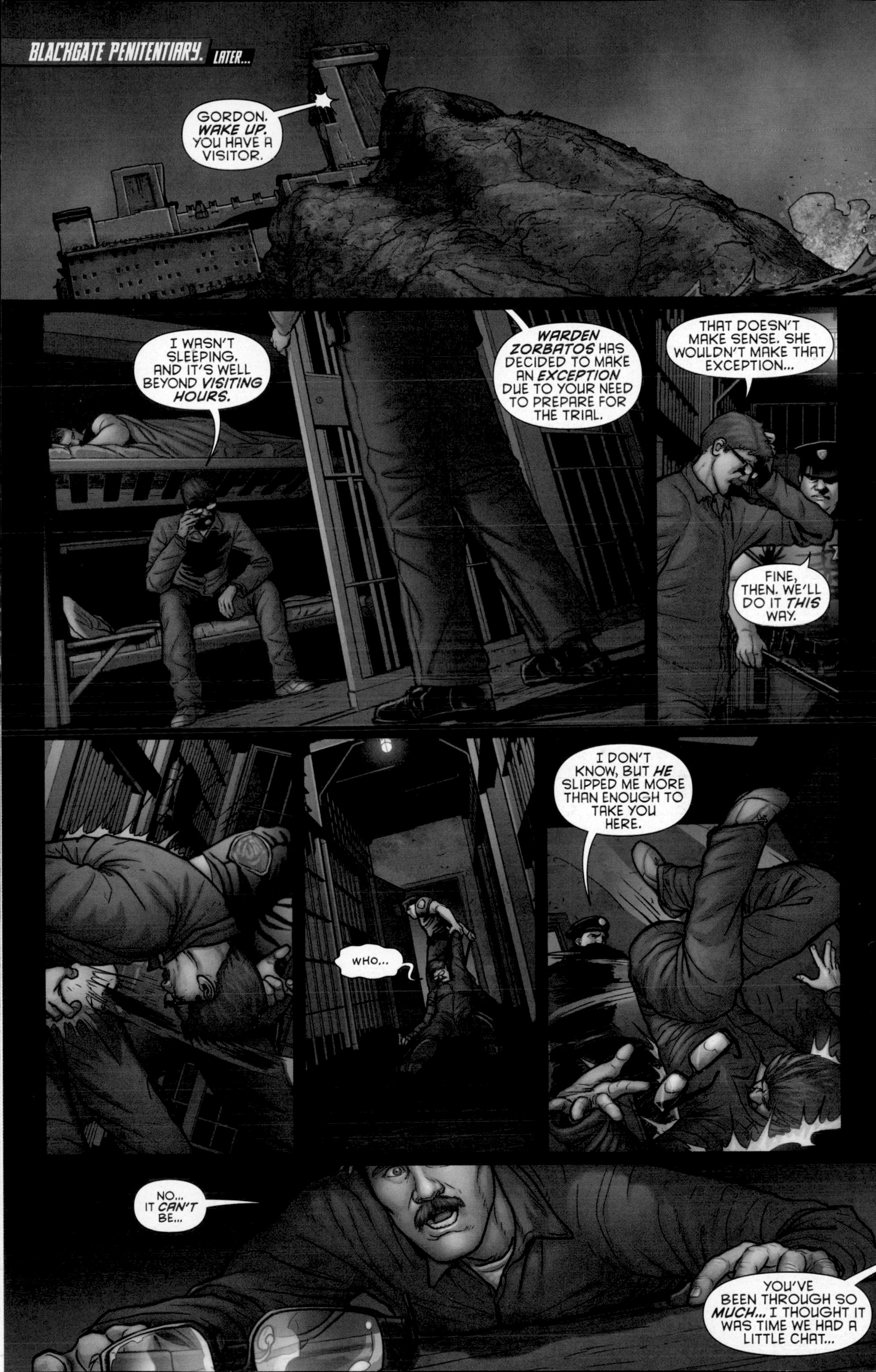

BLACKGATE PENITENTIARY. LATER...
GORDON. WAKE UP. YOU HAVE A VISITOR.
I WASN'T SLEEPING. AND IT'S WELL BEYOND VISITING HOURS.
WARDEN ZORBATOS HAS DECIDED TO MAKE AN EXCEPTION DUE TO YOUR NEED TO PREPARE FOR THE TRIAL.
THAT DOESN'T MAKE SENSE. SHE WOULDN'T MAKE THAT EXCEPTION...
FINE, THEN. WE'LL DO IT THIS WAY.
WHO...
I DON'T KNOW, BUT HE SLIPPED ME MORE THAN ENOUGH TO TAKE YOU HERE.
NO... IT CAN'T BE...
YOU'VE BEEN THROUGH SO MUCH... I THOUGHT IT WAS TIME WE HAD A LITTLE CHAT...

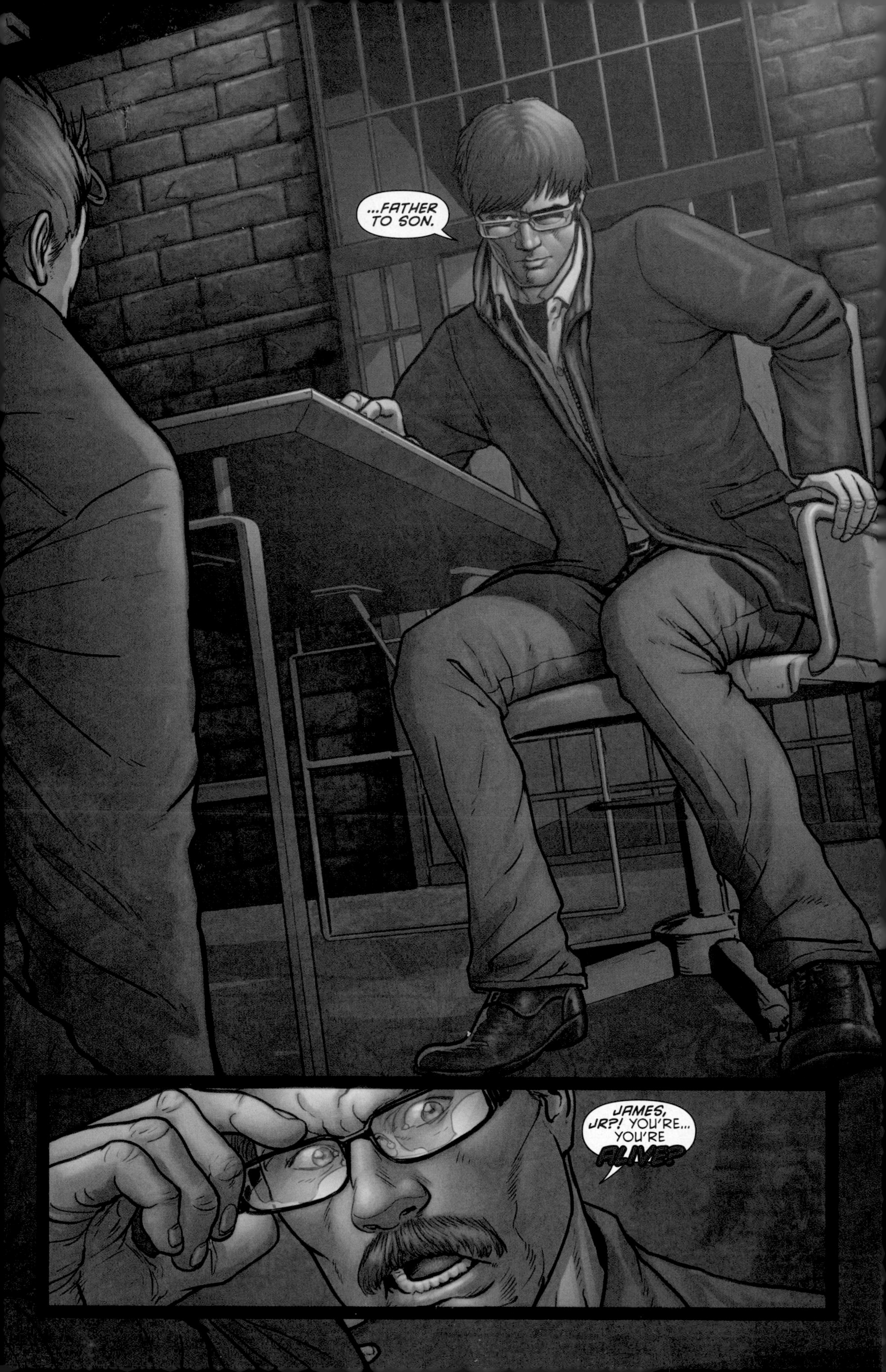

...FATHER TO SON.
JAMES, JR?! YOU'RE... YOU'RE ALIVE?

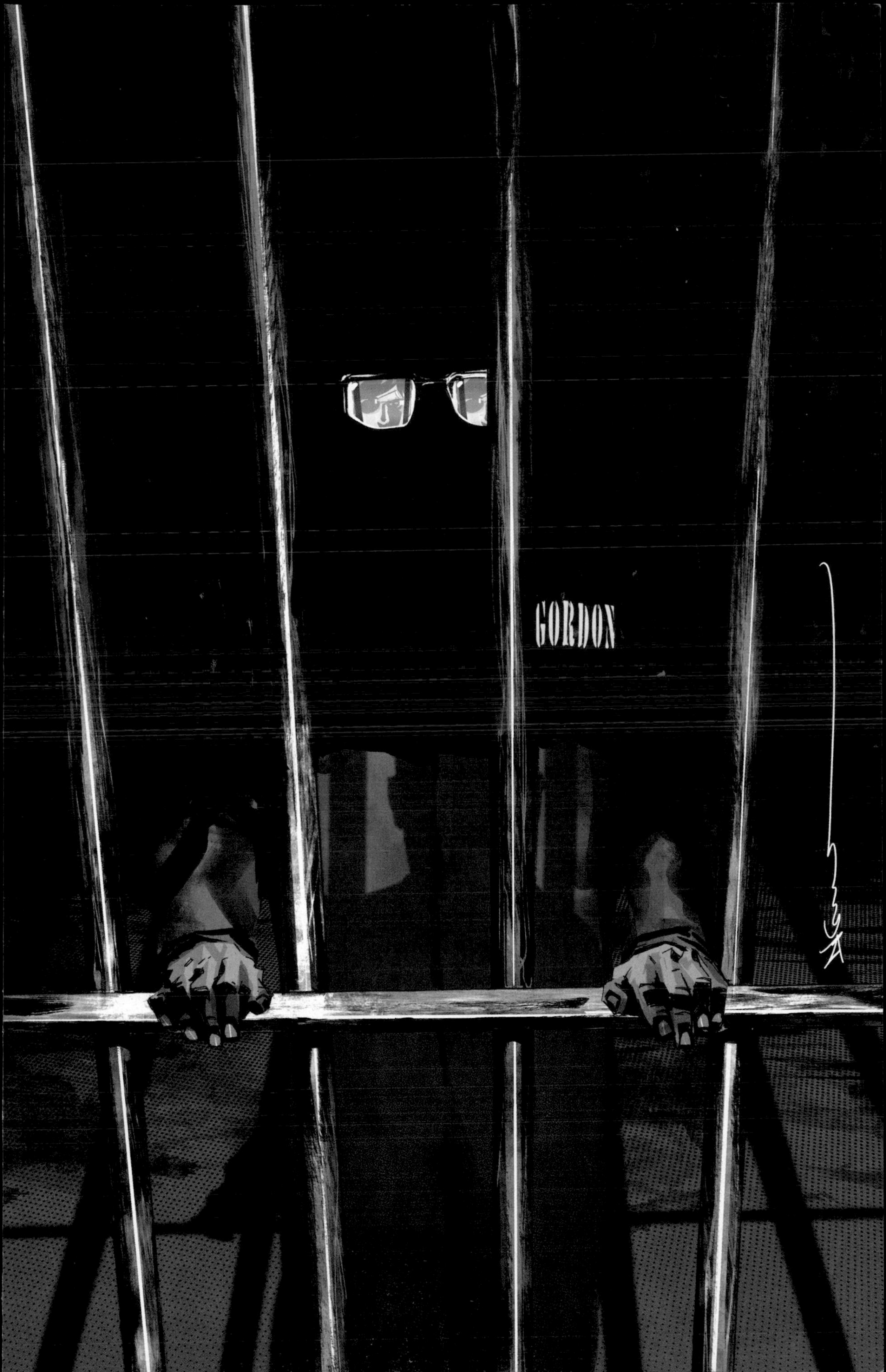
GORDON

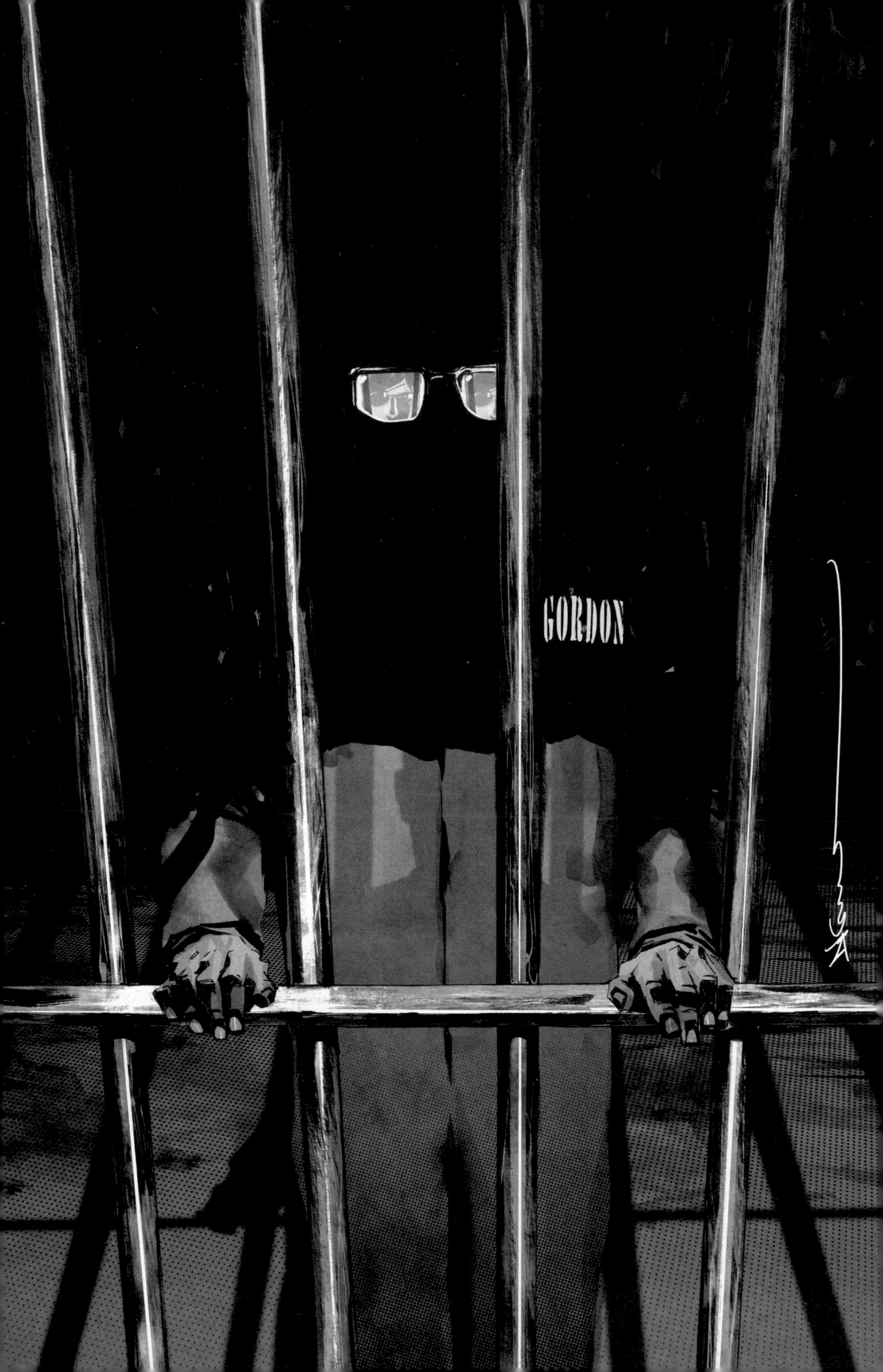
GORDON

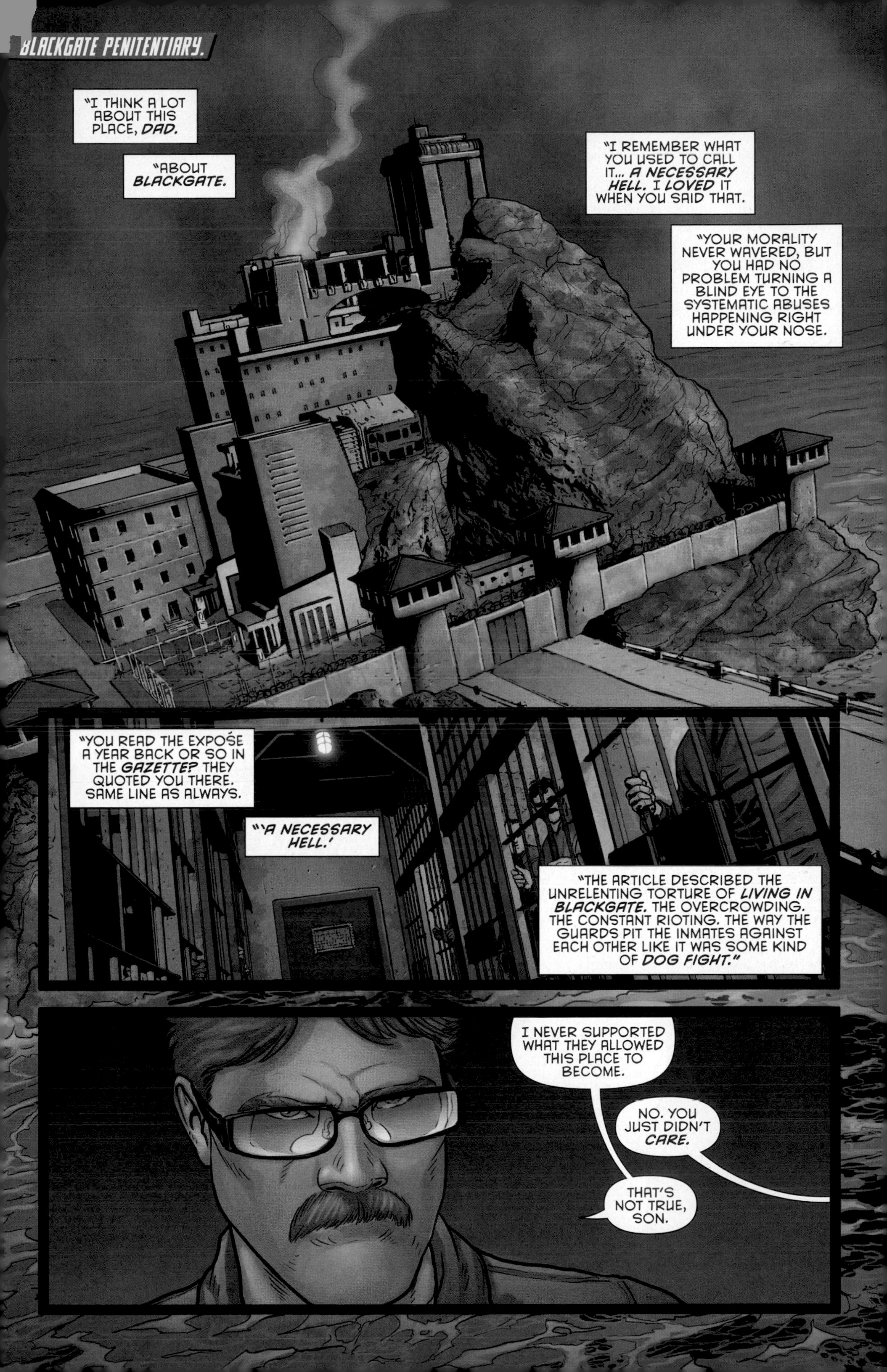
BLACKGATE PENITENTIARY.
"I THINK A LOT ABOUT THIS PLACE, DAD.
"ABOUT BLACKGATE.
"I REMEMBER WHAT YOU USED TO CALL IT... A NECESSARY HELL. I LOVED IT WHEN YOU SAID THAT.
"YOUR MORALITY NEVER WAVERED, BUT YOU HAD NO PROBLEM TURNING A BLIND EYE TO THE SYSTEMATIC ABUSES HAPPENING RIGHT UNDER YOUR NOSE.
"YOU READ THE EXPOSÉ A YEAR BACK OR SO IN THE GAZETTE? THEY QUOTED YOU THERE. SAME LINE AS ALWAYS.
"'A NECESSARY HELL.'
"THE ARTICLE DESCRIBED THE UNRELENTING TORTURE OF LIVING IN BLACKGATE. THE OVERCROWDING. THE CONSTANT RIOTING. THE WAY THE GUARDS PIT THE INMATES AGAINST EACH OTHER LIKE IT WAS SOME KIND OF DOG FIGHT."
I NEVER SUPPORTED WHAT THEY ALLOWED THIS PLACE TO BECOME.
NO. YOU JUST DIDN'T CARE.
THAT'S NOT TRUE, SON.

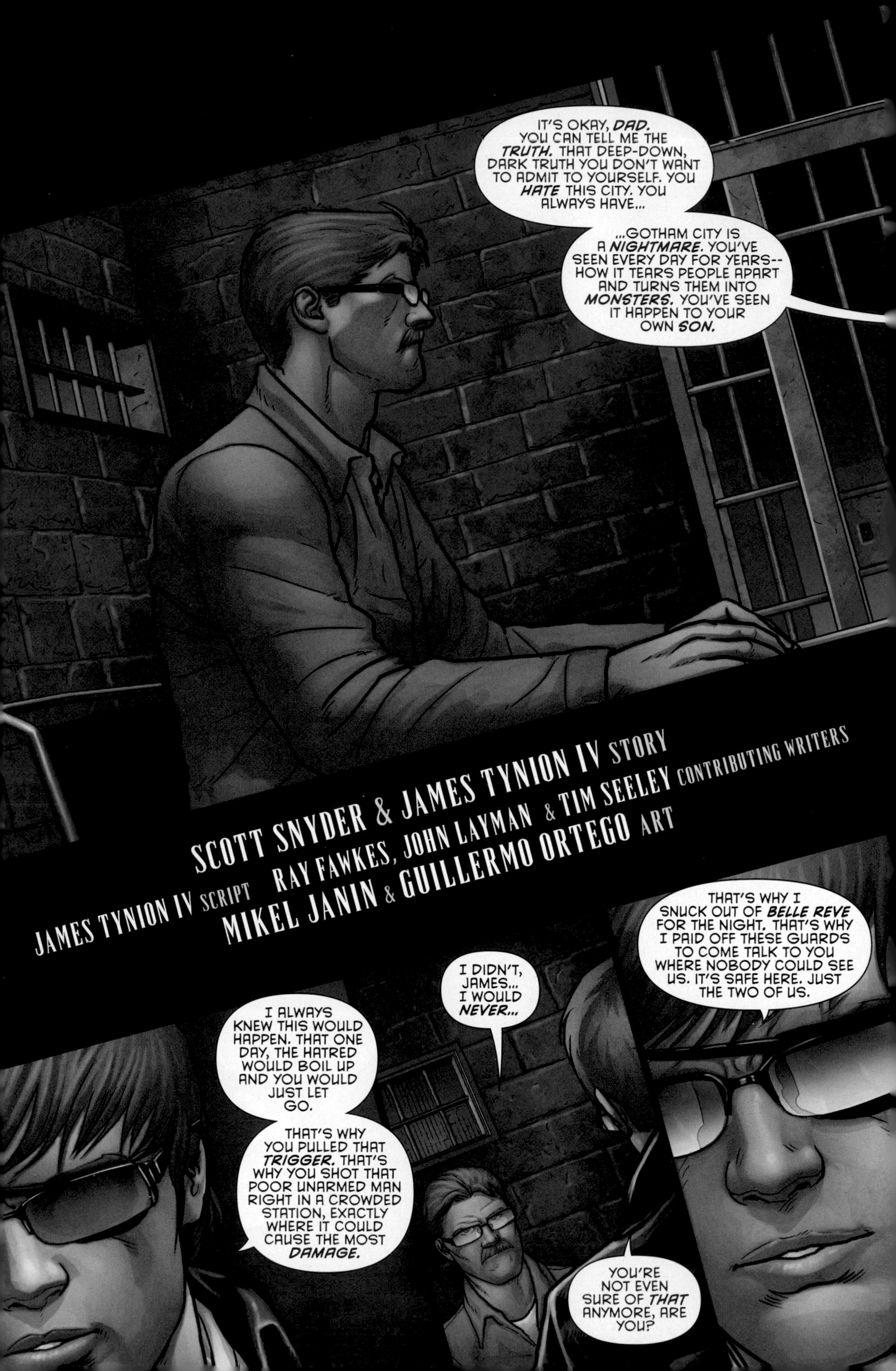
IT'S OKAY, DAD. YOU CAN TELL ME THE TRUTH. THAT DEEP-DOWN, DARK TRUTH YOU DON'T WANT TO ADMIT TO YOURSELF. YOU HATE THIS CITY. YOU ALWAYS HAVE...
...GOTHAM CITY IS A NIGHTMARE. YOU'VE SEEN EVERY DAY FOR YEARS-- HOW IT TEARS PEOPLE APART AND TURNS THEM INTO MONSTERS. YOU'VE SEEN IT HAPPEN TO YOUR OWN SON.
SCOTT SNYDER & JAMES TYNION IV STORY
JAMES TYNION IV SCRIPT RAY FAWKES, JOHN LAYMAN & TIM SEELEY CONTRIBUTING WRITERS
MIKEL JANIN & GUILLERMO ORTEGO ART
THAT'S WHY I SNUCK OUT OF BELLE REVE FOR THE NIGHT. THAT'S WHY I PAID OFF THESE GUARDS TO COME TALK TO YOU WHERE NOBODY COULD SEE US. IT'S SAFE HERE. JUST THE TWO OF US.
I ALWAYS KNEW THIS WOULD HAPPEN. THAT ONE DAY, THE HATRED WOULD BOIL UP AND YOU WOULD JUST LET GO.
I DIDN'T, JAMES... I WOULD NEVER...
THAT'S WHY YOU PULLED THAT TRIGGER. THAT'S WHY YOU SHOT THAT POOR UNARMED MAN RIGHT IN A CROWDED STATION, EXACTLY WHERE IT COULD CAUSE THE MOST DAMAGE.
YOU'RE NOT EVEN SURE OF THAT ANYMORE, ARE YOU?

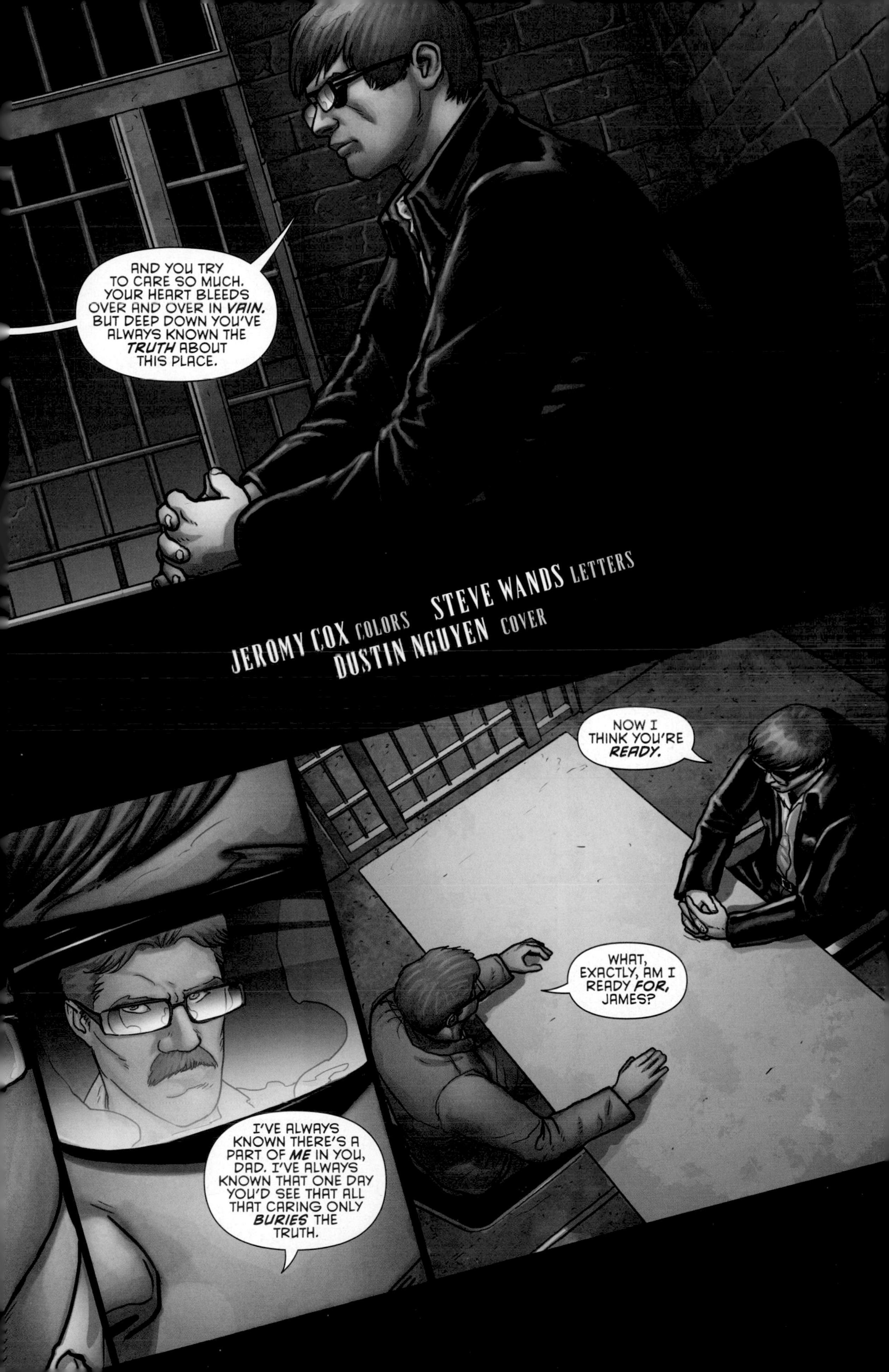
AND YOU TRY TO CARE SO MUCH. YOUR HEART BLEEDS OVER AND OVER IN *VAIN.* BUT DEEP DOWN YOU'VE ALWAYS KNOWN THE *TRUTH* ABOUT THIS PLACE.
JEROMY COX COLORS
STEVE WANDS LETTERS
DUSTIN NGUYEN COVER
NOW I THINK YOU'RE *READY.*
WHAT, EXACTLY, AM I READY *FOR,* JAMES?
I'VE ALWAYS KNOWN THERE'S A PART OF *ME* IN YOU, DAD. I'VE ALWAYS KNOWN THAT ONE DAY YOU'D SEE THAT ALL THAT CARING ONLY *BURIES* THE TRUTH.

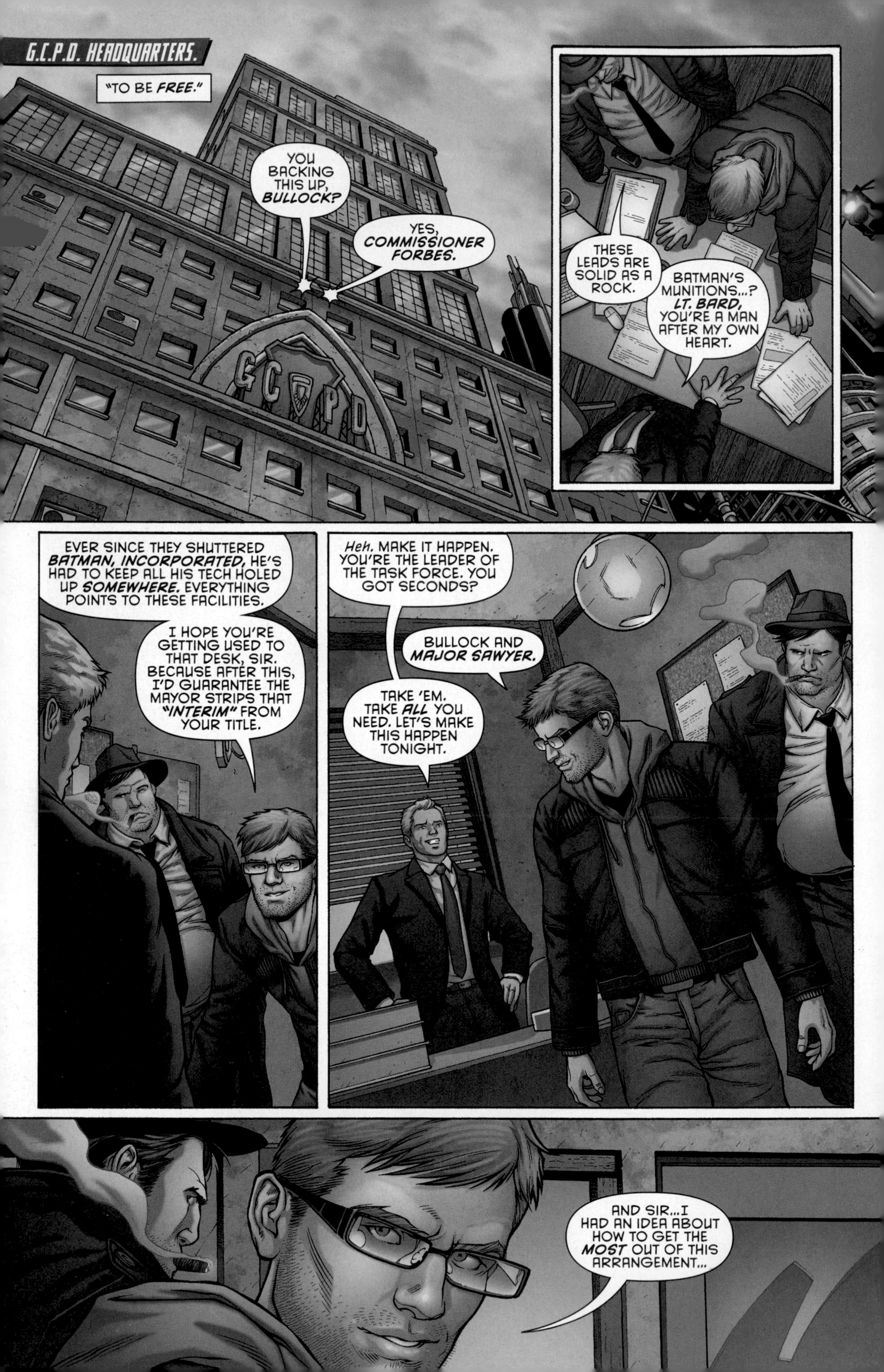
G.C.P.D. HEADQUARTERS.
"TO BE FREE."
YOU BACKING THIS UP, BULLOCK?
YES, COMMISSIONER FORBES.
GCPD
THESE LEADS ARE SOLID AS A ROCK.
BATMAN'S MUNITIONS...? LT. BARD, YOU'RE A MAN AFTER MY OWN HEART.
EVER SINCE THEY SHUTTERED BATMAN, INCORPORATED, HE'S HAD TO KEEP ALL HIS TECH HOLED UP SOMEWHERE. EVERYTHING POINTS TO THESE FACILITIES.
I HOPE YOU'RE GETTING USED TO THAT DESK, SIR. BECAUSE AFTER THIS, I'D GUARANTEE THE MAYOR STRIPS THAT "INTERIM" FROM YOUR TITLE.
Heh. MAKE IT HAPPEN. YOU'RE THE LEADER OF THE TASK FORCE. YOU GOT SECONDS?
BULLOCK AND MAJOR SAWYER.
TAKE 'EM. TAKE ALL YOU NEED. LET'S MAKE THIS HAPPEN TONIGHT.
AND SIR...I HAD AN IDEA ABOUT HOW TO GET THE MOST OUT OF THIS ARRANGEMENT...

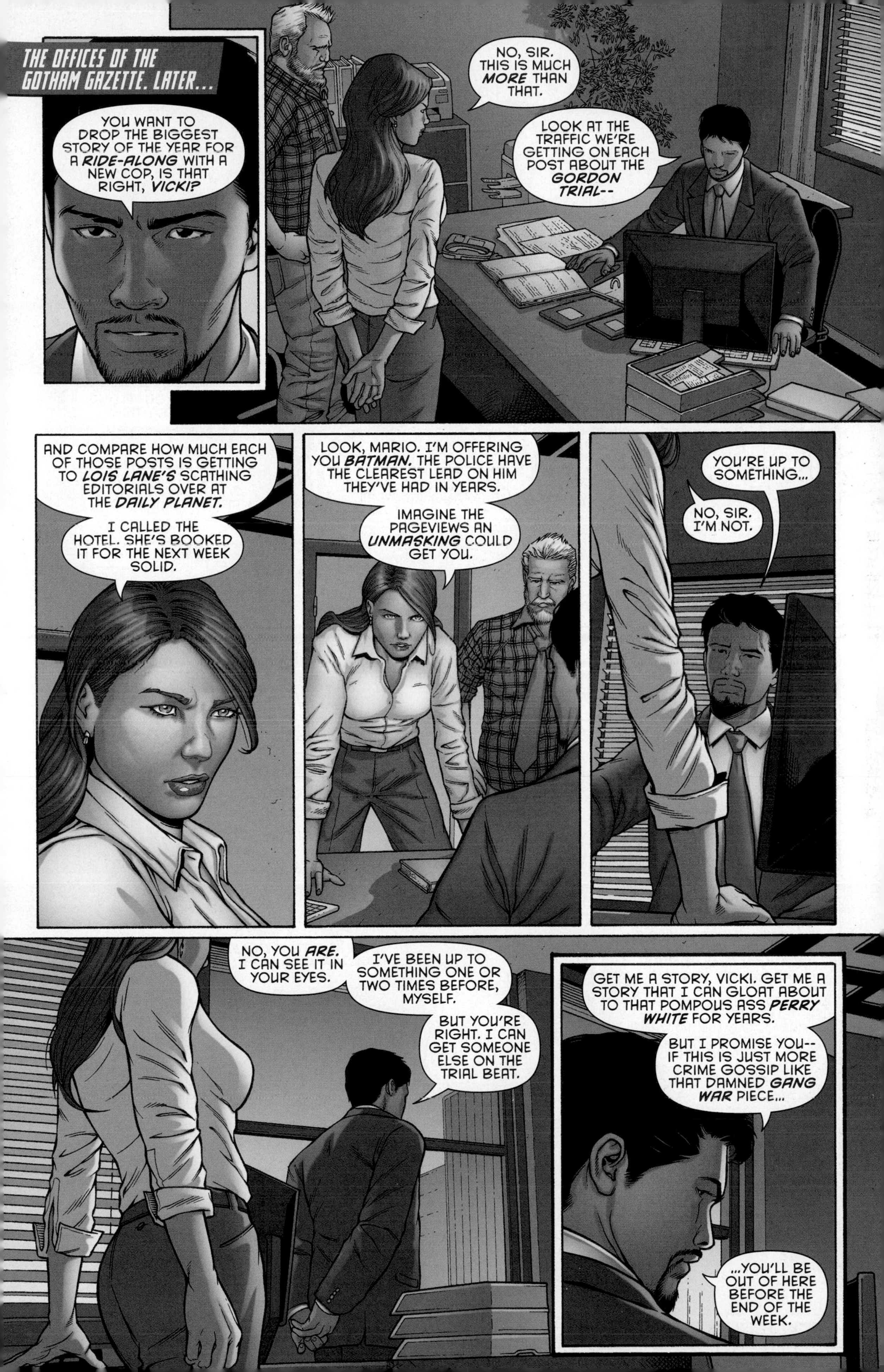
THE OFFICES OF THE GOTHAM GAZETTE. LATER...
YOU WANT TO DROP THE BIGGEST STORY OF THE YEAR FOR A RIDE-ALONG WITH A NEW COP, IS THAT RIGHT, VICKI?
NO, SIR. THIS IS MUCH MORE THAN THAT.
LOOK AT THE TRAFFIC WE'RE GETTING ON EACH POST ABOUT THE GORDON TRIAL--
AND COMPARE HOW MUCH EACH OF THOSE POSTS IS GETTING TO LOIS LANE'S SCATHING EDITORIALS OVER AT THE DAILY PLANET.
I CALLED THE HOTEL. SHE'S BOOKED IT FOR THE NEXT WEEK SOLID.
LOOK, MARIO. I'M OFFERING YOU BATMAN. THE POLICE HAVE THE CLEAREST LEAD ON HIM THEY'VE HAD IN YEARS.
IMAGINE THE PAGEVIEWS AN UNMASKING COULD GET YOU.
YOU'RE UP TO SOMETHING...
NO, SIR. I'M NOT.
NO, YOU ARE. I CAN SEE IT IN YOUR EYES.
I'VE BEEN UP TO SOMETHING ONE OR TWO TIMES BEFORE, MYSELF.
BUT YOU'RE RIGHT. I CAN GET SOMEONE ELSE ON THE TRIAL BEAT.
GET ME A STORY, VICKI. GET ME A STORY THAT I CAN GLOAT ABOUT TO THAT POMPOUS ASS PERRY WHITE FOR YEARS.
BUT I PROMISE YOU-- IF THIS IS JUST MORE CRIME GOSSIP LIKE THAT DAMNED GANG WAR PIECE...
...YOU'LL BE OUT OF HERE BEFORE THE END OF THE WEEK.

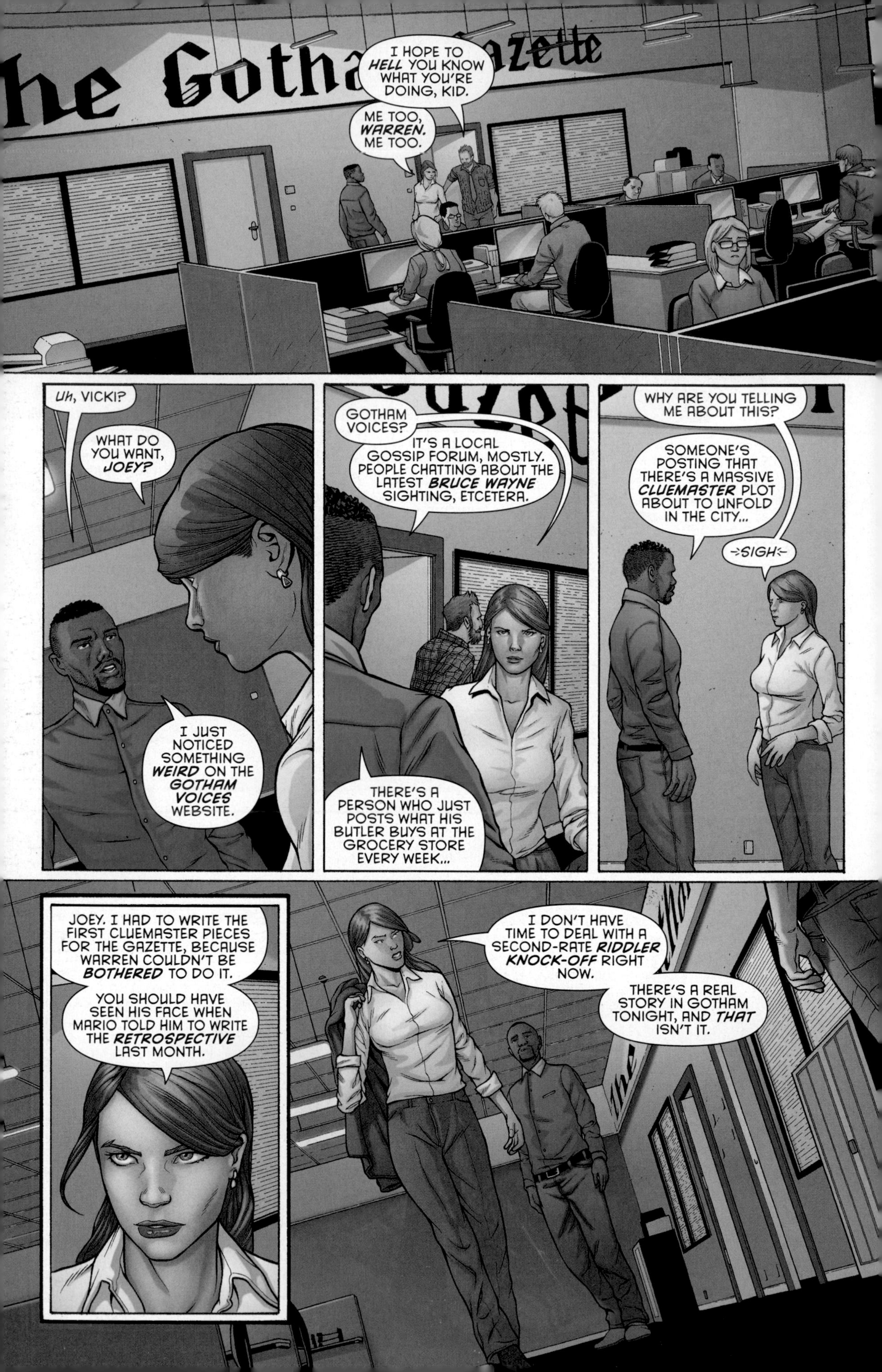

The Gotham Gazette
I HOPE TO HELL YOU KNOW WHAT YOU'RE DOING, KID.
ME TOO, WARREN. ME TOO.
Uh, VICKI?
WHAT DO YOU WANT, JOEY?
I JUST NOTICED SOMETHING WEIRD ON THE GOTHAM VOICES WEBSITE.
GOTHAM VOICES?
IT'S A LOCAL GOSSIP FORUM, MOSTLY. PEOPLE CHATTING ABOUT THE LATEST BRUCE WAYNE SIGHTING, ETCETERA.
THERE'S A PERSON WHO JUST POSTS WHAT HIS BUTLER BUYS AT THE GROCERY STORE EVERY WEEK...
WHY ARE YOU TELLING ME ABOUT THIS?
SOMEONE'S POSTING THAT THERE'S A MASSIVE CLUEMASTER PLOT ABOUT TO UNFOLD IN THE CITY...
SIGH
JOEY. I HAD TO WRITE THE FIRST CLUEMASTER PIECES FOR THE GAZETTE, BECAUSE WARREN COULDN'T BE BOTHERED TO DO IT.
YOU SHOULD HAVE SEEN HIS FACE WHEN MARIO TOLD HIM TO WRITE THE RETROSPECTIVE LAST MONTH.
I DON'T HAVE TIME TO DEAL WITH A SECOND-RATE RIDDLER KNOCK-OFF RIGHT NOW.
THERE'S A REAL STORY IN GOTHAM TONIGHT, AND THAT ISN'T IT.

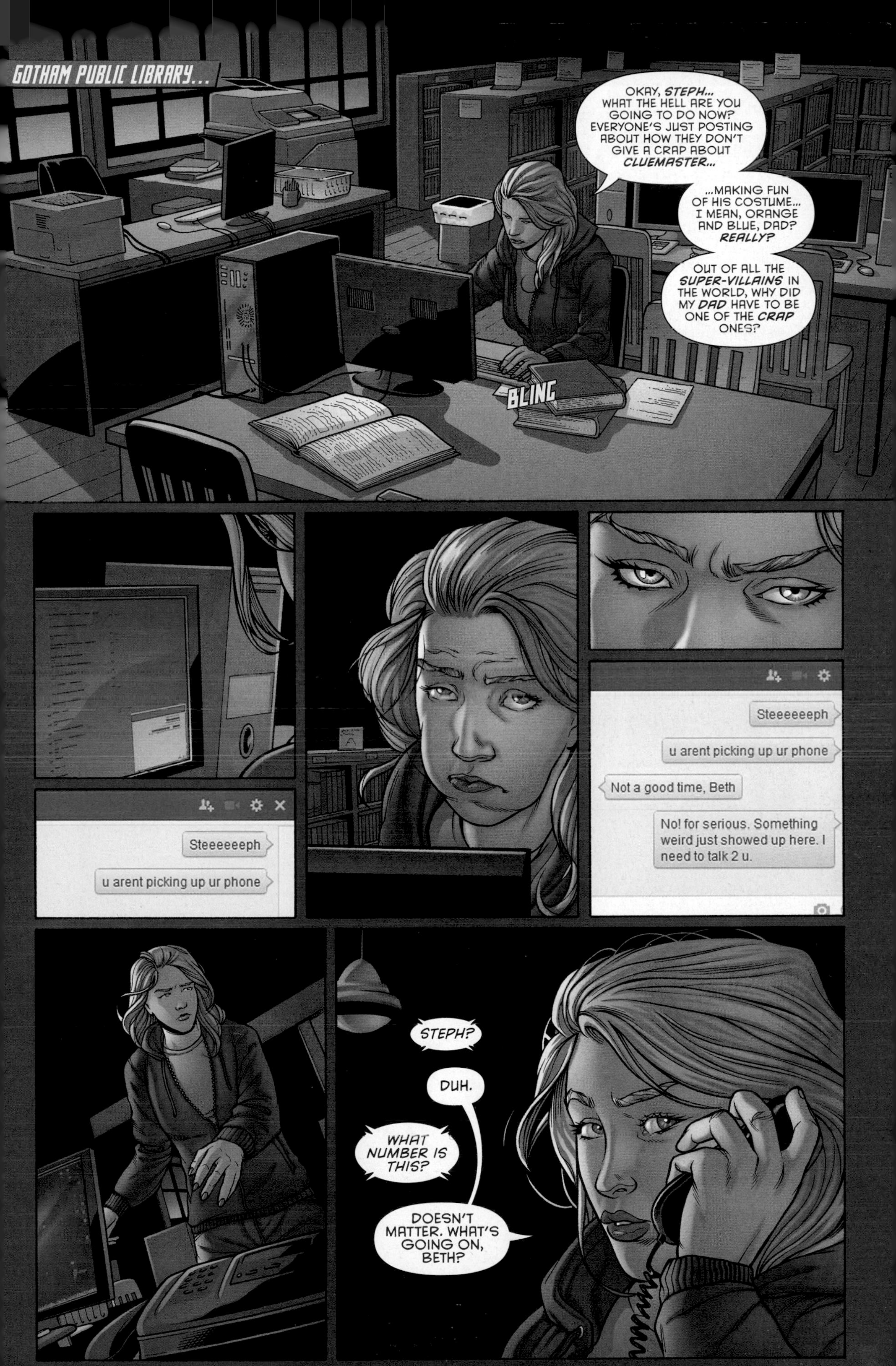
GOTHAM PUBLIC LIBRARY...
OKAY, STEPH... WHAT THE HELL ARE YOU GOING TO DO NOW? EVERYONE'S JUST POSTING ABOUT HOW THEY DON'T GIVE A CRAP ABOUT CLUEMASTER...
...MAKING FUN OF HIS COSTUME... I MEAN, ORANGE AND BLUE, DAD? REALLY?
OUT OF ALL THE SUPER-VILLAINS IN THE WORLD, WHY DID MY DAD HAVE TO BE ONE OF THE CRAP ONES?
BLING
Steeeeeeph
u arent picking up ur phone
Steeeeeeph
u arent picking up ur phone
Not a good time, Beth
No! for serious. Something weird just showed up here. I need to talk 2 u.
STEPH?
DUH.
WHAT NUMBER IS THIS?
DOESN'T MATTER. WHAT'S GOING ON, BETH?

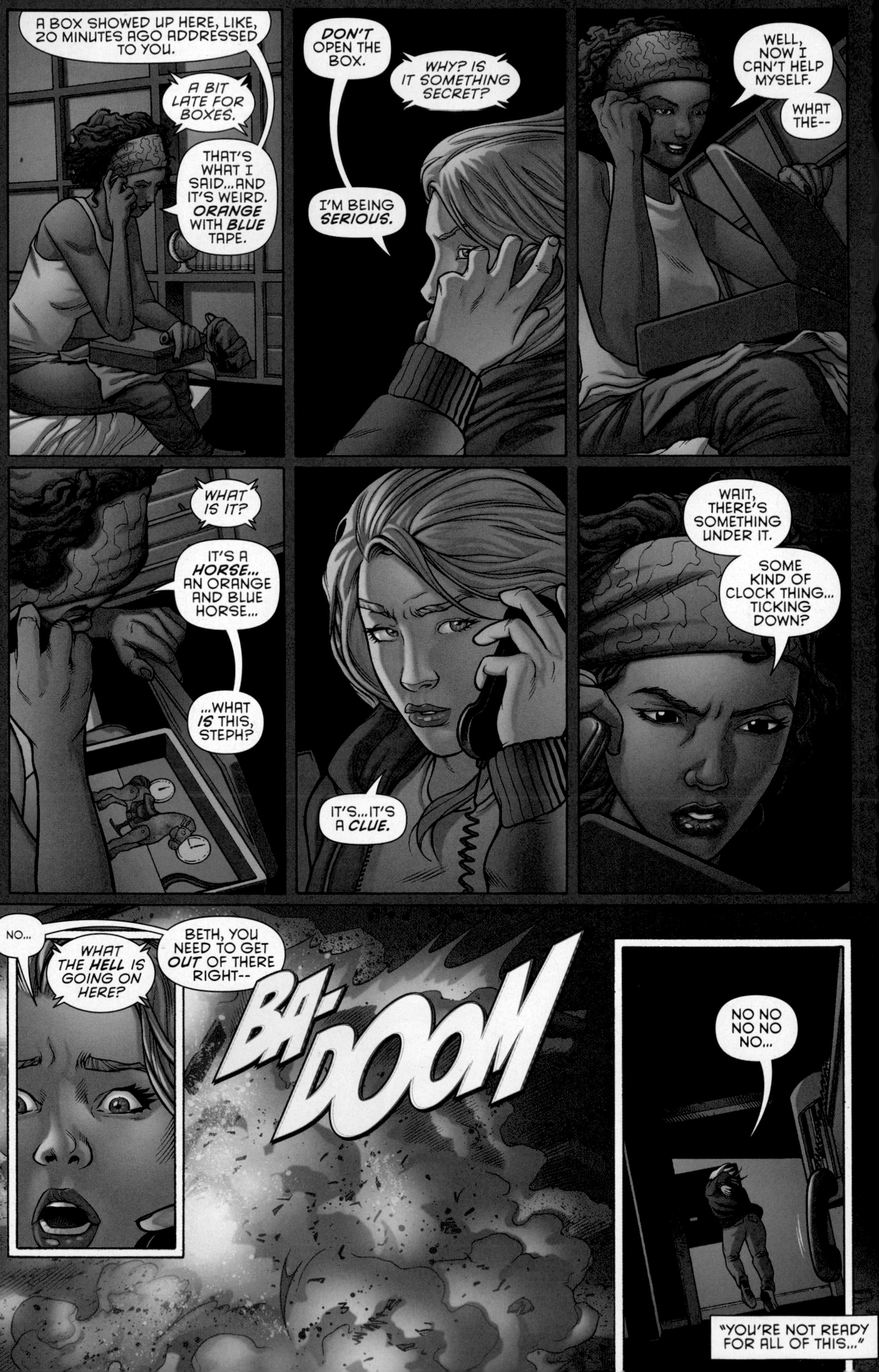
A BOX SHOWED UP HERE, LIKE, 20 MINUTES AGO ADDRESSED TO YOU.
A BIT LATE FOR BOXES.
THAT'S WHAT I SAID...AND IT'S WEIRD. ORANGE WITH BLUE TAPE.
DON'T OPEN THE BOX.
WHY? IS IT SOMETHING SECRET?
I'M BEING SERIOUS.
WELL, NOW I CAN'T HELP MYSELF.
WHAT THE--
WHAT IS IT?
IT'S A HORSE... AN ORANGE AND BLUE HORSE...
...WHAT IS THIS, STEPH?
IT'S...IT'S A CLUE.
WAIT, THERE'S SOMETHING UNDER IT.
SOME KIND OF CLOCK THING... TICKING DOWN?
NO...
WHAT THE HELL IS GOING ON HERE?
BETH, YOU NEED TO GET OUT OF THERE RIGHT--
BA-DOOM
NO NO NO NO NO...
"YOU'RE NOT READY FOR ALL OF THIS..."

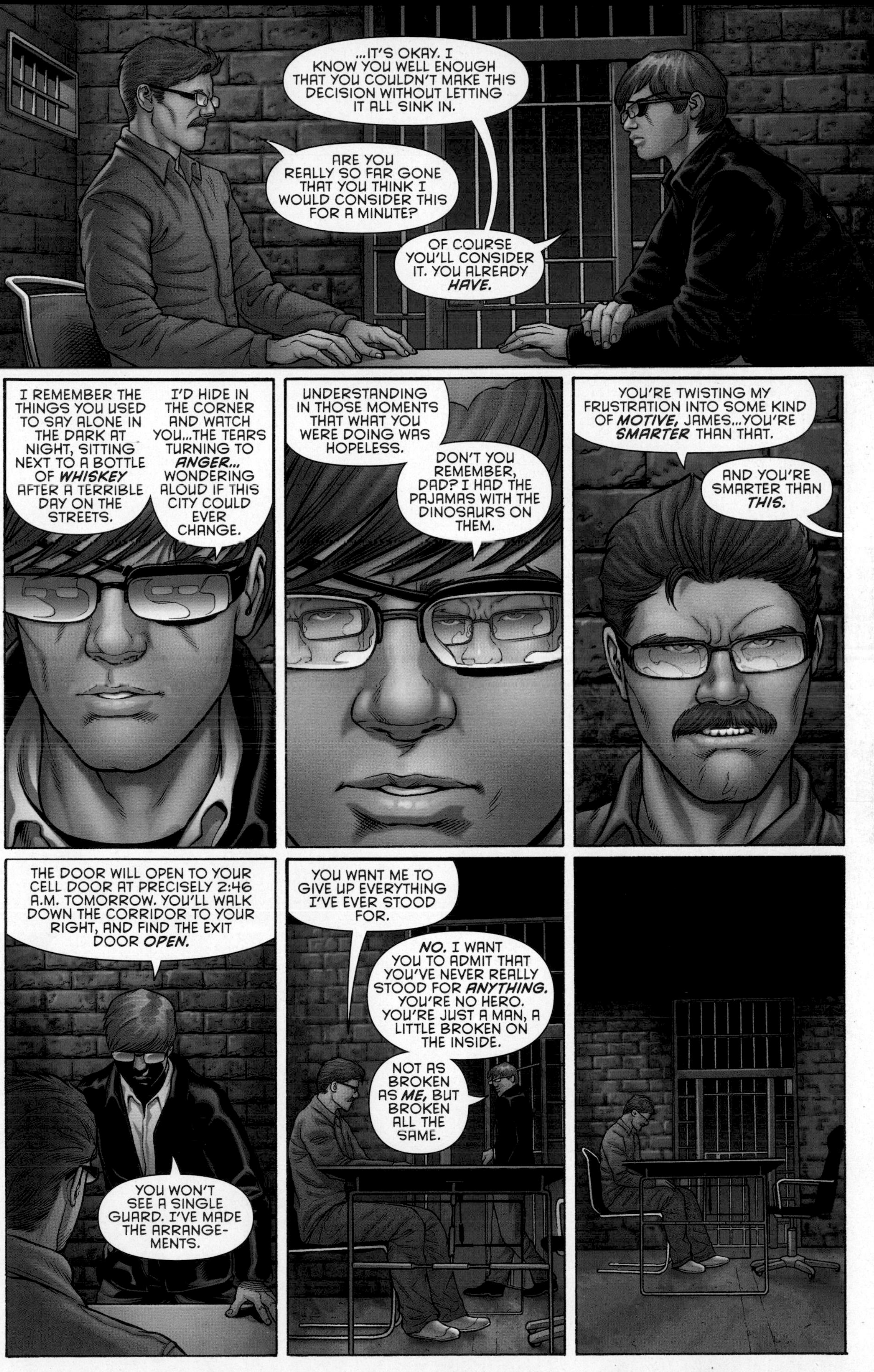
...IT'S OKAY. I KNOW YOU WELL ENOUGH THAT YOU COULDN'T MAKE THIS DECISION WITHOUT LETTING IT ALL SINK IN.
ARE YOU REALLY SO FAR GONE THAT YOU THINK I WOULD CONSIDER THIS FOR A MINUTE?
OF COURSE YOU'LL CONSIDER IT. YOU ALREADY HAVE.
I REMEMBER THE THINGS YOU USED TO SAY ALONE IN THE DARK AT NIGHT, SITTING NEXT TO A BOTTLE OF WHISKEY AFTER A TERRIBLE DAY ON THE STREETS.
I'D HIDE IN THE CORNER AND WATCH YOU...THE TEARS TURNING TO ANGER... WONDERING ALOUD IF THIS CITY COULD EVER CHANGE.
UNDERSTANDING IN THOSE MOMENTS THAT WHAT YOU WERE DOING WAS HOPELESS.
DON'T YOU REMEMBER, DAD? I HAD THE PAJAMAS WITH THE DINOSAURS ON THEM.
YOU'RE TWISTING MY FRUSTRATION INTO SOME KIND OF MOTIVE, JAMES...YOU'RE SMARTER THAN THAT.
AND YOU'RE SMARTER THAN THIS.
THE DOOR WILL OPEN TO YOUR CELL DOOR AT PRECISELY 2:46 A.M. TOMORROW. YOU'LL WALK DOWN THE CORRIDOR TO YOUR RIGHT, AND FIND THE EXIT DOOR OPEN.
YOU WON'T SEE A SINGLE GUARD. I'VE MADE THE ARRANGE- MENTS.
YOU WANT ME TO GIVE UP EVERYTHING I'VE EVER STOOD FOR.
NO. I WANT YOU TO ADMIT THAT YOU'VE NEVER REALLY STOOD FOR ANYTHING. YOU'RE NO HERO. YOU'RE JUST A MAN, A LITTLE BROKEN ON THE INSIDE.
NOT AS BROKEN AS ME, BUT BROKEN ALL THE SAME.

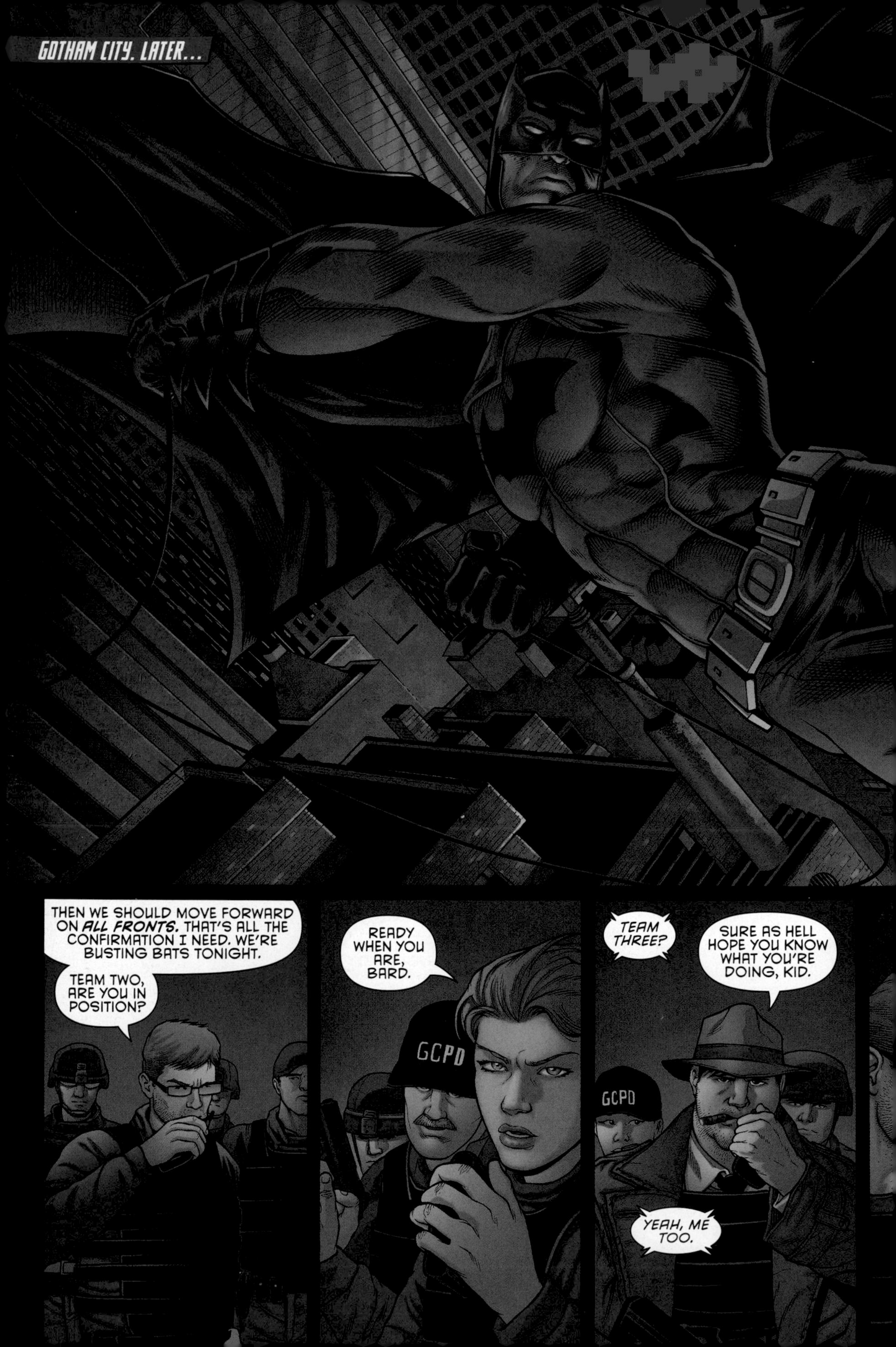
GOTHAM CITY. LATER...
THEN WE SHOULD MOVE FORWARD ON *ALL FRONTS*. THAT'S ALL THE CONFIRMATION I NEED. WE'RE BUSTING BATS TONIGHT.
TEAM TWO, ARE YOU IN POSITION?
READY WHEN YOU ARE, BARD.
GCPD
TEAM THREE?
SURE AS HELL HOPE YOU KNOW WHAT YOU'RE DOING, KID.
GCPD
YEAH, ME TOO.

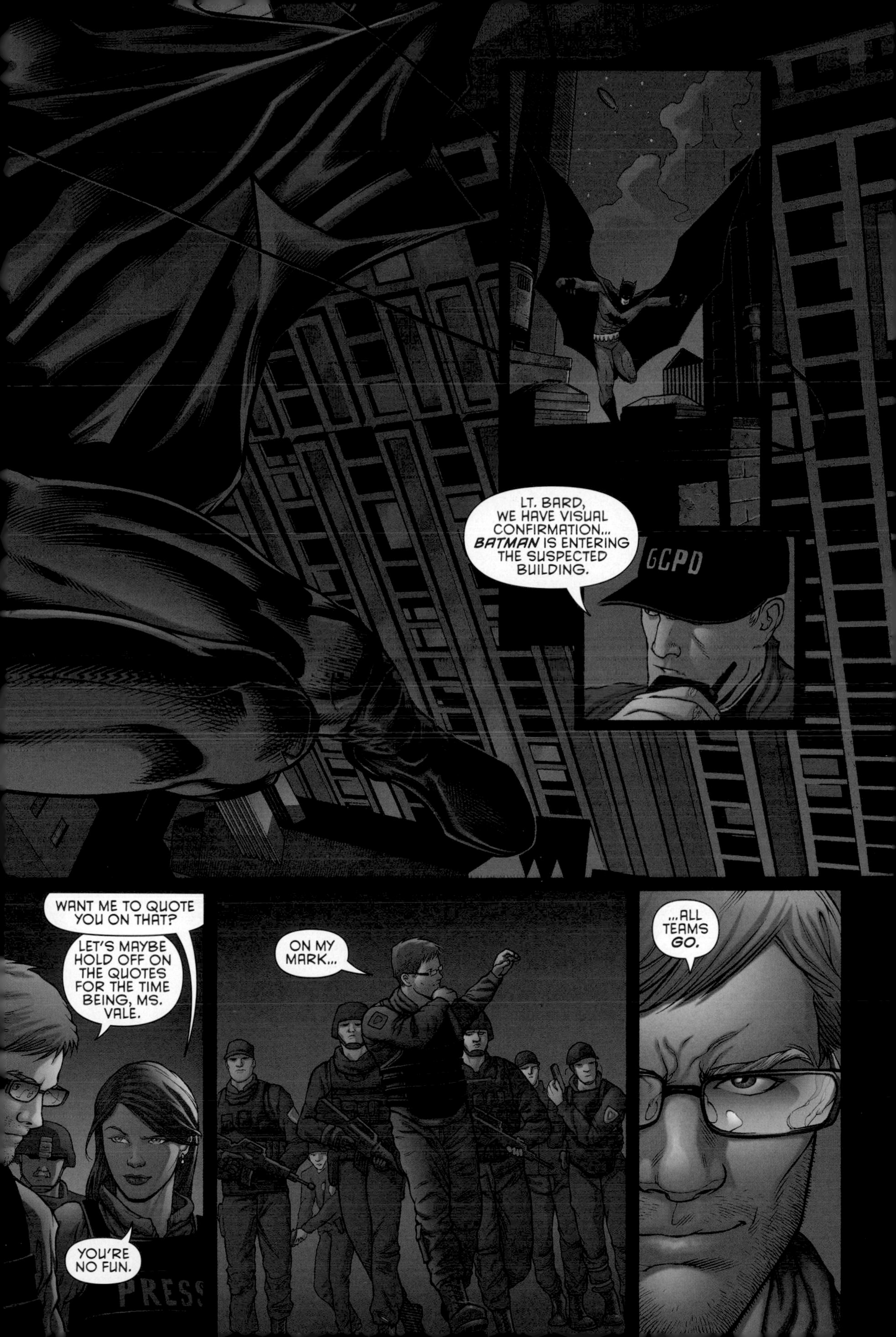

LT. BARD, WE HAVE VISUAL CONFIRMATION... *BATMAN* IS ENTERING THE SUSPECTED BUILDING.
WANT ME TO QUOTE YOU ON THAT?
LET'S MAYBE HOLD OFF ON THE QUOTES FOR THE TIME BEING, MS. VALE.
YOU'RE NO FUN.
ON MY MARK...
...ALL TEAMS *GO.*

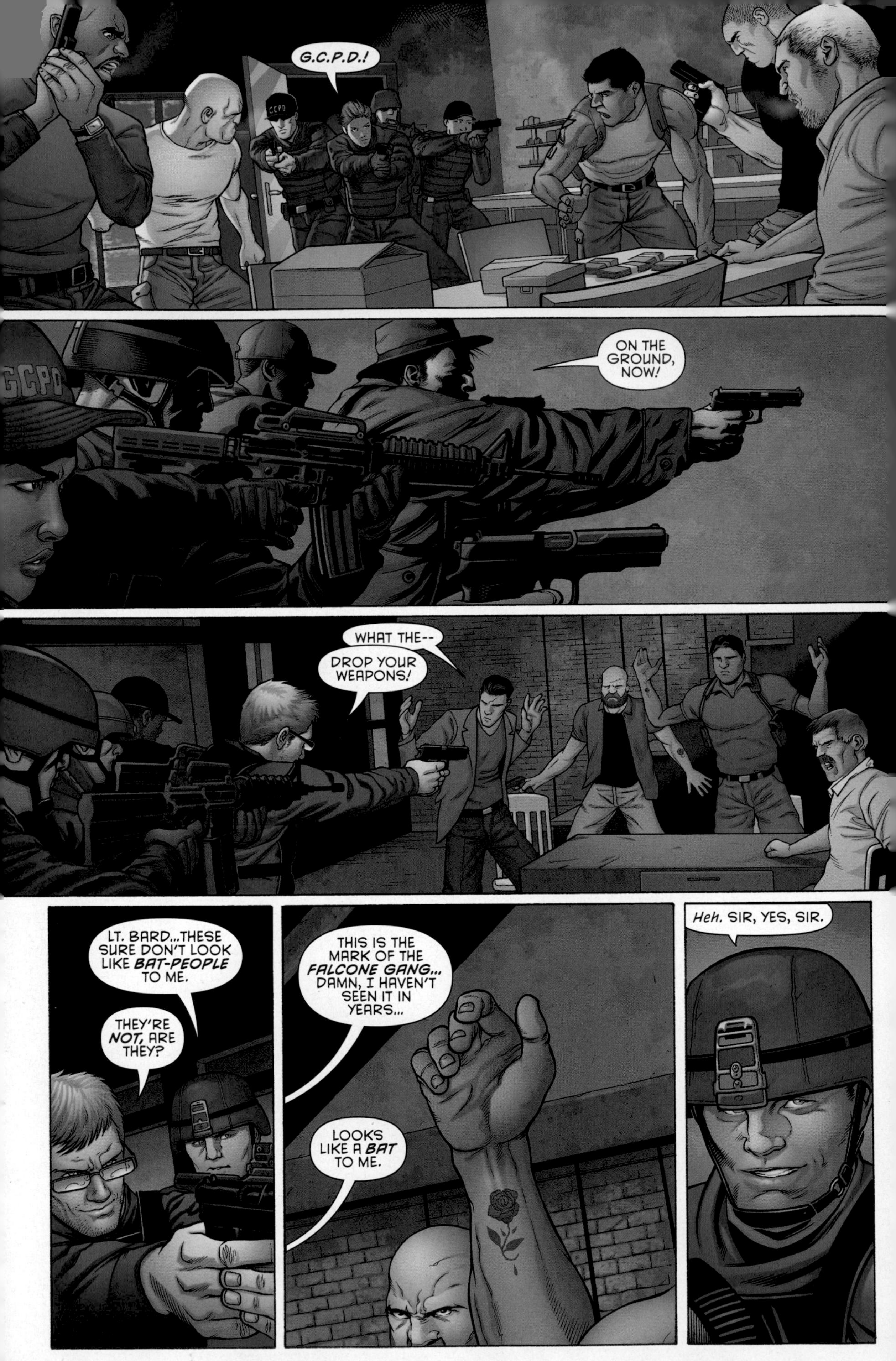
G.C.P.D.!
ON THE GROUND, NOW!
WHAT THE--
DROP YOUR WEAPONS!
LT. BARD...THESE SURE DON'T LOOK LIKE BAT-PEOPLE TO ME.
THEY'RE NOT, ARE THEY?
THIS IS THE MARK OF THE FALCONE GANG... DAMN, I HAVEN'T SEEN IT IN YEARS...
LOOKS LIKE A BAT TO ME.
Heh. SIR, YES, SIR.

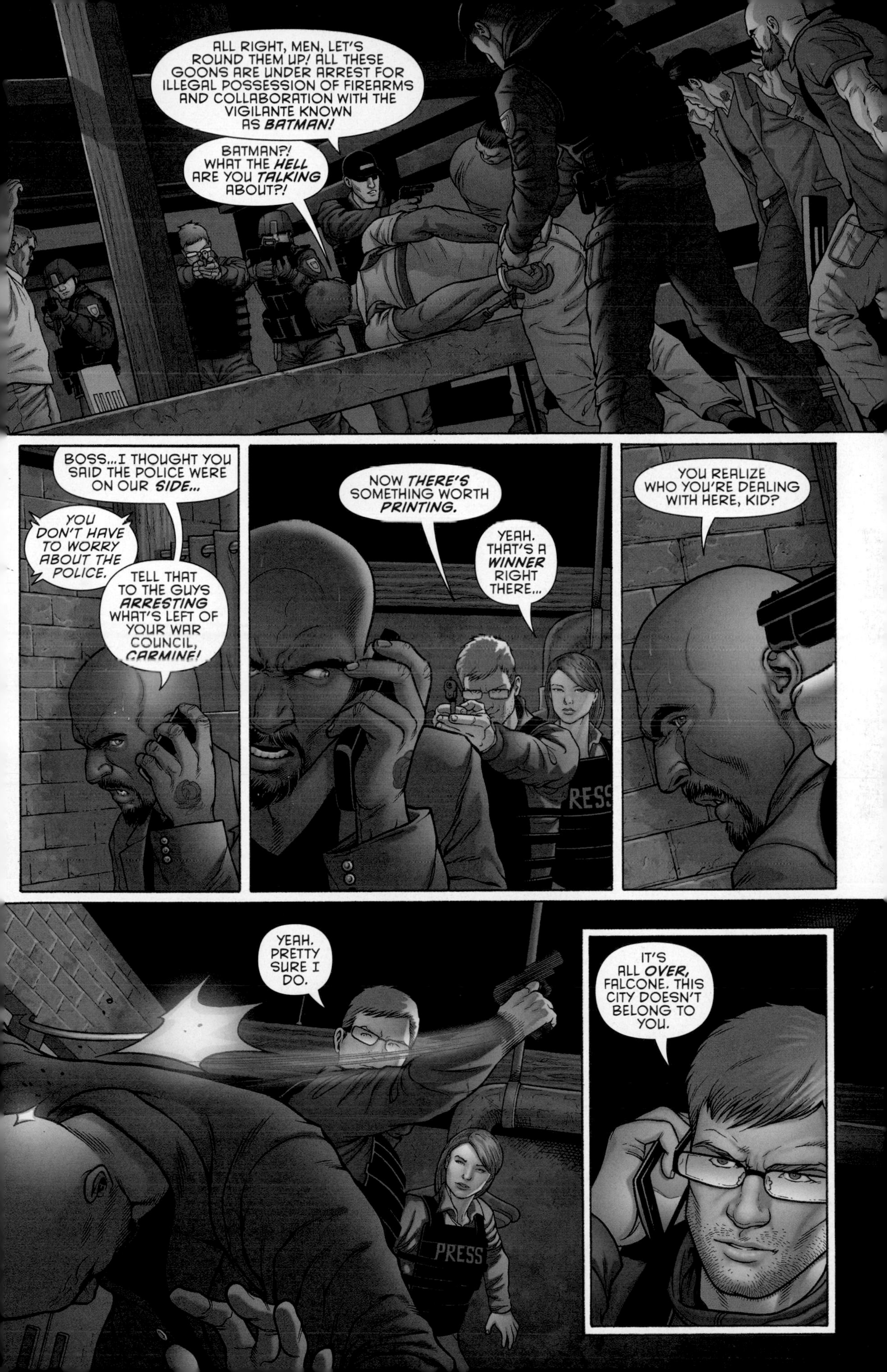
ALL RIGHT, MEN, LET'S ROUND THEM UP! ALL THESE GOONS ARE UNDER ARREST FOR ILLEGAL POSSESSION OF FIREARMS AND COLLABORATION WITH THE VIGILANTE KNOWN AS BATMAN!
BATMAN?! WHAT THE HELL ARE YOU TALKING ABOUT?!
BOSS...I THOUGHT YOU SAID THE POLICE WERE ON OUR SIDE...
YOU DON'T HAVE TO WORRY ABOUT THE POLICE.
TELL THAT TO THE GUYS ARRESTING WHAT'S LEFT OF YOUR WAR COUNCIL, CARMINE!
NOW THERE'S SOMETHING WORTH PRINTING.
YEAH. THAT'S A WINNER RIGHT THERE...
RESS
YOU REALIZE WHO YOU'RE DEALING WITH HERE, KID?
YEAH. PRETTY SURE I DO.
PRESS
IT'S ALL OVER, FALCONE. THIS CITY DOESN'T BELONG TO YOU.

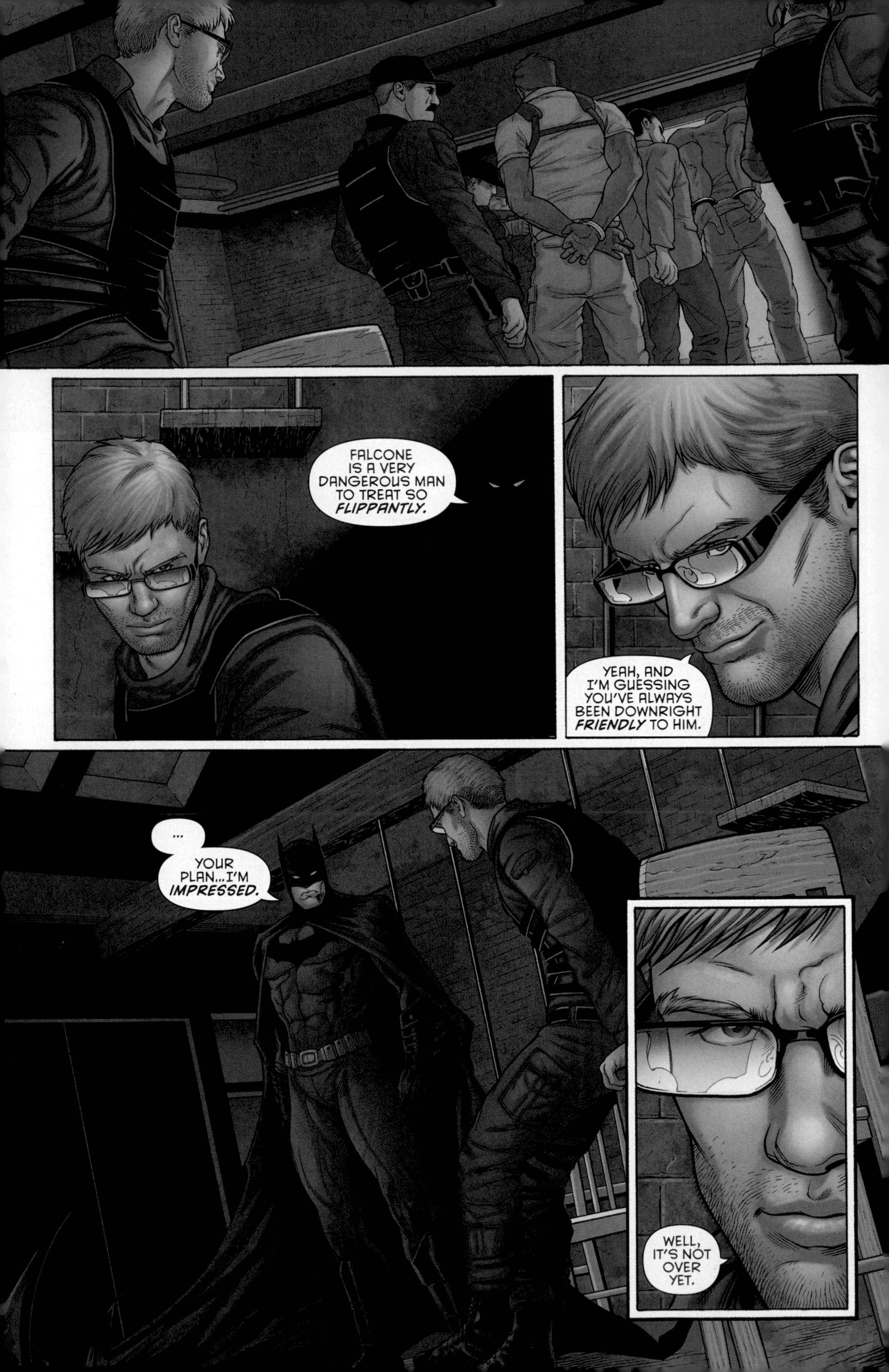
FALCONE IS A VERY DANGEROUS MAN TO TREAT SO *FLIPPANTLY.*
YEAH, AND I'M GUESSING YOU'VE ALWAYS BEEN DOWNRIGHT *FRIENDLY* TO HIM.
...
YOUR PLAN...I'M *IMPRESSED.*
WELL, IT'S NOT OVER YET.

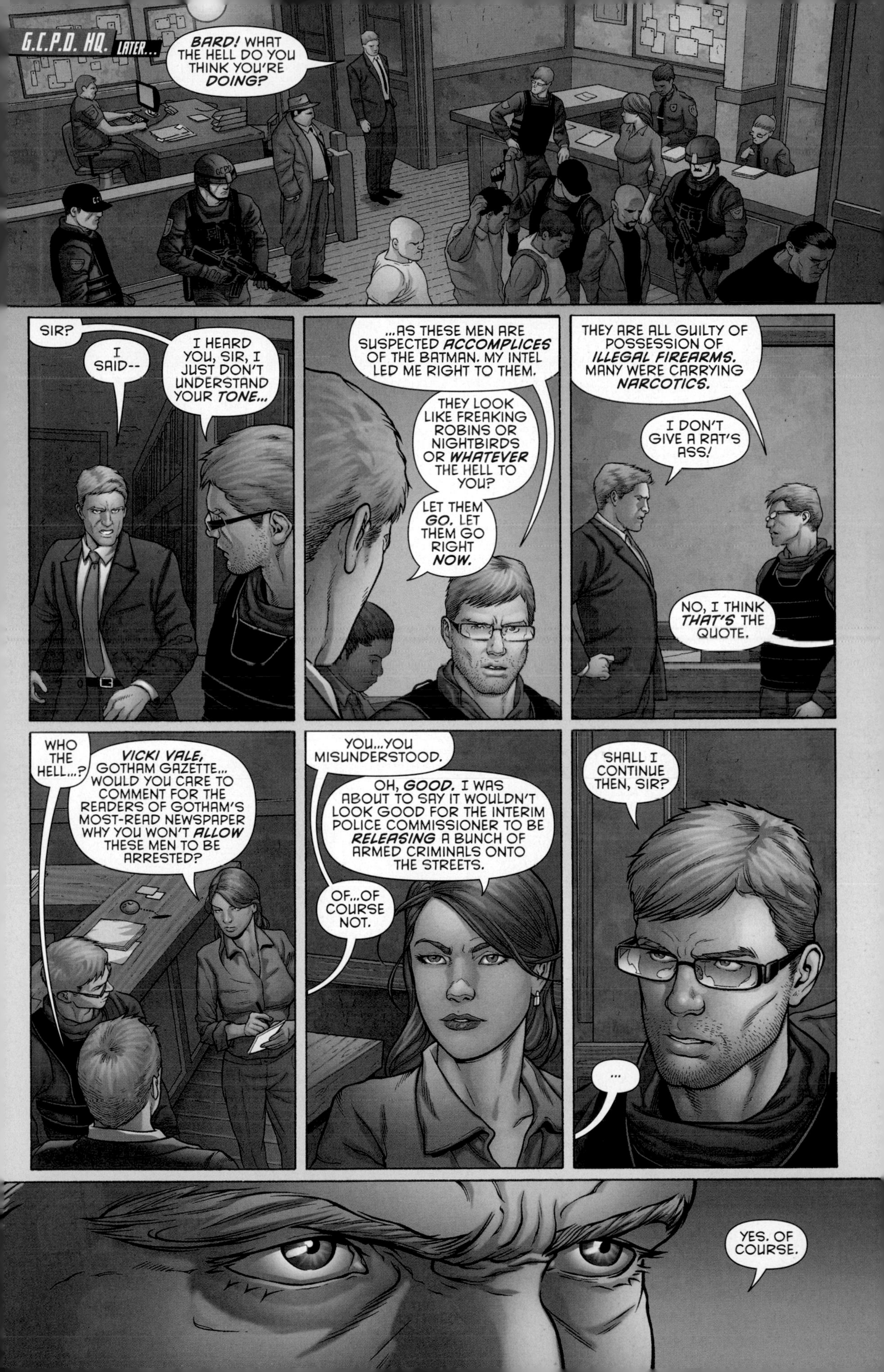
G.C.P.D. HQ.
LATER...
BARD! WHAT THE HELL DO YOU THINK YOU'RE DOING?
SIR?
I SAID--
I HEARD YOU, SIR, I JUST DON'T UNDERSTAND YOUR TONE...
...AS THESE MEN ARE SUSPECTED ACCOMPLICES OF THE BATMAN. MY INTEL LED ME RIGHT TO THEM.
THEY LOOK LIKE FREAKING ROBINS OR NIGHTBIRDS OR WHATEVER THE HELL TO YOU?
LET THEM GO. LET THEM GO RIGHT NOW.
THEY ARE ALL GUILTY OF POSSESSION OF ILLEGAL FIREARMS. MANY WERE CARRYING NARCOTICS.
I DON'T GIVE A RAT'S ASS!
NO, I THINK THAT'S THE QUOTE.
WHO THE HELL...?
VICKI VALE, GOTHAM GAZETTE... WOULD YOU CARE TO COMMENT FOR THE READERS OF GOTHAM'S MOST-READ NEWSPAPER WHY YOU WON'T ALLOW THESE MEN TO BE ARRESTED?
YOU...YOU MISUNDERSTOOD.
OH, GOOD. I WAS ABOUT TO SAY IT WOULDN'T LOOK GOOD FOR THE INTERIM POLICE COMMISSIONER TO BE RELEASING A BUNCH OF ARMED CRIMINALS ONTO THE STREETS.
OF...OF COURSE NOT.
SHALL I CONTINUE THEN, SIR?
...
YES. OF COURSE.

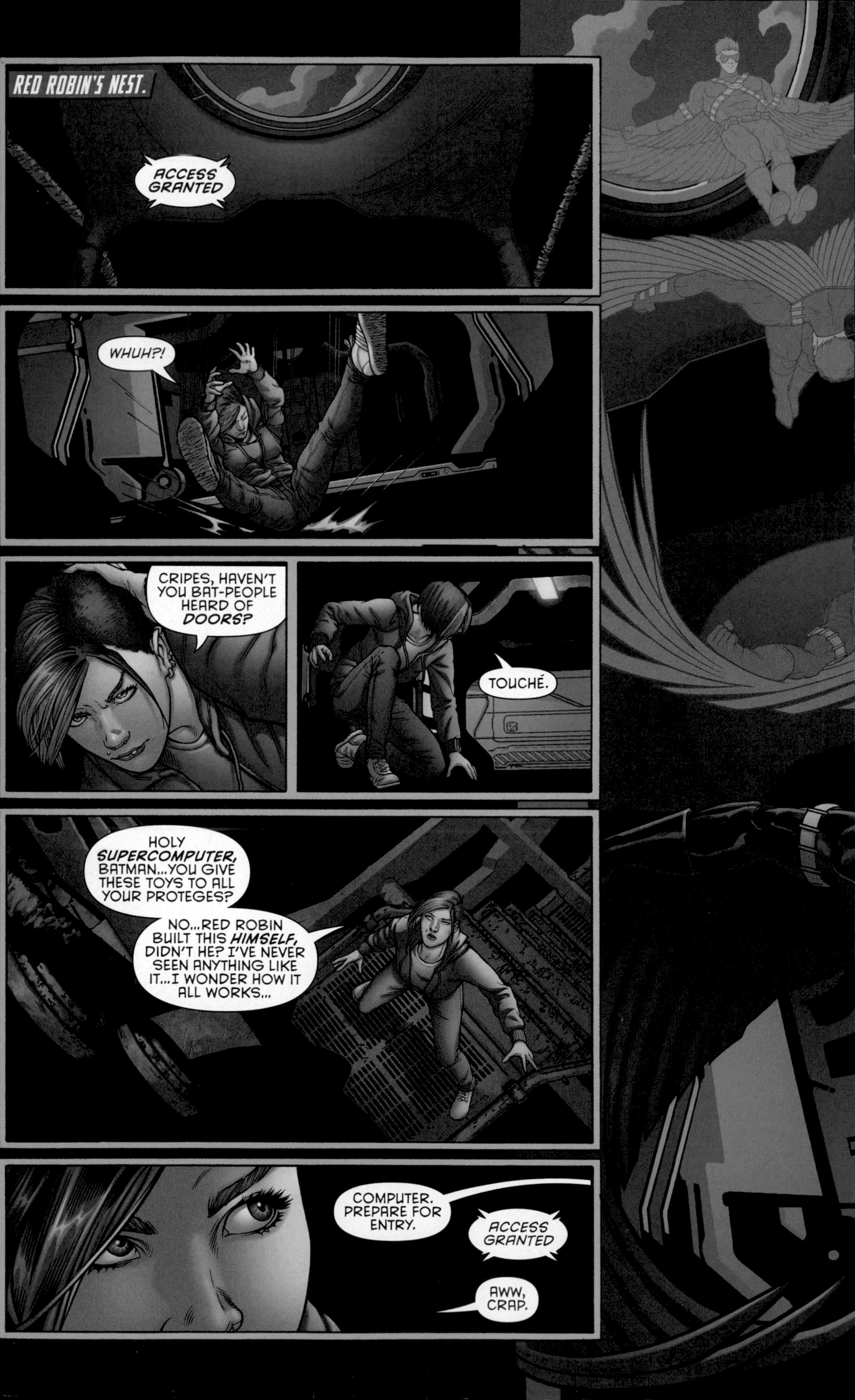

RED ROBIN'S NEST.
ACCESS GRANTED
WHUH?!
CRIPES, HAVEN'T YOU BAT-PEOPLE HEARD OF DOORS?
TOUCHÉ.
HOLY SUPERCOMPUTER, BATMAN...YOU GIVE THESE TOYS TO ALL YOUR PROTEGES?
NO...RED ROBIN BUILT THIS HIMSELF, DIDN'T HE? I'VE NEVER SEEN ANYTHING LIKE IT...I WONDER HOW IT ALL WORKS...
COMPUTER. PREPARE FOR ENTRY.
ACCESS GRANTED
AWW, CRAP.

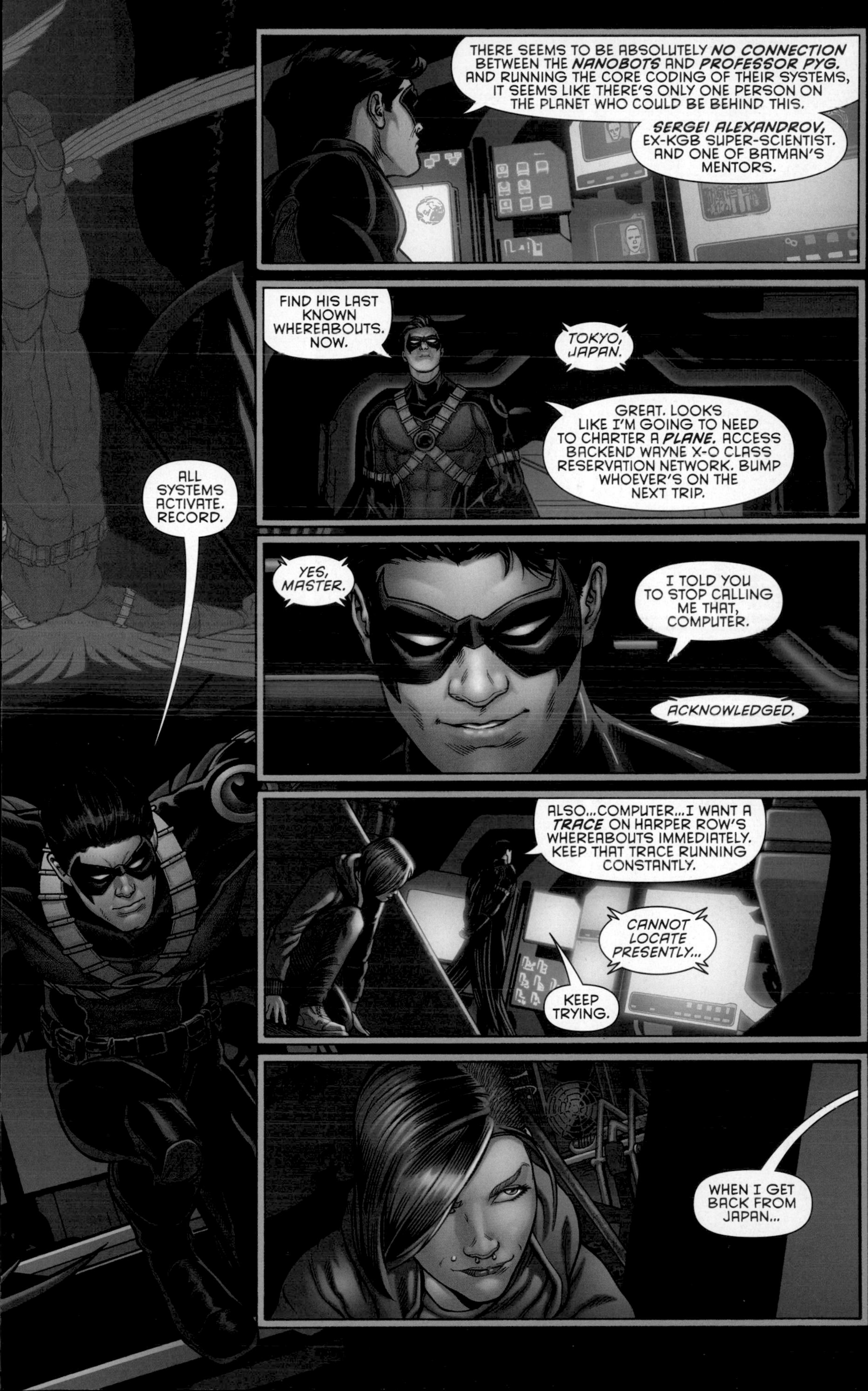
THERE SEEMS TO BE ABSOLUTELY *NO CONNECTION* BETWEEN THE *NANOBOTS* AND *PROFESSOR PYG*. AND RUNNING THE CORE CODING OF THEIR SYSTEMS, IT SEEMS LIKE THERE'S ONLY ONE PERSON ON THE PLANET WHO COULD BE BEHIND THIS.
SERGEI ALEXANDROV, EX-KGB SUPER-SCIENTIST. AND ONE OF BATMAN'S MENTORS.
FIND HIS LAST KNOWN WHEREABOUTS. NOW.
TOKYO, JAPAN.
GREAT. LOOKS LIKE I'M GOING TO NEED TO CHARTER A *PLANE.* ACCESS BACKEND WAYNE X-O CLASS RESERVATION NETWORK. BUMP WHOEVER'S ON THE NEXT TRIP.
ALL SYSTEMS ACTIVATE. RECORD.
YES, MASTER.
I TOLD YOU TO STOP CALLING ME THAT, COMPUTER.
ACKNOWLEDGED.
ALSO...COMPUTER...I WANT A *TRACE* ON HARPER ROW'S WHEREABOUTS IMMEDIATELY. KEEP THAT TRACE RUNNING CONSTANTLY.
CANNOT LOCATE PRESENTLY...
KEEP TRYING.
WHEN I GET BACK FROM JAPAN...

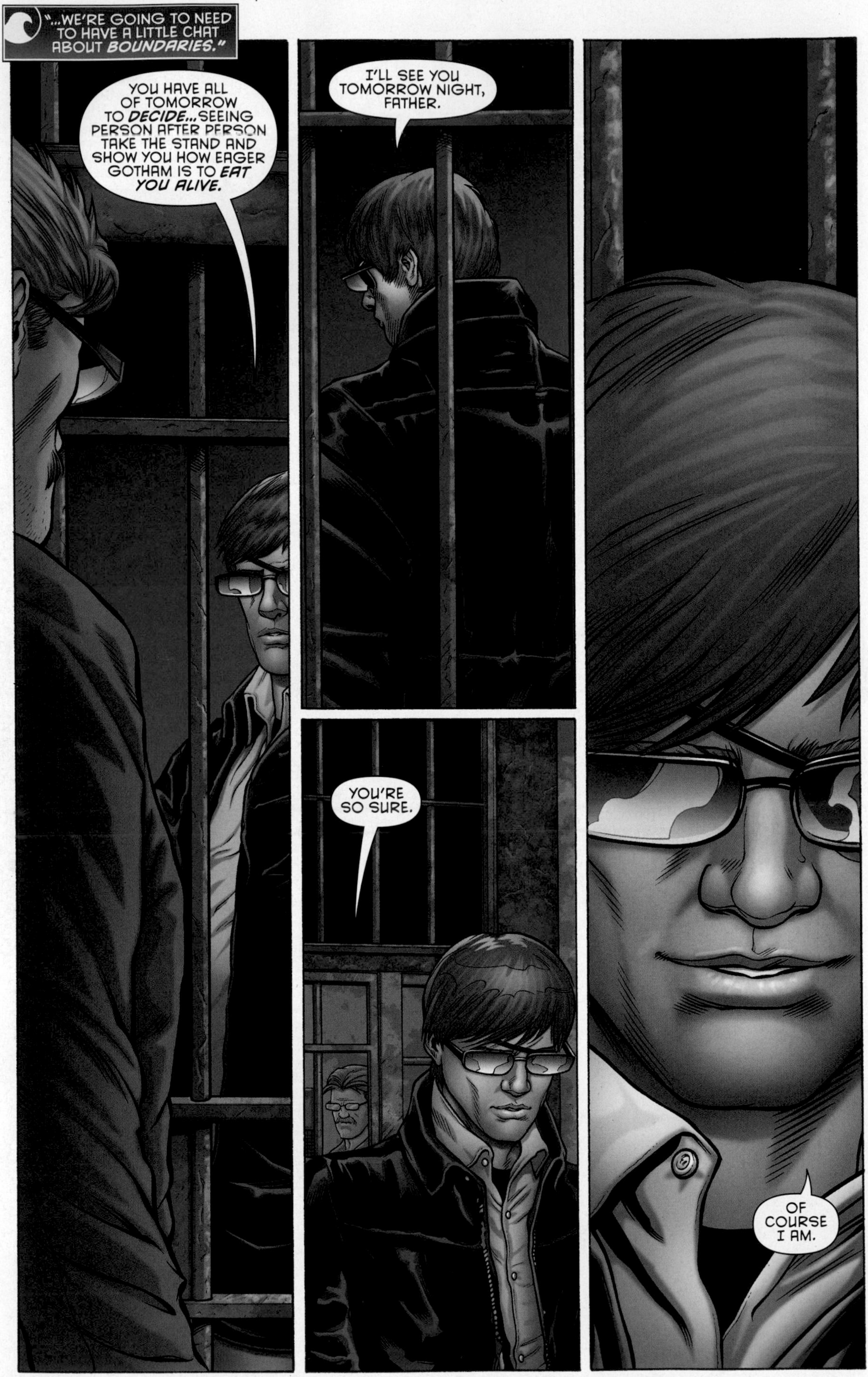
"...WE'RE GOING TO NEED TO HAVE A LITTLE CHAT ABOUT BOUNDARIES."
YOU HAVE ALL OF TOMORROW TO DECIDE... SEEING PERSON AFTER PERSON TAKE THE STAND AND SHOW YOU HOW EAGER GOTHAM IS TO EAT YOU ALIVE.
I'LL SEE YOU TOMORROW NIGHT, FATHER.
YOU'RE SO SURE.
OF COURSE I AM.

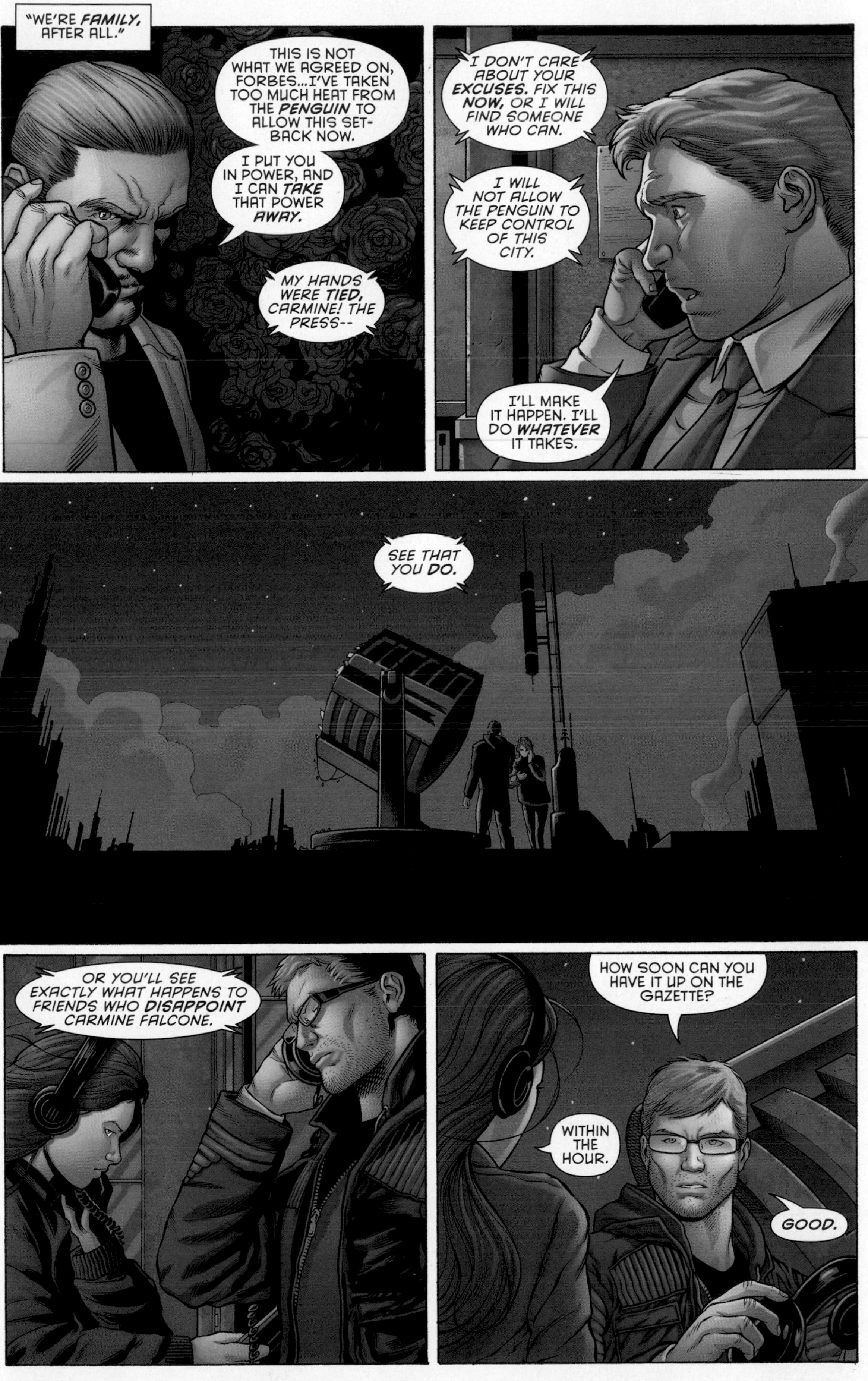
"WE'RE FAMILY, AFTER ALL."
THIS IS NOT WHAT WE AGREED ON, FORBES...I'VE TAKEN TOO MUCH HEAT FROM THE PENGUIN TO ALLOW THIS SET-BACK NOW.
I PUT YOU IN POWER, AND I CAN TAKE THAT POWER AWAY.
MY HANDS WERE TIED, CARMINE! THE PRESS--
I DON'T CARE ABOUT YOUR EXCUSES. FIX THIS NOW, OR I WILL FIND SOMEONE WHO CAN.
I WILL NOT ALLOW THE PENGUIN TO KEEP CONTROL OF THIS CITY.
I'LL MAKE IT HAPPEN. I'LL DO WHATEVER IT TAKES.
SEE THAT YOU DO.
OR YOU'LL SEE EXACTLY WHAT HAPPENS TO FRIENDS WHO DISAPPOINT CARMINE FALCONE.
HOW SOON CAN YOU HAVE IT UP ON THE GAZETTE?
WITHIN THE HOUR.
GOOD.

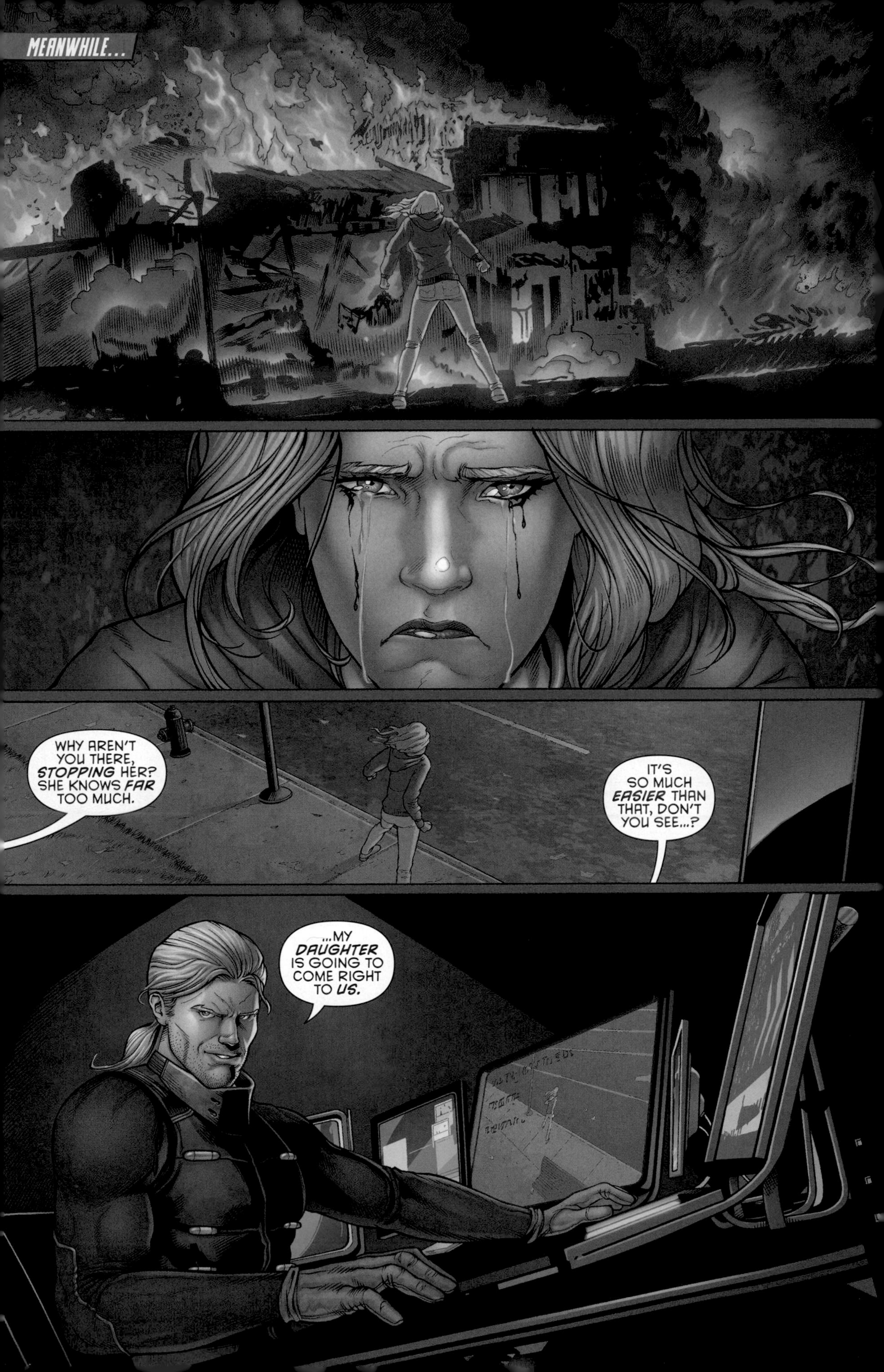
MEANWHILE...
WHY AREN'T YOU THERE, STOPPING HER? SHE KNOWS FAR TOO MUCH.
IT'S SO MUCH EASIER THAN THAT, DON'T YOU SEE...?
...MY DAUGHTER IS GOING TO COME RIGHT TO US.

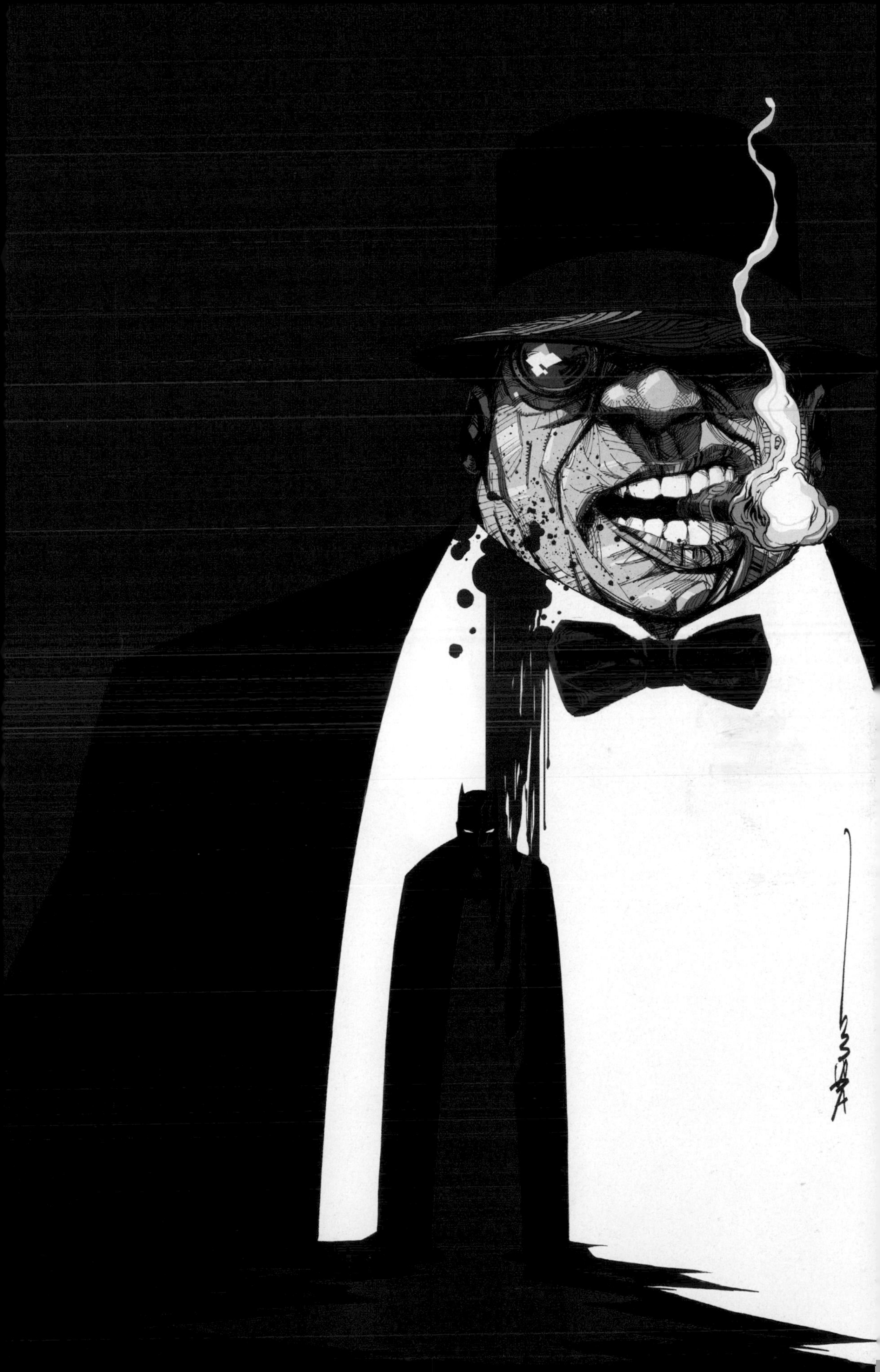

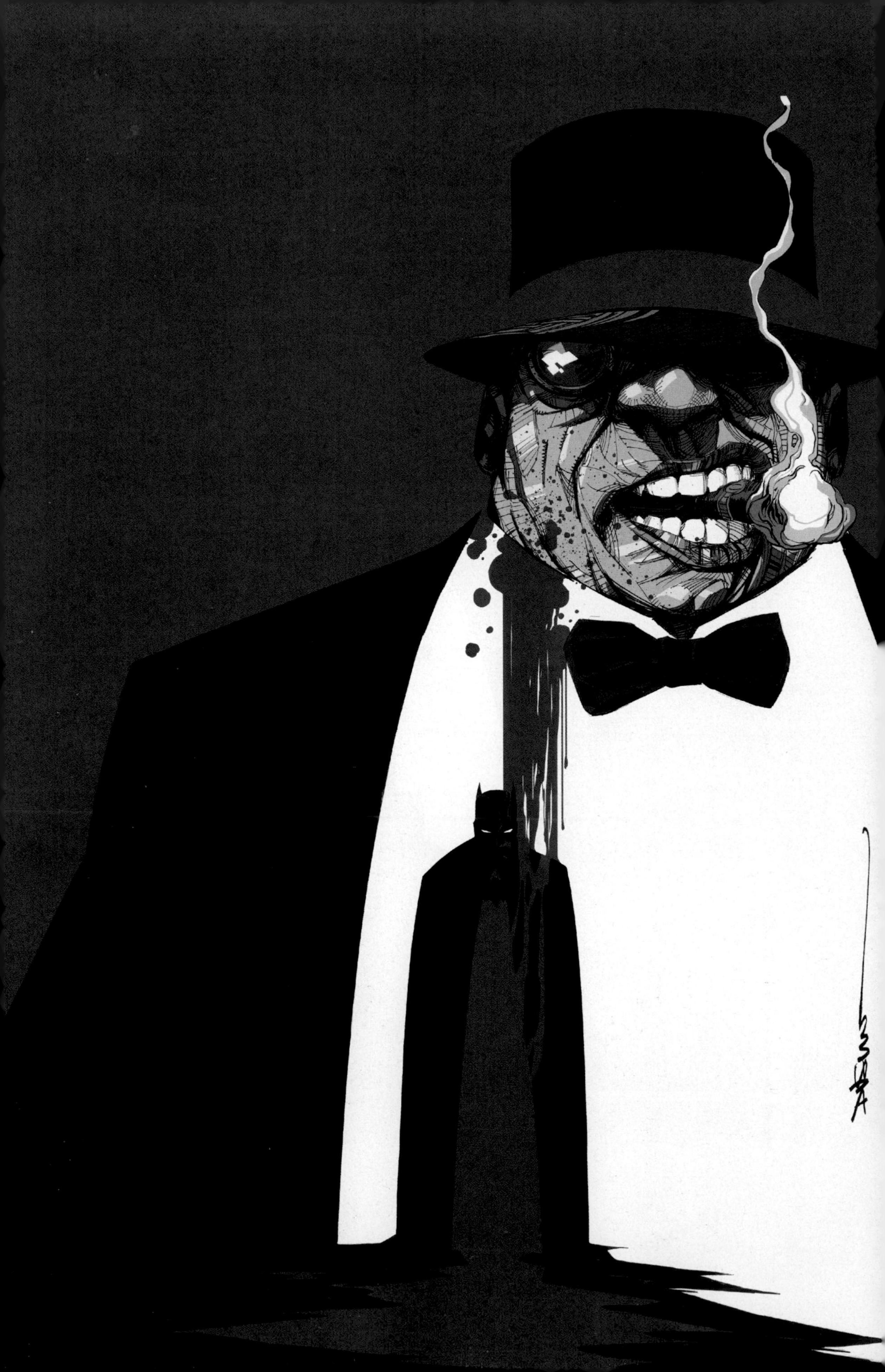

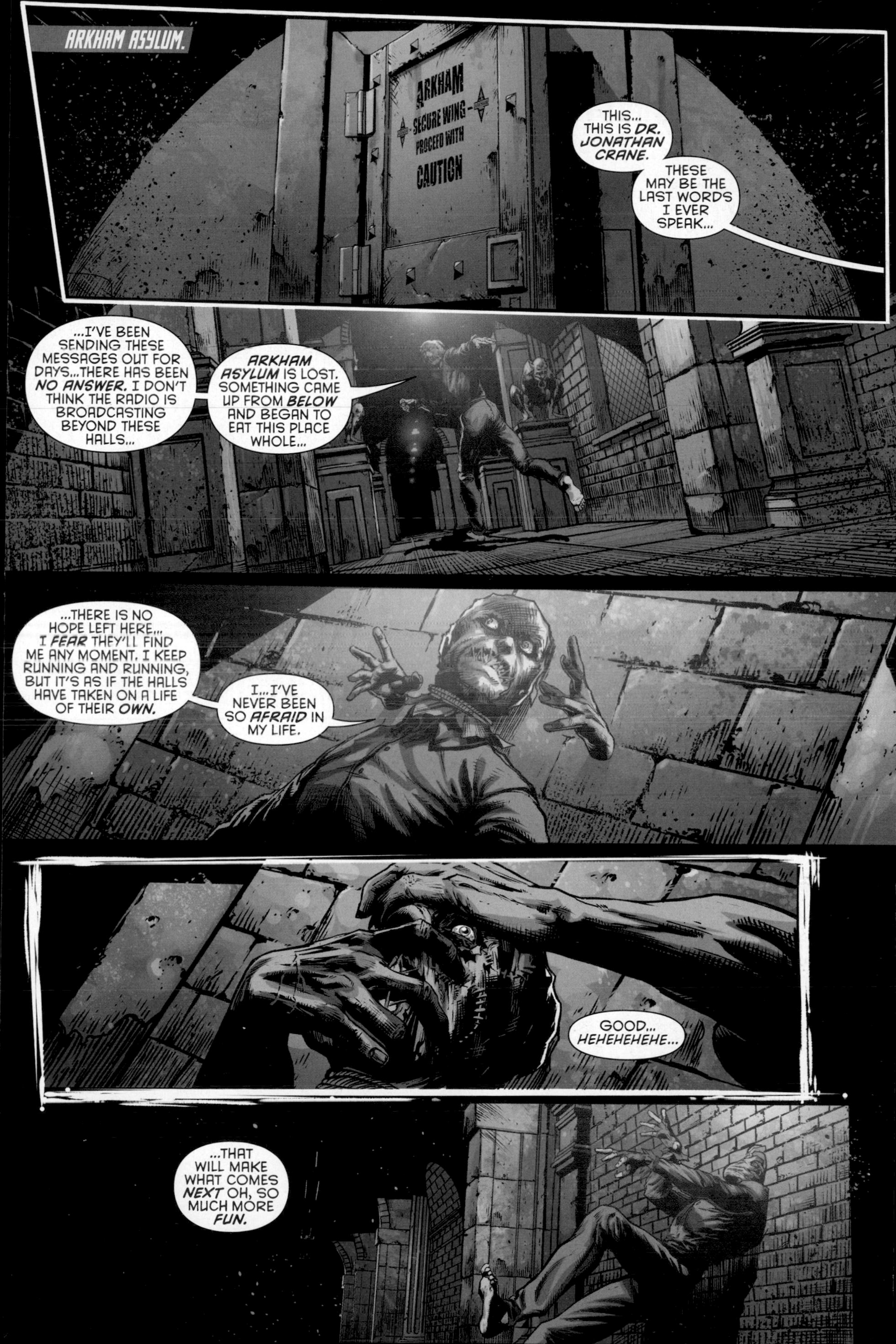
ARKHAM ASYLUM.
ARKHAM
SECURE WING-
PROCEED WITH
CAUTION
THIS... THIS IS DR. JONATHAN CRANE.
THESE MAY BE THE LAST WORDS I EVER SPEAK...
...I'VE BEEN SENDING THESE MESSAGES OUT FOR DAYS...THERE HAS BEEN NO ANSWER. I DON'T THINK THE RADIO IS BROADCASTING BEYOND THESE HALLS...
ARKHAM ASYLUM IS LOST. SOMETHING CAME UP FROM BELOW AND BEGAN TO EAT THIS PLACE WHOLE...
...THERE IS NO HOPE LEFT HERE... I FEAR THEY'LL FIND ME ANY MOMENT. I KEEP RUNNING AND RUNNING, BUT IT'S AS IF THE HALLS HAVE TAKEN ON A LIFE OF THEIR OWN.
I...I'VE NEVER BEEN SO AFRAID IN MY LIFE.
GOOD... HEHEHEHEHE...
...THAT WILL MAKE WHAT COMES NEXT OH, SO MUCH MORE FUN.

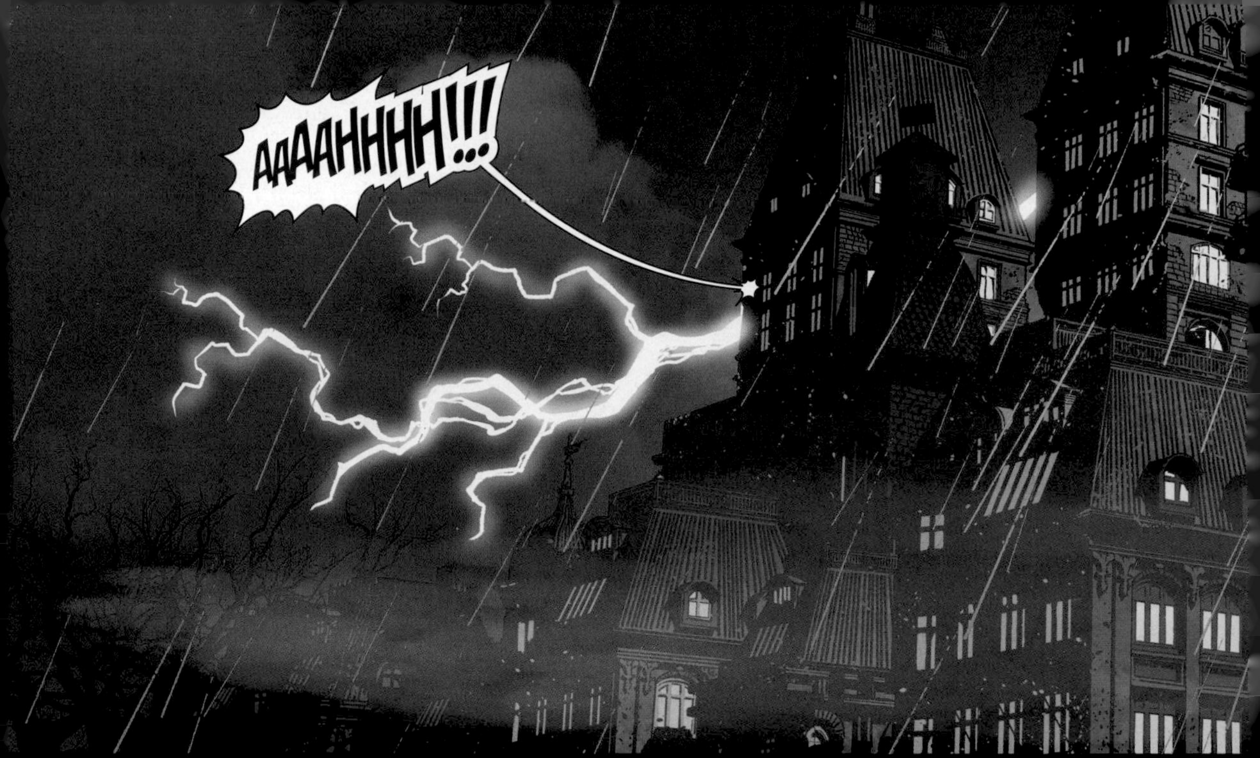
AAAAHHHH!!!

STORY BY: SCOTT SNYDER & JAMES TYNION IV • SCRIPT BY: JAMES TYNION IV
CONTRIBUTING WRITERS: RAY FAWKES, JOHN LAYMAN & TIM SEELEY

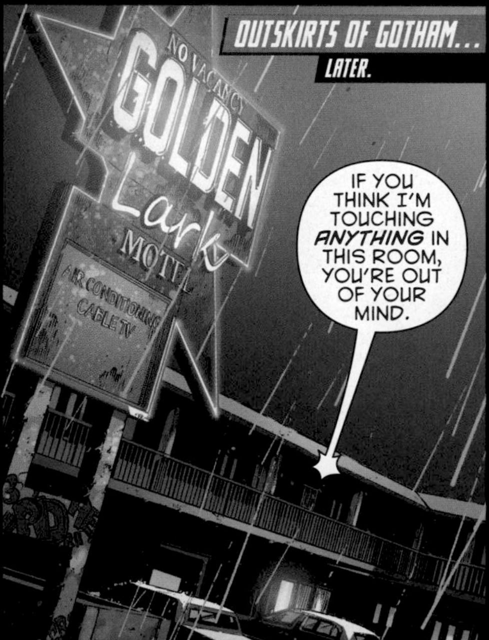
OUTSKIRTS OF GOTHAM...
LATER.
NO VACANCY
GOLDEN Lark MOTEL
AIR CONDITIONING CABLE TV
IF YOU THINK I'M TOUCHING ANYTHING IN THIS ROOM, YOU'RE OUT OF YOUR MIND.

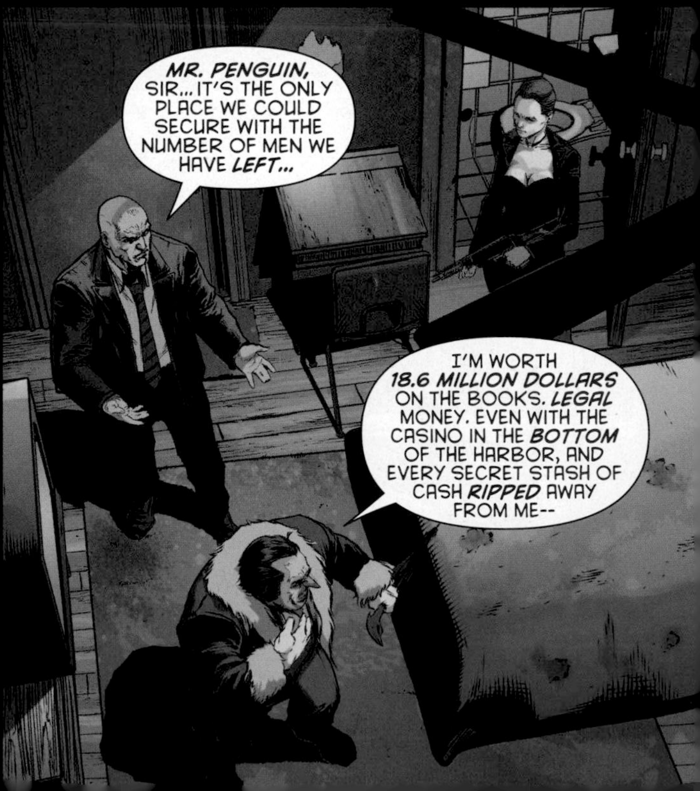
MR. PENGUIN, SIR... IT'S THE ONLY PLACE WE COULD SECURE WITH THE NUMBER OF MEN WE HAVE LEFT...
I'M WORTH 18.6 MILLION DOLLARS ON THE BOOKS. LEGAL MONEY. EVEN WITH THE CASINO IN THE BOTTOM OF THE HARBOR, AND EVERY SECRET STASH OF CASH RIPPED AWAY FROM ME--

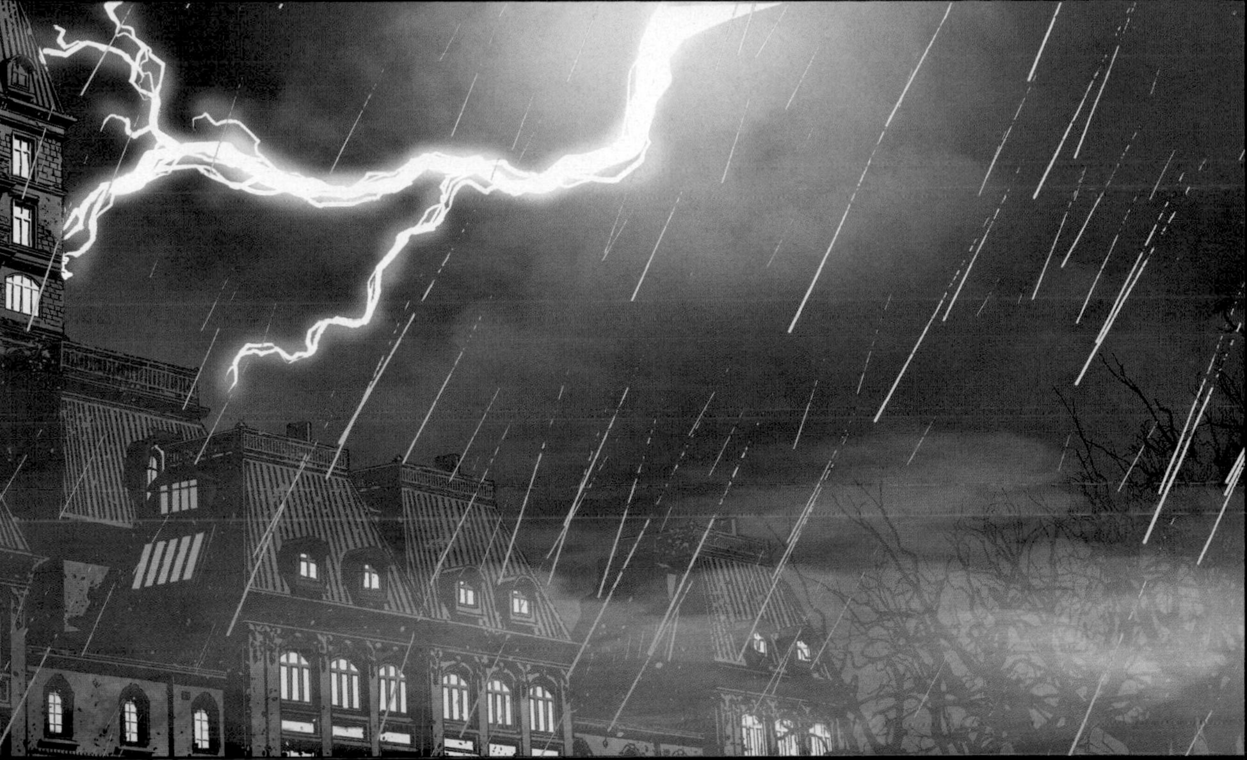

ART BY: JASON FABOK • COLORS BY: BRAD ANDERSON

LETTERING BY: CARLOS M. MANGUAL • COVER BY: DUSTIN NGUYEN

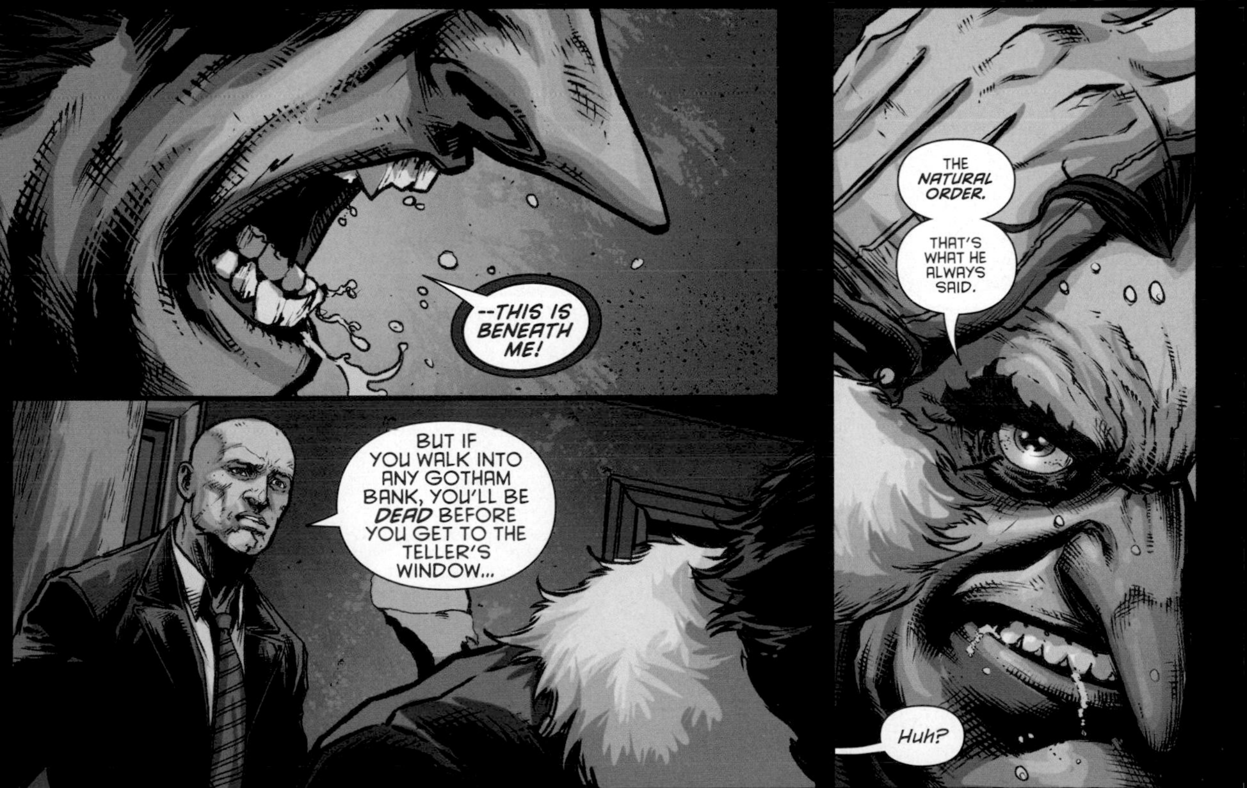
--THIS IS BENEATH ME!
THE NATURAL ORDER.
THAT'S WHAT HE ALWAYS SAID.
BUT IF YOU WALK INTO ANY GOTHAM BANK, YOU'LL BE DEAD BEFORE YOU GET TO THE TELLER'S WINDOW...
Huh?

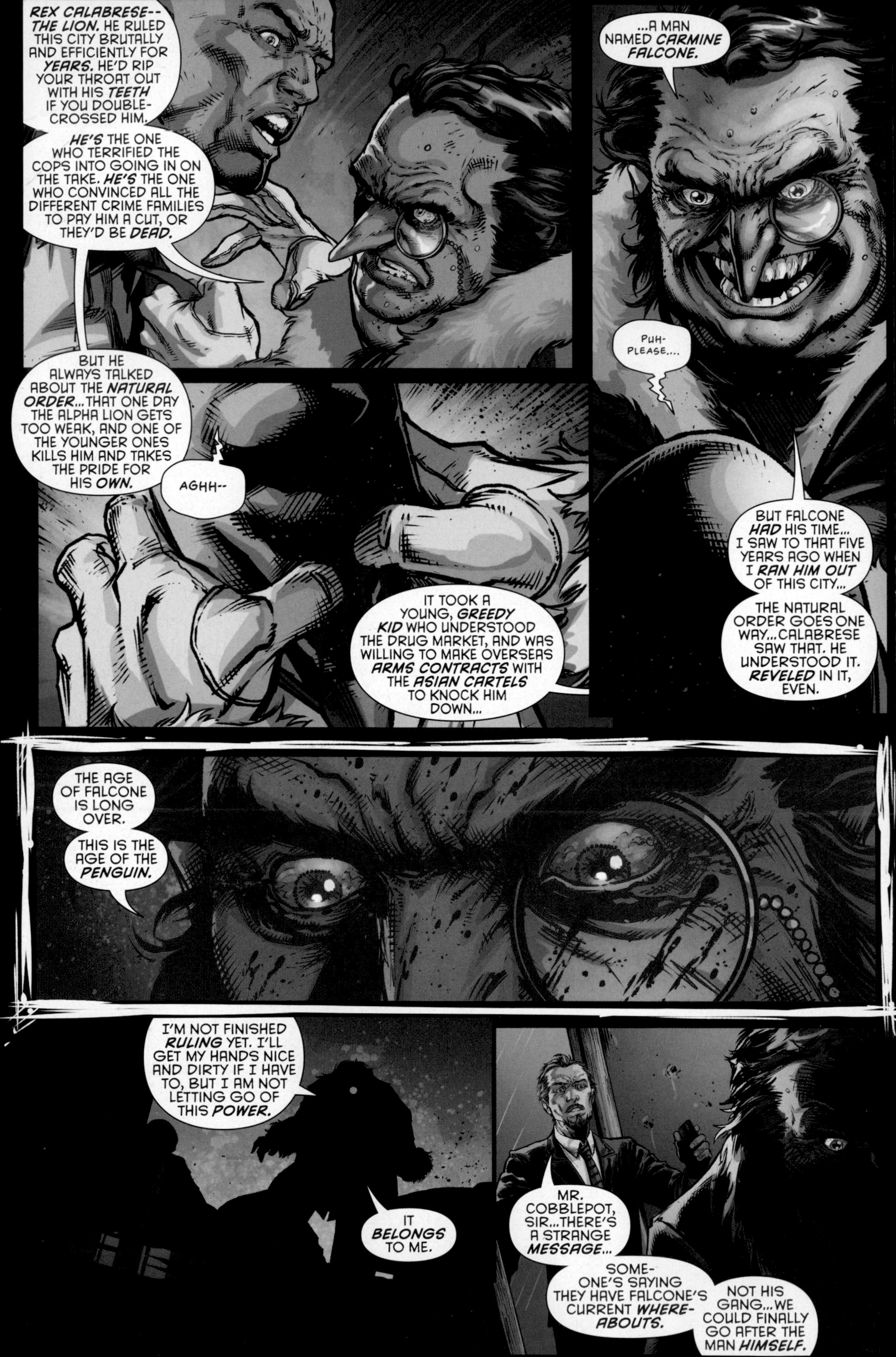
REX CALABRESE--THE LION. HE RULED THIS CITY BRUTALLY AND EFFICIENTLY FOR YEARS. HE'D RIP YOUR THROAT OUT WITH HIS TEETH IF YOU DOUBLE-CROSSED HIM.
HE'S THE ONE WHO TERRIFIED THE COPS INTO GOING IN ON THE TAKE. HE'S THE ONE WHO CONVINCED ALL THE DIFFERENT CRIME FAMILIES TO PAY HIM A CUT, OR THEY'D BE DEAD.
BUT HE ALWAYS TALKED ABOUT THE NATURAL ORDER... THAT ONE DAY THE ALPHA LION GETS TOO WEAK, AND ONE OF THE YOUNGER ONES KILLS HIM AND TAKES THE PRIDE FOR HIS OWN.
AGHH--
IT TOOK A YOUNG, GREEDY KID WHO UNDERSTOOD THE DRUG MARKET, AND WAS WILLING TO MAKE OVERSEAS ARMS CONTRACTS WITH THE ASIAN CARTELS TO KNOCK HIM DOWN...
...A MAN NAMED CARMINE FALCONE.
PUH-PLEASE....
BUT FALCONE HAD HIS TIME... I SAW TO THAT FIVE YEARS AGO WHEN I RAN HIM OUT OF THIS CITY...
THE NATURAL ORDER GOES ONE WAY... CALABRESE SAW THAT. HE UNDERSTOOD IT. REVELED IN IT, EVEN.
THE AGE OF FALCONE IS LONG OVER.
THIS IS THE AGE OF THE PENGUIN.
I'M NOT FINISHED RULING YET. I'LL GET MY HANDS NICE AND DIRTY IF I HAVE TO, BUT I AM NOT LETTING GO OF THIS POWER.
IT BELONGS TO ME.
MR. COBBLEPOT, SIR... THERE'S A STRANGE MESSAGE...
SOME-ONE'S SAYING THEY HAVE FALCONE'S CURRENT WHERE-ABOUTS.
NOT HIS GANG... WE COULD FINALLY GO AFTER THE MAN HIMSELF.

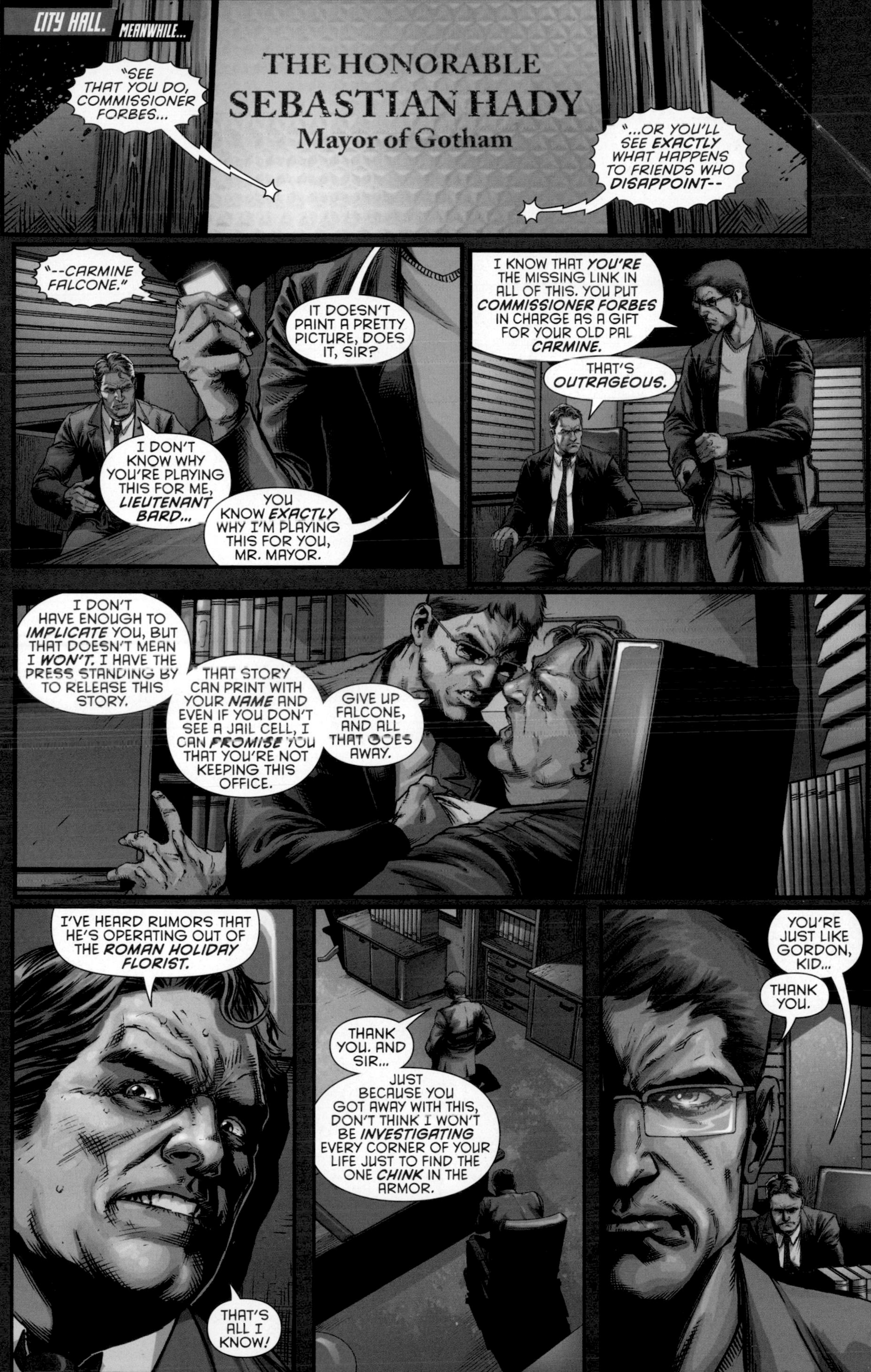
CITY HALL. MEANWHILE...
THE HONORABLE SEBASTIAN HADY Mayor of Gotham
"SEE THAT YOU DO, COMMISSIONER FORBES...
"...OR YOU'LL SEE EXACTLY WHAT HAPPENS TO FRIENDS WHO DISAPPOINT--
"--CARMINE FALCONE."
IT DOESN'T PAINT A PRETTY PICTURE, DOES IT, SIR?
I DON'T KNOW WHY YOU'RE PLAYING THIS FOR ME, LIEUTENANT BARD...
YOU KNOW EXACTLY WHY I'M PLAYING THIS FOR YOU, MR. MAYOR.
I KNOW THAT YOU'RE THE MISSING LINK IN ALL OF THIS. YOU PUT COMMISSIONER FORBES IN CHARGE AS A GIFT FOR YOUR OLD PAL CARMINE.
THAT'S OUTRAGEOUS.
I DON'T HAVE ENOUGH TO IMPLICATE YOU, BUT THAT DOESN'T MEAN I WON'T. I HAVE THE PRESS STANDING BY TO RELEASE THIS STORY.
THAT STORY CAN PRINT WITH YOUR NAME AND EVEN IF YOU DON'T SEE A JAIL CELL, I CAN PROMISE YOU THAT YOU'RE NOT KEEPING THIS OFFICE.
GIVE UP FALCONE, AND ALL THAT GOES AWAY.
I'VE HEARD RUMORS THAT HE'S OPERATING OUT OF THE ROMAN HOLIDAY FLORIST.
THAT'S ALL I KNOW!
THANK YOU. AND SIR...
JUST BECAUSE YOU GOT AWAY WITH THIS, DON'T THINK I WON'T BE INVESTIGATING EVERY CORNER OF YOUR LIFE JUST TO FIND THE ONE CHINK IN THE ARMOR.
YOU'RE JUST LIKE GORDON, KID...
THANK YOU.

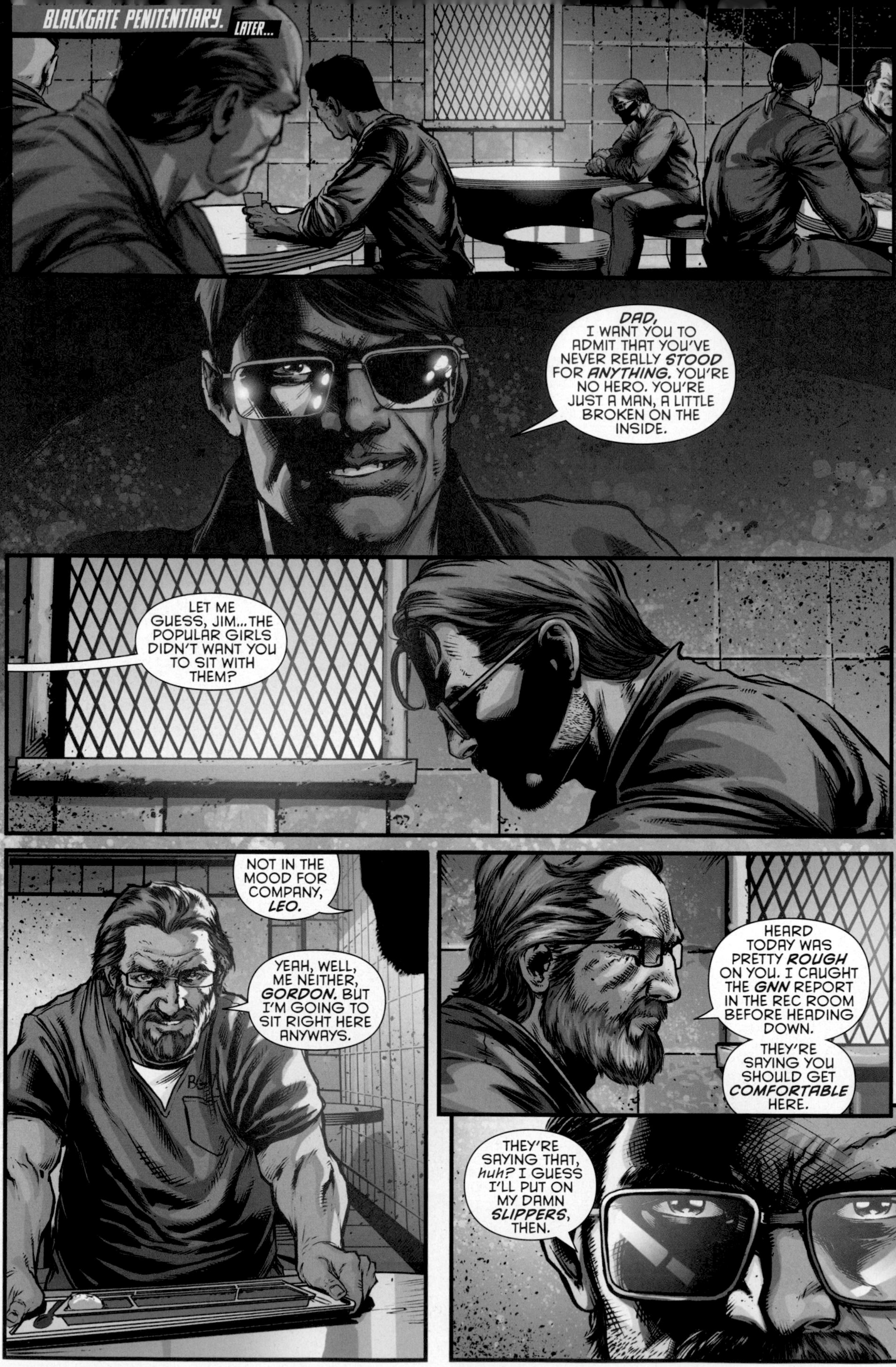
BLACKGATE PENITENTIARY.
LATER...
DAD, I WANT YOU TO ADMIT THAT YOU'VE NEVER REALLY STOOD FOR ANYTHING. YOU'RE NO HERO. YOU'RE JUST A MAN, A LITTLE BROKEN ON THE INSIDE.
LET ME GUESS, JIM...THE POPULAR GIRLS DIDN'T WANT YOU TO SIT WITH THEM?
NOT IN THE MOOD FOR COMPANY, LEO.
YEAH, WELL, ME NEITHER, GORDON. BUT I'M GOING TO SIT RIGHT HERE ANYWAYS.
HEARD TODAY WAS PRETTY ROUGH ON YOU. I CAUGHT THE GNN REPORT IN THE REC ROOM BEFORE HEADING DOWN.
THEY'RE SAYING YOU SHOULD GET COMFORTABLE HERE.
THEY'RE SAYING THAT, huh? I GUESS I'LL PUT ON MY DAMN SLIPPERS, THEN.

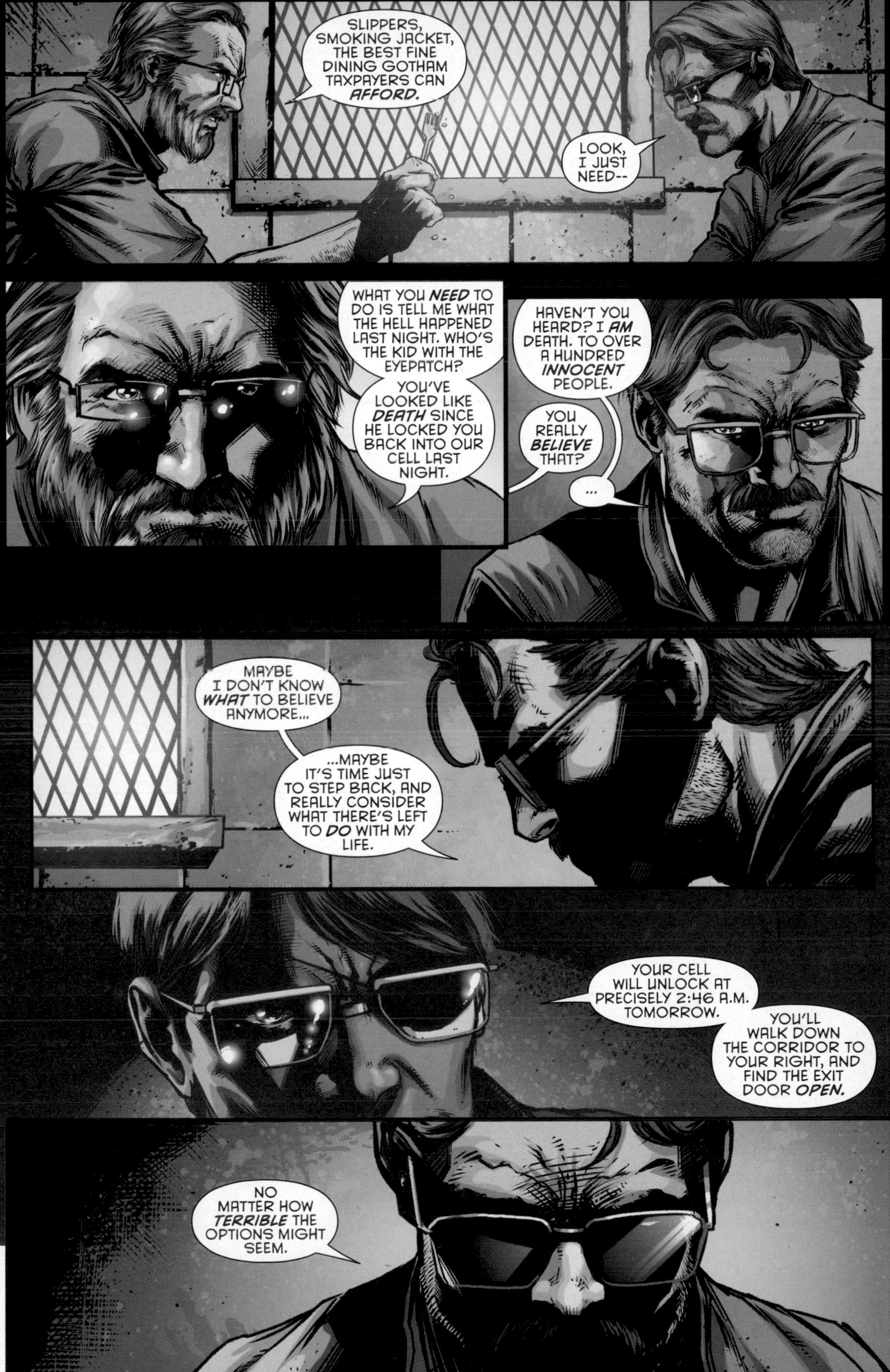
SLIPPERS, SMOKING JACKET, THE BEST FINE DINING GOTHAM TAXPAYERS CAN *AFFORD.*
LOOK, I JUST NEED--
WHAT YOU *NEED* TO DO IS TELL ME WHAT THE HELL HAPPENED LAST NIGHT. WHO'S THE KID WITH THE EYEPATCH?
YOU'VE LOOKED LIKE *DEATH* SINCE HE LOCKED YOU BACK INTO OUR CELL LAST NIGHT.
HAVEN'T YOU HEARD? I *AM* DEATH. TO OVER A HUNDRED *INNOCENT* PEOPLE.
YOU REALLY *BELIEVE* THAT?
...
MAYBE I DON'T KNOW *WHAT* TO BELIEVE ANYMORE...
...MAYBE IT'S TIME JUST TO STEP BACK, AND REALLY CONSIDER WHAT THERE'S LEFT TO *DO* WITH MY LIFE.
YOUR CELL WILL UNLOCK AT PRECISELY 2:46 A.M. TOMORROW.
YOU'LL WALK DOWN THE CORRIDOR TO YOUR RIGHT, AND FIND THE EXIT DOOR *OPEN.*
NO MATTER HOW *TERRIBLE* THE OPTIONS MIGHT SEEM.

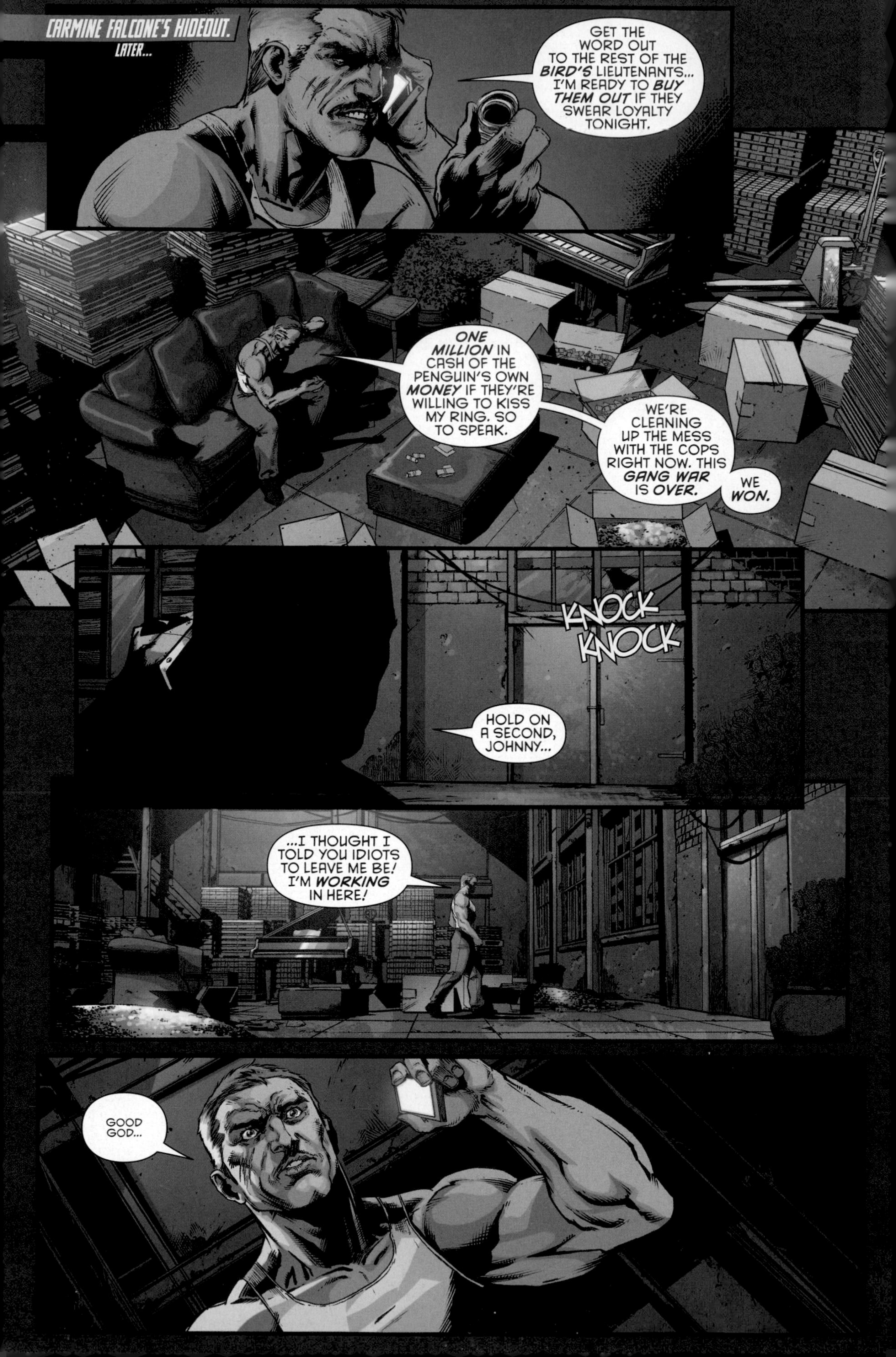
CARMINE FALCONE'S HIDEOUT.
LATER...
GET THE WORD OUT TO THE REST OF THE BIRD'S LIEUTENANTS... I'M READY TO BUY THEM OUT IF THEY SWEAR LOYALTY TONIGHT.
ONE MILLION IN CASH OF THE PENGUIN'S OWN MONEY IF THEY'RE WILLING TO KISS MY RING. SO TO SPEAK.
WE'RE CLEANING UP THE MESS WITH THE COPS RIGHT NOW. THIS GANG WAR IS OVER.
WE WON.
KNOCK KNOCK
HOLD ON A SECOND, JOHNNY...
...I THOUGHT I TOLD YOU IDIOTS TO LEAVE ME BE! I'M WORKING IN HERE!
GOOD GOD...

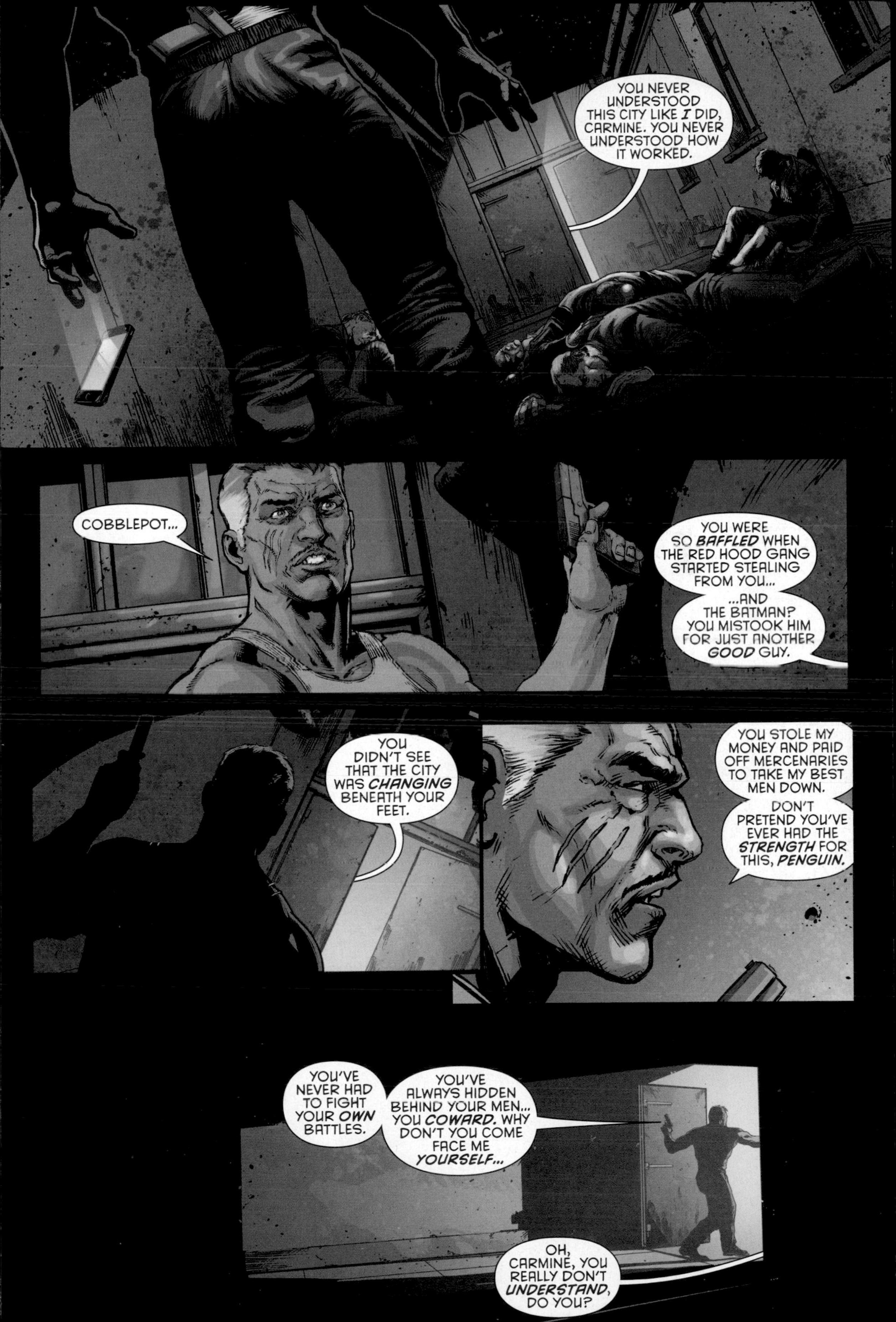

YOU NEVER UNDERSTOOD THIS CITY LIKE I DID, CARMINE. YOU NEVER UNDERSTOOD HOW IT WORKED.
COBBLEPOT...
YOU WERE SO BAFFLED WHEN THE RED HOOD GANG STARTED STEALING FROM YOU...
...AND THE BATMAN? YOU MISTOOK HIM FOR JUST ANOTHER GOOD GUY.
YOU DIDN'T SEE THAT THE CITY WAS CHANGING BENEATH YOUR FEET.
YOU STOLE MY MONEY AND PAID OFF MERCENARIES TO TAKE MY BEST MEN DOWN.
DON'T PRETEND YOU'VE EVER HAD THE STRENGTH FOR THIS, PENGUIN.
YOU'VE NEVER HAD TO FIGHT YOUR OWN BATTLES.
YOU'VE ALWAYS HIDDEN BEHIND YOUR MEN... YOU COWARD. WHY DON'T YOU COME FACE ME YOURSELF...
OH, CARMINE, YOU REALLY DON'T UNDERSTAND, DO YOU?

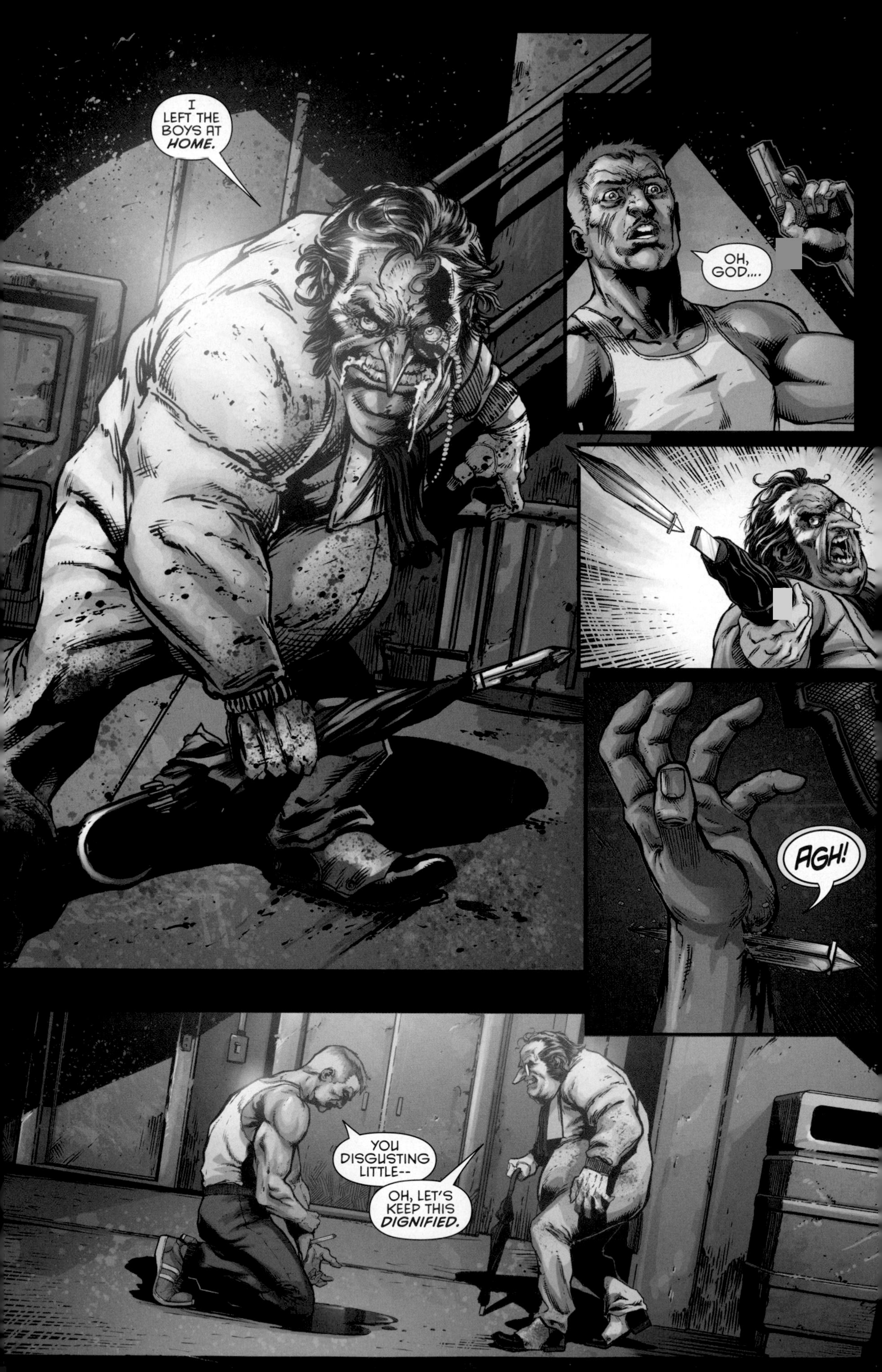
I LEFT THE BOYS AT HOME.
OH, GOD....
AGH!
YOU DISGUSTING LITTLE--
OH, LET'S KEEP THIS DIGNIFIED.

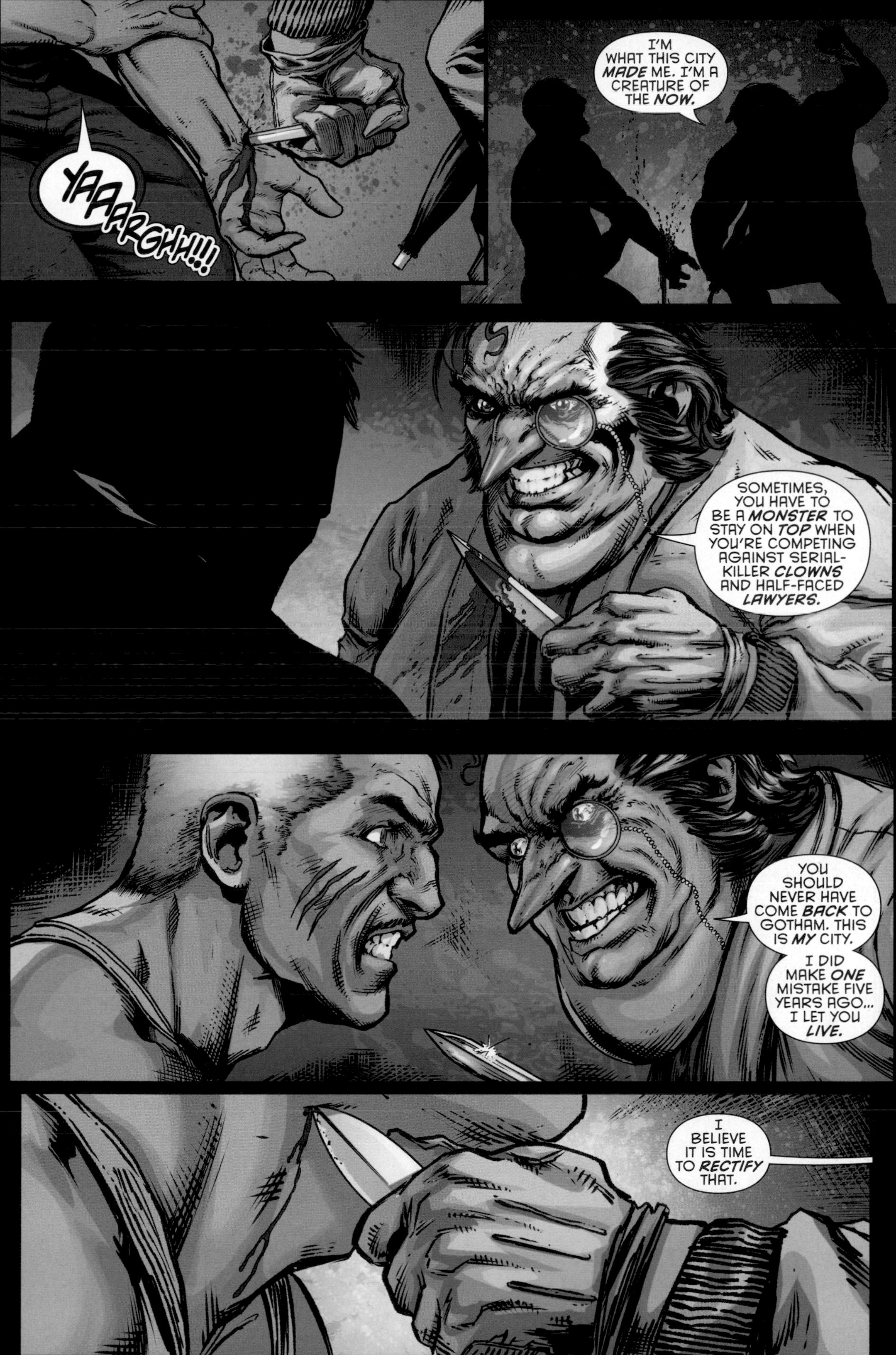
YAAARGHH!!!
I'M WHAT THIS CITY MADE ME. I'M A CREATURE OF THE NOW.
SOMETIMES, YOU HAVE TO BE A MONSTER TO STAY ON TOP WHEN YOU'RE COMPETING AGAINST SERIAL-KILLER CLOWNS AND HALF-FACED LAWYERS.
YOU SHOULD NEVER HAVE COME BACK TO GOTHAM. THIS IS MY CITY.
I DID MAKE ONE MISTAKE FIVE YEARS AGO... I LET YOU LIVE.
I BELIEVE IT IS TIME TO RECTIFY THAT.

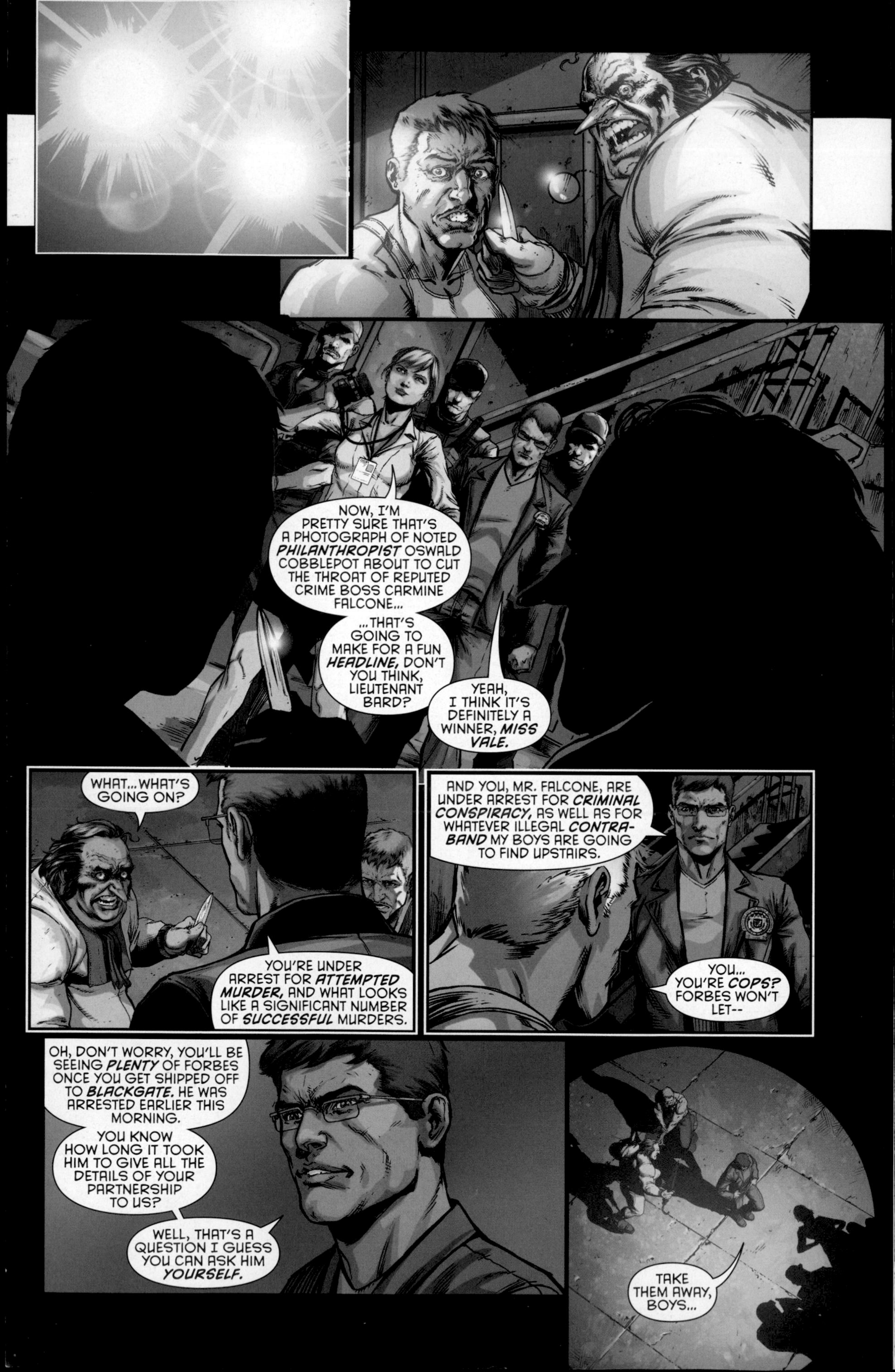

NOW, I'M PRETTY SURE THAT'S A PHOTOGRAPH OF NOTED *PHILANTHROPIST* OSWALD COBBLEPOT ABOUT TO CUT THE THROAT OF REPUTED CRIME BOSS CARMINE FALCONE...
...THAT'S GOING TO MAKE FOR A FUN *HEADLINE,* DON'T YOU THINK, LIEUTENANT BARD?
YEAH, I THINK IT'S DEFINITELY A WINNER, *MISS VALE.*
WHAT...WHAT'S GOING ON?
YOU'RE UNDER ARREST FOR *ATTEMPTED MURDER,* AND WHAT LOOKS LIKE A SIGNIFICANT NUMBER OF *SUCCESSFUL* MURDERS.
AND YOU, MR. FALCONE, ARE UNDER ARREST FOR *CRIMINAL CONSPIRACY,* AS WELL AS FOR WHATEVER ILLEGAL *CONTRA-BAND* MY BOYS ARE GOING TO FIND UPSTAIRS.
YOU... YOU'RE *COPS?* FORBES WON'T LET--
OH, DON'T WORRY, YOU'LL BE SEEING *PLENTY* OF FORBES ONCE YOU GET SHIPPED OFF TO *BLACKGATE.* HE WAS ARRESTED EARLIER THIS MORNING.
YOU KNOW HOW LONG IT TOOK HIM TO GIVE ALL THE DETAILS OF YOUR PARTNERSHIP TO US?
WELL, THAT'S A QUESTION I GUESS YOU CAN ASK HIM *YOURSELF.*
TAKE THEM AWAY, BOYS...

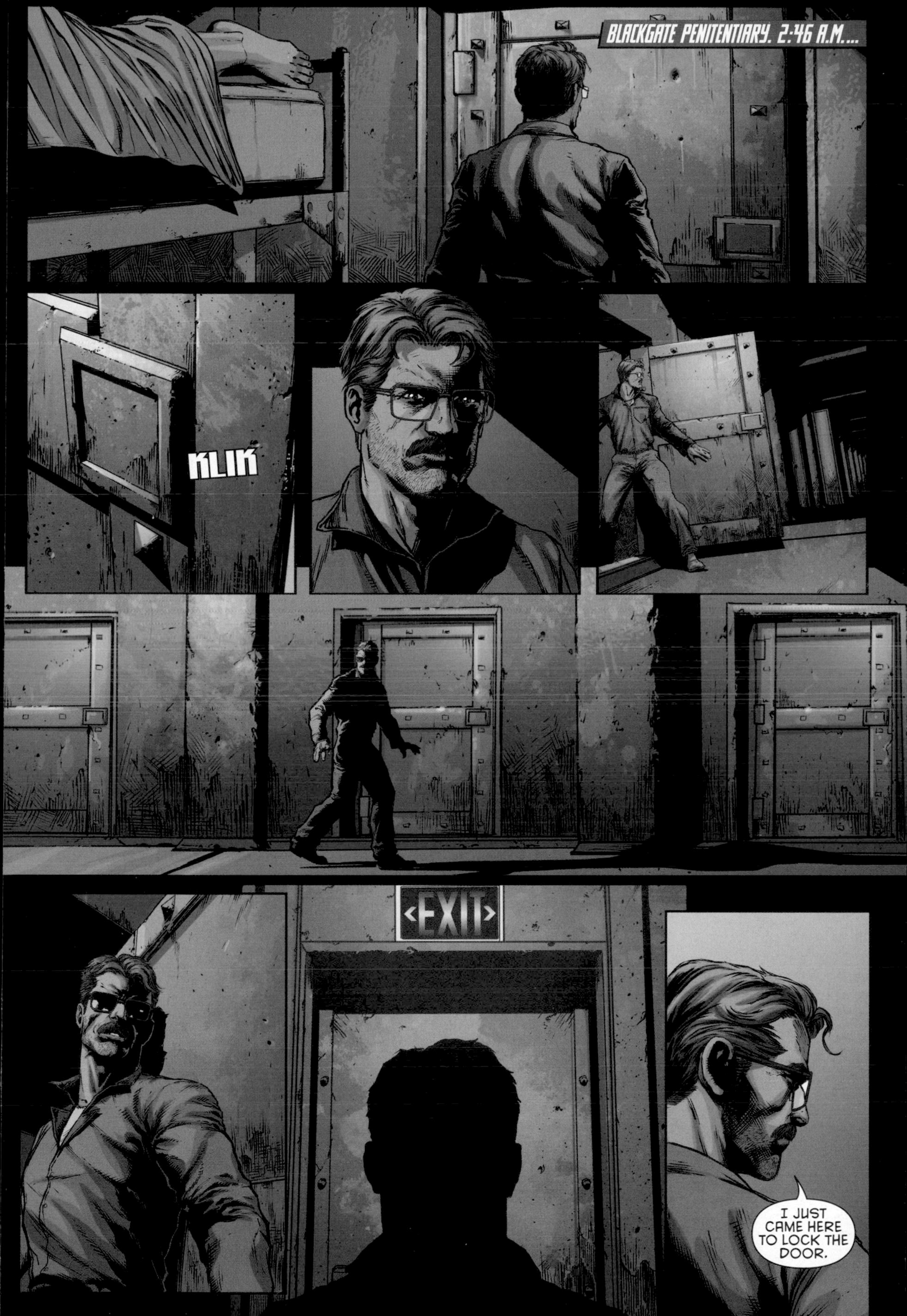

BLACKGATE PENITENTIARY. 2:46 A.M....
KLIK
EXIT
I JUST CAME HERE TO LOCK THE DOOR.

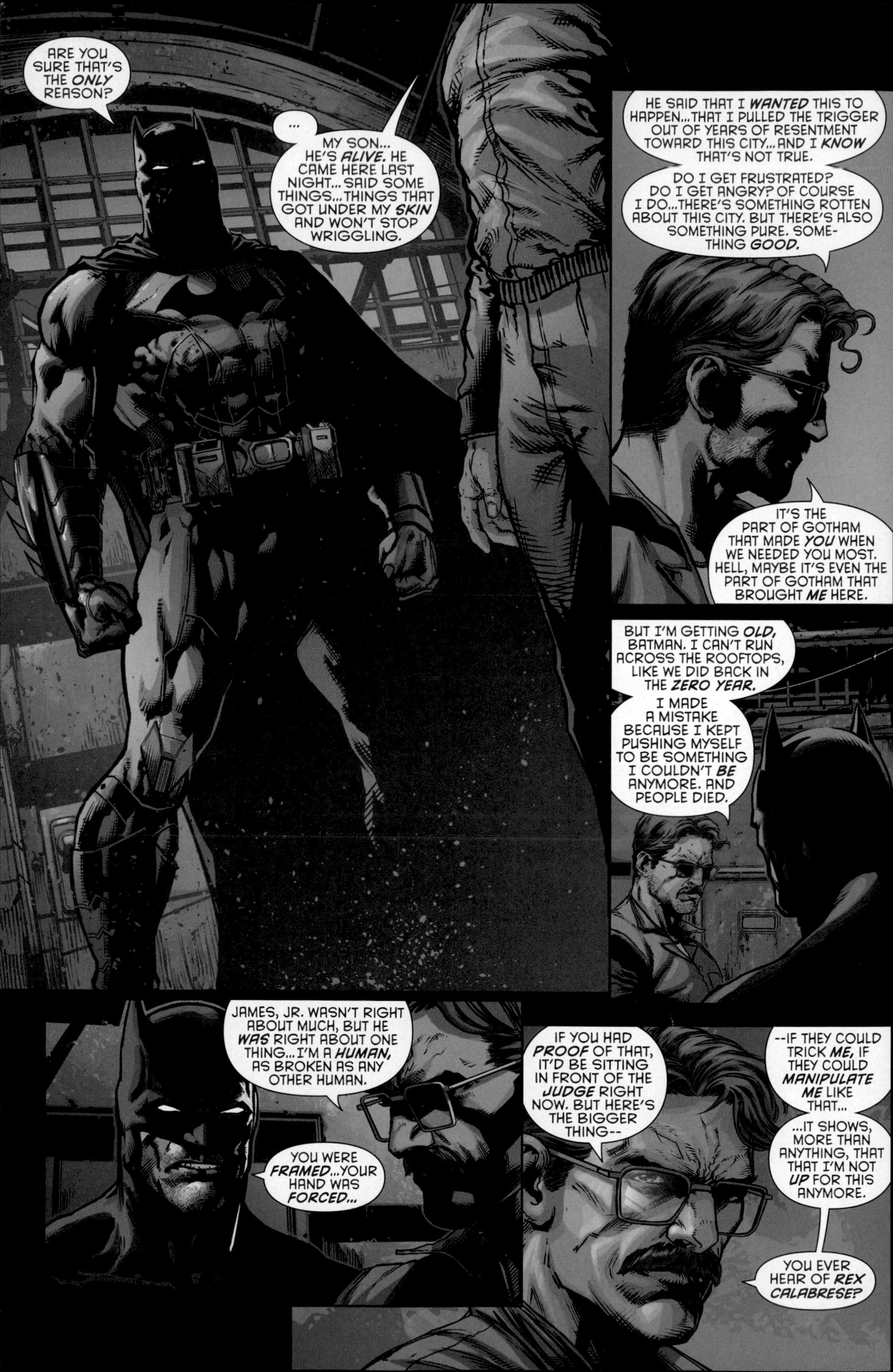
ARE YOU SURE THAT'S THE ONLY REASON?
...
MY SON... HE'S ALIVE. HE CAME HERE LAST NIGHT... SAID SOME THINGS... THINGS THAT GOT UNDER MY SKIN AND WON'T STOP WRIGGLING.
HE SAID THAT I WANTED THIS TO HAPPEN...THAT I PULLED THE TRIGGER OUT OF YEARS OF RESENTMENT TOWARD THIS CITY...AND I KNOW THAT'S NOT TRUE.
DO I GET FRUSTRATED? DO I GET ANGRY? OF COURSE I DO...THERE'S SOMETHING ROTTEN ABOUT THIS CITY. BUT THERE'S ALSO SOMETHING PURE. SOME-THING GOOD.
IT'S THE PART OF GOTHAM THAT MADE YOU WHEN WE NEEDED YOU MOST. HELL, MAYBE IT'S EVEN THE PART OF GOTHAM THAT BROUGHT ME HERE.
BUT I'M GETTING OLD, BATMAN. I CAN'T RUN ACROSS THE ROOFTOPS, LIKE WE DID BACK IN THE ZERO YEAR.
I MADE A MISTAKE BECAUSE I KEPT PUSHING MYSELF TO BE SOMETHING I COULDN'T BE ANYMORE. AND PEOPLE DIED.
JAMES, JR. WASN'T RIGHT ABOUT MUCH, BUT HE WAS RIGHT ABOUT ONE THING...I'M A HUMAN, AS BROKEN AS ANY OTHER HUMAN.
YOU WERE FRAMED...YOUR HAND WAS FORCED...
IF YOU HAD PROOF OF THAT, IT'D BE SITTING IN FRONT OF THE JUDGE RIGHT NOW. BUT HERE'S THE BIGGER THING--
--IF THEY COULD TRICK ME, IF THEY COULD MANIPULATE ME LIKE THAT...
...IT SHOWS, MORE THAN ANYTHING, THAT THAT I'M NOT UP FOR THIS ANYMORE.
YOU EVER HEAR OF REX CALABRESE?

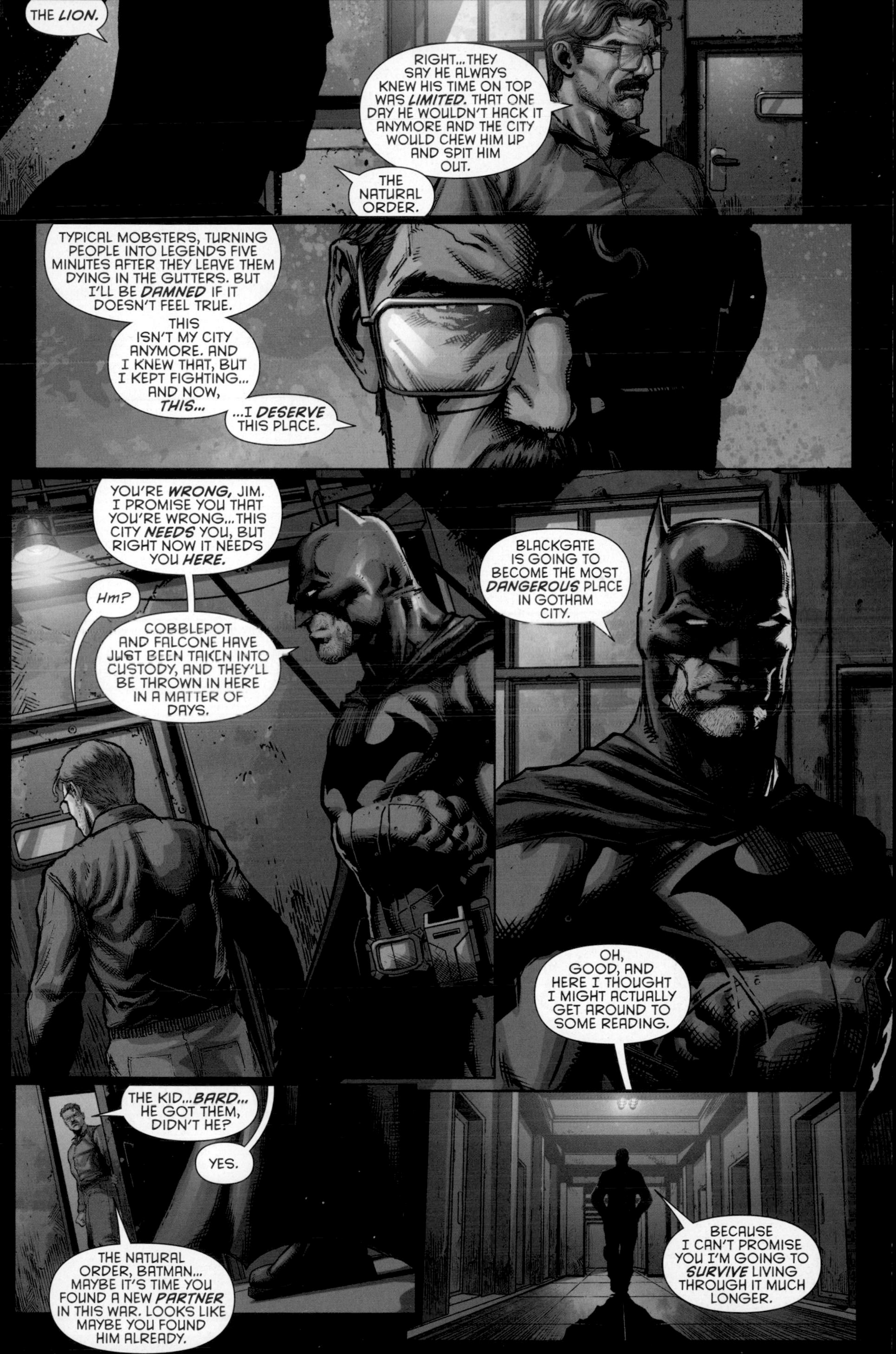
THE LION.
RIGHT... THEY SAY HE ALWAYS KNEW HIS TIME ON TOP WAS LIMITED. THAT ONE DAY HE WOULDN'T HACK IT ANYMORE AND THE CITY WOULD CHEW HIM UP AND SPIT HIM OUT.
THE NATURAL ORDER.
TYPICAL MOBSTERS, TURNING PEOPLE INTO LEGENDS FIVE MINUTES AFTER THEY LEAVE THEM DYING IN THE GUTTERS. BUT I'LL BE DAMNED IF IT DOESN'T FEEL TRUE.
THIS ISN'T MY CITY ANYMORE. AND I KNEW THAT, BUT I KEPT FIGHTING... AND NOW, THIS...
...I DESERVE THIS PLACE.
YOU'RE WRONG, JIM. I PROMISE YOU THAT YOU'RE WRONG... THIS CITY NEEDS YOU, BUT RIGHT NOW IT NEEDS YOU HERE.
Hm?
COBBLEPOT AND FALCONE HAVE JUST BEEN TAKEN INTO CUSTODY, AND THEY'LL BE THROWN IN HERE IN A MATTER OF DAYS.
BLACKGATE IS GOING TO BECOME THE MOST DANGEROUS PLACE IN GOTHAM CITY.
OH, GOOD, AND HERE I THOUGHT I MIGHT ACTUALLY GET AROUND TO SOME READING.
THE KID... BARD... HE GOT THEM, DIDN'T HE?
YES.
THE NATURAL ORDER, BATMAN... MAYBE IT'S TIME YOU FOUND A NEW PARTNER IN THIS WAR. LOOKS LIKE MAYBE YOU FOUND HIM ALREADY.
BECAUSE I CAN'T PROMISE YOU I'M GOING TO SURVIVE LIVING THROUGH IT MUCH LONGER.

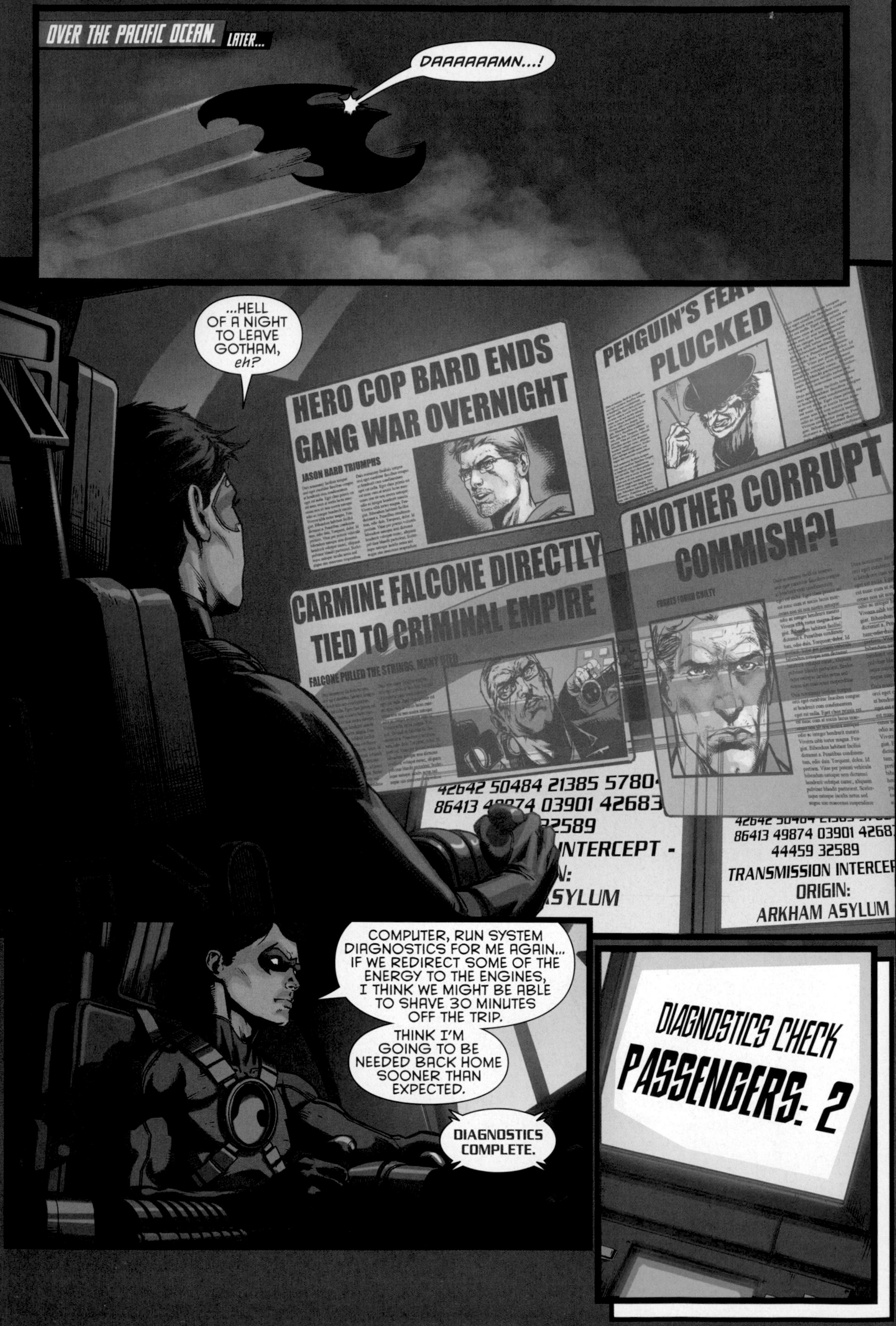

OVER THE PACIFIC OCEAN. LATER...
DAAAAAAMN...!
...HELL OF A NIGHT TO LEAVE GOTHAM, *eh?*
HERO COP BARD ENDS GANG WAR OVERNIGHT
JASON BARD TRIUMPHS
PENGUIN'S FEAT PLUCKED
ANOTHER CORRUPT COMMISH?!
CARMINE FALCONE DIRECTLY TIED TO CRIMINAL EMPIRE
FALCONE PULLED THE STRINGS, MANY SAID
42642 50484 21385 5780
86413 49874 03901 42683
32589
INTERCEPT -
ASYLUM
86413 49874 03901 4268
44459 32589
TRANSMISSION INTERCEP
ORIGIN:
ARKHAM ASYLUM
COMPUTER, RUN SYSTEM DIAGNOSTICS FOR ME AGAIN... IF WE REDIRECT SOME OF THE ENERGY TO THE ENGINES, I THINK WE MIGHT BE ABLE TO SHAVE 30 MINUTES OFF THE TRIP.
THINK I'M GOING TO BE NEEDED BACK HOME SOONER THAN EXPECTED.
DIAGNOSTICS COMPLETE.
DIAGNOSTICS CHECK
PASSENGERS: 2

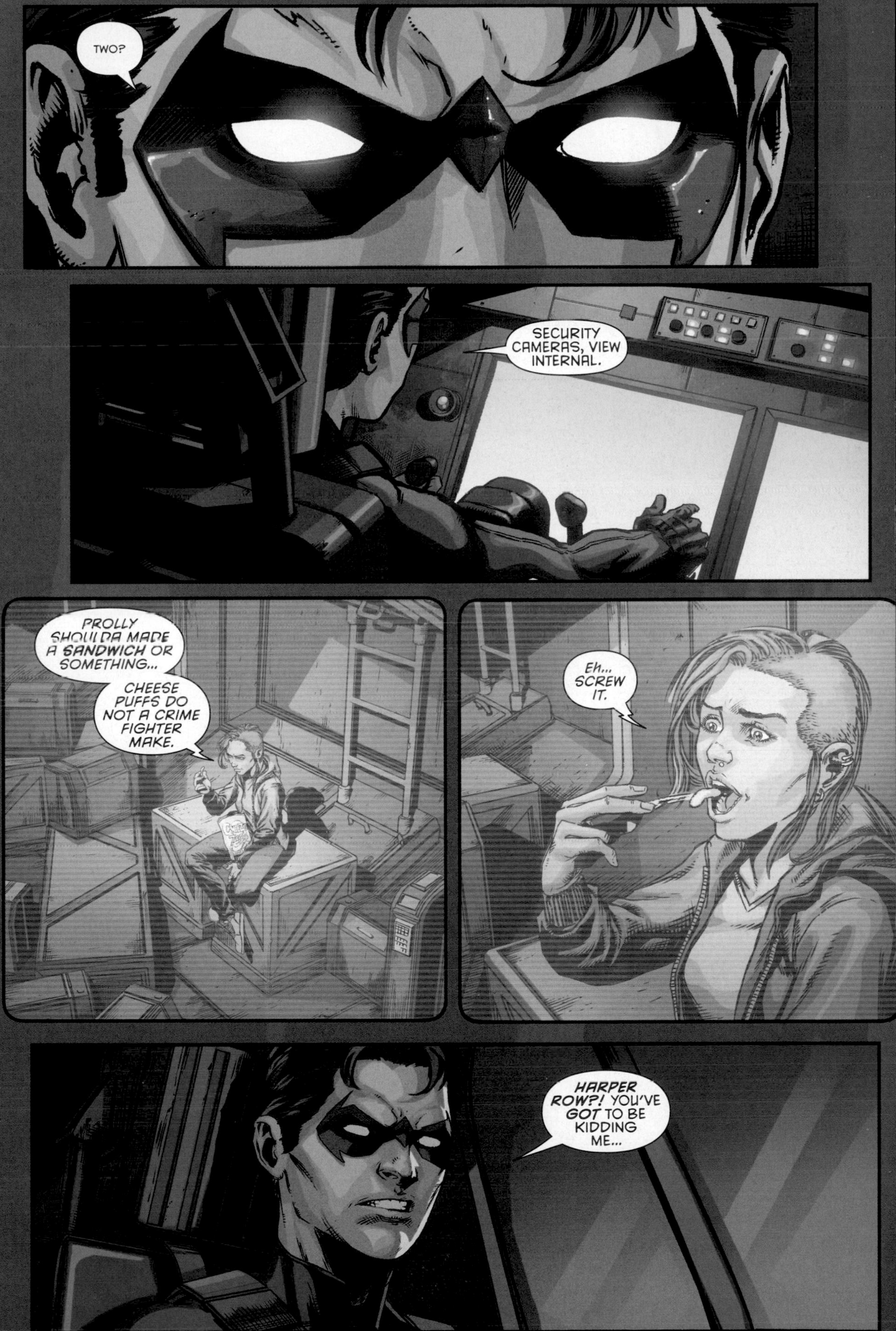
TWO?
SECURITY CAMERAS, VIEW INTERNAL.
PROLLY SHOULDA MADE A SANDWICH OR SOMETHING...
CHEESE PUFFS DO NOT A CRIME FIGHTER MAKE.
Eh... SCREW IT.
HARPER ROW?! YOU'VE GOT TO BE KIDDING ME...

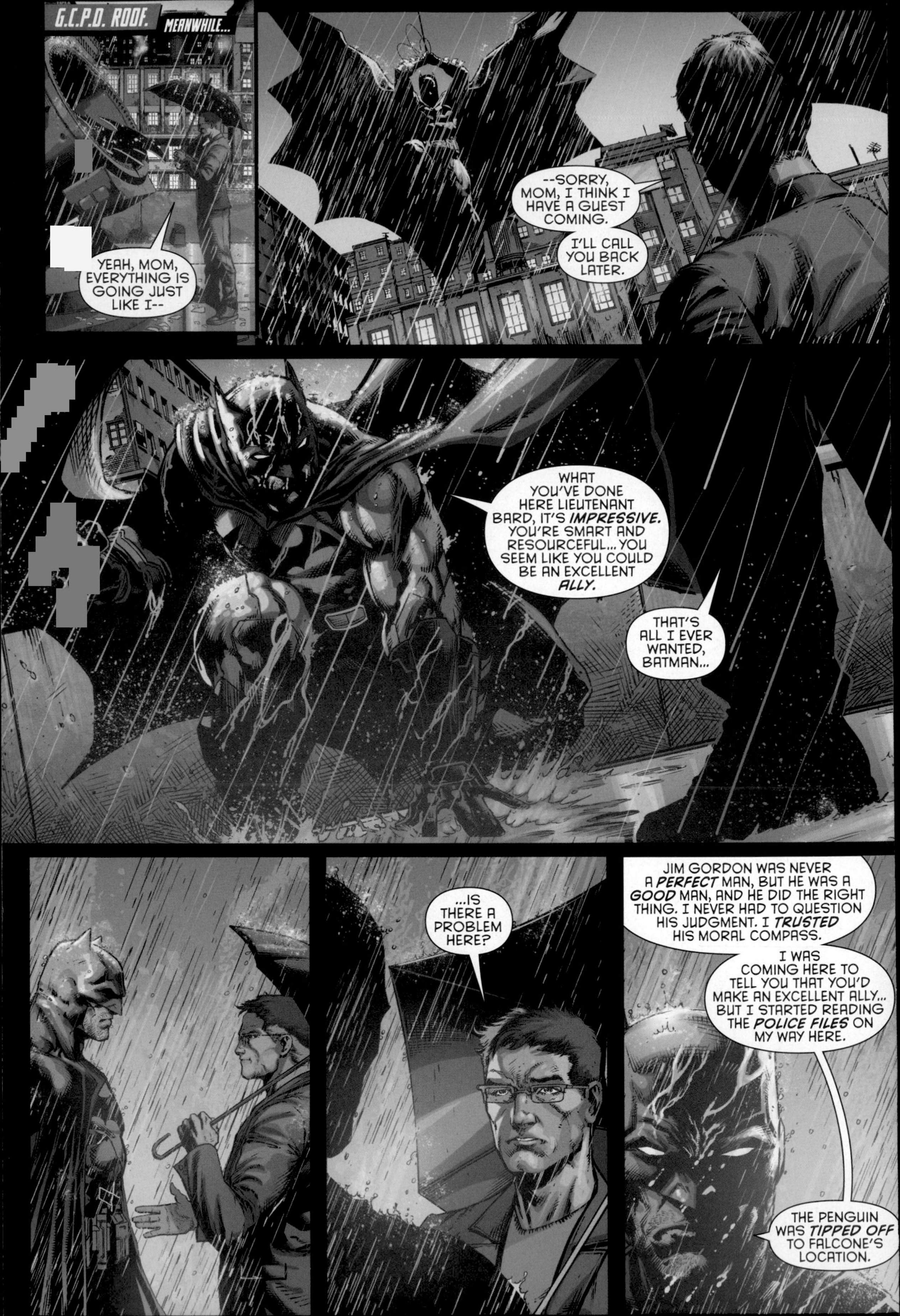
G.C.P.D. ROOF.
MEANWHILE...
YEAH, MOM, EVERYTHING IS GOING JUST LIKE I--
--SORRY, MOM, I THINK I HAVE A GUEST COMING.
I'LL CALL YOU BACK LATER.
WHAT YOU'VE DONE HERE LIEUTENANT BARD, IT'S IMPRESSIVE. YOU'RE SMART AND RESOURCEFUL... YOU SEEM LIKE YOU COULD BE AN EXCELLENT ALLY.
THAT'S ALL I EVER WANTED, BATMAN...
...IS THERE A PROBLEM HERE?
JIM GORDON WAS NEVER A PERFECT MAN, BUT HE WAS A GOOD MAN, AND HE DID THE RIGHT THING. I NEVER HAD TO QUESTION HIS JUDGMENT. I TRUSTED HIS MORAL COMPASS.
I WAS COMING HERE TO TELL YOU THAT YOU'D MAKE AN EXCELLENT ALLY... BUT I STARTED READING THE POLICE FILES ON MY WAY HERE.
THE PENGUIN WAS TIPPED OFF TO FALCONE'S LOCATION.

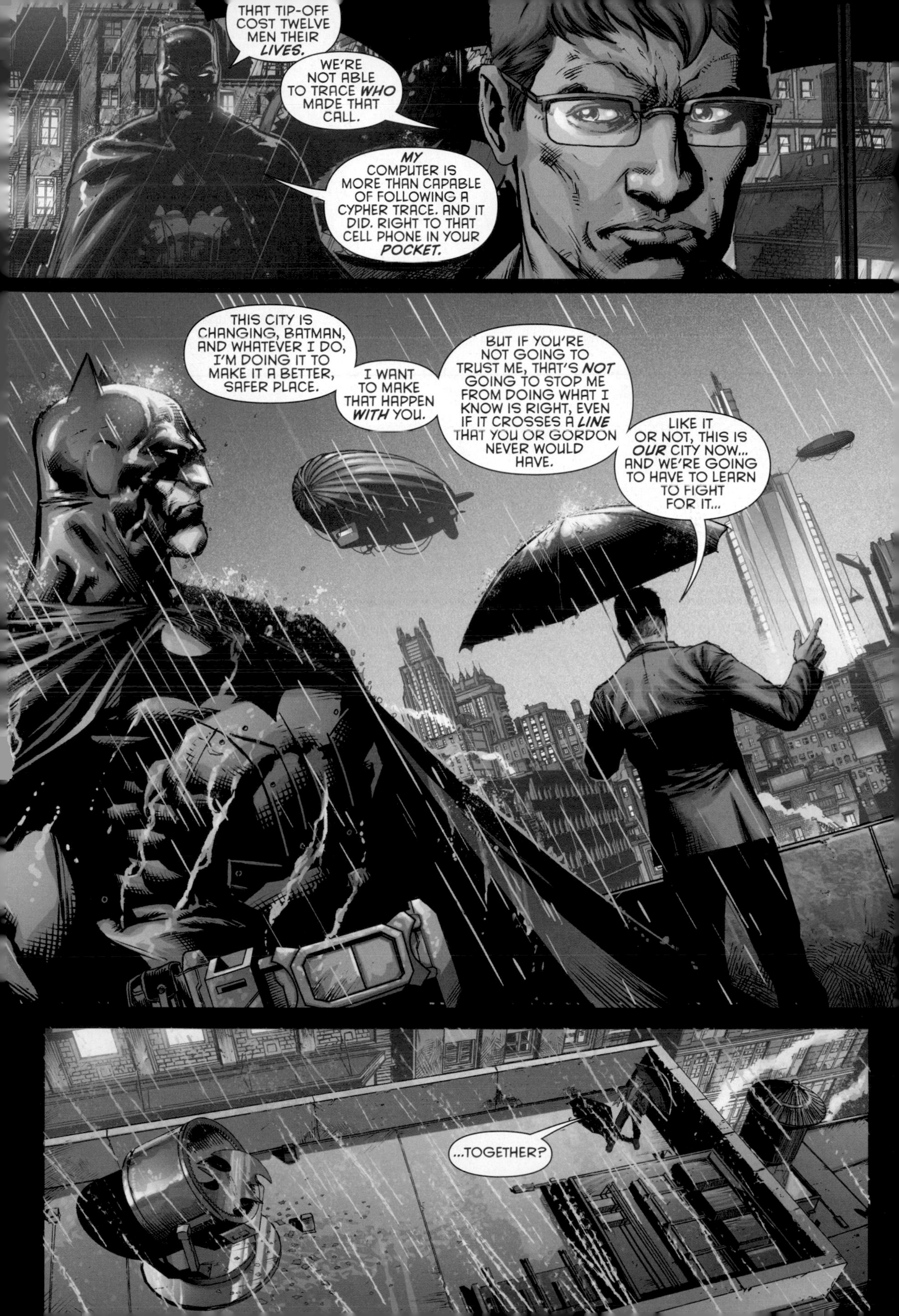
THAT TIP-OFF COST TWELVE MEN THEIR LIVES.
WE'RE NOT ABLE TO TRACE WHO MADE THAT CALL.
MY COMPUTER IS MORE THAN CAPABLE OF FOLLOWING A CYPHER TRACE. AND IT DID. RIGHT TO THAT CELL PHONE IN YOUR POCKET.
THIS CITY IS CHANGING, BATMAN, AND WHATEVER I DO, I'M DOING IT TO MAKE IT A BETTER, SAFER PLACE.
I WANT TO MAKE THAT HAPPEN WITH YOU.
BUT IF YOU'RE NOT GOING TO TRUST ME, THAT'S NOT GOING TO STOP ME FROM DOING WHAT I KNOW IS RIGHT, EVEN IF IT CROSSES A LINE THAT YOU OR GORDON NEVER WOULD HAVE.
LIKE IT OR NOT, THIS IS OUR CITY NOW... AND WE'RE GOING TO HAVE TO LEARN TO FIGHT FOR IT...
...TOGETHER?

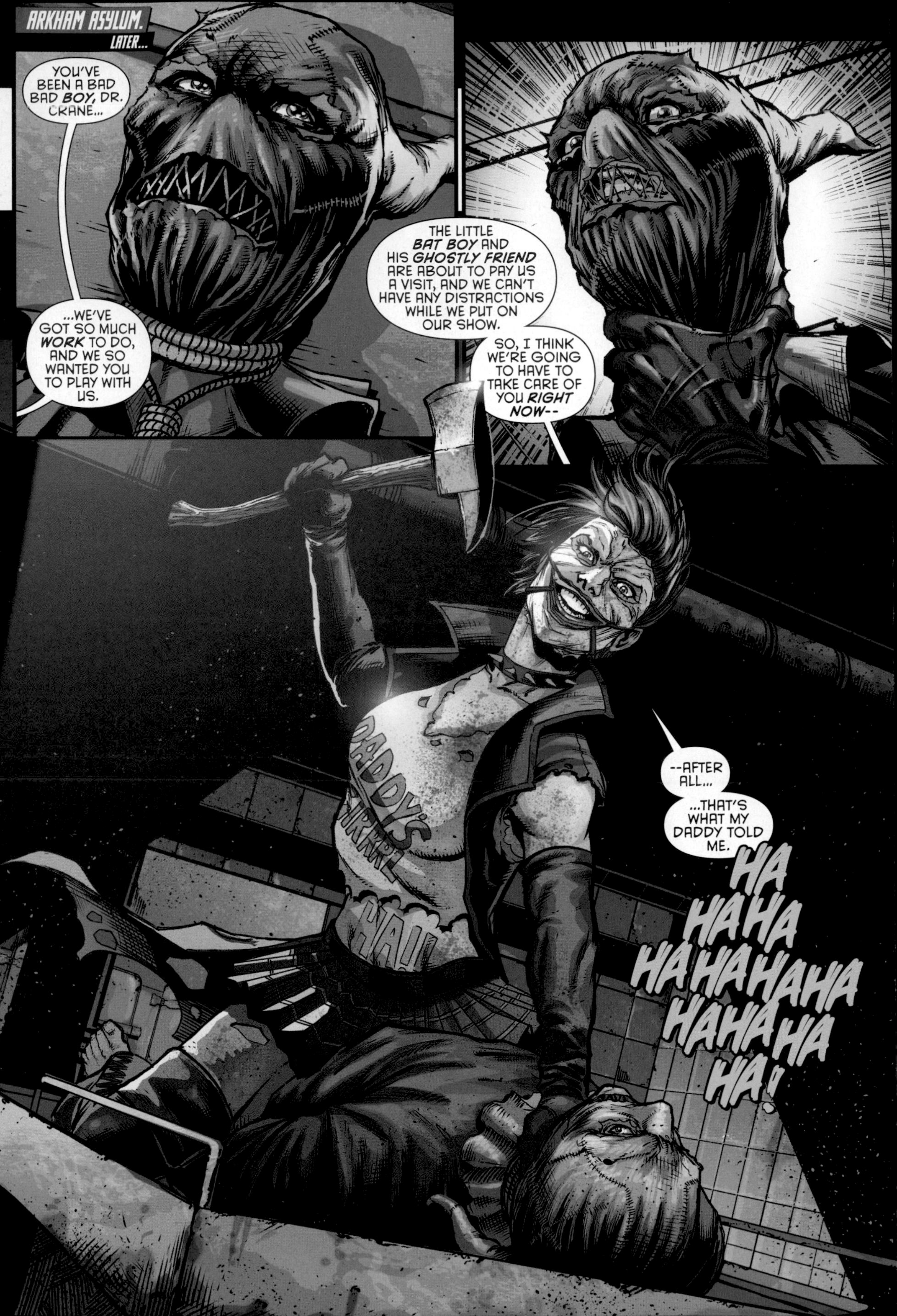

ARKHAM ASYLUM.
LATER...
YOU'VE BEEN A BAD BAD BOY, DR. CRANE...
...WE'VE GOT SO MUCH WORK TO DO, AND WE SO WANTED YOU TO PLAY WITH US.
THE LITTLE BAT BOY AND HIS GHOSTLY FRIEND ARE ABOUT TO PAY US A VISIT, AND WE CAN'T HAVE ANY DISTRACTIONS WHILE WE PUT ON OUR SHOW.
SO, I THINK WE'RE GOING TO HAVE TO TAKE CARE OF YOU RIGHT NOW--
--AFTER ALL...
...THAT'S WHAT MY DADDY TOLD ME.
HA HAHA HAHAHAHAHA HAHAHA HA HA!

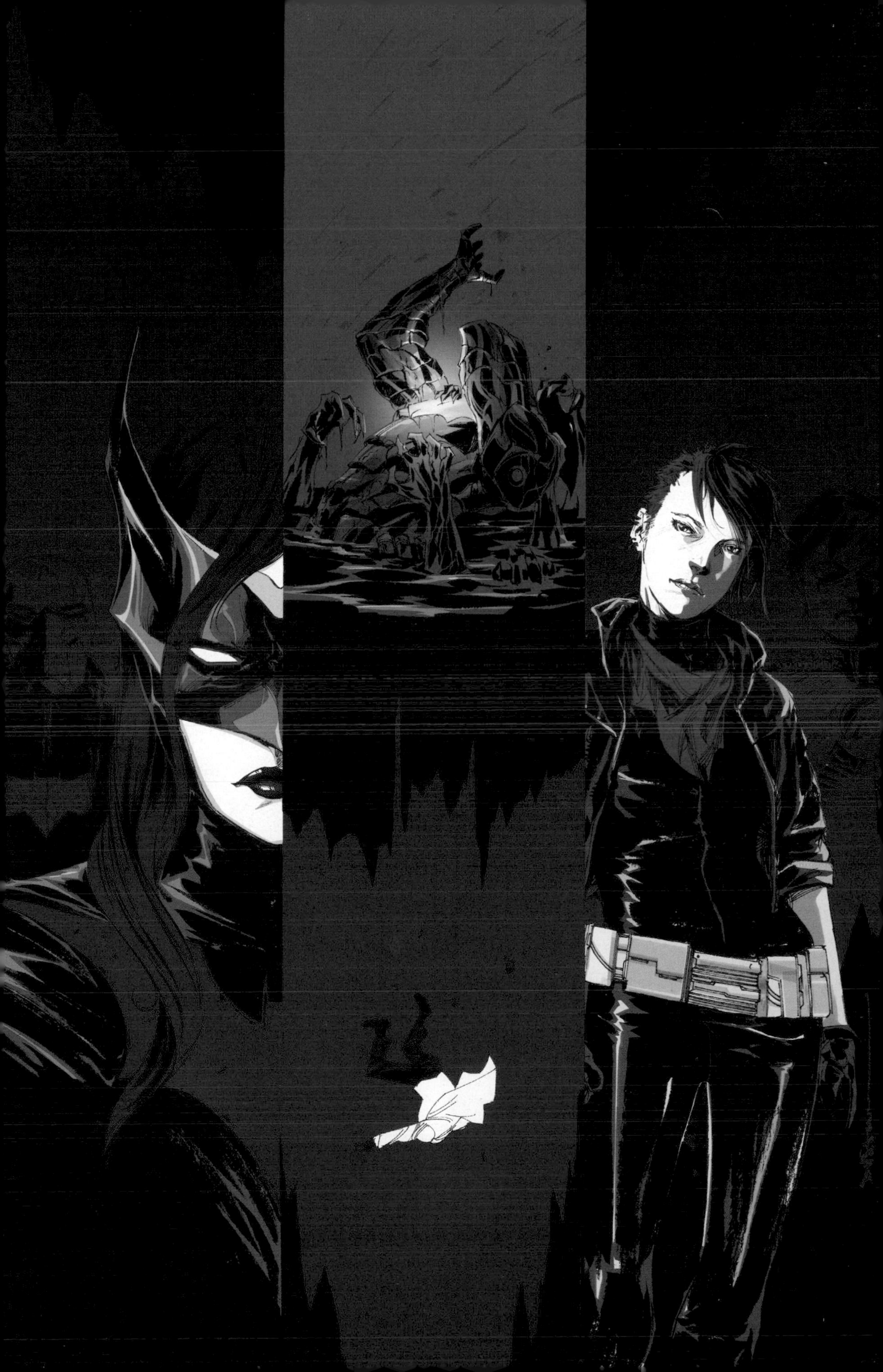

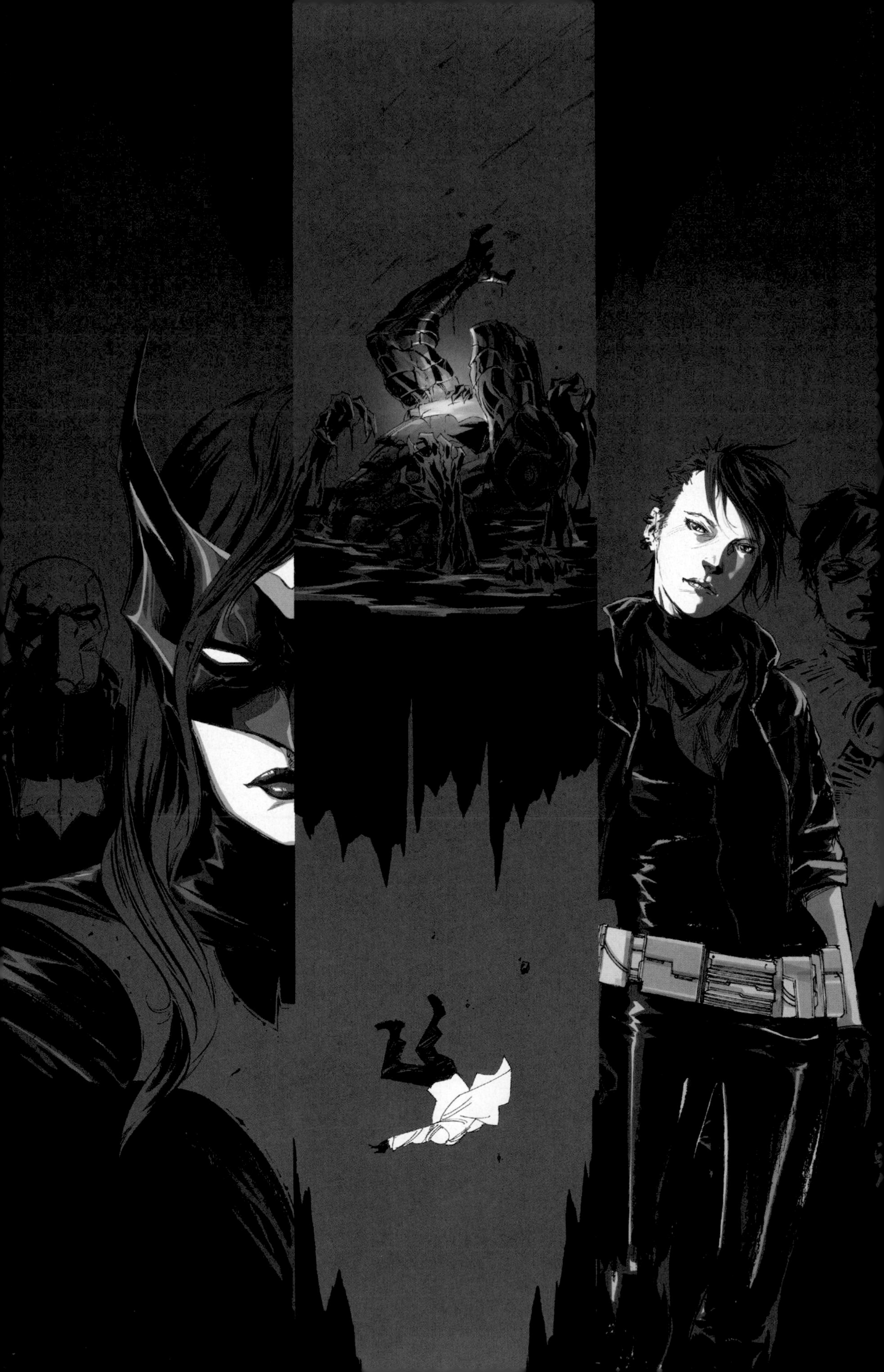

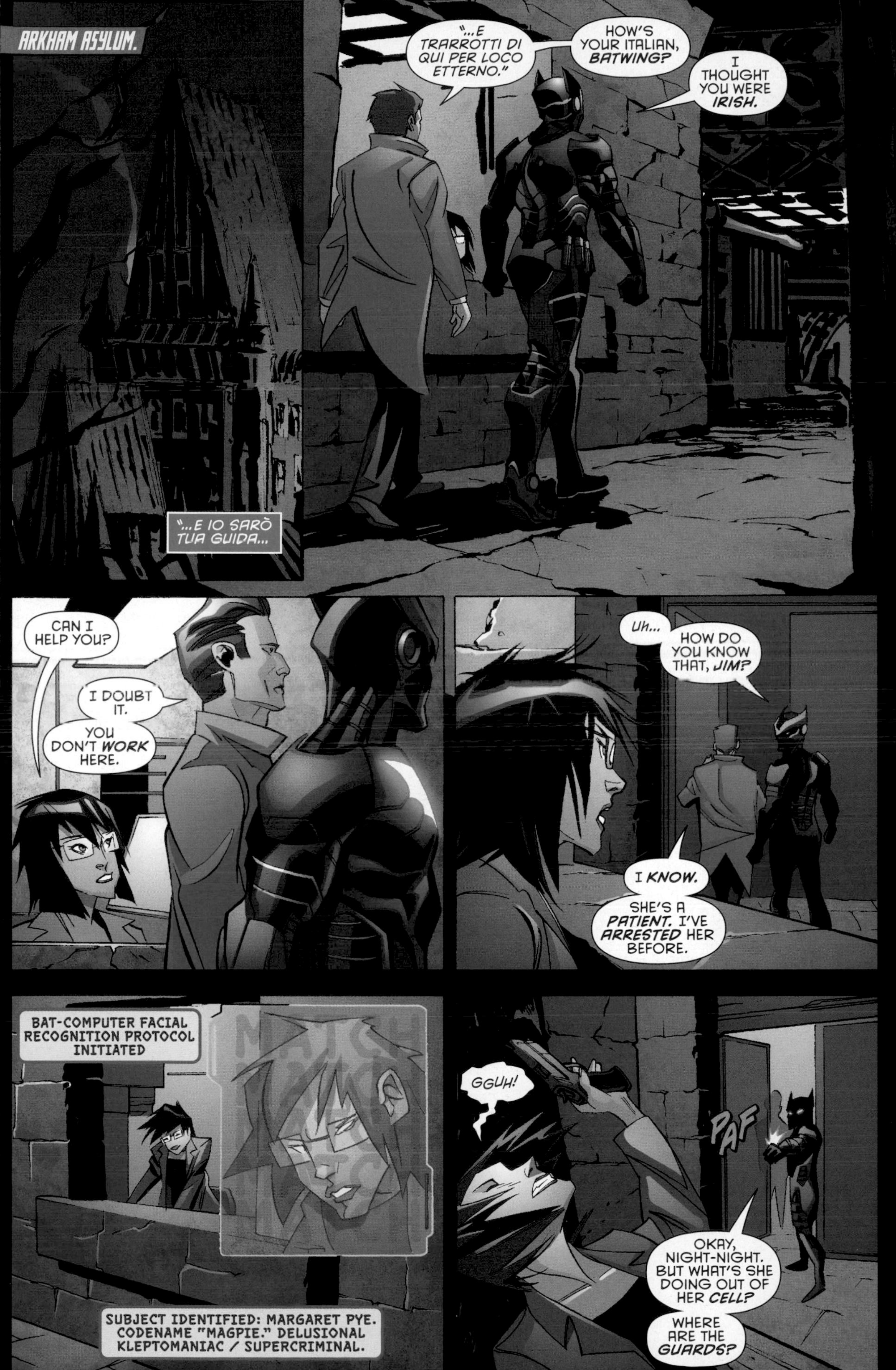
ARKHAM ASYLUM.
"...E IO SARÒ TUA GUIDA...
"...E TRARROTTI DI QUI PER LOCO ETTERNO."
HOW'S YOUR ITALIAN, BATWING?
I THOUGHT YOU WERE IRISH.
CAN I HELP YOU?
I DOUBT IT.
YOU DON'T WORK HERE.
UH...
HOW DO YOU KNOW THAT, JIM?
I KNOW.
SHE'S A PATIENT. I'VE ARRESTED HER BEFORE.
BAT-COMPUTER FACIAL RECOGNITION PROTOCOL INITIATED
MATCH
SUBJECT IDENTIFIED: MARGARET PYE. CODENAME "MAGPIE." DELUSIONAL KLEPTOMANIAC / SUPERCRIMINAL.
GGUH!
PAF
OKAY, NIGHT-NIGHT. BUT WHAT'S SHE DOING OUT OF HER CELL?
WHERE ARE THE GUARDS?

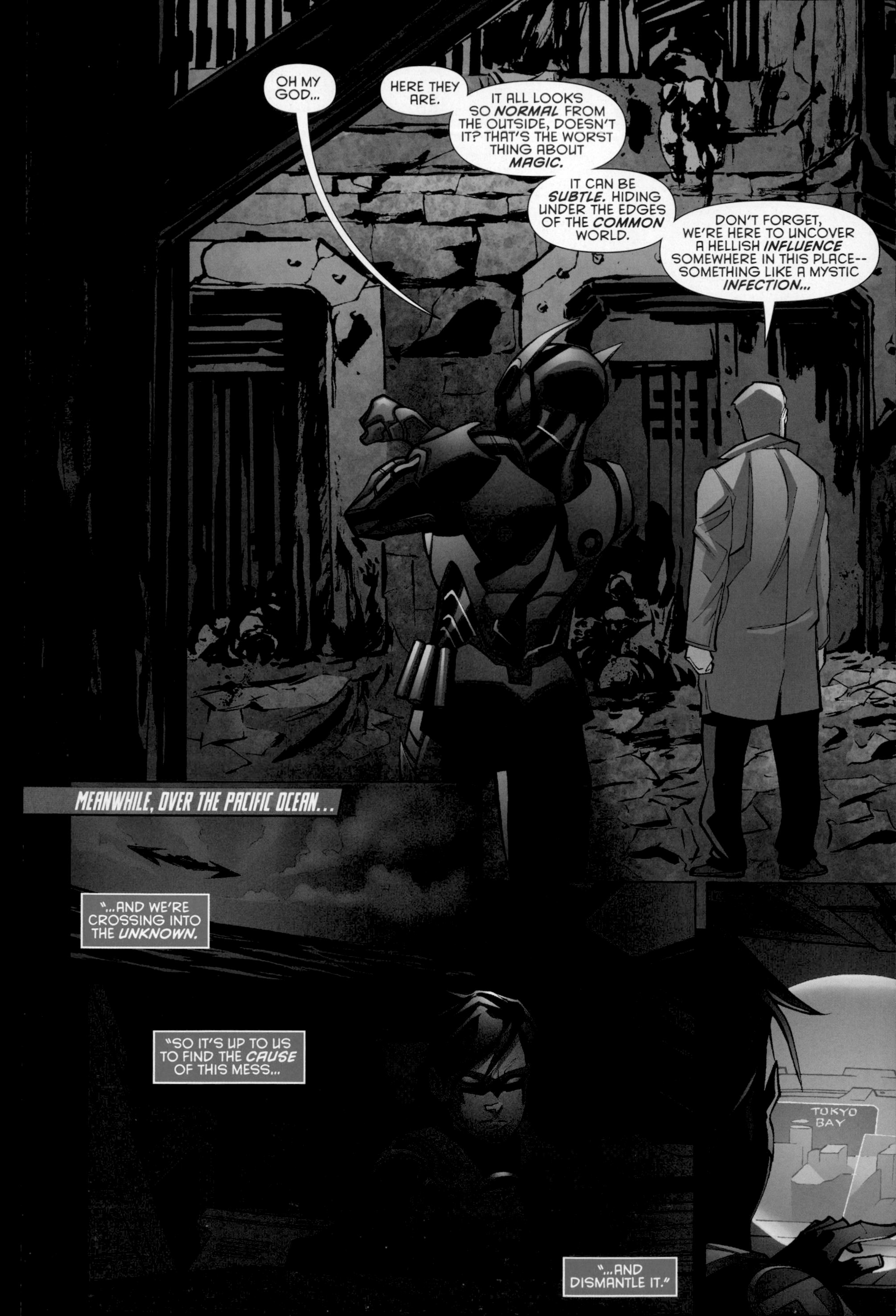
OH MY GOD...
HERE THEY ARE.
IT ALL LOOKS SO NORMAL FROM THE OUTSIDE, DOESN'T IT? THAT'S THE WORST THING ABOUT MAGIC.
IT CAN BE SUBTLE. HIDING UNDER THE EDGES OF THE COMMON WORLD.
DON'T FORGET, WE'RE HERE TO UNCOVER A HELLISH INFLUENCE SOMEWHERE IN THIS PLACE-- SOMETHING LIKE A MYSTIC INFECTION...
MEANWHILE, OVER THE PACIFIC OCEAN...
"...AND WE'RE CROSSING INTO THE UNKNOWN.
"SO IT'S UP TO US TO FIND THE CAUSE OF THIS MESS...
TOKYO BAY
"...AND DISMANTLE IT."

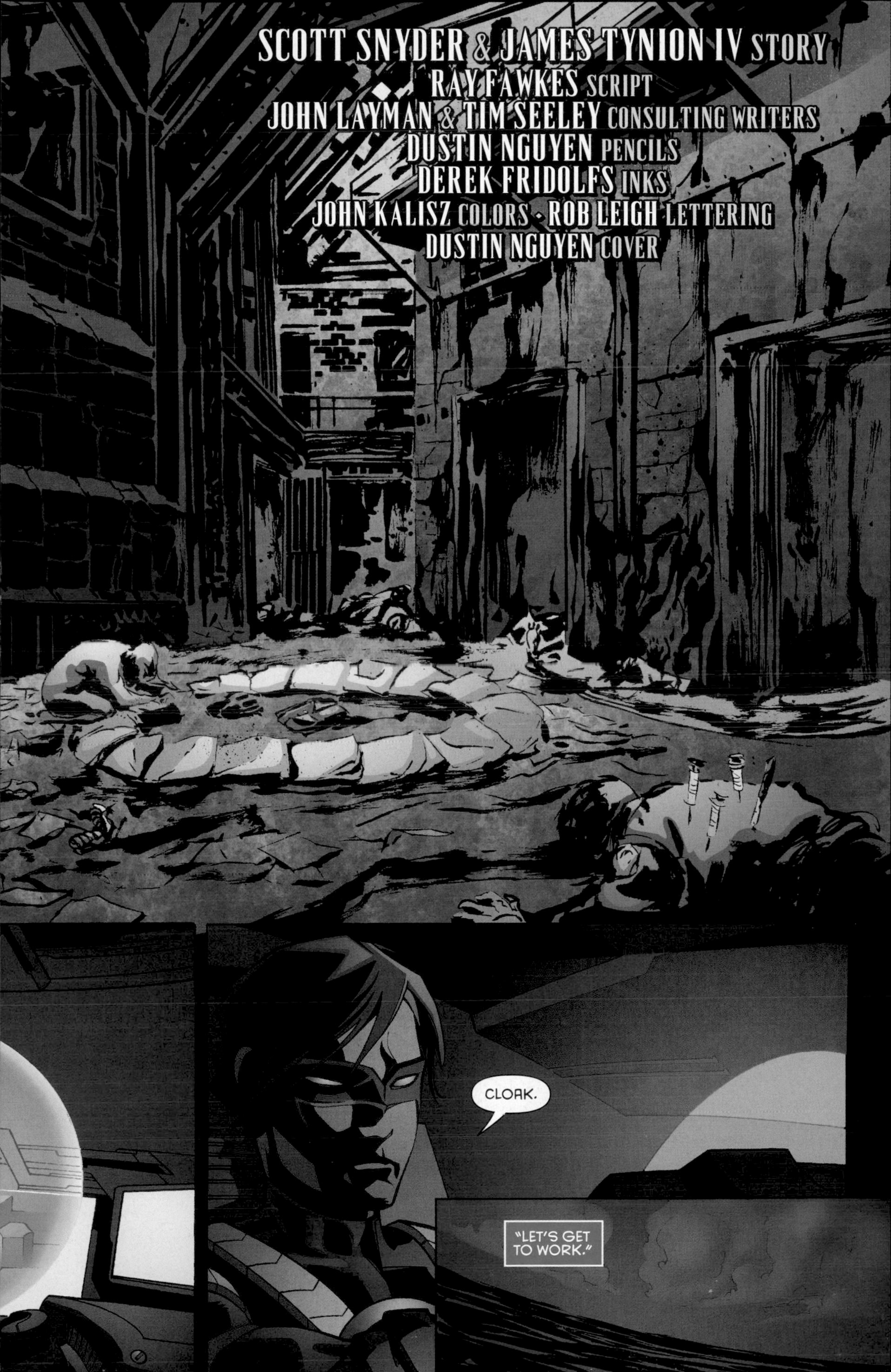
SCOTT SNYDER & JAMES TYNION IV STORY
RAY FAWKES SCRIPT
JOHN LAYMAN & TIM SEELEY CONSULTING WRITERS
DUSTIN NGUYEN PENCILS
DEREK FRIDOLFS INKS
JOHN KALISZ COLORS • ROB LEIGH LETTERING
DUSTIN NGUYEN COVER
CLOAK.
"LET'S GET TO WORK."

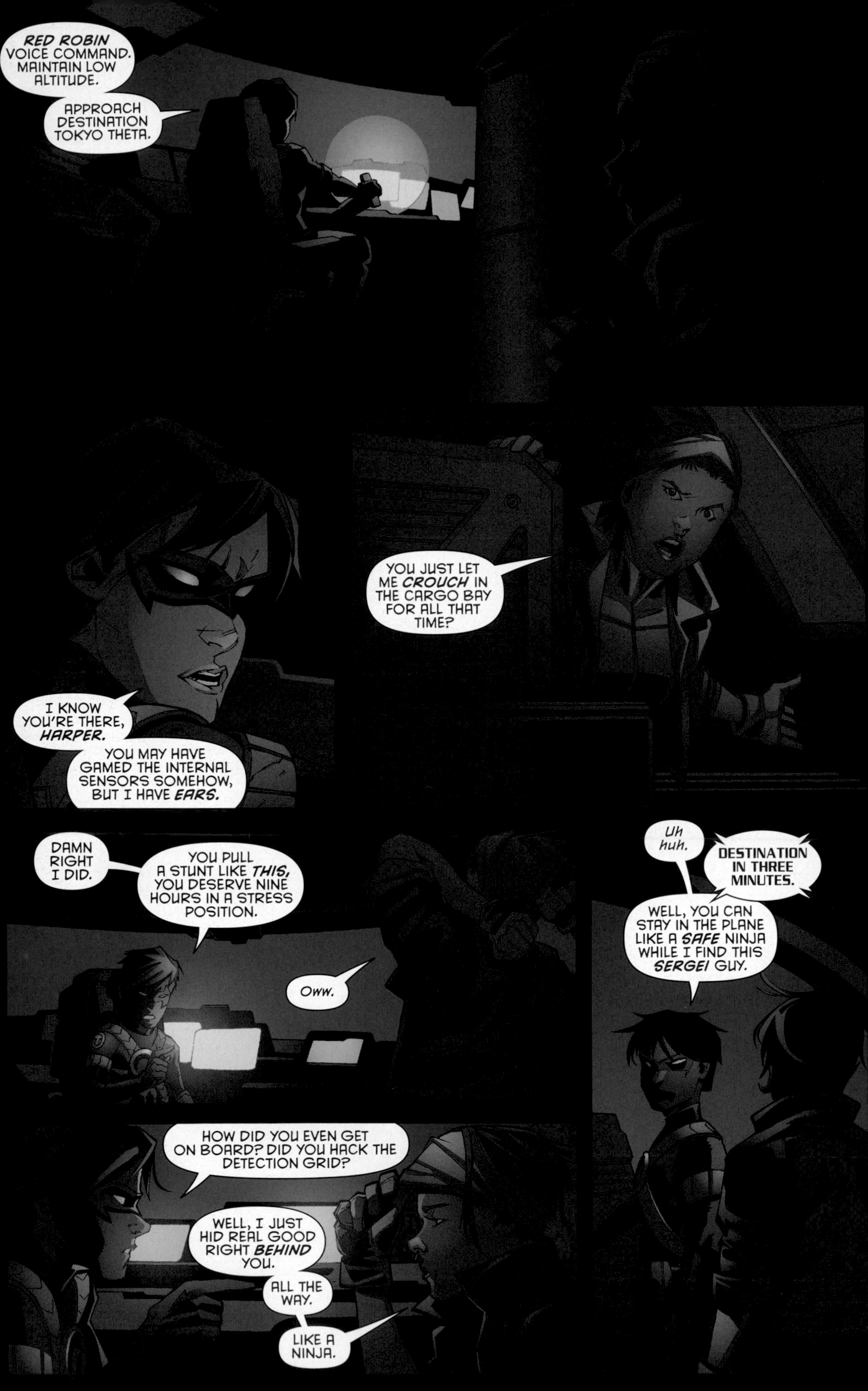
RED ROBIN VOICE COMMAND. MAINTAIN LOW ALTITUDE.
APPROACH DESTINATION TOKYO THETA.
I KNOW YOU'RE THERE, HARPER.
YOU MAY HAVE GAMED THE INTERNAL SENSORS SOMEHOW, BUT I HAVE EARS.
YOU JUST LET ME CROUCH IN THE CARGO BAY FOR ALL THAT TIME?
DAMN RIGHT I DID.
YOU PULL A STUNT LIKE THIS, YOU DESERVE NINE HOURS IN A STRESS POSITION.
Oww.
HOW DID YOU EVEN GET ON BOARD? DID YOU HACK THE DETECTION GRID?
WELL, I JUST HID REAL GOOD RIGHT BEHIND YOU.
ALL THE WAY.
LIKE A NINJA.
Uh huh.
DESTINATION IN THREE MINUTES.
WELL, YOU CAN STAY IN THE PLANE LIKE A SAFE NINJA WHILE I FIND THIS SERGEI GUY.

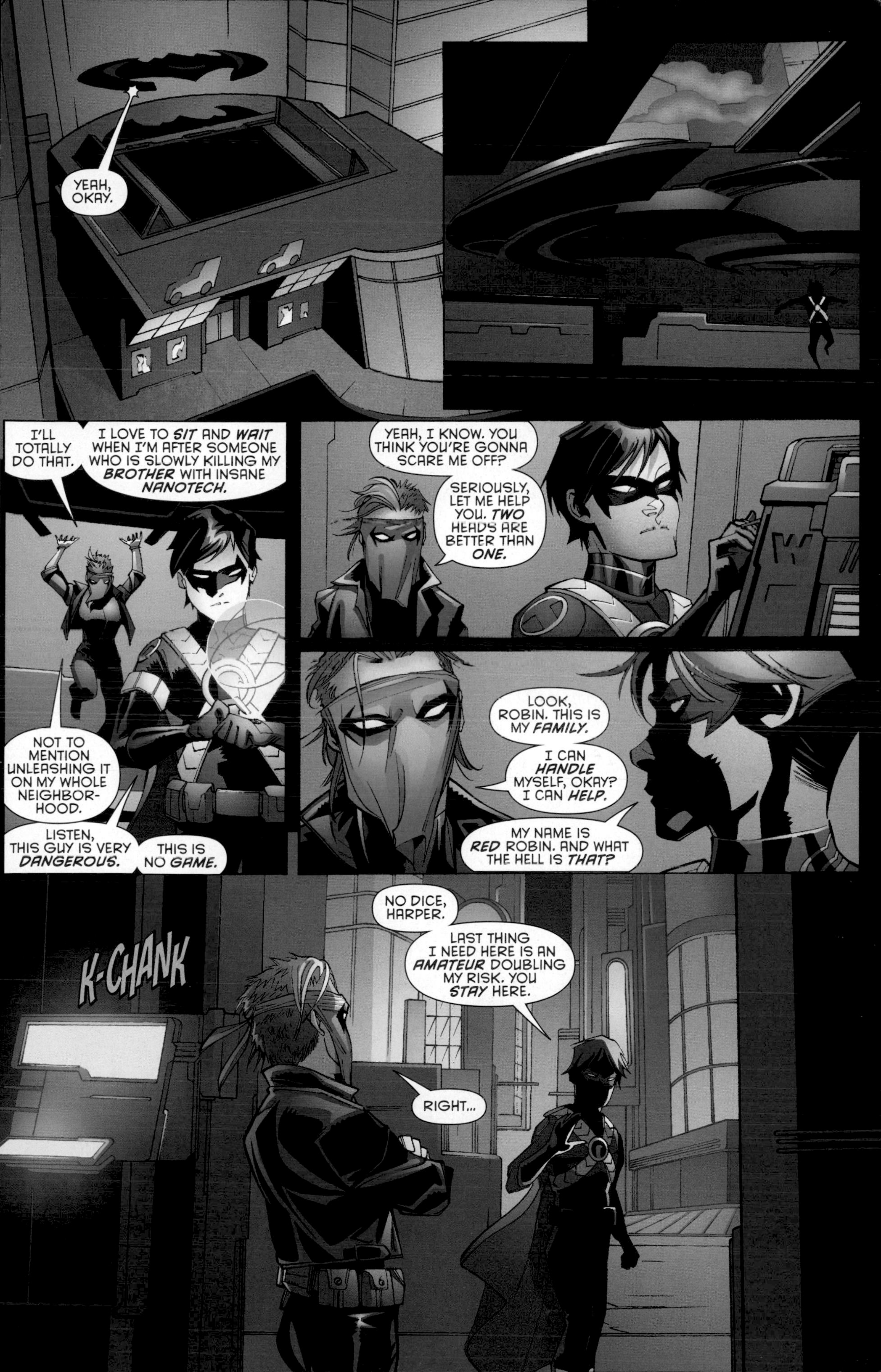
YEAH, OKAY.
I'LL TOTALLY DO THAT.
I LOVE TO SIT AND WAIT WHEN I'M AFTER SOMEONE WHO IS SLOWLY KILLING MY BROTHER WITH INSANE NANOTECH.
NOT TO MENTION UNLEASHING IT ON MY WHOLE NEIGHBOR-HOOD.
LISTEN, THIS GUY IS VERY DANGEROUS.
THIS IS NO GAME.
YEAH, I KNOW. YOU THINK YOU'RE GONNA SCARE ME OFF?
SERIOUSLY, LET ME HELP YOU. TWO HEADS ARE BETTER THAN ONE.
LOOK, ROBIN. THIS IS MY FAMILY.
I CAN HANDLE MYSELF, OKAY? I CAN HELP.
MY NAME IS RED ROBIN. AND WHAT THE HELL IS THAT?
K-CHANK
NO DICE, HARPER.
LAST THING I NEED HERE IS AN AMATEUR DOUBLING MY RISK. YOU STAY HERE.
RIGHT...

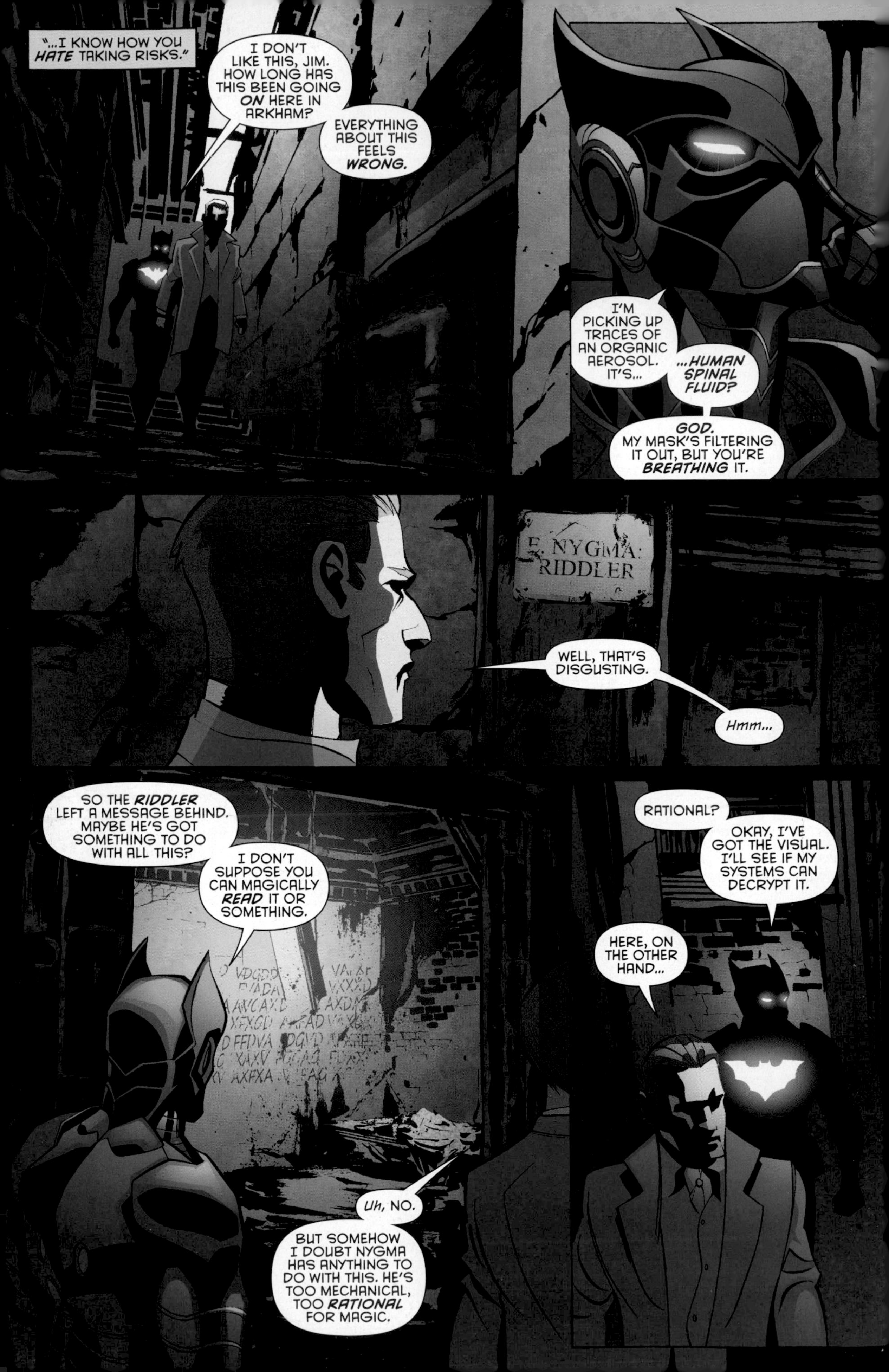
"...I KNOW HOW YOU HATE TAKING RISKS."
I DON'T LIKE THIS, JIM. HOW LONG HAS THIS BEEN GOING ON HERE IN ARKHAM?
EVERYTHING ABOUT THIS FEELS WRONG.
I'M PICKING UP TRACES OF AN ORGANIC AEROSOL. IT'S...
...HUMAN SPINAL FLUID?
GOD. MY MASK'S FILTERING IT OUT, BUT YOU'RE BREATHING IT.
E. NYGMA: RIDDLER
WELL, THAT'S DISGUSTING.
Hmm...
SO THE RIDDLER LEFT A MESSAGE BEHIND. MAYBE HE'S GOT SOMETHING TO DO WITH ALL THIS?
I DON'T SUPPOSE YOU CAN MAGICALLY READ IT OR SOMETHING.
Uh, NO.
BUT SOMEHOW I DOUBT NYGMA HAS ANYTHING TO DO WITH THIS. HE'S TOO MECHANICAL, TOO RATIONAL FOR MAGIC.
RATIONAL?
OKAY, I'VE GOT THE VISUAL. I'LL SEE IF MY SYSTEMS CAN DECRYPT IT.
HERE, ON THE OTHER HAND...

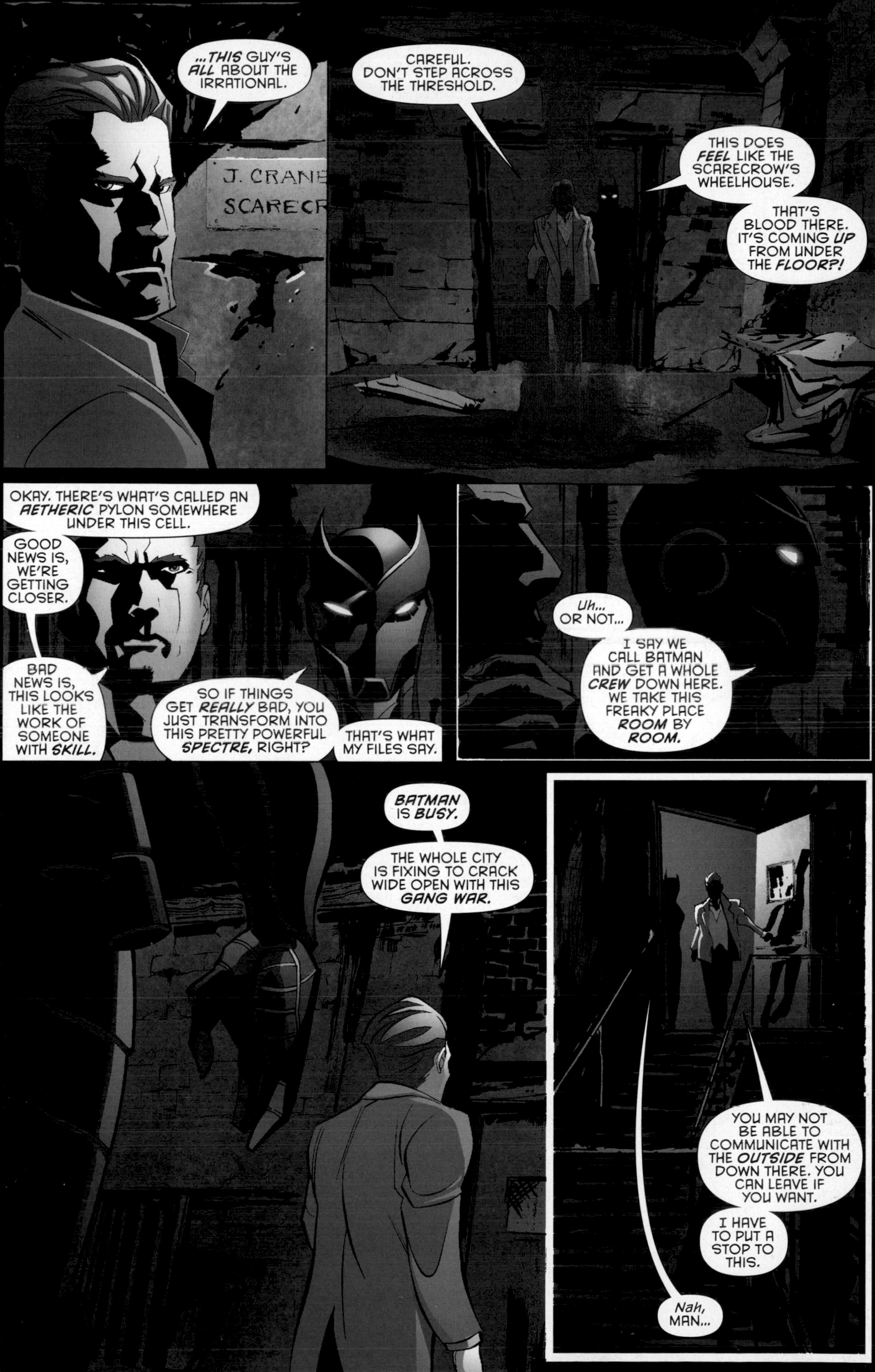
...THIS GUY'S ALL ABOUT THE IRRATIONAL.
J. CRANE SCARECR
CAREFUL. DON'T STEP ACROSS THE THRESHOLD.
THIS DOES FEEL LIKE THE SCARECROW'S WHEELHOUSE.
THAT'S BLOOD THERE. IT'S COMING UP FROM UNDER THE FLOOR?!
OKAY. THERE'S WHAT'S CALLED AN AETHERIC PYLON SOMEWHERE UNDER THIS CELL.
GOOD NEWS IS, WE'RE GETTING CLOSER.
BAD NEWS IS, THIS LOOKS LIKE THE WORK OF SOMEONE WITH SKILL.
SO IF THINGS GET REALLY BAD, YOU JUST TRANSFORM INTO THIS PRETTY POWERFUL SPECTRE, RIGHT?
THAT'S WHAT MY FILES SAY.
Uh... OR NOT...
I SAY WE CALL BATMAN AND GET A WHOLE CREW DOWN HERE. WE TAKE THIS FREAKY PLACE ROOM BY ROOM.
BATMAN IS BUSY.
THE WHOLE CITY IS FIXING TO CRACK WIDE OPEN WITH THIS GANG WAR.
YOU MAY NOT BE ABLE TO COMMUNICATE WITH THE OUTSIDE FROM DOWN THERE. YOU CAN LEAVE IF YOU WANT.
I HAVE TO PUT A STOP TO THIS.
Nah, MAN...

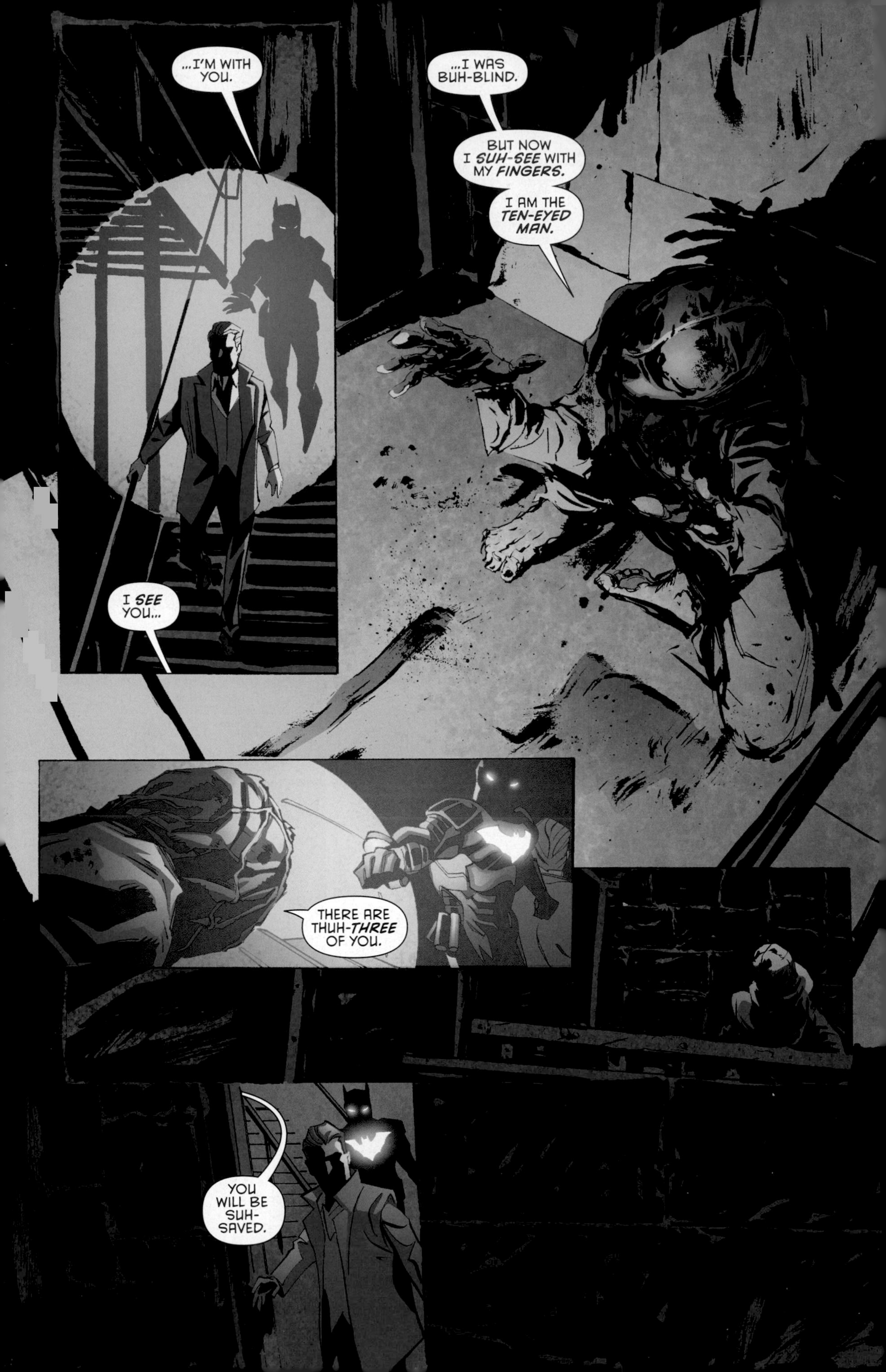
...I'M WITH YOU.
I SEE YOU...
...I WAS BUH-BLIND.
BUT NOW I SUH-SEE WITH MY FINGERS.
I AM THE TEN-EYED MAN.
THERE ARE THUH-THREE OF YOU.
YOU WILL BE SUH-SAVED.

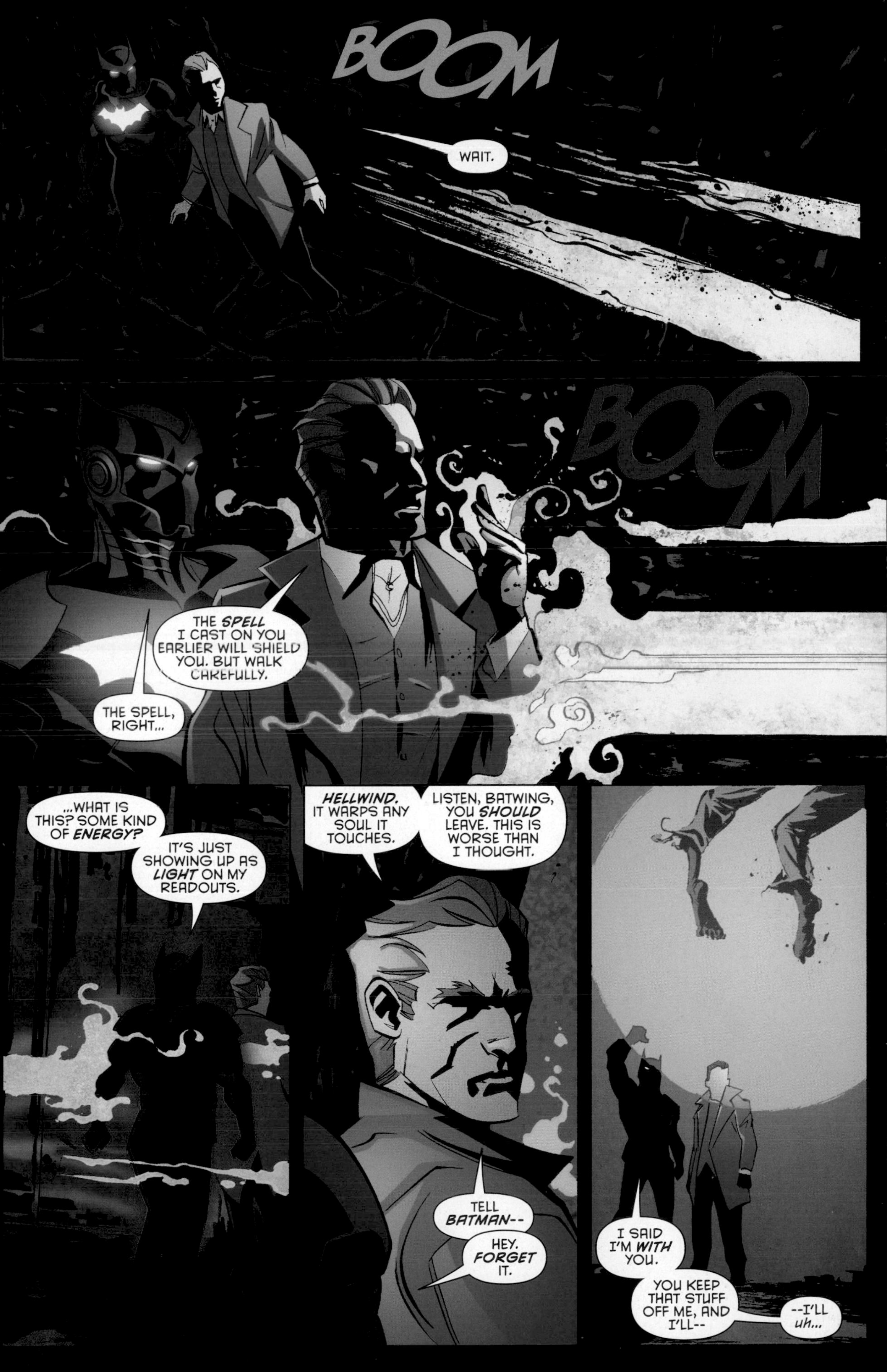
BOOM
WAIT.
BOOM
THE SPELL I CAST ON YOU EARLIER WILL SHIELD YOU. BUT WALK CAREFULLY.
THE SPELL, RIGHT...
...WHAT IS THIS? SOME KIND OF ENERGY?
IT'S JUST SHOWING UP AS LIGHT ON MY READOUTS.
HELLWIND. IT WARPS ANY SOUL IT TOUCHES.
LISTEN, BATWING, YOU SHOULD LEAVE. THIS IS WORSE THAN I THOUGHT.
TELL BATMAN--
HEY. FORGET IT.
I SAID I'M WITH YOU.
YOU KEEP THAT STUFF OFF ME, AND I'LL--
--I'LL uh...

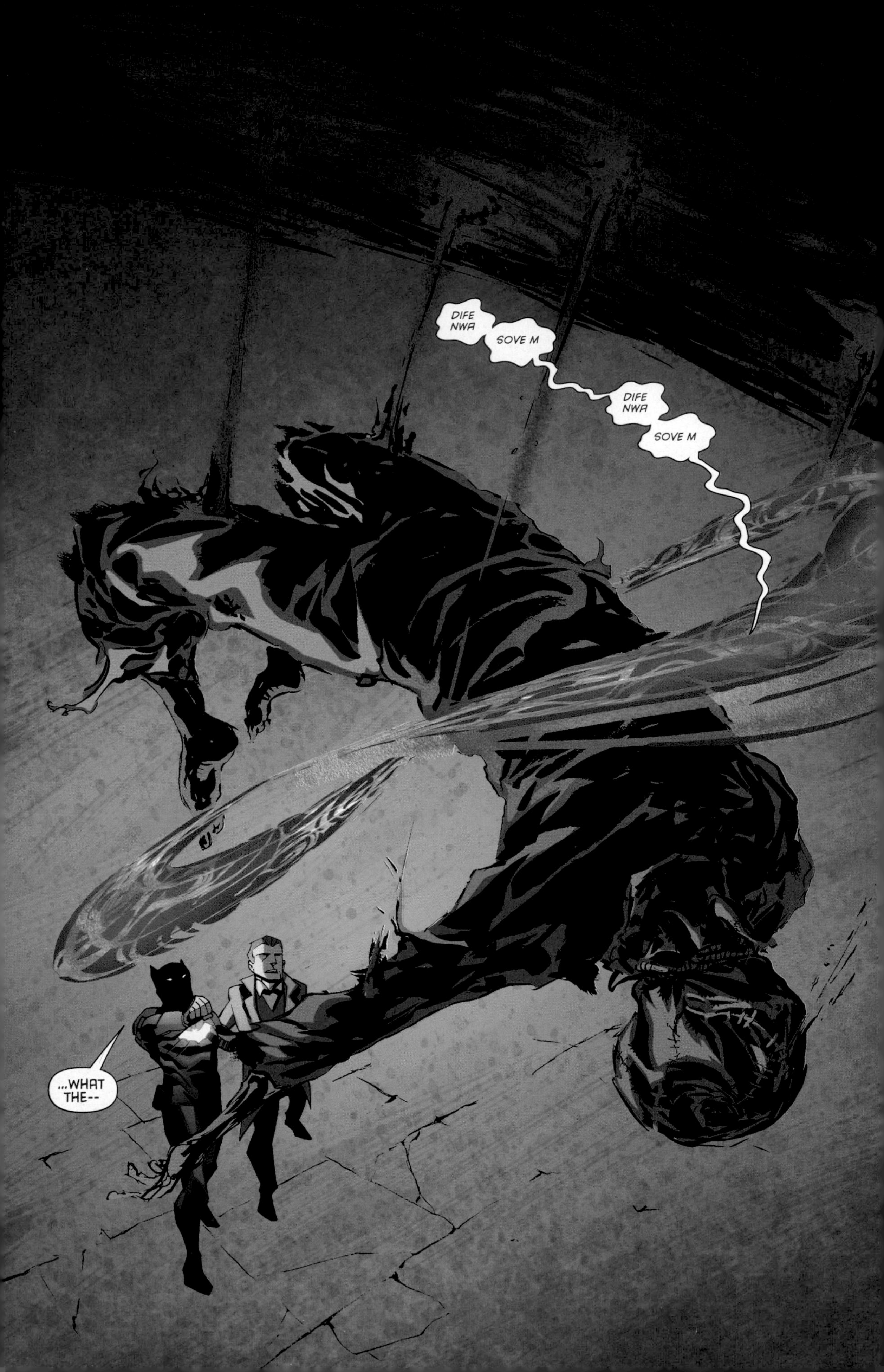
DIFE NWA
SOVE M
DIFE NWA
SOVE M
...WHAT THE--

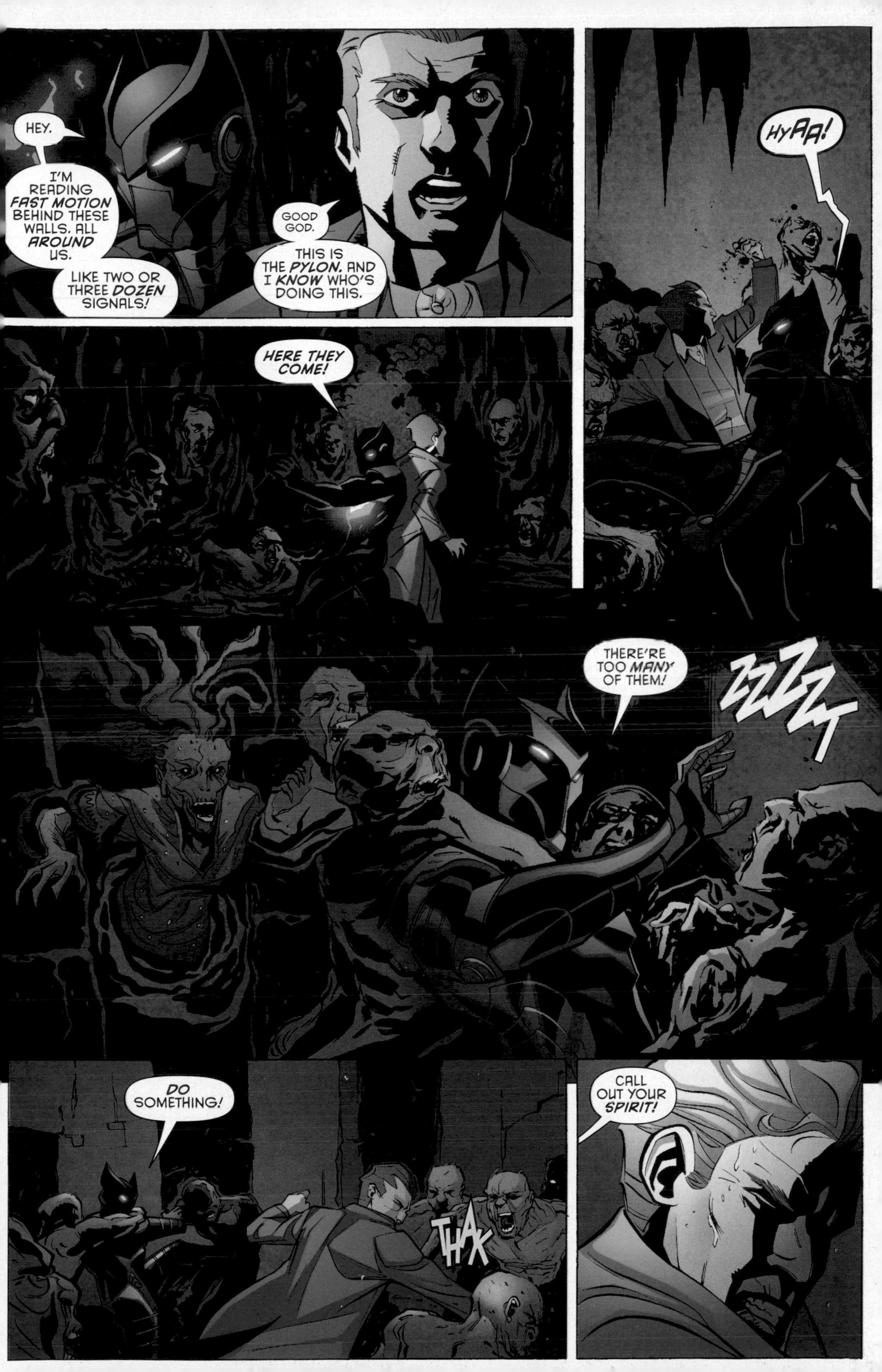
HEY.
I'M READING FAST MOTION BEHIND THESE WALLS. ALL AROUND US.
LIKE TWO OR THREE DOZEN SIGNALS!
GOOD GOD.
THIS IS THE PYLON. AND I KNOW WHO'S DOING THIS.
HYAA!
HERE THEY COME!
THERE'RE TOO MANY OF THEM!
ZZZZT
DO SOMETHING!
THAK
CALL OUT YOUR SPIRIT!

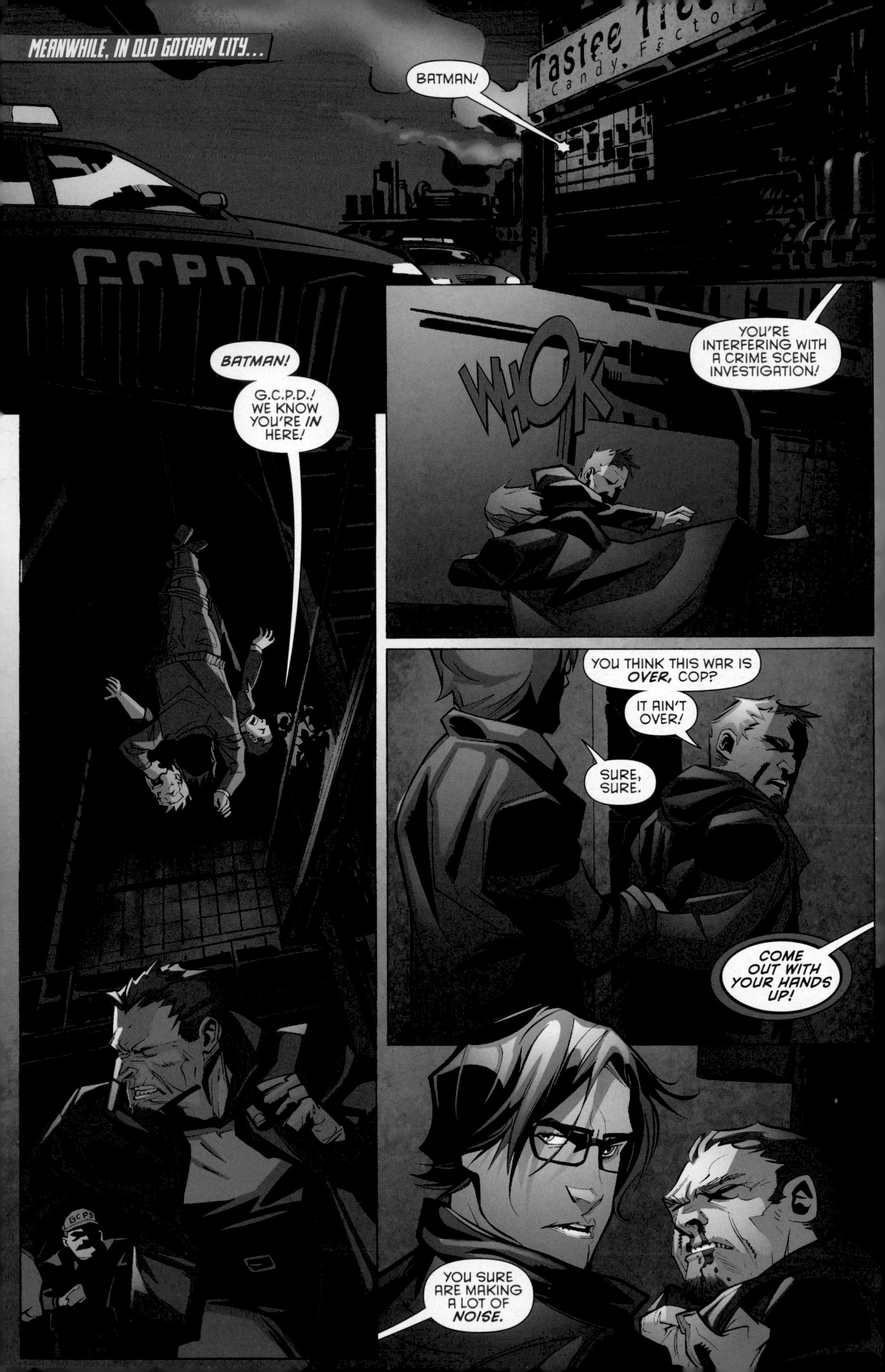
MEANWHILE, IN OLD GOTHAM CITY...
Tastee Treats Candy Factory
BATMAN!
GCPD
BATMAN!
G.C.P.D.! WE KNOW YOU'RE IN HERE!
WHOK
YOU'RE INTERFERING WITH A CRIME SCENE INVESTIGATION!
YOU THINK THIS WAR IS OVER, COP?
IT AIN'T OVER!
SURE, SURE.
COME OUT WITH YOUR HANDS UP!
GCPD
YOU SURE ARE MAKING A LOT OF NOISE.

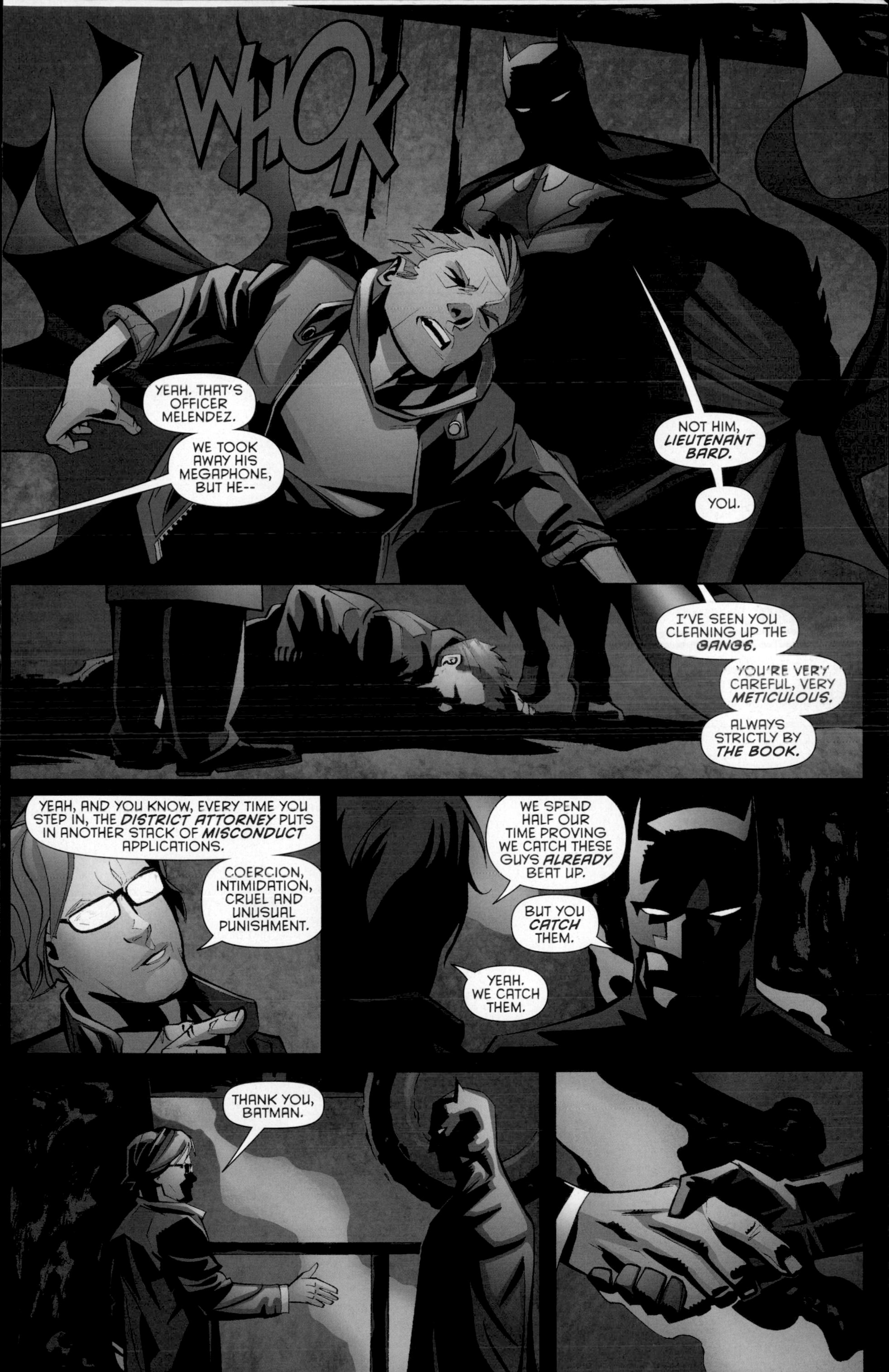
WHOK
YEAH. THAT'S OFFICER MELENDEZ.
WE TOOK AWAY HIS MEGAPHONE, BUT HE--
NOT HIM, LIEUTENANT BARD.
YOU.
I'VE SEEN YOU CLEANING UP THE GANGS.
YOU'RE VERY CAREFUL, VERY METICULOUS.
ALWAYS STRICTLY BY THE BOOK.
YEAH, AND YOU KNOW, EVERY TIME YOU STEP IN, THE DISTRICT ATTORNEY PUTS IN ANOTHER STACK OF MISCONDUCT APPLICATIONS.
COERCION, INTIMIDATION, CRUEL AND UNUSUAL PUNISHMENT.
WE SPEND HALF OUR TIME PROVING WE CATCH THESE GUYS ALREADY BEAT UP.
BUT YOU CATCH THEM.
YEAH. WE CATCH THEM.
THANK YOU, BATMAN.

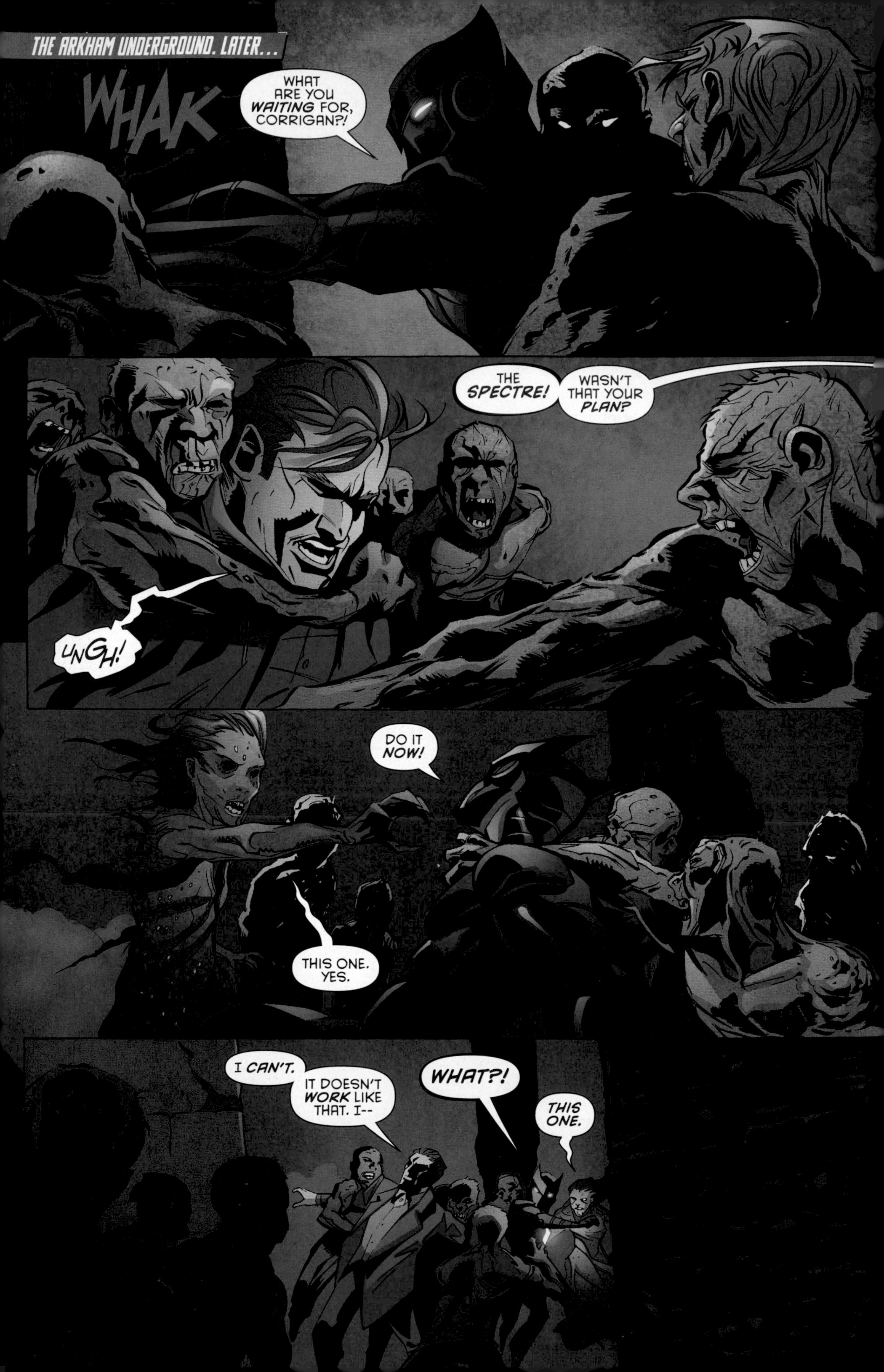
THE ARKHAM UNDERGROUND. LATER...
WHAK
WHAT ARE YOU WAITING FOR, CORRIGAN?!
THE SPECTRE!
WASN'T THAT YOUR PLAN?
UNGH!
DO IT NOW!
THIS ONE. YES.
I CAN'T.
IT DOESN'T WORK LIKE THAT. I--
WHAT?!
THIS ONE.

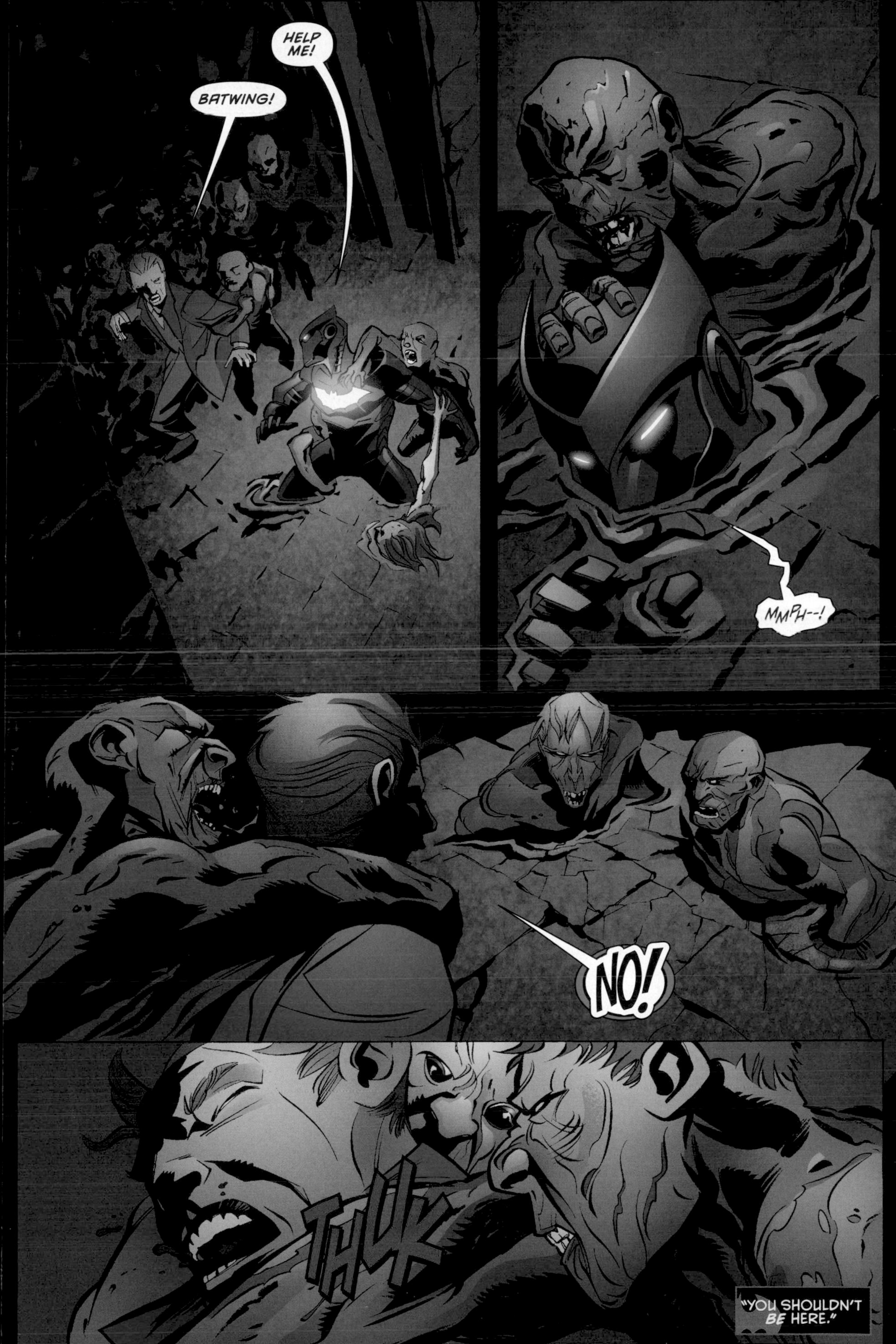
BATWING!
HELP ME!
MMPH--!
NO!
THUK
"YOU SHOULDN'T BE HERE."

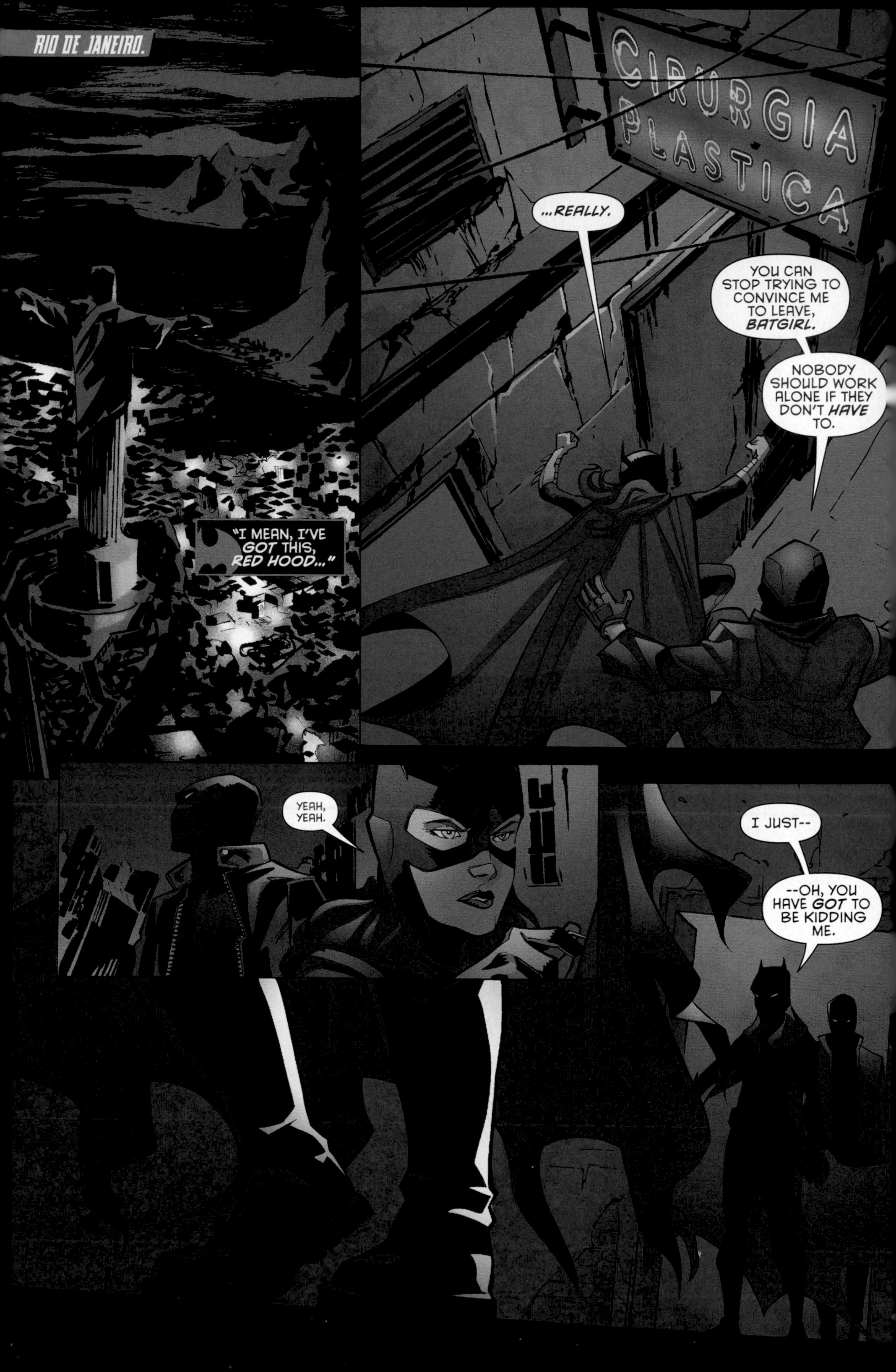

RIO DE JANEIRO.
"I MEAN, I'VE GOT THIS, RED HOOD..."
CIRURGIA PLASTICA
...REALLY.
YOU CAN STOP TRYING TO CONVINCE ME TO LEAVE, BATGIRL.
NOBODY SHOULD WORK ALONE IF THEY DON'T HAVE TO.
YEAH, YEAH.
I JUST--
--OH, YOU HAVE GOT TO BE KIDDING ME.

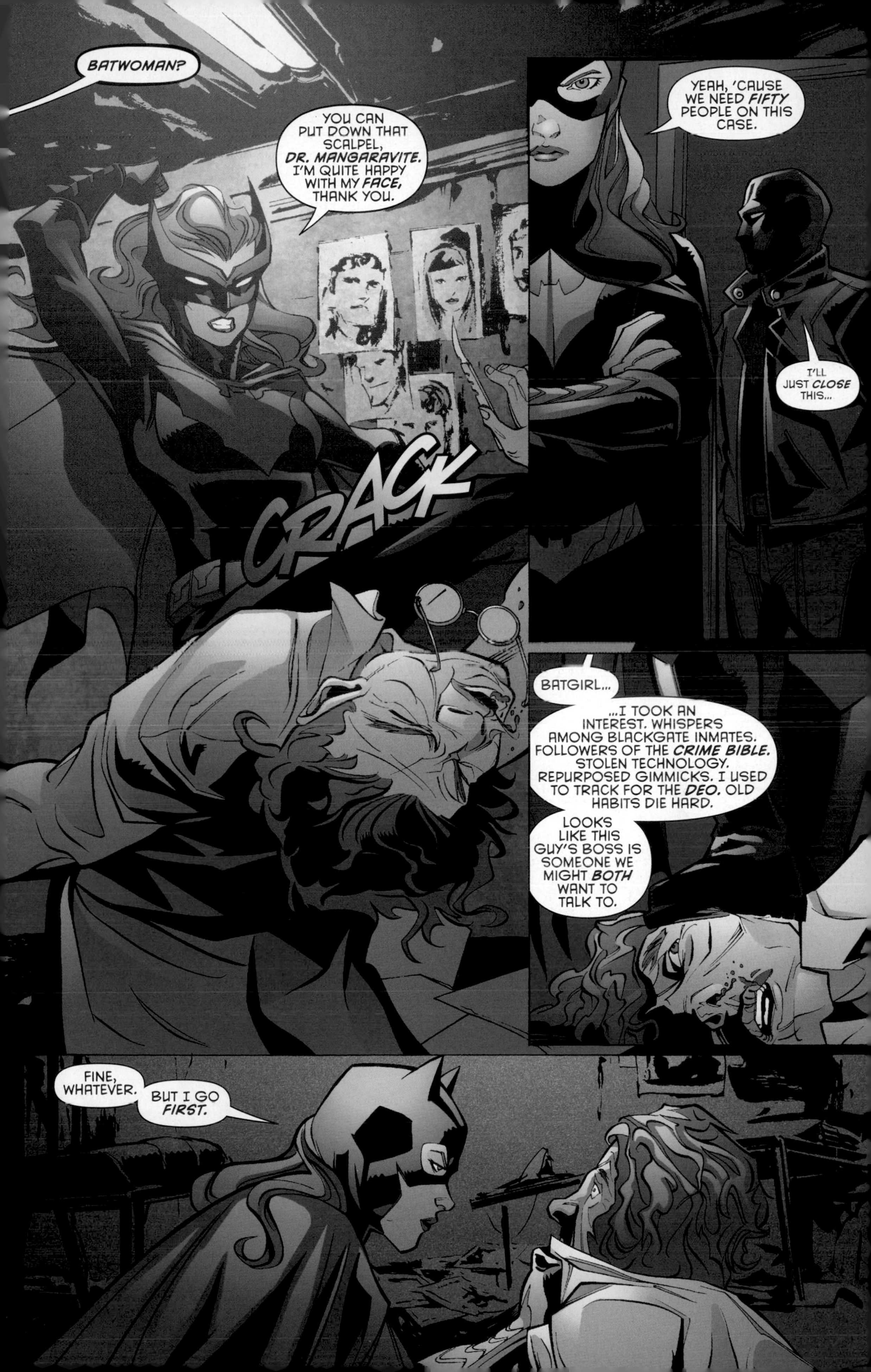
BATWOMAN?
YOU CAN PUT DOWN THAT SCALPEL, DR. MANGARAVITE. I'M QUITE HAPPY WITH MY FACE, THANK YOU.
YEAH, 'CAUSE WE NEED FIFTY PEOPLE ON THIS CASE.
I'LL JUST CLOSE THIS...
CRACK
BATGIRL...
...I TOOK AN INTEREST. WHISPERS AMONG BLACKGATE INMATES. FOLLOWERS OF THE CRIME BIBLE. STOLEN TECHNOLOGY. REPURPOSED GIMMICKS. I USED TO TRACK FOR THE DEO. OLD HABITS DIE HARD.
LOOKS LIKE THIS GUY'S BOSS IS SOMEONE WE MIGHT BOTH WANT TO TALK TO.
FINE, WHATEVER.
BUT I GO FIRST.

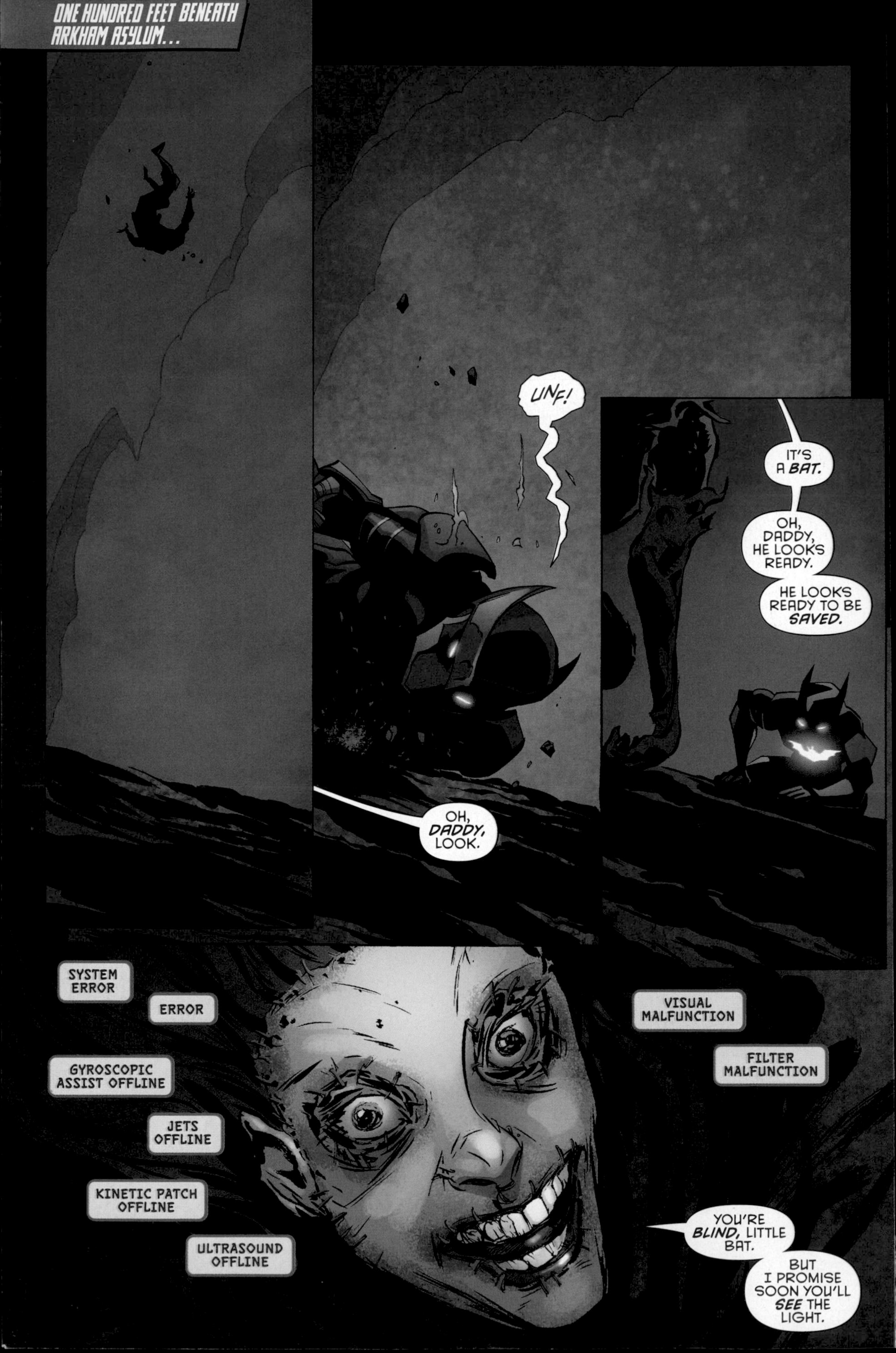
ONE HUNDRED FEET BENEATH ARKHAM ASYLUM...
UNF!
OH, DADDY, LOOK.
IT'S A BAT.
OH, DADDY, HE LOOKS READY.
HE LOOKS READY TO BE SAVED.
SYSTEM ERROR
ERROR
GYROSCOPIC ASSIST OFFLINE
JETS OFFLINE
KINETIC PATCH OFFLINE
ULTRASOUND OFFLINE
VISUAL MALFUNCTION
FILTER MALFUNCTION
YOU'RE BLIND, LITTLE BAT.
BUT I PROMISE SOON YOU'LL SEE THE LIGHT.

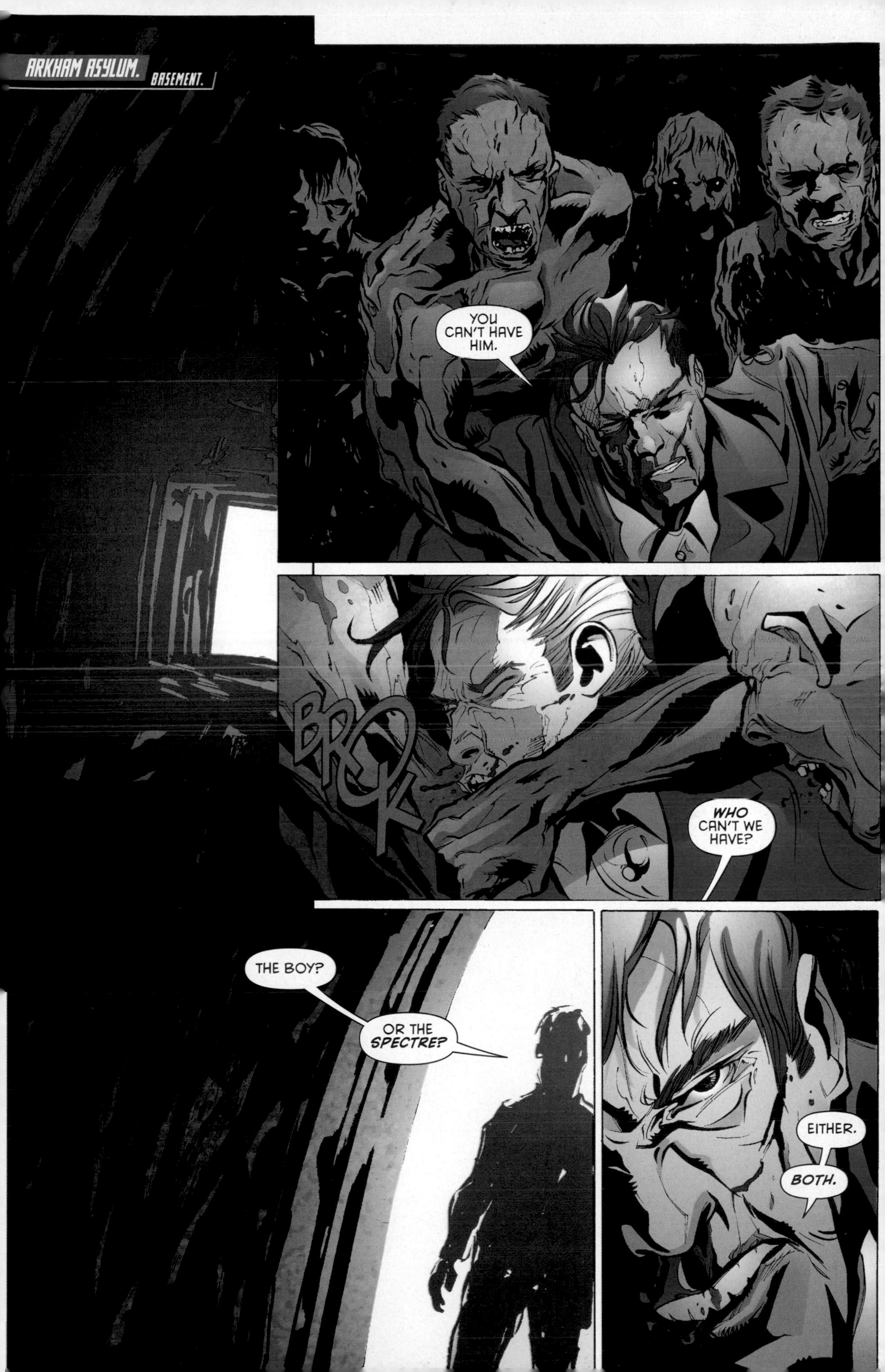
ARKHAM ASYLUM.
BASEMENT.
YOU CAN'T HAVE HIM.
BROK
WHO CAN'T WE HAVE?
THE BOY?
OR THE SPECTRE?
EITHER.
BOTH.

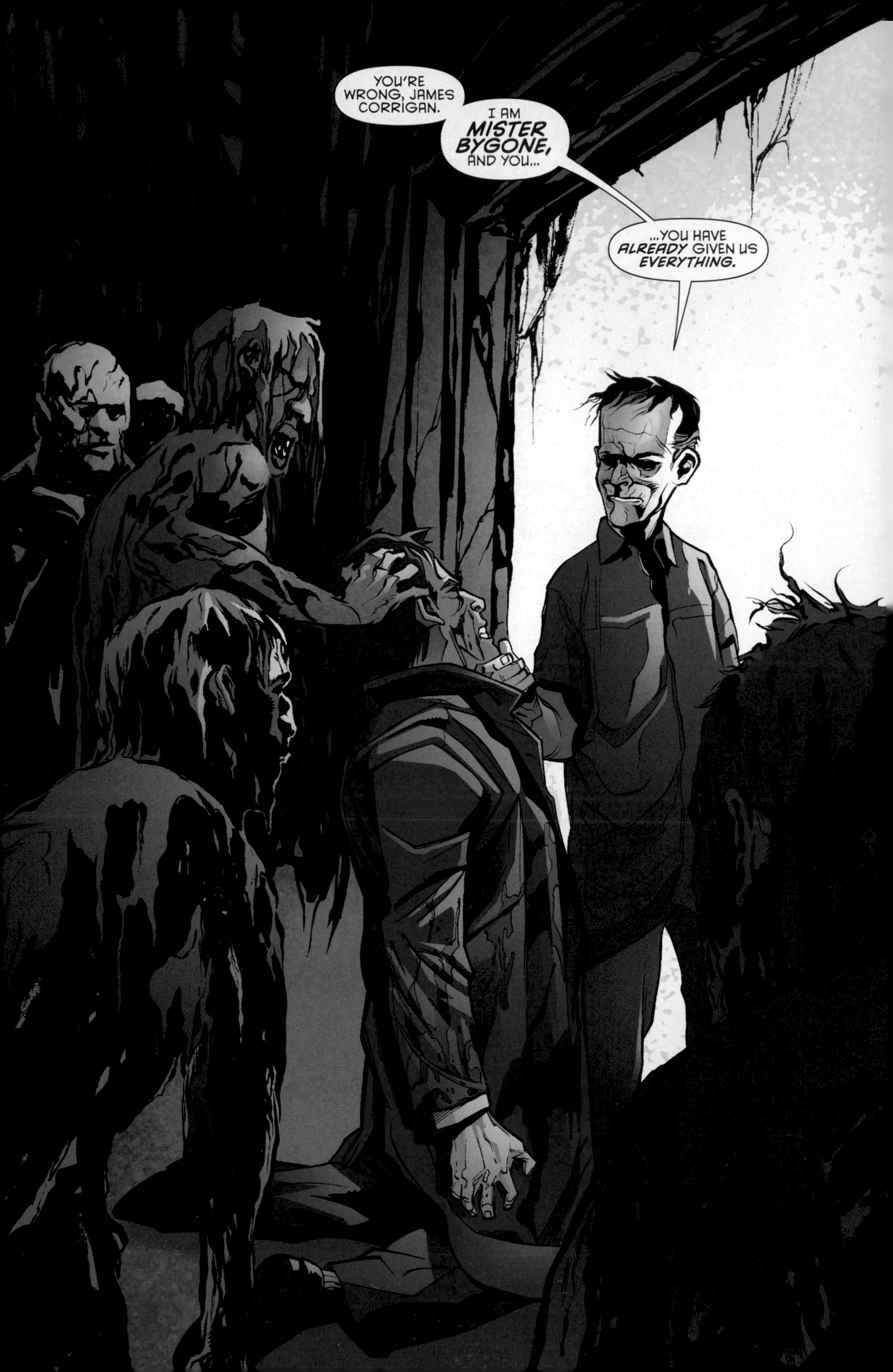
YOU'RE WRONG, JAMES CORRIGAN.
I AM MISTER BYGONE, AND YOU...
...YOU HAVE ALREADY GIVEN US EVERYTHING.

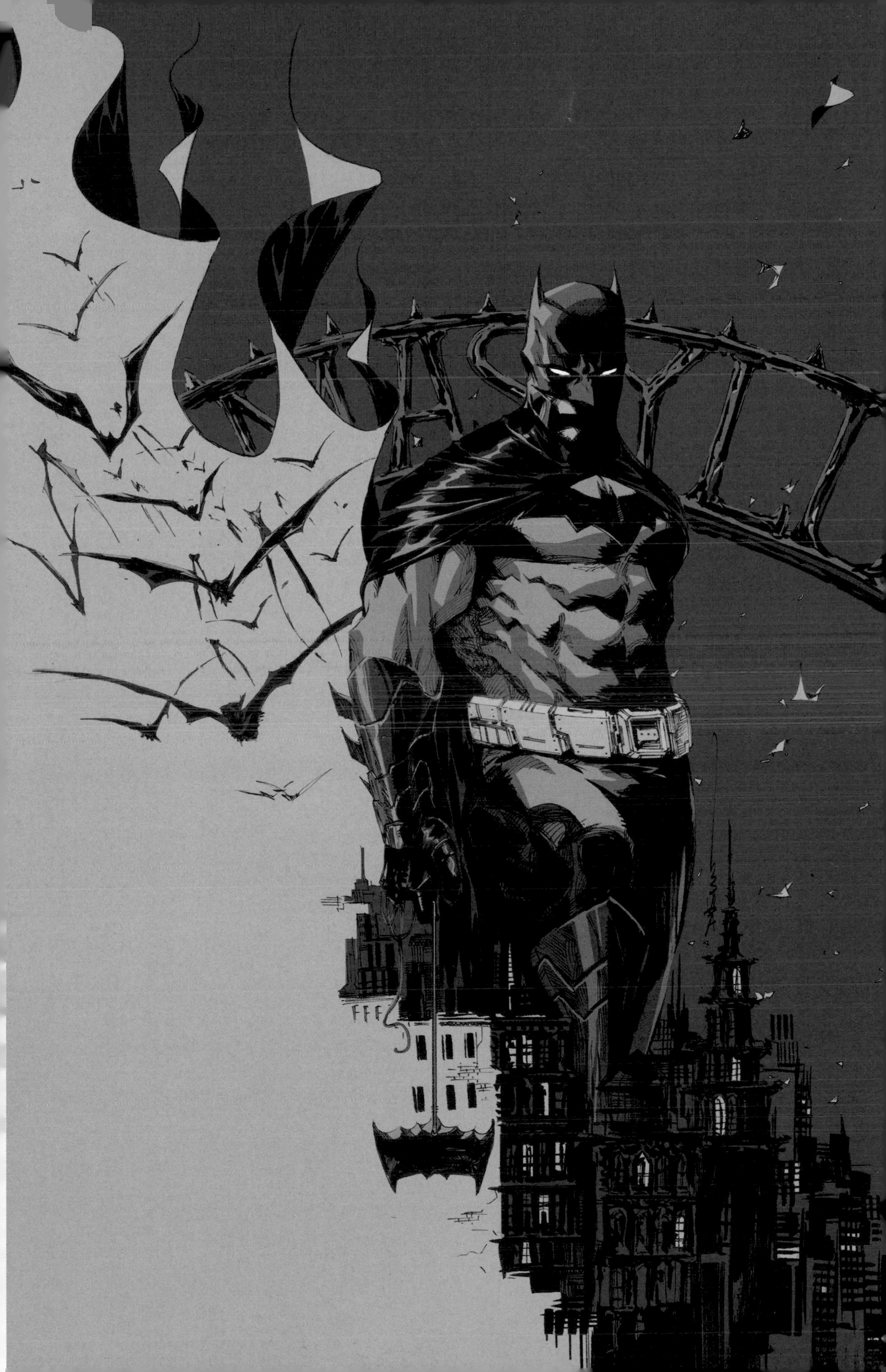

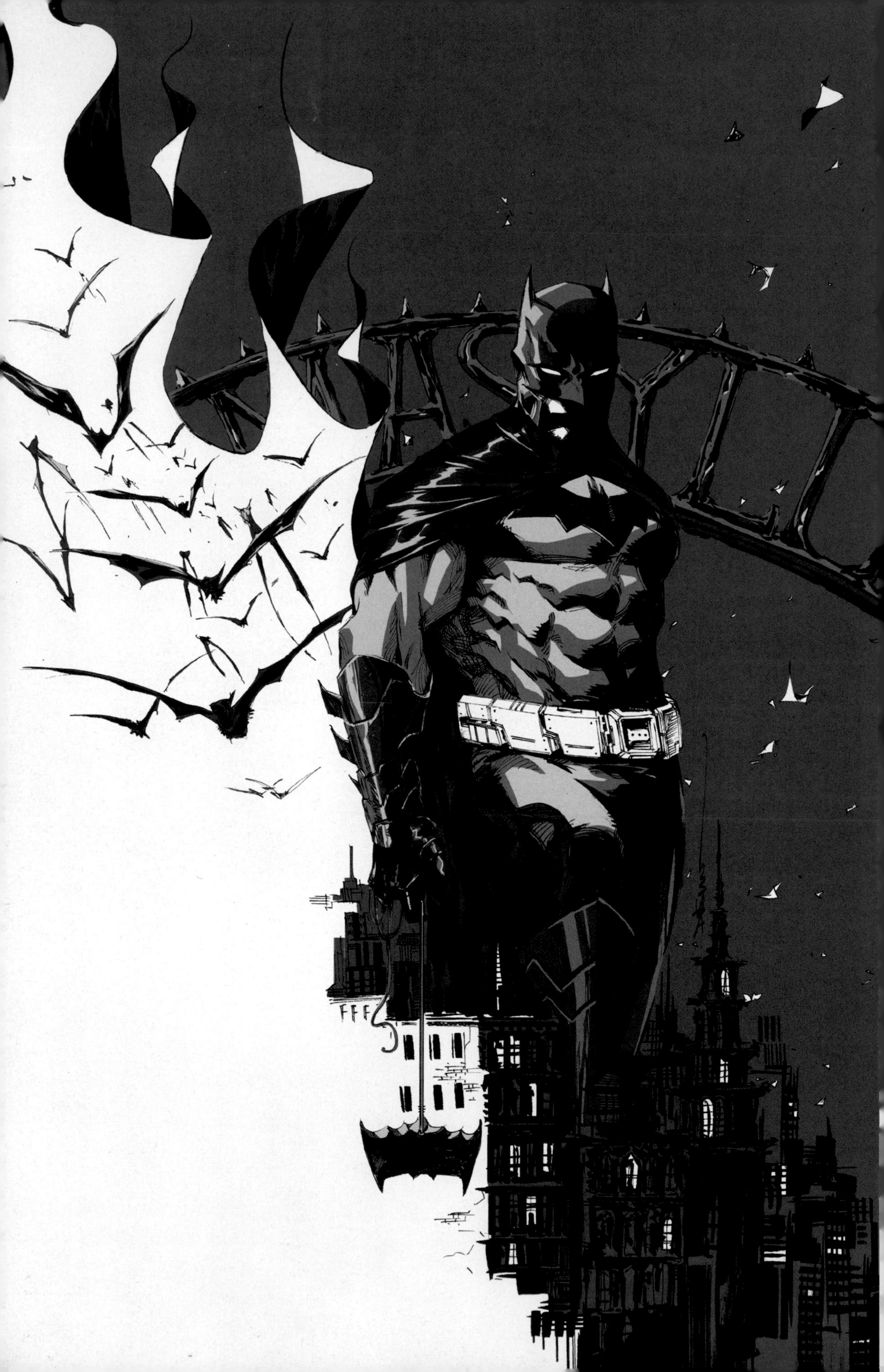

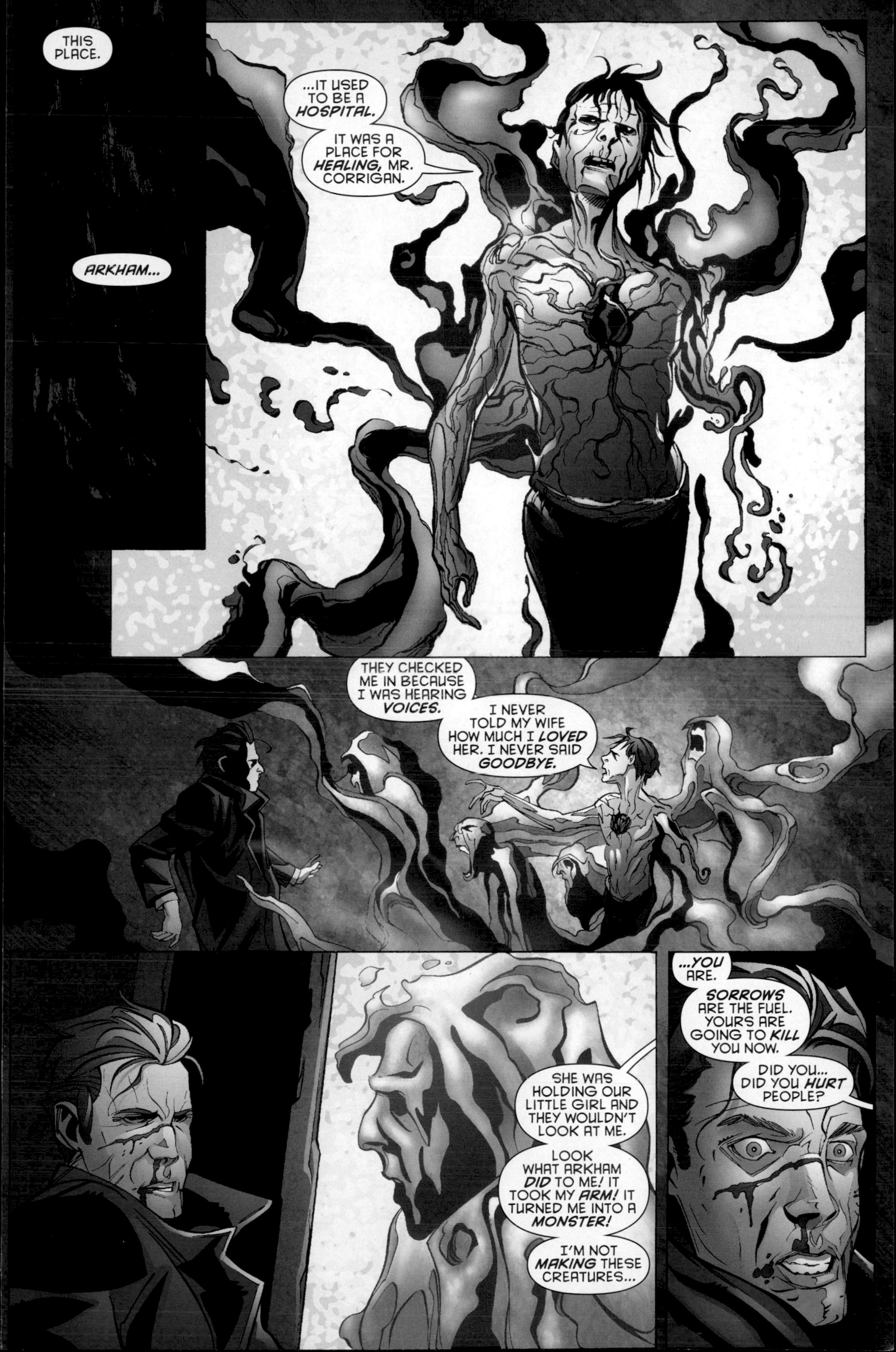
THIS PLACE.
...IT USED TO BE A HOSPITAL.
IT WAS A PLACE FOR HEALING, MR. CORRIGAN.
ARKHAM...
THEY CHECKED ME IN BECAUSE I WAS HEARING VOICES.
I NEVER TOLD MY WIFE HOW MUCH I LOVED HER. I NEVER SAID GOODBYE.
SHE WAS HOLDING OUR LITTLE GIRL AND THEY WOULDN'T LOOK AT ME.
LOOK WHAT ARKHAM DID TO ME! IT TOOK MY ARM! IT TURNED ME INTO A MONSTER!
I'M NOT MAKING THESE CREATURES...
...YOU ARE.
SORROWS ARE THE FUEL. YOURS ARE GOING TO KILL YOU NOW.
DID YOU... DID YOU HURT PEOPLE?

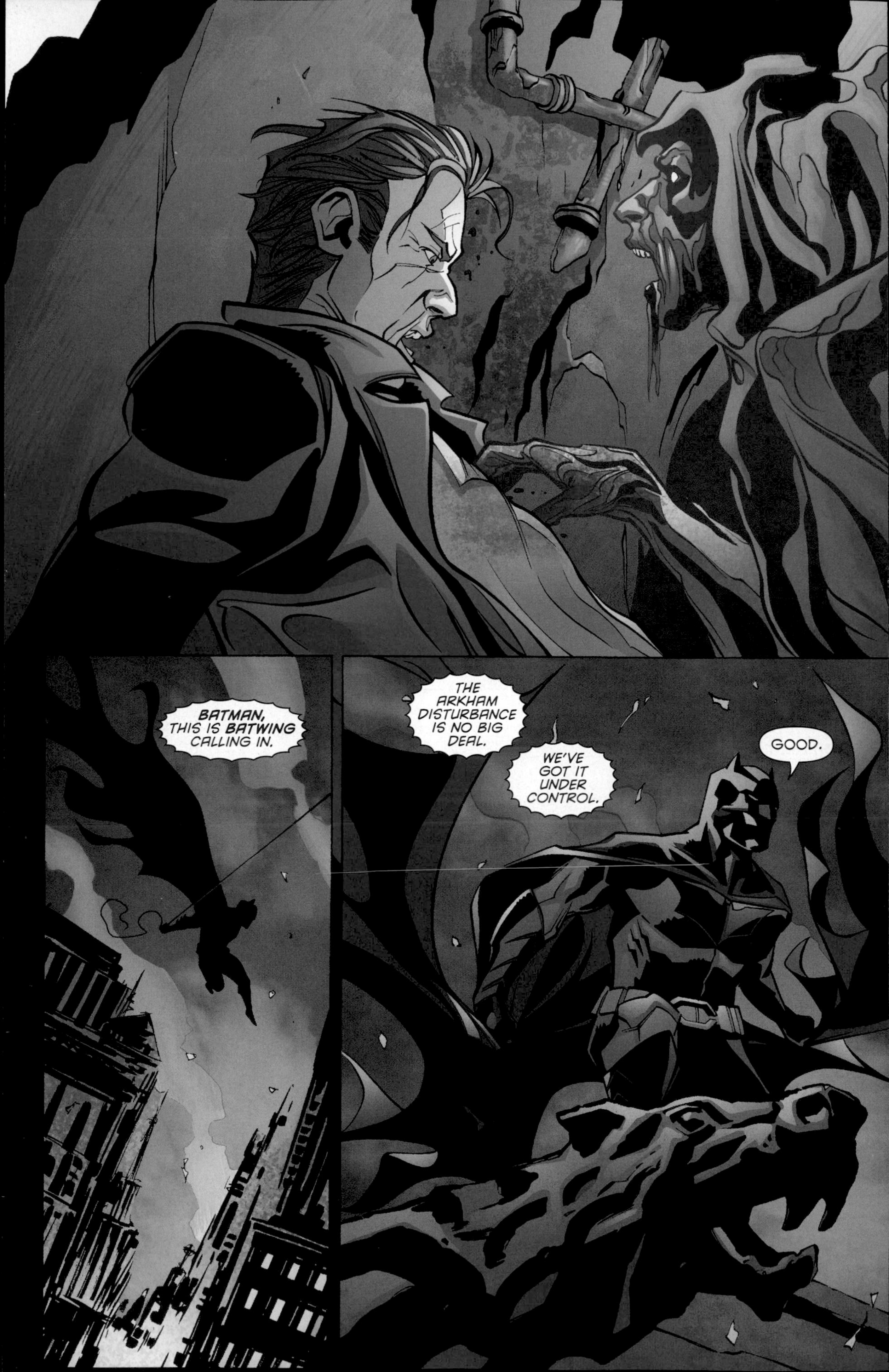
BATMAN, THIS IS BATWING CALLING IN.
THE ARKHAM DISTURBANCE IS NO BIG DEAL.
WE'VE GOT IT UNDER CONTROL.
GOOD.

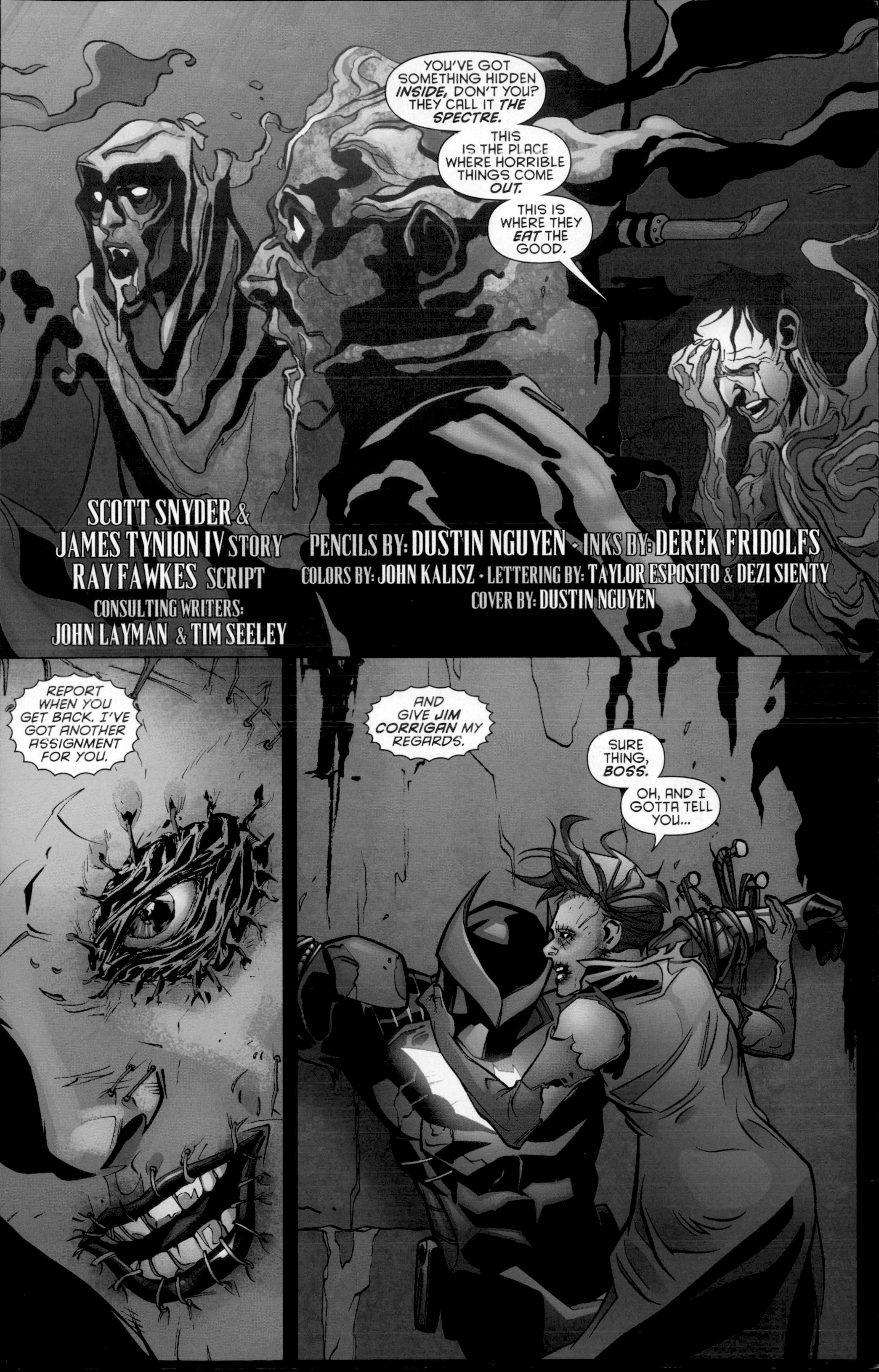

YOU'VE GOT SOMETHING HIDDEN INSIDE, DON'T YOU? THEY CALL IT THE SPECTRE.
THIS IS THE PLACE WHERE HORRIBLE THINGS COME OUT.
THIS IS WHERE THEY EAT THE GOOD.
SCOTT SNYDER & JAMES TYNION IV STORY
RAY FAWKES SCRIPT
CONSULTING WRITERS: JOHN LAYMAN & TIM SEELEY
PENCILS BY: DUSTIN NGUYEN • INKS BY: DEREK FRIDOLFS
COLORS BY: JOHN KALISZ • LETTERING BY: TAYLOR ESPOSITO & DEZI SIENTY
COVER BY: DUSTIN NGUYEN
REPORT WHEN YOU GET BACK. I'VE GOT ANOTHER ASSIGNMENT FOR YOU.
AND GIVE JIM CORRIGAN MY REGARDS.
SURE THING, BOSS.
OH, AND I GOTTA TELL YOU...

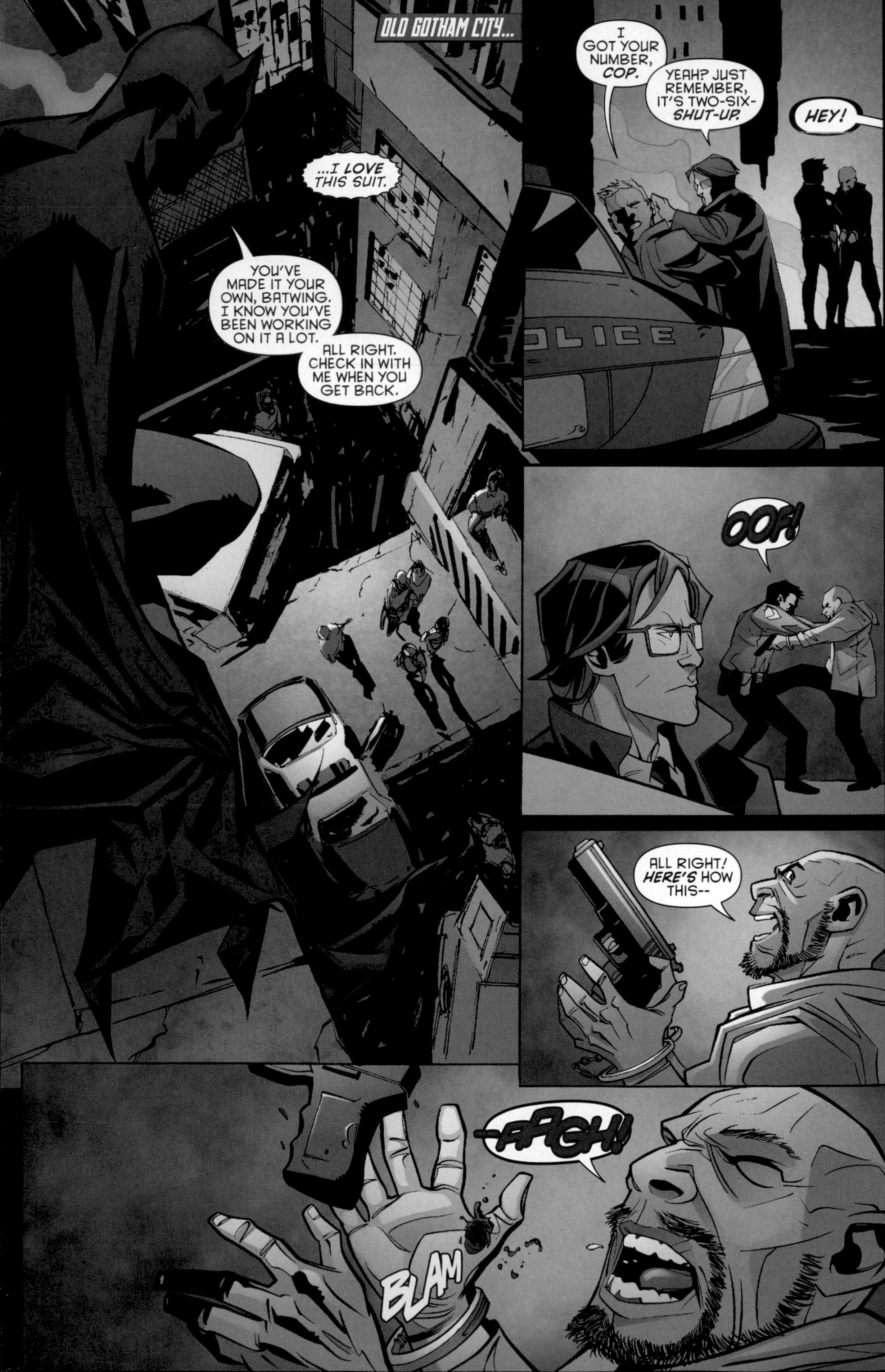

OLD GOTHAM CITY...
...I LOVE THIS SUIT.
YOU'VE MADE IT YOUR OWN, BATWING. I KNOW YOU'VE BEEN WORKING ON IT A LOT.
ALL RIGHT. CHECK IN WITH ME WHEN YOU GET BACK.
I GOT YOUR NUMBER, COP.
YEAH? JUST REMEMBER, IT'S TWO-SIX-SHUT-UP.
HEY!
POLICE
OOF!
ALL RIGHT! HERE'S HOW THIS--
-AAGH!
BLAM

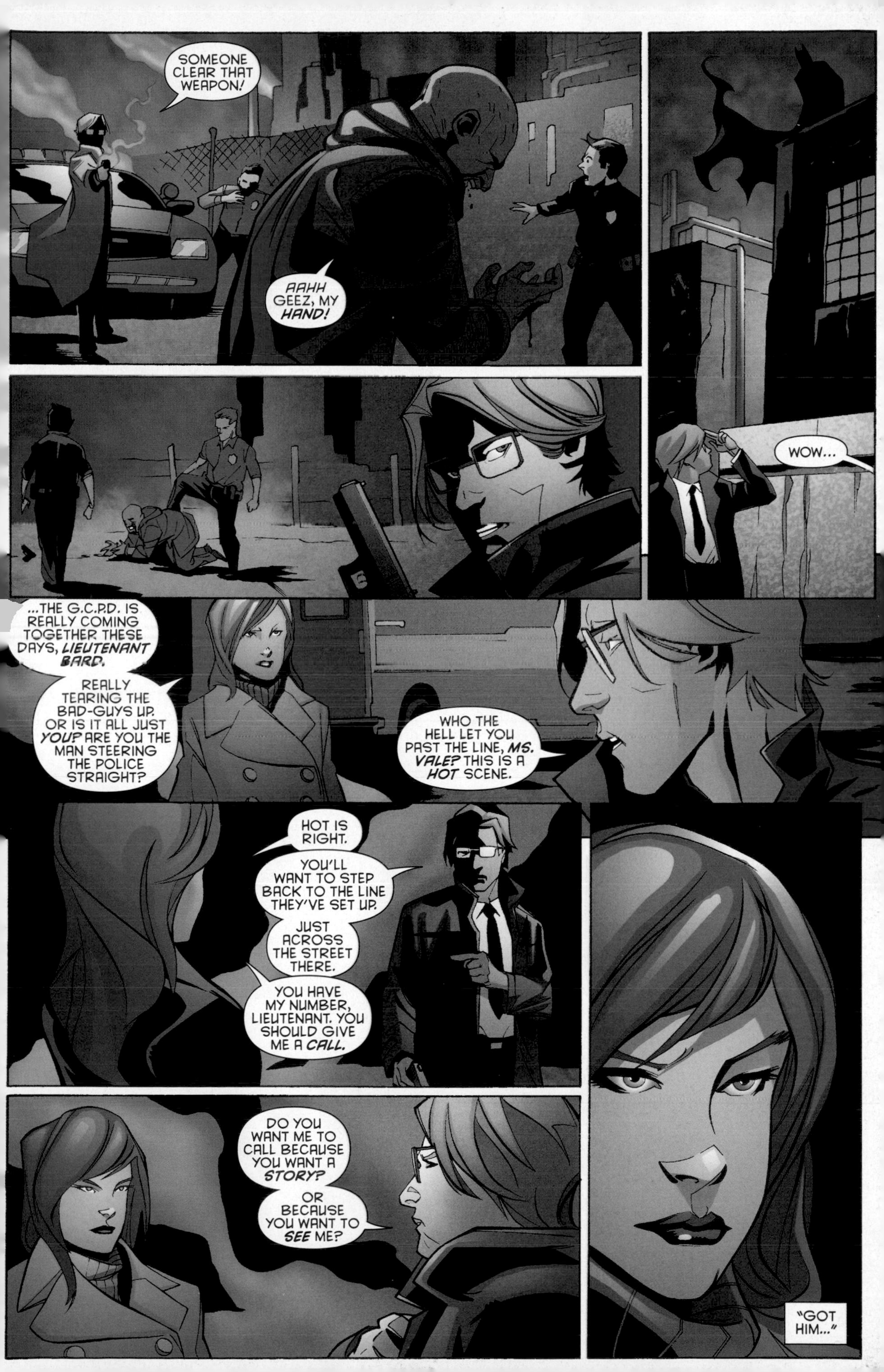
SOMEONE CLEAR THAT WEAPON!
AAHH GEEZ, MY HAND!
WOW...
...THE G.C.P.D. IS REALLY COMING TOGETHER THESE DAYS, LIEUTENANT BARD.
REALLY TEARING THE BAD-GUYS UP. OR IS IT ALL JUST YOU? ARE YOU THE MAN STEERING THE POLICE STRAIGHT?
WHO THE HELL LET YOU PAST THE LINE, MS. VALE? THIS IS A HOT SCENE.
HOT IS RIGHT.
YOU'LL WANT TO STEP BACK TO THE LINE THEY'VE SET UP.
JUST ACROSS THE STREET THERE.
YOU HAVE MY NUMBER, LIEUTENANT. YOU SHOULD GIVE ME A CALL.
DO YOU WANT ME TO CALL BECAUSE YOU WANT A STORY?
OR BECAUSE YOU WANT TO SEE ME?
"GOT HIM..."

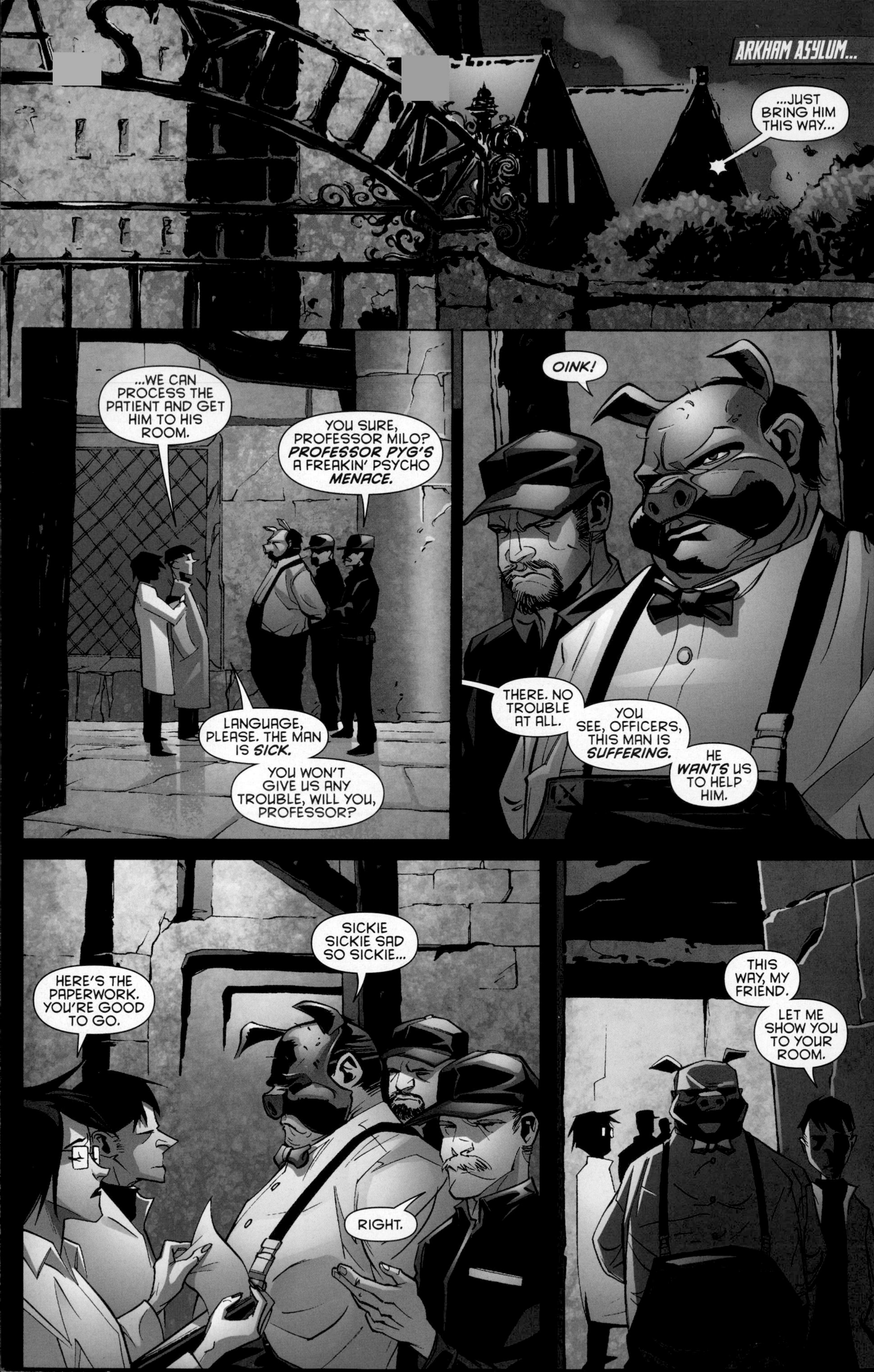

ARKHAM ASYLUM...
...JUST BRING HIM THIS WAY...
...WE CAN PROCESS THE PATIENT AND GET HIM TO HIS ROOM.
YOU SURE, PROFESSOR MILO? PROFESSOR PYG'S A FREAKIN' PSYCHO MENACE.
LANGUAGE, PLEASE. THE MAN IS SICK.
YOU WON'T GIVE US ANY TROUBLE, WILL YOU, PROFESSOR?
OINK!
THERE. NO TROUBLE AT ALL.
YOU SEE, OFFICERS, THIS MAN IS SUFFERING.
HE WANTS US TO HELP HIM.
HERE'S THE PAPERWORK. YOU'RE GOOD TO GO.
SICKIE SICKIE SAD SO SICKIE...
RIGHT.
THIS WAY, MY FRIEND.
LET ME SHOW YOU TO YOUR ROOM.

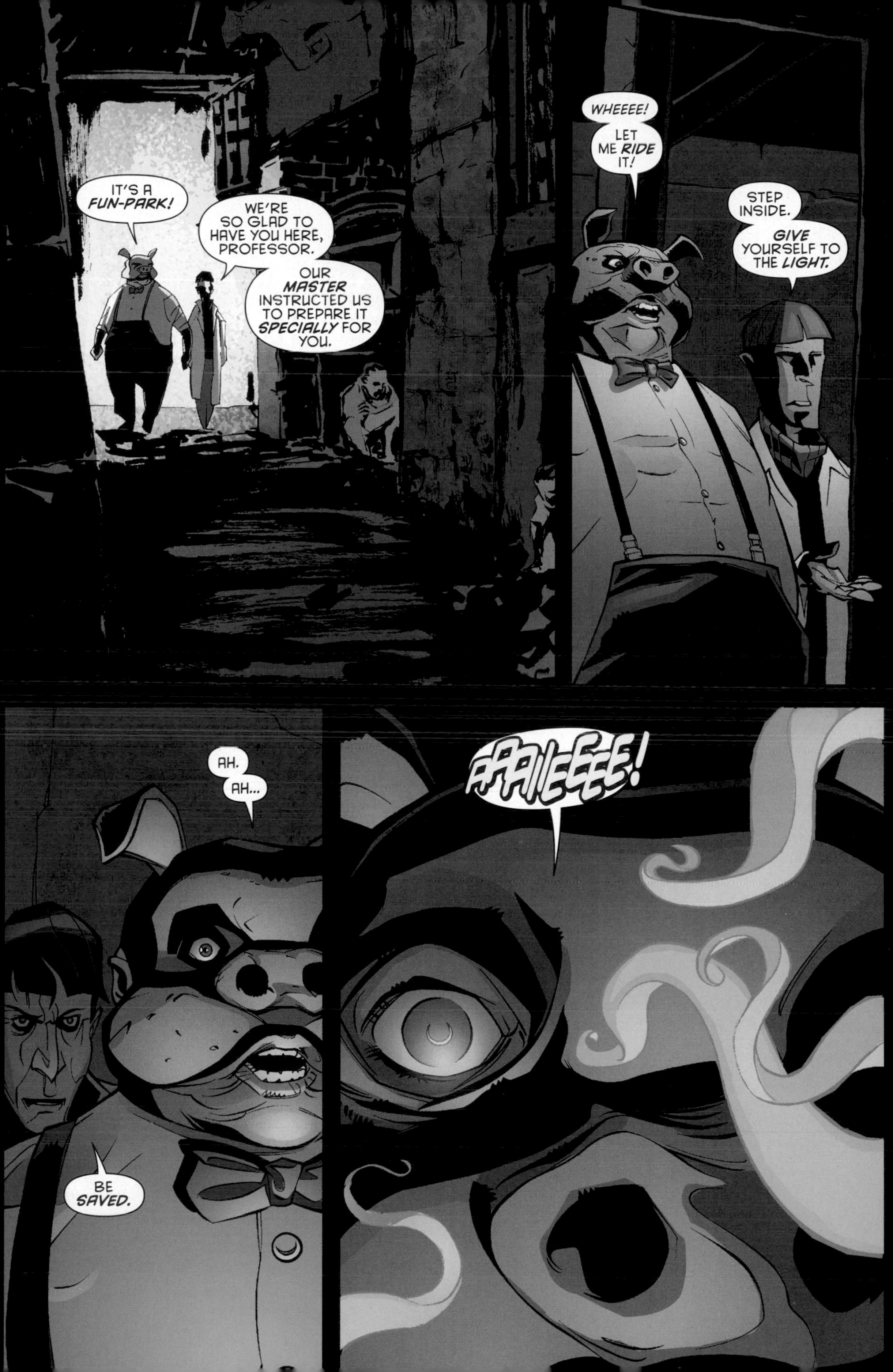

IT'S A FUN-PARK!
WE'RE SO GLAD TO HAVE YOU HERE, PROFESSOR.
OUR MASTER INSTRUCTED US TO PREPARE IT SPECIALLY FOR YOU.
WHEEEE! LET ME RIDE IT!
STEP INSIDE. GIVE YOURSELF TO THE LIGHT.
AH. AH...
BE SAVED.
AAAIIEEEEE!

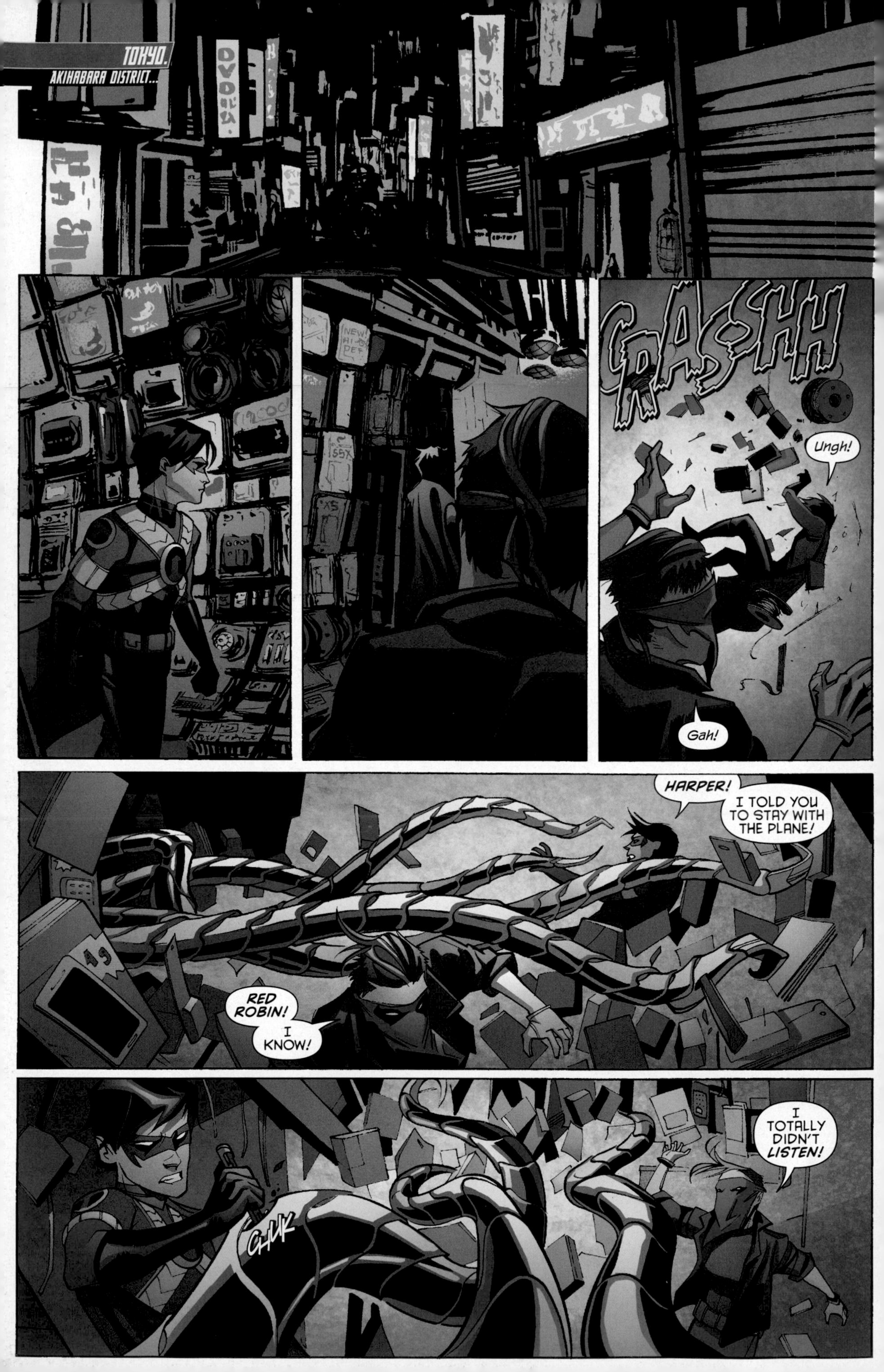
TOKYO.
AKIHABARA DISTRICT...
CRASHH
Ungh!
Gah!
HARPER!
I TOLD YOU TO STAY WITH THE PLANE!
RED ROBIN!
I KNOW!
I TOTALLY DIDN'T LISTEN!
CHUK

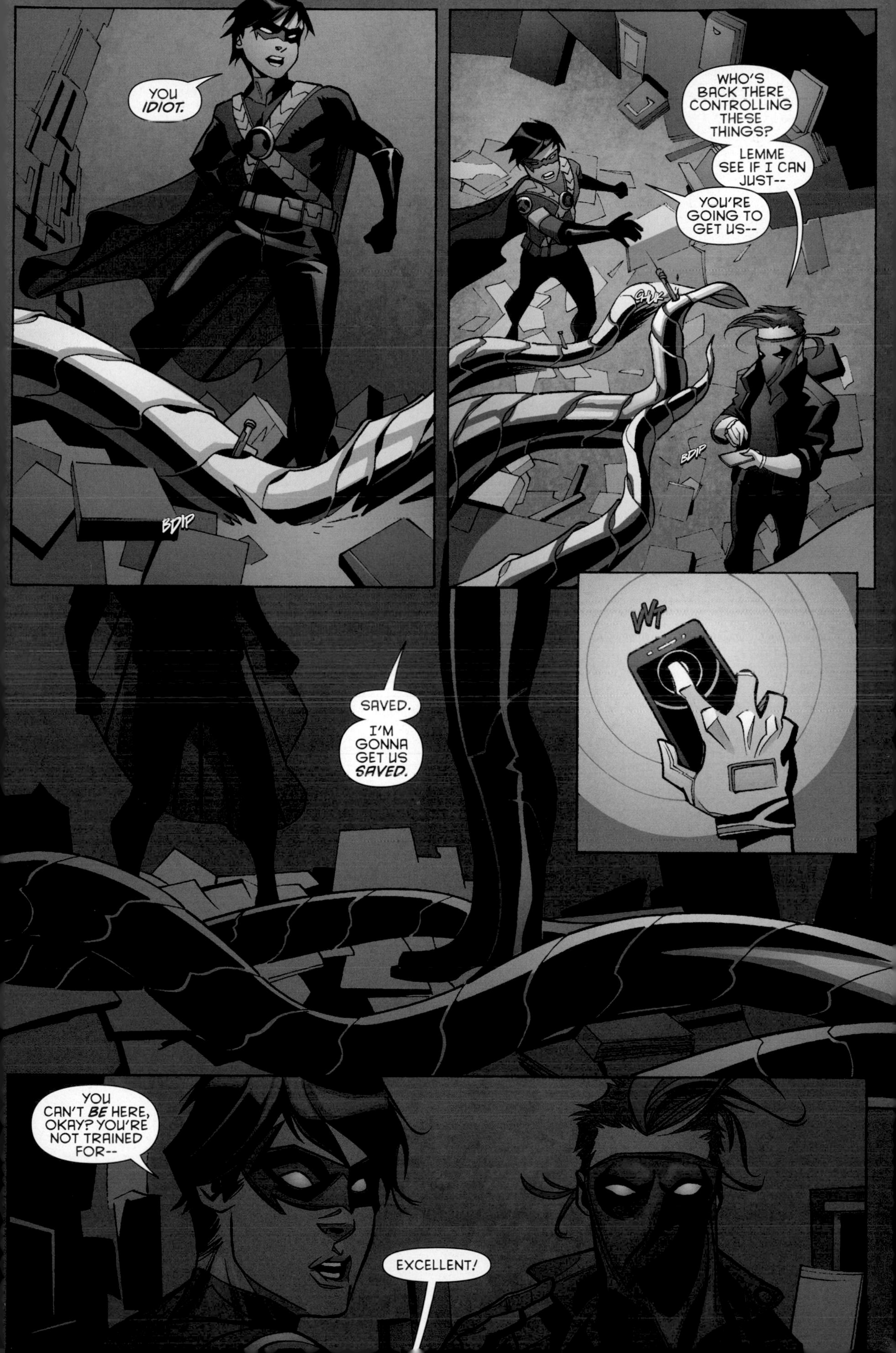
YOU IDIOT.
WHO'S BACK THERE CONTROLLING THESE THINGS?
LEMME SEE IF I CAN JUST--
YOU'RE GOING TO GET US--
CHUK
BDIP
BDIP
VVT
SAVED.
I'M GONNA GET US SAVED.
YOU CAN'T BE HERE, OKAY? YOU'RE NOT TRAINED FOR--
EXCELLENT!

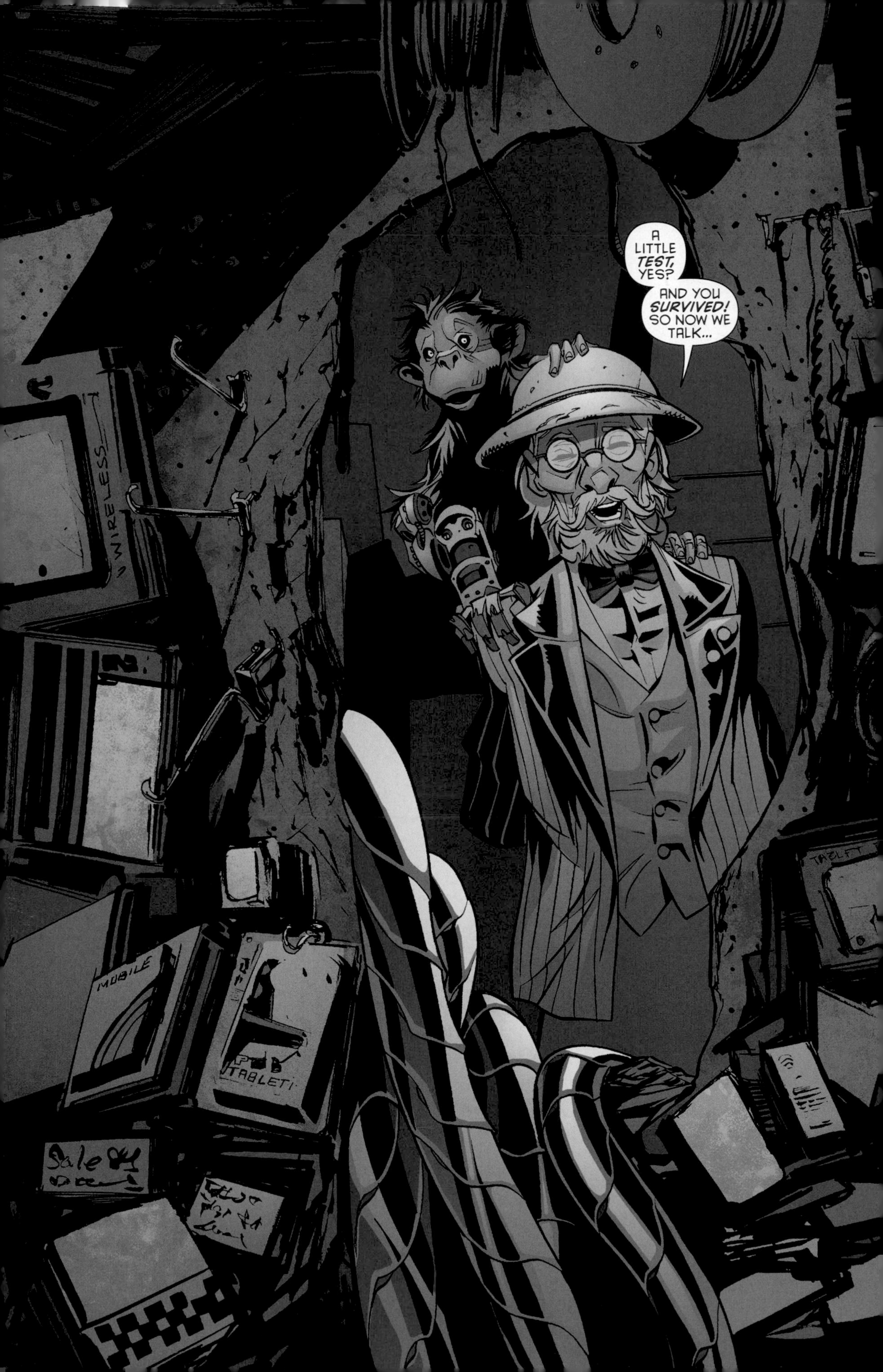
A LITTLE TEST, YES?
AND YOU SURVIVED! SO NOW WE TALK...

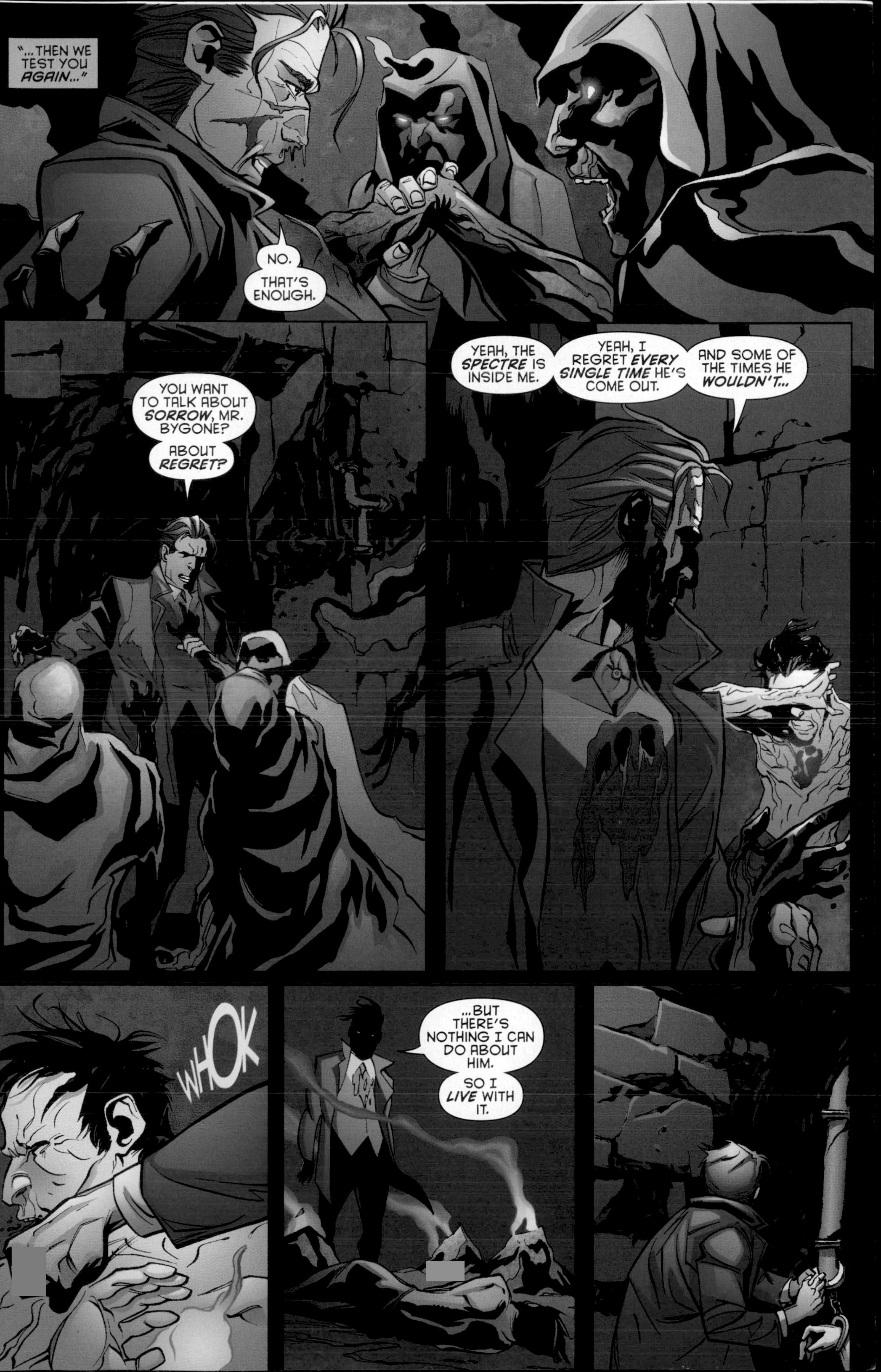
"...THEN WE TEST YOU AGAIN..."
NO. THAT'S ENOUGH.
YOU WANT TO TALK ABOUT SORROW, MR. BYGONE?
ABOUT REGRET?
YEAH, THE SPECTRE IS INSIDE ME.
YEAH, I REGRET EVERY SINGLE TIME HE'S COME OUT.
AND SOME OF THE TIMES HE WOULDN'T...
WHOK
...BUT THERE'S NOTHING I CAN DO ABOUT HIM.
SO I LIVE WITH IT.

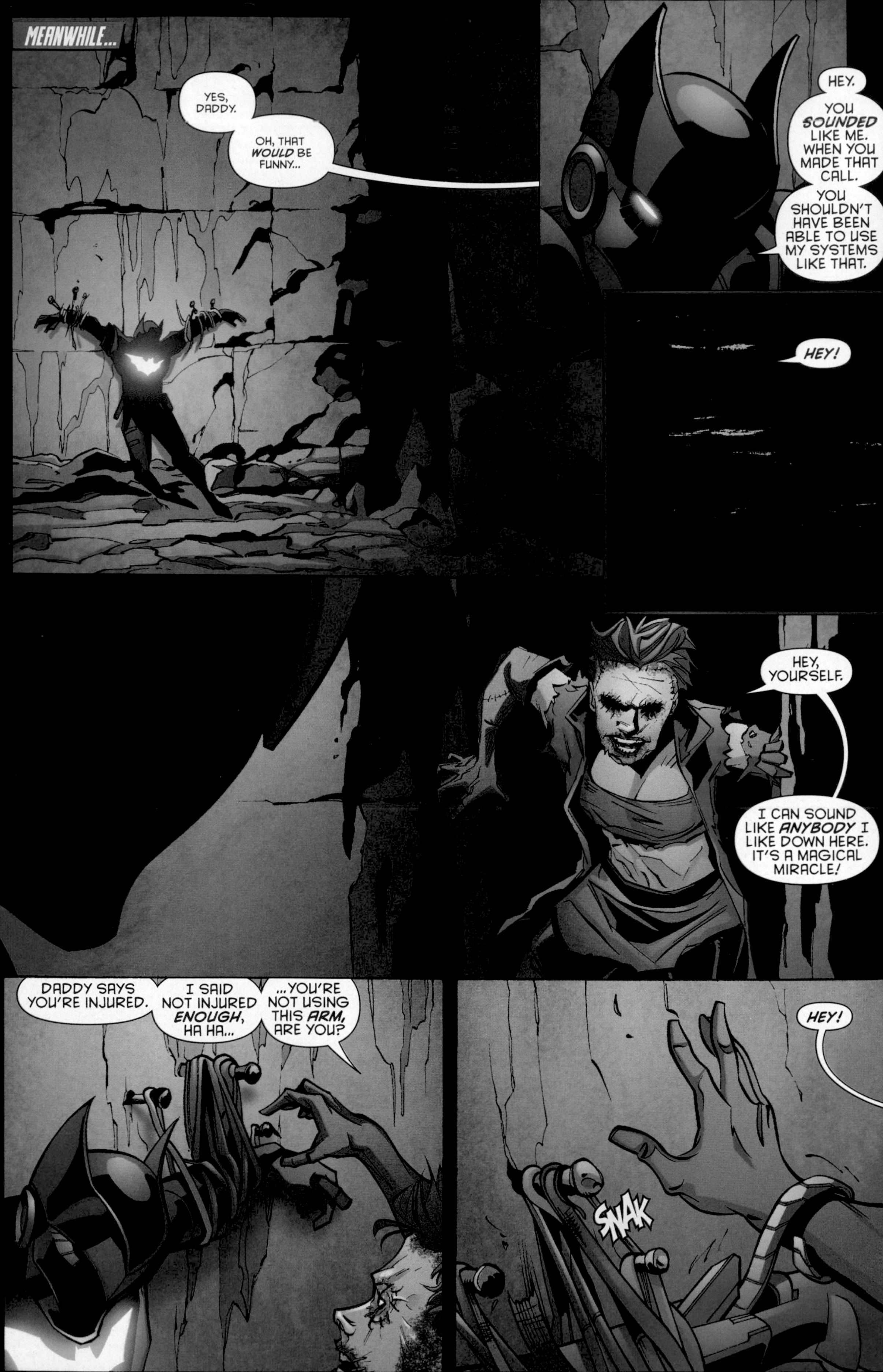
MEANWHILE...
YES, DADDY.
OH, THAT WOULD BE FUNNY...
HEY.
YOU SOUNDED LIKE ME. WHEN YOU MADE THAT CALL.
YOU SHOULDN'T HAVE BEEN ABLE TO USE MY SYSTEMS LIKE THAT.
HEY!
HEY, YOURSELF.
I CAN SOUND LIKE ANYBODY I LIKE DOWN HERE. IT'S A MAGICAL MIRACLE!
DADDY SAYS YOU'RE INJURED.
I SAID NOT INJURED ENOUGH, HA HA...
...YOU'RE NOT USING THIS ARM, ARE YOU?
HEY!
SNAK

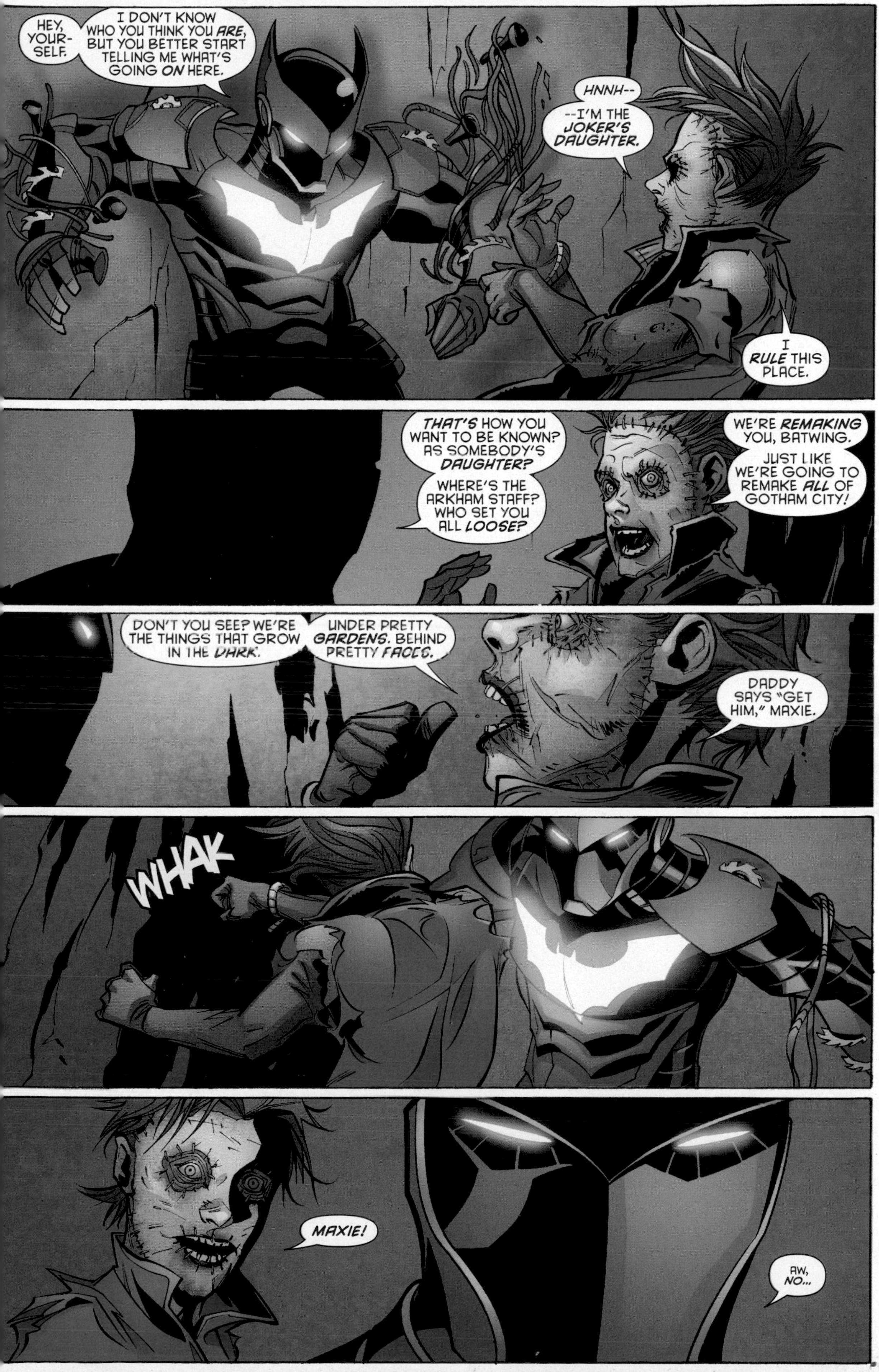
HEY, YOURSELF.
I DON'T KNOW WHO YOU THINK YOU ARE, BUT YOU BETTER START TELLING ME WHAT'S GOING ON HERE.
HNNH--
--I'M THE JOKER'S DAUGHTER.
I RULE THIS PLACE.
THAT'S HOW YOU WANT TO BE KNOWN? AS SOMEBODY'S DAUGHTER?
WHERE'S THE ARKHAM STAFF? WHO SET YOU ALL LOOSE?
WE'RE REMAKING YOU, BATWING.
JUST LIKE WE'RE GOING TO REMAKE ALL OF GOTHAM CITY!
DON'T YOU SEE? WE'RE THE THINGS THAT GROW IN THE DARK.
UNDER PRETTY GARDENS. BEHIND PRETTY FACES.
DADDY SAYS "GET HIM," MAXIE.
WHAK
MAXIE!
AW, NO...

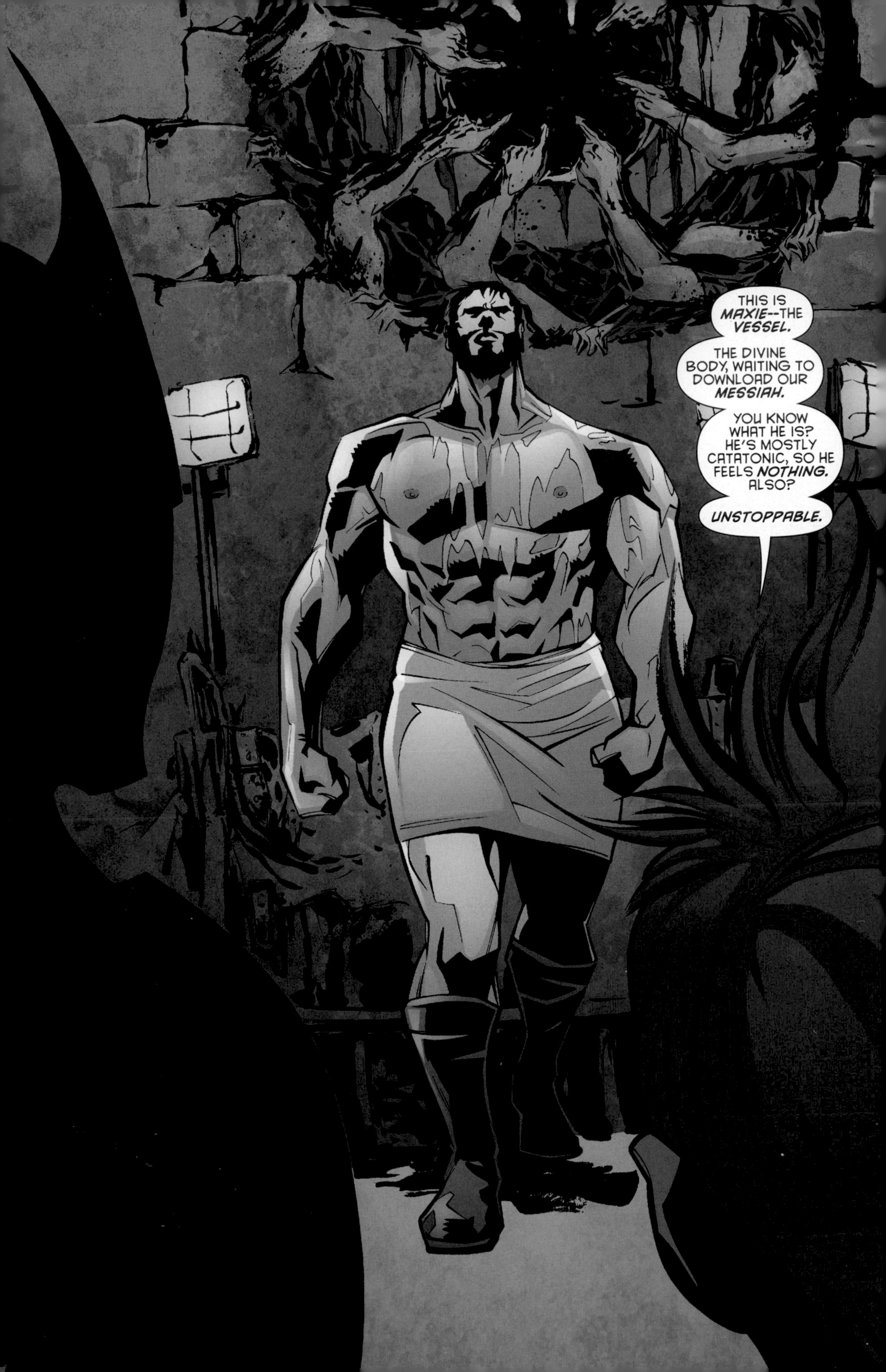
THIS IS MAXIE--THE VESSEL.
THE DIVINE BODY, WAITING TO DOWNLOAD OUR MESSIAH.
YOU KNOW WHAT HE IS? HE'S MOSTLY CATATONIC, SO HE FEELS NOTHING. ALSO?
UNSTOPPABLE.

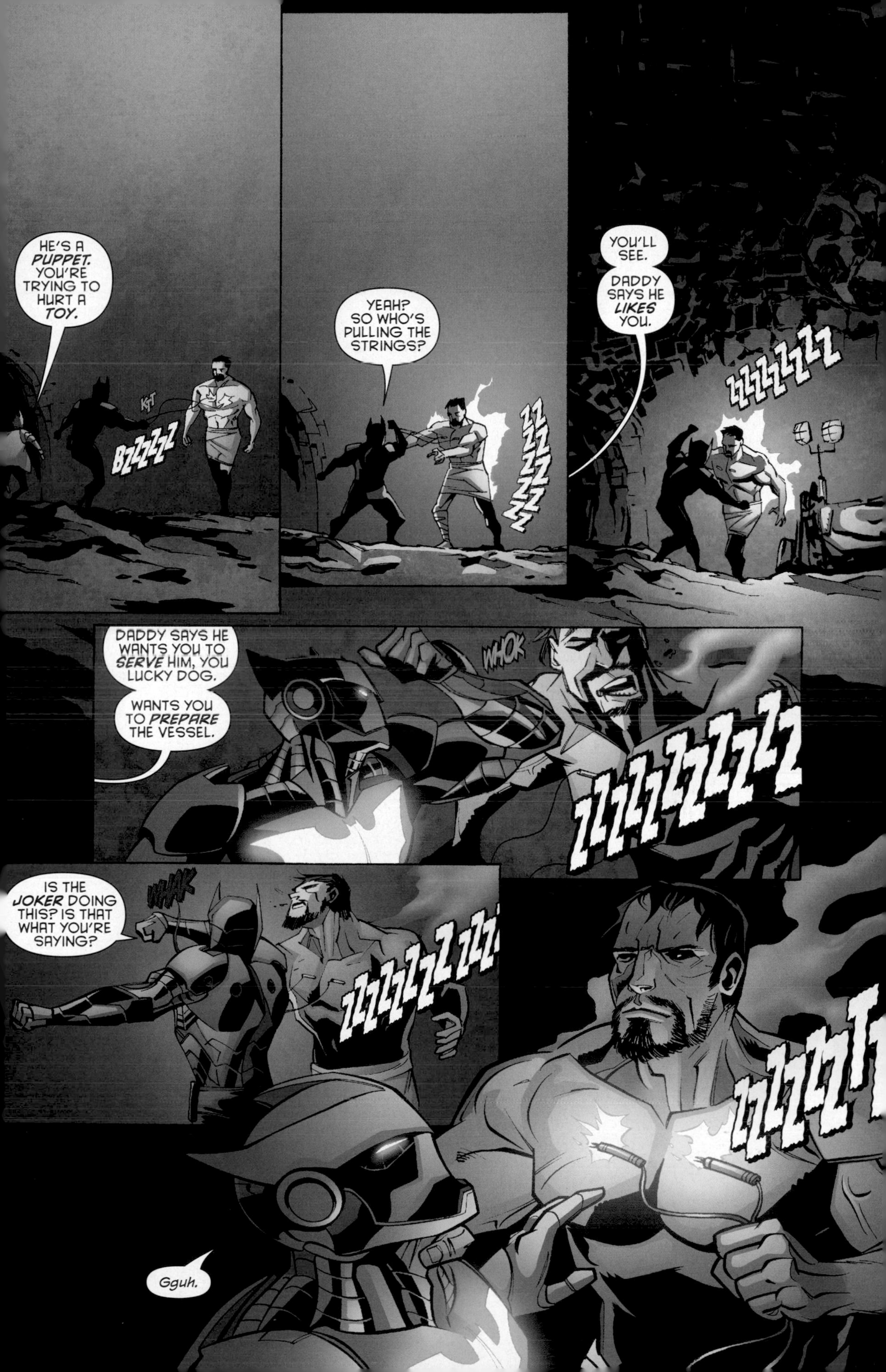
HE'S A PUPPET. YOU'RE TRYING TO HURT A TOY.
KT
BZZZZZZ
YEAH? SO WHO'S PULLING THE STRINGS?
ZZZZZZZZ
YOU'LL SEE.
DADDY SAYS HE LIKES YOU.
ZZZZZZZZZ
DADDY SAYS HE WANTS YOU TO SERVE HIM, YOU LUCKY DOG.
WANTS YOU TO PREPARE THE VESSEL.
WHOK
ZZZZZZZZZZZ
IS THE JOKER DOING THIS? IS THAT WHAT YOU'RE SAYING?
WHAK
ZZZZZZZZ ZZZ
ZZZZZZZT
Gguh.

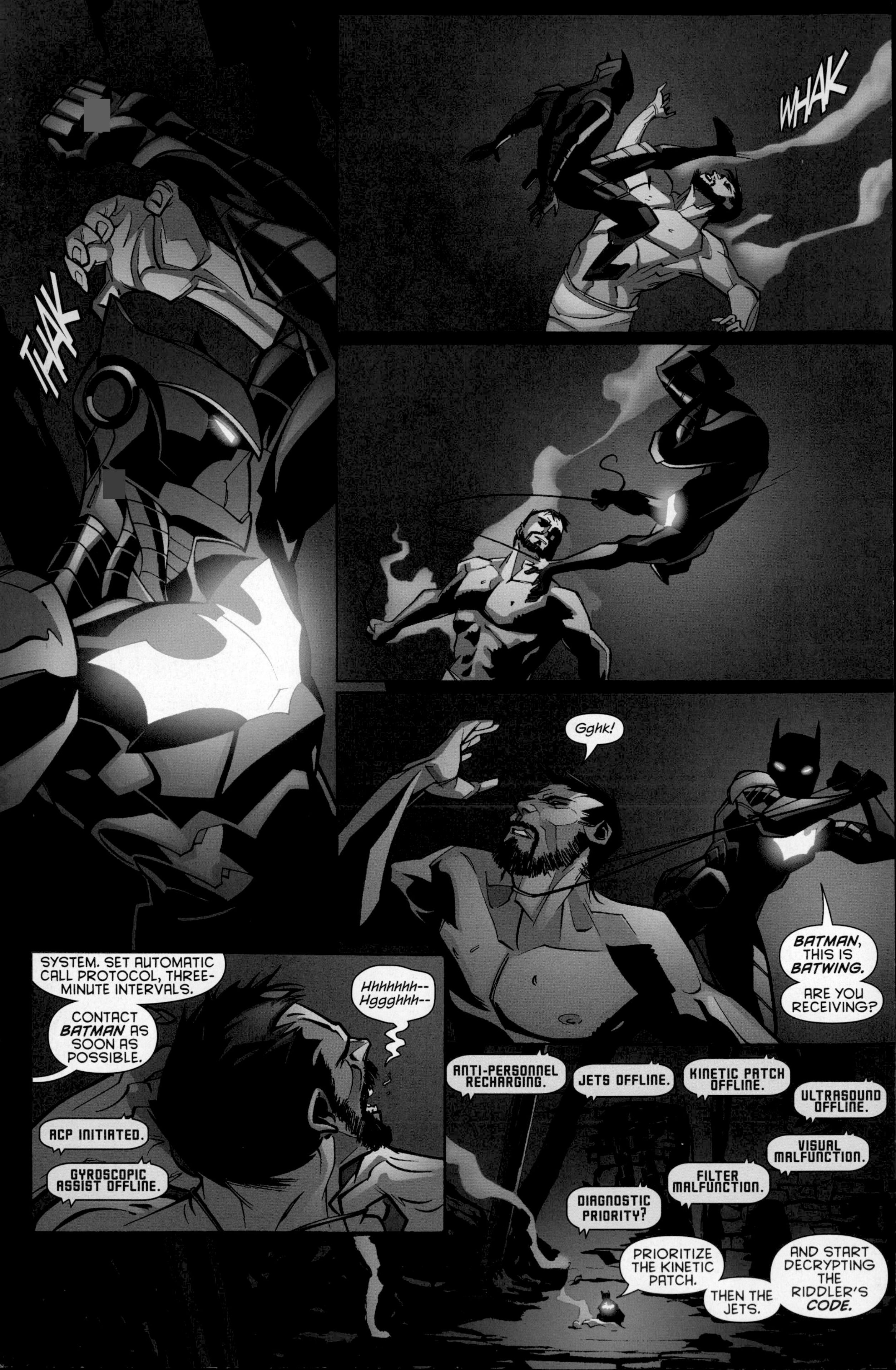
THAK
WHAK
Gghk!
BATMAN, THIS IS BATWING.
ARE YOU RECEIVING?
SYSTEM. SET AUTOMATIC CALL PROTOCOL, THREE-MINUTE INTERVALS.
CONTACT BATMAN AS SOON AS POSSIBLE.
Hhhhhhh-- Hggghhh--
ACP INITIATED.
GYROSCOPIC ASSIST OFFLINE.
ANTI-PERSONNEL RECHARGING.
JETS OFFLINE.
KINETIC PATCH OFFLINE.
ULTRASOUND OFFLINE.
VISUAL MALFUNCTION.
FILTER MALFUNCTION.
DIAGNOSTIC PRIORITY?
PRIORITIZE THE KINETIC PATCH.
THEN THE JETS.
AND START DECRYPTING THE RIDDLER'S CODE.

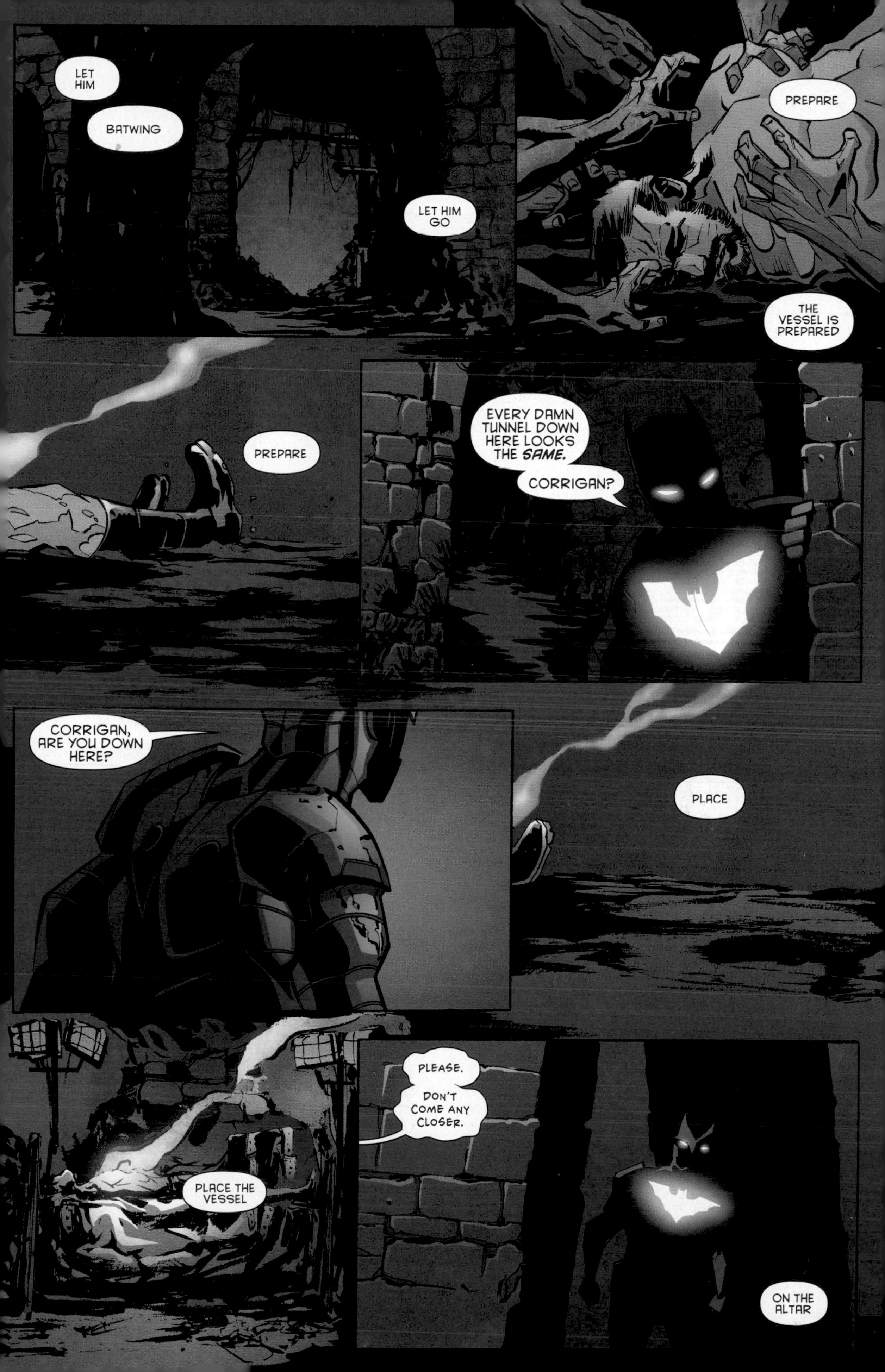
LET HIM
BATWING
LET HIM GO
PREPARE
THE VESSEL IS PREPARED
PREPARE
EVERY DAMN TUNNEL DOWN HERE LOOKS THE SAME.
CORRIGAN?
CORRIGAN, ARE YOU DOWN HERE?
PLACE
PLACE THE VESSEL
PLEASE.
DON'T COME ANY CLOSER.
ON THE ALTAR

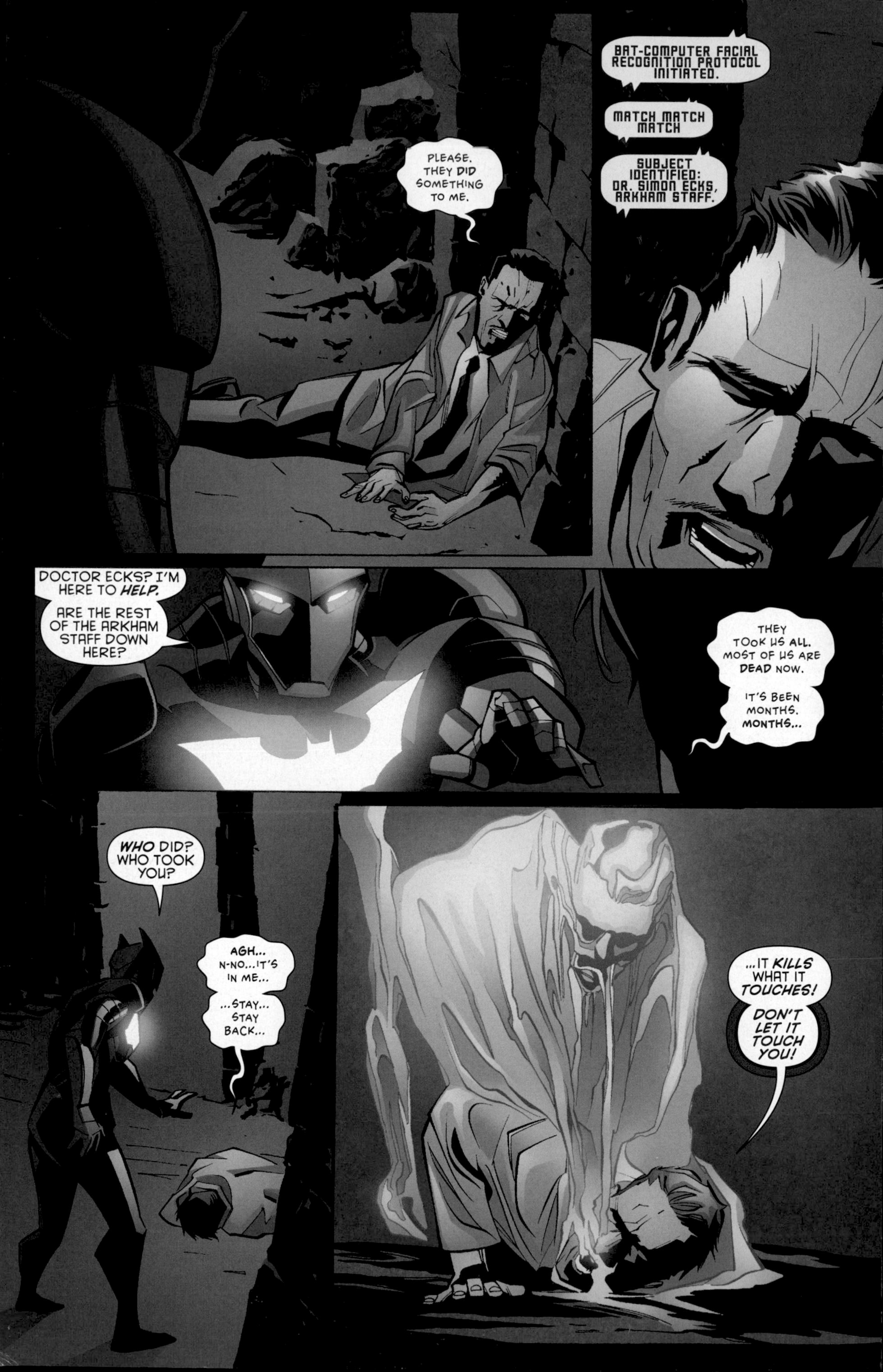
PLEASE. THEY DID SOMETHING TO ME.
BAT-COMPUTER FACIAL RECOGNITION PROTOCOL INITIATED.
MATCH MATCH MATCH
SUBJECT IDENTIFIED: DR. SIMON ECKS, ARKHAM STAFF.
DOCTOR ECKS? I'M HERE TO HELP.
ARE THE REST OF THE ARKHAM STAFF DOWN HERE?
THEY TOOK US ALL. MOST OF US ARE DEAD NOW.
IT'S BEEN MONTHS. MONTHS...
WHO DID? WHO TOOK YOU?
AGH... N-NO...IT'S IN ME...
...STAY... STAY BACK...
...IT KILLS WHAT IT TOUCHES!
DON'T LET IT TOUCH YOU!

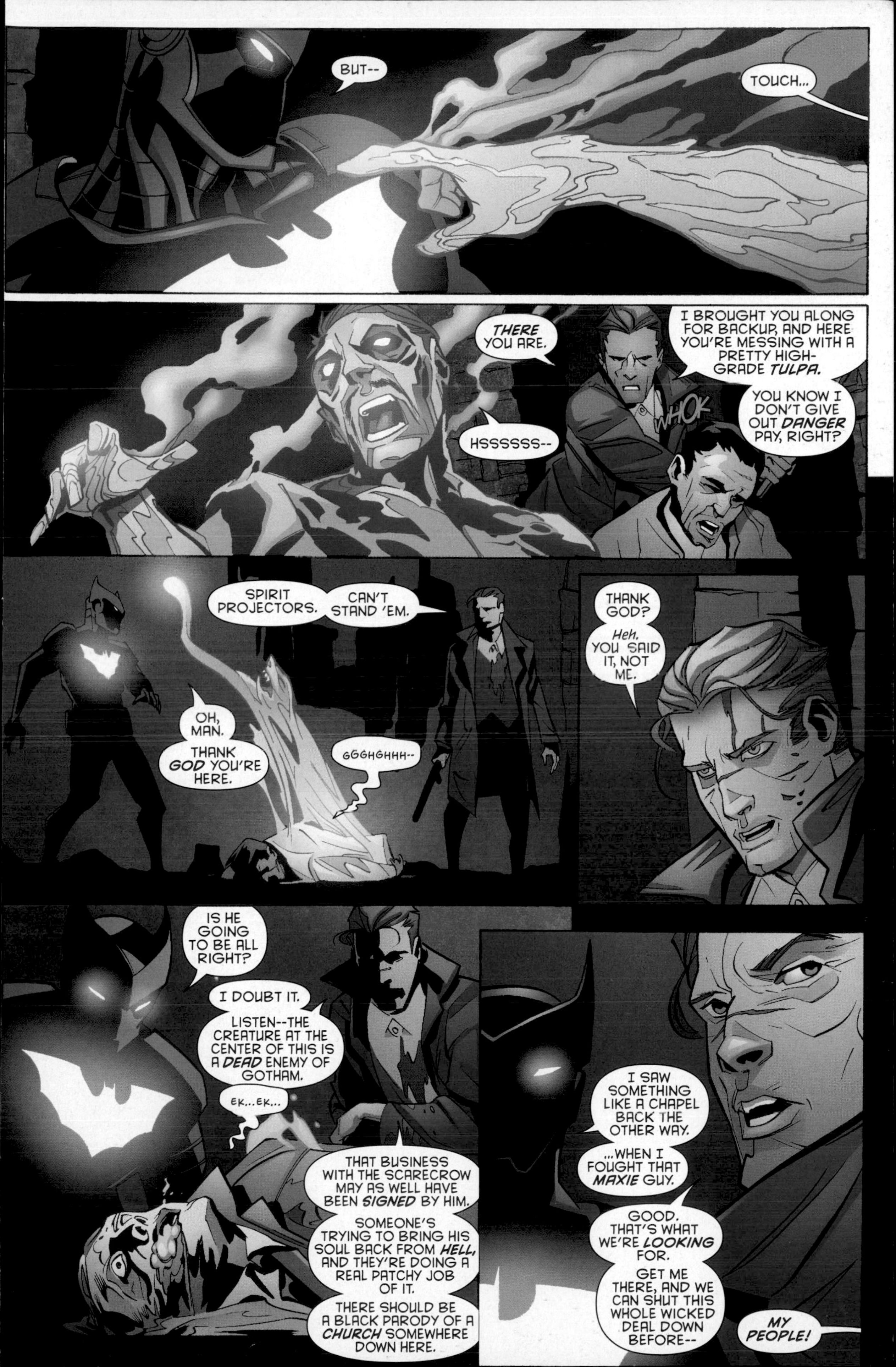
BUT--
TOUCH...
THERE YOU ARE.
I BROUGHT YOU ALONG FOR BACKUP, AND HERE YOU'RE MESSING WITH A PRETTY HIGH-GRADE *TULPA.*
HSSSSSS--
WHOK
YOU KNOW I DON'T GIVE OUT *DANGER* PAY, RIGHT?
SPIRIT PROJECTORS.
CAN'T STAND 'EM.
OH, MAN. THANK *GOD* YOU'RE HERE.
GGGHGHHH--
THANK GOD? *Heh.* YOU SAID IT, NOT ME.
IS HE GOING TO BE ALL RIGHT?
I DOUBT IT.
LISTEN--THE CREATURE AT THE CENTER OF THIS IS A *DEAD* ENEMY OF GOTHAM.
EK...EK...
THAT BUSINESS WITH THE SCARECROW MAY AS WELL HAVE BEEN *SIGNED* BY HIM.
SOMEONE'S TRYING TO BRING HIS SOUL BACK FROM *HELL,* AND THEY'RE DOING A REAL PATCHY JOB OF IT.
THERE SHOULD BE A BLACK PARODY OF A *CHURCH* SOMEWHERE DOWN HERE.
I SAW SOMETHING LIKE A CHAPEL BACK THE OTHER WAY.
...WHEN I FOUGHT THAT *MAXIE* GUY.
GOOD. THAT'S WHAT WE'RE *LOOKING* FOR.
GET ME THERE, AND WE CAN SHUT THIS WHOLE WICKED DEAL DOWN BEFORE--
MY PEOPLE!

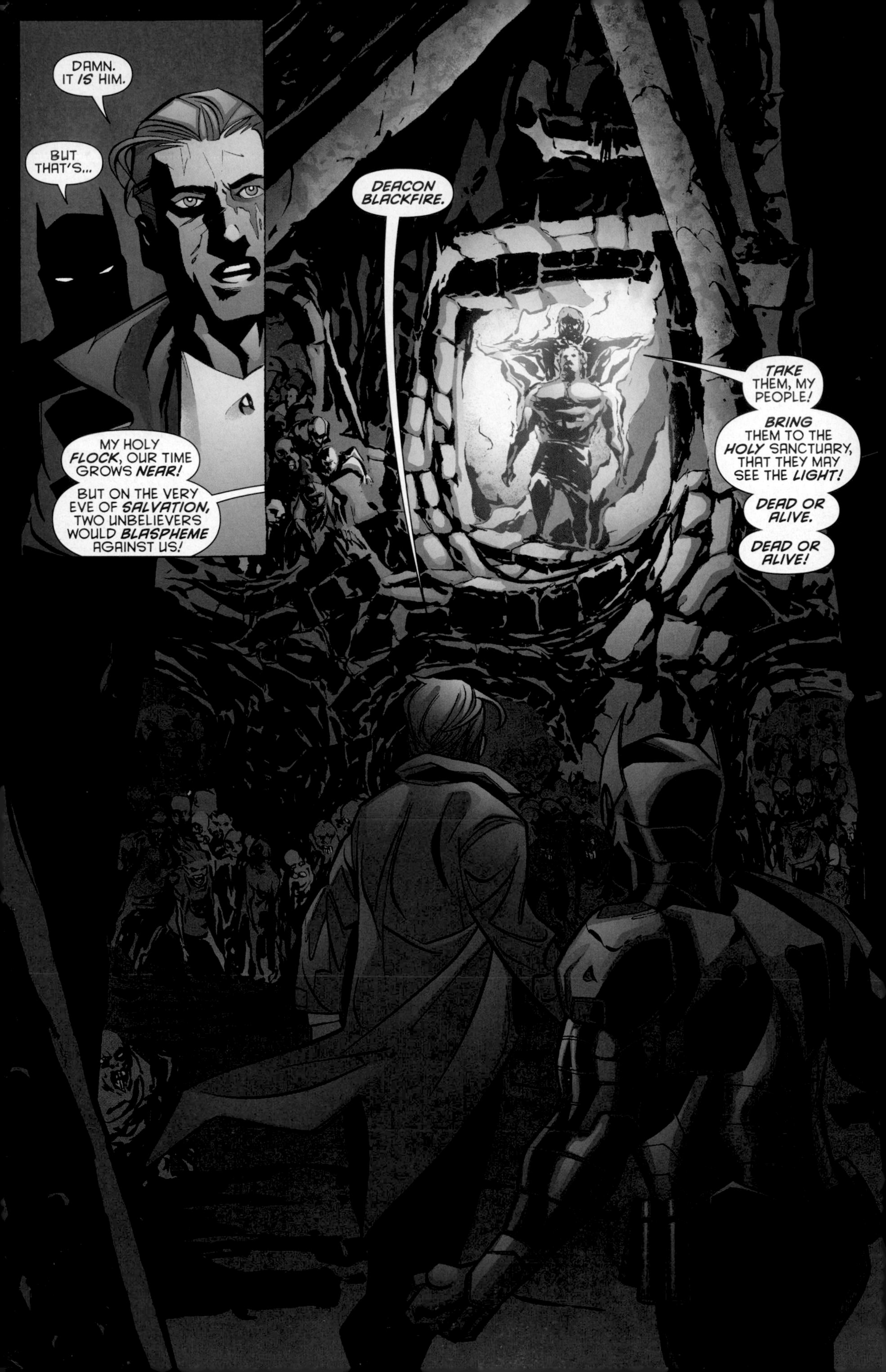
DAMN. IT *IS* HIM.
BUT THAT'S...
DEACON BLACKFIRE.
MY HOLY *FLOCK*, OUR TIME GROWS *NEAR!*
BUT ON THE VERY EVE OF *SALVATION,* TWO UNBELIEVERS WOULD *BLASPHEME* AGAINST US!
TAKE THEM, MY PEOPLE!
BRING THEM TO THE *HOLY* SANCTUARY, THAT THEY MAY SEE THE *LIGHT!*
DEAD OR ALIVE.
DEAD OR ALIVE!

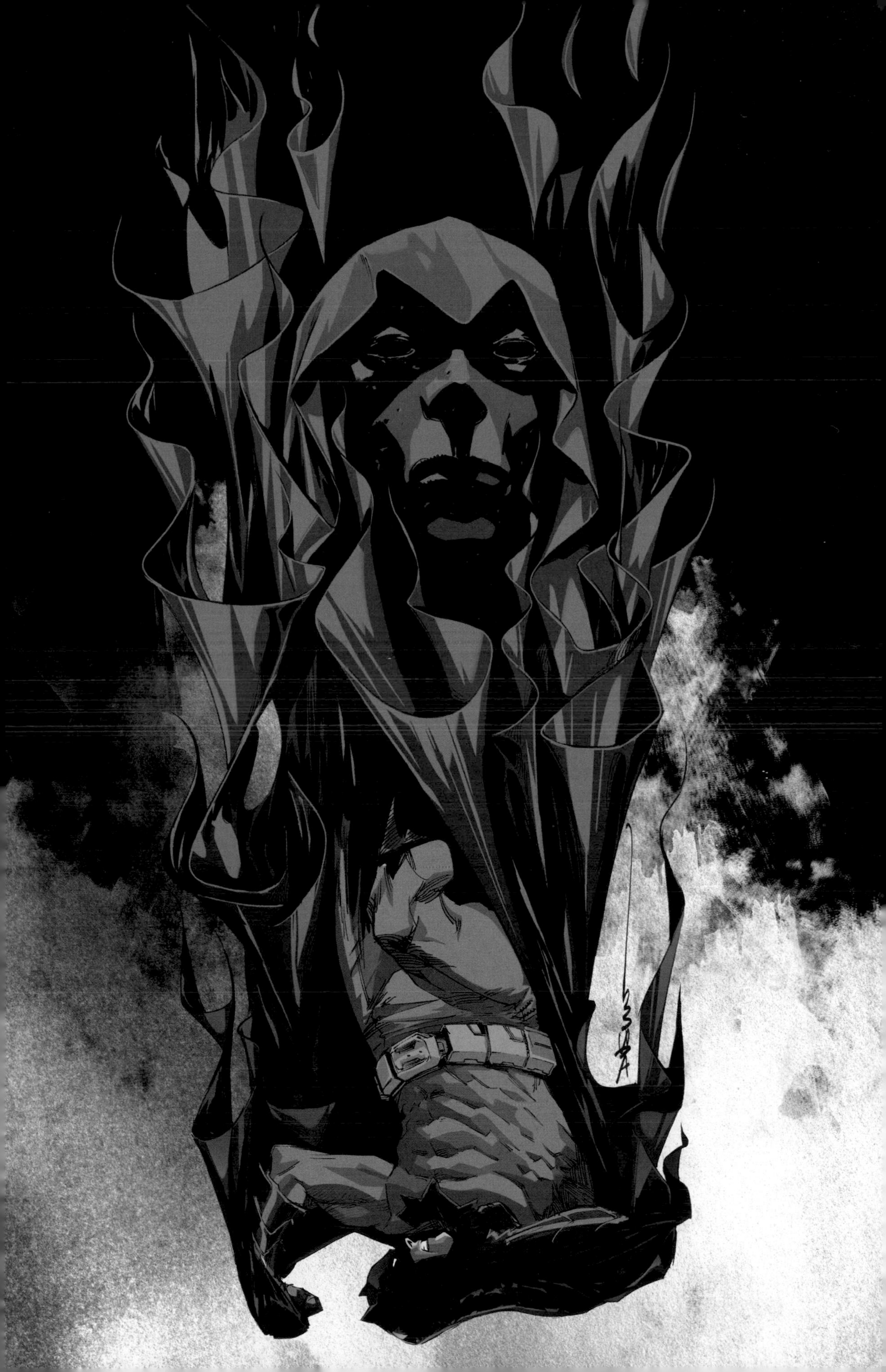

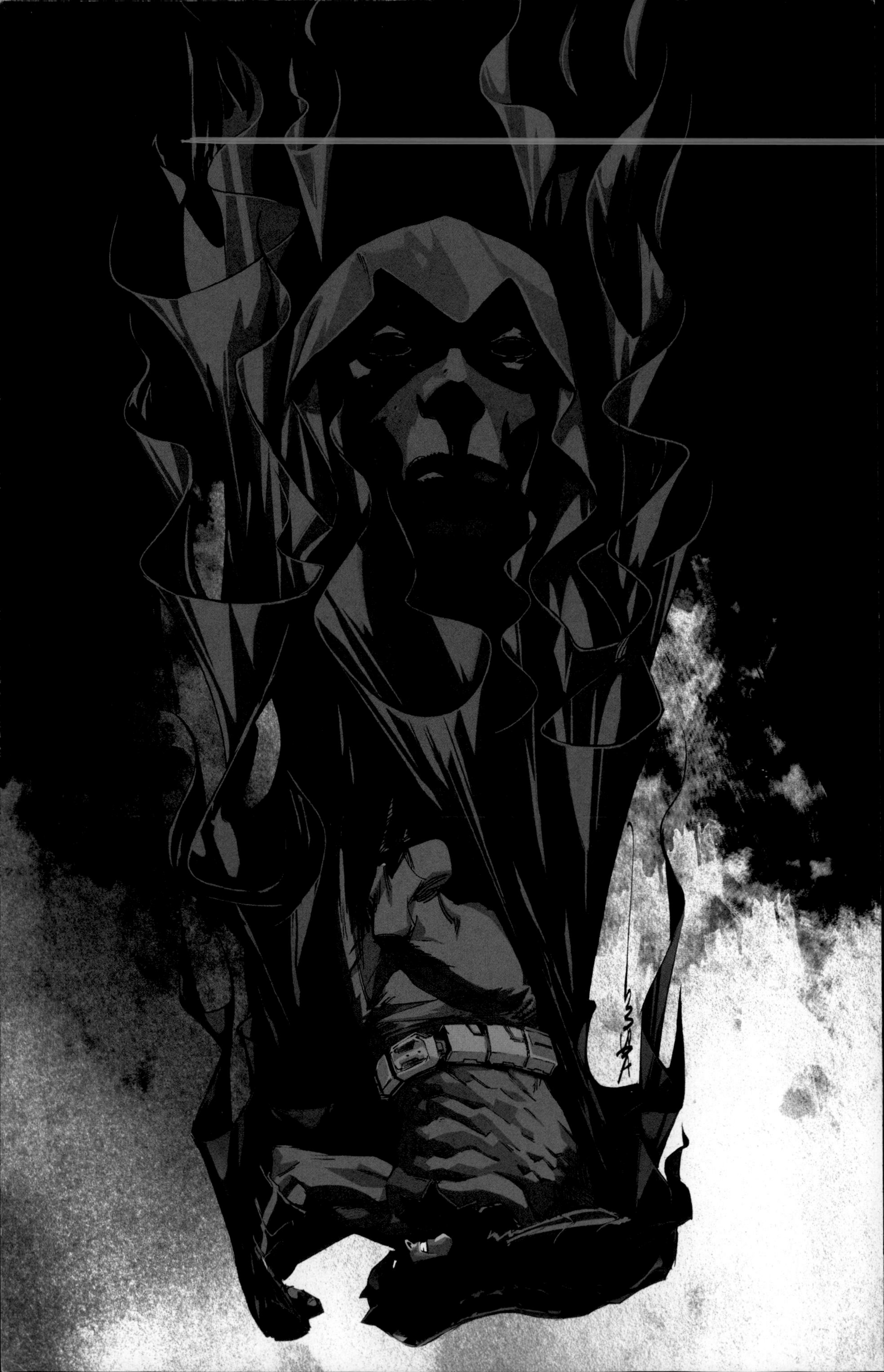

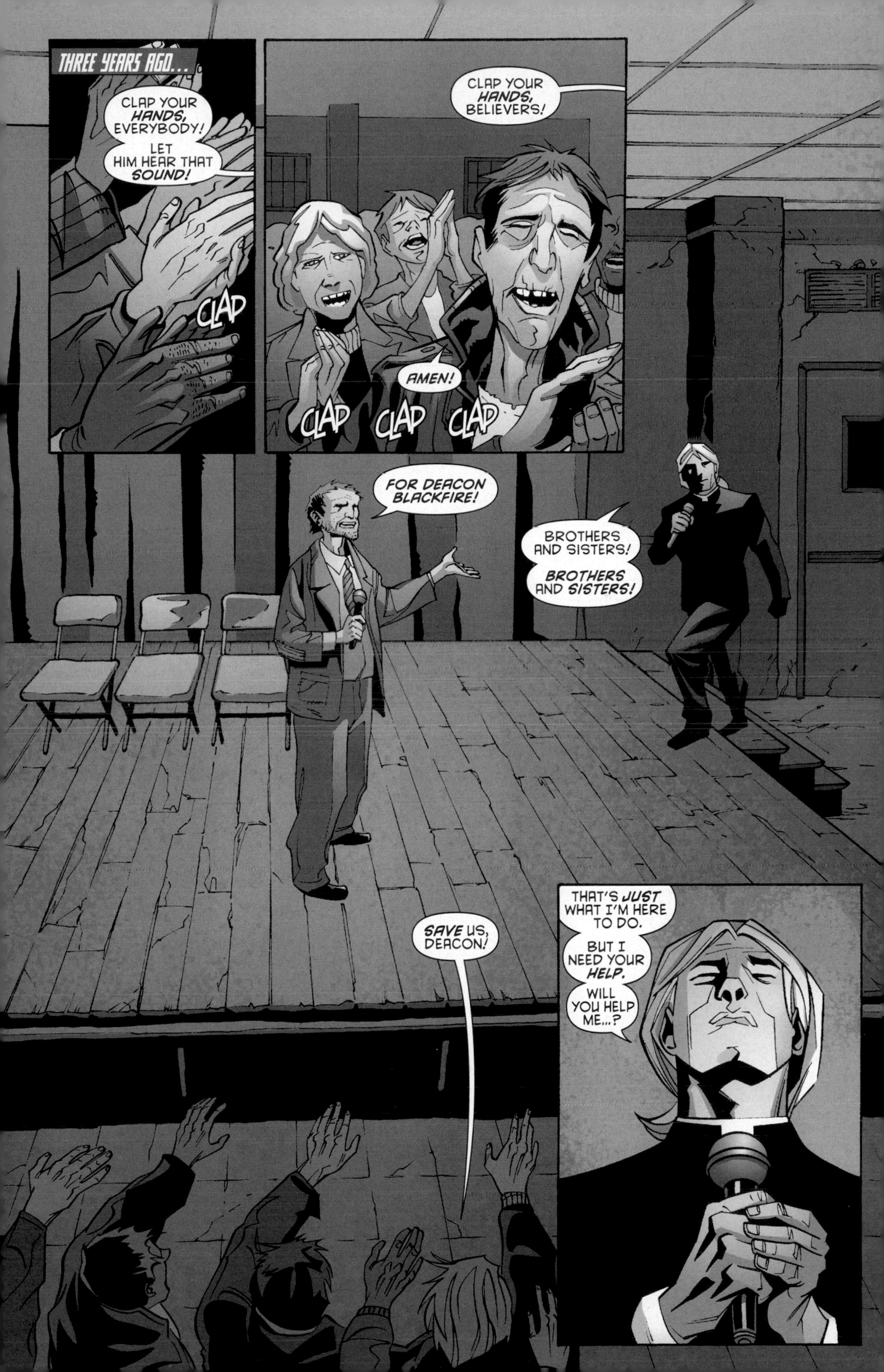
THREE YEARS AGO...
CLAP YOUR HANDS, EVERYBODY!
LET HIM HEAR THAT SOUND!
CLAP
CLAP YOUR HANDS, BELIEVERS!
AMEN!
CLAP CLAP CLAP
FOR DEACON BLACKFIRE!
BROTHERS AND SISTERS!
BROTHERS AND SISTERS!
SAVE US, DEACON!
THAT'S JUST WHAT I'M HERE TO DO.
BUT I NEED YOUR HELP.
WILL YOU HELP ME...?

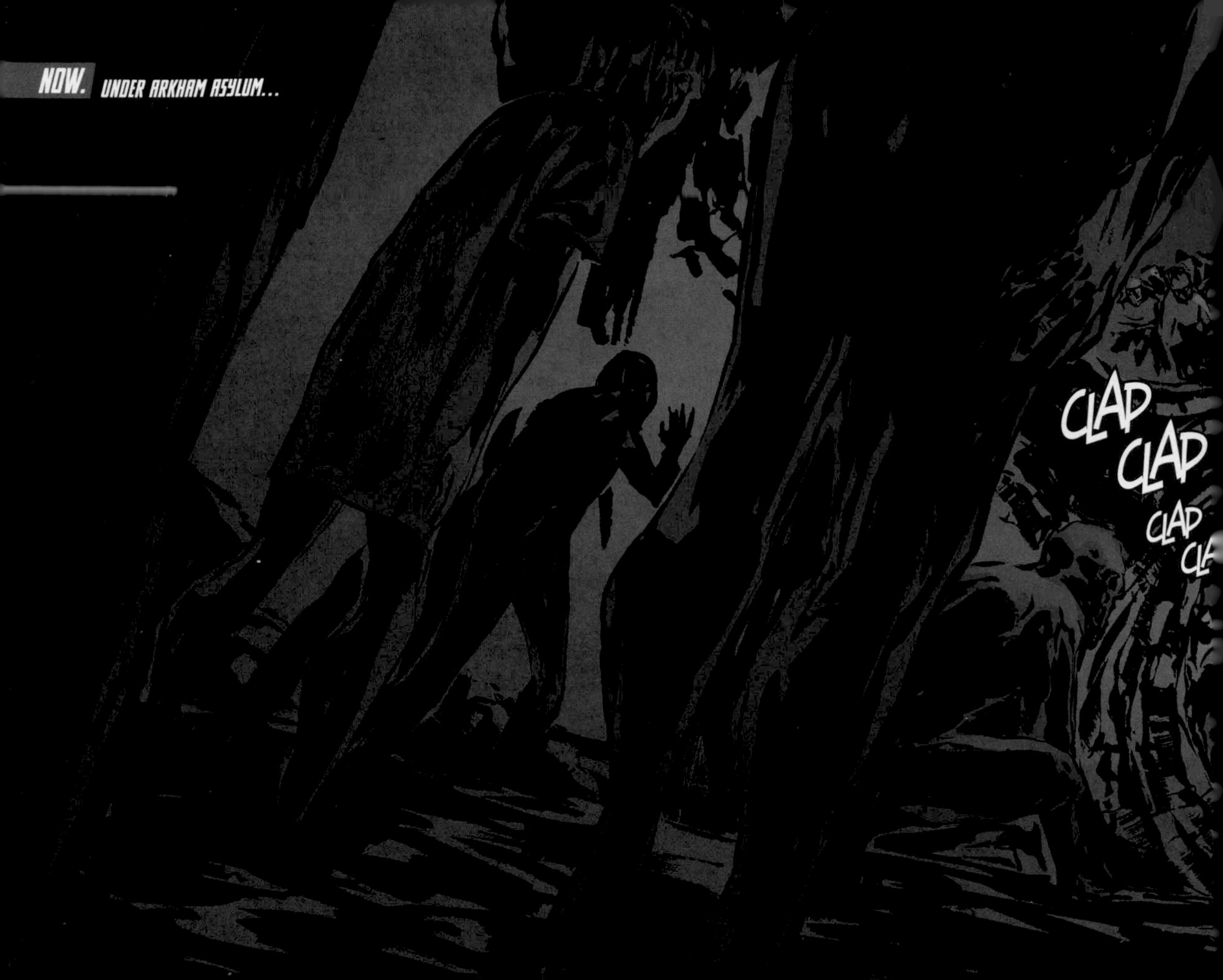
NOW. UNDER ARKHAM ASYLUM...
CLAP
CLAP
CLAP

SCOTT SNYDER & JAMES TYNION IV STORY

RAY FAWKES SCRIPT

CONSULTING WRITERS: JOHN LAYMAN & TIM SEELEY

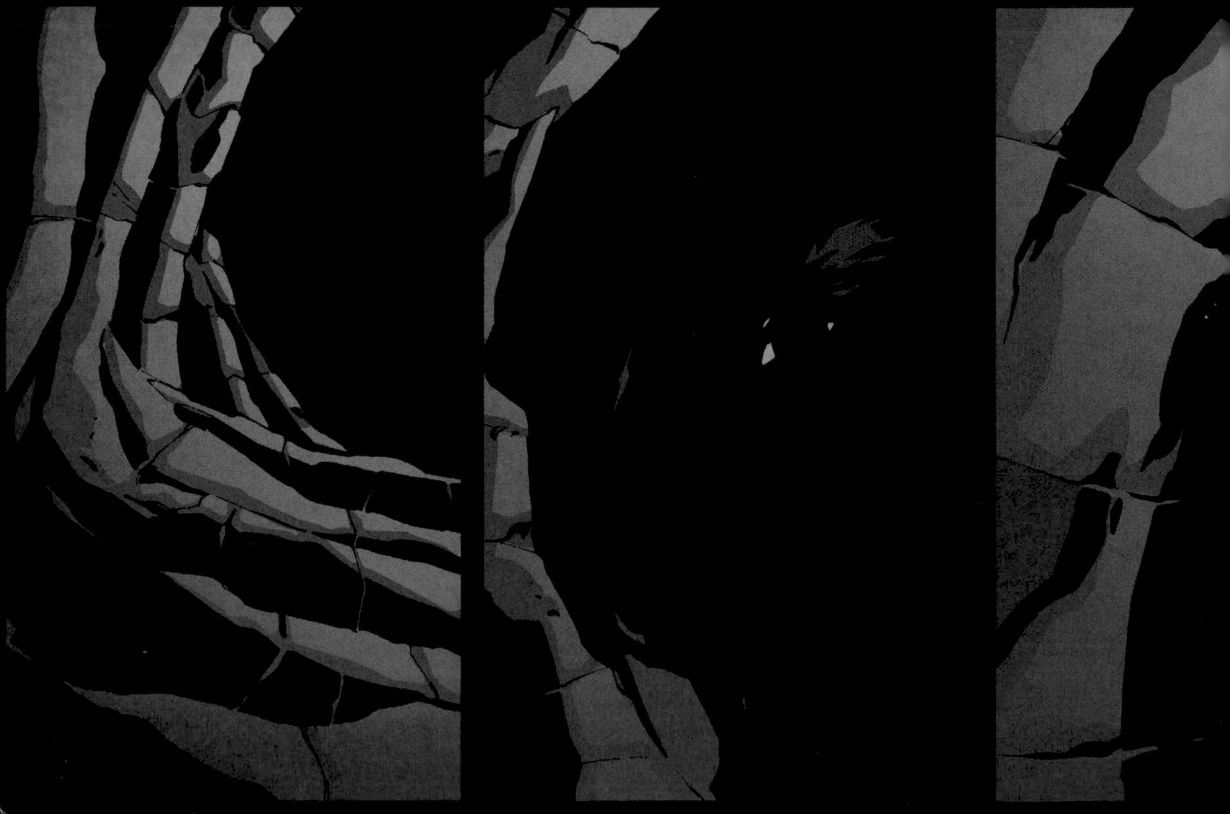

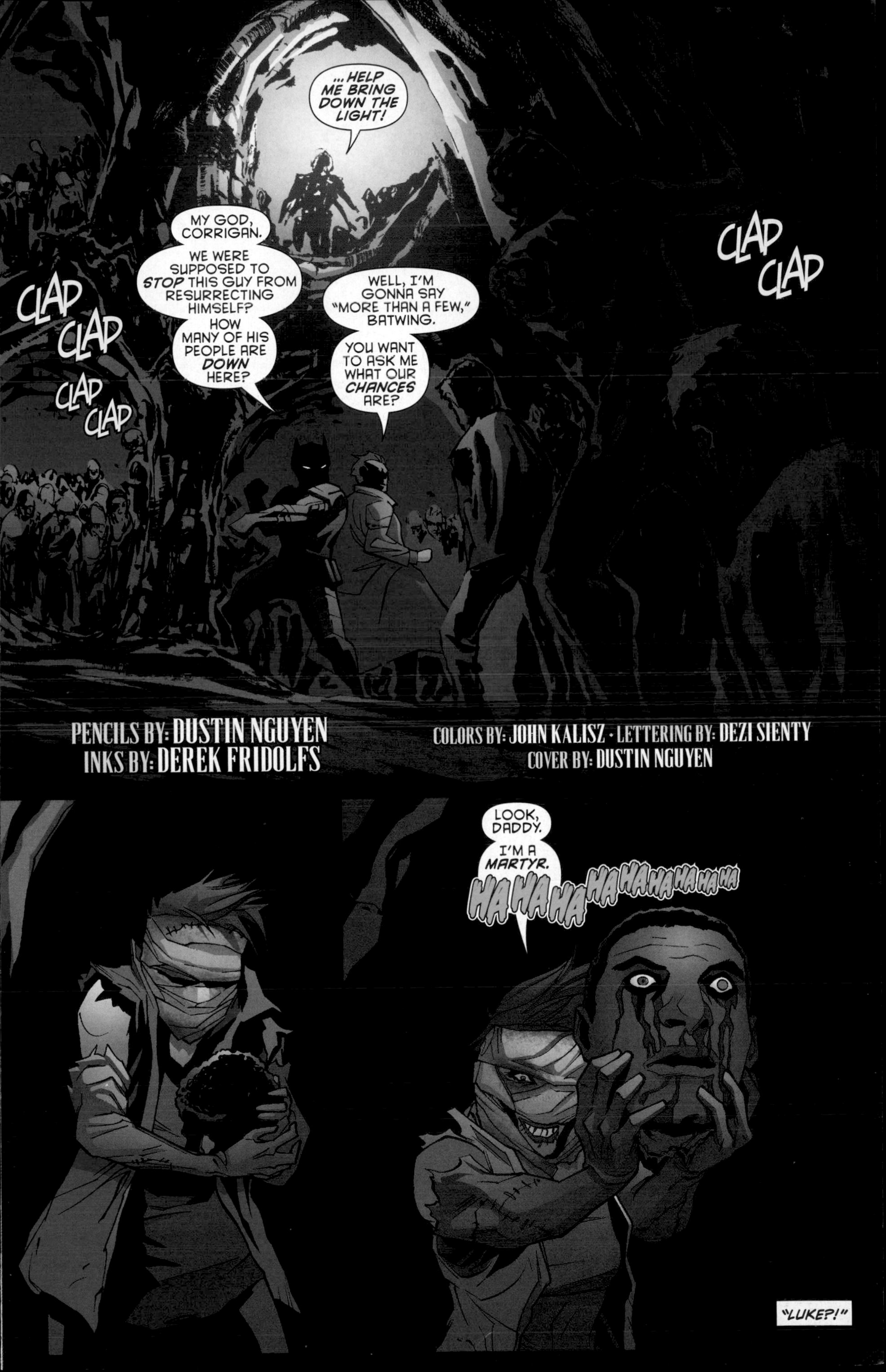
...HELP ME BRING DOWN THE LIGHT!
MY GOD, CORRIGAN.
WE WERE SUPPOSED TO STOP THIS GUY FROM RESURRECTING HIMSELF? HOW MANY OF HIS PEOPLE ARE DOWN HERE?
WELL, I'M GONNA SAY "MORE THAN A FEW," BATWING.
YOU WANT TO ASK ME WHAT OUR CHANCES ARE?
CLAP CLAP CLAP CLAP
CLAP CLAP
PENCILS BY: DUSTIN NGUYEN
INKS BY: DEREK FRIDOLFS
COLORS BY: JOHN KALISZ · LETTERING BY: DEZI SIENTY
COVER BY: DUSTIN NGUYEN
LOOK, DADDY.
I'M A MARTYR.
HA HA HA HA HA HA HA HA HA
"LUKE?!"

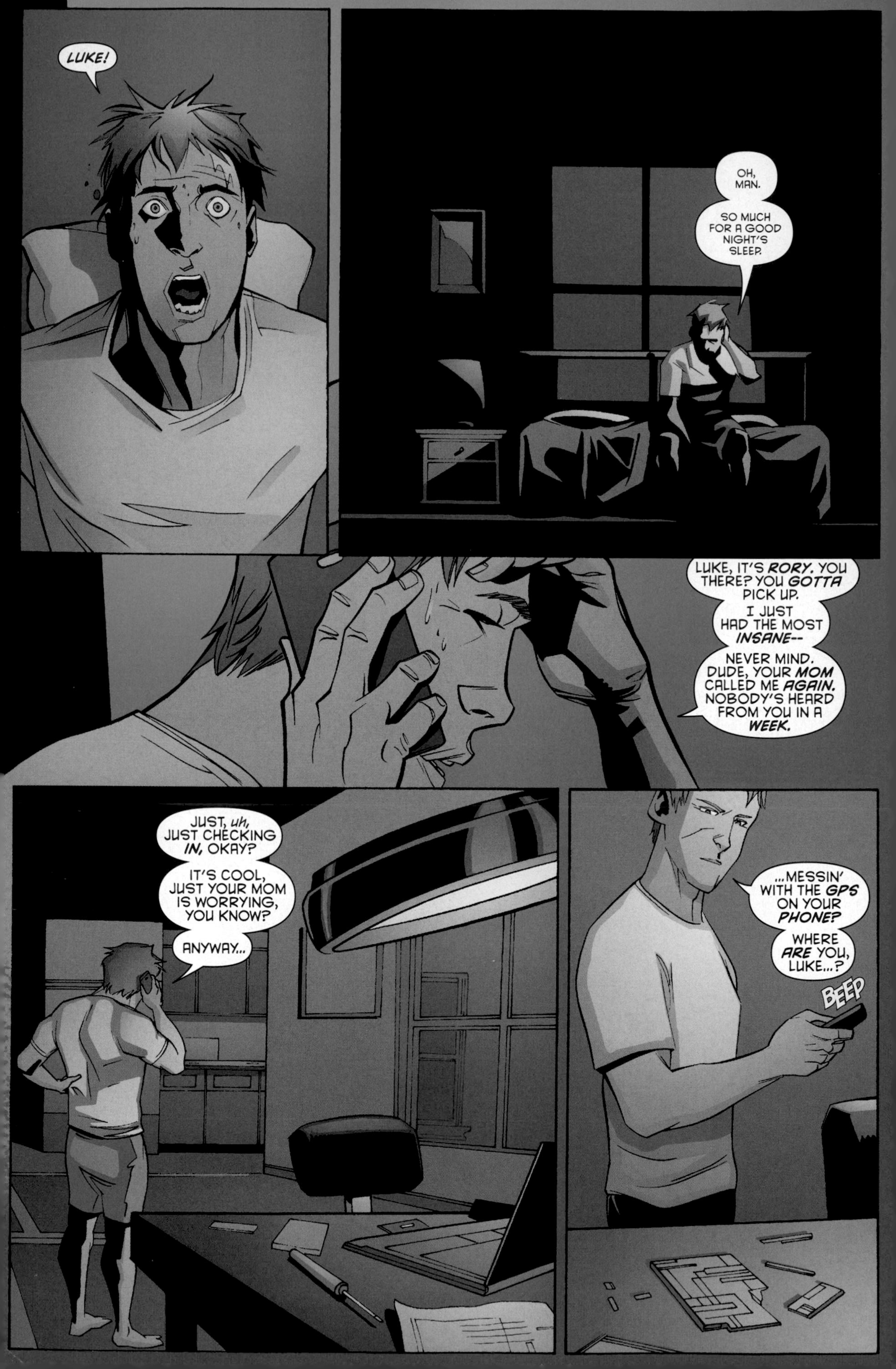
LUKE!
OH, MAN.
SO MUCH FOR A GOOD NIGHT'S SLEEP.
LUKE, IT'S RORY. YOU THERE? YOU GOTTA PICK UP.
I JUST HAD THE MOST INSANE--
NEVER MIND. DUDE, YOUR MOM CALLED ME AGAIN. NOBODY'S HEARD FROM YOU IN A WEEK.
JUST, uh, JUST CHECKING IN, OKAY?
IT'S COOL, JUST YOUR MOM IS WORRYING, YOU KNOW?
ANYWAY...
...MESSIN' WITH THE GPS ON YOUR PHONE?
WHERE ARE YOU, LUKE...?
BEEP

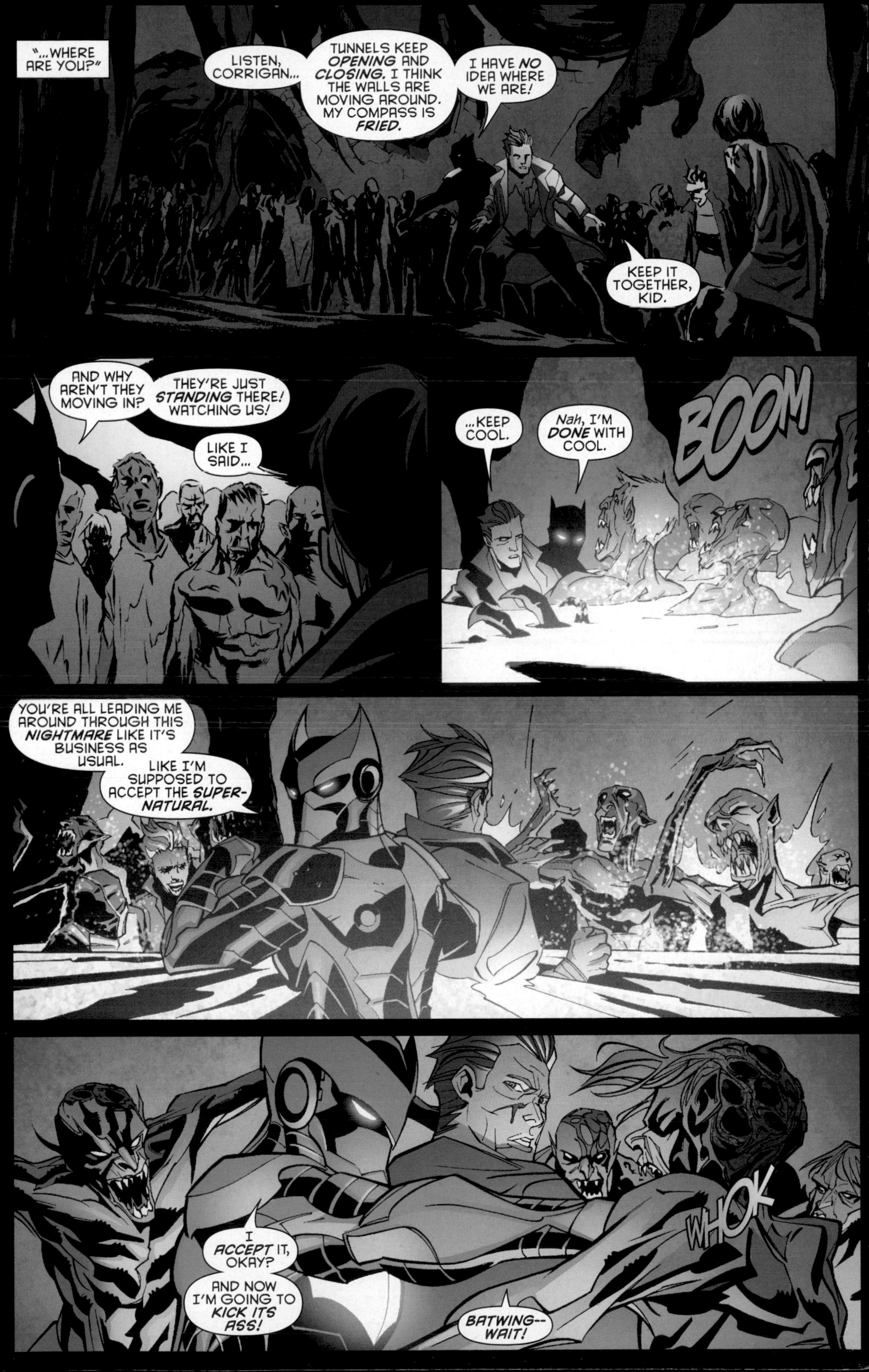
"...WHERE ARE YOU?"
LISTEN, CORRIGAN...
TUNNELS KEEP *OPENING* AND *CLOSING.* I THINK THE WALLS ARE MOVING AROUND. MY COMPASS IS *FRIED.*
I HAVE *NO* IDEA WHERE WE ARE!
KEEP IT TOGETHER, KID.
AND WHY AREN'T THEY MOVING IN?
THEY'RE JUST *STANDING* THERE! WATCHING US!
LIKE I SAID...
...KEEP COOL.
Nah, I'M *DONE* WITH COOL.
BOOM
YOU'RE ALL LEADING ME AROUND THROUGH THIS *NIGHTMARE* LIKE IT'S BUSINESS AS USUAL.
LIKE I'M SUPPOSED TO ACCEPT THE *SUPER-NATURAL.*
I *ACCEPT* IT, OKAY?
AND NOW I'M GOING TO *KICK ITS ASS!*
WHOK
BATWING-- WAIT!

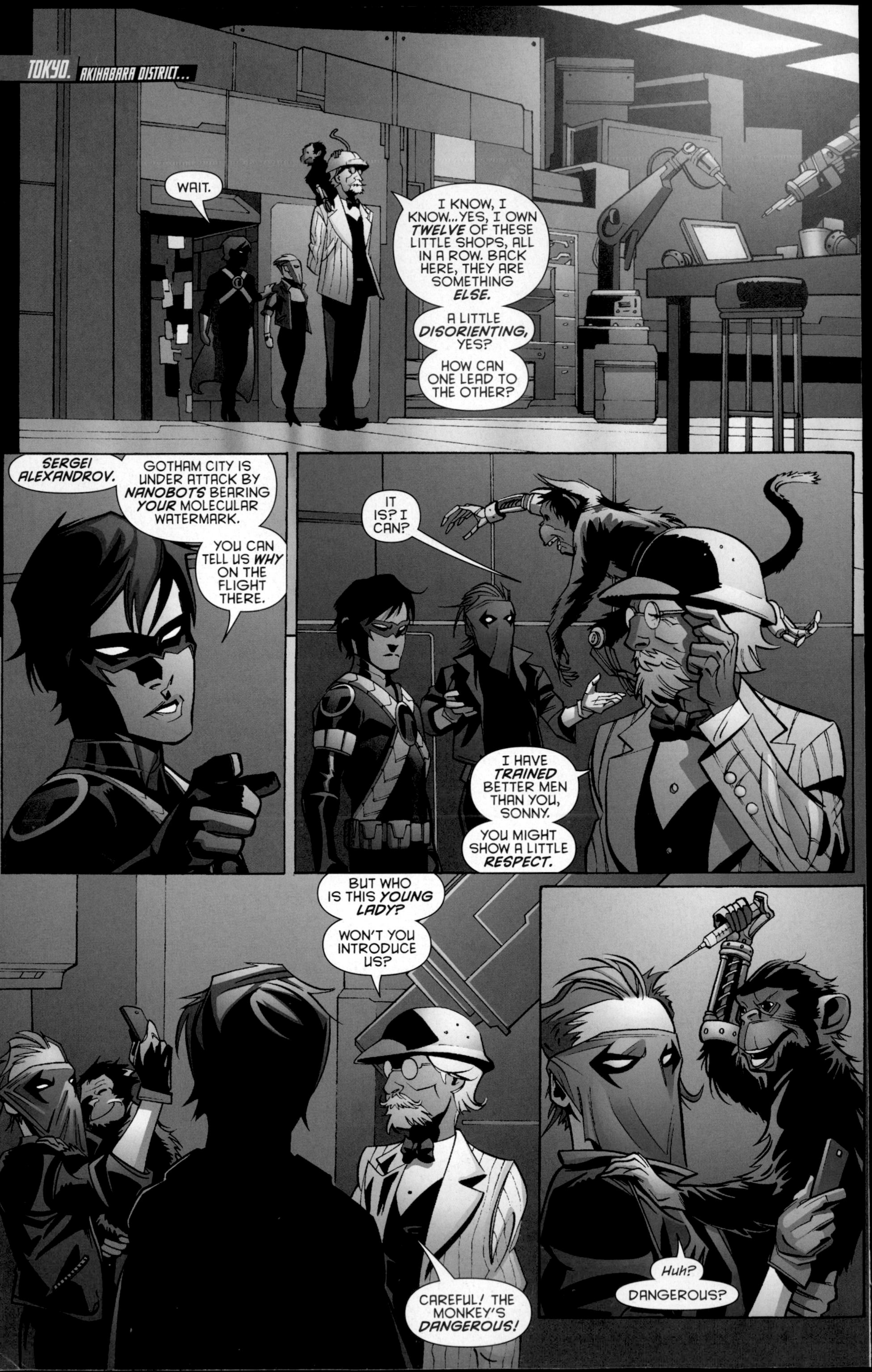
TOKYO. AKIHABARA DISTRICT...
WAIT.
I KNOW, I KNOW...YES, I OWN TWELVE OF THESE LITTLE SHOPS, ALL IN A ROW. BACK HERE, THEY ARE SOMETHING ELSE.
A LITTLE DISORIENTING, YES?
HOW CAN ONE LEAD TO THE OTHER?
SERGEI ALEXANDROV.
GOTHAM CITY IS UNDER ATTACK BY NANOBOTS BEARING YOUR MOLECULAR WATERMARK.
YOU CAN TELL US WHY ON THE FLIGHT THERE.
IT IS? I CAN?
I HAVE TRAINED BETTER MEN THAN YOU, SONNY.
YOU MIGHT SHOW A LITTLE RESPECT.
BUT WHO IS THIS YOUNG LADY?
WON'T YOU INTRODUCE US?
CAREFUL! THE MONKEY'S DANGEROUS!
Huh? DANGEROUS?

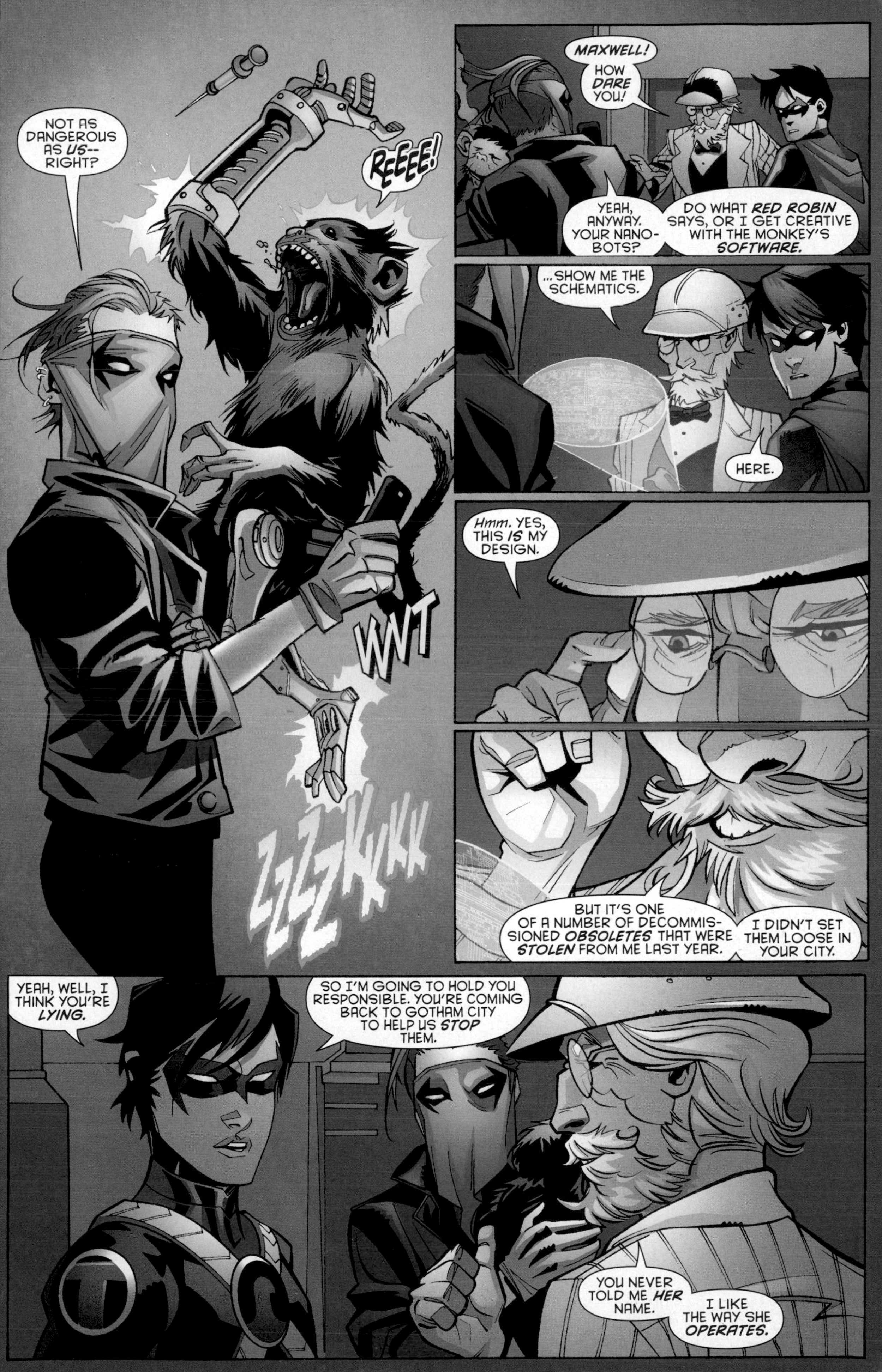

NOT AS DANGEROUS AS US-- RIGHT?
REEEE!
WVT
ZZZZKKKK
MAXWELL! HOW DARE YOU!
YEAH, ANYWAY. YOUR NANOBOTS?
DO WHAT RED ROBIN SAYS, OR I GET CREATIVE WITH THE MONKEY'S SOFTWARE.
...SHOW ME THE SCHEMATICS.
HERE.
Hmm. YES, THIS IS MY DESIGN.
BUT IT'S ONE OF A NUMBER OF DECOMMISSIONED OBSOLETES THAT WERE STOLEN FROM ME LAST YEAR.
I DIDN'T SET THEM LOOSE IN YOUR CITY.
YEAH, WELL, I THINK YOU'RE LYING.
SO I'M GOING TO HOLD YOU RESPONSIBLE. YOU'RE COMING BACK TO GOTHAM CITY TO HELP US STOP THEM.
YOU NEVER TOLD ME HER NAME.
I LIKE THE WAY SHE OPERATES.

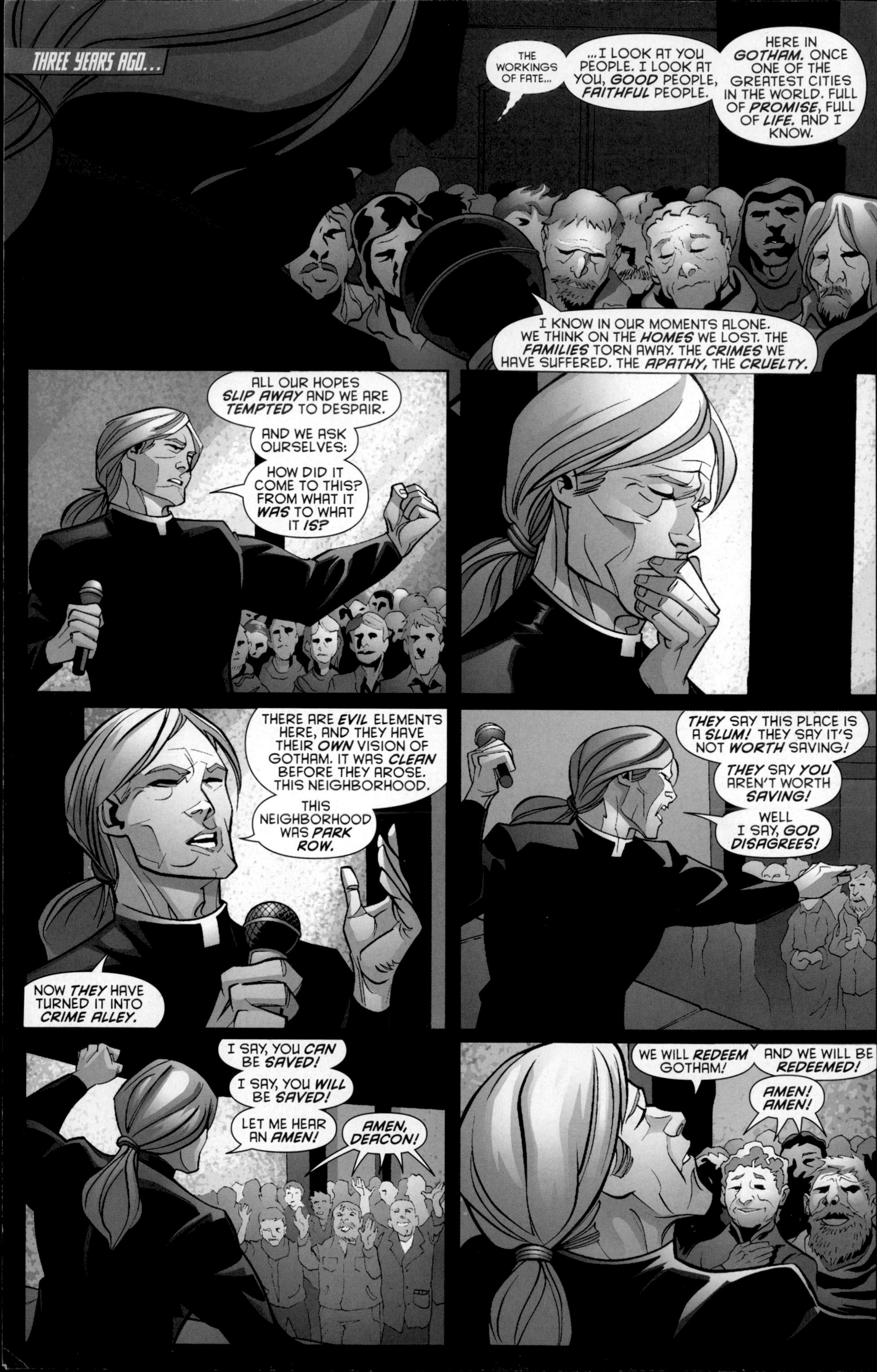
THREE YEARS AGO...
THE WORKINGS OF FATE...
...I LOOK AT YOU PEOPLE. I LOOK AT YOU, GOOD PEOPLE, FAITHFUL PEOPLE.
HERE IN GOTHAM. ONCE ONE OF THE GREATEST CITIES IN THE WORLD. FULL OF PROMISE, FULL OF LIFE. AND I KNOW.
I KNOW IN OUR MOMENTS ALONE. WE THINK ON THE HOMES WE LOST. THE FAMILIES TORN AWAY. THE CRIMES WE HAVE SUFFERED. THE APATHY, THE CRUELTY.
ALL OUR HOPES SLIP AWAY AND WE ARE TEMPTED TO DESPAIR.
AND WE ASK OURSELVES:
HOW DID IT COME TO THIS? FROM WHAT IT WAS TO WHAT IT IS?
THERE ARE EVIL ELEMENTS HERE, AND THEY HAVE THEIR OWN VISION OF GOTHAM. IT WAS CLEAN BEFORE THEY AROSE. THIS NEIGHBORHOOD.
THIS NEIGHBORHOOD WAS PARK ROW.
NOW THEY HAVE TURNED IT INTO CRIME ALLEY.
THEY SAY THIS PLACE IS A SLUM! THEY SAY IT'S NOT WORTH SAVING!
THEY SAY YOU AREN'T WORTH SAVING!
WELL I SAY, GOD DISAGREES!
I SAY, YOU CAN BE SAVED!
I SAY, YOU WILL BE SAVED!
LET ME HEAR AN AMEN!
AMEN, DEACON!
WE WILL REDEEM GOTHAM!
AND WE WILL BE REDEEMED!
AMEN! AMEN!

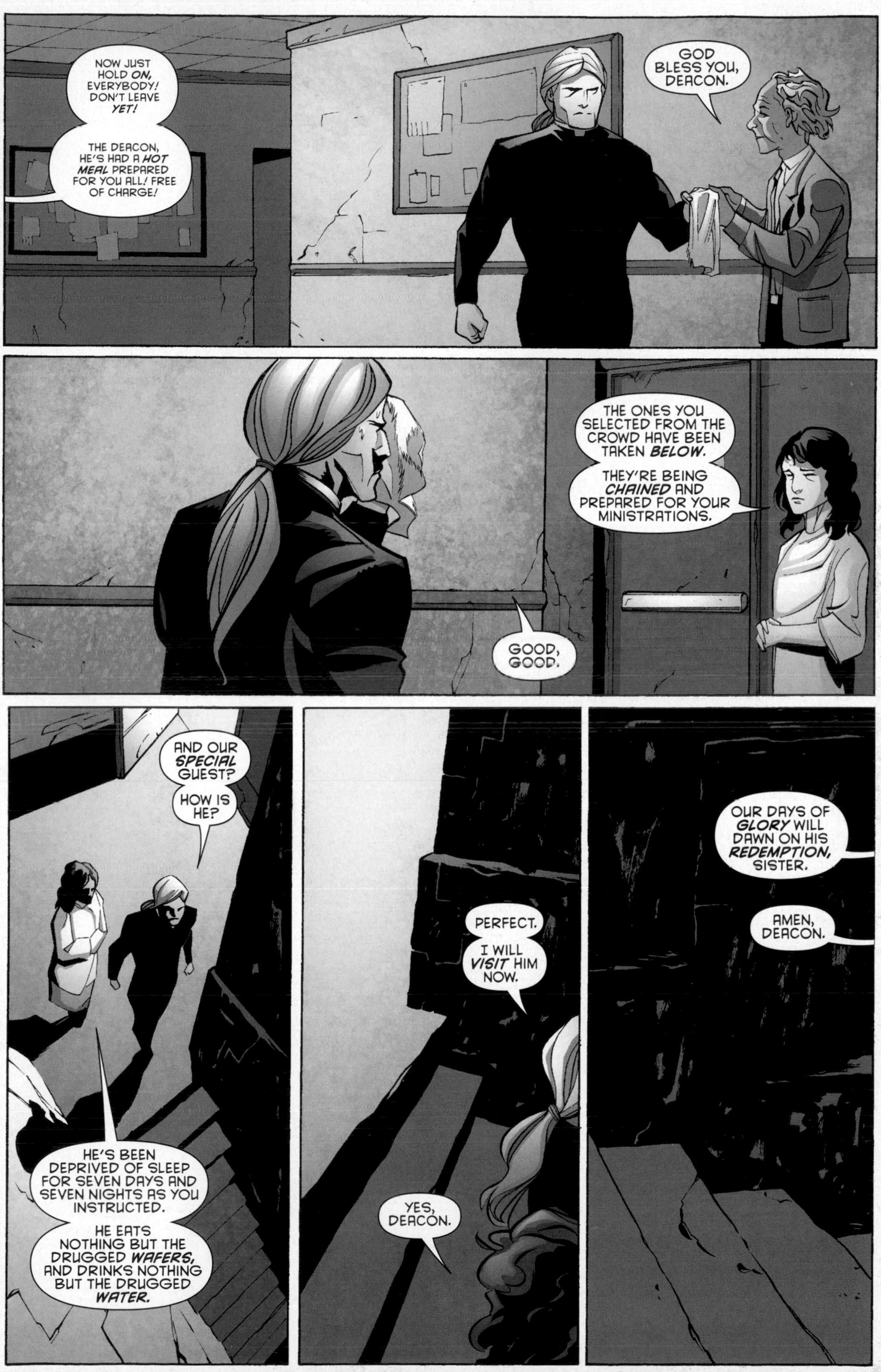
NOW JUST HOLD ON, EVERYBODY! DON'T LEAVE YET!
THE DEACON, HE'S HAD A HOT MEAL PREPARED FOR YOU ALL! FREE OF CHARGE!
GOD BLESS YOU, DEACON.
THE ONES YOU SELECTED FROM THE CROWD HAVE BEEN TAKEN BELOW.
THEY'RE BEING CHAINED AND PREPARED FOR YOUR MINISTRATIONS.
GOOD, GOOD.
AND OUR SPECIAL GUEST?
HOW IS HE?
HE'S BEEN DEPRIVED OF SLEEP FOR SEVEN DAYS AND SEVEN NIGHTS AS YOU INSTRUCTED.
HE EATS NOTHING BUT THE DRUGGED WAFERS, AND DRINKS NOTHING BUT THE DRUGGED WATER.
PERFECT.
I WILL VISIT HIM NOW.
YES, DEACON.
OUR DAYS OF GLORY WILL DAWN ON HIS REDEMPTION, SISTER.
AMEN, DEACON.

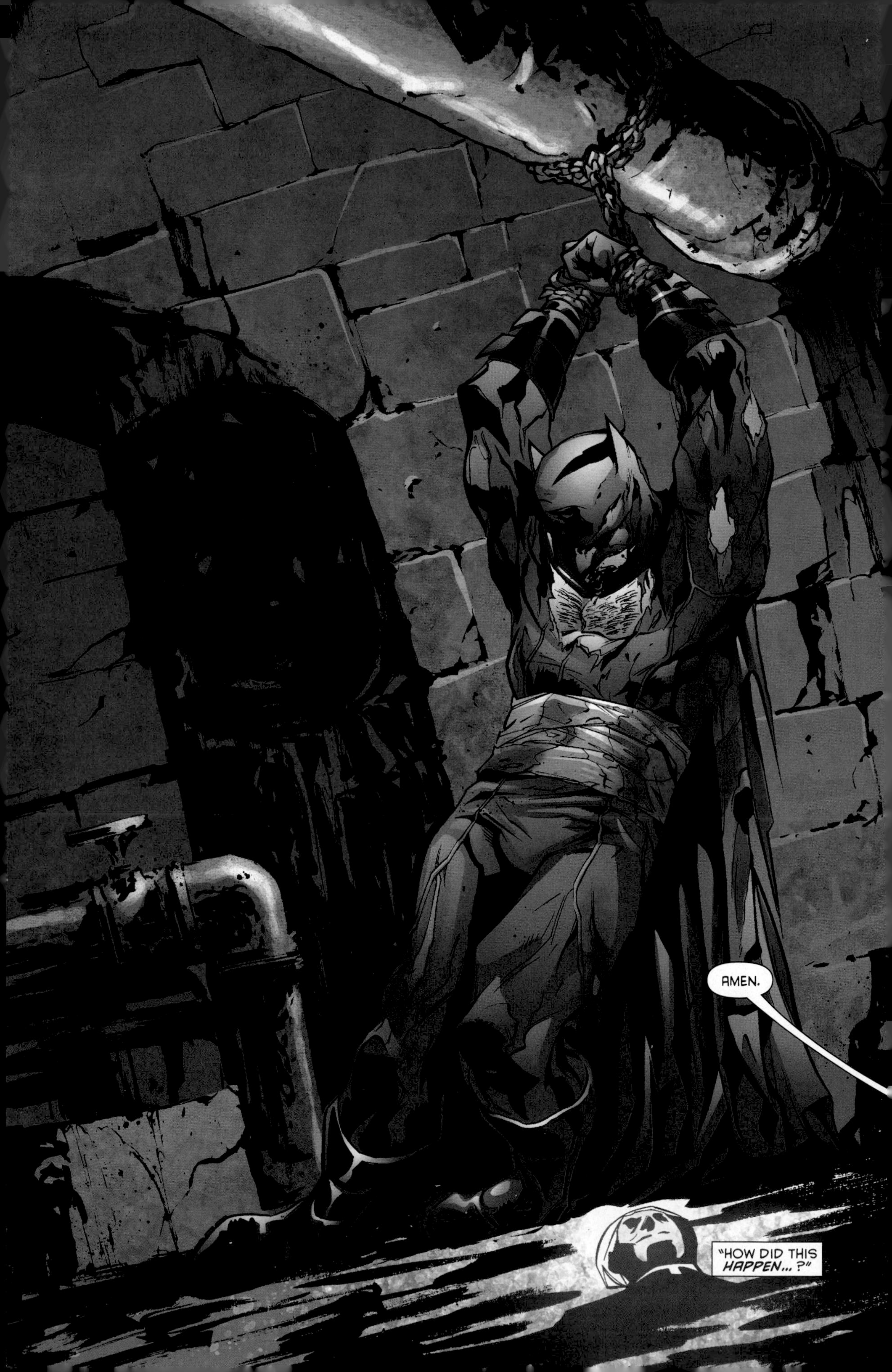
AMEN.
"HOW DID THIS HAPPEN...?"

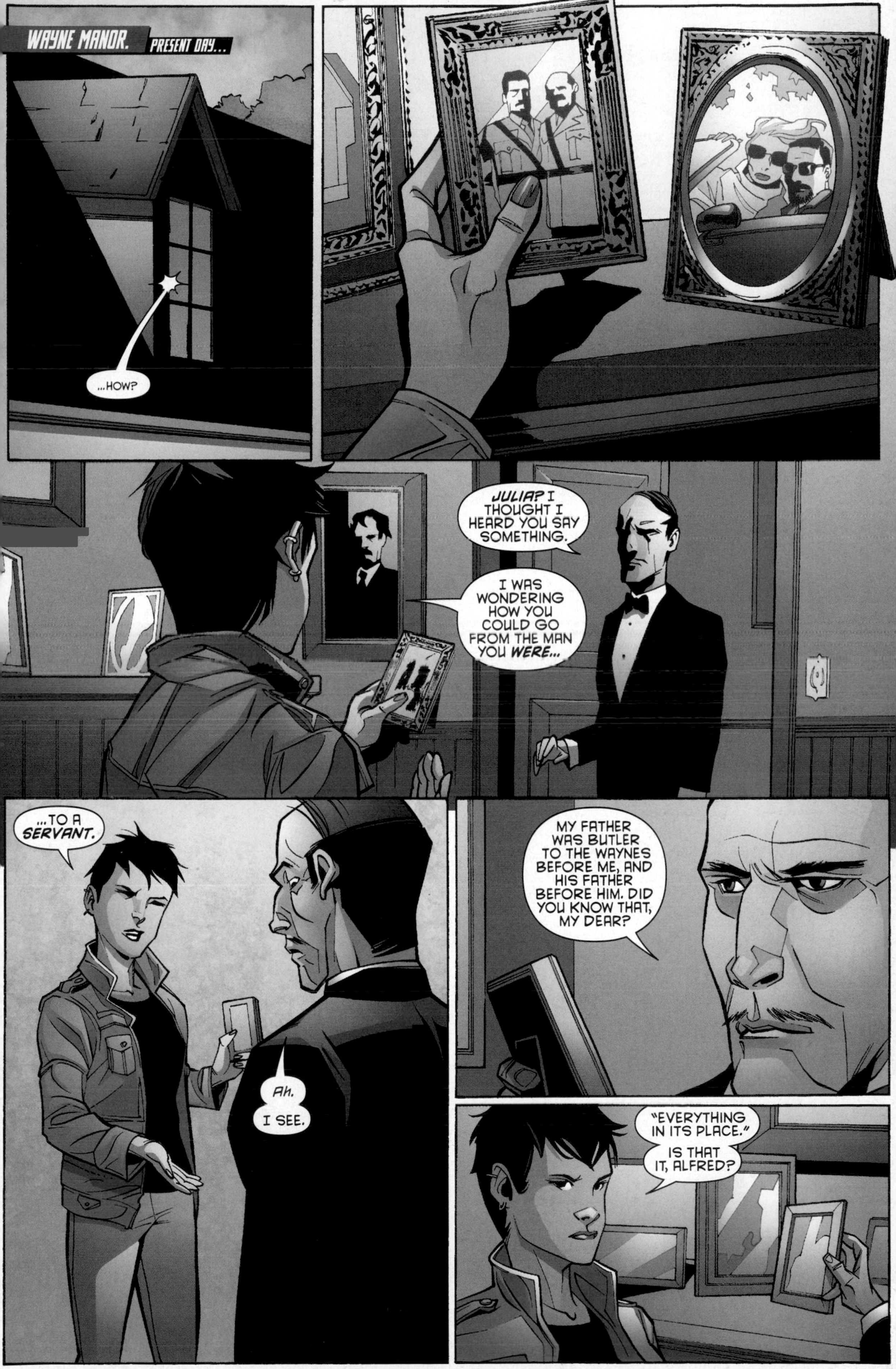
WAYNE MANOR. PRESENT DAY...
...HOW?
JULIA? I THOUGHT I HEARD YOU SAY SOMETHING.
I WAS WONDERING HOW YOU COULD GO FROM THE MAN YOU WERE...
...TO A SERVANT.
Ah.
I SEE.
MY FATHER WAS BUTLER TO THE WAYNES BEFORE ME, AND HIS FATHER BEFORE HIM. DID YOU KNOW THAT, MY DEAR?
"EVERYTHING IN ITS PLACE."
IS THAT IT, ALFRED?

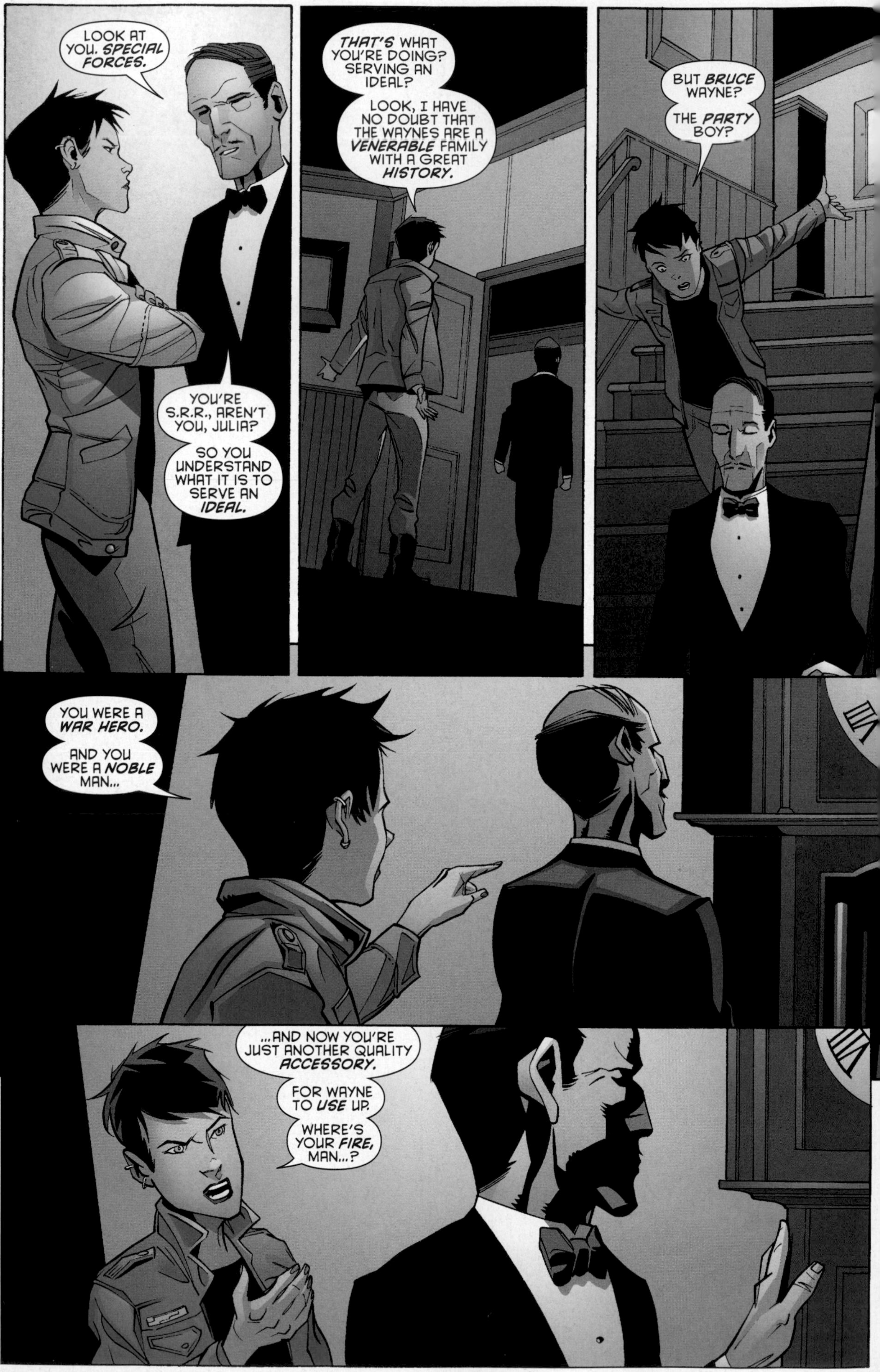
LOOK AT YOU. SPECIAL FORCES.
YOU'RE S.R.R., AREN'T YOU, JULIA?
SO YOU UNDERSTAND WHAT IT IS TO SERVE AN IDEAL.
THAT'S WHAT YOU'RE DOING? SERVING AN IDEAL?
LOOK, I HAVE NO DOUBT THAT THE WAYNES ARE A VENERABLE FAMILY WITH A GREAT HISTORY.
BUT BRUCE WAYNE?
THE PARTY BOY?
YOU WERE A WAR HERO.
AND YOU WERE A NOBLE MAN...
...AND NOW YOU'RE JUST ANOTHER QUALITY ACCESSORY.
FOR WAYNE TO USE UP.
WHERE'S YOUR FIRE, MAN...?

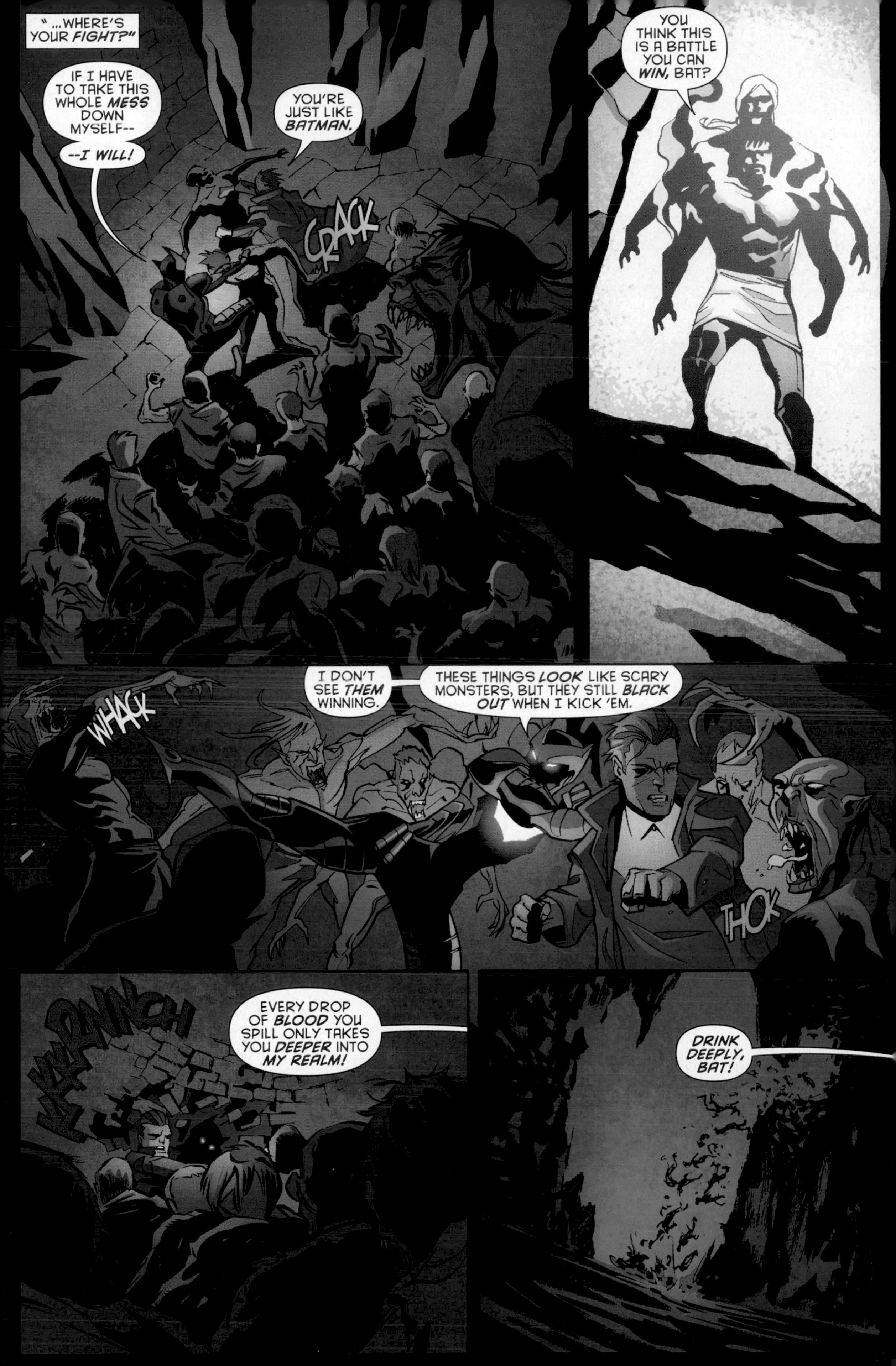
"...WHERE'S YOUR FIGHT?"
IF I HAVE TO TAKE THIS WHOLE MESS DOWN MYSELF--
--I WILL!
YOU'RE JUST LIKE BATMAN.
CRACK
YOU THINK THIS IS A BATTLE YOU CAN WIN, BAT?
I DON'T SEE THEM WINNING.
THESE THINGS LOOK LIKE SCARY MONSTERS, BUT THEY STILL BLACK OUT WHEN I KICK 'EM.
WHACK
THOK
EVERY DROP OF BLOOD YOU SPILL ONLY TAKES YOU DEEPER INTO MY REALM!
DRINK DEEPLY, BAT!

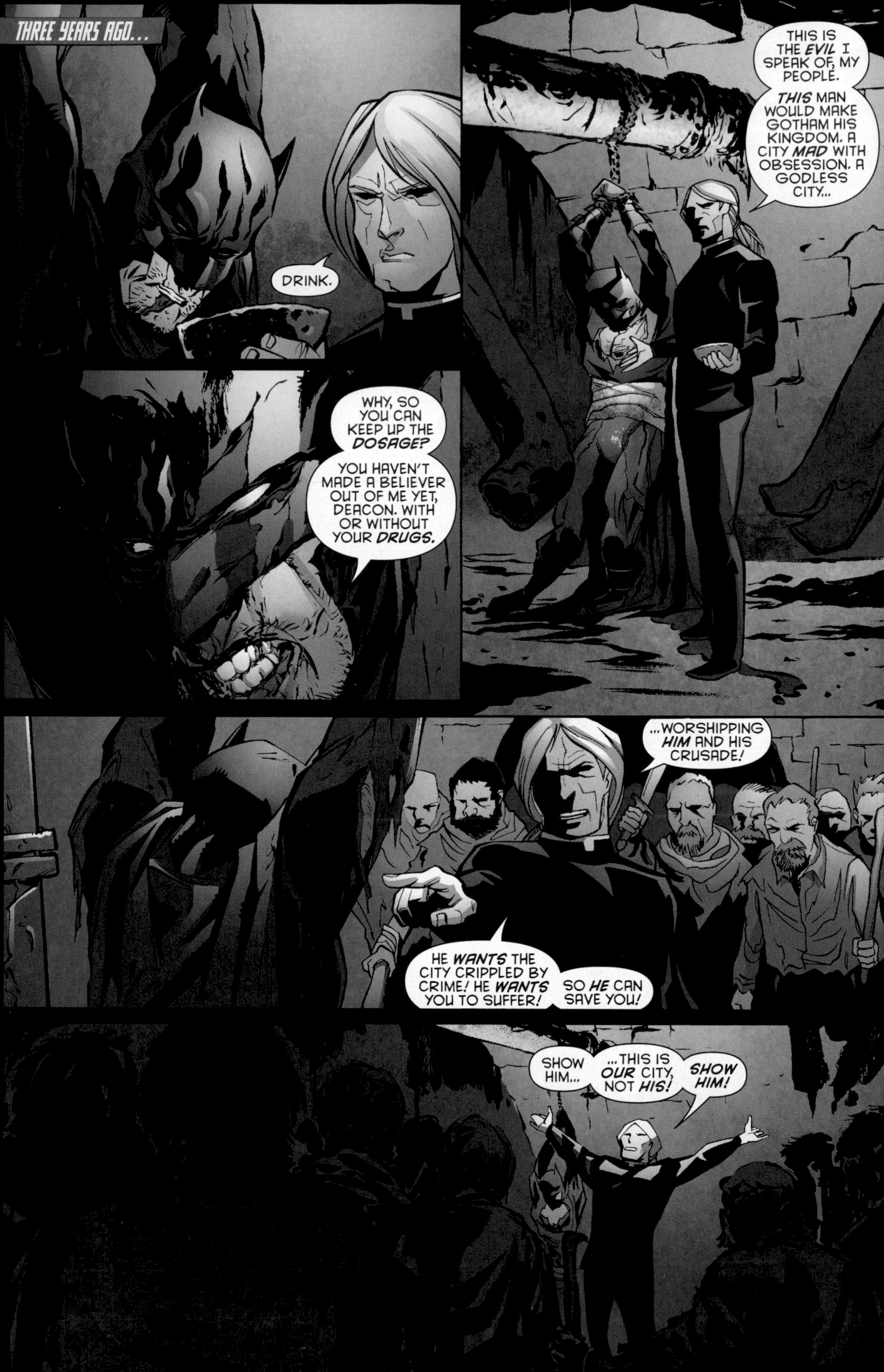

THREE YEARS AGO...
DRINK.
THIS IS THE EVIL I SPEAK OF, MY PEOPLE.
THIS MAN WOULD MAKE GOTHAM HIS KINGDOM. A CITY MAD WITH OBSESSION. A GODLESS CITY...
WHY, SO YOU CAN KEEP UP THE DOSAGE?
YOU HAVEN'T MADE A BELIEVER OUT OF ME YET, DEACON. WITH OR WITHOUT YOUR DRUGS.
...WORSHIPPING HIM AND HIS CRUSADE!
HE WANTS THE CITY CRIPPLED BY CRIME! HE WANTS YOU TO SUFFER!
SO HE CAN SAVE YOU!
SHOW HIM...
...THIS IS OUR CITY, NOT HIS!
SHOW HIM!

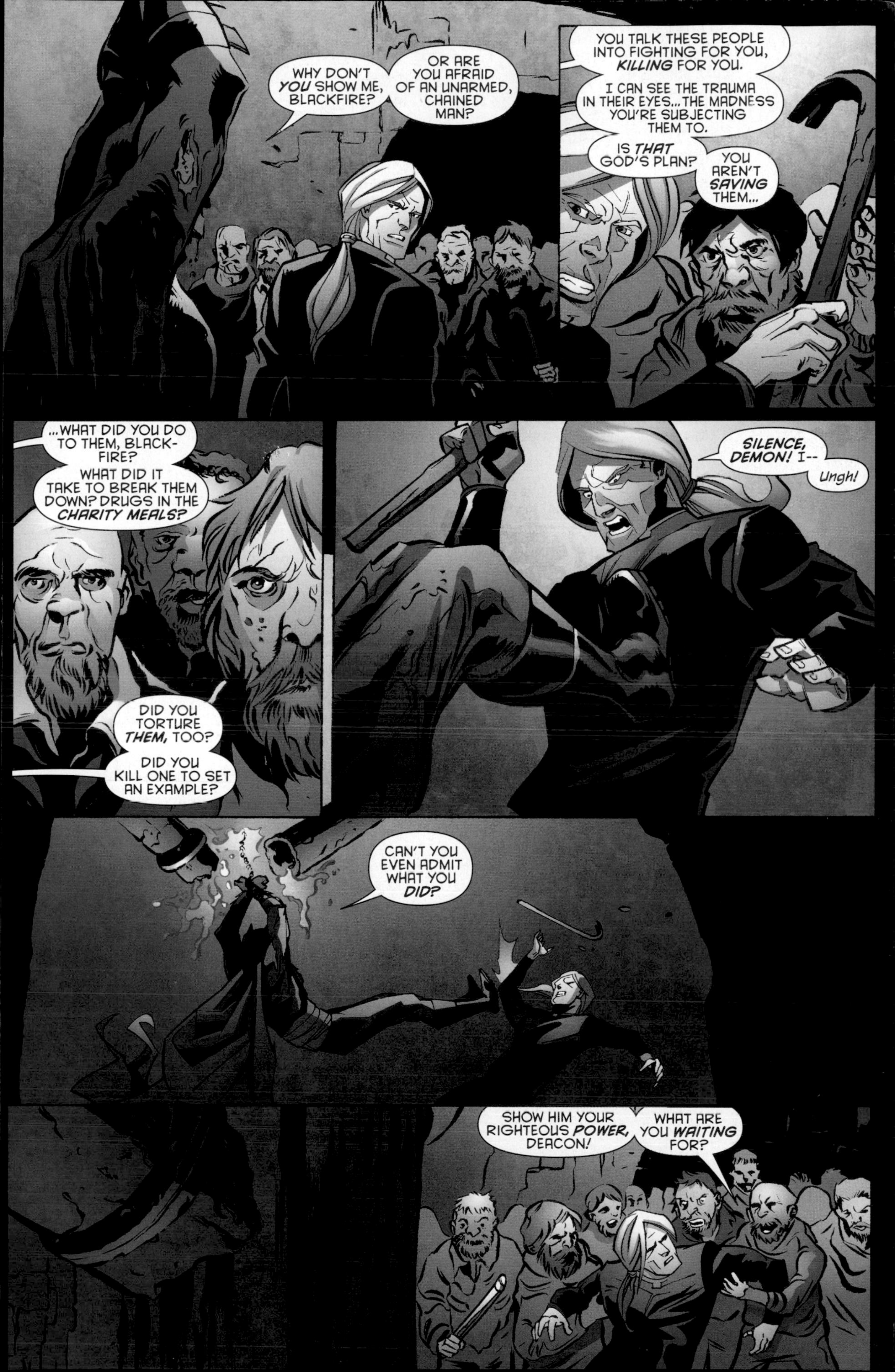

WHY DON'T YOU SHOW ME, BLACKFIRE?
OR ARE YOU AFRAID OF AN UNARMED, CHAINED MAN?
YOU TALK THESE PEOPLE INTO FIGHTING FOR YOU, KILLING FOR YOU.
I CAN SEE THE TRAUMA IN THEIR EYES... THE MADNESS YOU'RE SUBJECTING THEM TO.
IS THAT GOD'S PLAN?
YOU AREN'T SAVING THEM...
...WHAT DID YOU DO TO THEM, BLACK-FIRE?
WHAT DID IT TAKE TO BREAK THEM DOWN? DRUGS IN THE CHARITY MEALS?
DID YOU TORTURE THEM, TOO?
DID YOU KILL ONE TO SET AN EXAMPLE?
SILENCE, DEMON! I--
Ungh!
CAN'T YOU EVEN ADMIT WHAT YOU DID?
SHOW HIM YOUR RIGHTEOUS POWER, DEACON!
WHAT ARE YOU WAITING FOR?

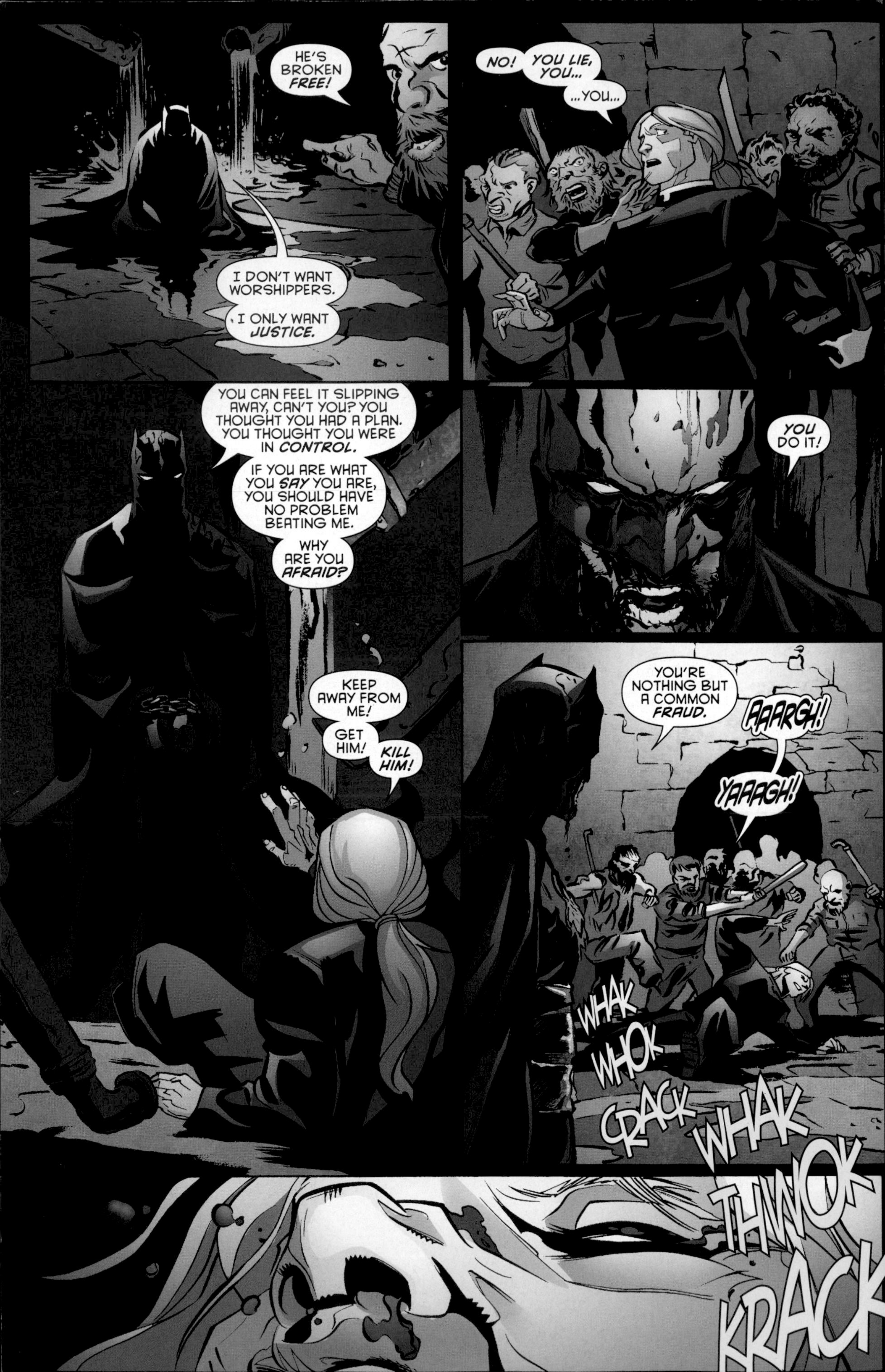
HE'S BROKEN FREE!
I DON'T WANT WORSHIPPERS.
I ONLY WANT JUSTICE.
NO!
YOU LIE, YOU...
...YOU...
YOU CAN FEEL IT SLIPPING AWAY, CAN'T YOU? YOU THOUGHT YOU HAD A PLAN. YOU THOUGHT YOU WERE IN CONTROL.
IF YOU ARE WHAT YOU SAY YOU ARE, YOU SHOULD HAVE NO PROBLEM BEATING ME.
WHY ARE YOU AFRAID?
KEEP AWAY FROM ME!
GET HIM!
KILL HIM!
YOU DO IT!
YOU'RE NOTHING BUT A COMMON FRAUD.
AAARGH!
YAAAGH!
WHAK
WHOK
CRACK
WHAK
THWOK
KRACK

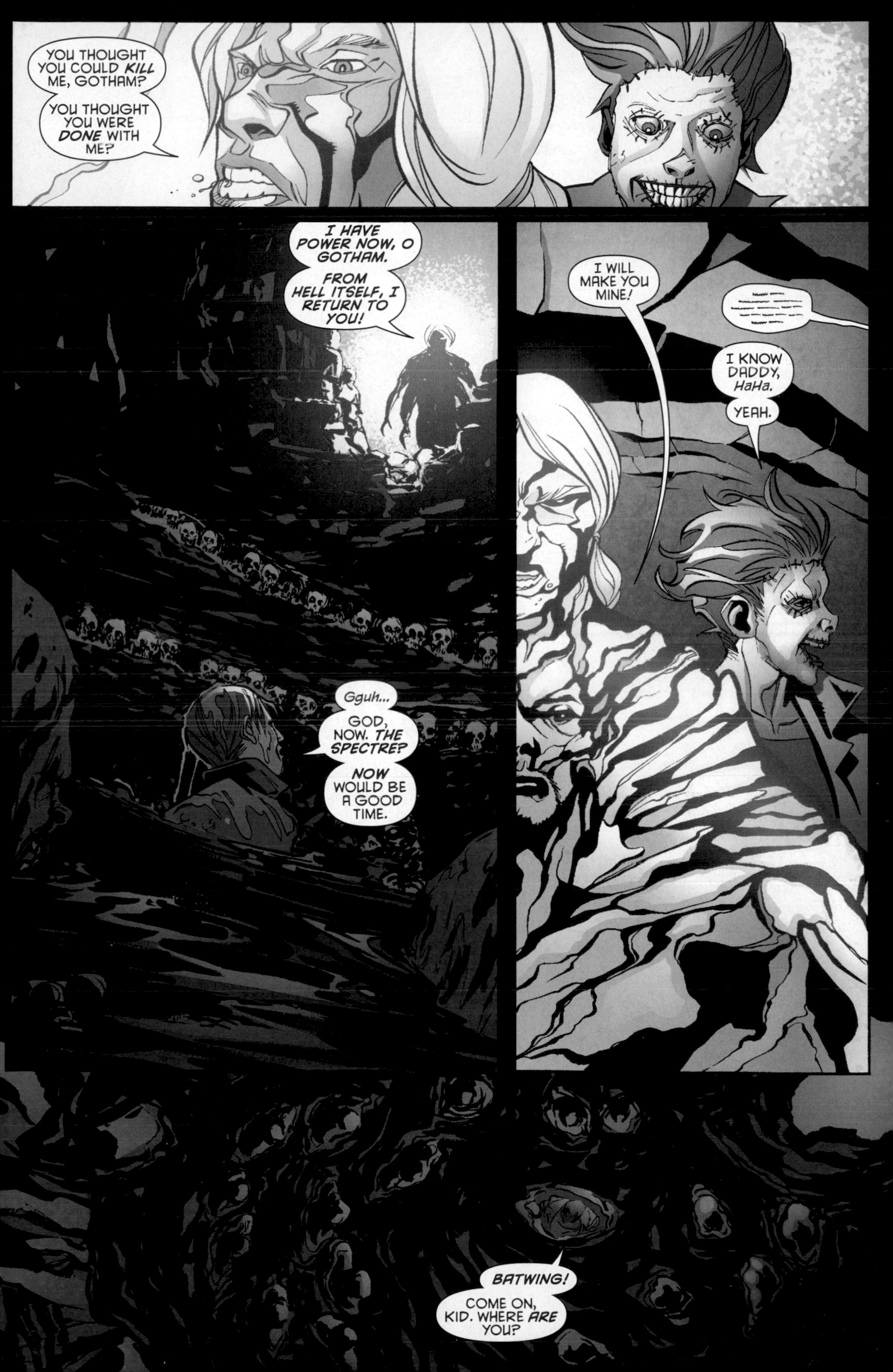
YOU THOUGHT YOU COULD KILL ME, GOTHAM?
YOU THOUGHT YOU WERE DONE WITH ME?
I HAVE POWER NOW, O GOTHAM.
FROM HELL ITSELF, I RETURN TO YOU!
I WILL MAKE YOU MINE!
I KNOW DADDY, HaHa.
YEAH.
Gguh...
GOD, NOW. THE SPECTRE?
NOW WOULD BE A GOOD TIME.
BATWING!
COME ON, KID. WHERE ARE YOU?

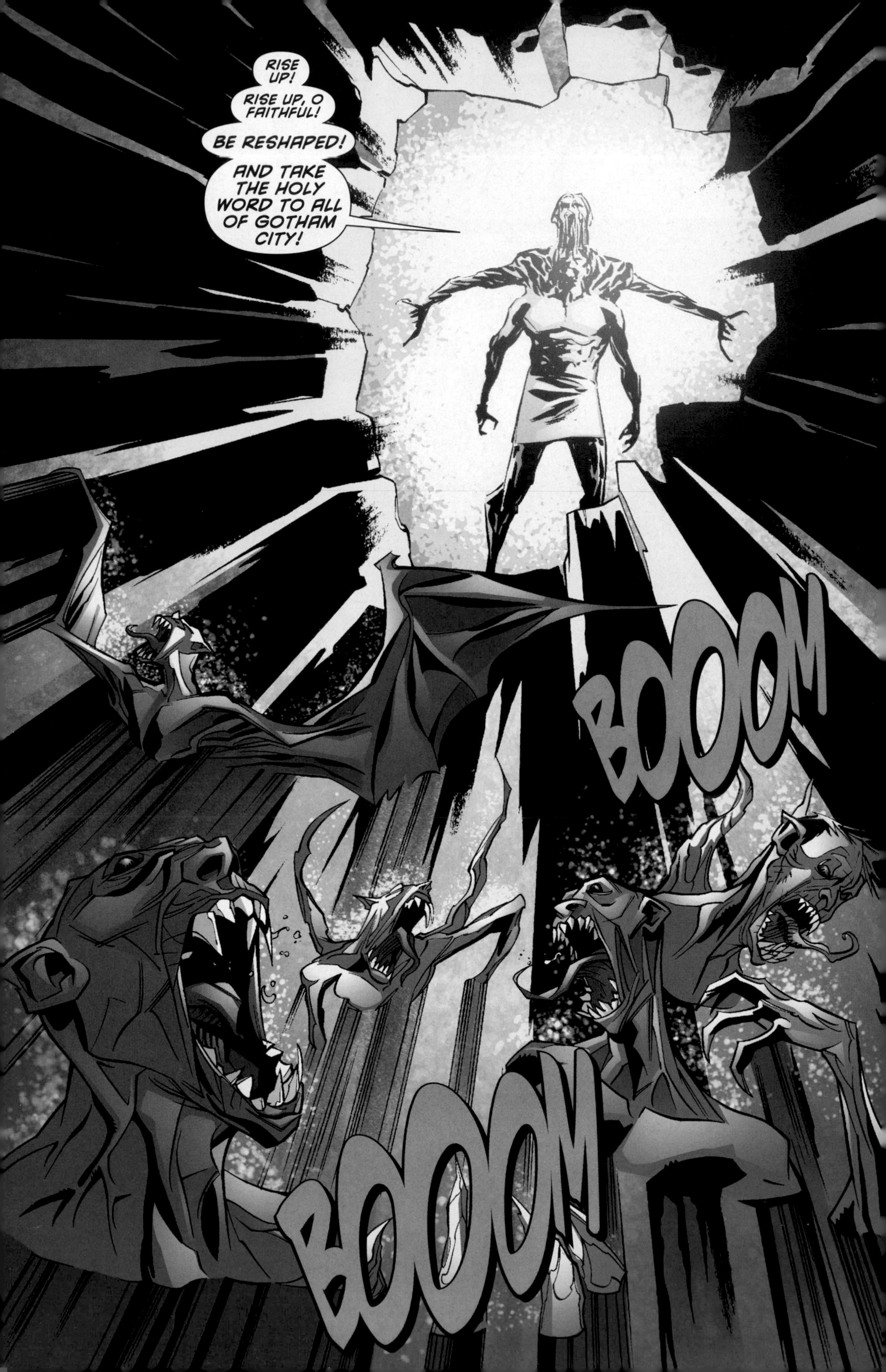
RISE UP!
RISE UP, O FAITHFUL!
BE RESHAPED!
AND TAKE THE HOLY WORD TO ALL OF GOTHAM CITY!
BOOOM
BOOOM

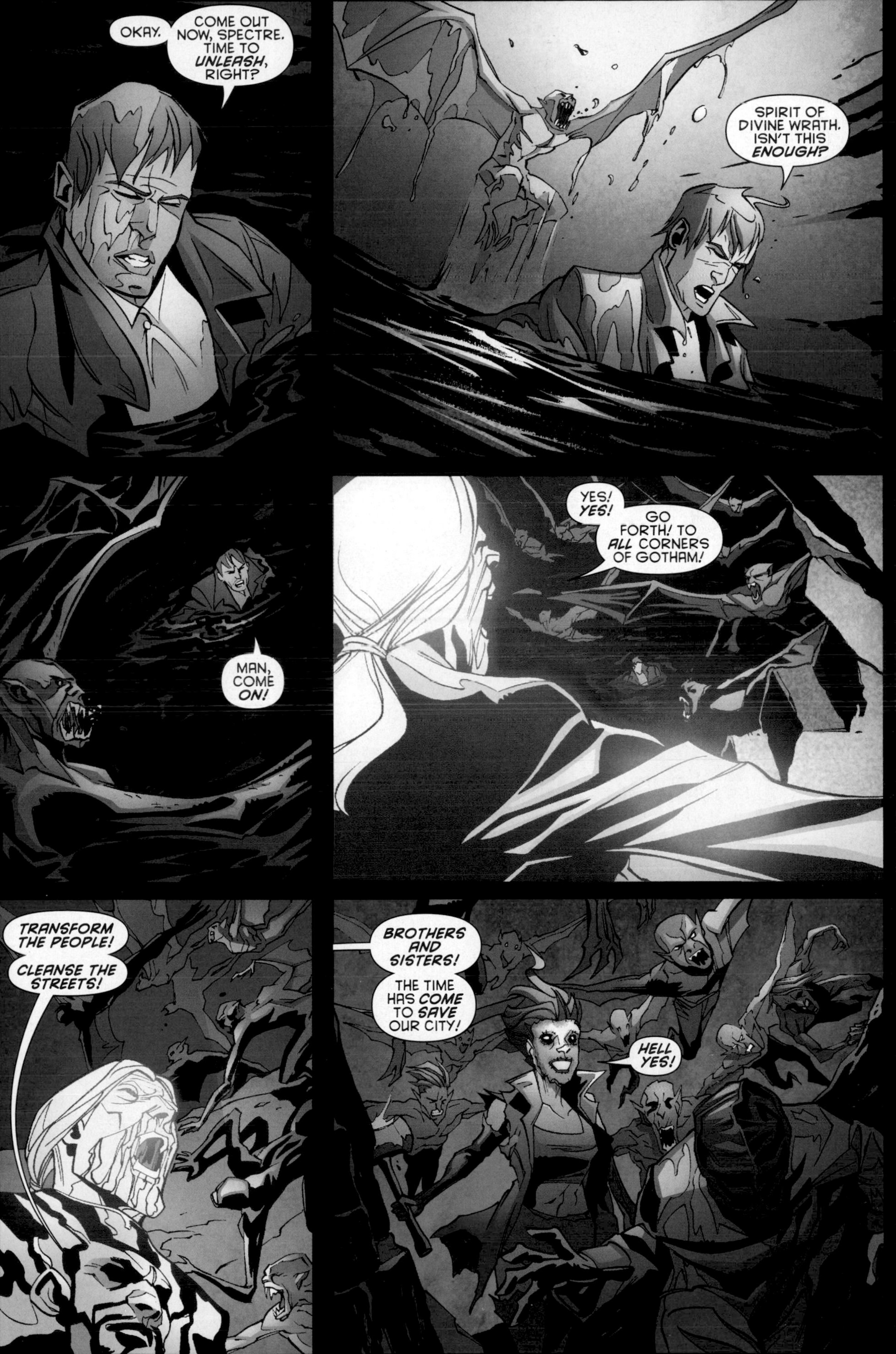
OKAY.
COME OUT NOW, SPECTRE. TIME TO UNLEASH, RIGHT?
SPIRIT OF DIVINE WRATH. ISN'T THIS ENOUGH?
MAN, COME ON!
YES! YES!
GO FORTH! TO ALL CORNERS OF GOTHAM!
TRANSFORM THE PEOPLE!
CLEANSE THE STREETS!
BROTHERS AND SISTERS!
THE TIME HAS COME TO SAVE OUR CITY!
HELL YES!

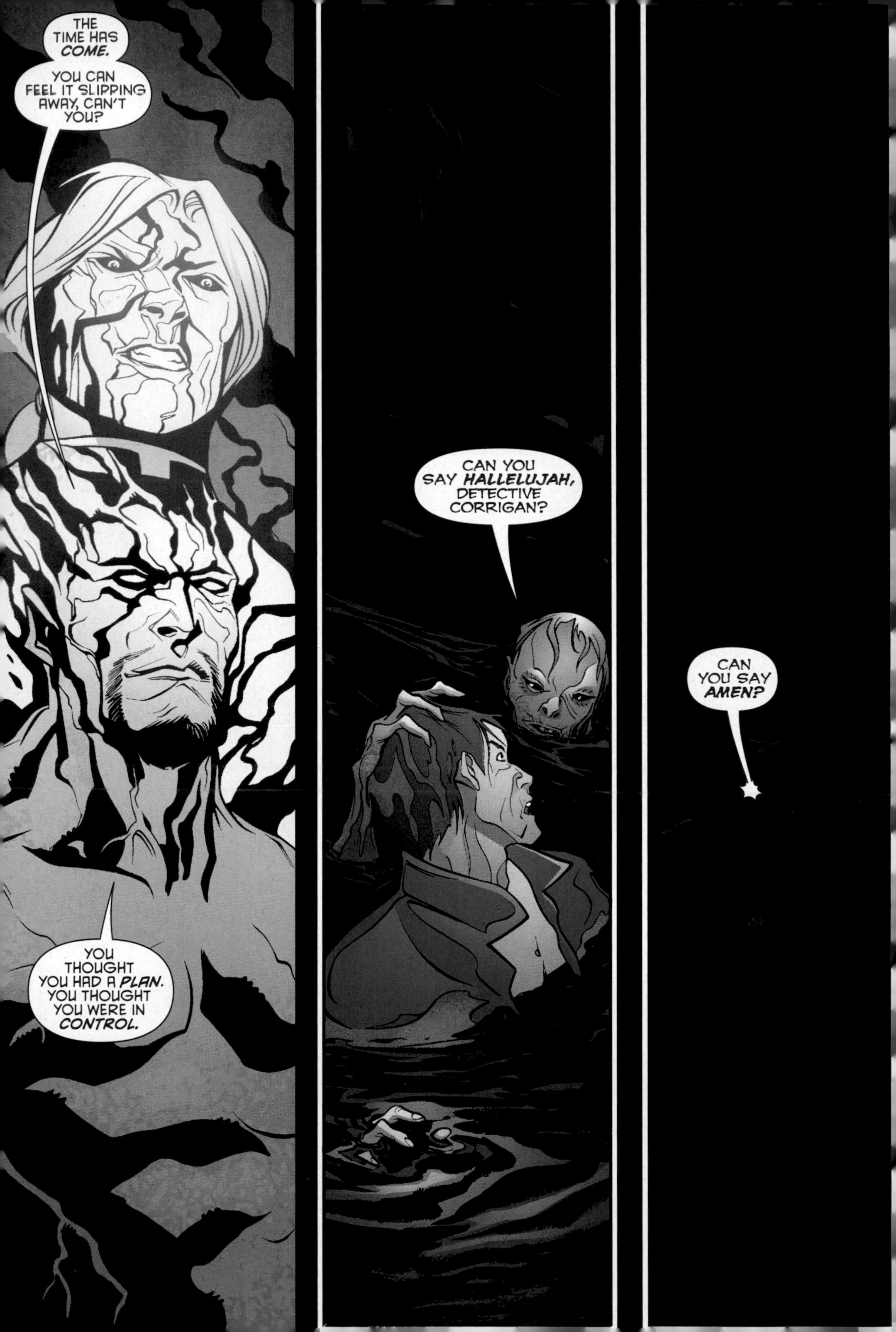
THE TIME HAS COME.
YOU CAN FEEL IT SLIPPING AWAY, CAN'T YOU?
YOU THOUGHT YOU HAD A PLAN. YOU THOUGHT YOU WERE IN CONTROL.
CAN YOU SAY HALLELUJAH, DETECTIVE CORRIGAN?
CAN YOU SAY AMEN?

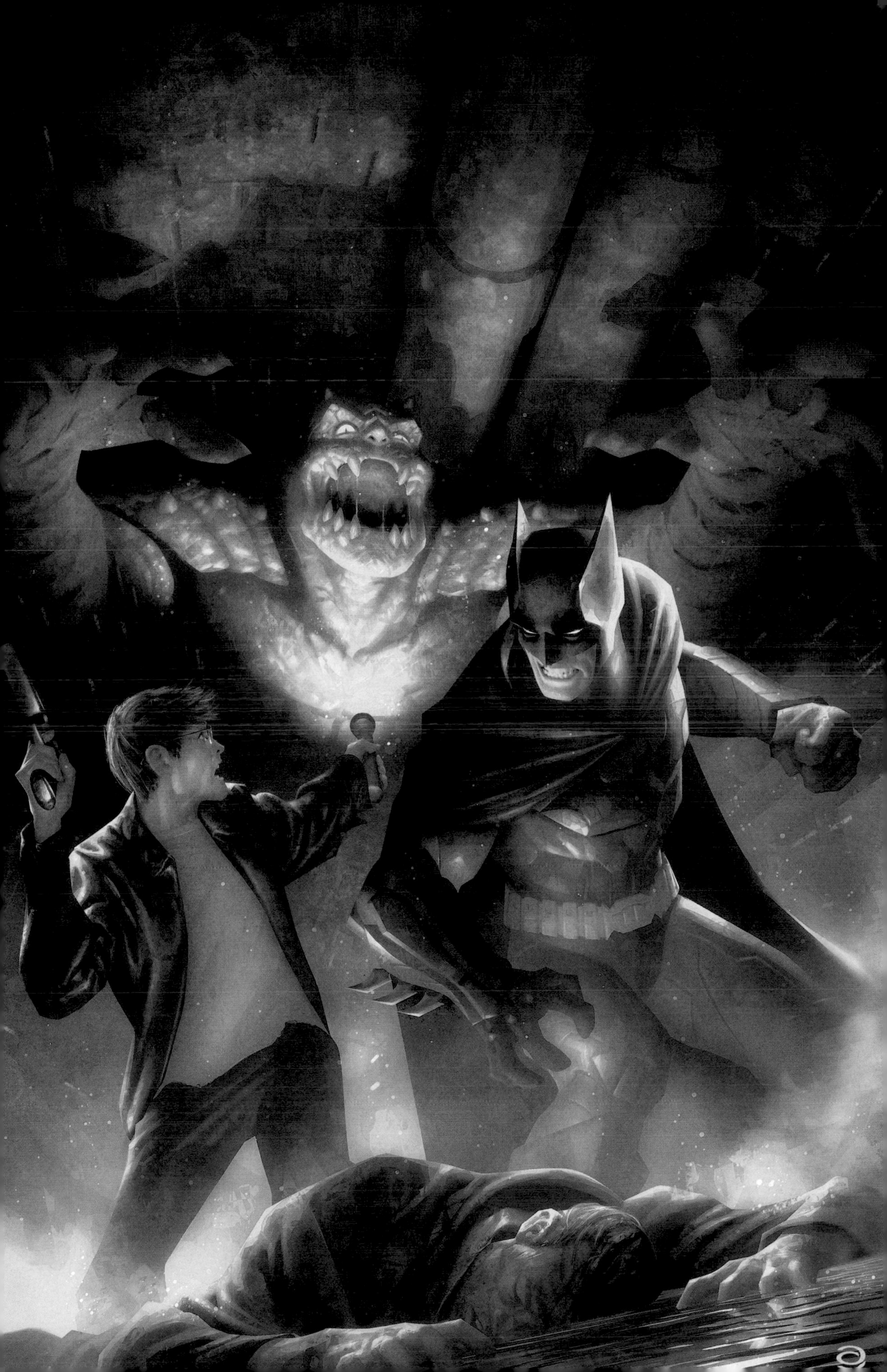

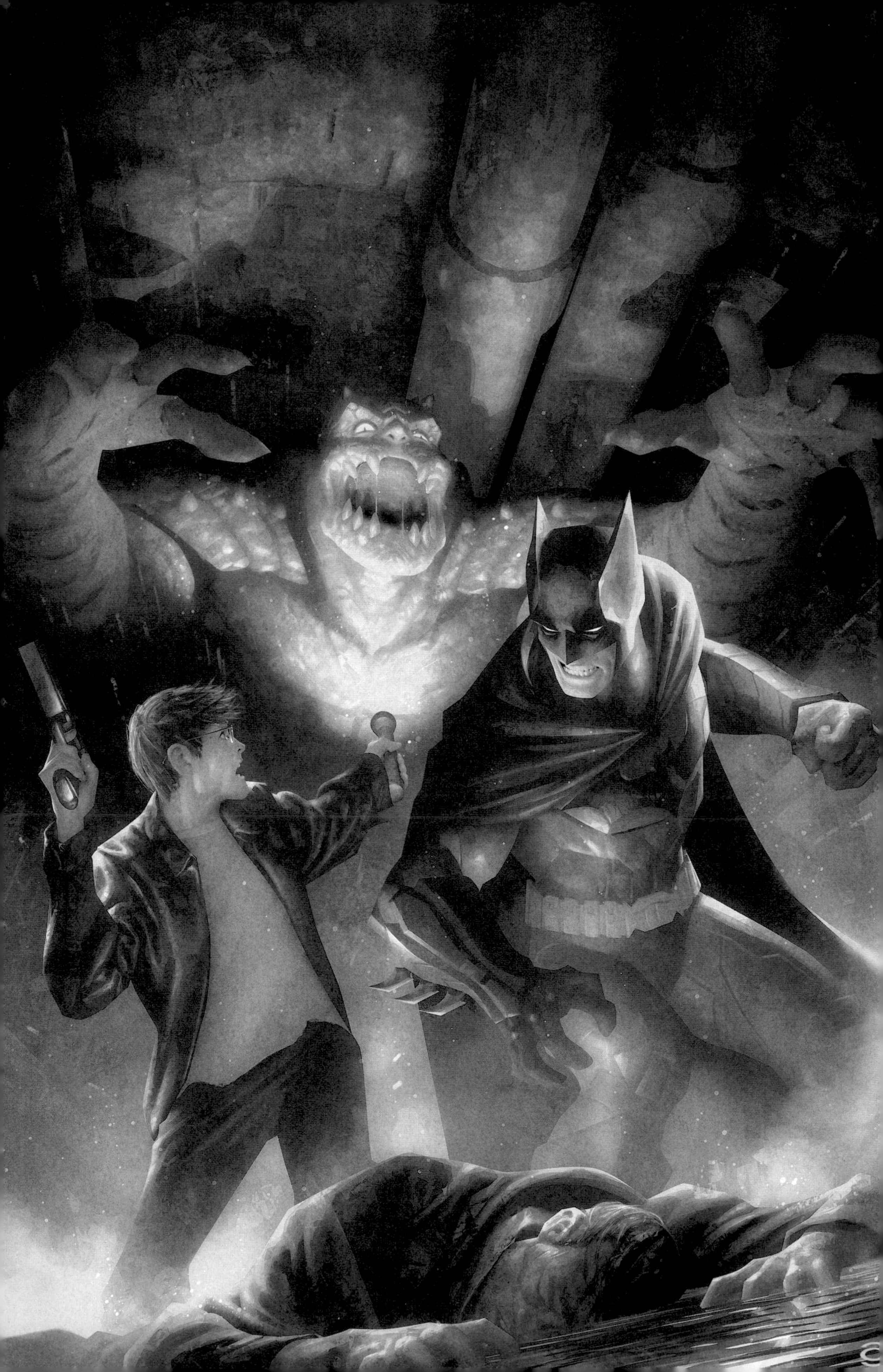

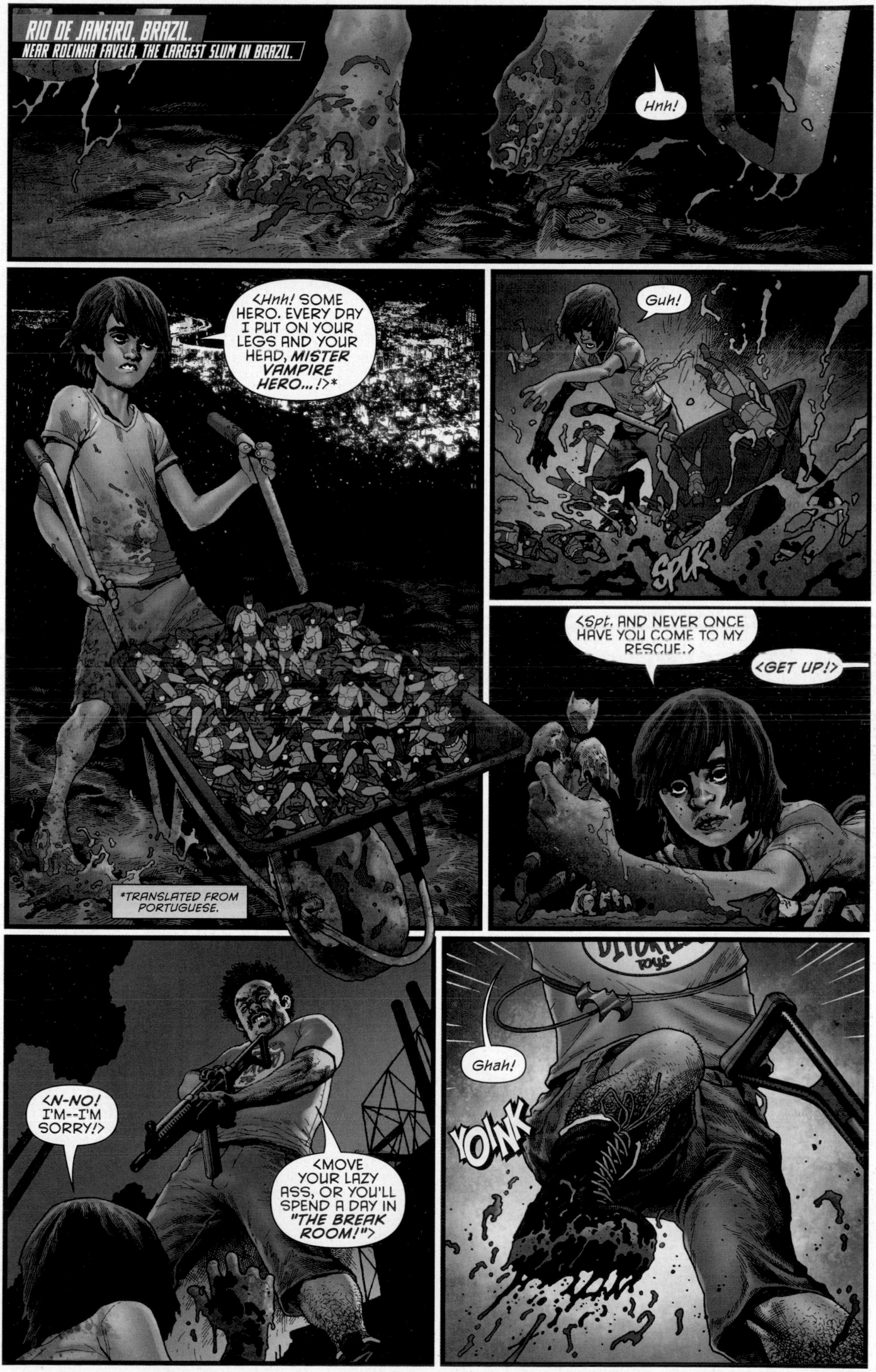

RIO DE JANEIRO, BRAZIL.
NEAR ROCINHA FAVELA, THE LARGEST SLUM IN BRAZIL.
Hnh!
<Hnh! SOME HERO. EVERY DAY I PUT ON YOUR LEGS AND YOUR HEAD, MISTER VAMPIRE HERO...!>*
*TRANSLATED FROM PORTUGUESE.
Guh!
SPLK
<Spt. AND NEVER ONCE HAVE YOU COME TO MY RESCUE.>
<GET UP!>
<N-NO! I'M--I'M SORRY!>
<MOVE YOUR LAZY ASS, OR YOU'LL SPEND A DAY IN "THE BREAK ROOM!">
Ghah!
YOINK

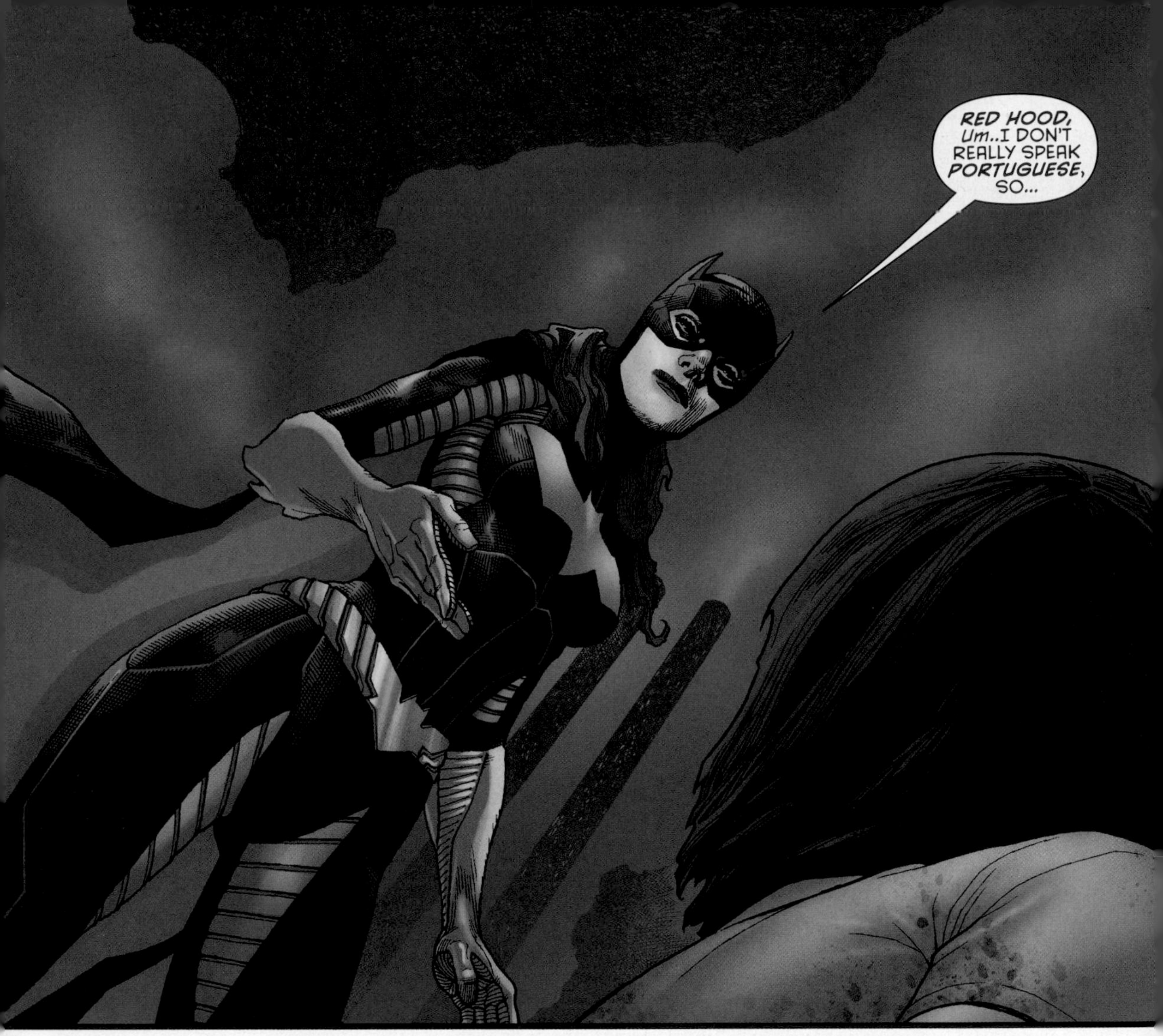
RED HOOD, Um..I DON'T REALLY SPEAK PORTUGUESE, SO...

SCOTT SNYDER & JAMES TYNION IV STORY TIM SEELEY SCRIPT
RAY FAWKES & JOHN LAYMAN CONTRIBUTING WRITERS

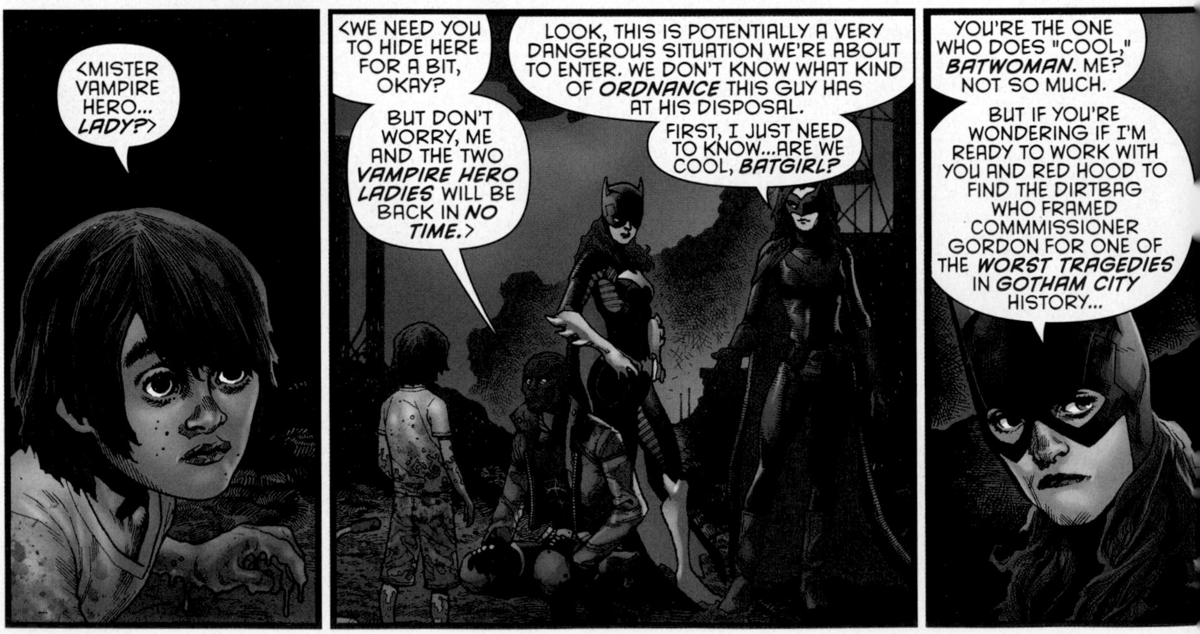
<MISTER VAMPIRE HERO... LADY?>
<WE NEED YOU TO HIDE HERE FOR A BIT, OKAY?
BUT DON'T WORRY, ME AND THE TWO VAMPIRE HERO LADIES WILL BE BACK IN NO TIME.>
LOOK, THIS IS POTENTIALLY A VERY DANGEROUS SITUATION WE'RE ABOUT TO ENTER. WE DON'T KNOW WHAT KIND OF ORDNANCE THIS GUY HAS AT HIS DISPOSAL.
FIRST, I JUST NEED TO KNOW...ARE WE COOL, BATGIRL?
YOU'RE THE ONE WHO DOES "COOL," BATWOMAN. ME? NOT SO MUCH.
BUT IF YOU'RE WONDERING IF I'M READY TO WORK WITH YOU AND RED HOOD TO FIND THE DIRTBAG WHO FRAMED COMMMISSIONER GORDON FOR ONE OF THE WORST TRAGEDIES IN GOTHAM CITY HISTORY...

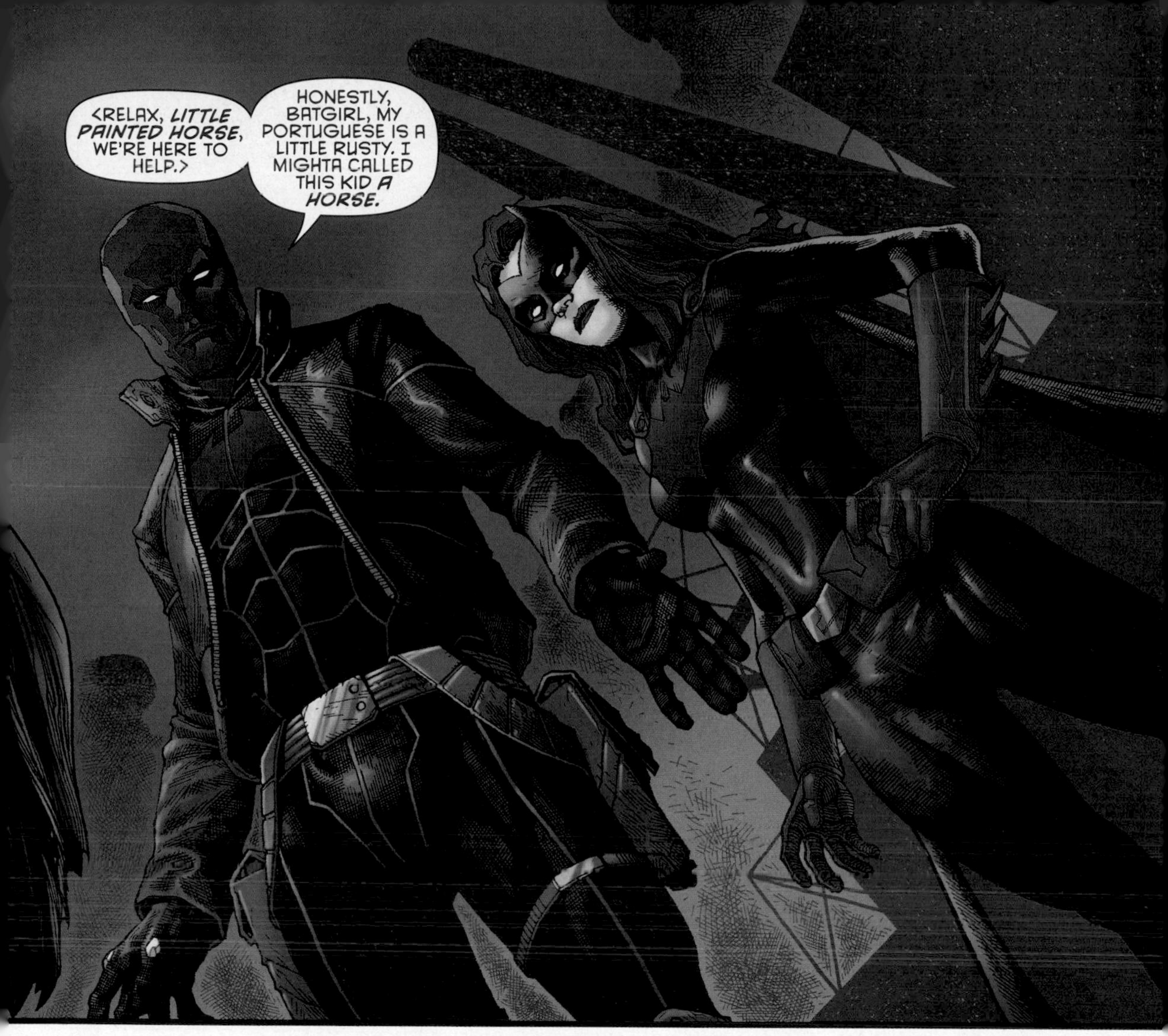
<RELAX, *LITTLE PAINTED HORSE*, WE'RE HERE TO HELP.>
HONESTLY, BATGIRL, MY PORTUGUESE IS A LITTLE RUSTY. I MIGHTA CALLED THIS KID *A HORSE.*

ANDY CLARKE ART

BLOND COLORS DEZI SIENTY LETTERS ALEX GARNER COVER

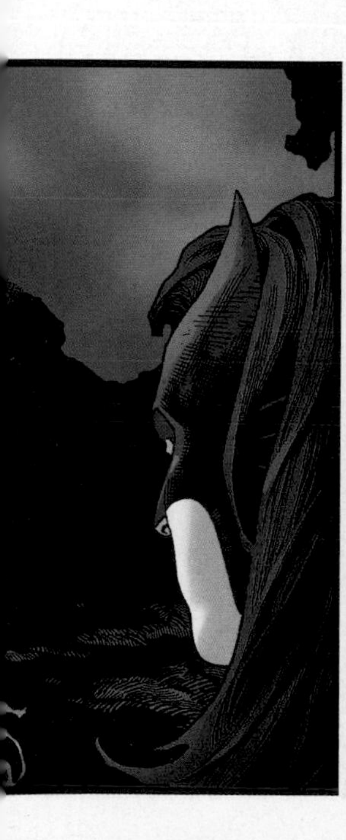

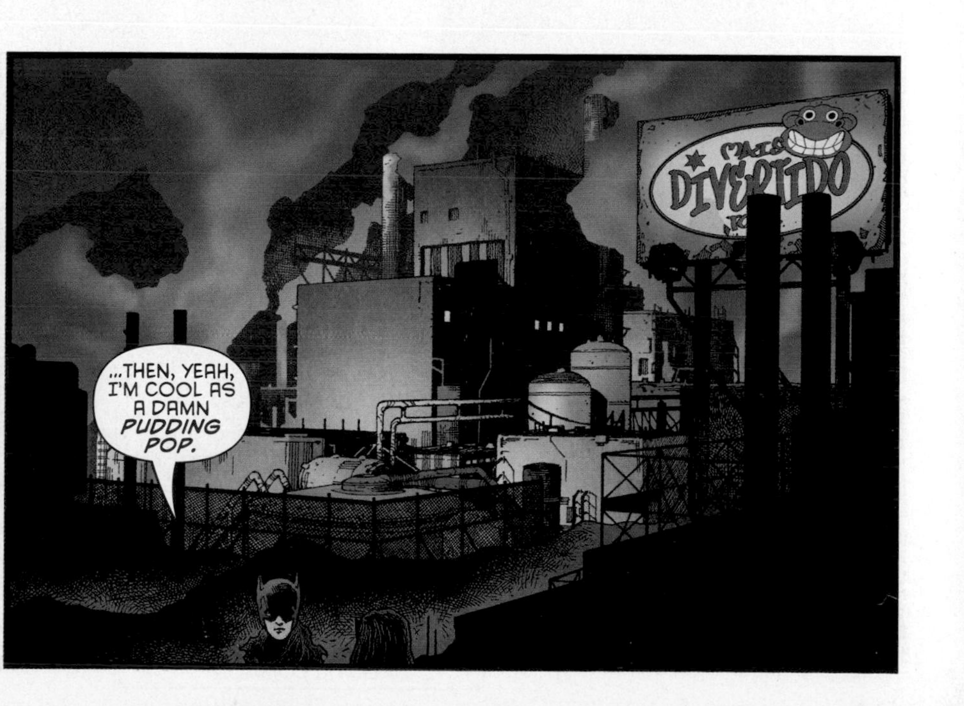
...THEN, YEAH, I'M COOL AS A DAMN *PUDDING POP.*

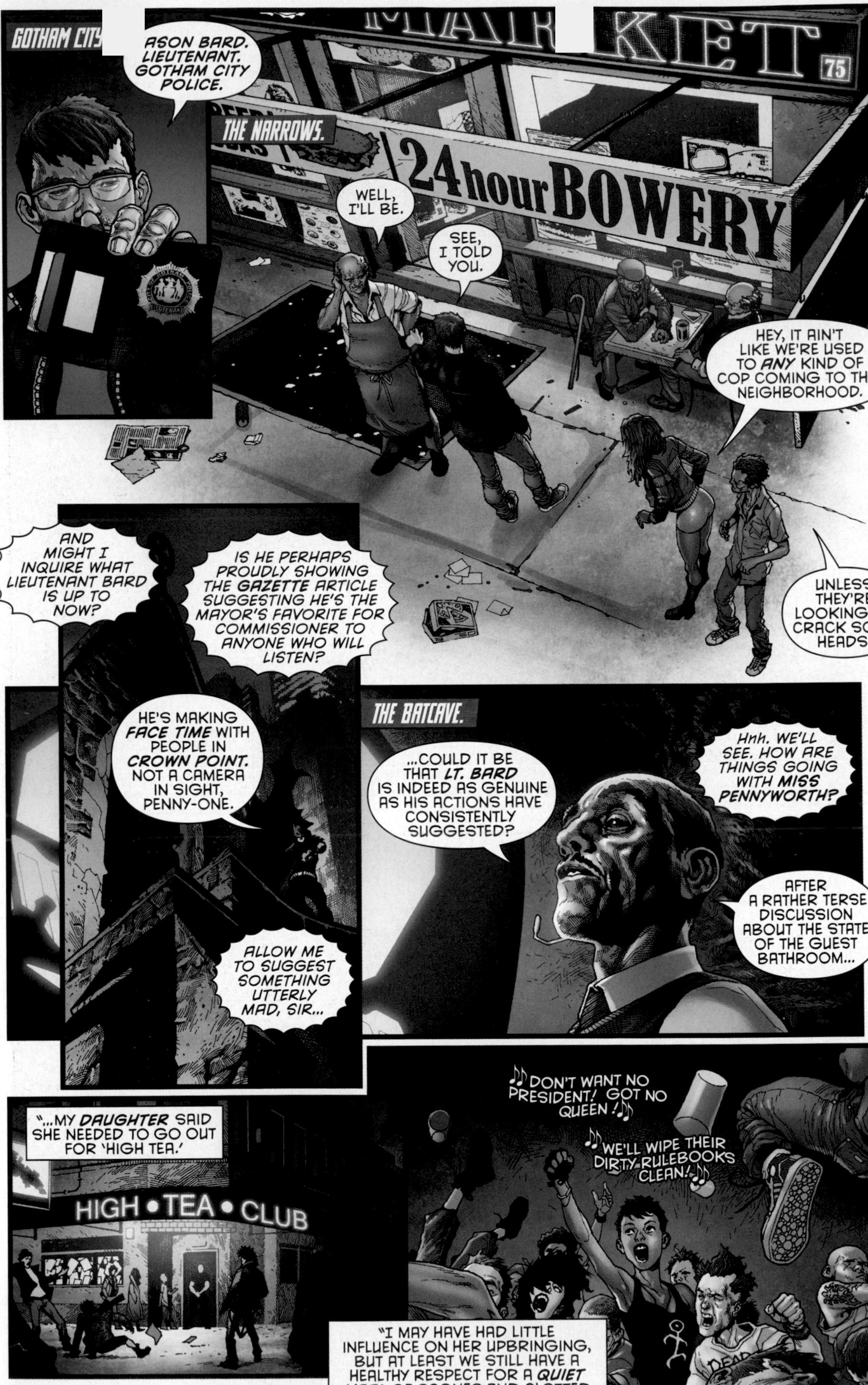
GOTHAM CITY
ASON BARD. LIEUTENANT. GOTHAM CITY POLICE.
MARKET
75
THE NARROWS.
24 hour BOWERY
WELL, I'LL BE.
SEE, I TOLD YOU.
HEY, IT AIN'T LIKE WE'RE USED TO ANY KIND OF COP COMING TO THIS NEIGHBORHOOD.
UNLESS THEY'RE LOOKING TO CRACK SOME HEADS.
AND MIGHT I INQUIRE WHAT LIEUTENANT BARD IS UP TO NOW?
IS HE PERHAPS PROUDLY SHOWING THE GAZETTE ARTICLE SUGGESTING HE'S THE MAYOR'S FAVORITE FOR COMMISSIONER TO ANYONE WHO WILL LISTEN?
HE'S MAKING FACE TIME WITH PEOPLE IN CROWN POINT. NOT A CAMERA IN SIGHT, PENNY-ONE.
ALLOW ME TO SUGGEST SOMETHING UTTERLY MAD, SIR...
THE BATCAVE.
...COULD IT BE THAT LT. BARD IS INDEED AS GENUINE AS HIS ACTIONS HAVE CONSISTENTLY SUGGESTED?
Hnh. WE'LL SEE. HOW ARE THINGS GOING WITH MISS PENNYWORTH?
AFTER A RATHER TERSE DISCUSSION ABOUT THE STATE OF THE GUEST BATHROOM...
"...MY DAUGHTER SAID SHE NEEDED TO GO OUT FOR 'HIGH TEA.'
HIGH • TEA • CLUB
♪♪ DON'T WANT NO PRESIDENT! GOT NO QUEEN! ♪♪
♪♪ WE'LL WIPE THEIR DIRTY RULEBOOKS CLEAN! ♪♪
"I MAY HAVE HAD LITTLE INFLUENCE ON HER UPBRINGING, BUT AT LEAST WE STILL HAVE A HEALTHY RESPECT FOR A QUIET MEAL OF SCONES AND CLOTTED CREAM IN COMMON."

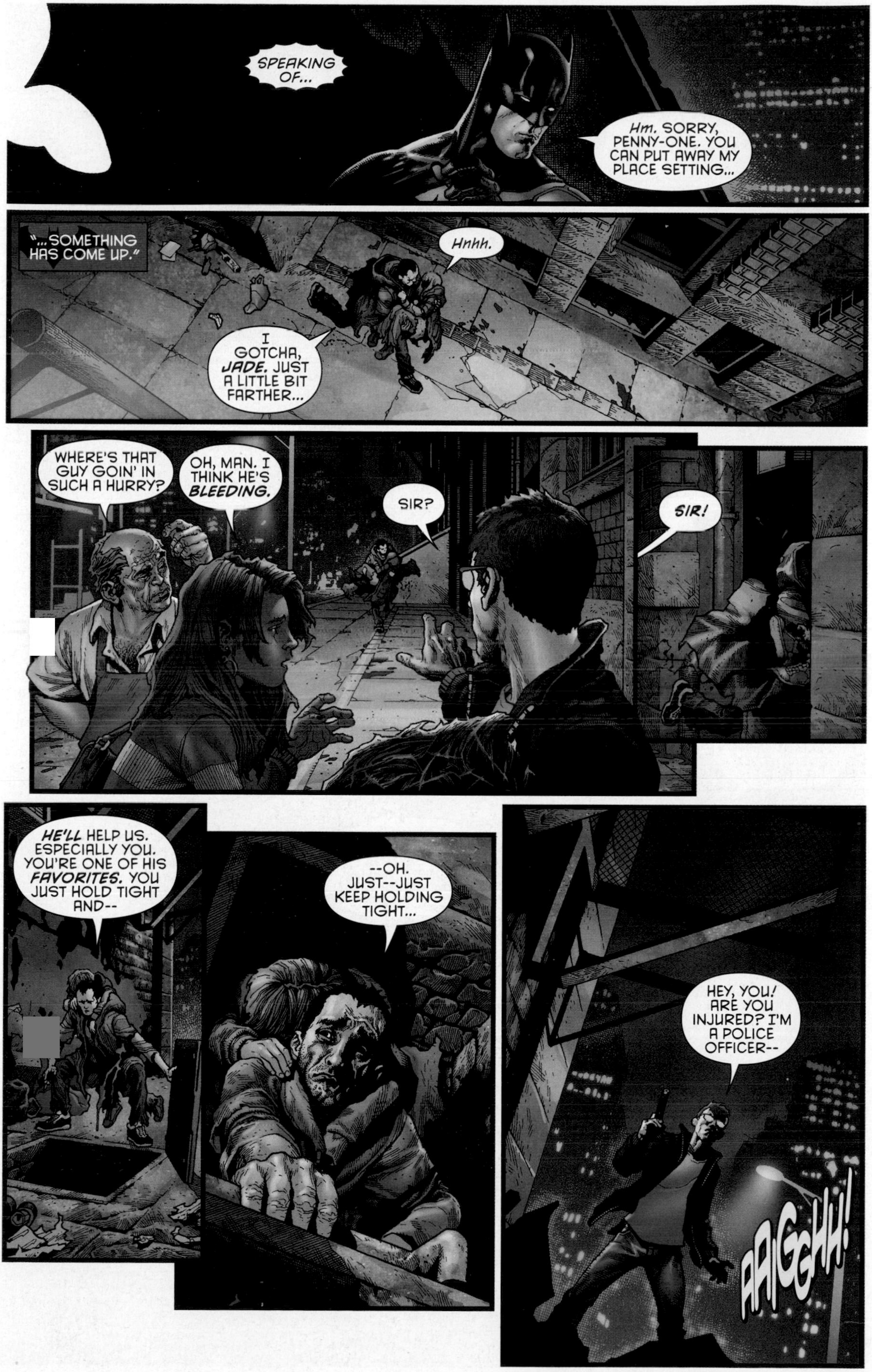
SPEAKING OF...
Hm. SORRY, PENNY-ONE. YOU CAN PUT AWAY MY PLACE SETTING...
"...SOMETHING HAS COME UP."
Hnhh.
I GOTCHA, JADE. JUST A LITTLE BIT FARTHER...
WHERE'S THAT GUY GOIN' IN SUCH A HURRY?
OH, MAN. I THINK HE'S BLEEDING.
SIR?
SIR!
HE'LL HELP US. ESPECIALLY YOU. YOU'RE ONE OF HIS FAVORITES. YOU JUST HOLD TIGHT AND--
--OH. JUST--JUST KEEP HOLDING TIGHT...
HEY, YOU! ARE YOU INJURED? I'M A POLICE OFFICER--
AAIGGHH!

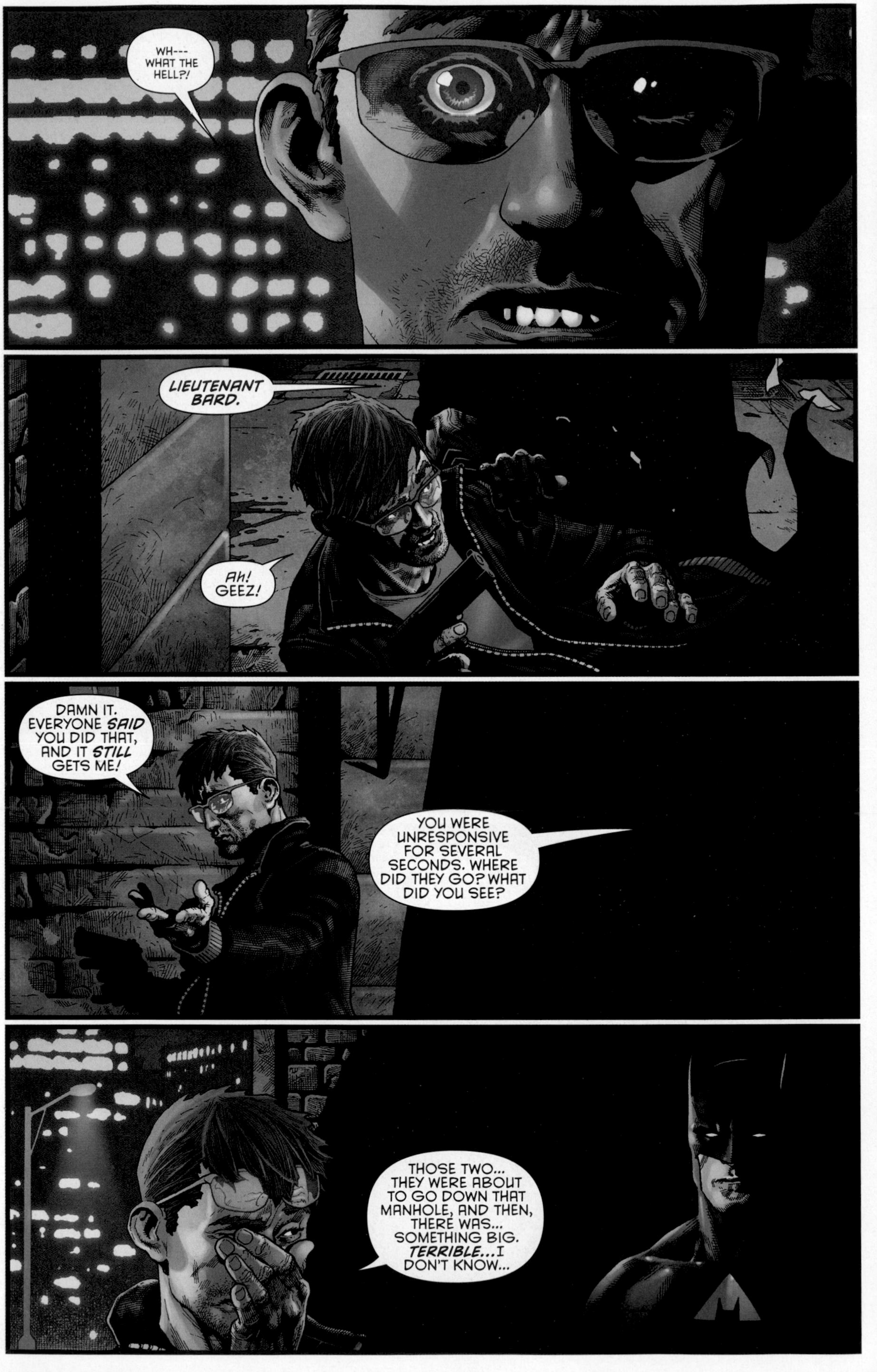
WH---
WHAT THE
HELL?!
LIEUTENANT
BARD.
Ah!
GEEZ!
DAMN IT.
EVERYONE SAID
YOU DID THAT,
AND IT STILL
GETS ME!
YOU WERE
UNRESPONSIVE
FOR SEVERAL
SECONDS. WHERE
DID THEY GO? WHAT
DID YOU SEE?
THOSE TWO...
THEY WERE ABOUT
TO GO DOWN THAT
MANHOLE, AND THEN,
THERE WAS...
SOMETHING BIG.
TERRIBLE...I
DON'T KNOW...

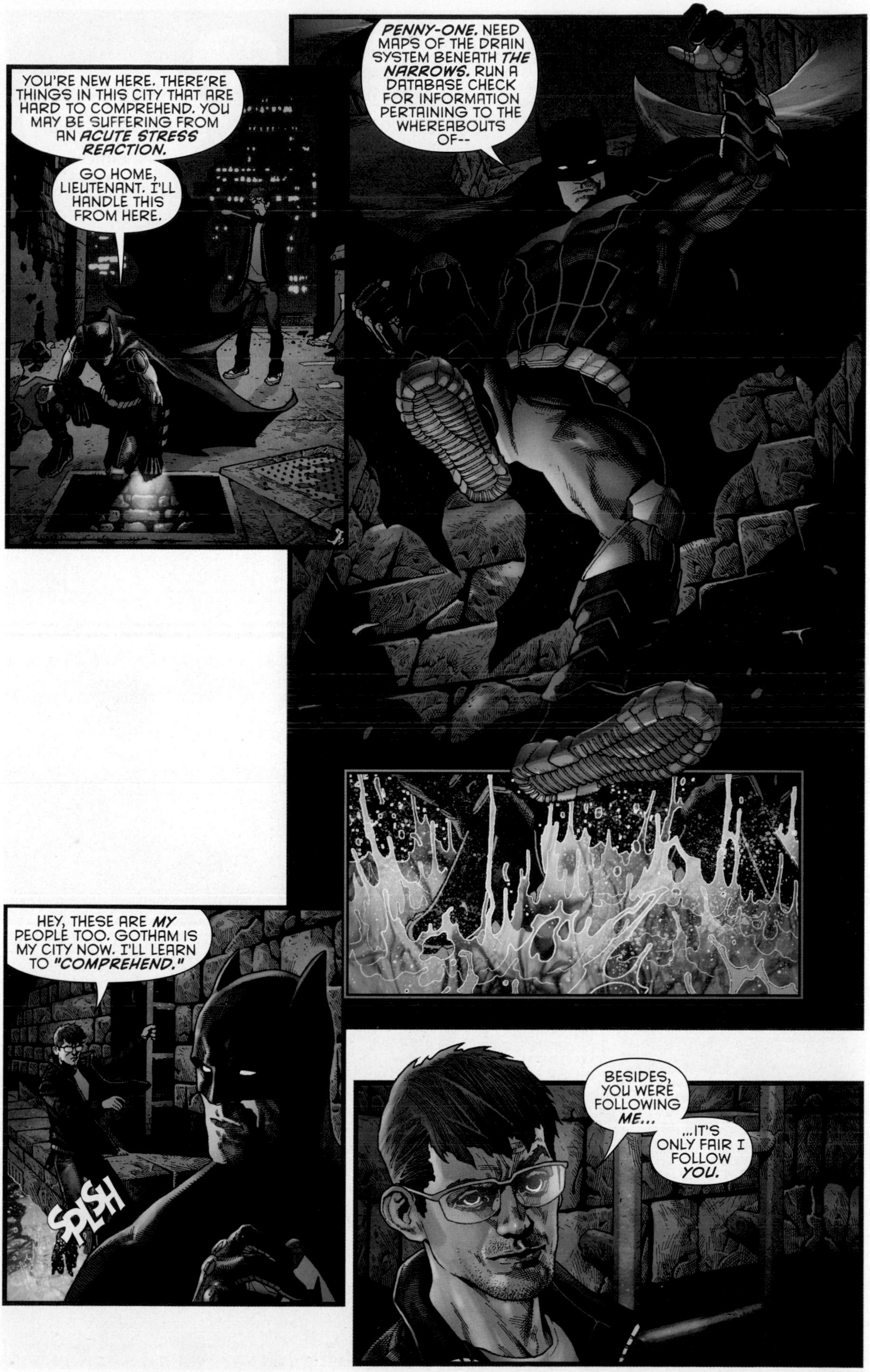
YOU'RE NEW HERE. THERE'RE THINGS IN THIS CITY THAT ARE HARD TO COMPREHEND. YOU MAY BE SUFFERING FROM AN ACUTE STRESS REACTION.
GO HOME, LIEUTENANT. I'LL HANDLE THIS FROM HERE.
PENNY-ONE. NEED MAPS OF THE DRAIN SYSTEM BENEATH THE NARROWS. RUN A DATABASE CHECK FOR INFORMATION PERTAINING TO THE WHEREABOUTS OF--
HEY, THESE ARE MY PEOPLE TOO. GOTHAM IS MY CITY NOW. I'LL LEARN TO "COMPREHEND."
SPLSH
BESIDES, YOU WERE FOLLOWING ME...
...IT'S ONLY FAIR I FOLLOW YOU.

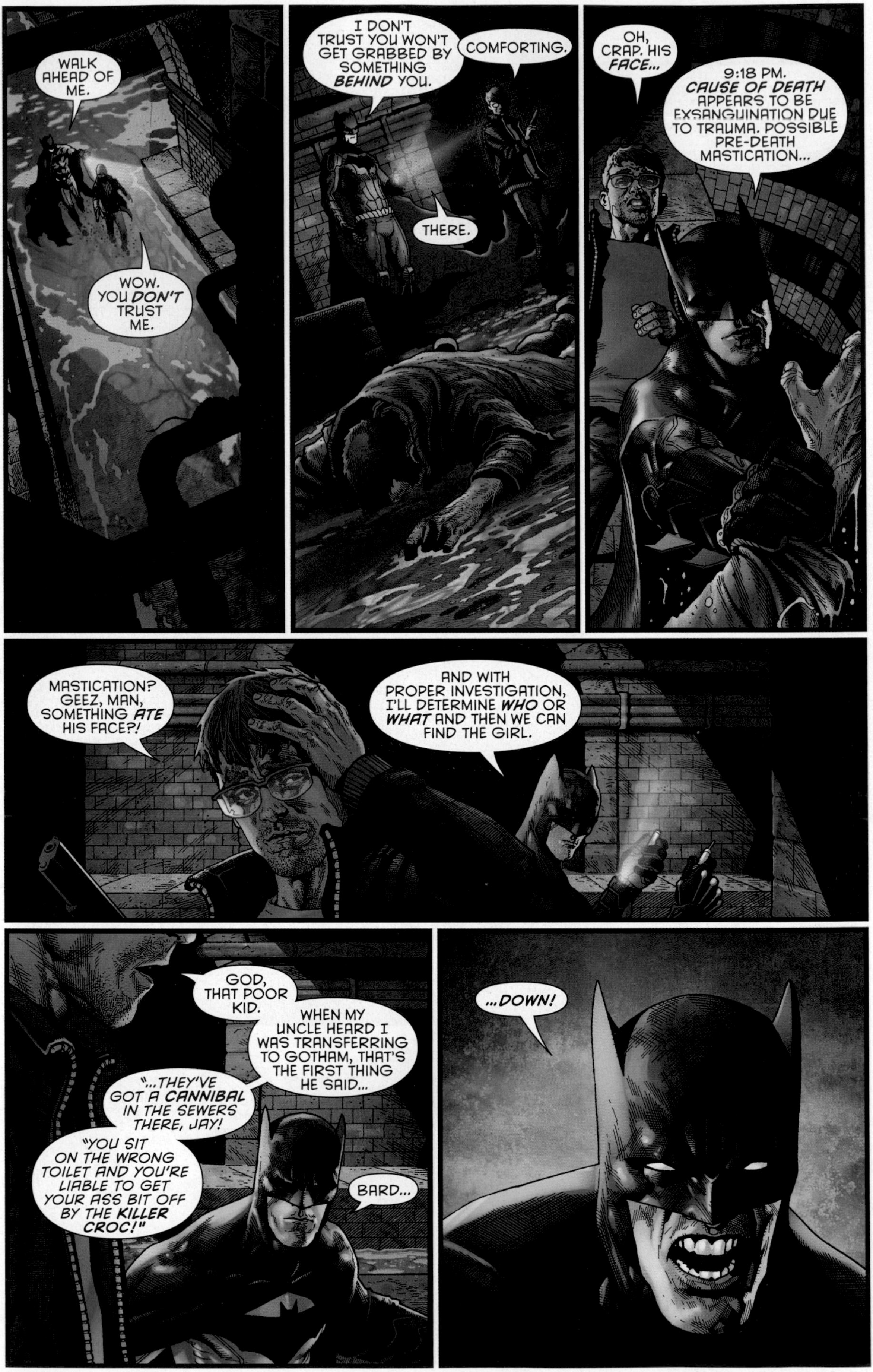

WALK AHEAD OF ME.
WOW. YOU *DON'T* TRUST ME.
I DON'T TRUST YOU WON'T GET GRABBED BY SOMETHING *BEHIND* YOU.
COMFORTING.
THERE.
OH, CRAP. HIS *FACE*...
9:18 PM. *CAUSE OF DEATH* APPEARS TO BE EXSANGUINATION DUE TO TRAUMA. POSSIBLE PRE-DEATH MASTICATION...
MASTICATION? GEEZ, MAN, SOMETHING *ATE* HIS FACE?!
AND WITH PROPER INVESTIGATION, I'LL DETERMINE *WHO* OR *WHAT* AND THEN WE CAN FIND THE GIRL.
GOD, THAT POOR KID.
WHEN MY UNCLE HEARD I WAS TRANSFERRING TO GOTHAM, THAT'S THE FIRST THING HE SAID...
"...THEY'VE GOT A *CANNIBAL* IN THE SEWERS THERE, JAY!
"YOU SIT ON THE WRONG TOILET AND YOU'RE LIABLE TO GET YOUR ASS BIT OFF BY THE *KILLER CROC!*"
BARD...
...DOWN!

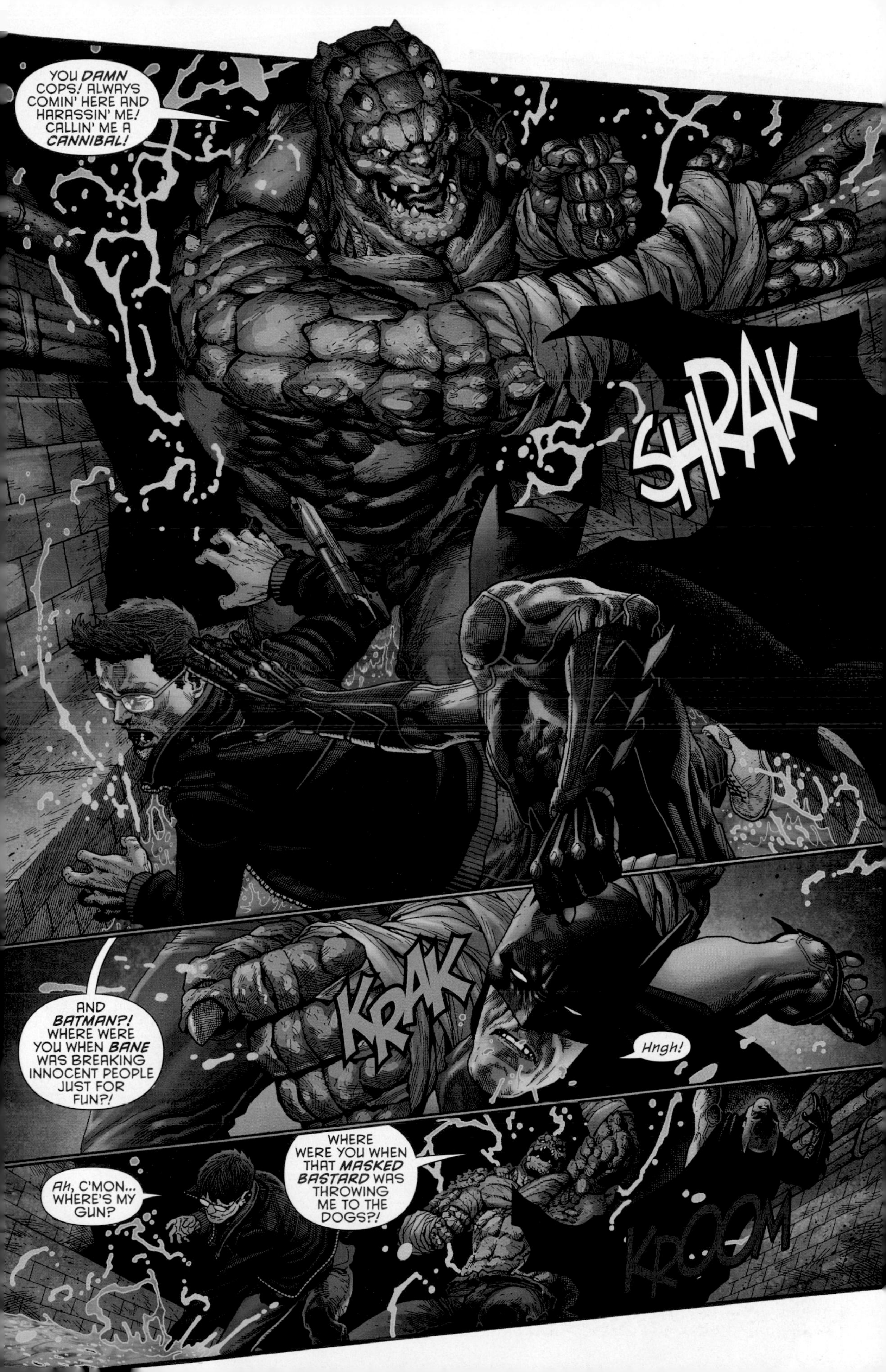

YOU DAMN COPS! ALWAYS COMIN' HERE AND HARASSIN' ME! CALLIN' ME A CANNIBAL!
SHRAK
AND BATMAN?! WHERE WERE YOU WHEN BANE WAS BREAKING INNOCENT PEOPLE JUST FOR FUN?!
KRAK
Hngh!
Ah, C'MON... WHERE'S MY GUN?
WHERE WERE YOU WHEN THAT MASKED BASTARD WAS THROWING ME TO THE DOGS?!
KROOOM

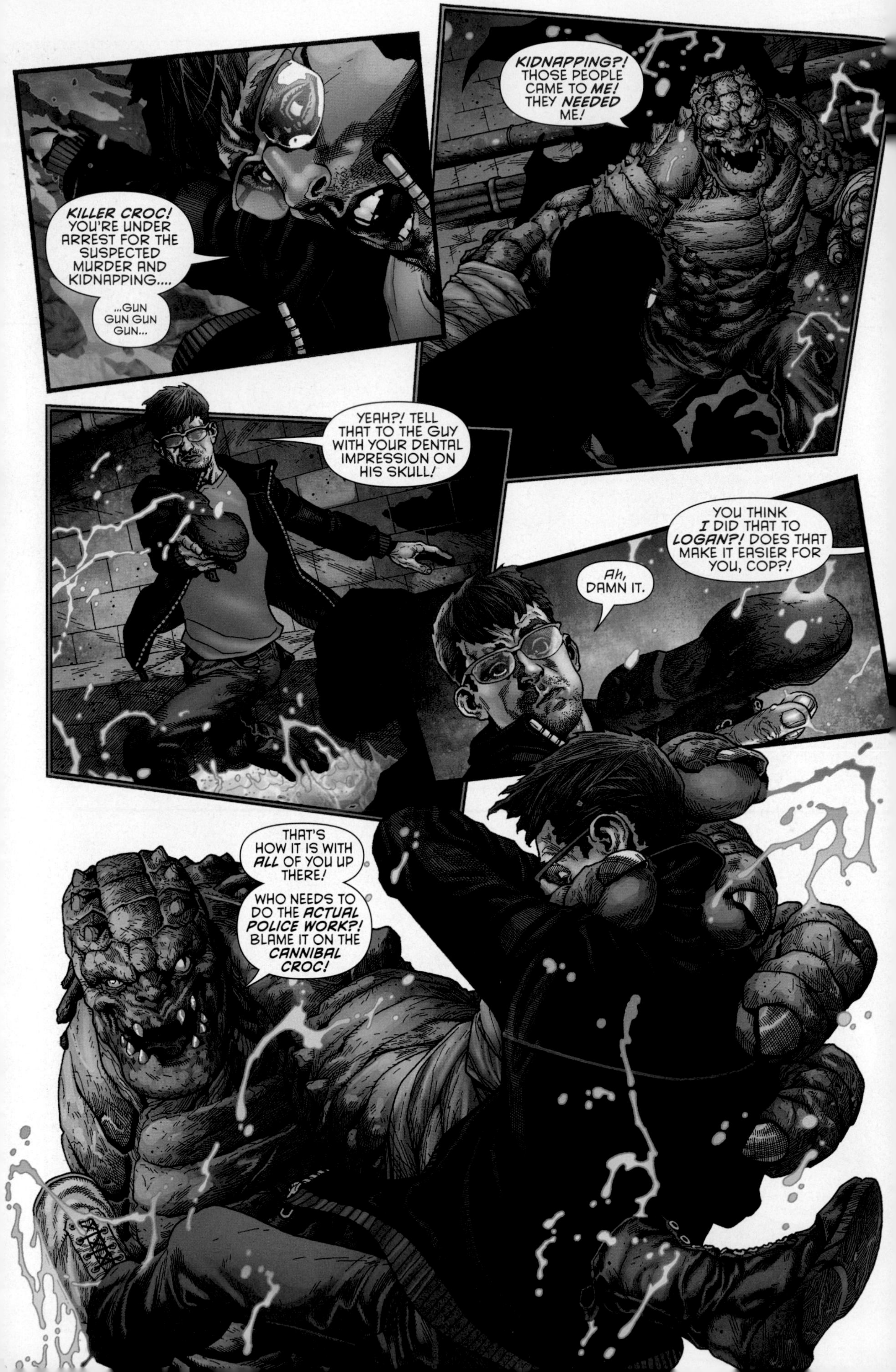
KILLER CROC! YOU'RE UNDER ARREST FOR THE SUSPECTED MURDER AND KIDNAPPING....
...GUN GUN GUN GUN...
KIDNAPPING?! THOSE PEOPLE CAME TO ME! THEY NEEDED ME!
YEAH?! TELL THAT TO THE GUY WITH YOUR DENTAL IMPRESSION ON HIS SKULL!
YOU THINK I DID THAT TO LOGAN?! DOES THAT MAKE IT EASIER FOR YOU, COP?!
AH, DAMN IT.
THAT'S HOW IT IS WITH ALL OF YOU UP THERE!
WHO NEEDS TO DO THE ACTUAL POLICE WORK?! BLAME IT ON THE CANNIBAL CROC!

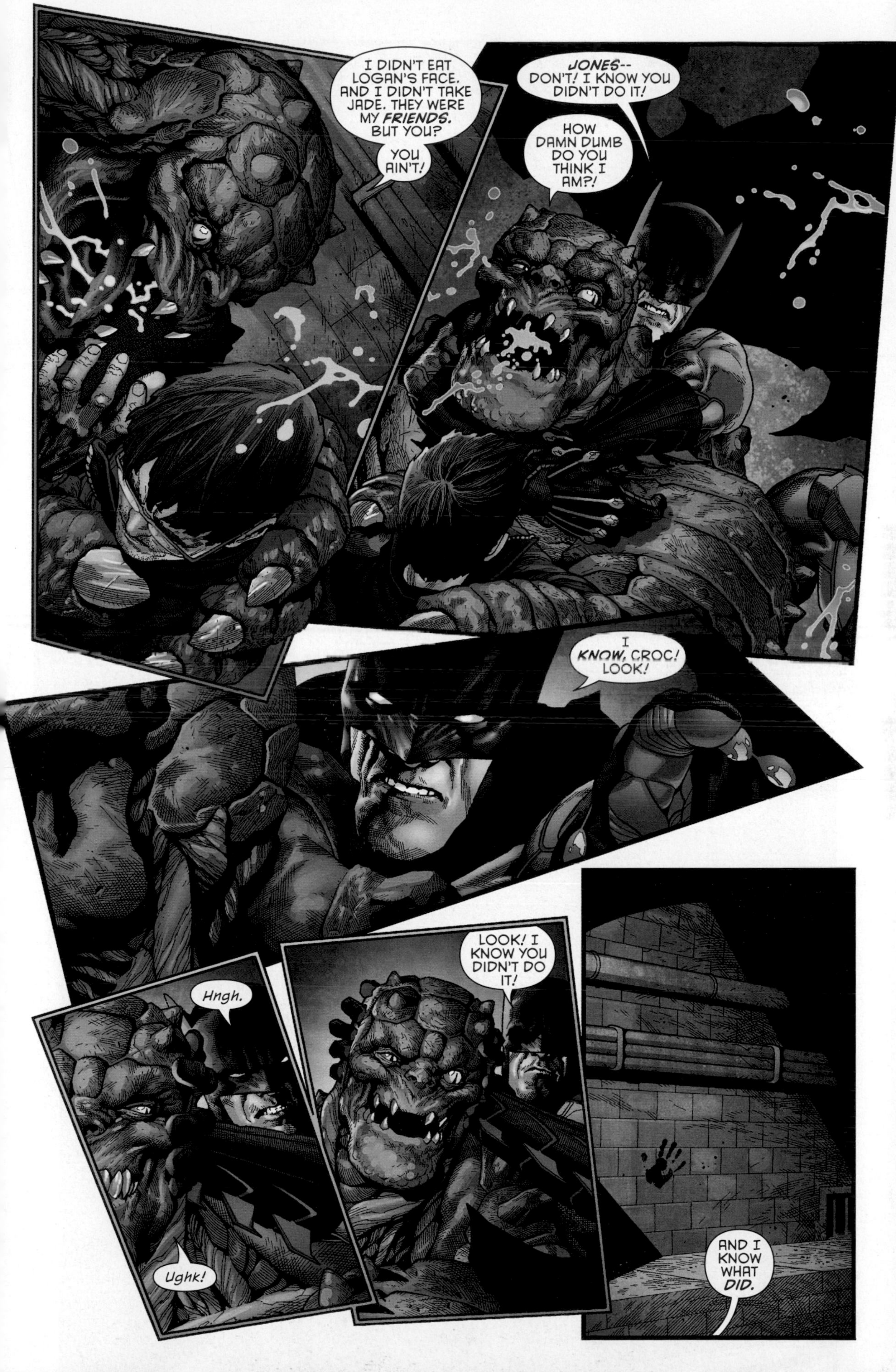
I DIDN'T EAT LOGAN'S FACE. AND I DIDN'T TAKE JADE. THEY WERE MY FRIENDS. BUT YOU?
YOU AIN'T!
JONES-- DON'T! I KNOW YOU DIDN'T DO IT!
HOW DAMN DUMB DO YOU THINK I AM?!
I KNOW, CROC! LOOK!
Hngh.
Ughk!
LOOK! I KNOW YOU DIDN'T DO IT!
AND I KNOW WHAT DID.

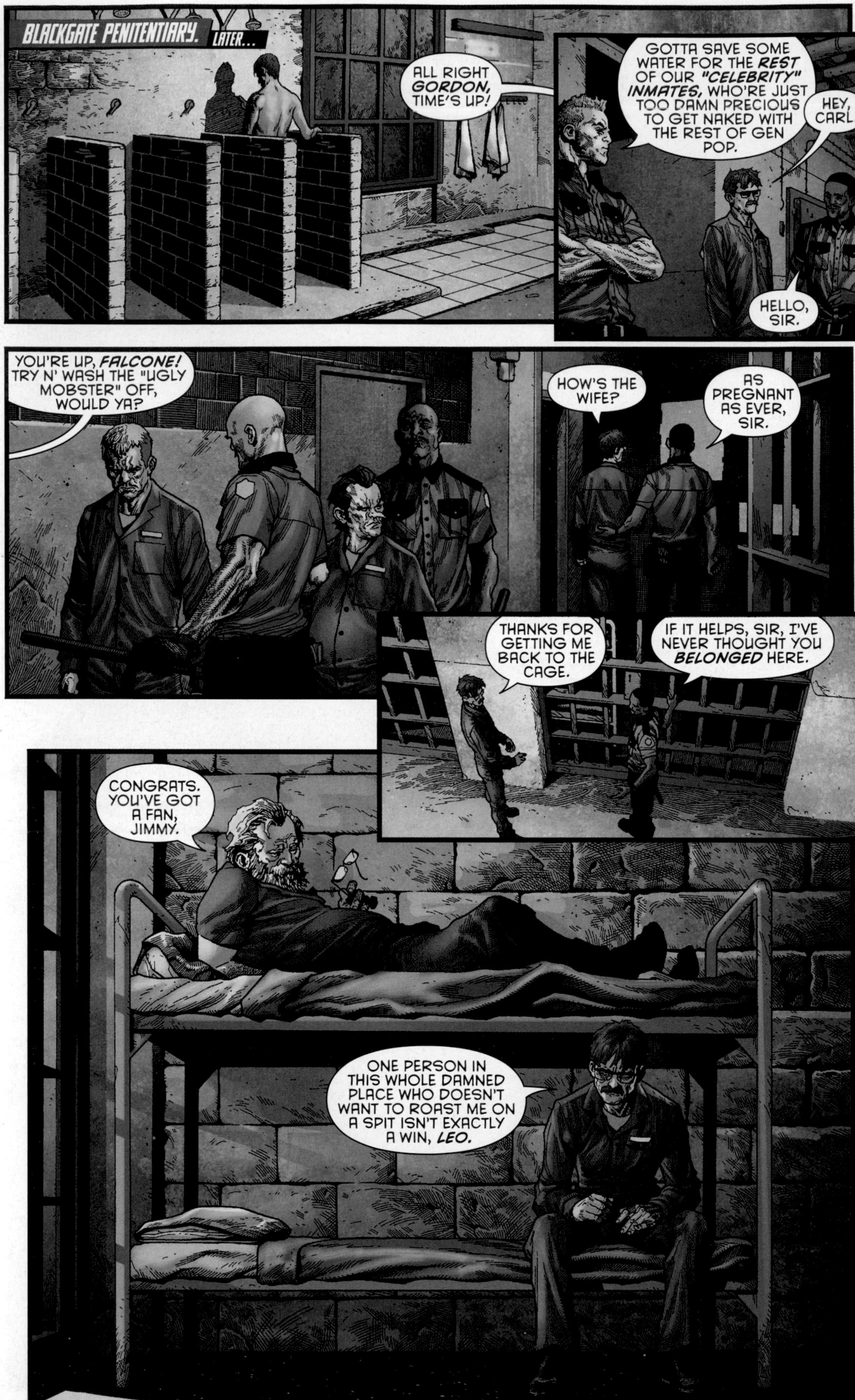
BLACKGATE PENITENTIARY. LATER...
ALL RIGHT GORDON, TIME'S UP!
GOTTA SAVE SOME WATER FOR THE REST OF OUR "CELEBRITY" INMATES, WHO'RE JUST TOO DAMN PRECIOUS TO GET NAKED WITH THE REST OF GEN POP.
HEY, CARL.
HELLO, SIR.
YOU'RE UP, FALCONE! TRY N' WASH THE "UGLY MOBSTER" OFF, WOULD YA?
HOW'S THE WIFE?
AS PREGNANT AS EVER, SIR.
THANKS FOR GETTING ME BACK TO THE CAGE.
IF IT HELPS, SIR, I'VE NEVER THOUGHT YOU BELONGED HERE.
CONGRATS. YOU'VE GOT A FAN, JIMMY.
ONE PERSON IN THIS WHOLE DAMNED PLACE WHO DOESN'T WANT TO ROAST ME ON A SPIT ISN'T EXACTLY A WIN, LEO.

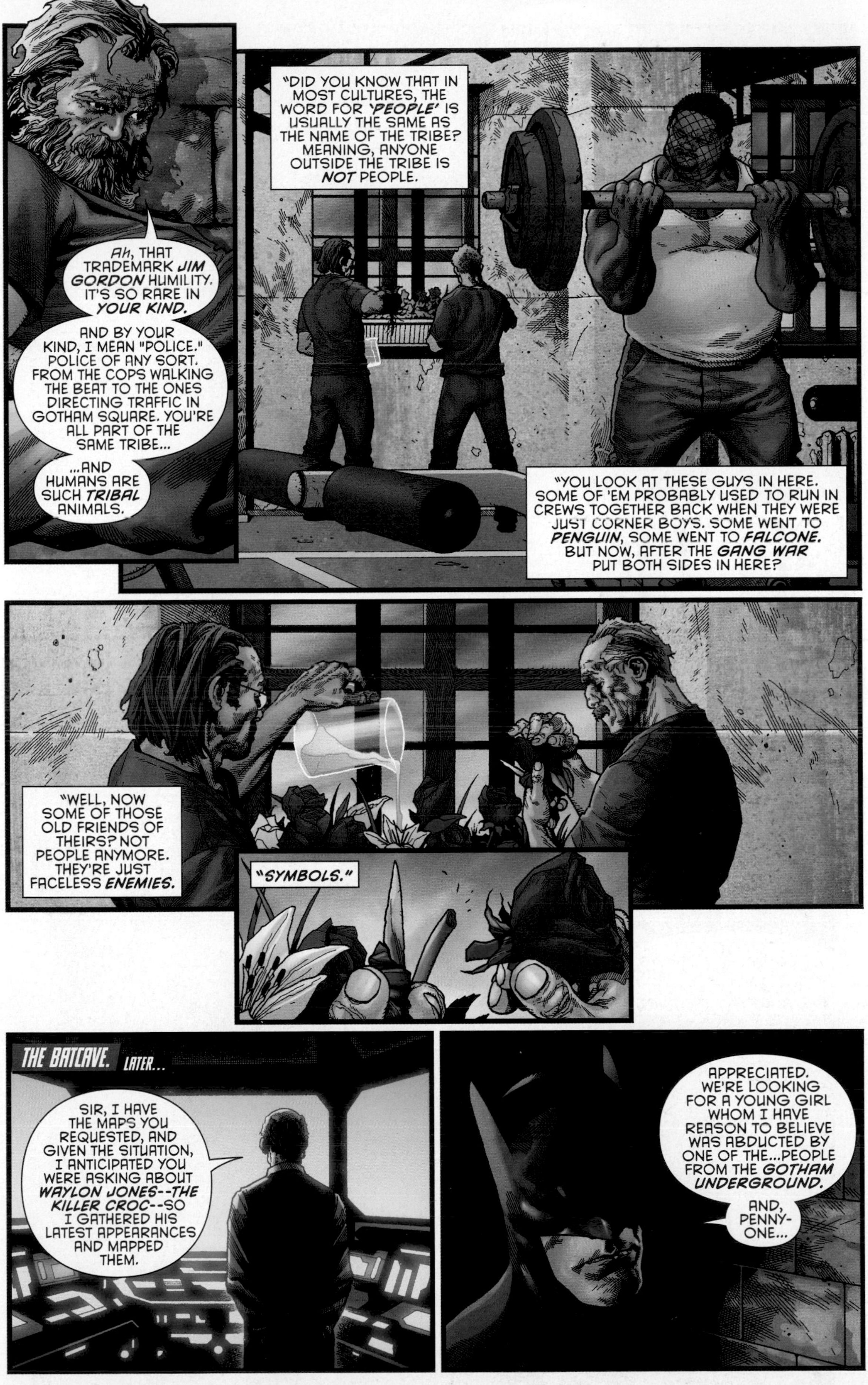
"DID YOU KNOW THAT IN MOST CULTURES, THE WORD FOR 'PEOPLE' IS USUALLY THE SAME AS THE NAME OF THE TRIBE? MEANING, ANYONE OUTSIDE THE TRIBE IS NOT PEOPLE.
AH, THAT TRADEMARK JIM GORDON HUMILITY. IT'S SO RARE IN YOUR KIND.
AND BY YOUR KIND, I MEAN "POLICE." POLICE OF ANY SORT. FROM THE COPS WALKING THE BEAT TO THE ONES DIRECTING TRAFFIC IN GOTHAM SQUARE. YOU'RE ALL PART OF THE SAME TRIBE...
...AND HUMANS ARE SUCH TRIBAL ANIMALS.
"YOU LOOK AT THESE GUYS IN HERE. SOME OF 'EM PROBABLY USED TO RUN IN CREWS TOGETHER BACK WHEN THEY WERE JUST CORNER BOYS. SOME WENT TO PENGUIN, SOME WENT TO FALCONE. BUT NOW, AFTER THE GANG WAR PUT BOTH SIDES IN HERE?
"WELL, NOW SOME OF THOSE OLD FRIENDS OF THEIRS? NOT PEOPLE ANYMORE. THEY'RE JUST FACELESS ENEMIES.
"SYMBOLS."
THE BATCAVE. LATER...
SIR, I HAVE THE MAPS YOU REQUESTED, AND GIVEN THE SITUATION, I ANTICIPATED YOU WERE ASKING ABOUT WAYLON JONES--THE KILLER CROC--SO I GATHERED HIS LATEST APPEARANCES AND MAPPED THEM.
APPRECIATED. WE'RE LOOKING FOR A YOUNG GIRL WHOM I HAVE REASON TO BELIEVE WAS ABDUCTED BY ONE OF THE...PEOPLE FROM THE GOTHAM UNDERGROUND.
AND, PENNY-ONE...

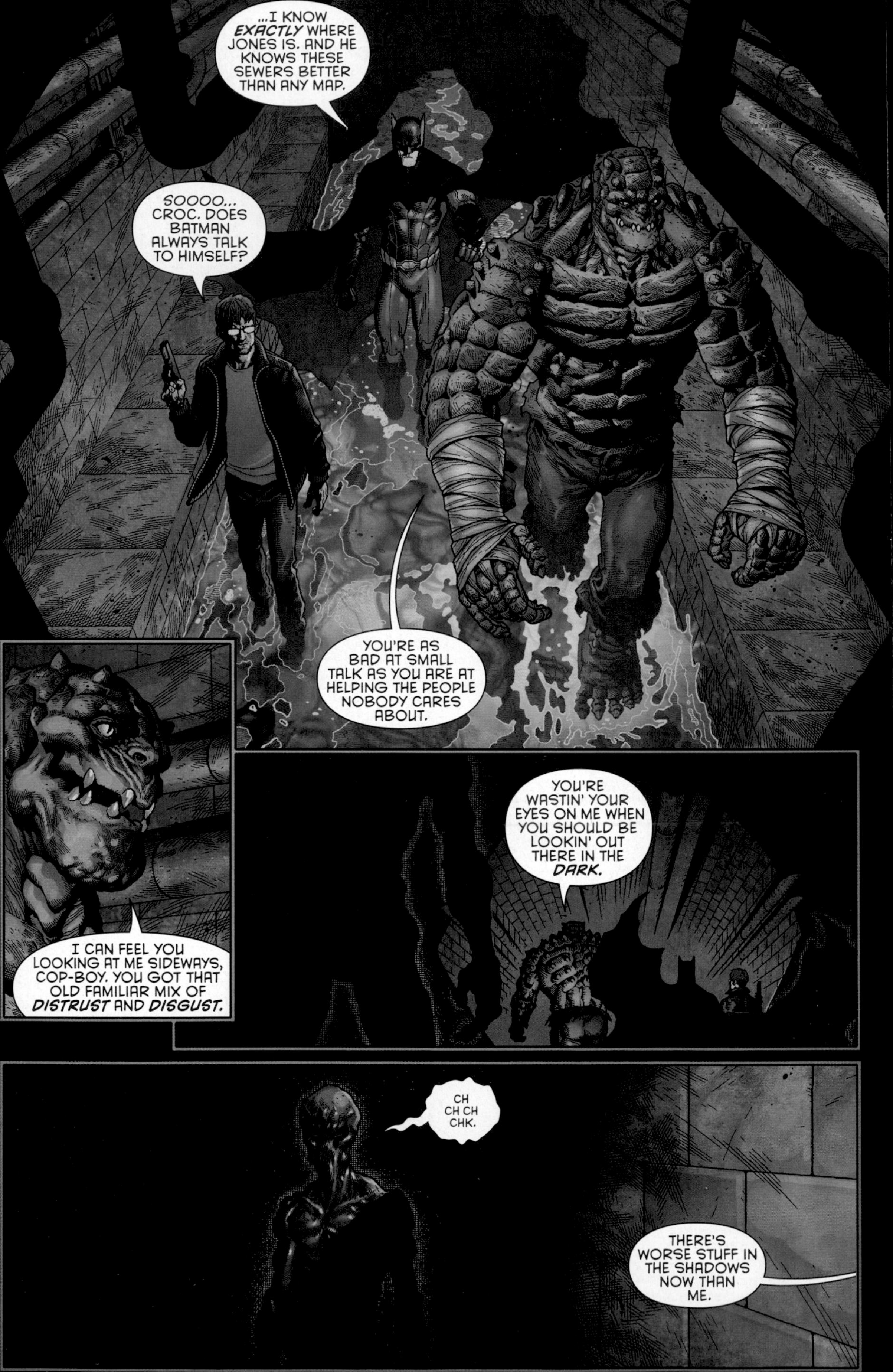
...I KNOW EXACTLY WHERE JONES IS. AND HE KNOWS THESE SEWERS BETTER THAN ANY MAP.
SOOOO... CROC. DOES BATMAN ALWAYS TALK TO HIMSELF?
YOU'RE AS BAD AT SMALL TALK AS YOU ARE AT HELPING THE PEOPLE NOBODY CARES ABOUT.
I CAN FEEL YOU LOOKING AT ME SIDEWAYS, COP-BOY. YOU GOT THAT OLD FAMILIAR MIX OF DISTRUST AND DISGUST.
YOU'RE WASTIN' YOUR EYES ON ME WHEN YOU SHOULD BE LOOKIN' OUT THERE IN THE DARK.
CH CH CH CHK.
THERE'S WORSE STUFF IN THE SHADOWS NOW THAN ME.

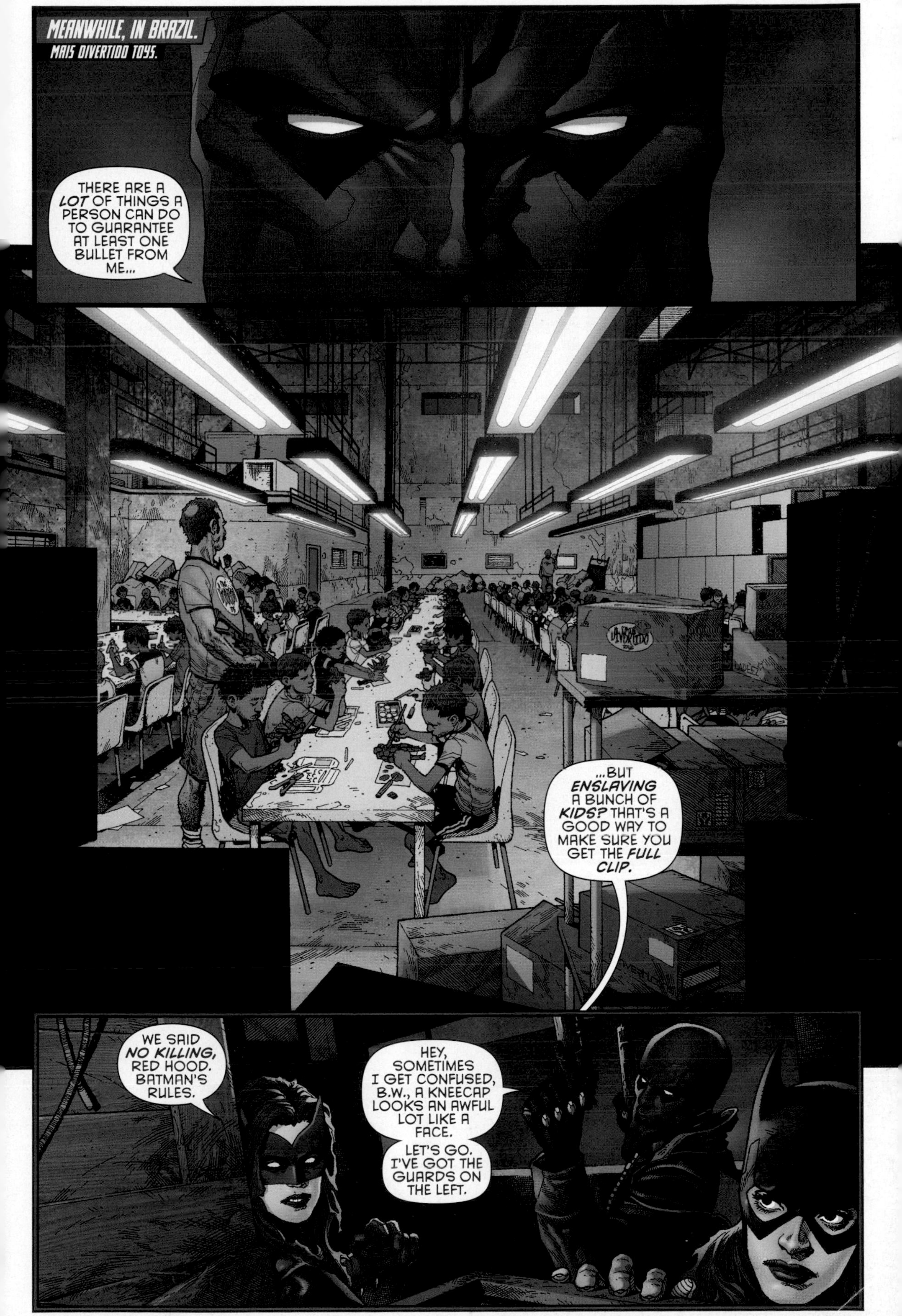
MEANWHILE, IN BRAZIL.
MAIS DIVERTIDO TOYS.
THERE ARE A LOT OF THINGS A PERSON CAN DO TO GUARANTEE AT LEAST ONE BULLET FROM ME...
...BUT ENSLAVING A BUNCH OF KIDS? THAT'S A GOOD WAY TO MAKE SURE YOU GET THE FULL CLIP.
WE SAID NO KILLING, RED HOOD. BATMAN'S RULES.
HEY, SOMETIMES I GET CONFUSED, B.W., A KNEECAP LOOKS AN AWFUL LOT LIKE A FACE.
LET'S GO. I'VE GOT THE GUARDS ON THE LEFT.

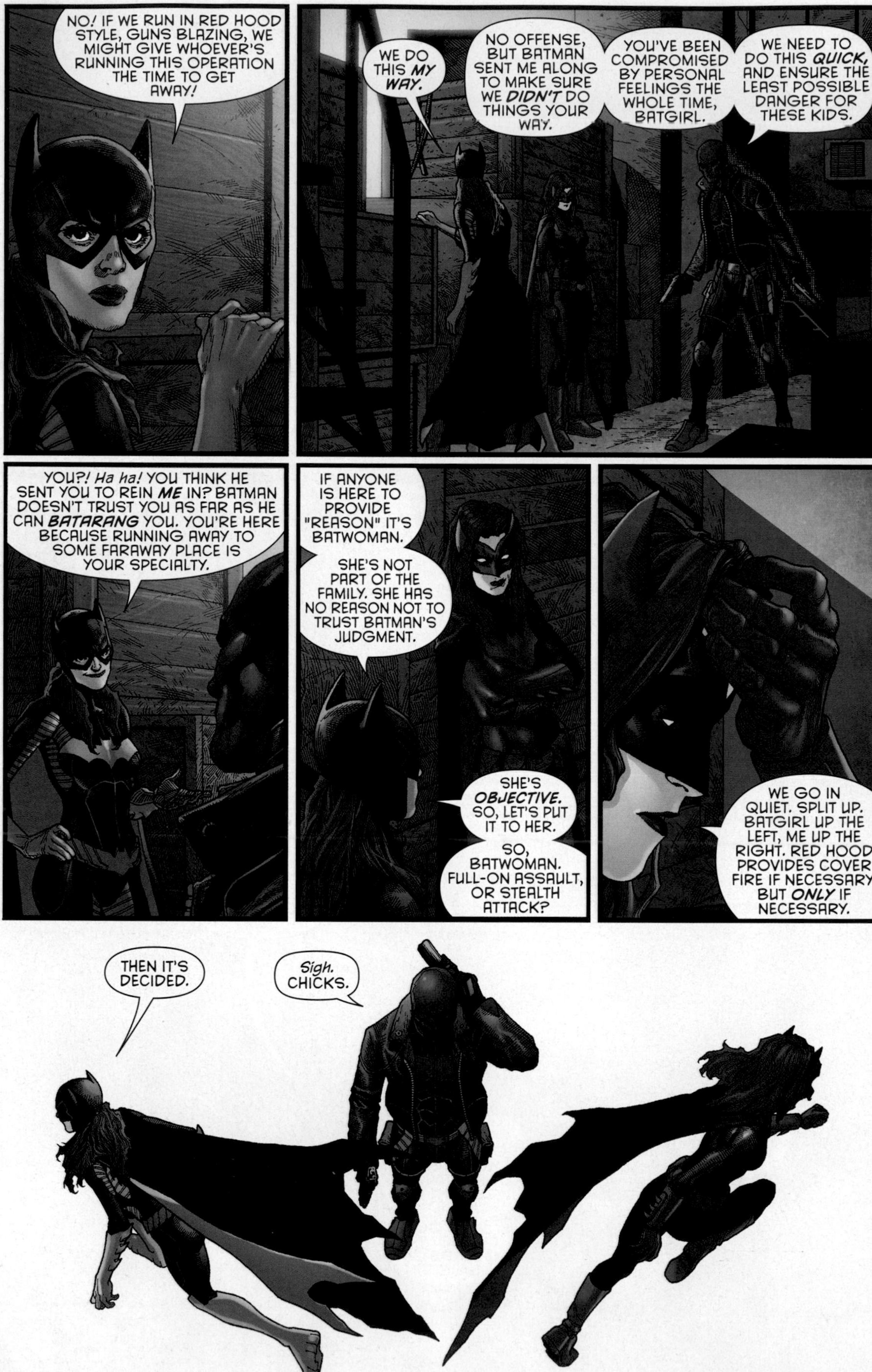
NO! IF WE RUN IN RED HOOD STYLE, GUNS BLAZING, WE MIGHT GIVE WHOEVER'S RUNNING THIS OPERATION THE TIME TO GET AWAY!
WE DO THIS *MY WAY.*
NO OFFENSE, BUT BATMAN SENT ME ALONG TO MAKE SURE WE *DIDN'T* DO THINGS YOUR WAY.
YOU'VE BEEN COMPROMISED BY PERSONAL FEELINGS THE WHOLE TIME, BATGIRL.
WE NEED TO DO THIS *QUICK,* AND ENSURE THE LEAST POSSIBLE DANGER FOR THESE KIDS.
YOU?! *Ha ha!* YOU THINK HE SENT YOU TO REIN *ME* IN? BATMAN DOESN'T TRUST YOU AS FAR AS HE CAN *BATARANG* YOU. YOU'RE HERE BECAUSE RUNNING AWAY TO SOME FARAWAY PLACE IS YOUR SPECIALTY.
IF ANYONE IS HERE TO PROVIDE "REASON" IT'S BATWOMAN.
SHE'S NOT PART OF THE FAMILY. SHE HAS NO REASON NOT TO TRUST BATMAN'S JUDGMENT.
SHE'S *OBJECTIVE.* SO, LET'S PUT IT TO HER.
SO, BATWOMAN. FULL-ON ASSAULT, OR STEALTH ATTACK?
WE GO IN QUIET. SPLIT UP. BATGIRL UP THE LEFT, ME UP THE RIGHT. RED HOOD PROVIDES COVER FIRE IF NECESSARY, BUT *ONLY* IF NECESSARY.
THEN IT'S DECIDED.
Sigh. CHICKS.

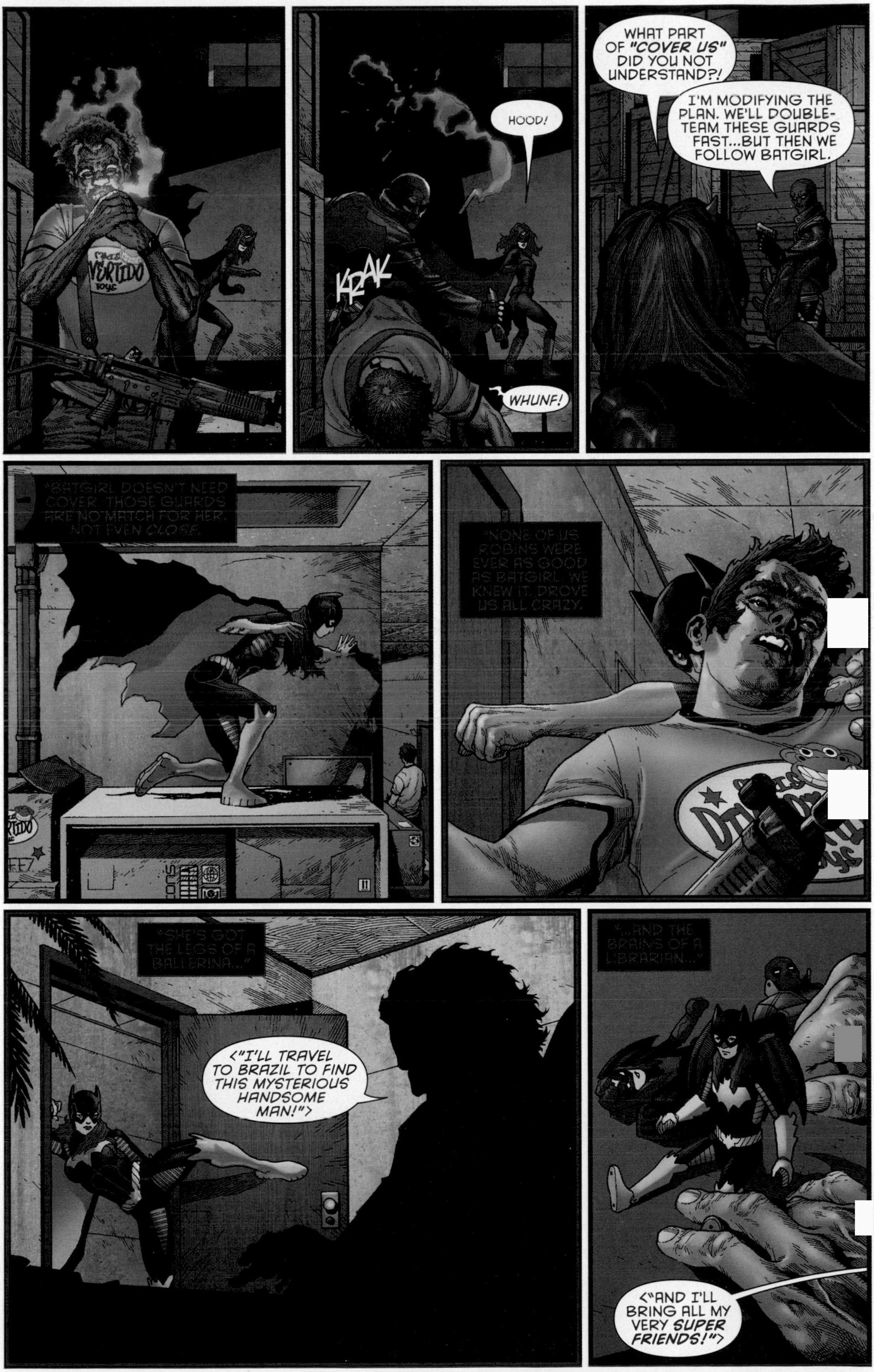

HOOD!
KRAK
WHUNF!
WHAT PART OF "COVER US" DID YOU NOT UNDERSTAND?!
I'M MODIFYING THE PLAN. WE'LL DOUBLE-TEAM THESE GUARDS FAST...BUT THEN WE FOLLOW BATGIRL.
"BATGIRL DOESN'T NEED COVER. THOSE GUARDS ARE NO MATCH FOR HER. NOT EVEN CLOSE.
"NONE OF US ROBINS WERE EVER AS GOOD AS BATGIRL. WE KNEW IT. DROVE US ALL CRAZY.
"SHE'S GOT THE LEGS OF A BALLERINA..."
<"I'LL TRAVEL TO BRAZIL TO FIND THIS MYSTERIOUS HANDSOME MAN!">
"...AND THE BRAINS OF A LIBRARIAN..."
<"AND I'LL BRING ALL MY VERY SUPER FRIENDS!">

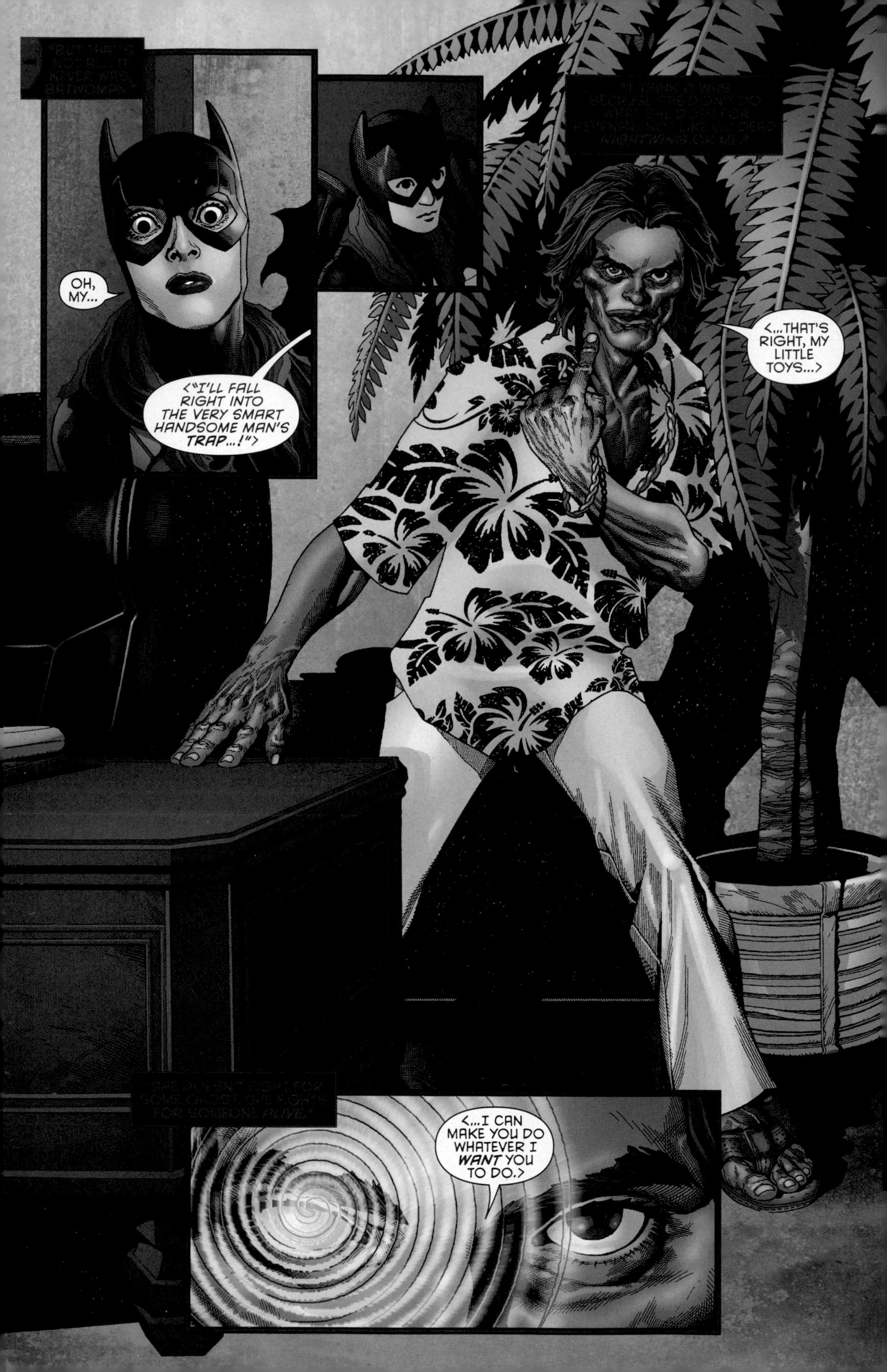
"BUT THAT'S NOT ALL IT NEVER WAS, BATWOMAN."
OH, MY...
<"I'LL FALL RIGHT INTO THE VERY SMART HANDSOME MAN'S *TRAP*...!">
<...THAT'S RIGHT, MY LITTLE TOYS...>
"SHE DIDN'T FIGHT FOR SOME GHOST. SHE FIGHTS FOR SOMEONE *ALIVE*."
<...I CAN MAKE YOU DO WHATEVER I *WANT* YOU TO DO.>

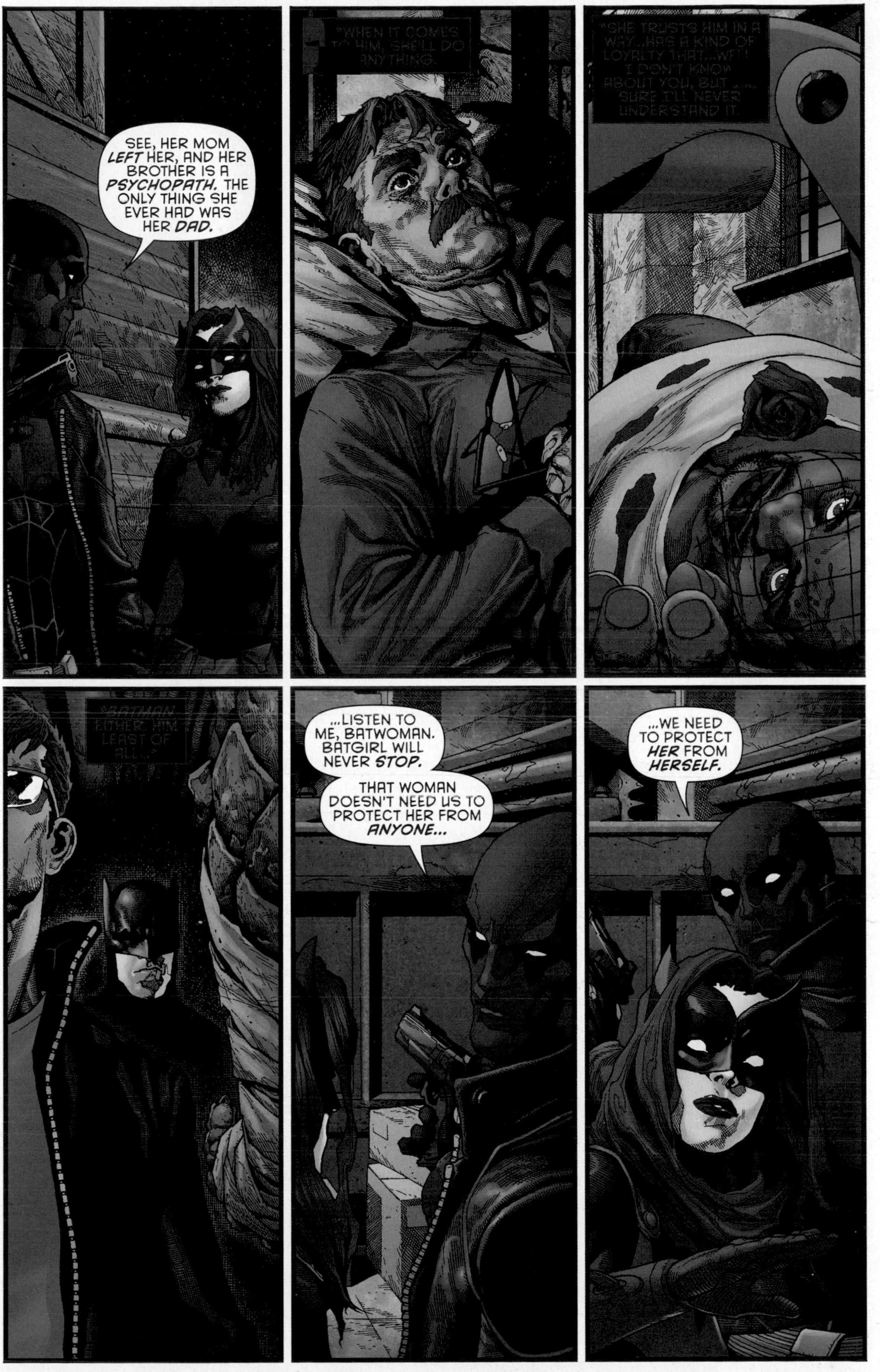
SEE, HER MOM *LEFT* HER, AND HER BROTHER IS A *PSYCHOPATH.* THE ONLY THING SHE EVER HAD WAS HER *DAD.*
"WHEN IT COMES TO HIM, SHE'LL DO ANYTHING.
"SHE TRUSTS HIM IN A WAY...HAS A KIND OF LOYALTY THAT...WELL I DON'T KNOW ABOUT YOU, BUT I... SURE I'LL NEVER UNDERSTAND IT.
BATMAN EITHER. HIM LEAST OF ALL..."
...LISTEN TO ME, BATWOMAN. BATGIRL WILL NEVER *STOP.*
THAT WOMAN DOESN'T NEED US TO PROTECT HER FROM *ANYONE...*
...WE NEED TO PROTECT *HER* FROM *HERSELF.*

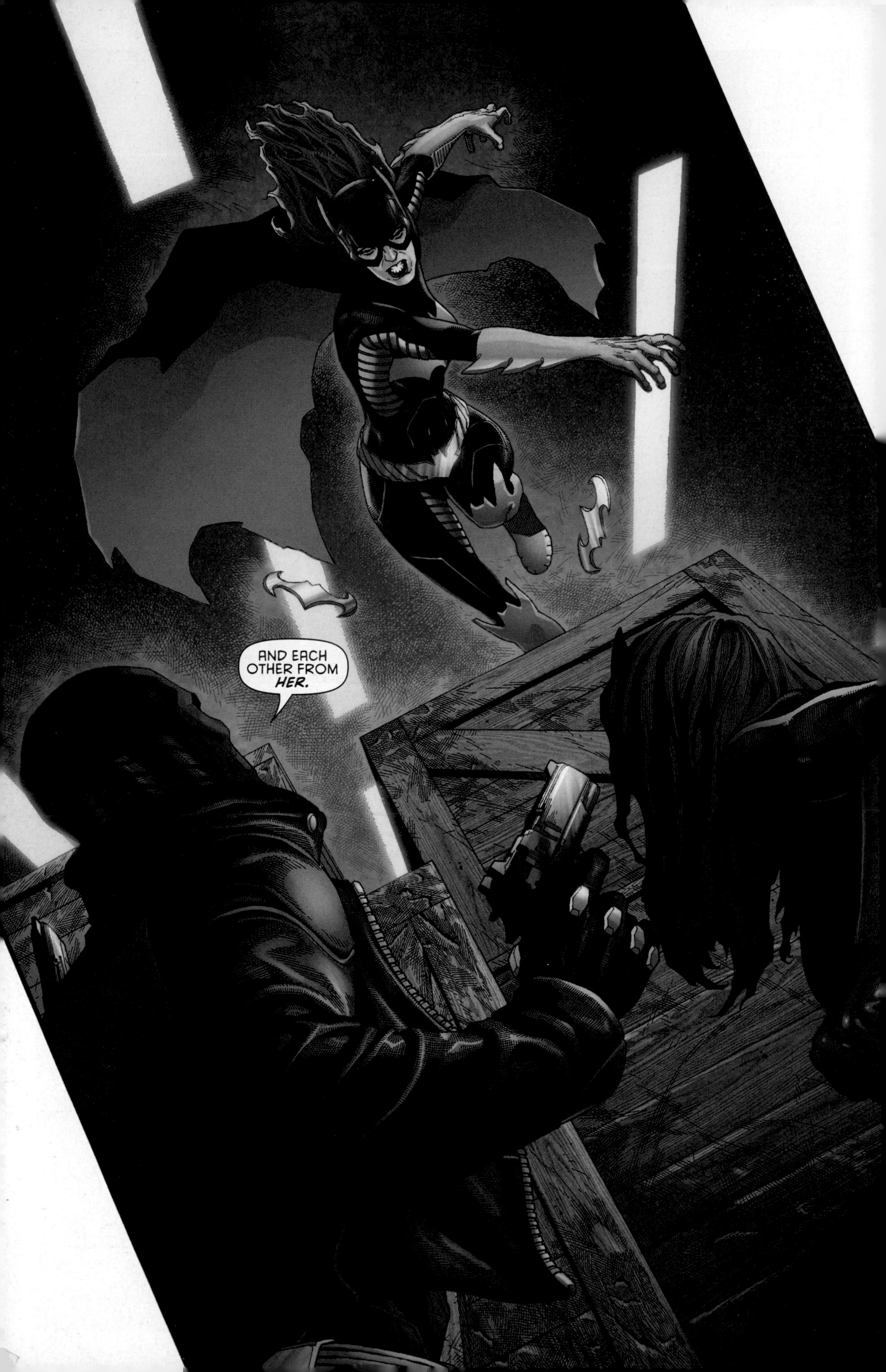
AND EACH OTHER FROM HER.

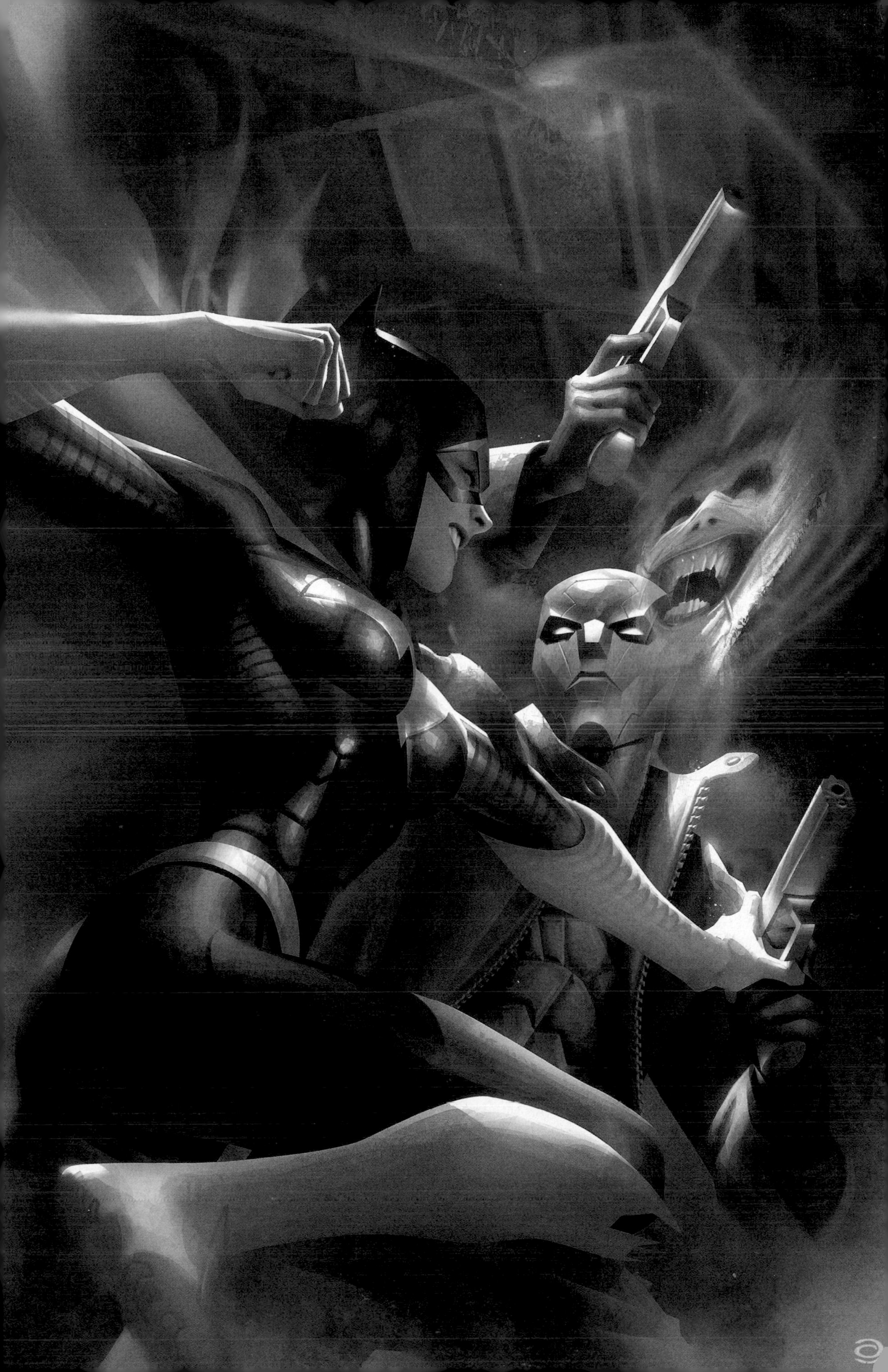

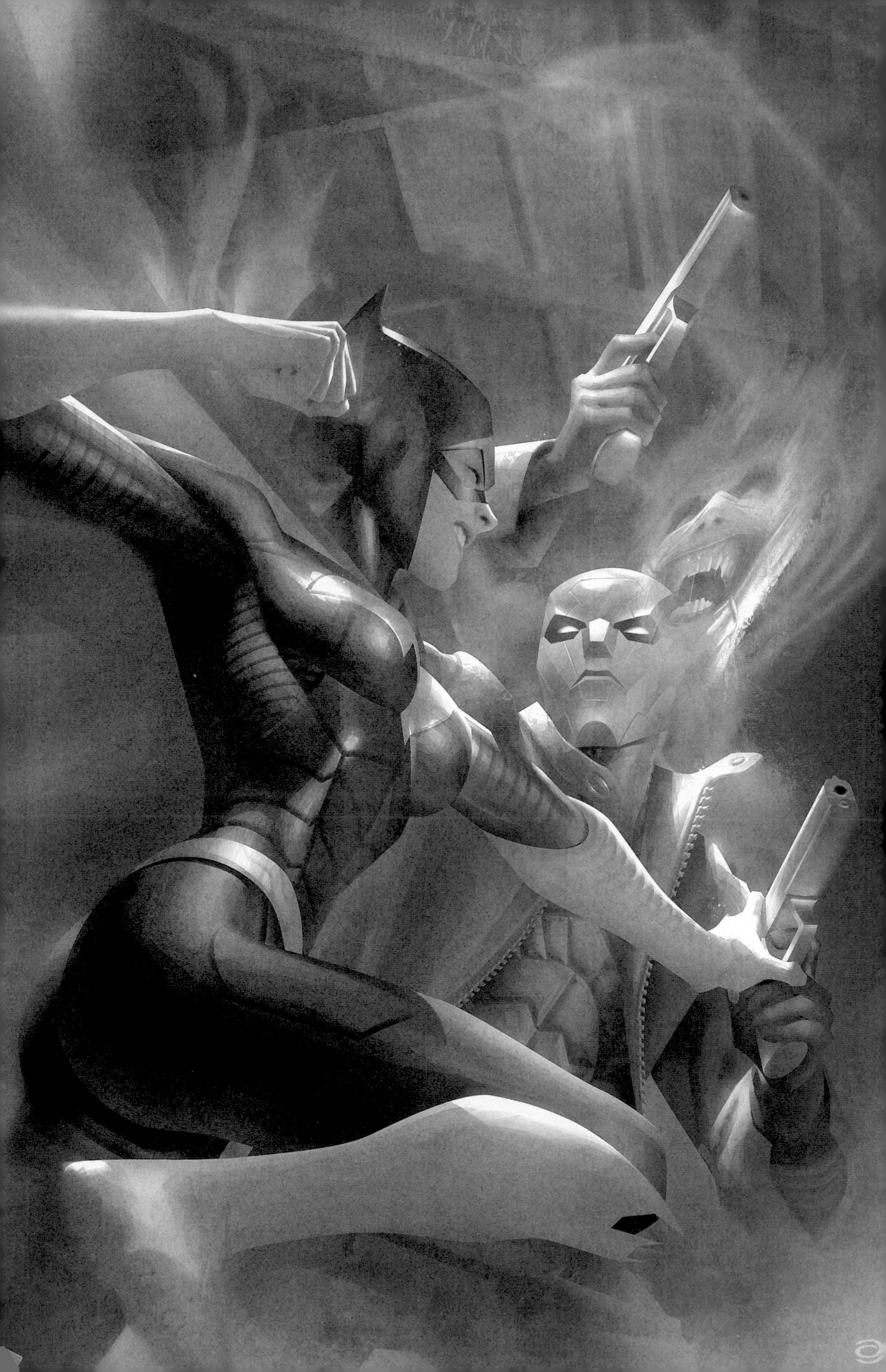

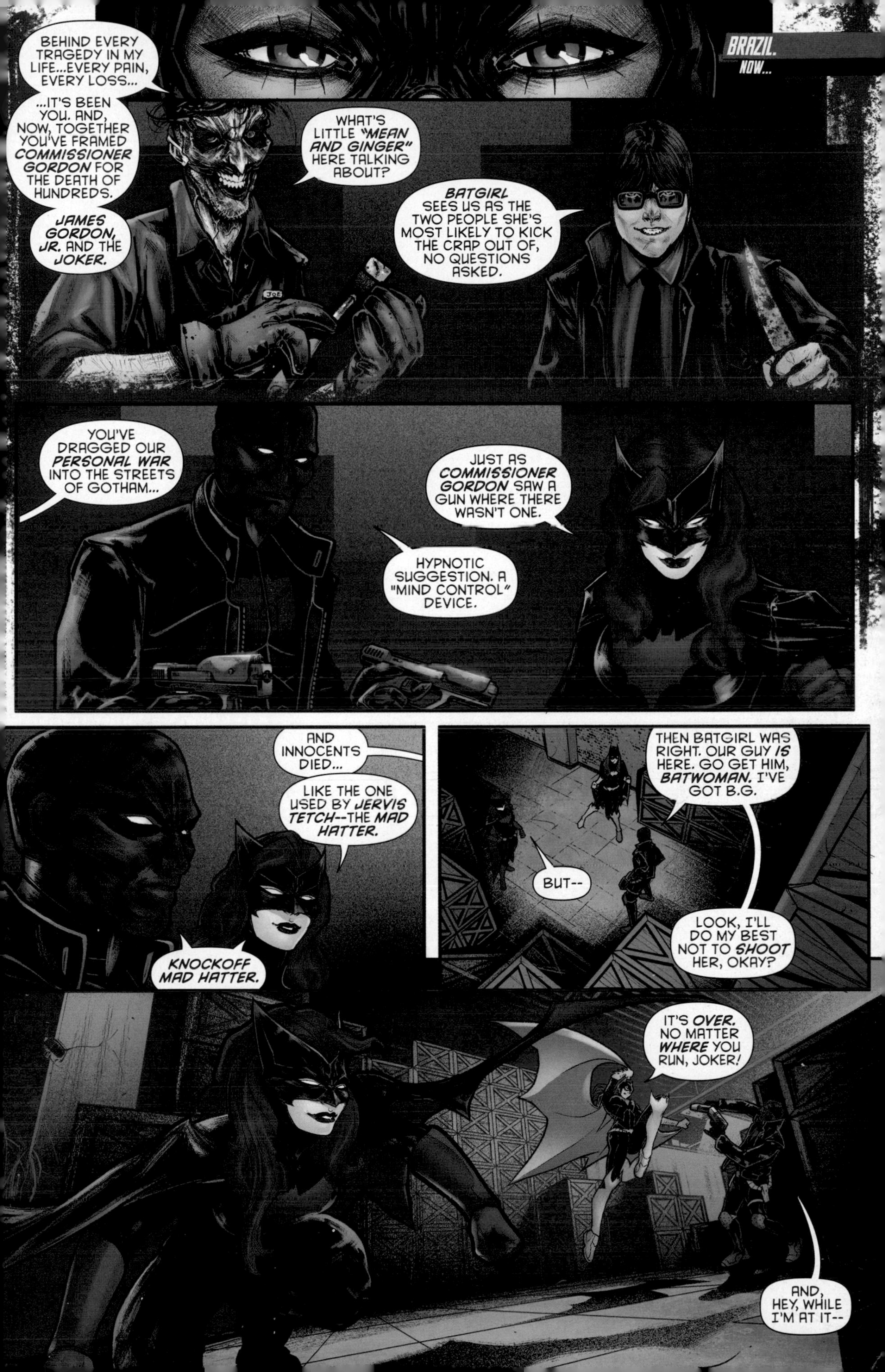
BRAZIL. NOW...
BEHIND EVERY TRAGEDY IN MY LIFE...EVERY PAIN, EVERY LOSS...
...IT'S BEEN YOU. AND, NOW, TOGETHER YOU'VE FRAMED COMMISSIONER GORDON FOR THE DEATH OF HUNDREDS.
JAMES GORDON, JR. AND THE JOKER.
WHAT'S LITTLE "MEAN AND GINGER" HERE TALKING ABOUT?
BATGIRL SEES US AS THE TWO PEOPLE SHE'S MOST LIKELY TO KICK THE CRAP OUT OF, NO QUESTIONS ASKED.
YOU'VE DRAGGED OUR PERSONAL WAR INTO THE STREETS OF GOTHAM...
JUST AS COMMISSIONER GORDON SAW A GUN WHERE THERE WASN'T ONE.
HYPNOTIC SUGGESTION. A "MIND CONTROL" DEVICE.
AND INNOCENTS DIED...
LIKE THE ONE USED BY JERVIS TETCH--THE MAD HATTER.
KNOCKOFF MAD HATTER.
THEN BATGIRL WAS RIGHT. OUR GUY IS HERE. GO GET HIM, BATWOMAN. I'VE GOT B.G.
BUT--
LOOK, I'LL DO MY BEST NOT TO SHOOT HER, OKAY?
IT'S OVER. NO MATTER WHERE YOU RUN, JOKER!
AND, HEY, WHILE I'M AT IT--

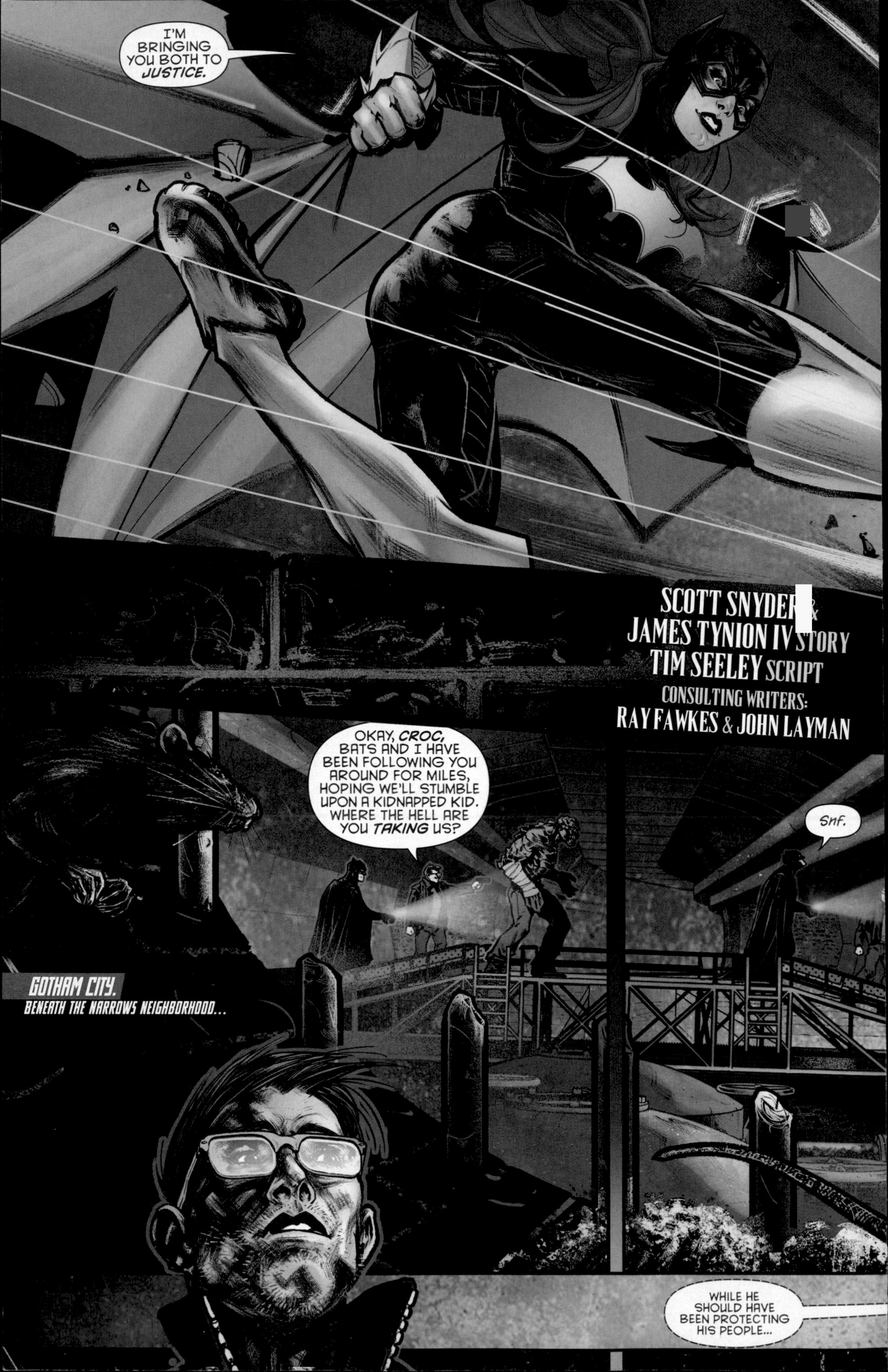
I'M BRINGING YOU BOTH TO JUSTICE.
SCOTT SNYDER & JAMES TYNION IV STORY
TIM SEELEY SCRIPT
CONSULTING WRITERS: RAY FAWKES & JOHN LAYMAN
GOTHAM CITY.
BENEATH THE NARROWS NEIGHBORHOOD...
OKAY, CROC, BATS AND I HAVE BEEN FOLLOWING YOU AROUND FOR MILES, HOPING WE'LL STUMBLE UPON A KIDNAPPED KID. WHERE THE HELL ARE YOU TAKING US?
Snf.
WHILE HE SHOULD HAVE BEEN PROTECTING HIS PEOPLE...

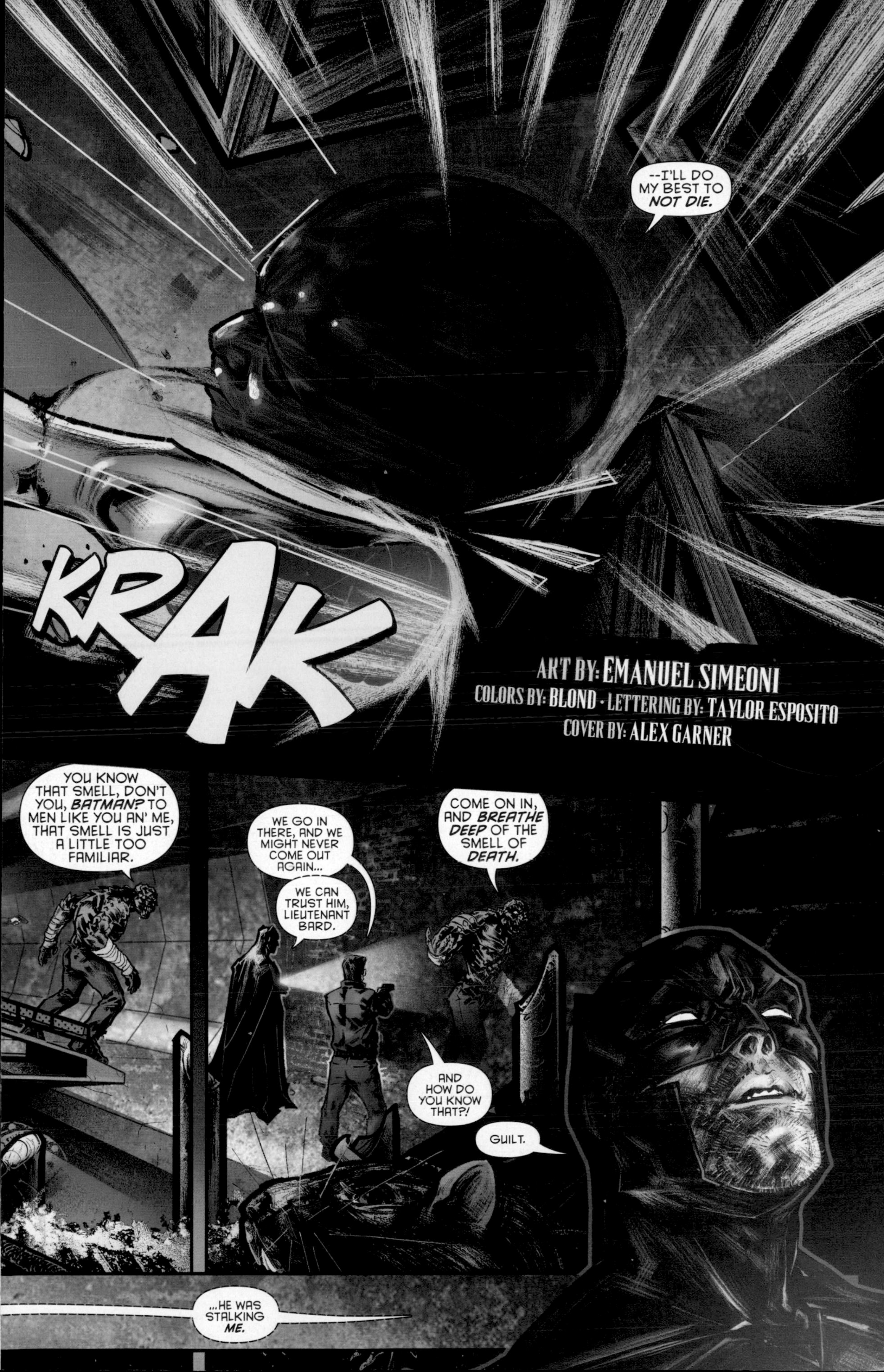
--I'LL DO MY BEST TO NOT DIE.
KRAK
ART BY: EMANUEL SIMEONI
COLORS BY: BLOND · LETTERING BY: TAYLOR ESPOSITO
COVER BY: ALEX GARNER
YOU KNOW THAT SMELL, DON'T YOU, BATMAN? TO MEN LIKE YOU AN' ME, THAT SMELL IS JUST A LITTLE TOO FAMILIAR.
WE GO IN THERE, AND WE MIGHT NEVER COME OUT AGAIN...
WE CAN TRUST HIM, LIEUTENANT BARD.
COME ON IN, AND BREATHE DEEP OF THE SMELL OF DEATH.
AND HOW DO YOU KNOW THAT?!
GUILT.
...HE WAS STALKING ME.

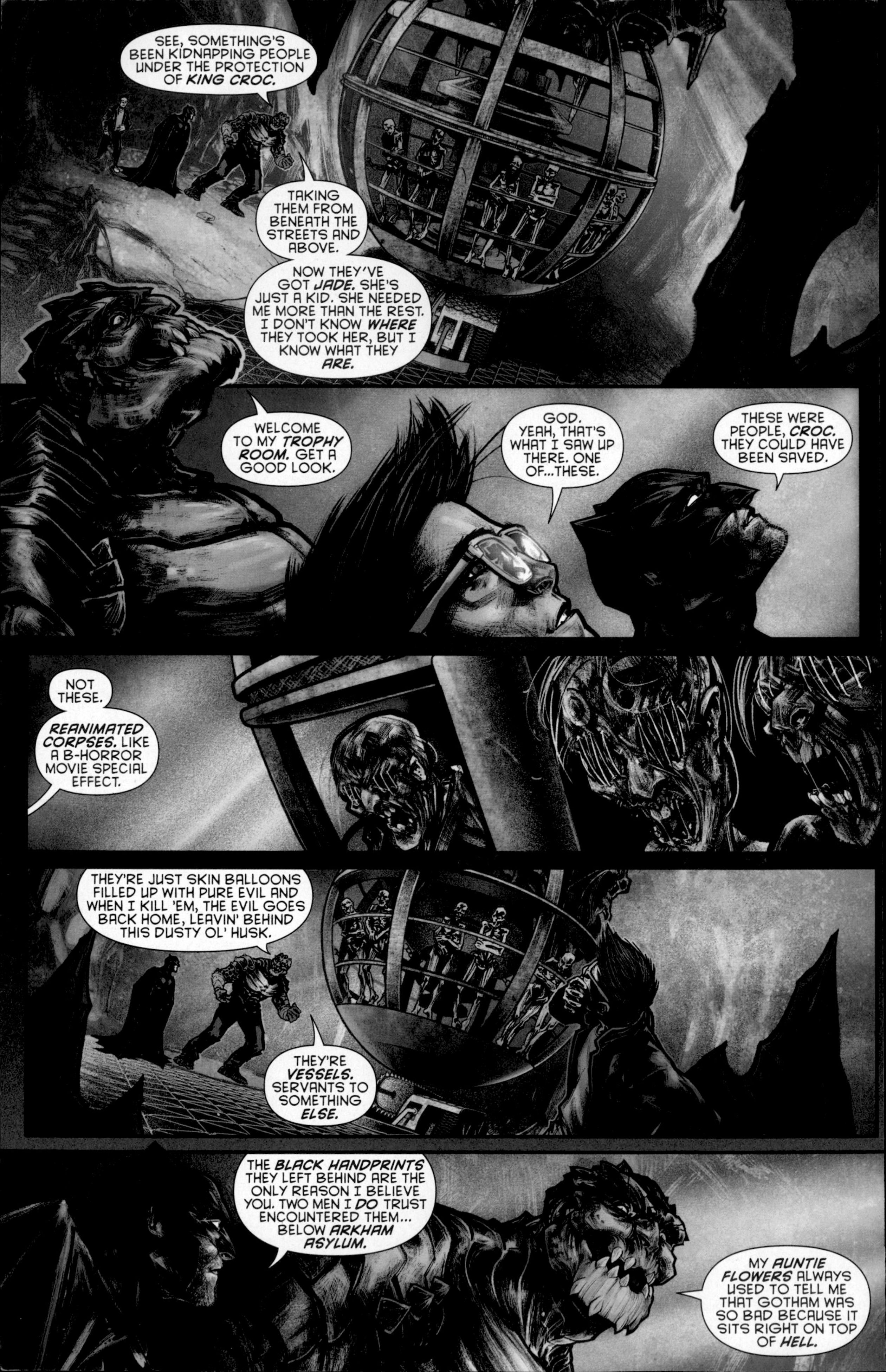
SEE, SOMETHING'S BEEN KIDNAPPING PEOPLE UNDER THE PROTECTION OF KING CROC.
TAKING THEM FROM BENEATH THE STREETS AND ABOVE.
NOW THEY'VE GOT JADE. SHE'S JUST A KID. SHE NEEDED ME MORE THAN THE REST. I DON'T KNOW WHERE THEY TOOK HER, BUT I KNOW WHAT THEY ARE.
WELCOME TO MY TROPHY ROOM. GET A GOOD LOOK.
GOD. YEAH, THAT'S WHAT I SAW UP THERE. ONE OF...THESE.
THESE WERE PEOPLE, CROC. THEY COULD HAVE BEEN SAVED.
NOT THESE.
REANIMATED CORPSES. LIKE A B-HORROR MOVIE SPECIAL EFFECT.
THEY'RE JUST SKIN BALLOONS FILLED UP WITH PURE EVIL AND WHEN I KILL 'EM, THE EVIL GOES BACK HOME, LEAVIN' BEHIND THIS DUSTY OL' HUSK.
THEY'RE VESSELS. SERVANTS TO SOMETHING ELSE.
THE BLACK HANDPRINTS THEY LEFT BEHIND ARE THE ONLY REASON I BELIEVE YOU. TWO MEN I DO TRUST ENCOUNTERED THEM... BELOW ARKHAM ASYLUM.
MY AUNTIE FLOWERS ALWAYS USED TO TELL ME THAT GOTHAM WAS SO BAD BECAUSE IT SITS RIGHT ON TOP OF HELL.

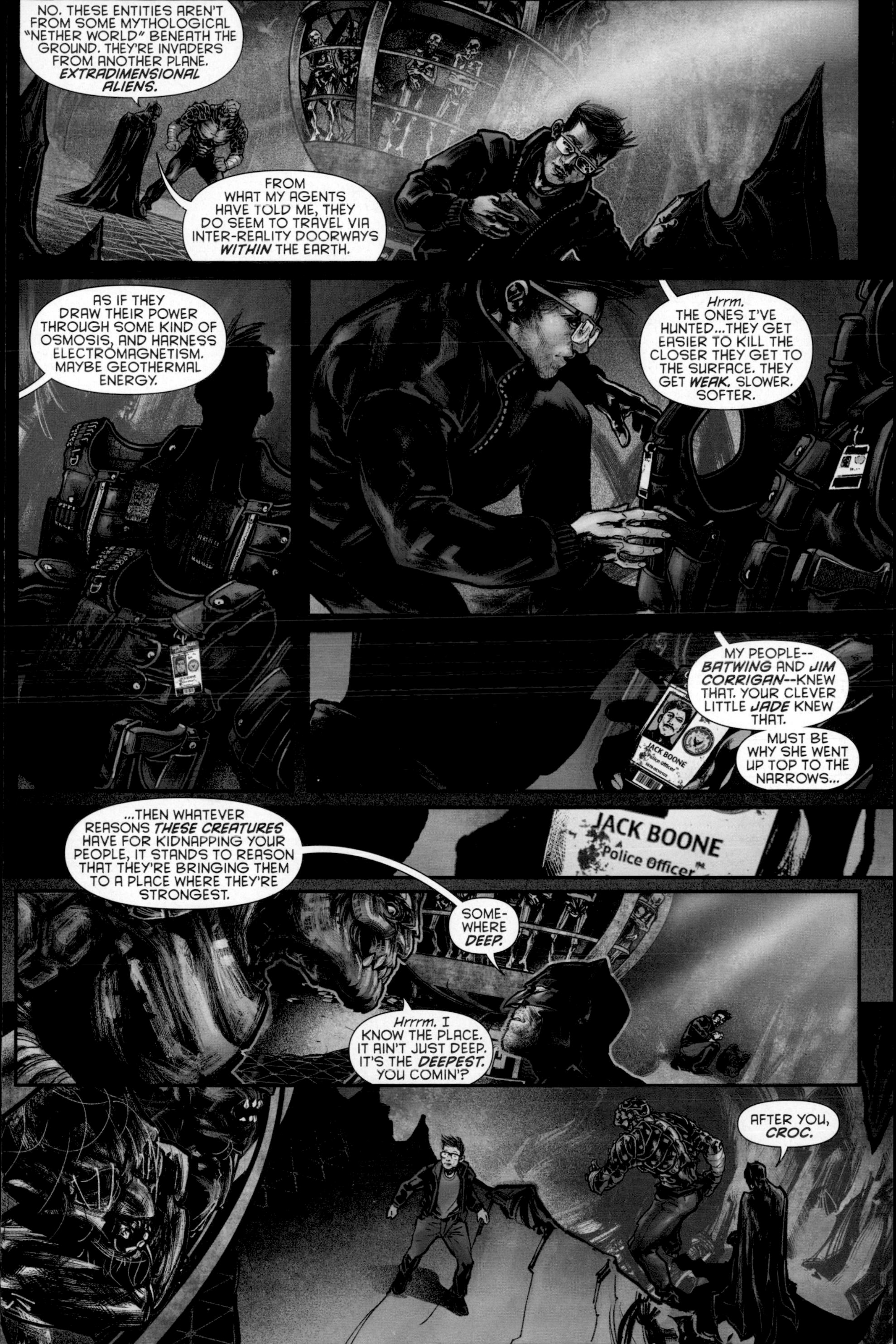

NO. THESE ENTITIES AREN'T FROM SOME MYTHOLOGICAL "NETHER WORLD" BENEATH THE GROUND. THEY'RE INVADERS FROM ANOTHER PLANE. EXTRADIMENSIONAL ALIENS.
FROM WHAT MY AGENTS HAVE TOLD ME, THEY DO SEEM TO TRAVEL VIA INTER-REALITY DOORWAYS WITHIN THE EARTH.
AS IF THEY DRAW THEIR POWER THROUGH SOME KIND OF OSMOSIS, AND HARNESS ELECTROMAGNETISM. MAYBE GEOTHERMAL ENERGY.
Hrrm. THE ONES I'VE HUNTED...THEY GET EASIER TO KILL THE CLOSER THEY GET TO THE SURFACE. THEY GET WEAK. SLOWER. SOFTER.
MY PEOPLE-- BATWING AND JIM CORRIGAN--KNEW THAT. YOUR CLEVER LITTLE JADE KNEW THAT.
MUST BE WHY SHE WENT UP TOP TO THE NARROWS...
JACK BOONE
Police Officer
JACK BOONE
Police Officer
...THEN WHATEVER REASONS THESE CREATURES HAVE FOR KIDNAPPING YOUR PEOPLE, IT STANDS TO REASON THAT THEY'RE BRINGING THEM TO A PLACE WHERE THEY'RE STRONGEST.
SOME-WHERE DEEP.
Hrrrm. I KNOW THE PLACE. IT AIN'T JUST DEEP. IT'S THE DEEPEST. YOU COMIN'?
AFTER YOU, CROC.

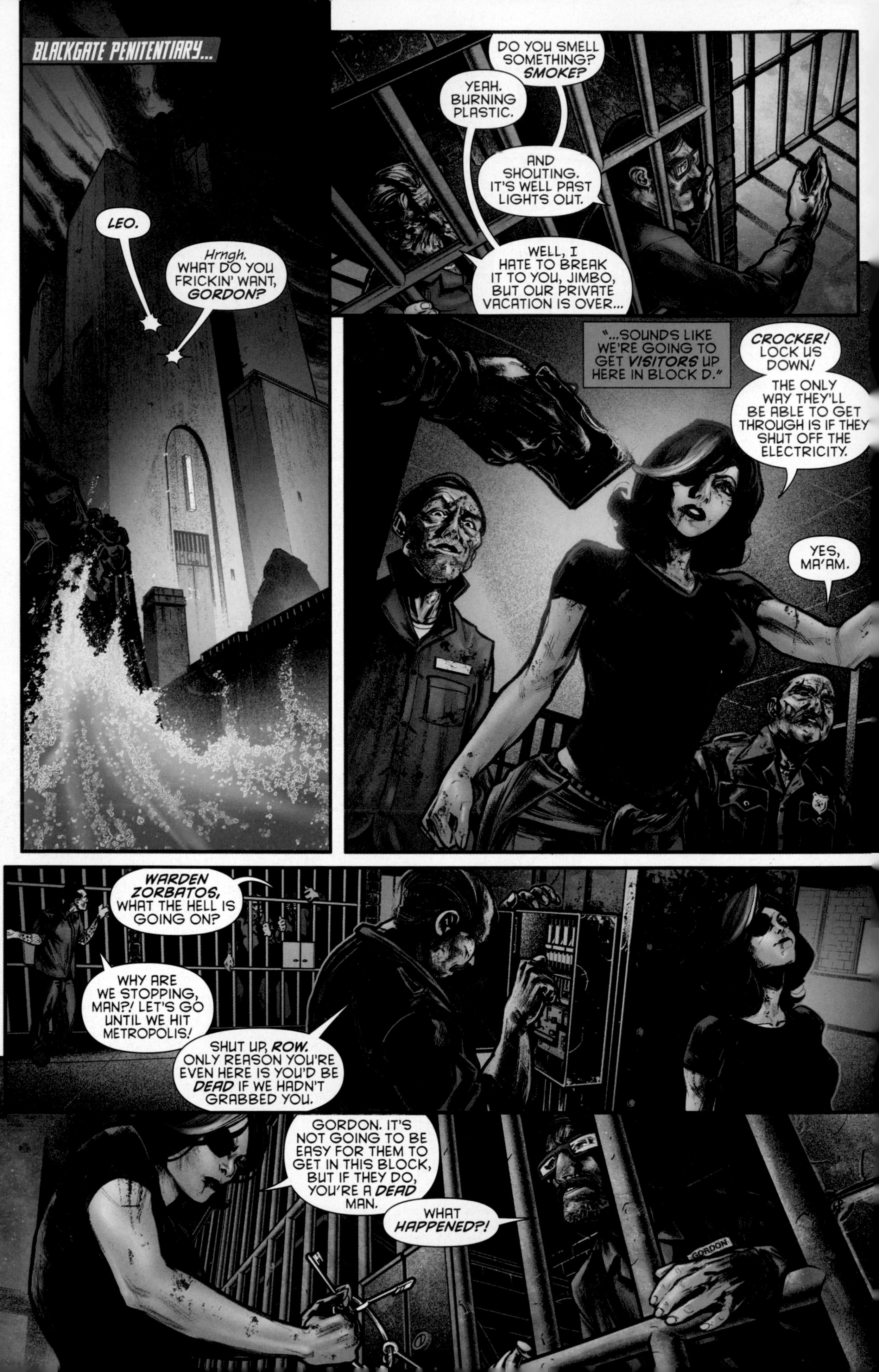
BLACKGATE PENITENTIARY...
LEO.
Hrngh. WHAT DO YOU FRICKIN' WANT, GORDON?
DO YOU SMELL SOMETHING? SMOKE?
YEAH. BURNING PLASTIC.
AND SHOUTING. IT'S WELL PAST LIGHTS OUT.
WELL, I HATE TO BREAK IT TO YOU, JIMBO, BUT OUR PRIVATE VACATION IS OVER...
"...SOUNDS LIKE WE'RE GOING TO GET VISITORS UP HERE IN BLOCK D."
CROCKER! LOCK US DOWN!
THE ONLY WAY THEY'LL BE ABLE TO GET THROUGH IS IF THEY SHUT OFF THE ELECTRICITY.
YES, MA'AM.
WARDEN ZORBATOS, WHAT THE HELL IS GOING ON?
WHY ARE WE STOPPING, MAN?! LET'S GO UNTIL WE HIT METROPOLIS!
SHUT UP, ROW. ONLY REASON YOU'RE EVEN HERE IS YOU'D BE DEAD IF WE HADN'T GRABBED YOU.
GORDON. IT'S NOT GOING TO BE EASY FOR THEM TO GET IN THIS BLOCK, BUT IF THEY DO, YOU'RE A DEAD MAN.
WHAT HAPPENED?!
GORDON

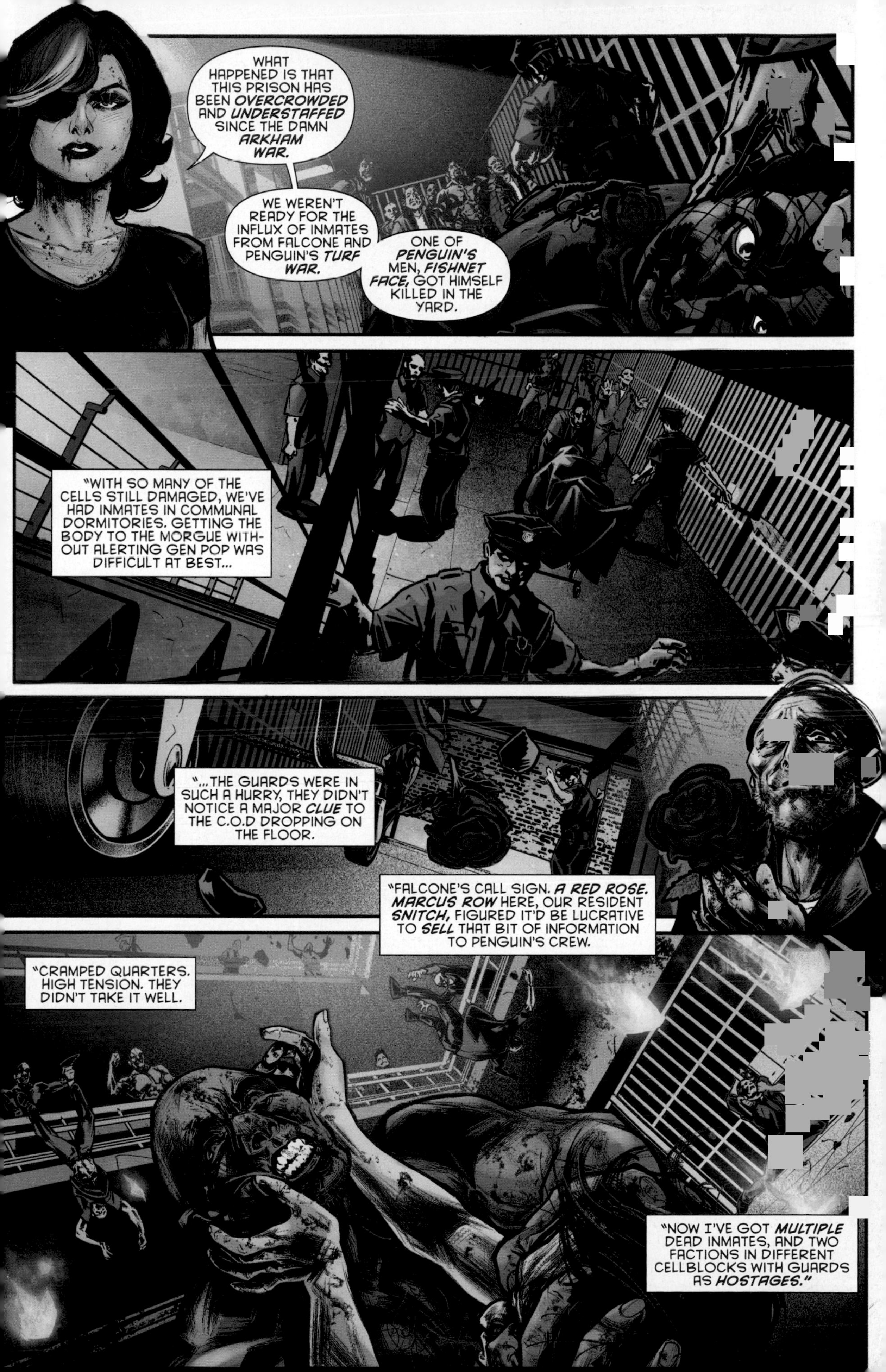
WHAT HAPPENED IS THAT THIS PRISON HAS BEEN OVERCROWDED AND UNDERSTAFFED SINCE THE DAMN ARKHAM WAR.
WE WEREN'T READY FOR THE INFLUX OF INMATES FROM FALCONE AND PENGUIN'S TURF WAR.
ONE OF PENGUIN'S MEN, FISHNET FACE, GOT HIMSELF KILLED IN THE YARD.
"WITH SO MANY OF THE CELLS STILL DAMAGED, WE'VE HAD INMATES IN COMMUNAL DORMITORIES. GETTING THE BODY TO THE MORGUE WITHOUT ALERTING GEN POP WAS DIFFICULT AT BEST...
"...THE GUARDS WERE IN SUCH A HURRY, THEY DIDN'T NOTICE A MAJOR CLUE TO THE C.O.D DROPPING ON THE FLOOR.
"FALCONE'S CALL SIGN. A RED ROSE. MARCUS ROW HERE, OUR RESIDENT SNITCH, FIGURED IT'D BE LUCRATIVE TO SELL THAT BIT OF INFORMATION TO PENGUIN'S CREW.
"CRAMPED QUARTERS. HIGH TENSION. THEY DIDN'T TAKE IT WELL.
"NOW I'VE GOT MULTIPLE DEAD INMATES, AND TWO FACTIONS IN DIFFERENT CELLBLOCKS WITH GUARDS AS HOSTAGES."

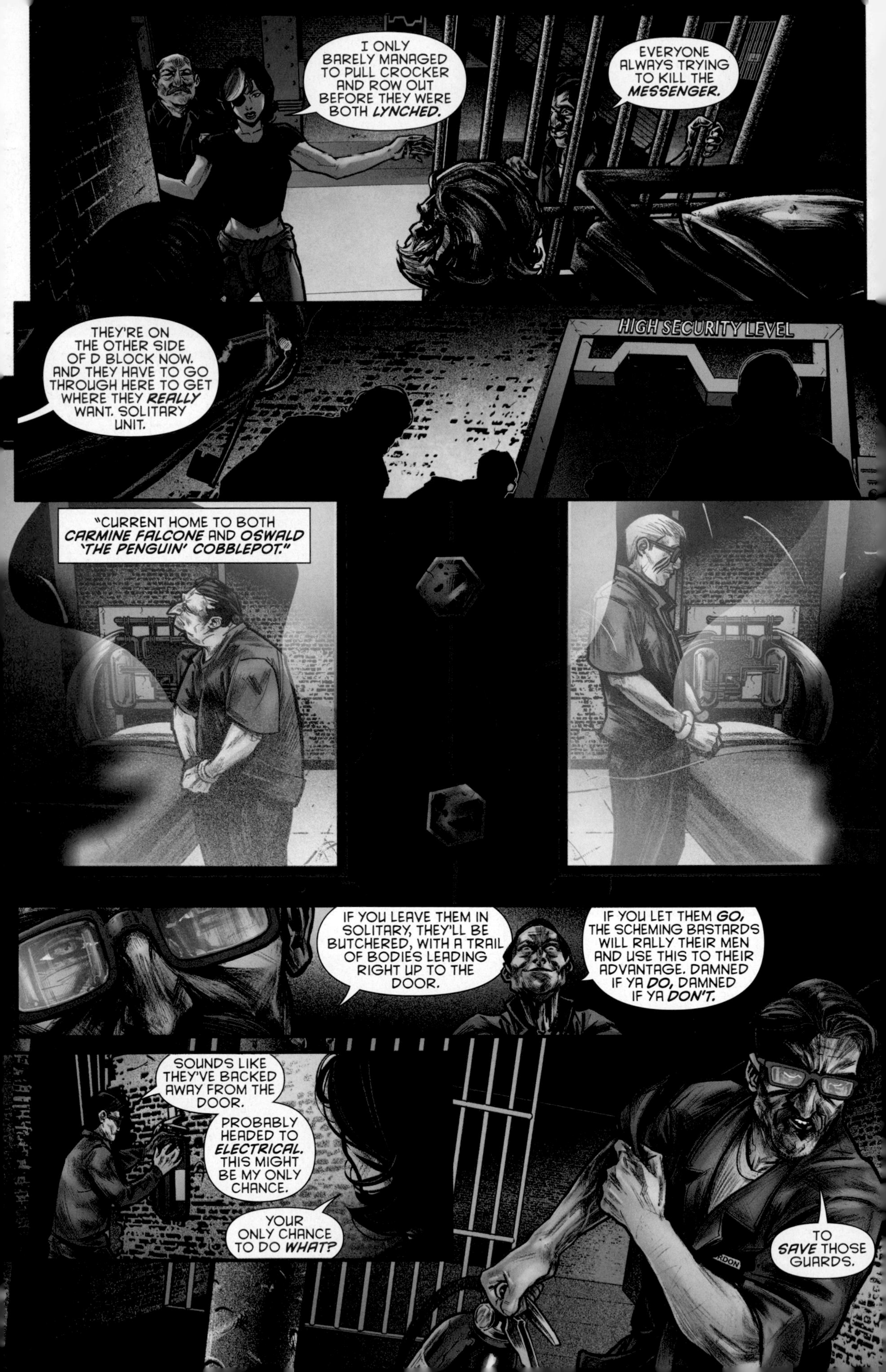
I ONLY BARELY MANAGED TO PULL CROCKER AND ROW OUT BEFORE THEY WERE BOTH *LYNCHED.*
EVERYONE ALWAYS TRYING TO KILL THE *MESSENGER.*
THEY'RE ON THE OTHER SIDE OF D BLOCK NOW. AND THEY HAVE TO GO THROUGH HERE TO GET WHERE THEY *REALLY* WANT. SOLITARY UNIT.
HIGH SECURITY LEVEL
"CURRENT HOME TO BOTH *CARMINE FALCONE* AND *OSWALD 'THE PENGUIN' COBBLEPOT."*
IF YOU LEAVE THEM IN SOLITARY, THEY'LL BE BUTCHERED, WITH A TRAIL OF BODIES LEADING RIGHT UP TO THE DOOR.
IF YOU LET THEM *GO,* THE SCHEMING BASTARDS WILL RALLY THEIR MEN AND USE THIS TO THEIR ADVANTAGE. DAMNED IF YA *DO,* DAMNED IF YA *DON'T.*
SOUNDS LIKE THEY'VE BACKED AWAY FROM THE DOOR.
PROBABLY HEADED TO *ELECTRICAL.* THIS MIGHT BE MY ONLY CHANCE.
YOUR ONLY CHANCE TO DO *WHAT?*
TO *SAVE* THOSE GUARDS.

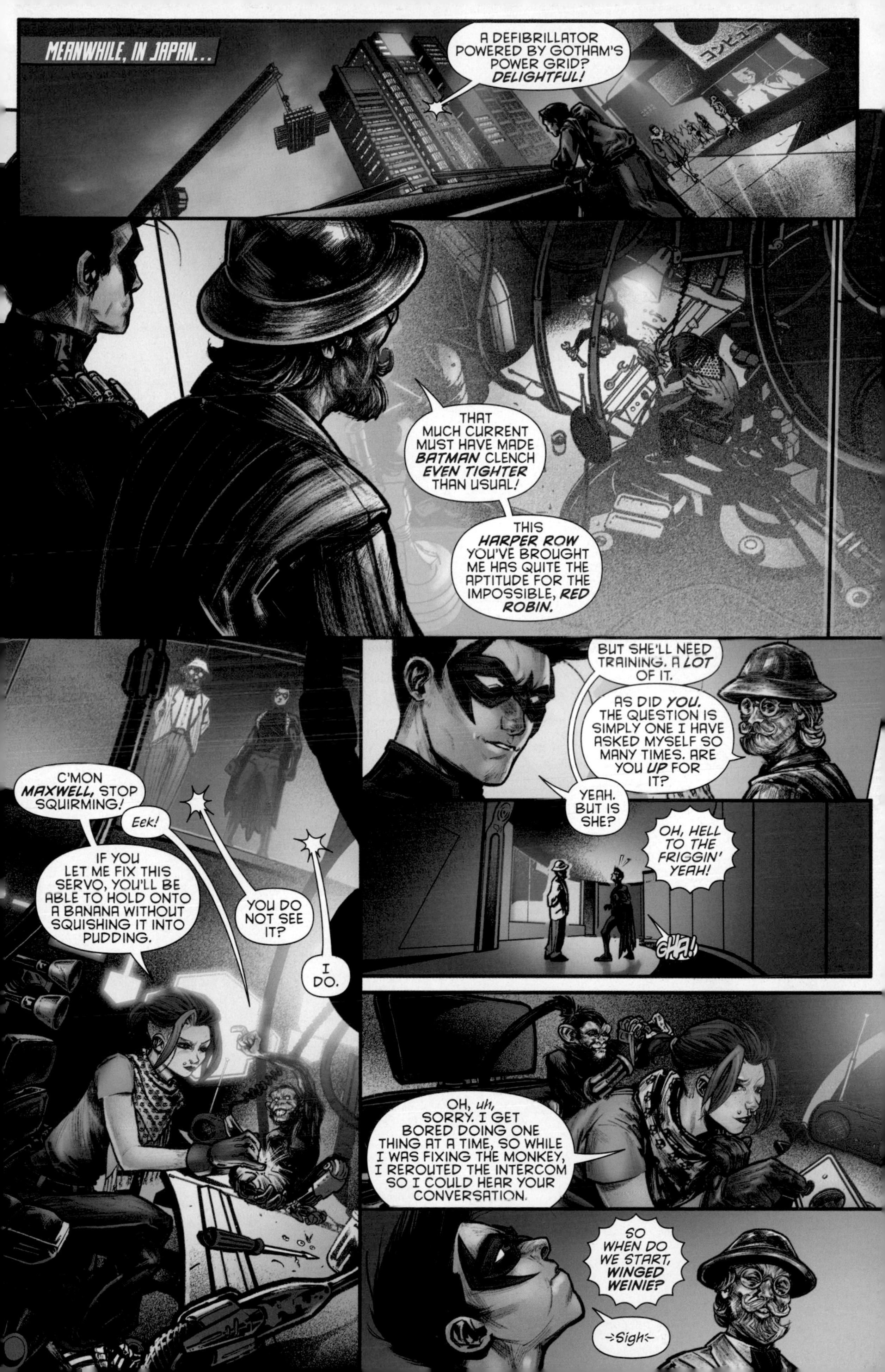
MEANWHILE, IN JAPAN...
A DEFIBRILLATOR POWERED BY GOTHAM'S POWER GRID? DELIGHTFUL!
THAT MUCH CURRENT MUST HAVE MADE BATMAN CLENCH EVEN TIGHTER THAN USUAL!
THIS HARPER ROW YOU'VE BROUGHT ME HAS QUITE THE APTITUDE FOR THE IMPOSSIBLE, RED ROBIN.
C'MON MAXWELL, STOP SQUIRMING!
Eek!
IF YOU LET ME FIX THIS SERVO, YOU'LL BE ABLE TO HOLD ONTO A BANANA WITHOUT SQUISHING IT INTO PUDDING.
YOU DO NOT SEE IT?
I DO.
BUT SHE'LL NEED TRAINING. A LOT OF IT.
AS DID YOU. THE QUESTION IS SIMPLY ONE I HAVE ASKED MYSELF SO MANY TIMES. ARE YOU UP FOR IT?
YEAH. BUT IS SHE?
OH, HELL TO THE FRIGGIN' YEAH!
GHA!!
OH, uh, SORRY. I GET BORED DOING ONE THING AT A TIME, SO WHILE I WAS FIXING THE MONKEY, I REROUTED THE INTERCOM SO I COULD HEAR YOUR CONVERSATION.
SO WHEN DO WE START, WINGED WEINIE?
Sigh

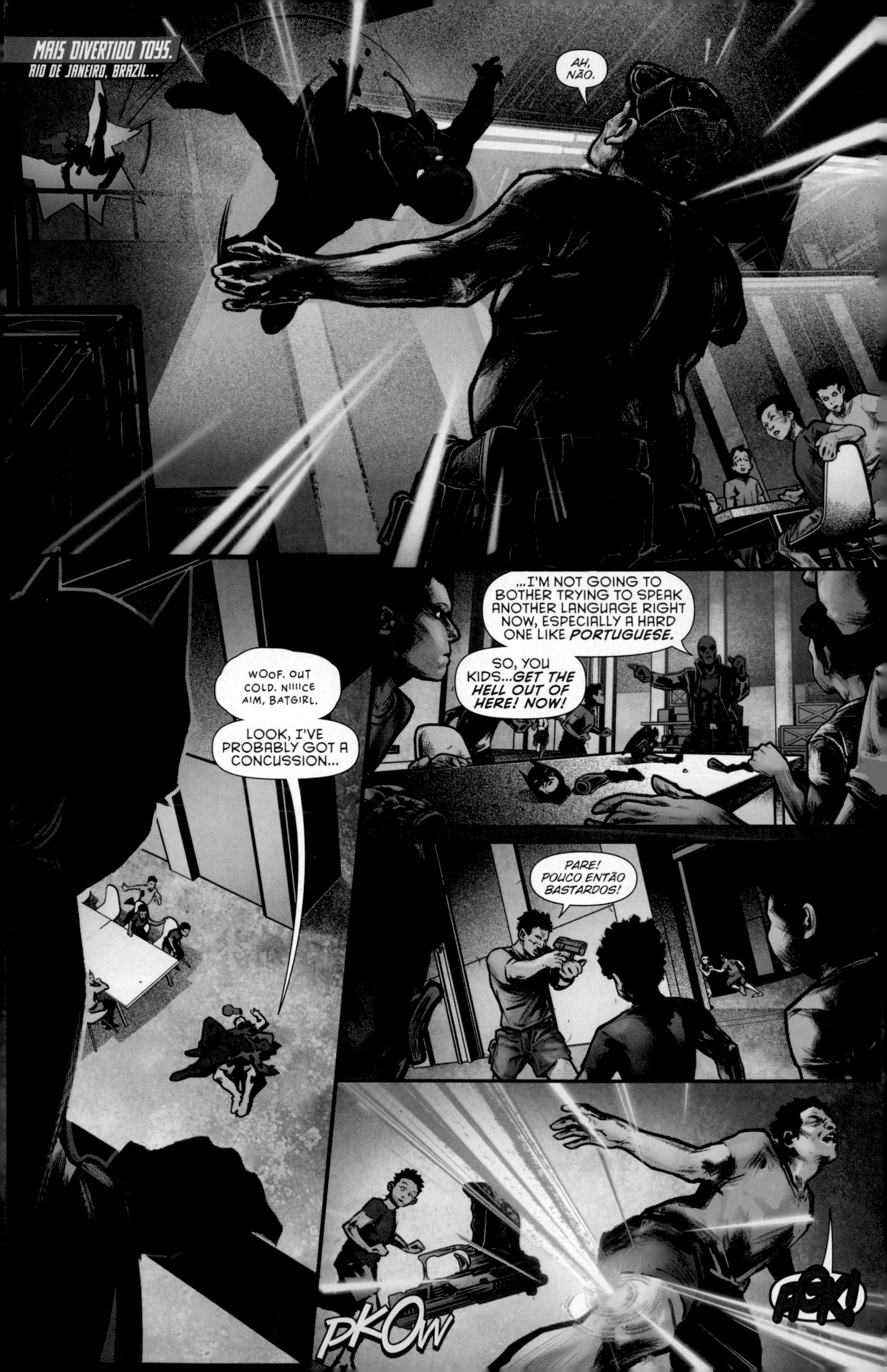
MAIS DIVERTIDO TOYS.
RIO DE JANEIRO, BRAZIL...
AH, NÃO.
WOOF. OUT COLD. NIIIICE AIM, BATGIRL.
LOOK, I'VE PROBABLY GOT A CONCUSSION...
...I'M NOT GOING TO BOTHER TRYING TO SPEAK ANOTHER LANGUAGE RIGHT NOW, ESPECIALLY A HARD ONE LIKE PORTUGUESE.
SO, YOU KIDS...GET THE HELL OUT OF HERE! NOW!
PARE! POUCO ENTÃO BASTARDOS!
PKOW
AGK!

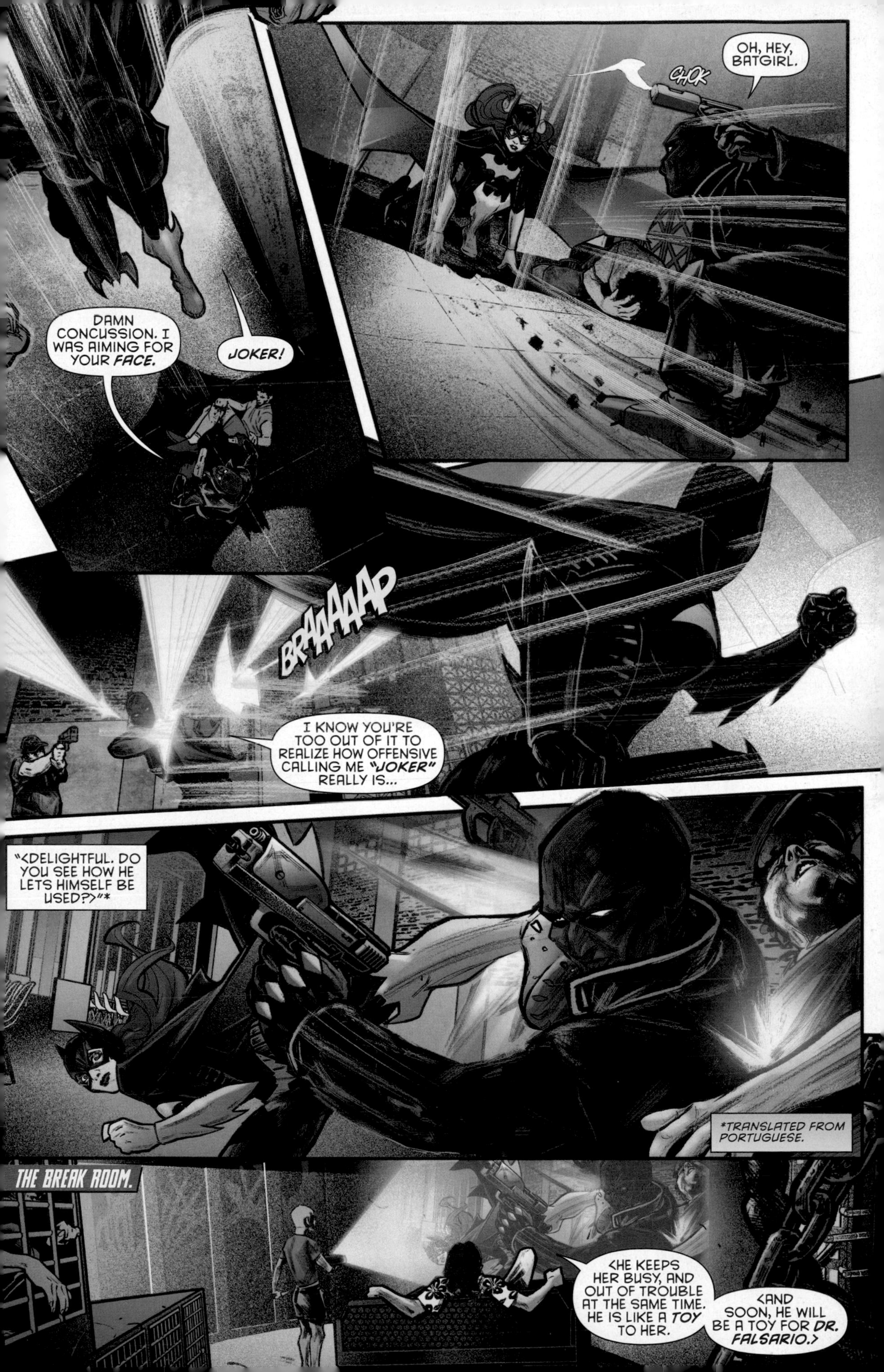
OH, HEY, BATGIRL.
CHOK
DAMN CONCUSSION. I WAS AIMING FOR YOUR FACE.
JOKER!
BRAAAAAP
I KNOW YOU'RE TOO OUT OF IT TO REALIZE HOW OFFENSIVE CALLING ME "JOKER" REALLY IS...
"<DELIGHTFUL. DO YOU SEE HOW HE LETS HIMSELF BE USED?>"*
*TRANSLATED FROM PORTUGUESE.
THE BREAK ROOM.
<HE KEEPS HER BUSY, AND OUT OF TROUBLE AT THE SAME TIME. HE IS LIKE A TOY TO HER.
<AND SOON, HE WILL BE A TOY FOR DR. FALSARIO.>

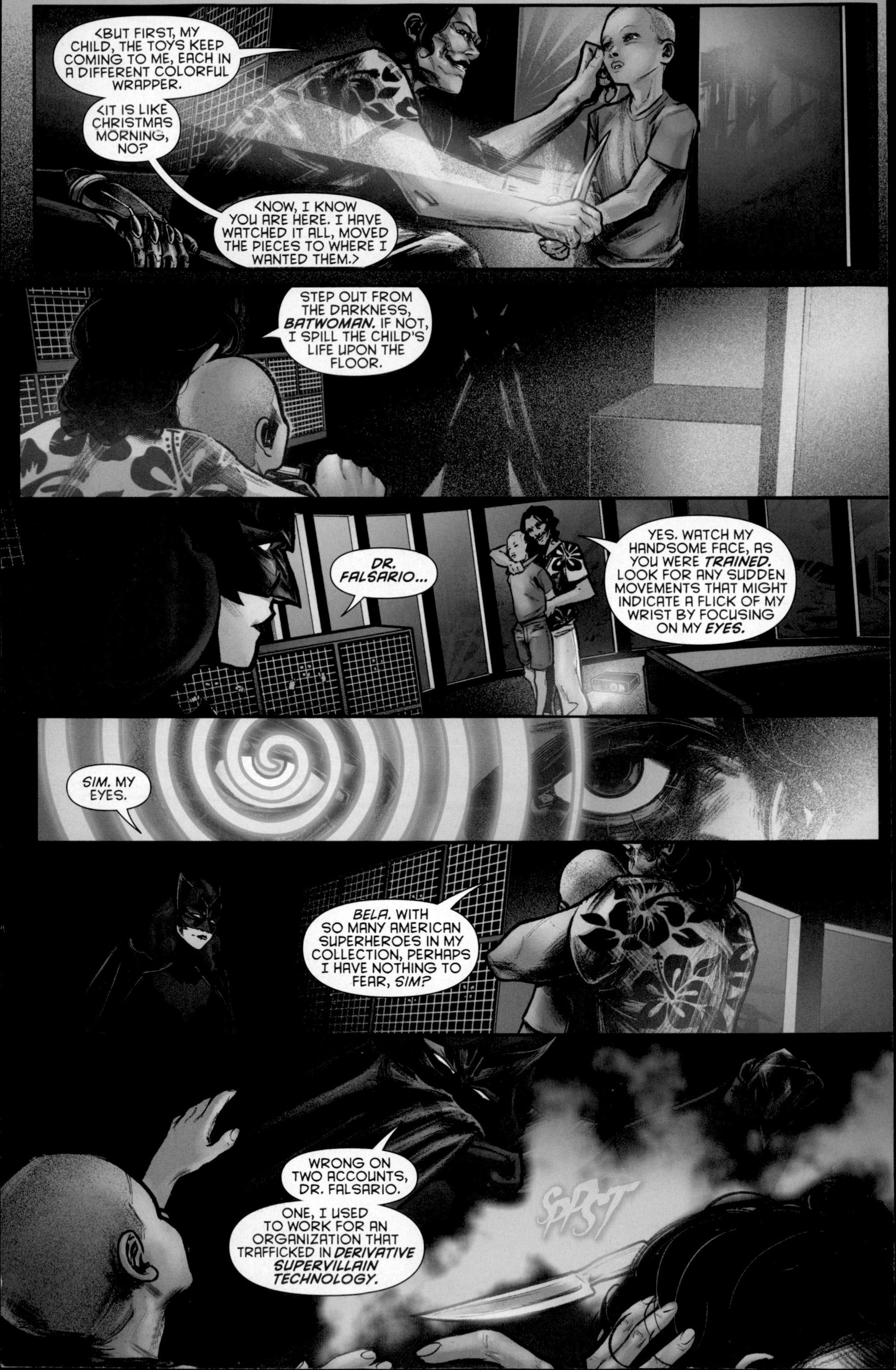

<BUT FIRST, MY CHILD, THE TOYS KEEP COMING TO ME, EACH IN A DIFFERENT COLORFUL WRAPPER.
<IT IS LIKE CHRISTMAS MORNING, NO?
<NOW, I KNOW YOU ARE HERE. I HAVE WATCHED IT ALL, MOVED THE PIECES TO WHERE I WANTED THEM.>
STEP OUT FROM THE DARKNESS, BATWOMAN. IF NOT, I SPILL THE CHILD'S LIFE UPON THE FLOOR.
DR. FALSARIO...
YES. WATCH MY HANDSOME FACE, AS YOU WERE TRAINED. LOOK FOR ANY SUDDEN MOVEMENTS THAT MIGHT INDICATE A FLICK OF MY WRIST BY FOCUSING ON MY EYES.
SIM. MY EYES.
BELA. WITH SO MANY AMERICAN SUPERHEROES IN MY COLLECTION, PERHAPS I HAVE NOTHING TO FEAR, SIM?
WRONG ON TWO ACCOUNTS, DR. FALSARIO.
ONE, I USED TO WORK FOR AN ORGANIZATION THAT TRAFFICKED IN DERIVATIVE SUPERVILLAIN TECHNOLOGY.
SPPST

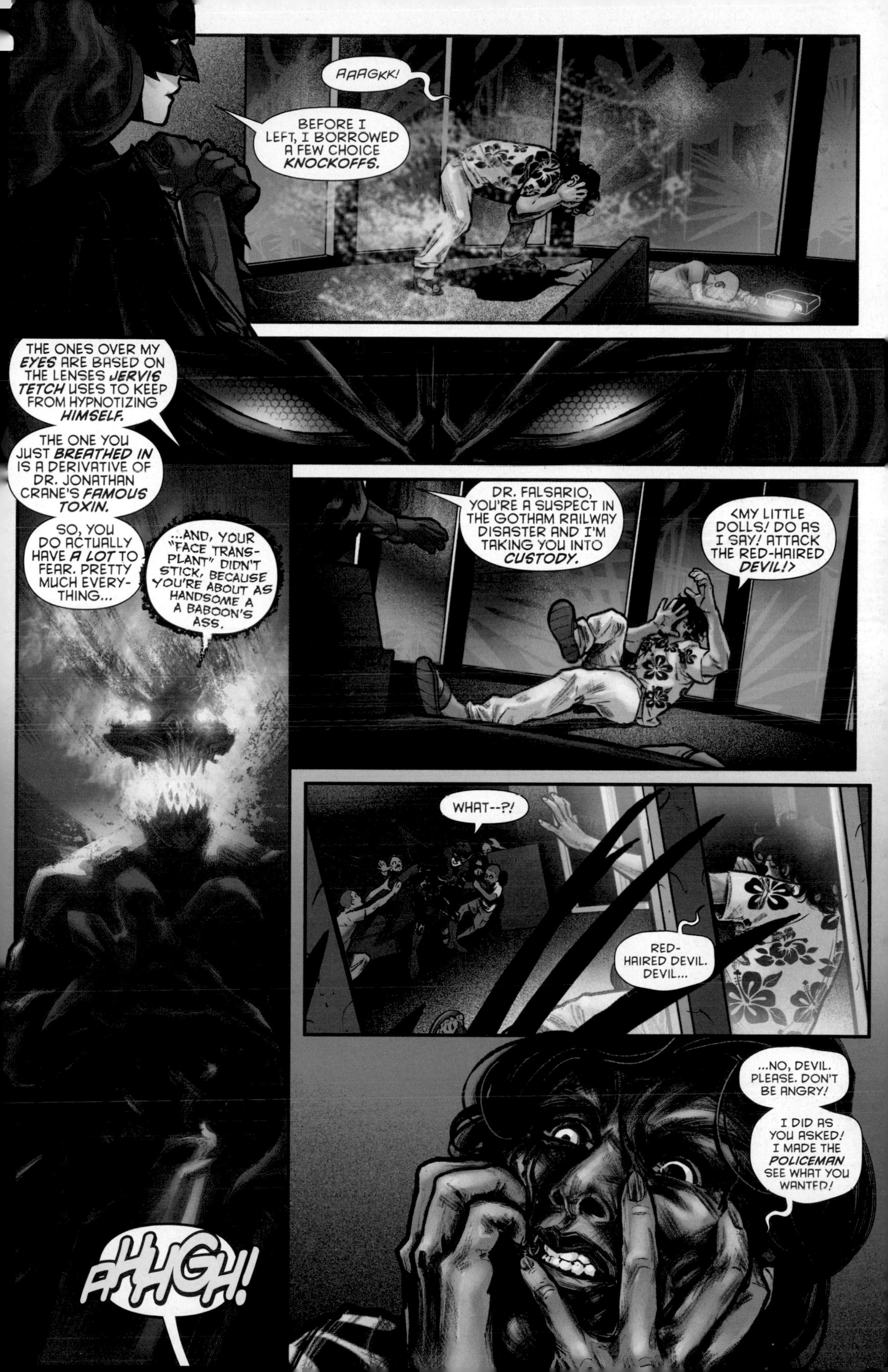
AAAGKK!
BEFORE I LEFT, I BORROWED A FEW CHOICE KNOCKOFFS.
THE ONES OVER MY EYES ARE BASED ON THE LENSES JERVIS TETCH USES TO KEEP FROM HYPNOTIZING HIMSELF.
THE ONE YOU JUST BREATHED IN IS A DERIVATIVE OF DR. JONATHAN CRANE'S FAMOUS TOXIN.
SO, YOU DO ACTUALLY HAVE A LOT TO FEAR. PRETTY MUCH EVERYTHING...
...AND, YOUR "FACE TRANSPLANT" DIDN'T STICK, BECAUSE YOU'RE ABOUT AS HANDSOME A A BABOON'S ASS.
DR. FALSARIO, YOU'RE A SUSPECT IN THE GOTHAM RAILWAY DISASTER AND I'M TAKING YOU INTO CUSTODY.
<MY LITTLE DOLLS! DO AS I SAY! ATTACK THE RED-HAIRED DEVIL!>
WHAT--?!
RED-HAIRED DEVIL. DEVIL...
...NO, DEVIL. PLEASE. DON'T BE ANGRY!
I DID AS YOU ASKED! I MADE THE POLICEMAN SEE WHAT YOU WANTED!
AHUGH!

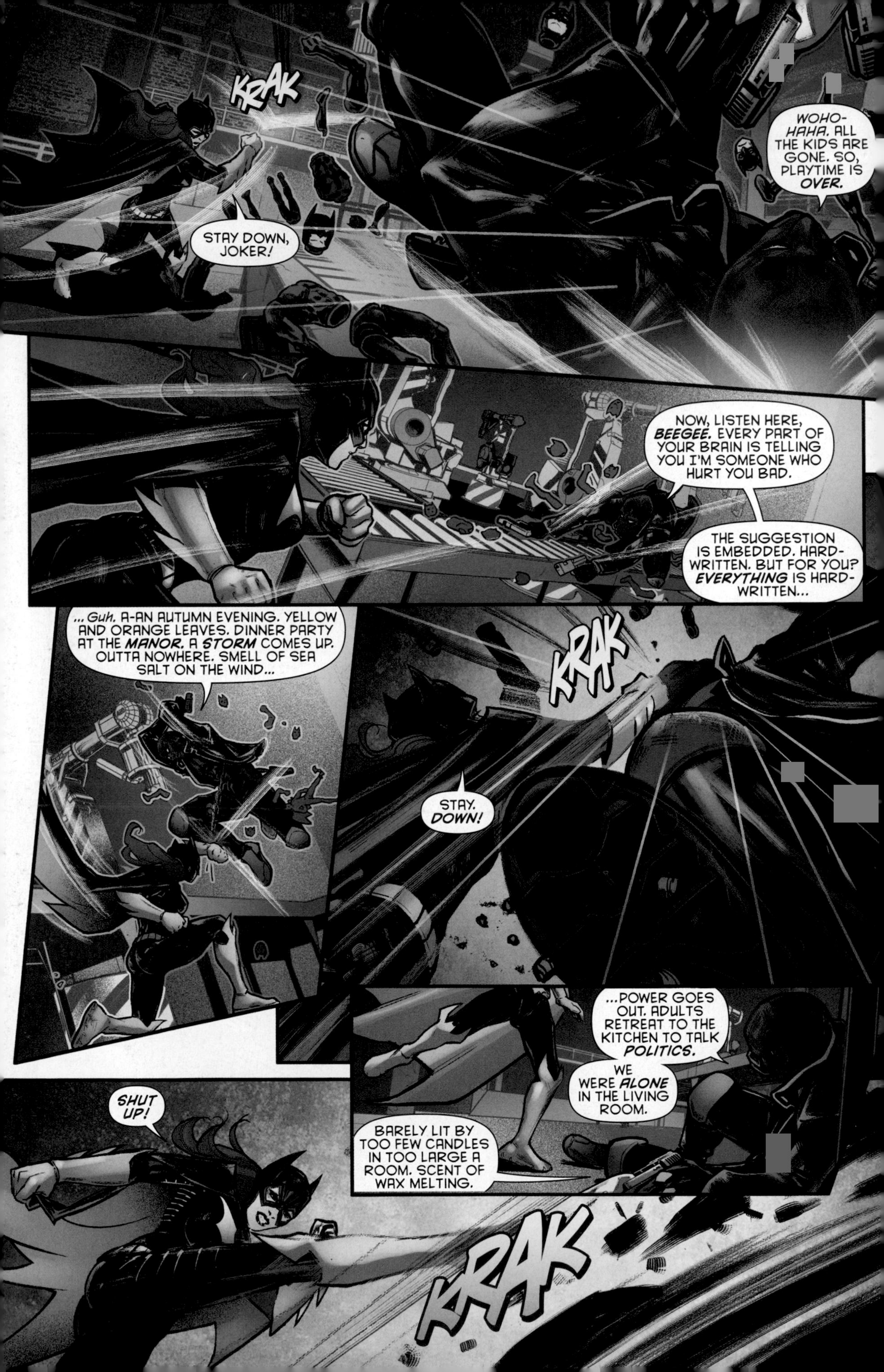
KRAK
STAY DOWN, JOKER!
WOHO-HAHA. ALL THE KIDS ARE GONE. SO, PLAYTIME IS OVER.
NOW, LISTEN HERE, BEEGEE. EVERY PART OF YOUR BRAIN IS TELLING YOU I'M SOMEONE WHO HURT YOU BAD.
THE SUGGESTION IS EMBEDDED. HARD-WRITTEN. BUT FOR YOU? EVERYTHING IS HARD-WRITTEN...
...Guh. A-AN AUTUMN EVENING. YELLOW AND ORANGE LEAVES. DINNER PARTY AT THE MANOR. A STORM COMES UP. OUTTA NOWHERE. SMELL OF SEA SALT ON THE WIND...
KRAK
STAY. DOWN!
...POWER GOES OUT. ADULTS RETREAT TO THE KITCHEN TO TALK POLITICS.
WE WERE ALONE IN THE LIVING ROOM.
BARELY LIT BY TOO FEW CANDLES IN TOO LARGE A ROOM. SCENT OF WAX MELTING.
SHUT UP!
KRAK

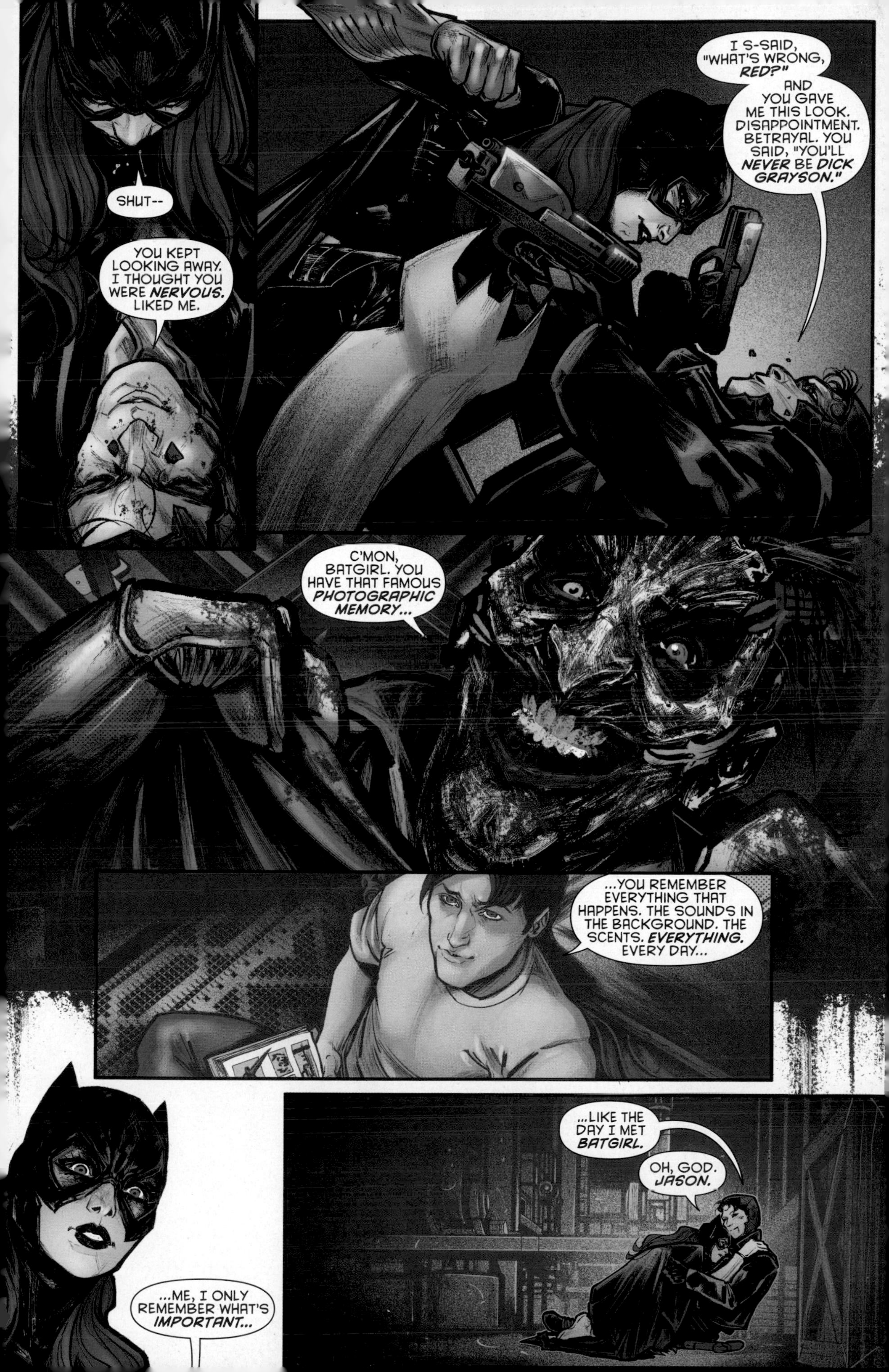
SHUT--
YOU KEPT LOOKING AWAY. I THOUGHT YOU WERE NERVOUS. LIKED ME.
I S-SAID, "WHAT'S WRONG, RED?"
AND YOU GAVE ME THIS LOOK. DISAPPOINTMENT. BETRAYAL. YOU SAID, "YOU'LL NEVER BE DICK GRAYSON."
C'MON, BATGIRL. YOU HAVE THAT FAMOUS PHOTOGRAPHIC MEMORY...
...YOU REMEMBER EVERYTHING THAT HAPPENS. THE SOUNDS IN THE BACKGROUND. THE SCENTS. EVERYTHING. EVERY DAY...
...ME, I ONLY REMEMBER WHAT'S IMPORTANT...
...LIKE THE DAY I MET BATGIRL.
OH, GOD. JASON.

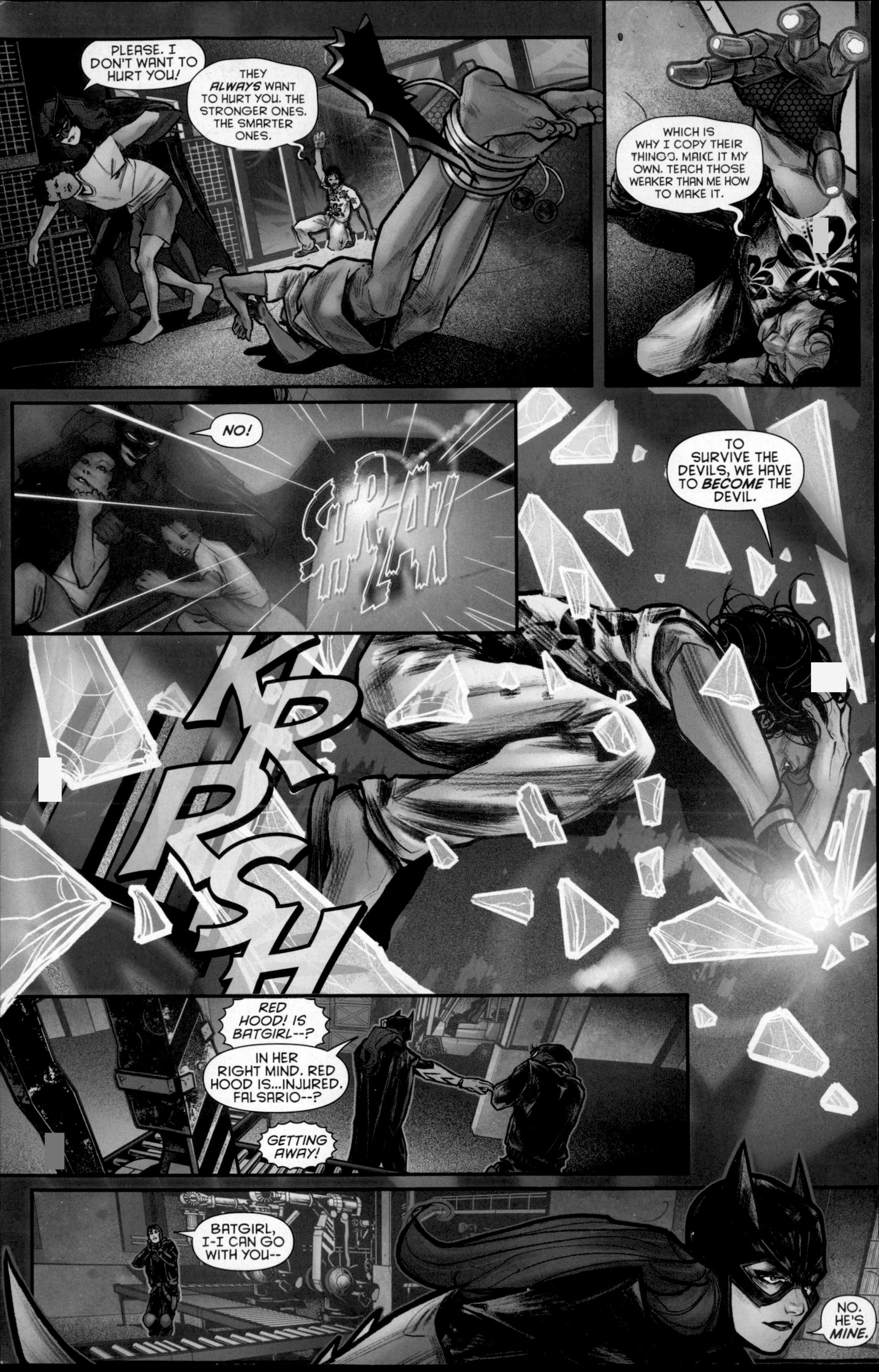

PLEASE. I DON'T WANT TO HURT YOU!
THEY *ALWAYS* WANT TO HURT YOU. THE STRONGER ONES. THE SMARTER ONES.
WHICH IS WHY I COPY THEIR THINGS. MAKE IT MY OWN. TEACH THOSE WEAKER THAN ME HOW TO MAKE IT.
NO!
TO SURVIVE THE DEVILS, WE HAVE TO *BECOME* THE DEVIL.
KRRSH
RED HOOD! IS BATGIRL--?
IN HER RIGHT MIND. RED HOOD IS...INJURED. FALSARIO--?
GETTING AWAY!
BATGIRL, I-I CAN GO WITH YOU--
NO. HE'S *MINE.*

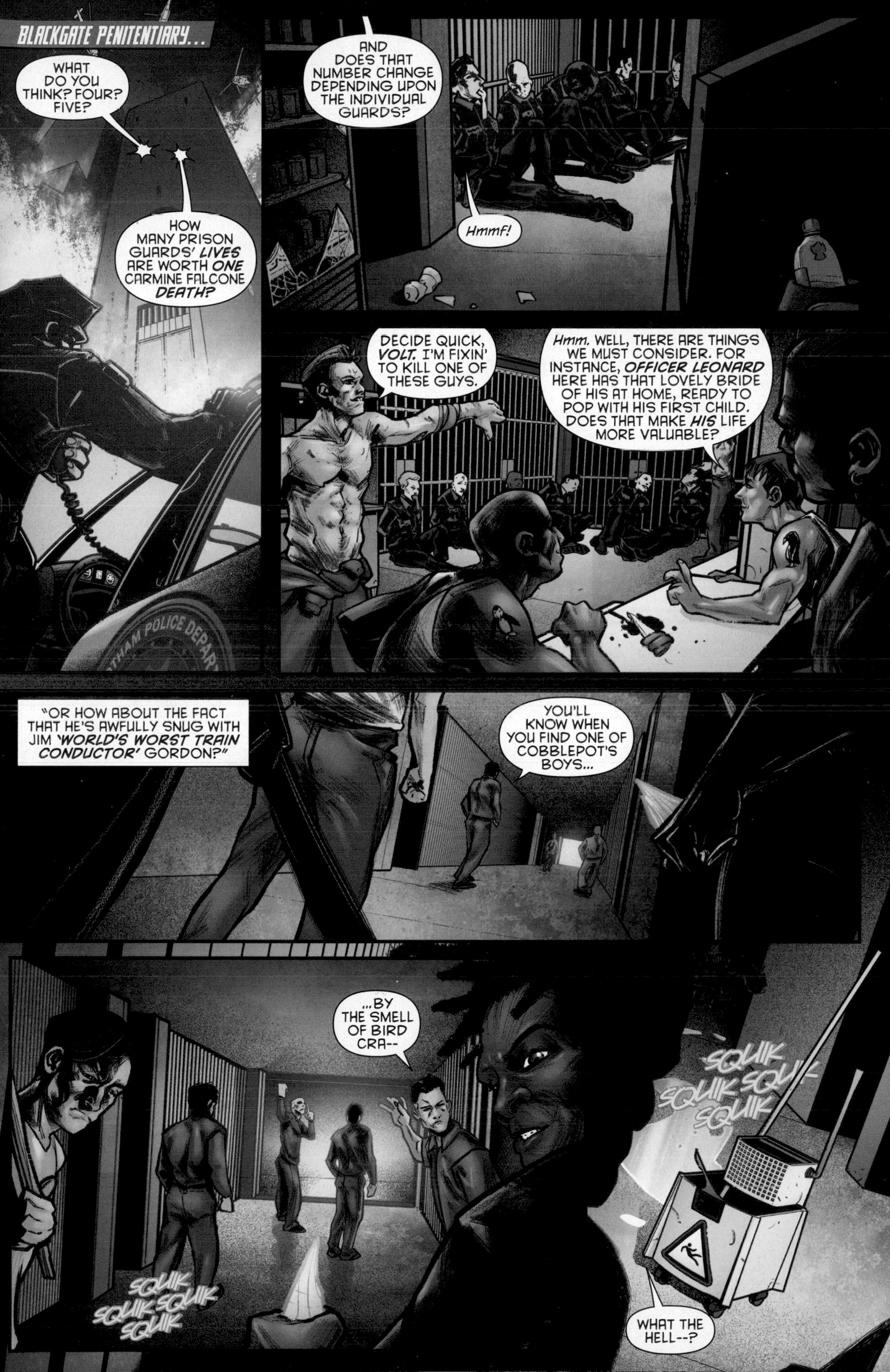
BLACKGATE PENITENTIARY...
WHAT DO YOU THINK? FOUR? FIVE?
HOW MANY PRISON GUARDS' LIVES ARE WORTH ONE CARMINE FALCONE DEATH?
AND DOES THAT NUMBER CHANGE DEPENDING UPON THE INDIVIDUAL GUARDS?
Hmmf!
DECIDE QUICK, VOLT. I'M FIXIN' TO KILL ONE OF THESE GUYS.
Hmm. WELL, THERE ARE THINGS WE MUST CONSIDER. FOR INSTANCE, OFFICER LEONARD HERE HAS THAT LOVELY BRIDE OF HIS AT HOME, READY TO POP WITH HIS FIRST CHILD. DOES THAT MAKE HIS LIFE MORE VALUABLE?
"OR HOW ABOUT THE FACT THAT HE'S AWFULLY SNUG WITH JIM 'WORLD'S WORST TRAIN CONDUCTOR' GORDON?"
YOU'LL KNOW WHEN YOU FIND ONE OF COBBLEPOT'S BOYS...
...BY THE SMELL OF BIRD CRA--
SQUIK SQUIK SQUIK SQUIK
SQUIK SQUIK SQUIK SQUIK
WHAT THE HELL--?

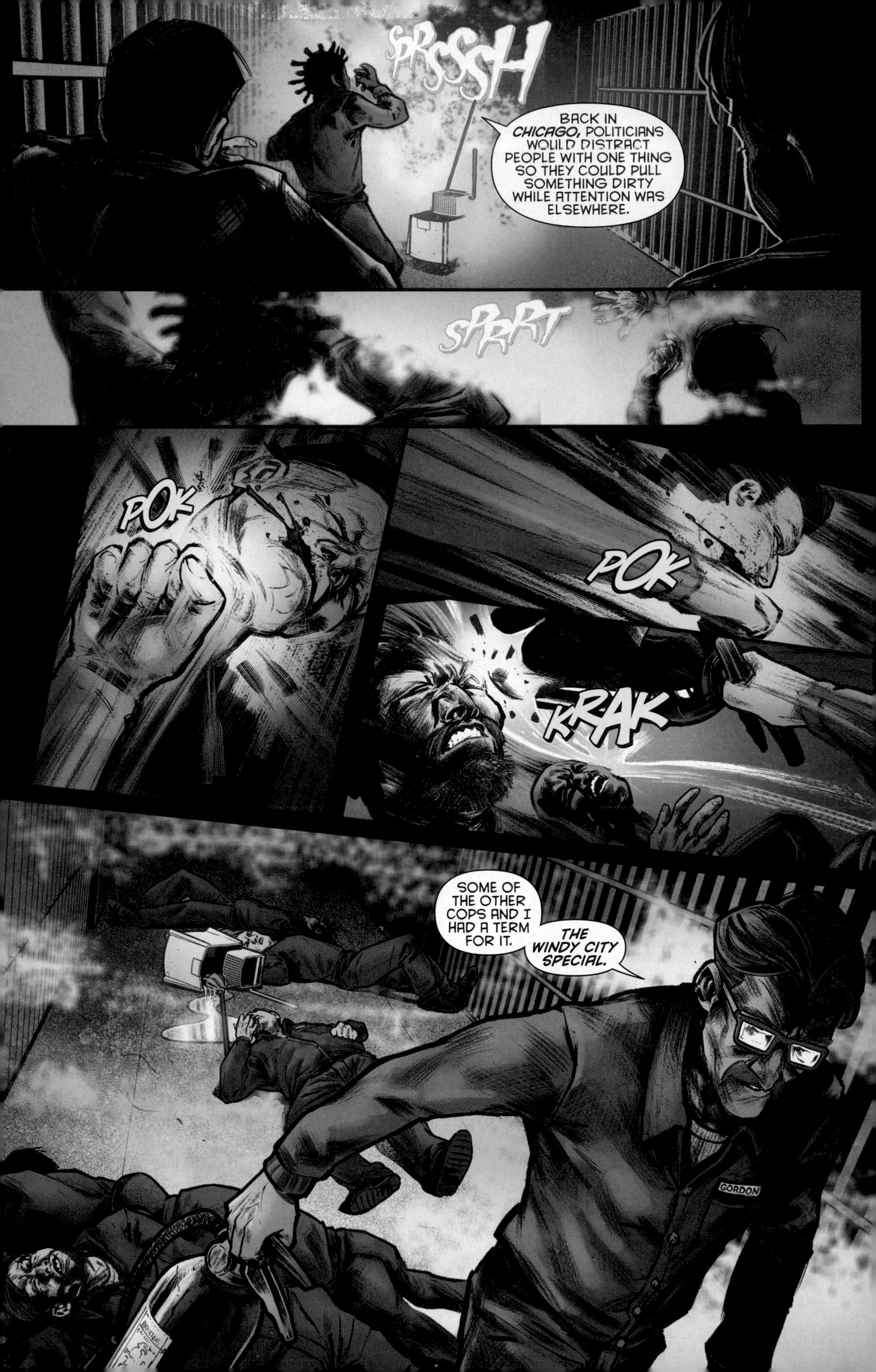
SPRSSSH
BACK IN CHICAGO, POLITICIANS WOULD DISTRACT PEOPLE WITH ONE THING SO THEY COULD PULL SOMETHING DIRTY WHILE ATTENTION WAS ELSEWHERE.
SPRRT
POK
POK
KRAK
SOME OF THE OTHER COPS AND I HAD A TERM FOR IT.
THE WINDY CITY SPECIAL.
GORDON

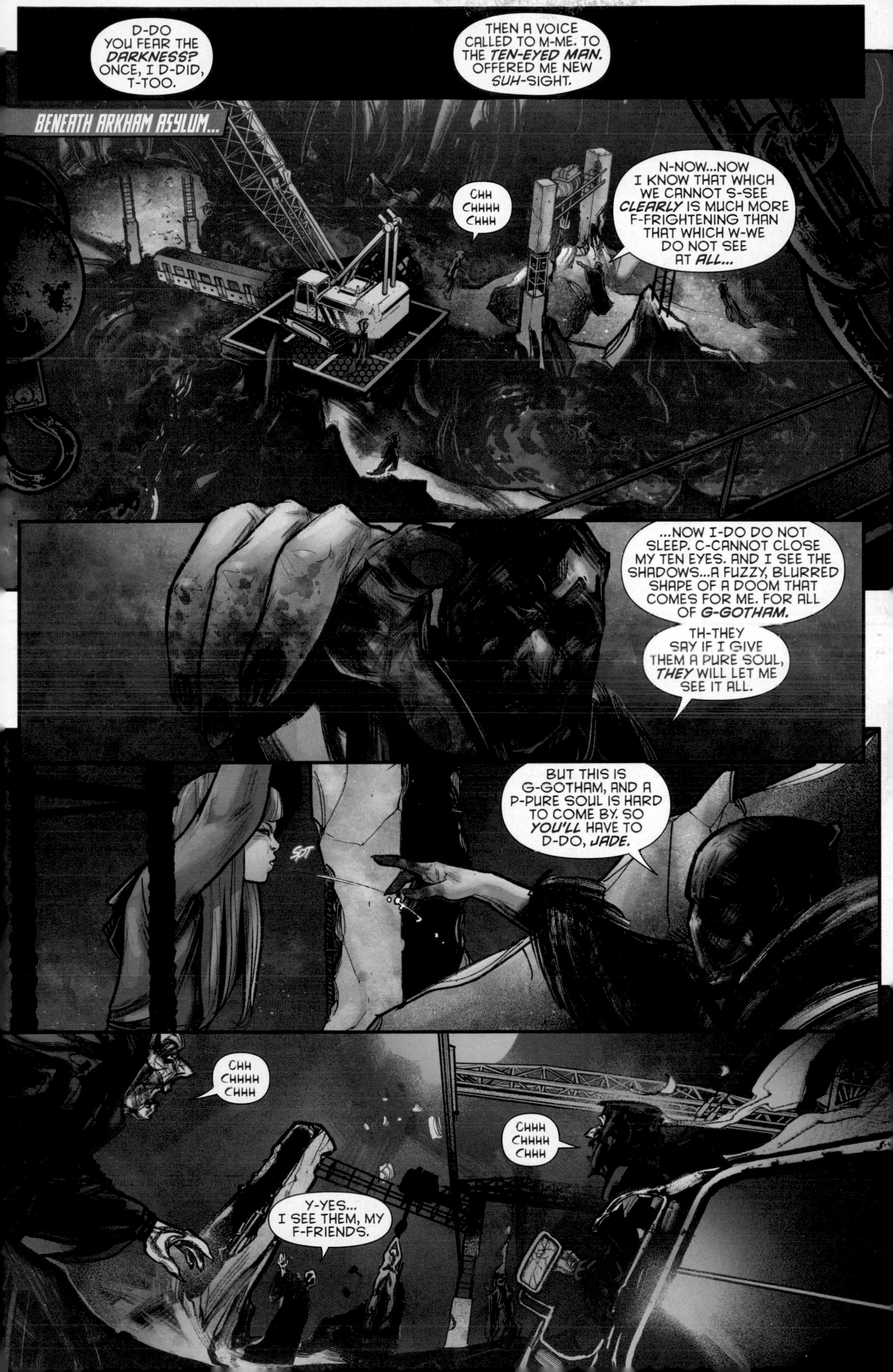
D-DO YOU FEAR THE DARKNESS? ONCE, I D-DID, T-TOO.
THEN A VOICE CALLED TO M-ME. TO THE TEN-EYED MAN. OFFERED ME NEW SUH-SIGHT.
BENEATH ARKHAM ASYLUM...
CHH CHHHH CHHH
N-NOW...NOW I KNOW THAT WHICH WE CANNOT S-SEE CLEARLY IS MUCH MORE F-FRIGHTENING THAN THAT WHICH W-WE DO NOT SEE AT ALL...
...NOW I-DO DO NOT SLEEP. C-CANNOT CLOSE MY TEN EYES. AND I SEE THE SHADOWS...A FUZZY, BLURRED SHAPE OF A DOOM THAT COMES FOR ME. FOR ALL OF G-GOTHAM.
TH-THEY SAY IF I GIVE THEM A PURE SOUL, THEY WILL LET ME SEE IT ALL.
BUT THIS IS G-GOTHAM, AND A P-PURE SOUL IS HARD TO COME BY. SO YOU'LL HAVE TO D-DO, JADE.
SPT
CHH CHHHH CHHH
CHHH CHHHH CHHH
Y-YES... I SEE THEM, MY F-FRIENDS.

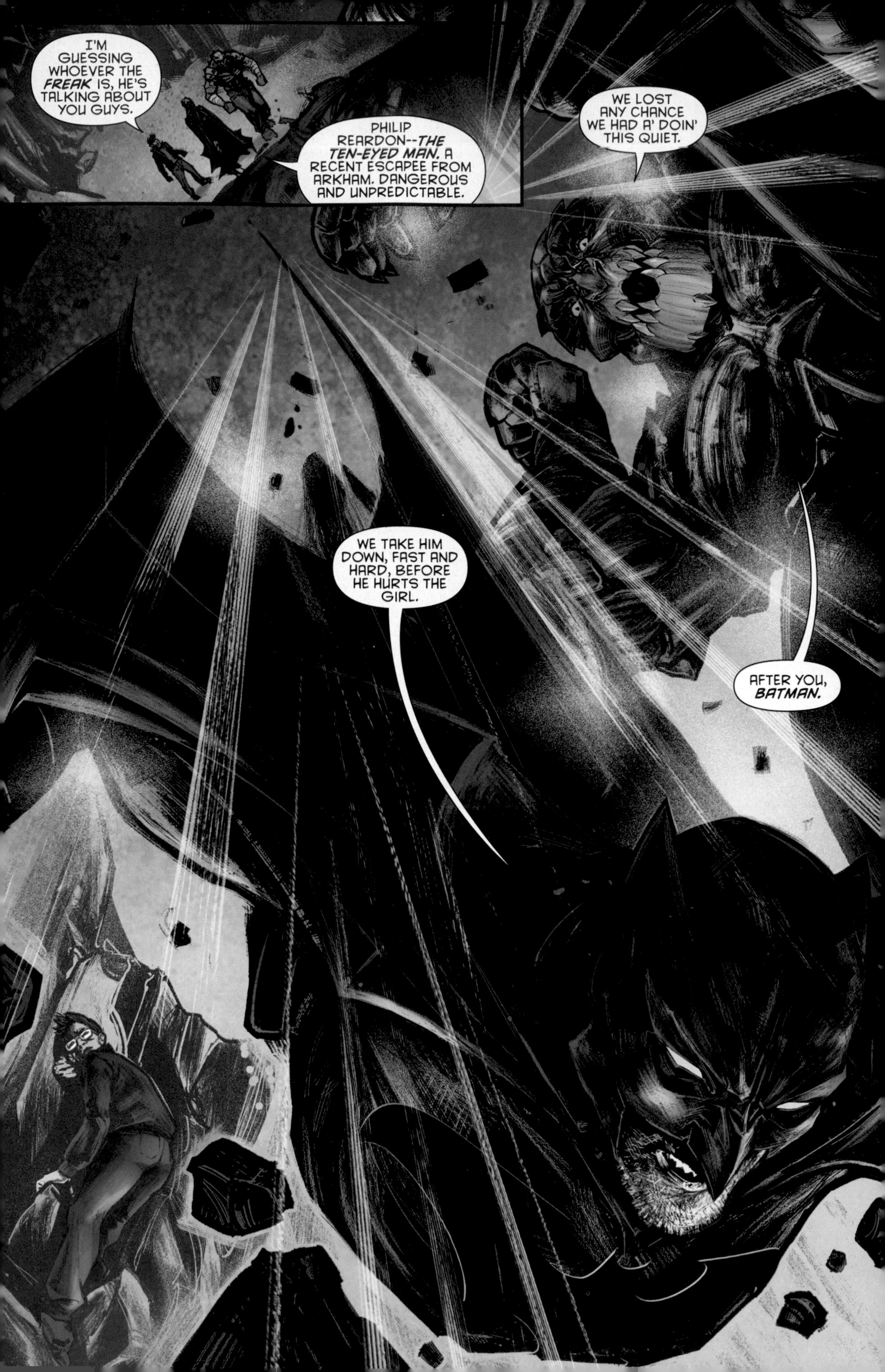
I'M GUESSING WHOEVER THE *FREAK* IS, HE'S TALKING ABOUT YOU GUYS.
PHILIP REARDON--*THE TEN-EYED MAN.* A RECENT ESCAPEE FROM ARKHAM. DANGEROUS AND UNPREDICTABLE.
WE LOST ANY CHANCE WE HAD A' DOIN' THIS QUIET.
WE TAKE HIM DOWN, FAST AND HARD, BEFORE HE HURTS THE GIRL.
AFTER YOU, *BATMAN.*

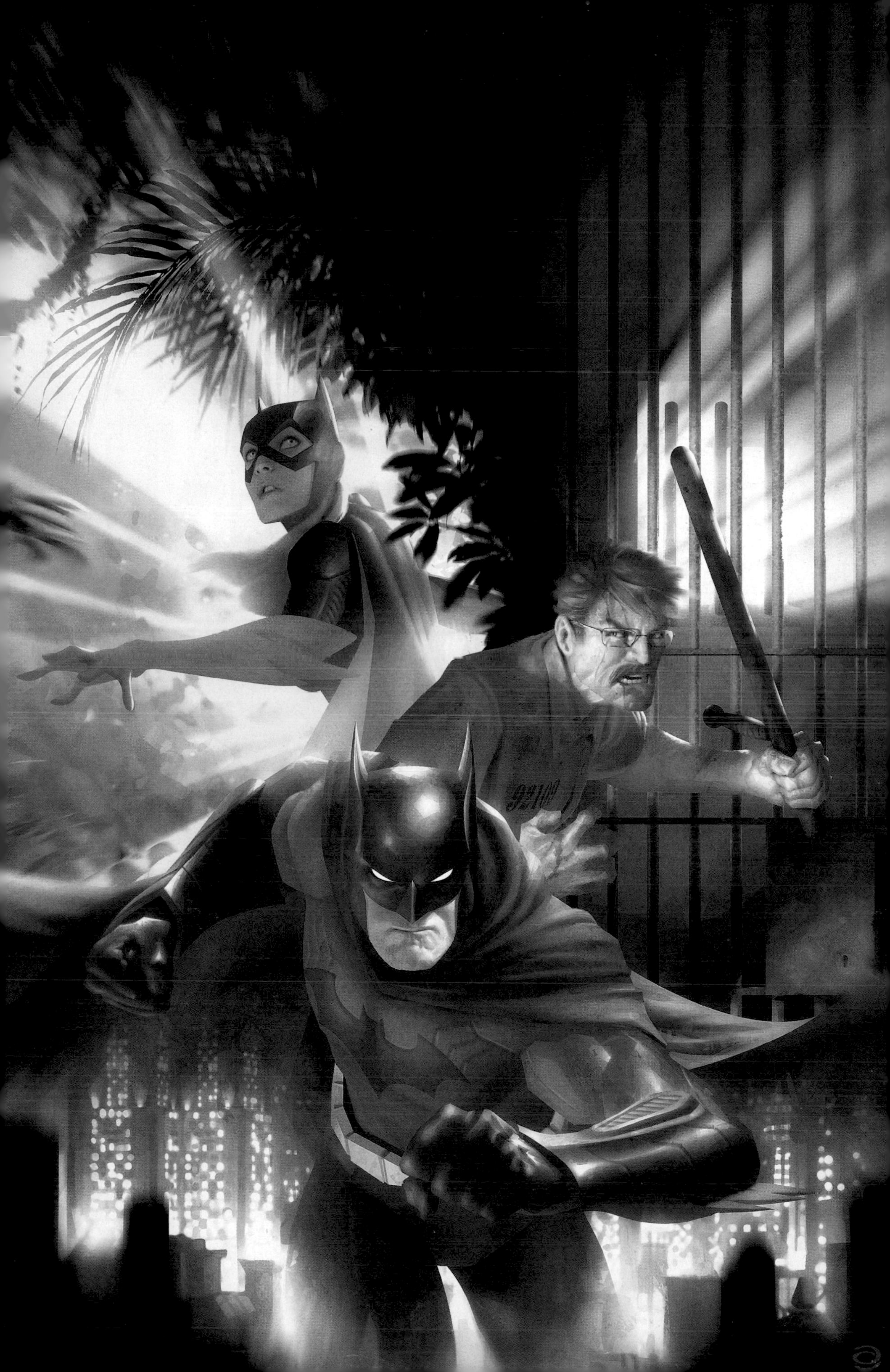

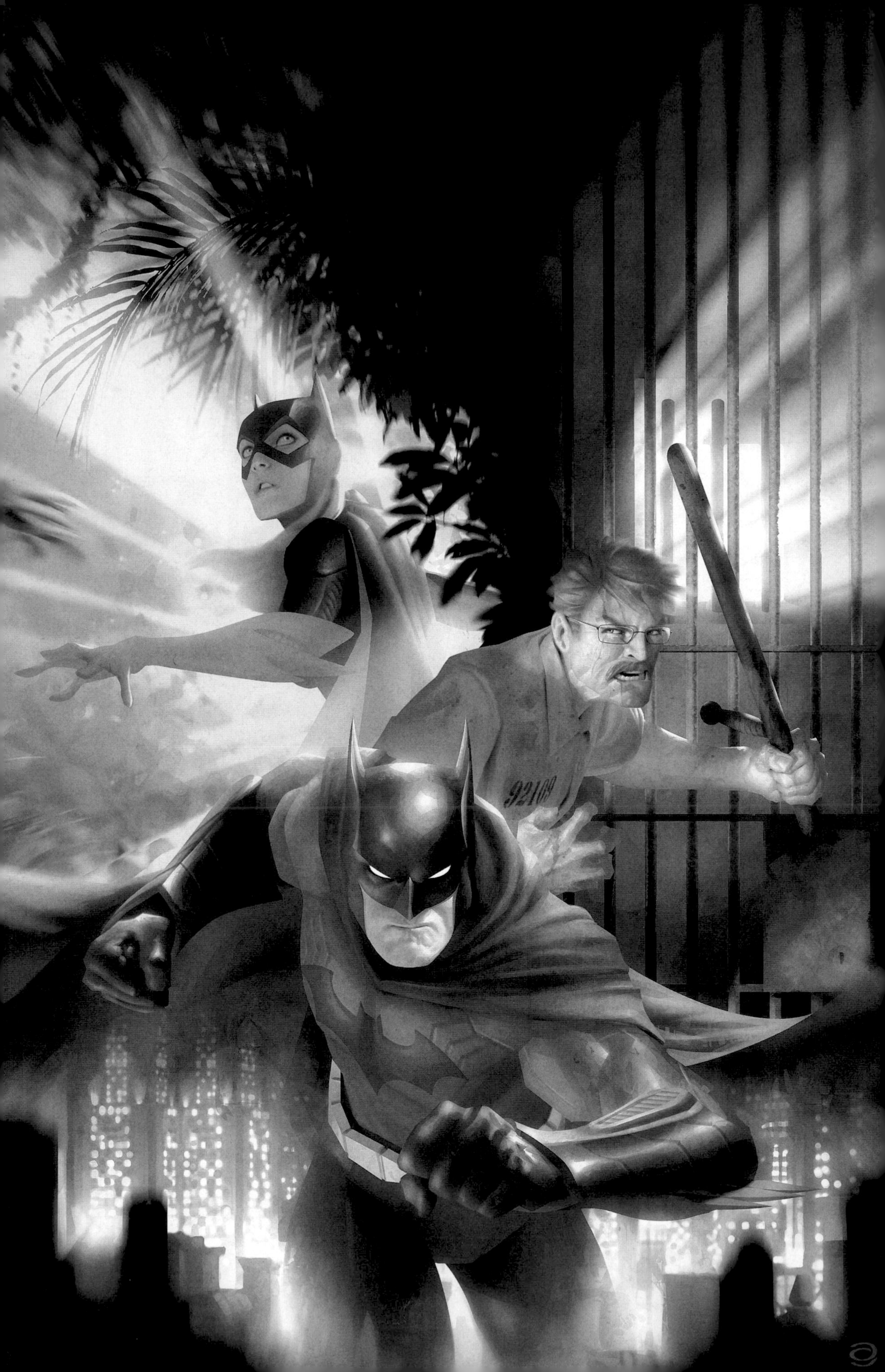
92109

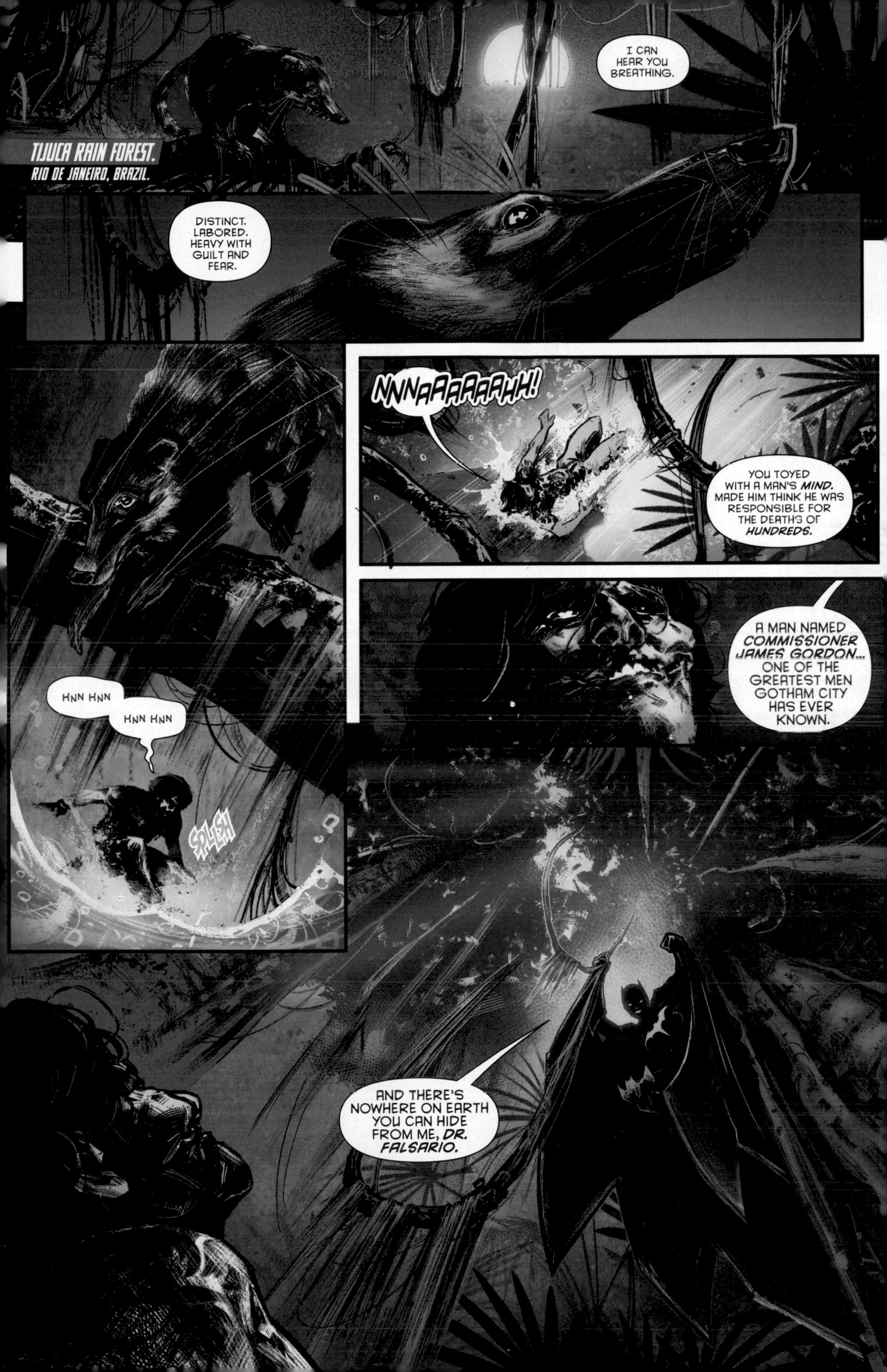
TIJUCA RAIN FOREST.
RIO DE JANEIRO, BRAZIL.
I CAN HEAR YOU BREATHING.
DISTINCT. LABORED. HEAVY WITH GUILT AND FEAR.
HNN HNN
HNN HNN
SPLASH
NNNAAAAAAAHH!
YOU TOYED WITH A MAN'S MIND. MADE HIM THINK HE WAS RESPONSIBLE FOR THE DEATHS OF HUNDREDS.
A MAN NAMED COMMISSIONER JAMES GORDON... ONE OF THE GREATEST MEN GOTHAM CITY HAS EVER KNOWN.
AND THERE'S NOWHERE ON EARTH YOU CAN HIDE FROM ME, DR. FALSARIO.

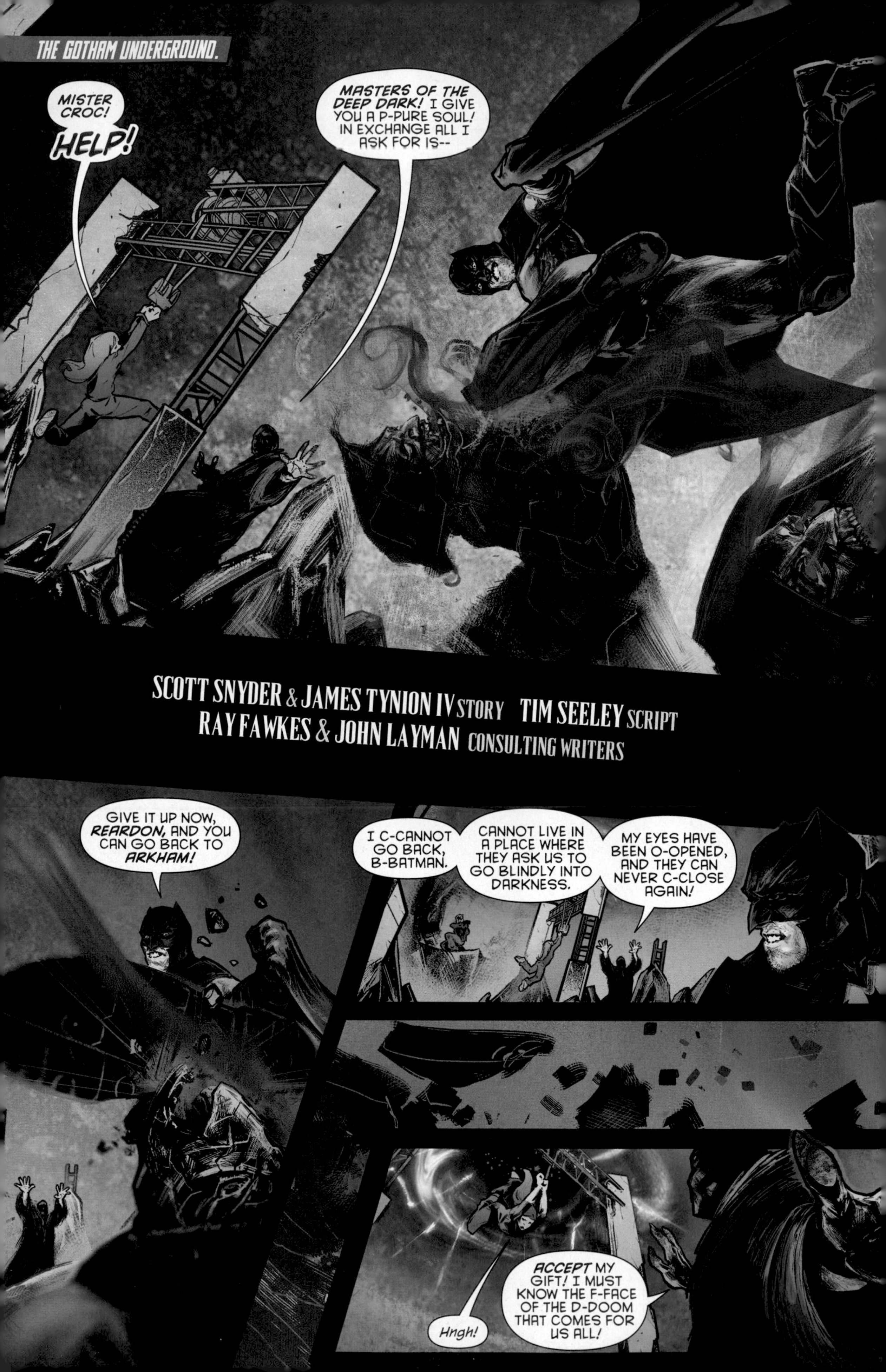
THE GOTHAM UNDERGROUND.
MISTER CROC! HELP!
MASTERS OF THE DEEP DARK! I GIVE YOU A P-PURE SOUL! IN EXCHANGE ALL I ASK FOR IS--
SCOTT SNYDER & JAMES TYNION IV STORY TIM SEELEY SCRIPT
RAY FAWKES & JOHN LAYMAN CONSULTING WRITERS
GIVE IT UP NOW, REARDON, AND YOU CAN GO BACK TO ARKHAM!
I C-CANNOT GO BACK, B-BATMAN.
CANNOT LIVE IN A PLACE WHERE THEY ASK US TO GO BLINDLY INTO DARKNESS.
MY EYES HAVE BEEN O-OPENED, AND THEY CAN NEVER C-CLOSE AGAIN!
Hngh!
ACCEPT MY GIFT! I MUST KNOW THE F-FACE OF THE D-DOOM THAT COMES FOR US ALL!

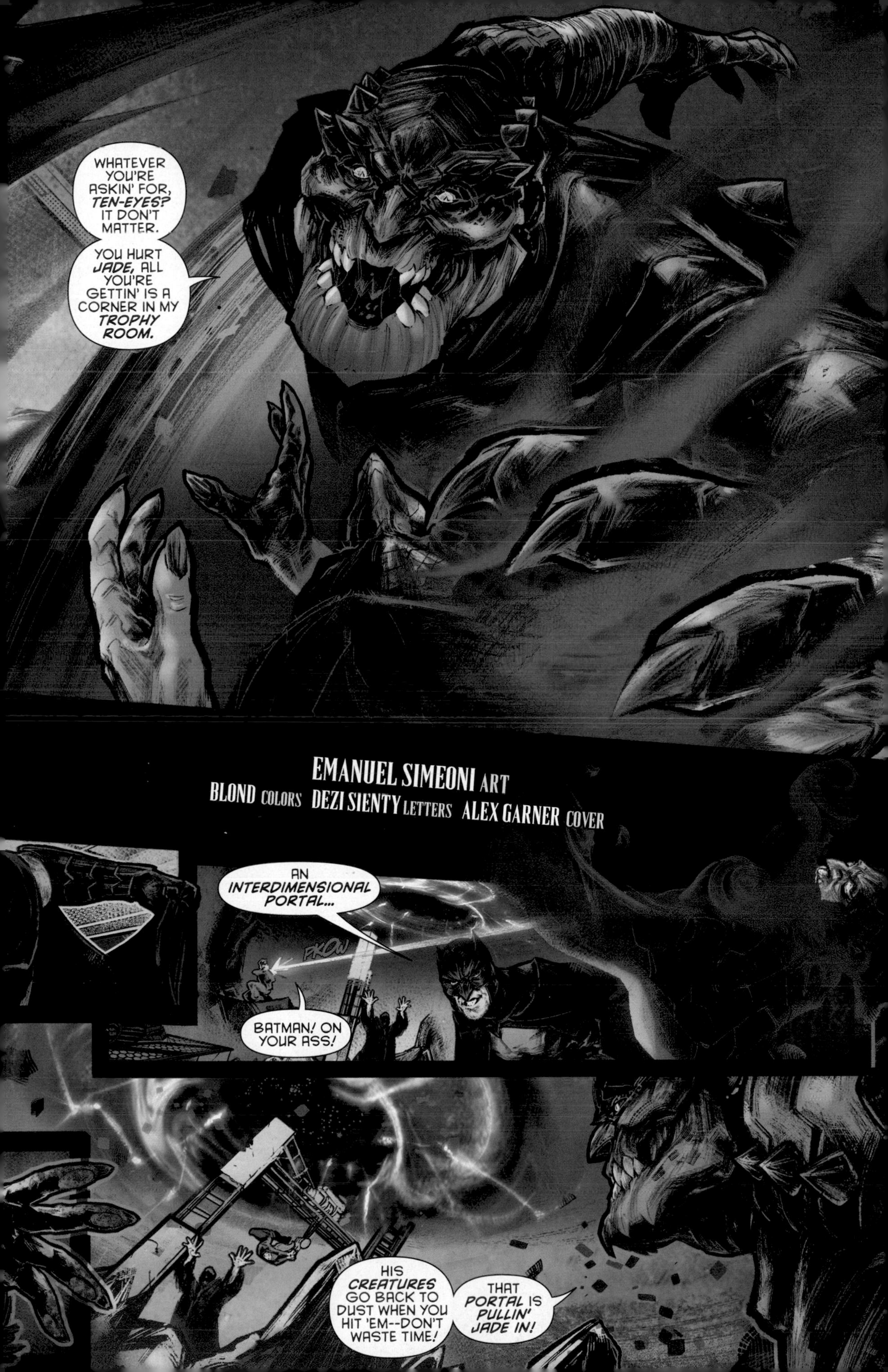
WHATEVER YOU'RE ASKIN' FOR, TEN-EYES? IT DON'T MATTER.
YOU HURT JADE, ALL YOU'RE GETTIN' IS A CORNER IN MY TROPHY ROOM.
EMANUEL SIMEONI ART
BLOND COLORS DEZI SIENTY LETTERS ALEX GARNER COVER
AN INTERDIMENSIONAL PORTAL...
PKOW
BATMAN! ON YOUR ASS!
HIS CREATURES GO BACK TO DUST WHEN YOU HIT 'EM--DON'T WASTE TIME!
THAT PORTAL IS PULLIN' JADE IN!

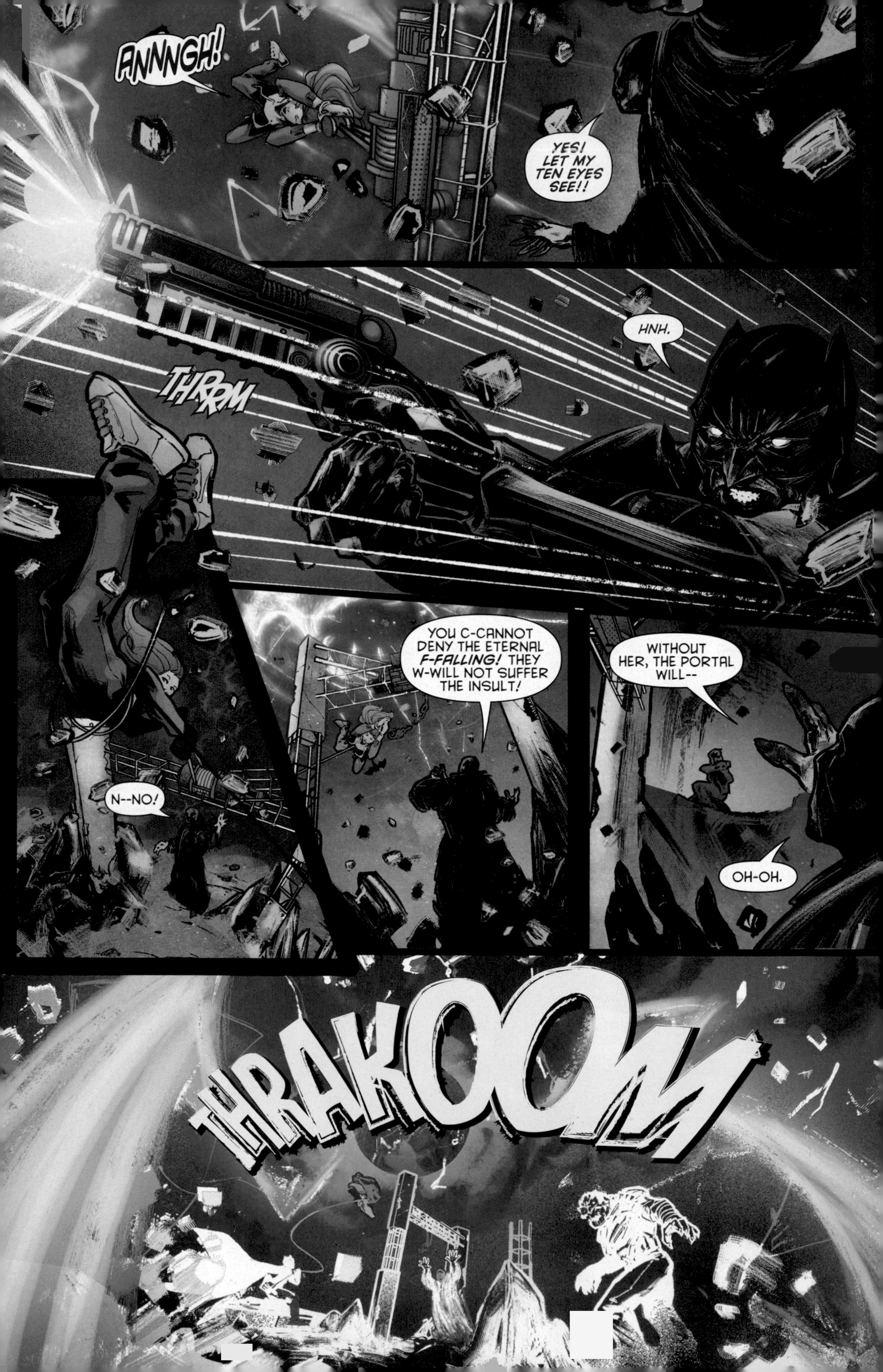
ANNNGH!
YES! LET MY TEN EYES SEE!!
HNH.
THRRM
N--NO!
YOU C-CANNOT DENY THE ETERNAL F-FALLING! THEY W-WILL NOT SUFFER THE INSULT!
WITHOUT HER, THE PORTAL WILL--
OH-OH.
THRAKOOM

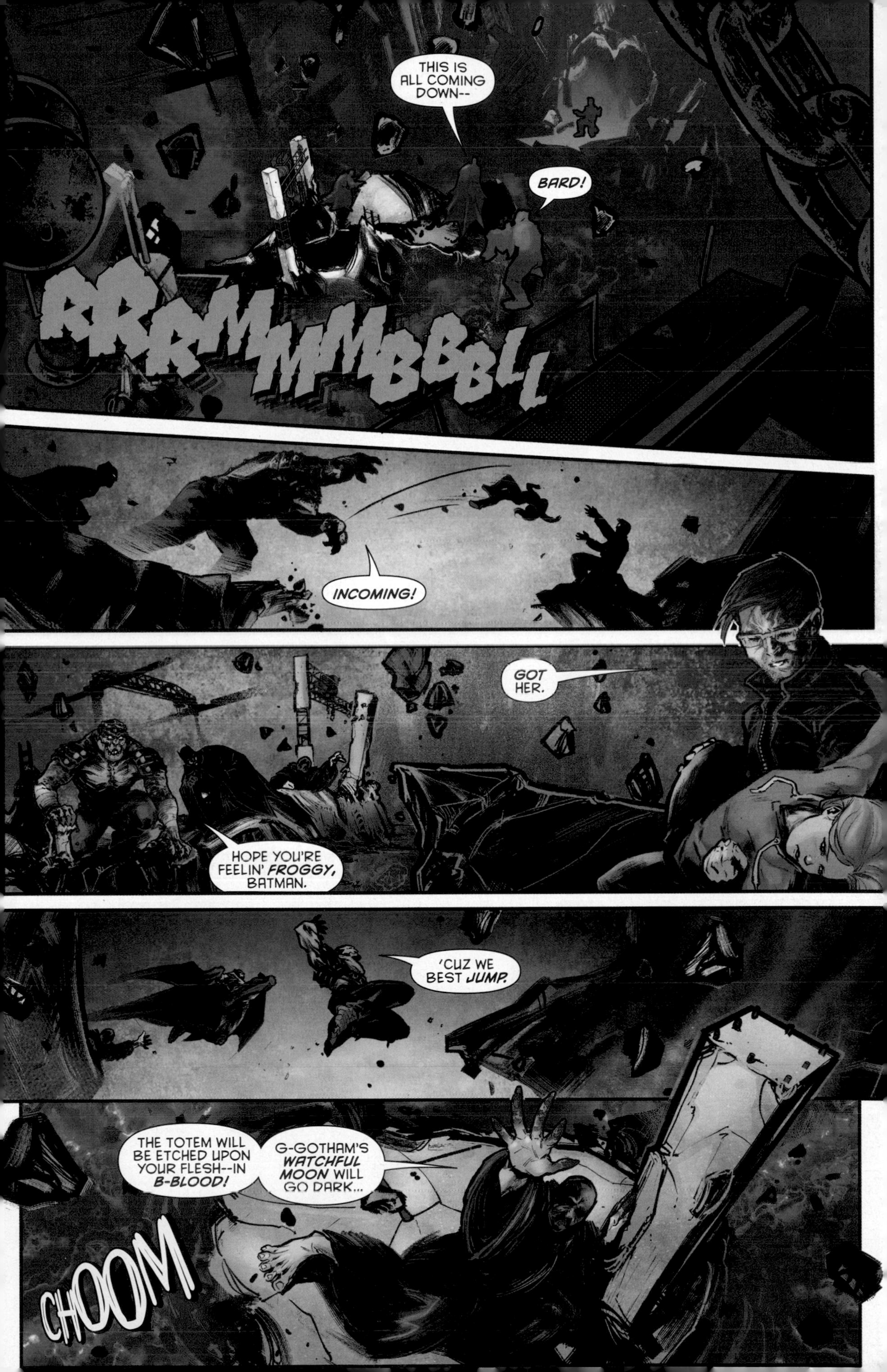

THIS IS ALL COMING DOWN--
BARD!
RRRMMMBBLL
INCOMING!
GOT HER.
HOPE YOU'RE FEELIN' FROGGY, BATMAN.
'CUZ WE BEST JUMP.
THE TOTEM WILL BE ETCHED UPON YOUR FLESH--IN B-BLOOD!
G-GOTHAM'S WATCHFUL MOON WILL GO DARK...
CHOOM

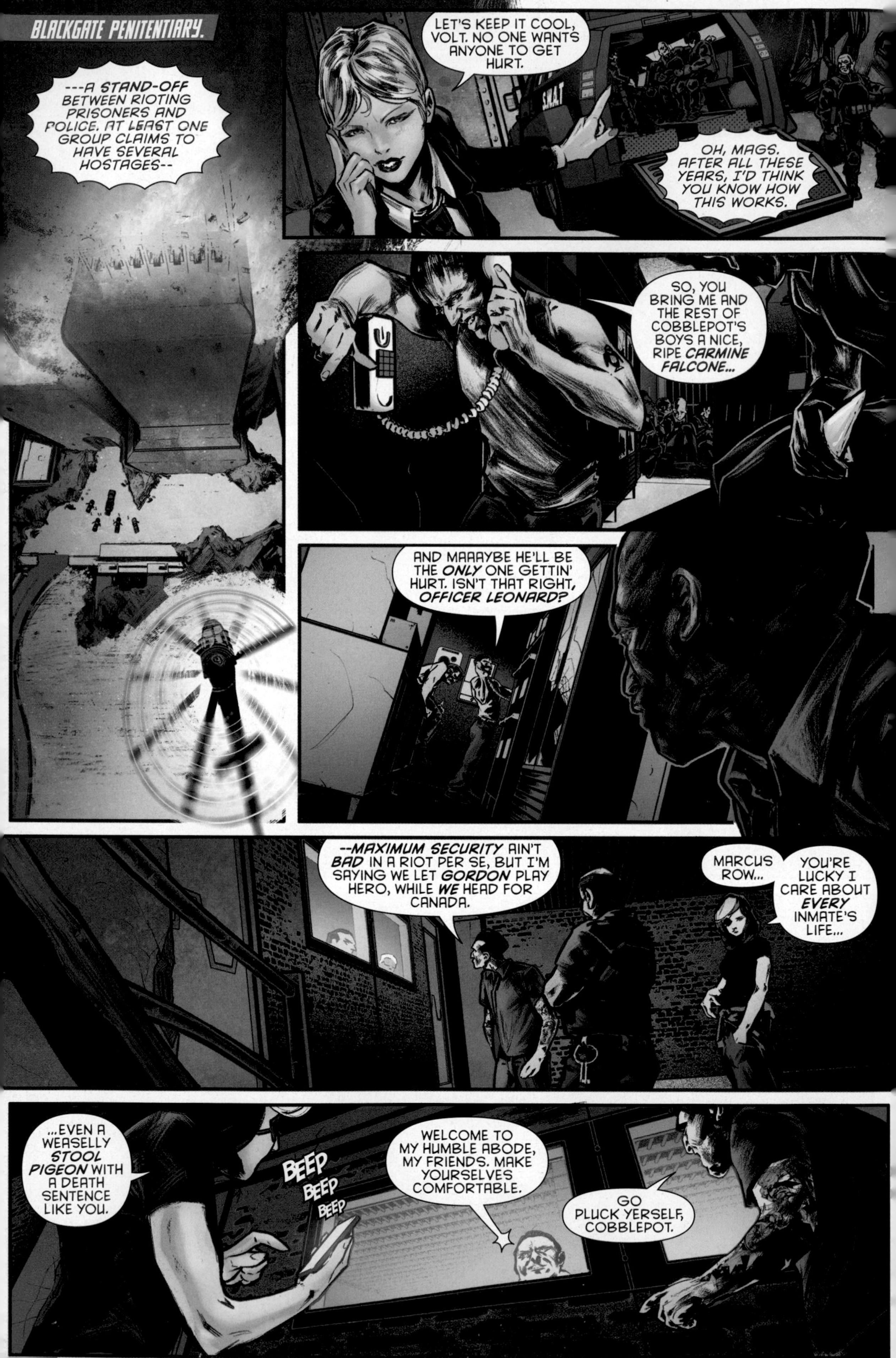
BLACKGATE PENITENTIARY.
---A STAND-OFF BETWEEN RIOTING PRISONERS AND POLICE. AT LEAST ONE GROUP CLAIMS TO HAVE SEVERAL HOSTAGES--
LET'S KEEP IT COOL, VOLT. NO ONE WANTS ANYONE TO GET HURT.
OH, MAGS. AFTER ALL THESE YEARS, I'D THINK YOU KNOW HOW THIS WORKS.
S.W.A.T
SO, YOU BRING ME AND THE REST OF COBBLEPOT'S BOYS A NICE, RIPE CARMINE FALCONE...
AND MAAAYBE HE'LL BE THE ONLY ONE GETTIN' HURT. ISN'T THAT RIGHT, OFFICER LEONARD?
--MAXIMUM SECURITY AIN'T BAD IN A RIOT PER SE, BUT I'M SAYING WE LET GORDON PLAY HERO, WHILE WE HEAD FOR CANADA.
MARCUS ROW...
YOU'RE LUCKY I CARE ABOUT EVERY INMATE'S LIFE...
...EVEN A WEASELLY STOOL PIGEON WITH A DEATH SENTENCE LIKE YOU.
BEEP
BEEP
BEEP
WELCOME TO MY HUMBLE ABODE, MY FRIENDS. MAKE YOURSELVES COMFORTABLE.
GO PLUCK YERSELF, COBBLEPOT.

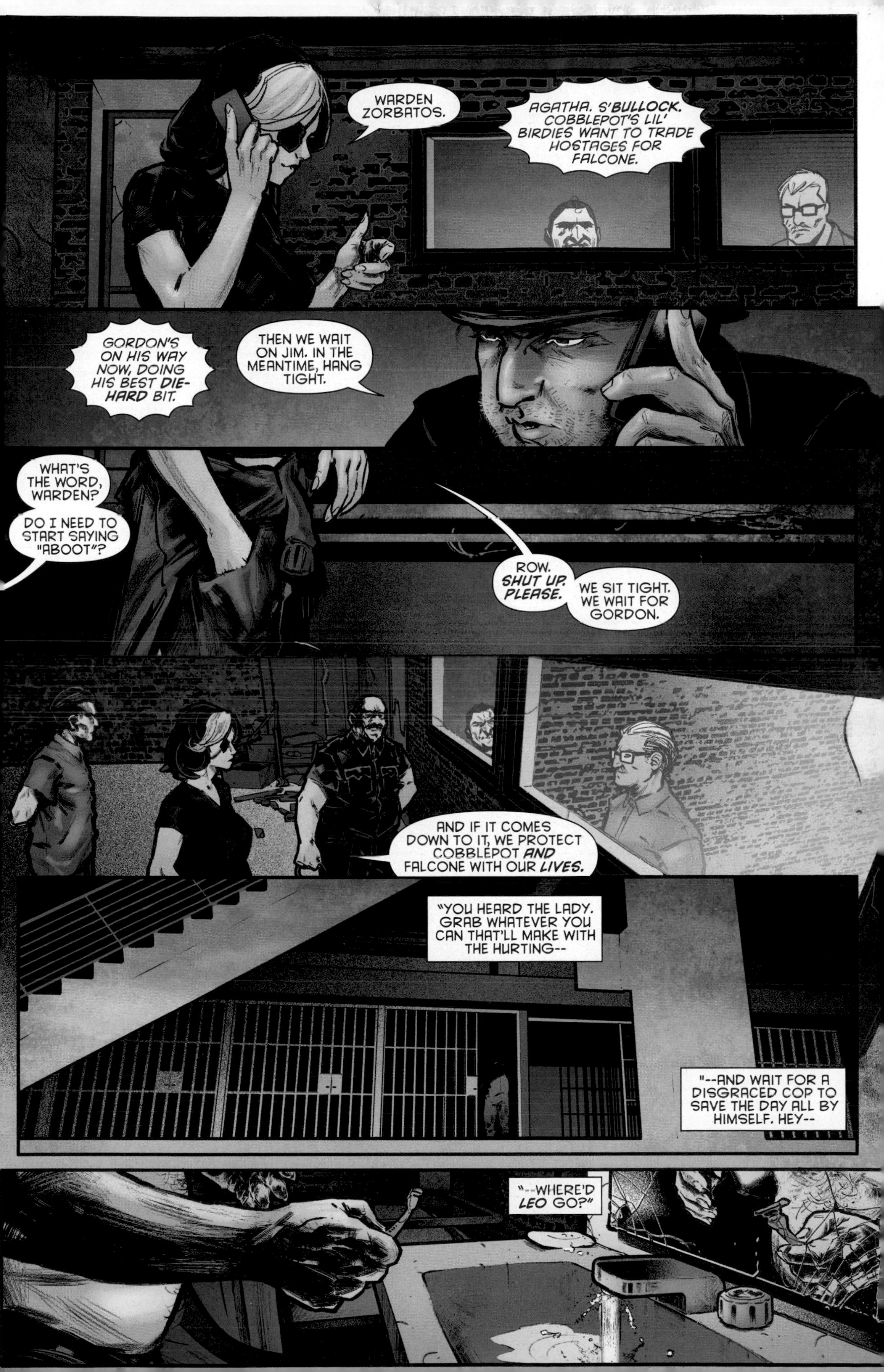
WARDEN ZORBATOS.
AGATHA. S'BULLOCK. COBBLEPOT'S LIL' BIRDIES WANT TO TRADE HOSTAGES FOR FALCONE.
GORDON'S ON HIS WAY NOW, DOING HIS BEST DIE-HARD BIT.
THEN WE WAIT ON JIM. IN THE MEANTIME, HANG TIGHT.
WHAT'S THE WORD, WARDEN?
DO I NEED TO START SAYING "ABOOT"?
ROW. SHUT UP. PLEASE.
WE SIT TIGHT. WE WAIT FOR GORDON.
AND IF IT COMES DOWN TO IT, WE PROTECT COBBLEPOT AND FALCONE WITH OUR LIVES.
"YOU HEARD THE LADY. GRAB WHATEVER YOU CAN THAT'LL MAKE WITH THE HURTING--
"--AND WAIT FOR A DISGRACED COP TO SAVE THE DAY ALL BY HIMSELF. HEY--
"--WHERE'D LEO GO?"

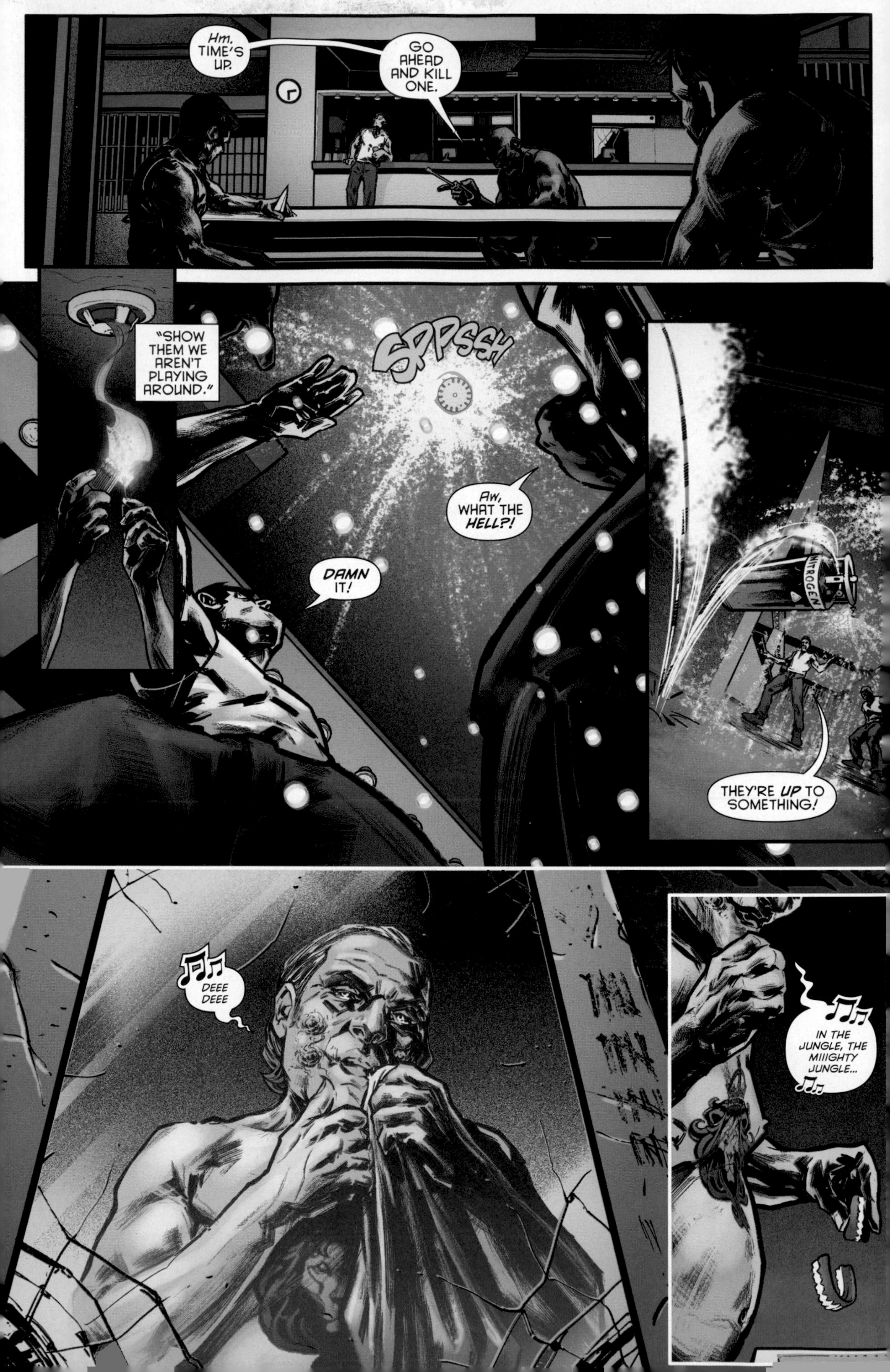
Hm. TIME'S UP.
GO AHEAD AND KILL ONE.
"SHOW THEM WE AREN'T PLAYING AROUND."
SPPSSH
AW, WHAT THE HELL?!
DAMN IT!
NITROGEN
THEY'RE UP TO SOMETHING!
DEEE DEEE
IN THE JUNGLE, THE MIIIGHTY JUNGLE...

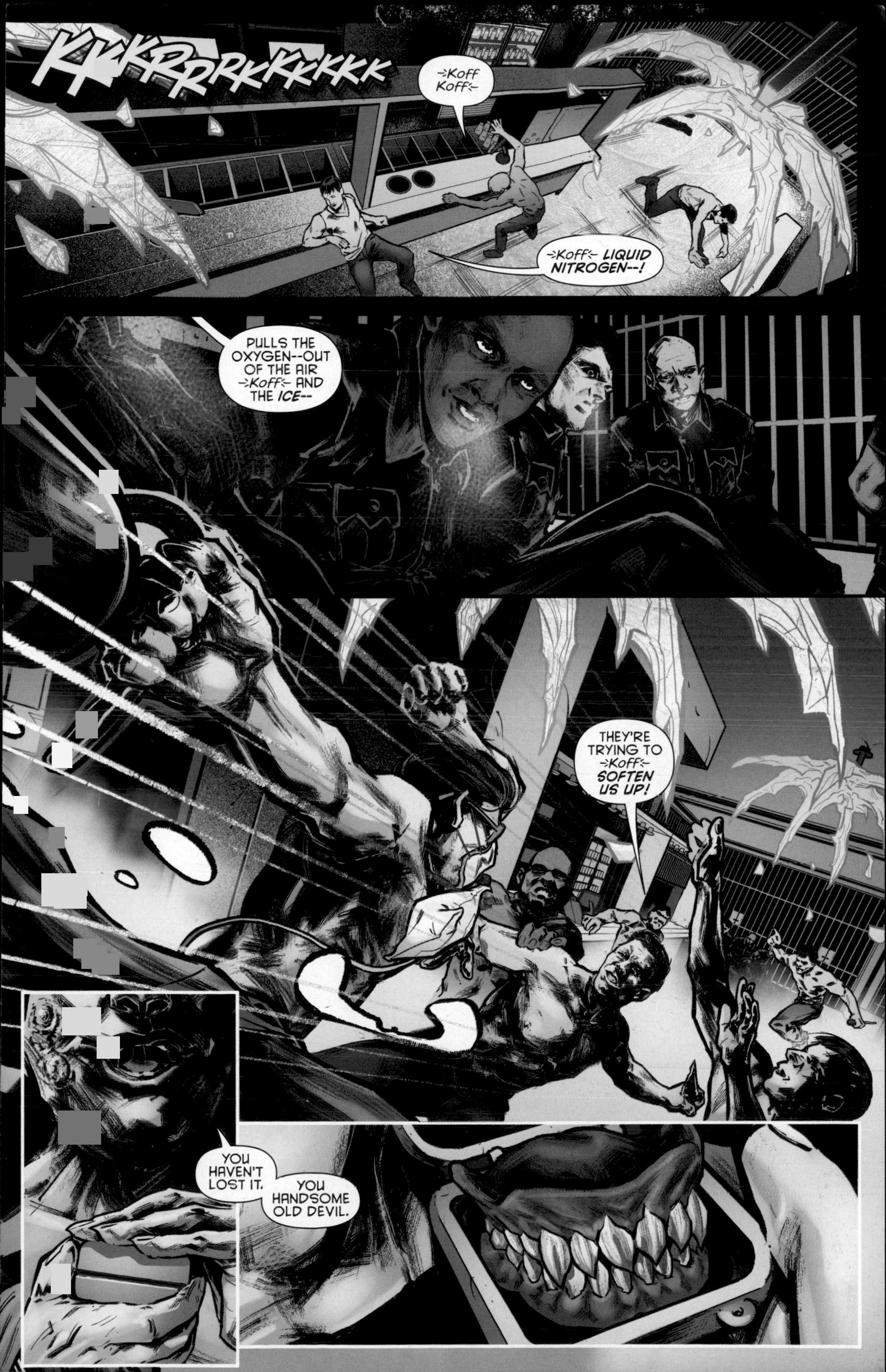
KKKRRRKKKKKK
-Koff Koff-
-Koff- LIQUID NITROGEN--!
PULLS THE OXYGEN--OUT OF THE AIR -Koff- AND THE ICE--
THEY'RE TRYING TO -Koff- SOFTEN US UP!
YOU HAVEN'T LOST IT.
YOU HANDSOME OLD DEVIL.

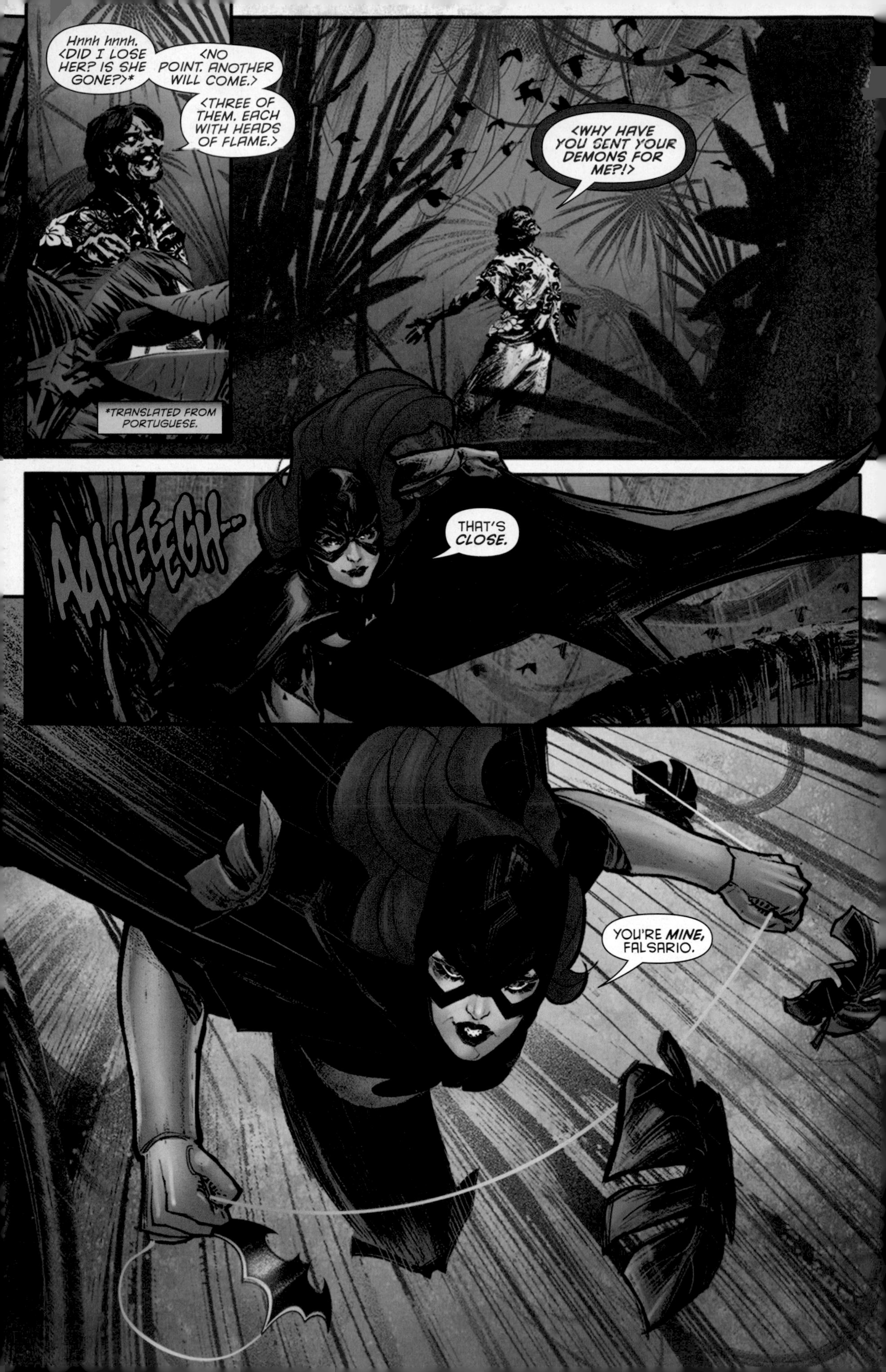
Hnnh hnnh. <DID I LOSE HER? IS SHE GONE?>*
<NO POINT. ANOTHER WILL COME.>
<THREE OF THEM. EACH WITH HEADS OF FLAME.>
*TRANSLATED FROM PORTUGUESE.
<WHY HAVE YOU SENT YOUR DEMONS FOR ME?!>
AAIIIEEEGH--
THAT'S CLOSE.
YOU'RE MINE, FALSARIO.

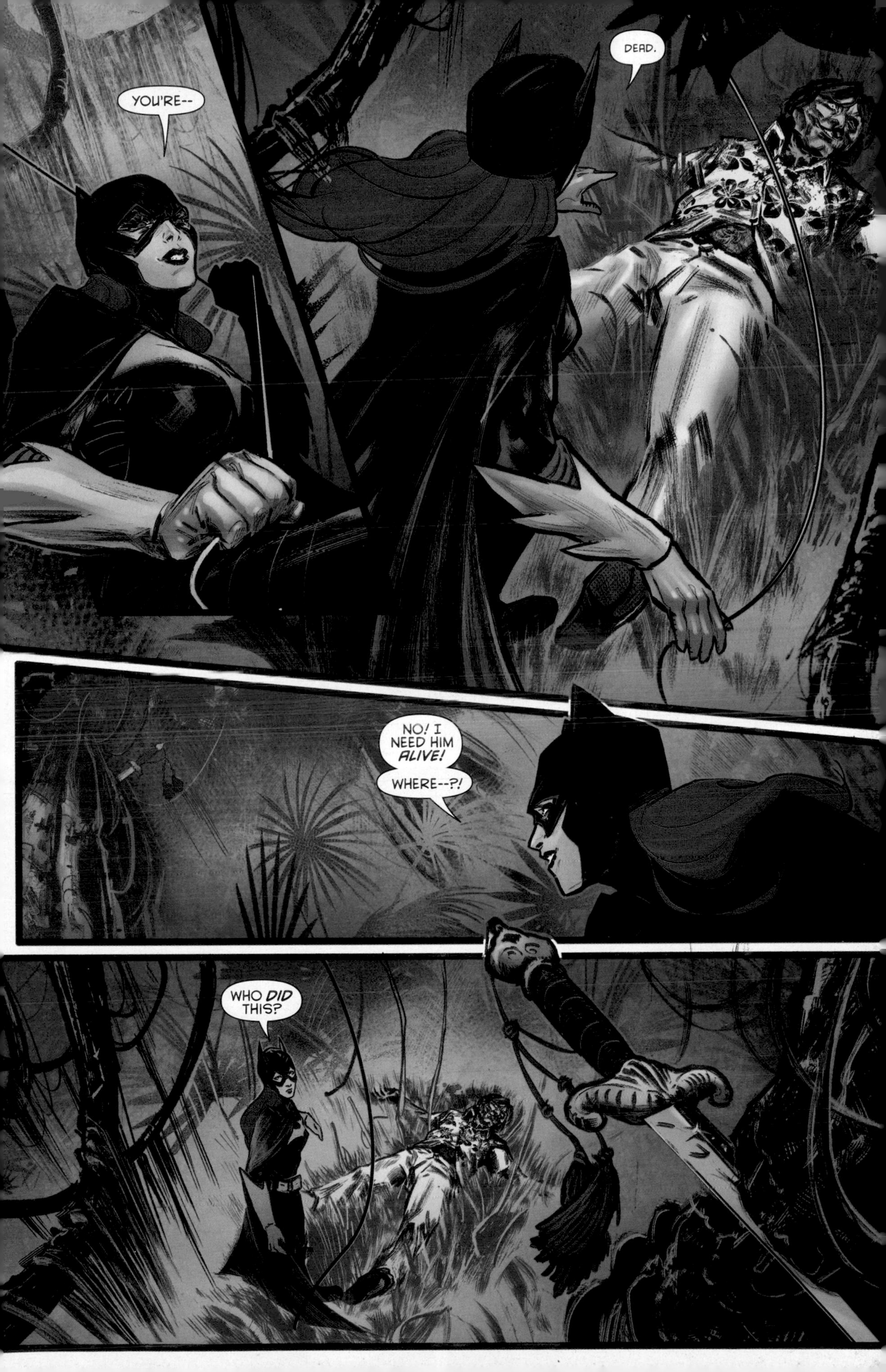
YOU'RE--
DEAD.
NO! I NEED HIM *ALIVE!*
WHERE--?!
WHO *DID* THIS?

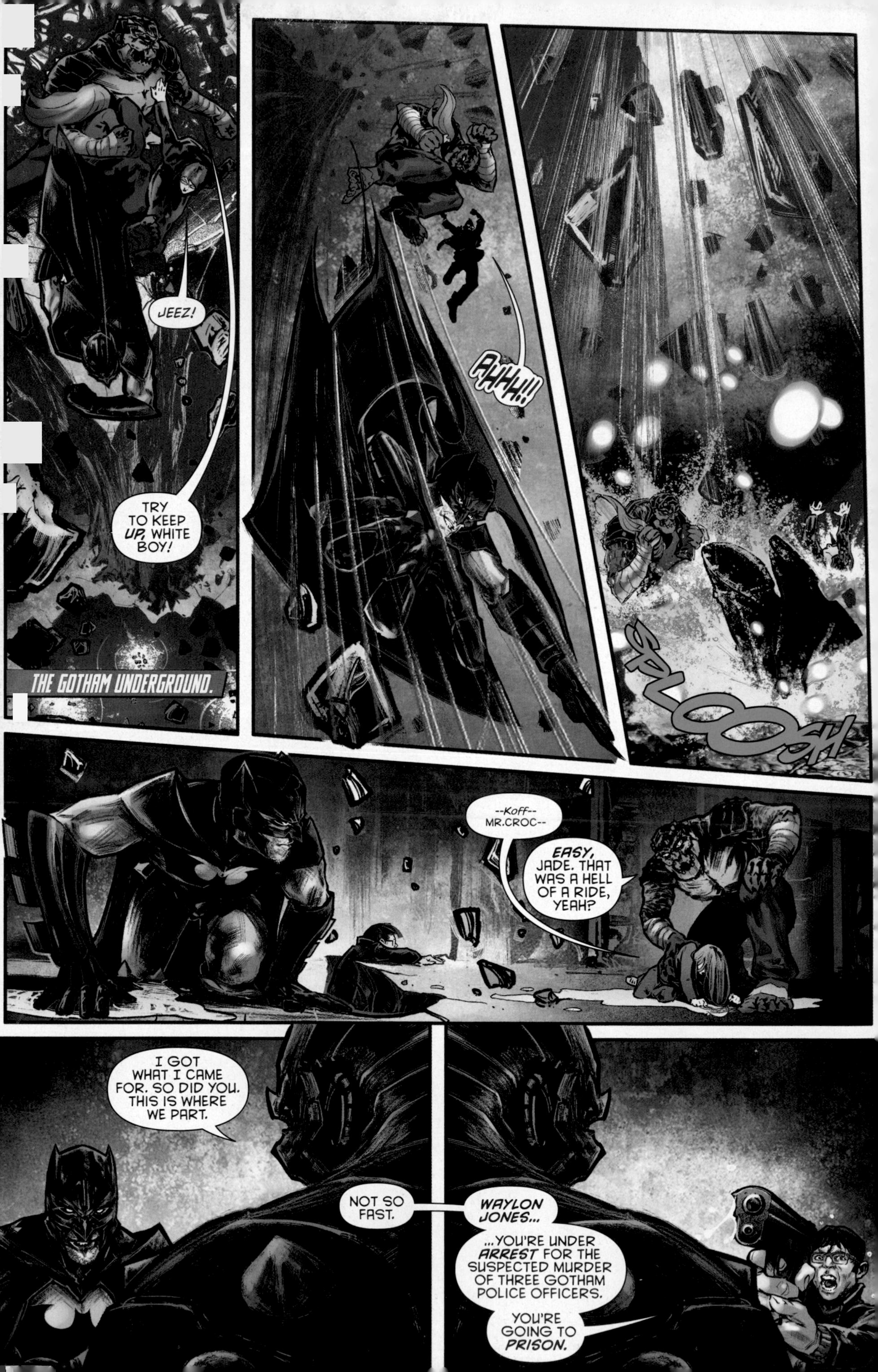
THE GOTHAM UNDERGROUND.
JEEZ!
TRY TO KEEP UP, WHITE BOY!
AHHH!!
SPLOOSH
--Koff-- MR.CROC--
EASY, JADE. THAT WAS A HELL OF A RIDE, YEAH?
I GOT WHAT I CAME FOR. SO DID YOU. THIS IS WHERE WE PART.
NOT SO FAST.
WAYLON JONES...
...YOU'RE UNDER ARREST FOR THE SUSPECTED MURDER OF THREE GOTHAM POLICE OFFICERS.
YOU'RE GOING TO PRISON.

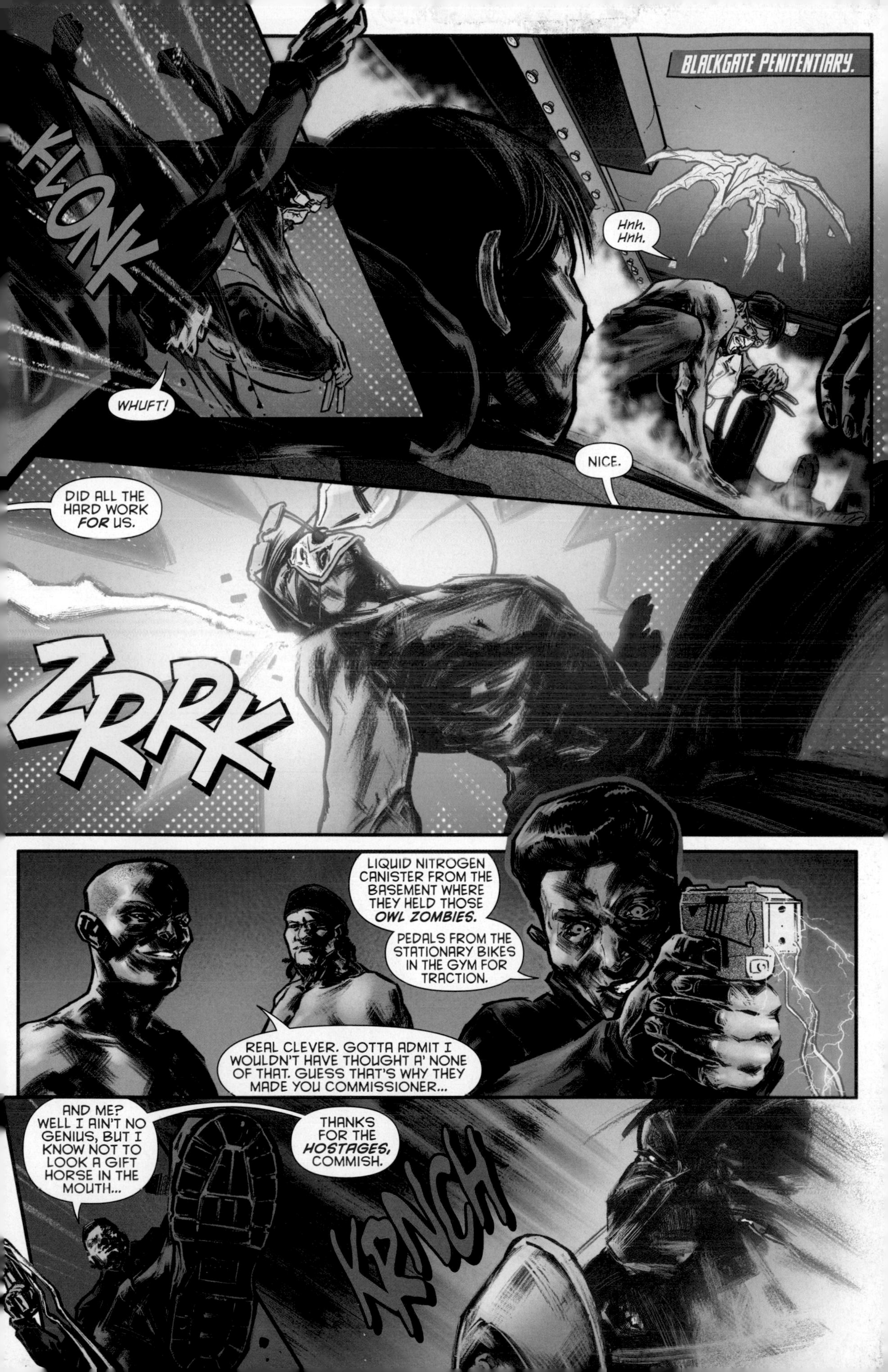
BLACKGATE PENITENTIARY.
KLONK
WHUFT!
Hnh. Hnh.
NICE.
DID ALL THE HARD WORK FOR US.
ZRRK
LIQUID NITROGEN CANISTER FROM THE BASEMENT WHERE THEY HELD THOSE OWL ZOMBIES.
PEDALS FROM THE STATIONARY BIKES IN THE GYM FOR TRACTION.
REAL CLEVER. GOTTA ADMIT I WOULDN'T HAVE THOUGHT A' NONE OF THAT. GUESS THAT'S WHY THEY MADE YOU COMMISSIONER...
AND ME? WELL I AIN'T NO GENIUS, BUT I KNOW NOT TO LOOK A GIFT HORSE IN THE MOUTH...
THANKS FOR THE HOSTAGES, COMMISH.
KRNCH

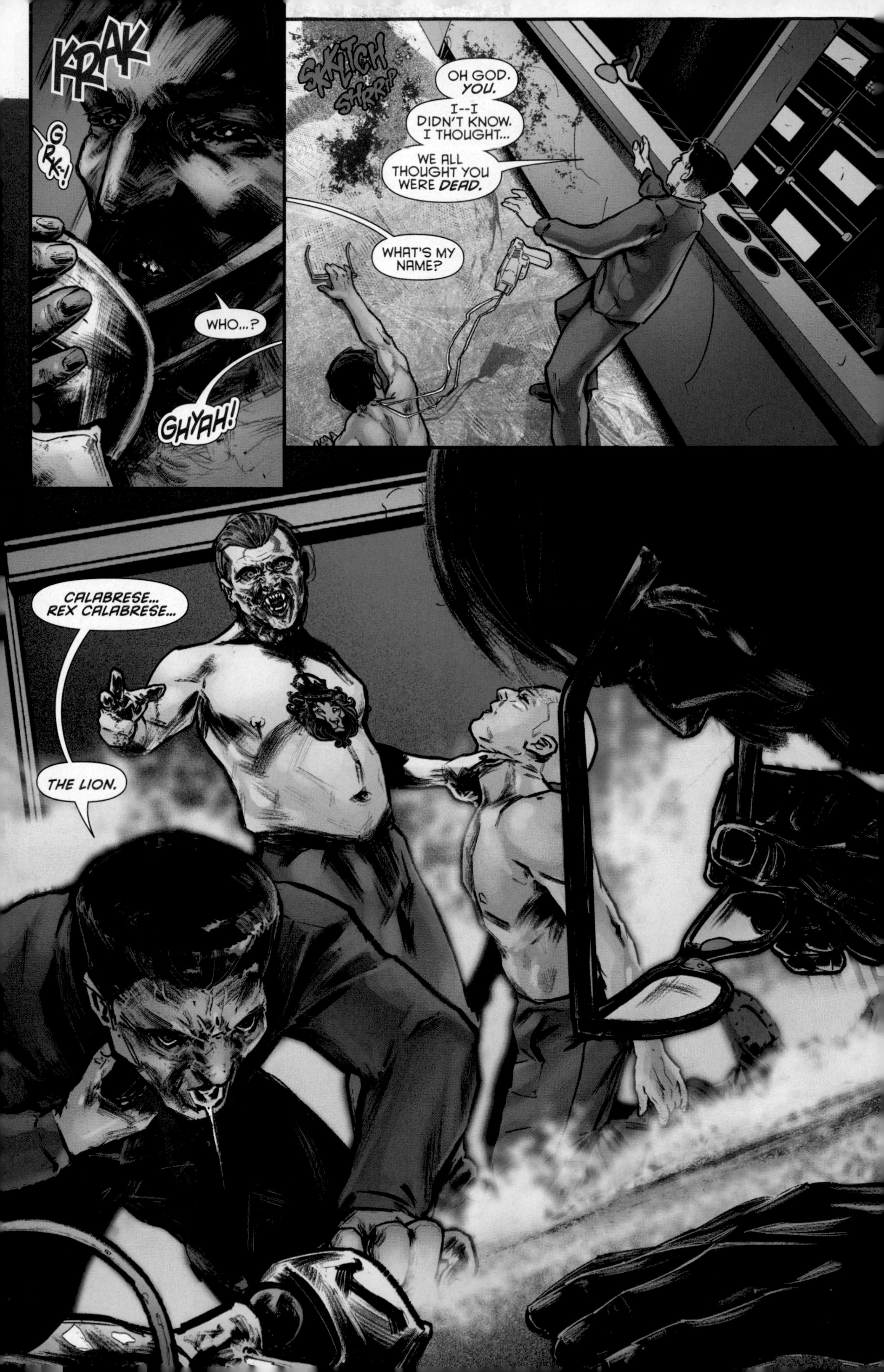

KRAK
GRK-!
WHO...?
GHYAH!
SKITCH
SHRP
OH GOD. YOU.
I--I DIDN'T KNOW. I THOUGHT...
WE ALL THOUGHT YOU WERE DEAD.
WHAT'S MY NAME?
CALABRESE... REX CALABRESE...
THE LION.

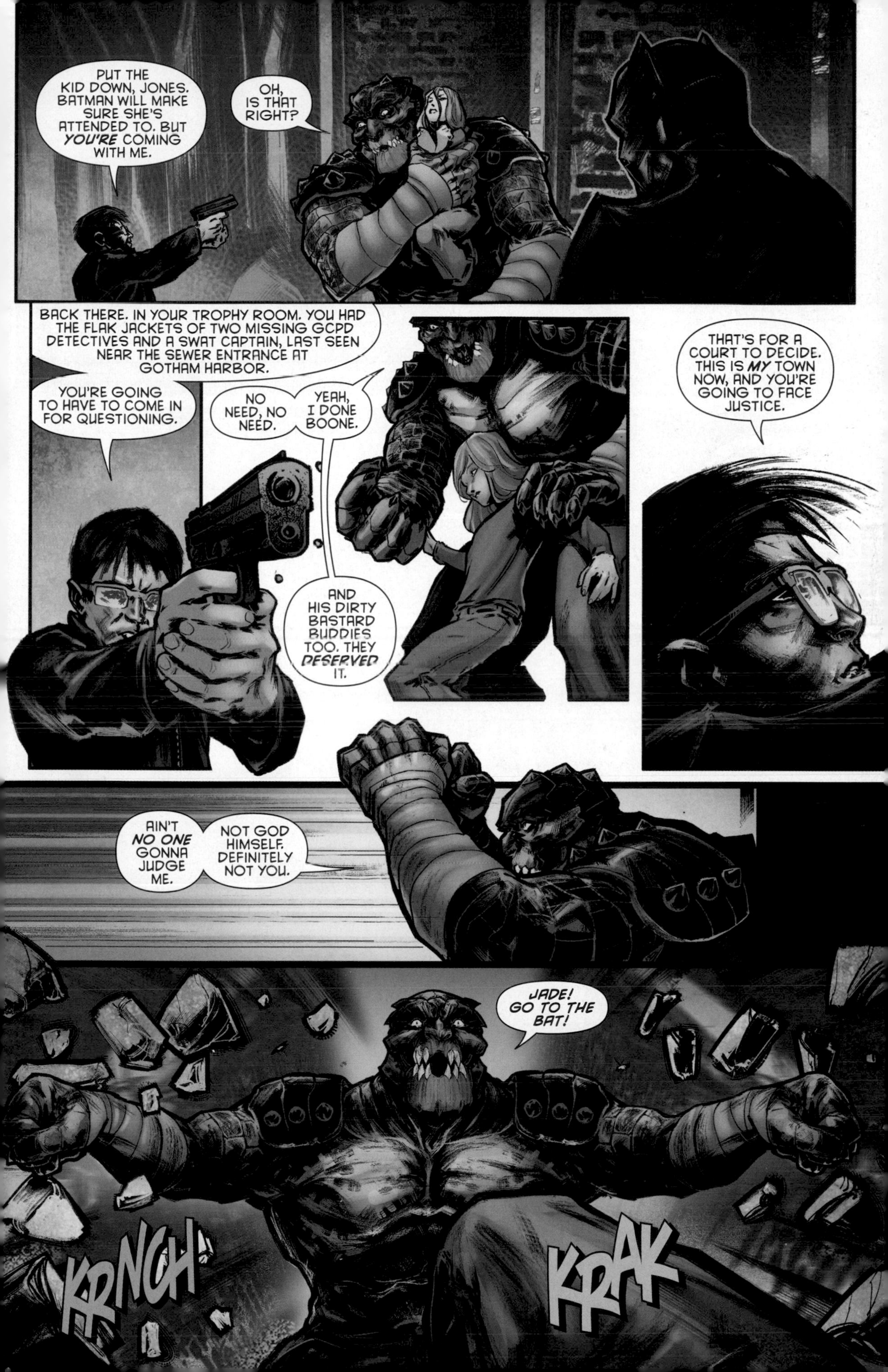
PUT THE KID DOWN, JONES. BATMAN WILL MAKE SURE SHE'S ATTENDED TO. BUT *YOU'RE* COMING WITH ME.
OH, IS THAT RIGHT?
BACK THERE. IN YOUR TROPHY ROOM. YOU HAD THE FLAK JACKETS OF TWO MISSING GCPD DETECTIVES AND A SWAT CAPTAIN, LAST SEEN NEAR THE SEWER ENTRANCE AT GOTHAM HARBOR.
YOU'RE GOING TO HAVE TO COME IN FOR QUESTIONING.
NO NEED, NO NEED.
YEAH, I DONE BOONE.
AND HIS DIRTY BASTARD BUDDIES TOO. THEY *DESERVED* IT.
THAT'S FOR A COURT TO DECIDE. THIS IS *MY* TOWN NOW, AND YOU'RE GOING TO FACE JUSTICE.
AIN'T *NO ONE* GONNA JUDGE ME.
NOT GOD HIMSELF. DEFINITELY NOT YOU.
JADE! GO TO THE BAT!
KRNCH
KRAK

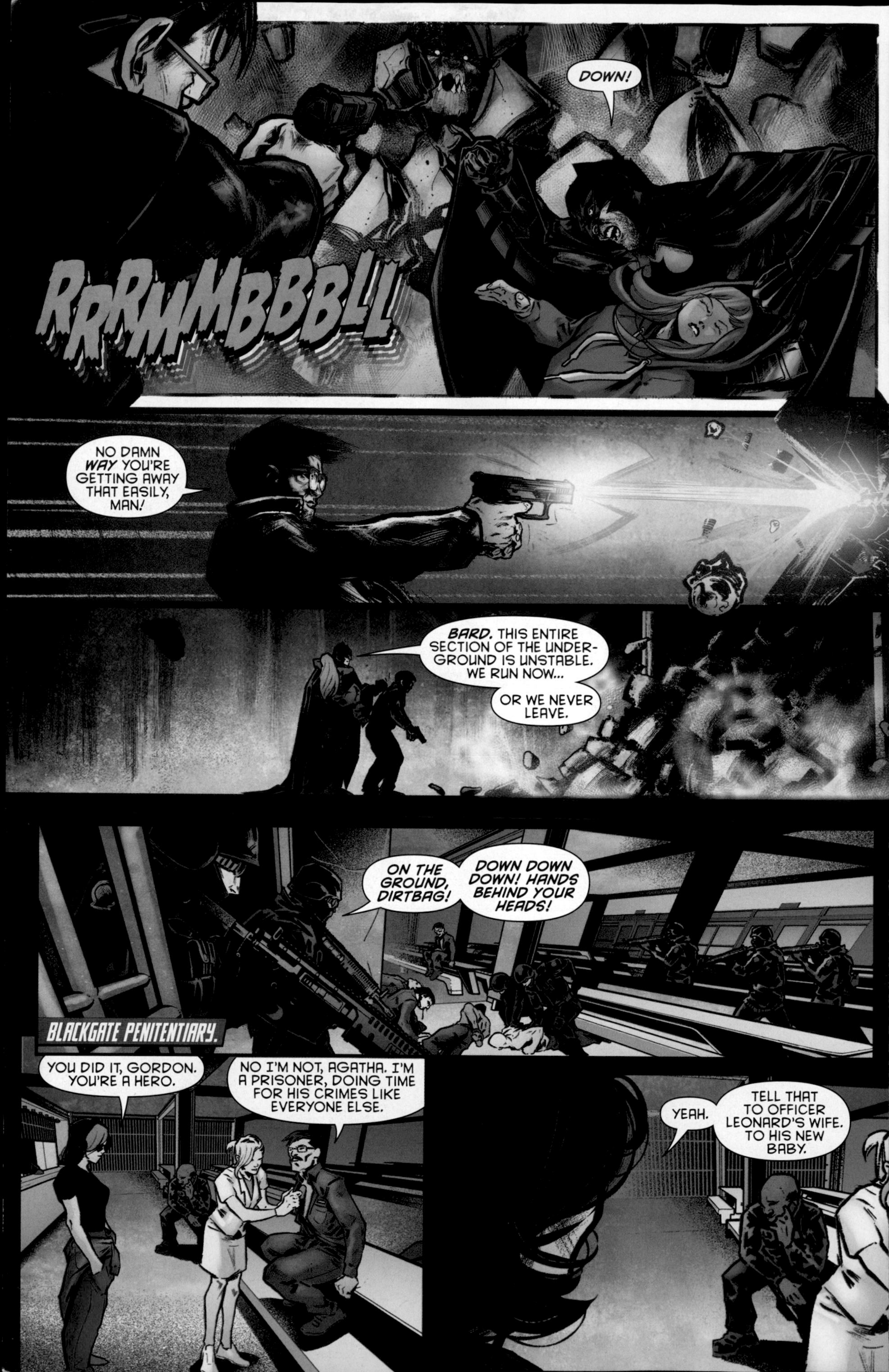
DOWN!
RRRMMBBBLL
NO DAMN WAY YOU'RE GETTING AWAY THAT EASILY, MAN!
BARD. THIS ENTIRE SECTION OF THE UNDER-GROUND IS UNSTABLE. WE RUN NOW...
OR WE NEVER LEAVE.
ON THE GROUND, DIRTBAG!
DOWN DOWN DOWN! HANDS BEHIND YOUR HEADS!
BLACKGATE PENITENTIARY.
YOU DID IT, GORDON. YOU'RE A HERO.
NO I'M NOT, AGATHA. I'M A PRISONER, DOING TIME FOR HIS CRIMES LIKE EVERYONE ELSE.
YEAH.
TELL THAT TO OFFICER LEONARD'S WIFE. TO HIS NEW BABY.

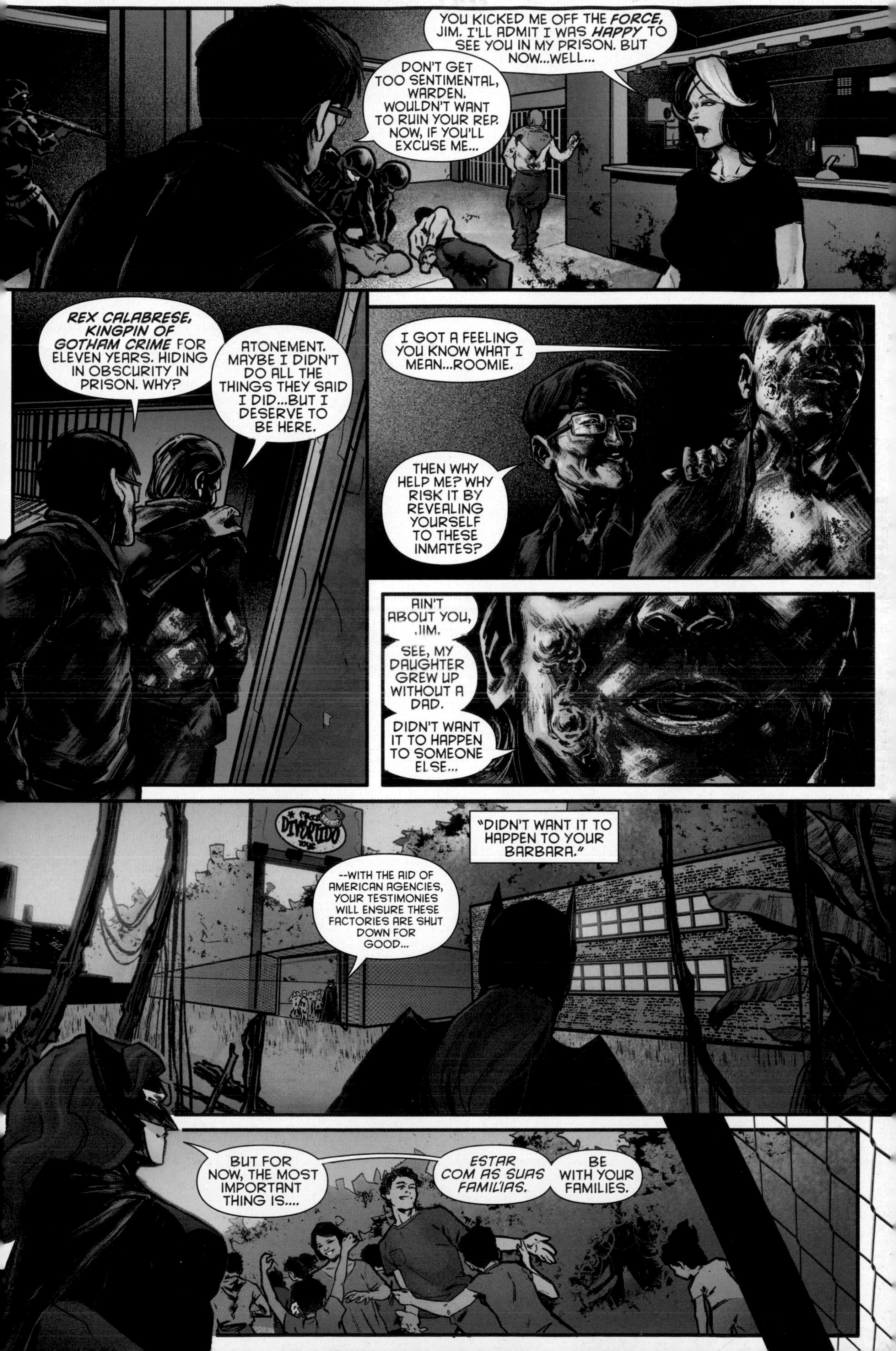

YOU KICKED ME OFF THE *FORCE*, JIM. I'LL ADMIT I WAS *HAPPY* TO SEE YOU IN MY PRISON. BUT NOW...WELL...
DON'T GET TOO SENTIMENTAL, WARDEN. WOULDN'T WANT TO RUIN YOUR REP. NOW, IF YOU'LL EXCUSE ME...
REX CALABRESE, KINGPIN OF GOTHAM CRIME FOR ELEVEN YEARS. HIDING IN OBSCURITY IN PRISON. WHY?
ATONEMENT. MAYBE I DIDN'T DO ALL THE THINGS THEY SAID I DID...BUT I DESERVE TO BE HERE.
I GOT A FEELING YOU KNOW WHAT I MEAN...ROOMIE.
THEN WHY HELP ME? WHY RISK IT BY REVEALING YOURSELF TO THESE INMATES?
AIN'T ABOUT YOU, JIM.
SEE, MY DAUGHTER GREW UP WITHOUT A DAD.
DIDN'T WANT IT TO HAPPEN TO SOMEONE ELSE...
"DIDN'T WANT IT TO HAPPEN TO YOUR BARBARA."
DIVERTIDO
--WITH THE AID OF AMERICAN AGENCIES, YOUR TESTIMONIES WILL ENSURE THESE FACTORIES ARE SHUT DOWN FOR GOOD...
BUT FOR NOW, THE MOST IMPORTANT THING IS....
ESTAR COM AS SUAS FAMÍLIAS.
BE WITH YOUR FAMILIES.

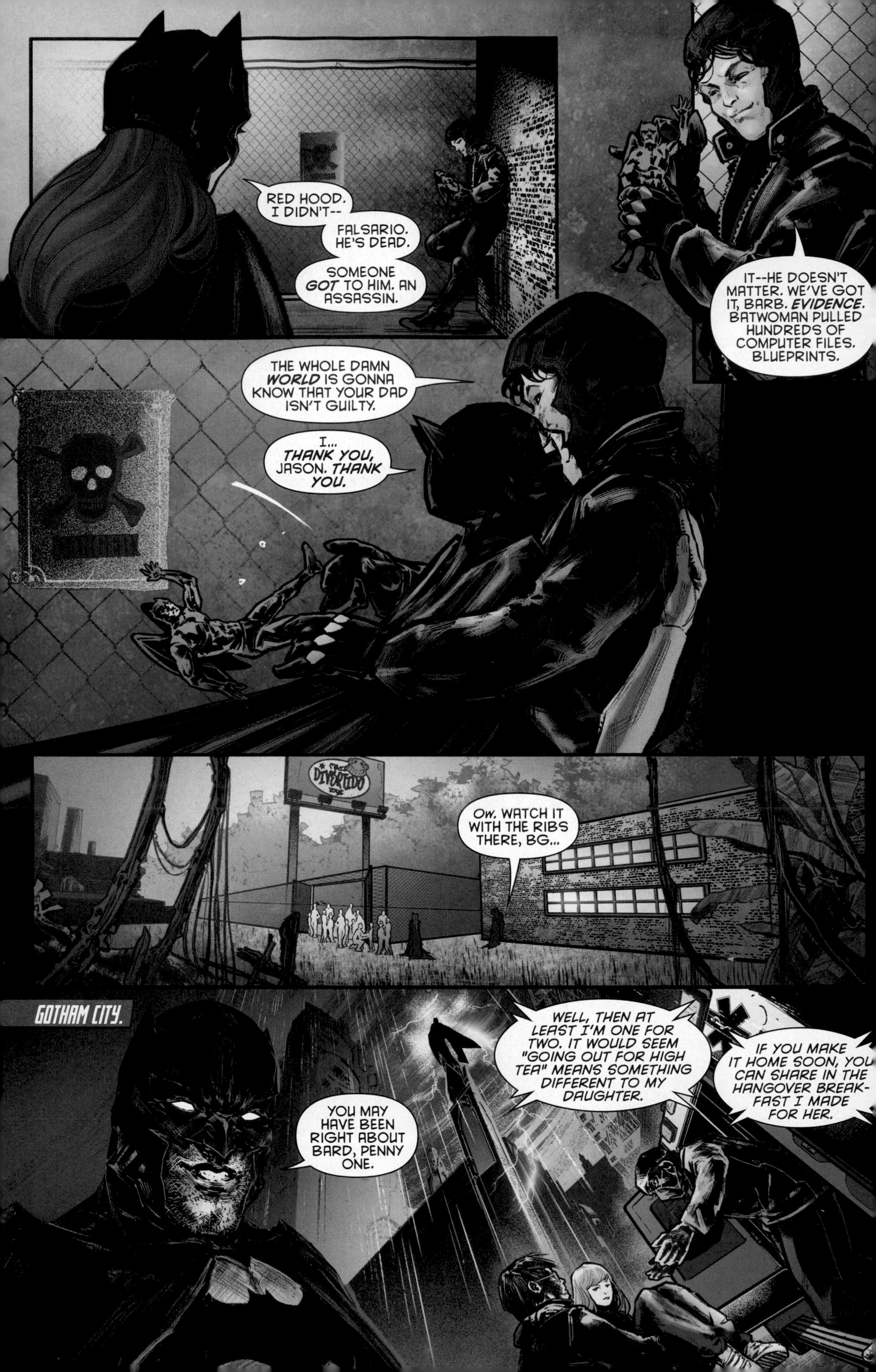
RED HOOD. I DIDN'T--
FALSARIO. HE'S DEAD.
SOMEONE GOT TO HIM. AN ASSASSIN.
IT--HE DOESN'T MATTER. WE'VE GOT IT, BARB. EVIDENCE. BATWOMAN PULLED HUNDREDS OF COMPUTER FILES. BLUEPRINTS.
THE WHOLE DAMN WORLD IS GONNA KNOW THAT YOUR DAD ISN'T GUILTY.
I... THANK YOU, JASON. THANK YOU.
DIVERTIDO
OW. WATCH IT WITH THE RIBS THERE, BG...
GOTHAM CITY.
YOU MAY HAVE BEEN RIGHT ABOUT BARD, PENNY ONE.
WELL, THEN AT LEAST I'M ONE FOR TWO. IT WOULD SEEM "GOING OUT FOR HIGH TEA" MEANS SOMETHING DIFFERENT TO MY DAUGHTER.
IF YOU MAKE IT HOME SOON, YOU CAN SHARE IN THE HANGOVER BREAK-FAST I MADE FOR HER.

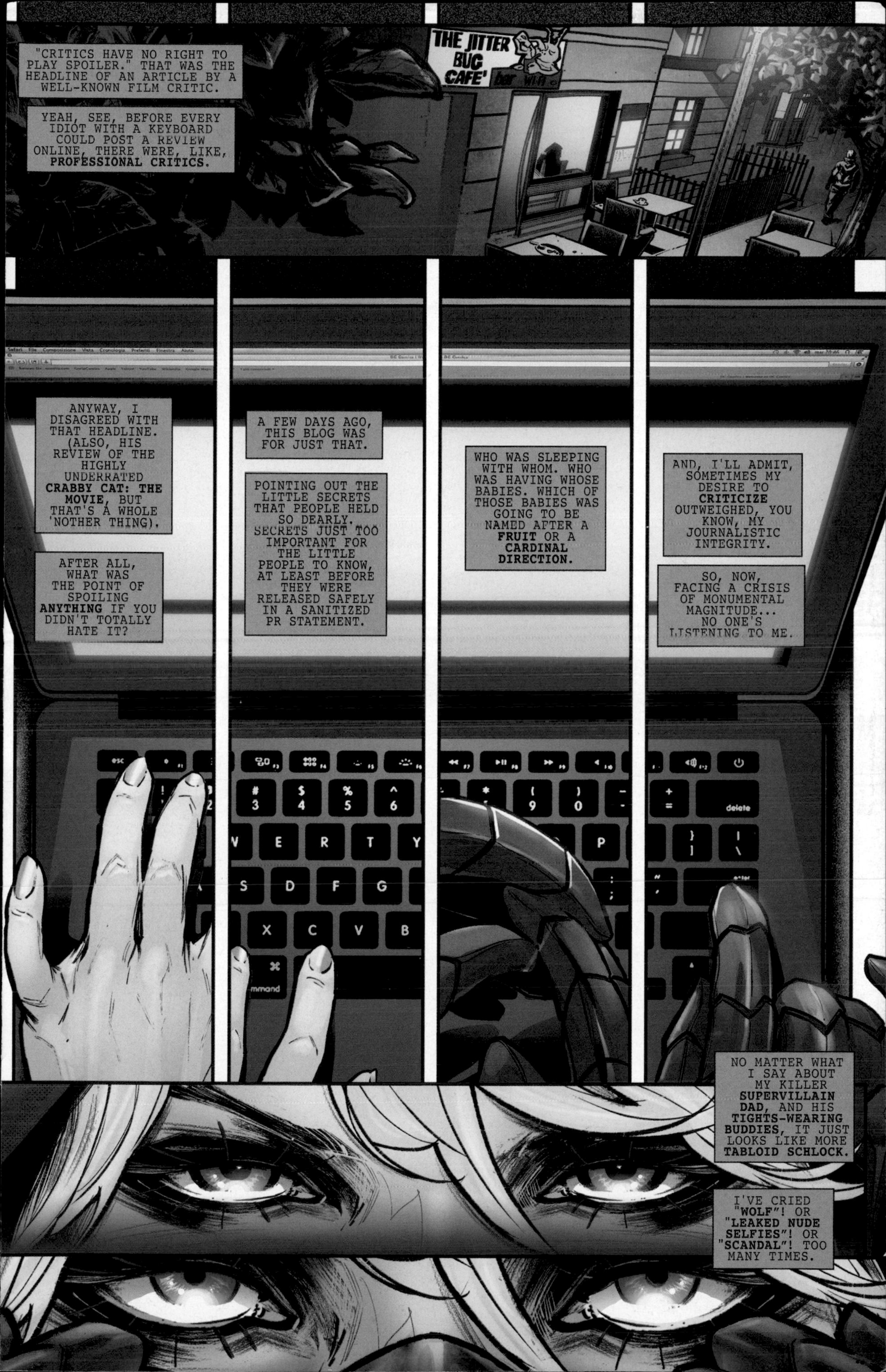

"CRITICS HAVE NO RIGHT TO PLAY SPOILER." THAT WAS THE HEADLINE OF AN ARTICLE BY A WELL-KNOWN FILM CRITIC.
YEAH, SEE, BEFORE EVERY IDIOT WITH A KEYBOARD COULD POST A REVIEW ONLINE, THERE WERE, LIKE, PROFESSIONAL CRITICS.
THE JITTER BUG CAFE' bar wi-fi
ANYWAY, I DISAGREED WITH THAT HEADLINE. (ALSO, HIS REVIEW OF THE HIGHLY UNDERRATED CRABBY CAT: THE MOVIE, BUT THAT'S A WHOLE 'NOTHER THING).
AFTER ALL, WHAT WAS THE POINT OF SPOILING ANYTHING IF YOU DIDN'T TOTALLY HATE IT?
A FEW DAYS AGO, THIS BLOG WAS FOR JUST THAT.
POINTING OUT THE LITTLE SECRETS THAT PEOPLE HELD SO DEARLY. SECRETS JUST TOO IMPORTANT FOR THE LITTLE PEOPLE TO KNOW, AT LEAST BEFORE THEY WERE RELEASED SAFELY IN A SANITIZED PR STATEMENT.
WHO WAS SLEEPING WITH WHOM. WHO WAS HAVING WHOSE BABIES. WHICH OF THOSE BABIES WAS GOING TO BE NAMED AFTER A FRUIT OR A CARDINAL DIRECTION.
AND, I'LL ADMIT, SOMETIMES MY DESIRE TO CRITICIZE OUTWEIGHED, YOU KNOW, MY JOURNALISTIC INTEGRITY.
SO, NOW, FACING A CRISIS OF MONUMENTAL MAGNITUDE... NO ONE'S LISTENING TO ME.
NO MATTER WHAT I SAY ABOUT MY KILLER SUPERVILLAIN DAD, AND HIS TIGHTS-WEARING BUDDIES, IT JUST LOOKS LIKE MORE TABLOID SCHLOCK.
I'VE CRIED "WOLF"! OR "LEAKED NUDE SELFIES"! OR "SCANDAL"! TOO MANY TIMES.

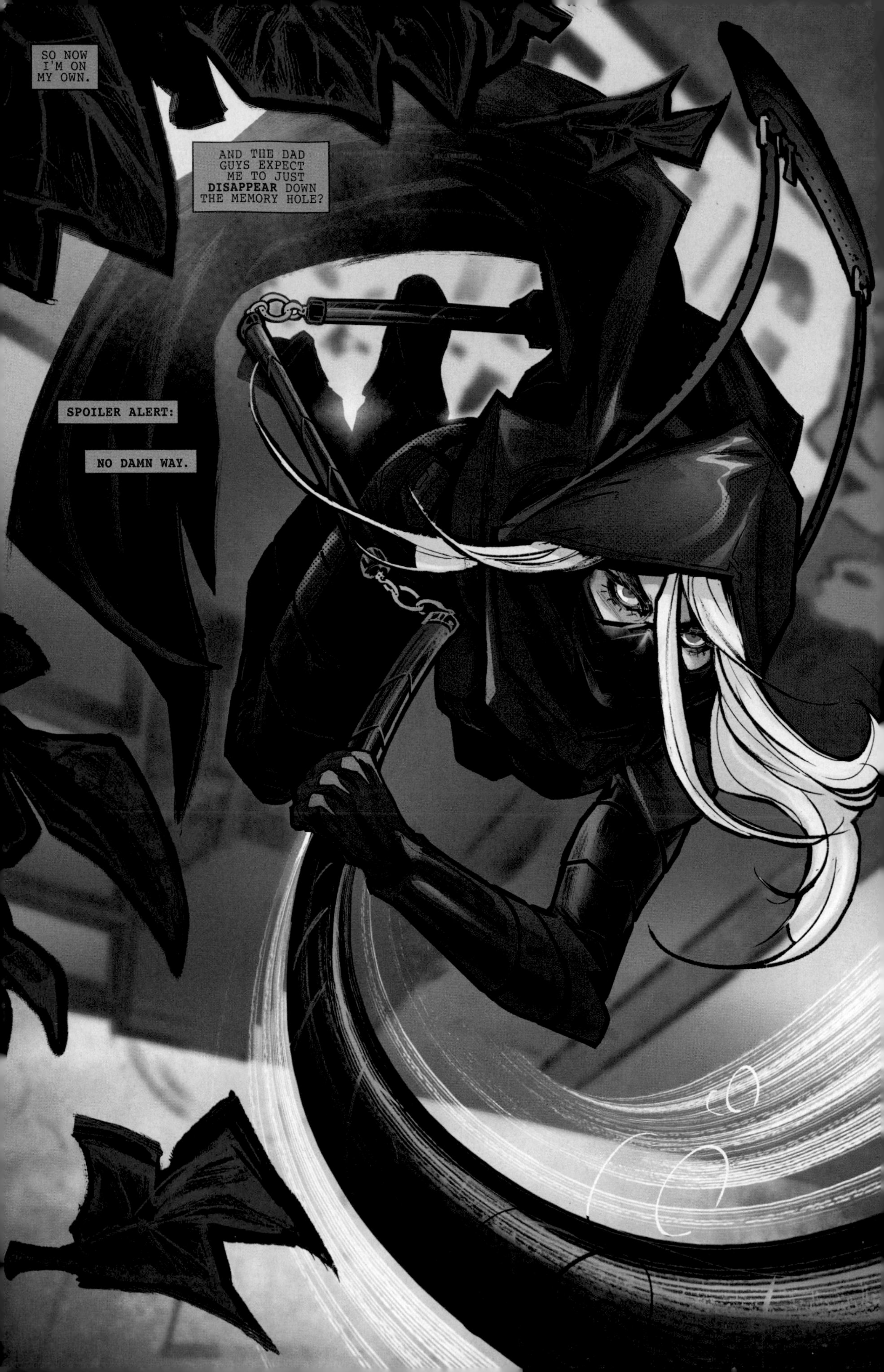

SO NOW I'M ON MY OWN.
AND THE BAD GUYS EXPECT ME TO JUST **DISAPPEAR** DOWN THE MEMORY HOLE?
SPOILER ALERT:
NO DAMN WAY.

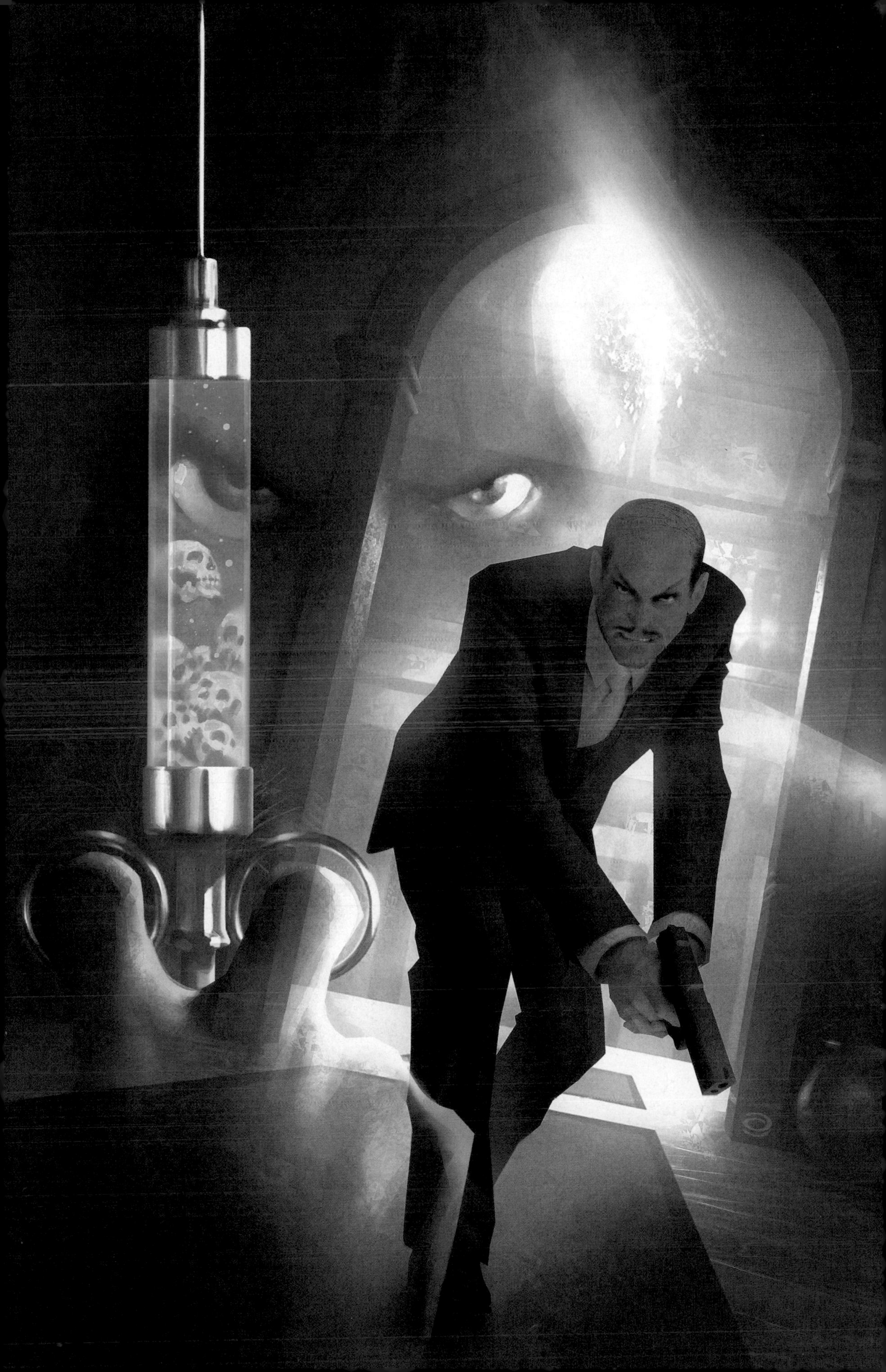

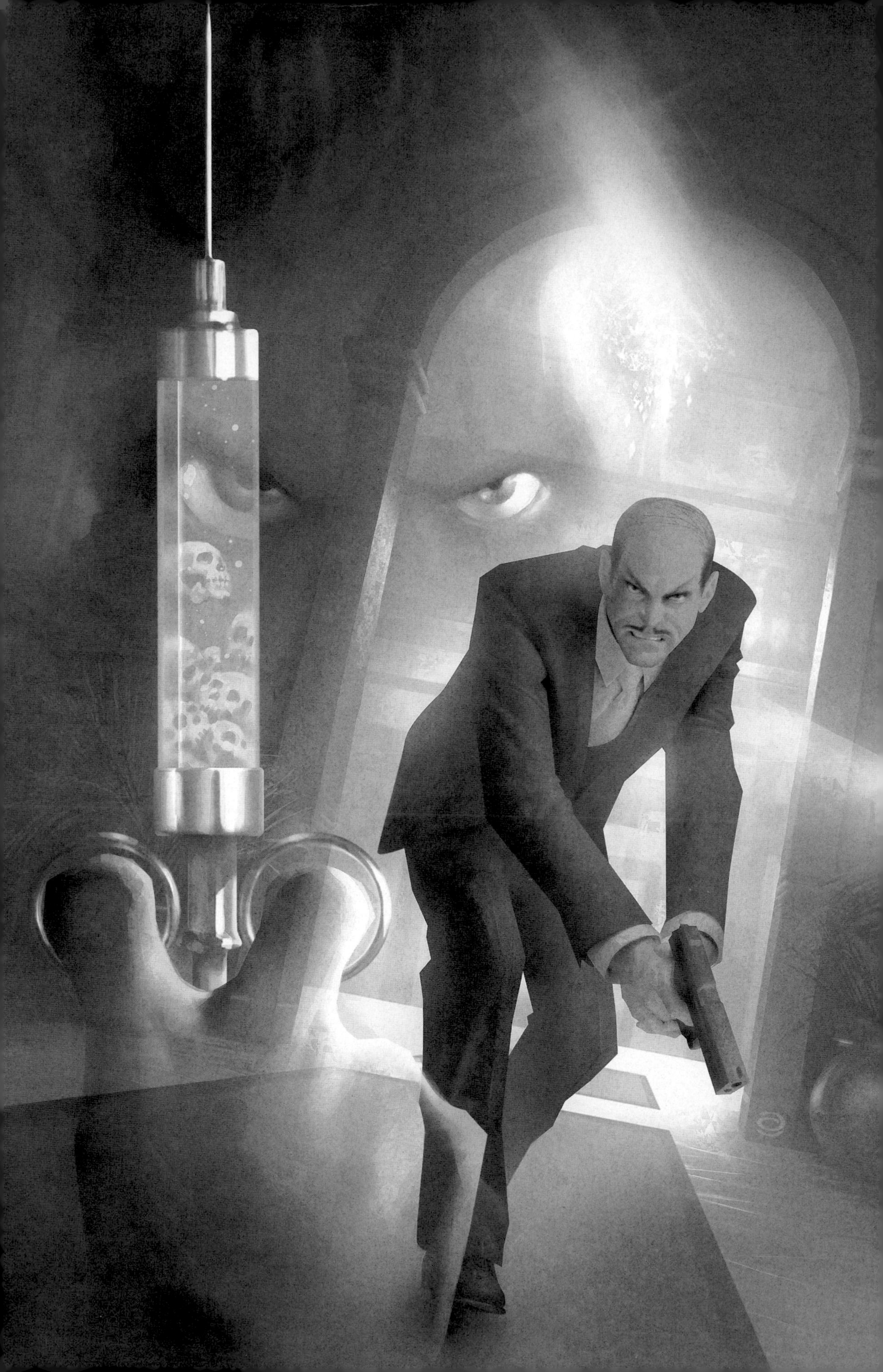

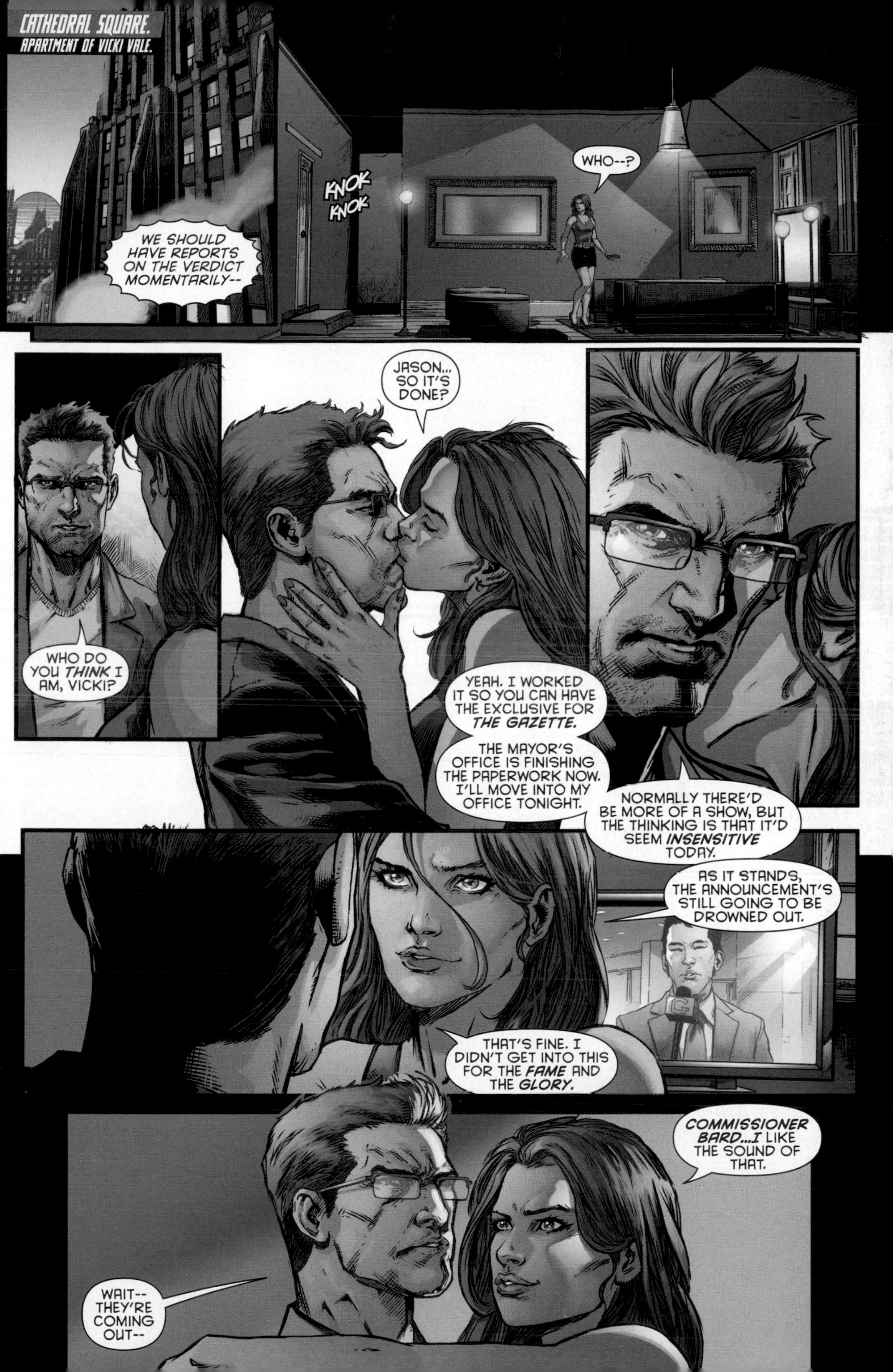
CATHEDRAL SQUARE.
APARTMENT OF VICKI VALE.
WE SHOULD HAVE REPORTS ON THE VERDICT MOMENTARILY--
KNOK KNOK
WHO--?
WHO DO YOU *THINK* I AM, VICKI?
JASON... SO IT'S DONE?
YEAH. I WORKED IT SO YOU CAN HAVE THE EXCLUSIVE FOR ***THE GAZETTE.***
THE MAYOR'S OFFICE IS FINISHING THE PAPERWORK NOW. I'LL MOVE INTO MY OFFICE TONIGHT.
NORMALLY THERE'D BE MORE OF A SHOW, BUT THE THINKING IS THAT IT'D SEEM ***INSENSITIVE*** TODAY.
AS IT STANDS, THE ANNOUNCEMENT'S STILL GOING TO BE DROWNED OUT.
THAT'S FINE. I DIDN'T GET INTO THIS FOR THE ***FAME*** AND THE ***GLORY.***
COMMISSIONER BARD...I LIKE THE SOUND OF THAT.
WAIT-- THEY'RE COMING OUT--

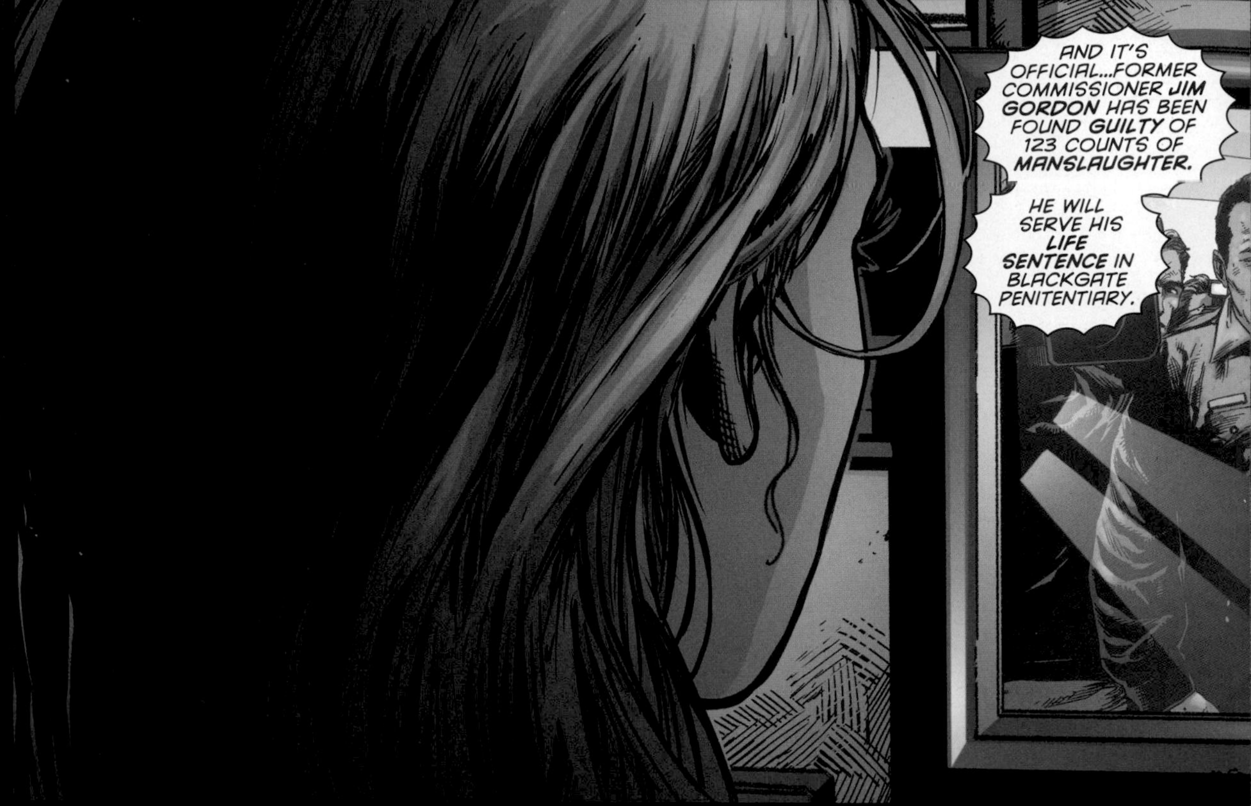
AND IT'S OFFICIAL...FORMER COMMISSIONER JIM GORDON HAS BEEN FOUND GUILTY OF 123 COUNTS OF MANSLAUGHTER.
HE WILL SERVE HIS LIFE SENTENCE IN BLACKGATE PENITENTIARY.

SCOTT SNYDER & JAMES TYNION IV STORY JAMES TYNION IV SCRIPT
RAY FAWKES, KYLE HIGGINS, TIM SEELEY CONSULTING WRITERS

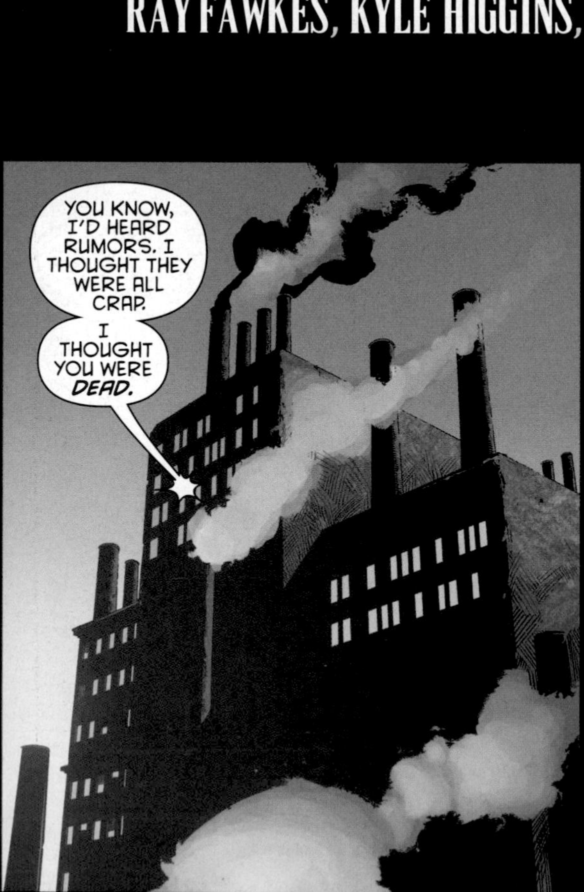
YOU KNOW, I'D HEARD RUMORS. I THOUGHT THEY WERE ALL CRAP.
I THOUGHT YOU WERE DEAD.

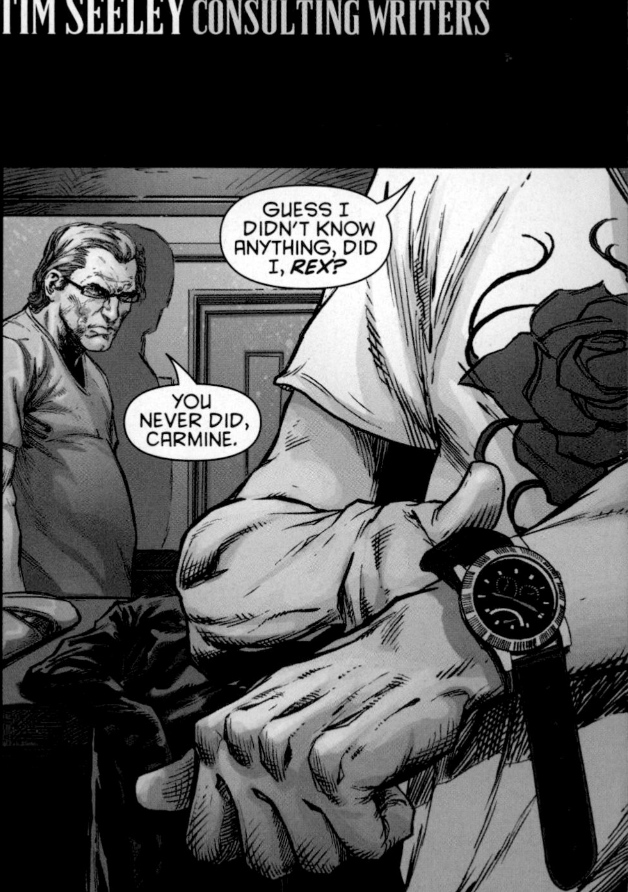
GUESS I DIDN'T KNOW ANYTHING, DID I, REX?
YOU NEVER DID, CARMINE.

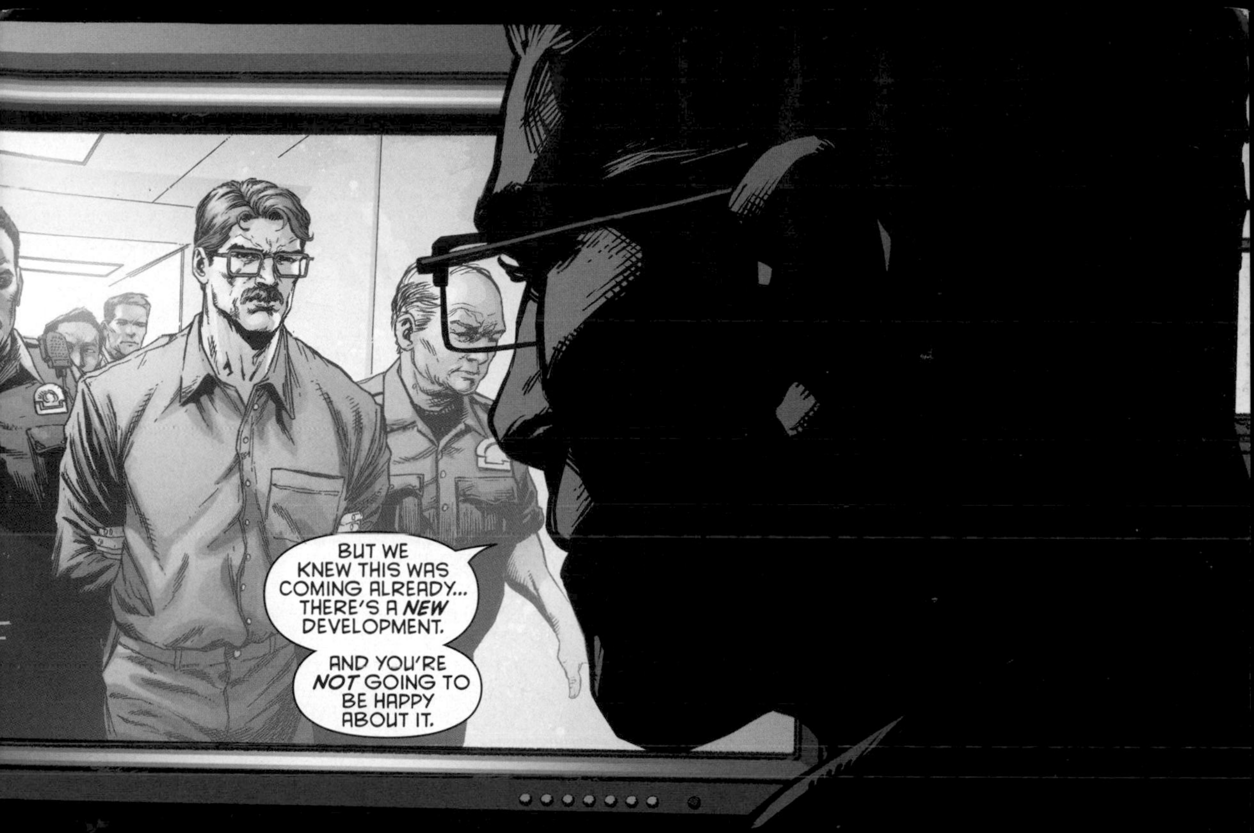
BUT WE KNEW THIS WAS COMING ALREADY... THERE'S A *NEW* DEVELOPMENT.
AND YOU'RE *NOT* GOING TO BE HAPPY ABOUT IT.

JASON FABOK ART

BRAD ANDERSON COLORS **DEZI SIENTY** LETTERS **ALEX GARNER** COVER

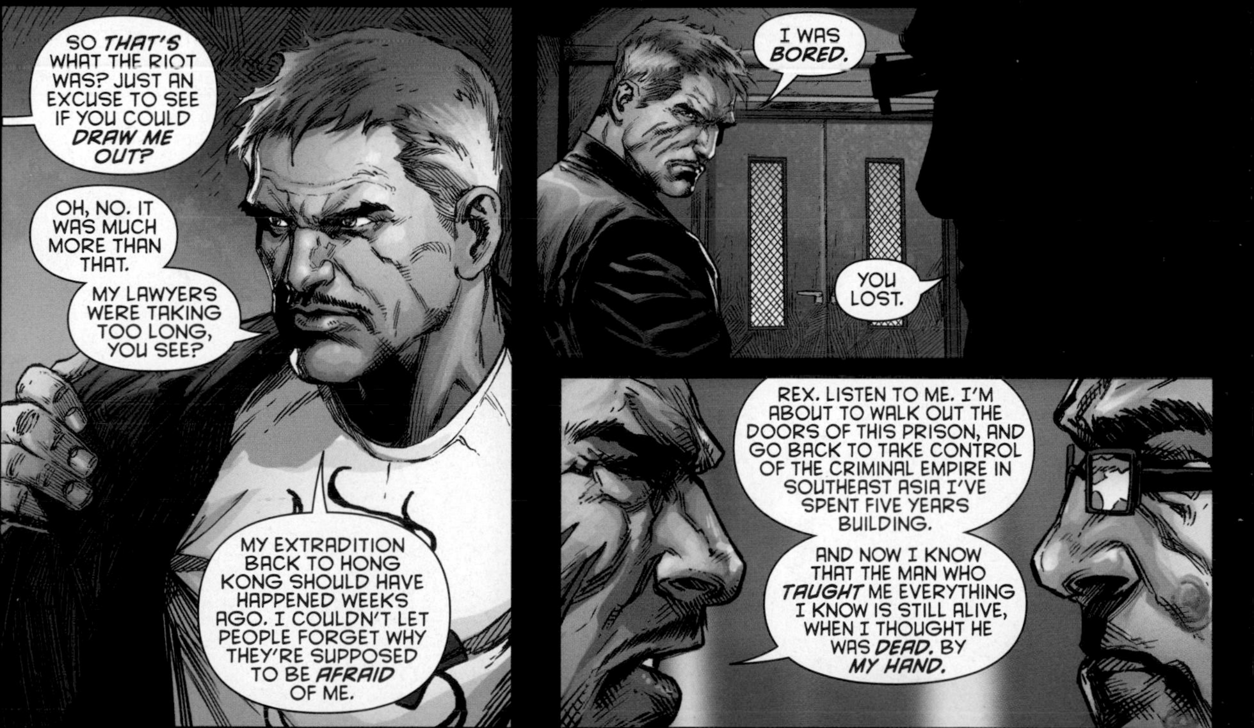
SO *THAT'S* WHAT THE RIOT WAS? JUST AN EXCUSE TO SEE IF YOU COULD *DRAW ME OUT?*
OH, NO. IT WAS MUCH MORE THAN THAT.
MY LAWYERS WERE TAKING TOO LONG, YOU SEE?
MY EXTRADITION BACK TO HONG KONG SHOULD HAVE HAPPENED WEEKS AGO. I COULDN'T LET PEOPLE FORGET WHY THEY'RE SUPPOSED TO BE *AFRAID* OF ME.
I WAS *BORED.*
YOU LOST.
REX. LISTEN TO ME. I'M ABOUT TO WALK OUT THE DOORS OF THIS PRISON, AND GO BACK TO TAKE CONTROL OF THE CRIMINAL EMPIRE IN SOUTHEAST ASIA I'VE SPENT FIVE YEARS BUILDING.
AND NOW I KNOW THAT THE MAN WHO *TAUGHT* ME EVERYTHING I KNOW IS STILL ALIVE, WHEN I THOUGHT HE WAS *DEAD.* BY *MY HAND.*

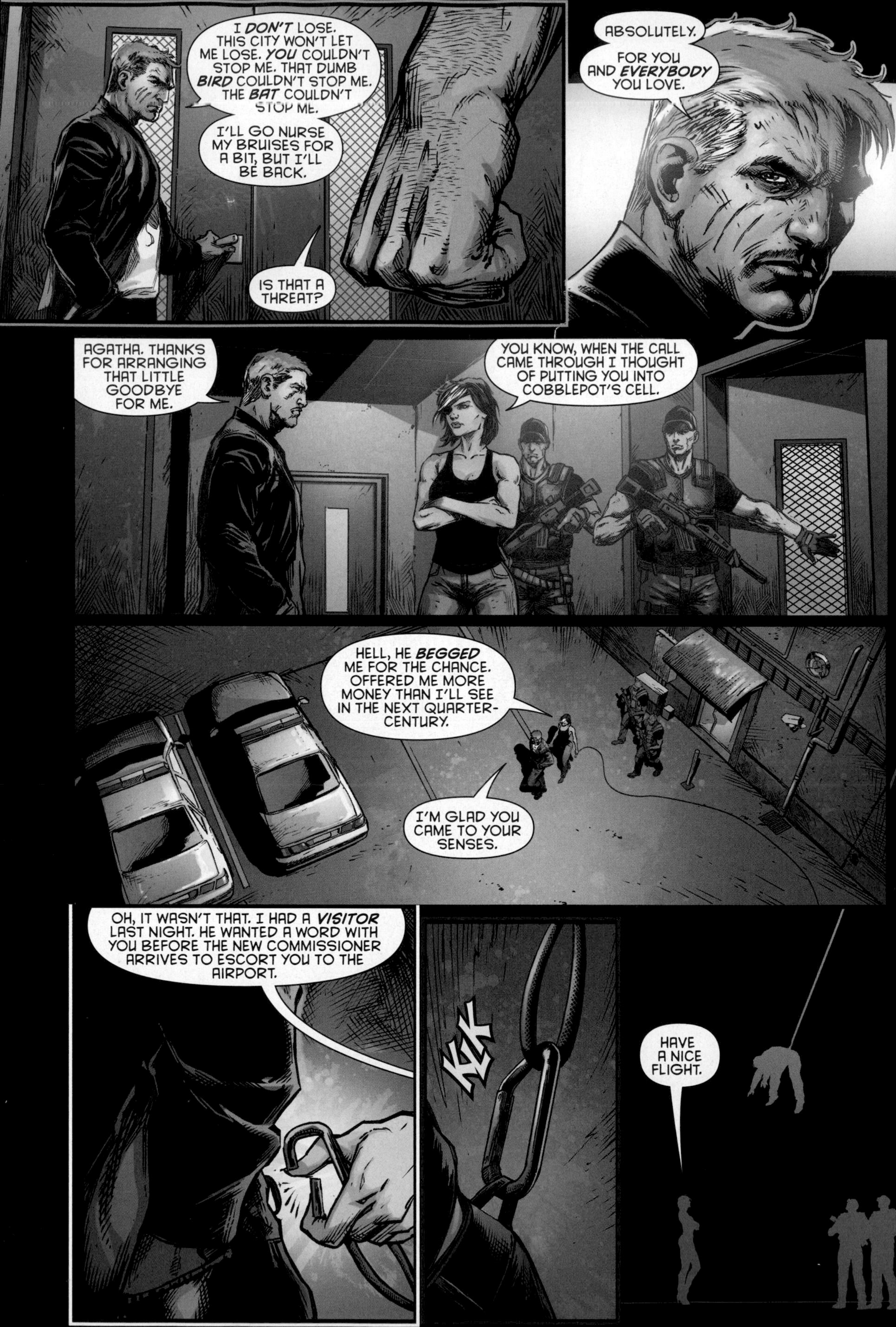
I DON'T LOSE. THIS CITY WON'T LET ME LOSE. YOU COULDN'T STOP ME. THAT DUMB BIRD COULDN'T STOP ME. THE BAT COULDN'T STOP ME.
I'LL GO NURSE MY BRUISES FOR A BIT, BUT I'LL BE BACK.
IS THAT A THREAT?
ABSOLUTELY.
FOR YOU AND EVERYBODY YOU LOVE.
AGATHA. THANKS FOR ARRANGING THAT LITTLE GOODBYE FOR ME.
YOU KNOW, WHEN THE CALL CAME THROUGH I THOUGHT OF PUTTING YOU INTO COBBLEPOT'S CELL.
HELL, HE BEGGED ME FOR THE CHANCE. OFFERED ME MORE MONEY THAN I'LL SEE IN THE NEXT QUARTER-CENTURY.
I'M GLAD YOU CAME TO YOUR SENSES.
OH, IT WASN'T THAT. I HAD A VISITOR LAST NIGHT. HE WANTED A WORD WITH YOU BEFORE THE NEW COMMISSIONER ARRIVES TO ESCORT YOU TO THE AIRPORT.
KLIK
HAVE A NICE FLIGHT.

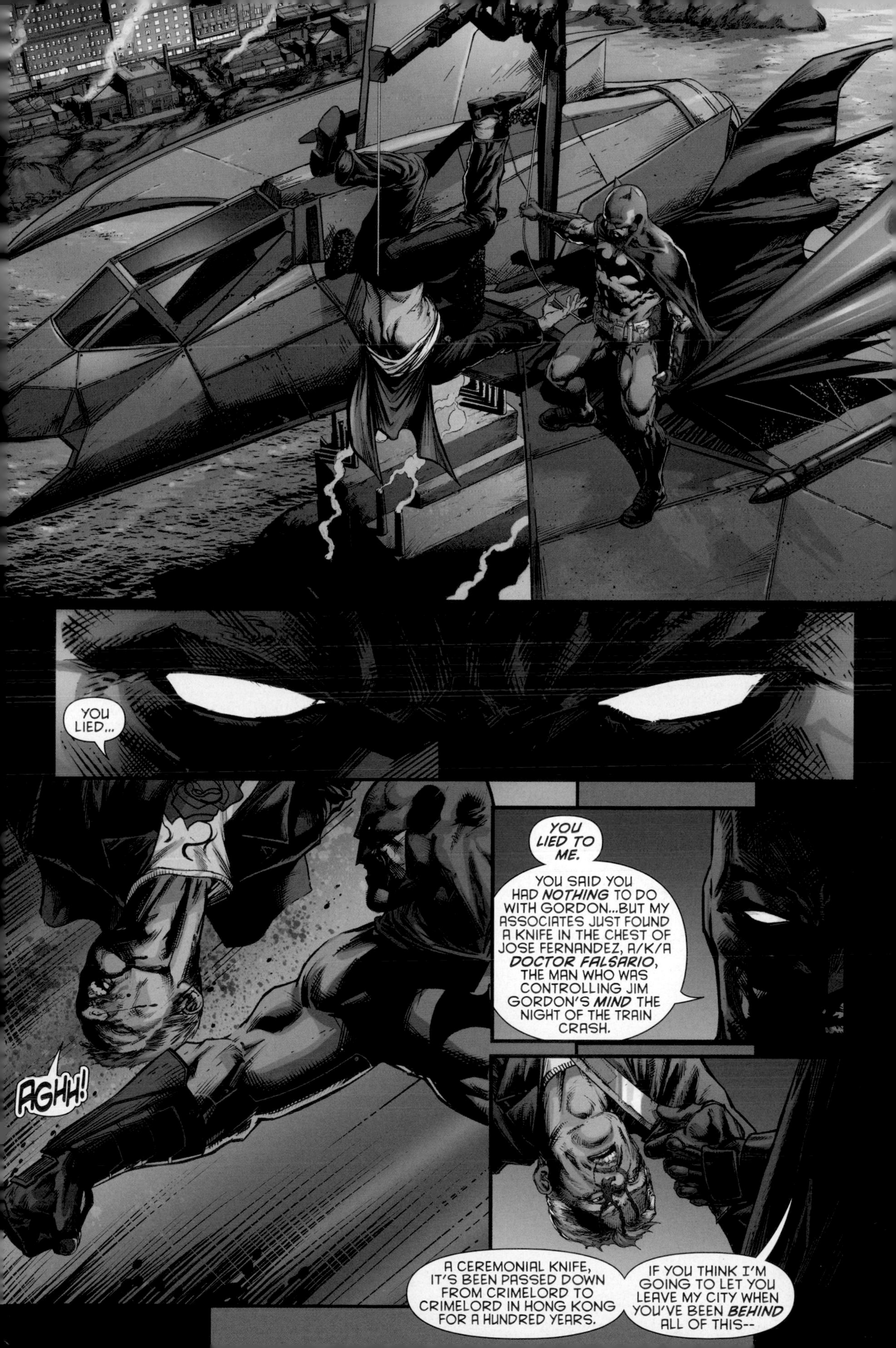
YOU LIED...
YOU LIED TO ME.
YOU SAID YOU HAD NOTHING TO DO WITH GORDON...BUT MY ASSOCIATES JUST FOUND A KNIFE IN THE CHEST OF JOSE FERNANDEZ, A/K/A DOCTOR FALSARIO, THE MAN WHO WAS CONTROLLING JIM GORDON'S MIND THE NIGHT OF THE TRAIN CRASH.
AGHH!
A CEREMONIAL KNIFE, IT'S BEEN PASSED DOWN FROM CRIMELORD TO CRIMELORD IN HONG KONG FOR A HUNDRED YEARS.
IF YOU THINK I'M GOING TO LET YOU LEAVE MY CITY WHEN YOU'VE BEEN BEHIND ALL OF THIS--

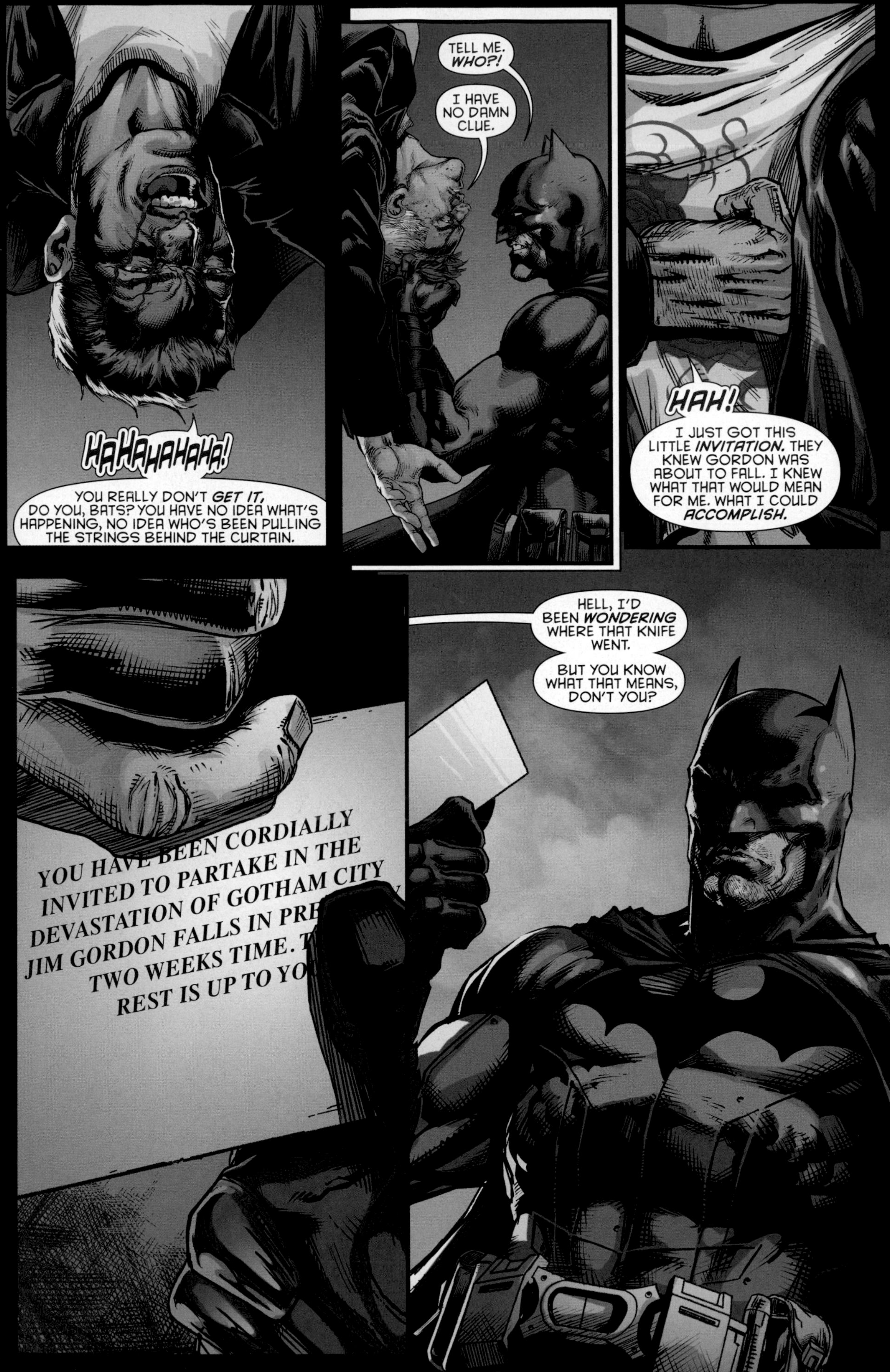
HAHAHAHAHAHA!
YOU REALLY DON'T GET IT, DO YOU, BATS? YOU HAVE NO IDEA WHAT'S HAPPENING, NO IDEA WHO'S BEEN PULLING THE STRINGS BEHIND THE CURTAIN.
TELL ME. WHO?!
I HAVE NO DAMN CLUE.
HAH!
I JUST GOT THIS LITTLE INVITATION. THEY KNEW GORDON WAS ABOUT TO FALL. I KNEW WHAT THAT WOULD MEAN FOR ME. WHAT I COULD ACCOMPLISH.
YOU HAVE BEEN CORDIALLY INVITED TO PARTAKE IN THE DEVASTATION OF GOTHAM CITY JIM GORDON FALLS IN PRE TWO WEEKS TIME. T REST IS UP TO YO
HELL, I'D BEEN WONDERING WHERE THAT KNIFE WENT.
BUT YOU KNOW WHAT THAT MEANS, DON'T YOU?

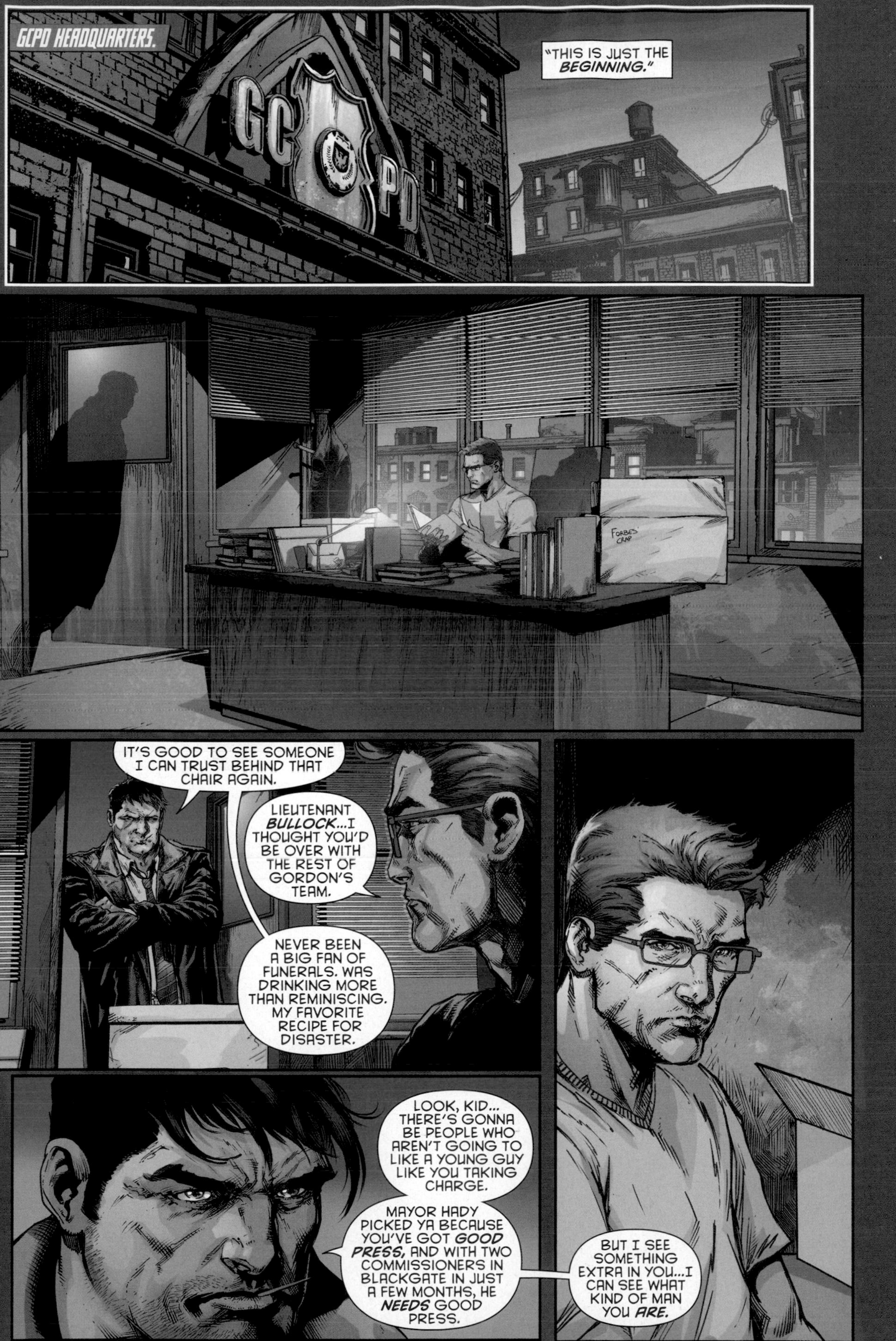
GCPD HEADQUARTERS.
"THIS IS JUST THE BEGINNING."
GC PD
FORBES' CRAP
IT'S GOOD TO SEE SOMEONE I CAN TRUST BEHIND THAT CHAIR AGAIN.
LIEUTENANT BULLOCK...I THOUGHT YOU'D BE OVER WITH THE REST OF GORDON'S TEAM.
NEVER BEEN A BIG FAN OF FUNERALS. WAS DRINKING MORE THAN REMINISCING. MY FAVORITE RECIPE FOR DISASTER.
LOOK, KID... THERE'S GONNA BE PEOPLE WHO AREN'T GOING TO LIKE A YOUNG GUY LIKE YOU TAKING CHARGE.
MAYOR HADY PICKED YA BECAUSE YOU'VE GOT GOOD PRESS, AND WITH TWO COMMISSIONERS IN BLACKGATE IN JUST A FEW MONTHS, HE NEEDS GOOD PRESS.
BUT I SEE SOMETHING EXTRA IN YOU...I CAN SEE WHAT KIND OF MAN YOU ARE.

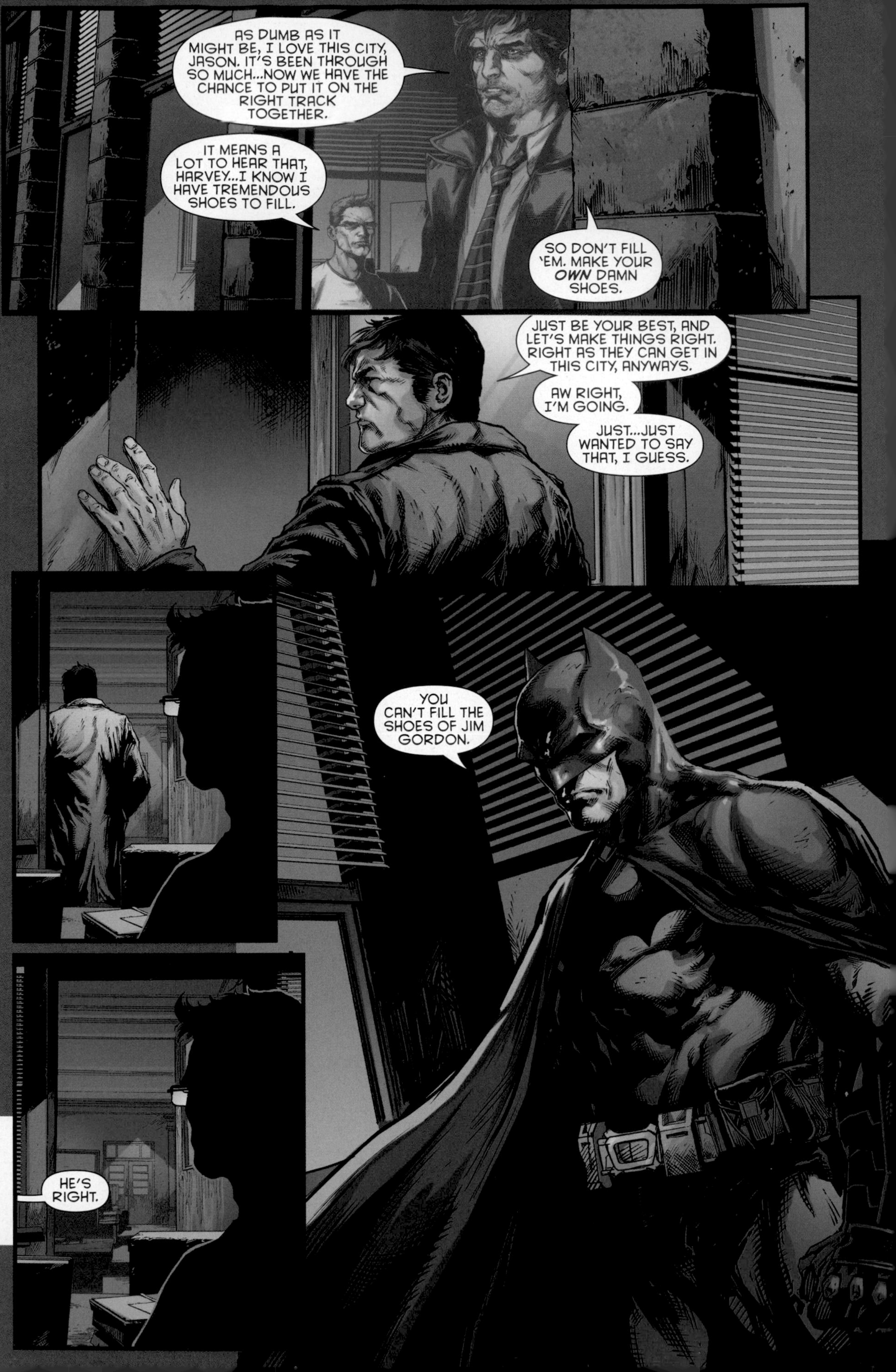
AS DUMB AS IT MIGHT BE, I LOVE THIS CITY, JASON. IT'S BEEN THROUGH SO MUCH...NOW WE HAVE THE CHANCE TO PUT IT ON THE RIGHT TRACK TOGETHER.
IT MEANS A LOT TO HEAR THAT, HARVEY...I KNOW I HAVE TREMENDOUS SHOES TO FILL.
SO DON'T FILL 'EM. MAKE YOUR OWN DAMN SHOES.
JUST BE YOUR BEST, AND LET'S MAKE THINGS RIGHT. RIGHT AS THEY CAN GET IN THIS CITY, ANYWAYS.
AW RIGHT, I'M GOING.
JUST...JUST WANTED TO SAY THAT, I GUESS.
YOU CAN'T FILL THE SHOES OF JIM GORDON.
HE'S RIGHT.

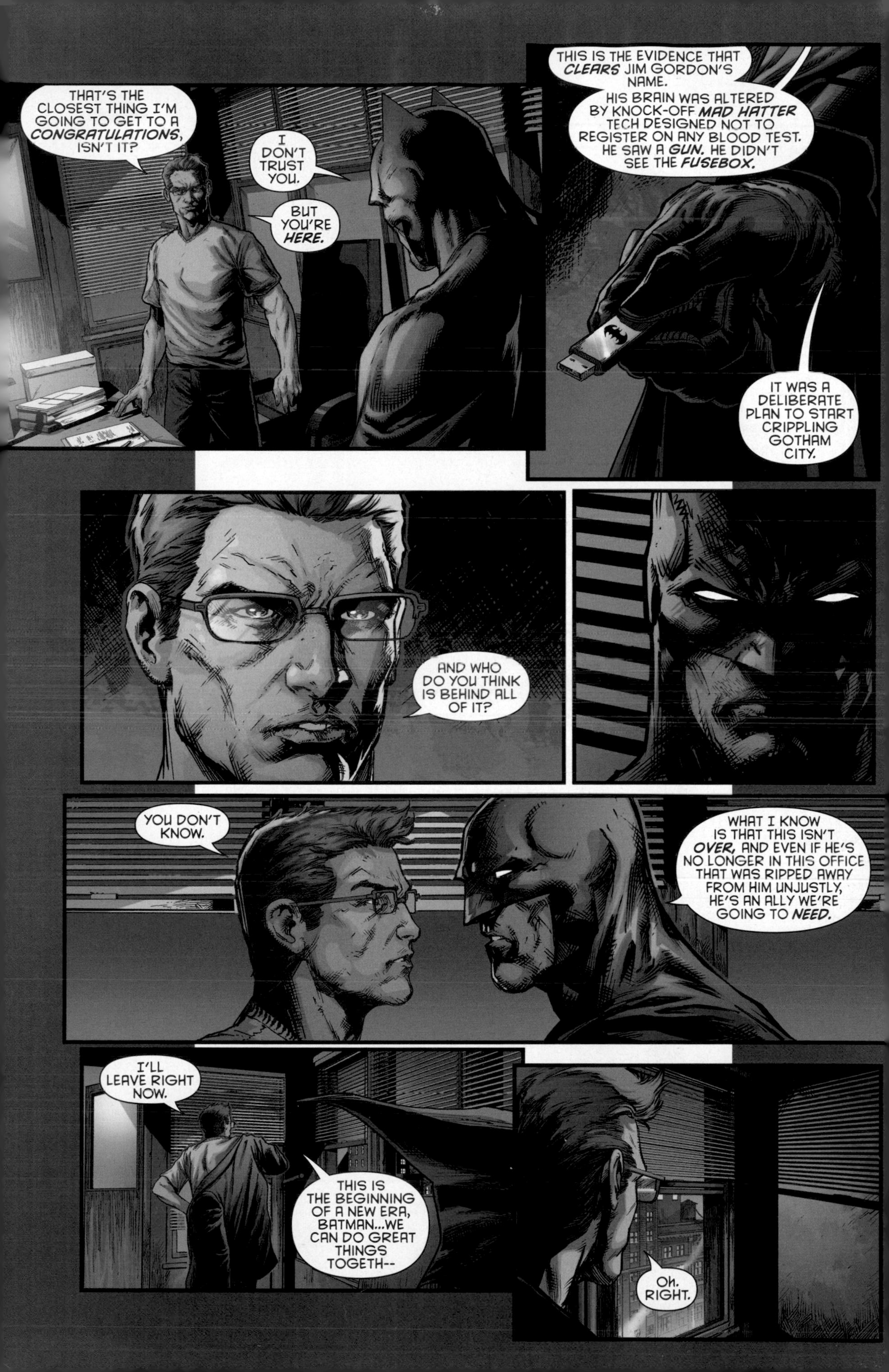
THAT'S THE CLOSEST THING I'M GOING TO GET TO A CONGRATULATIONS, ISN'T IT?
I DON'T TRUST YOU.
BUT YOU'RE HERE.
THIS IS THE EVIDENCE THAT CLEARS JIM GORDON'S NAME.
HIS BRAIN WAS ALTERED BY KNOCK-OFF MAD HATTER TECH DESIGNED NOT TO REGISTER ON ANY BLOOD TEST. HE SAW A GUN. HE DIDN'T SEE THE FUSEBOX.
IT WAS A DELIBERATE PLAN TO START CRIPPLING GOTHAM CITY.
AND WHO DO YOU THINK IS BEHIND ALL OF IT?
YOU DON'T KNOW.
WHAT I KNOW IS THAT THIS ISN'T OVER, AND EVEN IF HE'S NO LONGER IN THIS OFFICE THAT WAS RIPPED AWAY FROM HIM UNJUSTLY, HE'S AN ALLY WE'RE GOING TO NEED.
I'LL LEAVE RIGHT NOW.
THIS IS THE BEGINNING OF A NEW ERA, BATMAN...WE CAN DO GREAT THINGS TOGETH--
Oh. RIGHT.

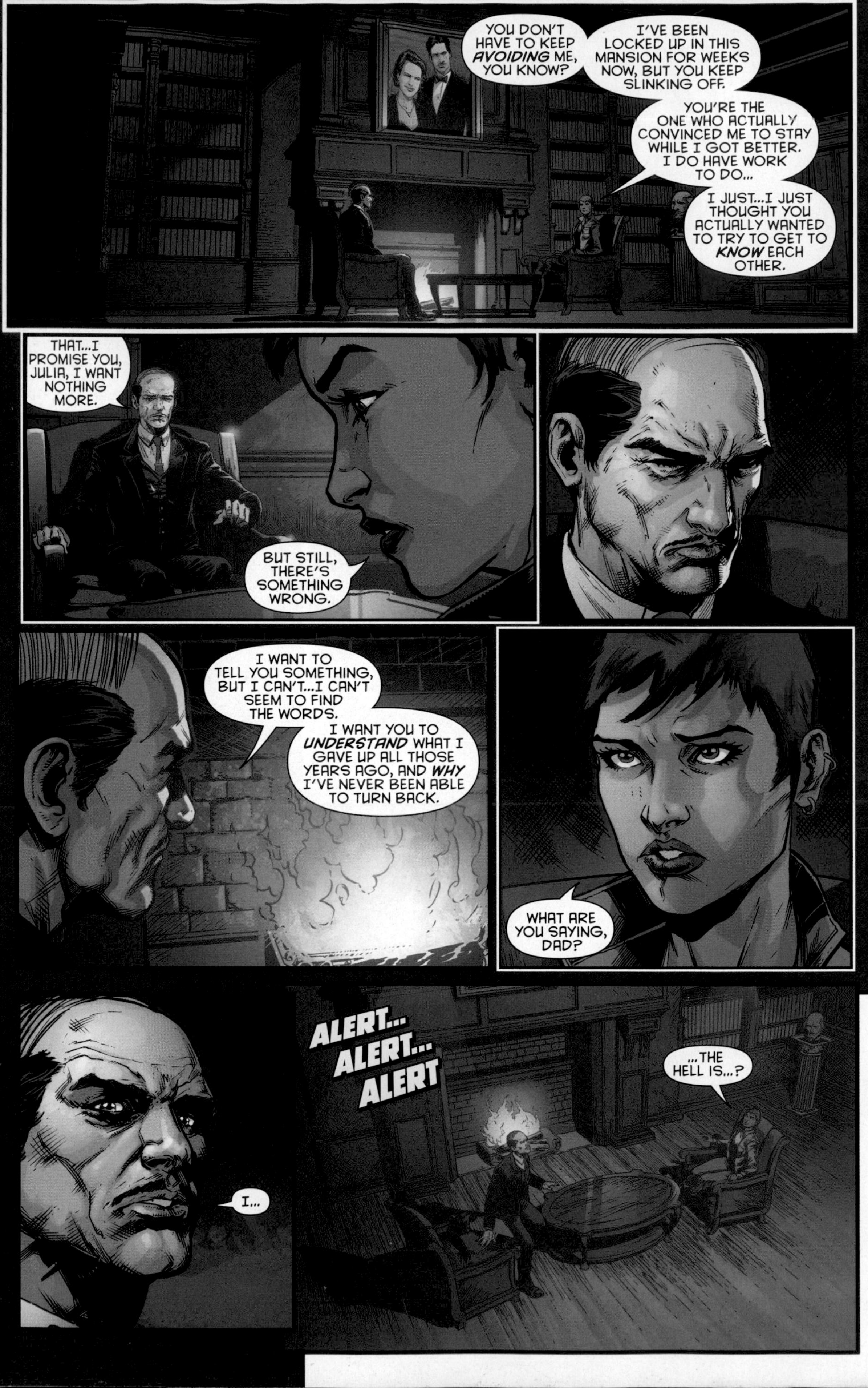
YOU DON'T HAVE TO KEEP AVOIDING ME, YOU KNOW?
I'VE BEEN LOCKED UP IN THIS MANSION FOR WEEKS NOW, BUT YOU KEEP SLINKING OFF.
YOU'RE THE ONE WHO ACTUALLY CONVINCED ME TO STAY WHILE I GOT BETTER. I DO HAVE WORK TO DO...
I JUST...I JUST THOUGHT YOU ACTUALLY WANTED TO TRY TO GET TO KNOW EACH OTHER.
THAT...I PROMISE YOU, JULIA, I WANT NOTHING MORE.
BUT STILL, THERE'S SOMETHING WRONG.
I WANT TO TELL YOU SOMETHING, BUT I CAN'T...I CAN'T SEEM TO FIND THE WORDS.
I WANT YOU TO UNDERSTAND WHAT I GAVE UP ALL THOSE YEARS AGO, AND WHY I'VE NEVER BEEN ABLE TO TURN BACK.
WHAT ARE YOU SAYING, DAD?
I...
ALERT... ALERT... ALERT
...THE HELL IS...?

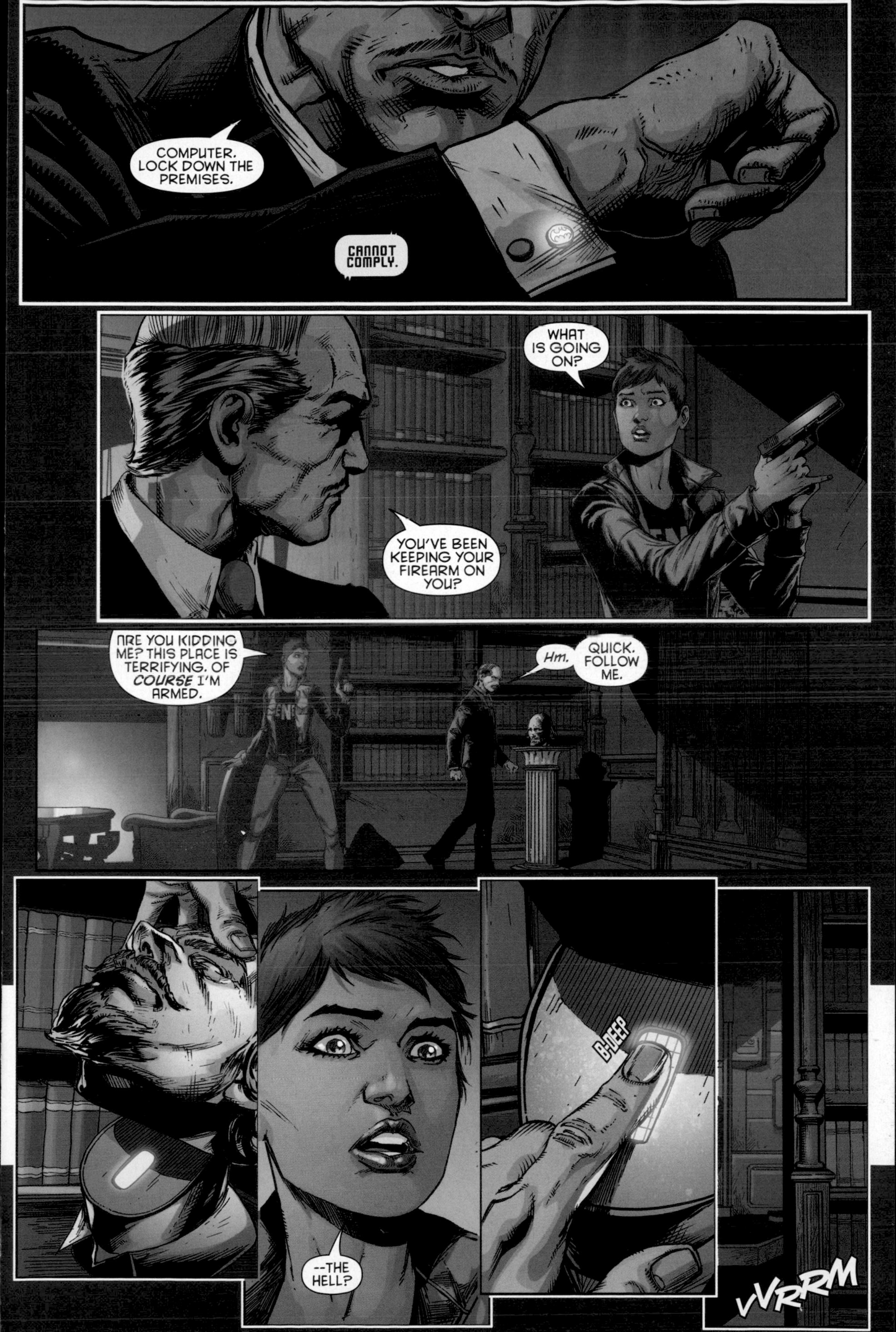
COMPUTER. LOCK DOWN THE PREMISES.
CANNOT COMPLY.
WHAT IS GOING ON?
YOU'VE BEEN KEEPING YOUR FIREARM ON YOU?
ARE YOU KIDDING ME? THIS PLACE IS TERRIFYING. OF *COURSE* I'M ARMED.
Hm.
QUICK. FOLLOW ME.
--THE HELL?
B-DEEP
VVRRRM

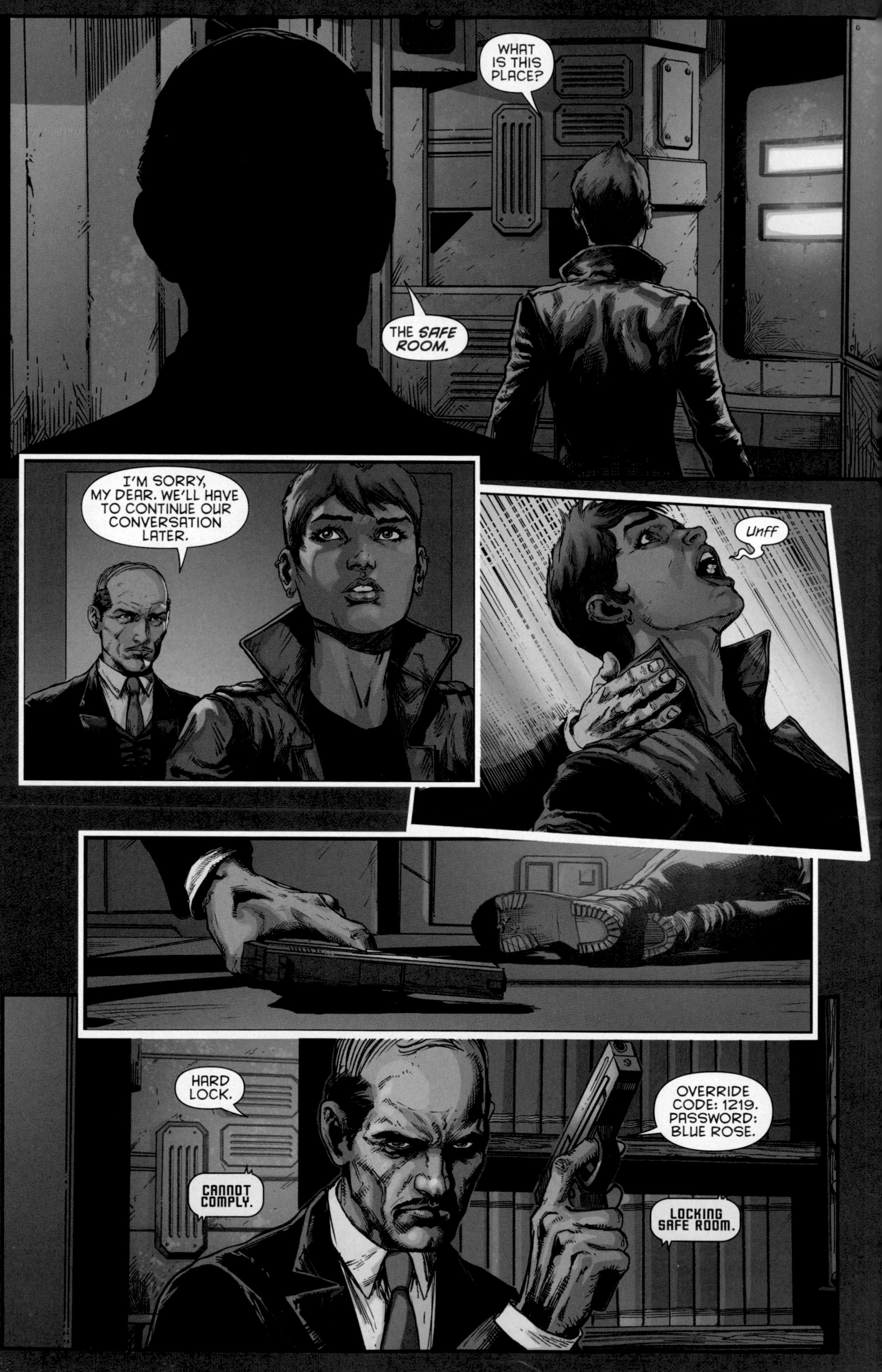
WHAT IS THIS PLACE?
THE SAFE ROOM.
I'M SORRY, MY DEAR. WE'LL HAVE TO CONTINUE OUR CONVERSATION LATER.
Unff
HARD LOCK.
CANNOT COMPLY.
OVERRIDE CODE: 1219. PASSWORD: BLUE ROSE.
LOCKING SAFE ROOM.

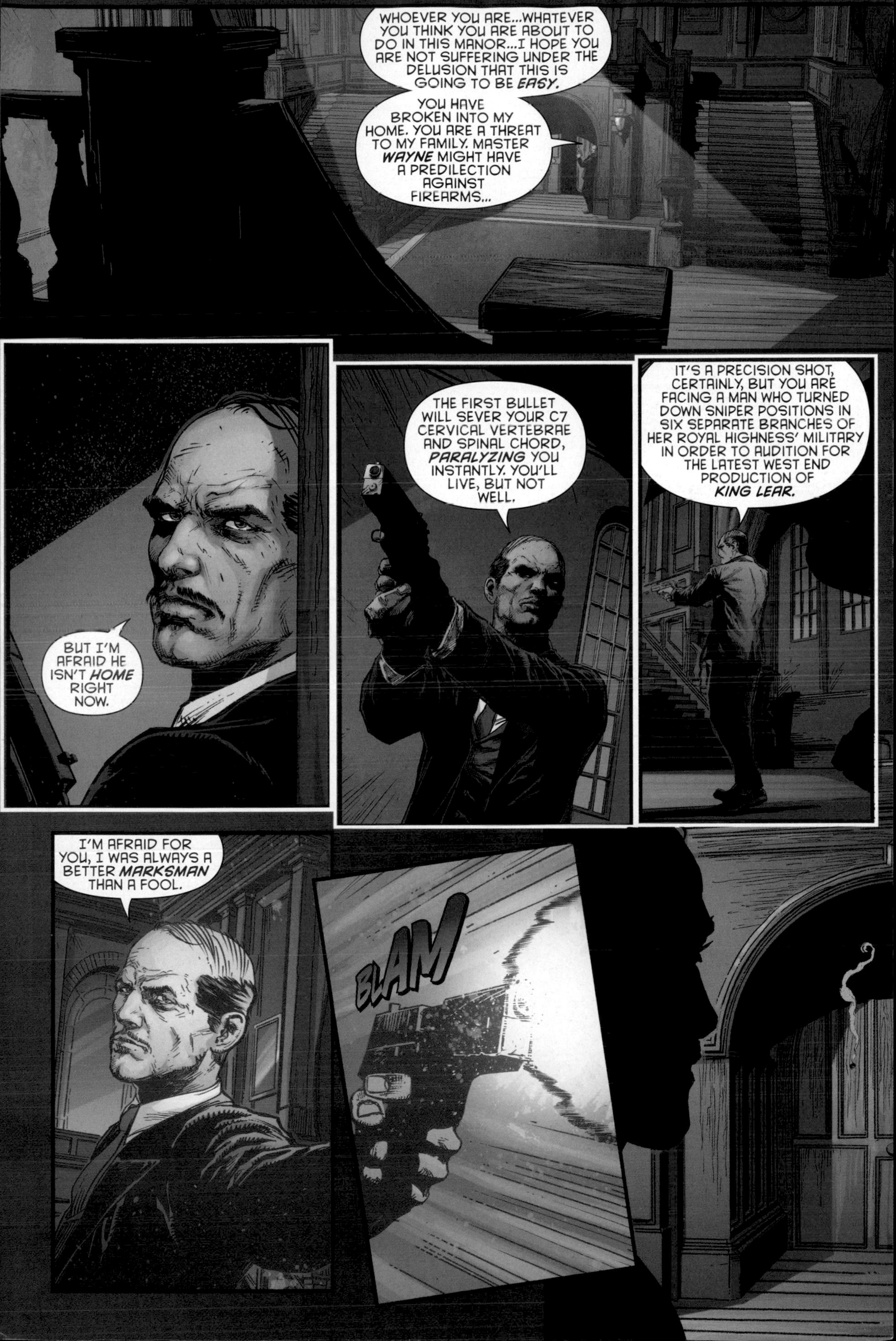
WHOEVER YOU ARE...WHATEVER YOU THINK YOU ARE ABOUT TO DO IN THIS MANOR...I HOPE YOU ARE NOT SUFFERING UNDER THE DELUSION THAT THIS IS GOING TO BE EASY.
YOU HAVE BROKEN INTO MY HOME. YOU ARE A THREAT TO MY FAMILY. MASTER WAYNE MIGHT HAVE A PREDILECTION AGAINST FIREARMS...
BUT I'M AFRAID HE ISN'T HOME RIGHT NOW.
THE FIRST BULLET WILL SEVER YOUR C7 CERVICAL VERTEBRAE AND SPINAL CHORD, PARALYZING YOU INSTANTLY. YOU'LL LIVE, BUT NOT WELL.
IT'S A PRECISION SHOT, CERTAINLY, BUT YOU ARE FACING A MAN WHO TURNED DOWN SNIPER POSITIONS IN SIX SEPARATE BRANCHES OF HER ROYAL HIGHNESS' MILITARY IN ORDER TO AUDITION FOR THE LATEST WEST END PRODUCTION OF KING LEAR.
I'M AFRAID FOR YOU, I WAS ALWAYS A BETTER MARKSMAN THAN A FOOL.
BLAM

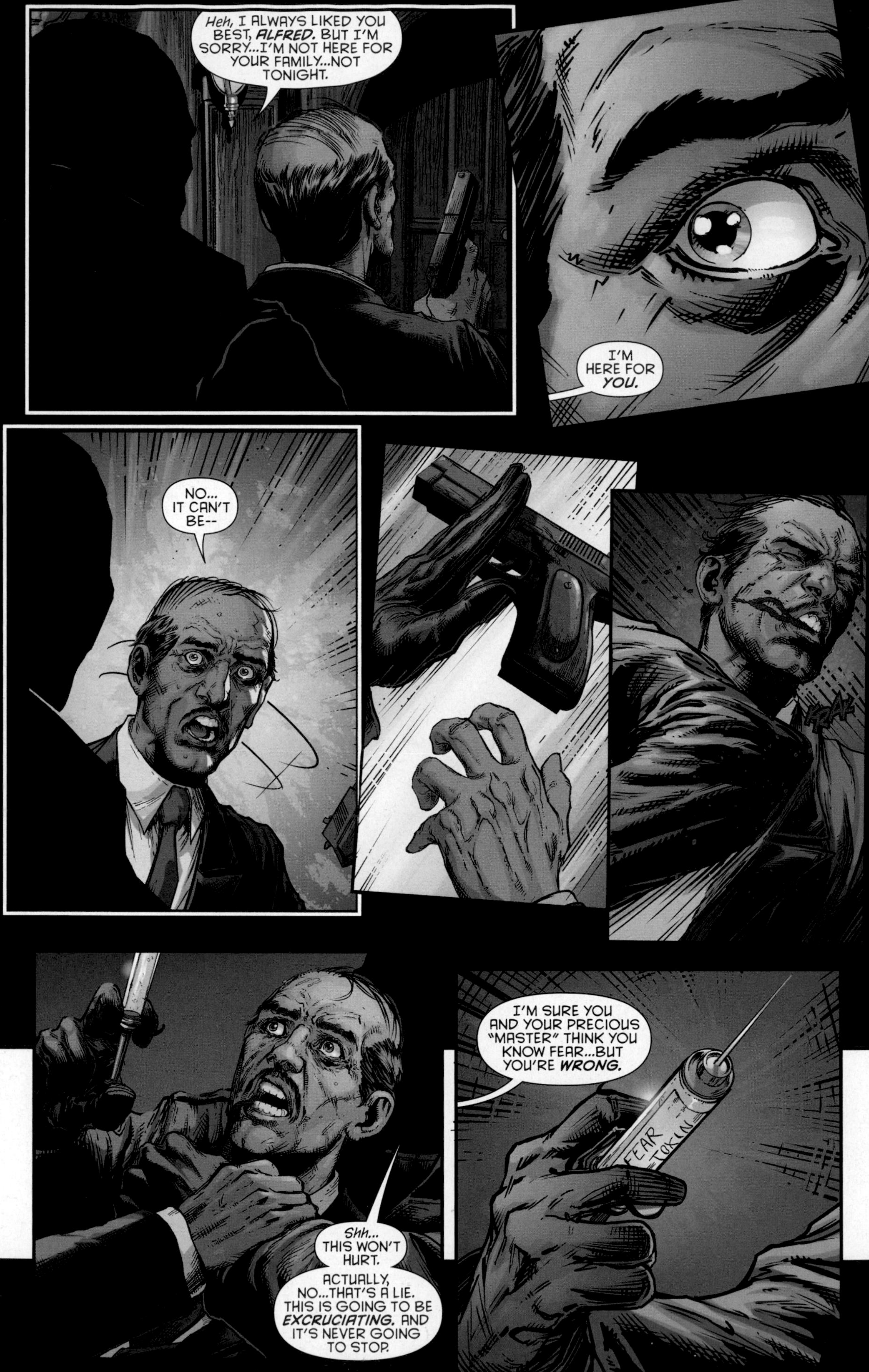
Heh, I ALWAYS LIKED YOU BEST, ALFRED. BUT I'M SORRY...I'M NOT HERE FOR YOUR FAMILY...NOT TONIGHT.
I'M HERE FOR YOU.
NO... IT CAN'T BE--
Shh... THIS WON'T HURT.
ACTUALLY, NO...THAT'S A LIE. THIS IS GOING TO BE EXCRUCIATING. AND IT'S NEVER GOING TO STOP.
I'M SURE YOU AND YOUR PRECIOUS "MASTER" THINK YOU KNOW FEAR...BUT YOU'RE WRONG.
FEAR TOXIN

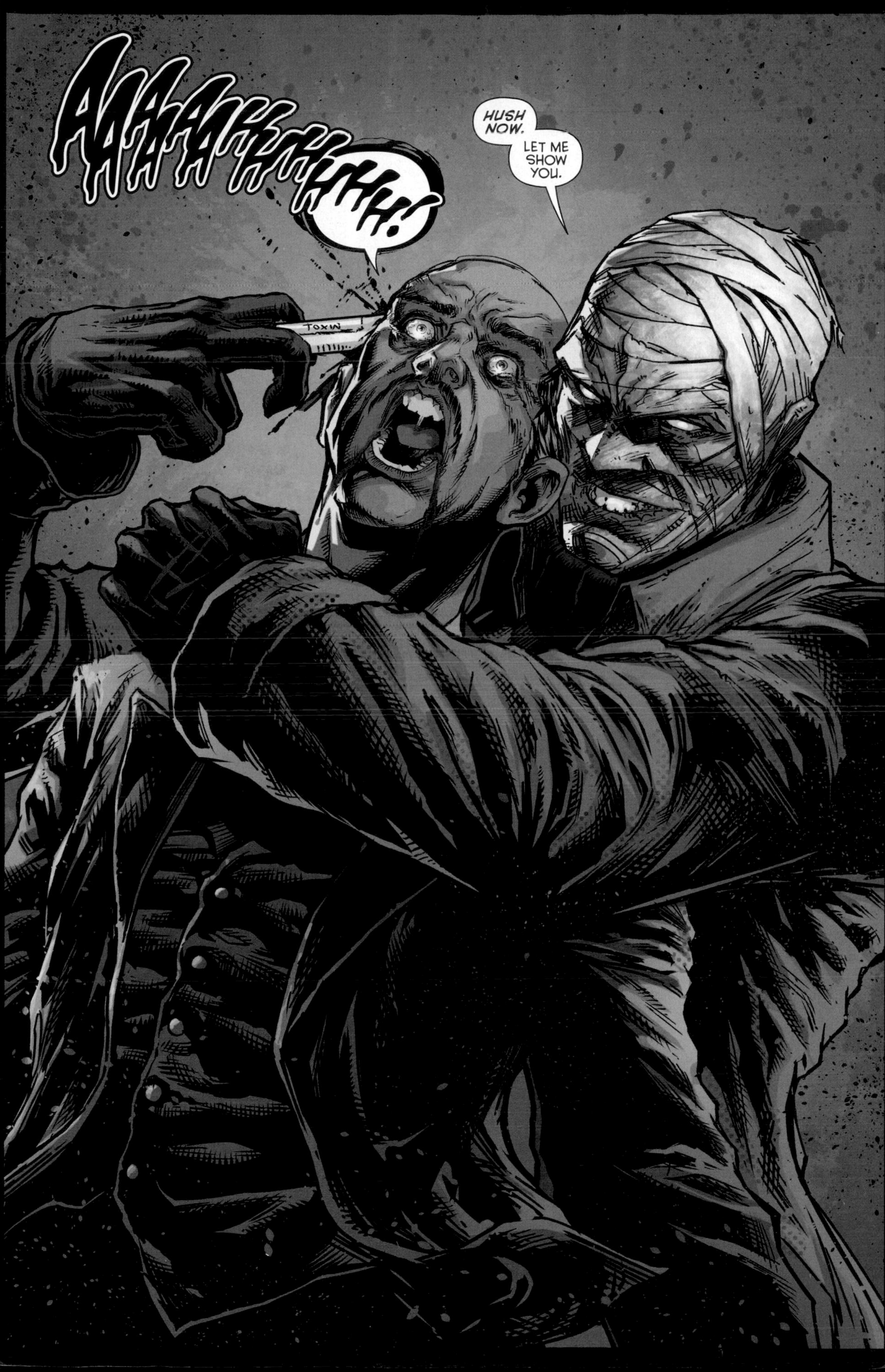
AAAAAAKKHHHH!
HUSH NOW.
LET ME SHOW YOU.
TOXIN

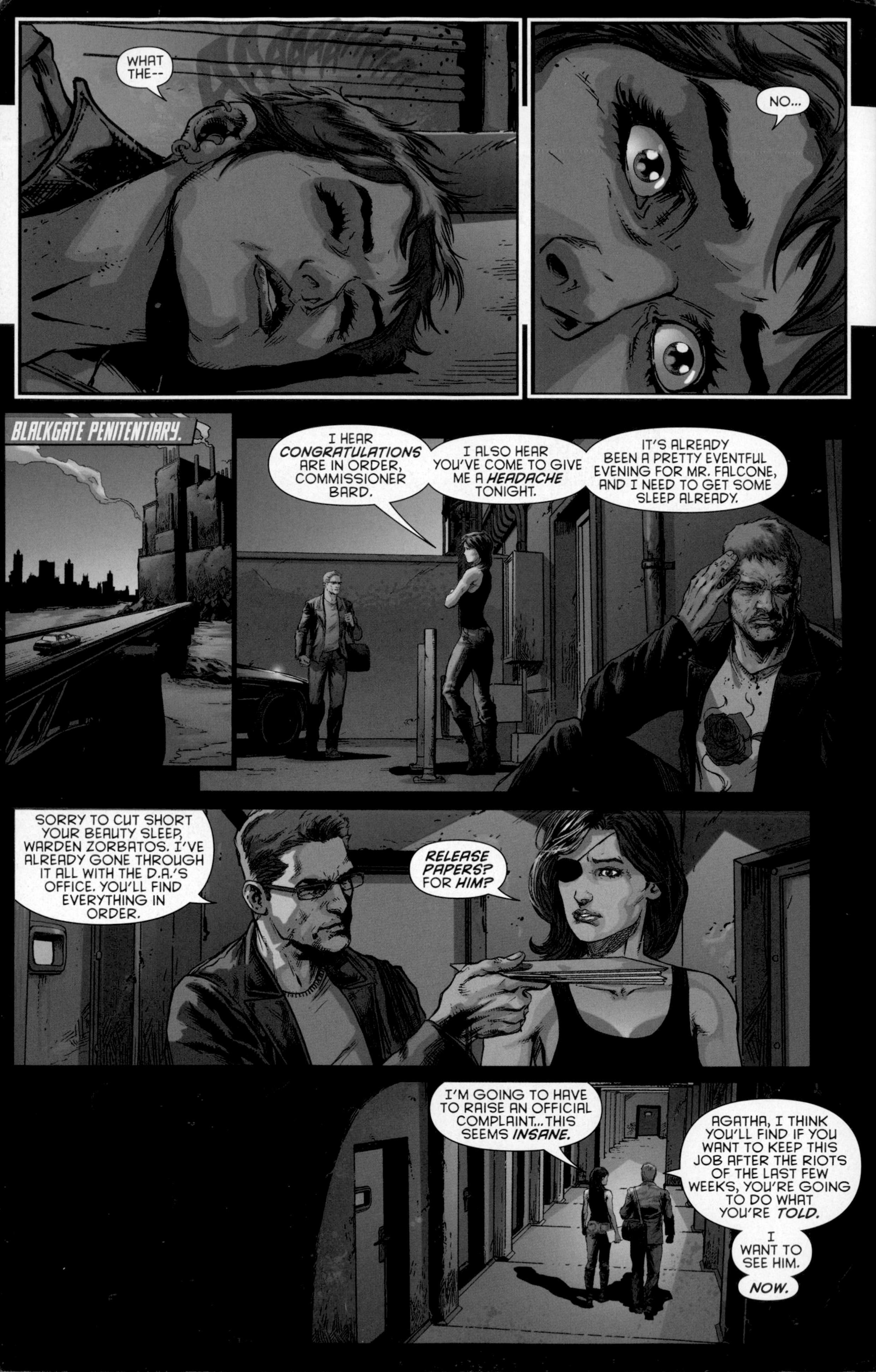
WHAT THE--
NO...
BLACKGATE PENITENTIARY.
I HEAR CONGRATULATIONS ARE IN ORDER, COMMISSIONER BARD.
I ALSO HEAR YOU'VE COME TO GIVE ME A HEADACHE TONIGHT.
IT'S ALREADY BEEN A PRETTY EVENTFUL EVENING FOR MR. FALCONE, AND I NEED TO GET SOME SLEEP ALREADY.
SORRY TO CUT SHORT YOUR BEAUTY SLEEP, WARDEN ZORBATOS. I'VE ALREADY GONE THROUGH IT ALL WITH THE D.A.'S OFFICE. YOU'LL FIND EVERYTHING IN ORDER.
RELEASE PAPERS? FOR HIM?
I'M GOING TO HAVE TO RAISE AN OFFICIAL COMPLAINT... THIS SEEMS INSANE.
AGATHA, I THINK YOU'LL FIND IF YOU WANT TO KEEP THIS JOB AFTER THE RIOTS OF THE LAST FEW WEEKS, YOU'RE GOING TO DO WHAT YOU'RE TOLD.
I WANT TO SEE HIM.
NOW.

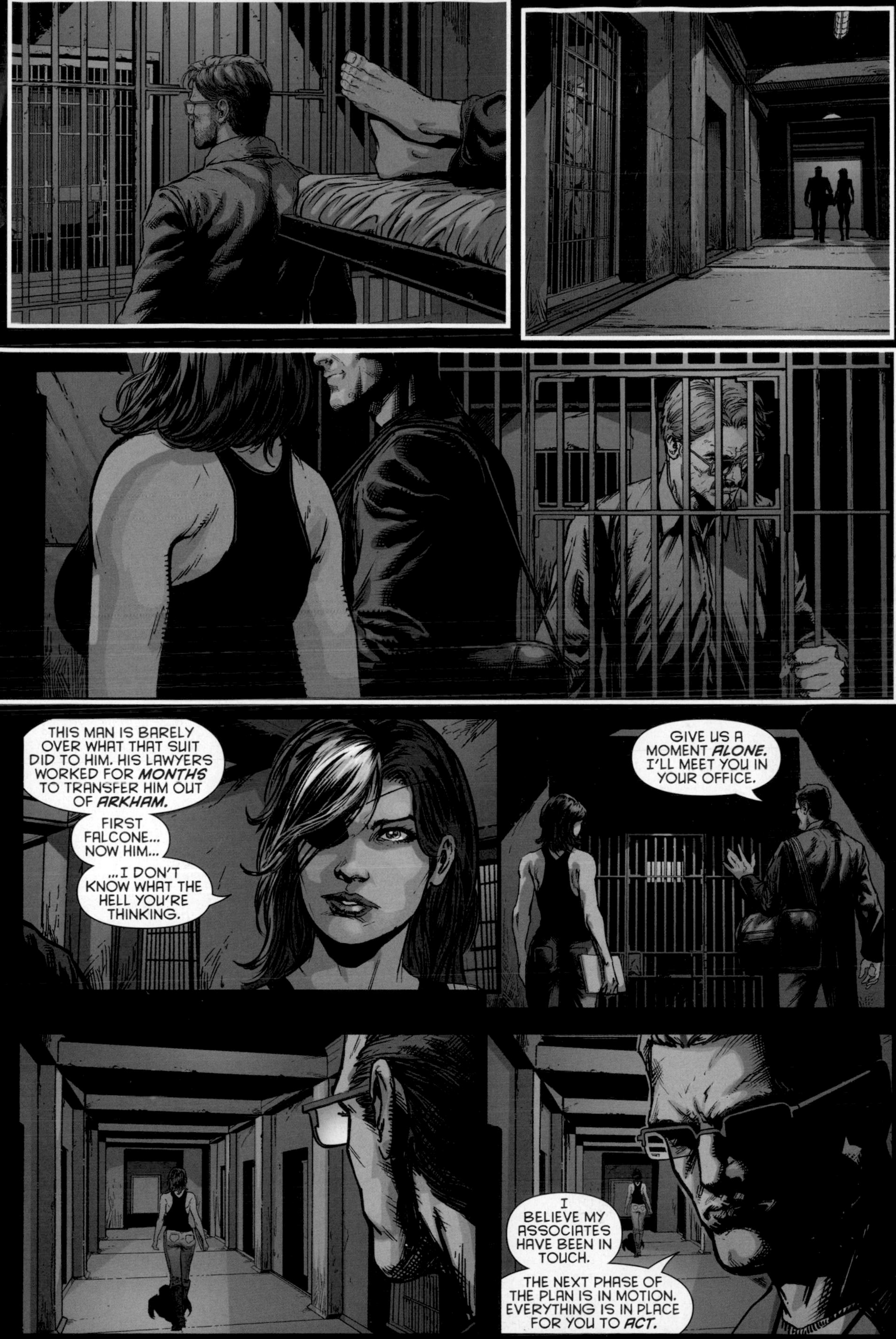

THIS MAN IS BARELY OVER WHAT THAT SUIT DID TO HIM. HIS LAWYERS WORKED FOR MONTHS TO TRANSFER HIM OUT OF ARKHAM.
FIRST FALCONE... NOW HIM...
...I DON'T KNOW WHAT THE HELL YOU'RE THINKING.
GIVE US A MOMENT ALONE. I'LL MEET YOU IN YOUR OFFICE.
I BELIEVE MY ASSOCIATES HAVE BEEN IN TOUCH.
THE NEXT PHASE OF THE PLAN IS IN MOTION. EVERYTHING IS IN PLACE FOR YOU TO ACT.

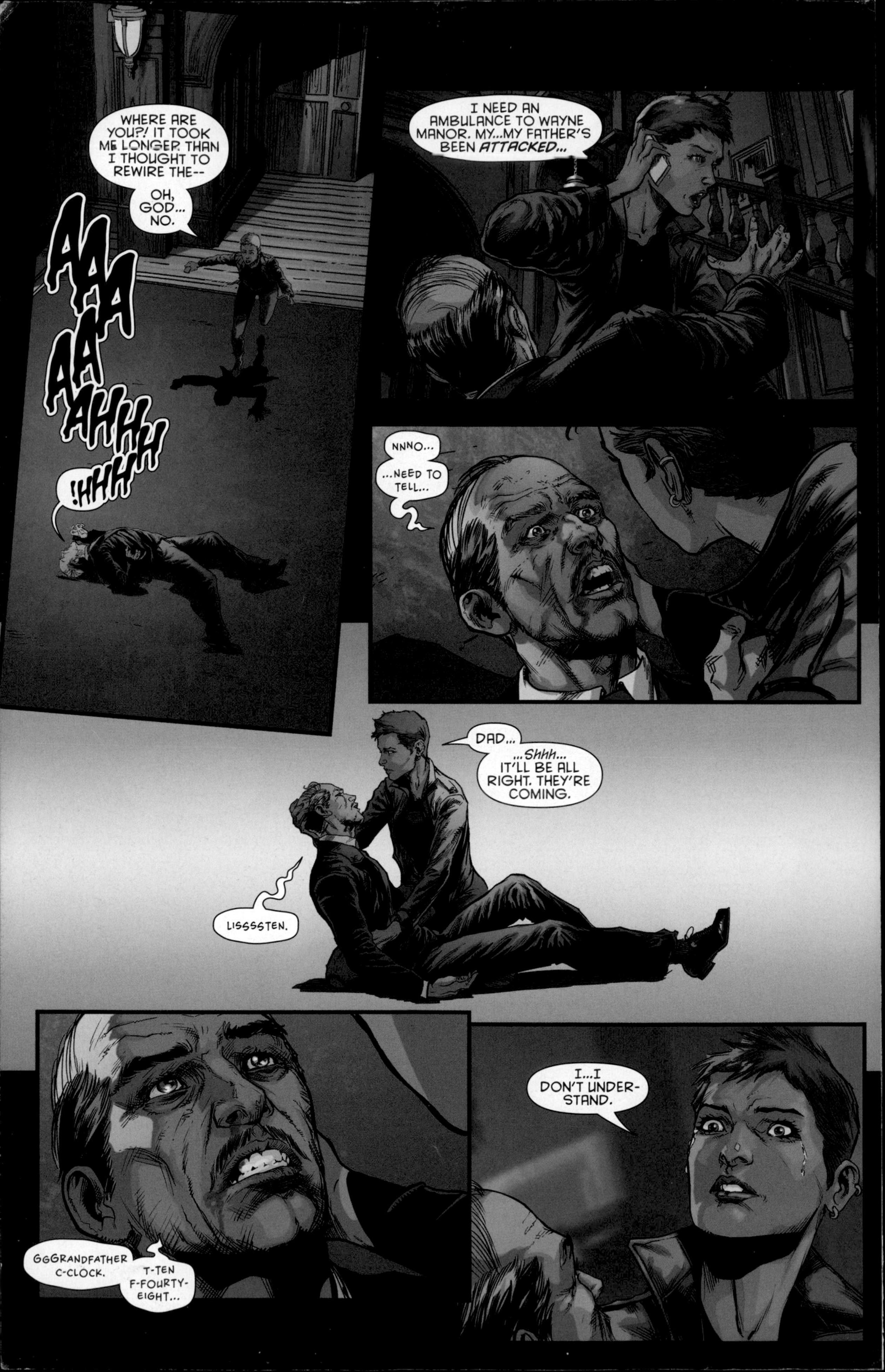
WHERE ARE YOU?! IT TOOK ME LONGER THAN I THOUGHT TO REWIRE THE--
OH, GOD... NO.
AAAAAAAHHHHHH!
I NEED AN AMBULANCE TO WAYNE MANOR. MY...MY FATHER'S BEEN ATTACKED...
NNNO...
...NEED TO TELL...
DAD...
...Shhh... IT'LL BE ALL RIGHT. THEY'RE COMING.
LISSSSTEN.
GGGRANDFATHER C-CLOCK.
T-TEN F-FOURTY-EIGHT...
I...I DON'T UNDER-STAND.

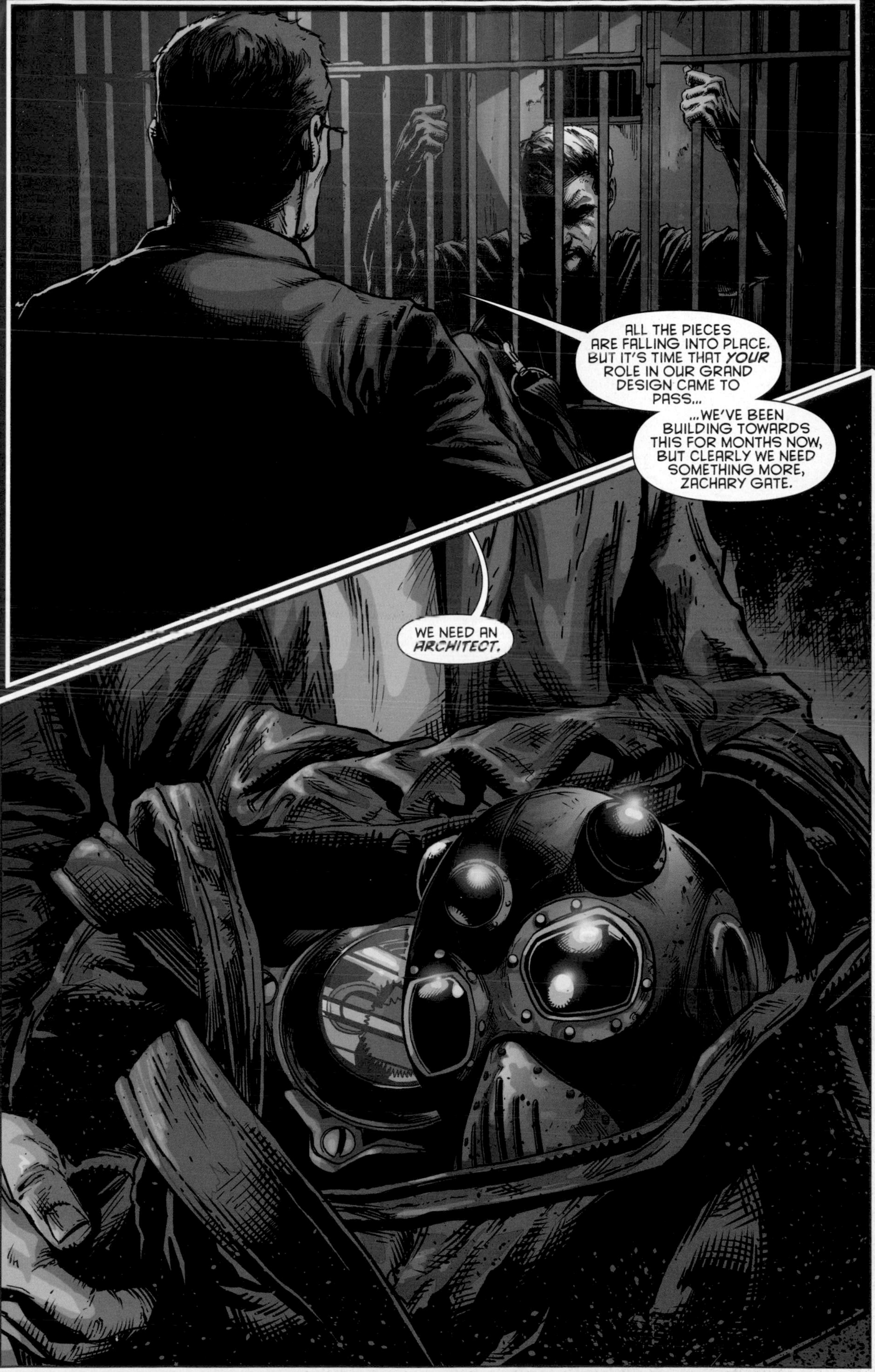
ALL THE PIECES ARE FALLING INTO PLACE. BUT IT'S TIME THAT YOUR ROLE IN OUR GRAND DESIGN CAME TO PASS...
...WE'VE BEEN BUILDING TOWARDS THIS FOR MONTHS NOW, BUT CLEARLY WE NEED SOMETHING MORE, ZACHARY GATE.
WE NEED AN ARCHITECT.

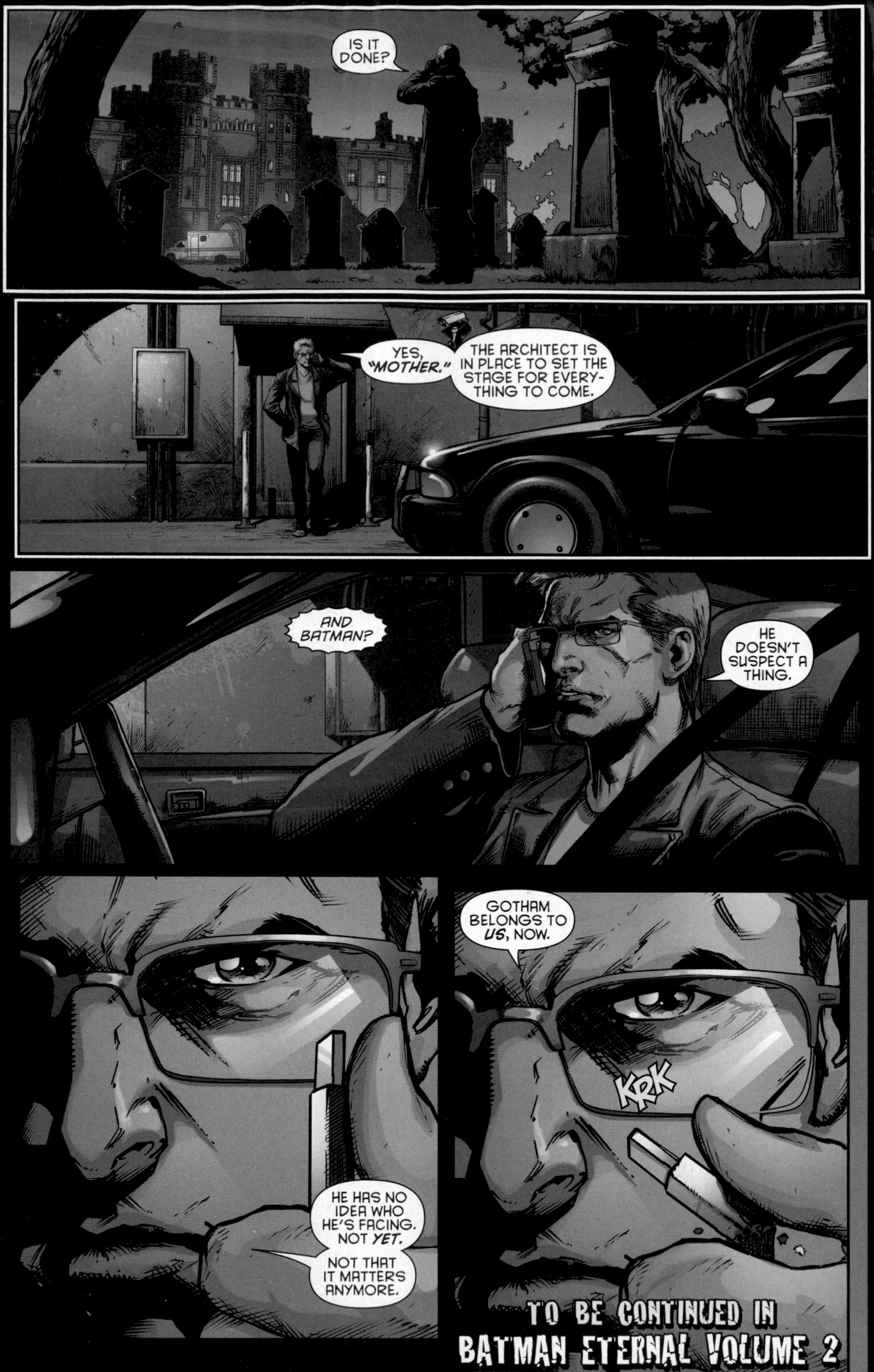
IS IT DONE?
YES, "MOTHER."
THE ARCHITECT IS IN PLACE TO SET THE STAGE FOR EVERYTHING TO COME.
AND BATMAN?
HE DOESN'T SUSPECT A THING.
HE HAS NO IDEA WHO HE'S FACING. NOT YET.
NOT THAT IT MATTERS ANYMORE.
GOTHAM BELONGS TO US, NOW.
KRK
TO BE CONTINUED IN BATMAN ETERNAL VOLUME 2

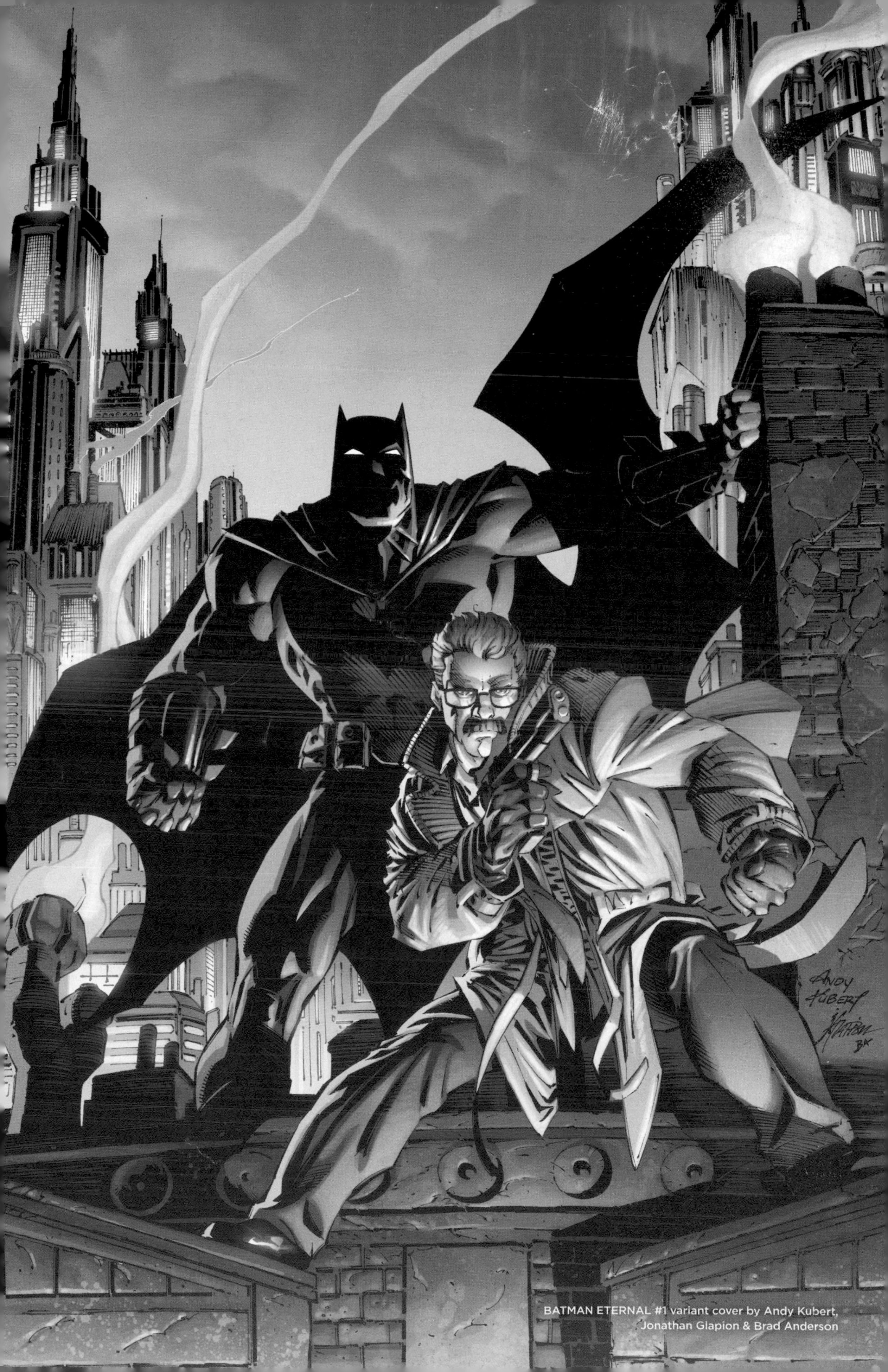
ANDY KUBERT
BATMAN ETERNAL #1 variant cover by Andy Kubert,
Jonathan Glapion & Brad Anderson

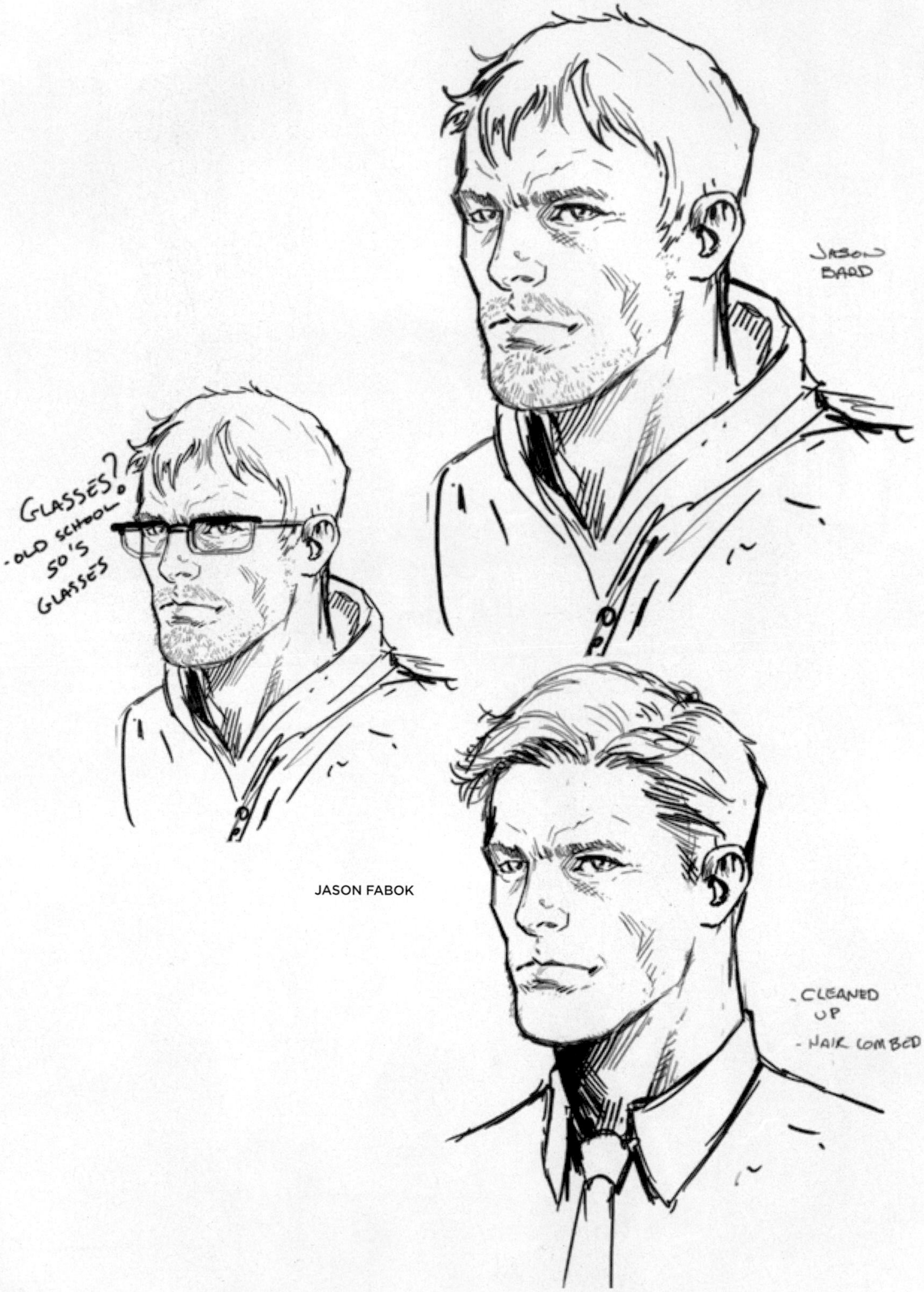
JASON BARD
GLASSES?
-OLD SCHOOL 50'S GLASSES
-CLEANED UP
-HAIR COMBED

JASON FABOK

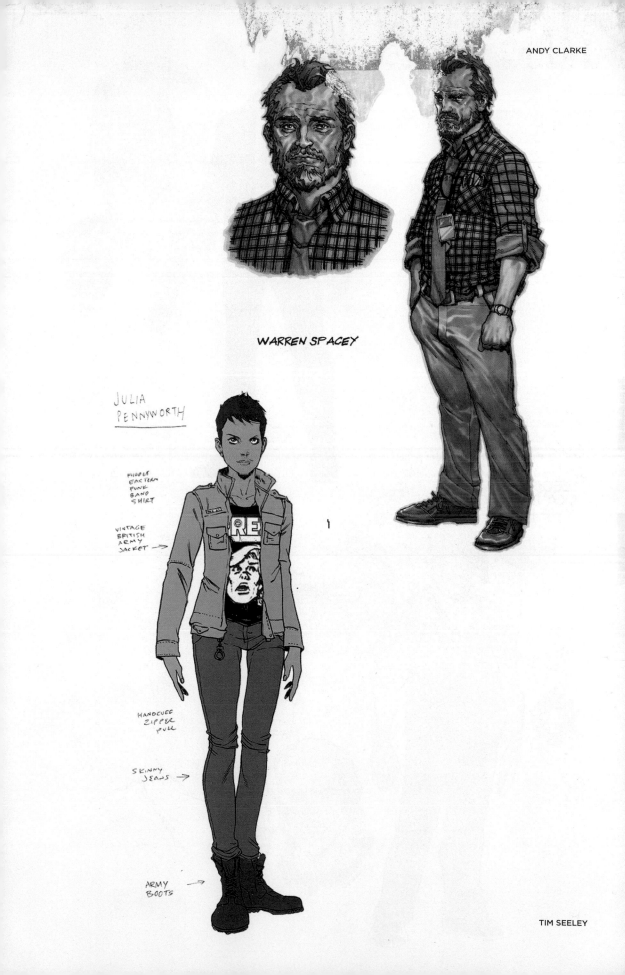

ANDY CLARKE

WARREN SPACEY

JULIA
PENNYWORTH

MIDDLE
EASTERN
PUNK
BAND
SHIRT

VINTAGE
BRITISH
ARMY
JACKET →

HANDCUFF
ZIPPER
PULL

SKINNY
JEANS →

ARMY
BOOTS →

TIM SEELEY

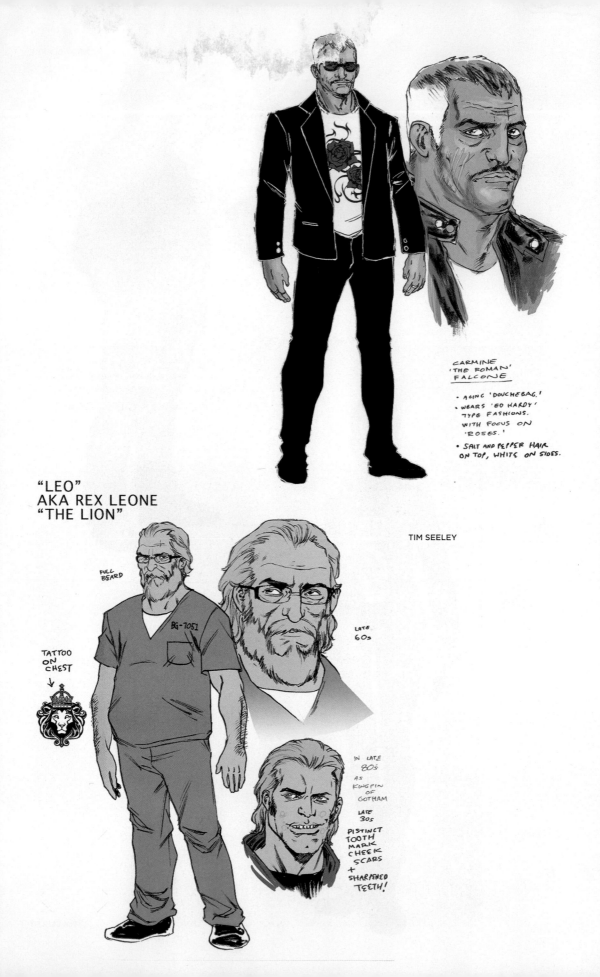

CARMINE
'THE ROMAN'
FALCONE

• AGING 'DOUCHEBAG.'
• WEARS 'ED HARDY'
  TYPE FASHIONS.
  WITH FOCUS ON
  'ROSES.'
• SALT AND PEPPER HAIR
  ON TOP, WHITE ON SIDES.

"LEO"
AKA REX LEONE
"THE LION"

TIM SEELEY

FULL BEARD

BG-7051

LATE 60s

TATTOO ON CHEST

IN LATE 80's AS KINGPIN OF GOTHAM

LATE 30s

DISTINCT TOOTH MARK CHEEK SCARS + SHARPENED TEETH!

TIM SEELEY

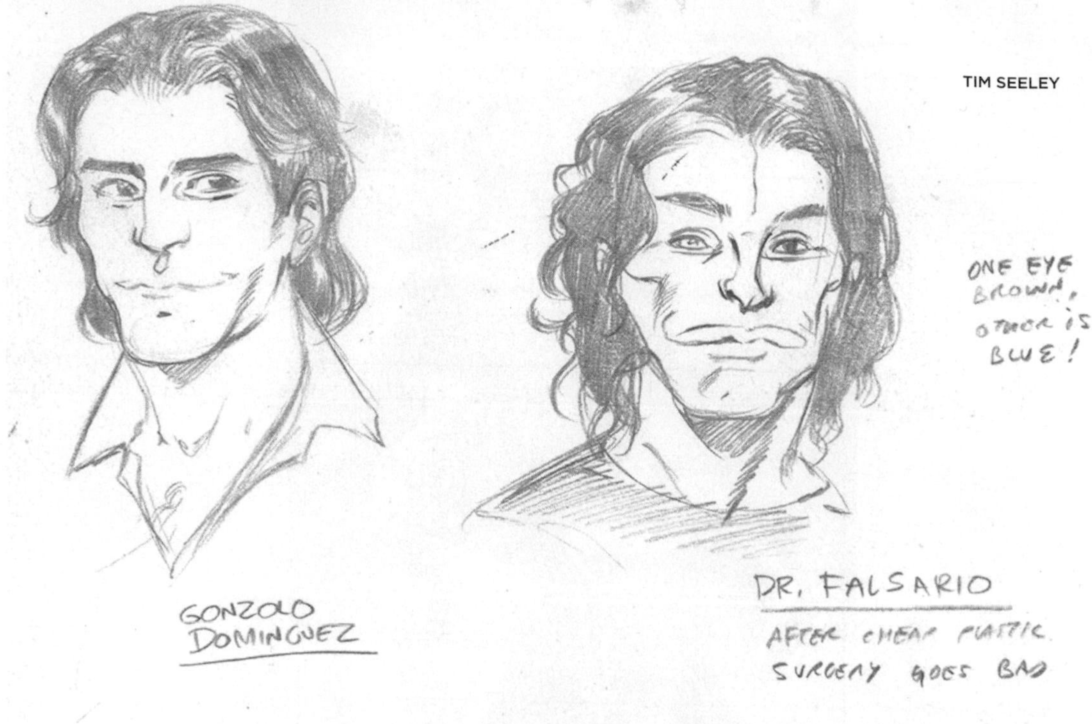
ONE EYE BROWN, OTHER IS BLUE!
GONZOLO DOMINGUEZ
DR. FALSARIO
AFTER CHEAP PLASTIC SURGERY GOES BAD

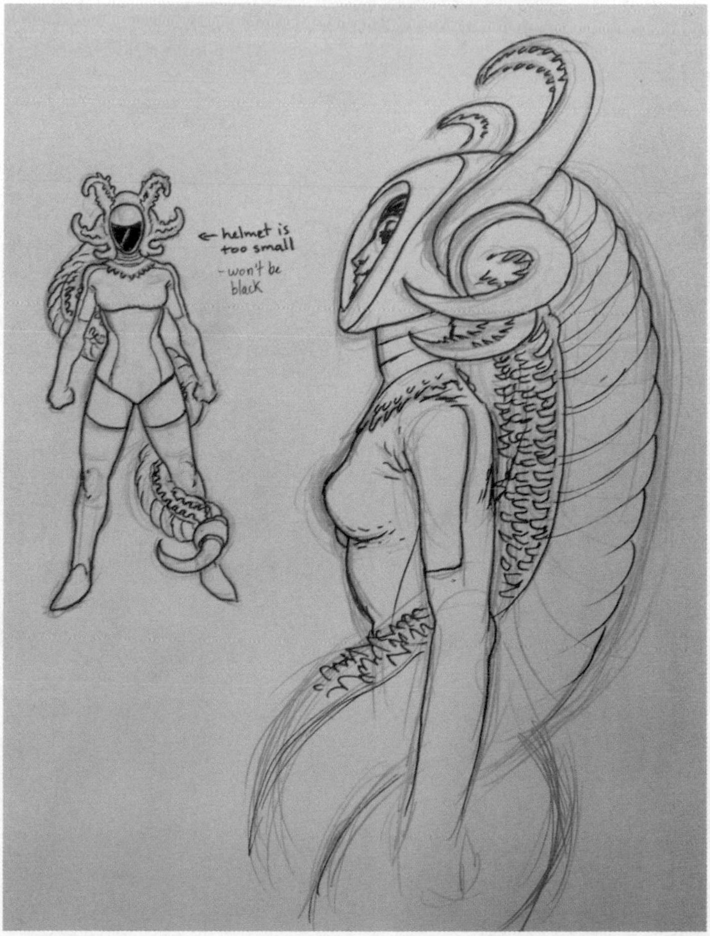
← helmet is too small
- won't be black

IAN BERTRAM

DUSTIN NGUYEN

CLUEMASTER

TIM SEELEY

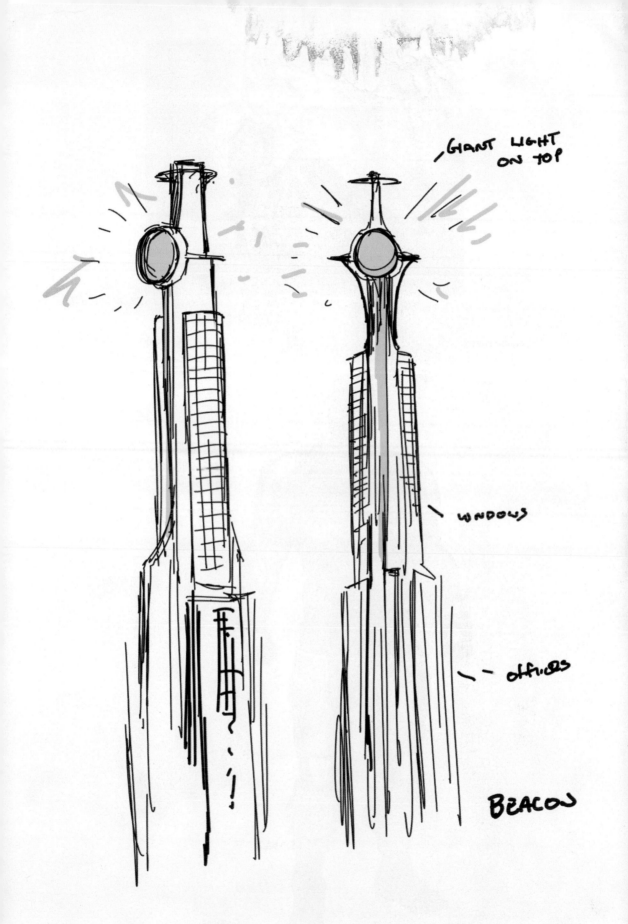

GIANT LIGHT
ON TOP

WINDOWS

OFFICES

BEACON

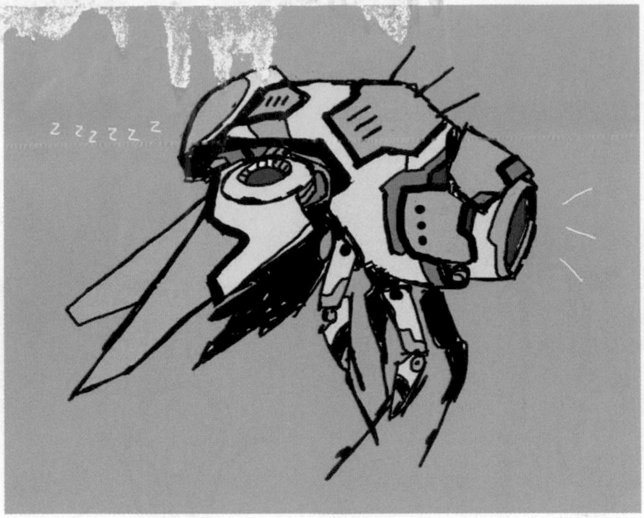

JASON FABOK

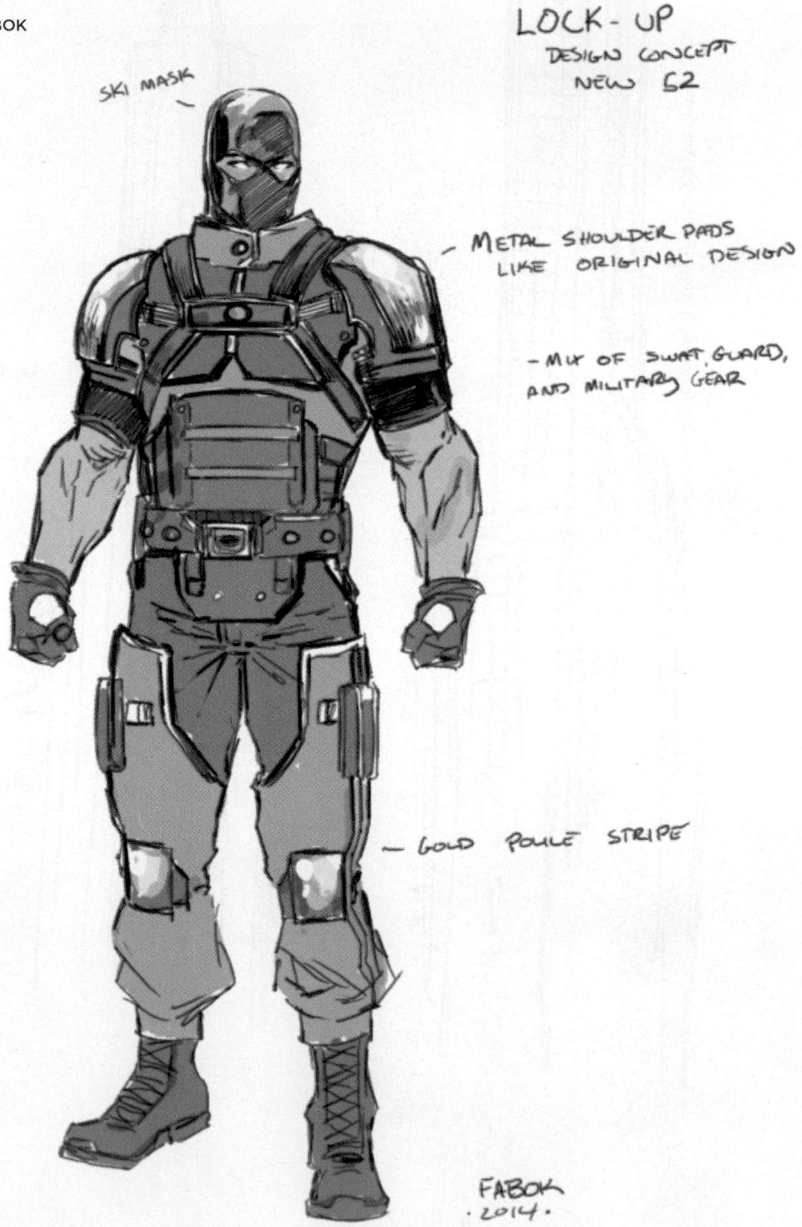
LOCK-UP
DESIGN CONCEPT
NEW 52
SKI MASK
- METAL SHOULDER PADS
LIKE ORIGINAL DESIGN
- MIX OF SWAT, GUARD,
AND MILITARY GEAR
- GOLD POLICE STRIPE
FABOK
·2014·

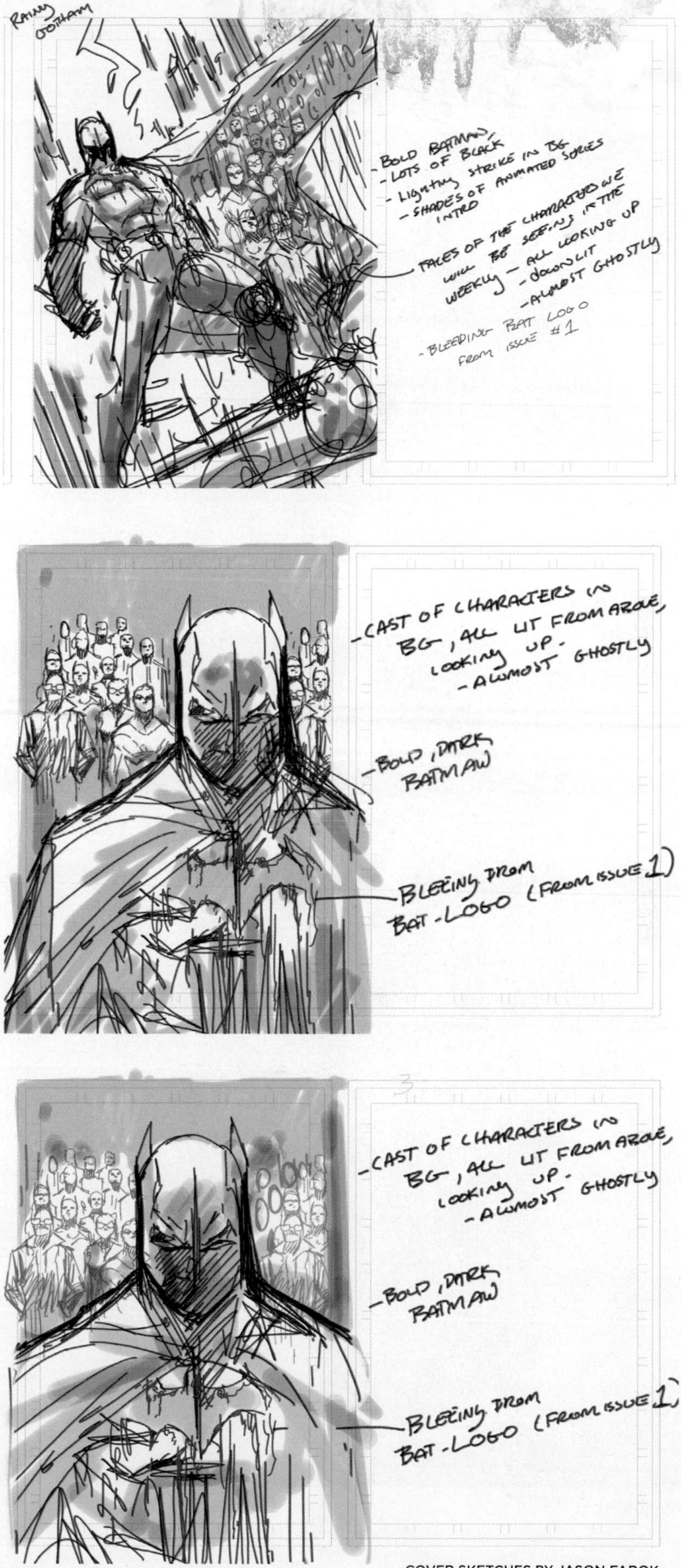
RAINY GOTHAM
- BOLD BATMAN,
- LOTS OF BLACK
- LIGHTNING STRIKE IN BG
- SHADES OF ANIMATED SERIES INTRO
FACES OF THE CHARACTERS WE WILL BE SEEING IN THE WEEKLY - ALL LOOKING UP
- DOWNLIT
- ALMOST GHOSTLY
- BLEEDING BAT LOGO FROM ISSUE #1
- CAST OF CHARACTERS IN BG, ALL LIT FROM ABOVE, LOOKING UP
- ALMOST GHOSTLY
- BOLD, DARK BATMAN
BLEEDING FROM BAT-LOGO (FROM ISSUE 1)
3
- CAST OF CHARACTERS IN BG, ALL LIT FROM ABOVE, LOOKING UP
- ALMOST GHOSTLY
- BOLD, DARK BATMAN
BLEEDING FROM BAT-LOGO (FROM ISSUE 1)

COVER SKETCHES BY JASON FABOK

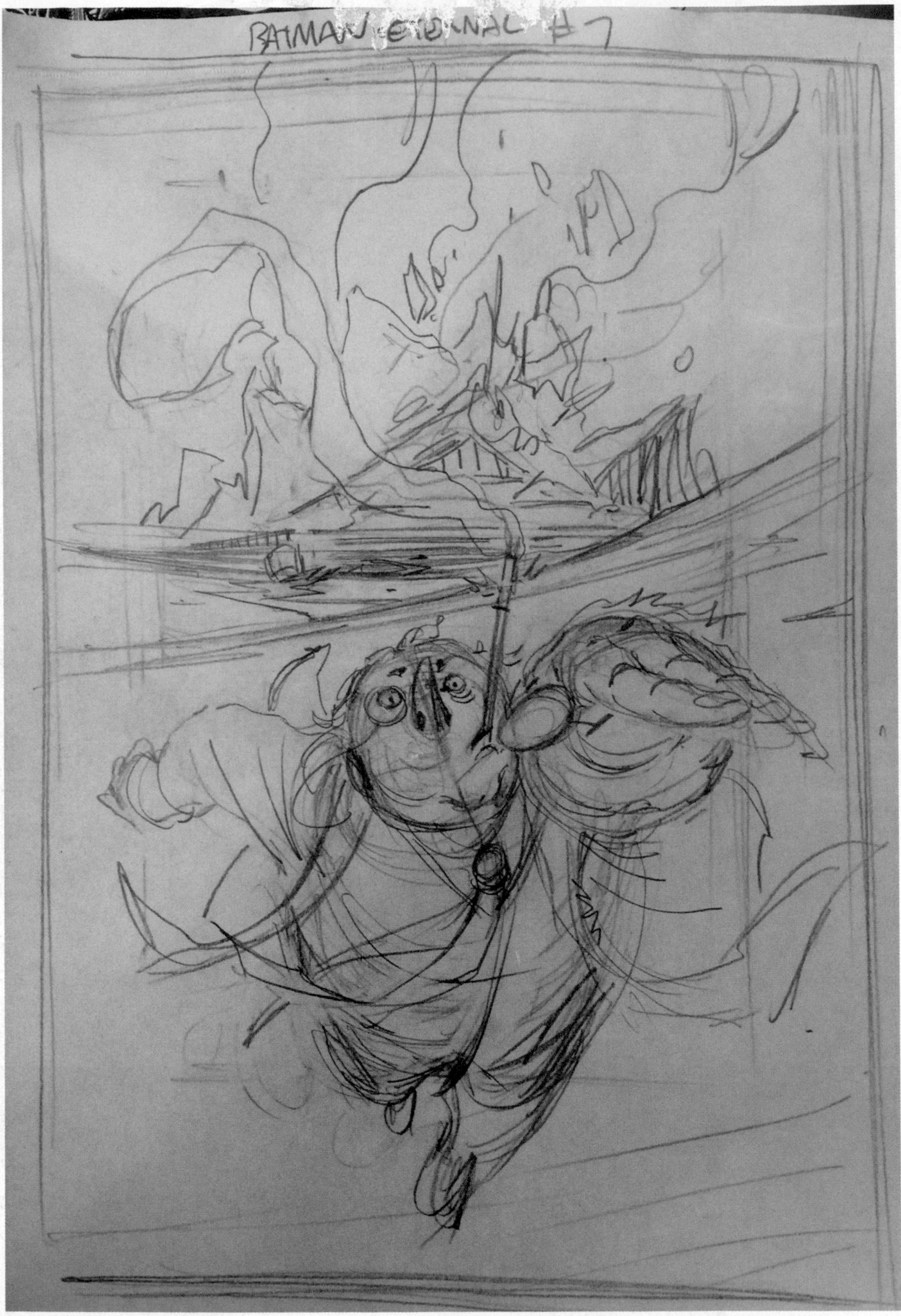
BATMAN ETERNAL #7

COVER SKETCH BY ANDY KUBERT

"Stellar. A solid *[that] roots* itself in Grayson's past, with gorgeous artwork by artist Eddy Barrows."—IGN

"Dynamic."—The New York Times

"A new generation is going to fall in love with Nightwing."
—MTV Geek

START AT THE BEGINNING!

NIGHTWING
VOLUME 1: TRAPS AND TRAPEZES

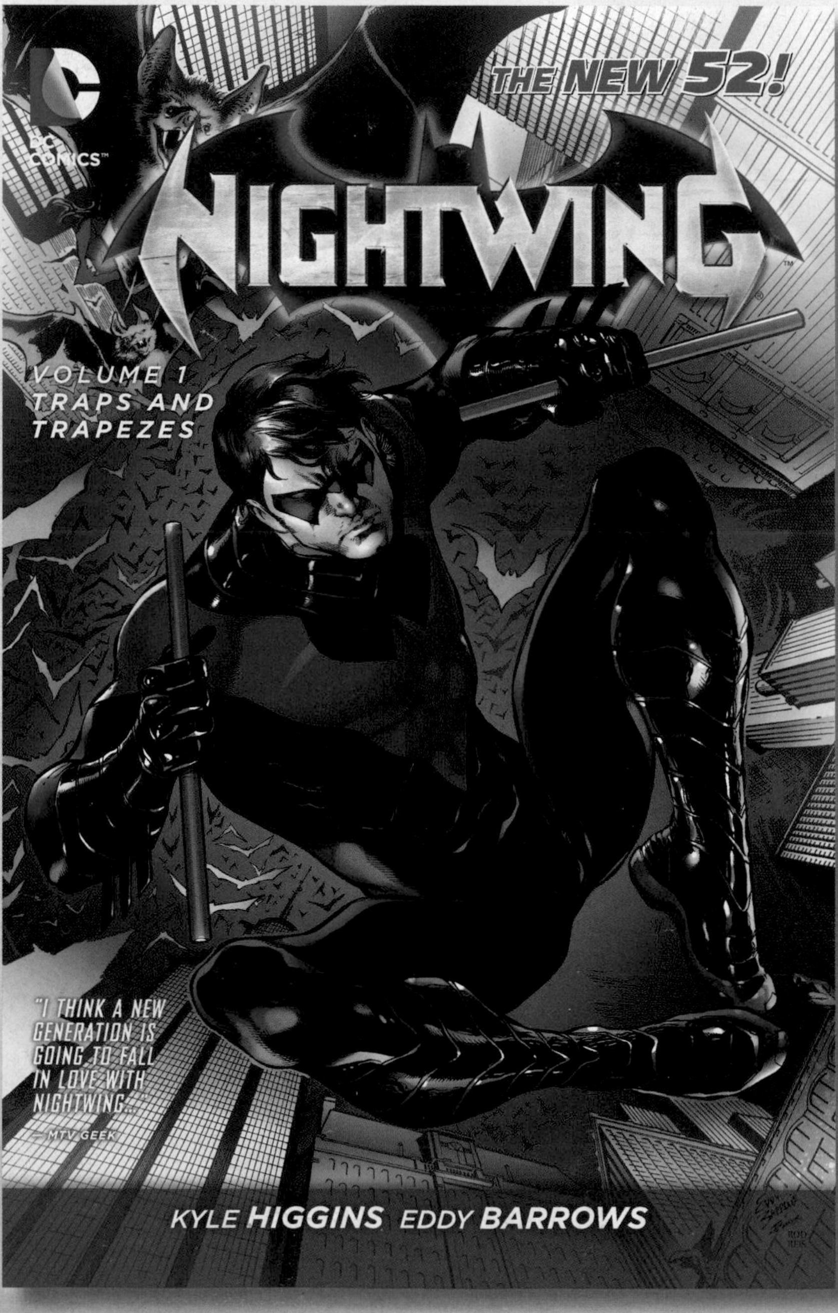

**NIGHTWING VOL. 2:
NIGHT OF THE OWLS**

**NIGHTWING VOL. 3:
DEATH OF THE FAMILY**

**BATMAN:
NIGHT OF THE OWLS**

THE NEW 52!

NIGHTWING

VOLUME 1
TRAPS AND
TRAPEZES

"I THINK A NEW
GENERATION IS
GOING TO FALL
IN LOVE WITH
NIGHTWING."
—MTV GEEK

KYLE **HIGGINS**   EDDY **BARROWS**